Thirteenth Ed

# SUPERVISION

## CONCEPTS AND PRACTICES OF MANAGEMENT

Thirteenth Edition

# SUPERVISION

## CONCEPTS AND PRACTICES OF MANAGEMENT

**EDWIN C. LEONARD, JR., PH.D.**
Professor Emeritus of Management and Marketing
Doermer School of Business
Indiana University—Purdue University, Fort Wayne (IPFW)
and
Visiting Distinguished Professor of Leadership
Trine University

**KELLY A. TRUSTY, PH.D.**
Assistant Professor
School of Public Affairs and Administration
Western Michigan University

Australia • Brazil • Canada • Mexico • Singapore • United Kingdom • United States

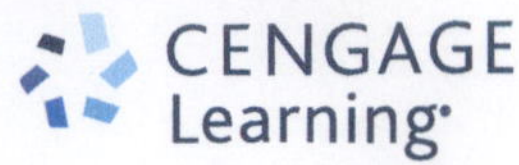

**Supervision: Concepts and Practices of Management, 13e**
**Edwin C. Leonard, Kelly A. Trusty**

Vice President, General Manager, Social Science & Qualitative Business: Erin Joyner

Product Director: Michael Schenk

Senior Product Manager: Mike Roche

Senior Content & Media Developer: Sally Nieman

Product Assistant: Brian Pierce

Marketing Manager: Emily Horowitz

Marketing Coordinator: Chris Walz

Art and Cover Direction, Production Management, and Composition: Lumina Datamatics, Inc.

Intellectual Property Analyst: Jennifer Nonenmacher

Project Manager: Amber Hosea

Manufacturing Planner: Ron Montgomery

Cover Image: © Bull's Eye/Imagezoo/Getty Images



Library of Congress Control Number: 2014951133

Student Edition ISBN: 978-1-285-86637-6

Loose-leaf Edition ISBN: 978-1-305-88487-8

**Cengage Learning**
20 Channel Center Street
Boston, MA 02210
USA

Cengage Learning is a leading provider of customized learning solutions with office locations around the globe, including Singapore, the United Kingdom, Australia, Mexico, Brazil, and Japan. Locate your local office at **www.cengage.com/global**

To learn more about Cengage Learning Solutions, visit **www.cengage.com**

Purchase any of our products at your local college store or at our preferred online store **www.cengagebrain.com**

Printed at CLDPC, USA, 09-20

Ed Leonard: *A mentor once told me, "You, Ed Leonard, are the richest man in the world because you have family and friends who love you and will do anything for you." I have been truly blessed! May you be blessed as you journey through life!*

Kelly Trusty: *To Tom, Blake, Evan, Jack & Bambi—the greatest support network ever! And, to my students, with encouragement to bloom where you are planted.*

# BRIEF CONTENTS

# CONTENTS

# PREFACE

One thing that has been constant in the early twenty-first century world is change. Widespread changes in technologies, organizational restructuring and economic, social, and political environments have affected every aspect of individual and corporate life. Offshoring, and the "China factor" have become a reality. Globalization is impacting competition, changes in technology and the skills that workers will need in the new digital age, and rising labor costs in the minimum wage and other employee benefits. Every day, the *Wall Street Journal*, *USA Today*, and trade publications feature articles about issues that affect organizations and individuals. Examples include the Affordable Care Act, Union-busting laws, the Target data breach, and RadioShack closing over 1,000 stores nationwide. Individuals and organizations will need to find ways to adapt to the ongoing volatility and uncertainty of our society.

Since the recession in 2008, the U.S. economy has grown at a slow rate. But we have hope that employers will focus on empowering their full-time, contingent and virtual employees to achieve high performance and interact effectively with customers, clients, and other stakeholders. Early in Professor Leonard's management career, a mentor said, "Every employee is a manager!" That notion is more appropriate today than at any time during his life. The skills, concepts and principles of management presented in this text are relevant for everyone in the workforce. Each and every person will be responsible for supervising someone or something at some time in his or her life. Therefore, we want to make sure that all students are well informed about the challenges of supervision and possess a solid skill foundation so that they can make informed decisions about the right things to do when necessary.

Throughout the 13th edition of *Supervision*, we have focused on ways in which leaders can engage their diverse workforce and effectively facilitate work teams. We believe that throughout the text we have described and demonstrated the supervisory skills that students will need to help them and their organizations meet the challenges of today and tomorrow.

## Organization of *Supervision*

Over the years, our students have told us that they need help becoming proficient in analysis, communication, decision-making, leadership, and working with dysfunctional bosses and co-workers, that is conflict resolution skills. To that end, every chapter begins with an opening, "You Make the Call!," a feature that gives students an opportunity to analyze a real-world situation and ponder courses of action. The Personal and Team Skill-Building activities at the end of each chapter reinforce the chapter's contents and give students opportunities to apply the skills and content in authentic situations. Students will also have opportunities to reflect back on the opening "You Make the Call!" features and make decisions about what needs to be done to keep employees, supervisors, and organizations moving in the right direction.

We have reorganized the 15 chapters of this edition of *Supervision: Concepts and Practices of Management* into four parts in order to facilitate the use of the text in a variety of instructional configurations including 8-week, 12-week, 15-week and 16-week course calendars. The parts are configured in the following way:

- Part 1: Supervisory Management Overview and Challenges. This part introduces the fundamentals of management, supervisory planning, and the diverse character of the workforce. We discuss the social, demographic, economic, technological and global challenges that managers will face every day in light of the big ideas and theories that have emerged over the past century to inform management thought. Students are introduced to the functions of management: planning, organizing, staffing, leading and controlling. Strategies for effective planning are presented, followed by the challenges and practices of supervising in a diverse workforce.
- Part 2: Essentials of Effective Supervision. The four chapters detail the key skills of leading, communicating and listening, motivating followers, solving problems and making decisions.
- Part 3: Organizing, Staffing, Managing and Measuring for Success. These four chapters provide the essentials for organizing work, empowering employees for success, building and facilitating effective teams, and improving employee performance.
- Part 4: Controlling and Managing Performance and Conflict. These three chapters provide guidance in establishing and using effective controls, resolving conflicts, and applying positive discipline in order to maintain a high-performing workforce.

## Text Features Are Application-Oriented

Our work with organizational behavior, management and leadership students at IPFW and Trine University, as well as with students of public administration at Western Michigan University continues to show us that students learn best when they have many opportunities to apply the concepts and practices of management in real-life contexts. Both of us divide our time among a range of activities that inform the development of the learning activities in the text. We work with private- and public-sector managers and supervisors in a variety of capacities, learning about their managerial challenges, discussing ideas with them, assessing their needs relative to the functions of management and helping them identify best-practice approaches to engage and empower employees. Also having managed employee groups and virtual teams over the past few decades, we have been fortunate to acquire first-hand knowledge of the problems managers face in supervising in a dynamic, complex environment.

We are honored to have the opportunity to share these personal and professional experiences with you by incorporating them into the chapter narratives and learning exercises in this edition of *Supervision*. As has been done in previous editions, the 13th edition of *Supervision* presents the concepts and practices of management from points of view of practicing managers, organizational theorists, employees, business owners and public sector administrators.

The perspectives are presented in ways that enable students to consider the "whys", "hows" and "what ifs" that real managers face through learning exercises and skill-building activities that have been field tested in classroom situations.

The most important question for an author to ask him or herself, as well as the users of a textbook, when approaching every new edition is "What tools do we want our students to add to their career toolbox as they use this text?" Students need to know the theories that explain management, leadership and behavioral practices so that they can understand why people and processes interact in organizations in the ways they do. Students should also be prepared to identify actionable supervisory situations in the workplace and have the knowledge and skills necessary to respond appropriately. This skills-based text provides a balance of theory and practice in chapter narratives that combines timely, relevant research and authentic examples of management concepts, as well as What Have You Learned higher-level thinking questions, Personal and Team Skill-Builders, critical incidents, opportunities for self-assessment, and a collection of Supervision in Action videos available on the student companion website that present students with many opportunities to sharpen their supervisory skills and put them to work. Some of the features we feel best facilitate student learning include the following:

- **An Integrated Teaching and Testing System.** The text and supplements are organized around Learning Objectives that form a comprehensive teaching and learning system. Each chapter begins with a set of Learning Objectives covering key concepts. The objectives then appear in the text margin, identifying where each objective is addressed. The key concepts are reinforced at the end of each chapter in a series of section summaries arranged by Learning Objective. Organization based on Learning Objectives continues into the supplement package, including the integrated lecture outlines in the Instructor's Manual, the chapter Power Point decks and the Test Bank.
- **Comprehensive Learning and Practice Activities.** Together with colleagues, students, practicing managers and others, we have prepared a convenient, challenging and realistic set of activities that will engage students in considering and addressing the issues and challenges that supervisors and employees face in today's workplace. Our goal in the 13th edition is to provide a series of learning activities to intellectually involve students, and, in some situations, to get them emotionally connected to their course work, our text, and the situations they are involved in. Thus, students will have a greater sense of responsibility for their learning.
- **"You Make the Call!" Opening Vignettes.** We begin each chapter with a problem faced by a supervisor or person impacted by a supervisor's choice of action or inaction, which will stimulate student interest about the chapter topics. Each presents a real supervisory situation that will challenge students to apply the concepts presented in the chapter. These case-like scenarios draw students into a problem and ask them to decide what to do.

  At the conclusion of each chapter, in either the Questions for Discussion or specific Skill-Builder activities, students can develop their own approach to the problems in the scenario by applying the concepts they just learned in the chapter. By applying chapter concepts to these opening problems and comparing their analysis and answers to questions we provided, students are more prepared to grapple with the challenging critical incidents presented at the end of each of the four parts of the textbook.

- **Contemporary Issues.** To better comprehend why organizations function the way they do in society, students must recognize and understand the complex issues that supervisors face. Throughout the text, we have integrated real people, real organizations and real situations to help students gain practical knowledge about supervisory and management situations.
- **Supervisory Tips.** Each chapter contains a "Supervisory Tips" box that draws from the authors' personal experiences, thorough reviews of research presented in business, public sector and academic publications, and discussions with practicing supervisors. These tips, together with skill-building activities, give students guidelines for addressing complex issues.
- **Pedagogical Features.** (1) Marginal Definitions of Key Terms: In an introductory supervision course, students must learn management vocabulary. Therefore, we have highlighted in **bold** print key terms where they are first used in the text and we have provided concise definitions in the margins of the text where they are first introduced. The key terms are also listed with the appropriate page number at the end of each chapter. (2) Summary Points: Major chapter concepts are summarized at the end of each chapter with reference to the Learning Objectives. By reviewing these summaries, students can quickly identify areas where they may need further review. Then, using the Learning Objectives number, students can easily locate the concepts they want to review. (3) Questions and Activities: At the end of each chapter is a series of discussion questions and individual and group exercises designed to help students check their understanding of chapter material and practice implementing key concepts. (4) References: The Endnotes section at the end of each chapter contains many current and foundational references. Relevant references are included for all the key concepts introduced in the book, as well as numerous additional sources of information and insights.
- **Skill Builders.** Each chapter contains several Personal and Team Skill Builders, which allow students opportunities to build their analytical thinking skills, including those identified in the "Supervisory Tips" boxes. The Skill Builders include a variety of application, role-play, and critical and creative "thinking outside the box" activities. In addition, all chapters include a "Technology Tool" Skill Builder and several chapters include exercises that introduce students to individuals who make life difficult for others in the workplace, hypothetical supervisors or employees whose behavior may create havoc in the organization. These mini-cases require students to assess and analyze a situation using concepts from the text and suggest solutions. We have found that testing the activities in the classroom helps students develop the competencies needed in today's fast-paced society.
- **Critical Incidents.** Instructors throughout the country have told us that our critical incidents, abbreviated case studies focusing on a specific supervisory situation or management decision point are excellent tools for teaching and learning supervisory skills. In response to this feedback, we have included 24 critical incidents in this edition, all of which are new or substantially revised. The critical incidents provide additional opportunities for students to engage with the learning objectives and content from their respective sections. Because the critical incidents involve concepts from more than one chapter, six incidents are presented at the end of each of the four parts of the text. Most of the critical incidents are short—some less than a page each—and are challenging without being overwhelming. Each is followed

by discussion questions that help students focus and synthesize their thinking. The critical incidents are based on actual experiences of supervisors and leaders in numerous work environments, and one critical incident in each part involves a highly-visible and well-known organizational or community leader.

The critical incidents can be used in several ways as fuel for class, seminar or online discussion, as written homework assignments, for team analysis and presentation, or as prompts for essay examinations. These assignments are excellent ways for students to practice their skills on a real supervisory problem and to assess their abilities to apply what they have learned.

## WATCH FOR THE ICONS

Our goal in the 13th edition of *Supervision* is to provide a series of learning activities through multiple modalities in order to actively involve students intellectually and accommodate a variety of learning styles. As in previous editions, we include icons for each modality to draw your attention to these special learning activities.

- 

**Internet Activities.** Internet-based exercises require students to search the World Wide Web for information, tools or strategies that may be associated with or included in the learning activity. Look for the "Internet Activity" icon.
- 

**Role Play Activities.** Several of the skill builders and end-of-part critical incidents have optional role-playing activities that involve small groups of students putting themselves in the place of a supervisor or employees. The "Role Play" icon is used to identify them.
- 

**Supervision in Action.** Video scenarios captured from authentic organizational environments offer effective, engaging learning opportunities for students. We now provide 15 real-world video vignettes, one for each chapter in the student companion website for this text, located at cengagebrain.com. A "Supervision in Action" icon at the end of each chapter prompts instructors and students to access the videos and accompanying discussion questions and activities online. We encourage use of the videos as catalysts for in-class discussion or enrichment of the online learning environment.

## New Perspectives and Expanded Topics

- The character of the text has transitioned to address a wider variety of supervisory environments. According to a 2014 Yconic.com study of over 1,000 millennial workers, nearly half would like to serve in the public sector in some capacity some time during their career. Further, many nonprofit organizations seek managers who can bring entrepreneurial and business skills to bear on pressing social problems, often finding candidates who wish to transition from the private sector. For these reasons, the 13th edition includes examples of supervisory challenges as they occur in all of these contexts and provide opportunities for students to apply concepts to a wide variety of organizational situations.

- New to this edition, we include at the end of each chapter an "Experiential Exercise for Self-Assessment." We believe that a quote from the 1963 speech prepared for John F. Kennedy, Jr., "Leadership and learning are indispensable to each other," holds true for all supervisors. In order to succeed in leading workers, supervisors must know their strengths and identify areas in which they can continue to grow. The Experiential Exercises give students opportunities to evaluate their personal and professional skills in order to identify their assets and learn some things that they can to do to make themselves more valuable in the workforce and in their communities.
- Throughout organizations, technology is transforming the ways in which workers work and supervisors manage. Accordingly, throughout the text we address these changes by describing supervisory functions that can now be augmented with technology. These changes are often accompanied by challenges, which we discuss as well, particularly the supervisor's responsibility to balance the demands of incorporating social media into stakeholder engagement efforts with the problem of employees' time-wasting technology behaviors.
- Also new in this edition, all of the chapters include a "Technology Tool" activity as one of the Personal or Team Skill-Builders. These activities provide students with opportunities to explore technology software applications and software use strategies that align with the functions of management. Business and social sector research tell us that when organizations align technology with their missions and goals, rather than simply using technology because it is available, they can improve the efficiency, effectiveness, quality, and overall performance of their organizations. The Technology Tools will help students identify ways in which they can facilitate this alignment by choosing tools that help organizations do what they're already doing, better.
- As our society recovers from the most recent economic recession, surveys have found that a lack of trust between workers and managers continues to affect productivity and employee engagement. In Chapter 5 we include an extended discussion of the importance of trust-building actions and behaviors supervisors should use to reverse this trend. Leadership ethics goes hand-in-hand with trust therefore we, provide recommendations to supervisors related to modeling and encouraging ethical behavior with specific mention of Character Counts™ Six Pillars of Character, which can be applied widely to organizations, communities, and personal ethical decisions.
- Followership, a required element in the leadership equation, is discussed in detail in Chapter 5.
- Previous editions' coverage of employee morale is augmented with new research findings and strategies for increasing employee engagement, a concept that more specifically delineates the extent to which supervisors and the organization play a role in building employee commitment to achieving organizational goals.
- Technology's inherent problem of data security and the increasing incidence of large-scale organizational data breaches are topics that merit specific mention in discussions of policy planning, positive discipline and resolving conflict.
- Organizational change is now included in Chapter 8 coverage of problem-solving and decision-making. Problem-solving drives the decision-making process; in order to solve a problem, often changes must be made. It is the

supervisor's responsibility to incorporate strategies for effectively facilitating change in order to maintain positive employee morale and engagement.

- Continued challenges of downsizing due to reorganization and the impact of technology are presented in Chapters 9 and 11, particularly the effects of layoffs on remaining workers who often must work through "survivor syndrome". Suggestions are provided in Chapter 11 for helping workers maintain productivity and morale during necessary transitions.
- The number of workers who telecommute and participate in virtual teams continues to increase. We provide updated suggestions for managing a virtual workforce.

## To the Instructor

First and foremost, this is a practitioner text. Using your personal career and life experiences along with the skill-building exercises and other experiential exercises from the text, you can help students identify problems and challenges by tapping into their life and organizational experiences. By coupling these past personal experiences with the concepts presented in the text, students are led to make recommendations for solutions or organizational improvement.

We believe that the greatest gift a professor has to give is to prepare students, inspire them to excel in the classroom, enable them to reach their full potential and encourage them to take risks. We are certain that your legacy will be that you invested wisely in your students, as they will be the ones that make our nation's future even brighter. The 13th edition of *Supervision: Concepts and Practices of Management* will help your students in the learning process and get them to recognize and understand the complex issues supervisors face.

## Supplements to Ease the Teaching Load

**Instructor's Manual.** Instructors always have more to do than there are hours in a day. To make class preparation easier, we have developed a comprehensive Instructor's Manual.

The Instructor's Manual includes suggestions for making the course "come alive" for your students. You will find that the integrated learning system that is found in the main text applies to the supplementary package as well. The Instructor's Manual is organized by Learning Objectives so that you can easily customize your lectures and emphasize the concepts your students need most. The extensive lecture outlines in the manual identify the materials that fulfill each objective so that you can be sure your lectures cover key concepts. In addition to the lecture outlines, the Instructor's Manual includes:

- Solution guidelines for all end-of-chapter discussion questions
- Commentaries on personal and team skill–builders, including suggested solutions and follow-up approaches
- Evaluation tools for assessing student presentation and teamwork contributions
- Commentaries and discussion guides for the "Supervision in Action" video clips

- Full commentaries on all critical incidents that can guide your classroom discussions
- Answers for the critical incident discussion questions that will also help you evaluate student written analyses.

**Test Bank.** Cengage Learning Testing Powered by Cognero is a flexible, online system that allows you to:

- author, edit, and manage test bank content from multiple Cengage Learning solutions.
- create multiple test versions in an instant
- deliver tests from your LMS, your classroom, or wherever you want.

Thoroughly revised, updated and certified for this edition, our comprehensive test bank contains an ample number of questions so that you can easily create several different versions of exams. Questions are linked to chapter Learning Objectives so that you can tailor your exams to complement your teaching emphasis. The number of multiple-choice questions has been increased, particularly with higher-level, application-based questions. And now, all questions are tagged according to level of difficulty, learning objective, two types of learning outcomes and Bloom's taxonomy so that you can search and find the perfect combination of questions to meet your needs. Test Bank items can be easily integrated with your institution's chosen learning management system (LMS).

**PowerPoint® slides created by Niclas Hulting.** Again reducing your lecture preparation time, a complete deck of PowerPoint® slides for every chapter will guide students through the key concepts and essential terms presented in the chapter material. The slides are completely correlated to the lecture outlines found in the Instructor's Manual. You can easily edit or add to each slide deck as needed to meet your personal presentation style.

**Instructor's Support Web Site.** At www.cengagebrain.com, instructors will find the entire suite of supplements—the Instructor's Manual, the PowerPoint® slides, and the Test Bank in various formats. And if you're looking for more critical incidents, you'll find them here! More than 25 cases—including many of your favorites from previous editions—are still available online.

**DVD.** Perhaps one of the most exciting and compelling bonus features of this program, these short and powerful video clips provide additional insights on the application of course concepts. A new set of video clips offers real-world organizational acumen and valuable learning experiences from an array of organizations.

## Supplements for Instructors and Students

**Product Support Web site.** The flashcards, Learning Objectives, and Glossary are available for quick reference on our complementary student product support Web site. Real-world video clips and corresponding questions and activities are available for viewing and offer valuable learning experiences. Web links and supporting materials corresponding to Experiential Exerices and Technology Tools for each chapter are also available on the student Web site.

## To the Student

We both like to greet our new classes with the following questions, "*Right now, what do you feel is the most important issue facing the United States?*" and "*Five years after graduation, what do you think will be the most important issue facing the United States?".* Then, we ask the same two questions with a slight variance, "*What is the greatest challenge you face today?*" and "*What is the most important challenge you will face five years after graduation?*" Then we ask two other questions, "*What do you want to know for when your days on earth have ended?*" and "*What strategy or plan do you have in place to get where you want to be?*" Reaction to those questions have been intense, extensive and varied in both of our classrooms. Not surprisingly, most students cannot grasp the challenges they might be facing in the future.

Historically, we have wanted this book to encourage *you*—the student—to think, communicate, and make decisions, unpleasant as those tasks may be at times. We have found these skills to be the ones that make the difference in the "real world," whether you work for a major corporation, a family business, a government agency, or a not-for-profit organization.

The Learning Objectives, listed at the beginning of each chapter, are what we expect you to learn or be able to do after completing the assigned readings and associated activities. We suggest that you "read with the end in mind." Read the Learning Objectives for the chapter, write them down on a sheet of paper or record them on your favorite electronic device; then read the chapter's summary. You will now have a feel for what the authors think are the most important concepts. Now that you have an overview, read the chapter. We believe that you learn much more when you read with a purpose. Our students have also found it beneficial to make a list of all the key concepts and terms prior to reading the chapter.

*Supervision* 13th edition was revised first and foremost with you, the student, in mind. Hopefully, your learning will be enhanced, and you will have great success in whatever you choose to do. If you have questions or concerns, you can email us: Professor Leonard, Leonard@ipfw.edu, and Professor Trusty, kelly.a.trusty@wmich.edu.

*We hope and pray that you will enjoy the journey as you travel through Supervision 13th edition.*

## Acknowledgments

In developing *Supervision: Concepts and Practices of Management,* 13th edition, and supplementary materials, we are indebted to so many individuals that it may not be possible to give them all credit.

We know that the authors are only one spoke in the wheel that drives a successful textbook. Simply stated, this edition has come about through the support and encouragement of many people. The authors give special thanks to their family members for their help and gracious encouragement and recognizing that there were things we were not able to do with them because we were doing research and working on the book.

We want to thank the Cengage/South-Western Learning team for their tremendous support and assistance. We especially thank Jennifer King (Managing Content Developer) and Sally Nieman (Sr. Media & Content Developer).

All of the opening *You Make the Calls* and *Critical Incidents* were developed by Professor Leonard. However, over the years, several colleagues have collaborated to present new You Make the Calls and Critical Incidents for this edition.

We would like to acknowledge all of the students at Trine University, Western Michigan University, and IPFW who were our field testers for the You Make the Calls, the Critical Incidents, the Technology Tools, and the Personal and Team Skill Builders that we have added to this edition.

Finally, we want to thank Barbara Liggett, Director, School of Public Affairs and Administration, Western Michigan University, for all she has done in the last four years to help Kelly Trusty finish her doctorate in 2013. Dr. Leonard would also like to thank Dr. Liggett, for allowing him to serve on Dr. Trusty's doctoral committee.

# MEET THE AUTHORS

Photo courtesy of Dr. Edwin Leonard

## EDWIN C. LEONARD, JR., PH.D.

Professor Emeritus of Management and Marketing
Doermer School of Business and Management Sciences
Indiana University—Purdue University, Fort Wayne (IPFW)
and
Distinguished Visiting Professor of Leadership
Studies Trine University

**Dr. Edwin C. Leonard, Jr.** received his bachelor's, master's, and doctoral degrees from Purdue University. After receiving the undergraduate degree, he worked for a construction company as a project manager. After serving in the military, where he taught at the Chemical, Biological, and Radiological Warfare School and served as commander of Headquarters Company, USAG and XVIII Airborne Corps (Fort Bragg, NC), he returned to graduate school.

Beginning in 1966, he held various administrative and faculty positions including manager of the NE Indiana Extension region, chair of the management/marketing department, and acting chair of the School of Public and Environmental Affairs. His primary teaching areas included organizational behavior and leadership, introduction to business/government/society, human resources/industrial relations, and strategic management. He received Emeritus status from

Indiana University in 2004. Currently, he is part of the Core Leadership Faculty and engaged in teaching and course development at Trine University.

Dr. Leonard has designed and conducted workshops and seminars for thousands of supervisors, managers, and executives. He has served as academic advisor and coordinator of Do-it-Best Corp.'s Management Training Course for 33 years. This comprehensive program is for management personnel of one of the nation's largest hardware and building material retailers. From 1970 through 2001, he had his own full-service management consulting firm.

Dr. Leonard's primary research interests are in the areas of employee involvement and motivation, organizational culture, climate and leadership, human resource interventions, and case development. He has published in numerous academic and professional journals, instructional supplement manuals, and conference proceedings. Dr. Leonard has received numerous "best paper" and "distinguished case" awards. His publication list (AACSB—The Association to Advance Collegiate Schools of Business—the national accrediting body for Schools of Business—refers to them as Intellectual Contributions) exceeds 60 since January 2000.

He served as Editor of ***The Business Case Journal (BCJ)*** for seven years. In addition to Supervision: Concepts and Practices of Management 13/e, he has authored or coauthored four other books:

- Edwin C. Leonard, Jr., and Roy A. Cook, ***Human Resource Management:*** *21st Century Challenges,* 1st Edition (Mason, OH: Thomson © 2005)
- Edwin C. Leonard, Jr., Claire McCarty Kilian, and Raymond L. Hilgert, ***Labor Agreement Negotiations***, 7th Edition (Mason, OH: Thomson Custom Publishing © 2003)
- Raymond L. Hilgert, Cyril C. Ling, and Edwin C. Leonard, Jr., ***Cases, Incidents and Experiential Exercises in Human Resource Management***, 3rd Edition (Houston, TX: Dame Publishing © 2000)
- Edwin C. Leonard, Jr., ***Assessment of Training Needs*** (Chicago, IL: The U.S. Civil Service Commission © 1973).

One of Dr. Leonard's early articles, "Answers to Your Questions about Case Writing," was reprinted in *The Business Case Journal* (Summer, 2011). An article with Roy Cook, "Teaching Tips: Teaching with Cases," appeared in the January–March 2010 (Volume 10, Number 1) *Journal of Teaching in Travel and Tourism*, (ISSN: 1531-3220). Several of his coauthored cases and critical incidents were adapted with permission for inclusion in the 12th edition of ***Supervision***.

Two articles co-authored with Dr. Trusty received the following awards: (1) the ***McGraw-Hill/Irwin 2012 Distinguished Paper Award*** for their "What to Do With a Druggie?" (2) the Society for Case Research ***2011 Best Critical Incident Award*** from "Unwelcomed Advances: Female to Male Harassment".

Dr. Leonard has served as president of the Society for Case Research (www.sfcr.org) and the Midwest Society of Human Resources/Industrial Relations (now the Midwest Management Association); as well as president of the Fort Wayne Area Chapter of the Society for Training and Development. During the 21st century, he has served on the board of directors of the Society for Case Research (SCR); the North American Case Research Association (NACRA); and the Management Association.

Dr. Leonard has received many teaching and service awards. Nearest to his heart are those awards he received from various student groups: Services for

Students with Disabilities (DASEL), the International Students Organization (ISO), and IPFW Honors Program. All of these awards were for his outstanding service to students.

He was the recipient of the ***Award of Teaching Excellence*** from the Indiana University School of Continuing Studies and the ***Faculty Service Award*** from the National University Continuing Education Association for his outstanding service to the professions.

In addition to inclusion in various "Who's Who?" Dr. Leonard was elected into ***Ordo Honorium*** of the Kappa Delta Rho Fraternity. This is a distinct honor bestowed by the Fraternity in recognition of the brother's outstanding service to their fraternity, their community, and their profession. This is the highest honor the Fraternity bestows on an alumnus.

Professor Ed Leonard received the IPFW Department of Consumer and Family Sciences' ***Hospitarian Award*** for his dedication and contributions to the program. The plaque reads "For displaying hospitality with a humanitarian heart."

In April of 2004, Ed Leonard received ***Distinguished Alumni Community Achievement Award*** from his alma mater, Purdue University. The award reads "For outstanding dedication to higher education and his community as a teacher, researcher, coach, and advisor". In 2005, he was inducted into his high school Hall of Fame. In 2009, he was inducted into the IPF W Athletics Hall of Fame for his outstanding contributions as a coach, administrator and supporter.

Dr. Leonard's contributions to the community go beyond the University and his Church: The Allen County Board of Commissioners bestowed upon him the title of ***Honorary County Commissioner***. The proclamation reads as follows: "Whereas, Dr. Leonard, recognizing that all work and no play makes for a colorless educational experience, initiated IPFW's basketball program (now an NCAA Division 1 program) and expanded its golf program (coached the first and only individual to represent the University in the NCAA Golf Championships), and helped to nurture a healthy economy in Allen County by training quality supervisors and managers; and teaching local businesses strategic management skills; and served as a member of many boards including the Allen County Tax Adjustment Board, the Indiana Labor Wage and Hour Board, March of Dimes/Birth Defects Foundation and the League for the Blind and Disabled as well as serving as chair or co-chair of several scholarship boards; NOW, THEREFORE, the Board of Commissioners of the County of Allen, Indiana hereby bestows upon Dr. Edwin C. Leonard, Jr., the title of **Honorary County Commissioner**.

In June 2014, Dr. Leonard received the Sagamore of the Wabash Award from Governor Michael Pence. The Sagamore of the Wabash Award is given to one who "has endeared himself to the Citizens of Indiana; one who is distinguished by his Humanity in Living, his Loyalty in Friendship, his Wisdom in Council, and his Inspiration in Leadership".

The Leonard family has endowed five college scholarships for needy and deserving students and created the Leonard Family Advised Fund within the Fort Wayne Community Foundation to provide spiritual and educational opportunities for needy and deserving youth under 14 years of age in Allen County, Indiana.

He and his wife, Ginger, have three children: Lori, Teo (wife Stacie), and Lisa (husband Gary Koss); and two grandchildren, Haley and Tyler Koss. The Leonards spend the winter months at their Jekyll Island, Georgia home.

## KELLY A. TRUSTY, PH.D.

Assistant Professor

School of Public Affairs and Administration

Western Michigan University

**Dr. Kelly A. Trusty** received her bachelor's degree from Purdue University, her master's degree from Ball State University and her doctorate degree from the Western Michigan University School of Public Affairs and Administration. A "pracademic" who began her career as a K-12 gifted and talented coordinator and elementary school teacher, Trusty then moved into the nonprofit sector to lead the growth of a grassroots coalition from a handful of passionate activists to a 501(c)3 corporation with a full paid staff, hundreds of volunteers, and a powerful action network. Her award-winning fieldwork in organizational management, leadership, strategic planning, evaluation and sustainability led to invitations to serve as a consultant to local, state and regional nonprofit, governmental and educational organizations. From 1997 to the present she has operated a consulting practice that focuses on helping organizations build their capacity to create, measure and sustain positive community change.

Moving into the higher education realm after nearly 20 years in the field was a natural transition. Dr. Trusty was invited to invest her expertise and practical experience in creating and directing the Master of Science in Leadership (MSL) program at Trine University, which became the largest graduate program in the institution's history. Along with leading the program, Trusty served as an assistant professor and lead faculty of the Nonprofit Organizational Studies concentration, teaching leadership, nonprofit management, organizational communication and capstone courses. She then returned to her alma-mater, Western Michigan University to teach in the School of Public Affairs and Administration, where her primary teaching areas include nonprofit and public agency leadership and management, human resource adminstration, grant writing and governance.

Dr. Trusty's research interests include the relationships between nonprofit strategy, technology/mission alignment and organizational outcomes, executive mentoring in the nonprofit environment, and the translational leadership necessary to bridge theory and practice. The conceptual model she developed to measure the relationships between strategy, IT/mission alignment maturity and nonprofit organizational outcomes, SIMO, is an example of such a bridge. Dr. Trusty's publications bridge community change and leadership theory and practice. She penned weekly columns in the *Journal Review* and *The Paper of Montgomery County* for eight years focusing on community mobilization and high-risk behavior prevention and she has authored award-winning case studies and critical incidents focusing on organizational management and human resources.

Dr. Trusty has presented practical leadership, strategic planning, sustainability, evaluation and teaching strategies at gatherings sponsored by the National Society for Leadership and Success, Trine University, Northwest Indiana Working Smarter Higher Education Consortium, Steuben County Community Foundation, Compassion Pregnancy Centers of Northeast Indiana, WIMC Radio, Montgomery County Division of Family and Children, the League of Women Voters and Indiana Tobacco Prevention and Cessation Agency. She has presented academic papers at a variety of national conferences and annual meetings, including the Association for Research on Nonprofit Organizations and Voluntary Action (ARNOVA), MBAA International, Society for Case Research, Business Society and Government Consortium, and IPFW Annual Teaching Conference.

She was the recipient of the 2012 Trine University Faculty Scholarship award for her case study research, she received the 2012 MBAA International McGraw-Hill/Irwin Distinguished Paper Award for "What to Do With a Druggie?", she received the Society for Case Research Best Critical Incident Award in 2011 for "Unwelcomed Advances: Female to Male Harassment", as well as the Thelma Cummins Vision Award from Cummins Behavioral Health Systems, Inc., the Governor's Commission for a Drug-Free Indiana Promising Practices Award and the Oustanding Indiana Economics Educator Award. She holds membership in Phi Kappa Phi, Kappa Delta Pi and Golden Key National Honor Societies.

Dr. Trusty and her family support educational programming in Haiti that empowers local youth with servant leadership and public service skills they can contribute to the ongoing rebuilding of their country. They also are committed to promoting and supporting the community asset-building value of local youth sports through coaching and fundraising. She and her brown dog, Mackey, also love to garden.

PART 1

ERIC PIERMONT/Getty Images

# Supervisory Management Overview and Challenges

Chapter 1

# The Supervisory Challenge

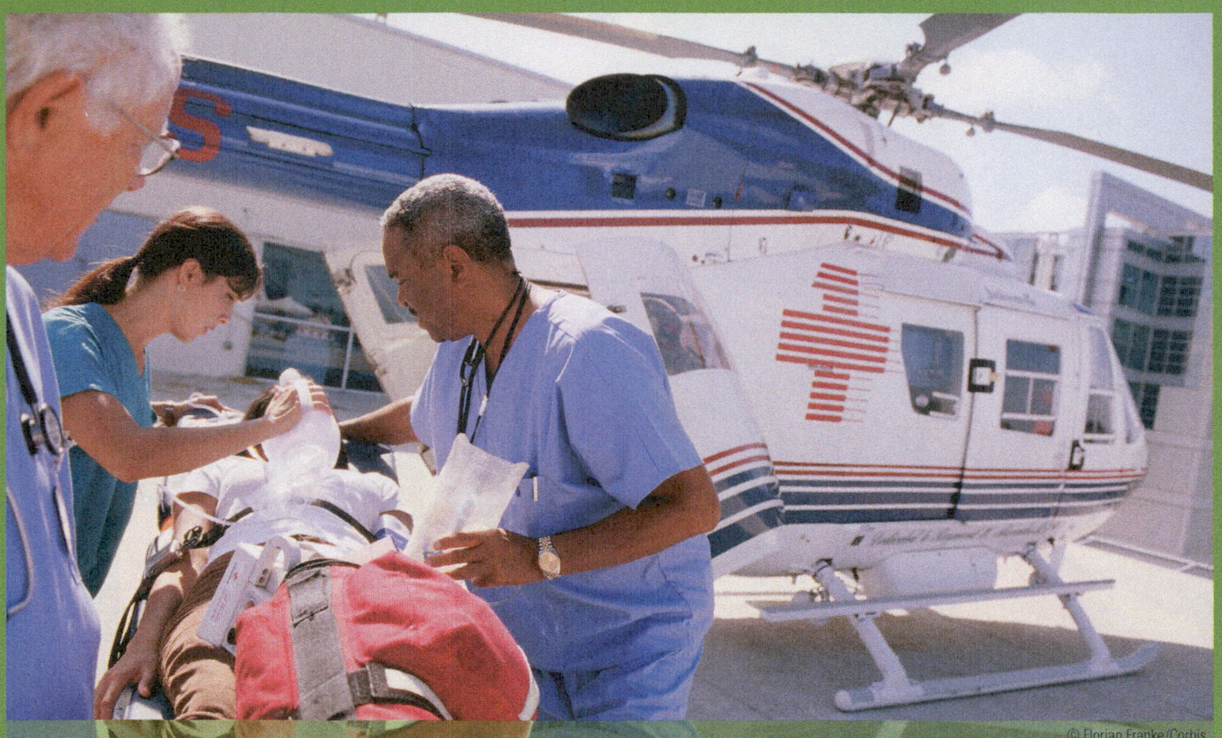

© Florian Franke/Corbis

**After studying this chapter, you will be able to:**

1. Understand that we are in difficult times.
2. Explain the demands and rewards of being a supervisor.
3. Describe the contributions of four schools of management thought.
4. Identify the economic, demographic, political, and social trends that will affect supervisors.
5. Explain why supervisors must continually grow and develop as professionals.
6. Recognize ways for getting into a supervisory position.

# YOU MAKE THE CALL!

*Every chapter in this book begins with a short case section titled "You Make the Call!" After reading each case, decide which decision(s) or course(s) of action the person described in the case should make or take. As you read each chapter, think about how the concepts apply to the opening problem.*

You are Charlotte Kelly, evening shift admitting services team leader at Community Medical Center's Pine Village. The Pine Village facility is located in a small Southern city located about 30 miles from its closest competitor and has 240 beds. (see Figure 1.7, "A sample values and belief statement"). In recent years there have been many changes in the healthcare industry. The implementation of the Affordable Care Act caused many companies to adjust their policies. The Pine Village facility recently announced that 22 positions were being eliminated and that one floor of the hospital was being closed due to the lack of need.

Charlotte, like many others at Pine Village, read the same recent *BusinessWeek* article that said, "In the next few years we will see an expansion of the number of people entering the healthcare system. In fact, by 2016, as many as 30 million more adults will have health insurance. Plus, each day, thousands of baby boomers will become eligible for Medicare."[1] She knew that more and more people will need care, but their stays in the hospital are only a few days. When her children were born, she was in a hospital for a week; now they may be in a day and out the next. New technology in healthcare has driven up the costs across the board. The article went on to talk about how to compare quality to cost. The Affordable Health Care Act, according to the Kaiser Family Foundation, has seen employers cost shifting, making employees pay a higher portion of the cost of dependent and spouse coverage.[2]

When you graduated from nursing school 30 some years ago, nursing jobs were plentiful. You began as a cardiac care nurse at a hospital in Greenville, South Carolina, where you met your future husband and began a family. Shortly after your youngest child graduated from high school, your husband was killed in an automobile accident. You moved to Pine Village to be near your sister and her family. As nursing jobs were scarce, Pine Village was looking for someone to be the admitting department's evening shift team leader, a job you accepted. As a shift team leader, you assumed summary supervisory responsibilities but you were limited in authority and were not part of the hospital's management team. The admitting department supervisor was Pat Graham.

Shortly after getting the job, you began attending classes at a local community college in the area. You received a certificate in medical records technology and decided to take a couple of courses in supervision and organizational leadership. One of your favorite professors was Bernie Ray, a middle-aged supervisor at one of the local companies. Mr. Ray usually began each class with a current problem or issue that required students to interact and expand upon their leadership perspectives. The textbook, *Supervision: Concepts and Practices of Management*, had critical incidents where you make the calls that were relevant to most of the people in the class. You liked the "team approach" to learning because your fellow classmates brought a variety of experiences to the class and you learned from each other.

Early Wednesday afternoon, your boss Pat Graham sent you a text message asking you to come in early that day and meet with her in her office. Much to your surprise, Norma Elward, human resource supervisor, and hospital administrator Larry Stuckey were also present. Stuckey began the conversation, "Charlotte we are pleased with the job that you have done as a team leader on the evening shift. You have been an excellent role model and from all reports, have communicated very well with your team members. You have a reputation as being someone who expects a lot and gets positive results because you expect no less from yourself. People tell me that you have encouraged your associates to get involved and to understand how their job performance affects patient care." Stuckey paused briefly then continued. "Charlotte, we want you to become the ER (emergency room) supervisor effective Monday morning to replace Amy Talmadge. You've taken classes in leadership and supervision and you have earned this promotion to our management team. We know that you will be able to handle this new assignment, even though you have not worked in the emergency services department previously.

Pat Graham then said, "Charlotte, because you have done a good job of cross training your associates, we want you to recommend your replacement. Please let us know by this time tomorrow which of your associates you are recommending and why. If you have any questions, I am always here."

You were exhilarated and a bit sobered by what had happened. "Wow," you thought to yourself. "This is a culmination of a five-year odyssey. It has been hard, but I knew right from the beginning that I wanted to be a supervisor. Pat Graham has been a great mentor. She shows interest in every employee and in increasing their skills, knowledge, and abilities. I learned a lot from her and also from Mr. Ray's classes. But I wonder if I have the right stuff for this supervisory and leadership position? And do I really want all the headaches, responsibilities and pressures that this job will create?"

Late on Friday afternoon you reflected on the events of the last two days. You had recommended Ken Morrison and Louise Turner as two possible candidates to replace you. In your opinion, both would be very capable.

You have just learned that Amy Talmadge was fired as the ER supervisor earlier in the day. You know that the ER department had become the butt of many employee jokes, and turnover in the department had been extremely high. Amy had the reputation of being an autocratic, very demanding, and insensitive person. Word had it that she expected her employees to do as she commanded, and at times she was known to criticize and embarrass her employees in public. The ER department consisted of a very diverse group of employees, and the ER department was operational 24/7. Friday nights, Saturdays, and Sundays were times the ER department had many people show up, and often some of them were brought in by the local police because of alcohol or other substance abuses.

As you sit at your desk contemplating the situation, you think, "I know some things not to do, but I don't know if I can make this transition to this challenging leadership position. Where do I go from here?"

**Disclaimer:** The above scenario presents a supervisory situation based on real events to be used for educational purposes. The identities of some or all individuals, organizations, industries, and locations, as well as financial and other information may have been disguised to protect individual privacy and proprietary information. In some cases details have been added to improve readability and interest.

**YOU MAKE THE CALL!**

**1 Understand that we are in difficult times.**

## What Does It Mean to Be a Supervisor in Uncertain Times?

The opening years of this century have been the most chaotic, uncertain, and unpredictable years in the authors' lives. Virtually every aspect of contemporary life has undergone major changes during the past few years. The first years of the twenty-first century have certainly been the times that try men's souls.

What happened yesterday is not relevant unless it can be used as a learning experience. Think back to when you were in the fifth grade. What was your world like? No doubt it was a lot different from your parents' world. Today, with the technology available, it is very easy to look up various employment, economic, and other demographic statistics to compare our lot in life with that of others and to see how we are progressing from one year to the next. But what else is new? Look at Figure 1.1 to get a glimpse of how things were just 20 years ago.

The twenty-first century will be noted in the future by those who experienced them as "another day of infamy"—except that the day turned into weeks, months, and years. Where were you on September 11, 2001? Do you remember what thoughts went through your mind as you heard the early reports of the planes crashing and the days of uncertainty that followed? What were you doing on April 14, 2007, when a murderer wreaked havoc on the Virginia Tech campus? What were your thoughts as you watched the following events unfold?

November 2009: A U.S. Army Major went ballistic and killed 13 people at Fort Hood, Texas. On April 2, 2014, again at Fort Hood, a soldier killed three soldiers and wounded 16 before killing himself.

April 2010: The BP oil disaster resulted in the largest marine oil spill in history. Eleven men working on the platform were killed, and the 205.8 million gallons of crude oil caused extensive damage to marine and wildlife habitats as well as to the Gulf's fishing and tourism industries.

January 2011: A college dropout killed six people and wounded 14 in Tucson, Arizona. Among the injured was Congresswoman Gabrielle Giffords.

March 2011: A powerful earthquake rocked Japan, followed by a tsunami resulting in massive devastation and thousands of deaths. At the time, Japan's economy was challenged by debt, economic stagnation, and depopulation.

July 2012: At the midnight premiere of *The Dark Knight Rises* in Aurora, Colorado, a 22-year-old opened fire, killing 12 and wounding 58.

**FIGURE 1.1 The year 1995—What a difference 20 years makes**

**In the year 1995**

- A postage stamp cost $0.32.
- A gallon of gas cost $1.35.
- A new car cost $12,800.
- The federal government spending was $1519.13 billion.
- The median household income was $34,076.
- Unemployment was 5.6%.
- President Bill Clinton invoked emergency powers to extend a $20 billion loan to help Mexico avert a financial crisis.
- Congress was controlled by Republicans for the first time in 20 years.
- An earthquake in Japan killed 6,434 people while an earthquake in Russia killed over 2,000.
- In February, the Dow Jones closed at 4,033, a new record. In November, the Dow closed at 5,023.
- The first search engine service, Yahoo!, was founded.
- Microsoft released Windows 95.
- 168 people were killed in the Oklahoma City bombing.
- Prodigy Internet service offered access to the World Wide Web.
- eBay was founded.
- In November, the federal government shut down because of a budget standoff between Democrats and Republicans.
- Pope John Paul II visited the United States in a whirlwind tour.
- Fighting resumed in Bosnia and Croatia.
- The Million Man March drew millions of black men to Washington.
- Women held 9.6% of Fortune 500 board seats.
- Forrest Gump won the Best Picture Award.
- O. J. Simpson was found not guilty of murder charges.
- December 16–January 6 (1996): the federal government had another shutdown as budget disagreements continued.



September 2012: In Minnesota, an employee went on a shooting rampage after losing his job, killing five co-workers and then himself.

December 2012: In Newtown Connecticut, a 21-year-old shot and killed his mother at their home, then drove her car to Sandy Hook Elementary where he killed 20 six- and seven-year-old students and six adults before killing himself.

April 2013: Bombs near the finish line of the Boston Marathon killed three and injured 264 others.[3]

June 2013: Nineteen Arizona firefighters lost their lives fighting a wildfire northwest of Phoenix.

March 8, 2014: Malaysia Airlines Flight 370 disappeared with 239 souls on board.[4]

March 2014: A catastrophic mudslide destroyed homes and blocked a mile-long stretch of highway in Oso, Washington, killing more than 40.[5]

As you watched the newscasts during the past several years, you had a hard time seeing the "good news" but 10 years ago (February 2004), Mark Zuckerberg created Facebook in his Harvard dorm room. In February 2014, Facebook shares rose to record levels and to celebrate their 10th anniversary, users were able to create videos from their top posts. A month later, Twitter celebrated its eighth birthday by sending its users back to their first tweets #Twitterisborn. The stock markets continue to break new barriers.

Yet, consumer confidence is low. Oil and food prices continue to rise. The unemployment rate in Detroit is 15.1 percent and the city has billions of dollars in long-term obligations that may never be paid.[6] Data breaches (hacking) in companies such as Target have caused distrust among shoppers.[7] Recalls of vehicles by General Motors, Nissan, and Toyota have led to congressional hearings.[8] As of March 2014, the unemployment rate in the United States has gone down almost one percentage point over the past year but there are still over 10.5 million workers unemployed and the job market remains weak.[9]

For many employees, these past 10 years have been a time of employers imposing work-rule concessions, wage freezes,[10] or pay cuts, and asking them to pay for a larger percentage of their healthcare costs—if they even had healthcare insurance.[11] The governors of several states have pushed what some described as a "union-busting strategy" (i.e., right-to-work laws) by trying to make it illegal to require an employee to join a union or remain a member of the union.[12] Along with that, many employees report significant increases in job responsibilities over the past three years.[13]

The news is filled with stories of middle-aged employees who expected to be in their peak earning years but now face the stark reality of looking for work, no doubt in a service industry that pays substantially less than what they made at their previous employment. Manufacturing jobs are no longer the gateway for high-school graduates to enter the middle class,[14] and shifts in shopping trends are causing companies to close their brick-and-mortar stores while trying to increase online sales.[15] A recent Manpower survey reported that 83 percent of employees are actively seeking new job opportunities in 2014.[16] A word of caution: It is easier to find a new job when you already have one.

The search for jobs has become very competitive. Many downsized employees have reverted to temporary work. In March 2014, about 2.8 million workers were currently in temporary or contract positions.[17] Susan Houseman, senior economist at Upjohn Institute for Employment Research, says this current pattern of hiring temporary workers does not fit the historical norm. "It's typical for temporary hiring to rise initially as the economy recovers, before businesses are ready to commit to hiring full-time employees. Right now we're seeing something interesting. We've seen it surpass its previous highs, so it looks like there could be a structural shift going on, too. There's a reason to believe we might see some increase in the use of temporary help in general."[18]

There is little doubt that major changes will continue to take place in our society during the coming years, and continuing change will challenge every person in every organization.

**2 Explain the demands and rewards of being a supervisor.**

**Supervisors**
First-level managers in charge of entry-level and other departmental employees

If managers and their organizations are to survive, managers at all levels will be at the forefront of planning and coping with trends, factors, and problems requiring attention and more effective management. This book focuses primarily on the first tier of management, which is generally called the supervisory level, or supervisory management. **Supervisors** are first-level managers who are in charge of entry-level and other departmental employees. In *The Effective Executive*, the management authority Peter F. Drucker defined an executive as "any member of the organization who makes decisions that materially affect the capacity of the organization to perform and obtain results."[19] Figure 1.2 is a tribute to Drucker and presents an overview of his thoughts and ideas.

**FIGURE 1.2 A tribute to Peter F. Drucker, father of modern management**

Peter Drucker was a writer, teacher, and consultant specializing in strategy and policy for businesses and not-for-profit organizations. He wrote for most of the contemporary business publications and authored books that set the foundation for this and other texts.

Drucker was born in 1909 in Vienna and was educated there and in England. After working as an economist for an international bank, Drucker came to the United States in 1937. He began his teaching career at Bennington College, taught for more than 20 years at the Graduate Business School of New York University, and was Clarke Professor of Social Studies at Claremont Graduate University. Its Graduate Management School was named after him in 1984. To say that he revolutionized business by systematizing the study of management would be an understatement.

*USA Today* perhaps said it best: "Peter Drucker, who died Friday, 11 days short of his 96th birthday, was his own best advertisement for the concept of the knowledge worker, which he identified more than 40 years ago; those who work with their minds, and thus own their means of production."[1] In 1997, Drucker was featured on the cover of *Forbes magazine* under the headline "Still the Youngest Mind," and *BusinessWeek* called him "the most enduring management thinker of our time." In 2002, President George W. Bush honored him with the Presidential Medal of Freedom.

In the early 1940s, General Motors invited Drucker to study its inner workings. That experience led to his 1946 book *Concept of the Corporation*. He went on to write more than 30 books. His books and thoughts are available at http://www.peter-drucker.com/. A few of Drucker's comments follow:

- A manager is responsible for the application and performance of knowledge.
- Company cultures are like country cultures. Never try to change one. Try, instead, to work with what you've got.
- Efficiency is doing things right; effectiveness is doing the right things.
- In a period of upheaval, such as the one we are living in, change is the norm.
- Making good decisions is a crucial skill at every level.
- The most important thing in communication is hearing what isn't being said.
- The most efficient way to produce anything is to bring together under one management as many as possible of the activities needed to turn out the product.
- Most of what we call management consists of making it difficult for people to get their work done.
- There are an enormous number of managers who have retired on the job.
- Time is the scarcest resource, and unless it is managed, nothing else can be managed.
- We now accept the fact that learning is a lifelong process of keeping abreast of change. The most pressing task is to teach people how to learn.

*Sources:* Bruce Rosenstein, "Visionary Writer Mined the Mine," *USA Today* (November 11, 2005), p. B3. Also see William Cohen, "A Class with Drucker—The Lost Lessons of the World's Greatest Management Teacher," AMACOM, 2007; http://www.peter-drucker.com; http://www.leadertoleader.org. It is hard to select from among Drucker's books, but I recommend the following: *The Practice of Management* (New York: Harper Collins Publishing, 1954); *The Effective Executive* (New York: Harper & Row, 1964, 1986); *Management Challenges for the 21st Century* (New York: Harper Collins, 1999); *The Daily Drucker: 366 Days of Insight and Motivation for Getting the Right Things Done* (New York: Harper Collins, 2004).

© Bettmann/Corbis

Peter Drucker, considered the father of modern management, contributed many important ideas about management theory and practices that are still relevant today

Most managers and supervisors, whether they are in factories, nursing care units, business offices, the hospitality industry, retail stores, or government agencies, realize that authoritarian direction and close control usually do not bring about the desired results. Managers everywhere will continue to expect supervisors to obtain better performance from their human resources and to do so in a constantly changing environment.

In many organizations, much of the supervisory work is performed by individuals who may not officially or legally be considered part of management. Although these individuals perform many of the supervisory functions discussed in this book, they usually have limited authority and are typically **working supervisors**. Other designations for these individuals include foreman/forewoman, group/team leader, lead person, coach, or facilitator. For brevity, we use the term *supervisor* to identify all first-level individuals who carry out supervisory functions. The concepts and principles discussed in this text generally apply to such individuals, whom we consider to be managers, even though officially or legally they are not part of the recognized management structure.

**Working supervisors**
First-level individuals who perform supervisory functions but who may not be legally or officially be part of management

Most people obtain their first management experience in supervisory management positions. Supervisory work has become more complex, sophisticated, and demanding, and it requires professional and interpersonal skills.[20]

Although the systematic study of management has largely been a twentieth-century phenomenon—thanks, in part, to Drucker's contributions—some knowledge of the past is helpful when looking to the future. Furthermore, a brief overview of the major schools, or approaches, to management theories and practices can provide some foundation and perspective for the supervisory concepts and practices presented in this book.

This book is intended for both practicing and potential supervisors, especially students who see the field of management as one of their career choices. At the end of this chapter is a "Supervisory Tips" section that helps those who are seeking supervisory or management positions to identify and discuss some important factors when job hunting. This section includes a number of career tips that are essential for those aspiring to be supervisors. They probably are vital to almost any type of career planning, regardless of one's choice of position or organization.

**3 Describe the contributions of four schools of management thought.**

## Schools of Management Thought

Management practices can be traced throughout history. The Great Wall of China, the Pyramids of Egypt, the Roman Coliseum, the Eiffel Tower, and the Statue of Liberty all resulted from the application of management principles. Many early schools of thought still influence the way people approach the supervisory task. Although there is no universally accepted theory of management, a common thread runs through the various theories that have been proposed over the years. Each theory attempts to answer the question, "What is the best way to manage the task at hand?" While there is little agreement on the number and nomenclature of the various management theories, four approaches deserve special mention: (1) the scientific management approach, (2) the functional approach, (3) the human relations/behavioral approach, and (4) the quantitative/systems approaches.[21]

## THE SCIENTIFIC MANAGEMENT APPROACH

One of the first approaches to the study of management in the twentieth century was the **scientific management approach**, which focused on determining the most efficient ways to increase output and productivity. Frederick Winslow Taylor, the father of scientific management, believed that managers should plan what, when, where, and how employees should produce the product. He felt a manager's job was to perform mental tasks, such as determining the "one best way" to do a job. The employees' jobs, then, would be to perform the physical tasks of their jobs. To this end, Taylor developed certain principles to increase productivity.

**Scientific management approach**
School of management thought that focuses on determining the most efficient ways to increase output and productivity

Taylor believed that many workers did not put forth their best effort and that, as a result, production often suffered. While observing workers in a steel plant, Taylor was shocked at the lack of systematic procedures, output restrictions among groups of workers, and the fact that ill-equipped and poorly trained workers typically were left on their own to determine how to do their jobs. Taylor believed that engineering principles could be applied to make people perform somewhat like machines—efficiently, mindlessly, and repetitively. By eliminating choice, operations could be standardized. In brief, Taylor's principles of scientific management include the following:

1. Analyze the tasks associated with each job. Use the principles of science to find the one best way to perform the work.
2. Recruit the employee best suited to perform the job; that is, choose the person who has the skills, aptitude, and other attributes to do the job.
3. Instruct the worker in the one best way to perform the job.
4. Reward the accomplishment of the worker. Taylor believed that workers were economically motivated and would, therefore, do the job the way they were instructed if rewarded with money.
5. Cooperate with workers to ensure that the job matches plans and principles.
6. Ensure an equal division of work and responsibility between managers and workers.

Similarly, other leaders of the early twentieth-century scientific management movement focused on determining ways to improve productivity through the systematic study and application of engineering principles. Some of you have seen the classic version or the 2003 version of the movie *Cheaper by the Dozen*, an adaptation of the book of the same name about how the Gilbreths managed their home. Frank and Lillian Gilbreth pioneered the use of time and motion studies of job operations, through which efficient ways to perform a job could be determined and time standards could be developed. These standards would then be used to improve productivity and to compensate employees appropriately.[22]

## THE FUNCTIONAL APPROACH

In the early 1900s, Henri Fayol, a French industrialist, identified 14 principles of management that he believed could be applied universally. Some writers have referred to this concept as the universality of management, which suggests that basic functions, principles, and their applications in management are similar, regardless of an organization's nature. In general, Fayol believed that a manager's authority should equal that manager's responsibility, and that the direction and flow of authority through an organization should be unified.

**Functional approach**
School of management thought that asserts that all managers perform various functions in doing their jobs, such as planning, organizing, staffing, leading, and controlling

Fayol introduced the **functional approach** to the study of management. This approach defined the manager's role and proposed that managers do their jobs by performing various functions. Fayol identified five functions as critical to managerial effectiveness:

1. Planning: Setting down a course of action
2. Organizing: Designing a structure, with tasks and authority clearly defined
3. Commanding: Directing subordinates' actions
4. Coordinating: Pulling organizational elements toward common objectives
5. Controlling: Ensuring that plans are carried out

Other writers built on these ideas. This textbook is organized around the more current version of the functional approach to the study of management: planning, organizing, staffing, leading, and controlling.

## THE HUMAN RELATIONS/BEHAVIORAL APPROACH

The contributions of Taylor and others gave rise to the notions that (1) if managers used the principles of scientific management, worker efficiency would increase and productivity increases would follow, and (2) if managers strove to improve working conditions, productivity would increase. The studies at the Hawthorne, Illinois, plant of Western Electric provided some of the most interesting and controversial results in the study of management.

Elton Mayo and Fritz Roethlisberger, leaders of a Harvard research team, conducted a series of illumination experiments from 1924 to 1936 at Western Electric. They hypothesized that if lighting improved, then productivity would increase. Contrary to expectations, productivity rose in both the control group (no change in working conditions) and the experimental group (working conditions varied). Numerous variations in working conditions were introduced, and no matter what change was introduced, productivity continued to rise until it stabilized at a relatively high level.

**Hawthorne effect**
The fact that personalized interest shown in people may cause them to behave differently

The researchers concluded that the workers performed differently than they normally did because the researchers were observing them. This reaction is known as the **Hawthorne effect**. Other phases of the Hawthorne studies emphasized the attitudes and behaviors of workers in small, informal groups and how those aspects can significantly influence performance and productivity in positive or negative directions.

**Human relations movement / behavioral science approach**
Approach to management that focuses on the behavior of people in the work environment

The experiments at the Hawthorne plant gave rise to what was known as the **human relations movement** and later as the **behavioral science approach**. This approach focuses on the behavior of people in organizations. Contributions from psychologists, sociologists, and other behavioral disciplines have provided numerous insights into individual and group behavior in work settings and the impact of supervisory practices and procedures on employee motivation and work performance. Chapter 7, which discusses employee motivation in relation to supervisory approaches, mentions various social and behavioral scientists and their contributions to understanding and managing human behavior in organizations.

## THE QUANTITATIVE/SYSTEMS APPROACHES

**Quantitative/systems approaches**
Field of management study that uses mathematical modeling as a foundation

While somewhat beyond the scope of this text, **quantitative/systems approaches** to management rely heavily on mathematical modeling. Through such models, which attempt to quantitatively describe the interrelationships of variables through data, data can be manipulated and outcomes predicted. Quantitative approaches are often closely connected with systems approaches, in which mathematical models are developed as a series or collection of interrelated variables or parts that can be analyzed and used in decision making.[23]

Quantitative/systems approaches are frequently found in large organizations where sales, costs, and production data are analyzed using computer technology. Mathematical modeling typically is used to build "what-if" situations (e.g., what would be the effect on sales if we reduce our employment level by 10 percent? 20 percent?). A number of planning concepts introduced in Chapter 3 rely on these types of approaches.

## Factors and Trends Affecting the Role of the Supervisor

**4 Identify and discuss the major demographic and societal trends that will affect supervisors.**

In the foreseeable future, supervisors will have to understand and address many complex environmental factors and trends. Therefore, let us examine some major demographic and societal factors and trends that are likely to affect the supervisory management position. Figure 1.3 illustrates many of the challenges a supervisor faces. Although every supervisor is responsible for managing numerous resources, unquestionably the most important, overriding aspect of supervision

**FIGURE 1.3 Effective supervisors must be adaptable and be able to maintain their perspective in the face of rapidly changing conditions**

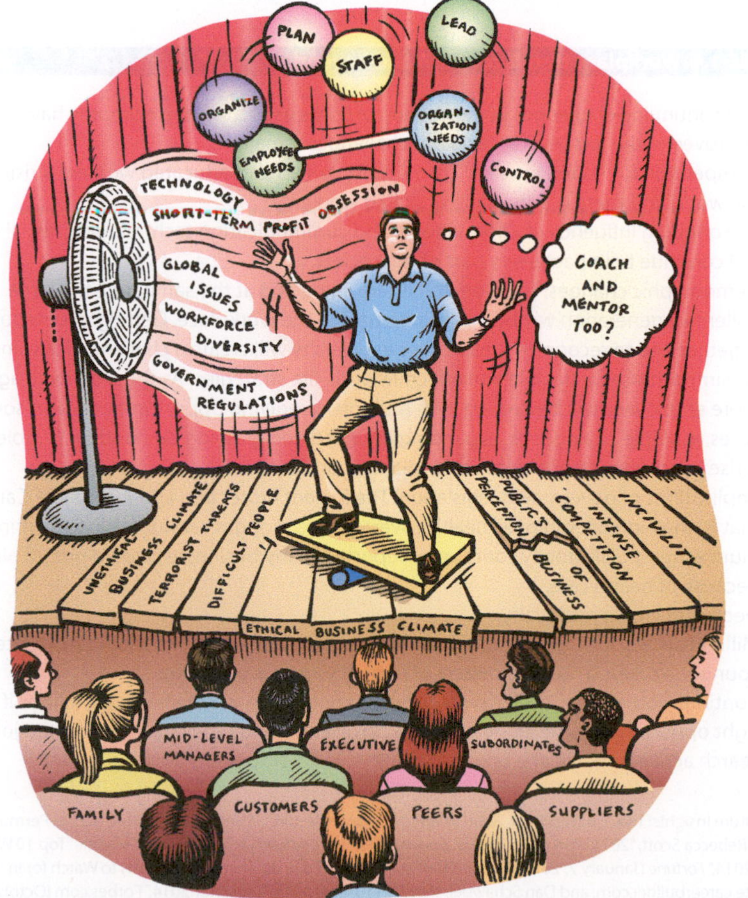

is the management of people. Therefore, the nature of the workforce should be of vital concern to the supervisor who plans for the future. Finding qualified employees and **onboarding** new hires (meaning engaging them in a continuous process of assimilation and growth within the organization) have always been among the most important supervisory responsibilities.[24] There are numerous reports and studies projecting trends that may impact an organization's and supervisor's ability to manage in the coming years (see Figure 1.4). A word of caution: These are projections, the accuracy of which can be likened to forecasting the weather.

**Onboarding**
A continuous process of assimilation and growth within the organization for new hires

The traditional challenges of attracting and retaining the most qualified employees may be superseded by the more acute challenge of leading and motivating an increasingly changing workforce. The most significant characteristic of this changing workforce will be its **diversity**. Work groups will be composed of employees with different cultural, ethnic, gender, age, educational level, racial, and lifestyle characteristics. The supervisor will need to get people from many different cultures to work together.

**Diversity**
The cultural, ethnic, gender, age, educational level, racial, and lifestyle differences of employees

## POPULATION AND WORKFORCE GROWTH

Despite the United States' rather low birthrate in recent decades, both the population and the workforce will continue to grow.

Immigration has accounted for, and will continue to account for, a considerable share of the nation's population and workforce growth. Some employment

**FIGURE 1.4 Workplace trends for 2014 and beyond**

1. The continuing challenges in the economy: Some aspects of the economy have improved in the last several years but challenges remain.
2. Competition for skilled workers: The need for skilled and educated workers is rising in the world and there is a shortage of skilled workers.
3. The ongoing influence of informational and communication technologies: Social media will continue to impact every part of the society.
4. Demographic changes: The work forces are aging and at the same time the large millennial generation will be making its mark in the workplace. Getting people to work together and to recognize the increase in diversity will create a challenge for some.
5. The importance for flexible and effective work–life strategies: As the workforce ages, more employees will be dealing with multiple caregiving opportunities and in some cases, multiple paying jobs, expanding the need and growing demand for flexible work.
6. A rise in economic uncertainty and volatile markets.
7. Implications of government legislation: The Patient Protection and Affordable Care Act, that is, the high of employee health coverage; the thoughts about raising the minimum wage; a CNNMoney.com survey reported many businesses would put off hiring because of health care.
8. Decline in employee loyalty.
9. Millennials account for 36% of the workforce. New opportunities should be created for younger workers as large numbers of baby boomers are retiring.
10. Continual job-search: 73% of workers would not have a problem changing jobs if the right opportunity came along and 48% of millennials say they have conducted job search activities while at work.

*Sources:* "Future Insights: The Top Trends for 2014," *SHRM*; "Workplace Vision." *SRHM Issues* 1 (2014); Rachel Permuth, Kevin Rettle, and Rebecca Scott, "2014 Workplace Trends." *Sodexo Quality of Life Service* (2014); Robin Madell, "Top 10 Workplace Trends for 2014," *Fortune* (January 7, 2014); Deanna Hartley, "U.S. Job Forecast and Hiring Trends to Watch for in 2014," http://thehiringsite.careerbuilder.com; and Dan Schawbel, "The Top 10 Workplace Trends for 2014," Forbes.com (October 24, 2013).

analysts advocate granting an increased number of immigration visas to meet the growing demand for information technology (IT) workers, professionals, and other highly skilled workers.[25] The growth in the number of new immigrants (refugees, legal or illegal) may expand certain interracial and intercultural problems that supervisors face in managing diverse workforces. As of May 2014, it is reported that there are 11.5 million illegal immigrants in the United States.[26] The debate about illegal immigrants will continue. Some would argue that the illegal immigrants are doing jobs that no one else wants to do.

Although managing a diverse workforce presents some difficulties, it also presents numerous opportunities for supervisors to build on the strengths of individuals and groups. In the following sections, we intend not only to create an awareness of the expected differences but also to "raise consciousness." Supervisors must understand the rights of both their employees and their employers, regardless of workforce differences. Supervisors must recognize the value of a diverse workforce and their own need to become more adaptable to change. Perhaps more than ever, supervisors will have to be scrupulously fair in supervising diverse groups of employees through nondiscriminatory and progressive actions.

## CHANGING AGE PATTERNS

Both the population and the labor force are getting older. The percentage of older Americans (55 and older) in the workforce is increasing. The number of women over age 60 in the workforce is rising dramatically. By 2016, the number of workers between 16 and 24 will decline and that of "prime-age" workers between 25 and 54 is expected to increase slightly.[27] However, the number of workers over age 60 will increase by 50 percent from 2000,[28] and by 2022, over 25 percent of the workforce is projected to be age 55 and over.[29]

The growth in the number of people in these mature age categories will provide an ample supply of experienced individuals who can be promoted to supervisory and other management positions. Yet it is interesting that almost half of these workers over age 55 are not with the same employer that they were with when they were 40. A recent study reported that the median tenure for employees staying in the same job was 4.6 years.[30] Apparently, job mobility is not exclusive to any one age group. At the same time, because there are so many older workers, there may be a glut of younger employees waiting for job opportunities. This possible mismatch in many firms between the number of employees desiring advancement and the number of opportunities available may lead to dissatisfaction, causing younger workers to leave and seek positions elsewhere. However, many factors will determine when the "boomers" retire and, if some projections are accurate, there will be many opportunities for those seeking supervisory positions.

Various worker categories have been proposed. Ann Clurman and J. Walker Smith, for example, define the population in three major categories: (1) "generation Xers," those born between 1964 and 1981; (2) "boomers," those born between 1946 and 1963; and (3) "matures," those born before 1945. Members of generation X will be replacing matures, but generation Xers have fundamentally different ideas about work, loyalty, and commitment than matures. In general, generation Xers have far less concern about staying with companies for long periods. They tend to want more personal and leisure time, and they harbor considerable skepticism about management's values and management's concerns for employees.[31] The authors fall into two of these categories—the "matures" and the Gen Xers. Dr. Leonard fits with the "beyond mature" group and is often described by his grandchildren as being "nostalgic"—one of those who is longing for the "good old days," wanting to be prepared for the unexpected, and resisting the frivolous. He has personally found that health, safety, and security are increasingly important to those in his group. We strongly urge you not to judge a book by its cover but to look at each individual as an individual and to view him or her from the inside out.

What about those born since 1982? Neil Howe and William Strauss, authors of the book *Millennials Rising*, state that these young people prefer group activities and want clear rules set for them—a combination that is distinctly different from their mostly boomer parents. Howe and Strauss believe that this group of new entrants to the workforce, called by some "Gen Y" or "millennials," are more spiritual and less individualistic than their parents.[32]

Some have described this group as having a short attention span—"flippers" on the remote control. Supervisors should be aware of a noticeable cultural phenomenon: Every generation of young people goes through a period in which it questions and even rejects the beliefs and values of its parent generation. There is little question that the success of supervisors will depend to a considerable extent on their abilities to tap into the interests and motivations of all members of the workforce.

## WOMEN IN THE WORKFORCE AND RELATED ISSUES

Perhaps the most dramatic change in the last several decades has been the increase in both the number and percentage of women in the U.S. workforce. Currently, some 60 percent of adult women are employed, and women constitute almost half the U.S. labor force. At the same time, nearly 60 percent of those unemployed in the United States are women and most of them have children under the age of 18. Furthermore, in 2014, the unemployment rate for all women was 6.6 percent but jumped to 12.8 percent for those women under the age of 25.[33] In recent years, women have assumed many jobs formerly dominated by men. Regardless of perceptions that women are stealing jobs formerly held by men, the reality is that women hold very few of the top management positions.[34]

While the Equal Pay Act was designed to narrow the gap between the pay rates of males and females, studies show that women's earnings on average are substantially less than those of men. Some account for the disparity by pointing out that fewer women than men major in engineering, business, and other fields that traditionally lead to higher paying jobs.[35] The movement of women into the workforce has affected employers with respect to women's roles as both employees and mothers.

A recent Pew Research study found the following: 13.7 million U.S. households with children under 18 now include mothers who are the main breadwinners; of those, 37 percent are married, while 63 percent are single. The income gap between the groups is large: $80,000 in median family income for married couples versus $23,000 for single mothers. Both groups have breadwinner moms.[36] Substantially higher percentages of African American and Hispanic families are headed by women, and many of them are single working mothers.[37]

Not surprisingly, many employees bring their family problems to work. Supervisors must understand that their employees' work performance may be impeded by conflicts between job and family obligations. To attract and retain qualified employees, more employers need to provide quality childcare facilities or help employees make suitable childcare arrangements. Employees will continue to experiment with different types of workdays and workweeks, such as **flextime**, in which employees choose their work schedules within certain limits; **job sharing**, in which two or more employees share a job; **telecommuting**, in which the employee works at home and is linked to the office by computer and modem; and 4-day, 10-hour-a-day workweeks.

**Flextime**
Policy that allows employees to choose their work hours within stated limits

**Job sharing**
Policy that allows two or more employees to perform a job normally done by one full-time employee

**Telecommuting**
Receiving work from and sending work to the office from home via a computer and modem

A recent study indicates that working mothers go to great lengths to keep family matters out of the workplace. Instead it is more likely that work-related issues will intrude on their home lives. A demanding job leaves almost half of parents too tired to do things with their children. Sixty percent of working mothers say they have to put work ahead of family at least some of the time and feel less successful in their relationships with spouses, children, and friends. Efforts to help employees balance the responsibilities of home and job will require better supervisory coordination, planning skills, and training to help managers handle work–life issues.[38]

Another major challenge for supervisors will be to ensure that sexual harassment does not occur in the work environment. Sexual harassment has been perpetrated against both men and women, but more attention has focused on the latter. Many court decisions have reiterated the implications for supervisors, who are obligated to take action to prevent harassment and to take steps to remedy reported incidents of harassment. The topics of sexual harassment and other discriminatory actions are explored in greater detail in Chapter 4.

## MINORITIES IN THE WORKFORCE

To what extent racial minorities will enter the workforce is a guess at best. One issue is very real. Many people believe that illegal immigrants and businesses that hire them are lawbreakers. The current debate about what to do with the millions of illegal and undocumented workers who have entered the labor force in recent years is not expected to be resolved quickly. Should they be identified, rounded up, prosecuted, and deported? Or should they be given a chance to keep their jobs and apply for legal status? One thing we do know for certain is that often they are working in jobs that many Americans would consider too difficult or too low paying to accept.

Supervisors know that many of their employees are natives of different countries and that English is most likely not their primary language. For example, the United States has the world's fifth largest Spanish-speaking population. Many recent immigrants are not fluent in English. The challenge for supervisors will be to learn cultural, racial, and language differences and to develop strategies for promoting cooperation among racially and ethnically diverse groups. English is the dominant language of technology, although many different languages and dialects are spoken daily in today's workplace. Most native English-speaking U.S. citizens are not proficient in another language because they haven't had to be—the rest of the world is learning English.[39]

## BARRIERS FOR WOMEN AND MINORITIES

Progress in upgrading the status of women and minorities has been mixed. Some firms still seem to relegate women and minorities to lower-skilled and lower-paying jobs and have not fully realized the contributions many have to offer. Thus, while some forward strides have been made, women and minorities remain concentrated in lower-level jobs. There appears to be an invisible

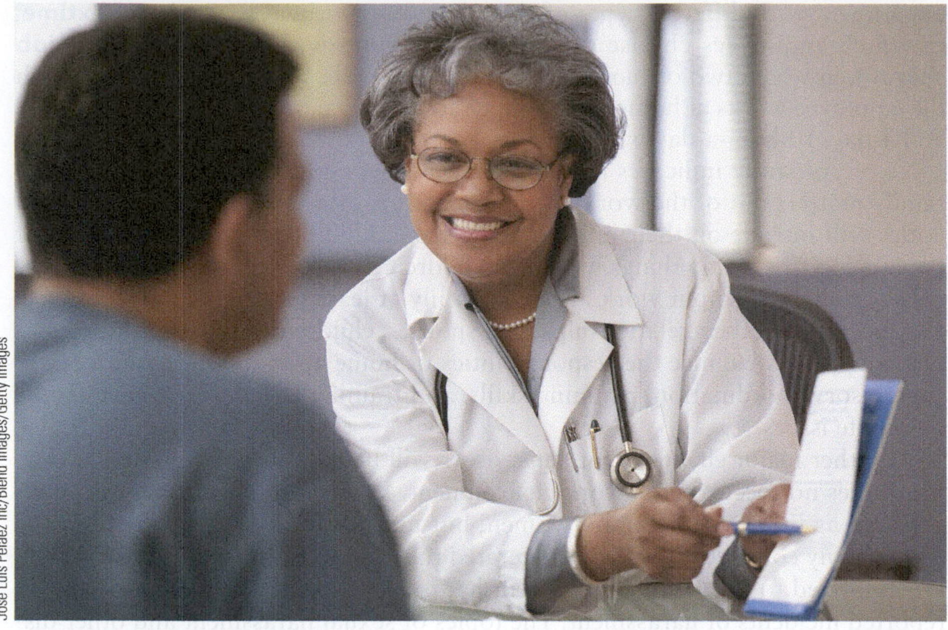

*Although glass ceilings still exist in many industries, more and more women and minorities are moving into positions of authority and leadership*

Jose Luis Pelaez Inc/Blend Images/Getty Images

**Glass ceiling**
Invisible barrier that limits the advancement of women and minorities

**Glass walls**
Invisible barriers that compartmentalize women and minorities into certain occupational classes

barrier—a "**glass ceiling**"—that limits advancement. To compound the problem, many organizations have placed women and minority employees in certain specialized occupations, such as human resources and accounting. These **glass walls** that segment employees can deny them the opportunity to develop the variety of skills needed to advance.[40]

A recent study reported what most males have long suspected: that women employ a different leadership style than men and their leadership style might actually be more effective than men's. The study states that women executives "demonstrate more empathy, better listening skills, and a more inclusive style of leadership. And successful female leaders tend to be more assertive, more persuasive, and more willing to take risks than their male counterparts."[41] But if women are actually better at leadership, why are so few of them in key executive positions? Is it that women and minorities are unwilling to fight to shatter the glass ceiling?[42] Or is it that the "old boys' network" still controls the path to the top? You can draw your own conclusions.

Minority and women employees will continue to need an effective combination of educational and job-related experiences to provide them with opportunities to develop their talents. Organizations will be expected to design programs to attract and develop women and minority employees and to provide these employees with the full range of opportunities open to everyone else.

## EDUCATIONAL PREPARATION

Accompanying the changes in the racial and ethnic composition of the workforce are educational-preparation factors that also will challenge supervisors in the future. The ability to read and use documents is essential in today's global economy. Yet one-third of the U.S. population has below-basic or basic document literacy, causing communication problems.[43]

**Underemployment**
Situations in which people are in jobs that do not use their SKAs

The competition for jobs and the increase in low-level service-industry jobs will probably create underemployment. **Underemployment** occurs when employees bring a certain amount of skills, knowledge, and abilities (**SKAs**) to the workplace and find that their jobs lack meaning and/or the opportunities to fully use their SKAs. A challenge for many supervisors will be to enhance workplace environments to satisfy the underemployed. The current abundance of college graduates presents corporate recruiters with a distinct challenge to select the best candidates available.

**SKAs**
A person's skills, knowledge, and abilities

We must keep in mind the other side of the picture: namely, that millions of workers in the workforce will not have completed a secondary school education. Of those who complete high school, many will receive an inferior education because their schools do not offer the variety or quality of classes that other schools offer. In addition, many individuals entering the workforce will have had considerable formal education, but this education will not have prepared them with the specific skills that apply directly to the job market.

An organization seeking to obtain a **competitive advantage** can do so by hiring qualified and adaptable people, training those people thoroughly, and then making appropriate use of those people's skills. Unfortunately, many job applicants lack proper workplace attitudes and skills. To this end, companies will be required to spend more time and effort training employees, particularly those who are unprepared and unskilled and those who need to develop their latent talents if they are to be successful and motivated to work. Supervisors will be required to allocate more time for on-the-job employee training and to ensure that employees are encouraged to capitalize on all opportunities for continuing education.

**Competitive advantage**
The ability to outperform competitors by increasing efficiency, quality, creativity, and responsiveness to customers and effectively using employee talents

## OCCUPATIONAL AND INDUSTRY TRENDS

Imagine reading this newspaper headline as you prepare to finish your college work and embark on a new career search: "Employment expectations down substantially in manufacturing, up in service sector. New-hire compensation growth slows in both manufacturing and service sectors." Yet, in reality, one company reported outsourcing jobs because they could not find people with the technical abilities to do the needed jobs. A 2014 survey reported that a high percentage of job seekers are ill-prepared in basic skills, including computer skills and math skills.[44]

We have found that students with technical backgrounds who can manage and supervise products, relationships, and people will find themselves of particular value to their organizations. At the same time, low-paying jobs will be on the rise. Millions of new service workers, such as cashiers at campus bookstores, servers and washers at local restaurants, and home healthcare workers, will be needed. Unfortunately, many of these service workers will find themselves in low-paying jobs.

Déjà vu—a sense that you have previously seen, heard, or experienced something that is, in fact, new to you—is presented in the next few paragraphs. The Bureau of Labor Statistics (BLS) projects that the labor force will grow more slowly because of economic conditions and that employment growth will be concentrated in the service sector. They estimate that service-providing industries will generate almost all of the employment gain from 2011 through 2016. It should not be a surprise, but manufacturing jobs are expected to decline substantially.[45] When was the last time you heard anyone encourage job seekers to explore an apprentice program, such as carpentry, plumbing, or electrical? These are well-paying skilled jobs, but fewer and fewer people want to be "Bob the Builder."

Not surprisingly, many Bobs have gone to vocational schools or community colleges to get a certification in repairing air-conditioning and heating systems, or to obtain other service skills.

During the past decade, many of the nation's largest industrial corporations have eliminated thousands of jobs.[46] More and more companies are outsourcing certain functions or requiring major departments to trim their budgets. Departments or services such as call centers, data processing, human resources, public relations, and accounting are especially vulnerable to outsourcing or downsizing. During the past few years, major U.S. corporations have added more jobs offshore. Even McDonald's growth has been driven by increased sales in Asia. By 2015, it is expected that McDonald's will have more than 2,000 restaurants in China. Yum Brands, Inc., currently has over 4,400 restaurants in China.[47] As we look around the classroom, not surprisingly, many of our students are wearing the Nike "swoosh." A recent *Wall Street Journal* article detailed that the Nike world has about one million workers in factories worldwide. Would it surprise you that none of these factories are in the United States?[48]

While the media and popular press tend to focus on large-scale businesses, small and midsize firms are expected to create most of the job growth in the coming decade. Many small businesses and not-for-profit organizations can provide unique opportunities for new college graduates. Many supervisors have found that they can gain broader and more diverse experiences in these organizations than in large companies where they may be assigned to specialized areas.

## CHANGING TECHNOLOGY AND BUSINESS CONDITIONS

In 2010, *Time* magazine recognized Mark Zuckerberg, CEO of Facebook, as its Man of the Year. "What does it take to be on top? The ability to create opportunities out of turmoil!"[49]

In 2004, Zuckerberg created a Web site, which he called "The Facebook." In May 2012, Facebook went public, offering 421 million shares at a price to investors of $38. Within the first few months, the share price dropped to $19. Most investors had lost 50 percent of their investment. Go online and find the price of one share of Facebook stock today.[50] Ask your instructor or your parents what social network they used when they were your age. We suspect that Facebook, Twitter, Instagram, Snapchat, Tumblr, Flickr, and LinkedIn were not in their vocabulary. The meteoric rise of Facebook, Twitter, and other social networking sites has altered the traditional mode of face-to-face communication and the way things are done.

A major problem that is likely to worsen is that of too much information (TMI).[51] With the growth of communication capabilities, including e-mail, text messaging, voice mail, telephone, and social media, supervisors are being inundated with hundreds of messages sent and received every day. Many individuals have difficulty with the extra work generated by these messages, many of which simply waste time. However, according to a recent survey, 46 percent of workers claim social media tools have increased their productivity.[52] The ability to manage information properly is another of the many demanding responsibilities of supervisors, and will continue to be so in the future.

Consider the events that have occurred since the turn of the century: a volatile stock market; 9/11; wars in Iraq and Afghanistan; Russia's annexation of Crimea; the rise of gasoline prices to record highs; cheap and easy credit creating a housing and financial institution crisis; the decline of the dollar against world currencies; the need of banks and other financial institutions for bailouts; airline mergers and fare increases; soaring food prices; auto company production cuts and plant shutdowns; natural calamities; terrorism on college campuses; and a rise in workplace violence, just to name a few. Collectively, these events, along with technological advances, changing markets, and other competitive influences, have forced businesses to adjust their way of doing business. Most consumers have felt the pain in their wallets as organizations have passed higher energy and raw material costs on to consumers in the form of higher prices for goods and services.

Because it is difficult to forecast specifically when and how technological change will impact a supervisor's position, every supervisor will have to be broadly educated. Supervisors will have to prepare themselves and their employees, both technologically and psychologically, for changes. Supervisors who keep up to date with changes unquestionably will be more valuable to their organizations.

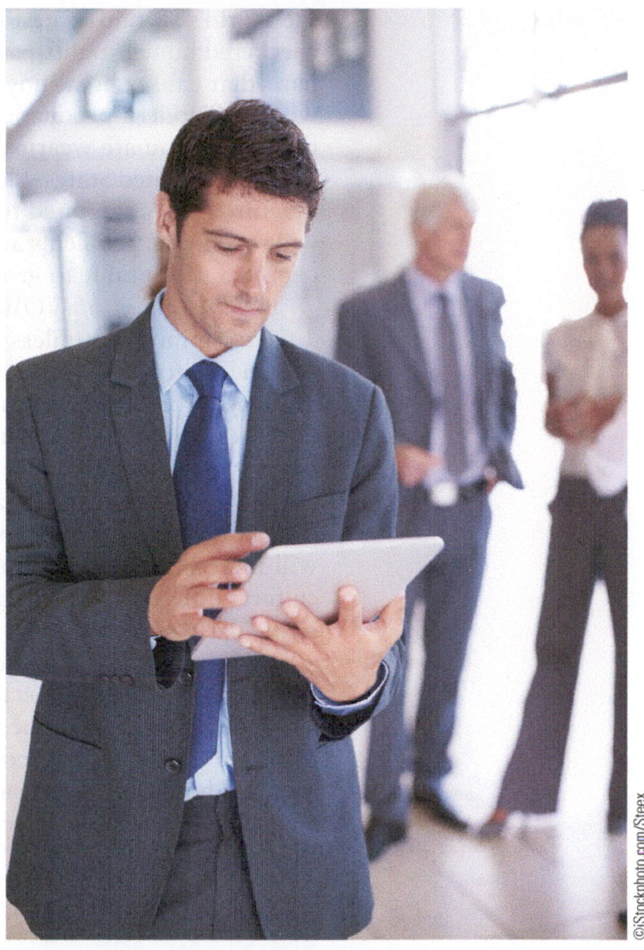

©iStockphoto.com/Steex

*Access to and timely management of information through the use of current technology has become a key supervisory responsibility*

## GLOBAL CHALLENGES

Global challenges will continue to impact the supervisor. The Saudis, Chinese, British, Germans, Swiss, Canadians, Japanese, and others have invested substantially in U.S. firms. Carlos Brito, CEO of InBev NV, the Belgian brewer of Stella Artois, stated that the acquisition of Anheuser-Busch Company "will create a stronger, more competitive, sustainable global company which will benefit all stakeholders." This acquisition came shortly after Miller, the "tastes great—less filling" beer became part of London's SAB-Miller PLC.[53] In 2014, ABInBev had over 150,000 employees worldwide and generated over $43 billion in sales. The world's largest brewing company in April 2014 acquired Chinese brewer Siping Ginsber.

Identifying the cultural and value systems and work-ethic differences of these phenomena is beyond the scope of this text. However, the supervisor must recognize that management practices in these firms differ culturally and structurally from practices in U.S.-owned and -operated firms.

The production facilities of U.S. firms are being drawn to China, India, South Korea, Eastern Europe, South America, Africa, Mexico, and other locations by low wages and other factors that help create a competitive advantage. When one corporate executive was asked why his company had outsourced work to the low-wage countries, he responded: "The customers we supply have plants in those countries. Even though we have a high turnover rate among employees, we still enjoy a tremendous cost advantage."

Then throw in the China factor. While many of us view China's economy as backward, we should think about the Great Wall, which stretches farther than the distance from New York to Los Angeles, as a symbol of China's potential. The People's Republic of China with more than 1.4 billion people has become the world's second largest economy after the U.S. economy. While China has a checkered human rights past, a history of clamping down on dissent, and a toxic haze that causes breathing difficulties, it has a seemingly unlimited number of workers, modern production facilities, and untapped mineral resources. Look at the clothes you are wearing or the light bulbs overhead. Where were they made? Not in the United States. Electronics, heavy-equipment, furniture, and other manufacturers have migrated to China and other Asian countries. Even with worldwide economic problems and increased transportation costs, China's exports are expected to continue to grow.[54]

In *The Pursuit of WOW!*, management consultant Tom Peters wrote that the "it's not important unless it happens here [in the United States]" attitude has become a problem. To be successful in foreign countries, U.S. firms must make a strong effort to understand the cultural customs in these environments. Over half the world's population lives in Asia, and a majority of that population is under the age of 25, which is dramatically different from the rest of the world. As new entrants to the Asian labor force become more literate, everything will change.[55] International opportunities for technically competent U.S. supervisors will increase. However, transplanted U.S. supervisors will need to learn about cultural differences and find ways to adapt to nontraditional management styles, particularly telecommuting techniques.

Outsourcing of high-end manufacturing and information technology jobs to low-cost countries is expected to continue. Outsourcing is not new, as companies have long sought to reduce operating costs and capital expenditures. The next time you have to call to complain about a product not working properly or to inquire about a warranty, ask where the employee you are talking to is located. Chances are that the call center is located in India or the Philippines—not in the United States.

## WORK SCHEDULING AND EMPLOYMENT CONDITIONS

General working conditions have changed and will continue to evolve. Only about one-third of employed Americans over the age of 18 still work a traditional Monday-through-Friday workweek. In the future, even fewer Americans will be working a standard 9-to-5 day shift because of the projected growth in jobs with evening, night, and weekend requirements.

**Contingent workforce**
Part-time, temporary, or contract employees who work schedules dependent primarily on employer needs

Another phenomenon that is likely to continue is the **contingent workforce**. The contingent workforce consists primarily of part-time and temporary or contract employees. According to the BLS, there are approximately 3 million contract and temporary workers in the United States. This is a type of "interim" workforce consisting of people who can be called in and sent home depending on the employer's needs. Employers have used these types of workers in an effort to reduce the wages and benefits that usually are paid to full-time employees. Temporary or contract employees often are supplied to employers by temporary agencies. It is likely that temporary and contract employment will continue because of the economic advantages to employers who use such services. Recruitment, training, and other associated costs are minimal, even though the per-hour cost of contract labor may be higher than that for regular employees. When the project is completed, the temporary employees can easily be dismissed.[56] On the negative side for business owners, supervisors often find it difficult to motivate temporary employees who consider themselves transient. These employees work at firms only until something better comes along. Furthermore, a number of

**FIGURE 1.5 It is easier to find a job when you have one**

"I'M BETWEEN JOBS . . . THE ONE I DIDN'T WANT AND THE ONE I COULDN'T GET."

*Source:* Adapted from SHRM Workplace Forecast (SHRM 2011), p. 4.

studies have indicated that lower productivity and increased accidents can occur when employees are not fully committed to their jobs, which, of course, is complicated by the contingent workforce situation.

Yet more employment factors are likely to complicate the supervisor's job in the future. Report after report indicates substantial cutbacks in consumer spending. With the rise in food and energy costs, along with the decline in quality job opportunities, more and more employees are being pushed to work multiple part-time jobs to try to make ends meet. Imagine the plight, for example, of the single parent with several school-aged children who is trying to balance work life responsibilities. How can he or she devote full attention to job requirements when worried about stretching a household budget? We are all aware of the turnover rate in the fast food industry. It is not unusual for a shop with 40 employees to experience a 100 percent or higher turnover rate. Figure 1.5 shows the dilemma faced by one employee who left his job prematurely.

Work scheduling problems caused by employees demanding greater flexibility to attend to family needs are likely to accelerate during the foreseeable future.[57] Still another thorny issue is the growing disparity in executive compensation as compared to the income of most employees. What impact does it have on morale and dedication to work when the employee reads that his or her CEO is making mega-millions while he or she is struggling to make ends meet? Clearly, the disparity of income between executives and employees in companies can erode morale and, consequently, performance.

# CORPORATE CULTURE AND ETHICAL CONDUCT

## Social Responsibility, Corporate Culture, and Ethical Conduct

**Corporate social responsibility (CSR)** is a concept whereby organizations consider the interests of society by taking responsibility for the impact of their actions on employees, customers, suppliers, shareholders, and other stakeholders as well as the environment and communities in which they operate. Author Archie

**Corporate social responsibility (CSR)**
A notion that organizations consider the interests of all stakeholders

Carroll developed a four-part definition of CSR that provides a medium for analyzing a company's responsibilities.

- Legal responsibilities. To comply with statutory obligations, that is, to play by the rules of the game.
- Economic responsibilities. To be profitable, that is, to make money for the shareholders.
- Ethical responsibilities. To do what is right, just, and fair.
- Philanthropic responsibilities. To contribute resources to improve the community and society at large.[58]

**Corporate culture**
Set of shared purposes, values, and beliefs that employees hold about their organization

**Corporate culture** is the set of shared purposes, values, and beliefs that employees have about their organization. Top-level management creates the overall vision and philosophy for the firm. To provide a foundation for the type of corporate culture that is desired, many companies develop mission statements and ethical conduct statements.

Figure 1.6 is an example of a values and beliefs statement that was developed by the top management of Community Medical Center (CMC). Throughout the present text, there are several CMC "You Make the Calls" and end-of-part cases that will feature situations arising at CMC. You can use these examples as a reference point for many of the decisions that will confront you. Supervisors exert major influences in determining the direction of the corporate culture in their departments. They play significant roles in informing, educating, and setting examples for ethical behavior. Although ethical behavior and fair dealing have always been the foundations for good management, it is clear that ethical conduct has become one of the most challenging issues confronting U.S. business. The daily news is filled with reports of people misusing business power and believing that corrupt business practices are the primary way to make profits. Ethics and

**FIGURE 1.6 A sample values and belief statement**

Every Community Medical Center (CMC) employee is important. With mutual respect, trust, and open communication, we will work together to create an organization that consistently meets or exceeds the expectations of patients, visitors, physicians, employees, and other stakeholders. We believe that when employees are actively engaged in their work, they will work with passion because they know that they can positively impact the quality of patient care.

CMC is dedicated to providing consistently superior services to all our customers. We believe in fostering an environment that encourages superior service and performance.

We believe that superior service and performance result from

- a clear understanding of goals and clear job expectations;
- knowing that every job is important and doing the job right the first time;
- effective communication;
- proper application of skills, knowledge, and abilities;
- wise use of resources;
- high standards of conduct that embody "trust" and "integrity";
- a safe and aesthetically pleasing work environment;
- shared involvement in attaining goals; and
- opportunities for personal and professional growth.

morality are back on the front page as a result of widespread illegal and unscrupulous behavior. The public consistently gives business managers low marks for honesty.

The **Society of Human Resources Management's (SHRM)** core principle of professional responsibility should apply for all those in supervisory positions. "We are responsible for adding value to the organization we serve and contributing to the ethical success of those organizations. As supervisors, we must accept professional responsibility for our individual decisions and actions."[59] In the future, as never before, it will be important that ethical behavior and fair dealing are at the forefront of good management practices, beginning at the supervisory level. A supervisor's personal ethics also can be an important guide for making decisions when facing ethical problems in the workplace. Chapter 8 further discusses the importance of the ethical standards that can serve as decision-making guides.

**SHRM**
The Society for Human Resource Management, a professional organization for HR professionals

## GOVERNMENTAL AND SOCIETAL ISSUES

Other emerging governmental and societal issues will continue to complicate the supervisory management position. For example, numerous environmental concerns continue to be serious long-term problems for business, government, and the general public. Energy availability and costs may be determined by international and domestic political and economic changes. These types of issues and societal pressures often become part of business planning and operations.

Figure 1.7 reviews the federal legislation affecting the supervisor's job. State and local governments also have laws and regulations that impact businesses. Such legislation can prove quite costly for organizations, often requiring changes in their methods of operation in order to comply.

Supervisors are influenced both directly and indirectly by such governmental requirements, and they must continue to stay abreast of any legislation that may influence their operations. Furthermore, supervisors must be sensitive to

*"Going green" means that individuals and organizations voluntarily take steps to conserve energy and behave in environmentally friendly ways*

**FIGURE 1.7 Overview of federal employment legislation affecting supervisors**

**Family and Medical Leave Act (FMLA) (1992).** Provides for up to 12 weeks of unpaid leave for certain personal and family health-related circumstances. http://www.dol.gov/esa/whd/fmla.

**Americans with Disabilities Act (ADA) (1990).** Prohibits discrimination based on physical and mental disabilities in places of employment and public accommodation. http://www.usdoj.gov/crt/ada/adahom1.htm.

**Worker Adjustment and Retraining Act (WARN) (1988).** Requires firms employing 100 or more workers to provide 60 days' advance notice to employees before shutting down or conducting substantial layoffs. http://www.doleta.gov/layoff/warn.cfm.

**Pregnancy Discrimination Act (1978).** Requires employers to treat pregnancy, childbirth, or related medical conditions the same as any other medical disability if the employers have medical and hospitalization benefit programs for employees. http://www.eeoc.gov/facts/fs-preg.html.

**Occupational Safety and Health Act (OSHA) (1970).** Designed to protect the safety and health of employees; holds employers responsible for providing workplaces free of safety and health hazards. Created the Occupational Safety and Health Administration to carry out the Act's provisions. http://www.osha.gov.

**Title VII of the Civil Rights Act, as amended (1964).** Prohibits discrimination in hiring, promotion, discharge, pay, benefits, and other aspects of employment on the basis of race, color, religion, gender, or national origin. The Equal Employment Opportunity Commission (EEOC) has the authority to bring lawsuits against employers in federal courts. http://www.eeoc.gov/policy/vii.html.

**Labor Management Relations Act (Taft–Hartley) (1947).** Amended the Wagner Act; specified unfair labor practices for unions, provided for Federal Mediation and Conciliation Service (FMCS) to assist in resolving labor–management disputes, and more clearly identified requirements for bargaining in good faith. (On the NLRB home page, http://www.nlrb.gov, click on *What Is the National Labor Relations Act; Employee Rights;* and *Read the NLRA.*)

**Fair Labor Standards Act (FLSA) (1938).** Established that employers covered by the act must pay an employee (1) at least a minimum wage and (2) time and a half for all hours worked in excess of 40 in a given week. Classified a person working in a job that is not subject to the provisions of the act as "exempt" from the overtime pay provisions. The change effective August 2004 set forth new criteria for determining overtime. http://www.dol.gov/elaws/flsa.htm.

**National Labor Relations Act (Wagner Act) (1935).** Gave workers the right to unionize and bargain collectively over hours, wages, and other terms and conditions of employment. Specified five unfair labor practices for employers. Created the National Labor Relations Board (NLRB) to (1) certify labor unions as the sole bargaining representatives of employees and (2) investigate unfair labor practices. (Go to http://www.nlrb.gov to review the National Labor Relations Act, court decisions, employee rights, and employer responsibilities.)



*Notes:* See the following U.S. Department of Labor Web sites for additional information on employment laws and applications: www.dol.gov.osbp (for those that relate to small businesses); www.dol.gov (click on summary of major laws); and www.dol.gov/elaws. (Students have found that this site provides easy-to-understand information on federal employment law.)

pressures exerted by special interest groups. Consumer groups, in particular, have demanded better products and services from business, labor, and government. Environmentalists seek to influence business decisions that may adversely impact the environment. "**Going green**" could become a more important issue as more organizations are volunteering to operate in a more environmentally responsible way. Some local governments are providing incentives to encourage businesses to become greener.

**Going green**
Voluntary steps taken by organizations and individuals to conserve energy and protect the environment

Some employees, especially the parents of young children or employees who have elderly parents, will expect their employers to provide daycare facilities so that they can better combine their family and job responsibilities. It seems likely that numerous other permanent and temporary special-interest groups will continue to make community and political demands on firms in ways that will affect how supervisors will operate in the future.

All indications are that these pressures will remain intense. A utility company supervisor said recently, "I have to be more of a lawyer, cop, teacher, accountant, political scientist, and psychologist these days than a manager!" Although this supervisor's comment is a bit overstated, it reflects a realistic aspect of every supervisor's contemporary role.

## WORKPLACE INCIVILITY AND PEOPLE WHO MAKE LIFE DIFFICULT

The typical employee will spend most of his or her waking hours going to, at, or coming home from work. It is logical to expect that whenever people convene in one place for so long their different personalities, expectations, values, and needs may clash from time to time. Many students can relate to this reality by thinking back to the playground bullies of their childhoods. In some instances, the playground bully has grown up and now works alongside us. The dilemma for many employees is, "How can you expect me to get along with that troublemaker?" A number of studies report that "rude behavior is on the rise in the workplace and can undermine an organization's effectiveness."[60]

Almost everyone has been on the receiving end of a rude person's temper or a bully's wrath. Whether crude or impolite behavior takes place behind closed doors or out in the open, it directly affects the recipients and lowers group morale. Who are these difficult people? In his book, *Coping with Difficult People*, Robert M. Bramson writes:

> *They are the hostile customers or coworkers, the indecisive, vacillating bosses, and the over agreeable subordinates of the world who are constant headaches to work with. Although their numbers are small, their impact is large. They are responsible for absenteeism, significant losses in productivity, and lost customers or clients. They frustrate and demoralize those unlucky enough to have to work with them, and they are difficult to understand. Worst of all, they appear immune to all the usual methods of communication and persuasion designed to convince them or help them to change their ways.*[61]

Throughout this text, we have identified some people who might make life difficult for you. Typically, employees arrive in an organization with little or no foundation for how to handle these types of people. We believe that it is crucial that you understand how to deal with incivility and difficult people. As such, we introduce you to some of these co-workers, associates, or supervisors in subsequent chapters. Unfortunately, you may find one or two whom you know fairly well.

### The Three E's—Engagement, Empowerment, and Employee Participation in Decision Making

How do you get people off the bench and into the game? How do you get diverse groups of people to work together? These questions have been with us since the beginning of time. Some employees will demand a greater voice in workplace decision making, while others will adopt the "what-how-when" attitude: "Just tell me what you want done, how you want it done, and when you want it done." Many employees will want more from their jobs and will demand a voice in decisions concerning their employment. This does not have to be objectionable to a supervisor. In fact, once supervisors realize that their employees have something to contribute, they will welcome employee participation in decisions rather than fear it.

What kind of employee would you like to work with and have work for you? A supervisor who prefers a "telling style" would want the employee with the "what-how-when" attitude. It is our contention, however, that most employees want more than that—they want to be engaged in the place where they spend most of their waking hours. In his book, *Getting Engaged: The New Workplace Loyalty*, Tim Rutledge explains that the "truly engaged employees are attracted to, inspired by ('I want to do this'), committed to ('I am dedicated to the success of what I am doing'), and fascinated by their work ('I love what I am doing')."[62]

The *Conference Board* review of employee engagement research identified certain factors that need to be present for employees to further both their own self-interests and the interests of their organization. These are as follows:

- Do I believe that my job is important?
- Do managers communicate expectations, provide regular feedback, and lead by example?
- Is the job mentally stimulating?
- Is there a direct connection between what I do and the organization's performance—quality, service, bottom line?
- Are there opportunities for personal and professional growth?
- Am I willing to work with a passion because I am connected to what the organization stands for?
- Is there a climate of open and honest communication between the manager, team members, and myself?
- Have I been empowered to make decisions that impact what I do and how I do it?[63]

*An employee is engaged when he or she feels totally connected, needed, appreciated, committed, and thus, willing to put forth his or her best effort for the good of the organization*

Andy Sacks/The Image Bank/Getty Images

As you review the bulleted points, it should become clear that **engaged employees** are those who are enthused about what they do, where they do it, and who they do it with. They are fully involved because they have been engaged. **Empowerment** means giving employees the authority and responsibility to achieve objectives. Opportunities to make suggestions and participate in decisions affecting their jobs can and should be supported. However, some supervisors become worried when workers challenge what have traditionally been management rights, thinking that certain areas should be beyond employee challenge. Many quality circles and other participatory management approaches of the last decade failed, in part, because managers failed to listen to the suggestions of employees, did not act on those suggestions in a timely fashion, or felt threatened by those suggestions. Nevertheless, employees, labor unions, minorities, and other groups will continue to pressure for more influence in decisions pertaining to the workplace.

**Engaged employees**
An employee who has a strong emotional bond to his or her organization and is committed to its objectives

**Empowerment**
Giving employees the authority and responsibility to accomplish their individual and the organization's objectives

Many supervisors have become accustomed to the practice of **participative management**, which essentially means a willingness to permit employees to influence or share in managerial decisions. If supervisors learn to react to this practice in a positive way, it should improve their own and their company's performance. Although forecasts are, at best, precarious, experienced supervisors will recognize that these trends have already begun. Supervisors must understand and plan for them.

**Participative management**
Allowing employees to influence and share in organizational decision making

## Supervision: A Professional Perspective

**5 Explain why supervisors must continually grow and develop as professionals.**

The primary responsibility of most supervisors is to manage their firms' most important resources—human resources. Managing people starts with selecting and training individuals to fill job openings, and it continues with ongoing development, motivation, leadership, and preparation of employees for promotion.

Thus, supervisors will have to become true professionals with a growing professional perspective, and they will have to develop as innovators and idea people. They must look to the future with a professional awareness of the trends influencing human behavior and observe how those trends impact the management of people in a complex society.

In all of this, it is imperative to take the professional perspective, which recognizes the need for constant self-improvement and self-renewal. No amount of formal or informal education can ever be enough to fulfill a supervisor's personal program of self-improvement. Supervisors must recognize that they, too, can become obsolete unless they constantly take measures to update their own skills and knowledge through a program of continuous self-development.

Students, as well as practicing managers, need to understand that "As long as you live, keep learning to live," should be a guide for all of us to live by.[64] Stephen Covey, author of *The Seven Habits of Highly Effective People*, presented the following illustration:

> *Suppose you were to come upon someone in the woods working feverishly to saw down a tree.*
>
> *"What are you doing?" you ask.*
>
> *"Can't you see?" comes the impatient reply. "I'm sawing down the tree."*
>
> *"You look exhausted!" you exclaim. "How long have you been at it?"*
>
> *"Over five hours," he returns, "and I'm beat! This is hard work."*

*"Well, why don't you take a break for a few minutes and sharpen the saw?" you inquire. "I'm sure it would go a lot faster."*

*"I don't have time to sharpen the saw," the man said emphatically. "I'm too busy sawing."*[65]

Both newly appointed and experienced supervisors should begin each day by asking, "What can I do to sharpen my saw?" Throughout the text, through skills building activities, experiential exercises, case studies, and other learning opportunities, we will provide you with numerous ways to sharpen your saw.

Supervisors who master the managerial concepts and skills discussed in this textbook should make considerable progress in terms of personal development, but just knowing concepts and approaches is not enough. Supervisors must constantly seek new ways to apply this knowledge in the challenging, complex, and dynamic situations they will encounter.

No one is certain what the future will bring, but we see reasons to be optimistic. When the time comes, will you—our students of today—be prepared so that you can achieve your dreams? At the beginning of each term, we ask students to look back, to take time to reflect on the past and learn from the mistakes that others have made; to look up, to contemplate what meaning they want from life; and to look ahead, to develop strategies for getting to where they want to be. We issue the same challenge to you!

**6 Recognize ways for getting into a supervisory position.**

## Getting into Supervision

Job hunting is not usually easy. The last several years have been the worst for new graduates, as many employers have cut back their hiring plans. Some graduates who would ordinarily expect to get multiple offers only got one, if any. Many college graduates have modified their expectations and job search criteria owing to the rocky job market. For some people, opportunities appear when they least expect them. For others, the road appears to be steep.

Many individuals are promoted to their first supervisory positions from nonsupervisory jobs in the same organization. It may be in the same department or in another area. They may have formally applied for the position or had a manager recommend them. In either case, the organization made a conscious effort to promote from within. The author is familiar with many middle-aged managers who did not continually find ways to sharpen their saws. Often, they felt they had "paid their dues" by being loyal to a particular firm for a long period of time.

If you are employed while going to school, it can be tough to find the time to do an effective job search for a position outside your current firm. In addition, you will have the added burden of being discreet. Many employers take a dim view of employees who are seeking employment elsewhere; their loyalty and commitment are questioned. Do not make or receive job-search-related calls at work. Advise prospective employers to contact you at home or through the college placement office. Schedule your interviews before or after work or on your days off. In today's difficult economy, do not leave your job until you have a new one and then, if possible, give two weeks' notice. We don't want you to burn any bridges; leave on good terms.

Consider the situation of one former student who stated that she had sent her résumé to a blind advertisement—neither the firm nor its address was listed. Her immediate supervisor informed her that he had received her resume and was wondering why she was unhappy with her current position. She had applied for a job similar to the one she currently had, but the advertisement listed broader responsibilities and sounded challenging. She was at a loss for words. She later left the organization, not for a better job but because she felt the supervisor never gave her a chance after that.

## WHERE TO LOOK FOR INFORMATION

Students in need of more detailed information, additional career opportunities, and salary information can refer to the latest *Occupational Outlook Handbook* or the *Career Guide to Industries* published by the U.S. Department of Labor (the *Handbook* and the *Career Guide* are available online at http://www.bls.gov/ovo and http://www.bls.gov/coc/cg). Check with your college placement office to see what pamphlets or suggestions they have for helping you to get the job you want.

Many students find that networking is a useful strategy. Numerous studies have reported that employee referrals were the single largest source of new hires.[66] That is substantially more than the number of people hired through job listings. Your strategy should be to meet and talk to many personal and professional colleagues and friends to help you identify potential opportunities. Networking through school, church, family members, or other associations to gather information and referrals should be part of your strategy. You might say, "I'm finishing my degree in June and am thinking about making a change," or "Your company has a reputation for being a good place to work. Do you know of any opportunities there?" Such an approach could be a good networking start.

A visit to the Internet will turn up many sources of information about an organization, such as annual reports, press releases, and news articles. This information will give you a good picture of the company's financial position, management style, and future. Increasingly, employers list jobs online and describe their products and services on company Web sites. Figure 1.8 contains a partial listing of online services. You can submit your résumé to databases that feed search engines used by employers to find candidates.

While many job opportunities can be found in the classifieds and on Web sites, the vast majority of positions never get advertised. We suggest that you make a list of organizations for which you would like to work. Most firms with Web sites prefer e-recruiting. Complete their online application and e-mail your cover letter and résumé. Make sure you have correctly spelled the name and title of the person who is to receive your letter. A well-written cover letter gives the reader a quick overview of you, your history, and your expectations. Usually, it is the only factor that determines whether or not the résumé gets read. Many HR professionals report that grammatical and spelling errors are the first thing that places an applicant in the "do not go further category."

Most colleges have an Office of Career Services to assist students and alumni in the job search process. Some colleges coach students in résumé writing, the art of interviewing (particularly Internet and telephone interviewing), and anything else their students need to know to pass the recruiting process. A word of caution: E-mail is now the preferred format for receiving résumés and cover letters. Check the organization's requirements carefully because some companies will not accept résumés submitted as attachments. Before you send it, e-mail it to yourself so you can double-check the formatting and appearance. You might even have a friend review it and make suggestions for improvement. We have found that many students have a generic résumé that they send to all. A suggestion: Tailor your résumé to the job you are seeking.[67]

**FIGURE 1.8 Sources for online job searches**

The list of online sources is far from complete. There are always new Web sites, bulletin boards, databases, and job search information on the Internet. Once you are familiar with the Internet job search progress, you can access information quickly. If you need help with your Internet search, your college placement office will provide help. Enjoy the journey!

***AARP*** (http://aarp.ogr/money/careers) offers tips to assist with career transitions. This site includes information on starting your own business, charting a career change, reentering the job market, and coping with work–life issues.

***The Bureau of Labor Statistics*** (http://stats.bls.gov) offers data and economic information, including wage/salary surveys for various job classifications.

***CareerBuilder.com*** (http://www/careerbuilder.com) allows you to search for jobs or careers using 13 different criteria, or lets you post your résumé so that employers with job openings can find you. It also provides salary information and tips on job hunting and résumé writing.

***CareerJournal.com*** (http://www.careerjournal.com) is maintained by the *Wall Street Journal*, and you can browse sections on salary and hiring information, job hiring advice, and managing your career.

***Monster.com*** (http://www.monster.com) is one of the largest online recruiting sites.

***Salary.com*** (http://www.salary.com) allows you to research job titles, descriptions, and salaries in your area.

In his book, *Cracking the Hidden Job Market: How to Find Opportunity in Any Economy*, Donald Asher says, "Sadly, applying for posted openings is how most job-seekers spend their time. It's hard to stand out in a pile of thousands of resumes; we need to get out of the pile. Half the jobs are filled before they are ever posted or advertised. You need to insert yourself in the process before a position is advertised."

*Sources:* Donald Asher, *Cracking the Hidden Job Market: How to Find Opportunity in Any Economy*, Ten Speed Press, 2010; Michelle Archer, "Cracking the Hidden Job Market," *USA Today*, January 18, 2011, p. 5b.

## MAKE YOURSELF MORE VALUABLE

In general, we believe the best way to get a supervisory position or to prosper in your current position is to find ways to make yourself more valuable. Always try to improve yourself. For example, if you are a student, make yourself available for internships and co-ops, or perhaps volunteer for some type of meaningful activity. Volunteer experiences in community groups can increase your networking opportunities, give you ideas and practical experiences, and help you become more comfortable working with and leading groups of diverse people. Get involved in one or more student organizations on your campus. Seek opportunities to apply your expertise and use such opportunities to enhance your communication and leadership skills. These experiences can be valuable. Try it; you might like it! We want you to be successful.

Remember, too, that continuing your educational preparation is an ongoing challenge. Finishing an academic degree is only a start; consider going further by enrolling in graduate study degree and non-degree programs that may enhance your technical, managerial, supervisory knowledge. Increasingly, colleges and universities are offering distance learning or online programs that can be taken at a remote location via computer.

Look in the mirror. What SKAs do you have in your toolbox? What experiences do you have that can add value to the organization? How might the SKAs

## SUPERVISORY TIPS

### Career Tips: Keep on Knocking!

1. Look for a job in the right places.
   - Network
   - College placement office
   - Job boards or Web sites
   - Newspaper classifieds
   - Job fairs
   - Recruiting firms
   - Temporary help agencies
   - Individual employers
2. Think like an employer.
   Ask yourself the following question: "If you were the one hiring for a position, what would you want to see in a résumé?"
   - Who are you?
   - What do you know?
   - What have you done?
   - What have you accomplished?
   - What can you do to add value to this organization?
   - Who can give you a good recommendation?
3. Prepare for the interview.
   - Research the company.
   - What business is this company really in?
   - What does the company's past, present, and future look like?
   - What can you learn by reading its annual report?
   - Who are the company's major competitors, and how do they compare?
   - What is the company's reputation?
   - Is the company a leader in the field?
   - Is the company regarded as a good place to work? Why or why not?
   - Find the gatekeepers, those people who may be in touch with those doing the hiring.
4. Be proactive.
   - Have a professional e-mail address. gottahock-aloogie@GHI.com will most likely not garner any interview requests. (*Note*: This was an actual first part of an e-mail address sent in a professional capacity!)
   - Clean up your social networking Web pages (most companies check).
   - Prepare your résumé with the job you are applying for in mind.
   - Prepare short statements on how your experience and training match the job. Rehearse prior to the interview. Prepare mentally for what the interviewer may ask.
   - Dress for success. First impressions count a lot. Your dress, manners, posture, and self-confidence will or will not make you an attractive candidate.
   - Have your questions prepared in advance. Ask questions about the job or the company (e.g., Which qualifications are most important for this position? What are the expectations of the ideal person for this job?) *Note*: Don't ask questions that you could have answered yourself by researching them on the Internet or by carefully reading the information the company may have previously provided. It is okay to ask for clarification, however.
   - Make sure you ask the right question of the right person at the right time.
   - Listen carefully during the interview. Watch the interviewer's body language and make sure your own conveys interest and enthusiasm.
   - Sell yourself—demonstrate how you can use your SKAs to help the organization achieve its goals.
   - Use each minute of the interview to sell yourself: Listen! Ask questions! Answer the questions that are asked!
5. Follow up.
   - Write a thank-you note to the interviewer(s).
6. Continuously seek ways to "sharpen your saw." We suggest that students do several practice interviews to gain experience.

and experiences be matched to a particular job opportunity? Remember that when applying for any position, particularly a supervisory position, you must discover the specific needs of the hiring organization and show how you can add value to the firm. Our message to you: Be assertive enough, bold enough, and knock on enough doors (see the accompanying Supervisory Tips box).

## SUMMARY

1. The challenges of this century have been unbelievable. It seems that if something could happen it did. Threats of terrorism, incivility, massive unemployment, financial markets on a roller coaster, plants and businesses closing, housing and commercial properties in foreclosure, natural disasters, and other factors that the typical person has little or no control over have caused grave concerns. In addition, major environmental factors impact everything the organization does. These factors are not static. The whole world is changing rapidly, and while some people do not want to deal with change, most do not know how to deal with it.

2. Supervisors are the first tier of management. They manage entry-level and other departmental employees. In the face of a rapidly changing environment, successful supervisors will find ways to balance the requirements for high work performance with the diverse needs of the workforce.

   Supervisory management focuses primarily on the management of people. For many people, being a supervisor provides a variety of satisfying experiences, notably, the challenge of getting diverse people to work together, the increased responsibility that comes with climbing the management hierarchy, the unpredictable nature of the job, and the sense of accomplishment from doing a job well. Conversely, some people avoid supervisory responsibility. Being a supervisor is a demanding position that often places the supervisor in the middle of organizational pressures and conflict. A supervisor must endeavor to reconcile the needs of the organization and the needs of employees, which often is an elusive target.

3. There is no one universal school of management thought. The scientific management approach attempts to find the most efficient or "one best way." In this approach, the manager's primary function is to plan the work. Time and motion study and other industrial engineering principles are used to analyze the work to be done. The functional approach assumes that there are essential functions that all managers should perform. The human relations movement/behavioral science approach emphasizes that managers must understand what causes employees to behave the way they do. This approach began with the Hawthorne studies at Western Electric Company. The quantitative/systems approaches apply mathematical models to help solve organizational problems. An understanding of the various schools of management thought gives supervisors a foundation on which to build their own supervisory philosophies.

4. Many factors and trends in the workforce will impact how most organizations operate. The workforce is expected to become more racially and ethnically diverse. Some of the baby boomers are expected to be leaving the labor market, but with the current economy being so anemic, most will need to continue to work. Women and minorities will continue to enter the workforce in increasing numbers, and they will be used more fully than they have been in the past, including in supervisory and management positions. Substantial numbers of contingent workers will be found in the workplace. The more diverse workforce will create numerous problems (e.g., multicultural and multilingual problems, family obligations versus job obligations). The workforce generally will consist of more college graduates, but millions of people will not be prepared educationally to qualify for many employment opportunities. The growth of the Latino population and other immigrants will have a profound effect on the organizations in which they work and the culture and traditions in the communities where they reside. We fully expect that immigration issues will be debated endlessly and, perhaps eventually, a solution will be found for the millions of illegal immigrants.

   Most manufacturers have or are in the process of downsizing, outsourcing, or offshoring their production activities. Although many jobs are becoming more complex because of the technology involved, the fastest growth will take place in the service sector. Occupational and industry trends, changing technology and business conditions, and the competition from the global marketplace will be significant influences on supervisory management. Government laws and regulations will continue to have a major impact on the policies and activities of most organizations.

   China, China, China! What does the future hold as China becomes an even more formidable force in the world's economy? China's gross domestic product ranks it second in the world only behind the United States. Many U.S. and European manufacturers have found China an attractive place because of its abundance of willing workers and its few environmental restrictions.

   Corporate social responsibility (CSR) implies that organizations must be both profitable and responsible to their various stakeholder groups. Supervisors need to look at each decision by asking two questions: (1) who will be impacted by the decision, and (2) is it fair to all concerned?

   Because of increased incivility, workplace violence, and the threat of terrorism, firms will establish programs and procedures to help supervisors recognize the symptoms of troubled employees.

Supervisors will have to be sensitive to existing and expected employee trends. For example, more employees will expect their jobs to have greater personal meaning to them as individuals. Many will want to be engaged or at least more involved through participation in their organizations. Employees will continue to expect a greater voice in workplace decision making, and they will expect to be empowered. Therefore, supervisors will likely have to be somewhat flexible in their approaches to managing.

5. The habits of highly effective people can be developed. Supervisors who want to be more effective will put themselves in situations in which they can practice new techniques. Finally, supervisors who aspire to become more effective leaders need a professional outlook and must recognize the need for a personal program of continuous self-development. *Get off the bench and into the game!*

6. Searching for a job is never easy. But it's easier to find a job when you have one (see Figure 1.5). The better you know yourself—your skills, your knowledge, your abilities, your priorities, and what you can do to help the organization to achieve its goals—the better your chances of landing that dream job!

## KEY TERMS

behavioral science approach (p. 10)
Competitive advantage (p. 17)
Contingent workforce (p. 20)
Corporate culture (p. 22)
Corporate social responsibility (CSR) (p. 21)
Diversity (p. 12)
Empowerment (p. 27)
Engaged employee (p. 27)
Flextime (p. 15)
Functional approach (p. 10)
Glass ceiling (p. 16)
Glass walls (p. 16)
Going Green (p. 24)
Hawthorne effect (p. 10)
Human relations movement (p. 10)
Job sharing (p. 15)
Onboarding (p. 12)
Participative management (p. 27)
Quantitative/systems approaches (p. 10)
Scientific management approach (p. 9)
SKAs (p. 17)
Society for Human Resource Management (SHRM) (p. 23)
Supervisors (p. 6)
Telecommuting (p. 15)
Underemployment (p. 16)
Working supervisors (p. 8)

## WHAT HAVE YOU LEARNED?

1. Please interview one practicing manager/supervisor in an organization or industry that you are not really familiar with. Ask him or her to identify the one thing he or she likes best about being a supervisor, then ask the manager to describe the most difficult aspect of his or her job. Compare your findings with those of another student. What are the similarities? Differences?
2. Based on your findings from question 1: What are some advantages to being a supervisor? What are some disadvantages?
3. From the standpoint of the supervisor, what is the significance of the following?
   - Taylor's scientific management
   - Fayol's functions of management
   - The Hawthorne studies
   - Behavioral science
   - The quantitative/systems approaches
4. Of those factors or trends projected to reshape the workplace and the economy, how might the changes over the next year or two affect you, your lifestyle, and the work of your organization? Which will create the greatest challenge for supervisors? Why?
5. Some people have postulated that the "hand of government should be invisible" in the marketplace. What are some arguments for having the federal, state, and/or local governments regulate business?
6. At the end of the day, how do you measure whether you have been successful?

## EXPERIENTIAL EXERCISES FOR SELF-ASSESSMENT

### EXPERIENTIAL EXERCISE FOR SELF-ASSESSMENT 1-1: Who are you? Who Do You Really Want To Be?

| 1 | 2 | 3 | 4 | 5 |
|---|---|---|---|---|
| Courageous | Thoughtful | Smart | Honest | Resourceful |
| Intriguing | Daring | Fearless | Impulsive | Ordinary |
| Curious | Bold | Consistent | Humorous | Boring |
| Comforting | Intense | Dependable | Informed | Supportive |
| Visionary | Fun | Strong | Intelligent | Contemporary |
| Credible | Authentic | Informative | Romantic | Forgiving |
| Confident | Mature | Interesting | Innovative | Trailblazer |
| Influential | Genuine | Relevant | Unpredictable | Trustworthy |
| Surprising | Provocative | Exciting | Committed | Independent |
| Informed | Predictable | Timely | Brave | Unique |
| Dynamic | Undaunted | Focused | Solid | Results-oriented |

a. From the list of adjectives, select two from each column (1, 2, 3, 4, 5) that you think best describe you.

b. Make six copies of the list above, give one copy each to six people, and ask them to circle the two adjectives in each column that best describe you and check the two items in each column that describe you least. (In our classroom experience, we have found it to be most effective if you give them the list and suggest they ponder the list for a day or two before completing the exercise. Include a variety of people in your survey, such as a family member, a friend, a co-worker or two, or someone from a non–work group that you belong to)

c. After the survey is returned, compile the data to determine how others view you. Are the perceptions of others consistent with how you perceive yourself? Why or why not?

d. Think of the most effective (successful) supervisor whom you have ever known. Which ten traits from the list would you use to describe him or her? (*Note*: You are not restricted to two from each column. Just select the ten traits regardless of which column they are in.) How do (a) your self-analysis (b) and how others perceive you compare with those attributes you identified for the most effective supervisor?

e. Now identify those 10 attributes that you would like to add to your toolbox or improve upon. Then create a self-development action plan for enhancing your skills, knowledge, and abilities (SKAs). As we will emphasize throughout this text, visualize (see what it is you want to achieve), develop an action plan, and do it. Write down your self-improvement plan and refer to it on a regular basis—Plan the work! Work the plan! Make adjustments as necessary!

(*Note*: This exercise was developed by Professor Ed Leonard and Professor Karen Moustafa Leonard and is reproduced here with permission. © 2008.)

## PERSONAL SKILL BUILDING

### PERSONAL SKILL BUILDER 1-1: What Call Did You Make?

Review this chapter's opening "You Make the Call!"

1. Make a complete list of the major concerns that face Charlotte Kelly as she begins this new assignment.
2. Prioritize the items on your list.
3. Review the three major concerns you have listed, then write suggestions that might help Charlotte Kelly deal with those concerns.
4. FOOD FOR THOUGHT QUESTION Why is it important for new supervisors such as Charlotte Kelly to make a list of concerns that they may face in their new assignment?

## PERSONAL SKILL BUILDER 1-2: Making a difference.

After reading this chapter, we want you to think about four people that we think have made a difference in the world during the twenty-first century:

- Steve Jobs—an American entrepreneur, marketer, and inventor who was the co-founder and CEO of Apple, Inc.
- Nelson Mandela—a South African anti-apartheid revolutionary, politician, and philanthropist who served as president of South Africa from 1994 to 1999
- Warren Buffett—an American business magnate, investor, and philanthropist
- Pope Francis—the current pope of the Catholic Church.

Choose one. Go to one of the following Web sites (or any other reputable site) to learn more about his life and how he made or is making a difference in the world.

a. https://www.google.com/search?q=steve+jobs&oq
b. https://www.google.com/search?q=nelson+mandela&oq
c. https://www.google.com/search?q=warren+buffett&oq (You may also want to review Anupreeta Das, "Buffett: Keeping Things Simple," *The Wall Street Journal* (March 1–2, 2014), b2.)
d. https://www.google.com/search?q=pope+francis&oq (*Time*'s Person of the Year, 2013) (See Howard Chua-Eoan and Elizabeth Dias, "The People's Pope," *Time* (December 23, 2013), pp. 46–75)

1. What differences has he made in the world?
2. Based upon your research what skills did he use (or is he using) to make these differences?
3. What did he do or is he doing to engage others to get off the bench and get in the game?
4. What did you learn after reading about this person's achievements that will help you meet challenges in the days ahead?

## PERSONAL SKILL BUILDER 1-3: Assessing Your Toolbox—What Do I Need to Get into Supervision?

Before you begin this exercise, you are encouraged to carefully read Section 6: Recognize Ways to Get into Supervision.

Each employee brings a "toolbox" to work each day. The toolbox consists of skills, knowledge, abilities, and experiences. Below, we have listed two supervisory jobs. Carefully read each one and then pick the one that most interests you. Then:

1. Make a list of the requirements (skills, knowledge, abilities, experiences) needed for the job.
2. Make a list of your strengths (SKAs) and compare them with the requirements for each job.
3. Determine what you need to do to add to your toolbox (i.e., sharpen your saw) in order to improve your chances of getting the job.
4. Outline a plan for adding those essential ingredients to your toolbox.
5. Explain how you will put the plan into action.
6. Refer to your plan once a week to assess your progress, and make changes as necessary.

**Opening #1: Supervisor Wanted**

A manufacturer of plastic containers for the food industry has a third-shift production supervisor position to fill. This position will direct the daily activities of hourly production personnel to accomplish production, safety, and quality goals. The successful candidate will possess strong people skills and good communication skills and will demonstrate leadership and problem-solving techniques. An associate degree with a minimum of two years' experience in a manufacturing environment is required for this position. Experience in the plastics industry would be a plus. We offer a competitive wage and benefits package. Interested candidates should send their résumés and salary histories to ABC@abc.net

**Opening # 2: Restaurant—Management Trainee Position**

A rapidly growing restaurant chain with operations in 10 southeastern states is looking for motivated people to join our management training program. Previous customer service experience is required. Our extensive training program is one of the best in the nation. We are seeking dynamic, motivated, detail-oriented persons who have the potential to lead their own teams in our facilities. Must be well-organized, have the ability to multitask, and be able to work without supervision.

We offer a competitive salary, vacation incentives, weekly bonuses, and promotion opportunity after 90 days. Send cover letter, résumé, and three references to DEF@xxx.net

7. These were actual advertisements appearing in want ads. Increasingly, firms are using the Web. For the sake of this exercise, we have used letters rather than the actual organization contact. Select the one that you are most interested in, and write a cover letter expressing your interest in the position. Your instructor may want to see your cover letter as a graded assignment or have you share it with a classmate—you critique his or her cover letter while he or she critiques yours. In the latter case, make constructive and cogent suggestions.
8. If you have not done so, develop a résumé. See the suggestions on writing a résumé given earlier in this chapter.
9. Develop a list of questions you would ask if you were selected for a job interview.
10. Visit your college placement office to see what services it provides students. Start your journey now—work to develop the skills and expertise desired by employers.

### PERSONAL SKILL BUILDER 1-4: Technology Tools—What's in Your Toolbox?

In order to take full advantage of the Technology Tool activities that are included at the end of each chapter of the text, the authors encourage you to engage in a quick self-assessment of your technology to ensure you have the basic tools necessary to access and complete the activities. As directed by your instructor, complete and submit the questionnaire below. If you are unsure of how to answer any of the questions, arrange a time to meet with a member of your institution's information technology (IT) help desk to receive guidance in securing the software necessary to access the Internet, open PDF documents and compose, save, and submit documents using a word processor.

1. Do you have access to an Internet connection?
2. What is the name of your Internet browser?
3. Can you find information using a search engine such as Google or Yahoo?
4. Can you download and save files, such as documents or PDFs, from the Internet?
5. What is the name of the program that opens portable document files (PDFs)?
6. Do you have a PDF reader program on your computer?
7. Do you have Microsoft Word or comparable word processing software on your computer?
8. Does your word processing software have automatic grammar and spell check functions? (If the software does have that function, please make sure it is turned on and that you use it when composing any written work).
9. Can you save files to your hard drive or a removable storage device, such as a CD or a flash drive?
10. Can you log into your student e-mail account and read and send e-mail messages?
11. Can you attach a file to an e-mail message?
12. If this course is Web-based or Web-enhanced, what is the Web site address (URL) for your online course room or learning management system (LMS)?
13. Can you upload a file to your online course room or learning management system (LMS)?
14. What is the name of the technology help center at your institution?
15. What is the Web site for the technology help center at your institution?
16. What is the phone number for the technology help center at your institution?
17. What is the e-mail address for the technology help center at your institution?
18. Do you have other specific technology questions related to this course for which you would like assistance to find answers?

## TEAM SKILL BUILDING

### TEAM SKILL BUILDER 1-1: You Make the Call

This chapter's You Make the Call! can be used as a team role-play exercise. We recommend dividing the class into groups of three for this exercise. If you have an odd number, let one or two students fill the role of an observer recorder.

One student can play the role of Charlotte Kelly, another Pat Graham, and another should be Larry Stuckey, the hospital administrator. Refer to Personal Skill Builder 1-1. Each student in the group should list the major concern that they had on their list. Working as a group, develop strategies that Charlotte should use to deal with her concerns.

1. Working as a group, are your suggestions for Charlotte's concerns better than the ones that you individually developed.
2. Thinking back upon your group experience, did all of you participate equally? Did a leader emerge? If so, who was the leader of your group and why were the rest of you willing to allow that person to become the leader?
3. The previous supervisor in the ER department was somewhat autocratic. Based upon your group experiences, why was this leader's style not appropriate for the ER department?
4. Charlotte appears to be an admired manager. Each of you in the group should identify your most admired manager and share what it was that he or she did that made you admire them. Does Charlotte have some of those same characteristics?
5. As a group, write a paragraph describing what you learned from this skill application. If time permits, the instructors may have students share those to see what commonalities there are within a class.

## TEAM SKILL BUILDER 1-2: The Best Companies to Work For!

In 2014, *Fortune* identified "The World's Most Admired Companies" (See Caroline Fairchild, "The World's Most Admired Companies" (March 17, 2014), pp. 123–130.)

The top 10 were Apple, Amazon.com, Google, Berkshire Hathaway, Starbucks, Coca-Cola, Walt Disney, FedEx, Southwest Airlines, and General Electric.

NOTE TO INSTRUCTORS. We suggest that you divide your students into groups of 3–8 for this Team Skill Builder.

Each student in the group should select one of the aforementioned companies, and go to the Web to get sources of information about their chosen company.

1. Based upon what you learned about your chosen company, how would you describe their management philosophy?
2. What does the leader of the company do to guide employees to be the best they can be?
3. Assume that you were to shadow the CEO of this company for a day. What do you think you would learn?
4. What challenges do you think the company is facing today?
5. Would you like to work for the company? Why or why not?

After you have answered these questions for your chosen company, share your findings with the other members of your group.

Working together as a group, write a two-page paper explaining the advantages of seeking a job in these organizations. Your final paragraph should identify three things that you learned that will help you get a job in one of these companies.

## TEAM SKILL BUILDER 1-3: Food for Thought

In 2014, President Obama and congressional Democrats are pushing to increase the federal minimum wage from $7.25 to $10.10 an hour. Several states have already passed legislation for wage increases. For example, Maryland has increased the rate to $8 for January 2015 and 50 cent increases until it peaks at $10.10 by July 2018. Indiana University recently increased its minimum wage for its employees, many of whom are student workers.

We suggest that you review, Eliza Gray/Washington, "Wage Warrior," *Time* (March 10, 2014), pp. 38–41; Rick Hampson, "Raise the Minimum Wage?" *USA Today* (February 11, 2014), p. 4A; and other articles about the pending wage increase.

Students working together in groups of 3 to 6 should respond to the following questions:

1. What impact will higher wages have on employee satisfaction?
2. What impact will the minimum wage increase have on the price of products?
3. What impact will the increase in minimum wages have on unemployment?
4. After sharing your thoughts on these questions, as a group, write a 60-word paper identifying why the group agrees or disagrees with the proposed wage increase.

## SUPERVISION IN ACTION

SUPERVISION IN ACTION

The video for this chapter can be accessed from the student companion website at www.cengagebrain.com. (Search by authors' names or book title to find the accompanying resources.)

## ENDNOTES


1. Nick Leiber, "The Obamacare Dividend," *Bloomberg BusinessWeek* (February 10–16, 2014), pp. 45–46; John Tozzi, "Losing Patience and Patients," *Bloomberg BusinessWeek,* (April 14–20, 2014), p.30.
2. See "As Workers' Insurance Costs Rise, Bosses (Sometimes Wrongly) Blame Obamacare," http://www.kaiserhealthnews.org (January 9, 2014). Also see Drew Altman, "Obamacare: The Metrics in the News are Mostly Wrong," http://KFF.org/health-reform (March 2014).
3. G. Jeffrey MacDonald, "A Year Later, Boston Marathon Tributes a Delicate Task," *USA TODAY* (April 1, 2014), p. 3A.
4. Andy Pasztor and Rachel Pannett, "U.S., U.K. Providing Data on Plane Search," *The Wall Street Journal* (March 24, 2014), p. A9; Mahi Ramakrishnan, Gary Stoller, and Gary Strauss,"'None…On Board Survived,' " *USA TODAY* (March 25, 2014), p. 1A; Rem Rieder, "TV Coverage Excessive for Some, but Not CNN," *USA TODAY* (March 25, 2014), p. 2A.
5. Joel Millman and Zusha Elinson, "Mudslide's Toll Still Unclear," *The Wall Street Journal* (March 25, 2014), p. A3; Heather Graf, "176 Missing in Wash. Landslide," *USA TODAY* (March 25, 2014), p. 1A; John Emshwiller and Joel Millman, "Mud 15 Feet Deep Hampers Search for Victims of Slide," *The Wall Street Journal* (March 24, 2014), p. A3;
6. Eileen Norcross, "Cities' Shiny Fake Future Collapses," *USA TODAY* (March 13, 2014), p. 9A.
7. Hadley Malcolm, "Shoppers Not Hitting the Target," *USA TODAY* (March 12, 2014), p1B; Paul Ziobro, "Tech Executive at Target Resigns After Data Breach," *The Wall Street Journal* (March 6, 2014), p.B3; Danny Yadron, Paul Ziobro, and Devlin Barrett, "Target Staff Had Warnings," *The Wall Street Journal* (February 15 &16, 2014), p. B1; Paul Ziobro and Robin Sidel, "Target Tried Anti-Theft Cards," *The Wall Street Journal* (January 21, 2014), pB1.
8. James R. Healey, "Key Questions Stalking Barra," *USA TODAY* (April 1, 2014), p.1B; Jeff Bennett, "Barra Assures Owners GM's Cars Are Safe," *The Wall Street Journal*, (March 27, 2014), p. B3.
9. Paul Davidson, "Stocks Jump After Yellen Says Jobs Weak," *USA TODAY* (April 1, 2014), p. 1B; http://data.bls.gov/ and http://www.bls.gov/cps/
10. "Boeing Said They Would Freeze Pensions for 68,000 Non-union Employees," *The Wall Street Journal* (March 7, 2014), p. B3.
11. See Sudeep Reddy, "Downturn's Ugly Trademark: Steep, Lasting Drop in Wages," *The Wall Street Journal* (January 11, 2011), pp. A1, A14; "Economic Body Blows," *BusinessWeek* (June 9, 2008), p. 2, and Paul J. Lim and Susie Poppick, "How to Invest in a Scary Economy," *Money* (September 2011), pp. 108–113.
12. Steve Benen, "Union-busting Efforts Move Forward in Mississippi, Michigan," *MSNBC* (April 1,2014), http://www.msnbc.com/rachel-maddow-show/union-busting-efforts-move-forward; Sylvester Schieber and Phillip Longman, "The Fallacy of Union Busting," *The Washington Monthly* (May/June 2011), http://www.massaaflcio.org
13. Jae Yang and Karl Gelles, "Taking on More Work," *USA TODAY* (February 3, 2014), p. 1B.
14. Charles Kenny, "Factory Jobs Are Gone. Get Over It," *Bloomberg BusinessWeek* (January 27–February 2, 2014), pp. 12, 13.
15. Paul Davidson, "Staples to Close 225 Stores, Push Online Sales," *USA TODAY* (March 7, 2014), p. 2B.
16. "Employers Advised to Connect Engagement to Performance to Retain Top Talent in the New Year," Manpower.com (November 19, 2013), http://www.manpowergroup.com
17. The Bureau of Labor Statistics, http://www.bls.gov
18. Martha White, "For Many Americans, 'Temp' Work Becomes Permanent Way of Life," http://www.firstcoastnews.com (April 21, 2014).
19. See Peter Drucker, *The Effective Executive* (New York: Harper & Row, 1964, reprinted 1986).
20. See "Special Report: The Best & Worst Managers of the Year," *BusinessWeek* (January 10, 2005), pp. 55–86. Also see Timothy D. Schellhardt, "Off the Ladder: Want to Be a Manager? Many People Say No, Calling Job Miserable," The *Wall Street Journal* (April 4, 1997), p. A1; Joe B. Hill, "Strategies of Successful Managers," *Supervision* (February 2005), pp. 10–13; Joseph Cottringer, "Being the Kind of Supervisor Every Employer Loves," *Supervision* (June 2005), pp. 8–10.
21. An overview of the evolution of management thought is provided in J. Baughman, *The History of American Management* (Englewood Cliffs, NJ: Prentice-Hall, 1969); C. George, *The History of Management Thought* (Englewood Cliffs, NJ: Prentice-Hall, 1972). The principles of scientific management are described in Frederick W. Taylor, *Shop Management* (New York: Harper & Brothers, 1911); Frank G. Gilbreth and Lillian M. Gilbreth, *Applied Motion Study* (New York: Sturgis & Walton, 1917); and Edwin A. Locke, "The Ideas of Frederick W. Taylor: An Evaluation," *Academy of Management Review* (January 7, 1982), pp. 22–23. See Henri Fayol, *General and Industrial Management*, trans. Constance Storrs (London: Pitman Publishing Corp. 1949) for the functional approach to describing and analyzing management principles. Additional information on the human relations/behavioral science school of thought can be found in E. Mayo, *The Human Problems of Industrial Civilization* (New York: Macmillan, 1933); Fritz J. Roethlisberger and W. J. Dickson, *Management and the Worker* (Boston: Harvard University Press, 1939); and J. A. Sonnenfeld, "Shedding Light on the Hawthorne Studies," *Journal of Occupational Behavior* 6(1985), pp. 111–130.

    For a discussion of the problems of developing universal agreement on management approaches, see the classic article by Harold Koontz, "The Management Theory Jungle Revisited," *Academy of Management Review* 5(1980), pp. 175–188.
22. For a most interesting insight into the principles of scientific management, see *Cheaper by the Dozen*. Either version will provide you with many laughs as the family puts the principles of scientific management into practice. The movies were based on the lives of Professors Lillian and Frank Gilbreths who were disciples of Taylor.
23. Harold R. Kerzner, *Project Management—A Systems Approach to Planning, Scheduling, & Controlling,*11th ed. (New York: Wiley, 2013). Specifically, see Dr. Kerzner's 16 Points to Project Management Maturity.

24. Talya N. Bauer, "Onboarding New Employees: Maximizing Success," *SHRM Foundation*, (2010).
25. Scott Whipple, "Focus on Manufacturing: Skilled Workers Needed," www.newbritainherald.com (April 23, 2014); "Canada—Federal Skilled Worker Program Accepting 25,000 New Applicants," www.cicnews.com (April 21, 2014); Miriam Jordan, "Factories Turn to Refugee Workers," *The Wall Street Journal* (May 6, 2008), p. A1; Dave Montgomery, "Illegal Immigration in U.S. Bringing out 'Deep-Seated' Anger," *The Jacksonville, FL Times-Union* (August 19, 2007), pp. A1, A6.
26. www.foxnews.com
27. Statistics and projections included in this and other sections are drawn from James C. Franklin, "An Overview of BLS Projections to 2016," *Monthly Labor Review Online* 130, No. 11 (November 2007), pp. 3–12. Also see "Employment Projections: 2006–2016 Summary," Bureau of Labor Statistics (December 4, 2007). For more current projections, see http://www.bls.gov/emp/emppub01.htm. Also go to http://www.bls.gov/emp/optd/home.htm. To access the Census Bureau's population estimates, go to http://factfinder.census.gov
28. Gary Burtless, "Is an Aging Workforce Less Productive?" www.brookings.edu/blogs/ (June 10, 2013).
29. "Share of Labor Force Projected to Rise for People age 55 and Over and Fall for Younger Age Groups," Bureau of Labor Statistics (January 24, 2014), http://www.bls.gov/opub/ted/2014/ted_20140124.htm#bls-print; "Labor Force Participation Projected to Fall for People under age 55 and Rise for Older Age Groups," Bureau of Labor Statistics (January 6, 2014), http://www.bls.gov/opub/ted/2014/ted_20140106.htm#bls-print.
30. Vicki Elmer, "50-plus Years on the Job: An Extremely Rare Bird," *CNN Money* (February 28, 2014), http://management.fortune.cnn.com; Employee Tenure Summary (September 18, 2012), http://bls.gov/news.release/tenure.nr0.htm; "Time Typical Worker Stays in Any One Job," *USA Today Snapshots* (August 3, 2010), p. 1A. Note: 17 percent of workers have been with the same employer for 15 years or longer.
31. See Adrienne Fox, "Mixing it Up," *HR Magazine* (May 2011), pp. 22–27; J. Walker Smith and Ann Clurman, *Generation Ageless* (New York, HarperCollins 2007); Anne Houlihan, "When Gen-X Is In Charge," *Supervision* (April 2008), pp. 11–13; and Houlihan, "The New Melting Pot: How to Effectively Lead Different Generations in the Workplace," *Supervision* (September 2007), pp. 10–12; and James A. Johnson and John Lopes, "The Intergenerational Workforce, Revisited," *Organizational Development Journal* 26, No. 1 (Spring 2008), pp. 31–36. Workforce classifications described in this article were from Ann S. Clurman and J. Walker Smith, *Rocking the Ages: The Yankelovich Report on Generational Marketing* (New York: HarperBusiness, 1997). See also Julius Steiner, "Six Steps to Guaranteeing Generation Y Productivity," *Supervision* (July 2007), pp. 6–7.
32. Neil Howe and William Strauss, *Millennials Rising: The Next Generation* (New York: Vintage Books, 2000), p. 45. See Sommer Kehrli and Trudy Sopp, "Managing Generation Y: Stop Resisting and Start Embracing the Challenges Generation Y Brings to the Workplace," *HR Magazine* (May 2006), pp. 113–119.
33. http://countryeconomy.com/unemployment/usa
34. Valorie Burton, *Happy Women Live Better*, (Eugene OR: Harvest House Publishers, 2013). You may also want to see Elaine Meryl Brown, Marsha Haygood, and Rhonda Joy McLean, *The Little Black Book of Success: Laws of Leadership for Black Women* (New York: Random House, 2010).
35. Carol Hymowitz, "On Diversity, America Isn't Putting Its Money Where Its Mouth Is," *The Wall Street Journal* (February 25, 2008), p. B1. A McKinsey Global Survey found a majority of executives believe there is a direct connection between a company's gender diversity and its financial success. (*Moving Women to the Top*, McKinsey & Company, 2010). Also see Herminia Ibarra, Nancy M. Carter, and Christine Silva, "Why Men Still Get More Promotions than Women," *Harvard Business Review* (September 2010), pp. 80–85; Julie Bennett, "Women Get a Boost up That Tall Leadership Ladder," *The Wall Street Journal* (June 10, 2008), p. D6, and Alice Eagly and Linda Carli, "Women and the Labyrinth of Leadership," *The Harvard Business Review* (September 2007).
36. Hope Yen, "Working Mothers Now Top Earners in Record 40 Percent of Households with Children: Pew," www.huffingtonpost.com, (May 29, 2013); Jonathan House, "Record Number of Women in Workforce," *The Wall Street Journal* (November 18, 2013), p A5.
37. Over 10 million single mothers living with children under 18 years old and 55 percent of women with infant children are in the labor force. See http://www.census.gov/population/socdemo/hh-fam/tabFM-2.pdf for additional workforce data. Also review the Census Bureau Facts and Figures that were prepared to commemorate Mother's Day (May 11, 2008). The author believes that it is imperative that employers adopt family-friendly policies and procedures to accommodate these worker needs.
38. From the Families and Work Institute as reported by Alison Ashton, "When It's Work vs. Family, Work Usually Wins," *Working Mother* (December 2001/January 2002), p. 10. Also see Sue Shellenbarger, "How Stay-at-Home Moms Are Filling an Executive Niche," The *Wall Street Journal* (April 30, 2008), p. D1. See www.workingmother.com for information on the strategies and programs companies use to help employees balance work and life and the "2010 Working Mother 100 Best Companies."
39. Camille Ryan, "Language Use in the United States: 2011," census.gov (August 2013).
40. "Empowering Women in Business," http://www.feminist.org/research/business/ewb_glass.html; Feminist Majority Foundation (2014); and "The Glass-Ceiling Index," http://www.economist.com (March 8, 2014).
41. See Ann Pomeroy, "Executive Briefing: Female Executives Lead Differently from Men," *HR Magazine* (June 2005), p. 24. Also see Martha White, "Women in Business Leadership: Up Against a Second Glass Ceiling," www.nbcnews.com (April 2014),; Steve Bates, "Women vs. Men: Which Make Better Leaders?" *SHRM Home* (November 11, 2005), and Del Jones, "What Glass Ceiling?" *USA Today* (July 20, 1999), p. 18.
42. Sheryl Sandberg with Nell Scovell, *Lean In: Women, Work, and the Will to Lead* (New York: Alfred A. Knopf, 2013). You may also want to see the 2014 McKinsey Global Survey Results, "Moving Mind-sets on Gender Diversity," mckinsey.com.

43. See the National Center for Educational Statistics (http://nces.ed.gov) and the Bureau of Labor Statistics for additional data on the educational attainment of the workforce. Also see Jessica Brown, "National Dropout, Graduation Rates Improve, Study Shows," *USA TODAY*, (January 22, 2013).

44. See the report at www.lhh.com. You may also want to see Jennifer Schramm, "Planning for Population Shifts," *HR Magazine* (February 2011), p. 80; and "Employment Projections: 2006–2016 Summary," Bureau of Labor Statistics (December 4, 2007).

45. Ibid. Also see Jennifer Schramm, "Slow Recovery Threatens Skills," *HR Trendbook* (2011), pp. 55–57.

46. John Lechleiter, "The Fix To America's Manufacturing Decline Stands Right Before Us," (02/13/2014), http://www.forbes.com; "Declining Manufacturing and the Middle Class" (February 3, 2014), http://america.aljazeera.com/watch/shows/real-money-with-alivelshi/Real-Money-Blog; Robert D. Atkinson, Luke A. Stewart, Scott M. Andes, and Stephen Ezell, "Worse than the Great Depression: What the Experts Are Missing about American Manufacturing Decline" (March 19, 1012), http://www2.itif.org/

47. Lorene Yue, "Can China Rescue McDonald's?" www.chicagobusiness.com (February 1, 2014); Panos Mourdoukoutas, "McDonald's Big Challenge at Home and Abroad," www.forbes.com, (July 22, 2013).

48. Shelly Banjo, "Inside Nike's Struggle to Balance Cost and Worker Safety," *The Wall Street Journal* (April 22, 2014) pp. A1, A12. *Note*: The whole notion of cheap labor is accountable for the Bangladesh boom. Thirty years ago, Bangladesh was making no ready-to-wear garments. Today they are exporting more than $21 billion yearly to the rest of the world. Currently, Nike has four factories and over 21,000 workers in Bangladesh.

49. "Time Honors Facebook Founder as Person of the Year," Associated Press (December 16, 2010), p. 8A. Also see, Peter Newcomb, "Mark Zuckerberg # 4," *Fortune* (December 6, 2010), p. 138 and Brad Stone, "Fight for Tomorrow," *Bloomberg BusinessWeek* (April 28–May 4, 2014), pp. 14–15.

50. Reed Albergotti, "Facebook Net Triples," *The Wall Street Journal* (April 24, 2014), p. B1, B12; John Kell, "Mark Zuckerberg Managed With a Bit Less in 2013," *The Wall Street Journal* (April 1, 2014), p. B3; Brad Stone and Sarah Frier, "Facebook's Next Decade," *Bloomberg BusinessWeek* (February 3–9, 2014), pp. 44–49.

51. Barrett Sheridan, "The Cure for Information Overload," *Bloomberg BusinessWeek,* (June19, 2012).

52. Reported in Entrepreneurs, Ilya Pozin, "4 Surprising Truths About Workplace Productivity," http://www.forbes.com (April 17, 2014).

53. See "Welcome to Our 2012 Global Citizen," www.AB-InBev.com/go/social-responsibility/. See also "Anheuser Discloses Early-Retirement Plans," *TheWall Street Journal* (August 13, 2008), p. B6; Heidi N. Moore, "Will Dollar Rise Hurt Mergers?" *The Wall Street Journal* (August 12, 2008), p. C3; David Kesmodel and Matthew Karnitschnig, "InBev UnCorks Anheuser Takeover Bid," *The Wall Street Journal* (June 12, 2008), p. A1, A14.

54. See Dexter Roberts, "China's Sentimental Journey Back to Mao," *Bloomberg BusinessWeek* (January 17–23, 2011), pp. 9–10; Jennifer Reingold, "P&G's New Mission: Make Money in Places Where People Earn $2 a Day," *Fortune* (January 17, 2011), p. 16.

55. Adapted from "Conversations with Tom Peters," *Quality Digest* (November 1996), pp. 37–38.

56. Motoka Rich, "Temporary Work Here to Stay?" *The Columbus Dispatch* (December 25, 2010). pp. A14–A15. Also see, Ed Frauheim, "Contingent Workers: Why Companies Must Make Then Feel Valued," workforce.com (August 2012); Rita Zeidner, "Heady Debate: Rely on Temps or Hire Staff," *HR Magazine* (February 2010), pp. 28–33.

57. Bill Leonard, "Employees Want More Quality Time with Families," *HR Magazine* (June 1999), p. 28.

58. Adapted from Archie B. Carroll and Ann K. Buchholtz, *Business & Society: Ethics Sustainability and Stakeholder Management*, 8th ed. (Cincinnati: Cengage/South-Western, 2012), chap. 2. Also see, Carroll, "The Pyramid of Corporate Social Responsibility," *Business Horizons* (July–August 1991), p. 39–48.
Also see Adrienne Fox, "Corporate Social Responsibility Pays Off," *HR Magazine* (August 2007), pp. 42–47; and A. Fox, "Be an Insider on Social Responsibility," *HR Magazine* (February 2008), pp. 49–51.

59. Go to www.shrm.org to see a listing of the expectations, responsibilities, and professional code of conduct for human resource (HR) professionals.

60. See Jack Wallen, "10 Rudest Behaviors in the Workplace," http://www.techrepublic.com/blog/10-things (November 2013); Erika Andersen, "Why Being Rude Is Bad For Business (and What to Do About It)," www.forbes.com (August 27, 2013); Casey Gueren, "The Nasty Workplace Epidemic," www.womenhealthmag.com (February 6, 2013); "Research Shows Rude Behavior at Work Is Increasing and Affects the Bottom Line," www.newswise.com/articles/research-shows-rude-behavior-at-work-is-increasing-and -affects-the-bottom-line (January 30, 2013); Kathy Gurchiek, "Workplace Violence on the Upswing," *HR Magazine* (July 2005), pp. 27–32; Christine M. Pearson, Lynn M. Andersson, and Christine L. Porath, "Assessing and Attacking Workplace Incivility," *Organizational Dynamics* 29, No. 2 (2000), pp. 123–137; Jenny McCune, "Civility Counts," *Management Review* (March 2000), pp. 6–8; and Michael A. Verespej, "A Call for Civility," *Industry Week* (February 12, 2001), p. 17.

61. Robert M. Bramson, *Coping with Difficult People* (New York: Dell Publishing Co., 1989).

62. Tim Rutledge, *Getting Engaged: The New Workplace Loyalty* (Scarborough, ON: Mattanie Press (October 2005). Also see Kay Greasley, et al., "Understanding Empowerment from an Employee Perspective: What Does It Mean and Do They Want It?" *Team Performance Management* 14, No.1/2 (2008), pp. 39–55; Nancy R. Lockwood, "Leveraging Employee Engagement for Competitive Advantage," *HR Magazine* (March 2007), p. 11; John Gibbons, "Employee Engagement: A Review of Current Research and Its Implications," *The Conference Board of New York* (November 2006), pp. 1–18; Gerald H. Seijts and Dan Crin, "The Ten C's of Employee Engagement," *Ivey Business Journal* 70, No. 4 (March/April 2006), pp. 1–5; and Alison M. Konrad, "Engaging Employees through High-Involvement Work Practices," *Ivey Business Journal* 70, No. 4 (March/April 2006), pp. 6–11.

63. See *Employee Engagement: A Review of Current Research and Its Implications* (New York: The Conference Board, November 2006), pp.1–18. Also see *2008 Employee Engagement Report* (New York: Blessing White Research, April 2008); and Patricia Soldati, "Employee Engagement: What Exactly Is It?" *Management-Issues On line* (March 8,

2007). You may also want to see Elizabeth Kampf, "Can You Really Manage Engagement without Managers?" http://businessjournal.gallup.com (April 2014).

64. The statement "As long as you live, keep learning to live" is from Seneca as quoted in Burton E. Stevenson, *The Home Book of Quotations, Classical and Modern*, 10th ed. (New York: Dodd, Mead, 1967), p. 1131.
65. Stephen R. Covey, *The Seven Habits of Highly Effective People: Restoring the Character Ethic* (New York: Simon & Schuster, 1989), p. 287. Also see Covey's *Principle-Centered Leadership* (New York: The Free Press 1992) and *First Things First: To Live, to Love, to Learn, to Leave a Legacy* (New York: Simon & Schuster, 1994).
66. See Nancy Collamer, "6 Ways to Crack the Hidden Job Market!" www.forbes.com (August 12, 2013).
67. Donna Fuscaldo, "College Grads: Don't Make these Job Search Mistakes," http://www.foxbusiness.com (August 7, 2013); Jeremy S. Hyman and Lynn F. Jacobs, "10 Tips for College Students Looking for a Job in a Tough Market," http://www.usnews.com (March 31, 2010).

Chapter 2

# The Managerial Functions

mediacolor's / Alamy

**After studying this chapter, you will be able to:**

1. Identify the difficulties supervisors face in fulfilling managerial roles.
2. Explain why effective supervisors should have a variety of skills.
3. Define management and discuss how the management functions are interrelated.
4. Discuss the important characteristics of the supervisor as a team leader.
5. Explain the difference between management and leadership.
6. Discuss the concept of authority and power as it relates to being a good supervisor.
7. Explain the need for coordination and cooperation and how they lead to good performance.
8. Identify how labor unions affect the management functions.

## YOU MAKE THE CALL!

*You are Dee Sikora, supervisor of housekeeping services at the Benevolent General Hospital, a 300-bed hospital located in Tennessee. You are responsible for the overall housekeeping services. You have several assistants (working supervisors) who report to you. There are 60 full-time and 22 part-time workers in your department.*

In recent weeks, rumors had been circulating about a major organizing campaign being undertaken by the Service Employees International Union (SEIU; http://www.seiu.org/our-union/). SEIU is the fastest-growing union in the United States with a focus on healthcare and healthcare properties services. There have been union organizers reported at several of the hospitals in the area, but you have not noticed any union organizers at your hospital and there has not been any word or discussions about this from the hospital administration.

The hospital is currently at 60 percent capacity and patients are staying for shorter times. However, the emergency room has a long waiting time most days of the week, and the rooms are filled to capacity most of the time. Early this morning, Charmaine, one of your assistants, gave you a copy of a *Boston Globe* article that talked about how the North Adams Regional Hospital located in the southwest corner of Massachusetts for the last 129 years would be shutting its doors on Friday. The move came in response to the hospital's worsening financial crisis. The move will create job woes for the 530 full- and part-time employees. The article went on to say that the Massachusetts Nurses Association and the SEIU will fight the decision to close. You wondered if something like that could happen here.

Later in the day, Tom Mays, one of your best employees who has worked for you for seven years, came into your office. This is what he had to say:

"Dee, I need your advice. Several of my co-workers have confronted me on three occasions, trying to get me to sign a union authorization card. They're trying to organize all of the housekeeping employees into a union bargaining unit. They are saying that we need a union to protect their jobs, and that we are not being fairly treated, both in wages and benefits, and we need a union to get a fair shake. They even have been going after me and others while we're trying to get our work done at the hospital. Maybe we do need a union here to protect our jobs. I really don't know who to believe. I know the names of most of the individuals who want a union here at the hospital. Perhaps you can talk to them to see how you can resolve some of their complaints. What should I do in the meantime?"

How should you respond to Tom? What should you say and do?

**Disclaimer:** The above scenario presents a supervisory situation based on real events to be used for educational purposes. The identities of some or all individuals, organizations, industries, and locations, as well as financial and other information may have been disguised to protect individual privacy and proprietary information. In some cases details have been added to improve readability and interest.

YOU MAKE THE CALL!

## The Person in the Middle

**1 Identify the difficulties supervisors face in fulfilling managerial roles.**

The supervisory position is a difficult and demanding role. Supervisors are "people in the middle"—the principal links between higher-level managers and employees. See Figure 1.3 in Chapter 1 for an overview of the responsibilities and difficult challenges faced by supervisors. A supervisor is a first-level manager, that is, a manager in charge of entry-level and other departmental employees. Every organization, whether a retail store, fast-food restaurant, manufacturing firm, hospital, or government agency, has someone who fills this role.

Throughout this textbook, we use the terms *worker*, *employee*, *associate*, *team member*, and *subordinate* interchangeably to refer to individuals who report to supervisors or managers. Regardless of the term used, employees may view their supervisors as the management of the organization, since the supervisor is their primary contact with management. Employees expect a supervisor to be technically competent and to be a good leader who can show them how to get the job done.

The supervisor must also be a competent subordinate to higher-level managers. In this role, the supervisor must be a good follower. Moreover, the supervisor is expected to maintain satisfactory relationships with supervisors in other departments. Therefore, a supervisor's relationship to other supervisors is that of a colleague who must cooperate and must coordinate his or her department's efforts with those of others in order to reach the overall goals of the organization.

In general, the position of any supervisor has two main requirements. First, the supervisor must have a good working knowledge of the jobs to be performed. Second, and more significant, the supervisor must be able to manage the department. It is the supervisor's managerial competence that usually determines the effectiveness of his or her performance.

**2 Explain why effective supervisors should have a variety of skills.**

## Managerial Skills Make the Difference

Most organizations have some supervisors who appear to be under constant pressure and continuously do the same work as their subordinates. They are getting by, although they feel overburdened. These supervisors endure long hours, may be devoted to their jobs, and are willing to do everything themselves. They want to be effective, but they seldom have enough time to supervise. Other supervisors appear to be on top of their jobs, and their departments run smoothly in an orderly fashion. These supervisors find time to sit at their desks at least part of the day, and they keep their paperwork up to date. What is the difference?

Of course, some supervisors are more capable than others, just as some mechanics are better than others. If we compare two maintenance supervisors who are equally good mechanics, have similar equipment under their care, and operate under approximately the same conditions, why might one be more effective than the other? The answer is that effective supervisors manage their departments in a manner that gets the job done through their people instead of doing the work themselves. The difference between a good supervisor and a poor one, assuming that their technical skills are similar, is the difference in their managerial skills and how they apply them.

The managerial aspects of the supervisor's position too often have been neglected in the selection and development of supervisors. Typically, people are selected for supervisory positions based on their technical competence, their seniority or past performance, and their willingness to work hard. Often newly promoted supervisors are expected to jump right into their new management positions. Hopefully, new supervisors will have a chance to develop some of the skills that would be necessary in their new assignments. In an ideal world, the organization would groom prospective supervisory candidates and provide them with opportunities to grow and to develop and hone certain skills.

Many managers do not do a good job of cross-training and delegating. These are two activities that create problems for many experienced supervisors. Early in our careers, we were blessed because we had managers who saw mentoring and employee development as a key part of their job. It was important that our bosses had confidence in us and us in them. Think back on your work-life experiences; were there people who provided you with opportunities for growth by coaching and delegating tasks, which allowed you to add skills to your personal toolboxes? Have you thanked them for what they did?

Unfortunately, many organizations do not adequately prepare prospective supervisors for these responsibilities or equip them with the necessary skills. While new supervisors begin their new assignments with great enthusiasm, they often become disenchanted when the first sign of trouble appears or when they

**FIGURE 2.1 Making your mark as a new supervisor.**

mismanage a situation. Figures 2.1 and 2.2 will help you take some smart first steps down the supervisory path.

What will your supervisory legacy be?
Do you want people to say you made the organization better?
If so, it is your job to put the pieces of the puzzle together.
Your first moves as a new supervisor are the most
important ones you'll ever make!
Focus on the Employee's Heart
Target Organizational Goals
© 2016 Cengage Learning®

Employees wanting to move into supervisory or upper-level management positions must make a conscious effort to develop their managerial skills by learning from their own managers, by completing company training programs, and by taking other avenues available to them. Remember, in today's economy, you must gain experience. "Where can I get that experience?" you may ask. Some possibilities include getting involved in student organizations, visiting the college placement office to see what kinds of unpaid internships are available, and volunteering in any number of not-for-profit organizations.

At this point you may want to go back and reread Chapter 1's "You Make the Call!" Charlotte took the initiative to learn. She earned her certificate in medical records technology and took college classes in supervision and organizational leadership. She gained an understanding of group dynamics and motivational techniques. Through the team approach to learning, not only did she learn things that effective supervisors need to do, she also learned about some supervisory methods that were ineffective.

**FIGURE 2.2 Winning moves a supervisor should make**

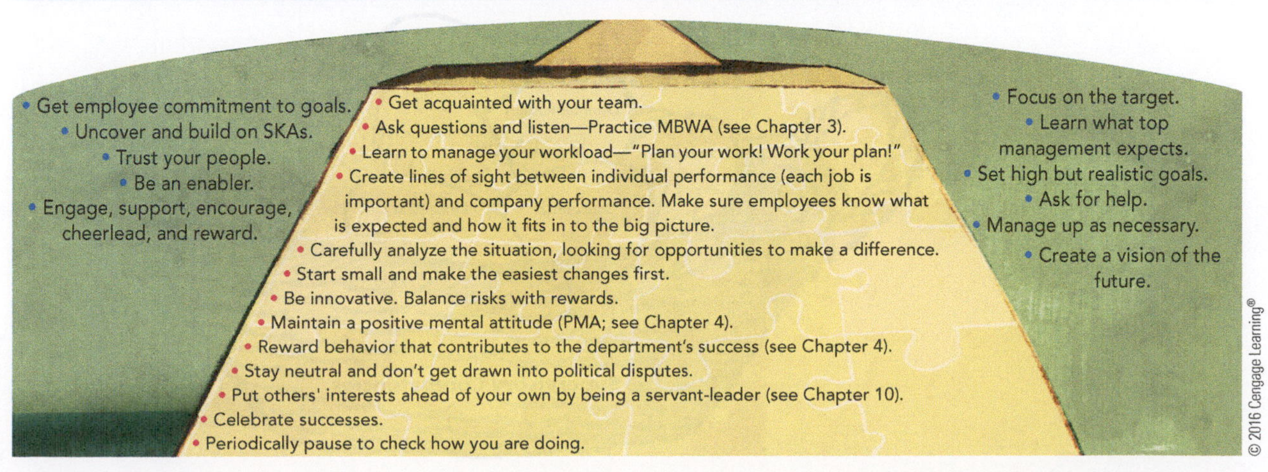

• Get employee commitment to goals.
• Uncover and build on SKAs.
• Trust your people.
• Be an enabler.
• Engage, support, encourage, cheerlead, and reward.
• Get acquainted with your team.
• Ask questions and listen—Practice MBWA (see Chapter 3).
• Learn to manage your workload—"Plan your work! Work your plan!"
• Create lines of sight between individual performance (each job is important) and company performance. Make sure employees know what is expected and how it fits in to the big picture.
• Carefully analyze the situation, looking for opportunities to make a difference.
• Start small and make the easiest changes first.
• Be innovative. Balance risks with rewards.
• Maintain a positive mental attitude (PMA; see Chapter 4).
• Reward behavior that contributes to the department's success (see Chapter 4).
• Stay neutral and don't get drawn into political disputes.
• Put others' interests ahead of your own by being a servant-leader (see Chapter 10).
• Celebrate successes.
• Periodically pause to check how you are doing.
• Focus on the target.
• Learn what top management expects.
• Set high but realistic goals.
• Ask for help.
• Manage up as necessary.
• Create a vision of the future.
© 2016 Cengage Learning®

To this end, we have grouped the managerial skills supervisors need into the following eight major classifications:

**Technical skills**
The ability to do the job

**Human relations skills**
The ability to work with and through people

**Communication skills**
The ability to give—and get—information

**Administrative skills**
The ability to plan, organize, and coordinate activities

**Conceptual skills**
The ability to obtain, interpret, and apply information

**Leadership skills**
The ability to engage followers in all aspects of the organization

**Servant leadership**
The notion that the needs of followers are looked after so they can be the best they can be

**Political skills**
The ability to understand how things get done outside of formal channels

**Emotional intelligence skills**
The ability to use your emotions intelligently

1. **Technical skills**: The ability to perform the jobs in the supervisor's area of responsibility.
2. **Human relations skills**: The ability to work with and through people; these skills include open-mindedness and the ability to motivate team members.
3. **Communication skills**: The ability to give—and get—information.[1]
4. **Administrative skills**: The ability to plan, organize, and coordinate the activities of a work group.
5. **Conceptual skills**: The ability to obtain, interpret, and apply the information needed to make sound decisions.
6. **Leadership skills**: The development of a leadership style that emphasizes collaboration, trust, and empathy; engages followers in all aspects of the organization; and helps followers to better themselves—that is, **servant leadership**.[2]
7. **Political skills**: The savvy to ascertain the hidden rules of the organizational game and to recognize the roles various people play in getting things done outside of formal organizational channels.
8. **Emotional intelligence skills**: The "intelligent use of your emotions to help guide your behavior and thinking in ways that enhance your results. You can maximize your emotional intelligence by developing good communication skills, interpersonal relationships, and mentoring relationships."[3]

People no longer grant automatic deference to those in positions of authority. The only way to earn their respect and trust is by appropriately using these skills. Your challenge is presented in Figure 2.3.

The notion of knowing oneself is not new, nor is it the only thing that supervisors need to master. Supervisors such as Dee Sikora, supervisor in this chapter's You Make the Call!, must strive to understand and manage the moods and emotions of others.[4] Chess master Bruce Pandolfini stresses that there are two basic forms of intelligence: (1) the ability to read other people and (2) the ability to understand one's self.[5]

Unfortunately, it was not too many years ago that corporate America believed you could take the best mechanics or the best salespeople and give them the title

**FIGURE 2.3 Your goals are to put all of your skills in one basket and be able to use them effectively**

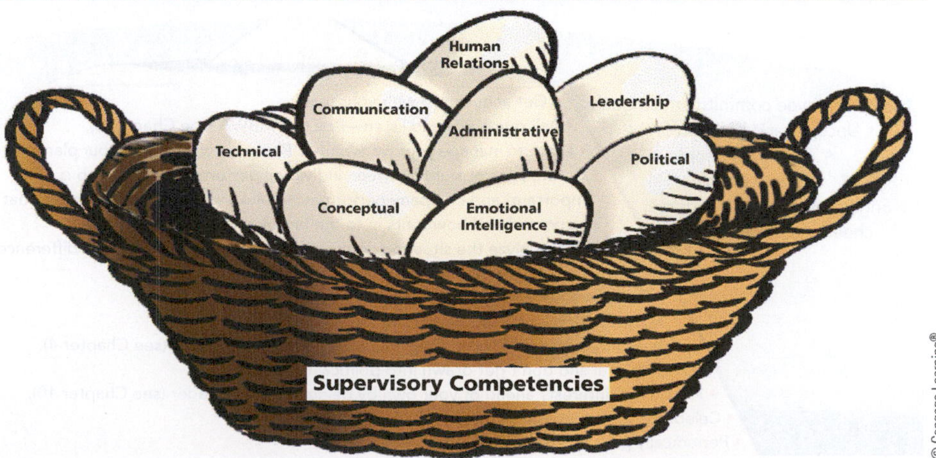

of supervisor or manager, and success would automatically follow. You may have heard horror stories about the supervisors who did their homework, did everything aboveboard, and called on the aforementioned skills, but somehow something went wrong. These supervisors made judgment errors; others would say they lacked common sense.

## MANAGERIAL SKILLS CAN BE LEARNED AND DEVELOPED

Many people believe that good managers, like good athletes, are born, not made. Much research has proven this belief to be generally incorrect, even though it is true that people are born with different potentials and that, to some degree, heredity plays a role in intelligence. An athlete who is not endowed with natural physical advantages is not likely to run 100 yards in 10 seconds flat. On the other hand, many individuals who are so-called natural athletes also have not come close to that goal.

Most superior athletes have developed their natural endowments into mature skills with practice, training, effort, and experience. The same holds true for a good manager. The skills involved in managing are as learnable as the skills used in playing tennis or golf, for example. It takes time, effort, and determination for a supervisor to develop managerial skills. Supervisors will make mistakes, but people learn from mistakes as well as from successes. By applying the principles discussed in this textbook, the supervisor can develop the skills that make the supervisory job a challenging and satisfying career.

Simply talking about supervisory management is somewhat like Mark Twain's comment about the weather: "Everybody talks about it, but no one does anything about it." Therefore, throughout this textbook we present tips, suggestions, and activities that are designed to reinforce concepts. However, these tools alone do not guarantee supervisory success. For example, if you wanted to learn to play golf or play the game better, you might strive to emulate the games of some of the greatest golfers of all time. Hopefully, for you, supervision will not be a spectator sport. Once you gain a supervisory position, if that is your dream, it will require your total commitment to be successful. We encourage you to take your talents to new heights.

However, if you really want to learn to play golf, you should take lessons from the coaches who provided the best with the solid fundamentals of the game. The great golfers—like great supervisors—have used multiple coaches during their careers. Unfortunately, their teachers might not have the time, and you might not have the money to pay what they might charge for the lessons. Then you would take another course of action—find someone who has knowledge of the fundamentals and the ability and willingness to instruct. Select a coach or mentor who will help you uncover your desires and help you chart a course of action to achieve them.

Think again of the game of golf. The goal of most golfers, whether they are in a competitive event, a friendly match, or just trying to beat their personal best, is to shoot lower scores.[6] The novice golfer would want to have multiple coaches because no one is best in teaching all facets of the game. Ideally, beginners who aspire to lofty goals would want a fitness coach, a driving coach, a short-game coach, a putting coach, and a mental attitude coach. They would want a coach who would help them stretch beyond "just being good enough"

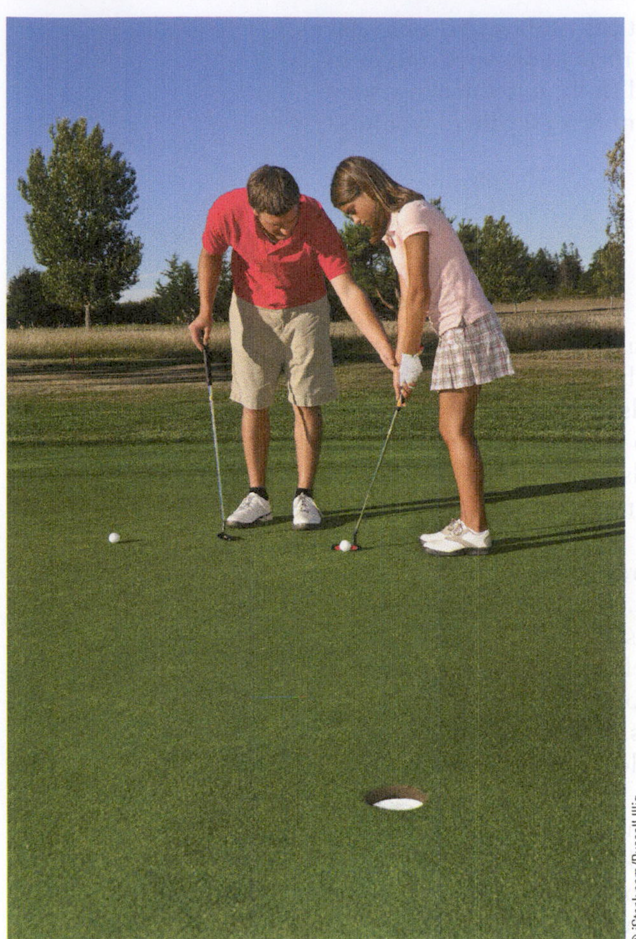
© iStock.com/Russell Illig

*Great supervisors—like great athletes—rely on coaches to help them develop and enhance their skills and abilities*

to being the "best they can possibly be." It is doubtful that one could do it on their own. We all know of some individuals who would prefer to go it alone, that is, they have the I-can-do-it-myself mentality. They might use self-teaching techniques such as viewing videos, trying to emulate the more successful players, or reviewing a series of *Golf Digest* instructional tips. Being a great golfer, like being a great supervisor, takes a lot of hard work. One has to master all aspects of the game. It does one no good to be able to hit the ball 300 yards straight down the middle of the fairway if he has the "yips"—the tendency to miss short putts on a regular basis. All of one's skills and functions have to work in combination. In the supervisory position—like the game of golf—there are no do-overs.

You would also need the proper tools (such as the right clubs) and the time to practice, learn from your mistakes, and make corrections. There is one major difference between the beginning golfer and the newly appointed supervisor. Unlike beginning golfers, who can go to the driving range or the practice green to work on their games, newly appointed supervisors are on the job. Supervisors go through a learning curve that offers very little room for trial and error. The supervisor cannot hit it out of bounds and tee it up again for another chance. To get the job done the right way, the supervisor must avoid some common mistakes. Consider our supervisory tips and remember that the challenge for any professional is to stay on the path of continuous improvement.

Even the best continually seek ways to sharpen their skills. Remember, golf, like successful supervision, requires one to control the "choke factor" (the ability to play under pressure). Supervision is not a spectator sport, and supervisors, like golfers, will occasionally find themselves in uncomfortable positions.

**3 Define management and discuss how the primary managerial functions are interrelated.**

## Functions of Management

**Management**
Getting objectives accomplished with and through people

The term *management* has been defined in many ways. In general, **management** is the process of getting things accomplished with and through people by guiding and motivating their efforts toward common objectives.

Successful managers will assure you that their employees are their most important asset. Most successful managers recognize that they are only as good as the people they supervise. In most endeavors, one person can accomplish relatively little. Therefore, individuals join forces with others to attain mutual goals. In all organizations, top-level managers or administrators are responsible for achieving the goals of the organization, but success requires the efforts of all subordinate managers and employees. Those who hold supervisory positions significantly

## SUPERVISORY TIPS

### The E-Z Route for Supervisory Succcess

- Above all, supervisors should do all of the things necessary to **Enable** employees to be the best they can be at their assigned tasks.
- Supervisors must foster and sustain a commitment to **Excellence**.
- Employees need to know what is **Expected** in the way of performance.
- Supervisors should **Establish** common goals and purpose.
- Employees must be **Educated**; that is, they must acquire the requisite job skills through coaching and/or training.
- Employees must be **Equipped** with the necessary tools, supplies, and equipment to do the job.
- Employees need to be **Encouraged** to see things that need to be done and to do them.
- Employees should be **Empowered** so that they have the authority and responsibility to achieve objectives.
- Supervisors should nurture an **Exciting** workplace where employees can find meaning and fulfillment of their individual needs.
- Employees should **Experience** a variety of tasks and thus become experienced in many areas that use a variety of skills.
- Supervisors should attempt to create a climate that fully **Engages** their employees in the organization. Open, honest, two-way communication is essential.
- Supervisors should understand and manage their **Emotions**.
- Supervisors should possess **Empathy**; that is, they should understand their employees' feelings, needs, and concerns.
- Supervisors should **Enthusiastically Exalt** employees when the job is well done.

influence the effectiveness with which people work together and use resources to attain goals. In short, the managerial role of a supervisor is to make sure that assigned tasks are accomplished with and through the help of employees.

With this in mind, we believe the term **enabler** more closely defines the new role of the manager.[7] Clearly, the foundation for success is built when the manager clarifies what is expected in the way of performance and specifies the behaviors that are acceptable in the work group. Then the role of the supervisor is to do all those things that enable employees to be the best they can be (in other words, effectively and efficiently achieve organizational objectives). The better the supervisor manages, the better the departmental results. In addition, the supervisor who manages well becomes capable of handling larger and more complicated assignments, which could lead to more responsibility and higher-paying positions in the organization. (See the accompanying "Supervisory Tips" box for some tips on becoming a successful supervisor.)

**Enabler**
The person who does the things necessary to enable employees to do the best possible job

## THE MANAGERIAL FUNCTIONS ARE THE SAME IN ALL MANAGERIAL POSITIONS

The managerial functions of a supervisory position are similar, whether they involve supervision of a production line, a sales force, a laboratory, or a small office. The primary managerial functions are also the same regardless of the level in the hierarchy of management: first-level supervisor, middle-level manager, or top-level manager. Similarly, the type of organization does not matter. Managerial functions are the same whether the supervisor is working in a profit-making firm, a nonprofit organization, or a government office. Supervisors, as well as other managers, perform the same basic managerial functions in all organizations. In this textbook, we classify these functions under the major categories of planning, organizing, staffing, leading, and controlling. The following description of these functions is general and brief since most of the book is devoted to discussing the applications of these concepts, particularly at the supervisory level.

## PLANNING

**Planning**
Determining what should be done

The initial managerial function—determining what should be done in the future—is called **planning**. It consists of setting goals, objectives, policies, procedures, and other plans needed to achieve the purposes of the organization. In planning, the manager chooses a course of action from various alternatives. Planning is primarily conceptual. It means thinking before acting, looking ahead and preparing for the future, laying out in advance the road to be followed, and thinking about how the job should be done. It includes collecting and sorting information from numerous sources and using that information to make decisions. Planning includes not only deciding what, how, when, and by whom work is to be done, but also developing what-if scenarios. A word of caution: Regardless of how well a supervisor like Dee Sikora (in You Make the Call!) plans, situations will occur that will be viewed as crises. In an ideal world, Dee would have observed or anticipated the employee dissatisfactions before Tom visited her office with his concerns. Supervisors must anticipate crisis situations and consider what they will do if this or that happens.

Many supervisors find that they are constantly confronted with crises. The probable reason for this situation is that these supervisors neglect to plan; they do not look much beyond the day's events. It is every supervisor's responsibility to plan; this task cannot be delegated to someone else. Certain specialists, such as human resource managers, accountants, production schedulers, or engineers, may help the supervisor plan, but it is up to each supervisor, as the manager of the department, to make specific departmental plans that coincide with the general objectives established by higher-level management.

Planning is the managerial function that comes first. As the supervisor proceeds with other managerial functions, planning continues, plans are revised, and alternatives are chosen as needed. This is particularly true as a supervisor evaluates the results of previous plans and adjusts future plans accordingly.

## ORGANIZING

**Organizing**
Arranging and distributing work among members of the work group to accomplish the organization's goals

Once plans have been made, the organizing function primarily answers the question, "How will the work be divided and accomplished?" The supervisor defines various job duties and groups these duties into distinct areas, sections, units, or teams. The supervisor must specify the duties, assign them, and, at the same time, give subordinates the authority they need to carry out their tasks. **Organizing** means arranging and distributing work to accomplish the organization's goals.

## STAFFING

The managerial tasks of recruiting, selecting, orienting, and training employees may be grouped in the function called **staffing**. This function includes appraising the performances of employees, promoting employees as appropriate, and giving employees opportunities to develop. In addition, staffing includes devising an equitable compensation system and rates of pay. In many companies, most activities involved in staffing are handled by the human resources (HR) department. For example, if the HR department and top-level managers establish the compensation system, then supervisors do not perform this task. However, day-to-day responsibility for the essential aspects of staffing remains with the supervisor.

**Staffing**
The tasks of recruiting, selecting, orienting, training, appraising, promoting, and compensating employees

## LEADING

**Leading** means guiding the activities of employees toward accomplishing objectives. The leading function of management involves guiding, teaching, and supervising subordinates. This includes developing employees to their potential by directing and coaching those employees effectively. It is insufficient for a supervisor just to plan, organize, and have enough employees available. The supervisor must attempt to motivate employees as they go about their work. Leading is the day-to-day process around which all supervisory performance revolves. Leading is also known as directing, motivating, or influencing because it plays a major role in employee morale, job satisfaction, productivity, and communication. It is through this function that the supervisor seeks to create a climate that is conducive to employee satisfaction and, at the same time, achieves the objectives of the department. Finding ways to satisfy the needs of a diverse employee workforce is a significant challenge. Figure 2.4 shows the differences between men and women when it comes to finding job satisfaction.

**Leading**
The managerial function of guiding employees toward accomplishing organizational objectives

Few employees are willing to blindly obey. They no longer grant automatic deference to the person in charge. We all know about the top-down hierarchical, autocratic leader. But as you will see in subsequent chapters, we have a strong preference for the servant-leader style.[8] In fact, most of a supervisor's time normally is spent on leading. It is the function around which departmental performance revolves.

**FIGURE 2.4 Job Satisfaction Differences for Men and Women**

| Top Drivers for Job Satisfaction | |
|---|---|
| Women | Men |
| 1. Compensation/pay | 1. Opportunity to use skills/abilities |
| 2. Job security | 2. Job security |
| 3. Relationship with immediate supervisor | 3. Compensation/pay |
| 4. Opportunity to use skills/abilities | 4. Organization's financial stability |

Adapted from *Employee Job Satisfaction and Engagement* survey report. Society for Human Resource Management (SHRM). *HR Magazine* (April 2014), p. 96

## CONTROLLING

**Controlling**
Ensuring that actual performance is in line with intended performance and taking corrective action

The managerial function of **controlling** involves ensuring that actual performance is in line with intended performance and taking corrective action as needed. Here, too, the importance of planning as the first function of management is obvious. It would be impossible for a supervisor to determine whether work was proceeding properly if there were no plans against which to check. If plans or standards are superficial or poorly conceived, the controlling function is limited. The supervisor must have the wisdom and foresight to take corrective action when necessary to achieve the planned objectives. It also means revising plans as circumstances require.

## THE CONTINUOUS FLOW OF MANAGERIAL FUNCTIONS

The five managerial functions can be viewed as a circular, continuous movement. If we view the managerial process as a circular flow consisting of the five functions (Figure 2.5), we can see that the functions flow into each other and that each affects the others. At times, there is no clear line to mark where one function ends and the other begins. Also, it is impossible for a supervisor to set aside a certain amount of time for one or another function because the effort spent in each function varies as conditions and circumstances change. Undoubtedly, planning must come first. Without plans, the supervisor cannot organize, staff, lead, or control.

Remember, all managers perform essentially the same managerial functions, regardless of the nature of their organizations or their levels in the hierarchy. The time and effort involved in each of these functions varies depending on which rung of the management ladder the manager occupies, the type of tasks subordinates perform, and the scope and urgency of the situation.

**FIGURE 2.5 The circular concept illustrates the close and continuous relationship between the five management functions**

## The Supervisor as Team Leader

4 **Discuss the important characteristics of the supervisor as team leader.**

Many organizations have implemented a team-based organizational structure focused on customer satisfaction, productivity, profitability, and continuous improvement. In Chapter 11, we will discuss the impact of teams in greater detail. Teams are a means to an end, and that end is superior performance to what team members would achieve working as individuals.[9] Author, trainer, and consultant Fran Rees identified several reasons for the increasing use of teams:

- Given the complexity of jobs and information, it is nearly impossible for managers to make all the decisions. In many cases, the person closest to the job is the one who should decide.
- The focus on quality and customer satisfaction has increased attention on the importance of each employee's work.
- The shift from a homogeneous workforce to a diverse one requires managers to work effectively with multiple employee perspectives.
- There is a growing realization that an autocratic, coercive management style does not necessarily result in productive, loyal employees. The fact that people support what they help create is behind the team approach.
- People are demanding strong voices in their work lives, as well as meaningful work, respect, and dignity.[10]

One example of how well teams perform is illustrated in the movie *Apollo 13*. The five little words "Houston, we have a problem" caused a diverse group of ground-crew specialists at Mission Control—working against the clock, borrowing and fabricating resources, and working against the odds—to figure out a way to bring the astronauts home.

## Managers and Leaders: Are They Different?

5 **Explain the difference between management and leadership.**

In the years since the classic *Harvard Business Review* article "Managers and Leaders: Are They Different?" appeared, debate has abounded among scholars regarding the differences between managers and leaders.[11] Not surprisingly, hundreds of articles and books have tried to clear up the confusion. Although some have contended that only labels or semantics separate managers and leaders, others have identified more substantive differences. For example, author Stephen Covey wrote, "Leadership is not management. Leadership deals with the top line—what are the things."[12] Covey also proclaimed, "Management is efficiency in climbing the ladder of success; leadership determines whether the ladder is leaning against the right wall." Another noted writer on leadership, Warren Bennis, has pointed out other differences between managers and leaders (see Figure 2.6).[13]

**FIGURE 2.6 Who does what?**

- The manager does things right; the leader does the right thing.
- The manager relies on control; the leader inspires trust.
- The manager focuses on systems and structures; the leader focuses on people.
- The manager administers; the leader innovates.
- The manager asks how and when; the leader asks what and why.
- The manager accepts the status quo; the leader challenges it.

*Source:* Adapted from Warren Bennis, Basic Books, a member of the Perseus Books Group.

Harvard professor John P. Kotter draws a similar distinction between leadership and management. He contends that management involves keeping the current system operating through planning, budgeting, staffing, controlling, and problem solving, while leadership is the development of vision and strategies, the alignment of relevant people behind those strategies, and the empowerment of people to make the vision happen. Kotter states:

> *The point here is not that leadership is good and management is bad. They are simply different and serve different purposes. Strong management with no leadership tends to entrench an organization in a deadly bureaucracy. Strong leadership with no management risks chaos; the organization might walk off a cliff.*[14]

When people have the title of manager, does it necessarily follow that they will be leaders? Clearly, the answer is no—title alone does not guarantee success. On the other hand, when people have the title of team leader, does it mean they will display the SKAs to excel in that position? Again, the answer is no. What does it take for an individual to be both a good manager and a good leader? Is it possible for individuals to learn to be both good managers and good leaders? In subsequent chapters, we clearly identify the necessary ingredients—the managerial skills necessary for success and we devote Chapter 5 to further discussion of leadership and followership.

**6 Discuss the concept of authority and power as it relates to being a good supervisor.**

## Managerial Authority

**Authority**
The legitimate right to direct and lead others

Does the individual have the authority to perform managerial functions? If the answer is no, the individual cannot perform well as a manager (see Figure 2.7). **Authority** is the legitimate or rightful power to lead others, the right to order and to act.[15] It is the formal, positional right by which a manager can require subordinates to do or not to do a thing the manager deems necessary to achieve organizational objectives. Managerial authority is not granted to an individual, but rather to the position the individual holds at the time. When individuals leave their jobs or are replaced, they cease to have that authority. When a successor assumes the position, that person then has the authority.

Included in positional managerial authority is the right and duty to delegate authority. The delegation of authority is the process by which the supervisor receives authority from a higher-level manager and, in turn, makes job assignments and entrusts related authority to subordinates. Having managerial authority means the supervisor has the power and the right to issue directives in order to accomplish the tasks assigned to the department. This authority includes the power and right to reward and discipline, if necessary. When a subordinate performs well, the supervisor has the power to give that subordinate a raise or another reward, within company guidelines. If a worker refuses to carry out a directive, the supervisor's authority includes the power and right to take disciplinary action, even to the extent of discharging the subordinate. Of course, this power, like all authority, is limited.

**Acceptance theory of authority**
Theory that holds that the manager only possesses authority when the employee accepts it

The **acceptance theory of authority** states that a manager does not possess real authority until and unless the subordinate accepts it. For example, a supervisor may instruct an employee to carry out a certain work assignment. The employee has several alternatives from which to choose. Although such a response is not likely, the employee can refuse to obey, thereby rejecting the supervisor's authority. Alternatively, the employee may grudgingly accept the supervisor's direction and carry out the assignment in a mediocre fashion. The supervisor should

FIGURE 2.7 To be effective, a manager must be able to use the managerial functions and possess requisite SKAs, power, and authority

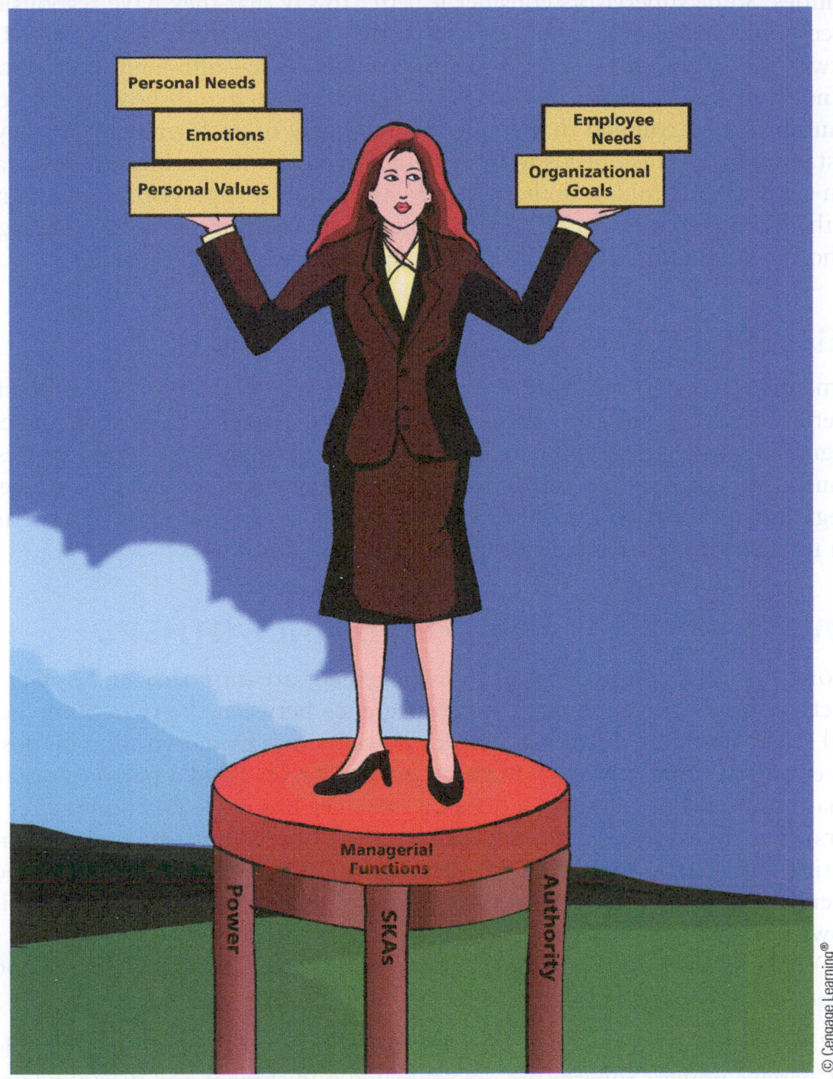


expect to experience resistance from some of their employees. When some employees reject the supervisor's authority, they will have no choice but to impose disciplinary action on those employees. When a new supervisor is announced to the team, their manager or top management should lay the foundation for his or her acceptance. Every manager requires the support of his or her boss.

Numerous limitations to authority exist—union contract provisions, government or regulatory agency restrictions, company policies, and ethical considerations. Generally, supervisors find there are limits to their authority to use resources and to make certain managerial decisions.

## AVOIDING RELIANCE ON MANAGERIAL AUTHORITY

Most successful supervisors know that to motivate workers to perform their duties, it is usually best not to rely on formal managerial authority but to employ other approaches. Generally, it is better for a supervisor not to display power and formal authority. In practice, many supervisors prefer to avoid even speaking about their authority. Instead, they want to speak of their responsibilities, tasks, or duties. Some supervisors consider it better to say that they have responsibility for certain activities instead of saying that they have authority in that area. Using the words *responsibility*, *tasks*, and *duties* in this sense—although these certainly are not the same as *authority*—helps the supervisor to avoid showing the "club" of authority. We contend that employees are likely to perform better if they understand why the task needs to be done and have a voice in how to do it rather than simply being told to do it.[16] Regardless of how a supervisor applies authority, the point to remember is that the supervisory position must have managerial authority. Without it, a supervisor cannot perform well as a manager.

## DELEGATING AUTHORITY

**Delegation**
The process of entrusting duties and related authority to subordinates

As mentioned previously, the **delegation** of authority is the process by which the supervisor receives authority from a higher-level manager and, in turn, makes job assignments and entrusts related authority to subordinates. Just as the possession of authority is a required component of any managerial position, the process of delegating authority to lower levels in the hierarchy is required for an organization to have effective managers, supervisors, and employees.

## POWER—THE ABILITY TO INFLUENCE OTHERS

**Position power**
Power derived from the formal rank a person holds in the chain of command

**Personal power**
Power derived from a person's SKAs and how others perceive that person

Among the most confused terms in management are *authority* and *power*. The effective supervisor understands the difference between the two. Some behavioral scientists contend that a manager's power comes from two sources: position power and personal power.[17] **Position power** derives from a person's organizational position. For example, a division manager has more position power than a first-line supervisor. **Personal power**, on the other hand, emanates from the relationship a supervisor has with other people. A supervisor's personal power depends to a greater extent on the followers' perceptions of that supervisor's knowledge, skill, and expertise.

Other theorists, such as John French and Bertram Raven, assert that power arises from the following five sources:

1. Reward power: Supervisors have reward power if they can grant rewards.
2. Coercive power: Supervisors who threaten punishment and discipline use coercive power.
3. Legitimate power: Some supervisors gain compliance by relying on their position or rank (e.g., "I'm the boss—do it my way").
4. Expert power: Knowledge or valuable information gives a person expert power over those who need that information.
5. Referent or charismatic power: People are often influenced by another person because of some tangible or intangible aspect of another's personality.[18]

Effective supervisors understand the effect their power has on others. Research indicates that reward power, coercive power, and legitimate power often force employees to comply with directives but do not get those employees' commitment to organizational objectives. Accordingly, supervisors who use expert power and referent power effectively have the greatest potential for achieving organizational goals.[19]

The acceptance theory of authority is also relevant to the application of power. For example, you can be an expert in computer applications, but if others do not need that knowledge, you will have very little influence over them. Therefore, two supervisors can hold the same title, occupy the same level in the hierarchy, and have equal authority, yet have different degrees of power, depending on their abilities and how others perceive them.

## Coordination

**7 Explain the need for coordination and cooperation and how they lead to good performance.**

Management has generally been defined as a process of getting things done through and with the help of people by directing their efforts toward common objectives. In a sense, all levels of management could be broadly visualized as involving the coordination of efforts of all the members and resources of an organization toward overall objectives. Some writers have therefore included the concept of coordination as a separate managerial function.

**Coordination** is the orderly synchronization (or putting together) of efforts of the members and resources of an organization to accomplish the organization's objectives. Coordination is not a separate managerial function; it is an implicit, interrelated aspect of the five major managerial functions previously cited. That is, coordination is fostered whenever a manager performs any of the managerial functions of planning, organizing, staffing, leading, and controlling. In a sense, coordination can best be understood as being a direct result of good management rather than as a managerial function in and of itself. The ability to communicate clearly and concisely is essential for coordination.

**Coordination**
The synchronization of employees' efforts and the organization's resources toward achieving goals

Achieving coordination typically is more difficult at the executive level than at the supervisory level. Top management has to synchronize the use of resources and human efforts throughout numerous departments and levels of the organization. A supervisor of one department has the responsibility to achieve coordination primarily within the department. However, this too can be difficult to achieve, especially during periods of rapid change and economic hardships.

### COOPERATION AS RELATED TO COORDINATION

**Cooperation** is the willingness of individuals to work with and help each other. It primarily involves the attitudes of a group of people. Coordination is more than the mere desire and willingness of participants. For example, consider a group of workers who are attempting to move a heavy object. They are sufficient in number, willing and eager to cooperate with each other, and trying their best to move the object. They are also fully aware of their common purpose. However, in all likelihood their efforts will be of little avail until one of them—the supervisor—gives the proper orders to apply the right amount of effort at the right place at the right time. Then the group members can move the object. It is possible that by sheer coincidence some cooperation could have brought about the desired result in this example, but no supervisor can afford to rely on such a coincidental occurrence.

**Cooperation**
The willingness of individuals to work with and help one another

While cooperation is helpful and the lack of it could impede progress, its presence alone will not necessarily get the job done. Efforts must be coordinated toward the common goal.

*Cooperation, coordination, and communication lead to success*

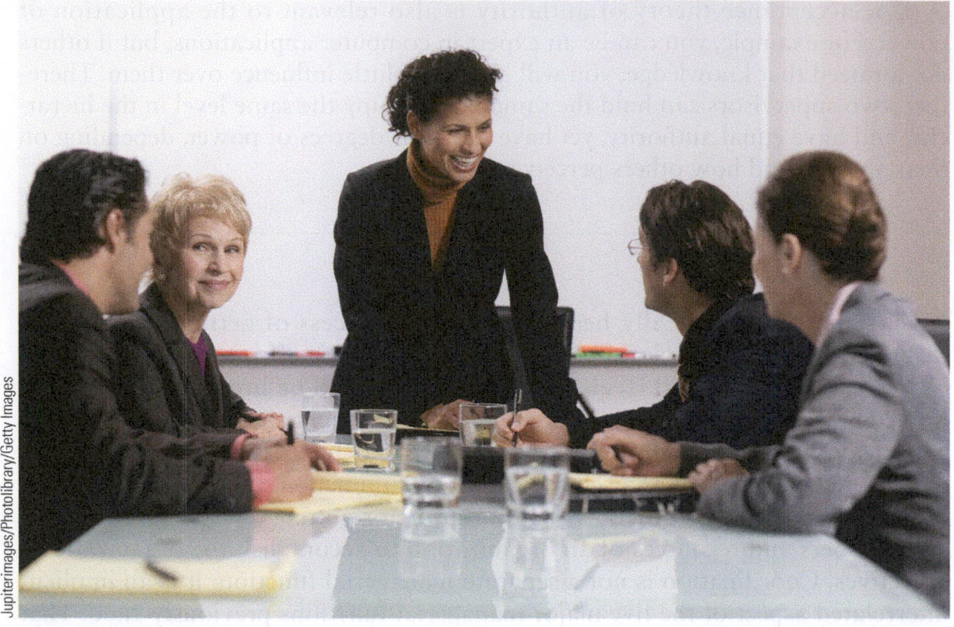
Jupiterimages/Photolibrary/Getty Images

## ATTAINING COORDINATION

Coordination is not easily attained, and the task of achieving coordination is becoming more complex. As an organization grows, coordinating the many activities of various departments becomes an increasingly complicated problem for high-level managers. At the supervisory level, as the number and types of positions in a department increase, the need for coordination to obtain desired results similarly increases. Every supervisor's primary focus should be on getting the desired results from his or her people. This era of rampant organizational downsizing has forced supervisors to do a better job of planning and coordinating.

The complexities of human nature present added coordination problems. For example, every employee comes to the workplace with a baggage cart. Loaded on that baggage cart are all of his or her off-the-job issues. We remind employees to leave their personal problems at the door when they come to work and to leave their work-related issues at the door when they leave. While it sounds good, in reality it doesn't happen. Many employees understandably are preoccupied with their own work and their personal baggage. In the final analysis, they are evaluated primarily on how they do their individual jobs. Therefore, employees tend not to willingly become involved in other areas and often are indifferent to the fact that their activities may affect other departments.

Supervisors can achieve coordination by building networks focused on attaining common objectives. According to *Merriam Webster's Collegiate Dictionary*, a network is "a fabric or structure of cords or wires that cross at regular intervals and are knotted or secured at the crossings." Think of it this way. A person's relationships are the knots, and the strength of the relationships equals the strength of the network.

Refer back to the chapter's opening You Make the Call! and think of all the individuals who have a stake in what housekeeping services does and how well it performs. *Dee is the proverbial person in the middle.* There are patients, their families, physicians, insurers who may pay for the care, government and other regulatory agencies, and a myriad of departments within the medical center.

Networking is essential to Dee as she carries out her supervisory responsibilities. She should develop networks with others, both inside and outside the organization. Also, she must understand that network members must give as well as receive. When Dee had a problem, she attempted to contact the HR director and her immediate supervisor for help. When they were not readily available, having a network inside the hospital would provide her with additional resources. Networking will allow Dee to balance autonomy on one hand and dependence on the other. **Networking** facilitates the flow of ideas across organizational barriers and thereby eases the coordination effort.

**Networking**
Individuals or groups linked by a commitment to a shared purpose

## COORDINATION AS PART OF THE MANAGERIAL FUNCTIONS

While performing the managerial functions, the supervisor should recognize that coordination is a desired result of effective management. Proper attention to coordination within each of the five managerial functions contributes to overall coordination.

Initially, the supervisor must ensure that the various plans are aligned with the right people. For example, a supervisor may wish to discuss departmental job assignments with the employees who are to carry them out. In this way, the employees can express their opinions or objections, which need to be reconciled in advance. Furthermore, employees may be encouraged to make suggestions and to discuss the merits of proposed plans and alternatives. When employees are involved in initial departmental planning, the supervisor's chances of achieving coordination usually improve. The purpose of establishing who is to do what, when, where, and how is to achieve coordination. For example, whenever a new job is to be done, a supervisor assigns that job to the unit with the employees best suited to the work. Therefore, whenever a supervisor groups activities and assigns subordinates to those groups, coordination should be uppermost in the supervisor's mind. Achieving coordination also should be of concern as a supervisor establishes authority relationships within the department and among employees. Clear statements as to specific duties and reporting relationships in the department foster coordination and prevent duplicate efforts and confusion.

When leading, the supervisor is significantly involved in coordination. The essence of giving instructions is to coordinate the activities of employees in such a manner that the overall objectives are reached in the most efficient way possible. In addition, a supervisor must assess and reward the performance of employees to maintain a harmonious work group.

The supervisor is also concerned with coordination when performing the controlling function. By checking, monitoring, and observing, the supervisor makes certain that activities conform to established plans. If there are any discrepancies, the supervisor should take immediate action to reprioritize or reassign tasks. In so doing, the supervisor may achieve coordination at least from then on. The very nature of the controlling process contributes to coordination and keeps the organization moving toward its objectives.

## COORDINATION WITH OTHER DEPARTMENTS

Not only must supervisors coordinate activities within their own departments, but they also must coordinate the efforts of their departments with those of others. For example, a production department supervisor must meet with supervisors of scheduling, quality control, maintenance, and shipping to coordinate various activities. Similarly, an accounting supervisor typically meets with supervisors from production, sales, and shipping to coordinate cost accounting, inventory records, and billing. Achieving coordination is an essential component of the supervisory management position.

### Cooperation and Coordination—Easier Said than Done

A group of employees becomes a team when its members share values and a purpose. How well the objectives are achieved depends on the supervisor's coordination and team-building skills. The move toward increased employee participation, broader spans of control, and fewer managerial levels causes a greater need for coordination skills. Meanwhile, many supervisors have higher aspirations; they eventually want to be promoted to positions of increased responsibility. In reality, competition among supervisors may impede cooperation.

**8 Identify how labor unions affect the managerial functions.**

## Labor Unions Are Part of Supervisory Concerns

Unions remain an important element of the workforce that supervisors should know about and be prepared to deal with appropriately. Most employees in the private sector of the U.S. workforce have legal rights to join or not to join labor unions under the National Labor Relations Act as amended. Federal government workers have their collective bargaining rights established under the Civil Service Reform Act. The rights of other public-sector workers generally are covered by state and local government legislation. (See http://www.flra.gov/statue; click on *Read the National Labor Relations Act* or *What Is the NLRA?* to gain some tips for dealing with a unionized workforce.) Although the strength and influence of labor unions has declined considerably in recent years, labor unions nevertheless continue to be a major influence on the manager's right to manage.[20]

The current economy has made for interesting times in union and management relations. A February 2014 vote against unionization by auto workers at the Volkswagen plant in Chattanooga, Tennessee, along with a recent ruling by the NLRB that Northwestern football players have the right to unionize are examples of where unions are in America today.[21] Sixty years ago, 35 percent of the American workforce was unionized—mostly in the private sector. Today, about half those unionized are government workers.

**Austerity**
Harsh and severe times requiring a tightening of the belt and budget

**Labor union / labor organization**
Legally recognized organization that represents employees and negotiates and administers a labor agreement with an employer

**Labor agreement**
Negotiated document between union and employer that covers the terms and conditions of employment for represented employees

Teachers' unions and other public-sector groups have been the target of cuts as states and local governments face budget shortfalls. **Austerity** in all aspects of state and local government's activity might be the appropriate word for the years ahead.

We use the terms **labor union** and **labor organization** interchangeably to describe any legally recognized organization that exists for the purpose of representing a group or bargaining unit of employees. The union negotiates and administers a labor agreement with the employer. A **labor agreement**, also called a union contract, is the negotiated document between the union and the employer that covers terms and conditions of employment for represented employees.

The labor agreement that management and union representatives have negotiated becomes the document under which both parties operate during the life of the agreement. Although no two labor agreements are exactly alike, most agreements cover wages, benefits, working conditions, hours of work, overtime, holidays, vacations, leave of absence rules, seniority, grievance procedures, and numerous other matters. The labor agreement outlines union–management relationships. In essence, it is a policy manual that provides rules, procedures, and guidelines—as well as limitations—for management and the union. To make it an instrument for fostering constructive relationships, the agreement must be applied with appropriate and intelligent supervisory decisions. The best labor agreement is of little value if it is poorly applied by the supervisor.

## COMPLYING WITH THE LABOR AGREEMENT

Wherever the labor agreement applies, supervisors are obliged to manage their departments within its framework. Therefore, supervisors should know the provisions of the agreement and how to interpret those provisions. One way to do this is for higher-level managers or the human resources department to hold meetings with supervisors to brief them on the contents of the agreement and to answer questions about any provisions. Copies of the contract and clarifications of various provisions should be given to supervisors so that the supervisors know what they can and cannot do while managing their departments (see Figure 2.8).

Supervisors should recognize that a labor agreement has been negotiated, agreed upon, and signed by both management and union representatives.

**FIGURE 2.8 The supervisor must know the provisions of labor agreements, how to interpret them, and how to apply them fairly and consistently**

Even if a provision in the agreement causes problems for a supervisor, the supervisor should not try to circumvent the contract in the hope of doing the firm a favor. For example, assume that a provision specifies that work assignments must be made primarily on the basis of seniority. While this provision may limit the supervisor in assigning the most qualified workers to certain jobs, the supervisor should comply with it or be prepared to face probable conflict with the union. If a labor agreement provision is clear and specific, the supervisor should not attempt to ignore it. When supervisors do not understand certain provisions, they should ask someone in higher-level management or the human resources department for help before trying to apply the provisions in question.

## ADJUSTING FOR THE UNION

A labor agreement does not fundamentally change a supervisor's position as a manager. Supervisors still must accomplish their objectives by planning, organizing, staffing, leading, and controlling. Supervisors retain the right to require employees to comply with instructions and to get their jobs done. The major adjustment required when a union is present is that supervisors must perform their managerial duties within the framework of the labor agreement. For example, a labor agreement may spell out some limitations to the supervisor's authority, especially in areas of disciplinary actions, job transfers, and assignments, or a labor agreement may specify procedures concerning the seniority rights of employees with regard to shift assignments, holidays, and vacations. Supervisors may not like these provisions. However, they must manage within them and learn to minimize the effects of contractually imposed requirements or restrictions by making sound decisions and relying on their own managerial abilities.

As members of management, supervisors have the right and duty to make decisions. A labor agreement does not take away that right. However, it does give the union a right to challenge a supervisor's decision that the union believes to be a violation of the labor agreement. For example, virtually all labor agreements specify that management has the right to discipline and discharge for "just" (or "proper") cause. The supervisor who follows **just cause** ensures that the disciplinary action meets certain tests of fairness and elements of normal due process, such as proper notification, investigation, sufficient evidence, and a penalty commensurate with the nature of the infraction. Therefore, disciplinary action remains a managerial responsibility and right, but it must meet the just-cause standard. Because a challenge from the union may occur, the supervisor should have a sound case before taking disciplinary action. If a supervisor believes that disciplinary action is called for when an employee breaks a rule, the supervisor should thoroughly examine all aspects of the problem, take the required preliminary steps, and think through the appropriateness of any action. In other words, unless there is a contractual requirement to the contrary, the supervisor normally will carry out the disciplinary action independent of union involvement. However, some labor agreements require that a supervisor notify a union representative before imposing discipline or that a union representative be present when the disciplinary action is administered. In Chapter 15, we will discuss in detail the handling of disciplinary matters in both union and nonunion work environments.

**Just or proper cause**
Standard for disciplinary action requiring tests of fairness and elements of normal due process, such as proper notification, investigation, sufficient evidence, and a penalty commensurate with the nature of the infraction

## RELATING SUPERVISORY DECISION MAKING TO THE LABOR AGREEMENT

In practice, the supervisor may amplify provisions of the labor agreement by decisions that interpret and apply those provisions to specific situations. In so doing, the supervisor might establish precedents that arbitrators consider when deciding grievances.

A **grievance** is a complaint that the union has formally presented to management and that alleges a violation of the labor agreement. Most labor agreements specify several steps as part of a grievance procedure before a grievance goes to arbitration. An **arbitrator** is someone who is selected by the union and management to render a final and binding decision concerning a grievance when the union and management cannot settle the grievance themselves. Procedures for arbitrating grievances are included in most labor agreements. The Supervisory Tips box in Chapter 14 provides guidance for resolving complaints and grievances in any situation.

**Grievance**
Formal complaint presented by the union to management that alleges violation of the labor agreement

**Arbitrator**
Person selected by the union and management to render a final and binding decision concerning a grievance

## MAINTAINING EMPLOYEES' COMPLIANCE WITH THE LABOR AGREEMENT

Grievances can be filed over any workplace issue that is subject to the collective bargaining agreement, or they can be filed over the interpretation and administration of the agreement itself. It is the supervisor's duty to act whenever employees do not comply with provisions of the labor agreement. Employees may interpret lack of action to mean that the provisions are unimportant or are not to be enforced. Supervisors should ensure that employees observe the labor agreement, just as supervisors must operate within the agreement. The supervisor's inaction could set a precedent or could be interpreted to mean that the provision has been set aside.

A few words of wisdom at this point:

- The management functions and their application are the same regardless of whether or not the organization is unionized.
- All employees need to have a clear vision of what is expected in the way of performance.
- Honest, sincere, authentic, daily feedback, and dialogue between the supervisor and employees is a must.
- Cooperation, coordination, and consistency may be more critical in a unionized environment.
- Supervisors must convey a clear description of what is going on and how "we are doing."
- All employees want praise and recognition for a "job well done."

The supervisor's daily relationships with employees and union representatives make the labor agreement a living document for better or worse. For the most part, the supervisor's involvement in union–management relations has two phases: learning what the labor agreement contains and applying it fairly and consistently on a daily basis.

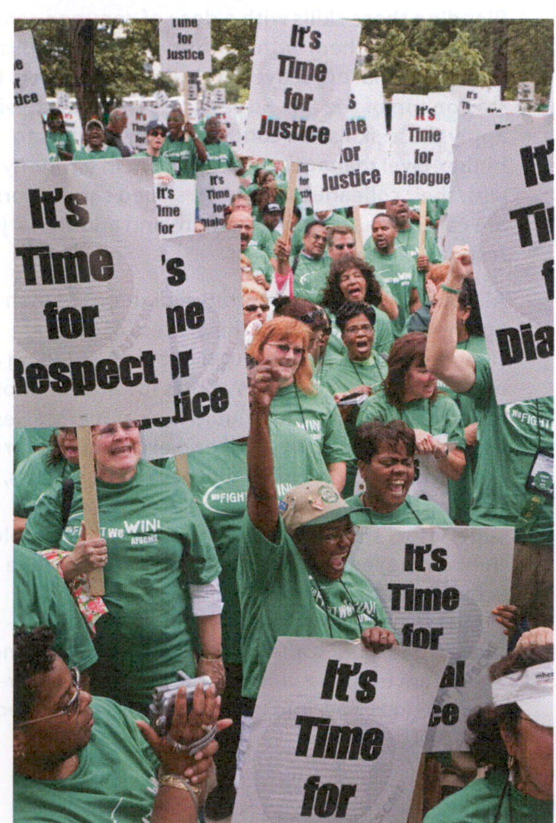

Jim West / Alamy

## SUMMARY

1. Supervisors are the "people in the middle." Employees see their supervisors as being management, but supervisors are subordinates to their own managers at higher levels. To supervisors of other departments, supervisors are colleagues who must cooperate with each other. Supervisors must have both good working knowledge of the jobs being performed in their departments and the ability to manage.

2. Effective supervisors must have technical, human relations, administrative, conceptual, and political skills. It is most critical that supervisors use their emotions intelligently. Supervisors must understand the technical aspects of the work being performed. When attempting to manage job performance, understanding employee needs is essential. "People skills" help supervisors accomplish objectives with and through people. It is equally important for supervisors to understand the dynamics of the organization and to recognize organizational politics.

   These skills are important to all levels of management. Most supervisors come to the job equipped with some of these skills. Supervisors have daily opportunities to apply managerial skills and must continually strive to develop them. Blending these skills with a dose of common sense and applying them with maturity help accomplish organizational objectives and allow supervisors to stay on top of the job. Supervisors who effectively apply these skills can contribute suggestions to higher-level managers and can work in harmony with their colleagues. In short, skilled supervisors are candidates for advancement and additional job responsibilities.

3. Although there are numerous definitions of management, we define it as the process of getting things accomplished through people by guiding and motivating those people's efforts toward common objectives. Supervisors should look at themselves as enablers, that is, by clarifying expectations for employees and giving employees the right tools, training, and opportunities to succeed. In short, supervisors should do all those things that enable their employees to be the best they can be while achieving organizational objectives.

   The five major managerial functions are planning, organizing, staffing, leading, and controlling. These functions are viewed as a continuous flow—the functions flow into each other, and each affects the others.

   Planning is the first function of management. The performance of all other managerial functions depends on it. The five managerial functions are universal regardless of the job environment, the activity involved, or a person's position in the management hierarchy. Typically, supervisors spend most of their time leading and controlling. A supervisor's planning covers a shorter time and narrower focus than that of a top-level executive.

4. Some companies have redefined the role of the supervisor as team leader. While team leaders must possess certain skills as identified earlier in the chapter, it is important to remember that teams are usually formed for such purposes as improving customer service, productivity, or quality. As such, developing a work environment in which team members share a purpose and goals is essential. Regardless of the term used, the first-line supervisor or team leader must be an enabler—helping others to be the best they can become in the continuous pursuit of organizational objectives. Information giving and information gathering allow team members to function most effectively.

5. Leadership and management go hand in hand. As one of the management functions identified in this text, leadership is concerned with establishing a vision, aligning people behind that vision, and empowering those people to accomplish the intended results (doing the right thing) while management is getting things done. The distinction is more than a semantic one.

6. A supervisor must have authority to perform well as a manager. Authority is the legitimate or rightful power to lead others. Authority is delegated from top-level managers through middle-level managers to supervisors who, in turn, delegate to their employees. All supervisors must be delegated appropriate authority to manage their departments.

   The acceptance theory of authority suggests that supervisors have authority only if and when their subordinates accept it. In reality, an employee's choice between accepting and not accepting a supervisor's authority may be the choice between staying in the job and quitting. Most supervisors prefer not to rely primarily on formal managerial authority but rather like to use other approaches for enhancing employee performance.

   Supervisors have power because of the positions they occupy. Position power increases as a person

**advances up the organizational hierarchy. Supervisors derive personal power from their relationships with others. Subordinates' perceptions of the supervisor's SKAs play an integral role in the supervisor's ability to influence those subordinates.**

**Theorists French and Raven identify five sources of power: reward, coercive, legitimate, expert, and referent or charismatic. Research indicates that supervisors who use expert power and referent power effectively have the greatest potential for achieving organizational goals. The supervisor's power is based largely on the willingness of the employee to accept it.**

**7.** **Coordination is the orderly synchronization of efforts of the members and resources of an organization toward attaining stated objectives. Cooperation—as distinguished from coordination—is the willingness of individuals to work with and help each other. While cooperation is helpful, it alone will not get the job done. Efforts must also be coordinated. Both coordination and cooperation are attainable through good management practices.**

**8.** **Unions are coming under attack from all sides. Union membership has declined substantially in the private sector. In several states, public-sector unions are facing politicians' attempts to reduce their collective bargaining rights.**

**Supervisors need to know how to apply the managerial functions when departmental employees are represented by a union. The supervisors are the key to good union–management relations because they apply the labor agreement from day to day. The presence of a labor union gives a formal mechanism for challenging a supervisor's actions.**

## KEY TERMS

Acceptance theory of authority (p. 54)
Administrative skills (p. 46)
Arbitrator (p. 63)
Austerity (p. 60)
Authority (p. 54)
Communication skills (p. 46)
Conceptual skills (p. 46)
Controlling (p. 52)
Cooperation (p. 57)
Coordination (p. 57)
Delegation (p. 56)
Emotional intelligence skills (p. 46)
Enabler (p. 49)
Grievance (p. 63)
Human relations skills (p. 46)
Just or proper cause (p. 62)
Labor agreement (p. 60)
Labor union/labor organization (p. 60)
Leadership skills (p. 46)
Leading (p. 51)
Management (p. 48)
Networking (p. 59)
Organizing (p. 50)
Personal power (p. 56)
Planning (p. 50)
Political skills (p. 46)
Position power (p. 56)
Servant leadership (p. 46)
Staffing (p. 51)
Technical skills (p. 46)

## WHAT HAVE YOU LEARNED?

1. Identify the major managerial skills every supervisor needs. Why are these skills important?
2. It is often said that planning is the most important managerial function. Do you agree? Why or why not?
3. Stephen Covey observed that "Effective leadership is putting first things first. Effective management is discipline, carrying it out."[22] Do you agree? Why or why not? What distinction have you observed between management and leadership? Why is the distinction important for one who desires to be a supervisor or team leader?
4. We suggest that supervisors should view themselves as enablers. The logical extension of this notion would be that the supervisor clarifies the objectives that must be obtained, provide the training and tools needed to complete the tasks, and get out of the way. Should "management by getting out of the way" be an appropriate philosophy of management? Why or why not?
5. What are the obstacles that the supervisor may encounter when trying to gain cooperation by coordinating the department's various activities? What could a mentor(s) or coach do to help a supervisor understand how cooperation, coordination, and communication have to work together to attain a satisfactory end result?
6. What might be some reasons that cause some employees to feel the need to join a labor union?

# EXPERIENTIAL EXERCISES FOR SELF-ASSESSMENT

## EXPERIENTIAL EXERCISE FOR SELF-ASSESSMENT 2.1: Measure Your Management Skills

The functions of management are driven by specific skills. In Chapter 2 you learned about eight different skill areas in which managers must be proficient in order to effectively perform their functions. If we drill down into the skill areas, we can identify competencies that are appropriate at different levels of management and supervision. Robert Katz described three such levels—supervisory management, middle management, and top management. He found in his research that successful supervisory managers showed the greatest competency in technical and human skills, middle managers had balanced competencies in technical, human, and conceptual skills, and top management were most proficient in using human and conceptual skills. Figure 2.9 below illustrates the distribution of skills across the three levels.

### Management Skills Inventory[23]

The self-assessment exercise below provides you with the opportunity to evaluate your level of technical, human, and conceptual skills, as well as consider which of these skill areas you prefer.

### Instructions

Read each of the items below and determine the level at which your feelings align with each item. Circle the number that corresponds with the level you chose for each item.

Key: 1= Not true 2=Seldom true 3=Occasionally true 4=Somewhat true 5=Very true

1 2 3 4 5 1. Getting all parties to work together is a challenge I enjoy.

1 2 3 4 5 2. I am good at completing the things I am assigned to do.

1 2 3 4 5 3. Creating vision and mission statements is rewarding work for me.

1 2 3 4 5 4. I am concerned with how my decisions affect the lives of others.

1 2 3 4 5 5. I appreciate routine tasks and procedures.

1 2 3 4 5 6. Thinking about organizational values and philosophy appeals to me.

1 2 3 4 5 7. Following directions and filling out forms comes easily for me.

1 2 3 4 5 8. I am intrigued by complex organizational problems.

1 2 3 4 5 9. One of my strongest skills is making things work.

1 2 3 4 5 10. My main concern is to have a supportive communication climate.

1 2 3 4 5 11. I would enjoy designing strategies to grow my organization.

1 2 3 4 5 12. I enjoy getting into the details of how things work.

1 2 3 4 5 13. As a rule, adapting ideas to people's needs is easy for me.

**FIGURE 2.9 Distribution of Skills across Levels of Management**

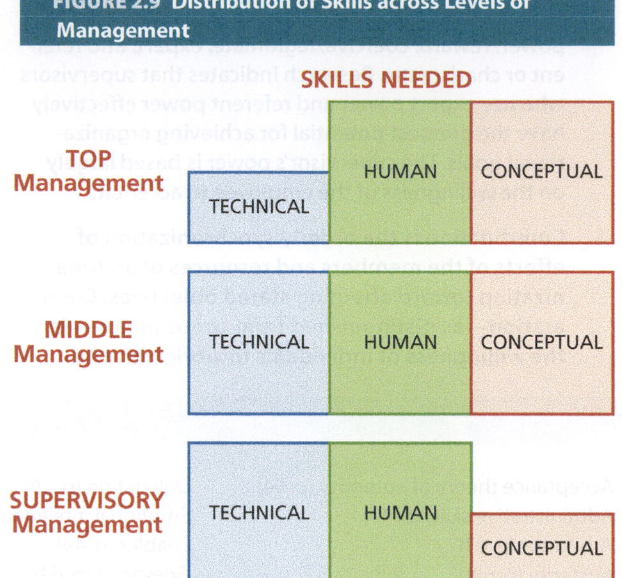


*Source: Adapted from Robert L. Katz, "Skills of an Effective Administrator,"* Harvard Business Review *33(1), pp. 33–42.*

1 2 3 4 5 14. I enjoy working with abstract ideas.

1 2 3 4 5 15. Understanding the social fabric of the organization is important to me.

1 2 3 4 5 16. Technical things fascinate me.

1 2 3 4 5 17. Being able to understand others is the most important part of my work.

1 2 3 4 5 18. Seeing the big picture comes easy for me.

### Scoring Procedure

This assessment measures respondents' level of interest in tasks that require technical, human, and conceptual skills. Score the inventory in the following way. First, add the responses on items 2, 5, 7, 9, 12, and 16 and record the score next to Technical skill. Next, add up the responses on items 1, 4, 10, 13, 15, and 17 and record the score next to Human skill. Finally, add up the responses on items 3, 6, 8, 11, 14, and 18 and record the score next to Conceptual skill. Then see the scoring interpretation.

### Scoring Interpretation

22–30: High Range

14–22: Moderate Range

6–13: Low Range

Your scores on the skills inventory provide information on your interest in three levels of management skills. As you compare the differences between the scores, you will identify management strengths and interests that may indicate areas of management that would best suit your skills.

PERSONAL SKILL BUILDER

## PERSONAL SKILL BUILDER 2-1: What Call Did You Make?

After reviewing this chapter's opening You Make the Call! and reviewing the National Labor Relations Act (http://flra.gov/statute) and the SEIU.org Web sites, respond to the following questions:

1. Supervisors, managers, and employees often have different viewpoints concerning what a labor union can do for its members. From the employee standpoint, what would be some of the benefits of union membership?
2. Based on Dee's style of management, how would having her employees represented by a labor union change her management style?
3. Based upon the concerns identified by Tom, how might Dee use her management skills to address those concerns?
4. What is the union's role in addressing the concerns expressed by Tom?
5. FOOD FOR THOUGHT QUESTION 1: Without a labor union, what chance will employees have to see their complaints handled fairly?
6. FOOD FOR THOUGHT QUESTION 2: Some organizations conduct training programs entitled "How to Avoid a Union." What might the hospital administration do to develop a program of this nature? What topics should be included?

## PERSONAL SKILL BUILDER 2-2: Great CEOs Put Themselves Last, or Do They?

INTERNET ACTIVITY

When Professor Leonard first began teaching, a colleague said that "the ultimate criterion of organizational worth is whether or not the organization survives." Today, we contend that survival is not the objective. We want to work and be affiliated with an organization that thrives and is thought of as being "Great!" In February 2014, *Fortune* published its list of the *50 Most Powerful Women Global Edition*. The top 10 were: Mary Barra, General Motors; Ginni Rometty, IBM; Indra Nooyi, Pepsico; Maria das Graças Silva Foster, Petrobras; Ellen Kullman, DuPont; Irene Rosenfeld, Mondelez International; Marilyn Hewson, Lockheed Martin; Meg Whitman, HP; Pat Woertz, Archer Daniels Midland; and Gail Kelly, Westpac.[24]

"Great CEOs also preside over innovation, lead through major transformations or crises, and improve financial performance. The one trait that distinguishes top CEOs is their deep sense of connectedness to the organizations they run, the employees they inspire, and the customers they serve."[25]

1. Conduct an Internet search to learn more about one of the women that made the *Fortune* list. Based on your research, write a one-page paper detailing what you learned about her, her leadership, and the success of the organization. In your concluding paragraph, briefly describe the strategies and style of your chosen CEO.
2. In your opinion, will the culture developed by your chosen leader allow the organization to continue to thrive after she steps aside? Why or why not?

## PERSONAL SKILL BUILDER 2-3: Technology Tool – Collaborate, Coordinate, Create, then Celebrate!

Coordinating work is a managerial function that incorporates a wide variety of skills. When employees, skills, and resources are brought together to complete a project, aligning them can sometimes feel like building a jigsaw puzzle. A variety of project management software applications can help streamline the coordination function so that a team can focus its time and effort on actually doing the work, rather than on coordinating. Project management software is particularly valuable to small organizations that do not have the financial resources to maintain a project manager staff position. While a software application cannot take the place of a well-organized manager, the difference between an estimated $50 a month software contract and a $3,000–4,000 a month manager frees up resources that can be invested in new projects.

The technology tools you will be exploring in this exercise each combine different applications and features in unique configurations that might work better for some projects than others. For this exercise, you should envision yourself as a team leader on one of five projects:

- A citywide health and wellness fair
- A new treadmill desk design
- A hospital facility reconfiguration
- A marketing campaign for a new bamboo bike
- An animal shelter fundraiser

With your project assignment in mind, use your Internet browser to search the keyword "project management software." Your search will result in links to specific software applications, such as AceProject, LiquidPlanner, Teamwork.com, and Wrike, as well as lists of reviews of several different tools.

Explore at least five different project management software applications by reviewing their Web sites, viewing preview videos or using demonstration or free versions of the software. As you examine each one, compose responses to the questions below as a "Project Management Software Review" memo:

1. What do you envision will be the major tasks that need to be coordinated for this project?
2. Which software tools did you review (include links to the company websites)?
3. What applications and features (e.g. file storage, task creation, communication, timers, calendars, file sharing, video sharing, customization of the platform, templates) do you feel will be most beneficial to managing the project?
4. Which software tools offer the features that best match your project management needs?
5. Beyond software features, what other things would you need to consider in order to choose a particular package (e.g. cost, user-friendliness)?
6. If you were going to purchase one of the products today, which would you choose and why?
7. Of the products you did not choose, which would you absolutely not purchase and why?
8. Once the team completes the project, how will they be rewarded for their hard work?

### PERSONAL SKILL BUILDER 2-4: Thinking Outside the Box

1. Using nine toothpicks, arrange them into three triangles as shown.
2. Your challenge is to try to make five triangles by moving only three toothpicks.
3. Your instructor has been provided with the correct response on the instructor support Web site.

*Source:* QCI International, from QCI International's Timely Tips for Teams, a monthly Internet newsletter (July 2005).

## TEAM SKILL BUILDING

### TEAM SKILL BUILDING 2-1: Attributes of a Successful Manager

1. Interview the most successful supervisors or managers you have ever known.
2. Ask them what they liked most about their jobs.
3. Ask them to identify what they believe to be the secret to successful supervision.
4. Connect with at least two other students and compare your findings. Make a composite list of (1) what the successful supervisors liked most about their jobs; and (2) their secrets to successful supervision.
5. Then your mission is to collaboratively develop a one-page paper that summarizes your group's findings.
6. In 40 words or less, describe why you could have done a better job of writing the paper yourself.
7. Why is it sometimes easier to do the assignment yourself?

### TEAM SKILL BUILDER 2-2: A Night at the Movies

In an era of endless restructuring, cutting off heads like Robespierre on a rampage is just average for many managers. They inflict pain by messing with your mind as well. Choose and watch one of the following movies: (1) 42, (2) *Nine to Five*, (3) *Norma Rae*, (4) *Saving Mr. Banks*, or (5) *The Wolf of Wall Street*. Find two to four other students who each watched a different film than you, and answer these questions:

1. In what ways was the management style ruthless? In what ways was it effective?
2. To what extent did the manager(s) correctly use the various managerial functions (plan, organize, staff, lead, control)?
3. What, if anything, did various managers do to guide and motivate the efforts of the subordinates toward common objectives?
4. Assume you are in a subordinate position, just below one of the primary managers in the movie. How did you feel about the way you were supervised? What would you have done about it? Why?
5. What did you learn about how to manage? About how not to manage?

## TEAM SKILL BUILDER 2-3: Labor Unions and You

After reviewing this chapter's You Make the Call! and the National Labor Relations Act (http://flra.gov/statute), your instructor will divide you into groups of three to five students. One of you will assume the role of Dee Sikora and the others should play the roles of her assistants.

PART 1: Working individually, respond to the following eight statements using this scale, Strongly Agree=4, Agree =3, Disagree = 2, Strongly Disagree=1:

________ 1. Unions are necessary to protect employees from job favoritism and discrimination.

________ 2. Job seniority is the fairest way to reward employees for their services.

________ 3. Unions are needed to ensure that workers are paid good wages and receive adequate benefits.

________ 4. Without a labor union, employees have little chance to have their complaints handled fairly.

________ 5. Every employee who benefits from the union should be required to join and support the union (i.e., a union shop).

________ 6. Most employees join a labor union because they want to join and they agree with the union's objectives.

________ 7. The best form of employee job participation occurs when a union can negotiate a labor agreement with an employer to cover the terms and conditions of employment.

________ 8. Stronger unions and wider representation of employees by unions are needed to counter corporate greed and management's indifference toward workers.

________ TOTAL (*add your score*)

Compare your total with the following:

8–15 You generally do not agree with or approve of labor unions.

16–23 You have mixed attitudes about labor unions.

24–32 You generally support unions and their objectives.

PART 2: Compare your results with the other members of your group. Is there a difference among your findings? How do you account for the difference?

PART 3: Working together as a group, discuss how a labor union workforce in the housekeeping services department might impact Dee's right to manage.

PART 4: The group should identify the aspects of Benevolent General Hospital's policies, procedures, and actions that might cause employees to seek a union.

PART 5: As a group, write a one page paper identifying what you learned from this exercise.

### FOOD FOR THOUGHT

How do you explain the differences that your group members had in working together on these Team Skill Builder activities but more importantly, what was the value of working together as a group?

## SUPERVISION IN ACTION

The video for this chapter can be accessed from the student companion website at www.cengagebrain.com. (Search by authors' names or book title to find the accompanying resources.)

## ENDNOTES

1. Robert Ramsey, "Supervising Volunteers Is Different," *Supervision* 74, No. 12 (December 2013), pp. 3–5.
2. Robert Greenleaf coined the phrase "servant-leader." "It begins with the natural feeling that one wants to serve, to serve first. That conscious choice brings one to aspire to lead." Visit http://www.greenleaf.org to access other insights and research on servant leadership. In their essay, "Servant-Leadership and Philanthropic Institutions," Larry Spears and John Burkhart list the 10 characteristics central to the development of servant-leaders: listening, empathy, healing, persuasion, awareness, foresight, conceptualization, commitment to the growth of people, stewardship, and building community. See "Leading by Serving," *Philanthropy Matters* (Spring 2008), pp. 8–10.
3. You can take a free emotional intelligence (EI) test. Go to http://www.queendom.com/test/access-page/index.htm. This will give you a free "snapshot" report.

   Also see Elizabeth J. Rozell and Wesley A. Scroggins, "How Much Is Too Much? The Role of Emotional Intelligence in Self-Managed Work," *Team Satisfaction and Group Processes* 16, No. 1/2 (2010), pp. 33–49 and review EI research by going to http://www.uh.edu/emotionalintelligence or the *Annual Review of Psychology* (2008).

Students may also want to review *Emotional Intelligence: Special Issue of the Journal of Organizational Behavior* 26, No. 4 (June 2005) for additional insights. Following on the works of others, Hendrie Weisinger identified four building blocks that help to develop skills and abilities, which are to: (1) accurately perceive, appraise, and express emotion; (2) access the ability or generate feelings on demand when they can facilitate understanding of yourself or another person; (3) understand emotions and the knowledge that derives from them; and (4) regulate emotions to promote emotional and intellectual growth. Also see Hendrie Weisinger, *Emotional Intelligence at Work* (San Francisco: Jossey-Bass, 1998), and Daniel Goleman, *Emotional Intelligence* (New York: Bantam Books, 1995).

4. See Jennifer George, "Emotions and Leadership: The Role of Emotional Intelligence," *Human Relations* 53, No. 8 (2000), pp. 1027–1055. Also see Gail Kinman and Louise Grant, "Exploring Stress Resilience in Training Social Service Workers: The Role of Emotional and Social Competencies," *British Journal of Social Work* 41, No. 2 (2011), pp. 261–274; Leonidas A. Zampetakis and Vassilis Moustakis, "Manager's Trait Emotional Intelligence and Group Outcomes," *Small Group Research* 42 (February 1, 2011), pp. 77–102; and Jae Uk Chun et al., "Emotional Intelligence and Trust in Formal Mentoring Programs," *Group and Organizational Behavior* 35 (August 1, 2010), pp. 421–455.
5. For additional information on Pandolfini's principles for making the right decisions under pressure, see "All the Right Moves," *Fast Company* (May 1999), p. 34. Also see Dave Kahle, "Characteristics of a Professional … Are You Serious about Your Job?" *SuperVision* (May 2007), pp. 12–14.
6. Adapted from the Titleist ad, "Which Ball Is Best for Your Game?" *Golf Digest* (September 8, 2008), pp. 5–6. Also, we suggest you review T. L. Stanley, "Running at Peak Performance," *Supervision* 74, No. 9 (September 2013),pp. 12–15.
7. The author first heard the term *enabler* used in the video *The Performance Appraisal*, produced and distributed by Business Advantage, Inc., of West Des Moines, Iowa. See the article by Robert T. Whipple, "Stop the Enabling: Confront Problem Employees before the Problems Overrun Your Ability to Deal with Them," *HR Magazine* (September 2010), pp. 114–115.
8. Op. cit. Servant-Leader (see end note 1 above).
9. Glenn M. Parker, *Cross-Functional Teams: Working with Allies, Enemies, and Other Strangers* (San Francisco: Jossey-Bass, 1998).
10. Fran Rees, *How to Lead Work Teams: Facilitation Skills* (San Diego: Pfeiffer & Co., 1991), pp. 1–2. Also see Kevin O'Connor, "Your Team-Building Exercises May Not Be Creating a Team," *Supervision* 74, No. 7 (July 2013) pp. 8–9; Nicholas Clarke, "Emotional Intelligence Abilities and Their Relationships with Team Processes," *Team Performance Management* 16, No. 1/2 (2010), pp. 6–32; Wolfgang Jenewein and Felicitas Morhart, "Navigating toward Team Success," *Team Performance Management* 13, No. 1/2 (2008), pp. 102+; Maria Isabel Delgado Pina, Ana Maria Romero-Martinez, and Luis Gomez Martinez, "Teams in Organization: A Review on Team Effectiveness," *Team Performance Management*, 13, No. 1/2 (2008), pp. 7–21; and Casimer DeCusatis, "Creating, Growing and Sustaining Efficient Innovation Teams," *Creativity and Innovation Management* 17, No. 2 (June 2008), pp. 155–164.
11. Thirty-plus years ago, Abraham Zaleznik, "Managers and Leaders: Are They Different?" *Harvard Business Review* (May–June 1977), pp. 126–135, set the stage for the debate of leader or manager. Also go to http://hrb.org/2004/01/managers-and-leadrs/ar/1 for a review of Zaleznik's work.

For a definitive description of managerial roles, see Henry Mintzberg, *The Nature of Managerial Work* (New York: Harper & Row, 1973) and Peter F. Drucker, *Management Challenges for the 21st Century* (New York, HarperBusiness, 1999).For additional review: Daniel Goleman, "The Focused Leader," *Harvard Business Review* 91, No. 12 (December 2013), pp. 50–60 and George Ambler, "Leaders vs Managers Are They Really Different?" Georgeambler.com (September 29, 2012), http://www.georgeambler.com/leaders-vs-managers-are-they-really-different/

12. Stephen R. Covey, *The Seven Habits of Highly Effective People* (New York: Simon & Schuster, 1989), p. 101; *The Speed of Trust* (New York: Free Press, 2007); *Principle-Centered Leadership: Strategies for Personal and Professional Effectiveness* (Bellevue: S&S Trade, 1992); and *The 8th Habit* (New York: Simon & Schuster, 2003). You may want to go to www.franklincovey.com for current insights into Covey's work.
13. See Noel Tichy and Warren Bennis, *Judgment: How Winning Leaders Make Great Calls* (New York: Portfolio-Penguin Group, 2007) and as discussed in *BusinessWeek* (November 18, 2007), pp. 68–72. Also see Adam Galinsky and Gavin Kilduff, "Be Seen as a Leader," *Harvard Business Review* 9, No. 12 (December 2013), pp. 127–130; Michael A. Roberto, *Why Great Leaders Don't Take Yes for an Answer* (New York: FT Press, 2013); Robert D. Harris, "Leadership Orientation," *Supervision* (August 2013), pp. 11–13; or Scott M. Patton, "It's about Leadership, Stupid," *Quality Digest* (March 2008), p. 56. A 2007 study by the Forum Corporation found that most leaders weren't equipped with the skills necessary to execute their companies' growth strategies, as reported in Pamela Babcock, "Survey: Many Leadership Development Programs too Tactical," *SHRM News* (May 2008). Also see Bennis, *On Becoming a Leader* (Reading, MA: Addison-Wesley, 1994) for insights into the differences between managers and leaders. Also, visit the Center for Creative Leadership (www.ccl.org).
14. Adapted from John P. Kotter, *John P. Kotter on What Leaders Really Do* (Boston: Harvard Business School Press, 1999). You may also want to see Kotter, *Accelerate: Building Strategic Agility for a Faster-Moving World* (2014) and Kotter's *Leading Change* (2012).
15. One of Henry Fayol's 14 principles of management defined formal authority as the "right to give orders." Henri Fayol, *General and Industrial Management*, trans. Constance Storrs (London: Sir Isaac Pitman & Sons, 1949), pp. 19–43.
16. See W. H. Weiss, "The Art and Science of Managing," *SuperVision* (October 2007), pp. 16–20; and Julian Birkinshaw, "Reinventing Management," *Ivey Business Journal* January/February 2010, http://www.iveybusinessjournal.com: Birkinshaw, *Reinventing Management: Smart Choices for Getting Work Done* (San Francisco: Jossey-Bass, 2010); Katharine Giacalone, "Five Concepts New Managers Often Forget," *SHRM Management Tools* (March 2010), www.shrm.org. Oliver W. Cummings, "What Do Manufacturing Supervisors Really Do on the Job?" *Industry Week* 259, No. 2 (February 2010), p. 53, David Sirota, Louis A. Mischkind, and Michael Irwin Meltzer, "Stop Demoting Your Employees!" *Harvard Management Update*, 11, No. 1 (January 2006). In about 85 percent of companies, employee morale sharply declines after only six months on the job. Sirota, Mischkind, and Meltzer's research shows how an individual manager's style of supervision contributes to the problem.
17. Much has been written about power. For additional information on position power and personal power, see Amitai Etzioni, *A Comparative Analysis of Complex Organizations* (New York: The Free Press, 1961), pp. 4–6; and John P. Kotter, "Power, Dependence, and Effective Management," *Harvard Business Review* (July–August 1977), pp. 131–136.

18. John R. P. French and Bertram Raven, "The Bases of Social Power," in *Studies in Social Power*, ed. Dorwin Cartwright (Ann Arbor: University of Michigan Press, 1959), pp. 150–167. Also see A. J. Stanhelski, D. E. Frost, and M. E. Patch, "Uses of Socially Dependent Bases of Power: French and Raven's Theory Applied to Working Group Leadership," *Journal of Applied Social Psychology* (March 1989), pp. 283–297.
19. See Timothy R. Hinkin and Chester A. Schriesheim, "Relationships between Subordinate Perceptions and Supervisor Influence Tactics and Attributed Bases of Supervisory Power," *Human Relations* (March 1990), pp. 221–237. Also see K. S. Cameron, D. Bright, and A. Carza, "Exploring the Relationships between Organizational Virtuousness and Performance," *American Behavior Scientist* 47, No. 6 (February 1, 2004), pp. 766–790.
20. As of February 2014, 11.3 percent of the total workforce was unionized, mostly in the public sector. That is down from 20.1 percent in 1983, a drop of nearly 9 percent. We suggest that you secure a copy of a *Guide to Basic Law and Procedures under the National Labor Relations Act* (Washington, DC: U.S. Government Printing Office, NLRB; or visit the National Labor Relations Board Web site (http://www.nlrb.gov/nlrb/legal/manuals/rules/act.asp) for an overview of labor law. You may also want to see Melanie Trottman, "Organized Labor Held Steady in '13,'", *The Wall Street Journal* (January 25–26, 2014), pA5.
21. Neal E. Boudette, "VW Bid to Grow in U.S. Is Hurt by UAW Fight," *The Wall Street Journal* (March 14, 2014), p. B3. George Will, "UAW Wants to Turn the South into Detroit," *Washington Post* (February 23, 2014), p. G-5. Lydia DePillis, "AFL-CIO Director Works to Stop Decline of Unions," *Washington Post* (November 24, 2013), p. 1; H. Kevin Trahan, "Football Players Win First Round in Union Bid," *USA Today* (March 27, 2014), p. 2C. Jason Gay, "The NCAA's Imperfect Union," *The Wall Street Journal* (March 28, 2014), p. D10; "Volkswagen's Lasting Lesson for Labor," *Bloomberg Businessweek* (February 24 to March 2, 2014), p. 8; "Fast-Food Workers of the World, Unite!" *Bloomberg Businessweek* (December 9 to 15, 2013), p. 20; Douglas Belkin, Melanie Trottman and Rachel Bachman, "College's Football Team Can Unionize," *The Wall Street Journal* (March 27, 2014), p. A2.
22. Stephen R. Covey as quoted at http://quotations.about.com/od/stillmorefamouspeople/a/StephenCovey1/.htm.
23. Adapted from Peter Northouse, "Skills Inventory," in *Leadership Theory and Practice*, 6th ed. (Thousand Oaks, CA: Sage Publications, 2013), pp. 68–70. NEED PERMISSION
24. See Rupali Arora, Catherine Dunn, Beth Kowitt, Colleen Leahey, Patricia Sellers, and Anne Vandermey, "50 Most Powerful Women Global Edition," *Fortune* (February 24, 2014) for a complete listing of the top 50.
25. "The 10 Greatest CEOs of All Time," *Fortune* (July 21, 2003), pp. 54–68.

Chapter

# 3 Supervisory Planning

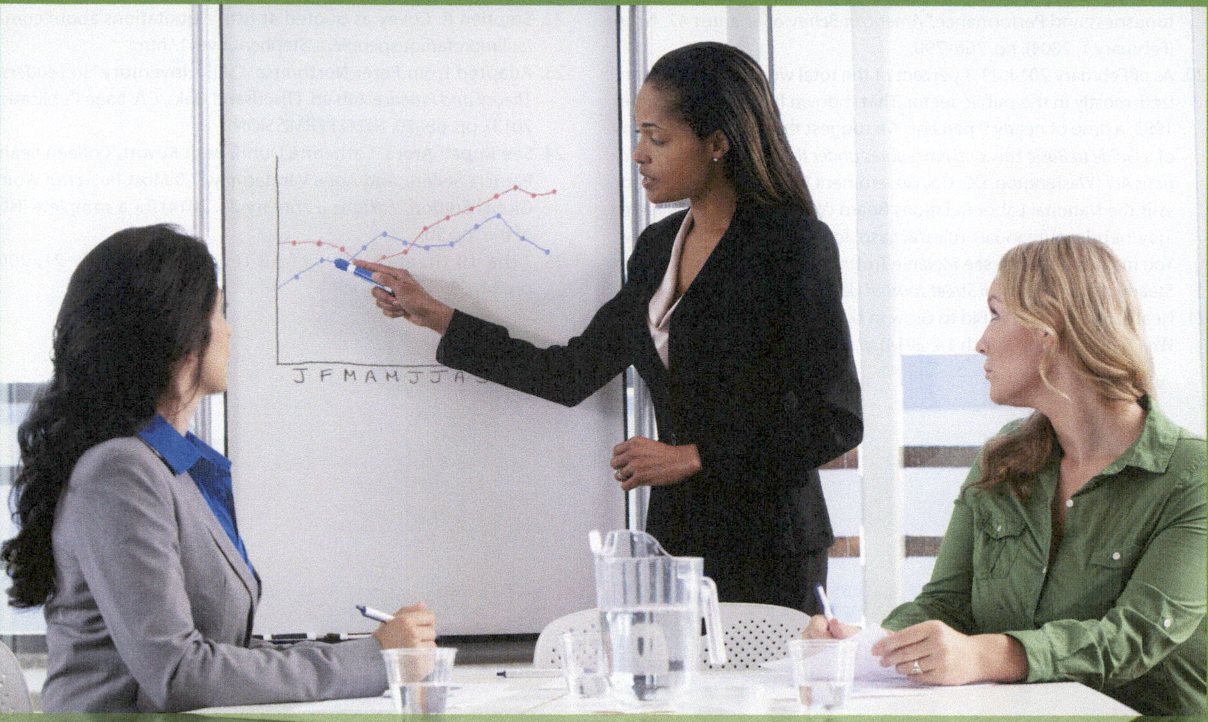


©Monkey Business Images / Shutterstock.com

**After studying this chapter, you will be able to:**

1. Define planning and explain why all management functions depend on planning.
2. Explain how visioning and mission statements provide the foundation for strategic planning.
3. Discuss the need for well-defined organizational goals and objectives, particularly as they relate to the supervisor.
4. Describe the supervisor's role in synchronizing his or her plans with organizational plans.
5. Summarize management by objectives (MBO).
6. Identify the major types of standing and single-use plans and explain how these plans help supervisory decision making.
7. Describe how the supervisor plans for efficient and effective resource use.
8. Cite the key advantages of planning for quality.
9. Recognize the importance of planning for the unthinkable (crisis management).

## YOU MAKE THE CALL!

*You are Shannon O'Neill, transportation supervisor for the Homestead School Corporation. Your basic responsibilities include hiring, training, and evaluating the employees in your department; scheduling bus utilization; ordering all fuels and maintenance supplies; coordinating extracurricular activity transportation; and safely transporting 6,000 children to and from school each day. The school district covers about 400 square miles, and most of the kids take the school bus to get to school.*

You developed a comprehensive planning system to schedule transportation requirements and preventive maintenance. The Homestead School Corporation has substantially lower per-pupil transportation costs than other schools and thus is able to use the savings to provide enrichment experiences for the district's children. You are frequently called to describe the benefits of your system to other school corporations, and last year you were invited to address the school administrators association's annual conference.

You are highly regarded as a supervisor. Employee turnover is minimal, and the list of people wanting to work for you is long. Open communication, trust, and transparency are values your team shares. The employees meet with you every Tuesday morning to review progress, identify potential problem areas, and make recommendations for improvement. Your department gets together informally once each month to celebrate accomplishments.

The foundation for your leadership style was inherited from your father, whose favorite saying was "Plan your work, then work your plan!" Every evening before you leave work, you develop your "Plan for Tomorrow." You list all the things that need to be done the next day in order of priority. You list the time of day that each task will need to be done and who is responsible for its accomplishment, then you post the list on the message board in the center of the office. Your employees conscientiously review the list at the beginning of each workday and align their daily calendars accordingly. When issues arise, everyone willingly works together to address them. This process has worked very well.

A new superintendent of schools arrived in the fall and announced a program of continuous improvement. At his first meeting this morning with all supervisors the superintendent strongly challenged the group to question their supervisory practices and find ways to improve them. Each supervisor was instructed to develop a list of three strategies to improve his or her areas of responsibility and submit them in two weeks.

You believe that your leadership and planning style has worked very well and that your system for continuous improvement is already in place. How will you respond to the superintendent's request?

**Disclaimer:** The above scenario presents a supervisory situation based on real events to be used for educational purposes. The identities of some or all individuals, organizations, industries, and locations, as well as financial and other information may have been disguised to protect individual privacy and proprietary information. In some cases details have been added to improve readability and interest.

YOU MAKE THE CALL!

## Management Functions Begin with Planning

**1 Define planning and explain why all management functions depend on planning.**

Management scholars and practitioners disagree about the number and designation of managerial functions. However, the consensus is that the first, and probably the most crucial, managerial function is planning.

**Planning** means deciding what is to be done in the future. It includes analyzing a situation, forecasting events, establishing objectives, setting priorities, and deciding which actions are needed to achieve those objectives. Logically, planning precedes all other managerial functions because every manager must project a framework and a course of action before trying to achieve the desired results. For example, how can a supervisor organize a department's operations without a plan? How can a supervisor effectively staff and lead employees without knowing which avenues to follow? How can a supervisor control employee activities without standards and objectives? All managerial functions depend on planning.

**Planning**
The process of deciding what needs to be done by whom and when

Planning is a managerial function every supervisor must perform every day. It should not be a process used only occasionally or when the supervisor is not engrossed in daily chores. By planning, the supervisor realistically anticipates and analyzes problems and opportunities, examines the probable effects of various alternatives, and chooses the course of action that should lead to the most desirable results. Of course, plans alone do not bring about desired results, but without good planning, activities would be random, thereby producing confusion and inefficiency.

**2 Explain how visioning and mission statements provide the foundation for strategic planning.**

## The Strategic Planning Process

Turbulent and rapid changes in economic conditions and technology, coupled with increasing domestic and international competition, have forced organizations to plan more thoroughly and systematically. The loss of quality manufacturing jobs to lower-cost countries has produced an era of pessimism that has not been experienced during this author's lifetime. Figure 3.1 is not a lighthearted reflection on the current state of affairs.

As the first function of management, planning must start at the top level of management and permeate all levels of the organization. For the organization as a whole, this means top management must develop an outlook and plans that guide the organization. We call this process **strategic planning**, which essentially means establishing goals and making decisions that enable an organization to achieve its long- and short-term objectives.

**Strategic planning**
The process of establishing goals and making decisions that enable an organization to achieve its long- and short-term objectives

For many years, noted management scholar Peter Drucker stressed that every organization's leadership must think through the firm's reason for being and constantly ask five important questions:

- What is our mission?
- Who is our customer?
- What does our customer value?
- What are our results?
- What is our plan?[1]

Only by asking these questions can an organization set goals and objectives, develop strategies, and make decisions that lead to success. Drucker emphasized that answering these questions has to be done by that part of the organization that can see the entire business, balance all current objectives and needs against tomorrow's needs, and allocate resources to achieve key results.

Peter Skarzynski and Linda Yates, co-founders of Strategos, a global strategy innovation firm, have echoed Drucker's assertions with their own emphasis on innovation as the guiding principle for all companies in the future. They write:

> *Getting to the future first ... requires organizations and their leaders to be courageous and farsighted. The company that wins the race to the future is driven by innovation. Not an innovation, but a conscious,*

**FIGURE 3.1 "Freshly Squeezed" By Ed Stein**

Universal Uclick

*built-in, continuous process of innovation that keeps an organization on a pathbreaking streak. Innovation must become, like the quality revolution of twenty years ago, the right and responsibility of every individual in a company, not the pet project of the executive suite. Companies that eat and breathe innovation never suffer from prosperity-induced slumbers. They are not predicting the future; they are inventing it.*[2]

In most organizations, top-level managers are primarily responsible for developing and executing strategic or long-term plans. However, once strategic goals and plans have been identified, middle managers and supervisors must be involved in the corresponding planning activities of the organization.[3] These employees must plan their work units' policies and activities to achieve the organization's overall goals. A supervisor likely becomes involved in developing and carrying out certain overall strategic plans for the corporation. Often, supervisors will not be a part of the organization's budget decisions, but they will certainly be involved in developing strategies, plans, policies, and procedures that impact the budget.

Strategic planning need not be a burdensome, voluminous undertaking. Strategic planning principles apply to small businesses as much as they do to major corporations. Time limitations and lack of strategic planning knowledge are often impediments for small business owners. The benefits of strategic management in directing the organization as a whole are just as important to small business. Regardless of the size or nature of the organization, managers must be involved in strategy formulation because their participation in the strategic planning process is essential to gaining employee commitment for the chosen directions and strategies. Remember, the inability to create a vision and develop plans is the sure route to failure.

## MISSION STATEMENTS AND VISIONING

Effective strategic planning usually begins with the development of a **mission statement** that reflects the philosophy and purpose of the organization as defined by its top leadership. An organization's mission is usually understood to be the purpose or reason for the organization's existence. While many organizations historically had voluminous mission statements that left people scratching their heads and wondering what business they're really in, the trend is toward more precise statements.

**Mission statement**
A statement of the organization's basic philosophy, purpose, and reason for being

How would you account for the fact that highly unionized Southwest Airlines (SWA) has consistently been the most profitable of U.S. airlines and has not strayed from its core business strategy of flying point to point? Colleen Barrett, former president of Southwest Airlines, proudly pointed to the fact that SWA's mission statement added up to less than 100 words:

1. *"The mission of Southwest Airlines is dedication to the highest quality of Customer Service delivered with a sense of warmth, friendliness, individual pride, and Company Spirit."*
2. *"We are committed to providing our Employees a stable work environment with equal opportunity for learning and personal growth. Creativity and innovation are encouraged for improving the effectiveness of Southwest Airlines. Above all, Employees will be provided the same concern, respect, and caring attitude within the organization that they are expected to share with every Southwest Customer."*[4]

Historically, SWA has worked very, very hard to keep their employees informed and motivated as a means to keep their customers satisfied. SWA treats their internal customers (employees) the way they are being asked to treat their external customers (passengers).

SWA's mission statement is well known to all employees and the customers who fly Southwest. Top management, from SWA president Gary Kelly to the line supervisors, is responsible for providing the leadership that sets the desired patterns for employees' behavior. As such, the mission statement serves as a springboard or basis for assessing the company's performance and results.[5]

The concept of visioning goes beyond that of a mission statement. Visioning is the process of developing a mental image of what the firm or organization could become; it seeks to define what it is that distinguishes the organization and what will make it better. The **vision statement** reflects this mental image and can become the foundation for all of a firm's activities. There is, of course, some overlap in vision statements and mission statements. See Figures 1.8 and 15.2 for other examples of vision, mission, value, and code of conduct statements.

**Vision statement**
Management's view of what the company should become; reflects the firm's core values, priorities, and goals

Visioning and vision statements should not be mere "advertising slogans" that primarily laud the organization and its accomplishments. Rather, the vision statement should reflect the firm's core values, priorities, and goals, which can be translated into concrete plans and actions.[6]

As mentioned previously, visioning should not be thought of as solely the responsibility of top management. In fact, effective supervisors use visioning to guide their parts of the organization. For example, considering the You Make the Call! section of this chapter, you can solicit ideas from fellow students as well as from other stakeholders who might be impacted by such a scenario of how Shannon might engage her department in creating a vision statement to drive continuous improvement. Proactive supervisors will glean the "best practices of the best" and figure out how to take those practices to a higher level for their areas of responsibility.

Widespread participation in visioning is crucial to realizing the vision. Using contacts and networks, the task force members should strive not only to generate ideas about what should be included in the policy and procedure documents, but also to set the stage for acceptance of the final project. The task force has an opportunity to shape the future.

When we look at the more successful organizations, we see a common thread: "Top management has clearly created a vision, defined what they want to be, identified their competitive edge, and involved employees in quality improvement efforts." It appears clear that those organizations that diligently work to eliminate ineffective processes and implement customer-first quality improvement programs are increasing their chances for success.

**3 Discuss the need for well-defined organizational goals and objectives, particularlyas they relate to the supervisor.**

## Organizational Goals and Objectives

Now that we have created a vision of what and where we want to be, the next major step in planning is to develop a general statement of goals and objectives that identifies the overall purposes and results toward which all plans and activities are directed. Setting overall goals is a function of top-level management, which must define and communicate to all managers the primary purposes for which the business is organized. These overall goals usually reflect the vision of upper-level managers with regard to such things as the production and distribution of products or services, obligations to the customer, being a good employer and responsible corporate citizen, profit as a just reward for taking risks,

**FIGURE 3.2 Mission statement and corporate objectives**

Qwik Home Center and Lumber Company, Inc.

Qwik Home Center and Lumber Company, Inc., depends on the respect and support of four groups: (1) its customers, (2) its employees, (3) its shareholders, and (4) the public, which includes the citizens of each community in which we do business. For us to have a satisfactory future, we must continuously earn the support, respect, and approval of all four of these groups. We believe in fostering an environment that encourages superior products, service, and performance. This requires each employee to clearly understand our corporate objectives.

**CORPORATE OBJECTIVES**

1. We will, by August 31, 2015, become the low-cost provider of lumber products.
2. We will reduce the number of customer complaints (as measured by merchandise returns) by 10 percent this year.
3. We will reduce accounts receivable by 50 percent in the next six months.
4. We will develop plans for revitalizing one-fourth of our stores during the next two years.
5. We will institute a profit-sharing plan for our employees by the end of the year.
6. A program of Customer Retention Management (CRM) will be instituted in the next six months.
7. Our long-term same-store sales growth is expected to increase by 7 percent per year for each of the next three years, while cost of goods sold are reduced to below the industry average.

This continuing long-term growth in earnings and record of financial stability is expected to attract to our organization the capital required to support its growth.



research and development, and legal and ethical obligations. Figure 3.2 presents a statement that combines the vision, mission, and objectives in an easy to understand document.

In this text, we use the terms *goals* and *objectives* interchangeably. Either term expresses what one wants to accomplish within a certain timeframe.

First, the organization as a whole begins the planning process by determining what kind of organization it wants to be at some future point in time. Generally, making this determination addresses the questions suggested by Peter Drucker that are listed on page 74 related to the organization's mission, customers, value, results, and plans for the future.

The goals formulated for an organization as a whole lead to more specific objectives for divisional and departmental managers and supervisors. Each division or department must clearly set forth its own objectives as guidelines for operations. These objectives must be within the general framework of the overall goals, and they must contribute to achieving the organization's overall mission and purpose. Sometimes these objectives are established on a contingency basis—that is, some may depend on certain resources or may reflect changing priorities.

Objectives are usually stated in terms of what is to be accomplished, when, and by how much. In general, a department's "what by when by how much" statements are more specific than the broadly stated goals of the organization. While the higher-level goal may be to provide quality maintenance services for the entire organization, the maintenance supervisor's objective might be to reduce machine downtime ("what") by 12 percent ("how much") by year's end ("when"). While the organization's supervisory-level objectives are more specific than its broadly stated goals, they are consistent with, and give direction to, departmental efforts to achieve organizational goals.

Supervisors must remember two things when developing their departmental objectives: (1) department objectives must be aligned with the organization's goals and objectives, and (2) there must be a means to measure and document the department's contribution to the organization's bottom line. Not all goals are equally important. Thus, with the help of upper-level managers, the supervisor must prioritize departmental objectives according to the priority of organizational goals. All employees should know what is to be done, when it is to be done, and how to measure the results. Noted author Peter Senge has stated that there is a simple principle to guide you: "Measure quantitatively that which should be quantified; measure qualitatively that which should not be quantified."[7] Simply stated, **metrics** are standards of measurement.[8] For example, a hospital supervisor may use mortality rates as a metric, while a sales manager might use on-time delivery. Regardless of the scope of one's responsibilities, supervisors must keep an eye on the financial statements and other scorecards to ensure that goals and objectives become reality.

**Metrics**
A standard of measurement used to determine that performance is in line with objectives

Whenever possible, objectives should be stated in measurable or verifiable terms, "by how much," such as "to reduce overtime by 5 percent during the month," "to increase output per employee-hour by 10 percent during the next quarter," "to achieve a 10 percent increase in employee suggestions during the next year," and so on. Each of these objectives becomes a metric. Thus, a supervisor is able to evaluate performance against specific targets. This approach is an essential part of management by objectives programs, which many organizations have implemented as ways to plan and attain results. One tool often used by companies to facilitate monitoring of multiple metrics is a **dashboard**, a visual presentation of the current status of an organization's key performance metrics relative to its goals, which can take the form of a one-page, easy-to-read report updated weekly or monthly or a computer screen that shows performance in real time. Regardless of the form the data takes, the supervisor must know where to find it and check it regularly to ensure that the department is on track to achieve its objectives and, if it is not, make changes to increase performance.

**Dashboard**
A visual presentation of the current status of an organization's key performance metrics relative to its goals

**4 Describe the supervisor's role in synchronizing his or her plans with organizational plans.**

## All Management Levels Perform the Planning Function

The organization's vision, objectives, and strategies serve as the foundation for the supervisor's planning process. Remember, the magnitude of a manager's plans depends on the level at which those plans are intended to be carried out. Planning is far more far-reaching at the top level than at the supervisory level. The top-level executive is concerned with the overall operation of the enterprise and long-range planning for new facilities and equipment, new products and services, new markets, and major investments. At the supervisory level, the scope is narrower and more detailed. The supervisor is usually concerned with day-to-day plans for accomplishing departmental tasks, such as meeting production quotas for a particular day.

While planning always involves looking to the future, evaluating the past should be part of managerial planning. Every manager can plan more effectively by evaluating previous plans and trying to learn from past successes and failures. Although there is no recipe that guarantees success, the guidelines in the accompanying Supervisory Tips box are recommended for increasing the probability of reaching the intended target.

In formulating plans, a supervisor may find that certain aspects of planning call for specialized help, such as for implementing employment policies, computer and accounting procedures, or technical know-how. In such areas, the supervisor should consult with specialists in the organization to help carry out the required planning responsibilities. For example, a human resources staff specialist can offer useful advice concerning policies involving employees. A supervisor should use available help in the organization to plan thoroughly and specifically. This includes consulting with employees for their suggestions on how to proceed in certain situations. Employees like to be consulted, and their advice may help the supervisor develop day-to-day plans for running the department. In small firms, expertise may not be readily available, so the supervisor may want to draw on personal contacts or consultants from outside the firm. In the final analysis, each supervisor is personally responsible for planning (see Figure 3.3 for a list of questions to ask before developing plans).

## PLANNING PERIODS

For how long should a manager plan? Usually, a distinction is made between long-range and short-range planning. The definitions of long-range and short-range planning depend on the manager's level in the organizational hierarchy, the type of enterprise, and the kind of industry in which the organization is operating. Most managers define *short-range planning* as that which spans the next couple of months. For others, it might be developing plans to get through the day. Very short-range planning is involved, for example, in scheduling a production run or in staffing an end-of-summer sale in a department store. Many supervisors prefer to do this type of planning at the end of the day or at the end of the week when they can evaluate what has been accomplished. There are some activities, such as preventive maintenance, for which the supervisor can plan several months in advance. The plans a supervisor makes should be integrated and coordinated with the long-range plans of upper management. These long-range plans stem from the vision and mission of the firm and are often called the **strategic plan**.

**Strategic plan**
Long-term plans developed by top management

**FIGURE 3.3 Planning requires answering these questions**

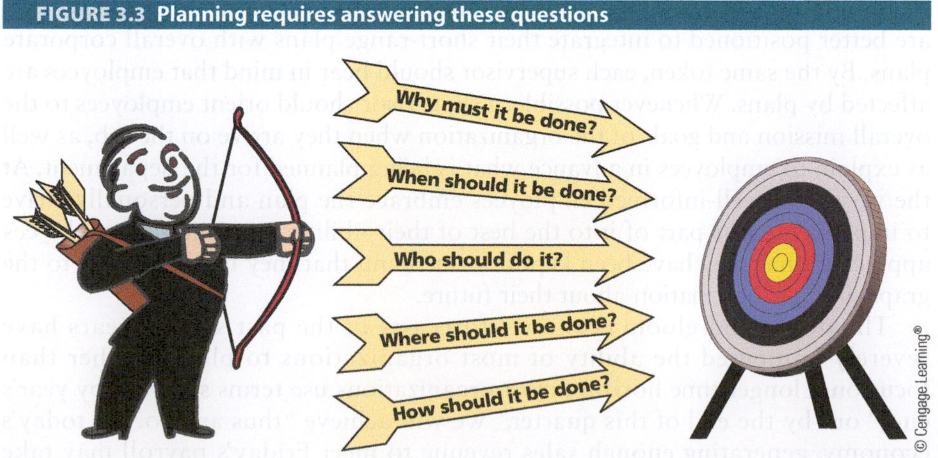
Why must it be done?
When should it be done?
Who should do it?
Where should it be done?
How should it be done?
© Cengage Learning®

## SUPERVISORY TIPS

### How to Reach Your Goal

1. Create a vision.
2. Develop a mission statement.
3. Involve others in setting SMART[1] goals and objectives:
   **S**tretching, yet attainable.
   **M**easurable by expressing it in a quantity.
   **A**ccountable by identifying the individual responsible for accomplishment.
   **R**ealistic, set in light of past performance, organizational resources, states of nature, and the competitive environment.
   **T**ime limited. This is often accomplished by expressing the objective in terms of the conditions or results to be achieved by a specific point in time. *What is to be done by when.*
4. Communicate goals/objectives to all those who must know.
5. Get commitment to the goals.
6. Develop plans and strategies for reaching the goal or objective.
7. Put the plan in writing.
8. Secure commitment to the plan.
9. Put the plan into action. Assign responsibility, accountability, and authority. (See Figure 3.3)
10. Establish feedback controls.
11. Monitor progress toward goal achievement.
12. Make changes, **as** necessary.

*Note:* (1) In earlier editions of this text, we stated that objectives should be specific, measurable, attainable, realistic as to organization resources, and time limited. I would like to thank Mike Lynch and Harvey Lifton for introducing me to the notion of evaluating objectives by applying their SMART criteria. See "Training Clips: 150 Reproducible Handouts: Discussion Starters and Job Aids," *HRD Press* (1998), p. 118.

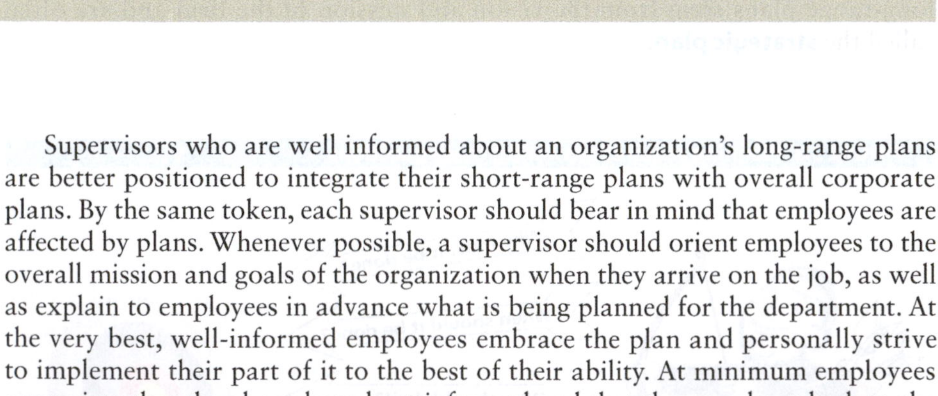

Supervisors who are well informed about an organization's long-range plans are better positioned to integrate their short-range plans with overall corporate plans. By the same token, each supervisor should bear in mind that employees are affected by plans. Whenever possible, a supervisor should orient employees to the overall mission and goals of the organization when they arrive on the job, as well as explain to employees in advance what is being planned for the department. At the very best, well-informed employees embrace the plan and personally strive to implement their part of it to the best of their ability. At minimum employees appreciate that they have been kept informed and that they need not look to the grapevine for information about their future.

The doom-and-gloom economic forecasts of the past several years have severely hampered the ability of most organizations to plan.[9] Rather than focus on a longer time horizon, most organizations use terms such as "by year's end," or "by the end of this quarter," we will achieve "thus and so." In today's economy, generating enough sales revenue to meet Friday's payroll may take precedence over focusing on long-term plans. In order to develop realistic and meaningful plans, managers must make assumptions about the future and make adjustments as necessary. Economic volatility and a rapidly changing competitive environment require constant monitoring and adjustments. Regardless of such challenges, it is essential that long-range plans be developed. Ask yourself these questions:

- Where do I see myself three months from now? A year from now? Three years from now?
- What will I be doing?
- Where will I be doing it?
- Who will I be doing it with?
- What do I want to be doing when I am 70 years old?
- How will I measure my success?

Remember: "Before individuals can decide in which direction to go, they must determine where they want to get to," or, as author Stephen Covey says, "Always begin with the end in mind."[10]

## Management by Objectives—A System for Participative Management

**5 Summarize management by objectives (MBO).**

**Management by objectives (MBO)** A process in which the supervisor and employee jointly set the employee's objectives and the employee receives rewards upon achieving those objectives

**Management by objectives (MBO)** is a management approach in which managers, supervisors, and employees jointly set objectives against which performance is later evaluated. It is a management system that involves participative management. MBO requires full commitment to organizational objectives, starting with top-level management and permeating throughout all levels. MBO is also called "managing by results" or "managing for performance."[11]

As Figure 3.4 shows, an effective MBO system has four major elements. The determination of specific, measurable, and verifiable objectives is the foundation of the system. The other three elements are (1) the inputs, or resources, needed for goal accomplishment; (2) the activities and processes that must be carried out to accomplish the goal; and (3) the results, which are evaluated against the

**FIGURE 3.4 Elements of the MBO approach**

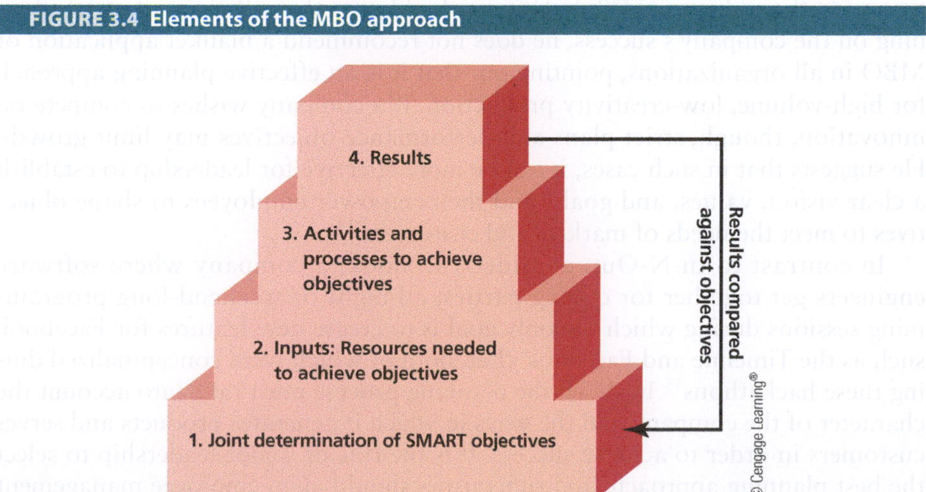

objectives. While MBO emphasizes results rather than the techniques used to achieve them, an effective MBO system is constructed such that all four of the aforementioned elements are integrated and support the others.

## WHY USE MANAGEMENT BY OBJECTIVES?

Regardless of what one calls the process, we all use an MBO approach in our lives. For example, a member of your study team suggests that you all do something together this weekend to take your minds off the midterm exams that are coming up. Remember, MBO is results-oriented. It requires thorough planning, organization, controls, communication, commitment, and dedication on the part of team members. Because all are involved in these activities, they should have a greater motivation to make sure that a good time will be had by all—the goal of the activity.

In an organizational setting, MBO provides a sound means of appraising individuals' performances by emphasizing objective criteria. Finally, MBO provides a more rational basis for sharing the rewards of an organization, particularly compensation and promotion based on merit.

A formalized MBO system helps high-level managers recognize the importance of delegating authority and responsibility to managers, supervisors, and employees if goals and objectives are to be achieved. Research has shown that employees will generally be more motivated to try to meet these objectives because they are "our goals" rather than "their goals." The advantage of a formal MBO system is that it ties together many plans, establishes priorities, and coordinates activities that otherwise might be overlooked or handled loosely in day-to-day business operations. A sound MBO program encourages the contributions and commitment of people toward common goals and objectives.

Stanford professor Michael Dearing gave an example of the successful results of MBO in his analysis of In-N-Out Burger, a company with 300 nonfranchised restaurants with the organizational goal to "generate exact reproductions" of its basic, Spartan menu.[12] The company has clearly stated quality, employee training, and growth goals that have produced the lowest employee turnover rate (the average manager stays on for 14 years), the highest-paid employees in the fast-food industry (always above minimum wage, with managers making upward of $100,000 a year), a cult-like customer following, and steadily growing competition for the industry.[13] While Dearing highlights the influence of strict planning on the company's success, he does not recommend a blanket application of MBO in all organizations, pointing out that it is an effective planning approach for high-volume, low-creativity production. If a company wishes to compete on innovation, though, strict plans and performance objectives may limit growth. He suggests that in such cases, it can be more effective for leadership to establish a clear vision, values, and goals, and then empower employees to shape objectives to meet the needs of markets and customers.[14]

In contrast to In-N-Out, consider Facebook, a company where software engineers get together for coding parties, all night or weekend-long programming sessions during which the only goal is to create new features for Facebook such as the Timeline and Facebook chat, both of which were conceptualized during these hackathons[15] In short, the planning process must take into account the character of the company and the ways in which it generates products and serves customers in order to achieve success. It is the role of senior leadership to select the best planning approach, and supervisors should align employee management practices with that approach.

## Types of Plans

6 **Identify the major types of standing and single-use plans and explain how these plans help supervisory decision making.**

After setting major goals and objectives, all levels of management participate in the design and execution of additional plans for attaining desired objectives. In general, such plans can be broadly classified as (a) standing or repeat-use plans, which can be used over and over as the need arises, and (b) single-use plans, which focus on one purpose or undertaking.

### PLANS

Many of the supervisor's day-to-day activities and decisions are guided by use of so-called **standing plans**, or repeat-use plans. Although terminology varies, these types of plans typically are known as policies, procedures, methods, and rules. All these plans should be designed to reinforce one another and should be directed toward the achievement of both organizational and work-unit objectives. Top-level managers formulate company-wide standing plans; supervisors formulate the necessary subsidiary standing plans for their work units.

**Standing plans**
Policies, procedures, methods, and rules that can be applied to recurring situations

In contrast to repeat-use plans are plans that are no longer needed or that become obsolete once the objective is accomplished or the period of applicability is over. These are **single-use plans**. For example, the conversion of a section of the student-union building into a coffeehouse/bookstore would require a single-use plan. Generally, the supervisor's role in establishing single-use plans is one of providing thoughts and suggestions.

**Single-use plans**
Plans to accomplish a specific objective or to cover a designated time period

### POLICIES

A **policy** is a general guide to thinking when making decisions. Corporate policies are usually statements that channel the thinking of managers and supervisors in specified directions and define the limits within which those staff must stay as they make decisions.[16]

**Policy**
A standing plan that serves as a guide to making decisions

Effective policies promote consistent decision making throughout an enterprise. Once policies are set, managers find it easier to delegate authority, because the decisions a subordinate supervisor makes are guided by policies. Policies enable supervisors to arrive at about the same decisions their managers would, or at least to make decisions within acceptable parameters. While policies should be considered guides for thinking, they do permit supervisors to use their own judgment in making decisions, as long as those decisions fall within the parameters of policy.

For example, most companies have policies covering employee conduct and other work-related issues. Do you know of any employees surfing the Internet rather than working?[17] The average employee is using the company's computer for some activities that are not work-related, and most organizations have instituted computer use policies. Look up your university's or organization's computer use and code of conduct policy. How clearly does it state the expectations for different groups in the organization? It should be noted that many organizations have installed systems that will show who is visiting which sites and when, and will track the number of keystrokes and other data.

**Origin of Policies.** Major company-wide policies are originated by top-level managers because policymaking is one of their important responsibilities. Top-level managers must develop and establish overall policies that guide the thinking of subordinate managers so that organizational goals can be achieved. Broad policies become the guides for specific policies developed within divisions and departments. Departmental policies established by supervisors must complement and coincide with the broader policies of the organization. In this regard, a firm's policy manuals should not become too excessive in concept, design, and detail. One corporate executive expressed his disdain for "bloated policy manuals" by replacing a multivolume manual at his company with two pages of "clear yet flexible guidelines." In his view, this turned his supervisors into decision makers who knew their responsibilities and acted accordingly.[18]

Small firms tend to have fewer policies than their large counterparts. On the one hand, the absence of policies gives the supervisor greater flexibility in dealing with situations as they occur. For example, many small firms do not have policies for drug or alcohol use; they prefer to handle problems on an individual basis if and when such problems occur. On the other hand, the absence of policies may cause inconsistent supervisory practices and lead to charges of unfairness or discrimination. Information concerning the kinds of policies and practices that exist in an area—especially those involving employee matters—is usually available through surveys conducted by employer associations. Such survey data can be helpful if a firm's management wants to make comparisons and perhaps adjust its policies and practices to align more closely with those of most other employers.[19]

In addition to policies formulated by top-level managers, some policies are imposed on an organization by external forces, such as government, labor unions, trade groups, and accrediting associations. The word *imposed* indicates compliance with an outside force that cannot be avoided. For example, to be accredited, schools, universities, hospitals, and other institutions must comply with regulations issued by the appropriate accrediting agency. Government regulations concerning minimum wage, pay for overtime work, and hiring of people without regard to race, age, and gender automatically become part of an organization's policies. Any policy imposed on the organization in such a manner is known as an externally imposed policy, and everyone in the organization must comply with it. Noncompliance can result in substantial fines and/or legal action, along with negative situations in an organization that the policies are designed to prevent.

**Written Policy Statements Promote Consistency.** Because policies are guides to decision making, they should be clearly stated and communicated to those in the organization who are affected by them. Although there is no guarantee that policies always will be completely followed or understood, they are more likely to be followed consistently if they are written. Few organizations have all of their policies in written form; some have few or no written policies, either because they simply never got around to writing them or because they would rather not state their policies publicly. However, the benefits of well-stated written policies usually outweigh the disadvantages. The process of writing policies requires managers to think through issues more thoroughly and consistently. Supervisors and employees can refer to a written policy as often as they wish. The wording of a written policy cannot be changed by word of mouth; when there is doubt or disagreement, the written policy can be consulted. In addition, written policies are available to supervisors and employees who are new to the organization so they can quickly acquaint themselves with the policies. Every policy should be reviewed periodically and revised or discarded as conditions or circumstances warrant.

**The Supervisor's Role.** Supervisors seldom have to issue policies. If a department is extremely large or geographically dispersed, or if several subunits exist within the department, the supervisor may find it appropriate to write departmental policies. For the most part, however, instead of writing policies, the supervisor will be called on to apply existing policies in making decisions. That is, most of the time, it is the supervisor's role to interpret, apply, and explain policies. Because policies guide supervisors in many daily decisions, supervisors must understand the policies and learn how to interpret and apply them.

A supervisor may occasionally experience a situation for which no policy exists or seems applicable. For example, suppose a group of employees asks the supervisor for permission to visit the user of their product to better understand how the product is used. To make an appropriate decision in this matter, the supervisor should be guided by a policy so that the decision will be in accord with other decisions regarding time away from work. If, upon investigation, the supervisor finds that higher-level management has never issued a formal policy to cover such a request, the supervisor needs guidance and should ask his or her manager to issue a policy—a guide for action. The supervisor can then apply the policy in this case as well as in the future so that there is consistency not only in the supervisor's particular department but also across the organization. After consulting with other supervisors who may have stakes in the issue, the supervisor may want to draft a suggested policy and present it to the manager. In large firms, it is unlikely that many such instances will happen because top-level management usually has covered the major policy areas. In small firms, where fewer policies exist, supervisors must use good judgment to determine when to make decisions themselves and when to consult their managers.

## PROCEDURES

A **procedure**, like a policy, is a standing plan for achieving objectives. It derives from policies but is more specific. Procedures define a chronological sequence of actions that carry out the terms and objectives of a policy. They promote consistency by listing the steps to be taken and the sequence to be followed. At times, procedures are combined with or incorporated into policy statements.

**Procedure**
A standing plan that defines the sequence of activities to be performed to achieve objectives

Another very common example is a company policy that requires supervisors to use the human resources department in the preliminary steps of hiring. This policy may contain several guidelines designed to meet nondiscriminatory hiring goals. To carry out this policy, management develops procedure governing the selection process. For example, the procedure to be followed by a supervisor who wants to hire a word processor might include completing a requisition form, specifying the job requirements, interviewing and testing potential candidates, and other such actions. In this way, the procedure details exactly what a supervisor must do or not do to comply with the company's hiring policies. All supervisors must follow the same procedure.

At the departmental level, the supervisor must often develop procedures to determine how work is to be done. When supervisors are fortunate enough to have only highly skilled employees to lead, they depend on the employees to a great extent to select efficient paths of performance. However, this situation is uncommon. Most employees look to the supervisor for instructions on how to proceed.

One advantage of preparing a procedure is that it requires an analysis of work to be done. Another advantage is that once a procedure is established, it promotes more uniform action, reduces the need for much routine decision making, and encourages a predictable outcome. Procedures also give the supervisor standards for appraising employees' work. To realize these advantages, a supervisor should devote considerable time and effort to devising departmental procedures to cover as many phases of operations as practical, such as work operations and work flow, scheduling, and personnel assignments.

## METHODS

**Method**
A standing plan that details exactly how an operation is to be performed

Like a procedure, a **method** is a standing plan for action, but it is even more detailed than a procedure. A procedure shows a series of steps to be taken, whereas a method is concerned with only one operation or one step, and it indicates exactly how that step is to be performed. For example, a departmental procedure may specify the chronological routing of work in the assembly of various components of a product. At each subassembly point, there should be a method for the work to be performed in that step.

For most jobs, there are usually "best methods," that is, the most efficient ways for the jobs to be done given existing technology and circumstances. Again, when a supervisor can rely on skilled workers, the workers often know the best method without having to be told. For the most part, however, the supervisor or someone in management must design the most efficient method for getting the job done. Much time should be spent devising methods, because proper methods have all the advantages of procedures. In devising methods, the supervisor may use the know-how of a methods engineer or a motion-and-time-study specialist if such individuals are available in the organization. These are specialists who have been trained in industrial engineering techniques to study jobs systematically to make those jobs more efficient. When such specialists are unavailable, the supervisor's experience and input from experienced employees actually doing the work should suffice to design work methods that are appropriate for the department.

In some activities, a supervisor need not be overly concerned with devising procedures and methods because employees have been trained in standard methods or procedures. For example, computer technicians are exposed to many years of education and training, during which proper procedures and methods of performing certain tasks are emphasized. Similarly, in the supervision of a department of highly skilled or professional employees, the supervisor's main concern is to ensure that generally approved procedures and methods are carried out in professionally accepted ways. However, most supervisors have employees who are not well trained and for whom procedures and methods must be established.

## RULES

A rule is different from a policy, procedure, or method, although it also is a standing plan that has been devised to attain objectives. A rule is not the same as a policy because it does not guide thinking or leave discretion to the involved parties. A rule is related to a procedure insofar as it is a guide to action and states what must or must not be done. However, a rule is not a procedure because it does not provide for a time sequence or a set of steps. A **rule** is a directive that must be applied and enforced wherever applicable. When a rule is a specific guide for the behavior of employees in a department, the supervisor must follow that rule,

**Rule**
A directive that must be applied and enforced wherever applicable

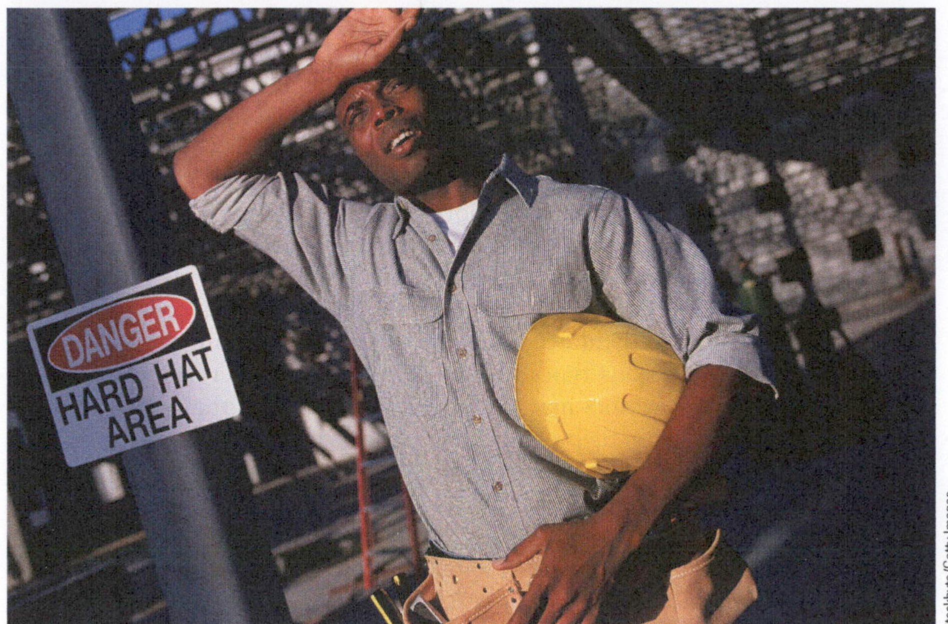


Stockbyte/Getty Images

There should be no deviation from this rule!

without deviation, wherever it applies. For example, "Safety equipment must be worn in posted areas" is a common organizational rule. It means exactly what it says, and there are no exceptions.

Occasionally, supervisors must devise their own rules or see to it that the rules defined by higher-level managers are obeyed. For example, rules concerning employee meal periods usually specify a certain amount of time employees can be away from their jobs for meals. Usually, high-level managers develop these rules, but often a supervisor must formulate departmental rules concerning the actual scheduling of meal periods. Regardless of who develops the rules, it is each supervisor's duty to apply and enforce all rules uniformly as those rules relate to each area of responsibility.

## BUDGETS

Although budgets are generally part of the managerial controlling function, a budget is first and foremost a plan. A **budget** is a plan that expresses anticipated allocations and results in numerical terms, such as dollars and cents, employee hours, sales figures, or units produced. It serves as a plan for a stated period, usually one year. All budgets are eventually translated into monetary terms, and an overall financial budget is developed for the entire firm. When the stated period is over, the budget expires; it has served its usefulness and is no longer valid. For this reason, a budget is a single-use plan.

**Budget**
A plan that expresses anticipated allocations and results in numerical terms, ultimately financial terms, for a stated period

As a statement of expected allocations and results, a budget is associated with control. However, preparing a budget is a planning process, and this again is part of every manager's responsibilities. Because a budget is expressed in numerical terms, it has the advantage of being specific rather than general. There is a considerable difference between just making general forecasts and attaching numerical values to specific plans. The figures that the supervisor finds in a budget are actual plans that become standards to be achieved.

**The Supervisor's Role in Budgeting.** Because supervisors must function within a budget, they should help prepare it. Supervisors should have the opportunity to propose detailed budgets for their departments or at least to participate in discussions with higher-level managers before departmental budgets are finalized. Supervisors must substantiate their budget proposals with their managers, and possibly with their financial managers, when budgets are being finalized.

Generally, business supervisors are more concerned about the expense side of the budget because business expenses can cut into profits. Nonprofit managers are often equally concerned with the revenue side, as nonprofit organizations must continually seek funding for their programs and services in order to sustain them. All supervisors are held accountable for variations from the established budget. There are numerous types of budgets in which supervisors can play a part. For example, supervisors may design budgets in which they plan the work hours to be used for jobs in their departments. Supervisors also may prepare budgets for materials and supplies, wages, utility expenses, and other departmental expenditures.

**Budget Review.** Most organizations schedule interim monthly or quarterly reviews during which the budget is compared to actual results. Therefore, a budget is also a control device. If necessary, the budget is revised to adjust to results and forecasts. This topic is discussed further in Chapter 13. Supervisors should carefully study and analyze significant variations from the budget to determine where and why plans went wrong, what and where adjustments need to be made, and what the revised budget should reflect, including new factors and any changes in the department. When an annual budget is about to expire, it becomes a guide for preparing the next year's budget. Thus, the planning process continues from one budget period to the next in a closely related pattern.

## COST-CUTTING

Reducing costs is a natural concern in all organizations. In recent years, many supervisors have had to find ways to cut costs. Imagine a blanket order that all departments must reduce operating costs by 10 percent by the end of the month. Such an order may present a hardship to the diligent, cost-conscious supervisor whose department is operating efficiently. Nevertheless, this supervisor will strive to take some action by looking at areas where there may be room to reduce expenses. This supervisor will call on his or her subordinates for suggestions. For example, perhaps some operations could be combined or eliminated. Or the supervisor might suggest a less expensive way of performing a task. Figure 3.5 provides an example of a hospital that initiated a creative cost-saving program involving employees as the key to success. Remember, it is wrong for an organization to focus only on cost reductions. Look constantly for ways to increase revenue. The best strategy for bottom-line improvement is a combination of both.

## PROJECT MANAGEMENT

**Project**
A single-use plan for accomplishing a specific, nonrecurring activity

Supervisors are typically more involved in planning projects. While a **project** may be part of an overall program, it is an undertaking that can be planned and fulfilled as a distinct entity, usually within a relatively short period. For example, the creation of a brochure by a public relations department to acquaint

**FIGURE 3.5 Example of a BAD program that works**

Pine Village Community Hospital (PVCH) was faced with escalating costs and shorter patient stays. Medicare, Medicaid, and insurance providers had placed severe financial constraints on revenue. The vice president of administrative services and an employee group worked together with a consultant to develop an employee suggestion program. The objective was to find ways to eliminate at least $500,000 in costs. While some organizations would have eliminated jobs, not filled positions as people retired or quit, or reduced hours and benefits, PVCH's management did not eliminate or explore those options. PVCH had been in a cooperative purchasing arrangement for about 15 years, and thus the purchasing area was one that could not generate great cost savings.

The program was dubbed the BAD program ("buck a day"). Each employee was given a new one-dollar bill and told to look for ways to reduce costs by that much each day. The reasoning for the program was that each employee could easily understand the "buck" (most people could not comprehend a half-million dollars). Department supervisors explained the program to employees. The program was straightforward and easily understood. BAD checklists were developed along with constant reminders and postings to employees to be on the lookout for things that cost money and were nonessential to quality patient care. Items on the checklist included the following:

1. Look at each process through the eyes of a stranger.
   - Why is it necessary?
   - Is it needed?
   - Could certain operations be simplified, combined, or eliminated?
2. Analyze each procedure to determine whether or not costs associated with procedure are necessary.
3. Look for ways to:
   - Eliminate idle time.
   - Eliminate handling time.
   - Eliminate indirect costs.
   - Eliminate costs by simplifying, combining, or eliminating operations.
   - Eliminate used inventory, machinery, equipment, or tools.
   - Eliminate overtime or extra-cost operations.
4. Analyze the workflow.
   - Would better coordination improve workflow?
   - What can we do to improve communication?
   - How can scheduling be more efficient?
5. Can we make better use of employees?
   - Are we using more employees on a job than are actually needed?
   - Are there occasions when not having enough employees on a job results in unnecessary overtime?
   - Are we using highly paid, skilled employees on jobs that lower-paid employees can do?
   - Do we fail to use skilled employees in their specialties for reasons of day-to-day expediency?
   - Are employees lacking in job knowledge because of our failure to provide on-the-job training?
   - Are some department supervisors not policing overtime?
   - Are we using our employees to their fullest potential?

*(continued)*

**FIGURE 3.5 *Continued***

Awards will be given for each suggestion. Employees are encouraged to work together to help PVCH get the biggest bang for the buck.

Every employee submitting a suggestion was entered into a drawing for a grand prize—a trip to the Indianapolis 500 or an Indianapolis Colts regular season game.

Review committees evaluated each suggestion and championed those ideas that were worthy of implementation. The net result was that over a two-year period the goal was met.



the public with the new facilities of a hospital expansion program would be a project. Arranging construction financing for the building expansion would be another project. Although these projects are connected with a major program, they can be handled separately.

An example of a project at the supervisory level is the design of a new inventory- control system by a warehouse supervisor. Two other examples are a research project conducted by a marketing department supervisor to determine the effectiveness of a series of television commercials and an art museum's implementation of a customer relationship management (CRM) system to keep track of donor activities. Projects such as these are a constant part of the ongoing activities at the departmental level. The ability to plan and carry out projects is another component of every supervisor's managerial effectiveness.

**7 Describe how the supervisor plans for efficient and effective resource use.**

## Supervisory Planning for Resource Use

Because supervisors are especially concerned with day-to-day planning, they must plan for the best use of all their resources. Making effective use of time is one of the most important supervisory activities. In addition to employees, another important resource is the supervisor's time. We all have the same amount of time. The adage time is money applies equally to the supervisor's and employee's time.

In the following sections, we will briefly discuss physical and human resources planning techniques.

### EFFICIENT SPACE USE

Supervisors must always plan for space allocation and use. They should determine whether too much or too little space is assigned to the department and whether that space is used efficiently. In most organizations, space demands typically far exceed the available office or plant space. Some firms have facilities managers or industrial engineers who can help the supervisor allocate space. Most supervisors, however, must assume this responsibility.

When planning space use, a floor-layout chart can be drawn and analyzed to determine whether there is sufficient space for the work to be performed and whether the space has been laid out appropriately. Consideration must also be given to the need for break areas and collaboration areas. Some organizations are experimenting with "open offices" in which all employees work in a common area so they can collaborate on projects, and private areas are used as needed for meetings and focused work.[20] The supervisor must determine, preferably with input from employees, the configuration that will result in the highest level of worker engagement and productivity. If the proposed layout indicates a need for additional space, the supervisor should include with the space request a thorough analysis of how the space is currently allocated. Chances are that the supervisor must compete with other departments that also need more room. Unless the supervisor plans thoroughly, the space request has little chance of being granted. Even if the request is denied, the supervisor's plans are useful. They alert the supervisor to some of the conditions under which employees are working and where improvements might be made.

## USE OF OTHER MAJOR PHYSICAL RESOURCES

Supervisors must plan for the efficient use of their departments' other major physical resources, such as tools, machinery, computers, and various types of equipment and furniture. Usually, these resources represent a substantial investment. When these items are poorly maintained or are inefficient for the jobs to be done, operating problems arise and employees' morale degrades. A supervisor does not always have the most desirable or advanced equipment, but any equipment, when adapted and properly maintained, usually suffices to do the job. Therefore, before requesting new equipment, supervisors should first determine whether employees are using their tools and equipment properly. Many times, when employees complain about poor equipment or technology, they are operating the equipment incorrectly or have not been trained to employ its full functionality. Therefore, supervisors should periodically observe their employees using equipment and technology and ask those employees whether the tools serve their purposes or need improvement. The supervisor is responsible for working closely with the maintenance department to plan the periodic maintenance of tools, equipment, and machinery, and the supervisor should also work with the information technology (IT) department to assess and maintain appropriate functionality of computers and software. Poorly maintained equipment may be blamed on the maintenance department in some cases, and the IT department shoulders the responsibility for computers working correctly, but supervisors share in the blame if they have not planned or scheduled maintenance and upgrades. The maintenance and IT departments can do only as good a job as other departments allow them to do.

The supervisor may sometimes decide that equipment must be replaced. In making this request, the supervisor should develop and submit to higher-level management a plan for disposing of the inefficient equipment. To determine when a major physical resource should be replaced, supervisors should review trade journals, listen to what salespeople say about new products, read literature circulated by distributors and associations, and generally keep up with field developments. When supervisors thoroughly study the alternatives and prepare to make recommendations based on several bids and models, they make stronger arguments to higher-level managers. Facts are more likely than emotions to persuade higher-level managers to support the supervisor's position.

Even when supervisors recommend equipment changes that are supported by well-documented reasons, higher-level managers may turn down those changes because they are not economically feasible. While supervisors should support those decisions, they should not hesitate to point out the decrease in productivity and morale that may result from failing to replace the equipment in question.

In the long term, a supervisor's plans for replacing or buying equipment probably will be accepted in some form. Even when they are not, the supervisor will be recognized as being on top of the job by planning for better use of the department's physical resources.

## USE AND SECURITY OF MATERIALS, SUPPLIES, MERCHANDISE, AND DATA

The economic downturn has led to an increase in loss and theft of materials, supplies, merchandise, and other company property, sometimes by employees. To prevent such losses, supervisors must make sure that adequate security precautions are taken to discourage individuals from theft and to make it difficult for items to be lost or stolen. For example, many supplies can be kept locked up, with someone assigned the responsibility for distributing them as needed. If the firm has its own security force, the supervisor should meet with security personnel to plan and implement security devices and procedures that are suited to the department. In retail establishments, this may mean removing the opportunity for theft and training employees to pay attention to customers' bags, clothing, carts, and boxes. Increased attention can often deter a theft or a fraudulent return or exchange. A supervisor may even request such assistance from local police or a private security agency.[21]

Another major concern of many firms has been the theft of data and information, mostly associated with computer break-ins and related thefts.[22] Just before Thanksgiving weekend in 2013, malicious software (malware) was installed by hackers on the Target department store's security and payments system, software which collected 40 million credit card numbers and contact information for 70 million shoppers during the holiday season and routed the data to servers located in Odessa, Ukraine, where it could be sold in an online marketplace for stolen credit-card data. Target was alerted to the data breach by federal investigators in mid-December and publicly alerted consumers that their credit card numbers, addresses, e-mail addresses, and phone numbers had possibly been in the hands of cybercriminals for nearly two weeks. Internal and external investigations after the breach illuminated serious problems in Target's security procedures. Target's computer security personnel failed to heed alerts from its data security software that malware was present on the servers, and for some reason the system function that automatically deletes malware was turned off. The fallout from the security breach included over 90 lawsuits brought by consumers and banks for compensatory damages and negligence. Analysts estimate that the breach could cost Target billions of dollars once all claims are made but, equally as disheartening for the retailer, holiday profits dropped 46 percent, indicating that Target lost the public's trust.[23]

Many managers do not believe that something like that could happen to them or their organization. No organization or sector is immune from cyber threats. In 2014, Korea Credit Bureau had 104 million electronic records stolen by data hackers. In 2013, LivingSocial and Cupid Media each had over 50 million records stolen, Target and Adobe Systems each experienced theft of over 100 million records, and Experian Corporation had 200 million records stolen. Similarly, the South Carolina Department of Revenue had 40 million personal and financial records stolen and the U.S. government had 1.7 million documents taken from its servers by National Security Agency contractor Edward Snowden.[24] In his confirmation hearing, secretary of defense, Leon Panetta, said, "There is a strong likelihood that the next Pearl Harbor could well be a cyber attack that cripples the U.S. power grid and financial and government systems. Cybersecurity will be one of my main focuses." If the growing number of data thefts is any indication of the threat, Panetta may be correct in his more recent remark, that the digital environment is "the battlefield of the future."[25]

Supervisors should work very closely with IT specialists to plan for limited access to certain data and to protect important hardware and software. They must also be very clear in presenting and enforcing rules and policies related to employee technology use.

While a supervisor's plans for the use and security of materials, supplies, merchandise, and data cannot eliminate all waste and loss, such planning usually reduces some waste and loss and promotes a more efficient and conscientious workplace.

## SAFE WORK ENVIRONMENT

Most managers and supervisors recognize that a safe work environment is one of their major responsibilities because such an environment is essential for employees' welfare and productivity. Safety data have long indicated that, due to carelessness, poor attitudes, inadequate training, and many other reasons, employees cause accidents more often than do faulty tools and equipment. The supervisor shares a major responsibility, ethically and legally, for doing everything possible to maintain the safest possible work environment. Of course, some job categories, by their very nature, are more hazardous than others. For example, supervisors in mining, construction, and heavy manufacturing face major challenges in working to reduce the potential for serious injuries and fatalities. By contrast, supervisors in the generally comfortable surroundings of an office usually do not have to worry about major injuries. Nevertheless, the potential for accidents exists in any situation if employees are not fully trained and reminded to follow safe work habits.

The 2012 Bureau of Labor Statistics (BLS) report showed that fatal work injuries were at their lowest level since the BLS has been reporting such data. That is the good news, but "Each year, more than 4 million workers in the United States suffer a workplace injury or occupational illness. More than 2 million workers are injured severely enough on the job that they miss work and need ongoing medical care." Agriculture, forestry, fishing and hunting is the most dangerous occupation sector, with a rate of 21.2 deaths per 100,000 workers, followed by mining, quarrying, and oil and gas extraction (15.6) and transportation and warehousing (13.3). The leading causes of deaths are vehicle accidents, violence, being struck by objects or equipment, falls, exposure to harmful elements, and machine accidents.[26]

**Workplace violence**
An act or threat of assault directed at another employee

The BLS defines **workplace violence** as violent acts, including physical assaults and threats of assault, directed at employees at work or on duty. Workers who exchange money with the public or work alone or in small groups are most at risk. The best protection employers can offer is to establish a zero-tolerance policy toward workplace violence against or by their employees. Unfortunately, all too often we hear about an employee "going postal." We might never know exactly why defense contractor Aaron Alexis shot and killed 12 people at the Washington Navy Yard in September 2013. After the incident, reports found that Alexis had an "aggressive streak" and he had been discharged from the military for misconduct. With this information, Navy personnel could have prevented the gunman from obtaining the security clearance necessary to be on the premises, but they "missed opportunities for intervention."[27]

©ostill / Shutterstock.com

*Supervisors can provide office workers with ergonomic equipment that will help ease strain and tension on eyes, neck, shoulders, wrists, and lower back*

Effective supervisors should be on the alert for unusual behaviors and seek assistance from the HR professional. Some organizations have telephone hotlines where one can report questionable behaviors. Unfortunately, it appears that "troubling gaps" in procedures contributed to tragedy at the Navy Yard. Ask the question, what can I and my organization learn from these examples? See the final section in this chapter, Crisis Management: Planning Required, for more information on planning for the unthinkable.

## OBSERVANCE OF OSHA AND OTHER SAFETY REGULATIONS

Both before and since passage of the Occupational Safety and Health Act (OSHA) of 1970, supervisors have been expected to devote major attention to reducing and preventing injuries and accidents on the job. OSHA has significantly impacted the scope and administration of safety programs in many organizations. It has expanded the responsibility of the supervisor in planning for and bringing about a safer work environment.

Regardless of the size of the firm, supervisors must plan to meet with managers, as well as with employees, union leaders, and even with government officials, if necessary, to do everything possible to maintain compliance with all safety regulations.

## SAFETY COMMITTEES

If they are not already in place, supervisors should endeavor to establish and participate in safety committees. The purpose of a safety committee is to help the supervisor develop safer work areas and enforce safety regulations. The supervisor and the safety committee can plan for periodic meetings and projects to communicate to employees the importance of safe work habits and attitudes.

**FIGURE 3.6 Inattention commonly causes accidents**

Labor unions have been quite vocal in asserting their concerns that safe work environments and safe work practices are monitored closely. Joint union/management safety committees invariably involve supervisors, and usually there is a concerted effort to reduce accidents and injuries. The impact of proactive safety committees has been well documented. Many safety committees have ongoing safety meetings and site walk-throughs in which safety committee representatives identify and correct various problems. To reinforce workers' awareness of proper safety practices and use of safety gear, supervisors and workers hold weekly "toolbox" safety meetings in which they discuss such subjects as storing tools and equipment to avoid tripping accidents, proper lifting techniques, the need for protective safety gear, and other areas over which employees have direct control.

The supervisor's constant attention to safety is mandatory if a safe work environment is to be maintained. Most accidents reported on the job are caused primarily by human failure (see Figure 3.6). The supervisor must emphasize safe work habits in daily instructions to employees and ensure that all equipment in the department is used properly and has ample protective devices.

A common half-truth is that a safety program is the responsibility of the safety department or the safety engineers. However, without the full support of supervisors and diligent supervisory observance of employee work practices in every department, almost any safety program will fail. In small organizations without a safety department, the responsibility for safety falls directly to leadership and supervisors. Safety planning and safety in practice are everyone's responsibility.

## FULL USE OF HUMAN RESOURCES

Our perspective throughout this book is that employees are a firm's most important resource. Planning for their full use should always be uppermost in every supervisor's mind. Using the workforce fully means getting employees to contribute to their fullest capabilities. This requires:

- Developing plans for recruiting, selecting, and training employees
- Searching for better ways to arrange activities

- Training employees in the proper and safe use of the materials associated with their jobs
- Supervising employees with an understanding of the complexities of human needs and motivation
- Communicating effectively with employees
- Appraising employees' performances
- Recognizing achievement
- Promoting deserving employees
- Adequately compensating and rewarding employees
- Taking just and fair disciplinary actions

These actions are ongoing aspects of a supervisor's plans for the full use of human resources.

Planning to use employees fully is at the core of effective supervision. It is mentioned here again only briefly because most chapters of this text are concerned in some way with this overall primary objective of supervisory management.

In addition to employees, another important resource is the supervisor's time. The adage "time is money" applies equally to the supervisor's and the employee's time.

## EMPLOYEE WORK SCHEDULES

To plan effective work schedules for employees, supervisors should operate from the premise that most employees are willing to turn in a fair day's work. Supervisors should not expect all employees to work continuously at top speed. They should establish a work schedule based on an estimate of what constitutes a fair, rather than a maximum, output. Allowances must be made for fatigue, unavoidable delays, personal needs, and a certain amount of unproductive time during the workday. Some supervisors may be able to plan employee time with the help of a specialist, such as a motion-and-time analyst. Even without such help, most supervisors have a good idea as to what they can expect, and they can plan reasonable performance requirements their employees will accept as fair. Such estimates are based on normal, rather than abnormal, conditions. In this regard, it may be unadvisable for a supervisor to schedule a department to operate at 100 percent capacity, which would leave no room for emergencies or changes in priorities and deadlines. Because some flexibility is needed to operate, only short periods of 100 percent capacity should be scheduled. Also, several rest periods are usually included in employee work schedules.

## OVERTIME AND ABSENCES

Occasionally, supervisors find it necessary to plan for overtime, although overtime primarily should be considered an exception or an emergency measure. As a general rule, supervisors should anticipate a reduction of between 5 and 10 percent in productivity from employees when they work overtime. If a supervisor finds that excessive overtime is required regularly, then alternative methods of doing the work should be found or additional employees should be scheduled or hired.

Supervisors also must plan for employee absences. Of course, a supervisor cannot plan for every employee absence due to sickness, injury, or personal problems.[28] However, the supervisor can plan for holidays, vacations, temporary layoffs, and other types of leaves or predictable absenteeism. Planning for anticipated absences ensures the smooth functioning of the department.

In recent years, some firms have established "leave sharing programs." These programs are paid-time-off sharing plans by which employees can donate some of their vacation days to a company pooled account, and an employee who is on an extended sickness or disability leave or are affected by a major disaster can draw on this account to receive income while off work.

How does the program work? Assume that Karen, a nurse making \$25 per hour, has 80 hours in her bank (80 hours × \$25 = \$2,000) and her good friend Rolf, another nurse making \$20 per hour develops cancer and has used up all his sick leave. Karen can donate her entire banked hours for Rolf. Rolf would receive 100 hours of paid leave from Karen (2,000 hours/\$20 per hour = 100 hours). The bookkeeping is not intensive, but the donation from Karen will appear on her W-2 form as a credit. This type of arrangement is usually not very costly for the employer, and it is a morale and team builder for the employees.[29]

## ALTERNATIVE WORK SCHEDULES AND TELECOMMUTING

Many organizations have adopted various work schedules for their employees, such as flextime, part-time work, job sharing, telecommuting, and other work-at-home arrangements, as well as unconventional hours. Alternative work-schedule plans are diverse. In some organizations, employees are scheduled for or may opt to work a four-day work week, which is usually a four-day, 10-hour-per-day arrangement. The most common form of alternative work scheduling is flextime, in which employees can choose, within certain limits, the hours they would like to work. Flextime usually involves permitting certain employees to select different starting and ending times within a five-day workweek. Alternative work arrangements are becoming more common, particularly in situations in which an employee's work is not closely interdependent or interrelated with that of other employees or departments.[30]

Supervisors have found that alternative work schedules create problems when they are trying to cover workstations and job positions, and that it may be difficult to exercise supervisory control at certain times of the workday. Nevertheless, supervisors who work with alternative work schedules learn to adapt within their departments and in their relations with other departments. Some supervisors may be in charge of different work groups on different days and at different times of the day as a result of flexible work scheduling. This situation requires supervisors on different shifts and in different departments to coordinate their activities if they are to achieve overall organizational effectiveness.

Telecommuting and other work-at-home arrangements present a number of different problems for supervisors. In general, time scheduling is not that important because work-at-home employees tend to make their own work schedules. However, supervisors must plan well in advance and communicate with these employees concerning such items as project work to be completed, deadlines, budget constraints, productivity expectations, and customer requirements. Some firms are making special efforts to train supervisors to manage telecommuters and other work-at-home employees.[31]

Most studies of alternative work-schedule plans have concluded that employees generally appreciate the opportunity to select their work schedules. Furthermore, flexible work schedules usually are associated with improvements in absenteeism rates, tardiness rates, retention, morale, and productivity.[32]

## PART-TIME AND TEMPORARY EMPLOYMENT

Contract workers, on-call workers, contingent workers, and other forms of temporary (temps) workers have accounted for over half of the job growth in the last few years.[33] Regardless of what we call them, the number of part-time and temporary employees is increasing. Retailers, service establishments, and health-care centers, in particular, often have large numbers of part-time workers.

Scheduling part-time employees requires considerable planning to match the needs of the department or business operation. Part-time work arrangements must be developed and monitored if they are to benefit employees and management. Some part-time employees are content to work limited schedules. Other part-time employees are eager to work as many hours as possible, and they also hope to obtain full-time employment, although this desire has been thwarted somewhat by the Affordable Care Act, which requires organizations to provide health insurance to all full-time workers, which adds significantly to the personnel budget.[34] Supervisors must accordingly assess the need for full- and part-time workers, as well as plan work schedules carefully to accommodate the special interests and needs of part-time workers without creating scheduling problems with full-time employees and departmental work requirements.

Another complicating factor for supervisors in work scheduling is the growing phenomenon of temporary employment. For the most part, temporary employees fall into two basic categories. The first type includes employees who are hired by agencies and are "farmed out" for short-term work assignments with various employers. Companies typically contact agencies to obtain individuals who have certain skills, and those companies pay the agencies for each employee who works. A supervisor who uses this type of temporary employee must schedule the employees with the sponsoring agency. The second type of temporary employee, called an interim employee, is hired directly by a firm for a specific need or project. Interim employees clearly understand that there is no guarantee of employment when the company's hiring need or project ends. Typically, the interim employee is paid a wage or salary with limited or no benefits.

*While the flexibility of telecommuting is popular with many employees, it can pose a challenge for their supervisors*

Ariel Skelley/Corbis Super RF/Alamy

While temporary employees are often justified to meet short-term staffing needs and cut costs, supervisors must be prepared to address their associated problems. These problems include a lack of commitment to the firm, especially as the project or interim period of employment nears completion. Temporary employees often leave jobs prematurely for other opportunities. They take with them knowledge and training, which can demoralize permanent employees, and they can leave companies in difficult situations.[35] In addition, temporary or contracted employees are, technically, employees of another organization, one which may have different screening and hiring processes than the companies for which its employees go to work. Accordingly, supervisors may be assigned workers about whom they have little background information, an unknown they must account for when assigning them to jobs with security clearances or specific skill requirements. For the most part, supervisors should try to give temporary employees job assignments that are very clearly defined, jobs they can do without disrupting the regular workforce. Supervisors should view temporary employees as team members who can help attain the department's objectives. Temporary employees can show by their performance that they are worthy of consideration for full-time positions. Therefore, temporary work situations can serve as trials that allow supervisors to determine whether temporary employees should be offered full-time status.[36]

A report from MIT projects that in a few years the work in many organizations will be "performed by autonomous teams of one to 10 people, set up as independent contractors or small firms, linked by networks, coming together in temporary combinations for various projects, and dissolving once the work is done."[37]

## IMPROVEMENT IN WORK PROCEDURES AND METHODS

Supervisors often are so close to the job that they may not recognize when work procedures and methods need updating. Therefore, supervisors should periodically try to look at departmental operations as strangers entering the department for the first time might view them. By looking at each operation from a detached point of view, the supervisor can answer such questions as:

- Is each operation needed?
- What is the reason for each operation?
- Can one operation be combined with another?
- Are the steps performed in the best sequence?
- Are there any avoidable delays?
- Is there unnecessary waste?

*Improvement* generally means any change in the way the department is doing something that will increase productivity, lower costs, or improve the quality of a product or service. Improvement in work procedures, methods, and processes usually makes the supervisor's job easier. Besides personally looking for ways to improve operations, the supervisor should solicit ideas from employees. Employees usually know their jobs better than anyone else in the organization. Alternatively, the supervisor may be able to enlist the help of a specialist, such as an industrial engineer or a systems analyst, if this type of person is available in the organization. When studying areas for improvement, a supervisor should concentrate on situations in which large numbers of employees are assigned; costs per unit are unacceptably high; or scrap figures, waste, or injury reports appear out of line. A good reason to concentrate on such areas is that it will be easier for the supervisor to convince employees and higher-level managers who recommended changes will bring about considerable improvement, savings, or other benefits.

Organizations must be more proactive in meeting the pressures of increasing competition. Every supervisor should consider the benefits of a methods improvement program, perhaps in conjunction with a firm's employee suggestion system if one is in place. At all times, a supervisor should urge employees to look for better ways to do their jobs.

The supervisor sometimes can apply work-sampling techniques to cut costs, save time, and increase employee efficiency. Broadly stated, work sampling involves inspecting a small amount of work from a job to determine areas for improvement. Generally, work-sampling techniques are the tools of the industrial engineer.[38] However, in small firms, supervisors usually perform this role. While work sampling is useful, every effort should be made to ensure that the sample typifies the whole.

## PLANNING INVENTORY

Maintaining large inventories of component parts, supplies, and finished goods is costly. It requires warehouse space that must be rented or bought, heated, and lighted. It also requires workers to store and track the materials. To reduce the costs of maintaining large inventories, many firms use inventory-control techniques that better plan the inflow of materials needed for production.

**Just-in-time (JIT) inventory-control system**
A system for scheduling materials to arrive precisely when they are needed in theproduction process

**Kanban**
Another name for a just-in-time (JIT) inventory-control system

A **just-in-time (JIT) inventory-control system**, also called **kanban**, is a system for scheduling the raw materials and components of production to arrive at the firm precisely when needed. This system avoids having to purchase and stock large amounts of items. JIT requires close coordination between the firm and its suppliers. For the system to work, suppliers must be willing and able to supply parts on short notice and in small batches. Also, so that suppliers can plan their production efficiently, the firm must keep suppliers well informed about its projected needs for their products.[39]

But more importantly, for the system to work, employees must be well trained, know their responsibilities, have timely and useful information, and be accountable for their actions. All of this seems like common sense to these authors.[40]

## SCHEDULING AND PROJECT PLANNING

Much supervisory time is spent planning projects. Supervisors must consider what must be done, which activities must be undertaken, the order in which activities must be done, who is to do each activity, and when activities are to be completed. This process of planning activities and their sequence is called scheduling. Two well-known project planning tools are Gantt charts and PERT.

**Gantt chart**
A graphic scheduling technique that shows the activity to be scheduled on the vertical axis and necessary completion dates on the horizontal axis

A **Gantt chart** is a graphic scheduling technique that shows the relationship between work planned and necessary completion dates.[41] Gantt charts are helpful in projects in which the activities are somewhat independent. For large projects, such as a complex quality improvement program, PERT is more applicable.

*To enjoy the benefits of a just-in-time inventory-control system, a supervisor needs to keep in close contact with employees regarding their needs*

Walter Hodges/The Image bank/Getty Images

**Program evaluation and review technique (PERT)** has been used successfully in many major production and construction undertakings. PERT is a flowchart-like diagram showing the sequence of activities needed to complete a project and the time associated with each. PERT goes beyond Gantt charts by clarifying the interrelatedness of the various activities. PERT helps a supervisor think strategically. A clear statement of goals serves as the basis for the planning process. PERT begins with the supervisor defining the project in terms of not only the desired goal but also all the intermediate goals on which the ultimate goal depends.

PERT is a helpful planning tool because it requires systematic thinking and planning for large, nonroutine projects. The development of PERT flowcharts by hand is time consuming, but use of Gantt charts and PERT is likely to increase because of the proliferation of commercially available computer software packages that can assist supervisors in planning, decision making, and controlling.

**Program evaluation and review technique (PERT)**
A flowchart for managing large programs and projects that shows the necessary activities, with estimates of the time needed to complete each activity and the sequential relationship of activities

## Planning for Quality Improvement and Knowledge Management

**8 Cite the key advantages of planning for quality.**

In recent decades, successful firms have shown an emerging commitment to quality. Many firms have turned to **total quality management (TQM)** and continuous improvement. In manufacturing firms, quality traditionally meant inspecting the product at the end of the production process. Today, the notion of total quality management means that the total organization is committed to quality—everyone is responsible for doing the job right the first time. TQM means a total effort toward meeting customer needs and satisfaction by planning for quality, preventing defects, correcting defects, and continuously building increased quality into goods and services as far as is economically and competitively feasible. TQM shares the characteristic of quality throughout the organization with a number of other management frameworks, including Lean, Six Sigma, Agile, and Quick Response Manufacturing (QRM), among others. While in-depth discussion of these quality management practices is beyond the scope of this book, it is important to note that each one of them can improve performance and add value in certain organizational contexts.[42] It is the role of leadership to determine whether adopting one of the frameworks can help the organization increase the quality of its processes and products. The supervisor, then, is responsible for ensuring that all employees understand and can apply the framework to their specific role in the organization.[43]

**Total quality management (TQM)**
An organizational approach involving all employees to satisfy customers by continually improving goods and services

Although not as widely known as TQM, many firms have been involved in planning and carrying out short- and long-term strategies for more effective knowledge management. The knowledge explosion, driven by computer technology, requires more systematic storage, retrieval, dissemination, and sharing of information in ways that are conducive to desired results. **Knowledge management** has been defined as

1. Adding actionable value to information by capturing, filtering, synthesizing, summarizing, storing, retrieving, and disseminating tangible and intangible knowledge.
2. Developing customized profiles of knowledge so that individuals can get at the kind of information they need when they need it.
3. Creating an interactive learning environment in which people transfer and share what they know and apply it to create new knowledge.[44]

**Knowledge management**
The systematic storage, retrieval, dissemination, and sharing of information

One does not have to look long or hard to find pronouncements about the innovative approaches organizations are adopting to improve customer satisfaction and product or service levels. Many of these approaches have been within, or similar to, other quality management efforts.

**Benchmarking**
The process of identifying and improving on the best practices of leaders

The increased emphasis on higher product and service quality has led many firms to follow guidelines or criteria developed by others. The process of identifying and improving on the best practices of the leaders in the industry or related fields is called **benchmarking**. Some executives even advocate benchmarking using best-in-the-world comparisons.[45] All of us have used benchmarking. When we evaluate the performance of our favorite sports team, we look to see how well that team is doing compared with the top team. We analyze the attributes of players of the top team, coaching styles, and so forth and conclude that our team could be just as good—if not better—if the owners and managers would change and copy the successful practices of top-team leaders.

The essence of benchmarking is to be as good as, or better than, the best in the field. Benchmarking follows these steps:

1. Determine what to benchmark (e.g., a process or procedure, quality, costs, customer service, employee development, compensation).
2. Identify comparable organizations inside and outside the industry.
3. Collect comparative performance data.
4. Identify performance gaps.
5. Determine the causes of the differences.
6. Ascertain the management practices of the best.

Once these steps are completed, management can develop plans for meeting or beating best-in-the-industry, or even best-in-the-world, standards.

**ISO 9001**
International quality standard

**Malcolm Baldrige National Quality Award**
America's highest quality award

In recent years, many firms have given serious attention to ways of achieving quality improvements. **ISO 9001** is the international standard for quality management.[46] You may notice that a business will proudly display signage proclaiming that it is an ISO 9001 or a **Malcolm Baldrige National Quality Award**.[47] Why do firms seek ISO 9001 certification? In short, does a firm show a commitment to quality, customers, and continuous improvement? Firms that want to compete internationally must produce products and services that conform to quality standards that only the best can meet.

**9 Recognize the importance of planning for the unthinkable (crisis management).**

## Crisis Management: Planning Required

**Crisis**
A critical point or threatening situation that must be resolved before it can cause more harm

We all face **crisis** situations each and every day. For some people, things like not hearing the alarm clock go off in the morning, leaving the car lights on, or being forced to take a detour to work are the most serious crises of their lives. In retrospect, these crises are, of course, minor.

For other people, an equipment failure during an important production run, not getting a desired job, or getting laid off have been major crises. Consider the father who must tell his children that their mother has a terminal illness or that their younger sibling was killed in an auto accident. Imagine the shock one of the authors got when he received a text message that his two neighbors were killed in a plane crash less than three hours after he had received an e-mail from them about a community board meeting the next week.[48]

What were your thoughts when you heard that two bombs placed near the finish line of the Boston Marathon exploded, killing three and injuring over 260 on April 15, 2013?[49] Do you know someone in Japan who was affected by the

Kimimasa Mayama /EPA/Landov

*Japan was struck by a huge earthquake and tsunami in March 2011, but the country's long-held crisis management plans helped the Japanese people recover more quickly*

earthquake and tsunami in March 2011?[50] Or what did you think when you saw clips from Newtown, Connecticut, where a former student entered Sandy Hook Elementary School in December 2012 with a semiautomatic rifle and killed 20 children and six staff members after killing his mother in her home?[51]

In each of these examples, the directly affected parties can often be heard to exclaim, "That is not possible! I can't believe it happened to me!" Others who are, at best, remotely connected to the people involved say, "Gosh, that's tough!" What one person views as a crisis is not necessarily a crisis to someone else. For those directly involved, each of the preceding events is perceived as a crisis that must be addressed.

The news is replete with situations that occur on what seems to be a daily basis: a customer gives the pharmacist a note demanding a get high drug; a robber brandishing a gun enters a bank; a ladle of molten steel falls on workers; a baseball fan falls to his death from the stands while trying to catch a ball; a bookkeeper steals from a church; a distraught worker carries a bomb into the workplace; a CEO is involved in a financial scandal; an unsafe product is designed, produced, and distributed; or a class-action lawsuit arises due to racial harassment in the workplace.

Often, events such as these may be described as a **tragedy**. Aristotle defined tragedy as "the imitation of an action that is serious and also as having magnitude, complete in itself. Tragedy is a form of drama exciting the emotions of pity and fear.[52]

**Tragedy**
A disastrous event or misfortune that negatively impacts the lives of people

Clearly, the impact of a crisis or tragedy varies depending on people's perspectives, perceptions, and the degree to which it impacts them. Crisis planning has become integral to every organization's long- and short-term planning.

Miles Everson, global head of Risk Services for PricewaterhouseCoopers, said it well: "Companies that are successful at seeing, taking and managing risk have an environment where their 'culture' is risk-aware and explicitly embraces practices that hold business unit leaders accountable for knowing the details of their business. This includes the risks they are taking and the implications of not managing to a proper-risk-and-return profile."[53] Without question, each of us must constantly look at every situation, event, action, and decision from the perceptive of risk-reward.

It is not surprising that most corporate executives report that computer security is now the single most critical attribute of corporate networks.[54] The greatest vulnerability appears to be from internal sabotage, espionage, or accidental mistakes. Twitter and other social networks, as harmless and superfluous as they may seem, are dangerous. The postings have cost people their jobs, including politicians, and have led to the demise of certain news media. Along with Target's epic hack discussed earlier in this chapter, one of the best examples of failure to properly manage risk is that of Rupert Murdoch's *News of the World*. Once the largest newspaper in the world with a circulation of over 2.8 million, the organization folded suddenly when faced with allegations that its employees had used hacking techniques to try to gain a competitive advantage. The *News* put out its final edition in July 2011 because its employees blurted out tweets without thinking.[55]

One never knows when such an event will occur, but when it does, management must react in a timely fashion. Today, more so than at any time in recent memory, supervisors must exercise due diligence and be prepared for the unexpected.

The most recognizable example of how to effectively deal with a crisis is Johnson & Johnson's (J&J's) Tylenol crisis of the 1980s. The unthinkable occurred when someone injected cyanide into Extra-Strength Tylenol™ capsules. In all, eight deaths were linked directly to cyanide-laced Tylenol capsules. The company recalled more than 30 million bottles of the product, with an estimated retail value of over $100 million. This voluntary recall was the first example of a corporation voluntarily assuming responsibility for its products. Because J&J's credo taught managers to focus on the company's responsibility to the public and to the consumer, the decision to recall was easy; the corporation's values were clear. J&J not only survived the crisis but came out of it with its reputation enhanced.[56] Hindsight is a wonderful thing for supervisors to have. Hopefully, the impact of catastrophic events and how various government agencies or organizations responded to them can provide insights into what to do and not to do when faced with potential dangers.

People face complicated issues all the time, some of which were once considered impossible. Ask an older person what they thought in 1961, when President John F. Kennedy gave the country a clear mandate: "Within the next ten years, we will send a man to the moon and return him home safely." At that time, most Americans viewed the task as impossible. But in July 1969, Neil Armstrong took "one giant step for mankind." Look at the space shuttle crises that occurred before that could happen. As a supervisor remarked to the author, "Over the years, I have learned what doesn't work. By learning from past mistakes, I now know what not to do! And knowing what not to do helps me discover options that will work!"

Every organization faces potential crisis situations. Regardless of the size or nature of the organization, supervisors must be involved in crisis-management planning. Every member of the management team, utilizing concepts as suggested in Figure 3.7, should plan for the unthinkable. Planning is primarily a mental process that enables the supervisor to anticipate what must be done as well as to adjust to changing circumstances and shifting priorities. It is not an overstatement to assert that effective planning is required for supervisors to succeed.

*What can you do to ease the potential pain?* Make sure you know that your organization has plans and procedures for crises. Be sure you and your employees know what to do when the unthinkable happens. Remember, too, that strategic

**FIGURE 3.7 Crisis management planning**

1. **Identify the *unthinkables*.** What are your areas of vulnerability? What has been happening to or in other organizations? Become a learning organization, and learn from the experiences of others. Also, do a walk-through assessment of your organization to identify areas that could invite criminal behavior, such as unsecured entrances and secluded areas. It must be made clear that every employee is responsible for reporting potential areas of concern and to do so promptly.
2. **Develop a plan for dealing with the *unthinkables*.** Ask "What if?" questions. For example, "If this happens, what should be done, and who should do it?" Learn from the mistakes of others. They are good indications of what not to do. Plans should include who will be the company's spokesperson in the event a crisis occurs. Speak with one voice to ensure consistent and uniform information.
3. **Develop contingency plans.** If Plan A does not work, then what should be done?
4. **Form crisis teams.** Have a team of qualified, well-trained individuals ready to go at a moment's notice. The events of 9/11 and the earthquake and tsunami in Japan in March 2011 illustrated the need to have several backup teams ready to go into action as soon as there was an indication that something might transpire.
5. **Simulate crisis drills.** As a child, your school probably had fire drills. Now, public school children practice responding to a variety of crises. Why? The school may have never experienced a crisis, but the potential for one exists. The exercises are repeated in schools so that all know what to do if a crisis occurs. Organizations can benefit from similar practices.
6. **Respond immediately,** if not sooner. Create a culture in your organization that empowers employees rather than compels them to send memos or e-mails and await approval. Many organizations have retreated when unthinkable situations arose. When the Fukushima Daiichi nuclear reactor in Japan failed after the 2011 tsunami and earthquake, Tokyo Electric Power Co. (TEPCO) was found criminally responsible for man-made disaster because the company admitted it had played down safety risks, afraid it would lead to plant shutdowns. Supervisors must share all they know as soon as they know it. Management professor James O'Toole maintains that "You can't get into trouble by admitting what you don't know or by giving people too much information."
7. **Do not be afraid to apologize.** Think about how you would like to be treated if something unthinkable happened to you. What would make it right? In many situations, nothing will make it right, but the right step is to apologize sincerely and to offer to make amends. As Professor Gerald Meyers says, "If you win public opinion, the company can move forward and get through it."
8. **Learn from the experience of others.** Learn from your own mistakes. Ask what you have learned from past crises and how you can integrate that knowledge into the planning process.
9. **Plan now!** There is no rewind button when a crisis occurs.

*Note*: Figure prepared by Professor Leonard. See the following for more information on crisis planning; Warren Bennis, Daniel Goldman, and James O'Toole, *Transparency: Creating a Culture of Candor* (San Francisco, 2008), pp. 45+; Jonathon Berstein at http://www.bernsteincrisismanagment.com; Andrea Sachs, "The New World of Crisis Management," *Time Business Magazine*, http://www.time.com (April 19, 2007); "Special Report: Lots of Blame—But It's No Game," *U.S. News & World Report* (September 19, 2005), pp. 26–38; "Japan Earthquake—Tsunami Fast Facts," CNN Library (February 20, 2014), http://www.cnn.com/2013/07/17/world/asia/japan-earthquake-tsunami-fast-facts/; Howard Paster, "Be Prepared," *The Wall Street Journal* (September 24, 2001), p. A24; Gerald Meyers and Susan Meyers, *Dealers, Healers, Brutes and Saviors* (New York: John Wiley and Sons, 2000), p. 253; and Norman Augustine, "Managing the Crisis You Tried to Prevent," *Harvard Business Review* (November–December 1995), pp. 147–158.

planning is certainly one of the major tools advocated by major corporations and management theorists. However, strategic planning alone is not a panacea for natural disasters or other catastrophic events. Constant monitoring of strategic plans and learning about what is happening in the world and how others have coped must be done. Making new plans and taking actions to deal with the unthinkable have never been more important.[57]

## SUMMARY

1. Planning is the managerial function that determines what is to be done. It includes analyzing the situation, forecasting events, establishing objectives, setting priorities, and deciding what actions are needed to achieve objectives. Planning is a function of every manager, from the top-level executive to the supervisor. Without planning, there is no direction to organizational activities.

2. The notion that "if you don't know where you want to go, then you may not be happy when you arrive" best illustrates why one needs to develop well-defined personal (and organizational) objectives. Setting the foundation for the creation of a vision are questions such as: "What businesses are we really in? What products, goods, or services do current or potential customers need? How can we best meet customer needs while making a reasonable return on our investment?"

   A mission/values statement identifies the purpose, philosophy, and direction for the organization. Visioning goes beyond the mission statement. Visioning is the process of developing a mental image of what the organization could become. Once defined, the mission and vision must be communicated so that everyone knows where the organization intends to be. Visioning can thus help focus company goals and objectives. The organization develops plans based on the vision.

3. When one has determined where one wants to get to, setting stretching, measurable, accountable, realistic, and time-limited (SMART) objectives is the next step. Although overall goals and objectives are determined by top-level management, supervisors formulate departmental objectives, which must be consistent with organizational goals and objectives. Objectives should state what should be done and when.

4. While overall organizational goals and objectives are determined by top-level management, supervisors must formulate objectives related to their areas of responsibility. The supervisors' plans must be consistent with those of upper-level management. Supervisors devote most of their attention to short-term (operational) plans that complement the organization's vision, mission, and overall strategies.

   Everyone is responsible for planning. Of course, the supervisor should consult with others to develop plans that are consistent with those of upper-level management. Supervisors devote most of their attention to short-term planning. The supervisor's short-term plans should be integrated and coordinated with the long-term plans of upper-level management. Supervisors must communicate to employees what is being planned in a timely fashion.

5. A management by objectives (MBO) approach relies on participative setting of objectives and using those objectives as the primary basis for assessing performance. The four-step process shown in Figure 3.4 begins with the development of SMART objectives.

   This step serves as the foundation for determining necessary resources, the activities that must be carried out, and the results that are to be worked toward. MBO ties planning activities together, establishes priorities, and provides coordination of effort. MBO-type approaches, which may be called other things, usually involve objectives being agreed upon by employees and their supervisor. Periodic reviews ensure that progress is being made. At the end of the appraisal period, results are evaluated against objectives, and rewards are based on this evaluation. Objectives for the next period are then set, and the process begins again.

6. To attain objectives, standing plans and single-use plans must be devised. Top-level managers typically develop company-wide policies, procedures, methods, and rules; supervisors formulate the necessary subsidiary standing plans for their work units.

   Policies are guides for decision making, and most originate with higher-level management. Most employees are familiar with their organization's human resources (HR) policies. The supervisor's primary concern is interpreting, applying, and staying within policies when making decisions for the department. Policies are more likely to be followed consistently if they are written.

Procedures, like policies, are standing plans for achieving objectives. Procedures specify a sequence of actions that guide employees toward objectives. The supervisor often develops procedures to determine how work is to be done. The advantages of procedures are that they require analysis of what must be done, promote uniformity of action, and provide a means of appraising employees' work.

In addition, the supervisor will be called on to design and follow methods and rules, which are essentially guides for action. Methods and rules are more detailed than procedures. A rule is a directive that must be applied and enforced wherever applicable.

Supervisors should help establish budgets for his or her areas of responsibility. These single-use plans are expressed in numerical terms. A budget serves as a control device that enables the supervisor to compare results achieved during the budget period against the budget plan.

Supervisors at times may play a small role in developing projects, which are single-use plans designed to accomplish specific undertakings on a one-time basis.

7. Planning serves to use human and physical resources to their potential. Planning how best to use a firm's material, capital, and human resources is essential. Supervisors must plan for the efficient use of the department's space and major physical resources. Such planning may include close coordination with the maintenance department and/or other staff.

A major problem has been the loss and theft of materials, supplies, merchandise, data, and other company property. Supervisors must ensure that adequate security precautions are taken to discourage individuals from misusing or stealing items. Issues with Internet freedom and easy access have led to many breaches of security, identity theft, and misinformation being posted.

Supervisors should have a general understanding of all safety requirements. Safety committees and safety programs help planning initiatives and bring about safe work environments.

Planning for the full use of employees is at the core of professional supervision. Planning work schedules for employees includes establishing reasonable performance requirements and anticipating overtime requirements and absences. Many organizations are experimenting with various types of alternative, part-time, and temporary work schedules.

Time is one of the supervisor's most valued resources. Everybody has the same amount of it, so time is not the problem; the problem is how we use it. Therefore, supervisors must plan and manage their own time if they are to be effective.

Supervisors wanting to improve work procedures and methods should continuously look for more efficient ways to achieve their objectives. Encouraging employees to look for better ways to do their jobs and evaluating periodic work samples may result in substantial savings for the organization.

Supervisors can use JIT inventory control systems to reduce inventory costs and ensure that materials and components arrive when needed. Gantt charts and PERT networks are graphic tools designed to aid supervisors in planning, organizing, and controlling operations.

8. Various quality-improvement concepts relate directly to planning. Total quality management (TQM) means planning for quality, preventing defects, correcting defects, and continuously improving quality and customer satisfaction. Knowledge management, which involves systematically planned approaches to storing and disseminating information, has increasingly become an important part of many organizational efforts to improve customer and employee services and satisfaction.

Benchmarking, the process of identifying and improving on the best practices of others, precedes plan development. Organizations that want to be as good as or better than the best in the world strive to attain national or international quality standards. Plans must be developed to establish, maintain, and increase product and service quality. Quality improvement does not just happen; it must be planned.

Organizations that want to be the best in the world will meet the quality standards established in ISO 9001 or the Baldrige Quality Awards. Quality improvement doesn't just happen; it has to be planned.

9. This century has witnessed many tragedies and crises that have, in some way, touched our lives and caused each of us to take a different look at how we plan. Today every individual and organization must prepare for the unexpected. Crisis management involves identifying the unthinkable, developing plans of action (POAs) for dealing with them, developing contingency plans, forming crisis teams, and stimulating crisis drills. Like Johnson & Johnson's response to the Tylenol crisis, organizations should respond proactively and quickly.

Planning helps supervisors anticipate possible unthinkable events and their consequences. Supervisors must use their information-getting and information-giving skills to help employees prepare for and address crisis situations. It is always appropriate to say "I am/We are sorry" and ask "What can be done to make it right?"

## KEY TERMS

Benchmarking (p. 102)
Budget (p. 87)
Dashboard (p. 78)
Crisis (p. 102)
Gantt chart (p. 100)
ISO 9001 (p. 102)
Just-in-time (JIT) inventory-control system (p. 100)
Kanban (p. 100)
Knowledge management (p. 101)
Malcolm Baldrige National Quality Award (p. 102)
Management by objectives (MBO) (p. 81)
Method (p. 86)
Metrics (p. 78)
Mission statement (p. 75)
Planning (p. 73)
Policy (p. 83)
Procedure (p. 85)
Program evaluation and review technique (PERT) (p. 101)
Project (p. 88)
Rule (p. 86)
Single-use plans (p. 83)
Strategic plan (p. 79)
Strategic planning (p. 74)
Standing plans (p. 83)
Total quality management (TQM) (p. 101)
Tragedy (p. 103)
Vision statement (p. 76)
Workplace violence (p. 93)

## WHAT HAVE YOU LEARNED?

1. Define planning. Why is planning primarily a mental activity rather than a "doing" type of function?
2. What is the importance of an organization's vision? What is your vision for the next 12 months?
3. Identify and discuss the important factors a supervisor should consider in planning the work of his or her areas of responsibility.
4. Discuss the step-by-step model for management by objectives (MBO). Explain why each step is crucial if MBO is to be successfully implemented.
5. If you were a supervisor in a small firm that had few policies and procedures and you believed that the organization needed to pursue a TQM program, how would you go about developing a plan to improve the company's production processes?
6. What do you see as the downside of a crisis management policy?

## EXPERIENTIAL EXERCISES FOR SELF-ASSESSMENT

### EXPERIENTIAL EXERCISE FOR SELF-ASSESSMENT— 3

**Planning for Personal Development**

We learned in this chapter that in order to achieve its goals and objectives, an organization must engage in planning for the future. Organizations use a variety of strategies for planning. It is valuable for individuals, also, to think about the future. Where do we want to go personally and professionally, and do we have a plan to get there? Personal development planning can help us create a roadmap to achieve short- and long-term goals. Before creating a plan, though, it is important to assess personal planning SKAs so we can have the appropriate tools in our personal toolbox. In this exercise, you will assess your level of personal planning knowledge and skills and identify ways in which you can build those skills.

For each of the following statements, rate your responses as follows:

0—agree

1—disagree

2—don't know

________ I know what personal development is (B)

________ I have good personal records of my life and achievements. (D)

________ I have clear life goals. (B)

________ I know what job I want to do. (A)

________ I know what courses I need to take to get the job I want. (A)

________ I know what extracurricular activities I need to do to help me get the job I want. (A)

________ I know what skills are required by employers for the kind of career that interests me. (A)

________ I have an up-to-date record of education and training. (D)

________ I have an up-to-date record of my employment history and work experience. (D)

________ I have an up-to-date profile of my skills and personal qualities. (C)

________ I know my personal qualities. (C)

________ I have a good understanding of personal health and safety issues. (F)

________ I have a good understanding of diversity and inclusion issues. (E)

________ I can easily give examples of where I demonstrate my personal qualities. (C)

________ I am confident about all aspects of applying for a job. (C)

________ I know what is meant by a competence-based job application. (A)

________ I have detailed personal records of my key competencies. (D)

________ I know what my priorities are for my personal development. (B)

________ I have an action plan for my personal development. (B)

________ I know the personal development planning opportunities that are open to me. (B)

________ I regularly monitor my own performance in areas of personal and professional interest. (D)

________ I regularly undertake a formal evaluation of my performance. (D)

________ I am good at structured reflection. (D)

________ I am clear about the range of personal development services offered by my school. (A, B)

________ I know where to go for more information about personal development planning. (A, B)

________ Total Score—Now double your score to get a percentage.

**Interpreting your score**

The percentage score above is an estimate of your personal development needs score.

Zero: You do not appear to need personal development planning presently. However, as your circumstances change, this may change. You may want to complete this assessment again in a few months.

1–30%: You have some personal development planning needs. Based on your current progress toward your personal and career goals, how essential is it to you to address these issues? If one or more seem to be keeping you from achieving your goals, it would be advantageous for you to start building your skills.

31–60%: Personal development planning would be of significant use to you. Once you make your prioritized list, create an action plan for the next month to address one of the high-priority areas. Then, create an action plan to address three more areas in the next three months. Follow that process to address the items in the assessment that you feel are most critical to achieving your goals.

61–100%: Your personal development planning needs appear to be high. The resources listed below may be helpful to you, but it may be valuable for you to first meet with your career advising department and share your list of personal development planning needs with them. They can help you devise an action plan for building your personal development planning skills.

The following steps will help you use that information to build your personal development planning skills:

1. Compare your percentage score to the interpretation key below to identify your level of personal development planning knowledge.
2. Then revisit the assessment items and circle those items you rated as "3."
3. Prioritize the items in the order you feel they are most important to you for future success.
4. Use the letter in parentheses (A–F) next to each item to identify the area of personal development planning identified by that item.

   A. Career preparation

   B. Goal Setting and Action Planning

   C. Interpersonal Skills

   D. Performance Monitoring

   E. Diversity and Inclusion

   F. Health and Safety
5. Visit the supplementary website for this textbook to access Internet links and other suggested resources that can help you build your personal development plan.

## PERSONAL SKILL BUILDING

### PERSONAL SKILL BUILDER 3-1 WHAT CALL WOULD YOU MAKE?

After reviewing this chapter's opening You Make the Call! respond to the following tasks:

1. Identify what Shannon does well.
2. Discuss her planning and time management techniques.
3. Evaluate the following statement. "Effective planning by Shannon does not create problems for her subordinates."

Now put yourself in the position of Shannon O'Neill, the transportation supervisor in this chapter's opening You Make the Call!

1. You have two weeks to develop three strategies for improvement in your department. What will you do to handle this challenge?
2. Your authors believe that total quality management can improve the quality of service by involving everyone in the process. Who should you involve to help you meet the superintendent's challenge?
3. Remember that you do not appear to have a system to evaluate the students', their parents', or the taxpayers' perceptions of quality. How would you get their input and how might that input help you develop a plan to improve the transportation system?

### PERSONAL SKILL BUILDER 3-1 Prior Planning

Some organizations have formed crisis management teams comprised of both hourly workers and supervisors to conduct risk assessments, develop action plans, and perform crisis interventions. Reports from school shooting locations Virginia Tech and Northern Illinois acknowledged that some students, staff, and faculty did not want to return to the buildings where the violence occurred. Consider the following scenario: *As your professor is passing back an exam paper, the person across the aisle from you crumples her exam before she throws it at him, runs toward the door, and screams, "That was the worst exam I've ever had. I could kick your butt!" as she storms from the room.*

a. Are you concerned that this might be a crisis situation—akin to an employee going postal in the workplace—waiting to happen? If so, what would you do? Why?
b. Should the university have a policy that would prohibit this student from returning to class? Why or why not?
c. Review your student handbook or code of conduct. Does your school have a policy and plan of action (POA) to cover incidents like this one? If so, do you think it is adequate to cover incidents like this one? If not, what recommendation would you make to improve the policy?
d. If your school does not have a policy to cover incidents like this, your mission is to develop a strategy to ensure that one is in place within the next three months. What plans would you develop to accomplish this assignment?

### PERSONAL SKILL-BUILDER 3-3 Technology Tools—Using Gantt and PERT Planning Software to Help the Community

Gantt and PERT charts are used in organizations to plan organization initiatives. Many online tools are available, some at no cost, that can be helpful in creating and sharing these kinds of charts. In this exercise you will make a plan and create a Gantt or PERT chart to illustrate the schedule and implementation steps of the plan.

*The scenario*: You are the marketing department manager for Thunder Sports, a small athletic apparel company. Your company has a strong corporate social responsibility (CSR) culture and has as one of its goals to engage in at least two community projects each year.

This year the CSR planning team, of which you are a member, worked with the local United Way to survey of all of the nonprofits and local elected officials in the community in order to identify the community's most pressing needs. The three top issues identified were funding for the food pantry, declining youth physical fitness, and overpopulation at the local animal shelter. The CSR planning team then surveyed all the company's employees to determine which of the three issues were most strongly embraced by the company. The employees expressed equal amounts of interest in all three issues. In order to evaluate which of the three issues the company could best address in its two community projects over the next year, the CSR team decided to create preliminary plans for projects that would address each one. The plans would then be aligned with the organization's goals and master calendar to find the best fits.

As a member of the CSR team, your assignment is to create a Gantt or PERT chart for one of the following three activities using an online planning tool:

- A Community 5K Run organized by Thunder Sports
- A Community Food Drive organized by Thunder Sports
- A Community Dog Wash organized by Thunder Sports

1. Choose the activity you will plan.
2. Create a rough draft of an action plan for the activity. The action plan should include the activities that will need to be done (volunteer recruitment, marketing, fund-raising, buying supplies, setup, implementation and clean-up, etc.), who will be responsible for each activity, the order in which the activities need to be accomplished, and the timeline for completing each activity. You may not know all the details for the activity, but include as many as you can.
3. Using your rough draft and one of the software applications listed below (or another application with which you are familiar), create either a Gantt or PERT chart and print it out to submit as an assignment.

- GanttProject, http://www.ganttproject.biz/
- PERT Chart, http://www.edrawsoft.com/PERT-Chart.php
- PERT Chart Expert, http://www.criticaltools.com/pertchart expertsoftware.htm
- Tom's Planner, http://www.tomsplanner.com/
- TeamGantt, http://teamgantt.com/
- TeamWeek, https://teamweek.com/

## TEAM SKILL BUILDING

### TEAM SKILL BUILDER 3-1 What Call Will You Make?

Your instructor will cluster the class into groups of 6 to 10 students depending on the class size. Each group should determine who will play the following roles: Abrigail Connealy, athletics director King, and other students who were selected to review the university's athletics programs and develop a plan of action (POA) for increasing student attendance and support of the program. (*Note*: Alternatively, students could devise a plan to increase attendance and support for music, dance, and other on-campus performing arts.)

1. Is there a problem with lack of student attendance and support of your school's athletics program?

   If so, what does your group think is the problem? If not, why are students engaged in these and other campus activities?
2. If there is a problem, what, if anything, can be done about it? As a group, your mission is to develop a strategy(s) for increasing attendance at campus activities. You may also create an action plan and Gantt or PERT using the Technology Tools listed in Personal Skill Builder 3-4.
3. Identify the variables and factors that might contribute to the lack of student support of campus activities, including the athletics program. Which of those can most easily be overcome? What strategies would you recommend to overcome the obstacles?
4. What difficulties did you encounter in identifying the problem, developing alternatives, and deciding on the action plan?
5. Working as a group, write a one-page paper describing how you felt about doing this project. Your concluding paragraph should affirm the advantages of group planning.

### TEAM SKILL BUILDER 3-2 Dealing with People You Might Appreciate: "THE ADVICE SEEKER!"

This is the fifth in a series of activities that introduces you to people you may encounter in the workplace. While the other stories involve people who might make your life difficult, the story of Bob Macon may provide you with the incentive to become a better supervisor.

In this Team Skill Builder, you are to partner with two or more of your classmates.

1. Read the following statements from and about Bob Macon, maintenance supervisor at Barry Automotives' nonunionized Camden plant.

   *It was the warmest summer on record, and with temperatures reaching triple digits for the sixth day in a row, the air-handling system at Barry Automotives' Camden plant put an extra demand on the area power grid. Maintenance supervisor Bob Macon and his staff were working around the clock to keep that overloaded system working. In a meeting with plant manager Stacey Proctor, Macon reported, "We're at a critical point where there's almost no more power to be given. We just need everybody to be conscious of their usage. We have asked employees to look for ways to cut back on usage. I could really use some input from you and engineering." Proctor and his staff are constantly seeking advice on ways that areas can be more cost effective.*

   *A meteorologist with the National Weather Service reported that the area had topped out at 104 degrees at 3:50 P.M. yesterday and that the forecast for the next five days was predicting no relief. Macon's staff is a critical component in Barry's efforts to maintain quality and timely production standards. Macon meets with his direct reports at the beginning of each week to share information and get their input on production issues.*

   *Macon shared the following with a supervisory training class at the local college: "When I started working at Barry, I learned a lot about what not to do and that there is always a better way. One of the most valuable lessons I learned was that workers should not second-guess management or vice versa. It's the sharing of ideas and information in a timely manner that will increase production quality and quantity and reduce costs. I am committed to asking and answering questions about how to make the best a little bit better each and every day."*

The Industry and the Camden Plant: The past few years have been difficult for the manufacturing industry. A recent Federal Reserve economic survey reported what everyone already knew: "The economy worsened in the past months, hampered by high employment, weak home sales, and signs of a slowdown in manufacturing." The same was not true for the Barry Camden plant. The closing of an Indiana plant resulted in Camden adding another shift and incorporating almost 200 transferred employees. The good news was that the Camden plant was ISO 9001 and consistently exceeded production and quality standards. The Camden plant is planning to spend about $9.2 million on new equipment in the next year and may create 35 to 70 new jobs.

Bob's most recent evaluation included the following statements:

- Bob, with the help of others, develops a clear vision of goals that are consistent with Barry's goals for quality and profitability.
- Bob is not afraid to get his employees excited and motivated.
- He involves others in developing plans and keeps them on a clear path to achieve those plans.
- He is able to see things from all sides and acknowledges that sometimes the best-made plans need to be changed.
- Bob organizes priorities and makes sure that his people do not spend their time working on something that is not a number one priority.
- Several employees stated: "I really look forward to coming to work and doing the best I can do. Bob helps to ensure that."

2. Identify what you think are the strengths and weaknesses of Bob Macon's supervisory leadership style. Would you like to work for Bob? Why or why not? If there are differences in your group, how do you account for the differences?
3. Discuss what Bob Macon can do to become a more effective supervisor. Exchange your group's recommendations with those of another group, and vice versa. What one suggestion did the other group(s) make that you would describe as a wow!
4. Explain the adage, "Effective planning by Bob Macon does not create emergencies or crises for his associates."
5. Evaluate the statement, "The quality of Bob Macon's planning is largely determined by the quality of his associates."
6. July 2011 was the warmest month on record in Camden. How might a supervisor like Bob plan for unexpected conditions like extremes in warm or cold temperatures?
7. As a group, write a one-page paper listing specific tips that you want to make to Bob Macon to overcome the issues created by the economy, the transferred employees, the weather, and the projected plant expansion.

## SUPERVISION IN ACTION

The video for this chapter can be accessed from the student companion website at www.cengagebrain.com. (Search by authors' names or book title to find the accompanying resources.)

## ENDNOTES

1. Coined by Peter F. Drucker, *The Five Most Important Questions You Will Ask about Your Organization* (Jossey Bass, 2008) are foundational to effective planning and organizational success. Drucker, "the man who invented management," has been the most influential person in the evolution of management thought. In *The Wall Street Journal Essential Guide to Management* by Allen Murray (2010), Drucker answers the question, What do managers do? He listed five basic tasks: set objectives, organize, motivate and communicate, measure, and develop people. Go to www.brainquote.com/quotes/authors/p/peter-drucker/html to see some of his one-line thoughts. Also see *Management: Tasks, Responsibilities, and Practices* (New York: Harper & Row, 1974), p. 611; *The Practice of Management* (New York: Harper Brothers, 1954), pp. 62–65, 126–129; "Plan Now for the Future," *Modern Office Technology* (March 1993), pp. 8–9; and Mike Johnson, "Drucker Speaks His Mind," *Management Review* (October 1995), pp. 11–14.
2. Linda Yates and Peter Skarzynski, "How Do Companies Get to the Future FIRST?" *Management Review* (January 1999), p. 17, or http://www.strategos.com/articles/futurefirst.htm. Also see Peter Skarzynski and Rowan Gibson, *Innovation to the Core: A Blue Print for Transforming the Way to Your Company Innovation* (Cambridge, MA: Harvard Business School Press, 2008). Also see Kyle Scott, "Do What's Right, or What's Right Now?" *Supervision* 72, No. 7 (July 2011), pp. 8–9; Rick Kash and David Calhoun, *How Companies Win: Profiting*

*from Demand-Driven Business Models No Matter What Business You're In* (New York: Harper Business, 2010); and C. K. Prahalad, "Seeing the Future First," *Fortune* (September 1994), pp. 64–70.
3. Robert S. Kaplan said that "priorities translate vision into action." See Kaplan's *What to Ask the Person in the Mirror* (Cambridge, MA: Harvard Business Review Press, 2011). Also see Andy Boynton and Bill Fischer, *Idea Hunter: How to Find the Best Ideas and Make Them Happen* (San Francisco: Jossey-Bass, 2011); Denny Strigl and Frank Swiatek, *Managers, Can You Hear Me Now? Hard-Hitting Lessons on How to Get Good Results* (New York: McGraw-Hill Professional, 2011); Byran Feller, "Death by Assumption: Why Great Planning Strategies Fail," *Supervision* 69, No. 2 (February 2008), p. 18; Audra Russell, "Strategic Objectives: Part of the Company's Strategy" (http://www.shrm.org, December 7, 2007); Bryan S. Schaffer, "The Nature of Goal Congruence in Organizations," *Supervision* 68, No. 8 (August 2007), pp. 13–17; and Michelle Labrosse, "Do You Know Where Your Goals Are?" *Supervision* 68, No. 6 (June 2007), pp. 16–17.
4. Southwest Airlines' (SWA) mission statement adds up to less than 100 words. See Colleen Barrett, president, SWA, *Spirit Magazine* (April 2008), p. 14. Barrett stepped down on July 16, 2008, and Gary Kelly assumed the roles of chairman and president. The fourth largest airline in the United States and repeatedly rated one of best companies to work for (2010–2014) by *Forbes*, Glassdoor.com, and others, Southwest Airlines emphasizes that the way the company treats its people is the secret to its success, according to founder Herb Kelleher in Max Nisen's "Ugly Airline Economics Are Hurting Southwest's Legendary Culture," *Quartz News* (April 8, 2014), http://qz.com/195599/the-airline-business-ugly-economics-is-hurting-southwests-legendary-culture/. Ongoing strategic planning is at the core of Southwest's high ratings and high success in serving customers, but it also provides the structure needed to stay afloat in rough times. For the first time in history, Southwest faced major labor conflict when forced to make contract changes, such as tightening sick time rules, freezing compensation, and increasing the number of part-time workers in order to cut costs. Leadership was not spared in the cuts, as top executives' salaries were frozen also, according to Mike Stone, "Southwest Airlines CEO's Compensation Flat at $4M," USAToday.com (April 7, 2014),http://www.usatoday.com/story/todayinthesky/2014/04/07/southwest-airlines-ceos-compensation-flat-at-4-million/7406795/. While union leaders were unhappy and some said the company is feeling more corporate and less like a family under President Kelly's leadership, workers have been able to keep their jobs to date in a still unstable economy, which provides evidence that planning, even tough love planning, helps businesses thrive.
5. Coauthor of the *One Minute Manager*, Ken Blanchard and Colleen Barrett's 2011 book, *Lead with LUV: A Different Way to Create Real Success: It Pays to Put Your People First* (Upper Saddle River, NJ: FT Press, Pearson Education, 2011) provides examples of how to put the concepts of customer service and servant leadership into practice. See also David Keonig and Elizabeth Gramling, "Kelleher Still Loves LUV," Associated Press (July 1, 2011), or Ginger Hardage, "Leading with LUV," *Spirit* (March 2011), p. 24.
6. See Jim Collins and Morten Hansen, *Great by Choice* (New York: Harper, 2011). My students have found that the *BusinessWeek* articles "How the Mighty Fall and How to Stay on Top," by Collins (May 25, 2009), pp. 26–38, and "Game Changing Ideas: There Is No More Normal" by Jena McGregor (March 23 and 30, 2008), pp. 30–34, provide valuable insights into the planning process in these uncertain times.
7. Peter M. Senge et al., *The Fifth Discipline Fieldbook: Strategies and Tools for Building a Learning Organization* (New York: Currency/Doubleday, 1994), p. 46. "There are times when an organization would have been better off with no measurement than with a faulty one."
8. The author likes revenue factors that can be measured to show how a particular aspect of the organization is contributing to the organization's bottom line, which is generally referred to as metrics. In recent years, it has been commonplace for CEOs and managers to talk about their metrics. With great pride they stress that "they are meeting their metrics." Investors, for the most part, only care about the financial bottom line and whether the company meets its quarterly forecast. Human resource managers, on the other hand, may use absence rate, healthcare costs per employees, turnover costs, and workers' compensation incident rates as part of their metrics. I like revenue factor (revenue divided by total full-time equivalent [FTE]) as a metric. In this case, employees are viewed as an investment, that is, capital. According to Forrest Breyfogle III, "The Balanced Scorecard and Beyond" (http://qualitydigest.com/IQedit/qdarticle), "Every metric will have an owner where the measurement's performance can be part of the manager's plan and review." This is the manager's scorecard.
9. See Dana O'Donovan and Noah Rimland Flower, "The Strategic Plan is Dead. Long Live Strategy," *Stanford Social Innovation Review* (January 10, 2013), http://www.ssireview.org/blog/entry/the_strategic_plan_is_dead._long_live_strategy. O'Donovan and Flower suggest that the turbulence of today's economy has taken the predictability out of the organizational environment. They suggest that organizations must shift from predictions to experiments, from data collection to pattern recognition and from top-down execution to execution by the whole while making ongoing strategic choices, rather than sticking to a hard-and-fast strategic plan. See also Glenda Eoyang and Royce Holladay, "But What if We Don't Love Chaos?" *PM Magazine* (January/February 2014), http://icma.org/en/press/pm_magazine/article/104127.
10. See Stephen R. Covey, *The Seven Habits of Highly Effective People: Powerful Lessons in Personal Change*, Silver Anniversary Edition (New York: Simon & Schuster, 2013), p. 104.
11. For additional information on MBO, see George S. Odiorne's (1965) foundational work inspired by Peter Drucker's management ideas, *Management by Objectives: A System of Managerial Leadership* (Pitman Publishing). See also a summary of the framework, "Management by Objectives," Economist.com (October 21, 2009), http://www.economist.com/node/14299761 and a history of conflicting views, David Halpern and Stephen Osofsky, "A Dissenting View of MBO," *Public Personnel Management* (Fall 1990), pp. 59–62 and John Dyer's "Does Management by Objectives Stifle Excellence," Industryweek.com (December 17, 2013), http://www.industryweek.com/mbo-stifle. *Author's note*: Much of what has been written about MBO in recent years focuses on its application in government and not-for-profit organizations. In the nonprofit sector, often the MBO framework is illustrated in a logic model. For more information on building and using logic models to enhance performance, see the University of Wisconsin Extension's Program Development and Evaluation resource page, http://www.uwex.edu/ces/pdande/evaluation/evallogicmodel.html.
12. Leigh Buchanan interviewed Michael Dearing and his Stanford colleagues to prepare "How Do You Go from This to This Without Losing What Makes You Great? Lessons in the Art of Scaling a Company," *Inc. (*March 2014), 31–37.
13. Ben Bowers, "The History of In-N-Out Burger," Gearpatrol.com (October 26, 2012), http://gearpatrol.com/2012/10/26/the-oral-history-of-in-n-out-burger/. See also Stacy Perman, "In-N-Out

Burger: Professionalizing Fast Food," *Bloomberg Businessweek* (April 8, 2009), http://www.businessweek.com/stories/2009-04-08/in-n-out-burger-professionalizing-fast-food
14. Leigh Buchanan, *Inc.*, p. 36.
15. Beth DeFalco, "Rich Kids 'Hack' to the Future," *New York Post* (May 18, 2012), http://nypost.com/2012/05/18/rich-kids-hack-to-the-future/.
16. New employees are often given an employee handbook that covers every conceivable HR policy, procedure, and rule that might someday have relevance to the employees. In many smaller firms, there may be a one-page sheet that says: "Management has the right to manage and if you have any questions, ask the boss." It is the responsibility of the organization, typically the HR department, to keep the handbook up-to-date relative to policies and laws. Susan Milligan provides suggestions for maintaining the employee handbook, "The Employee Handbook: A Perennial Headache," *HR Magazine* (April 1, 2014), http://www.shrm.org/hrdisciplines/employeerelations/articles/Pages/Employee-Handbook-Writing.aspx.
17. Many reports speculate that employees are spending more than an hour per day using social media for non-work-related things. A Robert Half Technology survey suggests that Web surfing, Facebook posts, tweets, and personal Internet use are still a no-no in most organizations. CIOs were asked, "Which of the following most closely describes your company's policy on visiting social networking sites, such as Facebook and Twitter, while at work?" Thirty-one percent prohibited completely; 51 percent permitted the sites for business purposes only; 14 percent for limited personal use; and 4 percent for any type of personal use (http://www.hrcompliance.ceridan.com). How did you learn the rules of the game from your most recent employer?
18. Jerre L. Stead (chairman and CEO, Ingram Micro, Inc., Santa Ana, CA), "Whose Decision Is It, Anyway?" *Management Review* (January 1999), p. 13. See also Sheila L. Margolis, "The Big-Picture View: Define the Why, How, and What of Your Organization to Provide Employees with the Big-Picture View," *HR Magazine* (June 2011), pp. 129–130.
19. For example, SHRM Research periodically conducts various surveys and issues reports, which cover current human resource policies and practices covering pay, benefits, working conditions, employment, and employee relations. Some of the reports are available to both the general public and SHRM members. To ascertain what might be available for your view, visit http://www.shrm.org/surveys.
20. See Jason Feifer and Anjali Mullany, "Are Open Offices Bad for Work?" *Fastcompany.com* (March, 2014), pp. 39–42.
21. The 2012–2013 Global Retail Theft Barometer reported that dishonest employees and shoplifters stole more the $113 billion globally from 157 companies in 16 countries including the United States, companies which generated more than $1.5 trillion in sales in 2013. Increases in shrink rates, or amount of theft, were reported in every country except the UK, Germany, and Hong Kong over 2011–2012's shrink rates. One might suspect that these organizations might have better theft prevention systems. Might the smaller firms be more vulnerable? Visit the Global Retail Theft Barometer (http://www.globalretailtheftbarometer.com) for more information.
22. Data theft and corruption are equally discouraging problems that are growing exponentially. According to a survey of 671 IT Pros, 80 percent believe mobile devices and laptops pose a severe security risk to their company's networks and data because they are not secure. Also, use of third party cloud computing applications is also a security risk perceived by 67 percent of respondents. Fifty-eight percent reported having more than 25 malware incidents (computer viruses and the like) every month capable of corrupting data. The 2013 State of the Endpoint technology risk survey from which these figures were retrieved can be viewed on the Ponemon Institute Web site, http://www.ponemon.org/library/2013-state-of-the-endpoint-1. Also see Alan Cohen, "To Stop a Thief," *Fortune* (March 21, 2011), p. 94; Bill Roberts, "Protect Data during Layoffs: Tough Times Demand Tough Scrutiny to Prevent Data Theft as Laid-off Employees Depart," *The HR Magazine* (July 2009), pp. 59–61; or Don Wilcox, "Teaching Your Employees to Recognize Waste Is the Smart Thing to Do," *Supervision* 69, No. 2 (February 2008), pp. 10–13.
23. The full extent of Target's security breech is chronicled by Michael Riley, Ben Elgin, Dune Lawrence, and Carol Matlack in "The Epic Hack: Target Ignored Its Own Alarms—and Turned Its Customers into Victims," *Bloomberg Businessweek* (March 13, 2014), 42–47. Also see Target's online Customer Response Center, *Data Breach FAQ*, https://corporate.target.com/about/shopping-experience/payment-card-issue-FAQ#q5888.
24. Riley et al., "The Epic Hack," p. 46. See also Derek Johnson's "State, Local Governments Turn Attention to Cybersecurity Capabilities," *Washington Post* (April 6, 2014), http://www.washingtonpost.com/business/capitalbusiness/state-local-governments-turn-attention-to-cybersecurity-capabilities/2014/04/04/8527c4b0-b912-11e3-899e-bb708e3539dd_story.html ; and Rory Carroll, "Snowden Used Simple Technology to Mine NSA Computer Networks," *The Guardian* (February 9, 2014), http://www.theguardian.com/world/2014/feb/09/edward-snowden-used-simple-technology-nsa.
25. As reported by Robert Burns and Lolita C. Baldor, Associated Press, "Data Stolen from Pentagon: Sensitive Information Lost in Cyberattack," the *Fort Wayne, IN Journal Gazette* (July 15, 2011), p. 9A and cited by David Stegon, "Panetta: Investment Needed to Prepare for 'Battlefield of the Future'," Fedscoop.com (March 12, 2014), http://fedscoop.com/panetta-cyber-symantec/.
26. Each year of this century, more than 4 million U.S. workers suffered a workplace injury, but the number of deaths has been declining. Go to the Bureau of Labor Statistics' *Injuries, Illnesses and Fatalities* Web page, http://www.bls.gov/iif/oshcfoi1.htm#2012, for current information. The Government Accountability Office (GAO) reported that employers minimize injury, accident, and illness because they are afraid of increasing workers' compensation costs. See Roy Maurer, "GAO: Workplace Injuries, Illnesses Underreported," *HR Magazine* (January 2010), p. 11. Employees themselves are hesitant to report injuries for fear of retaliation when they inform bosses that they are sick or injured. More than 100 cases of workman's compensation claim retaliation were decided in 2012, according to James R. Haggerty in "Workplace Injuries Drop, but Claims of Employer Retaliation Rise," *Wall Street Journal* (July 22, 2013), http://online.wsj.com/news/articles/SB10001424127887323664204578610133657300940.
27. On September 16, 2013, a former Navy reservist working as a civilian defense contractor updating computers at military installations was killed in a gun battle at Washington Navy Yard after he killed 12 civilians and injured 8. Investigation after the attack found that the shooter, Aaron Alexis, was discharged from the Navy for misconduct with a firearm in 2011, acquaintances described him as aggressive, and his family reported that he "had experienced anger management problems." These findings bring into question the screening policies and the processes for issuing security clearances that were in place at the time of the shooting. See Theresa Vargas, Steve Hendrix, and Marc Fisher, "Aaron Alexis, 34, Is Dead Gunman in Navy Yard Shooting, Authorities Say," *Washington Post* (September 17,

2013), http://www.washingtonpost.com/politics/aaron-alexis-34-is-dead-gunman-in-navy-yard-shooting-authorities-say/2013/09/16/dcf431ce-1f07-11e3-8459-657e0c72fec8_story.html. See also Ernesto Londono and Christian Davenport, "Navy Yard Shooting Might Have Been Prevented, Pentagon Review Shows," *Washington Post* (March 18, 2014), http://www.washingtonpost.com/world/national-security/navy-yard-shooting-might-have-been-prevented-pentagon-review-shows/2014/03/18/5d48cc70-aeac-11e3-9627-c65021d6d572_story.html. Also see Aliah D. Wright, "Extreme HR: Keep Employees Safe in Perilous Environments by Planning and Communicating," *HR Magazine* (May 2011), pp. 28–31.

28. 2013–14 data from the U.S. Bureau of Labor Statistics showed that nearly 3 million workers quit their jobs each month in the past year, an increase of almost a million from the previous year (http://www.bls.gov/news.release/jolts.nr0.htm). A late 2011 survey of U.S. workers by Mercer found that one in three employees are seriously considering leaving their current jobs to find greater advancement, recognition, or a boss who will empower them. See Alan Hall, "'I'm Outta Here!' Why 2 Million Americans Quit Every Month" (And 5 Steps to Turn the Epidemic Around)," *Forbes* (March 11, 2013), http://www.forbes.com/sites/alanhall/2013/03/11/im-outta-here-why-2-million-americans-quit-every-month-and-5-steps-to-turn-the-epidemic-around/.

    *Note*: According to the CIPD *Annual Survey Report 2013 of Absence Management*, the average worker misses 7.6 days of work due to unplanned absence, two-thirds of which are short-term, less than consecutive days. For every employee with perfect attendance, another employee misses twelve days of work per year. Those are days that he or she is scheduled to work and, for whatever reason, chooses not to show up. The average employee is scheduled to work 250 days per year. You can access the survey at http://www.psyccess.com/wp-content/uploads/2013/09/Absence-Management-Report-2013.pdf. Also see Investopedia's "The Causes and Costs of Absenteeism in the Workplace," *Forbes* (July 10, 2013), http://www.forbes.com/sites/investopedia/2013/07/10/the-causes-and-costs-of-absenteeism-in-the-workplace/.

29. With the current concerns about healthcare costs and coverage, leave sharing might be another way that organizations can help employees plan for unexpected healthcare issues. Guidance on creating a leave-sharing program is provided in the Society for Human Resource Management's (SHRM) how-to guide, "How to Create a Leave Donation Program" (September 6, 2013), http://www.shrm.org/templatestools/howtoguides/pages/howtocreatealeavedonationprogram.aspx

30. "Working 24/7 may be good for the organization, but it's bad for employee's health." Eric Barker provides suggestions of how to reduce time-on-the-job and regain balance in "How to Achieve Work-Life Balance in 5 Steps," *Time* (April 2, 2014), http://time.com/43808/how-to-achieve-work-life-balance-in-5-steps/. Rebecca Fraser-Thrill suggests a new approach to work–life balance in, "Forget Work-Life Balance: Aim for Blend Instead," *Huffington Post* (March 7, 2014), http://www.huffingtonpost.com/rebecca-fraserthill/success-and-motivation_b_4889295.html. See Jody Miller and Matt Miller, "Get a Life!" *Fortune* (November 28, 2005), pp. 108–124, for illustrations of how some organizations are helping employees balance work–life issues.

31. Adrienne Fox, "At Work in 2020," *HR Magazine* (January 2010), pp. 18–23, reported that 17.2 million people worked from remote locations at least once a month in 2008. That number jumped to 25 million in 2013, according to the Global Workplace Analytics survey, results of which are available at www.GlobalWorkplaceAnalytics.com/telecommuting_statistics. It is expected that the workforce of the future will be more independent but much more connected by the networks. Fox contends that a Chinese proverb in play for each of us: "The person who does not worry about the future will shortly have worries about the present."

    According to a SHRM survey, 37 percent of companies offer telecommuting or similar flexible work arrangements. Robert LeRose provides suggestions to its supervisors of how to effectively manage the growing virtual workforce in "Working Remotely: Setting Up and Managing a Telecommuting Workforce," Bank of America Small Business Community Web site (April 15, 2013), https://smallbusinessonlinecommunity.bankofamerica.com/community/running-your-business/human-resources/blog/2013/04/15/working-remotely-setting-up-and-managing-a-telecommuting-workforce. Planning for and securing appropriate technology for virtual workers is a critical consideration for their success. First steps in such planning are given by Sara Angeles in "Remote Workers' Success Starts with IT Support," BusinessNewsDaily.com (July 29, 2013), http://www.businessnewsdaily.com/4831-information-technology-managing-remote-workers.html.

32. For example, see Ed Frauenheim, "Research Backs Benefits of Flex Work for Workers—and Companies," Workforce.com (May 29, 2013), http://www.workforce.com/articles/research-backs-benefits-of-flex-work-for-workers-and-companies

33. See Adrienne Fox, "Part-Times: Make People Strategy Whole," *HR Magazine* (August 2010), pp. 28–33. Fox contends that adding part-time positions can give you and your employees much-needed flexibility.

34. See Gary B. Kushner, "Time to Get Strategic," *HR Magazine* (August 2013), 52–56.

35. Jennifer Taylor Arnold, "Managing a Nontraditional Workforce," *HR Magazine* (August 2010), pp. 75–77.

36. See Steve Taylor, "The Lowdown on Unpaid Internship Programs," *HR Magazine* (November 2010). pp. 46–48. All indications are that there will be an increasing demand for temporary workers.

37. As reported in Rita Zeidner, "Heady Debate: Rely on Temps or Hire Staff?" *HR Magazine* (February 2010), pp. 28–33.

38. For example, see Eric Krell, "Spreading the Workload: Planning How to Redistribute Work Is a Key Step to Engineering Layoffs," *HR Magazine* (July 2009), p 55; An example of how an industrial engineer would design a flexible work schedule is described by TC Chiang and Hsaio-Jou Lin, "A Simple and Effective Evolutionary Algorithm for Multiobjective Job Show Scheduling," *International Journal of Production Economics* 141, No. 1, 87–98. For more information on work-sampling techniques, see Richard B. Chase and Nicholas J. Aquilano, *Operations Management for Competitive Advantage*, 11th ed. (Boston: McGraw-Hill Irwin, 2005), pp. 181–205; or Lee J. Krajewski and Larry P. Ritzman, *Operations Management* (Upper Saddle, NJ: Pearson Prentice Hall, 2005).

39. Kanban, the foundation of just-in-time inventory management, is described in detail on the LeanKit Web site, http://leankit.com/kanban/what-is-kanban/. The Web site provides a free e-book that can guide the kanban strategy. An insightful case of the results of materials requirements planning (MRP) and just in time (JIT) purchasing strategies is presented by Colorado Department of Transportation Process Improvement Intern Marcus Ritosa, "MRP, 'Just-in-Time' Strategies Reduce Inventory by $1,932,428," (August 30, 2013), http://www.coloradodot.info/business/process-improvement/using-information-technology-to-improve-processes/mrp-just-in-time-strategies-reduce-inventory-by-1-932-428. Likewise, cost savings was combined with improved supply management in

Mayo Medical Laboratories as described by Joy Gomez, Ray Frick, Jerry Dietenberger, and Kari Solak in "Systematic Management of Laboratory Supplies," *Medical Lab Management* 2(4) (July–August, 2013), p. 2. See also Jack Wilson, "Real Life Examples of Successful JIT Systems," BrightHubPM.com (June 29, 2013), http://www.brighthubpm.com/methods-strategies/71540-real-life-examples-of-successful-jit-systems/

For a contrary opinion on JIT, see Susanna Ray and Thomas Black, "The Downside of Just-in-Time Inventory," *Bloomberg Businessweek* (March 24, 2011), http://www.businessweek.com/magazine/content/11_14/b4222017701856.htm

40. See Richard Bird, Jerry Durant, Michele Tomasicchio, and Lonnie Wilson, *Best Practices for Managing Just-in-Time (JIT) Production*, Focus Research (December 29, 2010), pp. 2–4.
41. For additional information on Gantt charts, see Andrew J. DuBrin, *Essentials of Management*, 9th ed. (Mason, OH: South-Western Thomson, 2012); or search the Internet for "Gantt charts." For additional information on PERT flowcharts, see Tyson Browning, "Managing Complex Project Process Models with a Process Architecture Framework," *International Journal of Project Management 32*(2), 229–241, or search the Internet for PERT.
42. Torbjorn Netland provides a comprehensive discussion of the organizational contexts for which these and other improvement frameworks are best suited in "The Concept Epicenters of Lean, TQM, Six Sigma & Co" (January 17, 2014), better-operations.com; http://better-operations.com/2014/01/17/concept-epicenters-lean-tqm-six-sigma/. See also MIT scholar Kirkor Bozdogan, *Towards an Integration of the Lean Enterprise System, Total Quality Management, Six Sigma and Related Enterprise Process Improvement Methods* (#ESD-WP-2010-05, ESD Working Paper Series) (Cambridge, MA: Massachusetts Institute of Technology Engineering Systems Division, 2010), http://esd.mit.edu/WPS/2010/esd-wp-2010-05.pdf
43. See Rita Zeidner, "Questing for Quality: For High-Performing Organizations, 'Good Enough' Is Not Good Enough," *HR Magazine* (July 2010), pp. 24–28. For additional information on TQM and continuous improvement, see H. James Harrington, "Six Sigma in Health Care: A New Prescription," *Quality Digest* (December 2007), p. 14; To view the Global Six Sigma Award winners, go to www.wcbf.com/quality/5081
44. Kimiz Dalkir provides a comprehensive overview of knowledge management in *Knowledge Management in Theory and Practice* (Burlington, MA: Elsevier Butterworth-Heinemann, 2013). See Lisa Quast, "Why Knowledge Management Is Important to the Success of Your Company," *Forbes* (August 20, 2012), http://www.forbes.com/sites/lisaquast/2012/08/20/why-knowledge-management-is-important-to-the-success-of-your-company/. See also a discussion of the role of power in knowledge management in Ray Gordon and David Grant, "Knowledge Management or Management of Knowledge? Why People Interested in Knowledge Management Need to Consider Foucault and the Construct of Power," *Tamara Journal for Critical Organization Inquiry* 3(2), (2004), 27–38.
45. For a comprehensive discussion of benchmarking, see Robert Damelio, *The Basics of Benchmarking*, 2nd ed. (New York, NY: Productivity Press, 2014). See also Micah Solomon, "An Unlikely Secret behind Great Customer Service: Benchmark The Experts In Manufacturing," *Forbes* (April 2, 2014), http://www.forbes.com/sites/micahsolomon/2014/04/02/to-create-great-customer-service-experiences-benchmark-the-experts-of-manufacturing/. Solomon describes instances of corporations looking not just at their own industry, but even outside of it. He shares Apple's strategy of looking to the best practices in the hospitality industry to improve their customer service.
46. ISO 9001 is a worldwide recognized quality standard (http://www.isogar.com/iso9001/qualintro.htm). Also see Craig Cochran, *ISO 9001 in Plain English* (Chico, CA: Paton Professional Books, 2011).
47. For information on the Malcolm Baldrige National Quality Award, go to www.quality.nist.gov/ or to http://www.baldrige.com for the balanced scorecard indices and a list of current winners. Sixty-nine organizations were vying for recognition in 2011. The applicants are evaluated on leadership; strategic planning; operations focus; measurement, analysis, and knowledge management; workforce focus; process management; and results. Among the seven 2010 winners were Advocate Good Samaritan Hospital of Downers Grove, Illinois, and the Studer Group of Gulf Breeze, Florida.
48. It is with sad heart that I share this story. At 4:25 p.m. on Friday, June 24, I received an e-mail from Kim Hatch reminding me of a meeting the next Tuesday morning. We serve on a nonprofit board together and are neighbors. She had just returned from a mission trip to help tornado victims in Joplin, Missouri, and was on her way to their cottage in Michigan. Less than four hours later their plane crashed. She and her husband, Steve, were killed. Son Austin, a University of Michigan basketball recruit, was severely injured. See "Plane on Instrument Approach before Michigan Crash," Associated Press (July 3, 2011), or Dominic Adams, "Fort Wayne Doctor, Wife Killed in Plane Crash; Son Critically Injured," *The Journal Gazette online* (June 25, 2011). One never knows exactly what the future will bring.
49. The shocking terror attack on the Boston Marathon on April 15, 2013, was orchestrated by two Chechen immigrants, brothers who planted two backpacks containing pressure-cooker bombs filled with nails and BBs among cheering crowds within yards of the marathon's finish line, then led police on a manhunt throughout the city of Boston, which ended with one brother dead and another captured. The surviving bomber faces the death penalty. See comprehensive coverage of the bombing provided by CNN at http://www.cnn.com/2013/06/03/us/boston-marathon-terror-attack-fast-facts/.
50. See "Japan's Meltdown," a special report on Earthquake, Tsunami, Nuclear Disaster, Resilience, *Time* (March 25, 2011), pp. 24–47; Drake Bennett et al., "Crisis in Japan," *Bloomberg Businessweek* (March 28–April 3, 2011), pp. 12–20; Chester Dawson, "Japan Plant Had Earlier Alert," *The Wall Street Journal* (June 15, 2011), p. A11; or you may want to read about the recovery efforts in Joplin, Missouri, after the deadliest U.S. tornado since 1947. See Alan Scher Zagier, "Joplin Recovery Gradual, Daunting," Associated Press (July 24, 2011). On April 27, 2011, tornadoes and cyclones raged through Alabama and other Southern states. You may also so want to see Reginald L. Bell, "Managing the Prodromal Crisis Situation: Two Techniques to Avoid Turning the Surge into a Mega-Tsunami," *Supervision* 72, No. 2 (February 2011), pp. 3–6.
51. Ray Sanchez, "Conn. Police Release Final Report on Newtown School Shooting," CNN.com (December 29, 2013), http://www.cnn.com/2013/12/27/justice/connecticut-newtown-shooting-report. A witness from the community shared in reports that the 20-year-old gunman, who had been diagnosed with significant mental health disorders, hated his mother and the school where she volunteered, feeling as though she "loved the students more than him." The gunman killed himself after committing the murders. See also Anna Almendrala, "The Harsh Dilemma of Preparing Kids for the Worst at School," *Huffington Post* (February 19, 2014), http://www.huffingtonpost.com/2014/02/19/active-shooter-drills-at-school_n_4785349.html; and Andrew Solomon, "The Reckoning: The Father of the Sandy Hook Killer Searches for Answers," *The New Yorker* (March 17, 2014), http://www.newyorker.com/reporting/2014/03/17/140317fa_fact_solomon?currentPage=all,

in which the killer's father warns, "I want people to be afraid of the fact that this could happen to them."

52. Adapted from Aristotle's *Poetics*, accessed at http://www.merriam-webster.com/dictionary/tragedy. Examples include the situation ended in tragedy when the gunman shot and killed two students; or the biggest tragedy is that the incident could have been prevented with prior planning.
53. Miles' leads PwC's U.S. Governance, Risk and Compliance Services division. He has authored several books on enterprise risk management. Quote found in "Today's PWC and Compliance Week Survey: How Are We Doing" (http://multivu.prnewswire.com/mnr'pwc/45949/).
54. See Michael Riley and Ashlee Vance, "The Code War," *Bloomberg Businessweek* (July 25–July 31, 2011), pp. 50–57; Cassell Bryan-Low and Siobhan Gorman, "Inside the 'Anonymous' Army of 'Hacktivist' Attackers," *The Wall Street Journal* (June 23, 2011), pp. A1–A14.

    Rhode Island recently put together a team whose mission it is to take down threats to cyber security and tackle cyberattacks before they happen. See Laura Crimaldi, "Rhode Island Cyber Security Team Announced," Associated Press (July 11, 2011) (accessed businessweek.com). Is your school prepared? How secure is your system?
55. One year after the BP Gulf of Mexico oil spill, the *News of World* published its last issue. After 168 years and 7.5 million readers, unethical practices led to its demise. The closing knocked billions of dollars off the value of Rupert Murdock's News Corp. Dow Jones & Co. and the *Wall Street Journal* are part of the Murdock chain. See *The Wall Street Journal* online (July 14, 2011) for Murdock's "sorry and we have handled the crisis extremely well." Only time will tell. Also see Catherine Mayer, "Tabloid Bites Man," *Time* (July 25, 2011), pp. 30–37; Ronald Grover and Felix Gillette, "Will Scandal Tame Murdoch?" *Bloomberg Businessweek* (July 25–July 31, 2011), pp. 18–20; Paul M. Barrett and Felix Gillette, "Ink-Stained Wretchedness," *Bloomberg Businessweek* (July 18–24, 2011), pp. 4–7; Raphael G. Slater, "Tabloids Tremble as World Ends!" www.journalgazette.net (July 10, 2011); and Jill Lawless, "Wall St. Journal Boss Quits!" www.journalgazette.net (July 16, 2011). As is stated in Figure 3.8, "respond immediately and do not be afraid to apologize."
56. Because of its proactive, consumer-oriented response to the Tylenol scare, Johnson & Johnson became one of the world's most respected companies. See Robert F. Hartley, *Management Mistakes and Successes*, 7th ed. (London: Wiley, 2002), Chapter ; Ian I. Mitroff and Gus Anagnos, *Managing Crises before They Happen* (New York: AMACOM, 2001); and Matthew Boyle, "The Shiniest Reputations in Tarnished Times," *Fortune* (March 4, 2002), pp. 70–82.

    However, J&J's product recall struggles continue as more than two dozen products have been recalled in the past five years. See *Fort Wayne, IN Journal Gazette* (July 20, 2011), p. 7B, as well as *New York Times* (September 12, 2013), http://www.nytimes.com/2013/09/13/business/new-recalls-by-johnson-johnson-raise-concern-about-quality-control-improvements.html.

    Also see the Society for Human Resource Management (SHRM) Managing Through Emergency and Disaster toolkit (March 25, 2013), https://www.shrm.org/TemplatesTools/Toolkits/Pages/ManagingEmergencyandDisaster.aspx; as well as employment law senior counsel Keisha-Ann G. Gray's "Best Practices for Dealing with Workplace Violence," Human Resources Executive Online (February 6, 2013), http://www.hreonline.com/HRE/view/story.jhtml?id=534354884; and Kathy Gurchiek, "Disaster Plans Put to the Test: We Moved Quickly," *SHRM Home* (October 29, 2007).
57. For additional information on crisis management, see Joe Mullich, "The 3-D View of Risk and Creating a Risk-Aware Culture," *The Wall Street Journal* (December 14, 2010), pp. B6–B8. Also see Valery Shemetov, "Crisis Management: Trade-off between Effectiveness and Timeliness," *The Business Review* 16, No. 1 (December 2010), pp. 1–10; Ahmad Areigat and Tawfiq AbdelHadi, "The Roles of R&D in Crisis Management," *Interdisciplinary Journal of Contemporary Research in Business* 2, No. 6 (October 2010), pp. 81–88; Tony Jaques, "Reshaping Crisis Management: The Challenge for Organizational Design," *Organizational Development Journal* 29, No. 1 (Spring 2010), pp. 9–17; and Michael Hargis and John D. Watt, "Organizational Perception Management: A Framework to Overcome Crisis Events," *Organizational Development Journal* 28, No. 2 (Spring 2010), pp. 73–87.

    The authors found it interesting that many companies operating in the Middle East do not have a crisis management or disaster recovery program. See "ME Firms Need Faster Crisis Management Schemes," *Khaleej Times Online* (July 9, 2011). Is your organization prepared?

Chapter 4

# Supervising a Diverse Workforce

Jetta Productions/Iconica/Getty Images

**After studying this chapter, you will be able to:**

1. Define the concept of workforce diversity and identify the major categories of legally protected employees and general guidelines for supervising a diverse workforce.
2. Explain the issues involved in supervising racial or ethnic minority employees.
3. Discuss factors that are particularly important when supervising female employees.
4. Identify and discuss the legal and other considerations of supervising employees with physical and mental disabilities.
5. Discuss the considerations of supervising older workers and managing an intergenerational workforce.
6. Provide examples of religious accommodation.
7. Describe the unique challenges of supervising globally dispersed employees.
8. Recognize several pressures faced by supervisors who are members of protected groups.
9. Explain the issue of reverse discrimination.
10. Understand how to best supervise a diverse workforce.

## YOU MAKE THE CALL!

*You are Ralph Adams, the purchasing department director at Global Manufacturing Company in Glendale, California. The company employs about 1,500 people and has several large government contracts. As such the company is subjected annually to an equal employment opportunity compliance review by a federal agency.*

Most of the buyers are college graduates or have had equivalent experience. Reporting to you are five supervisors, each having responsibility for purchasing various types of goods and services. Each supervisor has a staff of several buyers and one support staff person. Recently, Lewis Minardi applied for an opening in your department as a buyer. Minardi's resume showed that he had been an excellent college student, and that he had worked as a purchasing manager and keeper for a small retail chain in Illinois. Recently, Minardi had moved to the Glendale area to be close to family members.

Minardi had been frustrated in his efforts to obtain a job since relocating to the area. Minardi is a paraplegic. After receiving Minardi's and all other candidates' applications for the opening in your department, the human resources department screened applicants and then submitted résumés to you for review. You selected four applicants to be interviewed including Minardi. You decided that Antionette Hoczyk was the best person for your department.

After finding out that he had been turned down for this job, Minardi asked for a meeting with you and Dwight Johnson, Global's director of human resources. At this meeting, Minardi stated, "When I came in for the interview, I could not shake hands firmly. They saw me in a wheelchair. Those things stuck in their heads. They didn't ask me about my condition. I was struck by a drunk driver 4 years ago. I returned to my purchasing job after extensive rehabilitation. I moved here to be close to family and continue physical therapy. I have had several job interviews, but no one gives me a chance to describe how I can handle certain aspects of the job. I can be a very effective purchasing agent."

To reinforce his claims, Minardi described several technological adaptive aids he used for his work and showed Johnson papers that documented the long hours that he had put in his previous job. Minardi's former employer and supervisors spoke highly of his abilities in several reference letters that he shared with Johnson.

You and Johnson listened patiently, making notes as Minardi talked. You were both particularly startled by Minardi's last statement, "Everyone has disabilities, whether they are obvious like mine or the inability to get along with people or do the work required. Perhaps I need to see a lawyer."

After the meeting, you and Johnson pondered what course of action the two of you, on behalf of the company, might take.

**Disclaimer:** The above scenario presents a supervisory situation based on real events to be used for educational purposes. The identities of some or all individuals, organizations, industries, and locations, as well as financial and other information may have been disguised to protect individual privacy and proprietary information. Fictional details may have been added to improve readability and interest.

YOU MAKE THE CALL!

## Managing Diversity Is the Bottom-Line Concern

**1 Define the concept of workforce diversity and identify the major categories of legally protected employees and general guidelines for supervising a diverse workforce.**

In Chapter 1, we presented an overview of some of the principal demographic and societal trends that impact organizations in general and supervision in particular. We mentioned that the increasingly diverse characteristics of people in the workplace will continue to be among the major challenges facing managers at all levels. At the same time, a diverse workforce, effectively managed and empowered, can become an organization's greatest asset.[1]

The reality of diversity in the workplace, sometimes called the "multicultural workforce," was summarized rather well in two management journal articles:

> *Diversity is a reality. Just look around you. The American workforce is changing—in age, gender, race, national origin, sexual orientation, and physical ability. So are customers and suppliers. Minority populations are increasing in every part of our country. Workers 55 and older are the fastest-growing segment of the workforce. Communication and information technology is enabling more and more people with disabilities to enter the workforce.*[2]

> *Hispanics constitute the largest and fastest-growing minority in the United States. Projections call for the Hispanic population to nearly triple in size and account for most of the nation's population growth in the near future. Assisting language-challenged and culturally challenged Hispanics is a skill that many HR leaders and supervisors have never been trained for. All HR and supervisory activities must be adjusted for language and cultural integration.*[3]

Because of these and other factors, diversity management now encompasses many considerations, including legal, demographic, economic, and political. Managing a diverse workforce encompasses virtually all aspects of a firm's operations, especially on the supervisory level. Initiatives and efforts to better manage a diverse workforce are growing significantly, not just because of legal requirements or social considerations but also because there is a recognition that this has become an area of vital importance to a firm's long-term success and bottom-line results.[4] Figure 4.1 illustrates one company's recognition of the value of diversity.

## PROTECTED-GROUP EMPLOYEES AND SUPERVISING DIVERSITY

Throughout this book, we have stressed that employees are individuals shaped by various forces from within and without the organization. In Chapter 11, we discussed how employees form groups and why supervisors should be aware of group dynamics. In this chapter, we focus on the need for supervisors to develop a special awareness, sensitivity, and adaptability to *protected-group employees*, a term that we recognize in a legal sense but one that also has many human dimensions.

**Protected-group employees** Classes of employees who have been afforded certain legal protections in their employment situations

The identification of employees who have been afforded special legal protection comes primarily from civil rights legislation, equal employment opportunity (EEO) regulations, and numerous court decisions. Various laws and regulations that govern employment policies and practices appear in Chapter 1 (see page 24). Areas of lawful and potentially unlawful inquiry during the selection process of job applicants are presented in Chapter 10. For our purposes in this chapter, we use the term **protected-group employees** to identify classes of employees who

**FIGURE 4.1 The value of diversity**

Image Courtesy of The Advertising Archives

have been afforded certain legal protections in their employment situations. The underlying legal philosophy is that many individuals in these classes have been unfairly or illegally discriminated against or should be afforded special consideration to enhance their opportunities for fair treatment in employment.

Reports by the U.S. Justice Department indicate that alleged discrimination in the workplace escalated rapidly during the past two decades, but for the first time in five years it has dropped slightly. In 2013, U.S. Equal Employment Opportunity Commission (EEOC) resolved 93,727 charges of employment discrimination, down 6 percent from the previous year, yet still 15 percent higher than a decade prior. The largest number of claims came from allegations of retaliation (41.1 percent), racial discrimination (35.3 percent), sexual harassment/gender (29.5 percent), disability (27.7 percent), age (22.8 percent), and national origin (11.4 percent). While the rates of most of the categories have remained consistent over the past decade, retaliation charges have nearly doubled in the past decade and discrimination on the basis of disability has increased by nearly one-third.[5] Often, these cases allege employer discrimination in hiring, promoting, firing, pay and benefits, and opportunities for training due to a person's race, color, religion, gender, national origin, age, disability, or exercise of legal rights. The number of accusations of employer retaliation outnumbered racial discrimination allegations for the first time since the establishment of the EEOC in 1965.[6] What does that say about the workplace climate?

Plaintiffs in certain job bias cases have the right to a jury trial and can win compensatory and punitive damages. A review of lawsuits filed on behalf of employees who were allegedly discriminated against, harassed, or retaliated against for filing charges under the law has found many multimillion-dollar awards. Usually, the organization agrees to pay a sum of money and provide significant remedial relief to the aggrieved employees. The EEOC has vigorously prosecuted claims of harassment, especially cases involving teenagers, many of whom are in the workplace for the first time.

Because employment discrimination laws can at times be quite complicated, we will keep our discussion relatively simple.[7] Supervisors normally should refer compliance questions that are of a legal nature to higher management or to an appropriate human resources staff person. The human resources department usually will have the expertise to answer the supervisor's questions and to give appropriate advice. At times, human resources staff will seek outside legal counsel to determine what should be done regarding certain matters and to avoid legal difficulties.

## CLASSIFICATIONS OF PROTECTED-GROUP EMPLOYEES

The protected-group employees we discuss in this chapter are classified according to:

- Racial or ethnic origin
- Gender (women)
- Physical or mental disability
- Age (over 40)
- Religion
- Military service (such as Iraq war or other veterans)[8]

In this chapter, we do not directly discuss the emerging issues of gender orientation, such as discrimination against homosexuals. To date, homosexuality has not been given legally protected status by federal legislation. However, author Diane

FIGURE 4.2 Managing diversity means being aware of differences and managing employees as individuals. To manage diversity does not mean just recognizing and tolerating differences but also supporting and using the differences to the organization's advantage

Cadrain noted that "[i]t's worthwhile for employers to take the basic steps, such as worker education and company policy reviews, in trying to make their workplaces more open to gay, lesbian, bisexual and transgender (GLBT) employees."[9]

The supervision of protected-group employees is, by definition, part of a firm's efforts to manage diversity so as to benefit both the firm and the employees. Regardless of personal views, supervisors must be sensitive to possible illegal discriminatory actions and adjust their supervisory practices accordingly. More important, however, is that supervisors recognize the strengths and potential contributions of all employees and supervise in ways that do not limit employees' development for inappropriate reasons (see Figure 4.2). Stated another way, effective supervision of a diversified workforce can be viewed as an opportunity to draw on and use the differences of people in a positive, productive, and enriching manner.

As discussed in previous chapters, incivility in the workplace is on the rise. It is a sad commentary on our society that certain inappropriate behaviors continue unabated. Perhaps it is an escalation of the adage, "The squeaky wheel gets the grease." Indeed, rude, obnoxious, and inappropriate behavior appears to get more attention in the popular press and on late-night television talk shows than other, more important issues.[10] Harassment in the workplace has been unlawful for a long time, but it is still pervasive.

## THE OUCH TEST IN SUPERVISING EMPLOYEES

The OUCH test, which we discuss in Chapter 10 as a guideline for selecting employees, also applies to day-to-day supervision. Remember, the supervisor's actions should be objective, uniform in application, consistent in effect, and have job relatedness.

FIGURE 4.3 A myth occasionally voiced by some supervisors is that protected-group employees cannot be disciplined or discharged

For example, assume that an organization's policy specifies a disciplinary warning for being tardy three times in one month. The supervisor should give the same warning to every employee who is late the third time in one month, regardless of whether the employee is in a protected-group category. This supervisory approach would meet the OUCH test because tardiness is an observable behavior that is measured objectively for all employees. The penalty is the same for all employees, is consistent, and is clearly job-related.

A myth occasionally voiced by some supervisors is that certain categories of employees cannot be disciplined or discharged because of government regulations (Figure 4.3). This view is unfounded. Laws and regulations do not prevent a supervisor from taking disciplinary action against protected-group employees. However, they do require that such employees be treated the same as other employees whenever disciplinary actions are taken. Therefore, it is extremely important that supervisors be careful in meeting the OUCH test and in justifying their actions through adequate documentation. We discuss how to take appropriate disciplinary actions in considerable detail in Chapter 15.

## Supervising Racial and Ethnic Minorities

**2 Explain the issues involved in supervising racial or ethnic minority employees.**

The most frequently identified racial and ethnic minority populations in the United States are African Americans, Hispanics, Asian Americans, and Native Americans. With the passage of major civil rights legislation, most employers have developed nondiscrimination or affirmative-action policies or programs for employing people from racial and ethnic minority groups. A major thrust of these policies and programs is to ensure that minorities, as well as certain other protected-group individuals, receive special consideration in hiring and promotion decisions. The philosophy underlying affirmative-action plans is to overcome the impact of past discriminatory practices and to provide greater opportunities for underrepresented groups to participate more fully throughout the workforce. The long-term goal is to have a fully diversified workforce in which all employees are hired and supervised solely on the basis of their capabilities and performance.

While most organizations recognize the importance of integrating their workplaces, minority populations still face substantial barriers. A 2013 series of in-depth interviews with managers, workers, and stakeholders by the Joseph Rowntree Foundation indicated the following barriers for minorities:

- Lack of role models in leadership positions
- Language difficulties
- Lower education levels
- Low self-confidence
- Exclusion from informal networks
- Lack of organizational understanding of ethnic minority communities
- Unequal access to opportunities for training and development
- Prejudice and stereotyping
- Under-recognition of existing skills and experience[11]

These findings echo those found more than a decade earlier in a Society for Human Resource Management (SHRM) study, showing that barriers to inclusion and advancement of minority workers persist.[12] At present, only 5 percent of all white-collar workers are African American, although African Americans make up 12.7 percent of the workforce. Hispanics make up 7.6 percent of the workforce, but only hold 4 percent of professional positions.[13] A review of these barriers and their persistent effects warrants an important question: Why should qualified minority applicants join an organization when they can look and see that, in the past, no other minority has succeeded? If the adage "success begets success" holds—that is, if a company is known as a great place for women and minorities—it follows that other qualified minority applicants will be attracted to the company.

## UNDERSTANDING DISCRIMINATION'S EFFECTS

Minority employees who have experienced prejudicial treatment may resent supervisors of different racial or ethnic backgrounds. Even though nondiscrimination laws have been in place for several decades, annual data compiled by the EEOC show that minority group members file tens of thousands of complaints about unfair treatment because of their race. Typically, alleged discriminatory discipline and discharge have been the most frequent bases for these complaints, although some are based on incidents of direct harassment.[14]

Because the responsibility for initiating discipline and discharge actions usually rests with supervisors, such decisions play a significant role in discrimination charges.[15] Charge investigation requires the extensive time, effort, and involvement of supervisors, human resources and legal specialists, and others. Therefore, supervisors must be sensitive to the feelings of minority employees who may have experienced discriminatory treatment in the past or who believe that they are currently experiencing discrimination. Supervisors should not enter into racial debates with minority employees who display lingering resentment and suspicion.

Rather, supervisors always should strive to be fair and considerate when making decisions that affect these employees. By demonstrating that minority employees will be supervised in the same manner as other employees, a supervisor can reduce the negative effects of past discrimination. In the event that a minority employee's feelings of resentment interfere with job performance or department relations, the supervisor should refer the employee to the human resources department.

## APPRECIATING CULTURAL DIFFERENCES

A continuing debate about human behavior concerns how much heredity, as compared to environment, shapes an individual. Obviously, heredity is a major factor in the physical and ethnic makeup of a person. Moreover, because members of various races or ethnic origins often have different environmental experiences, unique subcultures have developed for each racial or ethnic minority group. For example, the ties that Native Americans have to their heritage reflect their subculture. People of Asian descent have distinctive values and traditions that reflect their heritage and cultures.

Unfortunately, differences in ethnic or cultural backgrounds can contribute to prejudicial attitudes and treatment of minority employees. For example, a minority employee's values regarding the importance of work and punctuality may differ from those of a supervisor. If a minority employee has not grown up in an environment that stresses the importance of punctuality, especially in a work situation, the supervisor must be prepared to spend extra time explaining to that employee the reasons for punctual attendance and the consequences of tardiness and absenteeism. Regardless of what cultural differences exist, it is the supervisor's job to exert special efforts to reduce the effects of these differences. By so doing, the supervisor can help the minority person learn to accept the requirements of the work environment and to meet the standards expected of all employees in the department.

As a result of the continuing news coverage of the tragic circumstances of September 11, 2001; current events in the Middle East, Afghanistan, and Pakistan; and the possibilities of additional terrorist attacks in the United States like the Boston Marathon bombing discussed in Chapter 3, many individuals of Arab or Islamic descent have been subjected to various forms of harassment and negative stereotyping.[16] More than a decade after 9/11, this cultural group still experiences workplace discrimination, threats, and perceived mistrust, which erodes their morale.[17] If Arab or Islamic employees are working in a department with other employees, the supervisor must endeavor to make sure that any harassing conduct is not tolerated or condoned. The supervisor may want to discuss with the employees the cultural backgrounds and customs of Arab or Islamic people and to emphasize their positive contributions in the workplace. The supervisor may need to use the services of the human resources department to do so. For example, if Arab or Islamic employees need dress, appearance, and scheduling accommodations, these needs must be explained to other employees so that those employees can understand and accept them.

## OVERCOMING LANGUAGE DIFFICULTIES

Another consideration in supervising minority employees relates to the different languages that may be spoken in a work environment. The U.S. Census's 2011

*Supervisors must be sensitive to past and present effects of racial discrimination.*

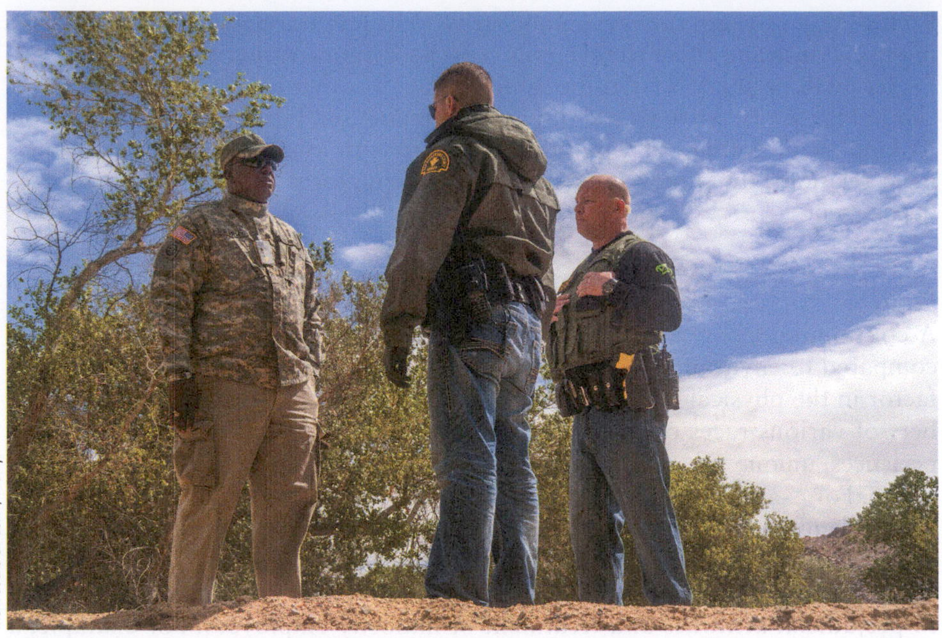

Marmaduke St. John / Alamy

American Community Survey reported that 21 percent of all U.S. residents spoke a language other than English at home. Another census report contended that many foreign-born and nonnative English-speaking people do not speak English well.[18] In an effort to familiarize non-English-speaking employees with the dominant language of the United States, an increasing number of employers sponsor English improvement and business English courses for minority employees. These programs focus on the writing and speaking skills needed for job improvement and advancement.[19] Some employers have held training programs to sensitize supervisors and managers to minority language patterns and to make those staff members more knowledgeable of the cultural and language backgrounds of certain minorities.

To accommodate non-English-speaking residents, states such as Indiana provide driver's license tests in the applicant's native language. The state also provides interpreters to assist in the process. Fort Wayne, Indiana, is home to a large number of Burmese immigrants, so several financial institutions there provide interpreters to assist with business dealings. Similarly, 25 percent of Shelby County, Kentucky's population is Hispanic. Since its opening in August 2007, the Citizens Union Bank branch in Shelby County has been operated by bilingual employees of Hispanic heritage, all of whom were involved in the branch's design. The branch has a different name, "Nuestro Banco," which means "Our Bank" in Spanish. Does it make good business sense to go this route?[20]

Yet, other employers are still attempting to institute English-only requirements in the workplace.[21] Consider the following illustrations. A manufacturing company's refusal to hire a Spanish-speaking worker on an assembly line might be ruled prejudicial because in that job, communication skills may be much less important than manual dexterity. However, for a salesperson in a department store or for a nurse working in an emergency room, adequate interpersonal language skills are essential. Is it reasonable for a retail store to require employees to speak English to customers? Yes, unless the customer wishes otherwise or unless the store is located in an area where a significant number of customers speak a native language other than English. In many parts of the United States, the English language is the minority language, and a bilingual person is a valuable asset. We encourage you to add more language skills to your toolbox.

## Supervising Women

**3 Discuss factors that are particularly important when supervising female employees.**

Throughout the past several decades, both the number and the percentage of women in the labor force have increased dramatically. While there is consensus that opportunities for women will increase during the first decade of the twenty-first century, barriers remain. These barriers include the lack of females at the executive board level, male-dominated corporate cultures, stereotypes or preconceptions about women, exclusion from informal networks, and lack of mentoring opportunities.[22] Yet several significant changes have taken place during the lifetime of the author, and they didn't come without sacrifice and effort. See Figure 4.4 for an overview of two women who made a difference.

Both male and female supervisors should be aware of a number of important concerns regarding the supervision of women. While not all-inclusive, the areas discussed here represent a range of issues supervisors should recognize and address appropriately.

### ENTRY OF WOMEN INTO MANY CAREER FIELDS

The combined effects of antidiscrimination laws, affirmative-action programs, and the increasing number of women in the workforce have led women into many jobs that were traditionally dominated by men. For example, in greater numbers than ever before, women are financiers, scientists, engineers, utility repair specialists, sales and technical representatives, accountants, and managers. However, a high percentage of women still work in clerical and service jobs.

The entry of women into jobs requiring hard physical labor and craft skills has been comparatively limited, but when women do assume craft or other physically demanding jobs, changes may occur. A number of firms have found that some equipment can be modified without excessive cost outlays. For example, changes have been made to the shape of some wrenches and other tools to accommodate women's smaller hands. Telephone companies have changed the mounting position for ladders on trucks used by outside repair employees to make those ladders easier for women to reach, and those companies have bought lightweight ladders that are easier to carry. Also, special clothing and shoes have been developed so that females can have the proper protective equipment.

While women have surmounted many of the barriers that previously limited their entry into male-dominated positions, problems still arise, especially at the departmental level. One common supervisory consideration when a woman takes a job traditionally held by a man is the reaction of male co-workers. Some men may resent and even openly criticize her.[23] The supervisor should be

**FIGURE 4.4 Two women who changed the world**

**"We hold these truths to be self-evident . . . that all men are created equal"**

—Thomas Jefferson (Preamble to the U.S. Constitution 2.1)

**Meet Rosie the Riveter**

J. Howard Miller/Corbis

Betty Hunter remembers her first job interview. It was the 1940s, and women were needed to fill jobs left vacant by men who had gone to war. But despite the demand for workers, management was reluctant to put an inexperienced woman on the factory floor. Millions of other women like Hunter worked in World War II defense industries and support services.

During World War II, Ford Motor Company's Richmond, California, factory was converted from automotive to tank production to support the war effort. Prior to 1940, only three women had worked at the plant—a daytime telephone operator and two typists. But as an increasing number of men headed off to war, Ford's managers quickly learned that women made excellent industrial workers. In certain tasks, they even concluded that women were superior to men. Betty Hunter, like thousands of other women, became known as Rosie the Riveter. According to Tom Butt, president of the Rosie the Riveter Historic Trust, "It was the first time in American history that women and minorities worked side by side with men for almost comparable wages." During the closing months of the war, Ford hired an increasing number of people of color and women as other workers who had migrated to California to work in wartime industries headed home.

It is no coincidence that Ford Motor Company was again named one of *Working Mother* magazine's *100 Best Companies for Working Mothers in 2008.*[1]

**Meet Rosa Parks**

Bettmann/Corbis

Rosa Parks, a grown woman of 42, refused to give up her seat on a bus in Montgomery, Alabama. She defied what was known as the Jim Crow laws—"white-only perquisites"—which limited blacks to segregated restrooms and drinking fountains (if any were available), entrance into stores through the rear door only, and seats in the back of the bus.

By refusing to move, Parks committed a deliberate act of civil disobedience. What would have happened if she had moved to the back of the bus as commanded? We will never know, but the inescapable truth is that Parks's actions let it be known that change was needed for America to "walk the talk." If the talk says that "all men (people) are created equal and have inalienable rights," then it was time to translate the talk into action.

Rosa Parks died in October 2005. President George W. Bush and members of Congress laid wreaths at her bier as it rested in the U.S. Capitol. Her legacy lives on today.[2]

*"Freedom is never voluntarily given by the oppressor; it must be demanded by the oppressed."*

—Martin Luther King Jr.

*Sources:* (1) "American Women I Have Always Understood, Advertisement," *Working Mother* (November 2003), p. 1–1. The Rosie the Riveter WWII Home Front National Historic Park commemorates and celebrates women's contributions to the war effort. Visit the Rosie the Riveter Historic Trust, a nonprofit organization in Richmond, California and http://www.RosieTheRiveter.org. Also go to www.workingmother.com and click on "Best Companies" to see their programs to help women to be the best they can be. (2) See Kiva Albin, "Rosa Parks: The Woman Who Changed a Nation" (1996 Interview); *Quiet Strength* (Grand Rapids, MI: Zondervan, 1994); and http://www.grandtimes.com/rosa.html. Parks's book is not to be confused with Tony Dungy's *Quiet Strength: The Principles, Practices, and Priorities of a Winning Life.* In November 1956, the U.S. Supreme Court ruled that segregation on public transport was unconstitutional.

prepared to deal with such attitudes to enable the woman to perform her job satisfactorily. The supervisor first should inform the men about the starting employment date of the woman so that her presence does not come as a surprise. Then, the supervisor should make it clear to the men that disciplinary action will be taken if this woman, or any female employee in the future, is ignored or subjected to abuse or harassment. The supervisor also should make it clear that any woman taking a previously all-male job will be afforded a realistic opportunity to succeed based on her ability to perform the job.

James Shaffer/PhotoEdit

*When women assume physically demanding jobs, some equipment and procedural changes may be needed.*

## BALANCING WORK–LIFE ISSUES

While less than one-fifth of Americans currently live in a "traditional" family composed of a married couple and their children,[24] the well-being of family is still critically important. In reality, whether one is a greeter at Wal-Mart, a Google CEO, or a waitress at Happy Burger, the issue is still the same—how to balance work–life issues. Meet Tanya, our hypothetical waitress mom.

> *Tanya is in my Wednesday night church group. She would like to attend Sunday services, but she has to work. A single parent with two children ages 8 and 14, Tanya is fighting to provide the basic needs for her family. She goes to work Tuesday through Friday at 5:30 A.M.—before her kids are off to school—and comes home at 2:30 P.M. She also works every Friday night from 4:30 P.M. to 10:00 P.M. and Sunday mornings from 5:30 A.M. to 3:00 P.M. The wages are low, but the tips are good. Of course, her employer does not provide medical or dental insurance, so she and the kids often don't go to the doctor when they are feeling sick. When 8-year-old Brittany ran a high fever last week, Tanya took her to Matthew 25—a free clinic where the waiting lines are long and you are exposed to additional germs in the waiting room. She rationalizes that it is better than nothing. Yet there is a stigma attached to the clinic.*
>
> *Tanya was thinking about going to the community college, but she doesn't have the time or the money. The issue for Tanya is not equal pay for equal work or discrimination in the workplace but one of being overwhelmed by the demands of job and family. As I looked over at Tanya during the service, I noticed that she often yawned and looked tired. I wondered what I could do to help the low-income, no-longer-married waitress mom.*

Tanya is among 72 percent of women who place work–life balance as the most important aspect of job satisfaction. By contrast, surveyed men placed that priority last and, according to an analysis of 4,000 interviews of executives done by Harvard Business School professor Boris Groysberg and his associate Robin Abrahams, male professionals still view work–life balance as a women's issue.[25] Look around any organization and see how many people face similar concerns. The problems that Tanya faces must be addressed if she is to be "the best employee she can be." Supervisors must be diligent and observant and aware of the life challenges that employees bring to the workplace. While not a member of a "protected class" of employees, Tanya and others like her need special accommodations, such as the flex time and time-off pools discussed in Chapter 3, so they can be productive employees. To that end, many large organizations and some smaller ones have developed a family-friendly culture that incorporates these benefits in order to facilitate work–life balance.

## SEXUAL-HARASSMENT AND SEXUAL-STEREOTYPING ISSUES

A growing number of civil rights and court cases in the United States have addressed the problems of sexual harassment. Sexual harassment usually means a female employee is subjected to sexual language, touching, or sexual advances by a male employee, a male supervisor, or a male customer. If a female employee resists or protests such behavior by a male supervisor, for example, she may fear retribution when the supervisor is considering pay raises or promotions. It is important to note that a female supervisor or a female employee can be charged with the sexual harassment of a male employee and that harassment can also occur when both parties are of the same sex.[26] However, sexual harassment of women by men has been the focus of most cases heard by federal agencies and the courts.

**Sexual harassment**
Unwelcome sexual advances, requests, or conduct when submission to such conduct is tied to the individual's continuing employment or advancement, unreasonably interferes with job performance, or creates a hostile work environment

Guidelines issued by the EEOC, which enforces the federal Civil Rights Act, define **sexual harassment** as sexual advances, requests for sexual favors, and other verbal or physical conduct of a sexual nature when

- submission to such conduct is explicitly or implicitly made a condition of an individual's employment;
- submission to or rejection of such conduct by an individual is used as the basis for employment decisions affecting that person; or
- such conduct has the purpose or effect of unreasonably interfering with an individual's work performance or creating an intimidating, hostile, or offensive working environment.[27]

Many firms have developed sexual harassment policy statements. Figure 4.5 is an example of such a statement by a printing company that defines harassment even beyond gender terms. This statement informs employees what to do if they encounter what they consider to be harassment.

Court decisions have generally held that an employer is liable if the sexual harassment of employees is condoned or overlooked or fails to lead to corrective actions by management. Reprimand and discipline of offending employees and supervisors are recommended courses of action.[28]

Supervisors should avoid and strongly discourage sexual language, innuendos, and behavior that is inappropriate in the work environment. Supervisors who use their positions improperly in this regard are engaging in conduct that is unacceptable and could cause their own dismissals.

In Chapter 9, we stress that "the best leaders have employees who would follow them anywhere." How would you feel if your highly compensated CEO is alleged to be romantically involved with a colleague? Consider the following situation involving past HP leader Mark Hurd:

**FIGURE 4.5 Illustration of a no-harassment policy statement**

**NO-HARASSMENT POLICY**

This company does not and will not tolerate harassment of our employees. The term ***harassment*** includes, but is not limited to, slurs, jokes, and other verbal, graphic, or physical conduct relating to an individual's race, color, sex, religion, national origin, citizenship, age, or handicap. Harassment also includes sexual advances; requests for sexual favors; unwelcome or offensive touching; and other verbal, graphic, or physical conduct of a sexual nature.

**VIOLATION OF THIS POLICY WILL SUBJECT AN EMPLOYEE TO DISCIPLINARY ACTION, UP TO AND INCLUDING IMMEDIATE DISCHARGE.**

If you feel you are being harassed in any way by another employee or by a customer or vendor, you should make your feelings known to your supervisor immediately. The matter will be thoroughly investigated, and, where appropriate, disciplinary action will be taken. If you do not feel you can discuss the matter with your supervisor, or if you are dissatisfied with the way your complaint has been handled, please contact the human resources director or the company president. Your complaint will be kept as confidential as possible, and you will not be penalized in any way for reporting such conduct. Please do not assume that the company is aware of your problem. It is your responsibility to bring your complaints and concerns to our attention so that we can help resolve them.



*Hewlett-Packard Co. ousted its CEO for allegedly falsifying documents to conceal a relationship with a former contractor and help her get paid for work she didn't do. . . . The Board of Directors said it learned about the relationship several weeks ago, when the woman, who did marketing work for HP, sent a letter accusing Hurd, 53, and the company of sexual harassment. An investigation found that Hurd falsified expense reports and other financial documents to conceal the relationship. The company said it found that its sexual harassment policy wasn't violated but that its standards of business conduct were.*[29]

Unfortunately, one study found that 37 percent of workers have had an office romance and another 11 percent of men and 4 percent of women would like to have an office romance if given the opportunity.[30]

Consensual workplace dating does not in and of itself constitute sexual harassment, but there may be harassment if the employee feels coerced to engage in or continue a relationship. Other employees who lose out on a promotion or pay raise that goes to the more favored person may also have discrimination claims against the organization. Worse yet, the organization may lose the faith and trust of its various stakeholders when the indiscretion becomes public knowledge.[31]

Because it is virtually impossible to monitor everything that happens in the workplace, many firms have required their managers, supervisors, and employees to attend training programs or seminars designed to prevent and address sexual harassment and inappropriate conduct. These programs are typically developed and presented by human resources staff or by outside training consultants. Information and discussions focus on prohibited types of conduct, how employees can deal with offensive comments and behavior, and remedies.[32] These programs also may cover certain aspects of sexual stereotyping that can be problematic.

**Gender stereotyping** involves the use of demeaning language, judgments, or behavior based on a person's gender. For example, a marketing department supervisor may suggest that men are more bull-headed and less open to creative

**Gender stereotyping**
Use of demeaning language, judgments, or behavior based on a person's gender

suggestions than women, or a factory floor supervisor may imply that women are more emotional, less rational, and less reliable than men. Many gender-specific assertions are inaccurate; for example, one large firm examined the absenteeism records of its male and female employees. This firm found no significant difference in absentee rates between the two genders, and it found that its female employees with children had a lower absentee rate than single men. Along with perpetuating inaccuracies, gender stereotyping can reduce employee motivation, perpetuate discrimination, and lead to perceived harassment.[33] Therefore, the supervisor should not make supervisory decisions based on sexual stereotypes, and the supervisor should discourage employees from stereotyping in their workplace interactions.

To avoid gender implications, many job titles have been changed. For example, the job title fireman is now firefighter, a mailman is now a letter carrier, and a stewardess is now a flight attendant.

## TRAINING AND DEVELOPMENT OPPORTUNITIES

Women employees should be offered equal access to training and development activities, and those employees with potential should be encouraged to develop their skills. This is especially important with regard to upgrading women to supervisory and other managerial positions.

Despite the entry of women into supervisory and lower-level management positions, upward mobility for women in organizations has been slow. White males still hold the majority of upper- and senior-level management positions. An Alliance for Board Diversity survey found that corporate boardrooms are still dominated by Caucasian men, in over 73 percent of the nation's top 100 companies.[34] As mentioned in Chapter 1, the barrier to the upward progression of women and minorities is called the glass ceiling. Firms that seriously try to bring more women and minorities into higher levels of management usually do so because their top management has strongly committed to diversity and inclusion initiatives within strategic business plans, but at the same time, women themselves are breaking through the glass ceiling by orchestrating their own personal strategic plans with SMART goals, targeted networking, and clearly defined action steps.[35]

In order to empower women, many firms find that well-conceived and well-implemented mentoring programs are essential. Mentoring efforts usually involve having both male and female senior-level managers serve as mentors or advisers for women and minority supervisors who have been identified as having the potential to hold higher management positions. The combined influence and participation of men and women as mentors is critical to a successful mentoring effort, since the percentage of senior-level women available as mentors is so small to begin with and women typically have more demands on their discretionary time. Mentors provide assistance in various ways, including feedback on job performance; career counseling; and networking with other mentors, advisees, and others to make them better known to people who can influence promotion and career decisions.[36]

## PREGNANCY AND FAMILY CARE

The Pregnancy Discrimination Act (PDA) of 1978, which amended the 1964 Civil Rights Act, requires that pregnancy be treated no differently from illnesses or health disabilities if an employer has medical benefits or a disability plan. Additionally, many states have laws that require certain pregnancy accommodations for employed women. In response, most employers have policies that allow a pregnant employee to work as long as she and her physician certify that it is appropriate. These policies also grant the pregnant employee a leave of absence until she can return to work. To prevent the abuse of pregnancy leaves or other types of disability leaves, many employers require a physician's statement to verify a continuing disability.

While supervisors must see to it that pregnant employees are treated in a nondiscriminatory manner, they are not required to give them easier job assignments, however they need to make mandated accommodations as requested (and with medical documentation where appropriate) such as allowing bottled water at a work station, providing breaks from standing or extra restroom breaks, or not assigning work on ladders near the end of pregnancy.[37] A more difficult problem for the supervisor is a pregnant employee's uncertainty about returning to work after her pregnancy leave is over. This affects supervisors in scheduling work and anticipating staffing needs. Supervisors may have to hire part-time or temporary help, schedule overtime work, or take other temporary actions until the employee definitely decides whether and when she will return to work. This is not unduly burdensome if a supervisor plans well in advance to accommodate the employee's temporary absence.

In Chapter 11, we briefly discuss the Family and Medical Leave Act (FMLA). The FMLA requires that an eligible employee (male or female) must be granted up to a total of 12 workweeks of unpaid leave during any 12-month period for the birth and care of the newborn child or placement with the employee of a child for adoption or foster care; to care for an immediate family member (spouse, child, or parent) with a serious health condition; or to take medical leave when the employee is unable to work because of a serious health condition. Healthcare coverage must be continued during this period, and the employee must be returned to his or her former position or a comparable position upon return to work.[38]

One of the well-recognized major problems that accompanied the growth of women in the labor force has been the conflict between the job demands placed on women and their family responsibilities. Women with children often must cope with demanding responsibilities at home, which are not always shared equally by their husbands.

Moreover, many women head single-parent households in which they are the primary provider. Because of concerns like these, many employers have adopted flexible policies concerning work schedules, leaves, and other arrangements to help employees, especially women, meet their obligations.[39] The FMLA also requires employers to grant unpaid leave to cover certain types of family-care situations, such as caring for a seriously ill child, spouse, or parent.

The conflict and tension between family and job responsibilities is one that employers and supervisors will have to address for many years to come. Supervisors should become familiar with their firm's policies regarding family and childcare assistance, and, whenever possible, they should try to solve those conflicts that interfere with employees' capacities to carry out their job responsibilities.

*Mother dropping off child at daycare center.*

Picture Partners / Alamy

## EQUITABLE COMPENSATION

Statistically, the pay received by women employees in the U.S. workforce generally has been below that of men. According to the U.S. Bureau of Labor Statistics, as of 2013 the weekly earnings of women working full-time were 80 percent of men working full-time.[40] This statistical disparity exists even though the Equal Pay Act of 1963 requires that men and women performing equal work must receive equal pay. For example, a female bookkeeper and a male bookkeeper in the same firm who have approximately the same seniority and performance levels must be paid equally. Although equal pay has not always been interpreted to mean "exactly the same," a firm would probably be in violation of the Equal Pay Act if it paid the female bookkeeper $1 an hour less than her male counterpart.

Despite the laws, disparities still exist.[41] A more complex reason for the disparity in the pay of men and women has been the issue of comparable worth. **Comparable worth** is a concept that jobs should draw approximately the same pay when they require similar skills and abilities. The issue arises when jobs that are distinctly different but require similar levels of skills and abilities have different pay scales, especially if one job is predominantly held by men and the other by women. For example, compare the job of medical technologist, which is held predominantly by women, with that of electrician, which is held mainly by men. Both jobs require licensing or certification, but medical technologists typically have more formal education. Now assume that the pay scales for medical technologists in a hospital are about one-third lower than those for electricians working in the same hospital. A comparison of these dissimilar jobs might suggest that unequal pay is being given for jobs of comparable worth.

**Comparable worth**
Concept that jobs should be paid at the same level when they require similar skills or abilities

A probable major cause for the difference in such pay scales is the labor market in the area. If unionized electricians are paid $28 per hour by other employers, the hospital would have to set its pay scale at that level to compete for electricians. Similarly, if the going rate for nonunionized medical technologists is $18 per hour, the hospital is likely to pay its medical technologists this rate. Also, the difference in pay may be attributable to numerous factors, including the supply or shortages of women in certain jobs. In the example cited, the job of electrician is held predominantly by men because in the past, few women sought or were permitted to become electricians. Only by providing training and entry opportunities for qualified women to become electricians will the disparity in pay be eliminated. Likewise, men with the appropriate interests and abilities could be encouraged to become medical technologists.

It is important for supervisors to understand the issue of comparable worth because it may become a major issue. It is even more important for supervisors to identify and support qualified women to train and develop for higher-paying jobs that have been held predominantly by men. They should be willing to encourage, select, and assist these women as they progress into higher-paying positions of greater skill and responsibility.

**4 Identify and discuss the legal and other considerations of supervising employees with physical and mental disabilities.**

## Supervising Employees with Disabilities

For decades, many organizations have made special efforts to provide employment opportunities for people with physical and mental disabilities. Many of these efforts were made voluntarily and from the conviction that it was the proper thing to do. However, as a result of a number of laws and government regulations, beginning with the Rehabilitation Act of 1973, people with disabilities were identified as a group that was to receive special consideration in employment and other organizational areas. The 1973 law used the term *handicapped* to define individuals with physical or mental impairments, but the preferred usage today is "individuals with disabilities." This law requires certain employers doing business with the federal government and federal agencies to develop affirmative-action programs and to reasonably accommodate the employment of such persons.

In 1990, the Americans with Disabilities Act (ADA) was passed.[42] It is the most significant legislation dealing with legal protection for a group since the Civil Rights Act of 1964. The ADA applies to employers with 15 or more employees and identifies coverage for people with disabilities. See Figure 4.6 for one company's ADA policy. The ADA requires employers to provide access to public spaces for people with disabilities and to make necessary alterations to public accommodations and commercial facilities for accessibility by people with disabilities.

The interpretation and application of the ADA has been the subject of a number of major court decisions. In one of its decisions, the U.S. Supreme Court took a somewhat restrictive view of what qualifies as a disability under the ADA. Generally, the court said the ADA does not protect from employment discrimination people with physical impairments such as poor eyesight or high blood pressure who can function normally when they wear glasses or take medication.[43] Nevertheless, supervisors should be familiar with major ADA provisions and, more important, ADA's implications for those supervising employees with disabilities.

**FIGURE 4.6 One company's ADA policy**

We are firmly committed to providing every employee and every applicant an equal opportunity to succeed in the workplace and during the application process. The company is committed to removing the barriers and obstacles that inhibit employees and applicants from performing to the best of their abilities, and giving them the opportunity to enjoy equal benefits and employment privileges.

It is our policy to provide reasonable accommodations to any qualified applicant or employee with a disability requesting such accommodation to complete the job application process or to perform the essential functions of his or her position. Reasonable accommodation may include, but is not limited to, making facilities accessible, restructuring jobs, modifying schedules, reassigning to a vacant position, acquiring or modifying equipment, or providing interpreters.

The Americans with Disabilities Act (ADA) defines a qualified individual with a disability as a person qualified to perform the essential functions of a position, with or without accommodation, who

- has a physical or mental impairment that substantially limits one or more of the person's major life activities;
- has a record of such an impairment; or
- is regarded as having such an impairment.

The company has developed, in cooperation with the Center for Independent Living, a Reasonable Accommodation Process to help management and employees handle reasonable accommodation issues. Additional information on this process can be obtained by contacting your human resources representative or the Center for Independent Living.

## WHO IS A QUALIFIED DISABLED INDIVIDUAL?

**Qualified disabled individual** Defined by the Americans with Disabilities Act (ADA) as someone with a disability who can perform the essential components of a job with or without reasonable accommodation

To be protected under the ADA employment provisions, an individual with a disability must be qualified. A **qualified disabled individual** is someone with a disability who can perform the essential components of a job with or without a reasonable accommodation on the part of the employer.[44] This means that a person with a disability must have the skills and other qualifications needed for the job to receive employment protection under the ADA.

The definition of a disabled person is very broad. By some estimates, one in six Americans could be considered disabled under the statute's definitions. The law exempts a number of categories from its definition of disability. However, the definition of disability covers most major diseases, including cancer, epilepsy, diabetes, and HIV/AIDS.[45] The concept of reasonably accommodating individuals with disabilities was established by the Rehabilitation Act of 1973. **Reasonable accommodation** means altering the usual ways of doing things so that an otherwise qualified disabled person can perform the essential duties of a job but without creating an undue hardship for the employer. Undue hardship means an alteration that would require a significant expense or an unreasonable change in activities on the part of the employer to accommodate the disabled person.

**Reasonable accommodation** Altering the usual ways of doing things so that an otherwise qualified disabled person can perform the essential job duties, but without creating an undue hardship for the employer

## COMPLYING WITH THE ADA

To comply with ADA provisions, many employers conduct training programs for supervisors who carry significant responsibility in making the necessary adjustments. In the employment process, for example, an employer cannot require a pre-employment medical examination to screen out applicants, with the exception of a drug test. An employer also cannot make any type of pre-employment inquiries about the nature of an applicant's disability. When discussing job requirements in a pre-employment interview, supervisors must be cautious not to mention the applicant's disability or medical record. However, after job offers have been made, applicants may be given medical examinations to determine whether they can physically perform the job. Most employers have reviewed their applications to ensure that improper questions are not included. Many employers also have revised their job descriptions to include the essential functions of each job.

Reasonable accommodation may take many forms. It typically means making buildings accessible by building ramps, removing such barriers as steps or curbs, and altering restroom facilities. Reasonable accommodation may mean that desks and aisles are altered to allow people in wheelchairs access to job locations. It could include modifying work schedules, acquiring certain equipment or devices, providing readers or interpreters, and other types of adjustments.

In some situations, job duties can be altered to accommodate people with disabilities. The supervisor, in consultation with upper management, as appropriate, should interact with employees to determine the accommodations needed. The courts have generally held that an interactive process is the hallmark of reasonable accommodation. In most cases, in order for the process to begin, an employee must request an accommodation, a change in the workplace environment that directly relates to his or her disability. It is not the responsibility of the employer to speculate about accommodation needs of employees. An employer may provide an accommodation without a request if it is evident that a disability exists, if the disability is affecting workplace performance, or if the disability prohibits a worker from requesting accommodation. If the employer offers accommodation and it is refused, then the employer will have fulfilled the requirements under ADA. It is critically important that the employer document accommodations and offers of accommodation made so that the documentation can be reviewed in the event that questions are raised about compliance.[46]

As an example, in one company an employee who assembled small-component units also was expected to place the completed units in a carton at the end of an assembly process. Several times a day, the full carton had to be carried to the shipping area. For an employee in a wheelchair to perform the subassembly job, the supervisor arranged for a shipping clerk to pick up the completed component units at designated times each day. This supervisor made a reasonable accommodation so that a physically impaired employee could handle the subassembly job. Another supervisor added a flashing warning light to equipment that already contained a warning buzzer so that an employee with a hearing impairment could be employed safely.

## SUPERVISOR AND EMPLOYEE ATTITUDES

The ADA is aimed at changing perceptions as well as actions in the workplace. The law encourages supervisors and employees to recognize the abilities, rather than the disabilities, of co-workers and others. As much as anything else, attitudes play an important role in organizational efforts to accommodate people with disabilities.[47]

It is important that supervisors and employees recognize that the ADA is the law and that they believe it is proper to follow it. Training programs are aimed at allowing open discussion about different disabilities and opportunities to air questions and feelings of discomfort. Employees should be aware that certain words may unintentionally carry negative messages. For example, the ADA uses the term *disability* rather than *handicap* because the former is the preference of most people with disabilities. Some training programs have used simulations in which nondisabled employees are required to experience certain types of mental, hearing, physical, or visual impairments (e.g., sitting in a wheelchair and trying to maneuver through a work area). This type of training helps employees to better understand the difficulties of coping with disabilities.

The type of disability an employee has may affect a supervisor's leadership style. For example, employees who are mentally disabled may require somewhat close and direct supervision. A physically disabled employee who uses a wheelchair and works as a proofreader probably should be supervised with a more general and participative style.

Much research has shown that individuals with disabilities make excellent employees, provided they are placed in jobs where their abilities can be adapted and used appropriately. As in so many other areas, the departmental supervisor is often the primary person to make this happen.

5 **Discuss the considerations of supervising older workers and managing an intergenerational workforce.**

## Supervising Older Workers

There are a number of protected-group categories in addition to racial and ethnic minorities, women, and people with disabilities. A discussion of all the aspects of these categories is beyond the scope of this book. In this section, we highlight some of the supervisory considerations for older employees and employees who have different religious beliefs.

### OLDER EMPLOYEES

Today, workers age 40 or older comprise about half of the nation's workforce. This large segment constitutes another legally protected group. The Age Discrimination in Employment Act (ADEA), as amended, which applies to employers with 20 or more employees, prohibits discrimination in employment for most individuals over age 40.[48] Consequently, mandatory retirement ages, such as age 70, are illegal for most employees. Many workers retire at age 65 or younger, in part because of improved retirement programs and pension plans, including plans that allow early retirement. Some early retirement plans permit employees who have 30 years of service to retire before age 60. However, as life expectancies increase, presently between 4 and 5 years longer now for individuals in their sixties than they were in 1950, people are working longer, often into their seventies. Also, as economic conditions fluctuate, some older workers have been forced to dip into retirement savings and do not have quite enough saved to retire; therefore they must continue working to make ends meet.[49] For varied reasons, many retired individuals decide to seek employment again, both part-time and full-time.

When deciding to hire, promote, or discharge, supervisors should be aware of the legal protections afforded to older workers. For example, selecting a 35-year-old person for a sales position instead of a 55-year-old with more selling experience might result in an age-discrimination lawsuit. Laying off a 50-year-old engineer while keeping a 30-year-old engineer during a reduction in force might be age discrimination, unless the younger engineer has superior abilities.

Supervisory decisions to demote or terminate older employees should be documented with sound, objective performance appraisals. Terminating a 62-year-old clerical worker simply for poor job performance might be discriminatory if the employee's work performance was not objectively measured and compared with that of all employees in the department. Some supervisors complain that greater costs and inefficiencies are incurred when they are required to carry older workers who can no longer do the job. Regardless of whether this complaint is valid, the supervisor must impartially and objectively appraise the performance of all employees before making decisions that adversely affect older workers. As emphasized in Chapter 12, performance appraisal is a significant part of any supervisor's job, but it is especially important when older workers are in the department. While many employees may believe they have been discriminated against because of their age, proving it has been difficult.[50]

Supervisors often express concern about older workers who show declines in physical and mental abilities. While some older people do lose some of their former strengths on the job, they may be able to compensate by using their experience. Even with a decline in physical strength due to age, most firms report that older workers tend to have better quality, safety, and attendance records than do younger employees.[51]

Moreover, it may be possible, within certain limits, for supervisors to make special accommodations for some older employees. Supervisors should not disregard years of dedicated and faithful service. Adjustments in the older employee's workload, scheduling, and the like can be reasonable allowances that others in the work group can understand and accept, particularly those who are themselves advancing in years and who recognize that someday their capabilities might also diminish.

It is common for newly elevated supervisors to supervise employees old enough to be their parents or perhaps older, which defines the proverbial "generation gap." Some older employees will reject the new supervisor and will resist changing their habits and learning new ways. In these situations, the supervisor must open the channels of communication, ask probing questions, avoid putting the older employees on the defensive, listen actively to the older employees' ideas—most older employees have a wealth of experience and information—and involve those employees in the decision-making process. Also, when differences exist in skill sets of younger and older workers, particularly technology skills, the supervisor should provide training and support necessary to help older workers build the skills necessary to remain productive. Supervisors must use common sense and sound supervisory practices with older employees.[52]

*Supervisors often manage employees older than themselves, so they must learn to be sensitive to the "generation gap."*

Older employees who are approaching retirement present another problem that requires sensitivity from supervisors. Some employees who have worked for 30 years or more look forward to retirement as a time to enjoy leisure activities. Others, however, view retirement with anxieties about losing the security of a daily routine, steady income, and established social relationships.

Supervisors should be supportive and understanding as older employees near retirement. These employees should be encouraged to take advantage of preretirement planning activities that may be available in the company or through outside agencies. Some companies allow employees nearing retirement age to attend retirement-related workshops during work hours, without loss of pay. A member of the human resources department or a benefits specialist may spend considerable time with each employee nearing retirement to discuss pensions, insurance, social security, and other financial matters. Supervisors should encourage recent retirees to attend company social functions and to maintain contact with their former supervisors and co-workers wherever possible. Such contacts are valuable aids for those transitioning to retirement.

## Accommodating Different Religious Beliefs

**6 Provide examples of religious accommodation.**

Under the Civil Rights Act, most employers are required to afford nondiscriminatory treatment to employees who hold different religious views. Although EEOC and court decisions have not always clearly defined religious discrimination, two principles have evolved, which are the following:

1. Employers must make reasonable accommodations for employees with differing religious beliefs.
2. An employee may not create a hostile work environment for others by harassing them about what they do or do not believe.[53]

Employers generally may not discriminate in employment practices because of an individual's religious beliefs, and employers are obligated to prevent practices or actions that might constitute a hostile environment for someone based on religion.[54] There are some exclusions from the coverage of the Civil Rights Act; for example, a Methodist Church may require that only members of that faith be employed in their operations.

Relatively speaking, charges of religious discrimination have been limited. Reasonable accommodation in holiday and other work scheduling has been the most recurring area in which employers have had some compliance problems. For example, employees who follow the orthodox Jewish faith consider Saturday, not Sunday, as the day of religious observance. Requiring such employees to work on Saturday would be the same as requiring employees who are members of some fundamentalist Christian sects to work on Sundays. A supervisor might be able to accommodate the religious views of such employees by scheduling their workweeks in ways that consider their religious preferences. Allowing Jewish employees to take holidays on Rosh Hashanah and Yom Kippur, instead of Christmas and Easter, is another example of accommodation, as is recognition of Ramadan for individuals of the Muslim faith.

Supervisors may confront situations in which it is difficult to accommodate all employees' religious preferences and still schedule the work. When this happens, supervisors should discuss the problem with their managers and with the human resources staff to determine whether scheduling alternatives that might accommodate the employees and yet not be too costly or disruptive are available. Labor law attorney Mary-Kathryn Zachary provides a succinct suggestion for supervisors regarding religious accommodation, "If an employer has any doubt that a request for an accommodation is religious in nature, the employer is allowed to make further inquiries of the [requestor]. An employer can not deliberately stay 'in the dark'."[55]

**7 Describe the unique challenges of supervising globally dispersed employees.**

## Managing Employees around the World

Increasing corporate globalization presents unique challenges for supervisors that can incorporate any of the above protected classes of workers employed in *multinational corporations*. A **multinational corporation** establishes locations, manages production, and delivers services in more than one country and most often directs management policies and practices from one home country. The multiplicity of people who interact in these organizations, and the diversity among them, increase the physical and interpersonal boundaries that supervisors must manage. Employees of multinational companies are sometimes assigned to specific countries; others split their time between locations; and some remain in their home country and communicate regularly with their international counterparts. In each of these situations, supervisors must recognize and consider the cultural and legal demands of managing geographically dispersed employees.

**Multinational corporation**
A company that establishes locations, manages production, and delivers services in more than one country and most often directs management policies and practices from one home country

## BUILDING SHARED UNDERSTANDING AND IDENTITY

Professor Rosabeth Moss Kanter contrasts this emerging trend with classic international trade, in which employees at each location remained relatively separate, with occasional contact among foreign counterparts during site visits by the corporate boss. Kanter indicates that in the growing global workplace, differences such as language, work methods and philosophies, cultural identities and practices, and biases about home-country power can pose challenges to supervisors charged with productively integrating their workforce. For example, corporate policies that originated in one country may not fit the cultural practices of acquired counterparts, as was the case in an Indian company that bought out a French company and suspended its corporate no alcohol rule across all locations in order to accommodate workers accustomed to having French wine during workday meals. Similarly, different approaches to technical processes may result in problems across work groups, problems that supervisors like those at Cemex, a building materials corporation, addressed by establishing common terminology and process approaches through a global training program.[56] Gender, age, and social conventions are unique to different cultures, and they all influence how employees interact and approach their work.

Professor Pankaj Ghemawat reinforces these challenges. He asserts that companies should appreciate cultural differences rather than trying to erase them and recognize that firms, their employees, and their customers have deep cultural roots. He claims that 90 percent of people will never leave the country in which they were born, only 2 percent of phone minutes used are international minutes, and 95 percent of the news people get is from their country's news sources. Accordingly, employees in global firms come to work each day with the perspective of their home culture, and not necessarily that of global citizenship. Ghemawat suggests that leaders and managers in these companies should be deliberate in helping employees develop a cosmopolitan attitude by establishing and promoting conceptual frameworks that reflect the appreciation of home-country cultures.[57]

Omron, a Japan-based company, developed the Omron Principles, which the company uses in dialogues across all its levels and locations to build understanding among all employees about its values and expectations.[58] Merck, a global pharmaceutical manufacturer, establishes the value of its workforce's individual differences in its corporate philosophy: "Many backgrounds. Many cultures. Many perspectives. One world. One Merck." It promotes this value to prospective employees in its recruiting literature,[59] setting the stage for mutual respect among colleagues.

## EMPLOYEE PROTECTIONS IN MULTINATIONAL CONTEXTS

Establishing a positive global climate is important; equally important is supervisors' understanding of the intricacies of employment and discrimination laws as they relate to U.S. and foreign employees of multinational companies. In some cases, workers in foreign countries are protected from discrimination by U.S. EEOC laws, whereas in others, workers are subject to the employment laws and practices of the local countries involved. Foreign laws can significantly influence employment and supervision practices, as illustrated by examples provided by the EEOC:

*Isaac is an African American U.S. citizen working in Africa for a U.S. employer as a customer service manager. Isaac alleges race discrimination after he was transferred to a less desirable and less public position. The new position involved a loss of pay and lack of upward career mobility opportunities. The employer admitted that it transferred Isaac because its predominantly white customers did not want to deal directly with non-whites. Customer preference is never a defense to violations of U.S. EEOC law. The transfer violates Title VII.*

*Sarah is a U.S. citizen. She works as an assistant manager for a U.S. employer located in a Middle Eastern country. Sarah applies for the branch manager position. Although Sarah is the most qualified person for the position, the employer informs her that it cannot promote her because that country's laws forbid women from supervising men. Sarah files a charge alleging sex discrimination. The employer would have a "Foreign Laws" defense for its actions if the law does contain that prohibition.*[60]

Supervisors should be aware of their company's obligations under EEOC laws, based on the structure of its operations, so that they can make appropriate decisions and effectively guide employee behavior.[61]

**8 Recognize several pressures faced by supervisors who are members of protected groups.**

## Protected-Group Supervisors

Thus far, we have discussed how the supervision of legally protected employees requires both awareness and sensitivity to various factors. Additional concerns can arise for supervisors who are themselves members of legally protected categories (e.g., minorities and women) and who may experience resistance and resentment in their supervisory positions.

For example, it is common to find a woman manager or supervisor whose subordinates primarily are men. Skepticism about the qualifications of the woman supervisor may be voiced in men's comments, such as, "She didn't deserve the job," or "She got it because she's female." A woman supervisor in such a situation may feel that she has to accomplish more than a male supervisor might be expected to achieve in a similar job. However, the experiences of many women supervisors indicate that once they have proven their competence, most initial skepticism fades.

Another example might be an African American production supervisor in a manufacturing plant who supervises African American employees. Because the supervisor is of the same race as the subordinates, some employees may try to take advantage of the situation, perhaps by taking more extended breaks than allowed. On the other hand, the supervisor may put greater pressure on African American employees to perform and to obey the rules so that no charge of favoritism can be justified.

Similarly, the female supervisor who feels obliged to accomplish more than her male counterparts and who wishes to avoid charges of favoritism toward female subordinates may put greater pressure on women employees. This tendency has led some women employees to say that they would rather work for male supervisors because female supervisors are tougher on them than are men.[62]

Generally, however, it is recognized that supervisors tend to communicate better with subordinates who are of the same race or the same sex. For example, an Asian American supervisor is likely to better understand the culture, speech patterns, and attitudes of Asian American employees.

Problems such as those cited here are not unusual, and they should even be anticipated by supervisors or potential supervisors. It is helpful when such issues are discussed openly in supervisory training and development meetings. In addition, protected-group supervisors, like all other supervisors, must have performance expectations, policies, and decisions that are applied consistently and uniformly to all employees, regardless of race, gender, age, and other such considerations.

## Understanding Reverse Discrimination

**9 Explain the issue of reverse discrimination.**

The reactions of employees who are not members of a legally protected group to hiring and promotion decisions are another challenge for supervisors. These employees may view the promotion of a protected-group employee as reverse discrimination. **Reverse discrimination** may be charged when a more senior or qualified person is denied a job opportunity or promotion because preference has been given to a protected-group individual who may be less qualified or who has less seniority.

**Reverse discrimination**
Preference given to protected-group members in hiring and promotion over more qualified or more experienced workers from nonprotected groups

In a Supreme Court case, the court ruled that the ADEA can't be used by younger workers when employers offer better contract terms to older employees. A General Dynamics unit and the United Auto Workers union agreed to stop providing healthcare coverage to future retirees except those current employees who were at least 50 years old, who would continue to be insured upon retirement. Younger workers sued, claiming they were being discriminated against. Writing for the majority opinion, Justice Souter said that the "notion of younger workers covered by the act bringing lawsuits was never contemplated by the Congress. We see the text, structure, purpose and history of ADEA . . . as showing that the statute does not mean to stop an employer from favoring an older employee over a younger one."[63]

EEO and affirmative-action programs most often impact white male employees. Some white males feel they lack an equal or a fair opportunity to compete for promotions or higher-paying jobs. They interpret the numerical goals of affirmative-action programs as quotas that must be met by hiring and promoting unqualified or less qualified women and minorities.[64]

Supervisors of integrated racial groups and male and female employees may be apprehensive of their situations. For example, supervisors may be reluctant to discipline anyone so as to avoid charges of favoritism or discrimination. Another difficulty is that conflicts and distrust among these various groups may arise and stress interpersonal relationships, thereby impeding the department's performance. Such problems are not easily overcome. Communication between the supervisor and all groups of employees is essential, and the supervisor should try to correct misperceptions about any employee's abilities and qualifications as they occur. Whether reverse discrimination exists is not really important. Rather, what is important is the supervisor's response to the feelings of all groups and individuals in an understanding, fair, and objective manner.

## Supervising Well: The Overriding Consideration

**10 Understand how to best supervise a diverse workforce.**

The issues discussed in this chapter will likely concern supervisors for years to come. Additional legislation and court decisions will specify and clarify other considerations for currently protected groups and, perhaps, for other groups to be identified in the future.

Although the diversity and complexity of the workforce varies, a supervisor can take several steps to reduce the likelihood of litigation and to deal with complaints and charges. The following Supervisory Tips box presents some suggestions for how supervisors can address diversity issues positively and professionally. Supervisors must adapt their ways of managing their departments to meet the considerations afforded legally protected employees. In this effort, supervisors should always recognize that the best way to manage all employees in their departments—protected or not—is to constantly apply the principles of good supervision as presented throughout this book.

## BEING FAIR IN ALL SUPERVISORY ACTIONS AND DECISIONS

Some minority employees are clustered in entry-level or service positions in which they see little potential for advancement. Others find themselves in job situations in which competition for better-paying and more challenging positions is keen. Tensions between majority and minority employees may be particularly noticeable when a minority employee alleges discrimination or unfair treatment in a job assignment, promotional opportunity, or disciplinary matter.

The supervisor must be diligent in his or her fairness. If a protected class employee complains of harassment or discriminatory treatment by a fellow employee, supervisor, or some other person, the supervisor must treat that complaint as a priority. In most cases, the supervisor should listen carefully to the nature of the complaint and report it to a higher-level manager or the human resources

### SUPERVISORY TIPS

#### Suggestions for Managing Diversity

- Incorporate consideration of diversity into all aspects of the organization by finding ways to include all workers' perspectives and skills into day-to-day operations and strategies for performance improvement.[65]
- Make sure that the organization's policy statement on discrimination and harassment is posted in a prominent, visible place in the department or elsewhere.
- Periodically review this policy statement with employees, including procedures to be followed if an employee wishes to report a perceived violation or to lodge a complaint. Assure employees that any such complaint will initially be handled confidentially.
- Discuss diversity issues with employees at departmental meetings. Provide examples of behaviors that are unacceptable and that will not be tolerated, as well as the consequences of violations.
- Whenever an employee alleges discrimination or harassment, investigate the matter thoroughly and identify the appropriate course of action. Seek assistance from higher management or the director of human resources, if needed.
- If a matter cannot be resolved at the supervisory level, expeditiously report the case to the director of human resources or other such person who is designated to handle discrimination complaints at the company or corporate level.
- Do not in any way react negatively or adversely to an employee who has filed a discrimination or harassment charge.
- Always supervise on a scrupulously fair and objective basis and with equitable performance standards. Try to find ways by which all employees have the same or comparable opportunities at work assignments and training and development programs.

department for further consideration and direction. In no way should a supervisor retaliate against the employee who has registered the complaint, even if the supervisor believes the discrimination or harassment allegation is without merit. The law protects a protected class employee's right to challenge management decisions and actions that the employee believes are discriminatory. The supervisor is responsible for making sure that this right is protected. In summary, supervising protected classes of employees requires understanding, sensitivity, and even extra fairness when the supervisor is not a member of that group.

We stated at the outset of this chapter that the management of a diverse workforce is a reality that affects most aspects of organizational operations and impacts a firm's bottom line.[66] Because of their importance, specialized training programs in diversity and inclusion have expanded. In our view, supervision of diversity and inclusion practices should not be viewed as something extra or separate. For all employees, but especially when protected class employees are part of the departmental work group, supervisors should develop *cultural competency*. **Cultural competency** means that the supervisor is scrupulously fair, yet can understand and adapt to a variety of cultural communities. When assigning work, affording training opportunities, conducting performance appraisals, or taking disciplinary actions—in virtually all supervisory actions and decisions—supervisors must make choices on objective and job-related grounds.

**Cultural competency**
The ability to understand and adapt to a variety of cultural communities

Further, organizations are encouraged to focus on **inclusion**, defined well by HP as creating and maintaining "a work environment where everyone has an opportunity to fully participate in creating success and where each person is valued for his or her distinctive skills, experiences and perspectives."[67] Creating an inclusive workplace, however, does not automatically follow putting diversity management practices into place. Effective inclusion begins at the top, with clear expectations, strategies, and accountability coming from leadership, but it is the responsibility of supervisors to recognize that promoting diversity and inclusion and managing a diverse workforce are integral and significant components of their ongoing responsibilities and challenges.[68]

**Inclusion**
Providing opportunities for every worker to fully participate and valuing every worker's skills, experiences and perspectives

## SUMMARY

**1.** **The diverse nature of the U.S. workforce requires supervisors to be prepared to manage a wide variety of people in the workforce who help achieve the firm's organizational goals, overall advantage, and bottom-line results. Diversity management can impact virtually all aspects of a firm's operations and should be viewed by supervisors as both a challenge and an opportunity. The major classifications of protected-group employees are by racial or ethnic origin, sex, age, physical and mental impairment, religion, and military service.**

**Specific legal protections are afforded to protected-group employees. Supervisors must be knowledgeable about these protections and understand that complying with legislation is part of the responsibility of supervising a diverse workforce.**

**All employees should be supervised in a consistent, fair, and objective manner that focuses on their talents, abilities, and potential contributions.**

**2.** **When supervising racial or ethnic minority employees, supervisors should try to reduce the impact of past discrimination. Awareness of cultural factors and recognition of language differences are important aspects of a supervisor's sensitivities to minority employees. Being scrupulously fair in all aspects of supervision and striving to prevent any type of discriminatory treatment toward minorities are essential.**

**3.** **Supervisors must try to ensure that women are provided fair opportunities as they move into a greater variety of career fields and positions. Avoidance of sexual harassment and stereotyping is mandatory. Human resources policies should stress training and development opportunities for women, nondiscriminatory treatment during pregnancy, flexibility in resolving family-care conflicts and problems, and equity in compensation.**

4. The Americans with Disabilities Act (ADA) prohibits employment discrimination against individuals with physical and mental disabilities. The ADA prohibits certain pre-employment inquiries and physical examinations of job applicants. It also requires employers to reasonably accommodate otherwise qualified disabled individuals who can perform the essential components of a job. People with disabilities who are placed in jobs that are consistent with their capabilities and who are given fair opportunities to perform by their supervisors typically become excellent employees.

5. The Age Discrimination in Employment Act prohibits discrimination against most employees older than 40 years. When making decisions concerning older employees, supervisors should appraise their qualifications and performance objectively. Supervisors should try to adjust to the reduced abilities of some older workers, if possible and, when appropriate, provide opportunities for older workers to learn new skills, particularly technology skills. Also, supervisors should help employees who are nearing retirement to prepare for it.

6. The principle of reasonable accommodation also should apply when supervising employees of different religious beliefs. Reasonable adjustments in work scheduling should be afforded individuals with certain religious requirements.

7. The growing number of multinational corporations presents unique management challenges. Differences in language, work methods, cultural identities, power, and legal systems and standards must be addressed, both in the employee's home country and corporate headquarters. Supervisors should engage employees in building shared understanding of these differences, help employees appreciate the differences, and involve them in establishing a shared identity within the company community. Having a clear understanding of how EEOC laws apply outside the United States is crucial to effective supervision multinational companies.

8. The supervisor who is a member of a protected group may encounter pressures from both protected-group and non-protected-group employees. These pressures typically involve questions about qualifications and fair treatment. The supervisor should act so that all employees are provided uniform and consistent or equal treatment and performance expectations.

9. Supervisors should be sensitive to the feelings of some employees—most often white males—about the issue of reverse discrimination. Employees may accuse the company of reverse discrimination if a protected-group person is hired or promoted over a more experienced or more qualified member of a nonprotected group.

10. No matter how future legislation and court decisions affect the issues related to protected groups, the best way to manage will always be to apply the principles of good supervision to all employees. In particular, supervisors should develop, model, and encourage cultural competency and inclusion practices in order for the organization and the workforce to benefit from all workers' skills and perspectives.

## KEY TERMS

Comparable worth (p. 134)
Cultural competency (p. 145)
Gender stereotyping (p. 131)
Inclusion (p. 145)
Multinational corporation (p. 140)
Protected-group employees (p. 120)
Qualified disabled individual (p. 136)
Reasonable accommodation (p. 136)
Reverse discrimination (p. 143)
Sexual harassment (p. 130)

## WHAT HAVE YOU LEARNED?

1. Why has management of a diverse workforce become both a reality and a business necessity for many firms? Some people view diversity management primarily as being politically correct. Do you agree or disagree with this type of assessment? Why?
2. Who are classified as protected-group employees? Discuss whether protected group means the same as a special group of employees, especially in view of affirmative-action requirements that may be present in a firm.
3. A recent survey indicates that nearly half of the 76 million U.S. baby boomers are experiencing some degree of hearing loss. During a recent performance appraisal meeting, an employee in the call center explained that the reason for his less than satisfactory performance rating was due to his hearing loss. Is that a legitimate excuse? Why or why not? What accommodation might be needed?

4. Give examples of harassment that you have experienced, observed, or heard about, and describe what should have been done to address such issues.
5. Discuss how women are affected by pregnancy and family-care situations and employer policies. What legal requirements are imposed, and not imposed, for employers in these areas?
6. How has the ADA expanded legal protections for individuals with disabilities? Discuss:
   a. The ADA's definition of a disabled person;
   b. What is meant by "reasonable accommodation" for someone with a disability to perform the essential functions of a job?
   c. Why will these areas be difficult for supervisors to comply with in certain job situations?
7. How does the concept of reasonable accommodation apply to older workers and to employees of different religious persuasions? Are there limits to reasonable accommodation? Discuss.
8. Imagine that a project director position becomes available in the company in which you are currently working as a project manager. The position is in India, and you currently work in Atlanta. You are very well qualified for the position, and it seems like a great opportunity for you to see the world. What questions about the company, its structure, its global workforce, and your new role should you ask before you take up the job?
9. Is it important for an organization to go beyond compliance with federal discrimination laws to create policies and practices that promote diversity and inclusion? Why or why not? What would be the benefits and challenges of creating and implementing such policies and practices?

## EXPERIENTIAL EXERCISES FOR SELF-ASSESSMENT

### EXPERIENTIAL EXERCISE FOR SELF-ASSESSMENT 4.1: Cultivating Cultural Sensitivity

Adapted with permission from University of Arkansas for Medical Sciences Diversity at UAMS Website, "Test Your Cultural Sensitivity," http://www.uams.edu/diversity/test.asp

Cultural sensitivity is something we all like to think we have. It is clearly tied to empathy—the capacity to put ourselves into another person's shoes and see the world from his viewpoint. Cultural sensitivity is an essential quality for peaceful and harmonious living in a society that admits, within the law, many different ways of thinking and behaving. Low cultural sensitivity is associated with authoritarian personalities and also with narrow and limited experience of the world. While it is easy to detect low cultural sensitivity in others, it is not so easy to pin it down in ourselves. This questionnaire, however, if answered honestly and accurately, will give you some pointers.

#### Instructions

1. Read each statement or question below and select the answer that best describes your thoughts and behaviors.
2. On a sheet of paper or Excel spreadsheet numbered 1–28, enter your answers to each question.
3. Using the Scoring Key below the questions, write the number of points you scored for each response.
4. Total your points to find your Cultural Sensitivity score.
5. Using your total, identify your level of Cultural Sensitivity by reading the description of each score range listed in the "Score Analysis" section below.
6. Consider how you can incorporate the suggestions from the analysis section into your own life.

#### Cultural Sensitivity Statements/Questions

1. When a friend does something you very much disapprove of, do you
   a. Break off the friendship
   b. Tell him how you feel, but keep in touch
   c. Tell yourself it is none of your business, and behave toward him as you always did.
2. Is it hard for you to forgive someone who has seriously hurt you?
   a. Yes
   b. No
   c. It is not hard to forgive him, but you don't forget.
3. Do you think that
   a. Censorship is vitally necessary to preserve moral standards?
   b. A small degree of censorship may be necessary (to protect children, for instance)?
   c. All censorship is wrong?
4. Are most of your friends people
   a. Very much like you?
   b. Very different from you and from each other?
   c. Like you in some important respects, but different in others?
5. You are trying to work and concentrate, but the noise of children playing outside distracts you. Would you
   a. Feel glad that they are having a good time
   b. Feel furious with them
   c. Feel annoyed, but acknowledge to yourself that kids do make noise

6. If you were traveling abroad and found that conditions were much less hygienic than you are used to, would you
   a. Adapt quite easily
   b. Laugh at your own discomfort
   c. Think what a filthy country it is
7. Which virtue do you think is most important?
   a. Kindness
   b. Honesty
   c. Obedience
8. Do you discuss critically one friend with others?
   a. Often
   b. Rarely
   c. Sometimes
9. If someone you dislike had something good happen to them, would you
   a. Feel angry and envious
   b. Wish it had been you, but not really mind
   c. Think "Good for him/her!"
10. When you have a strong belief, do you
   a. Try very hard to make others see things the same way as you
   b. Put forward your point of view, but stop short of argument or persuasion
   c. Keep it to yourself unless directly asked.
11. A friend is suffering from depression. Everything in his life seems to be fine, but he complains to you that he always feels depressed. Would you
   a. Listen sympathetically
   b. Tell him to pull himself together
   c. Take him out to cheer him up
12. Would you employ someone who has had a severe nervous breakdown?
   a. No
   b. Yes, provided there was medical evidence of complete recovery
   c. Yes, if he was suitable in other ways for the work
13. When you meet someone who disagrees with your views, do you
   a. Argue and lose your temper
   b. Enjoy a good argument and keep your cool
   c. Avoid argument
14. Do you ever read a periodical that supports political views very different from yours?
   a. Never
   b. Sometimes, if you come across it
   c. Yes, you make a special effort to read it
15. Which statement do you most agree with?
   a. If crime were more severely punished, there would be less of it
   b. A better society would reduce the need for crime
   c. I wish I knew the answer to the problem of crime
16. Do you think
   a. That some rules are necessary for social living, but the fewer the better
   b. That people must have rules because they need to be controlled
   c. That rules are tyrannical
17. If you are a religious believer, do you think
   a. That your religion is the only right one
   b. That all religions have something to offer their believers
   c. That nonbelievers are wicked people
18. If you are not a religious believer, do you think
   a. That only stupid people are religious
   b. That religion is a dangerous and evil force
   c. That religion seems to do good for some people
19. Do you react to the elderly with
   a. Patience and good humor
   b. Annoyance
   c. Sometimes a, sometimes b
20. Do you think the women's rights movement is
   a. Run by a bunch of aggressive and insecure people
   b. An important social movement
   c. A joke
21. Would you marry someone of a different race?
   a. Yes
   b. No
   c. Not without thinking carefully about the various problems involved.
22. If a brother or friend told you that he was a homosexual, would you
   a. Send him to a psychiatrist
   b. Feel shocked and accept him
   c. Feel shocked and reject him
23. When young people question authority, do you
   a. Feel uneasy
   b. Think that it is a good thing
   c. Feel angry
24. Which statement do you agree with
   a. Marriage is a bad institution
   b. Marriage is sacred and must be upheld
   c. Marriage is often difficult, but seems to meet the needs of many people
25. Do you think you are right in matters of belief rather than fact
   a. Always
   b. Often
   c. Rarely
26. If you stay in a household that is run differently from yours in matters of tidiness and regularity of meals, do you
   a. Fit in quite happily
   b. Feel constantly irritated by the chaos or the rigid orderliness of the place
   c. Find it fairly easy for a while, but not for too long

27. Do other people's personal habits annoy you
    a. Often
    b. Not at all
    c. Only if they are extreme
28. Which statement do you most agree with?
    a. We should not judge other people's actions, because no one can ever fully understand the motives of another.
    b. People are responsible for their actions and have to take the consequences.
    c. Even if it is tough on some people, actions have to be judged.

### Scoring Key

| Question # | Score for each answer choice | | |
|---|---|---|---|
| | A | B | C |
| 1 | 4 | 2 | 0 |
| 2 | 4 | 0 | 2 |
| 3 | 4 | 0 | 4 |
| 4 | 4 | 0 | 2 |
| 5 | 0 | 4 | 2 |
| 6 | 0 | 0 | 4 |
| 7 | 0 | 2 | 4 |
| 8 | 4 | 0 | 2 |
| 9 | 4 | 2 | 0 |
| 10 | 4 | 2 | 0 |
| 11 | 0 | 4 | 2 |
| 12 | 4 | 2 | 0 |
| 13 | 4 | 0 | 2 |
| 14 | 4 | 2 | 0 |
| 15 | 4 | 2 | 0 |
| 16 | 0 | 4 | 4 |
| 17 | 2 | 0 | 4 |
| 18 | 4 | 4 | 0 |
| 19 | 0 | 4 | 2 |
| 20 | 2 | 0 | 4 |
| 21 | 0 | 4 | 2 |
| 22 | 2 | 0 | 4 |
| 23 | 2 | 0 | 4 |
| 24 | 4 | 0 | 2 |
| 25 | 4 | 0 | 2 |
| 26 | 0 | 4 | 2 |
| 27 | 4 | 0 | 2 |
| 28 | 0 | 4 | 2 |

### Score Analysis

**Below 30:** If your score lies in this range, you are a particularly culture-sensitive person. You are exceedingly aware of others' problems and difficulties and you have a natural capacity for accepting then even when they offend you. You likely will be a preferred friend and colleague. You may find that other people take advantage of this sympathetic nature. Even then, you do not get very cross with them. However, it is important for you to be assertive in maintaining boundaries so that you do not get taken advantage of.

**31–60:** You are a culturally sensitive person, and people will recognize you as one. If your score is above 50, however, you are probably sensitive and broad-minded in a limited number of areas. Actually it is easy to be culturally sensitive if one does not hold very firm beliefs about anything. Look through the questions again and note where you picked up high rather than low scores. Were these questions in which personal comfort was directly concerned, or in which convictions or very strong ideological beliefs were touched upon?

**61–90:** You are not as culturally sensitive as many people, and if your score is higher than 80 you have a high level of insensitivity, which could be detrimental to work relationships and friendships. It could also mean that little things trouble you far more than they should and that you may waste emotional energy on what is really rather insignificant. A wider range of experiences in environments that are different from yours and genuine, authentic experiences with people from different cultures who hold different values and perspectives will help you become more culturally sensitive.

**Over 90:** This high score indicates that you have a very low level of cultural sensitivity. It is likely that you easily take offense to situations or people who are different from you, and it is difficult for you to accept the opinions or values of others. It would be very helpful for you to learn ways to build cultural sensitivity.

### For More Information and Further Study

Links to additional resources for building cultural sensitivity can be found in the Chapter Experiential Exercises for Self-Assessment section of the companion website for this textbook.

## EXPERIENTIAL EXERCISE FOR SELF-ASSESSMENT 4.2: Attitudes toward People with Disabilities and the Americans with Disabilities Act (ADA)

Below are a series of statements that relate to attitudes toward disabled people and the Americans with Disabilities Act (ADA). Mark each statement according to how much you agree or disagree with it, using the following scale:

Strongly Agree (SA) Agree (A)

Disagree (D) Strongly Disagree (SD)

_________ 1. Individuals with severe disabilities cannot compete for jobs that require demanding physical and mental capabilities.

_________ 2. Under the ADA, an employer can expect just as much from a disabled person as from anyone else.

_________ 3. People with disabilities are usually more conscientious and reliable at work than other employees.

_________ 4. Most people with severe disabilities expect others to show them sympathy and to give them extra help to hold a job.

_________ 5. Employers will find that the ADA is impossible to comply with in many situations without extraordinary costs and efforts.

_________ 6. The ADA will benefit attorneys far more than it will help people with disabilities.

_________ 7. Compliance with the ADA will cause considerable resentment toward people with disabilities.

_________ 8. The ADA is morally and ethically appropriate and helps qualified disabled individuals become more self-sufficient.

_________ 9. People with disabilities are usually more cheerful and enthusiastic on the job than other employees.

_________ 10. Reasonable accommodation under the ADA really means that people with disabilities receive preferential treatment.

After completing the survey, answer the following questions:

1. Why would awareness of attitudes toward people with disabilities and the ADA be important to supervisors?
2. Compare your responses to those of others. What common views do you have? What areas of difference? Discuss the basis for your differences of opinion.
3. If you were (are) a supervisor, how would you deal with negative attitudes toward people with disabilities and/or the ADA that might be held by other employees in a workgroup that includes a disabled person?
4. Write a 100-word paper describing what you learned from this self-assessment.

# PERSONAL SKILL BUILDING

## PERSONAL SKILL BUILDER 4-1: The Supervisor and Protected Groups

1. Look around, and what do you see? Is anyone different from you? How so?
2. From the information in this chapter, develop a list of the requirements and considerations that you believe are essential for effective supervision of protected-group employees.
3. Identify two practicing supervisors who would be willing to be interviewed. One should be a person who is nonprotected (such as a white male under 40 years of age); and the other one should be a member of a protected class (such as a person described in this chapter as a protected-class member). Ask each supervisor to identify what they believe to be the five most important requirements (or tips) for good supervision of protected-group employees within their departments.
4. Compare the supervisors' lists with your list. To what degree were the practicing supervisors' lists similar or different? If there are differences, what do you feel would be the most likely explanation?

## PERSONAL SKILL BUILDER 4-2: Test Your Knowledge and Practice Your Skills

1.

INTERNET ACTIVITY

You will confront many of the following situations. In reality, you will have a human resources professional or legal counsel to help guide your decision; however, for the skills application, you are the final arbiter. After reading each situation, use Internet resources to research the legal implications of the question. Then answer the questions at the end of each situation. You are the manager of the housekeeping services department at Anderson Memorial Hospital's Marion facility. Your department is responsible for 24/7 coverage.

**Situation 1**: Simonette has worked for you for the past seven months. During this time, she has worked slightly less than 1,400 hours. She wants to be off each Friday and Monday for the next few months to care for an ailing cousin who is dying of cancer. She has accumulated 36 hours of PTO (paid time off). She would like to take leave under FLMA. Would you allow her to take leave under the FLMA? Why or why not?

**Situation 2**: Due to the closing of a wing, you have had to reassign several employees from the first shift to the second and third shifts. This reassignment was done per hospital policy and past practice. Emily Pearson told you she would not accept the transfer to second shift (3:30 P.M. to 11:30 P.M.) because she claimed to be protected under the ADA and the organization must accommodate her request. In discussions with you, she brought in a medical slip that indicated that she suffered from colitis (an intestinal disorder), tiredness, nausea, and diarrhea. Emily claimed that due to her medical impairments, you must accommodate her request to remain on the first shift. Would you grant Emily's request for reasonable accommodation. Why or why not?

**Situation 3**: John Daniel "Jackie" Phillips works in the laundry. Jackie recently came out and has affirmed his sexuality by becoming an activist in the local gay rights movement. Jackie worked 2,018 hours during the past 12 months. He has requested that he be granted 12 weeks of leave to care for his companion who is dying of AIDS. Would you allow Jackie to take leave under FMLA? Why or why not?

2. Write a one-page paper listing the decision you made in each of these situations, and conclude with a statement highlighting what you learn from this personal skill builder.

*Source:* Adapted with permission from scenarios developed by Professor Leonard for inclusion in Edwin C. Leonard Jr. and Roy A. Cook, *Human Resource Management: 21st Century Challenges* (Mason, OH: Thomson Custom Publishing, 2005), pp. 190–191; 204–205.

## PERSONAL SKILL BUILDER 4-3: Can She Turn It Around?

INTERNET ACTIVITY

In Chapter 9, we introduce you to the "HP Way." Go to the Hewlett-Packard Web site and look at the company history.

1. Make a list of all the CEOs since 1990 and their terms of office.
2. Their first female CEO was Carly Fiorina. Make a list of her strengths and weaknesses, and explain why you think she was "shown the door."
3. In September 2011, the former CEO of PayPal, Meg Whitman, became HP's fourth CEO in less than seven years. During her tenure, what changes has Whitman made to "right the ship"? Were all of the changes successful? Why did some not turn out as expected?
4. In retrospect, was Meg Whitman the right person for the job? Why? Why not?

## PERSONAL SKILL BUILDER 4-4: Technology Tools—Do an Assessment of Assistive/Adaptive Technology

INTERNET ACTIVITY

As technology continues to evolve, new products are created every day that can help individuals with disabilities overcome workplace challenges. At some point in your career you may be asked to identify an appropriate accommodation for someone with a disability. In this exercise you will investigate just a few *adaptive/assistive technologies*, software applications designed to help a person compensate for an area of disability or impairment and have the same access to information as individuals who are not disabled or impaired.

Examples of adaptive/assistive software include speech recognition software, which allows a user to speak into a microphone and have their speech translated to text. Screen readers and magnifiers brighten, enlarge, or re-color text or read text aloud. Literacy programs assist writers by automatically checking grammar and spelling and suggesting improvements. Many features of current computer operating systems also have built-in assistive features such as speech-recognition and output, magnification, icon upgrades, grammar and spelling correction and prediction, color contrast adjustments, and alternate controls for peripherals like mouse and keyboard.[69] Assistive/adaptive technology also includes hardware, such as keyboards and monitors, Braille devices, headsets, magnifiers, scanners, and tactile enhancers, which create dimensional impressions of images so that a person with a visual impairment can feel the image's contours.[70]

Technologies such as these can help individuals who have visual impairment, motor skill impairment, learning disabilities, and fatigue, along with other disabilities, maintain their productivity.

1. Use your Internet Browser to locate and view the websites for at least two of the following adaptive/assistive technology software applications (or others you find during your search):
   - Screen Readers and Magnifiers
     - JAWS—Job Access with Speech
     - Window-Eyes
     - ZoomText
   - Speech Recognition
     - Dragon NaturallySpeaking
     - Kurzweil3000
     - SpeakQ
   - Literacy programs
     - WhiteSmoke
     - Read&Write
     - WordQ

2. View any demonstration videos or features on the website. If you wish, you may download a trial version of the software and try it yourself.
3. As you review each website, ask yourself the following questions:
   - How might this product help a person with a disability overcome workplace challenges?
   - Is this tool affordable for a small or medium-sized organization?
   - What are the major benefits of this product?
   - What might be some challenges to using this product?
4. Create an "Adaptive/Assistive Technology Software Review." List each of the products you reviewed, along with a link to each website and a 100-word summary of the products' potential for use, cost, benefits and challenges.

## TEAM SKILL BUILDING

### TEAM SKILL BUILDER 4-1: You Make the Call

ROLE PLAY

You Make the Call!

Refer to this chapter's You Make the Call! Your instructor will divide the class into groups of three or more. Choose one to play each of the roles: Adams, Johnson, and the company's legal advisor. Role-players should adapt the attitudes and values associated with their roles.

1. How should Adams and Johnson have responded to Minardi's closing statements?
2. Why is a problem of this nature extremely sensitive for all individuals involved?
3. What should the managers do in case Minardi pursues legal action against the company?
4. Using the Internet, ascertain the impact that the Americans with Disabilities Act (ADA) can have on business organizations. Explain how your findings may have held management to do things differently in this You Make the Call.
5. How might the company use this experience as a learning opportunity?
6. Why should supervisors and managers be knowledgeable about employment laws like ADA?
7. Working as a group, write a one-page paper describing what you learned from this skill builder.

### TEAM SKILL BUILDER 4-2: Working with People Who Make Your Life Difficult: "Bean the Bigot"

ROLE PLAY

This is another in the series of skills applications that introduces one of those people who make life difficult for others. For the purpose of this team skill-building application, place students into groups of three to eight. One student should be selected to play the role of Barbara Jones.

1. Read the following statement from Barbara Jones, one of the employees at Sanders Supermarkets Store 17:

   *I work part-time at one of the Sanders Supermarkets Stores, and I work with people of different races, religions, and ethnic backgrounds. Most of the associates and I get along very well with one another—except for a college freshman named Bryce Bean. Bean is very close-minded and dislikes anyone different from him. Even though he is relatively new to the organization—he started in August just before school started—he often makes degrading comments toward co-workers who aren't like him.*

   *Bean loves to make fun at the expense of others. Yesterday, his target was Charlie, one of the produce clerks. Charlie does look like he is pregnant, and his shirt is always sticking out in the back. In the break room, Bean grabbed Charlie's right arm and in a loud voice said, "Do you know what this is for? It's for pushing yourself away from the food table, you fatty." Several people laughed, but most of us did not find it funny.*

   *Last week, Bean's target was Angie. Without warning, he pointed his finger at her and shouted, "U-G-L-Y. You ain't got no alibi. You're the ugliest thing I've ever seen. How can you stand to look at yourself in the mirror in the morning?" Again, several associates chortled. Angie didn't respond to Bean's baiting, but she stormed out of the break room.*

   *The situation is no different when Bean is around an African American associate like me. He is known to have racial prejudices and will often spout comments like, "You wouldn't have a job if it wasn't for that affirmative-action crap," and he is known to make racist jokes.*

   *I know we'll encounter difficult people in life, but Bean is like a boxer. He constantly jabs at vulnerable individuals, hoping to bring them down. I'm really frustrated by his lack of sensitivity. I'd complain to management, but I don't think it would make a difference. I'm just a part-time employee, and I need this job. What should I do to make this work environment a bit more enjoyable?*

2.  Using the Internet, find at least three sources of information for working with people like "Bean the Bigot." Carefully review each site for suggestions on how to deal with bigotry and prejudice.

INTERNET ACTIVITY

3. Based on your findings, what suggestions would the group make to Barbara Jones on how to deal with Bean?
4. Have any of you ever worked with someone like Bean? If so, share with the group how you dealt with the situation. After the completion of this team skill-building application, do you now know of some better ways to cope with the situation?
5. Write a one-page paper explaining how this exercise increased your working knowledge of coping with the behaviors of this type of difficult person.

## SUPERVISION IN ACTION

SUPERVISION IN ACTION

The video for this chapter can be accessed from the student companion website at www.cengagebrain.com. (Search by authors' names or book title to find the accompanying resources.)

## ENDNOTES

Suggestions: The following references provide current information on the diversity of the U.S. workforce. (1) The Equal Employment Opportunity Commission (http://www.eeoc.gov). The EEOC issues a yearly workforce report. (2) *The Monthly Labor Review*. See Mitra Toossi, "A New Look at Long-Term Labor Force Projections to 2050" (November 2006). (3) "Selected Cross-Cultural Factors in Human Resource Management," *SHRM Research Quarterly* (Third Quarter 2008) (www.shrm.org).

October is National Disability Employment Awareness Month. See the U.S. Department of Labor's Office of Disability Employment Policy (ODEP) website (www.dol.gov/odep) for profiles on organizations that have successfully implemented strategies to hire, support, and empower employees with disabilities.

1. Glenn Llopis, "Diversity Management Is Outdated and Demands a New Approach," *Forbes* (January 7, 2013), http://www.forbes.com/sites/glennllopis/2013/01/07/diversity-management-is-outdated-and-demands-a-new-approach/
2. Adapted from Genevieve Capowksi, "Managing Diversity," *Management Review* (June 1996), pp. 13–19. For a comprehensive overview, see Rebecca Hastings, "SHRM 2007 State of Workplace Diversity Report: A Call to Action," *SHRM Workplace Diversity Library* (February 2008), p. 37; "The Conference Board Report: Middle Management: A Roadblock to Diversity Initiatives," *SuperVision* (July 2007), pp. 8–10. See also Jim Giulliano, "Diversity Programs: Reap the Benefits while Avoiding Problems," HRMorning.com (April 4, 2008, http://www.hrmorning.com/ diversity) identifies three lessons of avoiding the problems: (1) Make sure everyone gets a fair shake. (2) Commit to treating all people equally and with respect. (3) Make certain that no one group is provided with an advantage or penalized with a disadvantage. His suggestions sound like common sense, but then why do we still have problems?
3. Quote adapted from information contained in Susan J. Wells, "The Majority Minority," *HR Magazine* (September 2008), pp. 38–43. See also Parmy Olson's description of Duolingo, a free software application used by many workers to quickly and effectively learn a new language in order to perform effectively on the job in "Crowdsourcing Capitalists," *Forbes* (February 2014), pp. 40–42.
4. Dori Meinert, "Tailoring Diversity Practices Produces Different Results," *HR Magazine* (July 2013), p. 16. See also Ann Pomeroy, "A Passion for Diversity," *HR Magazine* (March 2008), pp. 48–49; Bill Leonard, "Measuring Diversity's Value Remains Elusive Task," *SHRM Home* (January 18, 2006); or Pamela Babcock, " Diversity—Down to the Letter," *HR Magazine* (June 2004), pp. 90–94.
5. Data gathered from http://www.eeoc.gov/eeoc/statistics/enforcement/charges.cfm(accessed March 2014).
6. As reported by Melanie Trotman, "Charges of Bias at Work Increase," *The Wall Street Journal* (January 12, 2011), p. A3. See also Allen Smith, "Retaliation Becomes Most Common Charge," *HR Magazine* (March, 2011), p. 16. Retaliation is a contentious issue, particularly when third parties are involved. The Supreme Court found cause for action regarding retaliation toward the fiancé of a woman who alleged sex discrimination against their mutual employer in "Supreme Court Considers Whether Claim for Third-Party Retaliation May Be Brought under Title VII," *SHRM* (December 8, 2010), http://www.shrm.org/LegalIssues/FederalResources/Pages/SupremeCourt-ThirdParty Retaliation.aspx. During the hearing, Chief Justice John Roberts questioned the relationship criteria of Title VII, asking, "How is the employer supposed to tell if someone is close enough or not?" See also Joanne Deschenaux, "Title VII Protects Third Parties from Retaliation," *HR Magazine* (March 2011), p. 16.
7. In 2007, employers paid out over $200 million in EEOC settlements. We would note that in 2004 Morgan Stanley alone paid $54 million to settle class-action claims that they underpaid and failed to promote women.

The volume of discrimination lawsuits in the workplace has been such that the EEOC has been trying different approaches to expedite and settle cases. See Jess Bravin, "Top Court Backs Workers Who Report Discrimination," *The Wall Street Journal* (May 28, 2008), p. A3.

8. For in-depth information, see "Federal Laws Prohibiting Job Discrimination: Questions and Answers," go to www.eeoc.gov/facts/qanda.html.
9. Diane Cadrain, "Sexual Equity in the Workplace," *HR Magazine* ( September 2008), pp. 44–50. Cadrain's suggestion of reviewing, revising, and strengthening organizational policies has been modeled by many companies. According to the Human Rights Campaign website, http://www.hrc.org/laws-and-legislation/federal-legislation/employment-non-discrimination-act, as of April 2013, 88 percent of Fortune 500 companies have strengthened their nondiscrimination policies by including sexual orientation, and 57 percent have incorporated gender identity into their policies. Several individual states have also passed laws prohibiting workplace discrimination based on sexual orientation (21 states) and gender identity (17 states).

   Similar adaptations were made to the 2011 National Football League (NFL) collective bargaining agreement. They added sexual orientation to its No Discrimination clause. NFL Players Association representative George Atallah justified the change with his assertion that the NFL has a tremendous social impact: "With something like discrimination of any kind, we just want to make sure we are a symbol for good," reported by Mike Jaccarino, "NFL Formally Prohibits Discrimination against Players Based on Sexual Orientation," *New York Daily News Football* (September 27, 2011), http://www.nydailynews.com/sports/football/2011/09/27.
10. There are many types of workplace aggression, but bullying is often subtle and not obvious to others. Comparing the consequences of bullying, other forms of workplace aggression, and sexual harassment, the researchers found that those who experience bullying are less satisfied with their jobs and more likely to quit than those who are sexually harassed. Regardless of who is doing what to whom, supervisors must respond and deal appropriately with these behaviors. See Sandy M. Hershcovis and Julian Barling, "Comparing Victim Attributions and Outcomes for Workplace Aggression and Sexual Harassment," *Journal of Applied Psychology 95* (5) (September 2010) pp. 847–888. See also Shana Lebowitz, "What's Behind a Rise in Workplace Bullying," *USA Today* (October 8, 2013), http://www.usatoday.com/story/news/health/2013/10/08/hostile-workplace-less-productive/2945833/, "Bullying Worse Than Sexual Harassment," *HR Magazine* (May 2008), p. 28, and *The No Asshole Rule: Building a Civilized Workplace and Surviving One That Isn't* (New York: Warner Business Books, 2007),

    The Society for Human Resource Management (SHRM)'s Roy Mauer describes steps workplaces and states have taken to reduce bullying through policies and legislation in "Workplace Bullying Laws on the Horizon," Society for Human Resource Management (July 16, 2013), https://www.shrm.org/hrdisciplines/safetysecurity/articles/pages/workplace-bullying-laws.aspx. The Workplace Bullying Institute suggests a three-step action plan employees can take if they are being bullied, http://www.workplacebullying.org/individuals/solutions/wbi-action-plan/. See also Carolyn Hirschman, "Giving Voice to Employee Concerns," *HR Magazine* (August 2008), pp. 50–53, who says that organizations should encourage employees to speak out on workplace issues by building channels to report concerns and working toward solutions.
11. Maria Hudson, Gina Netto, Filip Soesenko, Mike Noon, Phiomena de Lima, Alison Gilchrist, and Nicolina Kamenou-Aigbekaen facilitated the 2013 JRF survey, results of which are available from the JRF website, http://www.jrf.org.uk/publications/poverty-ethnicity-workplace-cultures. See also Dori Meinert, "Closing the Latino Education Gap," *HR Magazine* (May 2013), pp. 29–33.
12. "SHRM Diversity Study Reveals Long-Term Optimism," as reported in Special Advertising Section, *Fortune* (July 1999), pp. S17–S18. Also see Susan J. Wells, "Tips for Recruiting and Retaining Hispanic Workers," *HR Magazine* (September 2008), pp. 40–41.
13. Claire Andre, Manuel Velasquez, and Tim Mazur chronicle the progress of civil rights in "Affirmative Action: Twenty-five Years of Controversy," *Santa Clara University Ethics Home Page* (July 28, 2011), http://www.scu.edu/ethics/publications/iie/v5n2/affirmative.html.
14. The U.S. Court of Appeals for the District of Columbia Circuit delivered a ruling of hostile work environment on behalf of a Fannie Mae auditor, who was the only individual in his department of 12 who did not receive a raise or promotion; he received repeated negative reviews from his supervisor; an executive from the company stated, "For a young black man smart like you, we are happy to have your expertise; I think I'm already paying you a lot of money" and the supervisor referred to him, yelling, as the n-word. The employee was then forced to continue working with the supervisor for three months, even after filing a complaint with the company's ethics department. See Ginger McCauley, "Single 'N-Word' Use Could Create Hostile Environment," *HR Magazine* (July 2013), p. 58.
15. In fiscal year 2013, the EEOC received 33,068 charges of racial discrimination. Of this total, 24,175 were found to have no reasonable cause. See http://eeoc.gov/eeoc/statistics/enforcement/race.cfm for a detailed breakdown of discrimination charges. In September 2013, a complaint filed by the U.S. Department of Labor about racial discrimination in Bank of America's hiring practices resulted in the company being ordered to pay $2.18 million to over 1,100 African American job applicants. This was after the company settled with hundreds of African American Merrill Lynch & Company brokers for similar racial bias. Go to "Bank of America to Pay $2.18 Million in Racial Discrimination Case," *Huffington Post* (September 23, 2013), http://www.huffingtonpost.com/2013/09/23/bank-of-america-racial-discrimination_n_3977581.html.
16. In a 2013 Pew Research Center study, 1,504 respondents indicated that discrimination against Muslim Americans is higher than that of gays and lesbians, Hispanic Americans, African Americans, and women. The study, *After Boston, Little Change in Views of Islam and Violence* (May 7, 2013) is available at http://www.people-press.org/2013/05/07/after-boston-little-change-in-views-of-islam-and-violence/ On September 11, 2001, terrorists flew two hijacked planes into the twin towers of the World Trade Center, killing 2,752 people. Another hijacked plane struck the Pentagon, killing 18, and 40 others died when their plane crashed into a field near Shanksville, Pennsylvania. See Marco Grob's photo and video collection honoring the heroes of September 11 in, "Beyond 9/11: Portraits of Resilience," *Time* (April 8, 2014), http://content.time.com/time/beyond911/#. See also Tom Brokaw, "How We Remember," *Parade* (September 11, 2011), pp. 5–7.
17. Robert J. Grossman, "Muslim Employees: Valuable but Vulnerable," *HR Magazine* (March 2011) pp. 22–27.
18. amille Ryan, *Language Use in the United States:* 2011 (August 2013, Washington, DC: U.S. Census Bureau), http://www.census.gov/prod/2013pubs/acs-22.pdf. See also Patricia Graves, "Why Do Some Employees React Negatively When Co-workers Speak Languages Other Than English at Work," *HR Magazine* (May 2011), p. 21; Miriam Jordan, "Employers Provide Language Aid," *The Wall Street Journal* (November 8, 2005), p. B13.

19. See Howard Stutz, "Workplace ESL Solutions Teaches English to Employees, Instills Confidence On The Job," *Las Vegas Review-Journal* (June 24, 2013), http://www.reviewjournal.com/business/workplace-esl-solutions-teaches-english-employees-instills-confidence-job; Sandra L. Campbell, "How to Help Your Employees to Learn English," *Houston Chronicle* (2014), http://smallbusiness.chron.com/employees-learn-english-14805.html; Jill Coody Smits, "The Long View: Growing A Culture of Generosity Can Pay Dividends Down the Line," *Spirit* (March 2014), p. 64; and Kathryn Tyler, "I Say Potato, You Say Potato," *HR Magazine* (January 2004), pp. 85–87.
20. Reported by Susan Well, "Say Hola to the Majority Minority," *HR Magazine* (September 2008), pp. 38–43.
21. See Dana Wilkie, "English-Only Rules at Work: Discrimination or Business Necessity?" Society for Human Resource Management (November 14, 2013), https://www.shrm.org/hrdisciplines/Diversity/Articles/Pages/English-Only-EEOC.aspx; Allen Smith, "Draft English-Only Policies Carefully," Society for Human Resource Management (April 3, 2014), http://www.shrm.org/LegalIssues/FederalResources/Pages/English-only-policies.aspx; Miriam Jordan, "Testing 'English Only' Rules," *The Wall Street Journal* (November 8, 2005), pp. B1, B13.
22. "SHRM Diversity Study." See Ben Waber, "Gender Bias by the Numbers," *Bloomberg Businessweek* (February 3–9, 2014), pp. 8–9; Duane Morris, "Boys Just Want to Have Fun: Shut Down Boys' Clubs," *HR Magazine* (March 2013), pp. 73–75; Also see Carol Hymowitz, "Too Many Women Fall for Stereotypes of Selves, Study Says," *The Wall Street Journal* (October 24, 2005), p. B1.
23. One such example of sexual harassment is chronicled by Wayne L. Helsby, "Gender-Based Hostile Work Environment Claim Upheld," *HR Magazine* (November 2013), p. 64: The 6th U.S. Circuit Court of Appeals found Consumers Energy Co. liable under Title VII of the Civil Rights Act of 1964 because its employees created a gender-based hostile work environment. A female part-time mail clerk transferred to the transmission department and began working on electric lines, the only female in the department. Her co-workers called her names, isolated and ostracized her, and refused to allow her to use a restroom, insisting she, "pee like a guy." Then, she was subjected to an unexpected evaluation and made mistakes that led to her being dismissed from the department's training program. Although she complained about the harassment to her supervisor, a union representative, and an HR representative, her claims were not investigated. When she filed suit against the company, the first trial was decided in the favor of the company. She filed for a second trial and was awarded compensatory and punitive damages of $680,000 by a jury, who ruled the company was liable for damages because it did not respond to complaints or take action to stop the employees' harassment.
24. Emily Babay, "Census: Big Decline in Nuclear Family," *Philadelphia Inquirer* (November 26, 2013), http://www.philly.com/philly/news/How_American_families_are_changing.html.
25. Job satisfaction statistic cited by Aja Carmichael, "Professional Women Drawn to Corporations That Are Family-Friendly," *South Bend, Indiana Tribune* (July 5, 2003), p. 2L. The Harvard study is summarized in Boris Groysberg and Robin Abrahams, "Manage Your Work, Manage Your Life: Zero In on What Really Matters," *Harvard Business Review* (March 2014), pp. 2–10. Also see Ben Waber, "Gender Bias by the Numbers," *Bloomberg Businessweek* (February 3–9, 2014), pp. 8–9, which reinforces the finding "Research Finds 'Motherhood Penalty' in Employment Process," *SHRM Home* (August 12, 2005). The two sides of the "Women can have it all," work and family coin have been argued incessantly over the past few years. Read the arguments of the two thought leaders, Facebook COO Sheryl Sandburg, in her book *Lean In: Women, Work and the Will to Lead* (New York, NY: Knopf Doubleday, 2013) and a past director of policy planning at the State Department, Anne Marie-Slaughter, "Why Women Still Can't Have It All," *The Atlantic* (June 13, 2012), http://www.theatlantic.com/magazine/archive/2012/07/why-women-still-cant-have-it-all/309020/.

    The SHRM 2013 Employee Benefits Survey Report found that 20 percent of large corporations (500 or more employees) offer full-time telecommuting and 45 percent allow telecommuting on an as-needed basis. Access the SHRM survey at http://www.shrm.org/research/surveyfindings/articles/pages/2013employee-benefits.aspx. Increasingly organizations are offering telecommuting to employees as a way to help deal with high gasoline prices. See Euan Hutchinson, "'People People' Work at Home, Too," *HR Magazine* (September 2008), pp. 60–62.
26. Men constitute a majority of the workforce, but file less than 18 percent of all harassment claims, according to 2013 EEOC statistics (http://www.eeoc.gov/eeoc/statistics/enforcement/sexual_harassment_new.cfm). While men have historically been reluctant to file complaints because they had been considered more difficult to prove, changes in the workplace environment, particularly growth in antiharassment policies, may help protect males and females equally, according to Courtney Rubin, "Sexual Harassment Complaints by Men Surge," *INC* (July 6, 2010), http://www.inc.com/news/articles/2010/07/men%2527s-sexual-harassment-claims-on-the-rise.html.
27. See http://eeoc.gov and in the "Employers" pull-down, under "Discrimination by Type", click on "sex," "sexual harassment," and/or "retaliation" for additional information.
28. See Alexander Hamilton Institute "Employee Need Not Be a Saint to Claim Hostile Work Environment," *Business Management Daily* (November 1, 2010) www.businessmanagementdaily.com. Also see Mary-Kathryn Zachary, "Reputation and Sex Discrimination," *SuperVision* (December 2010), pp. 21–24; Jonathon A. Segal, "I Did It, But . . . Employees May Be as Innocent as They Say, But Still Guilty of Harassment," *HR Magazine* (March 2008), pp. 91–95.

    A hostile work environment for the purposes of an employee's harassment claim is a single event that may include conduct spanning years prior to the filing of a single charge, according to the 7th U.S. Circuit Court of Appeals (*Bright v. Hill's Pet Nutrition Inc.*, 7th Cir., No. 06–3827, December 21, 2007).

    Historically, employers were automatically liable for the harassing and discriminatory actions of their supervisors. However, in the following cases the Supreme Court offered some protection for employers. In *Faragher v. City of Boca Raton* (U.S. Supreme Court, No. 97-282, June 26, 1998) and *Burlington Industries, Inc. v. Ellerth (U.S.* Supreme Court, No. 97-569, June 26, 1998), the Court held that an employer may defend a harassment lawsuit not involving a tangible job detriment, that is, termination or demotion, by showing that it (the employer) exercised a reasonable care to prevent and promptly correct any harassing behavior, and that the employee suing unreasonably failed to take advantage of such preventive or corrective measures. In *Kolstad v. American Dental Association* (U.S. Supreme Court, No. 98-208, June 22, 1999), the Court found that while employers may be charged with punitive damages for international discrimination by supervisors, punitive damages for such unlawful conduct may be avoided if the employer has made "good-faith" efforts to prevent workplace discrimination. Clearly, supervisors must understand the organization's policies and procedures and their responsibilities to prevent workplace harassment. Policies and procedures must be clear and consistently applied. Supervisors must receive periodic training, and any action that might be considered harassment must be dealt with immediately. For additional information on legal issues, go to http://www.law.cornell.edu or http://www.findlaw.com/casecode.

29. Jordon Robertson and Rachel Metz,"HP CEO Mark Hurd Resigns after Sexual-Harassment Probe," www.huffingtonpost.com (August 6, 2010). In a similar situation, "Office Depot Fires Exec in Improper Relationship," the Associated Press reports that "the head of Office Depot Inc.'s international division was fired . . . for having an 'improper relationship' with a co-worker." CEO Neil Austrian explained, "The company has a zero tolerance policy in this regard." Retrieved from www.businessweek.com (September 26, 2011).
30. In a survey of over 5,200 workers, CareerBuilder found that "[n]early 40 percent of workers have flirted with romance on the job," www.theworkbuzz.com/jobs/employment-trends/office-romance (February 10, 2010). See also Jae Yang and Veronica Salazar, "Would You Date a Co-Worker?" *USA Today* (February 14, 2008), p. 1B, reported that 31 percent of men and 29 percent of women would not date a co-worker. Also see Sue Shellenbarger, "Getting Fired for Dating a Co-Worker: Office Romance Comes under Attack," *The Wall Street Journal* (February 19, 2004), p. D1.
31. A case in point—U.S.-based iGate Corporation and its CEO Phaneesh Murthy are embroiled in a collection of lawsuits that were precipitated by the CEO's alleged improper relationship with a subordinate. The first, a U.S. class action lawsuit, was filed against iGate by the company's stockholders when they learned Murthy had been fired for failing to report the relationship in disregard of company policy, which the stockholders alleged was a violation of federal security laws, particularly false and misleading statements and failure to disclose. "Murthy's improper conduct created a risk that he would be terminated from the company, jeopardizing the company's future success," the suit states, as chronicled in *Business Today* on June 18, 2013, http://businesstoday.intoday.in/story/igate-phaneesh-murthy-class-action-suit/1/195964.html. Murthy responded to his termination by bringing suit against the company, citing defamation and wrongful termination of employment, as reported by Anirban Sen in, "Phaneesh Murthy Files Defamation Suit against iGate," LiveMint.com (December 9, 2013), http://www.livemint.com/Companies/JTAM9avBCedHA4SWq7dA3O/Phaneesh-Murthy-files-defamation-suit-against-iGate.html. In response, iGate filed a countersuit aimed at Murthy, on the grounds that his behavior caused the company to suffer "significant financial damage,", as reported by IndiaWest, "iGate Counter Sues Former CEO Phaneesh Murthy for Damages" (March 5, 2014), http://www.indiawest.com/news/17357-igate-counter-sues-former-ceo-phaneesh-murthy-for-damages.html. While the circumstances above are all alleged at this point, it is important to note that they arose due to questionable relationship behavior. In situations like this, it pays to ask the question, "Is this really worth the risk?"
32. Bringing employees together for required training on harassment and discrimination, particularly in companies with multiple shifts or locations, can be a challenge. A variety of Web-based and prerecorded educational programs may meet companies' needs. An example of such a program can be found on the HRTrain website, http://www.hrtrain.com/preview/index.cfm (accessed March 2014). For prevention techniques, see Texas Employment Law, "5 Steps You Must Take to Prevent and Address Sexual Harassment," *Business Management Daily* (January 6, 2014), http://www.businessmanagementdaily.com/37080/5-steps-you-must-take-to-prevent-and-address-sexual-harassment. For suggested topics for supervisor training, see Chris Ceplenski, "Supervisor Training: Preventing Sexual Harassment," HR Daily Advisor (October 1, 2013), http://hrdailyadvisor.blr.com/2013/10/01/supervisor-training-preventing-sexual-harassment/. See also Paula McDonald, Sara Charlesworth, and Cerise Somali, "Below the 'Tip of the Iceberg': Extra-legal Responses to Workplace Sexual Harassment," *Women's Studies International Forum 34* (4) (July/August 2011) p. 278. For guidance on creating a sexual harassment policy and complaint procedure, see the Society for Human Resource Management (SHRM) website, http://www.shrm.org/TemplatesTools/Samples/Policies/Pages/CMS_000554.aspx.
33. For an insightful discussion of how gender stereotyping has decreased over the past 40 years, see Michael Kimmel, "How 'Free to Be' Heralded the Most Successful Revolution of Our—or Any—Era," *Huffington Post* (April 8, 2014), http://www.huffingtonpost.com/michael-kimmel/how-free-to-be-heralded-the-most-successful-revolution_b_5097715.html. See also Shankar Vedantam, "How Stereotypes Can Drive Women to Quit Science," *NPR* (July 12, 2012), http://www.npr.org/2012/07/12/156664337/stereotype-threat-why-women-quit-science-jobs and Rosalind C. Barnett and Caryl Rivers, "For Women, It's Not a Glass Ceiling but a Plugged Pipeline," *Los Angeles Times* (December 26, 2013), http://articles.latimes.com/2013/dec/26/opinion/la-oe-rivers-women-workplace-plugged-pipeline-20131226.
34. See the 2012 Alliance for Board Diversity Census, *Missing Pieces: Women and Minorities on* Fortune *500 Boards* (August 15, 2013), Catalyst, The Prout Group, The Executive Leadership Council, the Hispanic Association on Corporate Responsibility, and Leadership Education for Asian Pacifics, Inc., retrieved from http://theabd.org/2012_ABD%20Missing_Pieces_Final_8_15_13.pdf
35. See Sheryl Sandberg, *Lean In: Women, Work, and the Will to Lead* (New York: Knopf Doubleday, 2013); Michael Kimmel, "How Can We Help Women? By Helping Men," *Huffington Post* (January 17, 2014), http://www.huffingtonpost.com/michael-kimmel/how-can-we-help-women-by-helping-men_b_4611523.html; Dianne Jacobs, "Women in the Pipeline: Next Practice Actions," *Ivey Business Journal* (November/December 2010). Nancy Lockwood, "The Glass Ceiling: Domestic and International Perspectives," *2004 SHRM Research Quarterly* (June 2004). Also see "Glass Ceiling Report Is No Surprise to SHRM," *Mosaics* (April 1995), p. 4; Stephenie Overman, " Mentors Without Borders," *HR Magazine* (March 2004), pp. 83–86.

    Jae Yang and Alejandro Gonzalez, "Glass Ceiling," *USA Today* (April 22, 2008), p. 1B reported responses to the question: "Has the glass ceiling (i.e., limitations that prevent qualified women from being promoted to leadership positions) for women in the workplace shifted in the past ten years? The answers: 'Yes, it is less difficult 55%.' 'Yes, no more limitations 15%' 'Yes, it is more difficult 8%' and 'No, it's the same 22%.'" What do you think?
36. See Peggy Drexler, "Can Women Succeed Without a Mentor?" *Forbes* (March 4, 2014), http://www.forbes.com/sites/peggydrexler/2014/03/04/can-women-succeed-without-a-mentor/. The answer to Drexler's question is a resounding yes. Many women achieve great things without a mentor. However, in a mentor's absence it is helpful for women to build a network of colleagues at a variety of levels in an organization who can attest to their achievements and, rather than just "show them the ropes." promote their value to the higher ranks. See also Joann S. Lublin, "When Women Mentor Too Much," *Wall Street Journal* (October 11, 2013), http://online.wsj.com/news/articles/SB10001424052702303382004579129273775055280, in which Lublin explains the difficulty women have in balancing their own growth with bringing others up through the ranks. For a unique perspective on networking strategies, read Jay Kernis, "Women Create 'Stilleto Networks' to Help Each Other

Achieve Business Success," NBC News Rock Center (May 23, 2013), http://rockcenter.nbcnews.com/_news/2013/05/23/18448664-women-create-stiletto-networks-to-help-each-other-achieve-business-success?lite; See also Nancy D. O'Reilly, "Women Helping Women: How Mentoring Can Help Your Business," *SuperVision* 69, No. 1 (January 2008), pp. 12–13.

37. Several states have mandated accommodations for pregnant workers beyond the scope of ADA and PDA such as those listed in this chapter. At present such laws have been passed in California, Connecticut, Maryland, *Texas, and New York City,* as described by Rita Zeidner in "NYC Employers Must Accommodate Pregnant Employees," *HR Magazine* (March 2014), p. 17.
38. For information on FMLA, go to www.dol.gove/esa/whd/fmla. Students might find T*rierweiler v. Wells Fargo Bank,* 8th Cir., No. 10-1343 (April 2011) of interest.
39. The 2013 SHRM Employee Benefit Survey lists a variety of flexible working benefits offered by companies, based on a sample of 516 HR representatives. The benefits a company offers may include telecommuting (58% of respondent companies offer this benefit), flextime (53%), break arrangements (39%), mealtime flex (37%), compressed workweek (35%), shift flexibility (19%), seasonal scheduling (19%), job sharing (10%), among others. See the SHRM website, www.shrm.org/research/surveyfindings to download the survey and review a comprehensive list of flexible working benefits. See also Working Mother's 2013 100 Best Companies for Working Mothers, http://www.workingmother.com/best-companies/2013-working-mother-100-best-companies, to learn of creative ways organizations can support worker success and work–life balance. See Lisa Armstrong, "Success Redefined," WorkingMother.com (September, 2010) for a discussion of the *career lattice* strategy, a flexible alternative to the traditional career ladder, in which employees have the option to maintain upward momentum in their career journey at a pace that fits their lives and that provides margin for other priorities, like family. Also see James B. Thelen, "An Rx for FMLA Headaches," *HR Magazine* (May 2008), pp. 93–102; Stephanie Armour, "Day Care's New Frontier: Your Baby at Your Desk," *USA Today* (March 31, 2008), pp. 1A, 2A; Sue Shellenbarger, "More Women Pursue Claims of Pregnancy Discrimination," *The Wall Street Journal* (March 27, 2008).
40. Department of Labor, Fact Sheet: Closing the Gender Wage Gap, Equal Pay Tool Kit, http://www.dol.gov/wb/equal-pay/WH-Equal-Pay-fact-sheet.pdf (last visited August 30, 2013). See the Bureau of Labor Statistics "overview of BLS Statistics on Pay and Benefits," http://www.bls.gov/bls/wages.htm; Pamela Coukos, "Myth Busting the Pay Gap," U.S. Department of Labor Website (June 7, 2012), http://social.dol.gov/blog/myth-busting-the-pay-gap/; Orrick, Herrington & Sutcliffe, LLP, *The Pay Gap, the Glass Ceiling, and Pay Bias: Moving Forward 50 Years after the Equal Pay Act* (2013), http://www.jdsupra.com/legalnews/the-pay-gap-the-glass-ceiling-and-pay-94101/.
41. For information on comparable worth, go to http://payequity research.com/worth.htm; or http://womenshistory.about.com. See also, Paul Weatherhead, E. James Brennan, and Ann Bares, "The Pros, Cons and What You Really Need to Know about Comparable Worth," *Workspan* 53, No. 7 (July 2010), pp. 14–16. Wal-Mart, the nation's largest corporate employer, was accused of paying female employees less than men in parallel positions despite seniority and higher performance ratings, along with purportedly awarding fewer store-level management promotions to women than men. These claims were presented to the U.S. Supreme Court as the grounds for a class-action discrimination lawsuit initiated by six women on behalf of 1.5 million women employed by Wal-Mart and Sam's Club between 1998 and the present, as reported by Robert Barnes. See "Justices Take Wal-Mart Bias Case," *The Journal Gazette* (December 7, 2010). Upon review, the Court determined that there was no way for the plaintiffs to show that every woman was a victim of discrimination, as all raise and promotion decisions are made independently by managers at 3,400 Wal-Mart stores. While the Court did not question the act of discrimination itself, the bundling together of all of the employees into a single class "failed the test of commonality required in class actions," as reported by Daniel Fisher, "Supreme Court Dumps Wal-Mart Sex-Discrimination Class Action, *Forbes* (June 20, 2011), www.forbes.com.
42. For a concise guide to compliance with the ADA and interpretations, visit the U.S. Department of Justice Civil Rights Division www.ADA.gov website. For workplace-related guidance, visit the United States Department of Labor Americans with Disabilities Act Disabilities Resources website, http://www.dol.gov/dol/topic/disability/ada.htm.
43. *Employment disability is defined as a physical, mental, or emotional condition lasting six months or more that causes difficulty working at a job or business.* See Allen Smith, "Disabilities Rule Narrowed," *HR Magazine* (May 2011), p. 11; Rebecca Hastings, "Rule Focuses on Workers' Rights," *HR Magazine* (May 2011), p. 11; Susan J. Wells, "Counting on Workers with Disabilities," *HR Magazine* (April 2008), pp. 44–49; Allen Smith, "Supreme Court Dismisses ADA Lawsuit, Agrees to Hear Constitutional Claim," *SHRM Law* (January 14, 2008); "Supreme Court to Review Wal-Mart Policy of Hiring Only the Best," *SHRM Online Workplace Law Focus Area* (January 2, 2008).

    See Chuck Thompson, "Standard Should Not Have Been Applied to Hearing Test," *HR Magazine* (March 2008), p. 88 suggests that "the use of pre-employment tests to screen applicants has many pitfalls under various employment laws. Employers should proceed with great caution in using any broad tests that tend to exclude persons in any protected category and should be sure any test strongly relates to an important job function." See *Bates v. United Parcel Service Inc., 9th Cir,* No. 04-17295 (December 28, 2007).
44. See www.eeoc.gov.facts/ada18.html. Are you eligible for social security disability? Go to www.social.security-disability.org to find out.
45. The ADA Amendments Act, effective in 2009, expands protections for individuals with cancer or other diseases that are in remission. An example of these protections is provided in James E. Hall, Mark T. Kobata, and Marty Denis, "Disabilities Protections Expanded," *Workforce Management* (November 2010), p. 11. For an extensive discussion of protections for individuals with chronic and terminal illness, see the EEOC webpage on Disability Discrimination, Question and Answer Series, http://www.eeoc.gov/laws/types/disability.cfm. See also William F. Banta, *AIDS in the Workplace* (Lanham, MD: Lexington Books, 1993). Complacency," *Business Insurance* (July 23, 2001), pp. 1–14.

    Attorney Tim Bland recommends "employers to educate employees about HIV and the medically recognized means by which it is transmitted; and ensure that all employees adhere to OSHA's bloodborne pathogen regulations." See "Unfounded Fear of HIV Not Compensable," *HR Magazine* (December 2003), p. 118; and *Guess v. Sharp Manufacturing Co. of America,* Tennessee Supreme Court, No. W2002-00818-WC-R3-CV (August 27, 2003).
46. See EEOC Enforcement Guidance: Reasonable Accommodation and Undue Hardship Under the Americans with Disabilities Act, No. 915.002 (October 17, 2002), http://www.eeoc.gov/policy/docs/accommodation.html, as well as Tiffani L. McDonough, "Implementing the Interactive Process under the ADA," *Employment & Labor Relations Law* 12, No. 1 (Fall 2013), pp. 1–6; and Allen Smith, "Reasonable

ADA Accommodation Isn't One-Stop Shopping," *SHRM Home* (March 22, 2006). A disabled employee's awareness of a job's requirements before accepting a position does not override the employee's right to a reasonable job accommodation. See *Smith v. Henderson*, 6th Cir., No 02-6073 (July 15, 2004). Also see *Humphrey v. Memorial Hospitals Association (239 F.3rd 1128 (9th Cir. 2001)*, which reinforces the notion that the reasonable accommodation is an ongoing obligation.

47. Labor and employment attorney Kimberly S. LeBlanc describes attitudes that can lead to noncompliance with ADA requirements in, "Misperception Hinders ADA Compliance in the Workplace," *Insight Into Diversity* (November 2013), p. 18. LeBlanc suggests that "lack of awareness on how to provide accommodations; potential costs associated with such accommodations; and difficulty in assessing a disabled applicant's ability to perform job tasks" can all lead to noncompliance. She suggests that organizations provide firm-wide training on ADA and EEOC laws, specific training for supervisors on how to mitigate negative perceptions, involvement of legal counsel when dealing with accommodation requests, and building partnerships with organizations that serve individuals with disabilities in order to recruit and retain and create an inclusive work environment.
48. Adrienne Fox in "Mixing It Up," *HR Magazine* (May 2011), pp. 22–27, discussed the generations as follows: "Silent Generation or Traditionalists" (born before 1945); "Baby Boomers" (born 1946–1964); "Generation X" (born 1965–1980); Millennials or Gen Y" (born 1981–1995); and "Gen Z or Digital Numbers" (born since 1996). With five very different age groups in the workplace at one time, supervisors need to be familiar with ADEA. Go to www.eeoc.gov/laws/statues/adea.cfm.
49. John Wagonner, "Many Will Need to Work Well Past 65—If They Can," *USA Today* (December 7, 2010), p. A1.
50. See Robert J. Grossman, "Invest in Older Workers," *HR Magazine* (August 2013), pp. 20–25. Examples of age discrimination rulings illustrate the variety of contexts in which this type of discrimination takes place. *Miller v. Raytheon Col*, 5th Cir., No. 11-10586 (May 2, 2013) ruled that a reduction in force was tainted by willful age discrimination, as the company deliberately avoided rehiring a 53-year-old employee. In *Rick L. Roach v. Safeway, Inc.*, U.S. Dist. No. 12-cv-01239-RBJ (D. Col., April 18, 2013), a jury found that while the company claimed they fired a 60-year-old individual for using profanity, because other, younger, employees also used profanity, the decision to fire him was motivated by his age. See also James A. Johnson and John Lopes, "The Intergenerational Workforce, Revisited," *Organizational Development Journal* 26, No. 1 (Spring 2008), pp. 31–36.

    For a discussion on another issue affecting older workers, see Pamela Babcock, "Elder Care at Work: Many Employers Are Making a Business Case for Helping Employees with Sudden, Short-term Elder Care Needs," *HR Magazine* (September 2008), pp. 11–12.
51. According to the U.S. Department of Labor Bureau Statistics, workers over 55 are a third less likely than their younger associates to be injured at work seriously enough to lose work time. However, when they are seriously injured, older workers typically require two weeks to recover, about twice the amount needed by younger workers. See the BLS website for more information, http://stats.bls.gov/opub/ted/2013/ted_20131230.htm.
52. See Michael E. Pepe, "How to Bridge Generation Gaps: Precise Survey Research May Help HR Professionals Create More Understanding among Workers," *HR Magazine* (November 2013), pp. 40–43; "Winning the Generation Game," *The Economist* (September 28, 2013), pp. 59–60; and Kathryn Tyler, "New Kids on the Block: Millennial Employees Are Driving Changes in HR Practices," *HR Magazine* (October 2013), pp 35–40. For two divergent views, see Jeffrey Zaslow, "Baby Boomers, Gen-Xers Clash in Mentoring Environment," *The Wall Street Journal* (June 9, 2003), p. 5C; Also see Nancy R. Lockwood, "Leadership Styles: Generational Differences," *SHRM Research* (December 2004).
53. Judith A. Moldover, "Employers May Bar Religious Affinity Groups," *SHRM Home* (January 13, 2006); *Moranski v. General Motors Corp., 7th Cir., No. 05-1803* (December 29, 2005).
54. See Deb Levine, "Religious Beliefs," *HR Magazine* (July 2008), p. 29; Rebecca R. Hastings, "Continuing Communication Helps Religious Accommodation," *SHRM Diversity* (November 2007). Among cultures, alcohol use is an issue. See Mary-Kathryn Zachary, "Alcohol Use and Work: Part 1," *SuperVision* (April 2011), pp. 21–25; and "Part 2" (May 2011), pp. 21–25.
55. See Mary-Kathryn Zachary, "Religious Accommodation in the 21st Century," *SuperVision 75* (3), pp. 19–22.
56. Rosabeth Moss Kanter provides guidance for leaders in her discussion of the challenges that are emerging as companies expand across borders in "Leadership in a Globalizing World," excerpted from *Handbook of Leadership Theory and Practice: A Harvard Business School Centennial Colloquium*, Nitin Nohria and Rakesh Khurana, eds. (Boston: Harvard Business School Press, 2010), pp. 569–610.
57. Pankaj Ghemawat, professor of global strategy at IESE Business School in Barcelona, encourages companies to help managers and employees develop a perspective that appreciates diversity and distance. He suggests four things companies can do to help employees do so: create conceptual frameworks to illustrate the intricacies of the company's relationships; engage managers in *longer and deeper immersion* in other cultures, rather than sending them abroad for three-day board meetings once a year; frame deliverables within *projects and networks* that cross international borders; and use *assessment tools* to get a read on managers' and employees global SKAs. See "The Cosmopolitan Corporation: *Harvard Business Review* (May 2011) (http://hbr.org/2011/05/the-cosmopolitan-corporation/ar/1). See also Erin Meyer, "Navigating the Cultural Minefield," *Harvard Business Review* (May 2014), pp. 119–123, in which Meyer provides a set of behavioral scales, the "Culture Map", to help individuals navigate diverse management cultures. The behaviors Meyer found to have the greatest variations across cultures include communicating, evaluating, persuading, leading, deciding, trusting, disagreeing, and scheduling. Considering these differences can help workers in multinational cultures effectively build relationships and work well together.
58. Kanter, "Leadership in a Globalizing World."
59. Merck's philosophy was presented in a talent recruiting advertisement in the career opportunities section of *Fortune magazine* (October 18, 2010).
60. Adapted from "Employee Rights When Working for Multinational Employers" published by the U.S. Equal Employment Opportunity Commission (April 28, 2003), http://www.eeoc.gov/facts/multi-employees.html.
61. Attorney Tyler Paetkau discusses the current inconsistencies and confusion employers face when making multinational employment decisions relative to Title VII, ADEA and ADA legislation and exemptions allowed when foreign laws override these statutes. He warns, "As the global economy continues to develop rapidly, more and more courts will grapple with the contours of the so called 'foreign compulsion' defense." He then poses the question, "Does foreign law truly compel the U.S. employer to discriminate against U.S. Citizen, or is the U.S. employer instead using foreign law compulsion

defense as a smokescreen to legitimize discrimination?" See "When Does a Foreign Law Compel a U.S. Employer to Discriminate against U.S. Expatriates?: A Modest Proposal for Reform," *Littler Mendelson, P.C.* (2009), retrieved from LawMemo website,http://www.lawmemo.com/articles/foreignlaw.htm#_ftn51. See also "The Equal Opportunity Responsibilities of Multinational Employers," also published by the U.S. EEOC (April 28, 2003), http://www.eeoc.gov/facts/multi-employers.html for the most current EEOC compliance directives related to employment practices for global companies.

62. See Laura Giuliano, David I. Levine, and Jonathan Leonard, "Manager Race and the Race of New Hires," *Journal of Labor Economics* 27, No. 4 (2006) pp. 589–631; Lizzie Crocker, "Why Women Don't Like Lady Bosses," DailyBeast.com (November 13, 2013), shares finding from a recent Gallup poll that women would rather work for a man than another woman, but the poll suggests that as more women achieve executive roles, this preference will begin to even out. Full results of the Gallup poll, *2013 Gallup Work and Education Survey*, are available at http://www.gallup.com/poll/165791/americans-prefer-male-boss.aspx. Also see Ancella B. Livers and Keith Caver, "Dear White Boss," *Harvard Business Review* (November 2002); and *Leading in Black and White: Working across the Racial Divide in Corporate America* (New York: Wiley, 2002).
63. Robert S. Greenberger, "Justices Limit Use of Age-Bias Laws," *The Wall Street Journal* (February 24, 2005), p. D2. Also see Margaret M. Clark, "Workers Can Sue for Unintentional Age Bias," SHRM Home (March 30, 2005); and *Smith v. City of Jackson,* No. 03-1160 U.S. Supreme Court (2005).
64. See Michael I. Norton and Samuel R. Sommers, "Whites See Racism as a Zero-Sum Game That They Are Now Losing," *Perspectives on Psychological Science* 6, No. 3 (May 2011), pp. 215–218. See also John Blake, "Are Whites Racially Oppressed?" *CNN* (March 4, 2011), http://www.cnn.com/2010/US/12/21/white.persecution/; Mitchell Kapor, Freada Kapor-Klein, and Tae-Shin Kim, "Redefining Bias in the 21st Century," *Huffington Post* (June 29, 2009), http://www.huffingtonpost.com/mitchell-kapor/redefining-bias-in-the-21_b_222302.html; Rutherglen, George A., "The Origins of Arguments over Reverse Discrimination: Lessons from the Civil Rights Act of 1866," *Virginia Public Law and Legal Theory Research Paper No. 2014-14* (February 1, 2014).
65. Glenn Llopis, "Diversity Management Is Outdated and Demands a New Approach," *Forbes* (January 7, 2013), http://www.forbes.com/sites/glennllopis/2013/01/07/diversity-management-is-outdated-and-demands-a-new-approach/.
66. See *Forbes* Global Diversity and Inclusion report, *Fostering Innovation through a Diverse Workforce* (July 12, 2011), http://images.forbes.com/forbesinsights/StudyPDFs/Innovation_Through_Diversity.pdf
67. HP, "The Meaning behind the Words," http://www8.hp.com/us/en/hp-information/about-hp/diversity/meaning.html. See the Society for Human Resources (SHRM) template for creating a diversity and inclusion policy, http://www.shrm.org/templatestools/samples/policies/pages/diversitypolicy.aspx.
68. Douglas R. Conant, nonexecutive chairman of Avon Products and the founder of Kellogg Executive Leadership Institute recommends five strategies that managers and supervisors can use to promote and practice inclusion in "How to Make Diversity and Inclusion Real," *Harvard Business Review* (July 28, 2011), http://blogs.hbr.org/2011/07/how-to-make-diversity-and-incl/. The strategies include (1) confronting the brutal facts if the organization doesn't represent the population it serves; (2) create a discipline plan for advancing diversity and inclusion that includes recruiting, training, and incorporating diversity and inclusion into performance measures; (3) "declare yourself" all leaders should "be the change you want to see" relative to advancing inclusion; (4) educate the organization, especially on "micro-inequities," common behaviors and stereotypes that can undermine inclusion; (5) deploy mentors and support networks for affinity groups that can help workers build skills and advance.
69. Jennifer Taylor Arnold, "Give Employees with Disabilities an Assist," *HR Magazine* (August 2013), pp. 79–82. Also see the web version of the article, which is accompanied by a variety of links related to adaptive/assistive technology, http://www.shrm.org/0813-assistive-technology.
70. Indiana University Information Technology Services Adaptive Technology and Accessibility Centers' Adaptive Hardware at the ATAC list, http://www.indiana.edu/~iuadapts/technology/hardware/

# PART 1 Critical Incidents

The critical incidents below each present a supervisory situation based on real events to be used for educational purposes. The identities of some or all individuals, organizations, industries, and locations, as well as financial and other information may have been disguised to protect individual privacy and proprietary information. In some cases fictional details have been added to improve readability and interest.

Critical Incident 1-1

## THE OPPORTUNITY OF A LIFETIME?

Randy Harber, a 36-year-old construction crew chief, is employed by one of the largest mechanical contractors in the country. His employer operates in 44 states and 14 foreign countries. Randy and his spouse, Eileen, have two children, seven-year-old Kelly and three-year-old Jason. Eileen is a registered nurse and works part time in a family-practice office. Randy began his career in the construction field by entering the apprenticeship program immediately upon completing high school. He served as an officer in the local union and became a crew chief three years ago. His technical skills rank among the best. During the past two years, he has taken evening courses at the local community college to enhance his supervisory skills and to improve his chances of becoming a field superintendent. However, the construction industry has experienced no real growth, and opportunities for advancement are slim. During the past winter, Randy and others suffered reduced work weeks and had their use of the company truck severely restricted.

Randy Harber had been called to meet with Kevin Cook, vice president of field operations, in Cook's office. The following conversation took place:

KEVIN: Randy, you know that our revenues are down about 25 percent from last year.

RANDY: Yes. (Thinking to himself, "Here it comes: I'm going to get laid off.")

KEVIN: We've been trying to expand our base of operations and have bid on contracts all over the world. I think we have the opportunity of a lifetime, and you figure to be one of our key players. The United Methodist Church is collaborating in a joint venture in Liberia to build a hospital on the outskirts of Monrovia, the capital city. They have a medical missionary program there, and this hospital is a $23 million project. The general contractor will be out of Milan, Italy, and we have received the mechanical portion of the contract.

RANDY: That's great! We can use the work.

KEVIN: This project will give us a strategic advantage in the European—African corridor. Top management has talked it over, and we would like for you to be our field superintendent on this project. Not only is this a great opportunity for us, but it will give you invaluable experience. In addition, your salary will almost double. All the people on this project will be our very best. You'll be leaving in three weeks, and we'd expect you to be on-site for 14months. What do you think?

RANDY: Geez, that sounds fascinating. How soon do you need an answer?

KEVIN: Go home, think it over, talk to Eileen, and let's get back together tomorrow afternoon at about 3:00.

## QUESTIONS FOR DISCUSSION

1. Evaluate the offer made to Randy Harber. Do you agree that this is the opportunity of a lifetime? Why or why not?
2. What factors should Harber consider, and how should Harber evaluate his career options?
3. If you were Randy Harber, what would you do and why? (Before you answer these questions, you may want to check some Web sites to get information on the country's history, economy, business and governmental practices, policies, culture, language, and living conditions.)



## GOVERNMENT BRINGS REALITY CLOSE TO HOME

Critical Incident 1-2

As a manager of a fast food franchise, Franklin Hinton was concerned about the media reports he had been listening to about worker demands for wage increases that might soon become an economic reality. Even though Franklin's store was considered to be successful on every financial measure, doubling wages, without a doubt, would create a significant increase on menu prices which would result in financial disaster. Fast food employees in many parts of the country were picketing and getting lots of press to get their hourly wages significantly raised.

If Franklin was faced to raise menu prices to compensate for the increase in employee wages, he wondered how much customers would be willing to pay and whether his competition would follow with similar price increases. Franklin prided himself on hiring high school and college students from the local area and giving them a chance to learn valuable job skills. In recent years he had hired employees with developmental disabilities and some senior citizens who were having a hard time finding work. Some of these workers had stayed with him for years, and some had moved up into supervisory positions. If he was forced to pay more, would it still make sense to hire workers who had no previous experience or those who may take longer to train? His entry-level workers were currently making at least a dollar an hour above the federal minimum wage and any significant increase above that, if menu prices were not raised, would have to be made up through reduced hours or reduction in the number of employees.

More troubling was the thought of being forced to pay a higher minimum wage, which would also have an impact on supervisory salaries. Then there was the potential of increases in health care costs. Although Franklin was sure that his employees trusted him, some of the fast food restaurants in the area had been upset with their employees wanting to join a union. There was also the potential for losing business and getting unwanted negative publicity as many students at the local university seemed to always be willing to join in any type of social or political protest.

Franklin knew that he needed to plan and organize for the future as his current business model provided a comfortable living at a 9 percent profit margin for the owner, but all of that could change. He knew that outside groups would promise his employees more money, better benefits, and better working conditions, even though they often could not deliver on that promise. Franklin needed to plan and organize for the future success of his business and employees.

(This critical incident developed by Roy Cook and Ed Leonard for this edition of *Supervision*.)

## QUESTIONS FOR DISCUSSION

1. What external forces could impact the future of Franklin Hinton's fast food business?
2. Franklin needs a plan for future success. Define planning as it relates to his business.
   How will an effective plan help him and his employees be more effective in providing quality service to customers?
3. Regardless of the situation, employees must understand fully the mission and vision of the company. What do you suggest that Franklin might do to help his employees be the best they can be?
4. In your opinion, if the minimum wage in your state is increased to $10, $12, or $15 an hour, what impact will it have on the fast food industry? Will an increase in the minimum wage have an impact on customer service or quality of product? Discuss.
5. What should Franklin do to prepare for the possibility of a union attempt to organize his employees?
6. If you were Franklin, how would you deal with the uncertainties that could impact the future success of his business and employees?

## FOOD FOR THOUGHT QUESTION

One of the toughest jobs for supervisors is how to handle worker complaints, particularly when it deals with compensation. In Chapter 14, we discuss resolving complaints. After reading the ideas in Chapter 14, what suggestions do you have for Franklin regarding how he might deal with workers' complaints about their challenging jobs and minimal pay?

**Critical Incident 1-3**

# WHAT TO DO WITH A DRUGGIE?

## THE STAGE

As Mike Pearson drove from work to his grandson's tennis match, he contemplated the future. The economy showed no signs of recovery and his company's sales were down about 10 percent. Worse yet, the bottom line was less than 3 percent after taxes, the lowest level in the history of the company, Pearson Construction. His great-granddad had created the company 85 years ago and 18 years ago Mike succeeded his father as CEO. With more than 1,500 employees, he wondered whether he would have to make some personnel changes, and if so, how he would best approach that delicate task. "I'd better hurry or I will miss the start of the match. I'm so glad Billy took up tennis while we were on vacation last summer. He's doing a great job, and it's so good for him to be out on the court."

## ACT ONE

Donald Summer began work as an electrician's apprentice in 1988, and shortly after completing the program, he participated in a not-for-credit supervisory program offered by the company through the local community college. In 1999, Donald became a project supervisor, which was the perfect position for him. He spent most of his time out on the job, and he also acted as a strategic liaison between labor and management, who both respected his expertise and easy-going nature. His work performance was good and he received a number of PRIDE points, recognition given by the company based on employees' demonstration of productivity, responsiveness, innovation, dedication, and enthusiasm (PRIDE) as reported by clients, other contractors, and fellow employees.

Donald was an avid tennis player since high school, and he often played on the weekends or after work with Pearson's purchasing manager, Carl Stoye. Once in a while he and Carl played doubles against Carl's boss, Mike Pearson, and Mike's neighbor, George Coggins. Donald struggled for years to overcome the nagging pain of tennis elbow because he didn't want to quit playing. It seemed to be getting worse, so around 2010 he made a visit to his doctor, who prescribed oxycodone, a narcotic pain reliever, which seemed to take care of the chronic pain and helped him get his edge back on the court. Boy, he sure loved the game, and it gave him the opportunity to get out of the house and away from the quagmire of his home life. His wife constantly nagged at him about money, and his teenage boys seemed to be getting into trouble on what seemed like a weekly basis. Tennis, followed by a few gin and tonics at the club and maybe a line or two of coke with the club crew after Carl left, made him feel like he was on top of the world. If only he could stay there, or at work, where he was actually appreciated.

Donald loved his job, the money was great, and it kept him connected with the good life. He went to work every day and did his very best. No one at Pearson had any idea what he was going through or how he medicated and self-medicated his way through what seemed like a cold, muddy ditch of an existence at home. His wife knew, though. She found out everything one day while out shopping with one of the club wives. She stormed home to find Donald with gin and tonic in hand, arguing with the boys about the latest three-day suspension and how long it would be until his 14-year-old got his smartphone back. "Donald," she hissed through her teeth, "We need to talk. Can I see you in the den, please?" As he sunk into his desk chair, she proceeded to describe what he already knew, the three-hour cooldowns at the club bar, the coke, the girls—everything. His shoulders slumped, he sighed, looked up at her and asked, "Okay, what? What do you want me to do?"

"I have a mind to throw you out of this house right now. Maybe you could go live at the club. You seem to be right at home there. But, no, I'm not going to raise these boys by myself. They're your responsibility. We are your responsibility. I bet if you left right now, you'd spend all of our money on your boozing, your coke, your stupid tennis. No way. I won't even let that happen. Clean up your act, Donald. Quit it. All of it. Now. Or you're out of here, and I'll take you for every cent you have."

Well, that was pretty clear, Donald thought. So long, good life. He quit the club and complied with the demands. What else could he do?

In July 2013, Donald voluntarily entered an outpatient drug rehabilitation program. The program met on the weekends and did not interfere with his work schedule. He completed the program in October. His elbow pain was back and he couldn't stand it any longer, so he went to a different doctor about 30 miles away to get a new prescription for oxycodone, but for some reason the doctor would only suggest over-the-counter medication. One of the guys from the club texted him and invited him to a Halloween party for members and friends, and he was able to go because although he was no longer a member, he was invited. The coke came out around midnight after the "cronies" left, and he decided to head home at 2:00 A.M. with a few grams in his pocket, and 15 oxycodone pills someone offered to give him for his elbow. As he was leaving the party, one of the members gave him a guest pass to the tennis club, so he could go whenever he wanted and just pay court fees out of pocket, and buy drinks after, of course. In December, Donald and his wife filed Chapter 13 bankruptcy. Shortly thereafter, Pearson and other company employees became aware of Donald's financial problems when they read about his bankruptcy in the local paper. A week later, Mike Pearson became aware of Donald's participation in the rehab program during a discussion with a colleague. Mike and Pat Watts, Pearson's HR director, met with Donald to get his side of the story. They asked him to take a drug test. Donald suggested that he would test positive for drugs, but agreed to submit to the test. Pearson's employee handbook stated that anytime an employee was injured on the job he or she would submit to a drug and alcohol test. There was also a broad statement that company had the right to request alcohol and drug testing of suspected cause.

On April 5, 2014, Donald tests showed positive for cocaine and oxycodone. He was fired that day for violation of Pearson's drug policy. Donald believed that he could get clean and asked if in that case would they consider him for reemployment? Mike and the HR director basically said, "We will have to see when that time comes."

## INTERMISSION

Mike and the Pat Watts struggled with the decision to terminate a long-term employee and pondered if they might have done something different.

## ACT 2

In late April, Donald entered an inpatient drug rehabilitation program. Upon entering the program, he tested positive for cocaine and oxycodone, along with THC (marijuana), which he had started smoking at night out in his workshop, which was the only place he could escape anymore. He couldn't afford to leave the house. He completed the program a month later, and the report issued by his rehab counselor described his recovery prognosis as "guarded."

The day after he completed the program, Donald contacted Pat Watts, Pearson's HR director, and asked to return to work. In a meeting with Mike Pearson and Watts, Donald was told that the company was completing and thus ending a $130 million hospital project and with the current poor economy, they were forced to lay off over 100 employees. They told him that several supervisors would be laid off and others would have their hours reduced.

Donald's last words were, "You lied to me. I'm going to get a lawyer and sue you!"

Mike and Pat wondered if they had made a mistake. "He is over forty and a drug addict. Wonder what would be the basis for a law suit?" Mike and Pat pondered their actions and wondered if they had done the right thing?.

## QUESTIONS FOR DISCUSSION

1. What are the issues in this critical incident?
2. Did management do the "right thing" in firing Donald Summer for his actions? (i.e. testing positive for cocaine and oxycodone?) Why or why not?
3. What things might management have done before taking the disciplinary actions they did?
4. In today's diverse environment, did management treat Summer ethically?
5. What role, if any, should "reasonable accommodation" play into the decision that was made?
6. Is there any way that Summer's actions are protected by the law in your state?
7. In 50 words or less, highlight what you learned from this Critical Incident. Compare your findings with those of three or more classmates. Is there a difference?

---

## BLACK FRIDAY: AN ILLUSION OR REALITY?

Critical Incident 1-4

Hispanics, who make up about 16 percent of the U.S. population, are the fastest growing minority group, and they are more likely to be uninsured than any other minority group, according to the U.S. Census Bureau. It is estimated that only 10.2 million of the 53 million uninsured Hispanics in the United States will qualify for coverage under the new healthcare laws. (Visit the Kaiser Family Foundation and the Health Research and Information Trust for additional information.)

The Community Health Care Center, which has facilities in central North Carolina, has created innovations to address preventive care, chronic disease management, and other initiatives to help the population in their area. Unfortunately, the hospital is not equipped to deal with the emotions and productivity of its employees.

All employees received the following e-mail from Douglas O'Rourke, the CEO of Community Health Care Center. "Thankfulness is the beginning of gratitude. Gratitude is the completion of thankfulness. Thankfulness may consist merely of words. Gratitude is shown in acts. -- Henri Fredice Amiel.... Enjoy the Thanksgiving Holiday."

Unfortunately, a *Wall Street Journal* article the same week said, "Insurers would be cutting doctors pay under the new health care plans." The same week Lockheed Martin announced they would be restructuring their business and cutting 4,000 jobs, and H.J. Heinz Co's new owners announced they would eliminate 1,350 jobs and would be closing a South Carolina plant. The Heinz announcement came on top of the 600 layoffs in August. Several companies were planning to cancel their employees' healthcare plans under the new federal healthcare law.

Inna Genova, an Hispanic, began a new career at age 34. She went back to college and spent two years getting her nursing degree. The single mom with two children aged 15 and 12 had enjoyed the last three years at Community Health Care Center.

Her job was challenging and she worked 12-hour shifts around-the-clock seven days a week. She told the authors that she had appreciated the lack of micromanaging but in the last several weeks no one in administration has ever said thanks for a job well done. The Friday after Thanksgiving, the hospitals' HR department had announced that 84 jobs would be eliminated in the next three months. A friend gave her a copy of a November 18, 2013 article from the *Wall Street Journal*. The highlights of the article were startling to her: "Despite the fact that more women were obtaining college degrees than men, women were earning 76.5 cents for every dollar that men were earning." Like most women she knew, she felt that she had a lack of job mobility and would have difficulty breaking in to the traditionally male-dominated professions.

Inna thought to herself, "I like my job here, and I know that the hospital has a lot of applicants even though they are not hiring. Struggles are not new for me. I have had many struggles in my life. Many times I have been uncomfortable, but I have survived. The work and family pressures have been intense, but I have always focused on where I want to be. If I am to lose my job, it will be painful, but I will accept it. I just wish I knew what will happen next?"

## QUESTIONS FOR DISCUSSION

1. The planned elimination of jobs by Community Health Care Center will have a profound effect on employee morale. What would you recommend to the management of Community Health Care Center to minimize the impact of the downsizing on employee morale?
2. Using the Internet, find ways to identify what other organizations have done to soften the blow on their eliminated employees.
3. Review the previous chapters and make a list of six things that Community Health Care Center could do to empower the remaining employees to be the best they can be.
4. Using the Internet, find at least three sources to discuss the problems that organizations will face in developing effective teams and empowering employees for success when the work culture and the economic environment create stress that might impact employee performance in the workplace. Identify some strategies that management might use to help the survivors at Community Health Care Center keep their lives under control and do what is best for the patients.
5. What would you recommend to Inna Genova to ensure that her job is not eliminated?

---

**Critical Incident 1-5**

## I NEED TO MAKE A DIFFERENCE!

Luisa Chalfant is the supervisor of the shipping and receiving department at Tideway Corporation's manufacturing plant in rural Arkansas. The Tideway plant, a producer of paper products, is one of the few unionized plants in the area. Driven by competitiveness in the global marketplace and in order to provide greater returns on company equity, the corporate structure has changed and additional change is expected at a higher pace in the foreseeable future. Because of constantly changing market competition, the company has had to find ways to be more efficient.

Luisa has supervised the department for the last two years after having worked as an employee in the department for the previous eight years. Fourteen employees report to her, and all are members of the plants' labor union. Three months ago, the union steward registered a complaint about her supervisory style in a meeting (Luisa, her immediate manager, and the director of HR were in attendance.) The HR manager had her enroll in a four-week supervisory management course at the local community college. There she learned about strategies and models of supervisory leadership, especially those that emphasized a collaborative approach.

She was also taught techniques for giving directions to employees that were less authoritarian than she had used previously. Participative style was emphasized by the professor as being more effective than just giving out orders to employees.

In the four weeks since she attended the last class, she tried to implement some of what she had learned. On a number of occasions, she asked the employees—both individually and in groups—for their suggestions and opinions concerning what needed to be done to improve productivity in the workplace. Luisa tried to avoid giving direct orders and suggested to employees what needed to be done rather than spelling out their initiatives in detail. However, despite her best efforts, nothing seems to have changed. Workforce performance has not improved significantly, and some of the employees seem to be going through the motions of their job just as before.

The department shop steward told her this morning that she did not think that Luisa understood how employees felt and that she had forgotten what it was to be a worker.

Luisa pondered whether there was something wrong in her approach. She thought, "Is what I am doing and the way of doing it a waste of time? Do employees resent the fact that I was promoted to the supervisory position? I wonder what I need to do to get employees to change so that we can be better at what we do?"

## QUESTIONS FOR DISCUSSION

Visit the website of the AFL-CIO (http://www.aflcio.org) or The Change to Win website (http://changetowin.org), to learn more about the concerns and issues facing today's labor organization.

1. What are the benefits for Luisa Chalfant to belong to a labor organization?
2. What role did Luisa's early leadership style have on her employees' unwillingness to follow her direction? Explain your answer.
3. Why do you feel Luisa's new style did not have the impact that she thought it would?
4. What suggestions would you make to Luisa to help her get her employees to do a better job?

---

## THE BEST OF PHILANTHROPIST BILL GATES

Critical Incident 1-6

ERIC PIERMONT/Getty Images

At the age of 15, Bill Gates and Paul Allen developed "Traf-o-Data," the computer program that moderated traffic patterns in their hometown of Seattle. They netted $20,000 and wanted to start their own company, but Gates's parents wanted him to finish high school, go to college, and become a lawyer. In the fall of 1973, he enrolled at Harvard University and spent more time in the computer lab than going to class.

In the summer of 1974, Gates joined Allen at Honeywell. A year later, the two formed a partnership called Micro-Soft. In late 1978 they moved back to Washington. They renamed the company Microsoft and it grossed $2.5 million that year. Gates was 23 years old.

In 1986, they took Microsoft public with an initial offering (IPO) at $21 a share. Gates held 45 percent of the company's shares and his stake was estimated to be about $234 million.

Gates studied the philanthropic efforts of others and created the William H. Gates Foundation in 1994 dedicated to supporting education, world health, and investing in low-income communities. In 2000, Bill and Melinda Gates put in $28 billion to the Bill and Melinda Gates Foundation.

In February 2014, Gates announced that he was stepping down as chairman of Microsoft in order to spend more time as its technology advisor. At the same time, Microsoft CEO Steve Ballmer was replaced by Satya Nadella.

On July 17, 2014, Microsoft announced that it was laying off up to 18,000 employees.

## QUESTIONS FOR DISCUSSION

We suggest that you review the following:

Roose, Kevin. "Microsoft Just Laid Off Thousands of Employees With a Hilariously Bad Memo," nymag.com (July 17, 2014).

Ovide, Shira. "Microsoft Brings Office to the iPad," *The Wall Street Journal* (March 28, 2014), p. B1

Ovide, Shira and Steve Rosenbush. "Microsoft Preps Office for iPad; New Boss to Deviate From Windows-First Policy, Users Are Wary," *The Wall Street Journal* (March 27, 2014), p. B4.

Ovide, Shira and Spencer E. Ante. "Microsoft Pick: Change Agent?" *The Wall Street Journal* (February 3, 2104), p.B1, B4.

Ovide, Shira. "Why Is It So Hard to Find Microsoft's Next Chief Executive,"; *The Wall Street Journal* (January 4-5, 2014), p. B1.

Stone, Brad. "Bill Gates—Philanthropist,"; Bloomberg BusinessWeek (August 12–25, 2013), pp. 52–54.

Wingfield, Nick. "Microsoft to Lay Off Thousands, Most from Nokia Unit," www.nytimes.com (July 17, 2014).

http://en.wikipedia.org/wiki/Bill_Gates

http://www.biograhy.com/print/profile/bill-gates-9307520.

http://www.washingtonpost.com/blogs/right-turn/wp/2014/03/16/the-best-of-bill-gates/

1. Across the country, public education is struggling. What are some solutions that the Gates Foundation is looking at to provide the inner-city student and the suburban student with equal educational opportunities?
2. How does the Gates Foundation focus to reduce death rates in children?
3. Discuss ways that that the company you work for might encourage its employees to engage in volunteerism and philanthropic organizations?
4. What should Bill Gates do to develop and encourage Satya Nadella in his new role as CEO of Microsoft?
5. If you were the gatekeeper of your organization, what did you learn after reading about Bill Gates that might help you be the best you could be?
6. If your grandparents had bought you 10 shares of Microsoft stock when you were born and the dividends were used to purchase more stock, how much would that investment be worth today?
7. What impact will the lay-off of thousands of employees have on Microsoft's image?
8. If one of your best friends was one of the laid-off Microsoft employees, what suggestions would you give to him or her to find a job in today's job market?

PART 2

Lisa Werner/Alamy

# Essentials of Effective Supervision

Chapter

# 5 Leadership and Followership

Michael Ventura/Alamy

**After studying this chapter, you will be able to:**

1. Define leadership, explain its importance at the supervisory level, and describe elements of contemporary leadership thought.
2. Outline the importance of trust in the leadership process and the effects of lack of trust on employee engagement and productivity.
3. Discuss the critical nature of ethics in informing leaders' behaviors and influencing followers and organizational culture.
4. Explain the delegation process and describe its three major components.
5. Discuss why some supervisors do not delegate, and describe the benefits of delegation.
6. Compare the autocratic (authoritarian) approach to supervision with the participative approach.
7. Explain the role of followers in the leadership process and differentiate between different types of followers.

## YOU MAKE THE CALL!

*Professor Edwards's "Fundamentals of Supervision" class was in the fifth week, and the class was discussing servant leadership. Professor Edwards identified three things for the students to consider. "Leaders need to create a vision for their team that will create a future for the organization based on resilience. Leaders need to use the talents and skills of their team members to get the best results. Leaders need to find ways to engage their followers to be the best they can be in doing the job they were hired to do."*

The classroom door opened and someone the students did not know walked into the class. Professor Edwards introduced her as Alisha McDonald, a former student, who was now district manager for IHOP and active in the area Habitat for Humanity Women Build Projects. He said that she would share her story of how her work with Habitat had helped her.

Most of the students had never done or even heard about the "hammer" experience.

Alisha began her talk by saying that Professor Edwards had gotten her professional business fraternity, Delta Sigma Phi, to get off the bench and get in a game that none of the group had ever heard about.

*My fraternity got involved in building a home for Habitat for Humanity. It was the most fun project I had ever been involved in. Marketing and finance majors worked on securing funds for the build. Other majors worked on all aspects of the house.*

*Habitat for Humanity put on "Women Build" classes to give us some knowledge, skills, and familiarity with working on a Habitat project. The area Habitat affiliate is planning on building over 100 homes in the next four years and they need volunteers. Projects like this have not just allowed me to be a better person, but also gave me a real appreciation for the leadership and teamwork needed to help those who are truly in need. I knew nothing about building a home, but I learned lots about working with a diverse group of people. Projects like this one and others allowed me to develop and demonstrate my leadership and followership skills and to get others to do some things they never thought they would be able to do.*

*This year, we will begin our Women Build project on Friday, May 1, and conclude on Saturday, May 16. There is also a men's build at the same time. As a team leader I have a critical role in making the Women Build program a success. A Habitat build is fun and rewarding, and I want you there to help.*

*Habitat for Humanity also has a year-round program known as the Collegiate Challenge. Summer, fall, winter, and Spring Break trips are available for those of you who might like to travel out of the area and spend a week working in partnership with a local Habitat affiliate to eliminate poverty housing in their area. Last year, we took a group of students to Jacksonville, Florida, on Spring Break. More than 14,000 college students took part in the Collegiate Challenge last year. If you would be interested in doing that during your Spring Break, Professor Edwards will help you get in touch with me so that we can get you involved.*

*Habitat's Women Build program started in Charlotte, North Carolina, in 1991 with a home completely built by a crew of female volunteers. Women Build projects provide an environment where women can feel comfortable learning construction skills they might not otherwise have an opportunity to learn. Women all over the United States will participate in a Mother's Day build. I encourage you to become a volunteer to help those in need and change communities.*

*Each Habitat home is sponsored, and we use private funds to purchase building materials and land for the homes. Each home built has a cost of $75,000, and we ask that each volunteer secure a gift of at least $250 to ensure that the home is properly funded. Last year, Professor Edwards and his wife gave us $2000 for a Women Build project, and he has told me that they will do that again.*

*What questions do you have for me?*

**Disclaimer:** The above scenario presents a supervisory situation based on real events to be used for educational purposes. The identities of some or all individuals, organizations, industries, and locations, as well as financial and other information may have been disguised to protect individual privacy and proprietary information. Fictional details may have been added to improve readability and interest.

YOU MAKE THE CALL!

## Leadership: The Core of Supervisory Management

**1 Define leadership, explain its importance at the supervisory level, and describe elements of contemporary leadership thought.**

Harry S. Truman, 33rd president of the United States, once remarked that leadership is the ability to get people to do what they don't like to do and enjoy it.[1] Simple as it seems, there still is considerable misunderstanding concerning the supervisor's leadership role in influencing employee motivation and performance. This misunderstanding often stems from a misconception regarding the meaning of leadership itself. Occupying a position of responsibility and authority does not necessarily make someone a leader whom subordinates will follow.

## THE TEST OF SUPERVISORY LEADERSHIP

**Leadership**
The process of influencing the opinions, attitudes, and behaviors of others toward the achievement of a goal

**Leadership** is the process of influencing the opinions, attitudes, and behaviors of others toward the achievement of a goal. Anyone who can direct or influence others toward objectives can function as a leader, no matter what position that person holds.

In the workplace, members of a work group often assume leadership roles. The direction of informal employee leadership can be supportive of, or contrary to, the direction the supervisor desires. For example, employee resistance to changes in work arrangements, work rules, or procedures is a common phenomenon. Such resistance is usually the result of some informal leadership in the work group.

Therefore, leadership in the general sense is a process rather than just a positional relationship. Leadership includes what the followers think and do, not just what the supervisor does. The real test of supervisory leadership is how subordinates follow. Leadership resides in a supervisor's ability to obtain the work group's willingness to follow—willingness based on commonly shared goals and a mutual effort to achieve them (see Figure 5.1).

However, the willingness of others to follow is not enough by itself. The following questions might identify several other tests for leadership:

- Does the leader possess a clear vision of what needs to be done (continuous pursuit of excellence and worthwhile objectives)?
- Does the leader communicate that vision and get others "onboard"?
- Does the leader build a climate of mutual trust and respect?
- Does the leader create the proper infrastructure to support the vision?
- Does the leader enable the followers to be the best they can be?
- Does the leader leave the organization better than he or she found it?

Obviously, leadership effectiveness, like beauty, is in the eyes of the beholder, but the better leaders are known as great communicators and people of impeccable credibility.

## LEADERSHIP CAN BE DEVELOPED

Supervisors often believe that any definition of leadership should include basic traits. That is, they believe that effective leaders have some special qualities, and they point to certain successful supervisors as representing outstanding leadership.

**FIGURE 5.1 Supervisory leadership results in a work group's willingness to follow**
**Beetle, King Features Syndicate**

This flag...the symbol of the hopes of man. This cloth of dreams for freedom, justice and opportunity. Its stars are like beacons guiding us through the shoals of adversity. Its red stripes like wounds of struggle. The good in it cannot be had for nothing...like any garden it must be tended...like any loved one it must be held. Hold this flag high and keep its promise bright, for in it lies the best hope for all of us.
MORT WALKER 9-4


Beetle, King Features Syndicate

Dana White/PhotoEdit

*There is no significant relationship between leadership ability and such characteristics as age, height, weight, gender, race, and other physical attributes.*

Does a person need to have certain natural qualities to be an effective leader? Generally, leadership behaviors can be learned. Many studies have shown that there is no significant relationship between one's ability to lead and such characteristics as age, height, weight, sex, race, and other physical attributes. Although there are indications that successful supervisors tend to be somewhat more intelligent than the average subordinate, they are not so superior in intelligence that they cannot be understood. Intelligence is partially hereditary, but, for the most part, it depends on environmental factors, such as the amount of formal education and the diversity of experiences. Successful supervisors tend to be well-rounded in their interests and aptitudes. They are good communicators, are mentally and emotionally mature, and have strong inner drives. Most important, they tend to rely more on their conceptual and interpersonal skills than on their technical skills. These are essentially learned characteristics, not innate qualities.

Author Peter Senge objects to the notion of teaching leadership. He makes the following contention:

> *Teaching suggests that you have certain concepts you want to understand, and that's pretty useless in a domain like leadership. Leadership has to do with how people are. You don't teach people a different way of being, you create conditions so they can discover where their natural leadership comes from.*[2]

Viewed from this perspective, supervisory leadership is something people can develop when they want to be leaders and not just people in charge of groups. Where can the novice gain leadership experience? As noted in Chapter 1, you can volunteer in a number of service or religious organizations or seek internships through your college placement office. Imagine the dynamics that can take place among a Boy Scout or Girl Scout leader and a group of young scouts. Volunteering provides the opportunity to work on real projects and to accomplish real objectives with real people while practicing newly learned leadership knowledge and skills.

A few words of guidance are appropriate at this point. In a number of chapters we discuss the importance of finding a mentor. When you enter a volunteer experience, hitch your wagon to a star. Find an experienced, well-respected leader to work with, one who will enable you to observe, practice, and hone the skills necessary to be an effective leader. Look for ways to use what you've learned from your mentor, ask for feedback, and say thank you. When asked to serve as a mentor, a skilled leader will support, coach, protect, and provide opportunities for you to be in charge of meaningful projects or programs. You should seize every opportunity to become a more effective leader and continuously strive to develop your managerial and human relations capacities and skills.

## EFFECTIVE SUPERVISORY LEADERSHIP AS A DYNAMIC PROCESS

Good communication is the foundation of effective leadership, such as getting scouts to do things they have never done before. The ability to communicate, to keep the lines of communication open at all times, and to communicate in ways that meet workers' expectations and needs is essential for any supervisor to be a leader.

Generally, the larger the work group, the more important it is for the supervisor to be an effective planner, organizer, and coordinator. The larger the work group, the more the supervisor will have to delegate authority. The smaller the work group and the closer the supervisor's location to the employees, the more the supervisor must address the individual needs of those in the group.

Understanding employee expectations is vital to effective supervision. As discussed in other areas of the text, today's employees want to participate in decisions about their jobs. However, a supervisor must sometimes exercise authority and make decisions that may not be popular with the work group. The ability to assess employee expectations and the demands of the job situation and then act appropriately is a skill that can be developed with experience and practice.

## CONTEMPORARY THOUGHTS ON LEADERSHIP

Contemporary writings on leadership are filled with findings—and some contradictions. One of the most noted writers on leadership, Warren Bennis, has conducted extensive research on the subject and has identified four things people want from their leaders:

1. Direction—People want leaders to have a purpose. The leader has a clear idea of what is to be done. Leaders love what they do and love doing it. Followers want passion and conviction from a strong point of view.
2. Trust—Followers want to have faith in their leader. Integrity, competence, constancy, caring, candor, and congruity are essential elements of building a relationship of mutual trust.
3. Hope—Leaders believe, and they kindle the fire of optimism in followers.
4. Results—Leaders accomplish difficult tasks. Success breeds success.

In order to provide these things for followers, Bennis asserts that leaders must be intentional in their behaviors and interactions with employees. By establishing a vision, clear goals, and objectives, leaders can forge a clear path for those they are leading. If their behaviors and decisions are reliable and consistent, authentic relationships will grow because employees know what to expect. When leaders take action with energy, commitment, confidence, and creativity, employees are excited to go where they are being led, and typically they go the extra mile under the leader's guidance in order to achieve results.[3]

Noted leadership researchers James Kouzes and Barry Posner maintain that "leadership is an observable, learnable set of practices. Given the opportunity for feedback and practice, those with desire and persistence to lead can substantially improve their abilities to do so."[4] After examining the experiences of managers who were leading others to outstanding accomplishments, Kouzes and Posner identified five practices and 10 specific behaviors that managers can learn and use at all levels. These practices and behaviors include:

- Challenging the process (searching for opportunities, experimenting, and taking risks);
- Inspiring a shared vision (envisioning the future, enlisting the support of others);
- Enabling others to act (fostering collaboration, strengthening others);
- Modeling the way (setting an example, planning small wins); and
- Encouraging the heart (recognizing contributions, celebrating accomplishments).[5]

In short, leaders need followers who understand what is expected. Then leaders engage their followers in the pursuit of those goals. According to Gary Neilson, a Booz & Company executive, "Healthy organizations are good at execution—they get things done. Unhealthy organizations lack clear decision rights and don't share information effectively."[6] Surprisingly, research by one of this text's authors has shown that less than 40 percent of employees had a clear idea of what they were accountable for.[7] Another study reported that only 44 percent of U.S. workers could actually identify their organization's top three goals and more than 30 percent of workers said their work team couldn't stay focused on its most important goals.[8] Remember: If you don't know where you're supposed to go, how will you know when you get there? Further, how will your followers know where to go?

## SERVANT-LEADERSHIP

In his book *Good to Great*, author Jim Collins described "Level 5" leaders as those who facilitate, coach, and empower others to find their own direction.[9] We believe that there are times when the leader must provide direction and that there are situations in which subordinates should be enabled to pursue their own direction—as long as it is consistent with the overall vision for the organization.

Former AT&T executive Robert Greenleaf defined **servant-leadership** in this way:

**Servant-leadership**
The notion that the needs of followers are looked after such that they can be the best they can be

> *The servant-leader is a servant first. . . . It begins with the natural feeling that one wants to serve, to serve first. Then conscious choice brings one to aspire to lead. He or she is sharply different from the person who is leader first, perhaps because of the need to assuage an unusual power drive or to acquire material possessions. For such it will be a later choice to serve—after leadership is established. The difference manifests itself in the care taken by the servant-first leader to make sure that other people's highest-priority needs are being served.*[10]

Greenleaf concluded that authentic leaders are chosen by those they serve—their followers. Regardless of his or her level of competence, every employee needs guidance, and servant-leaders set up their employees for success. Professor Max

Douglas contends that servant-leaders treat co-workers as equals, affirm their worth, and match their performance to their espoused values.[11] Larry Spears, past CEO of the Greenleaf Center for Servant-Leadership, said, "Servant-leadership provides a strong set of values and ethics for people and organizations."[12] Figure 5.2 identifies the 10 keys (characteristics) central to the concept of servant-leadership.

Earlier in this chapter, we proposed that one of the tests of leadership is whether the leader enables the followers to be the best they can be. This is not to imply that leaders focus solely on serving the needs of others. Look back at the sample values-and-belief statement for the Community Medical Center (CMC) in Chapter 1 (Figure 1.8 on page 30). It clearly states that every employee is important and that employees must work together to meet or exceed the expectations of various stakeholder groups. Reflect for a moment on the following question: "If an employee is not treated as a very special person, how can you expect that employee to treat a customer as a very special person?"

Of all the keys to effective servant-leadership, whether service is focused on employees, customers, or other stakeholders, listening is the most essential. Kent Keith, current CEO of the Greenleaf Center, explains, "Servant leaders really are good at listening, they stay close to their colleagues, they have a good understanding of what their colleagues need to perform at a high level, and they work hard to get that to them." When leaders listen, they also learn what is important to customers in terms of programs, products, and services that will meet their needs.[13] Professor Bill George asserts that a leader can tell if they are serving their own interests or the interests of others by how much they listen to the people around them. A self-determined leader who carries the weight of the world on his shoulders is separate from the team, often because he isn't listening to his team members in order to become aware of the strengths and talents they are willing and able to contribute. Furthermore, a leader who doesn't look for ways to empower employees often ends up with a workforce with low morale and minimal commitment to organizational goals.[14] Companies such as FedEx, Starbucks, Southwest Airlines, and YUM Brands (KFC, Pizza Hut, Long John Silvers) have adopted servant leadership as one of their core values, a leadership choice that is reflected in their public images and their success.[15]

**FIGURE 5.2 The essence of servant-leadership. Use these keys to unlock your Employees' Potential***

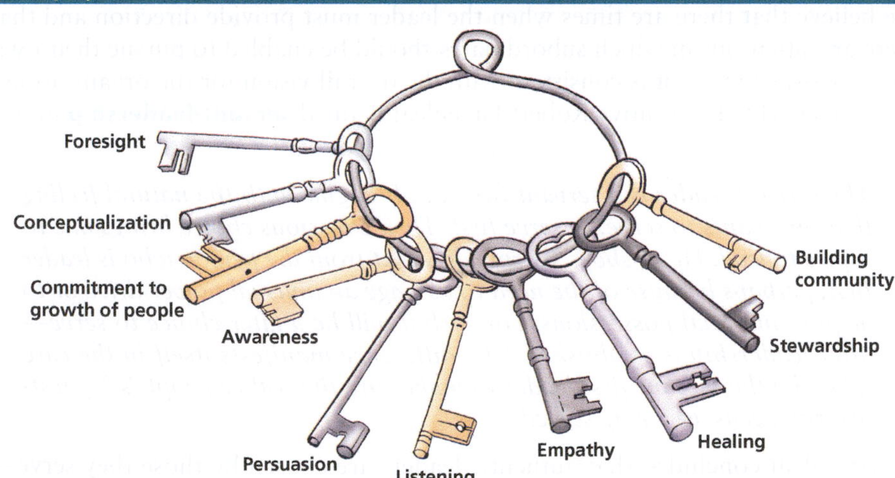


*Source:* Larry C. Spears and John C. Burkhardt Listed the Ten Characteristics Central to the Development of Servant-Leaders in Servant-Leadership and Philanthropic Institutions (Indianapolis, IN: The Greenleaf Center, 2006).

### LEADERSHIP STYLE DEPENDS ON MANY FACTORS

While researchers and theorists generally agree that leading is not the same as managing (see Chapter 2), there is still considerable debate regarding what the leader does and how the leader does it. Most supervisors and managers recognize that no one leadership style is effective in all situations. There is no simple set of do's and don'ts a supervisor can implement to achieve high motivation and excellent performance. Although leadership skills can be learned and developed, no one formula will apply in all situations and with all people. Considerable evidence suggests that an effective approach is contingent on numerous factors in any given situation. **Contingency-style leadership** proponents advocate that these considerations include such things as the supervisor, the organization, the type of work, the skill level and motivation of employees, and time pressures.

**Contingency-style leadership**
No one leadership style is best; the appropriate style depends on a multitude of factors

Some approaches promote good performance better than others. The concept of leadership has been studied and discussed for decades, and the consensus from dozens of leadership theories is that no one best style of leadership exists. The lesson for practicing supervisors is that the most effective leadership depends on a multitude of factors, including the supervisor, the organization, the type of work, the employees involved, their ability and willingness to accomplish a task, the amount of time available to complete a task, and the particular situation and its urgency. In general, we conclude that effective leaders must be able to establish standards, actively listen to employees to identify their challenges, needs and motivations, develop a climate in which people become self-motivated and adapt to constant change. The effective leader provides direction, instruction, guidance, support and encouragement, feedback and positive recognition, and enthusiastic help when necessary.

## Trust: The Basis of Effective Supervisory Relationships

**2 Outline the importance of trust in the leadership process and the effects of lack of trust on employee engagement and productivity.**

The concept of trust warrants specific attention because the ability to trust a leader is perhaps more important today than at any other time in recent history, when an uncertain workforce is experiencing a quaking economy and industries are in turmoil. When we tell someone, "I trust you," what does that phrase mean to the person saying it, and to the person hearing it? In a supervisory relationship, it means a great deal.

### TRUST IS A GROWING CONCERN IN THE WORKPLACE

While the words "us versus them" are common in the workplace, few managers would admit publicly that they do not trust their employees. Likewise, when asked whether they trust their bosses, most employees would be afraid to answer if they couldn't say "yes." **Trust**, according to Merriam-Webster, is the belief that someone is reliable, good, honest, and effective. Is trust alive and well in the workplace? In an American Psychological Association 2013 poll of nearly 1,600 U.S. workers, less than one in four employees said they don't trust their employer, only half believe their employer is upfront and open with them, and one-third shared that their employer is not always honest and truthful. In a similar survey of nearly 1,000 workers done by Forum Corp., more than one-third

**Trust**
The belief that someone or something is reliable, good, honest, and effective

of employees asserted that their level of trust has eroded over time; they trust their leaders less now than in the past. Attitudes of 2,900 workers collected by Maritz Research found that only 12 percent of workers strongly believe their leaders are honest and ethical, 7 percent strongly believe the actions of senior managers are consistent with their words, and 7 percent completely trust that their boss will look out for employees' best interests. Lack of trust is a growing concern in the workplace, which survey respondents attribute to senior leaders' lack of caring, perceived favoritism, poor communication, and inconsistent behavior.[16]

## THE IMPACT OF TRUST ON SUPERVISORY RELATIONSHIPS

Trust is the foundation of effective supervisory relations. Some years ago, a customer placed a special order for a child's bedroom set at a locally owned furniture store. When told the set would be delivered in three weeks, the customer asked, "Do you want me to give you some money as a deposit or sign something?" The owner said, "No problem. You told me you want it. If your word isn't any good, what good is your signature?" As Bennis and others imply, "We want to be able to trust others and to have others trust us."

Stephen R. Covey, author of *Principle-Centered Leadership*, notes that:

> *Trust bonds management to labor, employees to each other, customers to supplier, and strengthens all other stakeholder relationships. With low trust, developing performance is exhausting. With high trust, it is exhilarating. The principle of alignment means working together in harmony, going in the same direction, and supporting each other. Alignment develops the organizational trustworthiness required for trust. And if personal trustworthiness and interpersonal trust are to mature, hiring, promoting, training, and other systems must foster character development as well as competence.*[17]

A number of specific leadership behaviors can erode trust between supervisors and employees. A supervisor's lack of confidence and courage to stand up for employees; operating with hidden agendas; unwillingness to apologize for mistakes; unclear or untrue communication; self-centeredness; taking credit for others' ideas; inappropriate choices, inconsistent behavior; and resistance to getting his or her "hands dirty" by staying distanced from employees and the work they do can lower employees' trust that the supervisor has their best interests at heart.[18]

Relationships of mutual trust can be facilitated by leaders who are authentic, aligning their words and actions to demonstrate integrity and model it for their employees. Supervisors who share their expertise while also acknowledging their shortcomings earn the respect of employees. Honest communication, excellent listening skills, and a truly caring attitude, particularly in times of organizational change, reduce employees' fear of the unknown and encourage them to trust and support the leader's decisions when it comes to navigating uncharted waters. Two-way communication about organizational and personal values also goes a long way toward building reciprocal trust. In short, organizations build trust by treating employees well, placing clients and customers ahead of financial gain, and demonstrating ethical practices.

## Ethics: The moral fiber of leadership

**3 Discuss the critical nature of ethics in informing leaders' behaviors and influencing followers and organizational culture.**

Our society is host to increasingly gray areas of judgment and ethical breakdowns, a perception that is reinforced by news reports of corporate scandals, political improprieties, bribery, and government snooping, to name just a few.[19] The authors like to think that while some leaders may make poor decisions that can affect millions of people, some consistently make decisions based on strong ethics that benefit equally as many. **Ethics** is the system of moral principles that guide the conduct of an individual, group, or society.

**Ethics:** The system of moral principles that guide the conduct of an individual, group, or society

### ETHCAL VALUES COMPRISE CHARACTER

A person's ethics determine how they distinguish between right and wrong and good and evil relative to their own actions and character, as well as the actions and character of others. Accordingly, a person's ethics, which are derived from their culture, upbringing, and personal experiences, direct them to adopt certain values that drive their decisions. According to leadership thought leader James MacGregor Burns, ethical values are broad character traits that include honesty, integrity, fairness, reliability, reciprocity, and accountability. Similarly, the Josephson Institute of Ethics suggests that six key ethical values, the Six Pillars of Character, comprise a person's character: trustworthiness, respect, responsibility, fairness, caring, and citizenship, values which can be easily remembered with the acronym TRRFCC (and the reminder that good character is terrific).[20] If a person bases his or her decisions on ethical values, he or she can rest assured that he or she has done the right thing, regardless of the outcome. Civil rights leader Martin Luther King, Jr. reminds us that "the time is always right to do what is right."[21]

### ETHICAL VALUES INFORM LEADERSHIP AND INFLUENCE FOLLOWERS

Returning to our definition of leadership, in which leaders influence the opinions, attitudes, and behaviors of others, consideration of ethics becomes critical because when leaders choose to behave ethically and influence followers to do the same, organizational performance is higher, but when they choose not to, organizational culture suffers, performance drops, and followers can be put in compromising situations.[22] The 2013 *National Business Ethics Survey* of 6,420 U.S. workers found that in organizations that had strong ethical cultures, only 20 percent of workers observed misconduct, while in organizations with weak ethical cultures, 88 percent of workers said they regularly witnessed misconduct. Further, 60 percent of workplace misconduct was reported as manager choices and behaviors, particularly senior managers. When employees were asked about their response to observed misconduct, more than 20 percent said they were retaliated against when they reported it, and those who chose not to report it said they did not because they feared retaliation from their supervisor,[23] which shows that in some cases, employees felt forced to compromise their own ethics to protect themselves. This fear became a reality for several associates of Lance Armstrong, the disgraced cyclist whose seven Tour de France victories were stripped when he was found guilty of years of doping. According to reports, not only did many of them fail to report his illegal activity, but they "became foot soldiers in his deceptions."[24] Those who refused to do so or stepped forward to attest to the doping were bullied, threatened, and slandered relentlessly by Armstrong.

Equally as concerning, according to the 2014 *Edelman Trust Barometer*, only 21 percent of 30,000 employees surveyed worldwide believe that business leaders make ethical and moral decisions and 15 percent of government leaders make ethical and moral decisions.[25] The workforce does not presently have much confidence in the ethics of its leaders, however, leaders shoulder the primary responsibility for modeling and promoting ethical values in the workplace and holding employees accountable for upholding those values through their own behavior.

## BEING ETHICAL REQUIRES WALKING THE TALK

Even when an organization has mission and value statements that espouse strong ethics, there is no guarantee that those statements will hold true in practice. Starting at the top of an organization through every level of the workforce, ethical behavior, not just repeating the words on a page, must be expected. Ethics scholar Joanne Ciulla explains how ethical values are demonstrated by walking the talk:

> *You have to make a lot of assumptions to make a value do something. You have to assume that because people value something they act accordingly, but we know this isn't* [always] *the case. Value articulations of ethics often leave the door open for hypocrisy. Many people sincerely value truth, but often lie. People can also tell the truth, but not value it. The test lies in outcomes—real, intended and durable change (behavior).*[26]

## LEADERS—KNOW THYSELF AND THY ETHICAL VALUES

In Chapter 1, you were introduced to the importance of ethics as a cornerstone of good management, which the data above strongly reinforces. In Chapter 8, on pages 286–287 you will learn about ethical considerations that supervisors must make when solving problems and considering alternatives, and in Chapter 15 we will present examples of ethical codes and policies that supervisors can use guide employee behavior and positive discipline. However, before a leader can influence the ethical values of employees, the leader must first have a clear grasp of his or her own ethical values and how they drive personal behavior.

At the end of each chapter you have opportunities to engage in self-assessment, measuring aspects of your own personal supervisory skills, knowledge, and abilities. Leaders must also engage in self-assessment, particularly in the area of ethics, so they can establish a strong ethical foundation with which to influence followers and identify areas in which they need to strengthen their ability to behave ethically and make ethical decisions. Ciulla suggests that leaders ask themselves, and possibly ask a close friend or peer, several questions about how their leadership behaviors reflect ethical values. The questions test three areas of ethics: ethics of the means, the ethics of person, and the ethics of the ends.

- *Ethics of the means*: What does the leader use to motivate followers to obtain their goals? What is the moral relationship between leaders and followers? Do the leader's ethics of the means demonstrate honesty, integrity, trustworthiness, reliability, reciprocity, and accountability, or the Six Pillars of Character?
- *The ethics of person*: What are leaders' personal ethics? Are they motivated by self-interest or altruism, serving others? Do the leader's ethics of the means

demonstrate honesty, integrity, trustworthiness, reliability, reciprocity, and accountability, or the Six Pillars of Character?

- *The ethics of the ends*: What is the ethical value of a leader's accomplishments? Did his or her actions and the results of those actions serve the greatest good? What is the greatest good? Who is and isn't part of the greatest good? Do the leader's ethics of the means demonstrate honesty, integrity, trustworthiness, reliability, reciprocity, and accountability, or the Six Pillars of Character?[27]

If, after considering these questions, a leader realizes that some (or all) of his or her attitudes, behaviors, or decisions do not reflect ethical values, it is critical that those disparities are addressed through reflection, skill-building, mentoring, or other means of strengthening his or her ethical core. Demonstrating strong ethical values and influencing employees to do the same can potentially be the most beneficial things a supervisor can do to empower and engage employees to do their best and achieve organizational goals the right way (as well as the best way to stay out of jail and off the front page of the newspaper).

### EVERYDAY ETHICS

A person can lead ethically while among friends on the weekend, when volunteering in the community, and especially while interacting in the workplace, regardless of job title—the skills and knowledge needed for all situations are the same. The Community and Leadership Development Center at Indiana University suggests three things anyone can do to demonstrate ethical leadership:

1. *Be people-oriented*: Be aware of how your actions impact others and how people view your leadership. If you consistently demonstrate ethical values, people will see you as someone who is trustworthy and someone they would like to follow.
2. *Choose your values*: Know what you value and be unshakable in what you believe in. If you hold true to your values, you will be less likely to stray from them or influence others in a negative way.
3. *Motivate others to serve the greater good*: Help others in the group understand that putting the group's needs in front of individuals' needs not only demonstrates ethical values, but it also builds strong commitment toward shared goals and shared responsibility for the final outcome.[28]

## The Process of Delegation

**4 Explain the delegation process and describe its three major components.**

A major aspect of managerial leadership is managers' use of the authority inherent in their positions. Just as authority is a major component of management, the delegation of authority is essential to the creation and operation of an organization. In the broadest sense, **delegation** gives employees a greater voice in how the job is to be done; the employees are empowered to make decisions.[29] Unfortunately, some managers view delegation as a means of lightening their workloads. They assign unpleasant tasks to employees and subsequently find that the employees are not motivated to complete those tasks. The manager must look at delegation as a tool to develop employees' skills and abilities rather than as a way to get rid of unpleasant tasks.

**Delegation**
The process of entrusting duties and related authority to subordinates

A manager receives authority from a higher-level manager through delegation, but this does not mean that the higher-level manager surrenders all

**Accountability**
The obligation one has to one's boss and the expectation that employees will accept credit or blame for the results achieved in performing assigned tasks

accountability. **Accountability** is the obligation one has to one's boss and the expectation that employees will accept credit or blame for the results achieved in performing assigned tasks. When supervisors delegate, they are still ultimately accountable for the successful completion of work.

Delegation is a supervisor's strategy for accomplishing objectives. It consists of the following three components, all of which must be present:

1. Assigning duties to immediate subordinates
2. Granting permission (authority) to make commitments, use resources, and take all actions necessary to perform duties
3. Creating an obligation (responsibility) on the part of each employee to perform duties satisfactorily

Unless all three components are present, the delegation process is incomplete. They are inseparably related; a change in one requires change in the other two.

## ASSIGNING DUTIES

Each employee must be assigned a specific job or task to perform. Job descriptions may provide a general framework through which the supervisor can examine duties in the department to decide which tasks to assign to each employee. The assignment should indicate the scope of the task—what to do, how much to do, the level of quality expected, and when the task should be completed. Routine duties usually can be assigned to almost any employee, but there are other functions that the supervisor can assign only to employees who are qualified to perform them. There are also some functions that a supervisor cannot delegate—functions the supervisor must do. The assignment of job duties to employees is of great significance, and much of the supervisor's success depends on it.

## GRANTING AUTHORITY

The granting of authority means that the supervisor confers upon employees the right and power to act, to use certain resources, and to make decisions within the prescribed limits. Of course, the supervisor must determine the scope of authority

*A good manager uses delegation to develop employees' skills and abilities, not to avoid unpleasant tasks.*

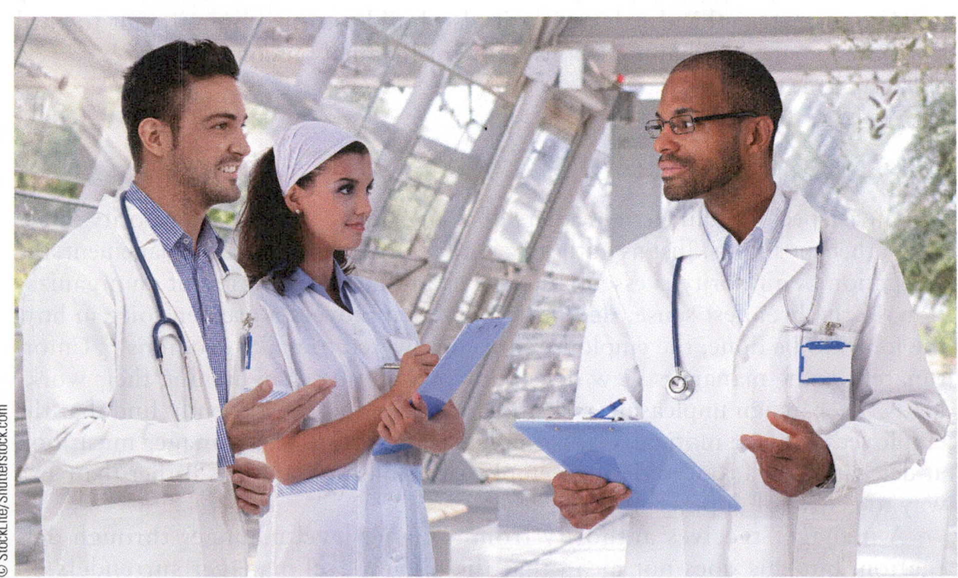

that is to be delegated. How much authority can be delegated depends in part on the amount of authority the supervisor possesses. The degree of authority is also related to the employees and the jobs to be done. For example, if a sales clerk is responsible for processing items returned to the store, that clerk must have the authority to give the customer's money back or provide a store credit or another item in exchange according to established policies with the understanding (limit) that the clerk should alert the supervisor if the returned item was obviously abused in some way. In every instance, enough authority must be granted to the employee to enable the employee to perform assigned tasks adequately and successfully. There is no need for the amount of authority to be larger than the tasks. Authority must be sufficient to meet the employee's obligations.

## DEFINING LIMITATIONS

Throughout the process of delegation, employees must be reassured that their orders and authority come from their immediate supervisor. A supervisor must be specific in telling employees what authority they have and what they can or cannot do. It is uncomfortable for employees to have to guess how far their authority extends. For example, an employee may be expected to order certain materials as a regular part of the job. This employee must know the limits within which materials can be ordered, perhaps in terms of time and costs, and when permission from the supervisor is needed before ordering additional materials. If the supervisor does not state this clearly, the employee will be forced to test the limits and learn by trial and error or return to the supervisor to gather more information, which decreases the effectiveness of the delegation process. If it becomes necessary to change an employee's job assignment, the degree of authority should be checked to ensure that the authority that is delegated is still appropriate. If it is less (or more) than needed, it should be adjusted.

## CREATING RESPONSIBILITY

The third component of the process of delegation is creating obligation on the part of the employee to perform assigned duties satisfactorily. Acceptance of this obligation creates responsibility; without responsibility, delegation is incomplete.

The terms *responsibility* and *authority* are closely related. Like authority, responsibility is often misunderstood. Supervisors commonly use expressions such as "holding subordinates responsible," "delegating responsibilities," and "carrying out responsibilities." Simply stated, **responsibility** is the subordinate's obligation to perform duties as assigned and required by the supervisor. By accepting a job or accepting an obligation to perform assigned duties, the employee implies the acceptance of responsibility. Responsibility in turn implies that the employee agrees to perform duties in return for rewards such as paychecks. The most important facet of the definition is that a subordinate must recognize and accept responsibility if delegation is to succeed.

**Responsibility**
The obligation to perform certain tasks and duties as assigned by the supervisor

## SUPERVISORY ACCOUNTABILITY CANNOT BE DELEGATED

Although a supervisor must delegate authority to employees to accomplish specific jobs, the supervisor's own accountability cannot be delegated. Assigning duties to employees does not relieve the supervisor of the responsibility for those duties. Therefore, when delegating assignments to employees, the supervisor remains accountable for the actions of the employees carrying out those assignments.

To reiterate, responsibility includes (1) the subordinate's obligation to perform assigned tasks and (2) the supervisor's obligation to his or her own manager, or accountability. For example, when a high-level manager asks a supervisor to explain declining performance in the department, the supervisor cannot plead that the responsibility was delegated to employees in the group. The supervisor remains accountable and must answer to the manager.

Regardless of the extent to which a supervisor creates an obligation on the part of employees to perform satisfactorily, the supervisor retains the ultimate responsibility, along with the authority, that is part of the supervisor's departmental position. As Figure 5.3 shows, effective delegation requires an appropriate mix of the assignment of tasks and the authority and responsibility needed to carry out those tasks.

That accountability cannot be delegated may worry some supervisors, but responsibility for the work of others goes with the supervisory position. Delegation is necessary for jobs to be accomplished—the supervisor cannot do everything. While a supervisor may use sound managerial practices, employees will not always use the best judgment or perform in superior ways. Therefore, allowances must be made for errors. Accountability remains with supervisors, but supervisors must be able to depend on their employees. If employees fail to carry out their assigned tasks, they are accountable to the supervisor, who must then redirect the employees as appropriate. When appraising a supervisor's performance, higher-level managers usually consider how much care the supervisor has taken in selecting, training, and supervising employees, and in controlling their activities.

**FIGURE 5.3 Effective delegation requires an appropriate mix of task assignments and the authority and responsibility to accomplish those tasks**

Implied in accountability is the notion that punishments or rewards will follow, depending on how well the duties are performed. However, the ultimate accountability to top-level managers lies with the supervisor who is doing the delegating. Supervisors are responsible and accountable not only for their own actions but also for the actions of their subordinates.

## Delegation by the Supervisor

**5 Discuss why some supervisors do not delegate, and describe the benefits of delegation.**

Every supervisor must delegate some authority to employees, which assumes that the employees can and will accept the authority delegated to them. However, many employees complain that their supervisors make all the decisions and scrutinize their work because they do not trust the employees to carry out assignments. These complaints usually describe supervisors who are unable or unwilling to delegate.

### REASONS FOR LACK OF SUPERVISORY DELEGATION

A supervisor may be reluctant to delegate for several reasons, some of which are valid and some not. Figure 5.4 shows some barriers the supervisor must overcome to achieve effective delegation.

### SHORTAGE OF QUALIFIED EMPLOYEES—"THEY CAN'T DO IT" MENTALITY

Some supervisors cite a lack of qualified employees as an excuse for not delegating authority. Actually, such supervisors feel that their employees cannot handle authority or are unwilling to accept it. If these supervisors refuse to delegate, employees will have little opportunity to obtain the experience they need to improve their judgment and to handle broader assignments. Supervisors must always remember that unless they begin somewhere they will probably always have too few employees who can and will accept more authority with commensurate responsibility.

**FIGURE 5.4 Supervisors must overcome the barriers to delegation**

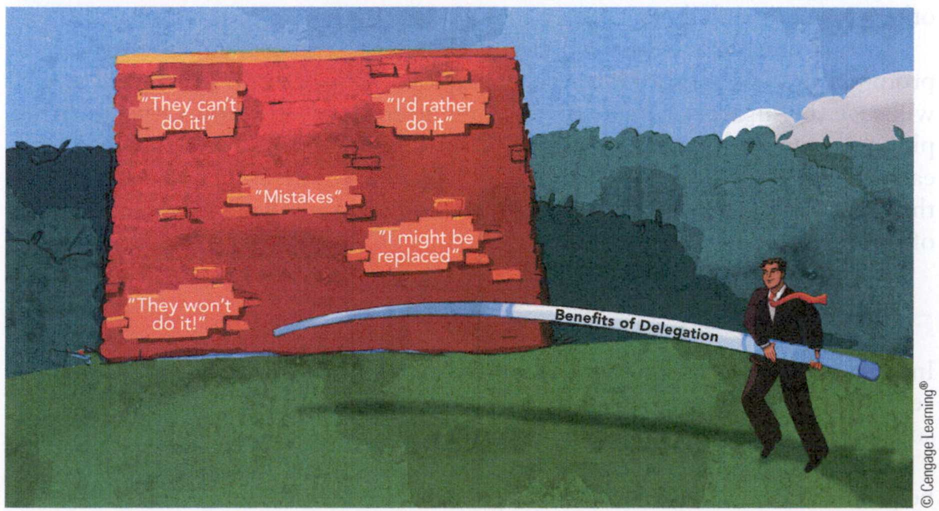

## FEAR OF MAKING MISTAKES

Some supervisors think it best to make most decisions themselves because, in the final analysis, they retain overall responsibility. Out of fear of mistakes, such supervisors are unwilling to delegate, and as a result, they continue to overburden themselves. However, indecision and delay often are more costly than the mistakes supervisors hope to avoid by refusing to delegate. Also, these supervisors may make mistakes by not drawing on employees for assistance in decision making.

## "I'D RATHER DO IT MYSELF" MENTALITY

The old stereotype of a good supervisor was that of one who pitched in and worked alongside employees, setting an example by personal effort. Even today, this type of supervision often occurs when a supervisor has been promoted through the ranks and the supervisory position is a reward for hard work and technical competence. The supervisors, therefore, resort to a pattern in which they feel secure by working alongside employees and doing tasks with which they are most familiar. Occasionally, the supervisor should pitch in, such as when the job is particularly difficult, when employees would benefit from demonstration and guidance, or when an emergency arises. With the trend toward eliminating management levels and consolidating operations, people will have to work together more closely. Under these conditions, the supervisor should be close enough to the job to offer help. Aside from emergencies and unusual situations, however, the supervisor should be supervising, and the employees should be doing their assigned tasks. Normally, it is the supervisor's job to get things done, not to do them.

## "IF IT IS TO BE DONE RIGHT—I HAVE TO DO IT" MENTALITY

Supervisors sometimes complain that if they want something done right, they have to do it themselves. They believe it is easier to do the job themselves than to correct an employee's mistakes, or they may simply prefer to correct an employee's mistakes rather than to clearly explain what should have been done. These attitudes interfere with a supervisor's prime responsibility, which is to supervise others to get the job done.

A good supervisor occasionally shows how a job can be done more efficiently, promptly, or courteously. However, an employee who does the job almost as well will save the supervisor time for more important jobs—for innovative thinking, planning, and more delegating. The effective supervisor strives to ensure that each employee, with each additional job, becomes more competent. Over time, the employee's performance on the job should be as good as or better than that of the supervisor.

## FEAR OF BEING REPLACED

Ineffective supervisors may fear that if they share their knowledge with employees and allow them to participate in decision making, the employees will become so proficient at making good decisions that the supervisor will be unnecessary. The fear of not being needed can be partially overcome if the supervisor cannot be promoted unless he or she has prepared at least two subordinates to take the supervisor's place.

## "THEY WON'T DO IT—YOU CAN KEEP IT" MENTALITY

Not everyone wants to take the responsibility for decisions. The supervisor must identify those employees who need the opportunity to grow and who want to be empowered. Employees may be reluctant to accept delegation because of their insecurity or fear of failure, or they may think the supervisor will be unavailable for guidance. Many employees are reluctant to accept delegation due to past managerial incompetence. For example, there is the "seagull manager" who, like the seagull, flies in, drops a load, and flies off. Too often, employees have had boring, mundane, and unpleasant tasks given to them from above.

Often, veteran employees will counsel new workers by saying, "Don't volunteer for anything, and if the boss gives you a new assignment, beg off." It is difficult for supervisors to create an environment of employee involvement and freedom to make decisions when their own managers do not allow them the same freedom. An environment for delegation and empowerment must be part of the organization's culture. Upper-level managers must advocate delegation at all levels.

## BENEFITS OF DELEGATION

Can supervisors realize the benefits of delegation if they have only a small number of employees and there is no real need to create subunits in a department? Many supervisors face this situation. Is delegation in this type of working situation worth its trouble and risks? In general, the answer is a strong yes.

The supervisor who delegates expects employees to make more decisions on their own. This does not mean that the supervisor is not available for advice. It means that the supervisor encourages the employees to make many of their own decisions and to develop self-confidence in doing so. This, in turn, should mean that the supervisor will have more time to manage. Effective delegation should cause employees to perform an increasing number of jobs and to recommend solutions that contribute to good performance. As the supervisor's confidence in employees expands, the employees' commitment to better performance also should grow. This growth may take time, and the degree of delegation may vary with each employee and with each department. However, in most situations, a supervisor's goal should be to delegate more authority to employees. This goal contributes to employee motivation and to better job performance.

Finally, it must be reiterated that some supervisory areas cannot be delegated. For example, it remains the supervisor's responsibility to formulate certain policies and objectives, to give general directions for the work unit, to appraise employee performance, to take disciplinary action, and to promote employees. Aside from these types of supervisory management responsibilities, the employees should be doing most of the departmental work.

## THE PROPER BALANCE OF DELEGATION

Although we have stressed the advantages of delegation that can be realized through general supervision, it is important to recognize that the process of delegation is delicate. It is not easy for a supervisor to part with some authority and still be left with the responsibility for the workers' performance. The supervisor must achieve a balance among too much, too little, and just the right amount to delegate without losing control. In some situations, supervisors must resort to their formal authority to attain the objectives of the department or provide direction to employees who require close supervision. Supervisors at times have to make decisions that are distasteful to employees. Delegation does not mean a supervisor should manage a department by consensus or by taking a vote on every issue.

**6 Compare the autocratic (authoritarian) approach to supervision with the participative approach.**

## Approaches to Supervisory Leadership

Most employees accept work as a normal part of life. In their jobs, they seek satisfaction that wages alone cannot provide. Most employees probably would prefer to be their own bosses or at least to have a degree of freedom to make decisions that pertain to their work. The question arises as to whether this freedom is possible if an individual works for someone else. Can a degree of freedom be granted to employees if those employees are to contribute to organizational objectives? This is where the delegation of authority can help. The desire for freedom and being one's own boss can be enhanced by delegation, which in the daily routine essentially means giving directions in general terms. It means that instead of watching every detail of the employees' activities, the supervisor is primarily interested in the results employees achieve and is willing to give them considerable latitude in deciding how to achieve those results.

### CLASSIFYING SUPERVISORY LEADERSHIP STYLES

Organizational behavior and management literature are replete with research studies and models that have sought to establish which leadership styles are most consistently associated with superior levels of performance. The magnitude of these studies is beyond the scope of this text, and their findings and concepts are neither consistent nor conclusive.[30]

Rather than debate the differences and nuances of various leadership theories, we believe that they all can be classified into two styles or approaches. These styles range from essentially autocratic or authoritarian supervisory styles (based on Theory X assumptions) to variations of general supervisory styles (based on Theory Y assumptions). These two styles can be presented as the extremes of a continuum (see Figure 5.5). However, in practice, a supervisor usually blends these approaches based on a number of considerations that include the supervisor's skill and experience, the employee or employees who are involved, the situation, and other factors. No one style of supervision has ever been shown to be correct in all situations. Consequently, supervisors must be sensitive to the needs and realities of each situation and must change their styles as necessary to accomplish objectives.

**Theory X**
Assumption that most employees dislike work, avoid responsibility, and must be coerced to do their jobs

**Theory Y**
Assumption that most employees enjoy work, seek responsibility, and can self-direct

Two theories developed by Douglas McGregor can help frame our understanding of supervisory styles, Theory X and Theory Y. We will introduce the assumptions of these theories in this chapter and then provide an expanded view of them in our discussion of motivation in Chapter 7. **Theory X** assumes that most employees dislike work, avoid responsibility, and must be coerced to work hard. **Theory Y** assumes that most employees enjoy work, seek responsibility, and can self-direct.[31] The theories are often illustrated in a supervisor's day-to-day approaches to leading employees. You may have even had a boss who operated with one of the assumptions or the other. While we focus primarily on supervisory leadership, we recognize that not everything that influences employee

**FIGURE 5.5 Leadership style continuum**

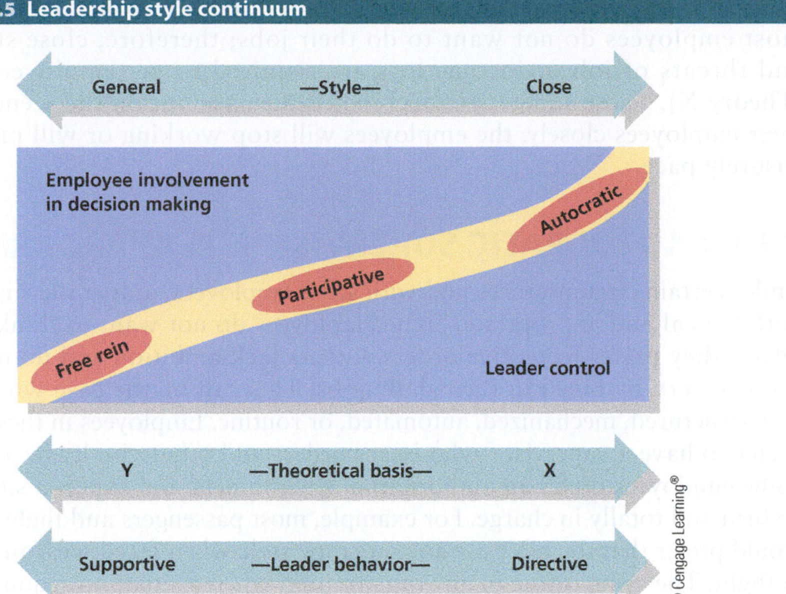


behavior is in response to a supervisory approach. With that said, consider how the assumptions presented in McGregor's theories might influence the supervisory approaches described later.

## AUTOCRATIC (AUTHORITARIAN) SUPERVISION

**Autocratic (authoritarian) supervision**
The supervisory style that relies on formal authority, threats, pressure, and close control

Many supervisors still believe that emphasizing formal authority, or **autocratic (authoritarian) supervision**, is the best way to obtain results. A supervisor of this type often uses pressure to get people to work and may even threaten disciplinary action, including discharge, if employees do not perform as ordered.[32] Employees sometimes call these managers "taskmasters." Autocratic supervision means close control of employees in which supervisors issue directives with detailed instructions and allow employees little room for initiative. Autocratic supervisors delegate very little or no authority. They believe that they know how to do the job better than their employees and that employees are not paid to think but to follow directions. Autocratic supervisors further believe that, because they have been put in charge, they should do most of the planning and decision making. Because such supervisors are quite explicit in telling employees exactly how and in what sequence things are to be done, they follow through with close supervision and are focused on the tasks to be done.

**Bureaucratic style of supervision**
The supervisory style that emphasizes strict compliance with organizational policies, rules, and directives

Autocratic supervision is sometimes associated with what has been called the **bureaucratic style of supervision**. This style emphasizes an organizational structure and climate that require strict compliance with managers' policies, rules, and directives throughout the firm. Because bureaucratic managers believe that their primary role is to carry out and enforce policies and directives, they usually adopt an authoritarian approach. Their favorite sayings are "It's policy," "Those are the rules," and "Shape up or ship out!"

Autocratic supervisors do not necessarily distrust their employees, but they firmly believe that without detailed instructions employees could not do their jobs. Some autocratic supervisors operate from the premise that most employees do not want to do their jobs; therefore, close supervision and threats of job or income loss are required to get employees to work (Theory X). These supervisors feel that if they are not on the scene watching their employees closely, the employees will stop working or will proceed at a leisurely pace.

## WHEN AUTOCRATIC SUPERVISION IS APPROPRIATE

Under certain circumstances and with some employees, autocratic supervision is both logical and appropriate. Some employees do not want to think for themselves; they prefer to receive orders. Others lack ambition and do not wish to become very involved in their daily jobs. This can be the case when jobs are very structured, mechanized, automated, or routine. Employees in these jobs may prefer to have a supervisor who issues orders and otherwise leaves them alone. Some employees prefer an authoritarian environment and expect a supervisor to be firm and totally in charge. For example, most passengers and flight attendants would prefer that the pilot use an autocratic style when faced with an emergency in flight. The same is true in any organization when a situation requires immediate attention.

Probably the major advantages of autocratic supervision are that it is quick and fairly easy to apply and that it usually gets rapid results in the short run. It may be appropriate when employees are new and inexperienced, especially if the supervisor is under major time pressures and cannot afford to have employees take time to figure out on their own how to get the work done.

## EFFECTS OF AUTOCRATIC SUPERVISION

For the most part, the autocratic method of supervision is not conducive to developing employee talents, and it tends to frustrate employees who have ambition and potential. Such employees may lose interest and initiative and stop thinking for themselves because there is little need for independent thought. Employees who strongly resent autocratic supervision may become frustrated rather than find satisfaction in their daily work. Such frustration can lead to arguments and other forms of discontent. In some cases, employees may become hostile toward an autocratic supervisor and resist the supervisor's directives. The resistance may not even be apparent to the supervisor when it takes the form of slow work, mistakes, and poor work quality. If the supervisor makes a mistake, these employees may secretly rejoice.

## GENERAL SUPERVISION AND PARTICIPATIVE MANAGEMENT

**General supervision**
The style of supervision in which the supervisor sets goals and limits but allows employees to decide how to achieve goals

Because of the potentially negative consequences associated with autocratic and close supervision, most supervisors prefer not to use it or to apply it sparingly. Is one leadership style better than another? Many research studies have suggested that effective supervisors tailor their leadership styles to situations and to the abilities and motivation of subordinates. Effective supervisors who want to guide employees to higher levels of performance recognize that they cannot rely solely on managerial authority. **General supervision** means that the supervisor sets goals, discusses those goals with employees, and fixes the limits within which the work must be done. Within this framework, employees have considerable freedom to decide how to achieve their objectives.

**Participative management** means that the supervisor discusses with employees the feasibility, workability, extent, and content of a problem before making a decision and issuing a **directive**. General supervision and participative management are grounded in Theory Y assumptions. Regardless of one's preference for a leadership style, the supervisor must issue directives and ensure that the assigned work gets done efficiently and effectively. The degree to which the supervisor uses directives will, in part, vary with the task to be performed; the skill level, experience, and willingness of the subordinate; and the urgency of the situation. The accompanying Supervisory Tips box offers five major characteristics for issuing good supervisory directives.

**Participative management**
Allowing employees to influence and share in organizational decision making

**Directive**
The communication approach by which a supervisor conveys to employees what, how, and why something is to be accomplished

A participatory style does not lessen a supervisor's authority; the right to decide remains with the supervisor, and the employees' suggestions can be rejected. Participative management involves sharing ideas, opinions, and information between the supervisor and the employees and thoroughly discussing alternative solutions to a problem, regardless of who originates the solutions. A high degree of mutual trust must be evident.

As discussed elsewhere in this text, the term *empowerment* has been used to describe an approach by which employees and work teams are given more responsibility and authority to make decisions about the jobs they do. Empowerment stems from the same philosophy of how to manage and supervise as participative management, and likewise is a matter of degree. Empowerment is a situational approach that involves the expectation of distinct amounts of participation by individuals in specific situations.

More important than approach is the supervisor's attitude. Some supervisors are inclined to use a pseudo-participatory approach simply to give employees the feeling that they have been consulted, asking for input even though a course of action has already been decided. They use this approach to manipulate employees to do what will be required, with or without employees' consultation. However, employees can sense superficiality, and when they believe their participation is contrived, the results may be worse than if the supervisor had practiced autocratic supervision.

If participative management is to succeed, the supervisor and the employees must want it. When employees believe that the supervisor knows best and that making decisions is none of their concern, an opportunity to participate is not likely to induce higher motivation and better morale. Further, employees should be consulted in those areas in which they can express valid opinions and in which they can draw on their knowledge. The problems should be consistent with employees' experiences and abilities. Asking for participation in areas that are far outside employees' scopes of competence may make employees feel inadequate and frustrated.

**SUPERVISORY TIPS**

### Guidelines for Issuing Good Directives

**Reasonable**—The supervisor should not issue a directive if the employee receiving it does not have the ability or experience and willingness to comply.
**Understandable**—The supervisor should make certain that an employee understands a directive by speaking in words that are familiar to the employee and by using feedback to ensure that the employee understands.
**Specific**—The supervisor should state clearly what is expected in terms of quantity and quality of work performance.
**Time-limited**—The supervisor should specify a time limit within which the work should be completed.
**Congruent**—Supervisory directives must be compatible with the philosophy, mission, policies, regulations, and ethical standards of the organization.

## ADVANTAGES OF PARTICIPATIVE MANAGEMENT AND GENERAL SUPERVISION

Perhaps the greatest advantage of participative management is that a supervisor's directive can be transformed into a solution for which employees feel shared ownership. Contributing to decisions and solutions leads employees to cooperate more enthusiastically in carrying out a directive, and their morale is apt to be higher when their ideas are valued. Still another advantage is that participative management permits closer communication between employees and the supervisor so that they learn to trust and respect each other better and, for the most part, the workplace can become more enjoyable with less tension and conflict.

General supervision means permitting employees, within prescribed limits, to work out the details of their daily tasks and to make many of the decisions about how tasks will be performed, with the assumption that employees want to do a good job and will find greater satisfaction in making decisions themselves. The supervisor communicates the desired results, standards, and limits within which the employees can work and then delegates accordingly.

For example, a school-maintenance supervisor might assign a group of employees to paint the interior walls of the school. The supervisor tells the group where to get the paint and other materials and reminds them that they should do the painting without interfering with normal school operations. Then, the supervisor suggests a target date for completing the project and leaves the group to work on its own. The supervisor may occasionally check back with the group to see whether group members are encountering any problems or need help. The advantages of participative management/general supervision are listed in Figure 5.6.

For general supervision to work, employees should know the routine of their jobs and which results are expected, but the supervisor should avoid giving detailed instructions that specify precisely how results are to be achieved. General supervision also means that the supervisor, or the supervisor and employees together, should set realistic standards or performance targets. These standards should be high enough to represent a challenge and may require employees to be innovative in their strategies to achieve them, but they should not be so high that

**FIGURE 5.6 The advantages of participative management/general supervision**

**FOR SUPERVISORS**

- Frees the supervisor from many details, which allows time to plan, organize, and control.
- Gives the supervisor more time to assume additional responsibility.
- Instills confidence that employees will carry out the work and develop suitable approaches to making decisions on the job when the supervisor is away from the department.
- The decisions made by employees may be better than the ones made by the supervisor because the employees are closest to the details.

**FOR EMPLOYEES**

- Have a chance to develop their talents and abilities by making on-the-job decisions.
- May make mistakes but are encouraged to learn from those mistakes and the mistakes of others.
- Are motivated to take pride in their decisions.
- May feel that they have a better chance to advance to higher positions.

they cannot be achieved. Such targets sometimes are known as **stretch targets**. Employees know that their efforts are being measured against these standards. If they cannot accomplish the targets, they are expected to inform the supervisor so that the standards can be discussed again and perhaps modified.[33]

**Stretch targets**
Targeted job objectives that present a challenge but are achievable

### PARTICIPATIVE MANAGEMENT AND GENERAL SUPERVISION AS A WAY OF LIFE

When practiced simultaneously, participative management and general supervision are a way of life that must be followed over time. A supervisor cannot expect sudden results by introducing these types of supervision into an environment in which employees have been accustomed to authoritarian, close supervision. It may take considerable time and patience before positive results are evident.

The successful implementation of participative management and general supervision requires a continuous effort on a supervisor's part to develop employees beyond their present skills. The participative supervisor spends considerable time encouraging employees to solve their own problems and to participate in and make decisions because they learn best from their own successes and failures.

As employees become more competent and self-confident, the supervisor has less need to instruct and watch them. A valid way to gauge the supervisor's effectiveness is to study how employees in the department function when the supervisor is away from the job. This is the essence of employee empowerment.

## Followership: An Equally Important Part of the Leadership Equation

**7 Explain the role of followers in the leadership process and differentiate between different types of followers.**

As we consider the role of leaders in the functions of supervision, it is equally important for us to consider the role of followers. The words General Douglas MacArthur spoke in 1961 still ring true today in any organization, "A general is just as good or just as bad as the troops under his command make him." As suggested earlier in this chapter, nearly anyone can learn leadership skills. But what makes a leader a leader is the presence of followers, people who choose to be guided and influenced by the leader, whether by accepting a job, participating in a committee or work group, volunteering in a community organization, joining a movement or even becoming one of a group of friends. The leader's effectiveness is reflected in how well followers perform, because it is their collective performance that ultimately achieves the goals of the group. So while leadership often gets the most attention in discussions of group and organizational success, followers can have an equally critical impact. Accordingly, an exploration of followership can help supervisors understand the implications their management choices have on their followers and how the whole group performs.

### WE ARE ALL FOLLOWERS

Mark Zuckerberg may have founded and continues to lead Facebook, but the company could not have achieved its level of success without the recruiters, coders, marketers, and other workers who show up to work each day. Likewise, the president of the United States issues countless executive orders, and thousands of public administrators, troops, and street-level workers engage in followership to put those orders into action. With no followers, there are no leaders.

**Followership**
The capacity or willingness to follow a leader

**Followership**, the capacity or willingness to follow a leader, completes the reciprocal process of leadership. Those who follow in response to the directives of a leader choose the extent to which they engage with and support the leader in order to complete a task. According to Harvard University public leadership lecturer Barbara Kellerman, followers are "low in the hierarchy and have less power, authority, and influence than their superiors."[34]

However, the position of a follower is not a static or a permanent position. Depending on the needs of an organization or a group, leadership and followership roles can be assumed by anyone because the follower is essentially a learner, a person who needs information or direction from someone else in order to proceed with the task at hand. For example, a Red Cross fundraising volunteer needs direction from the Director of Giving in order to know who to call, when to call, and how much to ask for during the annual fund drive. The director of giving needs to know the overall fundraising goal and timeline, which is provided by the executive director, who gets strategic directives from the Board of Directors. Three of the four employees in this scenario are followers, but three parties are also leaders.

In a completely different organizational context, the director of music for Fairview Church might receive his assignment to blow up and tie 200 balloon animals for the annual Fall Festival from the volunteer mom in charge. In both situations, someone has to lead and someone has to follow in order for the work to get done. The role determination is based on who has decision-making authority, who has expertise and who needs information, not the position on each person's name badge or business card. In the course of a traditional work day, however, the supervisor typically leads and subordinates follow, but not all followers follow in quite the same way.

## TYPES OF FOLLOWERS

A variety of followership behaviors can be observed in organizations. Carnegie Mellon University professor Robert E. Kelley suggests that followers can be categorized into five groups, based on the combination of their tendency to be passive or assertive in their actions and the extent to which they use independent, critical thinking. As illustrated in Figure 5.7, *passive* followers, termed sheep in some of Kelley's writings, are not very engaged with their organization. They aren't actively involved and they depend on others to make decisions for them. *Conformist* followers are the "yes men and women," who are supportive and involved, but they tend to go along with the crowd rather than making their own choices. Followers who are *alienated* are independent thinkers, but not in a positive way. They are disengaged from the organization's goals and remain distant from the leader, but they willingly share their ideas, which often come across as skeptical or cynical. The *exemplary* follower is often considered the star of the office, a creative, constructive, independent thinker who actively focuses energy toward group goals. The exemplary follower will back the leader 100 percent if he or she agrees with the current goal, but if not, that active, independent thinking could transform into alternative leadership and steer the group in another direction. *Pragmatist* followers assess the group situation and choose the followership style that best fits the task, as well as his or her current workload, attitude toward the goal, and presence of other followers that might fulfill other roles in the group.[35]

After learning about each of the different types of followers, imagine for a minute a workgroup or department comprised of all one type of follower. Nothing new would ever get done, either because everyone would be waiting for

**FIGURE 5.7 Followership style**

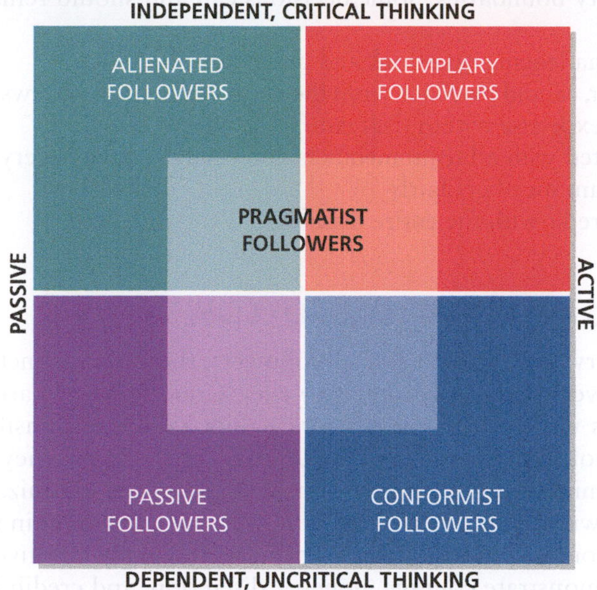


*Source:* Adapted from *The Power of Followership* by Robert E. Kelley, copyright © 1992 by Consultants to Executives and Organizations, Ltd. Used by permission of Doubleday, a division of Random House, Inc.

someone else to do it, everyone would criticize, everyone would agree, or everyone would try to be second in command. It shouldn't be the leader's goal to transform everyone into one type of follower; rather, the leader should use a variety of management strategies to engage each follower in a way that is most appropriate for his or her needs and style of followership.

Leaders need to be aware that followers also have the power to influence. Followers' influence can certainly be positive when it is focused on achieving shared goals, but some followers, termed toxic followers[36] by George Washington University psychology professor Lynn R. Offermann, use their influence to create unique leadership challenges. Strong-willed followers who have their own agenda can rally others in the group to form a competing majority with the intent to turn the course of action in another direction. Flattering followers do all they can to get on the boss's good side and shower him or her with praise and complements in order to get the best assignments or preferential treatment, but they often insulate the leader from organizational or performance problems because they don't want to be the bearer of bad news. Power mongers with their eyes on the leader's corner office use organizational information as a tool to make the leader dependent on them, while at the same time demonstrating their value to the organization, hoping it is recognized and rewarded. These strategies can undermine the leader's effectiveness, pollute organizational culture, and negatively impact organizational performance in significant ways. A leader should quickly stop toxic follower behaviors by addressing them one-on-one with the employee and providing guidance on more appropriate behaviors. Healthcare consultant Andrew Gibbons and performance specialist Danielle Bryant suggest strategies leaders should use to create an environment where all followers thrive:

- Lead by example, keeping vision and values front and center
- Explain why when making decisions

- Delegate responsibility appropriately
- Set authority boundaries. Some decisions can and should remain leadership decisions
- Welcome challenging questions and disagreement
- Seek regular, candid feedback from the team. Welcome bad news with the good
- Utilize the expertise within the team
- Be acquainted with all team members and engage equally everyone
- Treat all team members fairly
- Share the credit with the entire team[37]

## QUALITIES OF EFFECTIVE FOLLOWERS

Although supervisors should value all followers, there are distinct qualities that effective followers share, according to Kelley. Good followers are able to manage themselves well by using good work habits, taking responsibility for their actions, and holding themselves accountable for the work they are assigned. They are committed to the goals, vision, or cause of the organization, more so than to their own personal gain. Good followers are competent in their roles and they strive to continually build their competencies. Finally effective followers are ethical and demonstrate courage, honesty, discretion, and credibility.[38] The last quality is particularly valuable for two reasons. First, if the leader of a group engages in unethical, illegal, or discriminatory practices, followers need to be brave enough to stand up for what is right to protect themselves, their co-workers, and

**FIGURE 5.8 The ten rules of good followership**

1. Don't blame your boss for an unpopular decision or policy; your job is to support, not undermine.
2. Argue with your boss if necessary; but do it in private, avoid embarrassing situations, and never reveal to others what was discussed.
3. Make the decision, then run it past the boss; use your initiative.
4. Accept responsibility whenever it is offered.
5. Tell the truth and don't quibble; your boss will be giving advice up the chain of command based on what you said.
6. Do your homework; give your boss all the information needed to make a decision; anticipate possible questions.
7. When making a recommendation, remember who will probably have to implement it (that would be you). This means you must know your own limitations and weaknesses as well as your strengths.
8. Keep your boss informed of what's going on in the work group; people will be reluctant to tell him or her their problems and successes. You should do it for them, and assume someone else will tell the boss about yours.
9. If you see a problem, fix it. Don't worry about who would have gotten the blame or who now gets the praise.
10. Put in more than an honest day's work, but don't ever forget the needs of your family. If they are unhappy, you will be too, and your job performance will suffer accordingly.

*Source:* Adapted from Col. Phillip S. Meilinger, "The Ten Rules of Good Followership". In Richard I. Lester and A. Glenn Norton (Eds.), *Concepts for Air Force Leadership* (pp. 99–101). Maxwell AFB, AL: Air University Press.

the organization. Second, a leader's perspective is only one perspective. Followers can bring multiple points of view to a problem or task and share their insights in order to provide alternatives or a more appropriate solution. However, speaking up from a position of less authority can sometimes be risky, and followers need to have the courage to be honest and use their knowledge, with appropriate tact and discretion, to serve the best interests of the organization.

Followership may always be a second thought after leadership, but the truth is, without followers, there are no leaders. It is important for supervisors and employees to remember that everyone is a follower at some point, and learning to be a good follower is excellent preparation for becoming a good leader. Figure 5.8 shares practical suggestions the U.S. Air Force uses to build its cadre of good followers.

## SUMMARY

1. Supervisory management requires more than just a title. To effectively engage employees in their assigned tasks in order to get the desired results, supervisors must learn and use leadership knowledge, skills, and abilities. The leadership role entails interacting with a group of individuals in order to influence their opinions, attitudes, and performance. A leader's influence is reflected in whether employees follow willingly and achieve organizational goals.

   Contemporary leadership thought leaders include Warren Bennis, who suggests that people want four things from leaders: (1) direction, (2) trust, (3) hope, and (4) results. James Kouzes and Barry Posner believe that successful leaders engage in five practices: (1) challenging the process, (2) inspiring a shared vision, (3) enabling others to act, (4) modeling the way, and (5) encouraging the heart.

   Servant-leadership has also emerged as a popular practice with many global companies. It posits that in order to lead, one must first know how to serve. Robert Greenleaf and other proponents of this leadership style contend that service entails making sure that others' needs are met first, acting with integrity, listening to stakeholders, and empowering followers for success.

   While no one style of leadership is considered best, effective leaders demonstrate a number of common practices. They take responsibility for their followers' success by inspiring shared vision and values, holding employees accountable, and engendering mutual trust and respect through consistent candor, caring, and competency. Leaders create a supportive climate for people to develop new competencies, explore new roles, make decisions, adapt to change, and become leaders themselves.

2. Trust is a key element in interactions between leaders and followers, an element that Stephen Covey relates to alignment, the process of working together in harmony. Unfortunately, lack of trust is a growing concern in the workplace, which workers attribute to their leaders inconsistent behavior, lack of concern for workers, favoritism, and poor communication. Supervisors can build trust with employees by using excellent listening and communication skills, being authentic, and making sure that their words and actions reflect integrity.

3. Ethics determine how a person distinguishes between right and wrong in their own behavior and the behaviors of others. Individuals' ethical values drive their decisions and comprise their character. A leader's influence transmits his or her values to followers and the overall organizational culture. When an organization has an ethical culture, performance increases and misconduct decreases, and the converse is also true. Research has shown that leaders' misconduct in particular erodes organizational conduct, it negatively influences workers' morale, it increases fear of retaliation and it can force workers to compromise their own ethics. Leaders should assess their ethical values relative to how they influence their means of getting work done, their motivations, and their accomplishments. If the leaders' behaviors do not reflect ethical values, they should strive to change them in order to protect themselves, their followers, and their organization from the results of impropriety. Ethical leadership spans beyond the workplace. In every situation, leaders should be people oriented, choose their values, and motivate others to serve the greater good. The time is always right to do what is right.

4. Delegation is a process comprised of three elements: (1) assigning a job or duties, (2) granting authority, and (3) creating responsibility. Successful delegation depends on supervisors' discretion to identify the appropriate amount of authority and responsibility

an employee will need to accomplish assigned duties or directives. The three elements act as an interdependent equation—if one changes, the others must change as well. A supervisor should specifically describe the delegated duty in terms of the level of performance required and the decision-making authority the employee has relative to the duty. Regardless of the authority the supervisor delegates to employees, the supervisor is still accountable for successful completion of the task.

5. Supervisors can be reluctant to delegate tasks for a number of reasons. The company may have a shortage of qualified employees, and the supervisor may have a fear of making mistakes, or an I'd-rather-do-it-myself mentality. The supervisor may be afraid of not being needed, or there may be a lack of managerial support for delegation. Employees may be reluctant to take on new tasks, possibly because of their interaction with managers who have conditioned them to avoid receiving tasks from a supervisor who "dumps" rather than delegates.

When delegation is carried out effectively, it can be very beneficial to the entire work team. Employees learn new skills, gain confidence, and learn how to make appropriate decisions. The supervisor is freed up to empower more employees, departmental decisions are made with a wider range of input, and employee morale and job performance increase.

6. Some supervisors believe that autocratic supervision, using formal authority to get results, is more effective than general supervision. At times close supervision, detailed instructions, and a climate of strict compliance (Theory X tactics) are appropriate, but generally these practices result in low employee morale, resistance, discontent, and frustration.

Conversely, participative management and general supervision assume that workers are motivated to do their best (Theory Y assumptions). Therefore, both involve delegation and provide freedom for employees to choose how to go about their work once the supervisor issues directives. In participative management, workers are empowered to take the initiative through the provision of increased authority and responsibility, and they are encouraged to contribute ideas to the decision-making process. These management styles, when used in authentic contexts, benefit supervisors and employees. The supervisor saves time by empowering other members of the team to work independently. When employees gain experience in making decisions based on their own judgment, they become more competent and more promotable. A supervisor's goal should be to help employees move to the next level.

The extent to which a supervisor uses the general, autocratic, bureaucratic, or participative style requires a delicate balance. Ultimately, the supervisor is responsible for achieving departmental objectives. Therefore, the supervisor should consider the task and the individuals involved and choose the most appropriate style in order to get work accomplished.

7. Followership is the capacity or willingness to follow a leader. Followers can choose the extent to which they engage with and support a leader. The follower position is not static, and everyone is a follower at some point in their life. The determination of who leads and who follows is based on who has authority, who has expertise, and who needs information and guidance. Followers can be classified into groups based on their levels of assertiveness and independent thinking, which can be described as passive, conformist, alienated, exemplary, and pragmatist. The leader's goal should be to engage a variety of follower types in workgroups and use multiple strategies to help all followers thrive. Followers can exert influence, sometimes in a toxic way, which can undermine the leader's efforts and negatively impact organizational performance. Effective leaders have good self-management skills, they are committed to the organization; they are competent, and they demonstrate ethics, courage, honesty, discretion, and credibility. Followers can be of particular value to organizations when they share different perspectives and stand up for what is right, even if the leader does not.

## KEY TERMS

Accountability (p. 182)
Autocratic (authoritarian) supervision (p. 189)
Bureaucratic style of supervision (p. 189)
Contingency-style leadership (p. 177)
Delegation (p. 181)
Directive (p. 191)
Ethics (p. 179)
Followership (p. 194)
General supervision (p. 190)
Leadership (p. 172)
Participative management (p. 191)
Responsibility (p. 183)
Servant-leadership (p. 175)
Stretch targets (p. 193)
Theory X (p. 188)
Theory Y (p. 188)
Trust (p. 177)

## WHAT HAVE YOU LEARNED?

1. How would you define leadership?
   a. If there is one person (living or dead) whom you would really like to follow, who would it be? Why would you want to follow that particular person? What characteristics of servant-leadership did that person exhibit?
   b. Think of a person whom you would not have wanted to follow. Why? How would this person's knowledge of the characteristics of servant-leadership have helped the person to be a better leader?
   c. In your opinion, what perceptual factors distinguish followership from non-followership?
2. Why is it inappropriate to assume that a leadership style that works best in one situation will be just as effective in another?
3. Why is trust a key ingredient in the leadership equation?
   a. Considering the last place you worked, how would you characterize your level of trust of your employer?
   b. What did your employer do (or not do) to establish that level of trust?
   c. If you were (or are) a supervisor, what are some things you could do to build trust with your employees?
4. Returning to the ethical values listed in this chapter, which of the values would you say most strongly direct your behavior and decisions? How can a leader's ethical values influence his or her followers? How can those values influence organizational performance?
5. Why are the concepts of responsibility, authority, and accountability closely related? Why can't a supervisor's personal accountability be delegated? Why are many supervisors reluctant to delegate? What benefits typically accrue to a supervisor who learns to delegate?
6. Distinguish between autocratic (authoritarian) supervision, participative management, and general supervision. What theoretical differences are implied in these approaches? Relate these to concepts concerning the delegation of authority, motivation, and empowerment.
7. Explain the role of followers in the leadership process. Why is it important to be able to differentiate between different types of followers? How can a leader encourage good followership?

## EXPERIENTIAL EXERCISES FOR SELF-ASSESSMENT

### EXPERIENTIAL EXERCISE FOR SELF-ASSESSMENT—5.1: Evaluating Leadership Integrity

The assessment below is adapted from Craig and Gustafson's Perceived Leader Integrity Scale (PLIS), which measures your perception of someone else's integrity within a group or organizational setting. *Integrity* is the quality of possessing and steadfastly adhering to high moral principles or moral standards. In some organizations, this scale is used as a 360 degree assessment, through which several people are asked to rate one individual, typically a leader or supervisor, and then submit their ratings for scoring. An individual scores each scale then aggregates (puts together and averages) the scores to provide the leader with an integrity score that represents multiple perspectives. Other organizations assign partners to assess one another. In this exercise, you should use one of the methods described above or simply ask someone to complete the scale for you to evaluate your leadership integrity. Then reflect on your findings by responding to the questions below.

**Perceived Leader Integrity Scale Instructions**

The following items concern your perceptions of another person. Circle responses to indicate how well each item describes that person.

Response Choices: 1=Not at all 2=Somewhat 3=Very Much 4=Exactly

| Rating | Question |
|---|---|
| 1 2 3 4 | 1. Would use people's mistakes to attack them personally |
| 1 2 3 4 | 2. Always gets even |
| 1 2 3 4 | 3. Gives special favors to certain favorite friends |
| 1 2 3 4 | 4. Would lie to me or others |
| 1 2 3 4 | 5. Would risk other people to protect himself or herself in work matters |
| 1 2 3 4 | 6. Deliberately fuels conflict among employees or peers |
| 1 2 3 4 | 7. Is evil |
| 1 2 3 4 | 8. Would use a person's performance appraisal to criticize them as a person |
| 1 2 3 4 | 9. Has it in for someone or some people |
| 1 2 3 4 | 10. Would allow other people to be blamed for his/her mistakes |
| 1 2 3 4 | 11. Would falsify records if it would help his/her work situation |
| 1 2 3 4 | 12. Lacks high moral standards |
| 1 2 3 4 | 13. Ridicules people when they make mistakes |
| 1 2 3 4 | 14. Would deliberately exaggerate people's mistakes to make them look bad |
| 1 2 3 4 | 15. Is vindictive |
| 1 2 3 4 | 16. Would blame others for his or her own mistakes |
| 1 2 3 4 | 17. Avoids coaching someone because he or she wants him or her to fail |
| 1 2 3 4 | 18. Would treat people better if they were a different ethnicity, gender, or religion |

| Rating | Question |
|---|---|
| 1 2 3 4 | 19. Would deliberately distort what people say |
| 1 2 3 4 | 20. Deliberately makes people angry at each other |
| 1 2 3 4 | 21. Is a hypocrite |
| 1 2 3 4 | 22. Would limit others' training opportunities to prevent them from advancing |
| 1 2 3 4 | 23. Would blackmail an employee if he or she though he or she could get away with it |
| 1 2 3 4 | 24. Enjoys turning down requests |
| 1 2 3 4 | 25. Would make trouble for someone if they got on his or her bad side |
| 1 2 3 4 | 26. Would take credit for other people's ideas |
| 1 2 3 4 | 27. Would steal from the organization |
| 1 2 3 4 | 28. Is rude or uncivil to co-workers |
| 1 2 3 4 | 29. Would engage in sabotage against the organization |
| 1 2 3 4 | 30. Would try to damage someone's career because he or she doesn't like them |
| 1 2 3 4 | 31. Would do things which violate organizational policy and then expect other people to cover for him or her. |
| 1 2 3 4 | 32. Puts his or her personal interests ahead of the organization |
| 1 2 3 4 | 33. Cannot be trusted with confidential information |

Adapted from a version of the PLIS, authored by S. Bartholomew Craig and Sigrid B. Gustafson (1998), published in *The Leadership Quarterly* 9(2), pp. 143–144.

### Scoring

The PLS measures perceptions of another person's ethical integrity. Responses on the PLIS indicate the degree to which the scorer views the behavior of another person as ethical. If you had someone complete the scale for you, then the scale score will represent a perception of your ethical integrity. If you completed the scale for someone else, then the scale score will represent a perception of that person's ethical integrity.

Score the questionnaire by adding together the responses on all 33 items. A low score on the scale indicates that the scorer perceives the person being evaluated to be highly ethical. A high score indicates that the scorer perceives the person being evaluated to be very unethical. Interpretations of the scores are provided below.

### Scoring Interpretation

0–33: Highly ethical. Scores in this rage mean that the person being evaluated is perceived as highly ethical. The scorer's impression is that the person has high integrity and strong ethical principles.

34–46: Moderately ethical: Scores in this range mean that the person being evaluated is viewed as moderately ethical. The scorer's impression is that the person might engage in some unethical behaviors under certain circumstances.

47 or above: Low ethical: Scores in this range mean that the person being evaluated is viewed as having very weak ethical principles or as being unethical. The scorer's impression is that the person being evaluated does things that are unfair and dishonest whenever he or she has the opportunity to do so.

### Taking Action

If you had someone complete the scale for you, reflect on the findings. What did the scale tell you about your level of integrity? How do the findings make you feel about yourself as a leader? What can you do with the information you gained? What specific steps can you take to ensure that your behavior is consistently ethical, based on the results?

If you completed the scale for someone else, reflect on the findings and ask that person to reflect on the findings. What did that person learn about his or her level of integrity? Do they feel there is anything they can do with the information? Ask them what specific steps they might take to ensure that their behavior is consistently ethical, based on the results. How do the findings about the other person make you feel about them as a co-worker or peer?

### For More Information and Further Study

Links to additional ethics self-assessments can be found in the Chapter 5 Experiential Exercises for Self-Assessment section of the companion website for this textbook.

## PERSONAL SKILL BUILDING

### PERSONAL SKILL BUILDER 5-1: You Make the Call

1. 

INTERNET ACTIVITY

Go to the website of a Habitat for Humanity that serves your community or visit the Habitat for Humanity International website. What did you learn about Women Build and other Habitat volunteer programs from this website? Did any of them look interesting to you as a possible volunteer opportunity?

2. Refer to the opening You Make the Call! Make a list of at least three questions you would ask Alisha McDonald.
3. Now put yourself in Alisha's shoes and write a brief answer to the questions you have written.

## PERSONAL SKILL BUILDER 5-2: Supervisor's Style of Leading

1. Think of a supervisor, coach, or instructor you have known or observed who had the best SKAs and talent to lead others to achieve superior results. Make a list of those attributes and techniques they used that made you feel this person was effective.
2. Think of a supervisor, coach, or person (it may be someone living or dead) that you would not like to be a follower of. Make a list of the traits or attributes that the person displayed that got them at the top of your list.
3. Compare your lists to the "keys to unlock potential" in Figure 5.2. To what degree do they coincide or differ?
4. Write a 60-word or less paper describing what you learned from this Personal Skill Builder.

## PERSONAL SKILL BUILDER 5-3: Dealing with People Who Make Your Life Difficult: Roary—the Exploder!

This is another in a series of exercises that introduce one of those people who might make your life difficult. Roary is very challenging because he has the potential to lose control at any time.

1. Read the following statement from B. J. Karim, an employee at Poore Brothers, a plumbing supply and distribution company:

   *I have a boss, Ralph Poore, who is the consummate Dr. Jekyll and Mr. Hyde. On some days, Poore can be the nicest and kindest person, but on others—that's another story. Behind his back, we call him Roary because when he's angry, he speaks at such a loud volume that anyone within miles can hear him. He shows his impatience and displeasure by exploding at the drop of a hat. He has meetings where, if someone disagrees with him or delivers bad news about what is happening at the company, he will pound his hands on the table and yell at the top of his lungs. More than once, Poore has ended the meeting with one of these tirades, either by kicking everyone else out or by leaving.*

   *Once, Roary went into one of the salespeople's offices to ask if he had called on a contractor as asked. When the salesperson answered that the person was not there when he called but that he had sent a fax and a copy of some new fixtures the company had just gotten in, Poore stormed out of the office, shouting obscenities.*

   *When Poore hears bad news, it doesn't matter whose fault it is—he blows up at whoever is there. Another time, Poore was speaking to another of my co-workers about a delivery she needed to arrange. She told Poore that Crane's manufacturing facility was about three months behind in its production runs. We couldn't deliver the product because Crane hadn't produced it. Poore picked up a flower vase and threw it across the room.*

   *Poore is always right—in his mind. If anyone disagrees with him or tells him something he doesn't want to hear, he throws a tantrum. This man is a time bomb waiting for something to set him off. I haven't felt his wrath, but it's only a matter of time.*

2. Analyze Roary's leadership style. When might this style be appropriate? What might be some disadvantages of this style?
3. **INTERNET ACTIVITY** Using the Internet, find at least three sources of information on how to deal with people like Roary. Carefully review each site for suggestions on how to cope with this difficult person.
4. Based on your findings, what suggestions would you make to Karim on how to cope with Roary?
5. Write a one-page paper explaining how this exercise increased your working knowledge of coping with the behaviors of this difficult person.

## PERSONAL SKILL BUILDER 5-4: Look in the Mirror

The perceptions of great leaders vary greatly.

1. Look at the picture frame collage. Our leader list includes (from left to right) Ford Motor Company's Allen Mulally, DuPont's Ellen Kullman, Harlem Children Zone's Geoffrey Canada, and Pope Francis, Pontiff of the Catholic Church. By searching the Internet, learn about the background for each of these leaders.

© Darren Brode/Shutterstock.com

Prashanth Vishwanathan/Bloomberg/Getty Images

Bennett Raglin/Getty Images

© Martin Podzorny/Shutterstock.com

   a. For each leader, identify what you perceive to be their SKAs.
   b. For each leader, in 50 words or less, describe their leadership styles.

2. After reading the article by Robert J. Thomas, "Life's Hard Lessons: Recognizing and Discussing Moments in Both Your Professional and Personal Life Makes You a Better Leader," *HR Magazine* (June 2008), pp. 143–146, picture yourself in the vacant frame.
   a. Think about what you have accomplished.
   b. Would others call you a leader? Why or why not?
3. Now think for a minute about what you bring to any situation. Then answer the following questions:
   a. What are your SKAs?
   b. If a very close friend made a list of your SKAs, what would be on the list that would be different from your list? What accounts for the difference?
   c. How would you describe your leadership style?
   d. What changes in SKAs and leadership style would you have to make in order to fill the vacant frame?
4. Would you want to be on the "America's Best Leaders" list? Why or why not?

## TEAM SKILL BUILDING

### TEAM SKILL BUILDER 5-1: How to Get to the Other Side?

Divide students into groups of four. Working together, their mission is to get all four team members safely across the bridge within the time limits.

There are some issues that limited your mission. All four of you are one side of the bridge and only two can cross at a time, and it is so dark that a flashlight has to be used to light the way. There is only one flashlight. The team must determine the best method for getting everyone across safely in only seventeen minutes, when it takes:

Person #1, one minute to cross

Person #2, two minutes to cross

Person #3, five minutes to cross

Person #4, 10 minutes to cross

1. The team members should make a list of some of the barriers that group might face in getting everyone across safely and within the time parameters.
2. Working together, the team members must develop a strategy for completing the assigned task.

FOOD FOR THOUGHT QUESTIONS

1. How did your group develop a strategy for completing the task?
2. In retrospect, would there have been a better way to accomplish the task?
3. Did a leader emerge during this activity? If it was not you, why did you allow someone else to take command of the group?
4. How can you apply the lessons learned in this exercise to your life?

*Source:* Adapted with permission of QCI International, from QCI International's Timely Tips for Teams, a monthly Internet newsletter (August 2003).

### TEAM SKILL BUILDER 5-2: Get Connected and Build Servant Leadership Skills

Divide the class into groups of three to five students. Have each group member share a story of how they have volunteered in their community and the impact that the experience had on building their leadership and supervisory skills.

1. Every community has a variety of problems. Each student should share what they think is the number one problem facing their university or college community.
2. The group should come up with ideas of how to get others involved in doing the right things to make their community a better place to live.
3. After sharing their responses, each group should come up with at least three ideas that they can use to get others "off the bench and into the game" by inspiring them to volunteer to help with a community solution.

### TEAM SKILL BUILDER 5-3: Technology Tools—Become a Leadership Development Content Curator

INTERNET ACTIVITY

Assign students to groups of three or four for this exercise.

If your supervisor asked you to come up with a plan to develop the leadership skills of the people in your department, where would you start? Would you visit the library? Scan your textbooks? Ask your professors? Search the Internet?

As you are probably aware, the easiest place to start would probably be your Internet browser. If you were to type the keyword "leadership" into your browser, it is likely that you would receive more than 150 million hits. If you were to narrow your search down to "leadership development," the list would narrow slightly, to maybe around 100 million hits. The sheer volume of leadership development resources available on the Internet is staggering. However, not every one of the resources is worth the bandwidth it travels on. How does one even begin to choose? By learning to be a content curator.

Content curation is the process of sorting through the plethora of Web content using a targeted strategy to find the most relevant material available on a specific theme. Content curation is more than just making a list of links. It is a process of evaluating resources, organizing them within a context, and presenting them in a way that is engaging and easy to navigate. Nonprofit technology expert Beth Kanter likens the process to setting up a museum exhibit.[39] Kanter suggests that content curation consists of three steps:

- Seeking—defining topics, scanning resources and capturing those that are high quality
- Sensing—making sense of the content by organizing and annotating it in an interesting and thematic way
- Sharing—finding an audience and presenting the curated content on a consistent basis, such as in a blog, on Twitter or on Facebook.

In this exercise, your challenge is to curate content for a hypothetical department that wants to develop its leadership skills. The department does not have a budget for this project, so all resources must be free. The department can be oriented in any sector you wish (business, public agency, nonprofit, healthcare, etc.). Your job is to curate content that will introduce at least two leadership or management SKAs over a period of four weeks. You should present your curated content as either a Word Document describing the content and plan for delivery or an emailed link to a blog or website you set up for this purpose. Follow these steps to get started:

- Read Beth Kanter's blog post, "Content Curation Primer," http://www.bethkanter.org/content-curation-101/
- Select your topic or theme. You should narrow the topic down from leadership development to specific leadership skills like communication, change management, strategic planning, trust, ethics, or another topic presented in this chapter.
- Follow the three steps of content curation. You may use the list of links curated by the authors found in the Chapter 5 Technology Tools section of the companion website for this textbook (note the catchy title) as their top leadership development picks, to get started.
- Present a plan or a mock-up of your content curation strategy as directed by your instructor.

## SUPERVISION IN ACTION

SUPERVISION IN ACTION

The video for this chapter can be accessed from the student companion website at www.cengagebrain.com. (Search by authors' names or book title to find the accompanying resources.)

## ENDNOTES

Many students have found the article about Nelson Mandela to be inspirational. See Richard Stengel, "Mandela: His 8 Lessons of Leadership," *Time* (July 21, 2008), pp. 42–48.

The text author also recommends that you add the following to your reading list: A. G. Lafley and Ram Charan, *The Game-Changer* (New York: Crown Business, 2008). Lafley is CEO of Procter & Gamble, which is noted as an integrated innovative organization and as having tripled profits during the past seven years.

1. Harry S. Truman's (1884–1972) other famous quotes included: "The buck stops here" and "If you can't stand the heat, get out of the kitchen." All of these relate to the concepts introduced in this chapter. See the *Oxford Dictionary of Quotations*, 3rd ed. (New York: Oxford University Press, 1980).

   For general discussions on leadership, the following are recommended: Adrienne Fox, "Leading with the Brain," *HR Magazine* (June 2011), pp. 52–53; A. G. Lafley and Ram Charan, *The Game-Changer* (New York: Crown Books, 2008); Scott M. Paton, "It's about Leadership, Stupid," *Quality Digest* (March 2008), p. 56; Noel Tichy and Warren Bennis, "Judgment: How Winning Leaders Make Great Calls," *BusinessWeek* (November 18, 2007), pp. 68–72; Alison Stein Wellner, "Leadership: Creative Control—Even Bosses Need Time to Dream," *Inc.* (July 2007), pp. 92–97; John Wooden and Steve Jamison, *Wooden on Leadership* (New York: McGraw-Hill, 2005); Ellen Samic and Scott Campbell, *5-D Leadership* (Palo Alto, CA: Davies-Black, 2005); Phil Dourado and Phil Blackburn, *Seven Secrets of Inspired Leaders* (New York: Wiley, 2005); Trudy Jean Evans, "Entering Your New Leadership Position," *SuperVision* (August 2005), pp. 12–13.

   Also see Bryan Schaffer, "Leadership and Motivation," *SuperVision* 69, No. 2 (February 2008), pp. 6–9; Martin Wood, "The Fallacy of Misplaced Leadership," *Journal of Management Studies* (September 2005), pp. 1101–1122; Jane M. Howell and Boas Shamir, "The Role of Followers in the Charismatic Leadership Process: Relationships and Their Consequences," *Academy of Management Review* 30, No. 1 (2005), pp. 96–112; and David D. Henningsen, Mary Lynn Miller Henningsen, and Ian Bolton, "It's Good to be a Leader: The Influence of Randomly and Systematically Selected Leaders on Decision Making Groups," *Group Dynamics: Theory, Research and Practice* 8, No. 1 (2004), pp. 62–76. Remember, without followers, there can be no leaders or leadership.
2. Stratford Sherman, "How the Best Leaders Are Learning Their Stuff," *Fortune* (November 27, 1995), pp. 90–102. Also see Michael O'Neil, "Leading the Team," *SuperVision* (April 2011), pp. 8–10; Warren Bennis and Sharon D. Parks, *Leadership Can Be Taught* (Boston: Harvard Business School Press, 2005), in which they discuss the best ways to teach the skills needed to become a leader; Peter Senge, *The Fifth Discipline: The Art and Practice of the Learning Organization* (New York: Doubleday, 1990); and Senge et al., *The Fifth Discipline Handbook: Strategies and Tools for Building a Learning Organization* (New York: Doubleday, 1994).
3. The traits are described in detail in Warren Bennis, "The Leadership Advantage," *Leader to Leader* 12 (Spring 1999), pp. 20–22. You also may want to review, Rebecca Hastings, "Study: Employees' Trust in Leaders Has Declined," *HR Magazine* (September 2011), p. 15.
4. A more complete discussion can be found in James M. Kouzes and Barry Z. Posner, "Exemplary Leaders," *Executive Excellence* (June 2001), pp. 5–7; *The Leadership Challenge: How to Get Extraordinary Things Done in Organizations* (San Francisco: Jossey-Bass, 1987) and *Leadership Practices Inventory (LPI): A Self-Assessment and Analysis* (available from Pfeiffer & Company, San Diego).
5. James M. Kouzes and Barry Z. Posner, *The Leadership Challenge*, 4th ed. (San Francisco, CA: Jossey Bass, 2008). See also Kouzes and Posner's, *Credibility: How Leaders Gain and Lose It, Why People Demand It* (San Francisco: Jossey-Bass, 1993).
6. As quoted in Justin Bachman, "Healthy Companies," Associated Press, as reported in the *Fort Wayne, Indiana Journal Gazette* (November 11, 2005), p. 2C. Also see Gary Neilson and Bruce Pasternick, *Results: Keep What's Good, Fix What's Wrong, and Unlock Great Performance* (New York: Crown Business, 2005). Booz & Company conducts an annual *CEO Succession Survey*. The 2008 survey found that CEOs generally have six years to design and implement their strategies. Also see Neilson's website (http://www.orgdna.com), which provides tips, suggestions, and results of their research to uncover the DNA of successful organizations.
7. One of the text's authors conducted the following exercise in March 2008. Thirty-nine store managers were asked to identify their MPC (most preferred coworker) and list the three most important things for which the person was responsible. Then the MPCs were sent e-mails asking them to briefly describe the functions of their job and list the three most important things for which they were responsible. There was less than 10 percent agreement between manager and subordinate as to the most important aspects of the job. We have been conducting similar research each year since 1978, and the results are strikingly similar. "If you don't know what the boss expects you to do, how can you do it well?"

8. See the Center for Advanced Research, "Franklin Covey xQ Database Averages" (February, 2011) at their website (http://www.franklincoveyresearch.com/catalog/Summary_Table_for_FC_Database__as_of_Dec_31__2010___Units.pdf ), which provides annual summaries of the execution quotient (xQ) organizational health study, a survey of over 20,000 workers with responses broken down by global region and country.
9. See Jim Collins, *Good to Great: Why Some Companies Make the Leap . . . and Others Don't* (New York: HarperCollins, 2001). Collins wrote about great organizations benefiting from the flywheel effect where the power of continued improvement and the delivery of results create additional momentum. How things change: Circuit City, one of the companies featured in Collins's book, is no longer to be found, and Fannie May is in receivership. You may want to read, Collins and Morten Hansen, *Great by Choice* (New York: Harper, 2011), or visit his website (http://www.jimcollins.com) to look over the "good to great" toolkit and his latest findings.
10. Visit the Greenleaf Center of Servant Leadership (www.greenleaf.org) for their current research and thoughts on how to become a servant-leader. Also see Kent M. Keith, *The Case for Servant-Leadership* (Indianapolis, IN: The Greenleaf Center, 2005); and a review of Frank Hamilton's *Practicing Servant-Leadership: Succeeding through Trust, Bravery, and Forgiveness* in the *Academy of Management Review* (October 2005), pp. 875–877.
11. Max E. Douglas, "Service to Others," *SuperVision* (March 2005), pp. 6–9. Also see Voss W. Graham, "Shared Leadership," *SuperVision* (September 2007), pp. 3–4.
12. Interview with Larry C. Spears, CEO and president of the Greenleaf Center for Servant-Leadership in "Leading by Serving," *Philanthropy Matters* (Spring 2008), pp. 8–10.
13. Larry C. Spears and John C. Burkhardt listed the 10 characteristics central to the development of servant-leaders in *Servant-Leadership and Philanthropic Institutions* (Indianapolis, IN: The Greenleaf Center, 2006).
14. As quoted by Josh Spiro in "How to Become a Servant Leader," *Inc.* (August 31, 2010), http://www.inc.com/guides/2010/08/-how-to-become-a-servant-leader.html.
15. Josh Spiro, "How to Become a Servant Leader," *Inc.* (August 31, 2010), http://www.inc.com/guides/2010/08/how-to-become-a-servant-leader.html, summarized specific suggestions made by Bill George, professor of management at Harvard Business School and former CEO of Medtronic, of how leaders can build their practice of servant leadership and recognize signs that they aren't acting as servant leaders.

    Benjamin Lichtenwalner, senior manager of Internet and eCommerce at Whirlpool Corporation, maintains the Servant Leadership Companies List (http://modernservantleader.com/featured/servant-leadership-companies-list, updated August 21, 2010), which includes companies that demonstrate servant leadership, as evidenced by publicly documented reference to the organization and its view of, support for, or belief in servant-leadership principles.
16. As reported by Lauren Weber, "Those Corporate Trust Exercises Aren't Working," *Wall Street Journal* (April 22, 2014), http://blogs.wsj.com/atwork/2014/04/22/those-corporate-trust-exercises-arent-working/, which summarizes the American Psychological Association's *2013 Work and Well Being Survey*, the results of which can be found at the APA Center for Organizational Excellence website, https://www.google.com/url?q=http://www.apaexcellence.org/assets/general/2013-work-and-wellbeing-survey-results.pdf. The Forum Corp. *Global Leadership Pulse Survey* (2013) is available at http://go.forum.com/ForumLeadershipPulseSurvey2013-US. For comprehensive information about the Maritz 2012 Employee Engagement Poll, visit www.maritzresearch.com/employeeengagement-news.aspx.

    In a survey by Universum, college students were asked about what they wanted from work. The top three choices were: to achieve work–life balance, to be secure, and stable in their job, and to be dedicated to a cause. Supervisors must develop a climate of mutual trust and respect so that employees can develop their full potential. See "What U.S. Graduates Really Want," a summary of the 2013 research, available at http://universumglobal.com/2013/05/what-us-graduates-really-want/. We agree that mutual trust and respect are the foundation of effective supervision.

    The Association for Training and Development analyzed content of current business and leadership trade publication and identified 10 traits that consistently emerged as characteristics for successful leadership, "What Are the Characteristics of a Good Leader?" (September 19, 2013), http://www.astd.org/Publications/Blogs/ASTD-Blog/2013/09/What-Are-the-Characteristics-of-a-Good-Leader-Infographic. Not surprisingly, honesty was at the top of their list. Kevin Cashman, author of "Leadership from the Inside Out" (*Executive Excellence,* 1998), argues that there are three core qualities to leadership: (1) authenticity, (2) self-expression, and (3) value creation. Also see Donna Fenn, "Sometimes Even CEOs Have to Say They're Sorry," *Inc.* (October 2007), pp. 37–38; Eric Krell, "Do They Trust You?" *HR Magazine* (June 2006), pp. 59–63; as well as the review on Kathleen M. Sutcliffe's *Ethics, the Heart of Leadership* in the *Academy of Management Review* (October 2005), pp. 869–871.
17. Stephen R. Covey, "Principle-Centered Leadership," *Quality Digest* (March 1996), p. 21. Richard L. Daft and Robert H. Lengel, authors of *Fusion Leadership* (San Francisco: Berrett-Koehler, 1998), describe a method for bringing people together to accomplish mutual goals based on shared vision and values. The principles of fusion (joining together) rather than fission (splitting apart) support individual employee growth and ingenuity.
18. Glen Llopis, "7 Reasons Employees Don't Trust Their Leaders," *Forbes* (December 9, 2013), http://www.forbes.com/sites/glennllopis/2013/12/09/7-reasons-employees-dont-trust-their-leaders/2/. See also Chief Learning Officer, "Survey: Bosses Rarely Apologize, Inspire Less Trust," *CLO Media.com* (November 13, 2013), http://www.clomedia.com/articles/survey-bosses-rarely-apologize-inspire-less-trust
19. See Paul Holmes and Arun Sudhaman's "The Top 12 Crises of 2013," *The Holmes Report* (February 9, 2014; February 14, 2014), http://www.holmesreport.com/featurestories-info/14554/The-Top-12-Crises-Of-2013-Part-1.aspx, http://www.holmesreport.com/featurestories-info/14571/The-Top-12-Crises-Of-2013-Part-2.aspx, which summarize a number of these events, including the $13 billion fine assessed to JP Morgan for selling troubled mortgages during the financial crisis that began in 2007; the U.S. National Security Agency (NSA)'s alleged collection of private citizens' Internet and communications data; pharmaceutical company GlaxoSmithKline's payment of nearly $1.4 million in kickbacks to Chinese doctors to promote and prescribe their products; and Wal-Mart's Thanksgiving food drive to collect food for its own employees, many of whom earn wages that put them at poverty level. Similarly, the IRS reflected questionable ethics when it chose to target nonprofit groups that had "Tea Party" ties for compliance audits, as described by Alex Altman in "The Real IRS Scandal," *Time* (May 14, 2013), http://swampland.time.com/2013/05/14/the-real-irs-scandal/.

    For more information on these scandals, see Bill Chappell, "JPMorgan Chase will pay $13 Billion in Record Settlement," National Public Radio (November 19, 2013), http://www.npr.org/blogs/thetwo-way/2013/11/19/246143595/j-p-morgan-chase-will-pay-13-billion-in-record-settlement; Barton Gellman and Laura Poitras, "U.S., British Intelligence Mining Data from

Nine U.S. Internet Companies in Broad Secret Program," *Washington Post* (June 6, 2013), http://www.washingtonpost.com/investigations/us-intelligence-mining-data-from-nine-us-internet-companies-in-broad-secret-program/2013/06/06/3a0c0da8-cebf-11e2-8845-d970ccb04497_story.html; Ben Hirschler, "Bribery Scandal Slashes GlaxoSmithKline's Chinese Drug Sales," *Reuters* (October 23, 2013), http://www.reuters.com/article/2013/10/23/us-gsk-earnings-idUSBRE99M0DB20131023; and Rick Ungar, "Walmart Store Holding Thanksgiving Charity Food Drive—For Its Own Employees!" *Forbes* (November 18, 2013), http://www.forbes.com/sites/rickungar/2013/11/18/walmart-store-holding-thanksgiving-charity-food-drive-for-its-own-employees/

20. See James McGregor Burns's foreword in Joanne B. Ciulla, *Ethics, the Heart of Leadership* (Westport, CT: Greenwood Publishing Group, 2004), p. X; and Josephson Institute and Character Counts! founder Michael Josephson *Making Ethical Decisions* (Los Angeles, CA: Josephson Institute, 2002). Margaret M. Perlis, in "8 Ways to Assess Leadership," *Forbes* (September 16, 2012), http://www.forbes.com/sites/margaretperlis/2012/09/16/inside-excellence-character-8-ways-to-assess-leadership-and-your-candidates/, suggests eight pillars of character: fortitude, temperance/responsibility, prudence, justice/fairness, trustworthiness, respect, caring, and citizenship.
21. Martin Luther King, Jr., "The Future of Integration," speech delivered at Oberlin College, Oberlin, OH (October 22, 1964).
22. See Dori Meinert, "Creating an Ethical Culture," *HR Magazine* (April, 2014), pp. 23–27.
23. The 2013 *National Business Ethics Survey of the U.S. Workforce* is available for download at www.ethics.org/downloads/2013NBESFinalWeb.pdf.
24. See Teri Thompson, Nathanial Vinton, Michael O'Keeffe, and Christian Red, "Victims of Lance Armstrong's Strong-Arm Tactics Feel Relief and Vindication in the Wake of U.S. Anti-Doping Agency Report," *New York Daily News* (October 20, 2012), http://www.nydailynews.com/sports/more-sports/zone-lance-armstrong-bully-downfall-article-1.1188512 and Dan Wetzel, "Lance Armstrong, Arrogant and Unaware, Did Little to Repair His Image In Mea Culpa with Oprah," Yahoo Sports (January 18, 2013), http://sports.yahoo.com/news/lance-armstrong-arrogant-and-unaware-did-little-to-repair-his-image-in-mea-culpa-with-oprah-062222144.html
25. See also the results of the *2014 Edelman Trust Barometer* survey at http://www.edelman.com/insights/intellectual-property/2014-edelman-trust-barometer/about-trust/global-results/.
26. Joanne B. Ciulla, *Ethics: The Heart of Leadership* (Westport, CT: Greenwood Publishing Group, 2004), p. XI.
27. Ciulla, ibid., p. XVI.
28. Community and Leadership Development Center at Indiana University, "Ethical Leadership" (Snapshots of Leadership series, 2007), retrieved from http://www.cldc.indiana.edu/docs/snapshots/EthicalLeadership.pdf.
29. For general discussions on delegation and the benefits of effective delegation, the following are recommended: Ted Pollock, "How Well Do You Delegate?" *SuperVision* (April 2011), pp. 26–27; Ken Fracaro, "Making Delegation Work," *Supervision* (September 2004), pp. 14–16; *Manager's Toolkit: The 13 Skills Managers Need to Succeed* (Boston: Harvard Business School Publishing, 2004); H. A. Richardson et al., "CEO Willingness to Delegate to the Top Management Team: The Influence of Organizational Performance," *International Journal of Organizational Analysis* 10, No. 2 (2004), pp. 134–155.
30. Ronald E. Merrill and Henry D. Sedgwick, in their article "To Thine Own Self Be True," *Inc.* (August 1994), pp. 50–56, identified six styles of entrepreneurial management: (1) the classic, (2) the coordinator, (3) the craftsman, (4) the team manager, (5) the entrepreneur plus employee team, and (6) the small partnership.

    They contend that any one of them can be effective. For a discussion on seven essential leadership skills, see Kennard T. Wing, "Become a Better Leader," *Strategic Finance* (February 2001), pp. 65–68.

    You might want to review Marshall Marvin, "3 Keys to Building Trust between Managers and Employees," *SuperVision* (February 2011), pp. 10–12.
31. Douglas McGregor, *The Human Side of Enterprise* (New York: McGraw-Hill, 1960, pp. 45–57.
32. Much of this is based on the authors' personal observations, as well as a not-far-from-the-truth portrayal of awful supervisors in the 2011 film, "Horrible Bosses," which has inspired many in the business field to directly address of the reality of poor management skills and further illustrate what it might look like in the workplace. Read examples in articles by Eric Jackson, "31 Telltale Signs You Are a Horrible Boss," *Forbes* (July 27, 2012), http://www.forbes.com/sites/ericjackson/2012/07/27/31-telltale-signs-you-are-a-horrible-boss/; and Tasha Eurich, "If You Were a Horrible Boss, Would You Even Know It?" *Huffington Post* (January 31, 2014), http://www.huffingtonpost.com/tasha-eurich-phd/if-you-were-a-horrible-bo_b_4688478.html. Survival strategies for dealing with such supervisors are suggested by Harvey Deutchendorf in "5 Steps to Coping with A Horrible Boss," *Fast Company* (March 4, 2014), http://www.fastcompany.com/3027155/work-smart/5-ways-to-cope-with-a-horrible-boss. See also Jean Lipman-Blumen, *The Allure of Toxic Leaders: Why We Follow Destructive Bosses and Corrupt Politicians—and How We Can Survive Them* (New York: Oxford University Press, 2005).
33. See Robert D. Behn, "On the Value of Setting Stretch Targets," *Bob Behn's Performance Leadership Report* 10, No. 4 (December 2011), Harvard Kennedy School of Government, retrieved from http://www.hks.harvard.edu/thebehnreport/All Issues/December2011.pdf. Ron Ashkenas warns that bombarding employees with just stretch goals can be frustrating, and he suggests that supervisors provide opportunities for workers to strive for a combination of "quick wins" that can lead to achievement of longer-term, more challenging goals, in "Don't Dismiss Stretch Goals," *Harvard Business Review* [blog] (May 22, 2012), http://blogs.hbr.org/2012/05/how-quick-wins-can-become-stre/.
34. Barbara Kellerman, "What Every Leader Needs to Know about Followers," *Harvard Business Review* 85, No. 12 (December 2007), pp. 84–91. See also John S. McCallum, "Followership: The Other Side of Leadership," *Ivey Business Journal* (September/October 2013), http://iveybusinessjournal.com/topics/leadership/followership-the-other-side-of-leadership#.U2AeolfijRU; Ronald Riggio, Ira Chaleff, and Jean Lipman-Blumen, *The Art of Followership: How Great Followers Create Great Leaders and Organizations* (San Francisco, CA: Jossey-Bass, 2008).
35. Robert E. Kelley, *The Power of Followership* (New York: Doubleday Business, 1992).
36. Lynn R. Offermann, "When Followers Become Toxic," *Harvard Business Review* 82, No. 1 (January 2004), pp. 54–63.
37. Adapted from Andrew Gibbins and Danielle Bryant, "Followership: The Forgotten Part of Leadership," *MPS Casebook* 21, No. 2 (May 2013), http://www.medicalprotection.org/uk/casebook-may-2013/followership-the-forgotten-part-of-leadership
38. Robert E. Kelley, "In Praise of Followers," *Harvard Business Review 66* No. 6 (November–December, 1988), pp. 142–148.
39. Beth Kanter, "Content Curation Primer," Beth's Blog (October 4, 2011), http://www.bethkanter.org/content-curation-101/

Chapter 6

# Communicating in a Noisy World

©Flik47/Shutterstock.com

**After studying this chapter, you will be able to:**

1. Define communication and explain its importance in today's culture.
2. Discuss the implications of the new communications age.
3. Analyze the channels of communication available to the supervisor.
4. Identify and discuss the barriers to effective communication.
5. Describe ways to overcome communication barriers.
6. Explain how supervisors can better manage meetings with their own managers.

# YOU MAKE THE CALL!

*James Matthews is the departmental supervisor in the water maintenance department in the city of Middletown. Middletown is a medium-sized community that has renovated itself in the twenty-first century by aggressively pursuing new industry and businesses and by providing economic incentives to support expansions of the existing firms. The town has built a new high school and a new elementary school and demolished many structures and homes that had fallen into disrepair. However, the cost to city residents for services and taxes is now much higher than that of comparable cities. Nevertheless, the city is viewed to be a great place to live.*

Three months ago, James was promoted to day shift supervisor. His management style is MBWA ('Management by Wandering Around'). He is in his office from 8 to 4 Monday through Friday. But the employees know that as he wanders around he may show up at any of the four shifts—weekdays (7 A.M. to 3 P.M.), evenings (3 to 11 P.M.), mornings (11 P.M. to 7 A.M.), or weekends (7 A.M. to 7 P.M. or 7 P.M. to 7 A.M.). Seventy-five percent of the workforce is on the day shift with the remainder evenly divided among the skeletal crews in the evening, morning, and weekend shifts. Backup crews supplement these skeletal crews as needed.

James believes that he is familiar with all employees and knows their strengths and weaknesses. His employees know that he is willing to help out when needed even though he prefers to let employees work out their problems on their own.

One of his first actions was to move Alphonso Robas from evening shift supervisor to the day shift position and promote George Harris to the position of evening shift supervisor. About a month ago, James heard through the grapevine that Thomas Smith, an employee on the evening crew, had threatened Harris during a virtual confrontation witnessed by several employees. When James discussed the incident with Harris, Harris felt that he had resolved the disagreement. Harris further explained that Smith appeared to have some personal problems that were negatively affecting his work performance, and in the discussion about performance, Smith became angry. But Harris assured James that as he was extremely busy with his new supervisory responsibilities and the increasing workload of the evening shift, he had not bothered James with the incident.

Late yesterday (Wednesday), James again heard through the grapevine that Smith had been overheard to say, "I will shoot Harris!" Immediately, James went to Harris and divulged what he had heard through the grapevine. Harris assured him that the grapevine had blown the situation out of proportion. James was concerned and called Deborah Barnes, the director of human resources, but she would not be in her office till Friday. He pondered what actions he should take.

Shortly after midnight on Thursday, a ringing cell phone woke James from a sound sleep. The call was from the hospital emergency room police informing him that George Harris had been shot in the water maintenance parking lot and was pronounced dead at the scene.

A subsequent call from the desk sergeant informed James that Thomas Smith had strolled into the jail, admitting the shooting, and turned himself in. Smith, a 25-year city employee, had alleged waiting in the parking lot with a .22-caliber handgun. Police reported that Smith shot Harris three times, twice at close range and once—the fatal shot—while standing over Harris, who had fallen on the ground. Smith told police that Harris "was ruining his life and giving him a hard time."

Later on Friday, when James interviewed several employees, he realized that he did not know his workers as well as he thought. Not only were both Smith and Harris separated from their wives, but most employees knew more about the situation than he did. They knew both Smith and Harris had argued not about work-related issues but about women.

The local newspapers detailed additional information. Smith's attorney announced that a set of mitigating circumstances would weigh in his client's favor when the case went to trial. Smith had turned himself in almost immediately and had no past criminal record. Even though Smith and Harris had been friends for many years, Smith had accused Harris of having a relationship with his wife and had been hostile toward him since becoming a supervisor. Smith claimed that Harris was "obsessive" about Smith's wife and had sent her flowers on the day of the murder.

Now James is having trouble sleeping at night and wonders what he might have done to have prevented this tragedy.

**Disclaimer:** The above scenario presents a supervisory situation based on real events to be used for educational purposes. The identities of some or all individuals, organizations, industries, and locations, as well as financial and other information may have been disguised to protect individual privacy and proprietary information. Fictional details may have been added to improve readability and interest.

YOU MAKE THE CALL!

**1 Define communication and discuss its implications for effective supervisory management.**

**Communication**
The process of transmitting information and understanding

# Communication Has Changed in the Twenty-First Century

**Communication** is the process of transmitting information and understanding from one person to another. Effective communication means a successful transfer of information, meaning, and understanding from a sender to a receiver. In other words, communication is the process of imparting ideas and making oneself understood to others. While it is not necessary to have agreement, there must be mutual understanding for the exchange of ideas to be successful. Simply stated, there is no managerial function a supervisor can fulfill without effectively using his or her information-giving and -getting skills.

Most supervisory activities involve interacting with others, and each interaction requires skillful handling of the information process. Communication links all the managerial functions. Supervisors must explain the nature of work, instruct employees, describe what is expected of them, and counsel them. Supervisors also must report to their managers, both orally and in writing, and discuss their plans with other supervisors. All these activities require communication.

Noted author Peter Senge believes that people who develop and exchange information are not merely talking about the learning organization; they use the information as a springboard for experiments and initiatives. With each effort people make, they create a new facet of the overall image of what the learning organization can be. According to Senge:

> *If there is one single thing learning organization does well, it is helping people embrace change. People in learning organizations react more quickly when their environment changes because they know how to anticipate changes that are going to occur (which is different than trying to predict the future) and how to create the kinds of changes they want.*[1]

Sharing information takes effort on everyone's part, and the organization's effectiveness depends on good communication. Think of your own experiences. Who do you trust? Why? Does your answer, in part, revolve around the person's ability to communicate effectively? I suspect so. I would guess that your trustworthy person is one who has the ability to communicate honestly, openly, candidly, and in a timely fashion—and leave the door open for questions you might have. Remember, as the *Titanic* was rapidly sinking, the captain of the ship was telling everyone not to panic, to believe there was no problem, and to implicitly trust the ship's staff. Now, more than ever, mutual respect and trust is at the heart of effective communication.

Yet, in an era when more messages are being sent and received, the primary objective in every organization is "doing a better job of communicating."

## EFFECTIVE COMMUNICATION REQUIRES TWO-WAY EXCHANGE

The significant point is that communication always involves at least two people: a sender and a receiver. For example, a supervisor who is alone in a room and states a set of instructions does not communicate because there are no receivers. While the lack of communication is obvious in this case, it may not be so obvious to a supervisor who sends an e-mail message. Once he or she hits the "Send" button, the supervisor may believe that communication has taken place. However, this supervisor has not really communicated until and unless the e-mail has been

FIGURE 6.1 Communications does not take place unless information is transferred successfully

received and the information and understanding have been transferred successfully to the recipient (see Figure 6.1).

It cannot be emphasized too strongly that effective communication includes both sending and receiving information. Understanding is a personal matter between people. If an idea received has the same meaning as the one intended, then we can say that effective communication has taken place. If, however, the idea received by a listener or reader is not the one intended, then communication has not been effective. The sender has merely transmitted spoken or written words. This does not mean that the sender and receiver must agree on a message or an issue; it is possible to communicate and yet not agree. Author and Professor Chip Heath developed key principles for making an idea "stick." Heath says, "A sticky idea is one that people understand when they hear it, that they remember later on, and that change something about the way they think or act."[2]

One should always pause, think, and ponder the impact of a message on the intended receiver. Regardless of the medium used, say what you mean, and mean what you say. For some more thoughts on the importance of communication skills, see Figure 6.2.

**FIGURE 6.2 Thoughts on the importance of communication**

"Developing excellent communication skills is absolutely essential to effective leadership. The leader must be able to share knowledge and ideas to transmit a sense of urgency and enthusiasm to others. If a leader can't get a message across clearly and motivate others to act on it, then having a message doesn't even matter."[1]

"It is better to keep your mouth closed and let people think you are a fool than to open it and remove all doubt."[2]

"Wise men talk because they have something to say; fools, because they have to say something."[3]

"Kind words can be short and easy to speak, but their echoes are truly endless."[4]

"The trouble with talking too fast is you may say something you haven't thought about yet."[5]

"If you have brilliant ideas, but you can't get them across, your ideas won't get you anywhere."[6]

*Sources:* (1) Gilbert Amelio, former president and CEO of National Semicoductor Corporation and currently director of AT&T. (2) Mark Twain. (3) Plato. (4) Mother Teresa. (5) Ann Landers. (6) Lee Iacocca. The quotes were accessed March 2011 from "Power Performance: Motivational & Inspirational Corner: America's System for Success," Power Performance (www.motivational-inspiritial-corner.com); and "Leading Thoughts," Leadership Now (www.LeadershipNow.com).

An analysis of supervisory activities would likely show that more than half the supervisor's day involves giving and getting information. The supervisor's effectiveness depends on the ability to create an environment that fosters communication. Fortunately, the skills of communication can be developed. By using some of the techniques and suggestions in this chapter, we hope you will become a more effective communicator and, ultimately, a more effective manager.

**2 Discuss the implications of the new communications age.**

## A New Era in Communications

A few short years ago, no one could talk about using social media to post tweets, photos, and other information. Facebook, Twitter, LinkedIn, Instagram, and other social networks were not around. Figure 6.3 pokes fun at this new phenomenon, but ask someone in her forties: "What type of social media did you use to connect with your friends when you were 20?" A *USA Today* article reported that with all the use of social sites, "2010 was the year we stopping talking."[3]

Would you be surprised to know that Facebook's Mark Zuckerberg doesn't have an office? In early 2004, the 19-year-old Harvard sophomore used his dorm room to start a Web service. From humble beginnings, an institution was born that has changed the way we communicate. He "took a dream" and became a billionaire. Zuckerberg was described as "one who approaches conversation as a way of exchanging data as rapidly and efficiently as possible, rather than as a recreational activity undertaken for its own sake. He is formidably quick and talks rapidly and precisely, and if he has no data to transmit, he abruptly falls silent."[4]

The following question arises: Will Facebook and other social media sites decrease the need for face-to-face communications? Look at the technology at your school. Do you have the ability work in the classroom or access information from virtually anywhere? Some of you may be taking this course online and may have found that you have the ability to communicate with your instructor and fellow students from almost anywhere in the world. Just a few short years ago, that would not have been possible. Technology now facilitates a continuous flow of information.

One survey contends that employees are overloaded with a constant stream of information. Corporate social media users received over 100 messages a day in 2013. In the business setting social media users spend approximately 2.22 hours a day on e-mail and more than 30 minutes each on social networking sites and

**FIGURE 6.3 Everyone has problems communicating**

www.Blondie.com

instant messaging.[5] The level of information flow beyond just the workplace is astounding. The number of tweets sent out per day on Twitter has grown from 100 million in 2010 to 500 million 2014.[6] Over 350 million photos are uploaded to Facebook every day, and the YouTube video database increases by 100 hours of video every minute. The Internet provides access to over two zettabytes (2 zettabytes=2 trillion gigabytes) of information.[7]

As information flow has increased and social media has emerged, it has been said that the technology creates new costs in companies due to unnecessary interruptions because it is assumed by some bosses that users take time away from their work to tweet friends and check their Facebook pages.[8] However, as more and more businesses turn to social media as the best way to connect with an increasingly digital audience, workers are spending as much if not more time using social media to connect with markets, customers, and other stakeholders than they are connecting with friends, and in some cases the two blend together.[9] In fact, when one of the authors did an Internet search of the question, "How many tweets should I post per day," a majority of the first hundred hits were related to how often businesses should tweet out branding or engaging messages each day. (The recommended number of tweets ranged from 4 to 37, and the average suggested number of Facebook posts was 2.) Social media has become a key communication tool for organizations.

Have you noticed that sometimes when you open up a Web page, there is a pop-up advertisement that is targeted at you? The concern over privacy issues and tracking of Internet users has become an important issue for many organizations. The story of WikiLeaks caused many to rethink their computer security systems. The ability to access and download messages and information and make it available worldwide caused many organizations, including the U.S. government, to rethink how to create a cyber-defense system. Even so, in 2013 the nine largest Internet security breaches resulted in the theft of over 400 million usernames and passwords and at least 50 million e-mail addresses. In late 2010, Walgreens Co., McDonald's, and Twitter all reported unrelated security breaches on the very same day. "Hackers gained access to a list of Walgreen's customers' e-mail addresses and sent them spam directing customers to enter personal data into outside Web sites. Private information that customers supplied McDonald's when signing up for on-line promotions was breached when a subcontractor improperly handled the data."[10] If such things could happen to major corporations, are you not vulnerable, too? What have you done to secure your system?

## Channels of the Communication Network

**3 Analyze the major channels of communication available to the supervisor.**

In every organization, the communication network has four primary and equally important channels: (1) the formal, or official, channel of communication, (2) the informal channel, usually called the grapevine, (3) the Web or social networks, and (4) body language. The formal and informal channels carry messages from one person or group to another in organizations—downward, upward, and horizontally. The proliferation of social networks has not only opened new opportunities for enhancing the ability of supervisors to communicate with employees, but has created numerous problems. Supervisors should realize that their behavior on the job is an important means of communicating. **Body language** is the observable action of the sender or the receiver. Your body language may be worth a thousand words.

**Body language**
All observable actions of the sender or receiver

## FORMAL CHANNELS

Formal communication channels are established primarily by an organization's structure. Vertical formal channels can be visualized by following the lines of authority from the top-level executive down through the organization to supervisors and employees.

### Downward Communication

The concept of a downward formal channel of communication suggests that upper-level management issues instructions or disseminates information that managers or supervisors at the next level receive and pass on to their subordinates, and so on down the line. The downward channel is most often used by high-level managers to communicate. Downward communication, which helps to tie levels together, is important for coordination. Managers use it to start action by subordinates and to communicate instructions, objectives, policies, procedures, and other information. Generally, downward communication is informative and directive and requires subordinates to act. Downward communication from a supervisor involves giving instructions, explaining information and procedures, training employees, and engaging in other types of activities designed to guide employees in performing their work.

Unfortunately, in practice downward communication leaves much to be desired. Think back to your own experiences. Have your managers been "open and honest" when communicating with you? If you answered, "It depends," you are probably in a majority. Recall your first day in this class. The instructor no doubt handed you a syllabus that detailed the expectations, assignments, and other relevant information needed for you to be successful. No doubt, he or she gave you a printed copy, noted where updates would be posted in your electronic course room, and then clarified the information. You were even given an opportunity to ask questions. Information was provided about office hours so that you could meet face to face, and an e-mail address was provided in case you had any questions or concerns. The instructor, like the effective supervisor, used multiple channels of communication to help you be a success.

The very best supervisors use open, honest, sincere, and genuine communication, which guides employees down a path of excellence. Employees, like students, want to be told what they need to know, how they can learn it, what constitutes a job well done, and how they will be evaluated.

## UPWARD COMMUNICATION

Upward communication is equally important to the official network. Supervisors who have managerial authority accept an obligation to keep their superiors informed and to contribute their own ideas to management. Similarly, employees should feel free to convey their ideas to their supervisors and to report on activities related to their work. Managers and supervisors should encourage a free flow of upward communication.

Upward communication usually involves informing and reporting, including asking questions, making suggestions, and lodging complaints. This is a vital means by which managers can determine whether proper actions are taking place and can obtain valuable employee insight into the problems facing a unit. For example, employees may report production results and also present ideas for increasing production.

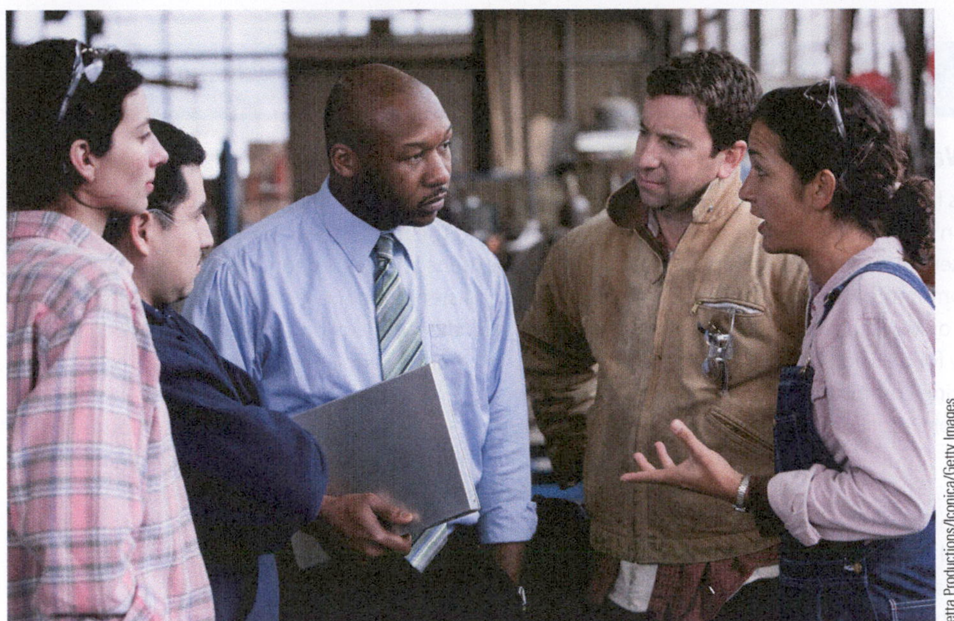
Jetta Productions/Iconica/Getty Images

*Frequently, no one knows the problems and possible solutions to those problems better than the employees who are doing the work*

Supervisors should encourage upward communication from employees and give ample attention to the information being transmitted. Supervisors must show that they want employee suggestions as well as the facts, and then those supervisors must evaluate information promptly. It has become clear that often no one knows problems—and possible solutions—better than the employees doing the work.[11] To tap into this important source of information, supervisors must convey a genuine desire to obtain and use the ideas suggested by employees. Many supervisors have told me that they don't know how to do this. The information in the accompanying "Supervisory Tips" box provides some ideas for improving getting-and-giving skills by using **MBWA (management by walking around)**, which involves going where the action is and asking others what you can do to help them be the best they can be. The key word is "probe." Ask questions such as, "How can we improve . . . ?" "What can we do better?" "What if . . . ?" and "What will make it work?" Effective supervisors develop rapport with their employees and other stakeholders, really listening to ideas and suggestions and acting on suggestions. A supervisor with effective information-getting skills usually wins the respect and admiration of colleagues and associates.

**MBWA (management by walking around)**
Going to where the action is. Ask employees, customers, and others what you can do to help them to be the very best they can be

Most supervisors acknowledge that it is often easier to converse with their subordinates than with their managers. This is particularly true when supervisors must tell their managers they failed to meet schedules or they made mistakes.

Nevertheless, it is a supervisor's duty to advise upper management whenever there are significant developments and to do so as soon as possible, before or after such events occur. It is quite embarrassing to a manager to learn important news elsewhere; this can be interpreted to mean supervisors are not abreast of their responsibilities.

A supervisor's upward communication should be sent on time and in a form that enables the manager to take necessary action. The supervisor should assemble and check facts before passing them on, though this may be quite difficult at times. A natural inclination is to "soften" information a bit so that things do not look quite as bad in the manager's eyes as they actually are. When difficulties

## SUPERVISORY TIPS

### Management by Walking Around (MBWA) Improves Communication

The most effective leaders have always led from the front line, where the action is.[1] Today, every leader who hopes to succeed must likewise lead from the trenches. Getting out and about (commonly known as "management by walking around," or MBWA) deals with gathering the information necessary for decision making, making a vision concrete, engendering commitment and risk taking, and caring about people.[2] But I do not know how to wander. How do I begin?

1. Get away from your workstation, your desk; get out of your cubicle and start talking with employees. Meet on their turf and try to learn something about them: Why did they decide to work here? What are their interests? Where do they want to be three years from now? What can you do to enable them to be the best they can be? In short, to get the job done the right way the first time, you need to know where they are coming from and be able to link that knowledge to buy-in to the goals of the organization.[3]
2. Learn about their problems and concerns. Ask for their ideas and suggestions on how to fix their problems.
3. Developing a climate of mutual trust and respect is critical to getting everyone committed to the common purpose.
4. MBWA means more than walking to where your employees are. It is not enough to advertise an open-door policy. It means being available to answer any questions that might arise. Accessibility is a crucial part of developing an effective corporate culture. It is important for you to stay in touch with everyone.
5. Tell people that you want feedback and be prepared to receive it. The technique of probing—asking the right questions and encouraging everyone to ask questions, listening to those affected by problems, learning all the facts, walking the talk—and acting on and incorporating suggestions as part of the process can lead to a more productive organization.
6. As you walk around, catch people doing something right. Tell them how good you feel about what they have done and encourage them to do more of the same. Make sure you link good performance to rewards people value.
7. Remember:
   - Be available to provide guidance and direction. Set aside a certain time when everyone knows you are accessible and able to listen to their ideas, suggestions, or concerns.
   - Do not walk around just for the sake of walking around. Have a purpose.
   - Walk around at different times and in different ways.
   - Look for opportunities to chat in informal settings, over coffee or at lunch.
   - Your work group is made up of individuals. Tailor the message to each person.
   - Tell people you want feedback and go out of your way to get it.
   - To be a good walker, you have to be a good listener. Stop what you are doing and listen.
   - When you can't answer a worker's question on the spot, get back to them with an answer within a specified period of time. Tell them when you will get back to them, and do it. This is one way to build credibility, trust, and loyalty.
   - Effective communication is the key to your success.

*Sources:* The authors' list would include (1) What are characteristics of a great leader? Most major business publications have developed their own methods of determining who fits that description. Our list would include Mohandas Gandhi, Alfred Sloan, Sam Walton, Jack Welch, General Colin Powell, and Colleen Barrett. Business publications such as *Fortune, BusinessWeek, Time,* and *Fast Company* publish their lists. (2) MBWA was developed by executives of Hewlett-Packard in the 1970s. Noted author Tom Peters popularized the concept in the book *In Search of Excellence: Lessons Learned from America's Best Run Companies* (New York: Harper & Row, 1982). In a subsequent book, Peters strongly advised that managers need to become highly visible and do a better job of listening to subordinates: *Thriving on Chaos* (New York: Alfred A. Knopf, 1988), pp. 423–440. (3) D. Michael Abrashoff, commander of the *USS Benfold*, sits down with his new crew members and tries to learn something from them. For more on Abrashoff's leadership style, see Polly LaBarre, "The Agenda—Grassroots Leadership," *Fast Company* (April 1999), pp. 114+.

arise, however it is best to tell the manager what is really going on, even if it means admitting mistakes. High-level managers depend on supervisors for reliable upward communication, just as supervisors depend on their employees for the accurate, upward flow of information.

## HORIZONTAL COMMUNICATION

A third direction of formal communication that is essential for efficient organizational functioning is lateral, or horizontal, communication between departments or people at the same levels but in charge of different functions. Horizontal communication must be open and freely flowing to coordinate functions among departments.

Horizontal communication typically involves discussions and meetings to accomplish tasks that cross departmental lines. For example, a production manager may have to contact managers of the marketing and shipping departments to ascertain progress on a delivery schedule for a product, or someone from the human resources department may meet with a number of supervisors to discuss how a new medical leave policy is to be implemented at the departmental level. Still another example is the cashier who pages the stock clerk to inquire when a particular item will be available. Without an open communication environment—upward, downward, and sideways—it would be virtually impossible to coordinate specialized departmental efforts toward a common purpose.

## INFORMAL CHANNELS—THE GRAPEVINE

Informal communication channels, commonly referred to as the **grapevine**, are a normal outgrowth of informal and casual groupings of people on the job, of their social interactions, and of their understandable desire to communicate with one

**Grapevine**
The informal, unofficial communication channel

RF Image Source/Getty Images

*Especially during periods of economic uncertainty, the grapevine carries bits of distorted information that flow quickly through the organization*

another. Every organization has its grapevine. This is a perfectly natural element because it fulfills employees' desire to know the latest information and to socialize. The grapevine offers members of an organization an outlet for imagining, as well as an opportunity to express apprehensions in the form of rumors.

## UNDERSTANDING THE GRAPEVINE

The grapevine can offer considerable insight into employees' thoughts and feelings. An alert supervisor acknowledges the grapevine and tries to take advantage of it whenever possible. The grapevine often carries factual information, but sometimes it carries half-truths, rumors, private interpretations, suspicions, and other bits of distorted or inaccurate information. Research indicates that many employees have more faith and confidence in the grapevine than in what their supervisors tell them.[12] In part, this reflects a natural human tendency to trust one's peers to a greater degree than people in authority, such as supervisors or parents.

The grapevine cannot be predicted because its path today is not necessarily the same as its path yesterday. Most employees hear information through the grapevine, but some do not pass it along. Any person in an organization may become active in the grapevine on occasion; some individuals are more active than others. Some people feel that their prestige is enhanced if they can pass along the latest news, and they do not hesitate to spread and embellish upon that news. Rumors serve, in part, as a release for emotions, providing an opportunity to remain anonymous and say whatever is wanted without being held accountable.

The grapevine sometimes helps clarify and supplement formal communication, and it often spreads information that could not be disseminated as well or as rapidly through official channels.

## THE SUPERVISOR AND THE GRAPEVINE

The supervisor should realize that it is impossible to eliminate the grapevine. It is unrealistic to expect that all rumors can be stamped out, and the grapevine is certain to flourish in every organization. To cope with the grapevine, supervisors should tune in to it and learn what it is saying. Supervisors should also determine who leads the grapevine and who is likely to spread its information.

Many rumors begin in the wishful-thinking stage of employee anticipation. In Team Skill Builder 6-2, you will read about the dilemma of Alice, a project engineer. She and others have a problem with their supervisor's communication skills. Suppose that she and the other employees start passing information (a rumor) though their communication networks that their boss, Mike, is on his way out. Nobody knows for certain where or how the rumor started, but the story spreads rapidly because many want to believe it. If such a story is spreading and the upper management is listening, they may investigate to see what the problem is. Action may or may not be taken. The best cure for rumors is to expose the facts to all employees and to give straight answers to all questions. Of course, morale suffers when hopes are built up in anticipation of something that does not happen.

Other frequent causes of rumors are uncertainty and fear. If business is slack and management is forced to lay off some employees, stories multiply quickly. The grapevine becomes more active during periods of insecurity and anxiety than at other times.

Often, rumors are far worse than reality. If a supervisor does not disclose facts to employees, those employees will make up their own "facts," which may be worse than reality. Thus, much of the fear caused by uncertainty can be eliminated or reduced if the truth of what will happen is disclosed. Continuing rumors and uncertainty may be more demoralizing than even the saddest facts presented openly.

Rumors also arise from dislike, anger, and distrust. Rumors spread through the grapevine can be about such topics as the company, working conditions, or the private or work life happenings of its members. The Web has accelerated access to the "truth" and "untruth." Think about some of the e-mails that have been forwarded to you. At first glance, they may even seem to be credible. Just take a trip to www.snopes.com to see some of the rumors that are spreading rapidly. Rumors, like gossip and storytelling, ease the boredom of organizational life and, in extreme cases, harm people. Occasionally, an employee grows to hate a company, supervisor, or fellow employee. This employee could fabricate a sensational story about the target of animosity.[13]

Rumors often start small but are spread quickly by a few who embellish those rumors. Others may be shocked to hear such rumors, and their trust and respect for the people in the rumors may erode. Unfortunately, there is no one best way for repudiating rumors and rebuilding credibility. If you mention a rumor without refuting it, some people may speculate that the rumor is at least partly true. Again, the best prescription is to state the facts openly and honestly. When supervisors lack all the information, they should admit it, try to assess the real situation, and report the situation to employees. One of the best ways to stop a rumor is to expose its untruthfulness. Supervisors should remember that the receptiveness of a group of employees to rumors is directly related to the quality of the supervisor's communication and leadership. When employees believe their supervisors are concerned about them and make every effort to keep employees informed, employees tend to disregard rumors and to look to their supervisors for answers.

The supervisor should listen to the grapevine and develop skills to address it. For example, an alert supervisor knows that certain events cause undue anxiety. In this case, the supervisor should explain immediately why such events have occurred. When emergencies occur, changes are introduced, or policies are modified, the supervisor should explain why and answer all employee questions as openly as possible. Otherwise, employees will make up their own explanations, and often these explanations will be incorrect. In some situations, supervisors do not have the facts. In these cases, supervisors should seek appropriate high-level managers to explain what is bothering employees and to ask for specific instructions as to what information may be given, how much may be told, and when. Also, when something happens that might cause rumors, it is helpful for supervisors to meet with their most influential employees to give them the real story. Then, those employees can spread the facts before anyone else can spread the rumors.[14]

## The Web and Social Networks

How often have you heard someone say, "It must be true, I found it on the Web"? Not surprisingly, much information is passed along as "fact," even though it lacks credibility.

Many people know of allegations, rumors, gossip, and old wives' tales that have found their way into homes and offices via the Internet. Not surprisingly, most of these pieces of information are passed along as "fact," even though they lack truth and scientific accuracy. Think about the e-mail messages you received this week: Were they fact, allegations, rumors, gossip, or old wives' tales? How many contained information that you could use to be a better student or a more valuable employee, or that added value to your toolbox?

Think of the e-mails that you sent this week. What was your purpose in sending them? Do you know the following people: The person who is texting when he or she should be listening to the lecture? The person whose cell phone goes off during a church service? The person who is not paying attention when driving because he is texting or using his mobile device? A person's date at a concert who is posting on Facebook? I know that you are not one of these people and that you always check your smartphone at the door. Not long ago, one of the authors of the text was at a wedding, and the ushers had baskets at the entrance to collect the devices. They didn't collect many, but it caused people to make sure theirs were turned off.

The headline story in *USA Today,* "2010: The Year We Stopped Talking," said that Americans are more connected than ever—just not in person.[15] Mobile device research shows the depth of this situation in the new era: 91 percent of Americans have cell phones or wireless; 56 percent of the cell phone users have smartphones; 5.1 trillion mobile text messages sent in the past 12 months; 93 percent of the global population has access to mobile networks.[16] As a supervisor, your access to relevant information in a timely fashion is critical, but the communications overload can have implications for how you manage your life and the lives of those you supervise. *Remember, success comes by letting people know how you want them to communicate to you and learning how they want you to communicate to them.*

## Your Body Language Is Communication

The supervisor's body language communicates something to employees, whether it is intended or not. Gestures, a handshake, a shrug of the shoulder, a smile, or

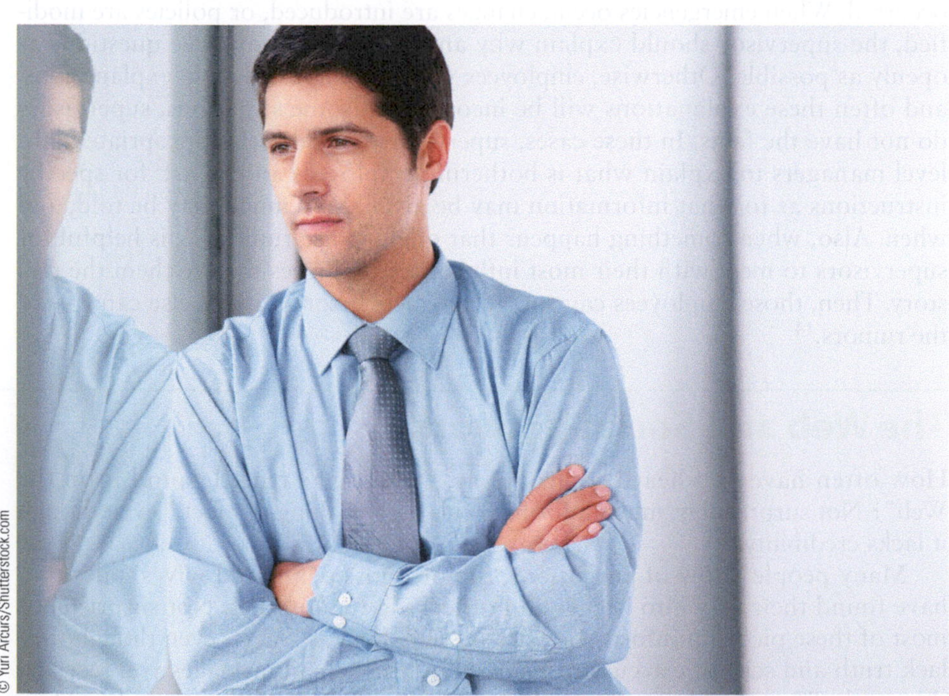

*We may think it's easy to read a person's body language but different gestures can mean different things*

even silence—all have meaning and may be interpreted differently by different people. For example, a supervisor's warm smile and posture slightly bent toward employees can send positive signals to employees. Particularly in an uncertain and sometimes chaotic world, smiling may be somewhat difficult, but it is definitely more effective than scowling. Conversely, a scowl on a supervisor's face may communicate more than 10 minutes of oral discussion, a printed page of information, or a quickly sent text message.

One of the problems with text messages and other modern communications media is that we are not able to read the true meaning because there is no body language or tone of voice to reinforce the important points of the message. We believe that one of the greatest advantages of face-to-face oral communication is that it can provide the sender an immediate opportunity to determine whether the communication is understood.

Body language is not universal. The messages sent by different expressions or postures vary from situation to situation and particularly from culture to culture. Touching, like the pat on the back, may be perceived differently by different people. The shaking of hands or hugging may not be appropriate for some. Think for a moment about the last time someone told you that they "loved you." What type of body language accompanied that verbal message? If they sent you a text proclaiming the same thing, did they include a little picture of a heart or other symbol to reinforce the meaning of the message? What could the person have done to make the message more meaningful?

Regardless of the channel the supervisor uses, his or her goal is to convey the message in a timely manner that is easily understood. To reiterate, the supervisor must always remember that effective communication takes place only when the meaning received by the intended audience is the same at that the sender meant to send. You must become familiar with the many barriers to effective communication. To that end, the next section seeks to clarify other barriers and provides suggestions on how to overcome them.

## Barriers to Effective Communication

**4 Identify and discuss the barriers to effective communication.**

Human differences and organizational conditions can create obstacles that distort messages between people. These obstacles can be called **noise**. Misunderstandings, confusion, and conflicts can develop when communication breaks down. These breakdowns not only are costly in terms of money but also create dilemmas that hurt teamwork and morale. Many supervisory human-relations problems are traceable to faulty communication. The ways supervisors communicate with their subordinates constitute the essence of their relationships.

**Noise**
Obstacles that distort messages between people

### TOO MUCH INFORMATION—TMI[17]

In today's business world, employees and supervisors are inundated with hundreds of bits of information every day. Many messages are long and wordy, which can cause misunderstanding and lost productivity. The typical written message is loaded with words that have little or no bearing on the message's purpose. Giving employees too much information results in information overload and causes employees to complain of being overwhelmed with irrelevant and redundant messages. How long does it take before employees consider all messages to be junk mail and discard them? Regardless of the medium used, you should use the **KISS technique**—keeping it short and simple means using as few words and sentences as possible.

**KISS technique**
An acronym that stands for *keep it short and simple*

With the advent of electronic forms of communication, it seems that employees should have all the information they need to do their jobs. On the one hand, companies want employees to have access to the best and latest information and resources to do a better job. On the other hand, Web use can become time-consuming for some employees and, if left unchecked, can impede productivity.

How much are employees using the Internet for personal use? Numerous studies have reported that U.S. workers are wasting at least two hours a day at work.[18] Increasingly organizations are developing policies and systems for monitoring employee Internet use, although design of such policies is becoming more and more difficult as social media becomes a critical element in organizations' efforts to engage and retain stakeholders.

## LANGUAGE AND VOCABULARY DIFFERENCES

People differ greatly in their abilities to convey meanings. Words can be confusing, even though language is the principal method used to communicate. Do you know of anyone who had to call an organization's customer-service center? Where was the person on the other end of the line? They may have been in another part of the world where the native language was not common for the person on the other end of the line, and vice versa. What was the reaction: patience, understanding, or frustration? Have you ever heard someone say, "Why can't we all speak the same language?"

In regions of the world that speak common languages, differences in cultures, accents, dialects, and word meanings can be profound.[19] Within the organization, an accounting department supervisor, for example, may use specialized words that may be meaningless when conversing with a computer technician. Similarly, if an information technologist uses technical terms when interfacing with the accounting department supervisor, the latter could be confused. This communication problem stems from the inappropriate use of what is known as **jargon**, or the use of words that are specific to a person's background or specialty.

**Jargon**
Words that are specific to an occupation or a specialty

Another consideration relates to the number of languages that may be spoken in a work environment. Some Hispanic or Latino workers may speak Spanish fluently but have difficulty with English. A native of Southeast Asia may speak Vietnamese but very little English. Technology provides a variety of solutions to address language needs. Productivity software, such as Microsoft Word, can now translate organizational materials into to multiple languages, although it is always a good practice to have a native speaker review the translation for accuracy. Also, organizations are increasingly providing multi-lingual websites on which users can choose to have content displayed in their preferred language, which, according to recent research, results in increased time spent on these sites, sometimes twice as long as if sites are only presented in English.[20] Avis Rent-A-Car, GE, and the U.S. Centers for Disease Control and Prevention (CDC) are just a few such organizations. Supervisors should take steps to identify and use tools that can help remove language barriers.

Another communication problem lies in the multiple meanings of words. Words can mean different things to different people, particularly in English, which is one of the most difficult languages in the world. The ways some words are used in sentences can cause people to interpret messages in ways other than intended. *Roget's Thesaurus*, a book of synonyms, identifies words with the same or similar meanings. When a word has multiple meanings, the desired meaning must be clarified because receivers tend to interpret words based on their perceptions, experiences, and cultural backgrounds.

The question is not whether employees *should* understand words; it is whether employees *do* understand. Supervisors should use plain, direct words in brief, simple statements. When needed, supervisors should restate messages to clarify the intended meaning or context.

## STATUS AND POSITION

An organization's structure, with its multilevel managerial hierarchy, creates a number of status levels among members of the organization. **Status** refers to the degree of responsibility and power afforded by a person's professional or social position. Status can affect attitudes the members of an organization hold toward a position and its occupant. The statuses of executive-level positions and supervisory-level positions, supervisors and employees, differ. Differences in status and position become apparent as one level tries to communicate with another. For example, a supervisor who tries to convey enthusiasm to an employee about higher production and profits for the company may find the employee indifferent. The employee may instead be concerned with achieving a higher personal wage and security. By virtue of their positions in the company, the supervisor and the employee represent different points of view, and these views may be obstacles to understanding.

**Status**
The degree of responsibility and power afforded by a person's professional or social position

When employees listen to a supervisor's message, several factors come into play. First, employees evaluate the supervisor's words in light of their own backgrounds and experiences. Second, they also consider the supervisor's personality, position, and status. It is difficult for employees to separate a supervisor's message from the feelings they have about the supervisor. As a result, employees may infer nonexistent motives in a message. For example, union members may be inclined to interpret a management statement in very uncomplimentary terms if they are convinced management is trying to weaken their union or change current practices and procedures.

Obstacles due to position and status also can distort the upward flow of communication when subordinates are eager to impress management. As was described in Chapter 5's discussion of followers, some employees may screen information passed up the line; they may tell their supervisor only what they think the supervisor likes to hear and omit or soften unpleasant details. This problem is known as **filtering**. By the same token, supervisors are eager to impress managers in higher positions. They may fail to pass on important information to their managers because they believe the information portrays their supervisory abilities unfavorably.

**Filtering**
The process of omitting or softening unpleasant details

## RESISTANCE TO CHANGE

Some people prefer things as they are; they do not welcome change in their work situations. It is normal for people to prefer their environments to remain unchanged. If a message is intended to convey a change or a new idea—something that will upset work assignments, positions, or the daily routine—employees may be inclined to resist the message. Why? People don't resist change, they resist being changed. If they have no input into the change process, employees will generally greet the change with suspicion.

Receivers usually hear what they want to hear. If a message is not consistent with their personal beliefs and values, the listeners may ignore it, reject it as false, or find a convenient way of twisting it to fit their own vantage point.

In today's economy, many receivers are insecure or fearful; these barriers become even more difficult to overcome. Employees become so preoccupied with their own thoughts that they attend only to those ideas they want to hear, selecting only those parts of the message they can accept. Employees brush aside, fail to hear, or explain away bits of information they do not like or that are irreconcilable with their biases. Supervisors must be aware of these possibilities, particularly when a message is intended to convey some change that may interfere with the normal routine or customary working environment.

## PERCEPTUAL BARRIERS

**Stereotyping**
The perception that all people in a group share attitudes, values, and beliefs

Barriers arise from deep-rooted personal feelings, prejudices, and physical conditions. The perception that all people in a group share attitudes, values, and beliefs is called **stereotyping**. Stereotyping influences how people respond to others. It becomes a barrier to effective communication as people are categorized into groups because of their gender, age, or race instead of being treated as unique individuals. Managers must be aware of stereotyping because it can impede communication.

Georgetown University professor Deborah Tannen has written several books on interpersonal communication and public discourse. In her *New York Times'* best-selling book *You Just Don't Understand—Women and Men in Conversation*, Tannen illustrates a common problem. In our society, if a woman's and a man's conversational styles differ, women—not men—are usually told to change. Consider one example from her book, which occurred between a couple driving home from a function:

> *The woman had asked, "Would you like to stop for a drink?" Her husband had answered truthfully, "No," and they hadn't stopped. He was later frustrated to learn that his wife was annoyed because she had wanted to stop for a drink. He wondered, "Why didn't she just say what she wanted? Why did she play games with me?" The wife was annoyed, not because she had not gotten her way but because her preference had not been considered. From her point of view, she had shown concern for her husband's wishes, but he had no concern for hers.*[21]

Tannen concluded: "Both parties have different but equally valid points. In understanding what went wrong, the man must realize that when she asks what he would like, she is not asking an information question but rather starting a negotiation about what both would like. The woman must realize that when he answers 'yes' or 'no' he is not making a nonnegotiable demand. Men and women must both make adjustments."[22] It is sad that neither party worked toward what was really important and targeted that goal with specific inquiries. Imagine how the conversation could have gone from the man's perspective: "No, I'm not really thirsty. But if you'd like to do that, it would be okay with me." Being considerate of other people and keeping an open mind go a long way toward improving understanding. Messages can be misunderstood because people perceive the situation or circumstances (i.e., the world) differently. Tannen's example clearly illustrates the importance of "saying what you mean and meaning what you say." You probably noted that either party could have paused and asked the other person questions to gain an understanding of what was really important to them.

## INSENSITIVE WORDS AND POOR TIMING

Sometimes, one party in a conversation uses so-called killer phrases. Comments like, "That's the stupidest idea I've ever heard!" "You do understand, don't you?" or "Do you really know what you're talking about?" can kill conversation. Often, the receiver of the killer phrase becomes silent and indifferent to the sender. Sometimes, the receiver takes offense and directs anger back to the sender. Insensitive, offensive language or impetuous responses can make understanding difficult. These exchanges happen in many workplaces. Often, the conflict that results impedes organizational goals.

Another barrier to effective communication is timing. Employees come to the workplace with "baggage"—events that happened off the job. It can be difficult to pay attention to a sender while anticipating a test, for example, or if an argument started at home before work is still simmering. An employee can pretend to listen politely but receive little to nothing. When other issues demand attention, responsiveness to work information will fail to meet the other party's expectations.

## INABILITY TO CREATE MEANING

Communication begins when the sender encodes an idea or a thought. For example, when managers set out to draft responses to issues, they address several questions, including:

- What conclusion have I formed about this issue?
- What claim do I want to make?
- What evidence or reasons can I offer in support of my claim?
- What data can I provide to back up my claim?[23]

Decoding is the receiver's version of encoding. During decoding, receivers put messages into forms they can interpret. To analyze a manager's position on an issue, an employee must find and weigh management's claim, evidence, and data, but the employee can ask more: "Does the manager's choice of words influence how I feel about this issue?" "Do I agree with management's basic premise or with the assumptions underlying management's position?" Often, the receiver's interpretation of a message differs from what the sender intended.

One of the authors recently saw a promotional piece on laundry detergent. The label read, "New and Improved." He wondered what it really meant and pondered the following: (1) If it's new, how can it be improved? (2) If it's improved, how can it be new? Have you ever wished that other people would say what they mean and mean what they say? We have.

*Differences in perception can lead to misunderstanding*

IS122/Image Source/Alamy

5 **Describe ways to overcome communication barriers.**

# Overcoming Barriers to Effective Communication

Most techniques for overcoming communication barriers are relatively easy and straightforward. Supervisors will recognize them as techniques they use sometimes but not as frequently as they should. A supervisor once remarked, "Most of these techniques are just common sense." The reply to this comment is simply, "Yes, but have you ever observed how uncommon common sense sometimes is?" The lesson is, "If you do not know, find out then follow up." In short, supervisors must proactively ensure that communication is effective.

## PREPARATION AND PLANNING

A first major step toward becoming a better communicator is to avoid speaking or writing until the message to be communicated has been thought through to the point that it is clear in the sender's mind. Only when supervisors can express their ideas in an organized fashion can they hope for others to understand. Therefore, before communicating, supervisors should know what they want and should plan the steps needed to attain their objectives (see Figure 6.4). Regardless

**FIGURE 6.4 Steps to achieving communication objectives**

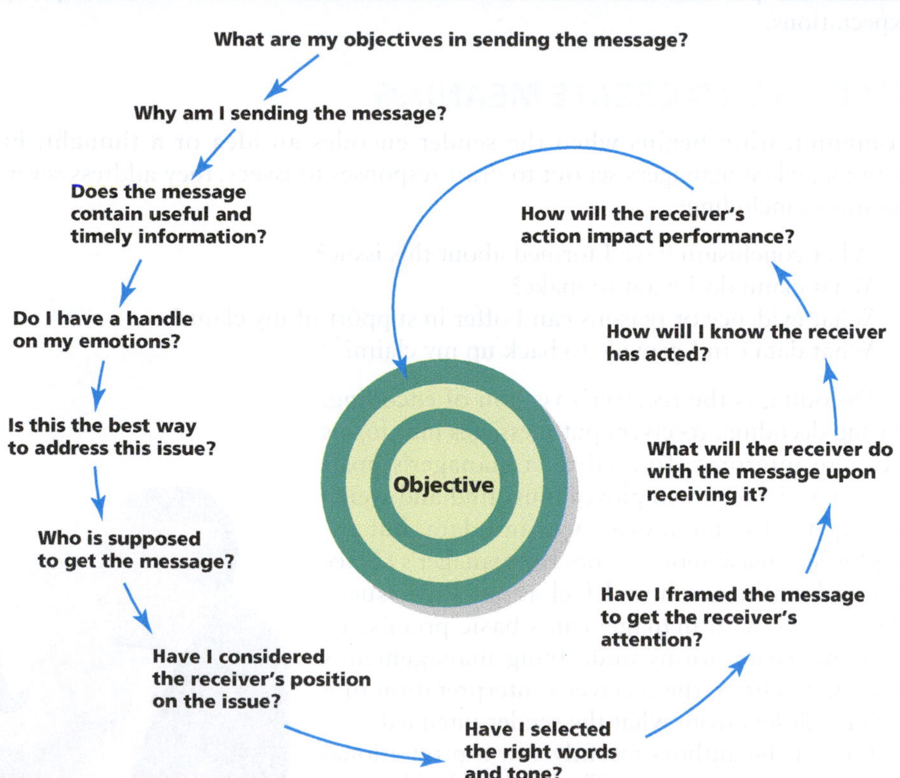

What are my objectives in sending the message?
Why am I sending the message?
Does the message contain useful and timely information?
Do I have a handle on my emotions?
Is this the best way to address this issue?
Who is supposed to get the message?
Have I considered the receiver's position on the issue?
Have I selected the right words and tone?
Have I framed the message to get the receiver's attention?
What will the receiver do with the message upon receiving it?
How will I know the receiver has acted?
How will the receiver's action impact performance?
Objective

*Sources:* From ideas in Curtis Sittenfeld, "How to WOW an Audience—Every Time," *Fast Company* (August 1999), pp. 86+; Carol Leonetti Dannhauser, "Shut Up and Listen," *Working Women* (May 1999), p. 41; Sean Morrison, "Keep It Simple," *Training* (January 1999), p. 152; Douglas Stone, Bruce Patten, and Sheila Heen, *Difficult Conversations: How to Discuss What Matters Most* (New York: Viking, 1999); Paul A. Argenti, "Should Business Schools Teach Aristotle?" *Strategy & Business* (Third Quarter, 1998), pp. 4–6; and A. Blanton Godfrey, "Quality Management: Getting the Word Out," *Quality Digest* (June 1996), p. 7.

of the method of communication used, supervisors must consider many elements before sending messages.

For example, when supervisors want to assign jobs, they should first analyze those jobs thoroughly so that they can describe them properly. An employee's ability to do a job depends on determining what information is important. Therefore, the supervisor needs to plan the method of communication—visual (body language), vocal (tone of voice), verbal (words), and emotional (feelings). When supervisors must give their bosses bad news, those supervisors should study the problems until they can explain the problems easily. Supervisors may even want to try to see the problems from their bosses' points of view. Supervisors should write down all important points to ensure they are covered.

A point of caution: Supervisors should only raise problems with their bosses after having formulated suggestions on how to solve or prevent problems.[24] When communication is to involve disciplinary action, supervisors should investigate the cases sufficiently and compile all relevant information before issuing penalties. Clearly, communication should not begin until supervisors know what they should say to achieve their goals.

## USING FEEDBACK

Among the methods for improving communication, feedback is by far the most important. In communication, **feedback** is the receiver's verbal or nonverbal response to a message. Feedback can be used to determine whether the receiver understood the message and to get the receiver's reaction to that message. The sender can initiate feedback by using questions, discussion, signals, and clues. Merely asking the receiver, "Do you understand?" and receiving "Yes" as an answer may not suffice. More information is usually required to ensure that a message was received as intended.

**Feedback**
The receiver's verbal or nonverbal response to a message

A simple way to obtain feedback is to observe the receiver and to judge that person's responses based on such nonverbal clues as expressions of bewilderment or understanding, raised eyebrows, frowns, and eye movement. Of course, this kind of feedback is possible only in face-to-face communication, which is one of the major advantages of this form of communication.

Perhaps the best feedback technique for ensuring that the sender's message is understood is for the sender to ask the receiver to paraphrase or play back the information just received. This approach is much more satisfactory than merely asking whether the instructions are clear. The process of restating all or part of the person's basic idea in the receiver's own words, rather than "parroting back verbatim" the sender's message, shows that communication has taken place. For example, the receiver might say, "Let me see if I understand correctly. Your understanding of the situation is thus and so." When the receiver states the content of the message, the sender knows the receiver has heard and understood the message. The receiver may then ask additional questions and request comments that the speaker can provide immediately. Do not ask questions that can be answered "yes" or "no." Phrase questions that force the other person to clarify and elaborate their position(s).

The feedback technique also applies when a supervisor receives a message from an employee or a higher-level manager. To clear up possible misunderstandings, a supervisor can say, "Just to make sure I understand what you want, let me repeat in my own words the message you just gave me." An employee or a manager will appreciate this effort to improve communication. A similar technique to paraphrasing is reflective feedback. This technique is used when the supervisor

**FIGURE 6.5 Why didn't you understand my instructions the first time?**

reflects the feelings (emotions) expressed by the sender. To illustrate, the supervisor might say, "You feel _____ because _____."

When a supervisor receives a written message and doubts any part of its meaning, that supervisor should contact the sender to discuss and clarify the message. In an amusing way, Figure 6.5 indicates that the teacher's original instructions were not received as intended. In a clear and direct way, the expectations are clarified.

## TIMELY AND USEFUL INFORMATION

Clearly, employees must be able to gather information. The key is that the information is pertinent and timely and helps employees do their jobs. Supervisors should begin by asking, "What information do my employees need to do their jobs?" The answer should be the foundation for gathering and giving information. Employees must know what is expected and what is and is not allowed. Figure 6.6 presents the six pillars for successful communication.

## DIRECT AND CLEAR LANGUAGE

Another sound approach to effective communication is to use words that are understandable and as clear as possible. Supervisors should avoid long, technical, complicated words. They should use language that receivers can understand easily. Jargon, or "shop talk," should be used only when receivers are comfortable with it.

## A CALM ATMOSPHERE

As mentioned earlier, tension and anxiety are serious barriers to effective communication. When supervisors try to communicate with employees who are visibly upset, the chance for mutual understanding is minimal. It is much better to communicate when both parties are calm and unburdened by unusual tension or stress. One of the best ways for supervisors to create the proper atmosphere for communicating with employees is to set times to meet in quiet rooms. This usually enables both parties to prepare to discuss problems calmly and unhurriedly.

Similarly, if supervisors want to discuss something with their managers, they should make appointments for times and places that allow calm, uninterrupted

FIGURE 6.6 The six pillars for successful supervisory communications

discussion. How (the tone), when (the time), and where (the place) are as important as the message.

Provide employees with timely and complete information.
Strive to be understood and to understand—feedback is vital to success.
Understand how your actions and body language influence others.
Keep messages short and simple—"manageable pieces for maximum impact."
Encourage everyone to ask questions.
Follow-up to make such that the message is doing what is intended

## TAKING TIME TO LISTEN

Listening is a very important part of the supervisor's job, whether in one-on-one conversations or in meetings. The ability to listen is critical to success as a supervisor. Therefore, supervisors should work to develop their listening skills every chance they get.

Figure 6.7 lists some helpful suggestions for supervisors to use for improving their listening skills. A supervisor should always listen patiently to what the employee has to say. Intensive listening helps reduce misunderstanding, and, by listening, the supervisor can respond in ways that are appropriate to the employee's concerns. Supervisors should provide feedback by restating employees' messages from time to time and by asking, "Is this what you mean?"

One of the worst things supervisors can do is to appear to be listening while their minds are elsewhere. Supervisors can avoid this situation by politely stating, "Right now is not a convenient time for us to have this discussion. It needs my full attention, and if we can reschedule this meeting for 10 in the morning, you will have my undivided attention." Attentiveness to the speaker goes a long way toward building trust.

To ensure that they have understood the message, supervisors must confirm it by restating in their own words what they have heard. In this way, they get

**FIGURE 6.7 The do's and don'ts of effective listening**

**DO'S OF LISTENING**

- Do adopt the attitude that you will always have something to learn.
- Do take time to listen, give the speaker your full attention, and hear the speaker out.
- Do withhold judgment until the speaker is finished. Strive to locate the main ideas of the message.
- Do try to determine the work meanings in the context of the speaker's background. Listen for what is being implied as well as what is being said.
- Do establish eye contact with the speaker. Read body language. Smile, nod, and give an encouraging sign when the speaker hesitates.
- Do ask questions at appropriate times to be sure you understand the speaker's message.
- Do restate the speaker's idea at appropriate moments to make sure you have received it correctly.

**DON'TS OF LISTENING**

- Don't listen with only half an ear by "tuning out" the speaker and pretending you are listening.
- Don't unnecessarily interrupt the speaker or finish the speaker's statement because of impatience or wanting to respond immediately.
- Don't fidget or doodle while listening. Don't let other distractions bother you and the speaker.
- Don't confuse facts with opinions.
- Don't show disapproval or insensitivity to the speaker's feelings.
- Don't respond until the speaker has said what he or she wants to say.
- Don't become defensive.



confirmation of the accuracy of the message, and both sender and receiver are on the same page of the playbook.

## REPETITION OF MESSAGES

It often helps to repeat a message several times, preferably using different words and different methods. For example, a new health insurance program for employees might be sent by snail-mail to employees' home, sent by e-mail, discussed in a message on the company Web site, or posted on the bulletin board in the employee break room. After the posting and distribution of the plan changes, ideally the human resource department representatives and top management will hold small-group discussions on the changes and the implications for the employees.

The degree of repetition should depend largely on the content of the message and the impact on the intended receivers. However, the message should not be repeated so much that it gets ignored because it sounds too familiar or boring. When in doubt, some repetition probably is safer than none.

## REINFORCING WORDS WITH ACTION

To succeed as communicators, supervisors must complement their words with appropriate and consistent actions. Supervisors communicate a great deal through their actions; actions do speak louder than words (see Figure 6.8. Therefore, one of the best ways to give meaning to messages is to act accordingly. When verbal

FIGURE 6.8 A supervisor communicates by actions as much as by words

announcements are backed by action, the supervisor is more credible. However, when a supervisor says one thing but does another, employees will eventually behave similarly.

## Managing Meetings with the Boss

6 Explain how the supervisor can do a better job of managing up!

Every manager has someone higher in the organization to whom they report. It is critical that supervisors understand the importance of communicating "up the organization."[25] For example, supervisors may want to report the most recent department/team meetings at their manager staff meetings. Supervisors should communicate not only the issues and items impacting their departments but also the positive contributions of their team members and other members of the organization.

As discussed earlier in this chapter, all managers should develop a climate that encourages a free flow of upward communication. However, in reality, the responsibility for upward communication typically falls on the supervisor. Increasingly, in an era of intense competition replete with organizational mergers, restructurings, and facility closings, supervisors must take the responsibility for keeping upper management informed and for managing the relationships with their own bosses. Supervisors also must be prepared to contribute suggestions, ideas, and opinions on a timely basis.

How many times have you heard someone say, "Treat others the way you want to be treated"? The same holds true for the supervisor's relationship with upper management. Most upward communication occurs in meetings between supervisors and their managers. Supervisors should try to build bonds with their bosses. Supervisors must clearly understand what their bosses expect of them, and the bosses must know what their subordinates need from them to achieve the organization's objectives. Each interaction that the supervisor has impacts the boss's perception of the supervisor, and vice versa. Obviously, how supervisors manage upward is vital to their careers. The following list provides insight on how the supervisor can more effectively manage meetings with the boss:

1. *Respect the boss's time.* Remember that "every boss has a boss" and, as such, has time demands of which you are not aware. Many bosses advocate an open-door policy, so be careful not to burden your boss with trivial issues or issues you can handle yourself. Choose a time when the boss is not busy and can give you and the issue undivided attention. A good approach might be, "I need about five minutes of your time to discuss _____ What would be a convenient time?" If the boss says, "two o'clock," be a few minutes early. It may sound basic, but think of the impression you make when you are late.
2. *Check your motives.* Is a meeting the best way to address the issue or problem and achieve your purposes? If the answer is no, the meeting may not be worth having. Don't barge in on the boss when you are angry and upset.
3. *Analyze the boss's listening style.* Some bosses are analytical listeners who like to hear the facts and draw their own conclusions. Others may be emotional listeners who want you to start with how you feel about the message, then present the factual information, and close with your suggestion or conclusion. Turn yourself 180 degrees, put yourself in the boss's shoes, and try to see the situation from his or her perspective. This will help you outline a plan.
4. Plan your agenda. To ensure you cover what you want in the meeting with the boss, have in front of you a few notes on the important points or issues. Managing upward successfully begins with preparation and planning. When planning the agenda, remember the KISS technique.
5. *Do not go to the boss "naked."* An effective manager encourages subordinates to develop alternatives, solutions, or suggestions to problems. No one wants a problem or an issue simply given to them to solve. You should start with a review of the situation and end with your suggestions. Bring suggestions on how to resolve the problem or prevent the situation from happening again. One manager the author knows only wants you to bring a problem to her after you have discussed it with others who have a stake in the outcome and have developed at least two viable options for solving it. You want to leave the boss with the feeling that you are on top of things, and this is one way to do it.
6. *Commit to the truth.* In *The Fifth Discipline*, author Peter Senge calls honesty a commitment to the truth, which he argues is necessary for the discipline of personal mastery.[26] We could not agree more. A meaningful relationship is built on mutual trust and respect. Explain your position on the issues objectively using facts, figures, and examples.
7. *Advertise success.* Make certain that upper management knows the successes of your work group and others you rely on to succeed. The supervisor who, in a meeting, tries to claim all credit loses respect.
8. *Learn to say no.* Upper managers can impose unrealistic workloads or deadlines. There may be tremendous pressure from above to "buy in." Do not over commit your team. The supervisor who does not learn to say "no" loses the respect of subordinates and ends up looking bad to the boss.
9. *Do not keep information from your boss.* Do not tell bosses only what they want to hear. Supervisors sometimes fail to pass along information because it might reflect unfavorably on them.
10. *Anticipate problems.* When you need the boss's help, ask for it in a timely fashion. The best time to get the help you need is at the beginning. A common

error supervisors make is to wait until they are overwhelmed by a project or job assignment or when failure is imminent.

11. *Meet periodically to clarify expectations.* In our fast-paced world, job requirements change rapidly. You must take responsibility for knowing what is expected from you. You may have to ask your boss to help you understand. Conversely, you need to analyze your job expectations and take the initiative to ensure that your boss knows what you need from him or her in order to succeed.
12. *Do not be a complainer.* As mentioned above, it is essential to apprise the boss of problems, but do not complain constantly. The supervisor who only approaches the boss to complain becomes part of the problem, not part of the solution.
13. *Do not put the boss on the defensive.* Supervisors can become upset or angry. They can attack the boss by demanding, pointing fingers, or venting their anger. These behaviors and words are an aggressive attack on the boss. Many people lack the ability to cope with attacks on them, and they attack back with vigor. The encounter then becomes antagonistic rather than favorable. In a favorable environment, colleagues focus on understanding the issues from the viewpoint of the other person and strive to reach agreement and to develop follow-up steps. Attack the problem, not the person.
14. *Leave on a positive note.* Get an agreement on a course of actions. Summarize the meeting in writing so that you have documentation that on a specific date, at a specific place, with specific individuals present, a specific issue was discussed and, from your perspective, the outcome was as you have stated. What is said and done day to day on the job is an important part of communication.
15. *Make a resolution.* Treat the boss as though you are a dedicated and competent employee, ready to make a difference. Resolve to manage upward effectively.

In conclusion, communication with the boss must be a two-way street. Most of us find it easy to tell others what to do, when to do it, and what they should have done. At the same time, we are used to receiving instruction and guidance from higher-ups. For many, it is not easy to go to the boss with our concerns. In many ways, it is like the teenager who will come to friends before going to their parents when they have a problem or concern. But the effective manager, like the great parent, sets the stage for the upward, honest, and open communication.

## SUMMARY

**1.** **Effective communication means that information transfers successfully and understanding takes place between a sender and a receiver. The ability to communicate effectively is one of the most important qualities of supervisory success.**

**Communication is a two-way process—getting and giving information. Communication succeeds only when the receiver understands the message. The receiver doesn't have to agree with the message, just understand it as the sender intended.**

**2.** **As the communication world has become more complex, it has become common for people to spend more and more time on the Web or texting. Now it is more important for people to seek ways to receive and manage information. Facebook, Twitter, LinkedIn, YouTube, and other social media sites have changed the way people can stay connected. Yet, the technology has created challenges for employees and employers alike. Numerous security breaches have taken place, and information that should have been secure has been compromised.**

**3.** **Four channels of communication are relevant to the supervisor: formal, information, the Web, and body language.**

**Formal channels of communication operate downward, upward, and horizontally. These**

communication channels primarily serve to link people and departments to accomplish organizational objectives. Supervisors communicate downward to their employees, but equally important is the supervisor's ability to communicate upward to management and horizontally with supervisors in other departments.

Every organization company has an informal channel called the grapevine. The grapevine can carry rumors as well as facts. MBWA is one technique for getting information and staying in touch with the employees. Supervisors should stay in touch with the grapevine and counteract rumors with facts, when necessary.

Employees and employers alike use the Web and various social networks to connect with each other and those outside the organization.

Body language—one's actions, gestures, or posture—is a powerful means of communication. Often, body language conveys more than written or spoken words.

4. Human differences and organizational conditions can create obstacles, called noise, which distort messages between people. TMI is just as bad as too little information. Information overload has become a major problem in today's society. Web sites and social networks contain lots of information, but not all of it is factual.

Not every employee has English as his or her primary language. Most supervisors are not fluent in a language other than English. And some of us have dialects that are confusing to others. Also, the use of jargon that receivers do not understand can impede communication. Because words have different meanings, the sender must ensure the receiver understands the intended meaning.

People at different status or position levels in an organization bring different points of view to interactions, which can distort meaning. People may filter out unpleasant information when communicating with their managers. Also, people's natural resistance to change can cause them to avoid hearing messages that upset the status quo or conflict with their beliefs.

Individuals perceive the world from the context of their backgrounds and prejudices. Perceptual barriers between sender and receiver, such as biases and stereotyping, can impede communication, as can conversation-killing phrases and poor timing.

The receiver's inability to properly analyze the content of a message causes misunderstanding. Misunderstanding may lead to suspicion and a lack of trust. Both sender and receiver share responsibility to ensure that information is successfully transferred.

5. To overcome communication barriers, supervisors should adequately prepare what they wish to communicate. During face-to-face communication, the receiver's verbal and nonverbal responses, called feedback, can help the supervisor determine whether the receiver understood the message. Asking the receiver to restate the message is one feedback technique that helps verify understanding. For written communication, the supervisor can obtain feedback by asking a colleague to comment on the message before it is sent and by discussing the message with receivers after it is sent.

Clear, direct language the receiver can understand facilitates communication. Also, both parties should agree on a time to talk when they are not overly stressed and have time to really listen to each other. Repeating the message in various words and formats can improve understanding if not done to excess. Also, to be effective, words must be reinforced with consistent actions.

Someone told me to remember that I was given two ears, two eyes, and only one mouth. There must be a reason for that. Listen to what is said and how it is being said, closely watch their body language.

6. Most people are not comfortable managing up. In today's fast-paced world, it is essential that supervisors keep higher management abreast of the developments and problems in their work areas. The tips for managing upward in this chapter blend practical applications with common sense. Supervisors who effectively manage meetings with higher management gain credibility and likely accomplish organizational goals.

## KEY TERMS

## WHAT HAVE YOU LEARNED?

1. What is meant by effective communication? What changes, if any, should you be making to improve your communication skills?
2. I am choking on all the e-mails and text messages I get every day. On most days, there are over 150. It seems like I am spending half of my waking hours reviewing and responding to those messages. My kids say, "It is the information age. Learn to cope with it." What is the best way to manage my e-mails and text messages? Give me some ideas. (*Note*: This question may require you to "go outside the box" to get some creative ideas for coping with communication overload.)
3. Think of the person to whom you would award the "World's Best Communicator." What does he or she do to deserve that title? What does he or she do to make sure that understanding takes place? If there is one thing he or she does that you would like to add to your toolbox, what would it be? What is your plan for adding it?
4. Discuss the types of communication barriers that exist in the typical college classroom. How can they be overcome? What specific steps do you need to improve your listening skills?
5. Do you agree with the old cliché that "actions speak louder than words?" Why or why not? Explain your rationale.
6. Think of your present or most recent work experiences:
   (1) How easy was it for you to offer suggestions for improving processes, production, customer service, or creating new products for new markets?
   (2) If you disagreed with one of the organization's policies, procedures, or actions how easy was it to express your views?
   (3) Based on your experiences, what could the organization do to improve communication?
   (4) Why didn't they ask you for suggestions?
7. If you were arrested and accused of being a good communicator, is there enough evidence to convict you? Why or why not?

## EXPERIENTIAL EXERCISES FOR SELF-ASSESSMENT

### EXPERIENTIAL EXERCISE FOR SELF-ASSESSMENT 6: The Communication Quiz

*Adapted from*: Mind Tools, "Communication Quiz," retrieved May 1, 2014, from http://www.mindtools.com/pages/article/newCS_99.htm

Each one of us has an important message to share, but we also have an important role to play in supporting others as they communicate. We all can become better communicators by, for example, being a better listener, explaining more clearly, or being more considerate to those who are different from us. This chapter's assessment will allow you to identify areas in which your communication skills are strong, and areas in which you can improve.

#### The Communication Quiz

**Instructions**

For each statement, select the number that corresponds with the rating that best describes you. Please answer questions as you actually are (rather than how you think you should be), and don't worry if some questions seem to score in the "wrong direction." When you are finished, please use the instructions below to tabulate and interpret your score.

Key: 1=Not at all 2=Rarely 3=Sometimes 4=Often 5=Very Often

1 2 3 4 5 1. I try to anticipate and predict possible causes of confusion, and I deal with them up front.

1 2 3 4 5 2. If I don't understand something, I tend to keep this to myself and figure it out later.

1 2 3 4 5 3. When I write a memo, e-mail, or other document, I give all of the background information and detail I can to make sure that my message is understood.

1 2 3 4 5 4. I'm sometimes surprised to find that people haven't understood what I've said.

1 2 3 4 5 5. I consider cultural, social, gender, and power barriers when planning my communications.

1 2 3 4 5 6. I can tend to say what I think, without worrying about how the other person perceives it. I assume that we'll be able to work it out later.

1 2 3 4 5 7. When people talk to me, I try to see their perspectives.

1 2 3 4 5 8. I use e-mail to communicate complex issues with people. It's quick and efficient.

1 2 3 4 5 9. When talking to people, I pay attention to their body language.

1 2 3 4 5 10. When I finish writing a report, memo, or e-mail, I scan it quickly for typos and so forth, and then send it off right away.

1 2 3 4 5 11. I use diagrams and charts to help express my ideas.

1 2 3 4 5 12. When someone's talking to me, I think about what I'm going to say next to make sure I get my point across correctly.

1 2 3 4 5 13. Before I communicate, I think about what the person needs to know, and how best to convey it.

1 2 3 4 5 14. Before I send a message, I think about the best way to communicate it (in person, over the phone, in a newsletter, via memo, and so on).

1 2 3 4 5 15. I try to help people understand the underlying concepts behind the point I am discussing. This reduces misconceptions and increases understanding.

### Scoring Instructions

First, reverse the ratings of statement numbers 2, 4, 6, 8, 10, and 12 (if your rating was a 1, change it to a 5; if your rating was a 3, keep the rating at 3, etc.). Next, add up all of your ratings. Then see the score interpretation below.

### Score Interpretation

**56–75**: Excellent! You understand your role as a communicator, both when you send messages, and when you receive them. You anticipate problems, and you choose the right ways of communicating. People respect you for your ability to communicate clearly, and they appreciate your listening skills.

**36–55**: You're a capable communicator, but you sometimes experience communication problems. Take the time to think about your approach to communication, and focus on receiving messages effectively, as much as sending them. This will help you improve.

**15–35**: You need to keep working on your communication skills. You are not expressing yourself clearly, and you may not be receiving messages correctly either. The good news is that, by paying attention to communication, you can be much more effective at work, and enjoy much better working relationships.

### For More Information and Further Study

Links to additional resources for improving communication skills can be found in the Chapter 6 Experiential Exercises for Self-Assessment section of the companion website for this textbook.

## PERSONAL SKILL BUILDING

### PERSONAL SKILL BUILDER 6-1: You Make the Call!

Listening is a two-way street. James Matthews clearly should have listened more intently to the grapevine and asked questions to understand what was really going on in the relationship between Thomas Smith and George Harris.

1. Unfortunately, at the end of this You Make the Call! James is at a point that when the incident happened, two valuable employees would be gone forever, and he cannot turn the clock back. What did you learn from this You Make the Call! that might help you improve your listening and questioning skills?
2. What aspects of the do's and don'ts of good listening did James violate?
3. In your opinion, what were the barriers that hindered James's ability to get at the problems that George Harris was having with Thomas Smith.
4. 

Using the Internet, find at least three sources of information that detail how a supervisor might better cope with workplace tragedy. What did you learn that might help you as you journey into the future?

### PERSONAL SKILL BUILDER 6-2: Do You Know How You Spend Your Time?

Information overload is a problem and time-waster for today's supervisor. Look at your lifestyle and how you spend your time. For the next 24 hours, keep a time-log that indicates how you spend your time.

1. Based on your time-log, how much time did you spend getting or giving information?
2. Are you on information overload? Why? Why not?
3. Evaluate your e-mail and texting practices. List five steps you can take to better manage your e-mail and Web activities.
4. What would prevent you from implementing those steps?
5. What changes could you make to improve your communication skills?

### PERSONAL SKILL BUILDER 6-3: Dealing with Employees Who Make Life Difficult—"Stretch"

All one has to do is to read a newspaper or magazine, listen to the radio, or watch television, and it becomes apparent that some people in the world are angry, hostile, uncaring, uncivil, or vociferous malcontents who are ready to do battle for any or no reason. There is always one or two of these people at work—you know them. They are the people who make your life difficult, and you must work with them. What do you do?

This is the first in a series of Personal Skill Building activities that will introduce you to some people who will make your life difficult. In the workplace, these characters share certain characteristics. First, they show up regularly in our lives. Second, there is no one best way to deal with them.

1. Consider the following statement from Alice, a project engineer at Supreme Electronics:

   *I report directly to Neil. He is one person who has the uncanny ability to stretch the truth. He selectively remembers things and uses his selective memory to nullify agreements or change things. On a proposal we submitted to a customer, we spelled out that a particular key team member would be leaving the project after two weeks, and Neil altered it to make it look like he would be running the whole thing. Another time, he cited his ability to develop people as the reason there was a high turnover rate in the department. In fact, most employees jump at a chance to transfer to other departments or to leave the organization. Not long ago, during a department meeting, my boss was talking about the importance of mental toughness. To illustrate the point, he told us about how he had played football in college against some greats who later played in the NFL. A co-worker got a copy of the school's media guide, and nowhere in the All-Time Roster List was our boss's name. When the co-worker confronted him, he said we had misunderstood. The guy is a compulsive liar. I'm locked into this job and can't afford to leave. I've repeatedly tried to transfer out of the department, but while my boss tells me to my face that "he'll support my efforts for advancement," I've found out that he continually stonewalls my requests. "With the current economic situation, I can't find work using my SKAs that would pay me near what I am earning here. I can't afford to leave!"*

2. Data indicates that 85 percent of current (2013) are considering leaving the organizations they work for.[27] If you were Alice, how bad would the job situation under supervisor Neil have to get before you would seriously consider taking a job with less responsibility and for less pay?
3. What are the advantages of working with someone like Neil?
4. What are the disadvantages of working with someone like Neil?
5. Using the Internet, find at least three sources of information for dealing with people who stretch the truth. Carefully review each of these sources for suggestions on how to deal with "stretch."
6. Based on your findings, what suggestions would you make to Alice on how to deal with Neil?
7. Write a paragraph of 60 words or less explaining how this Personal Skills Application increased your working knowledge of coping with the behaviors of this type of person.

## TEAM SKILL BUILDING

### TEAM SKILL BUILDER 6-1: Technology Tool—Be Strategic When Using Social Media

Students should work in groups of three or four to complete this activity.

We've discussed the use of social media quite a bit in this chapter, its benefits, and its challenges. You may be using social media applications in your personal life or as part of your job, but do you use them strategically? Typically when people use social media for personal purposes, they simply tweet to their followers or post to their Facebook or Instagram page if they have something fun or interesting to share. But what if, in the next staff meeting, the boss turns to you and says, "Hey, you're pretty tech savvy. Can you set us up on social media?" What does that mean?

It does *not* mean you should go back to your desk and create accounts for your organization on Twitter, LinkedIn, Facebook, or Instagram. Instead, it means you should carve out at least a full day to create a draft of a social media strategy for your organization, meet with the boss to get his or her approval, and then set to work implementing the plan.

A *social media strategy* is a plan that describes *why* and *how* you will use specific social media applications to connect your mission, product, or brand with your customers or stakeholders.

The importance of having a social media strategy cannot be understated, as many organizations suffer from *digital maximalization*[28] or trying to use every social media app to reach every conceivable population, which is impossible, frustrating, and it wastes valuable time and resources. Effective social media use connects organization with its stakeholders is aligned with the organization's mission or purpose and its existing goals. In other words, what is your organization doing now that social media could help it do better?

While creating a comprehensive social media strategy is beyond the scope of this text, we would like you to have a tool in hand that can help you if the boss puts social media on your to-do list. Your task in this exercise is to create a skeletal social media strategy for an organization of your choice. Using one of the resources from the list below, complete the exercise:

1. Within your group, choose an organization. It can be a business, a local government, a club or group.
2. Use your Internet browser to search for the strategy guides listed below. Use the title of the resource and the organization that publishes it as your search terms. Links to the strategy guides are also available in the "Technology Tools" section of the companion website for this textbook.
3. Each person in the group should read one of the strategy guides and summarize its suggested process for the group. Together, choose one of the guides to follow to create your strategy.
4. Create a one- to two-page outline that briefly describes the following aspects of why and how you would incorporate

social media into the organization's communication and outreach strategies.

a. The message or mission you want to promote—What is your message?
b. The audience of this organization—Who does it serve?
c. The typical social media outlets the audience uses—Where do they gather?
d. The goals of using social media for this organization—What do you want to accomplish—increase membership, share information, recruit employees?
e. How you will measure whether social media is reaching who you want it to reach—Is it working?
f. A description of two social media tools you would use and the way(s) you would use them.

**Sources for Social Media Strategy Guides**

- Convince & Convert suggests a straightforward process for creating a social media strategy for an organization in its blog post, "Social Media Strategy in 8 Steps."
- Hoot Suite provides a Social Media Strategy 5-step PDF guide.
- Nonprofit Technology Network offers a free, 2-session webinar that shows viewers "How to Develop A Social Networking Strategy For Your Organization."
- Salesforce provides free e-book that can help organizations or individuals conceptualize and set up a social media presence, "How To Develop a Social Media Strategy."

## TEAM SKILL BUILDER 6-2: Handling Unpleasant Situations

ROLE PLAY

Arrange students into groups of four. If there is an uneven number of students, select the others to be observers. Assign the students one of the following roles:

1. "I am currently unemployed and drawing unemployment compensation. I quit my job because the boss was constantly on my back about being on time."
2. "Find a home for these files, and then confirm my Friday flight to New Orleans. You did make the hotel reservation for the Mardi Gras, didn't you? My soul mate and I are really looking forward to this weekend."
3. "I know how to do this job better than anyone else. I'll do it my way . . . when I have the time."
4. "You know I was a great athlete. You can't believe how many awards I've won!"

Format: (1) The person selected for #1 should share his story. The others should first pause to ponder the context and the tone used by the sender then write on a three-by-five card what they thought about the message sent including the attitude of the speaker. Then repeat the process for the other three speakers. (2) After the fourth speaker, each person should pass his or her cards to the presenter. (3) After reviewing the cards, each presenter should make a list of how they could have done a better job of presenting the message. (4) Then you should discuss your observations among the group members. (5)

As part of the discussion process, select two of the following words that you think best describe each of the presentations.

| | | | |
|---|---|---|---|
| Showoff | Honest | Independent | Efficient |
| Bossy | Defiant | Insulting | Confident |
| Irresponsible | Arrogant | Polite | Condescending |

(6) As a group, develop a message for each of the presenters that would proclaim the same information but in a better way.

## SUPERVISION IN ACTION

SUPERVISION IN ACTION

The video for this chapter can be accessed from the student companion website at www.cengagebrain.com. (Search by authors' names or book title to find the accompanying resources.)

## ENDNOTES

1. Peter M. Senge, Art Kleiner, Charlotte Roberts, Richard B. Ross, and Bryan J. Smith, *The Fifth Discipline Handbook: Strategies and Tools for Building a Learning Organization* (New York: Doubleday, 1994), p. 11. Senge, in *The Dance of Change: The Challenge of Sustaining Momentum in Learning Organizations* (New York: Doubleday, 1999), stressed the importance of "open, honest, sincere, and genuine" communication to create change in organizations, foster real learning environments, and sustain a positive culture.

   For an interesting way to connect to customers, see Larry Kramer, "How the French Innovators Are Putting the 'Social' Back in Social Networking," *Harvard Business Review* (October 2010), pp. 121–114.
2. Lenny T. Mendonca and Matt Miller, "Crafting a Message That Sticks: An Interview with Chip Heath," *The McKinsey Quarterly—The Online Journal of McKinsey & Co.* (December 2007). Also see Chip Heath and Dan Heath, *Made to Stick: Why Some Ideas Survive and Others Die* (New York: Random House, 2007) for ideas and tips on how to sell your ideas and be a more effective presenter. Ted Pollock, in "9 Ways to Improve Communications," *SuperVision* (April 2008), p. 26, reports that the average manager spends at least 80 percent of his or her time communicating. *Inc.* magazine has curated a collection of articles written by communication experts and CEOs that can help supervisors improve their communication skills, titled "Better Communication with Employees and Peers," http://www.inc.com/guides/growth/23032.html, accessed April 30, 2014.

   Also see Adam M. Grant, Francesca Gino, and David A. Hoffman, "The Hidden Advantages of Quiet Bosses," *Harvard Business Review* (December 2010), p. 28; Barbara Hemphill, "Effective Information Is the Key," *SuperVision* (November 2010), pp. 15–16; Kathleen Brush, "Communicate as Though the World Is Your Stage," *SuperVision* (October 2010), pp. 13–16; Patricia M. Buhler, "Opening Up Management Communication: Learning from Open-Book Management," *SuperVision* (August 2010), pp. 15–17; Justin Scheck and Bobby White, "'Telepresence' Is Taking Hold," The *Wall Street Journal* (May 6, 2008), p. B8; Elizabeth Garone, "Managers Learn to Bond with Remote Workers," *Wall Street Journal* (May 6, 2008), p. D5; and N. Lamar Reinsch Jr., Jeanine Warisse Turner, and Catherine H. Tinsley, "Multi-Communicating: A Practice Whose Time Has Come," *Academy of Management Review* 33, 2 (April 2008), pp. 391–403.
3. Sharon Jayson, "2010: The Year We Stopped Talking," *USA Today* (December 30–31, 2010), pp. 1A–2A. See also Dan Travieso, "Wanted: For the Death of Communications! Technology" *SuperVision* 75, 2 (February 2014), pp. 15–17.
4. See Richard Stengel, "Person of the Year: Mark Zuckerberg, the Case," *Time* (December 27, 2010–January 3, 2011), p. 41. Also see Lev Grossman, "2010 Person of the Year Mark Zuckerberg," *Time* (December 27, 2010–January 3, 2011), pp. 44–57 and "Mark Zuckerberg Biography" on Biography.com, http://www.biography.com/people/mark-zuckerberg-507402
5. See the Radicati Group's *Business User Survey 2013*, http://www.radicati.com/?p=10037
6. Suzanna Kim, "Twitter's IPO Filing Shows 215 Million Monthly Active Users," ABCNews.go.com (October 3, 2013).
7. Cheryl Conner, "Who Wastes the Most Time at Work," *Forbes* (September 7, 2013), http://www.forbes.com/sites/cherylsnappconner/2013/09/07/who-wastes-the-most-time-at-work/.
8. Jon Swartz, "Communications Overload," *USA Today* (February 2, 2011), pp. 1B–2B. Also see William Arruda, "Three Elements of an Effective Social Media Strategy," *Forbes* (August 27, 2013), http://www.forbes.com/sites/williamarruda/2013/08/27/three-elements-of-an-effective-social-media-strategy/. Soumitra Dutta, "What's Your Personal Social Media Strategy," *Harvard Business Review* (November 2010), pp. 127–130; and Tracy Crevar Warren, "Can Facebook Kill Face-to-Face Networking," *CPA in Perspective* (Summer 2010), pp. 32–34.
9. See Scott MacFarland, "Transform Personal Social Media Talent to Business Social Media Talent," *Huffington Post* (February 25, 2014), http://www.huffingtonpost.com/scott-macfarland/transform-personal-social_b_4850906.html; Debra Askanase, "Social Media Convergence," CommunityOrganizer20.com (May 3, 2013); and Jay Baer, "How to Balance Your Personal and Professional Lives in Social Media," ConvinceandConverg.com (April 25, 2014).
10. See Lauren C. Williams, "The 9 Biggest Privacy and Security Breaches that Rocked 2013," ThinkProgress.org (December 31, 2013), http://thinkprogress.org/security/2013/12/31/3108661/10-biggest-privacy-security-breaches-rocked-2013/ and "Walgreen, McDonald's Databases Breached," *The Fort Wayne, IN, Journal Gazette* (December 14, 2010), p.6B. Also see Herb Weisbaum, "5 Lessons Learned from Target Security Breach," Today.com (December 27, 2013), http://www.today.com/money/5-lessons-learned-target-security-breach-2D11803343; Bryon Acohido, "Most Google, Facebook Users Fret over Privacy," *USA Today* (February 9, 2011), p. 1B. Also see Joseph L. Lieberman and Susan M. Collins, "How to Prevent the Next WikiLeaks Dump," *The Wall Street Journal* (January 13, 2011), p. A17.
11. Noted author Tom Peters has strongly advised managers to become highly visible and to do better jobs of listening to subordinates. We agree. For additional information on management by wandering around (MBWA), see Tom Peters, *Thriving on Chaos* (New York: Alfred A. Knopf, 1988), pp. 423–440. For an example of MBWA in practice, see Luis Martinez, "How to Manage by Walking Around," *Rochester Democrat & Chronicle* (March 7, 2014), http://www.democratandchronicle.com/story/RocNext/2014/03/07/how-to-manage-by-walking-around-2/6158545/; and Polly LaBarre, "The Agenda—Grassroots Leadership," *Fast Company* (April 1999), pp. 114+.
12. The grapevine cuts across the formal channels of communications. See Carol Kinsey Goman, "What Leaders Don't Know about the Rumor Mill," *Forbes* (November 30, 2013), http://www.forbes.com/sites/carolkinseygoman/2013/11/30/what-leaders-dont-know-about-the-rumor-mill/ and Vanada Singh and Neha Sharma, "Coping with Grapevine Communication," *VSRD International Journal of Technical and Non-Technical Research* 4, No. 7 (July 2013), pp. 157–158. The classic article on this subject is Keith Davis's "Management Communication and the Grapevine," *Harvard Business Review* (September–October 1953), pp. 43–49.

13. See Julia Angwin, "U.S. Seeks Web Privacy 'Bill of Rights,' " *The Wall Street Journal* (December 17, 2011), pp. A1–A2; Robert M. McDowell, "The FCC's Threat to Internet Freedom," *The Wall Street Journal* (December 20, 2010), p. A23; Nathan Becker, "Web Surfers Troubled by Tracking," *The Wall Street Journal* (December 22, 2010), p. B6.There were two 2007 court cases that dealt with free speech. In both cases, a student had written in his or her notebook or personal Web page threatening a "Columbine-style attack" or recalling "having a dream of shooting a teacher." The courts held that the students' free speech rights were not violated when the school system disciplined them. See *Ronce v. Socorro Independent School District* and *Boim v. Fulton County School District.*
14. For further discussion of informal channels of communication and the grapevine, see Rudolph F. Verderber and Kathleen S. Verderber, *Inter-Act: Using Interpersonal Communication Skills* (Belmont, CA: Wadsworth Publishing Company, 1995); William W. Hull, "Beating the Grapevine to the Punch," *SuperVision* (August 1994), pp. 17–19; "Stopping Those Nasty Rumors," *HR Focus* (November 1990), p. 22; J. Mishra, "Managing the Grapevine," *Public Personnel Management* (Summer 1990), pp. 21–28; Keith Davis and Curtis Sittenfield, "Good Ways to Deliver Bad News," *Fast Company* (April 1999), pp. 58+.
15. Jayson,"2010: The Year We Stopped Talking," p. 1A.
16. See Aaron Smith's summary of smartphone ownership data in "Smartphone Ownership 2013" (June 5, 2013) on the Pew Research Center's Internet & American Life Project Web site, http://www.pewinternet.org/2013/06/05/smartphone-ownership-2013/. See also Nielsen Co., "Text Message Statistics," StatisticsBrain.com (June 18, 2013), http://www.statisticbrain.com/text-message-statistics/. Global mobile access statistics are described in We Are Social's *Global Digital Statistics 2014* (January, 2014), retrieved from http://www.slideshare.net/wearesocialsg/social-digital-mobile-around-the-world-january-2014.
17. The term TMI was first brought to our attention in Rebecca Ganzel, "Editor's Notebook: Too Much Information," *Training* (February 1999), p. 6. You also might want to review, Dori Meinert, "Too Much Information," *HR Magazine* (January 2011), p. 19; and Paul Harvey and Kenneth J. Harris, "Frustration-based Outcomes of Entitlement and the Influence of Supervisor Communication," *Human Relations* (November 2010)., p. 1639.
18. Cheryl Conner, "Who Wastes the Most Time at Work," *Forbes* (September 7, 2013), http://www.forbes.com/sites/cherylsnappconner/2013/09/07/who-wastes-the-most-time-at-work/. Accounting Professional Ken Tysiac reports in "How to Keep Employees from Wasting Time," CGMA.org (February 7, 2014), http://www.cgma.org/magazine/news/pages/20149559.aspx, that non-business-related Internet use is the biggest time waster for workers. He provides four suggestions for reducing wasted worker time: (1) keep employees engaged; (2) have employees track their time for a day; (3) encourage and model productive use of social media; and (4) do not block social media on office computers because workers will simply use their smartphones and reduce productivity even further. What do you think of the last suggestion? Also see John Schaeffer, "The Root Causes of Low Employee Morale: Focusing on Communication Can Fix Them," *SuperVision* (April 2010), pp. 3–4.
19. Quality guru Joseph Juran used the simple explanation that managers needed to be bilingual—that is, they had to speak the language of both upper management and of the workforce. While English is generally recognized as the world's primary business language, not all employees will understand the common tongue.
20. Mikal E. Belicove, "How to Create a Multilingual Website," Entrepreneur.com, (December 5, 2012), http://www.entrepreneur.com/article/224742. See also Mark Grannan, Peter Sheldon, Lily Varon, (February 13, 2014), *Streamline Localization with Language Service Provider Offerings, Market Overview: Language Service Providers 2013.* Cambridge, MA: Forrester, retrieved from http://www.forrester.com/Streamline+Localization+With+Language+Service+Provider+Offerings/fulltext/-/E-RES112441?highlightTerm=languages&isTurnHighlighting=false.
21. See Deborah Tannen, *You Just Don't Understand: Women and Men in Conversation* (New York: William Morrow, 2007), pp. 13–15. Also see Tannen, *That's Not What I Meant! How Conversation Style Makes or Breaks Your Relations with Others* (New York: Morrow, 1992); *Talking from 9 to 5: Women and Men at Work* (New York: Quill, 2001); or *The Argument Culture: Stopping America's War of Words* (New York: Ballantine, 1999)
22. Ibid.
23. Kathleen H. Jamieson as quoted in *Critical Thinking about Critical Issues* (Williamsburg, VA: Learning Enrichment, 1995), p. 9; and Jamieson, *Dirty Politics: Deception, Distraction and Democracy* (Oxford, England: Oxford University Press, 1993), p. 38.
24. When one of the authors started his business career in the early 1960s, his style of management was such that when employees went to him with a problem, his job was to solve it for them. One day the author realized that he was spending all his time solving their problems. One of his coaches suggested that he try another approach: The next time an employee comes to you with a problem, pause, think about it for a second, and if it is not a crisis, then tell the employee to go back and think about the problem, identify who is affected by the problem and talk with them, and then come back with at least two recommendations on how to solve the problem. Then explore their options and help them make a decision. Then, if possible, give them permission to implement the solution, making sure they understand the need to get those others who have to live with the decision involved in the implementation. His coach stressed the notion of "ownership." Also see Jeff Kehoe, "How to Save Good Ideas: An Interview with John Kotter," *Harvard Business Review* (October 2010), pp. 129–132; Jill Jusko, "A Little More Conversation," *Industry Week* (March 2010), p. 19; Daisy Sanders, "Create an Open Climate for Communication," *SuperVision* 60, No. 1 (January 2008), pp. 6–8; and Rick Mathes, "Building Bridges through Effective Communication," *SuperVision* 68, No. 10 (October 2007), pp. 3–4.
25. The author cannot remember when he heard the term "Managing Up!" but the article by John J. Gabarro and John P. Kotter, "Managing Your Boss," *Harvard Business Review* (January–February 1980), pp. 92–100, still has relevance today as every boss has a boss. The ideas and suggestions in this list were derived from material on Meryl Natchez's Web site, "Managing Up: The Overlooked Element in Successful Management" (http://www.techprose.com/managing_up.html); Mike Lynch and Harvey Lifton's *Training Clips: 150 Reproducible Handouts, Discussion Starters, and Job Aids* (Amherst, MA: HRD Press, 1998), p. 16; and Douglas Stone, Bruce Patton, and Sheila Heen *Difficult Conversations: How to Discuss What Matters Most* (New York: Viking, 1999). Also see Andrew Park, "Taming the Alpha Exec (AKA: 'How to Tame the Boss from Hell')," *Fast Company*

(May 2006), pp. 86–90. For interesting approaches to managing the relationship with one's boss, see Sue Shellenbarger, "The Care and Feeding (and the Avoiding) of Horrible Bosses," *The Wall Street Journal* (October 20, 1999), p. B1; and Thomas J. Zuber and Erika H. James, "Managing Your Boss," *Family Practice Management* (June 2001), pp. 33–36.

26. Peter M. Senge, *The Fifth Discipline* (New York: Currency/Doubleday, 1980), pp. 159–161. Also see Mortimer Zuckerman, "How to Fight and Win the Cyberwar," *The Wall Street Journal* (December 6, 2010), p. A19.

27. According to the results of LinkedIn's Talent Trends 2014 survey, which involved over 18,000 employed professionals from 26 countries, only 15 percent of workers are completely satisfied with their jobs and do not want to move. The balance are actively looking for opportunities, talking to recruiters about other opportunities, or discussing opportunities with their personal networks. The Talent Trends report is available for download at http://business.linkedin.com/talent-solutions/c/14/3/talent-trends.html

28. William Powers, *Hamlet's Blackberry: A Practical Philosophy for Building a Good Life in the Digital Age* (New York: HarperCollins, 2010), p. 4.

Chapter 7

# Principles of Motivating Followers

©Snezana Ignjatovic/Shutterstock.com

**After studying this chapter, you will be able to:**

1. Recognize personal and situational factors that may cause employee job dissatisfaction.
2. Identify and discuss reasons people behave the way they do.
3. Understand the various motivational theories and appreciate their importance.
4. Explain how one might use the motivational theories to manage their own lives and the performance of others.
5. Appreciate ways to more effectively cope with people who make your life difficult.
6. Consider how the ABCs can be used to shape behavior.
7. Compare the assumptions and applications of Theory X and Theory Y in supervision.
8. Articulate how job redesign, multitasking, and participative management can be used to develop employee SKAs.

## YOU MAKE THE CALL!

*Don Davis is the director of reloading operations for Economy Moving and Storage, a large international shipping company. Due to a corporate reorganization, over 1,300 employees had their jobs eliminated. Don was recently transferred to the Dublin center, where he would be in charge of five front-line supervisors who direct the operations of 90 employees. Don was thankful for the opportunity and was looking forward to the challenge and responsibilities in his new position, but he would miss the camaraderie that he had at the previous location. Maintaining contact via Facebook and e-mail was not the same.*

In Don's first week on the job, it became obvious that the Dublin center had some serious problems that needed to be corrected quickly. He became aware that many customers were complaining that the packages shipped from the Dublin center arrived at their destinations late or in poor condition. For a company that prided itself on quality customer service and timely delivery, these conditions were not acceptable, and it was Don's responsibility to correct the situation.

The first thing Don did was gather information regarding the customer complaints. When he checked with Holly Henderson, the human resources director, to gather information on the employee characteristics at the Dublin center, Don discovered that his center had a high rate of employee turnover and lost time injury rates. Absenteeism and tardiness were running rampant, and the number of employee grievances had increased in the past six months. Realizing that unhappy employees equal poor customer service, Don decided to meet with the supervisors to understand why employees were performing below expectations.

During the meeting, Don illustrated the last three months' performance results to Amy, Steve, Joe, Sue, and Ryan and asked for their input. Amy, a long-term supervisor, pointed out that the conditions in which the employees work were sometimes terrible. "We have had record high temperatures during the month of June," she said. "Last week, it was over 100 degrees in here. How can you expect people to perform in such extreme heat? This place is not air-conditioned and it is awful!"

Ryan, the newest of the supervisors, added, "Most workers are part-time. Some of them have other part-time jobs or are working here while they attend school. They come here tired and with other things on their minds. Most of the injuries I see are directly related to a lack of concentration. They make stupid mistakes. Even during our safety meetings, many workers seem bored and do not seem to pay attention." Steve complained, "The job the employees perform is very repetitious. They seem bored and lack enthusiasm. In fact, on several occasions employees have pointed out that their work is mindless, not satisfying, and needs changes. If you ask me, boredom is the main problem with employee performance."

Steve said, "I think the performance of some of our employees is affected by a few 'bad apples.' Overall, most of our people are good workers. They want to do a good job. I've seen them getting frustrated because of a poorly performing co-worker who needs to be reprimanded. I can't do anything about it; we are often short staffed and if I discipline someone, he or she will probably quit. That's how it was last week when I leaned on Reuben about his job performance. He essentially said, 'take this job and shove it!' Our employees know what to do, but they sometimes just don't feel they need to do it or do it the right way. Even when I plead with them to improve or threaten to write them up, it doesn't work. If I could only get the poor performers motivated, I think the rest would fall in line and overall performance would improve."

Last, Sue chimed in, "I have trouble motivating my workers. Just yesterday, one of my best workers left with a knee injury and the others failed to pick up the slack. If we don't find a way to motivate our people and improve performance, none of us will have a job."

The real question is: "What can Don do to help his front-line supervisors do a better job of motivating their workers to perform better?" He knew that pay increases were not possible. He knows he will have to do something quickly. What should he do?

**Disclaimer:** The above scenario presents a supervisory situation based on real events to be used for educational purposes. The identities of some or all individuals, organizations, industries, and locations, as well as financial and other information may have been disguised to protect individual privacy and proprietary information. Fictional details may have been added to improve readability and interest.

YOU MAKE THE CALL!

## Where Can I Get Satisfaction?

**1 Recognize personal and situational factors that may cause employee job dissatisfaction.**

Some things never change. Aristotle said, "Happiness is the meaning and purpose of life, the whole aim and the end of human existence."[1] Thus, the fundamental question for each of us is, "What does it take to make you happy?"

Two popular songs of our early teaching years may still be relevant today. While the 1965 Rolling Stones hit song, *"(I Can't Get No) Satisfaction"* wasn't about job satisfaction, that message is still being sung in the hearts and minds of

**Satisfaction**
An emotional state or affective response toward various factors associated with one's work

many employees today.[2] **Satisfaction** is an emotional state or affective response toward various factors associated with one's work. The bitterness of a man who worked long and hard hours with no apparent rewards was expressed best in a 1978 Johnny Paycheck song, in which the lyrics insist, "Take this job and shove it, I ain't working here no more!"[3]

Job satisfaction surveys vary greatly in their statistics, but the conclusions are the same. The Conference Board has been conducting surveys since 1987, and their most recent study reported that although job satisfaction levels have come back from their lowest point realized during the recent economic recession, for the seventh year in a row, less than half of U.S. workers are satisfied with their jobs.[4] Economic, political, social, and personal factors may influence the findings, but unlike those factors, working conditions and other work-related factors probably contribute greatly to the dissatisfaction. Millions of U.S. jobs were lost during the recent recession, and some have gone to lower wage countries, although these losses are beginning to ebb.[5]

Why do employees leave their jobs? Figure 7.1 illustrates the differences between what employers believe and what the employees' actual reasons are. Employees typically state in exit interviews or tell others that they're leaving for a better job, more pay, or job security, but researchers have concluded that the real reasons are often a bad supervisor, a nonchallenging or unfulfilling work situation, problems with co-workers, and so on.

In an annual celebration of International Women's Day, the release of a 2014 study by Accenture revealed that less than half of the respondents were satisfied in their current jobs.[6] While the research data collected by various agencies varies in the degree of satisfaction or dissatisfaction, the conclusions are obvious. (1) The employee's perception of the organization's financial stability is related to satisfaction. (2) Job security is still very important. (3) When the economy begins to warm up, workers who are dissatisfied with their jobs go looking for new ones.[7]

Clearly, the economic climate has changed the way employees look at their employer, their current work, and other aspects of their lives. The data reported in Figure 7.2 might surprise you, but many employees still view their work as a career. Supervisors must work with human resources professionals and other members of the management team to ensure that their organization is known as a "great place to work." Throughout the remainder of the book, we will provide you with tips and suggestions on how to accomplish this goal in your organization.

**FIGURE 7.1 Reasons employees leave organizations**

| Employers' Speculations | Employees' Reasons |
|---|---|
| 1. Increased base pay | 1. Base pay |
| 2. Career advancement opportunity | 2. Greater job security |
| 3. Improved work–life balance | 3. Pension |
| 4. More flexible work location | 4. Improved work–life balance |
| 5. Greater job security | 5. Better health benefits |

*Source:* Based on 2010 Towers Watson Global Workforce Study, reported in *HR Magazine* (January 2011), p. 27.

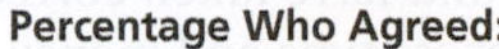
FIGURE 7.2 "I view my work as a career, not just a job"

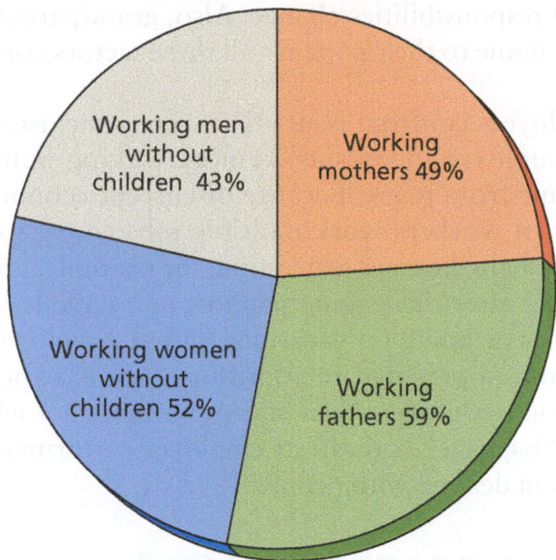


*Source:* Working Mother/Ernst & Young survey of workers, reported in *USA Today* (December 14, 2010), p. 1B.

## Determinants of Human Behavior

**2 Identify and discuss reasons people behave the way they do.**

In Chapter 2, we defined management as getting things accomplished with and through people by guiding and motivating their efforts toward common objectives. To manage effectively, as this definition suggests, supervisors must understand employee motivation and develop approaches that encourage employees to work to their full capabilities.

People are the most important resource that a supervisor is asked to manage. Human beings have values, attitudes, needs, and expectations that significantly influence their behaviors on the job. The feelings people have toward their supervisors, their job environments, their personal problems, and numerous other factors are often difficult to ascertain.[8] However, they have a tremendous impact on employee motivation and work performance.

What causes employees to behave in the ways they do? This question is difficult to answer because each individual is unique. The behavior of people is often rational, consistent, and predictable. However, people's behaviors at other times may seem irrational, inconsistent, and unpredictable. People tend to associate with others who are like themselves—"birds of a like feather flock together." This may lead to distrust and misunderstanding of those who are not of their "flock." Have you ever behaved differently because of the group you were in? Of course, you have. Was that behavior inconsistent with your family's or organization's expectations? If so, then problems arose for your parents, your supervisor, and eventually you. Remember, behavior is influenced by many forces, making it difficult for the supervisor to formulate simple principles that apply to every situation.

The forces that stimulate human behavior come from within individuals and from their environments. To illustrate, think about why parents' behavior changes when they become grandparents. One answer might be that the grandparents are older and perhaps more mature or experienced. They have received feedback on their earlier parenting efforts and have taken corrective action. Many grandparents appear to be willing to devote time and money to their grandkids. As grandparents, duties and responsibilities change. Also, grandparents can always send their grandchildren home to their parents. All these factors combined may lead to behavioral change.

Every day, employees confront issues that were nonexistent just a few years ago. The typical employee today spends more waking hours going to, being at, and coming home from work. Because of current economic conditions, an increasing number of workers work multiple jobs to try to make ends meet. Some workers in the baby boomer generation, for example, are caring for grandchildren and looking after their aging parents, and have less time to spend on leisure-time activities or going on vacations. Often, employees find themselves in intolerable or soured personal relationships. Many experienced managers speak about the people who were their star performers but who lost their luster. Understanding the "baggage" that affects employee performance is critical to the supervisor's success in dealing with people.

## DETERMINANTS OF PERSONALITY[9]

**Personality**
The knowledge, attitudes, and attributes that make up the unique human being

Every individual is the product of many factors, and it is the unique combination of these factors that results in an individual human personality. **Personality** is the complex mix of knowledge, attitudes, and attributes that distinguishes one person from all others.

Many people use the word "personality" to describe what they observe in another person. However, the real substance of human personality goes far beyond external behavior. The essence of an individual's personality includes his or her attitudes, values, and ways of interpreting the environment, as well as many internal and external influences that contribute to behavioral patterns. Several major schools of personality study can help explain the complexity of human behavior. First, we will discuss the primary determinants of personality, and then describe how some major theories relate these factors to employee motivation.

## PHYSIOLOGICAL (BIOLOGICAL) FACTORS

One major influence on human personality is physiological (or biological) makeup. Such factors as gender, age, race, height, weight, and physique can affect how a person sees the world. Intelligence, which is at least partially inherited, is another. Most biological characteristics are apparent to others, and they may affect the way in which a person is perceived. For example, a person who is tall is sometimes considered to have more leadership ability than a shorter person. While physiological characteristics should not be the basis for evaluating an employee's capabilities, they do exert considerable influence on an individual's personality as well as defining certain physical abilities and limitations.

## EARLY CHILDHOOD INFLUENCES

Many psychologists feel that the very early years of a person's life are crucial to an individual's development. The manner in which a child is trained, shown affection, and disciplined has a lifelong influence. Parents who encourage autonomy, independence, exploration, and the ability to deal with risk, while instilling a willingness to work with others, give the child valuable lessons. A person's background and previous experiences affect the way they are—and the way they act at work. A critical parent or teacher in one's younger years, for instance, may lead to insecurity in adult life. "Such folks often end up humiliating others, blaming them for their shortcomings, and taking credit for others' work."[10]

## ENVIRONMENTAL (SITUATIONAL) FACTORS

Sociologists and social psychologists emphasize the immediate situation or environment as being the most important determinant of adult personality. Education, income, employer, home, and many other experiences that confront an individual throughout life influence who that person is and eventually becomes. Have you ever talked about "the good old days"? Where you lived during your formative years and what you experienced during that time have, in part, shaped who and what you are today.

Each day's experiences contribute to an individual's makeup. This is particularly true in terms of the immediate working environment. For example, the personality of the blue-collar worker performing routine, manual labor on an assembly line is affected by work differently than the personality of a white-collar worker who performs primarily mental work involving thought and judgment. Stated another way, what a supervisor does in a work situation affects the personalities of the people being supervised and how they in turn treat others.

## CULTURAL (SOCIETAL) VALUES

Culture also influences personality. In the United States, such values as competition, rewards for accomplishment, equal opportunities, and similar concepts are part of a democratic society. Individuals are educated, trained, and encouraged to think for themselves and to strive to achieve worthwhile goals. However, some cultural values are changing. For example, for many years the workforce

David Grossman/Alamy

*Our daily experiences, such as our method of commuting to and from work, can influence our personality, outlook, and mood*

in the United States was relatively homogeneous, and the cultural values of most workers tended to be similar. During the past 10 years, however, the workforce has become increasingly diversified, reflecting many different subcultures and subgroups. The number of Asians, Hispanics, and Latinos in the workforce has increased dramatically. As the diversity of the workforce has increased, so has the effect of different cultural norms and values on the workplace. In particular, the values of certain ethnic, age, and other minority groups may be quite different among employees. By recognizing and respecting different cultural values, supervisors should become more adept in dealing effectively with people unlike themselves.

## EVERY EMPLOYEE HAS AN ATTITUDE[11]

Not long ago, a manager expressed to the text's author that her biggest challenge was an employee with an attitude problem. The employee constantly complained. The manager was upset with herself because she had taken the path of least resistance and avoided the employee. Supervisors must recognize that the positive or negative behavior of one person spills over—someone else now has either a positive or negative attitude. We have all seen situations where one employee with a bad attitude is like cancer and can affect the entire system if left unchecked. You and I don't have a bad attitude; it's all those other people.

**Positive Mental Attitude (PMA)**
Seeing the positive side of things, rather than the negative, which helps individuals deal with challenges and adapt more easily to changes.

How do others see you? Think about a person you know who has a **Positive Mental Attitude (PMA)** and tends to look on the bright side, rather than complaining and finding fault with people and situations. Is this person fun to be around (i.e., work with)? Is this person's attitude infectious? Does an employee with a PMA perform better in the workplace? How about you? Are you known for having a PMA? Do others see you as having a negative attitude? Team Skill Builder 7-1 at the end of this chapter gives you an opportunity to develop strategies for coping with this type of behavior.

**Rule of reciprocity**
The rule of reciprocity implies paying back a good deed or retaliating when one experiences a wrongdoing

Not surprisingly, there is a **Rule of reciprocity** that suggests that humans react and respond in like manner to the attitude and action of others. Consider these two scenarios:

- As we drive down the highway, we can see this rule in effect. Suppose someone is driving much slower than the speed limit and another person is in a hurry. What happens? The second driver may blast the horn, yell obscenities, and gesture until there is an opportunity to pass the slower driver. Who has the bad attitude? Now they both do.
- On the other hand, if a driver lets someone cut into a traffic flow, what happens? A wave of the hand, a mouthed "thanks," and perhaps a little later that person lets someone else into the traffic flow. The notion of "one good deed warrants another" comes into play.

**Emotional contagion**
Transfer of emotion and attitudes between people who are in close contact

Often our attitudes are caused by what others do and say. In *The Ripple Effect: Emotional Contagion and Its Influence on Group Behavior,* Sigal Barsade describes the phenomenon of **emotional contagion** as transfer of emotion and attitudes between people who are in close contact, and asserts that when a leader's bad mood permeates the office, employees' engagement and performance can be severely impacted.[12] Of course, leaders' and employees' positive attitudes can also rub off on one another. Remember an axiom of supervision: Focus on what the person does or does not do related to his or her job and, whenever possible, reinforce the positive.

### RECOGNIZING HUMAN DIFFERENCES AND SIMILARITIES

The many complexities of human personality have been discussed here only briefly because any number of factors cause a person's personality and attitude to change. Realistically, it is impossible to understand all the unique characteristics of a person's personality.

Supervisors can understand the unique needs and personality makeup of individual employees enough to adapt general approaches to individuals to some extent. Throughout the text, we will provide you with suggestions, strategies, and tips to help you lead a diverse group of employees toward achieving organizational goals.

## Understanding Motivation and Human Behavior

**3 Understand the various motivational theories and appreciate their importance.**

Too often, motivation is viewed as something one person can give to, or do, for another. Supervisors sometimes talk in terms of giving a worker a "shot" of motivation or of having to "motivate employees." However, motivating employees is not that easy, because human motivation really refers to an inner drive or impulse. Motivation cannot be given to another. In the final analysis, motivation comes from within a person. **Motivation** is a willingness to exert effort toward achieving a goal, stimulated by the effort's ability to fulfill an individual need. In other words, employees are more willing to do what the organization wants if they believe that doing so will result in a meaningful reward.

**Motivation**
A willingness to exert effort toward achieving a goal, stimulated by the effort's ability to fulfill an individual need

The supervisor's challenge is to stimulate that willingness and ensure that the rewards are commensurate with the results. The rewards need not always be money; they can be anything employees value.

### EMPLOYEE NEEDS (MASLOW AND OTHERS)

Most psychologists who study human behavior and personality are convinced that all behavior is caused, goal-oriented, and motivated. Stated another way, there is a reason for everything a person does, assuming the person is rational, sane, and in control (i.e., not under the influence of drugs or alcohol). People constantly strive to attain something that has meaning for them in terms of their needs and in relation to how those people see themselves and the environments in which they live. Often, we may be unaware of why we behave in a certain manner, but we all have subconscious motives that govern the ways we behave in different situations.

One of the most widely accepted theories of human behavior is that people are motivated to satisfy certain well defined and more or less predictable needs. In 1943, college professor and psychologist Abraham H. Maslow formulated the concept of a **hierarchy** (or priority) **of needs**.[13] He maintained that there were five clear stages of needs ranging from low-level to high-level needs, in an ascending priority. Maslow referred to other aspects of motivation, and over the years, others (including this author) have added cognitive, aesthetic, transcendence, and consistency to his original list. While Maslow referred to the first three of these, he did not include them as additional stages in his hierarchy of needs. Figure 7.3 presents an overview of the needs theory of motivation.

**Hierarchy of needs**
Maslow's theory of motivation, which suggests that employee needs are arranged in priority order such that lower-order needs must be satisfied before higher-order needs become motivating

FIGURE 7.3 Hierarchy of needs

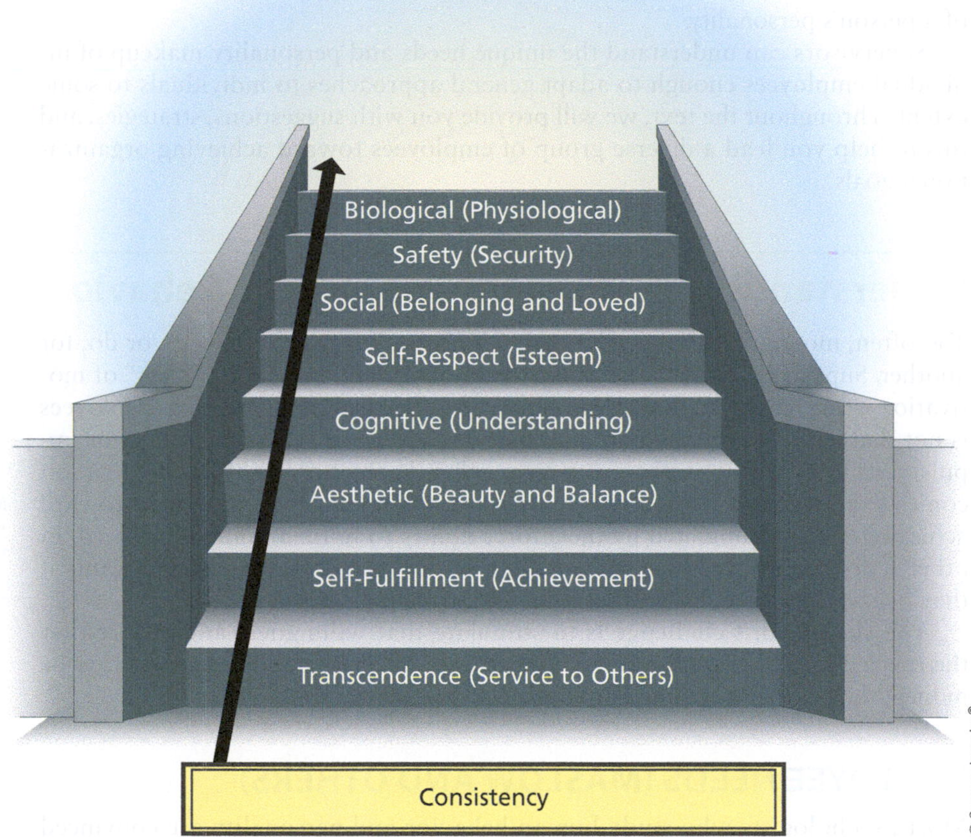




These needs actually overlap and are interrelated, and it may be preferable to consider them as existing along a continuum rather than as being separate and distinct from one another.

Maslow's theory of a hierarchy of human needs implies that people try to satisfy these needs in the order in which they are arranged in the hierarchy. Until the lowest, or most basic, needs are reasonably satisfied, a person will not be motivated strongly by the other levels. As one level of need is satisfied to some extent, the individual focuses on the next level, which then becomes the stronger motivator of behavior. Maslow even suggested that once a low level of need was reasonably satisfied, it would no longer motivate behavior, at least in the short term.

## BIOLOGICAL (PHYSIOLOGICAL) NEEDS

**Physiological needs** Basic physical needs (e.g., food, rest, shelter, and recreation)

On the first level of Maslow's hierarchy are **physiological** (or biological) **needs**. These are the needs everyone has for food, shelter, rest, recreation, and other physical necessities. Virtually every employee views work as a means of caring for these fundamental needs. A paycheck enables a person to buy the necessities vital to survival, as well as some of the comforts of life.

## SECURITY (SAFETY) NEEDS

Once a person's physiological needs are reasonably satisfied, other needs become important. The **security** (or safety) **needs** include the need to protect ourselves against danger and to guard against the uncertainties of life.[14] Most employees want some sense of security or control over their future. To satisfy such expectations, many employers offer various supplementary benefits. For example, medical, retirement, hospitalization, disability, and life insurance plans are designed to protect employees against various uncertainties and their possible serious consequences. Wage and benefit packages are designed to satisfy employees' physiological and safety needs. By fulfilling these basic needs, organizations hope to attract and retain competent personnel.

**Security needs**
Desire for protection against danger and life's uncertainties

## SOCIAL (BELONGING) NEEDS

Some supervisors believe that good wages and ample benefits suffice to motivate employees. These supervisors do not understand the importance of the higher-level needs of human beings, beginning with social (or belonging) needs. **Social needs** are needs people have for attention, for being part of a group, for being accepted by their family, friends, and peers, and for love. Many studies have shown that group motivation can be a powerful influence on employee behavior at work, either negatively or positively. For example, some employees may deliberately perform contrary to organizational goals to feel that they are accepted in an informal group. On the other hand, if informal group goals are in line with organizational goals, the group can influence individuals toward exceptional performance.

**Social needs**
Desire for love and affection and affiliation with something worthwhile

Think about these questions: Do you have friends? Or do you have a group of acquaintances? Do you have a group you can share a cup of coffee or a few jokes with, but then go your own way? Or do you have someone you can call at 3 A.M. to discuss a personal problem who will listen critically without passing

Jose Luis Pelaez Inc./Cusp /Corbis

*Some employers provide off-the-job social and athletic opportunities for their employees to help those employees satisfy their social needs and to build loyalty to the organization*

judgment? Think back to when you were 10 years old. Who was your very best friend? Where is that person today? Or ask someone who has been married for more than 25 years these questions: "Who was the best man or maid/matron of honor at your wedding? Where are they today? Are they still there for you? Have they stood alongside you (unconditionally, without strings attached)?" In some cases, the answer is "yes." Human connectedness is at the top of the list for some people. Unfortunately, most of us can provide many illustrations of the "here today–gone tomorrow" phenomenon.

We all know many people who like their jobs but not the people they work with and, as such, seek fulfillment of their social needs through off-the-job interactions.

## SELF-RESPECT (ESTEEM) NEEDS

**Self-respect needs**
Desire for recognition, achievement, status, and a sense of accomplishment

Closely related to social needs are **self-respect** (or esteem or ego) **needs**. These are needs everyone has for recognition, achievement, status, and a sense of accomplishment. Self-respect needs are very powerful because they relate to personal feelings of self-worth and importance. Supervisors should look for ways to satisfy these internal needs, such as providing varied and challenging work tasks and recognizing good performance. Something as simple as saying "good job" to someone can keep that person doing good work.

## COGNITIVE (UNDERSTANDING) NEEDS

**Cognitive needs**
One's need to know and understand

**Cognitive dissonance**
The state of being out of balance because of conflicting goals, job assignments, expectations, or knowledge

The previous needs are said to be extrinsic because satisfaction can come from factors external to the individual. Although it was not one of Maslow's original five, Maslow often referred to a person's needs to know and understand, which are known as **Cognitive needs**. At an early age, a child asks questions of his parents. Students should ask questions of their instructors. New employees often seek clarification of the job requirements and expectations. Why? In order to fulfill their needs to know and understand, they search for answers.

**Cognitive dissonance** is a feeling of being uncomfortable because two ideas conflict simultaneously.[15] Consider this example: An employee is scheduled to work on the day of the Kentucky Derby. He had never had access to tickets, nor did he feel that he could afford to buy them on e-Bay or Stub-Hub, but he had always dreamed of being there. Two days before the race, he received a text from a long-time friend inviting him to be his guest for the festivities. The employee knows that he is scheduled to work, and finding a substitute at this late day is not possible. What will he do? His thought processes might go like this: "I run the risk of getting a reprimand if I don't go to work on Derby Day. Or I might be fired in this tough economy. But I have always wanted to be there on Derby Day. I am a smart, intelligent person who needs to make the right choice." At that instant, the person has an uncomfortable feeling and experiences some tension because of the two conflicting options.

We often find ourselves in such situations. Hopefully, we will make the decision that allows minimum dissonance. A sidebar issue: Imagine yourself sitting in class during an exam. The answer to the question is one that you know almost as well as you know your name, but you just can't remember. "I know that cheating is wrong, but I have to do well on this exam." What will you do? Cognitive needs and cognitive dissonance come into play. We all have a need to know and understand, but we also have a need to be in balance.

## AESTHETIC (BEAUTY AND BALANCE) NEEDS[16]

"Wow! The Great Wall of China is a sight to behold." Imagine the tens of thousands of people working for centuries to make it happen and in an era when there were no computer programs available to design it. This is one example of the wall's designer fulfilling his **aesthetic needs** by using his creativity to create something useful and aesthetically pleasing. However, subjectivity needs to be factored in. Some would not find the Great Wall to have significance or value. Others, based on their senses and perceptions, would conclude otherwise.

**Aesthetic needs**
The need to create something that is useful and pleasing. Beauty is in the eyes of the beholder

A friend of one of the authors orders liver and onions every time the two of them go to a particular restaurant. Another friend does not have the same taste or appreciation of the choice. Tastes, appreciation, and enjoyment vary greatly among people. As Kant wrote, "Beauty is no quality in things themselves, it exists merely in the mind which contemplates them."[17]

Unfortunately, we have found that many college students strive to achieve balance in their lives, but lots of things get in the way. Meeting both the lower-level needs as well as higher-level needs, like aesthetic needs, can be challenging. Not long ago, a friend said that she was having problems finding balance between the things she had to do as an employee and mother; doing things for those people she loves; and doing things that she loved to do. She concluded by saying, "I wish there were 40 hours in each day, then I would get everything done that needs to be done!" It is not easy to offer help in such situations. Successful people learn to prioritize, determine what is most important, adjusting priorities and balancing the conflicts that occur between work, family, and self. The authors find this to be easier said than done.

## SELF-FULFILLMENT NEEDS

The term **self-fulfillment** (self-actualization) **needs** refers to the desires to use one's capabilities to their fullest. Maslow suggested that people want to be creative and to achieve within their capacities. Presumably, this need is not satisfied until people reach their full potential. As such, these needs persist throughout a person's life and can go unsatisfied. As we go through life, we have many options and choices available to us. Maslow contended that self-actualization is the process of making each decision a choice for growth and that striving for continuous improvement can lead to fulfillment.[18]

**Self-fulfillment needs**
Desire to use one's abilities to the fullest extent

Many jobs frustrate rather than satisfy this level of human needs. For example, many factory and office jobs are routine and monotonous, and workers must seek self-fulfillment in pursuits off the job and in family relationships. However, supervisors can provide opportunities for self-fulfillment on the job by assigning tasks that challenge employees to use their abilities more fully. The authors maintain that in today's world, you have to take responsibility for developing your own potential. You need to find ways to use your skills, knowledge, abilities, and talents in order to "do well those things that you really want to do."[19]

## TRANSCENDENCE NEEDS

Kant is given credit for introducing the term *transcendental*—that which goes beyond.[20] Later, Maslow took the field of psychology to new levels by introducing the notions of humanistic psychology and transpersonal psychology.

He maintained that humanistic psychology should examine what is right with people rather than focus on what is wrong with them. Maslow identified those who have gone beyond his own notion of self-actualization as those who are not only fulfilled but have transcended beyond. "For transcenders, peak experiences and plateau experiences have become the most important things in their lives."[21] Sometimes we hear about an individual who has gone above the normal or expected, fulfilling their **transcendence needs** by achieving even higher goals and peak experiences after realizing self-actualization. What causes someone to do that? Might it be that their lower-order needs have been fulfilled and that they want to do something simply because it is the right thing to do at the time; or could their actions feel like the next logical steps in striving for greatness? Numerous service clubs conduct a wide variety of projects to benefit others. Rotary International, for example, defines core values and priorities as "service before self." You might ask, why do people spend hours helping others? For these people, joy comes from using their SKAs to help those who are less fortunate.

**Transcendence needs**
Achieving even higher goals and peak experiences once all of the self-actualization needs have been met

## NEED FOR CONSISTENCY

One of the authors first became aware of this need when he was a high school student. A coach said, "Leonard, you need to be more consistent! More practice will make perfect!" But as much as I practiced, I could never make all my free throws. Then a friend said, "perfect practice makes perfect!" I searched for the person who was the best at shooting free throws, analyzed his methods, and practiced and practiced some more. As hard as I tried, I would still miss some shots. But I gave it my best shot.

Leon Festinger, among others, said, "When our inner systems (beliefs, attitudes, values) and our actions all support one another, we are in a state of comfort."[22] Some individuals' **Consistency needs**, the extent to which all areas of their life or all areas of their work environment are in harmony and free from variation and contradiction, are very high, so they must have consistency in order to be satisfied and productive. Think about people you know who thrive when they have clear, ethical guidelines, a clean desk, a set schedule, and a specific, predictable role to fill. Contrast them in your mind with people who are at their best in the middle of chaos—a messy desk, phone lighting up constantly with texts, overlapping commitments, and loud meetings fraught with controversy. The former have far stronger consistency needs than the latter, yet both can be equally successful.

**Consistency needs**
Being in harmony and free from variation and contradiction

Many years ago, there was a popular TV show called the *Sixty-four Thousand Dollar Question*. Not surprisingly to these authors, five years after they hit the jackpot some of these contestants were worse off financially than before. The same thing has happened to many lottery winners.[23] Why? Consistency was no longer in play for them. Spend, spend, spend had become their motto without regard to the consequences. The consistency of having, feeling, loving, believing, knowing, and so on is an important need because, in part, it helps to keep us in balance.

## ERG THEORY

Based on the works of Maslow and others, Clayton Alderfer introduced the **ERG Theory**.

**ERG Theory**
Existence, relatedness, and growth needs

- Existence: Physiological and safety needs
- Relatedness: Social and external esteem needs
- Growth: Self-actualization and internal esteem needs[24]

Alderfer believed that various levels of needs can be pursued at the same time and that the order is different for each individual. The notion of "different strokes for different folks" is relevant. This theory holds that if a higher-level need is largely unfulfilled, the person may regress to a lower-level that is easier to satisfy. He called this the ***frustration-regression* principle**.

***Frustration-regression* principle**
If higher-needs are not satisfied, individuals will regress to a lower-order need that is more easily fulfilled

## MCCLELLAND'S THREE-NEED THEORY[25]

David McClelland examined workplace needs for achievement, affiliation, and power. Setting and attaining challenging goals, completing difficult assignments, or doing something that had not been done before are examples of fulfilling achievement needs (nACH). Interestingly, research shows that those with high ACH needs prefer tasks of moderate difficulty, such as situations where performance is due to their own efforts and a lot of positive feedback is desired.

Some people take great pride in the groups to which they belong. The prestige of the group may be more important to them than what the group does or doesn't do. People with high affiliation needs (nAFF) join groups and spend lots of time and energy maintaining social relationships. They get great satisfaction from being liked and respected by others. Team harmony and cohesion are important to them. It is even better when the team achieves a task previously thought to be unachievable.

As we discussed in Chapter 2, power is the ability to influence others. Watch the evening news to see illustrations of those who have high **needs for power (nPOW)**. Yukl reviewed McClelland's work and suggested that "influencing others, defeating a competitor, winning every argument, and attaining a position of control over others to bolster their own position or status" were the motives for those with high power needs.[26]

**Needs for power (nPOW)**
The need to exert influence over others or to be in position of control

McClelland concluded that top managers should have a high need for power coupled with a low need for affiliation.[27] This author believes that balance (consistency) is important and that often, supervisors will seek opportunities to maintain a positive self-image. Which of McClelland's needs is most important to you at this point in your life?

## MOTIVATION-HYGIENE THEORY

Another theory of motivation is the **motivation-hygiene theory**, sometimes called the two-factor theory or the dual-factor theory, developed by Frederick Herzberg.[28] Herzberg's research has demonstrated that some factors in the work environment that were traditionally believed to motivate people actually serve primarily to reduce their dissatisfaction rather than motivate them.

**Motivation-hygiene theory**
Herzberg's theory that factors in the work environment primarily influence the degree of job dissatisfaction while intrinsic job content factors influence the amount of employee motivation

Herzberg and others have conducted numerous studies in which they asked people to describe events that made them feel particularly good or bad about their jobs. Other questions were designed to determine the depth of feelings, how long those feelings lasted, and the kind of situations that made employees feel motivated or frustrated. These studies were conducted with employees in various organizations and industries, including personnel at all levels and from different technical and job specialties. Interestingly, the general pattern of results was fairly consistent. All the studies revealed a clear distinction between factors that tend to motivate employees (motivation factors) and those that, while expected by workers, are not likely to motivate them (hygiene factors).

## MOTIVATION FACTORS

**Motivation factors**
Elements intrinsic to the job that promote job performance

Herzberg identified **motivation factors** as elements intrinsic to the job that promote job performance. Among the most frequently identified motivation factors were the following:

- Opportunity for growth and advancement
- Achievement or accomplishment
- Recognition for accomplishments
- Challenging or interesting work
- Responsibility for work

Stated another way, job factors that tend to motivate people are primarily related to higher-level needs and aspirations. These factors all relate to outcomes associated with the content of the job being performed. Opportunity for advancement, greater responsibility, recognition, growth, achievement, and interesting work are consistently identified as the major factors making work motivating and meaningful. The absence of these factors can be frustrating and nonmotivating. These motivation factors are not easily measured, and they may be difficult to find in certain types of jobs.

## HYGIENE FACTORS

**Hygiene factors**
Elements in the work environment that, if positive, reduce dissatisfaction but do not tend to motivate

Also called dissatisfiers, **hygiene factors** are elements of the work environment that, if positive, reduce dissatisfaction, but they do not tend to motivate. Herzberg identified the following hygiene factors:

- Working conditions
- Money, status, and security
- Interpersonal relationships
- Supervision
- Company policies and administration

The factors that employees complained about most in the work environment were the following:

- Poor company policies and administrative practices
- Lack of good supervision in both a technical and a human-relations sense
- Poor working conditions
- Inadequate wages and benefits

Herzberg concluded that these job-context factors tend to dissatisfy rather than motivate. In recent years, the conflict between work demands and personal life has been identified as another hygiene factor. When these factors are negative or inadequate, employees are unhappy. When these factors are adequate or even excellent, they do not, by themselves, promote better job performance. This does not mean that hygiene factors are unimportant. They are very important, but they serve primarily to maintain a reasonable level of job motivation, not to increase it.

Compassionate Eye Foundation/Ivan Hunter/Stockbyte/Getty Images

*One hygiene factor that is important to many people is having enough free time and money to pursue their personal interests*

## EXPECTANCY THEORY

**Expectancy theory** provides another interesting and practical way of looking at employee motivation.[29] This theory is based on the worker's perception of the relationships among effort, performance, and reward. According to expectancy theory, workers will be motivated to work harder when they believe their enhanced efforts will improve performance and that such improved performance will lead to desired rewards. Figure 7.4 illustrates how the expectancy theory model works when the rewards are something that the employee values.

**Expectancy theory**
Theory of motivation that holds that employees perform better when they believe such efforts lead to desired rewards

Expectancy theory is based on worker perceptions and on relationships called linkages. Employee motivation depends on workers being able to perceive that their effort(s) will lead to a certain level of performance, and that the performance will lead to a desired reward. When employees cannot clearly recognize that such linkages exist, they will not be highly motivated.

For example, if employees at Subway® restaurants do not receive adequate training in preparing sandwiches and do not receive feedback on their performance from their supervisor, and possibly raises in their hourly wages, they will not know what the expected performance is and they will not be able to perceive a relationship between their effort and their performance. Instead, they will conclude that no matter how much effort they expend, there will be no significant improvement in their job performance and no reward for doing their best. Or if they see that their high-performing co-workers are not being rewarded any more than average or even substandard performers, they will not believe that a performance–reward relationship exists. As a result, they will not be motivated to perform well.

In reality, expectancy theory is a simple notion: People will do what is in their best interest. Employees will be motivated to put forth more effort if they believe the additional effort will result in something of value. For example, if a student believes that more work (study time) will not lead to a better performance on the forthcoming test, then he or she will not study more. We have all known a

FIGURE 7.4 Expectancy theory

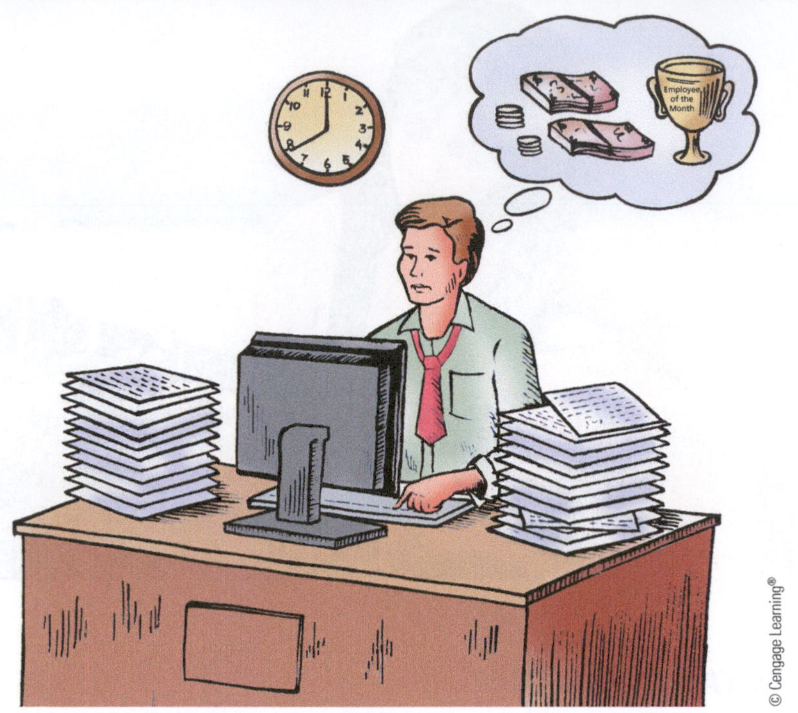




few students who are content to "just pass" a course. A grade of A or B is not sufficient enough reward for them to exert additional effort. Therefore, the motivational effort is low when perception of improved performance is low and the anticipated reward is low.

It does not matter how clearly supervisors view the linkages among effort, performance, and rewards. If the workers cannot see them, the linkages might as well be absent. Supervisors should strive to show employees that increased effort will improve work performance, which in turn will increase rewards. Rewards may be extrinsic, in the form of additional pay, or intrinsic, such as a sense of accomplishment or some type of praise or recognition. Probably the most important characteristic of a reward is that it is something the recipient desires and values.

## EQUITY THEORY

How many times have you heard the following: Ed, an employee, complains to anyone who will listen, "It's not fair! I've been here as long as Carl. We do the same job, but he gets paid more than I do." Ed's belief of inequity rests on the notion that his outcome–input ratio is lower than Carl's (see Figure 7.5). Inputs include such things as seniority, experience, age, skill, ability, job knowledge, and effort. Ed's exasperated statement suggests that Ed and Carl have similar inputs: They have both held the same job for the same amount of time. Inequity exists because Ed perceives that Carl evidently receives more outcomes (he is paid more than Ed). Outcomes can include salary, working conditions, degree of employee involvement and decision making, opportunity for advancement and promotion, challenging assignments, pay and benefits, and assorted forms of recognition.

**FIGURE 7.5 It's not fair!—Equity theory at work**

*Ed's inputs are the same as Carl's; they both have the same job. Carl has higher outcomes than Ed, because he gets paid more. This makes Carl's outcome/input ratio greater than Ed's, which creates a feeling of unfairness. Equity theory holds that Ed will be motivated to change the situation so that his and Carl's ratios are equal.*

**Equity theory** Explains how people strive for fairness in the workplace

Based on the works of J. Stacy Adams, **equity theory** is a theory of motivation that explains how people strive for fairness in the workplace. Since the beginning of time, people have compared themselves to others. They compare their own input/outcome ratios to those of others. When the ratios are unequal, there is inequity. This inequity will be followed by a motivation to achieve equity, or fairness, by making the outcome–input ratios equal.

Adams also stressed that what is important in determining motivation is the relative, rather than the absolute, level of outcomes a person receives and the inputs a person contributes.[30] In Figure 7.5, Ed compares himself to Carl, a person performing similar work in the same organization. It is important to realize that while Ed believes Carl is paid more, this may not be the case. However, inequity still exists because of what Ed believes, and Ed will still be motivated to achieve equity.

People can make a number of different kinds of comparisons with others in order to draw conclusions about fairness. We have seen that Ed compares himself to Carl, someone who has the same job. Ed might also be inclined to compare himself to individuals or groups of people in other departments in his organization, even if those people do different work than Ed. Ed might compare himself to his own expectations, such as where he expected to be at this stage of his career. Ed could even compare himself to an individual or a group in another organization. To illustrate, consider the following scenario, in which Ed uses a referent from another company:

Ed's next door neighbor, Carolyn, works at Magna Donnelly, the Holland, Michigan, manufacturer of mirrors, windshields, and other precision-glass products for the auto industry.[31] Part of Carolyn's work satisfaction comes from the way employees work together. The culture builds ownership and inspires employees. Magna Donnelly encourages innovation and teamwork.

Carolyn's factory is organized into small teams. These teams set their own goals and have broad discretion in how they do their work. A cooperative decision-making process is used that includes all team members. Each team chooses a representative to serve on the equity committee, which is a forum for the entire building. The equity (fairness) committee deals with pay structure, benefits, and grievances. One person from the equity committee is chosen as the representative to the Magna Donnelly Committee, whose members also include senior management. The Magna Donnelly Committee's power is limited to matters that concern employees directly. It solicits ideas from employees, studies solutions, debates issues, and develops plans for running the business in a way that is fair.

Carolyn continually provokes Ed by talking about how great she has it there. She says that her satisfaction comes from what she does, how she does it, and who she does it with. "Top management trusts us, we trust them, and we trust each other."

To an interested audience of coworkers, Ed laments, "You should see how Magna Donnelly listens to its employees and the input they have. No one listens to us. It's not fair!" In this case, Ed is comparing his work situation to his perceptions of the work environment of another organization. Ed's frustration with his situation inspires him to prepare a poster like that in Figure 7.6. Some employees express their displeasure in other ways. It is not uncommon to find expressions of "hate" on personal blogs, on personal Web pages, Facebook and other social networks.

**FIGURE 7.6 A disgruntled employee's response**

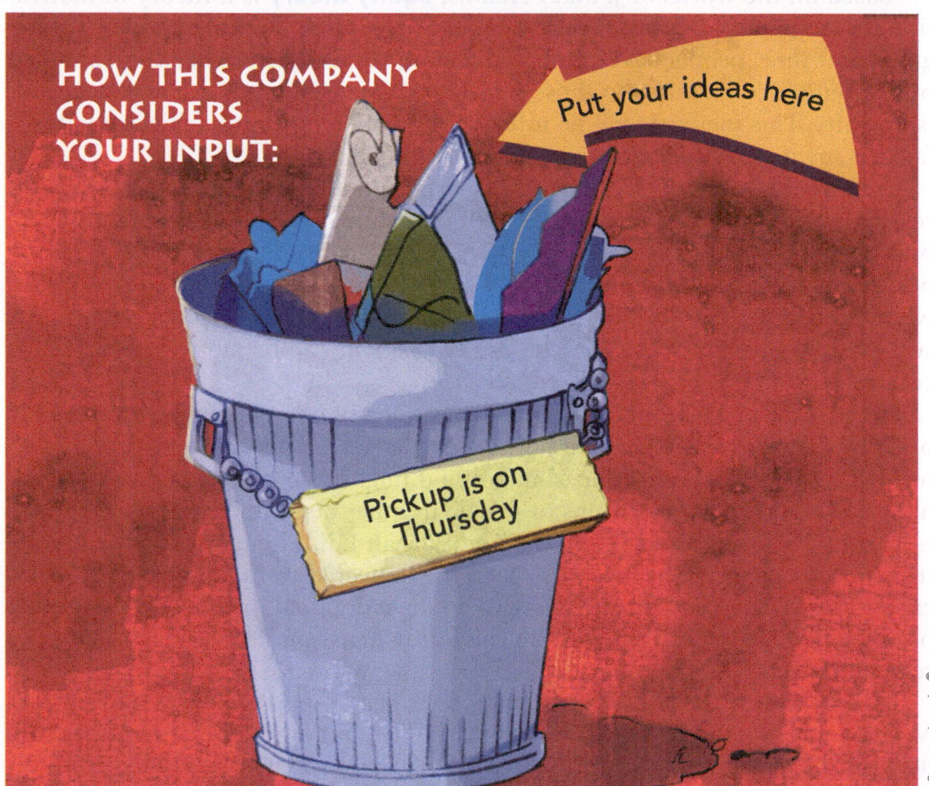

## Practical Suggestions for Using the Motivational Theories

**4 Explain how one might use the motivational theories to manage their own lives and the performance of others.**

Supervisors can use the hierarchy of human needs as a framework for visualizing the kinds of needs people have and for assessing the relative importance of those needs in motivating individuals in the workplace. The supervisor's challenge is to make individual fulfillment the result of doing a good job. For example, if the supervisor senses that an employee's most influential motivator is social needs, the employee is most likely to do a good job when assigned to work with a group and the whole group is rewarded for doing the job well. If an employee seems to be seeking self-respect, the supervisor might provide visible signs of recognition to influence this employee toward good performance, such as awarding a bonus or giving praise in front of the employee's peers at a departmental meeting. The key for the supervisor is to recognize where each employee is in the hierarchy so that the supervisor can determine which needs are driving the employee. Withholding praise and not recognizing employee accomplishment is a common pitfall.

Ultimately, all motivation is self-motivation. Therefore, a good supervisor structures the work situation and reward systems so that employees are motivated to perform well because good work performance leads to satisfaction of their needs.

We all know someone for whom work appears to be the only focus of their life. Others find work to be a source of comfort, security, and meaning. Their values combine Edison's "There is no substitute for hard work" and Emerson's "We put our love where we put our labor."[32] However, we challenge you to find someone who, when on his or her deathbed, says, "As I look back over my life, I wish I had spent more time at work."[33]

In some organizations, there may be some who subscribe to **employee entitlement** a belief that the organization owes them something regardless of the effort they make. This attitude manifests itself in the workplace in many ways: the poor performer who asks for a severance package after being fired, employees who fail to meet sales goals but demand bonuses anyway ("we got one last year"), or college professors who expect a substantial pay raise because they survived another year.[34]

**Employee entitlement** The belief that the organization "owes" them

### THE SUPERVISOR AND HERZBERG'S THEORY

To improve performance, Herzberg's theory suggests that the supervisor should implement strategies that target the motivation factors—that is, those that contribute to the satisfaction of employees' social, self-respect, and self-fulfillment needs. One of the supervisor's strategies should be to "catch people doing something right" and "give them credit when credit is due." A note of caution: Praise and other forms of recognition must be highly individualized and genuinely deserved to be effective. A key element in effective supervision is to give employees an opportunity to fulfill their needs as a result of good job performance.

Job security, money, benefits, good working conditions, and the like are extremely important, and organizations must strive continuously to be competitive in these areas.

## THE SUPERVISOR AND EQUITY THEORY

What are the implications of equity theory for the supervisor? First, it provides another explanation for how perceptions and beliefs about what is fair influence job performance. Second, it acquaints managers with the disasters that can occur when rewards are misaligned with performance. Ed's constant complaints about the unfair situation could negatively affect other employees. While some people like to distance themselves from negativists, others find solace in continuing claims of unfairness and jump on the bandwagon. The situation can get out of hand; factions can develop to threaten organizational effectiveness.

Effective supervisors must be vigilant for signs of unfairness and immediately address employee concerns. Questions such as "What is not fair?" "Why is it not fair?" and "What would it take to make it fair?" must be asked. In addition, the supervisor may give Ed information that will help him to better assess his own and Carl's outcomes or inputs. However, research indicates that rather than change perceptions about himself, Ed is more likely to change his perceptions of Carl's outcomes or inputs or change to another referent.

Often, employees like Ed feel they must go somewhere else because their organizations do not appreciate their contributions. How many times have you heard someone say, "I'm not happy with the way I was treated—it's not fair!" Supervisors need to use information-getting, probing-type questions to find out

### SUPERVISORY TIPS

Words alone will not motivate or produce employee commitment to the goals and objectives of the organization. The actions of management speak the true message.

#### Motivating Employees

- Prepare, coach, and equip employees with the SKAs so they can be the best. Employees want to work for a winning team.
- People need to know what is expected in the way of performance. Therefore, be sure to tell employees what they must do (the expectations you have for them) in order to receive reinforcement.
- Provide opportunities for employees to be engaged in projects or work they will enjoy.
- People want to know how they are doing. Therefore, provide immediate feedback on performance.
- People want recognition for a job well done. Therefore, when employees do their jobs well, reinforce their behavior with the consequences they desire and value.
- Don't reward all people the same—different strokes for different folks.
- Make the consequences equal to the behavior.
- Remember that failure to respond has reinforcing consequences.
- People need to know that it is okay to make mistakes. Therefore, create a learning organization that says to all employees, "We'll learn what not to do from the mistakes we make." The supervisor can say, "Everything I've learned, I learned from either the mistakes I've made or the mistakes of others."
- Don't punish people in front of others.
- Employees will do their best work for people they trust and respect. Therefore, treat your employees as you would want to be treated.

*Remember*: Be an **enabler**. Therefore, do the things that enable others to be the best they can be.

what the person sees as unfair and why he considers it unfair. Supervisors must find out what employees want, need, and perceive as just and equitable rewards for their contributions. Only then can the supervisors address the problem.

The "Supervisory Tips" box provides some generic tips that will help guide your employees on the path to success. The author has found that withholding praise for a job well done is the number one mistake made by more supervisors. Think about the person you are most fond of. When was the last time you told that person how much you loved him or her and appreciated the difference that he or she has made in your life?

## Coping with People Who Make Your Life Difficult[35]

**5 Appreciate ways to more effectively cope with people who make your life difficult.**

Everyone has a bad day once in a while. People get too little sleep, receive bad news, or carry family or personal problems. Some people blame others for their problems. Often, these blamers and complainers are referred to as "difficult people." A note of caution is warranted at this point: Do not hang a label on people; instead, focus on what they do that makes our lives difficult. We want to change their behavior.

Team Skill Builder 7-1 introduces you to another member of the cast of characters who makes your life difficult. Throughout the rest of this text, you will see that these people come in all sizes and shapes. Students always want to know, "What am I supposed to do when confronted by the person who makes my life difficult?" My response has always been the same: "Tell me what you mean." "Describe this person to me." "Tell me how the person makes your life difficult." These and other responses can be used to focus attention on what the "difficult" person does and how this behavior impacts others. Because there are many different variants of the people who make our lives difficult, and there is no cure-all prescription, we refer students to books and programs that are designed to guide people in successfully dealing with them. There is also a great deal of information on the Internet. Consult Figure 7.7 for some generic suggestions for dealing with people who make your life difficult.

One of the authors is often asked, "Why are some people so easy to get along with while others are so difficult?" After a brief pause, I ask them to describe their "best friend." What is it that he or she does that has solidified that friendship? Then I ask them to tell me about the other person. Generally, it is what the person does and how the person does or does not do it. What causes some people to be frustrating or not easy to get along with? Often, conditions that do not produce the fulfillment of a person's needs ultimately result in dissatisfaction and frustration. When their needs are not satisfied on the job, employees may resort to behavior patterns that are detrimental to their job performance and to the organization. A typical approach for frustrated employees is to resign themselves to just "getting by" on the job. They simply go through the motions and put in time without trying to perform in other than an average or marginal manner. Some employees involve themselves in off-the-job activities to fulfill their need for personal satisfaction. Others have been known to drown their sorrows by abusing alcohol or illegal substances. They may seek immediate, short-term pleasure outside of work. The popular press is full of illustrations of workers who have taken out their frustrations and anger by posting "unrepeatable stuff" and "nontruths" on the Web.

**FIGURE 7.7 Suggestions for coping with people who make your life difficult**

- Do not label people as difficult, no matter how difficult they make your life.
- Think in terms of difficult behaviors, not difficult people.
- The easiest way to cope with some people is to avoid them, but the easiest answer isn't always the best answer. Change your mindset and focus on what they do well.
- Accentuate the positive—build on their strengths.
- Take control of the situation. Get their attention by calling them by name.
- Talk with them in private; give them your undivided attention.
- Avoid accusations, ask open-ended questions, and listen to their side of the story.
- Factually provide one specific situation that illustrates the problem behavior.
- Clearly state that you expect the behavior to improve.
- Focus on changing what they do, not who they are.
- Establish deadlines and timetables for the behavior to cease.
- If the behavior does not change, consider asking upper management or human resources to step in.

*Remember*: There is no recipe for dealing with people who make your life difficult. Search the Internet, review the literature, continually learn about what people want and need, and develop strategies for getting the best out of people.



Some employees constantly find things that distract them from doing the job, and, at times, they even try to beat the system. They often are absent or tardy, or they break rules as a way of trying to get back at situations they find frustrating. Increasingly, employees resort to searching the Web or engaging in fantasy computer games.[36] Still other employees who are dissatisfied adopt aggressive behavior, which ultimately may cause these employees to leave the job. Examples of aggressive behavior are vandalism, theft, fighting, and temper outbursts. When the situation becomes intolerable, these employees quit or almost force their supervisors to fire them.

These types of reactions to job situations are undesirable and should be prevented. Employee turnover, absenteeism, tardiness, poor performance, and other unsatisfactory conduct on the job can cost an organization a great deal. The supervisor is responsible for dealing with these behaviors. Rather than just accepting an employee's behavior, a supervisor should endeavor to relieve frustration by providing more opportunities for need fulfillment.

**6 Consider how the ABCs can be used to shape behavior.**

## Using the ABCs to Shape Employee Behavior

Organizational behavior researchers have long debated the influence of job satisfaction on performance. We believe that employees who experience high levels of job satisfaction are more likely to engage in positive behaviors that influence organizational efficiency and productivity. Performance management expert Aubrey Daniels developed a practical guide for shaping employee behavior.[37] According to Daniels, "behavior (the B) cannot be separated from the antecedents (the A) that come before it and the consequences (the C) after it."[38] See Figure 7.8 for suggestions on how to use the ABCs.

**FIGURE 7.8 Steps in ABC analysis**

- Regularly monitor employee performance to uncover areas of low productivity and to identify the behavior leading to undesirable performance.
- Describe the performance you don't want and who is doing it.
- Record the specific behavior that needs to be changed.
- Determine all possible links between the antecedents, the undesirable behavior, and its consequences.
- Tell the employee what is expected in the way of performance (i.e., set specific goals).
- Set the stage for good performance (i.e., arrange antecedents so that the employee can achieve the desired behavior).
- Eliminate any consequence that is irrelevant to the employee.
- Ensure an appropriate linkage between desired behavior and consequences the employee values.
- Monitor performance.
- Provide support and feedback on performance.
- Reinforce the positive aspects of the employee's performance with consequences the employee values.
- Ensure that consequences are positive, immediate, and certain.
- Evaluate results and continue to reinforce desired behavior with desirable consequences.
- Experiment to find the most effective forms of reinforcement and rate of reinforcement.

**Remember:**

1. You cannot change people; you can change only their behaviors.
2. You will get the behaviors you consistently expect and reinforce. Therefore, only expect the best from your employees.
3. Employees need to know exactly what behaviors will be reinforced and precisely what they are doing that is right or wrong.

*Source*: Based, in part, on the book by Aubrey C. Daniels, Ph.D., *Performance Management* (Atlanta, GA: Performance Management Publications, Inc., 1989, 3rd ed.).

Common sense dictates that if supervisors expect good performance, they must set the stage so that the expected performance occurs. First, supervisors should clearly identify what they want the employee to do. Then, the employee must know what the job entails and what is expected in the way of performance. Ask someone you know to think back to his or her first day on the job. How did the person know what was expected? Many respondents will say it was a process of "trial and error"—that the supervisor never clearly explained what was expected. This has been particularly true in the current era of downsizings and outsourcings. The supervisor either does not sense the importance of expectations or is too busy to explain them.

In Chapter 2, we discussed the supervisor's role as an enabler. The enabler ensures that employees have all they need to do their jobs correctly the first time, including the appropriate instruction, training, tools, and materials. Unfortunately, this is seldom the way it works. If the supervisor does not set the stage (provide the proper antecedents), employee performance is likely to be unsatisfactory. Consequences can affect behavior in one of two ways. Thorndike's **law of effect**

**Law of effect**
Behavior with favorable consequences is repeated; behavior with unfavorable consequences tends to disappear

postulates that "behavior with favorable consequences tends to be repeated while behavior with unfavorable consequences tends to disappear."[39] Unfortunately, some supervisors assume that what would be a favorable consequence for them would also be a desirable consequence for others. Consider the following:

Question 1: When you do your job exceptionally well and your immediate supervisor knows you do your job exceptionally well, what happens?

Answer 1: "Nothing—absolutely nothing. My supervisor takes good performance for granted."

Implication 1: When good performance is ignored or goes unrecognized, what happens? Clearly, the lack of feedback and recognition for good performance can cause employee discontent. Also, the good performance is weakened because it is not reinforced. This process is called **extinction**.

**Extinction**
Good behavior occurs less frequently or disappears because it is not recognized

Question 2: When you do your job exceptionally well and your immediate supervisor knows you do your job exceptionally well, what happens?

Answer 2: "He gives me more work to do."

Implication 2: If the employee perceives that the additional work will require a variety of skills or fulfill higher-order needs, then the consequence is desirable. This is called **positive reinforcement**. Linking something the employee values or sees as pleasing to good performance strengthens behavior. As a result, good performance is likely to repeat itself. On the other hand, if the employee perceives the extra work to be boring, monotonous, or mundane, then the consequence of good performance is perceived to be **punishment**. The employee got something unwanted—an unfavorable consequence. The result is that the employee's good performance will decrease. Chapter 6 discusses punishment and discipline in greater detail.

**Positive reinforcement**
Making behavior occur more frequently because it is linked to a positive consequence

**Punishment**
Making behavior occur less frequently because it is linked to an undesirable consequence

Question 3: When you do your job exceptionally well and your immediate supervisor knows you do your job exceptionally well, what happens?

Answer 3: "We really appreciate the good job you did. I've recommended moving you from the six-person cubicle into your own office."

Implication 3: This response gets back to the perceptual problem previously identified. Sincere and genuine praise for a job well done is positive reinforcement. For many employees, the move from a six-person shared cubicle to a private office would be **negative reinforcement**. By removing a consequence that is unpleasant or undesirable, the employee's good performance is reinforced. The employee will continue to do a good job. Suppose the employee really enjoyed the close interaction with the other five employees of the cubicle. In this case, the relocation would be viewed as something the employee did not want (i.e., punishment).

**Negative reinforcement**
Making behavior occur more frequently by removing an undesirable consequence

Question 4: What happens when a co-worker, Charlie, fails to show up on time for work regularly?

Answer 4: "Nothing happens."

Implication 4: The chronically tardy employee continues to be tardy regularly. Ignoring bad performance tends to strengthen the behavior. Unintentionally, management sends a message to the employee that "it's okay to show up late for work." When management ignores "poor performance" in one employee, that employee usually has a cancerous impact throughout the entire work group. Others might assume, and rightfully so, that management has sanctioned showing up for work late (a desirable behavior).

Question 5: What happens when a co-worker, Charlie, fails to show up on time for work regularly?

Answer 5: "The employee was given an unpleasant task or made to stay late and complete necessary work."

Implication 5: The tardy employee perceives staying late as an undesirable consequence. Because of the punishment, the employee may make special efforts to get to work on time. Other employees also will see the linkage between performance and punishment. Remember: The process of removing undesirable consequences when an employee's behavior improves is called negative reinforcement.

Supervisors must continually be alert for what their employees perceive to be important, and, like so many things in life, timing is critical. Aubrey Daniels contends "that an intelligently timed consequence has much more influence than a random one."[40] Immediate feedback on performance and positive reinforcement are essential if the supervisor wants to shape employee behavior positively. Figure 7.9 presents an interesting picture of how workers' perceptions of consequences influence their behavior.

**FIGURE 7.9 Antecedents and consequences influence behavior**

Blondie-King Features Syndicate

*Reprinted with special permission of King Features Syndicate. Blondie-King Features Syndicate*

**7 Compare the assumptions and applications of Theory X and Theory Y in supervision.**

# Comparing Theory X and Theory Y

A continuous (and unresolved) question that confronts supervisors is what general approach, or style, best contributes to positive employee motivation. This age-old dilemma typically focuses on the degree to which supervisory approaches should be based on satisfying employees' lower-level and higher-level needs. This often becomes an issue of the degree to which supervisors should rely on their authority and position instead of trying to use human relations practices to provide more opportunities for employee motivation. In the following paragraphs and in Chapter 10, we will analyze approaches associated with various supervisory management styles. First, we will look at the contributions of Douglas McGregor.

## MCGREGOR'S THEORY X AND THEORY Y

In his book *The Human Side of Enterprise*, Douglas McGregor noted that individual supervisory approaches usually relate to each supervisor's perceptions about what people are all about. That is, each supervisor manages employees according to his or her own attitudes and ideas about people's needs and motivations. For comparison, McGregor stated that extremes in attitudes among managers could be classified as Theory X and Theory Y. Following are the basic assumptions of McGregor's Theory X and Theory Y.[41]

**Theory X**
Assumption that most employees dislike work, avoid responsibility, and must be coerced to do their jobs

**Theory Y**
Assumption that most employees enjoy work, seek responsibility, and can self-direct. The belief that well-designed jobs lead to increased motivation

**Theory X** *The assumption that most employees dislike work, avoid responsibility, and must be coerced to work hard.*

**Theory Y** *The assumption that most employees enjoy work, seek responsibility, and can self-direct.*

Supervisors who are Theory X–oriented have a limited view of employees' abilities and motivations. These supervisors feel that employees must be strictly controlled, closely supervised, and motivated based on money, discipline, and authority. Theory X supervisors believe that the key to motivation is in the proper implementation of approaches designed to satisfy employees' lower-level needs. Theory Y supervisors have a much higher opinion of employees' abilities. These supervisors feel that if the proper approaches and conditions can be implemented, employees will exercise self-direction and self-control toward the accomplishment of worthwhile objectives. According to this view, management's objectives should fit into the scheme of each employee's set of needs. Therefore, Theory Y managers believe that the higher-level needs of employees are more important in terms of each employee's personality and self-development.

The two approaches McGregor describes represent extremes in supervisory styles (see Figure 7.10). Realistically, most supervisors are somewhere between Theory X and Theory Y. Neither approach is right or wrong because the appropriateness of a given approach depends on the needs of the individuals involved and the demands of the situation. In practice, supervisors may sometimes take an approach that is contrary to their preferred approach. For example, even the strongest Theory Y supervisor may revert to Theory X in a time of crisis, such as when the department is shorthanded, when there is an equipment failure, when a serious disciplinary problem has occurred, or when a few employees need firm direction.

FIGURE 7.10 The two extremes of managerial approach are typified by Theory X and Theory Y

## ADVANTAGES AND LIMITATIONS OF THEORY X

Supervisors who adopt Theory X typically find that, in the short term, a job is done faster. Because the questioning of orders is not encouraged, it may appear that workers are competent and knowledgeable and that work groups are well organized, efficient, and disciplined.

A major disadvantage of Theory X is that there is little opportunity for employees' personal growth. Because supervision is close and constant, employees are unlikely to develop initiative and independence. Moreover, most workers resent Theory X supervision, and thus may be unmotivated to do the required work. In the long term, they may exit the job—physically or emotionally. Traditionally, supervisors who advocated the Theory X approach could get employees to do what they wanted by using the "carrot-and-stick" approach ("Do what I want you to do and you will be rewarded").[42] Punishments were applied when the job was not done. Many supervisors still use this approach. However, employees may rebel when confronted with the stick, and supervisors may not have sufficient rewards to motivate employees to subject themselves to this tight control.

## ADVANTAGES AND LIMITATIONS OF THEORY Y

An overriding advantage of Theory Y supervision is that it promotes individual growth. Because workers are given opportunities to assume some responsibility on their own and are encouraged to contribute their ideas in accomplishing their tasks, it is possible for these employees to partially satisfy their higher-level needs on the job.

While the Theory Y approach is often viewed as more desirable than Theory X, it is not without disadvantages. Theory Y can be time-consuming, especially in the short term. Because personal development is emphasized, supervisors must become instructors and coaches if they are to help their employees move toward the simultaneous attainment of organizational and personal goals. Some supervisors find the extreme application of Theory Y to be more idealistic than practical because some employees expect firm direction from their supervisors.

**8 Articulate how job redesign, multitasking, and participative management can be used to develop employee SKAs and motivation.**

## Supervisory Approaches for Attaining Positive Employee Motivation

Having reviewed several prominent theories of employee motivation, the next question is, how can these theories be applied in the most meaningful ways? There is no simple set of guidelines a supervisor can implement to achieve high motivation and excellent performance. Human beings are much too complex for that. Supervisory skills can be learned and developed, but they often need to be modified to fit individuals and situations.

Over the past few years, the workforce and work environment have changed greatly. Even in this depressed economy, employees still want a high quality of work life.

**Job enrichment**
Job design that helps fulfill employees' higher-level needs by giving those employees more challenging tasks and more decision-making responsibility for their jobs

Supervisors have used various forms of **job enrichment**, which means assigning more challenging tasks and giving employees more decision-making responsibility for their jobs.

To enrich jobs, the supervisor should assign everyone in a department a fair share of challenging and routine jobs and give employees more autonomy in accomplishing their tasks. Unfortunately, many supervisors prefer to assign the difficult or more challenging jobs only to their best employees and the dull jobs to the weaker employees. However, this practice can be defeating in the long term. The supervisor should give all employees opportunities to find challenging and interesting work experiences within the framework of the department's operations. For example, one Subway® supervisor enriched the jobs of associates by giving them a greater role in scheduling work and devising their own work rules for the group. The result was a schedule that better met employee needs and rules the employees were willing to follow because they helped create them. In its most developed form, job enrichment may involve restructuring jobs in such a way that employees are given direct control and responsibility for what they do.

What obstacles will the supervisor have to overcome in attempting to "enrich" employees' jobs? Overall, if job enrichment is practiced sincerely, subordinates usually assume an active role in making or participating in decisions about their jobs. The result can be better decisions and a more satisfied and motivated workforce.

In a sense, job enrichment involves the employees' assumption of some of the supervisor's everyday responsibilities. The supervisor remains accountable, however, for the satisfactory fulfillment of these obligations, which can pose something of a risk. Yet despite the risk, many supervisors endorse job enrichment because it works. Several techniques for enriching jobs are discussed in greater detail in the following paragraphs.

## JOB REDESIGN

It is generally believed that well-designed jobs lead to increased motivation, higher-quality performance, higher satisfaction, and lower absenteeism and turnover. These desirable outcomes occur when employees experience three critical psychological states:

1. They believe they are doing something meaningful because their work is important to other people.
2. They feel responsible for how the work turns out.
3. They learn how well they performed their jobs.

Many **Job redesign** programs are based on the model developed by Professors Hackman and Oldham. They contend that internal motivation is determined by three psychological factors: the experienced meaningfulness of work, responsibility for the work performed, and knowledge of the results. The more these factors are positive, the more effort the employee will put forth. According to this model, any job can be described in terms of the following five core job dimensions:

**Job redesign**
The belief that well-designed jobs lead to increased motivation

1. *Skill variety*: The degree to which an employee has an opportunity to do various tasks and to use a variety of skills and abilities.
2. *Task identity*: The completion of a whole, identifiable piece of work.
3. *Task significance*: The degree to which the job impacts the lives or work of others.
4. *Autonomy*: The amount of independence, freedom, and discretion an employee has in making decisions about the work to be done.
5. *Feedback*: The amount of information an employee receives on job performance.[43]

Jobs that have little of the above would be a prime candidate for job redesign. Suppose that close examination reveals that the task significance is relatively low. The supervisor could, for example, assign workers to go with a salesperson to visit end users of the company's products so that the workers will have a feel for how the customers use the end product. Job rotation could be used to increase both skill variety and task significance, thereby increasing the job's motivating potential.[44]

Think of your most recent work experience: What aspects of the job stimulated you to "go above and beyond that which was expected?" According to Hackman and Oldham's theory, internal motivation occurs because the employee is "turned on to [his or her] work because of the positive internal feelings generated by doing well, rather than being dependent on external factors (such as incentive pay, job security, or praise from the supervisor) for the motivation to work effectively."[45]

You've probably heard the expression, "Variety is the spice of life." What does that mean in the workplace? Variety and challenge can keep jobs from becoming monotonous and can fulfill employee needs.

There are ways to give employees new tasks and new work experiences by which the basic nature of the job can be broadened in scope and importance. The following job-redesign strategies are similar in the sense that each attempts to increase employee performance by improving job satisfaction.

## JOB ROTATION

Switching job tasks among employees in the work group on a scheduled basis is known as **job rotation**. Most supervisors can implement this process, which often is accompanied by higher levels of job performance and increased employee

**Job rotation**
The process of switching job tasks among employees in a work group

interest. Job rotation not only helps to relieve employees' boredom but also enhances employees' job knowledge. Although the different tasks may require the same skill level, learning different jobs prepares employees for promotion. A major side benefit to the supervisor is that job rotation results in a more flexible workforce, which can be advantageous during periods of employee absence. Moreover, job rotation should mean that employees share both pleasant and unpleasant tasks so work assignments are perceived as fair.

## MULTITASKING

**Multitasking**
When an employee performs several tasks simultaneously

When a person is able to perform more than one task at the same time, we say that he or she is **multitasking**.[46] Most students are familiar with this concept since they have learned to drive the car while talking on the cell phone, doing their laundry while reading this textbook, or washing dishes while listening to their favorite music.

In the organizational setting, another motivational strategy is when supervisors expand an employee's job with a greater variety of tasks. Multitasking can be a powerful motivational tool if the employees can see that the tasks give them a chance to use previously acquired SKAs or develop a new one. For example, tasks that were handled by several employees may be combined or consolidated into one or two enlarged jobs. Some employees respond positively to multitasking, and this positive attitude is reflected in their performance and in increased job satisfaction. In one furniture factory, for example, a number of routine jobs were changed so that each job required five or six operations rather than just one repetitive operation. Employees supported the change. Such comments as "My job seems more important now" and "My work is less monotonous now" were common.

There can be problems in implementing multitasking. In "Management Matters: The Myth of Multitasking," Elizabeth Newell contends that multitasking could be slowing you down because of "switchover time."[47] Think of the single mom with three kids ranging in age from 11 to 15, working 40+ hours per week, and taking two college classes online in an attempt to finish her associate's degree. Her challenge is to effectively manage multiple tasks (projects) in the most effective way. In order to do so, she needs to meticulously organize and methodically focus her activities as well as ask for help from her co-workers, bosses, children, and professors. Unfortunately, we all know that there will be switching costs as she goes from one assignment or task to another.

As a result of the economic downturn, many employees (usually the survivors of organizational downsizing) have been asked to do more and more. Some have found themselves stretched too thin, and, as a result, frustration and discontent have crept into the workplace.[48]

## PARTICIPATIVE MANAGEMENT

In his best-selling book *A Great Place to Work*, Robert Levering postulates that the high morale of great workplaces consists of pride in what you do (the job itself), enjoying the people you're working with (the work group), and trusting the people you work for (management practices and economic rewards).[49] Levering and others have been tracking the "best places to work." Historically, Dallas-headquartered Southwest Airlines (SWA) has ranked among everyone's Top 10.[50] Why Southwest? It is the largest airline in the world by number of passengers carried. During the past 10 years, the low-fare, highly unionized airline has consistently posted profits. It leads the industry in customer satisfaction. How is that done—by magic? If you have an opportunity to fly with SWA, I encourage you to ask any employee the following questions: (1) How long have you worked at SWA? (2) What do you like best about working at SWA?

I hope that their responses to you will be the same as those we have found over the years: "Working here is truly an unbelievable experience. They treat you with respect, pay you well, and empower you. They use your ideas to solve problems. They encourage you to be yourself. I love going to work! Every member of the management team has walked in my shoes. Our motto, 'LUV' says it all!" Do the comments from SWA employees translate to better company performance? Let us reaffirm our belief that "happy cows give more milk."

SWA, like many organizations, actively solicits employee input via formal suggestion programs. The open work environment allows employees to share their ideas and make suggestions without fear of retribution. While some suggestion systems provide monetary rewards for suggestions that are received and accepted, the monetary rewards are only part of the employee's overall compensation. Employees like to have their suggestions heard and answered. To some of them, the fact that a suggestion has been implemented may mean more than the monetary reward.

This supervisory approach, in which employees have an active role in decision making, has historically been called participative management. Delegation, discussed in greater detail in Chapter 5, is important to motivating employees. Delegation does not mean turning all decisions over to employees, nor does it mean just making employees believe they are participating in decisions. Rather, it means the supervisor should earnestly seek employees' opinions whenever possible and be willing to be influenced by employee suggestions and criticisms. When employees feel that they are part of a team and that they can influence the decisions that affect them, they are more likely to accept the decisions and seek new solutions to problems.

The major advantages of participative management are that decisions tend to be of higher quality and that employees are more willing to accept those decisions. One disadvantage is that this approach can be time-consuming. Also, participation makes it easier for employees to criticize, which some supervisors find threatening. On balance, however, participative management is widely recognized as an effective motivational strategy. Its advantages far outweigh its disadvantages.

Supervisors who practice participative management properly are aware of the importance of their information-giving and information-getting skills. They also know that it is vital to respond fully to subordinates' suggestions as soon as those supervisors have had sufficient time to consider them.

During the past two decades, most organizations have adopted various forms of participatory management programs. These types of programs often are known by other labels, such as employee-involvement programs, problem-solving teams, quality circles, or semiautonomous or self-directed work teams. King & Prince Seafood's program called *Perfect Service* collected more than 800 ideas from employees in 2010 and implemented many of them.[51] Each month they give $1,000 for the three best suggestions. At the end of the year, the company throws a gala and conducts a drawing from among the monthly winners. The grand prize winner gets either a $25,000 cash prize or a two-week trip to Namibia for the employee and a guest. Carolyn Bush, a line worker and the

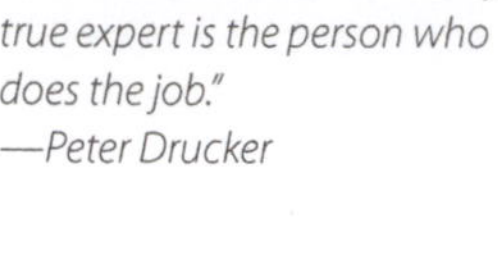
"Even in routine work the only true expert is the person who does the job."
—Peter Drucker

© iStock.com/Wavebreak

2010 winner, took the $25,000 and said, "It's a great program because everyone is involved. Sure the company pays out lots of money, but the savings from one idea more than paid for the program." The key is that the company implements the ideas as quickly as possible. The common denominator is employee involvement, engagement, and enthusiasm. Employees are encouraged to work together when submitting suggestions. Volker Kuntzsch, president of King & Prince, said, "The positive atmosphere this has created is phenomenal. Everyone wins!"[52] Regardless of what they are called, these programs are based on the belief that employees want to contribute to the long-term success of the organization and that managers have a strong commitment to participatory management as a way of organizational life.

## SUMMARY

**1.** **Every term students ask, "Where can I find a job that will provide me with the satisfaction I expect?" My response is always the same: "Tell me what it would take to make you satisfied?" In recent years, job security has moved toward the top of the list. Many factors contribute to employee dissatisfaction. Personal Skill-Builder 4-1 will give you an opportunity to evaluate the various work-related factors that may spark your job enthusiasm.**

**2.** **Each one of us is a unique individual, and one's behavior is influenced by many factors. Personality is the complex mix of skills, knowledge, abilities, attitudes, and other attributes that distinguishes one person from another. Prominent factors that interact to form the personality of each individual include physiological makeup, early childhood experiences, the immediate and continuing environment through life, and cultural values. The working environment is one of the almost unlimited number of influences that become part of an employee's personality. A person's attitude impacts everyone that person contacts, and often negatively or positively impacts the organization's performance.**

**Supervisors need to be sensitive to individual differences and similarities. A consistent supervisory approach based on similarities is a practical way to lead employees.**

**3.** **Motivation is a willingness to exert effort toward achieving a goal. Individuals have been found to put forth more effort if the reward fulfills their**

individual needs. According to Maslow, when a lower-level need is fulfilled, higher-level needs emerge that influence one's motivation. The need to know and understand is probably more important today. The need to seek balance is the essence of Festinger's cognitive dissonance theory. Figure 4.3 identified eight needs in ascending order of importance and showed that there is a need for consistency in knowing, feeling, believing, having, and experiencing.

Alderfer's ERG theory attempted to clarify Maslow's theory by categorizing the lower needs as existence. Relatedness and growth were additional categories. Alderfer's frustration-regression principle maintains that when high-order needs are not met, the individual will put more effort into fulfilling needs that can more easily be met.

McClelland identified the need for affiliation (nAFF), achievement (nACH), and power (nPOW). The need to be in control of various situations is a prime motivator for some.

Herzberg's motivation-hygiene research studies indicate that hygiene factors such as money, management policies, working conditions, and certain aspects of supervision must be adequate to maintain a reasonable level of motivation. Forces that stimulate good performance, called motivation factors, are intrinsic to the job. These motivation factors include the employees' needs for achievement, opportunity for advancement, challenging work, promotion, growth, and recognition.

Expectancy theory suggests that employees will be motivated if they perceive links between their efforts and performance and between their performance and rewards.

Equity theory of motivation explains how people strive for fairness based on an outcome–input ratio. Employees can compare themselves to many other people, even those who do not work in their organizations, to determine if perceived equity or inequity exists.

4. It is important for supervisors to recognize the different levels of need. Supervisors can influence employee motivation positively if they rely on supervisory approaches that promote higher-level need fulfillment. When employee needs are not satisfied on the job, job performance usually suffers. Some employees express their dissatisfaction through absenteeism. Others may display aggressive and disruptive behavior; still others may quit. The result is that the organization suffers from a decrease in production and a loss of quality.

   Every one of us is a unique individual, and accordingly we have different wants and needs. Effective supervisors must know the likes and dislikes and what "button to push" for each individual. "Different strokes for different folks" is the plan of action for effective supervisors.

5. Working conditions that do not fulfill employee needs ultimately cause dissatisfaction and frustration. The interaction between individuals creates the opportunity for conflict. Since the beginning of time, there have been people who made life difficult for others. Many factors may cause some people to do things that make other people's lives difficult. Incivility and other inappropriate behavior must be dealt with in a proper and timely manner.

6. The ABC model of behavior modification is built on the notion that the supervisor can use antecedents (those things that precede behavior) and consequences (the results of behavior) to condition desirable behavior or to extinguish undesirable behavior. The use of extinction, positive reinforcement, punishment, and negative reinforcement can make specific behavior occur more or less often. Feedback and positive reinforcement should be used regularly to shape employee behavior in the desired direction.

7. The Theory X supervisor believes primarily in authoritarian techniques, which relate to lower-level human needs. The Theory Y supervisor prefers to build motivation by appealing to employees' higher-level needs.

8. We provided a definitional and conceptual framework for strategies for enhancing employee morale and motivation.

   The major approaches include job design, job rotation, multitasking, job enrichment, participative management, and other opportunities for employees to be more involved. The job characteristics model has been used to guide job-redesign efforts.

   The advantages of participative management are that decisions tend to be of higher quality and employees are more willing to accept decisions. Employee participation programs are widely used and varied in application. Delegation strategies, suggestion programs, quality circles, and self-directed work teams are approaches that emphasize employee involvement. Getting people at all levels of the organization involved in objective setting and problem solving, rearranging duties and responsibilities, and creating ways to reward people for their accomplishments represent the essence of the approaches to motivating employees to perform. The supervisor must learn to implement different supervisory approaches that are appropriate for different people and settings.

## KEY TERMS

Aesthetic needs (p. 251)
Cognitive dissonance (p. 250)
Cognitive needs (p. 250)
Consistency needs (p. 252)
Emotional contagion (p. 246)
Employee entitlement (p. 259)
Equity theory (p. 257)
ERG theory (p. 252)
Expectancy theory (p. 255)
Extinction (p. 264)
Frustration-regression principle (p. 253)
Hierarchy of needs (p. 247)
Hygiene factors (p. 254)
Job enrichment (p. 268)
Job redesign (p. 269)
Job rotation (p. 269)
Law of effect (p. 263)
Motivation (p. 247)
Motivation factors (p. 254)
Motivation-hygiene theory (p. 253)
Multitasking (p. 270)
Negative reinforcement (p. 264)
Personality (p. 244)
Physiological needs (p. 248)
Positive mental attitude (PMA) (p. 246)
Positive reinforcement (p. 264)
needs for power (nPOW) (p. 253)
Punishment (p. 264)
Rule of reciprocity (p. 246)
Satisfaction (p. 242)
Security needs (p. 249)
Self-fulfillment needs (p. 251)
Self-respect needs (p. 250)
Social needs (p. 249)
Theory X (p. 266)
Theory Y (p. 266)
Transcendence needs (p. 252)

## WHAT HAVE YOU LEARNED?

1. a. Think of a time when you accomplished something that made you very proud. What caused you to react that way? What rewards or satisfactions came your way to reinforce those actions?
   b. Think of a time when you did something that made you ashamed. What caused you to behave that way? Have you repeated that behavior? Why or why not?
   c. How do you explain why people behave the way they do?
2. Compare and contrast each of the motivational theories discussed in this chapter. From the aspect of practical application, what are the benefits of each of the motivational theories discussed in this chapter?
3. What are the basic elements of Theory X and Theory Y? Can you think of any reasons Theory Y would be inappropriate for all supervisors?
4. With respect to the management problem of motivating subordinates to accomplish organizational goals, what conclusions can you draw from reading the material in this chapter?
5. Look in the mirror. (a) What are you doing well? (b) What needs a little work? (c) What incentives do you need to make "the best a little bit better?"

## EXPERIENTIAL EXERCISE FOR SELF-ASSESSMENT

### EXPERIENTIAL EXERCISE FOR SELF-ASSESSMENT 7.1—What Motivates Employees?

1. Rank the following 20 items in order of their importance to you. In the left-hand column, place the number 1 next to the most important item, the number 2 next to the second most important item, and so on through to the least important item (number 20).

   *Note*: If this skills application is used as an in-class exercise, to save time we suggest that you use the following scale rather than the rank order: Select the four items that are most important to you and place the number one (1) in the blanks to the left of those items. Select the four items that are least important to you and place the number three (3) in the blanks. From the remaining items, place the number two (2) in the blanks. After everyone has had time to complete the task, I ask for two student volunteers to be my counters. Using a simple show of hands, we tabulate the results, for example, "Everyone who has freedom to do my job in their top four raise their hands." The results may surprise you.
2. Make four copies of the 20 items and give one copy to four persons who are employed full-time. Have them give A's to the five items that are most important to them; B's to those five items that rank next in important; C's to those five that rank next in importance; and D's to those five items what are least important to them.
3. Compare your individual rankings with those of the four persons you asked to complete the survey.
   **a.** Are there differences?
   **b.** If so, how do you explain them?

4. THE JOB SATISAFACTION QUESTIONAIRE

_________ Freedom to do my job

_________ Supervisors who care about me as a person

_________ One-on-one team meetings so I can keep up to date

_________ Opportunity to learn and use new skills

_________ A work environment where others listen and act on my ideas and suggestions

_________ Job security

_________ A manager who lets me know what is expected—one who springs no surprises

_________ Interesting and challenging work

_________ Material, equipment, and resources to do the job right the first time

_________ Daily feedback on performance

_________ Good compensation and benefits

_________ Working for a company that is ethical, honest, and fair-dealing

_________ Praise and recognition for accomplishments

_________ Working for a company that is profitable

_________ Co-workers dedicated to achieving company goals

_________ Opportunity to make work-related decisions

_________ Opportunity to use a variety of skills

_________ Knowing what the future holds for me and the company

_________ Support and encouragement when I make a mistake

_________ A boss who allows me freedom to play to my strengths

*Source*: This instrument was developed by Edwin C. Leonard Jr. and Roy A. Cook, *Human Resource Management: 21st Century Challenges*, 1st ed. (Mason, OH: Thomson Custom Publishing, 2005), p. 237.

## PERSONAL SKILL BUILDING

### PERSONAL SKILL BUILDER 7.1: What Call Would You Make?

Consider this chapter's You Make the Call! and provide suggestions for Don and his supervisors.

1. It should be obvious that the road to employee motivation is not entirely clear to Don's five first-line supervisors. List specific illustrations from the You Make the Call! that support this observation.
2. Define motivation and explain how Don and his five direct reports can use it to get employees into the right game.
3. Why might some of the employees in today's economy not be willing to do the best job possible to preserve their job at Economy Moving and Storage?

### PERSONAL SKILL BUILDER 7.2: Employee Satisfaction

The Conference Board reported that between 1987 and 2009 four key indicators of job satisfaction declined dramatically; (a) Interest in their work, down 18.9 percent; (b) Job security, down 16.5 percent; (c) Interest in co-workers, down 11.6 percent; and (d) satisfaction with their supervisors, down 9.5 percent. (Reported in *HR Magazine*, February 2010, p. 13.) I would point out that in 2009 a substantial number of employees were paying more for their health insurance, if they even had insurance.

1. Using the Internet, search for at least three current research articles or reports on "what employees want from their jobs" or the "current state of employee morale." Write a one-page report summarizing your findings.

2. Write a two- or three-page paper that answers the following questions:
   a. Why do the perceptions of employees vary?
   b. Briefly identify the factors that account for the differences.
   c. Assume that you are Bob Felker, the Subway Systems' area supervisor. What three tips would you give each of your seven site managers to help their associates be even better at what they do?

## TEAM SKILL BUILDING

### TEAM SKILL BUILDER 7-1: Dealing with People Who Make Your Life Difficult—"The Whiner"

This is the second in a series of activities that introduces you to people who might make your life difficult.

1. Read the following statement from Steve Wright, a shipping department employee at Sanders Supermarket's Ashton Distribution Center:

   Nancy seemed really pleasant and nice when she interviewed for the job. She knew what was expected and was aware that the job was physically and mentally demanding at times. Most of the time, she gets her work done, but it's the baggage that comes with her that annoys me. Nancy brings her personal life to work. I see that in her daily conversations with me. Every day, I hear about her out-of-work husband, her lazy kids, and how she has to be a superwoman at home and at work. On top of that, every time the supervisor asks her to do something, she comes to me to tell me what a hard, nasty, hot job has been assigned to her. Every day is another poor, miserable, everything-bad-always-happens-to-me story. Nothing good ever happens to her. She never has a good day at work. Every day is the worst day of her life—much worse than yesterday.

   Nancy's whining is like cancer in the department. No one in the group wants to work with her on any quality or methods-improvement projects. When she's in a really bad mood, everyone avoids her. If she's miserable, everyone's supposed to be miserable. I've learned to deal with her by developing a positive mental attitude and smiling. I suspect this probably aggravates her more, but she just leaves my work area and looks for another shoulder to whine on.

   Nancy exhibits a negative attitude with a tendency to not do the work that needs to be done. Early on, I felt sorry for her predicament, but it began to wear on all of us. Because she cannot set aside her personal agenda during the day, she impedes everyone's performance. I don't think people are born unhappy, and I'm running out of sympathy for her. What should I do?

2. 
INTERNET ACTIVITY
Using the Internet, find at least three sources of information on how to deal with people who complain all the time. Carefully review each site for suggestions on how to deal with these people.

3. Pair up with at least three other classmates. (a) Briefly, share with each other the salient findings from your research on how to deal with "whiners." (b) Working together as a group, your assignment is to develop a strategy that Steve Wright can use to minimize his own discomfort with Nancy.

4. In 100 words or less, collaboratively write a paper offering suggestions to Steve to help him cope with Nancy's behavior.

FOOD FOR THOUGHT QUESTIONS

5. Reflect on the following: (a) One time in my life, I acted like a "whiner." What were the antecedents that caused me to behave that way? (b) These were the consequences of my behavior? (c) What impact did it have on the work that needed to be done? (d) What did you learn from that experience? (e) What made you change your behavior?

6. ROLE PLAY If time allows, you can assign one student to play the role of Steve Wright, another to play the role of the HR manager, and another to play the role of Wright's immediate supervisor. Steve should begin the conversation by talking about the frustration he is feeling. His immediate supervisor and the HR manager are to listen, seek clarification of the salient concerns, and offer suggestions. The other students can be observers and should be asked to state whether the supervisor and HR manager did well or could have done better.

7. Your instructor may wish to have you write a short paper identifying what you learned from this activity.

### TEAM SKILL BUILDER 7-2: Technology Tools—Motivate Employees with Online Incentives

INTERNET ACTIVITY

Most employees will do their best and give their all to their job if they know that their work will be appreciated by the boss, as well as recognized by the organization and its employees. People want to be "caught doing well," and they enjoy receiving a pat on the back. As discussed at the end of this chapter, one way to show workers they are appreciated is by recognizing them publicly for their achievement. Another is by providing them with incentives or rewards for achieving or surpassing specific organizational goals. Roy Saunderson, chief learning officer for Rideu Recognition Management Institute, described several trends that have emerged in employee recognition, practices that incorporate technology, or are available on the Web to make appreciating workers easier for employers, and often even more rewarding for employees.[53]

In this exercise, your task is to review the recognition trends listed below, search the Internet for examples of at least three tools using the descriptions below to identify search keywords, and then describe which strategy you feel would be the most effective tool to use to motivate employees. You should create an annotated list of the three tools you reviewed, including a link to information about the tool and a 100-word description of each, then a paragraph explaining why you would use one of the three, as opposed to the others. Then, meet with a group of three students to share your top choice. Discuss whether the choices each of you made would be motivating to others in the group.

1. Social media recognizes and rewards employees. Companies such as GiveAWow and Terryberry provide organizations with Facebook-like platforms to praise employee work.
2. Online courses that educate supervisors on how and why to provide meaningful recognition to employees. MindTools, Terryberry, and APA Excellence provide such trainings.
3. Customized gift cards that align with employees' interests, rather than generic restaurant cards.
4. Eco-friendly incentive packaging and gifts that demonstrate a company's commitment to "green" practices.
5. "Leaderboards" that display workers' progress against one another, to encourage friendly competition. The Employee Engagement Network is one such leaderboard.
6. Peer-to-peer recognition tools, which employees can use to recognize the contributions of those on their team or in their work group. Baudville provides such recognition tools for organizations.
7. Points redemption programs, in which employees earn points by achieving organizational milestones, which they can "cash in" for products they choose from an incentive Web site. AwardsNetwork, Intelispend, and AwardCo are a few examples of such services.

## SUPERVISION IN ACTION

The video for this chapter can be accessed from the student companion website at www.cengagebrain.com. (Search by authors' names or book title to find the accompanying resources.)

David Grossman/Alamy

*Our daily experiences, such as our method of commuting to and from work, can influence our personality, outlook, and mood.*

Jose Luis Pelaez Inc./Cusp/Corbis

*Some employers provide off-the-job social and athletic opportunities for their employees to help those employees satisfy their social needs and to build loyalty to the organization.*

Compassionate Eye Foundation/Ivan Hunter/Stockbyte/Getty Images

*One hygiene factor that is important to many people is having enough free time and money to pursue their personal interests.*

© iStock.com/Wavebreak

*"Even in routine work the only true expert is the person who does the job."*
*—Peter Drucker*

## ENDNOTES

1. "Happiness is the meaning and purpose of life, the whole aim and the end of human existence," Aristotle (384–322 BC), accessed at http://www.brainyquote.com. Compare with the statement by Nobel Laureate Bertrand Russell, "Man needs, for his happiness not only the enjoyment of this or that, but hope and enterprise and change." Also see Jennifer Schramm, "New Ways of Doing Good," *HR Magazine* (October 2010), p. 120.
2. "I Can't Get No Satisfaction" was a 1965 song by the English rock band, The Rolling Stones. It was written by Mick Jagger and Keith Richards. This was the Stones's first no. 1 hit in the United States. Watch the Stones's video production of the song; go to http://www.YouTube.com.
3. To watch a three-minute video of the song, go to http://www.YouTube.com and listen to "Take This Job and Shove It!," written by David Allen Coe in 1977 and popularized by artist Johnny Paycheck under the Epic Records label. Thirty-some years ago, in the movie *Network,* television news anchor Howard Beale urged his viewers to open their windows and yell, "I'm mad as hell, and I'm not going to take this anymore."
4. The most recent Conference Board found that only 47.3 percent of Americans reported they were satisfied with their jobs. For the first time since 1987, the downward trend in job satisfaction has leveled off. Like news anchor Beale, many employees would probably like to express these dissatisfactions but know that if they lost their job, they probably couldn't find one as good as a one they have.

   See Rebecca L. Ray, Thomas Rizzacasa, and Gad Levanon, "Job Satisfaction: 2013 Edition," *The Conference Board, Report Number: TCB_R-1524-13-RR* (June 2013). On the other hand, a Gallup poll reported that no more than 31 percent of workers were dissatisfied with any aspect of their job, with on-the-job stress, compensation level, and health insurance benefits showing the highest levels of dissatisfaction, retrieved from "Work and Workplace" survey data, August 7–11, 2013 (http://www.gallup.com/poll/1720/work-work-place.aspx#1). However, government workers' job satisfaction was recently rated at its lowest, 42.2 percent, by 781,047 federal employees since rating began in 2003. The rating has been dropping over the past three years, according to a report by the Partnership for Public Service and Deloitte based on data from the *2013 Federal Employee Viewpoint Survey* (2013, http://www.fedview.opm.gov/).

Also see Bill Roberts, "The Grand Convergence," *HR Magazine* (October 2011), pp. 39–48; or Adrienne Fox, "At Work in 2020: Shape Your Organization for the Future by Measuring Workforce Needs, Analyzing Trends and Being Open to New Working Relationships," *HR Magazine* (January 2010), pp. 18–23.

5. U.S. Bureau of Labor Statistics unemployment data are summarized by Adam Belz in, "Trends in Long-Term Unemployment," *Star Tribune* (January 7, 2014), http://www.startribune.com/blogs/3D_Economics.html and Jackie Northam reported that U.S. companies are beginning to "reshore" workers as labor costs rise overseas and the number of jobs appropriate for offshoring begin to decrease, in "As Overseas Costs Rise, More U.S. Companies Are 'Reshoring'" NPR.org (January 27, 2014). Even with unemployment leveling off, it remains a critical problem as reported by Rebecca Riffkin, "Unemployment Rises to Top Problem in the U.S.," Gallup.com (February 17, 2014), http://www.gallup.com/poll/167450/unemployment-rises-top-problem.aspx; Terry Terhark, "Needle in a Haystack: Uncovering the Reality of Skill Employee Shortages," *HR Magazine* (April 2011), p. 66; Nancy M. Davis, "The Great Recession's Lasting Legacy," *HR Magazine* (February 2010), p. 40.
6. In an effort to enhance their careers, 89 percent of women said that they will immediately take action to build their "career capital" by developing their SKAs and adding knowledge to their toolboxes in order to achieve their career objectives. See 2014 Women's Research—Career Capital, Accenture (http://www.accenture.com). Also see Naomi Chan and June Carbone, *Red Families v Blue Families: Legal Polarization and the Creation of Culture* (New York: Oxford University Press, 2010).
7. "One in Five Workers Plan to Change Jobs in 2014," an increase from 17 percent in 2013, according to a CareerBuilder survey of 3,000 full-time workers (CareerBuilder.com, January 9, 2014). This trend has emerged as the economy has bounced back in the postrecession era. See also Jennifer Schramm, "Post-Recession Job Dissatisfaction," *HR Magazine* (July 2010), p. 88. The SHRM *2014 Employee Job Satisfaction* survey (May 7, 2014) reported the following to be the most important contributors: (1) compensation/pay, 60 percent; (2) job security and opportunities to use skills/abilities, 59 percent; (3) relationship with immediate supervisor, 54 percent; (4) overall benefits package, 53 percent; (5) organization's financial stability, 53 percent; and (6) the work itself, 51 percent.
8. What is trust? What are the effects of trustworthy behavior? How do you react when a supervisor or manager unconditionally exhibits trust in their relationship with you? In part, does that cause you, in turn, to trust them? If so, this reflects what I call the "rule of reciprocity." L. Gordon Crovitz reported that only 37 percent of "informed people"—those with college degrees—had trust in the government to do the right thing; and only 45 percent trusted business leaders. See Crovitz, "The Business of Restoring Trust," *The Wall Street Journal* (January 31, 2011), p. A13. Contrast that finding with the findings reported in a 2013 survey by Blessing White, *Employee Engagement Research Update*, summarized by Elizabeth Lupfer (September 7, 2013) in which 74 percent of U.S. employees "trust" their immediate supervisor, but "trust" wanes the higher up the chain one goes. (Only 57 percent of employees trust their senior management.) Also see Benjamin Schneider and Karen B. Paul, "In the Company We Trust," *HR Magazine* (January 2011), pp. 40–43; J. Scott Colquitt and J. LePine, "Trust, Trustworthiness, and Trust Propensity: A Meta-analytic Test of Their Unique Relationships with Risk Taking and Job Performance," *Journal of Applied Psychology* 92, No. 4 (2007), pp. 909–927; and Michael Summers, "Purpose, Direction, and Motivation," *SuperVision* (June 2010), pp. 11–13.
9. Many companies rely, in part, on personality assessment programs to evaluate employees. One of the more widely recognized approaches to the identification of individual differences is the Myers-Briggs Type Indicators. If your college has the Myers-Briggs test, use it to identify your basic personality type. There are four dichotomies: Extraversion (E) or (I) Introversion; Sensing (S) or (N) Intuition; Thinking (T) or (F) Feeling; and Judgment (J) or (P) Perception. One's preference for E or I says something about attitudes. For additional information on personality development, see Robert Hogan, *Personality and the Fate of Organizations* (Mahwa, NJ: Lawrence Erlbaum Associates Publishers, 2007); J. M. George, "The Role of Personality in Organizational Life: Issues and Evidence," *Journal of Management* 18 (1992), pp. 185–213; and R. C. Carson, "Personality," *Annual Review of Psychology* 40 (1989), pp. 227–248.
10. Sandra A. Crowe as quoted in Rebecca Meany, "What a Pain?" *Successful Meetings* (February 2001), p. 72. Also see Crowe, *Since Strangling Isn't an Option . . . Dealing with Difficult People: Common Problems and Uncommon Solutions* (New York: Perigree, 1999). See *Rumors of Our Progress Have Been Greatly Exaggerated: Why Women's Lives Aren't Getting Any Easier—And How We Can Make Real Progress for Ourselves and Our Daughters* (New York: Rodale, Inc., distributed by Macmillan, 2008). Additional research supports the contention that early influence is important in leadership development and work performance. See Robert Anda, Vladimir Fleisher, Vincent Felitti, Valerie Edwards, Charles, Whitfiled, Shanta Dube, and David Williamson, "Childhood Abuse, Household Dysfunction, and Indicators of Impaired Adult Worker Performance," *The Permanente Journal* 8, No. 1 (Winter 2004), pp. 30–38.
11. The author first heard a coach 50 years ago tell a referee that he had a bad 'tude. The result was a technical foul. Then, who had the "bad 'tude?" See Noelle Nelson, "Don't Give Gripes Traction by Ignoring Them," SHRM.org, *Managing Smart* (May 2, 2014), http://www.shrm.org/Publications/ManagingSmart/winter07/Documents/story1.doc W. H. Weiss, "Attitude: A Major Managerial Challenge," *SuperVision* (August 2010), pp. 20–22; Paul Falcone, "When Employees Have a 'tude," *HR Magazine* (June 2001), pp. 189–194; and Jacquelyn Smith, "How to Manage a Moody Boss," *Forbes* (June 25, 2013), http://www.forbes.com/sites/jacquelynsmith/2013/06/25/how-to-manage-a-moody-boss/ for illustrations of how the supervisor's bad attitude impacts the organization.
12. Sigal G. Barsade, *The Ripple Effect: Emotional Contagion and Its Influence on Group Behavior*. (Cornell, NY: Cornell University, 2002). Anne Kreamer, *It's Always Personal: Navigating Emotion in the New Workplace* (New York: Random House, 2013). See also Lynn Taylor, *Tame Your Terrible Office Tyrant: How to Manage Childish Boss Behavior and Thrive in Your Job* (Hoboken, NJ: Wiley, 2009).

13. See Abraham H. Maslow, *Motivation and Personality*, 2nd ed. (New York: Harper & Row, 1970), Chapter 4. In his "A Preface to Motivation Theory," *Psychosomatic Medicine* 5 (1943), pp. 85–92, Maslow's conclusions included: (1) "The integrated wholeness of the organism must be one of the foundation stones of motivation theory." (2) "Motivation theory is not synonymous with behavior theory.The motivations are only one class of determinants of behavior." In *Drive: The Surprising Truth about What Motivates Us* (New York: Penguin Group, 2011), Daniel Pink asserts that employers can incorporate three critical elements to increase employee motivation: autonomy, mastery, and purpose. See also Micah Solomon, "To Motivate Employees, Apply This Scientific Rule of Leadership," *Forbes* (March 9, 2014), http://www.forbes.com/sites/micahsolomon/2014/03/09/motivate-customer-service/.
14. Job security has been indicated in past employment engagement surveys as the most important aspect of employees' job satisfaction, while feeling safe in the work environment has also been ranked as one of the top ten aspects. See *2010 Employee Job Satisfaction* survey (SHRM, 2010, Figure 2). Feeling safe at work was consistently ranked by women as one of the most important factors in job satisfaction. See Jennifer Schramm, "Feeling Safe," *HR Magazine* (May 2004), p. 152. See also "Women's Safety and Health Issues at Work," Centers for Disease Control National Institute for Occupational Safety and Health (NIOSH) information Web site (November 19, 2013), http://www.cdc.gov/niosh/topics/women/
15. See, Alice Andors, "You Can Cry If You Want To," *HR Magazine* (October 2011), p. 49; Wesley Harris, "Withering on the Vine: Ten Ways to Insure Your Employees Become Stagnant," *SuperVision* (December 2010), pp. 25–26; J. S. Atherton, "Cognitive Dissonance and Learning," *Learning and Teaching* (http://www.learningandteaching.info/learning/dissonance.htm); and Ross Norman, "Affective-Cognitive Consistency, Attitudes, Conformity," *Journal of Personality and Social Psychology* 32, No. 2 (1975), pp. 83–91.
16. For more information on aesthetic needs, see D. Martin and K. Loomis, *Building Teachers: A Constructive Approach to Introducing Education* (Belmont, CA: Wadsworth, 2007), pp. 72–75.
17. Kant's "transcendental aesthetic" gives meaning to the branch of study defined as the philosophy of the beautiful or taste or having to do with the fine arts. For a deeper overview, go to "Aesthetics: Love to Know 1911" at http://www.1911encyclopedia.org/Aesthetics.
18. For additional insights on Maslow's theories, see Maslow, *Motivation and Personality,* 2nd ed. (New York: Harper & Row, 1970). The March 1998 *Fortune* cover article entitled "Yo, Corporate America—I'm the New Organization Man," depicted the wants and needs of the new "gold collar worker." Expecting to be well paid, this generation of workers believed they were entitled to a job "that was fun, a job that was cool, a job that would let them discover who they really were." For this worker, work was not about paying the rent anymore—"It's about self-fulfillment." My! how times have changed, or have they?

    See R. Katzell and D. Thompson, "Work Motivation: Theory and Practice," *American Psychologist* (February 1990), pp. 144–153 for an overview of motivational theory.
19. See Ed Leonard and Roy Cook, *Human Resource Management:21st Century Challenges* (Mason, OH: Thomson Custom Publishing, 2005), p. 3. They expanded the skills to include technical, administrative, people, communication, emotional intelligence, political, and conceptual. They also enlarged the notion of SKAs to include personal attributes. Also see Ted Pollock, "Helpful Attitudes for Managers," *SuperVision* (September 2010), pp. 16–18.
20. Kant's *categorical imperative* basically says "people will think rationally and make a morally correct decision that is not based on their own personal desires." Thus, one's actions could not cause harm or inflict damage to another person. Also see "Kant's Moral Philosophy," *Stanford Encyclopedia of Philosophy* (April 6, 2008), accessed May 25, 2011.
21. The publication of Ralph Waldo Emerson's 1836 essay "Nature" is considered the foundation for transcendentalism (accessed at http://en.wikipedia.org/wiki/Transcendentalism). It is not clear whether the notion of transcendence should be attributed to Kant, Viktor Frankl, or Maslow. Maslow established the Association for Transpersonal Psychology. Maslow's notion of humanistic psychology seeks to examine what is really right with people while transpersonal psychology explores extreme wellness or optimal well-being (http://www.rare-leadership.org/Maslow_on_transpersonal_psychology.html).
22. Leon Festinger developed the theory of cognitive dissonance in the 1950s. See Festinger, *A Theory of Cognitive Dissonance* (Stanford, CA: Stanford University Press, 1957). Also see interview by Adrienne Fox, "Leading with the Brain, *HR Magazine* (June 2011), pp. 52–53; or G. Coppin et al., "I'm No Longer Torn after Choice," *Psychological Science* 21, No. 8 (2010), pp. 489–493.
23. See Joe Nocera, "The Bad Luck of Winning," *New York Times* (November 30, 2012), http://www.nytimes.com/2012/12/01/opinion/nocera-the-bad-luck-of-winning.html
24. C. P. Alderfer, "An Empirical Test of a New Theory of Human Needs," *Psychological Review* (March 1969), pp. 165–194. Also see Alderfer, "Existence, Relatedness, and Growth: Human Needs in Organizational Setting." You may also want to google "ERG theory" to glean more information.
25. David C. McClelland, *Human Motivation* (Glenville, IL: Scott, Foresman, 1985); *Power: The Inner Experience* (New York: Irvington, 1975); and McClelland and D. H. Burnham, "Power Is the Great Motivator," *Harvard Business Review* 54, No. 2 (1976), pp. 100–110.
26. G. A. Yukl, *Leadership in Organizations* (Englewood Cliffs, NJ: Prentice Hall, 1989).
27. McClelland stated that people with a high need for personal power may have little self-control and they exercise power impulsively. Those who use socialized power do so in positive ways that benefit others and the organization. They seek power because it is through power that the work of the organization is accomplished. See McClelland, op. cit. (1975), pp. 74–82.
28. The complete dual-factor theory is well explained in Frederick Herzberg, Bernard Mausner, and Barbara Bloch Snyderman, *The Motivation to Work*, 2nd ed. (New York: John Wiley & Sons, 1967); Herzberg's *Work and the Nature of Man* (New York: World, 1971), and Herzberg's classic article, "One More Time: How Do You Motivate Your Employees?" *Harvard Business Review* (January/February 1968), pp. 53–62. Also see "The BEST of HBR 1968," a reprint of Herzberg's 1968 article in *Harvard Business Review* 81, No. 1 (January 2003).
29. For a discussion of expectancy theory, see Victor H. Vroom, *Work and Motivation* (New York: John Wiley & Sons, 1964), and Terrence R. Mitchell, "Expectancy Models of Job Satisfaction, Occupational Preference, and Effort: A Theoretical, Methodological, and Empirical Appraisal," *Psychological Bulletin* 81 (1974), pp. 1053–1077.
30. J. Stacy Adams, "Toward an Understanding of Inequity," *Journal of Abnormal and Social Psychology* 67 (1963), pp. 422–436. Also see

Jerald Greenberg and Claire L. McCarty, "Comparable Worth: A Matter of Justice," in Gerald R. Farris and Kendrith M. Rowland, eds., *Research in Personnel and Human Resource Management* (Greenwich, CT: JAI Press, 1990), pp. 265–303; Greenberg, "Cognitive Reevaluation of Outcomes in Response to Underpayment Inequity," *Academy of Management Journal* (March 1989), pp. 174–184; or Robert P. Vecchio, "Predicting Worker Performance in Inequitable Setting," *Academy of Management Review* (January 1982), pp. 103–110.

31. Magna Donnelly's long-standing innovative approach to management has resulted in numerous awards and has been listed among the "Best Companies to Work for in America." John F. Donnelly, a former seminarian and former president of the company, believed in sharing profits with employees. This approach evolved into a participatory management style with work teams being involved in every aspect of the decision-making process. For more information on the company's culture and commitment to employees, visit their Web site (http://www.magna.com/magna/en/about/culture/default.aspx).
32. The quotes attributed to Thomas Alva Edison and Ralph Waldo Emerson were cited in Steve Vogel, "She Just Keeps Rolling Along," *The Washington Post* (June 4, 1998), p. D-1. Also see the *Oxford Dictionary of Quotations* (Oxford: Oxford University Press, 1980), pp. 199, 206–208 for other quotes attributed to these two distinguished persons.
33. This quote is a variation of Lee Iacocca's "No one says on their deathbed, 'I wish I had spent more time with my business.'" See Daisy Sanders, "Appreciate Your Employees Today & Everyday," *SuperVision* 68, No. 8 (August 2007), pp. 6–7.
34. See Rhonda R. Savage, "No Raises This Year? Secrets to Employee Retention in Difficult Times," *SuperVision* (July 2010), pp. 25–27; Kenneth Thomas, "The Four Intrinsic Rewards That Drive Employee Engagement," *The Ivey Business Journal: Workplace* (November/ December 2009). http://iveybusinessjournal.com/topics/the-workplace/the-four-intrinsic-rewards-that-drive-employee-engagement#.U6SOj7FBnRw; and Thomas, *Intrinsic Motivation at Work: What Really Drives Employee Engagement* (San Francisco: Berrett-Koehler, 2009). For a discussion of the factors that contribute to a culture of job entitlement, see Alison Stein Wellner, "Spoiled Brats," *HR Magazine* (November 2004), pp. 61–65. Also see Brian Fitzgerald, "What's the Best Way to Manage and Motivate Young Workers Who Have an Inflated Sense of Entitlement?" *Inc.* (September 2007), pp. 60–61.
35. Robert M. Bramson, *Coping with Difficult People* (New York: Doubleday, 1988). Also see Maurice A. Ramirez, "Outrage or Enthusiasm: The Choice Is Yours," *SuperVision* 69, No. 4 (April 2008), pp. 17–19; Cherie Carter-Scott, *Negaholics No More* (Shawnee Mission, KS: National Press Publications, 1999); Rick Brinkman and Rick Kirschner, *Dealing with People You Can't Stand* (New York: McGraw-Hill, 1994); and Muriel Solomon, *Working with Difficult People* (Englewood Cliffs, NJ: Prentice Hall, 1990).
36. One recent study found that the average college student was spending about 40 hours a week social networking and less than half that amount of time going to class and studying. Several surveys found that employees were spending at least two hours a day on non-work-related activities. Whatever it is today, it will increase tomorrow unless organizations establish guidelines and monitoring controls. Also see Vara Vauhini, "New Sites Make It Easier to Spy on Your Friends," *The Wall Street Journal* (May 13, 2008), pp. D1, D3.
37. The thoughts and ideas for the section on the ABCs were adapted from Aubrey C. Daniels, *Performance Management: Improving Quality and Productivity through Positive Reinforcement*, 3rd. ed. (Atlanta: Performance Management Publications, 1989).
38. Ibid., pp. 14, 75+.
39. E. L. Thorndike, *Educational Psychology: The Psychology of Learning*, Vol. II (New York: Teachers College Columbia University, 1913). B. F. Skinner built on the works of Thorndike and identified S-R and R-S behaviors. The latter is known as operant conditioning and implies that individuals behave, in large part, to receive desired consequences. See Skinner, *The Behavior of Organisms* (New York: Appleton-Century Crofts, 1938).
40. Daniels, *Performance Management*, p. 45.
41. Douglas McGregor, *The Human Side of Enterprise* (New York: McGraw-Hill, 1960), pp. 45–57.
42. See Nathan W. Harter, "The Shop Floor Schopenhauer: Hope for a Theory-X Supervisor," *Journal of Management Education* (February 1997), pp. 87+. Among other notions, Harter acknowledges that even McGregor conceded that coercion works reasonably well under certain circumstances.
43. J. Richard Hackman, Greg R. Oldham, Robert Janson, and Kenneth Purdy, "A New Strategy for Job Enrichment," *California Management Review* (Summer 1975), pp. 51–71; Hackman and Oldham, "Motivation through the Design of Work: Test of a Theory," *Organizational Behavior and Human Performance* 16, No. 2 (1976), pp. 250–270; Hackman and Oldham, *Work Redesign* (Reading, MA: Addison-Wesley, 1980); and Carol T. Kulik, Greg R. Oldham, and Paul H. Langner, "Measurement of Job Characteristics: Comparison of the Original and the Revised Job Diagnostic Survey," *Journal of Applied Psychology* (August 1988), pp. 462–466.
44. Hackman, Oldham, Janson, and Purdy, "A New Strategy for Job Enrichment," p. 58.
45. Ibid.
46. Multitasking is the ability of a person to perform more than one task at the same time. The research by Rubinstein, Meyer, and Evans shows that people lose time when they have to switch from one task to another and that time costs increased with the complexity of the tasks. David Meyer said that "For every aspect of human performance—perceiving, thinking, and acting—people have specific mental resources whose effective use requires supervision." See Joshua Rubinstein, David Meyer, and Jeffrey Evans, "Executive Control of Cognitive Processes in Task Switching," *Journal of Experiential Psychology: Human Perception and Performance* 27, No. 4 (August 2001), pp. 763–797.
47. Elizabeth Newell, "Management Matters: The Myth of Multitasking," Government Executive.com (June 1, 2011), http://www.govexec.com/story_page_pf.cfm?articleid=47904&printerfriendlyvers=1
48. Alison Overholt, "The Art of Multitasking," www.fastcompany.com (December 19, 2007). Also see Jonathan Katz, "Cozy Up to Customers: Employee Engagement with Clients Fosters a Sense of Worker Pride and Ownership," *Industry Week* (February 2010) p. 16; and Katz, "E-Z-Go Charts a Course for Competitiveness: Benchmarking Initiatives and Employee Engagement Help Increase Market Share and Profitability," *Industry Week* (January 2010), p. 28.
49. Robert Levering, *A Great Place to Work* (New York: Random House, 1988). Also see Robert Grossman, "The Care and Feeding of

High-Potential Employees," *HR Magazine* (August 2011), pp. 34–39; or Patrick Lencioni, *The Three Signs of a Miserable Job* (New York: Wiley, 2007).

50. As listed in *Fortune*'s "World's Most Admired Companies" in 2013, http://money.cnn.com/magazines/fortune/most-admired/2013/snapshots/2068.html; See Scott McCartney, "Delta Sends Its 11,000 Agents to Charm School," *The Wall Street Journal* (February 3, 2011), p D3. Delta finished 2010 with the highest rate of customer complaints and was second-to-last in on-time arrivals and baggage handling. Compare that performance with that of the industry leader, Southwest Airlines. See Ken Blanchard and Colleen Barrett, *Lead with LUV: A Different Way to Create Success* (New York: Free Press, 2011); Hal Lancaster, "Herb Kelleher Has One Main Strategy: Treat Employees Well," *The Wall Street Journal* (August 31, 1999), p. B1; Kevin Frieberg and Jackie Frieberg, *Nuts! Southwest Airlines' Crazy Recipe for Business and Personal Success* (Austin, TX: Bard Press, 1996); and Colleen Barrett, "Corner on Customer Service: The Voices of Southwest Airlines," *Southwest Airlines Spirit* (April 2005), p. A11.
51. See Shanessa Fakour, "Business Encourages Employee Participation with Incentives," *The Brunswick, GA News* (February 9, 2011), p. 13a.
52. Ibid.
53. Roy Saunderson, "Top 10 Trends for Employee Recognition in 2013," Incentive.com (December 10, 2012), http://www.incentivemag.com/Incentive-Programs/Expert-Opinions/Roy-Saunderson/Articles/Top-10-Trends-for-Employee-Recognition-in-2013/

Chapter 8

# Solving Problems, Making Decisions, and Managing Change

© 3Kzenon/Shutterstock.com

**After studying this chapter, you will be able to:**

1. Explain the importance of problem-solving and decision-making skills.
2. Describe and apply the basic steps and skills involved in the decision-making process.
3. Identify and describe various decision-making styles.
4. Discuss why a supervisor should not make hasty decisions.
5. Suggest approaches for introducing change to employees and for proposing change to higher-level managers.
6. Understand the formula for organizational renewal.

## YOU MAKE THE CALL!

*You are Brey Yancey, general manager of Kincaid Pharmacy's State Street store. Kincaid has pharmacies in Arkansas and Missouri, and business has been tough because of mail-order pharmacies, Wal-Mart, and the major pharmacies such as Rite Aid, Walgreens, and CVS. The pharmacist has responsibility for the pharmacy operations while you have total responsibility for the rest of the store. You report to Craig Ellis, vice president of operations for the 16-store chain. The pharmacy's philosophy emphasizes, "Customer service is your number one job. Do whatever is necessary to exceed the needs of the customer!" Your management style, in part, is based upon the following: "Brey will create a culture of high performance, satisfying customer needs and motivating employees. Brey will balance the employees' working life, so that the State Street store is an employer of choice."*

Molly, one of your cashiers, is a single parent with several school-age children. She has exhausted her vacation hours for the year and has no personal time left. On a day she was scheduled to work, her youngest daughter developed a high temperature and seemed very ill. Even though a relative was willing to look after her daughter, Molly preferred not to do that. About 15 minutes before her shift began, Molly called the store.

Molly: "Brey, I am not feeling well this morning. I think I might have a strain of the new flu that is going around. I would hate to spread it around to anyone else, particularly the customers. I will call you later in the day and let you know how I am feeling, because I am scheduled to work tomorrow also."

Brey knows that it will be difficult to get coverage at this late hour and that the pharmacy staffing is lean to begin with.

Brey: "I am sorry that you are not feeling well, Molly. Take good care of yourself and get it under control. Please let me know as soon as possible regarding tomorrow."

Molly: "Thanks for your understanding, I really appreciate it."

You contemplated the work ahead. You called several employees, and none would be available to fill in for Molly until later in the day. You pondered some of the things you can do to help your pharmacy team get through the day. You knew that you could make it work.

About a week after Molly had called in sick, Ronnie, a coworker asked to speak with you.

Ronnie: "Brey, Remember last week when Molly called in sick and you couldn't find anyone to cover for her. I really hate to bring this up, but Molly never goes the extra mile. She always seems to find ways to take advantage of you and us."

Brey: "What, specifically, do you mean?"

Ronnie: "I know the last time she called in about being sick she wasn't really, her daughter was. I don't want to work with her, she lies all the time, and I know she is very dishonest."

Brey: "Ronnie, I can understand your anger over this, and I appreciate your sharing this with me. Now, to be fair to you and all the other employees, let me investigate this. I would appreciate it if you would keep this communication between us. Thanks for being a good employee."

You check with Molly, and she admitted lying about her illness. She is in clear violation of company policy. According to the Kincaid Pharmacy Employee Handbook, dishonesty may result in discharge. Firing someone is something that you have never done. As a matter fact, you have never had to deal with a problem of this nature. On the other hand, if Ronnie suspects that Molly is lying about such things, what did the other employees think? If you discipline Molly, how will they feel? You ponder your alternatives.

The above scenario presents a supervisory situation based on real events to be used for educational purposes. The identities of some or all individuals, organizations, industries, and locations, as well as financial and other information may have been disguised to protect individual privacy and proprietary information. Fictional details may have been added to improve readability and interest.

YOU MAKE THE CALL!

## The Importance of Decision-Making Skills

**1 Explain the importance of problem-solving and decision-making skills.**

All human activities involve decision making. Each of us faces problems at home, at work, at school, and in social groups for which decisions must be made. Problems can be large or small, simple or complex, life-threatening or trivial. Some problems can be dealt with almost automatically. Consider the following illustration:

> *Lori, a college student, has been juggling school work with her clerking job at Wal-Mart. As soon as her 7:00 A.M.-to-3:30 P.M. shift is completed, she runs to her car so she can get to class a few minutes early to review for her midterm*

*exam that evening. The car won't start. She needs to get to campus quickly. She grabs her backpack out of the trunk and begs a coworker to give her a lift. "It shouldn't be too far out of your way, and I'm really in trouble if I miss this exam," she pleads. The coworker obliges and drops Lori off at the circle drive. Whew! Lori has solved one problem. It's almost 4:30 P.M., and she has just a few minutes to quickly review one last time before the exam. But now Lori is faced with another problem—answering the questions posed by the instructor. There are 30 multiple-choice questions, each one of which forces Lori to choose among four possible answers. The two essay problems require her to make additional choices. As the instructor collects the exam booklet, Lori heaves a sigh of relief. She really feels good about her performance on this test. As she walks out to the parking lot, she suddenly remembers that her car is back at the Wal-Mart parking lot. Even though Lori has solved several problems in the last few hours, there is another one waiting for her.*

All of us have encountered similar situations. Look at the events you experience each day. You constantly have to make choices. Some choices may be easier to make than others. Others seem to be insurmountable. In these tough times, the decisions made by upper management will affect a variety of stakeholders. Every day people face a fateful turn of events. Suppose a family member or your best friend lost his or her job or had a major health issue. Who could you turn to for help? Many events today impact our family and friends in negative ways. Many of us can recall the song, "If you got a problem, don't care what it is, I can help!"[1] But what kind of help do we need? Like Lori and her broken-down car, most of us face problems each and every day, and we look for guidance from others. Often, each of us would like to know which direction to take, but we sometimes give little thought to the consequences of our choices (see Figure 8.1).

How many decisions have you made today? Each of us has to make choices, and sometimes we do not make the "right" ones. Think back to a couple of your

**FIGURE 8.1 To make a decision, you must first know what you want to accomplish**

more recent decisions. Did you just "wing it?" Or did you use a systematic problem-solving approach? Decision making is an essential part of life and an integral part of all managerial functions. While it lies at the core of the planning function of management, we have placed this chapter on decision making in Part 2 of this text because the principles discussed here apply when supervisors carry out all their managerial functions and duties.

In work settings, when asked to define their major responsibilities, many supervisors respond that solving problems and making decisions are the most important components of what they do daily and throughout their ongoing supervisory management tasks. **Decision making** is the process of defining problems and choosing a course of action from among alternatives. The term *decision making* often is used together with the term *problem solving* because many supervisory decisions focus on solving problems that have occurred or are anticipated. However, the term *problem solving* should not be construed as being limited to decisions about problem areas. Problem solving also includes decisions about realistic opportunities that are present or available if planned for appropriately. Therefore, throughout the text, we use these terms interchangeably.

**Decision making**
Defining problems and choosing a course of action from among alternatives

Many of the problems that confront supervisors in their daily activities recur and are familiar; for these problems, most supervisors have developed routine answers. When supervisors are confronted with new and unfamiliar problems however, many find it difficult to choose courses of action.

Managers and supervisors at all levels are constantly required to solve problems that result from changing situations and unusual circumstances. Regardless of their managerial levels, supervisors should use a similar, logical, and systematic decision-making process. While decisions at the executive level are usually wider in scope and magnitude than decisions at the supervisory level, the decision-making process should be fundamentally the same throughout the management hierarchy.

Of course, once a decision is made, effective action is necessary. A good decision that no one implements is of little value. In this chapter, we are unconcerned with the problem of getting effective action. Instead, we discuss the process before action is taken that should lead to the best decision or solution.

If you were to draw a picture of a decision maker, what would your picture look like? I suspect that your drawing would portray a person at the moment of choice, ready to choose an alternative. Supervisors must understand that information gathering, analysis, and other processes precede the moment of selecting one alternative over others.

Decision making is an important skill that can be developed just as skill at any sport is developed—by learning the steps, practicing, and exerting effort. By doing these things, supervisors can learn to make more thoughtful decisions and can improve the quality of their decisions.

At the same time, supervisors should ensure that their employees learn to make their own decisions more effectively. A supervisor cannot make all the decisions necessary to run a department. Many daily decisions in a department are made by the employees who do the work. For example, employees often have to decide, without their supervisors, what materials to use, how a job is to be done, when a job is to be done, and how to coordinate activities with other departments.

This forward thinking is embodied in the notion of **appreciative inquiry (AI)**. Professor David Cooperrider explains that "AI is the cooperative search for the best in people, their organizations, and the world around them. AI involves the art and practice of asking questions that strengthen a system's capacity to heightened positive potential."[2] Numerous organizations have embraced the concept in

**Appreciative inquiry (AI)**
The cooperative search for the best in people, organizations, and the world around them

order to push performance to higher levels. What is appreciative inquiry? Read the following definitions to gain some insight.

- *Appreciate*: (1) To recognize the quality, significance, or magnitude of; (2) to be fully aware of; (3) to be thankful for; (4) to admire greatly; (5) to raise in value, especially over time. Synonyms: value, prize, esteem, treasure, cherish. These verbs mean to have a favorable opinion of someone or something.
- *Inquire*: (1) To seek information by asking a question; (2) to make an inquiry or investigation. Synonyms: discovery, search, study, systematic exploration.
- *Inquiry*: (1) The act of inquiring; (2) a question; (3) a close examination of a matter in the search for information or truth.[3]

According to Professor Cooperrider, "The excitement of discovering, dreaming, and designing can turn empowered employees into a revolutionary force for positive organizational change." Instead of relying on traditional managerial decision-making processes, AI assumes that every living system has many untapped resources and unexplored potentials and, as such, managers must believe that their employees want to be involved and will ultimately make decisions that are in the best interests of their organization.[4] Elsewhere in this text we discuss the importance of engaging, empowering, and encouraging employees. In practice, those companies that are the "best companies to work for" are giving employees more active roles in charting the future of their organizations.[5]

**2 Describe and apply the basic steps of the decision-making process.**

## The Decision-Making Process

**Decision-making process** A systematic, step-by-step process to aid in choosing the best alternative

When making managerial decisions, supervisors should avoid making choices on the fly without considering alternatives and consequences. Rather, they should follow a **decision-making process**, a logical series of steps to aid them in choosing the best alternative, the steps of which are described in detail in the next section (see Figure 8.2). First, supervisors must define the problem. Second, they must analyze the problem using available information. Third, they must establish decision criteria—factors that will be used to evaluate the alternatives. Next, after thorough analysis, supervisors should develop alternate solutions. After these steps, the

**FIGURE 8.2 Effective supervisors follow the decision-making process**

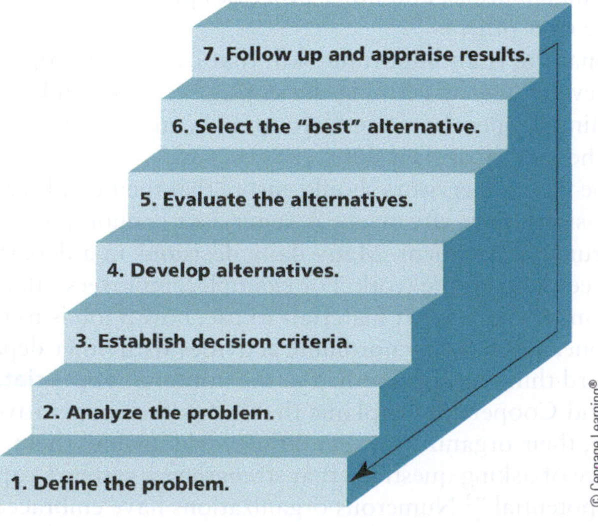
7. Follow up and appraise results.
6. Select the "best" alternative.
5. Evaluate the alternatives.
4. Develop alternatives.
3. Establish decision criteria.
2. Analyze the problem.
1. Define the problem.
© Cengage Learning®

supervisor should carefully evaluate the alternatives and select the solution that appears to be the best or most feasible under the circumstances. The concluding step in this process is follow-up and appraisal of the consequences of the decision.

## STEP 1: DEFINE THE PROBLEM

When confronted with a situation, the supervisor should step back, look at the situation, and specifically identify the real problem. Nothing is as useless as the right answer to the wrong question. Defining a problem is not easy. What appears to be the problem might merely be a symptom that shows on the surface. It is usually necessary to delve deeper to locate the real problem and define it.

Consider the following scenario. Tom Engle, an office supervisor, believes that his department has a problem of conflicting personalities. Two employees, Diana and Stuart, are continually bickering and cannot work together. Because of this lack of cooperation, their jobs are not being done in a timely manner. Engle must develop a clear, accurate problem statement. The problem statement should be brief, specific, and easily understood by others. A good problem statement addresses the following key questions:

- What is the problem?
- How do you know there is a problem?
- Where has the problem occurred?
- When has the problem occurred?
- Who is involved in, or affected by, the problem?

Expressing a problem through a problem statement can help the supervisor understand it. A careful review of the answers to key questions can lead to a problem statement, as shown in Figure 8.3. The statement reveals that the major problem is that the work is not getting done in a timely manner. When checking into this situation, the supervisor should focus on why the work is not getting done.

While defining a problem often can be time-consuming, it is time well spent. A supervisor should go no further in the decision-making process until the problem relevant to the situation has been pinpointed. Remember, a problem arises when there is a difference between the way things are and the way they should be. Effective supervisors use problem solving not only to take corrective action but also to improve the organization.

Unfortunately, many managers and supervisors do not spend the time necessary to frame the problems before them in proper terms. Often, they resort to making snap decisions and taking quick actions that do not solve the problems at hand.

## STEP 2: ANALYZE THE PROBLEM—GATHER FACTS AND INFORMATION

After the problem—not just its symptoms—has been defined, the next step is to analyze the problem. The supervisor begins by assembling facts and other pertinent information. This is sometimes viewed as the first step in decision making,

**FIGURE 8.3 Sample problem statement**

Bickering between employees detracts from the completion of work assignments. Last Monday and Tuesday, customer callbacks were not completed. Customers, other department employees, and the shipping department all are affected.

but until the real problem has been defined, the supervisor does not know what information is needed. Only after gaining a clear understanding of the problem can the supervisor decide how important certain data are and what additional information to seek.

Today so much information is available, and supervisors should understand the pitfalls and perils of using such data. The supervisor needs to pause and ponder whether the data are factual and relevant to the problem. Figure 8.4 illustrates the stress and frustration that occurs when needed information is not readily available.

Tom Engle, the office supervisor in Step 1, must find out why the work is not getting done. When he gathers information, he finds out that he never clearly outlined the expectations for his employees—where their duties begin and where they end. What appeared on the surface to be a problem of personality conflict was actually a problem caused by the supervisor. The chances are good that once the activities and responsibilities of the two employees are clarified, the friction will end. Engle must monitor the situation closely to ensure that the work is completed on time.

**FIGURE 8.4 The supervisor needs alternative sources of information**

Being human, a supervisor may find that personal opinion impacts decision making. This is particularly true when employees are involved in the problem. For example, if a problem involves an employee who performs well, the supervisor may be inclined to show that employee greater consideration than a poor performer. The supervisor should try to be as objective as possible in gathering and examining information.

Sometimes the supervisor does not know how far to go in searching for additional facts. A good practice is to observe reasonable time and cost limitations. This means gathering all information without undue delay and without excessive costs. In the process of analysis, the supervisor should try to think of intangible factors that play a significant role. Some intangible factors are reputation, morale, discipline, and personal biases. It is difficult to be specific about these factors, but they should be considered when analyzing a problem. As a general rule, written and objective information is more reliable than opinions and hearsay. Another way to depict Steps 1 and 2 of the decision-making process is the **fishbone technique (cause-and-effect diagram)**. As illustrated in Figure 8.5 and the appendix to this chapter, the technique will allow the problem solver not only to identify the various factors that have produced the problem but to consider the potential interrelatedness of the causes of the problem.[6]

**Fishbone technique (cause-and-effect diagram)**
Cause-and-effect approach to consider the potential interrelatedness of problem causes in decision making

## STEP 3: ESTABLISH DECISION CRITERIA

**Decision criteria** are standards or measures for evaluating alternatives; they are typically statements of what the supervisor wants to accomplish with the decision. Such criteria also can be used to determine how well the implementation phase of the process is going—that is, whether the decision is doing what it was intended to do. To illustrate, suppose that Tom Engle's initial actions do not remedy the situation. It will be appropriate to establish decision criteria. Figure 8.6 provides examples of the decision criteria that can be used to evaluate other courses of action.

**Decision criteria**
Standards or measures to use in evaluating alternatives

**FIGURE 8.5 Sample Fishbone (cause-and-effect) diagram**

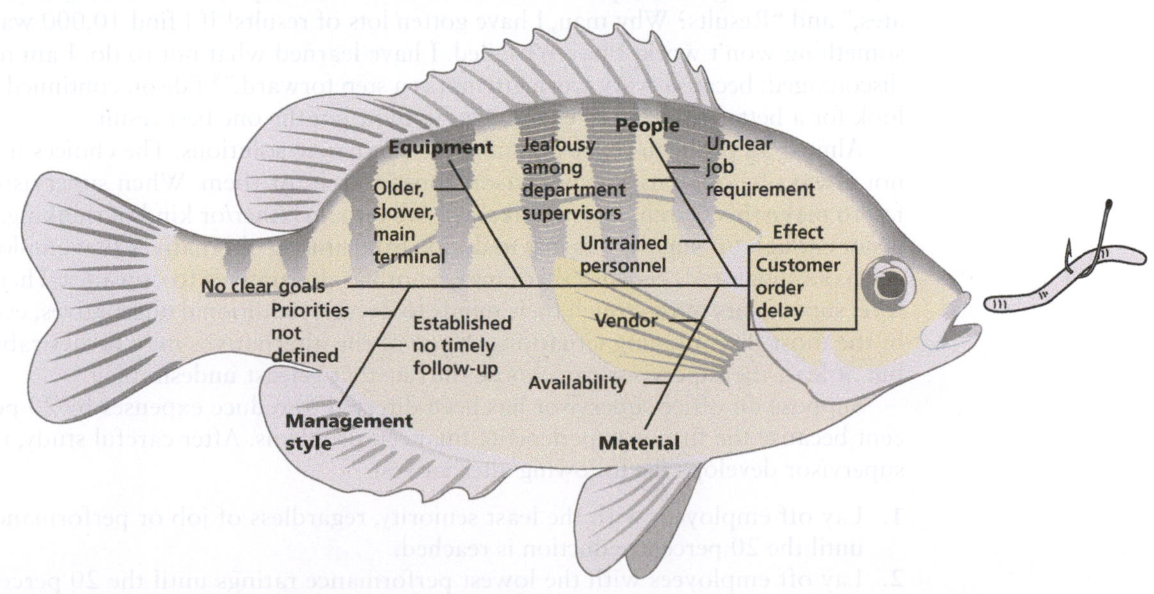


*Source:* Adapted from International Business Machines Corporation, (2011).

**FIGURE 8.6 Sample decision criteria**

**THE SOLUTION TO A PROBLEM**

- Should result in the work assignments being completed on time.
- Should incur no financial cost.
- Must not impede quality of service to the customer.
- Should put no employee's job in jeopardy.
- Should allow differentiation of product or service in the marketplace.
- Should have no negative impact on employees.
- Must alleviate the problem within one week.



Once the decision criteria are established, the supervisor must determine which criteria are necessary and must establish their order of priority. Because no solution alternative is likely to meet all the criteria, the supervisor must know which criteria are most important; thus alternatives can be judged by how many of those criteria the alternatives meet. The supervisor may want to consult with upper-level managers, peers, or employees when prioritizing criteria.

## STEP 4: DEVELOP ALTERNATIVES

After the supervisor has defined and analyzed the problem and established decision criteria, the next step is to develop alternative solutions. The supervisor should consider as many solutions as can reasonably be developed. By formulating many alternatives, the supervisor is less apt to overlook the best course of action. Roger von Oech identified several phases of creative thinking: The *explorer* is one who looks for ideas (alternatives), and the *artist* plays with those ideas.[7] Inventor Thomas Edison developed the incandescent electric light. Two of his many quotes are relevant here: "The electric light has caused me the greatest amount of study and has required the most elaborate experiments. Although I was never myself discouraged or hopeless of its success, I can not say the same for my associates," and "Results? Why man, I have gotten lots of results! If I find 10,000 ways something won't work, I haven't failed. I have learned what not to do. I am not discouraged, because every worn attempt is a step forward."[8] Edison continued to look for a better way and to experiment until he got the one best result.

Almost all problems have a number of alternative solutions. The choices may not always be obvious, so supervisors must search for them. When supervisors fail to make this search, they are likely to fall into an either/or kind of thinking. It is not enough for supervisors just to decide from among alternatives that employees have suggested, because there may be other alternatives to consider. Therefore, supervisors must stretch their minds to develop additional alternatives, even in the most discouraging situations. None of the alternatives may be desirable, but at least the supervisor can choose the one that is least undesirable.

Suppose an office supervisor has been directed to reduce expenses by 20 percent because the firm is experiencing financial problems. After careful study, the supervisor develops the following alternatives:

1. Lay off employees with the least seniority, regardless of job or performance, until the 20 percent reduction is reached.
2. Lay off employees with the lowest performance ratings until the 20 percent reduction is reached.

3. Analyze department duties and decide which jobs are essential. Keep the employees who are best qualified to perform those jobs.
4. Lay off no one and reduce work hours for all employees to achieve a 20 percent reduction.
5. Ask employees to take a reduction in wages and benefits to achieve a 20 percent reduction in costs.
6. Subcontract out the work to another organization or contract employees offshore, and lay off a significant portion of the employees until a 20 percent reduction in expenses is met.
7. Develop ways to increase the organization's revenues so that no employees must be laid off.

While alternative 7 is most attractive, it may not be realistic given the current economic situation. Unfortunately, we all know of organizations that have used options 5 and 6. While no other alternative may be the ideal one to solve this unpleasant problem, at least the office supervisor has considered several alternatives before making a decision. Remember, a decision is only as good as the best alternative identified.

## BRAINSTORMING AND CREATIVE PROBLEM SOLVING

When enough time is available, a supervisor should meet with a group of other supervisors or employees to brainstorm alternatives to a perplexing problem. Through the free flow of ideas in a group, with judgment suspended, the group should set out to identify as many alternatives as possible. Using this technique, the supervisor presents the problem, and the participants offer as many alternative solutions as they can in the time available. Any idea is acceptable—even one that may at first appear to be wild or unusual. Evaluation of ideas is suspended so that participants can give free rein to their creativity.

Of course, brainstorming requires an atmosphere that encourages creativity. When supervisors are unwilling to devote sufficient time to brainstorming, or

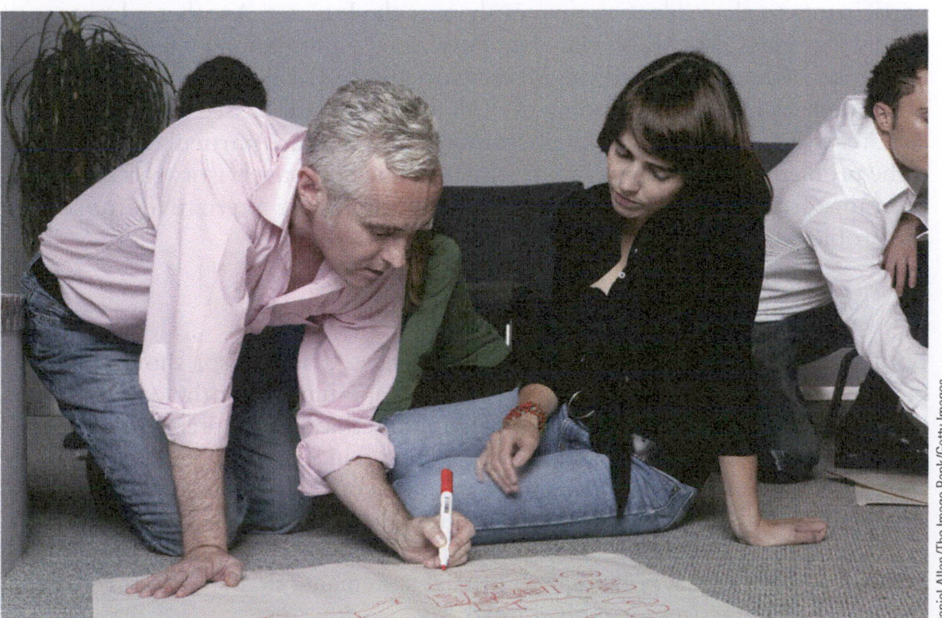

Daniel Allan/The Image Bank/Getty Images

*Using brainstorming, the supervisor presents the problem and the participants offer as many solutions as they can in the time available*

when supervisors try to dominate the process with their own opinions and solutions, the brainstorming effort is likely to fail.

Alex Osborn, an authority on creativity and brainstorming, suggests the following four guidelines for effective brainstorming:

1. Defer all judgment of ideas. During brainstorming, allow no criticism by the group. People suppress ideas consciously and subconsciously, and this tendency must be avoided. Even if an idea seems impractical and useless, it should not be rejected because rejection could inhibit the free flow of more ideas.
2. Seek many ideas. Idea fluency is the key to creative problem solving, and fluency means quantity. The more ideas that are generated, the more likely some ideas will be viable.
3. Encourage freewheeling. Being creative calls for a free-flowing mental process in which all ideas, no matter how extreme, are welcome. Even the wildest idea may, on further analysis, have some usefulness.
4. "Hitchhike" on existing ideas. Combining, adding to, and rearranging ideas often produce new approaches that are superior to the original ones. When creative thought processes slow down or stop, review some of the existing ideas and try to hitchhike on them with additions or revisions.[9]

The preceding guidelines apply to both individual and group brainstorming. When it involves a large group, unstructured brainstorming can become long, tedious, and unproductive because many ideas are simply not feasible and because conflicts may develop. The **nominal group technique (NGT)** involves having group members first write down their ideas and their alternatives to the problem. Then, group members share, discuss, evaluate, and refine their ideas. The group's final choice(s) may be made by a series of confidential votes in which a list of ideas is narrowed until consensus is attained.[10]

**Nominal group technique (NGT)**
A group brainstorming and decision-making process by which individual members first identify alternative solutions privately and then share, evaluate, and decide on an approach as a group

It may not be feasible or convenient to get employees together, and the manager may prefer to use the **electronic brainstorming system (EBS)**. EBS allows participants to share ideas anonymously over the Internet. Another advantage of EBS is that ideas may be evaluated and discussed without going face to face with the person who introduced the ideas. Proponents of EBS claim that this technique reduces many of the problems of brainstorming discussed above.[11]

**Electronic brainstorming system (EBS)**
Using technology to share and evaluate ideas

Creative approaches and **brainstorming** meetings are particularly adaptable if the problem is new, important, or strategic. Even the supervisor who takes time to brainstorm a problem alone is likely to develop more alternatives for solving the problem than one who does not brainstorm.

**Brainstorming**
A free flow of ideas in a group, while suspending judgment, aimed at developing many alternative solutions to a problem

## ETHICAL CONSIDERATIONS

Both when developing and evaluating alternatives, a supervisor should consider only those alternatives that are lawful and acceptable within the organization's ethical guidelines. Recall from our discussion of ethics in Chapter 5 that supervisors' decisions should also demonstrate strong ethical values for their employees. In recent years, many firms have become concerned that their managers, supervisors, and employees make ethical decisions because they recognize that, in the long term, good ethics is good business.[12] Consequently, many firms have developed handbooks, policies, and official statements that specify their ethical standards and practices, or **ethical "tests."**[13]

**Ethical "tests"**
Considerations or guidelines to be addressed in developing and evaluating ethical aspects of decision alternatives

The following guidelines for decision making are not comprehensive, but they are relevant when addressing the ethical aspects of most problem situations.

- *Legal/compliance test*: Laws, regulations, and policies are to be followed, not broken or ignored. The rationale and explanation that "everybody's doing it" and "everybody's getting away with it" are poor excuses if you get caught violating a law, policy, or regulation. If in doubt, ask for guidance from someone who knows the law or regulation. However, compliance should be only a starting point in most ethical decision making.
- *Public knowledge test*: What would be the consequences if the outcome of an alternative decision became known to the public, one's family, the media, or a government agency?
- *Long-term consequences test*: What would be the long-term versus short-term outcomes? Weigh these outcomes against each other.
- *Examine-your-motives test*: Do the motives for a proposed decision benefit the company and others, or are they primarily selfish and designed to harm or destroy other people and their interests?
- *Inner-voice test*: This is the test of conscience and moral values that has been instilled. If something inside you says the choice is or may be wrong, it usually is. It is then prudent to look for a different and better alternative.
- *Fairness test*: Are the decision and corresponding actions fair to all concerned such as the various stakeholders? Will they be beneficial to all concerned? When in doubt about the impact of the decision on various stakeholder groups, check and recheck the process used to arrive at the decision.
- *The four-way test*: For Rotarians, this test serves as the foundation for their actions. (1) Is it the truth? (2) Is it fair to all concerned? (3) Will it build goodwill and better friendships? (4) Will it be beneficial to all concerned? We might want to keep this test in mind when we are confronted with a decision-making opportunity.[14]

It cannot be stressed enough that when supervisors believe an alternative is questionable or might be unacceptable within the firm's ethical policies, they should consult their managers, the human resources department, or other staff specialists who can provide guidance on how to proceed. Many firms have an ethics hotline where individuals can call to seek assistance when confronted with ethical dilemmas. We believe that employees should have access to safe and confidential channels to raise concerns about possible ethics violations. It is not enough to just have an ethics policy. Supervisors are responsible for ensuring that the company's ethical policies aren't just nice words posted in the company handbook; they must be words to live by.

## STEP 5: EVALUATE THE ALTERNATIVES

The ultimate purpose of decision making is to choose the course of action that will provide the greatest number of wanted and the smallest number of unwanted consequences. After developing alternatives, supervisors can mentally test each of them by imagining that each has already been put into effect. Supervisors should try to foresee the probable desirable and undesirable consequences of each alternative. By thinking alternatives through and appraising their consequences, supervisors can compare the desirability of choices.

The usual way to begin is to eliminate alternatives that do not meet the supervisor's decision criteria and ethical standards. The supervisor should evaluate how many of the most important criteria each alternative meets. The successful alternative is the one that satisfies or meets the largest number of criteria at the highest priority levels. Often, there is no clear choice.

The supervisor is frequently required to choose a course of action without complete information about the situation. Because of this uncertainty, the chosen alternative may not yield the intended results, and, as a result, there is risk involved. Some supervisors consider the risk and uncertainty of each course of action. There is no such thing as a risk-free decision; one alternative may simply involve less risk than others.[15]

Time may make one alternative preferable, particularly if a difference exists between how much time is available and how much time is required to carry out an alternative. The supervisor should consider the available facilities, tools, and other resources. It is also critical to judge alternatives in terms of economy of effort and resources. In other words, which action will give the greatest benefits and results for the least cost and effort?

When one alternative clearly appears to provide a greater number of desirable consequences and fewer unwanted consequences than any other alternatives, the decision is fairly easy. However, the best alternative is not always so obvious. At times, two or more alternatives may seem equally desirable. Here, the choice may become a matter of personal preference. It is also possible that the supervisor may feel that no single alternative is significantly better than any other. In this case, it might be possible to combine the positive aspects of the better alternatives into one composite solution.

Sometimes, no alternatives are satisfactory; all have too many undesirable effects, or none will bring about the desired results. In such a case, the supervisor should begin to think of new alternative solutions or perhaps even start all over again by attempting to redefine the problem.

A situation might arise in which the undesirable consequences of all alternatives appear to be so overwhelmingly unfavorable that the supervisor feels the best solution is to take no action. However, this may be deceiving because taking no action does not solve the problem. Taking no action is as much a decision as is taking another action, even though the supervisor may believe an unpleasant choice has been avoided. The supervisor should visualize the consequences that are likely to result from taking no action. Only if the consequences of taking no action are the most desirable should it be selected as the appropriate course.

## STEP 6: SELECT THE BEST ALTERNATIVE

**Optimizing**
Selecting the best alternative

**Satisficing**
Selecting the alternative that meets the minimal decision criteria

Selecting the alternative that seems best is known as **optimizing**. However, the supervisor sometimes makes a **satisficing** decision, selecting an alternative that meets the minimal decision criteria. A famous management theorist, Herbert Simon, once likened the difference to finding a needle in a haystack (satisficing) and finding the biggest, sharpest needle in the haystack (optimizing).[16] Nevertheless, after developing and evaluating alternatives, the supervisor must make a choice.

Among the most prominent bases for choosing the best alternative are experience, intuition, advice, experimentation, and statistical and quantitative decision making. Regardless of the process, a supervisor rarely makes a decision that pleases everyone equally.

ColorBlind Images/Comet/Corbis

*A manager rarely makes a decision that pleases everyone*

## EXPERIENCE

When selecting from alternatives, the supervisor should rely on experience. Certain situations will recur, and the adage, "Experience is the best teacher," applies to a certain extent. A supervisor can often decide wisely based on personal experience or the experience of some other manager. Knowledge gained from experience is a helpful guide, and its importance should not be underestimated. On the other hand, it is dangerous to follow experience blindly.

When looking to experience as a basis for choosing among alternatives, the supervisor should examine the situation and the conditions that prevailed at the time of the earlier decision. It may be that conditions are nearly identical to those that prevailed on the previous occasion and that the decision should be similar to the one made then. More often than not, however, conditions change considerably, and the underlying assumptions change. Therefore, the new decision probably should not be identical to the earlier one.

Experience can be helpful when supervisors are called on to substantiate their reasons for making certain decisions. In part, this may be a defense, but there is no excuse for following experience in and of itself. Experience must always be viewed with the future in mind. The circumstances of the past, the present, and the future must be considered realistically if experience is to help supervisors select from alternatives.

## INTUITION

At times, supervisors base their decisions on intuition. Some supervisors even appear able to solve problems by subjective means.[17] However, a deeper search usually reveals that the so-called intuition on which the supervisor appeared to have based a decision was really experience or knowledge stored in the supervisor's memory. By recalling similar situations that occurred in the past, supervisors may be better able to reach decisions, even though they label doing so as having hunches.

Intuition may be particularly helpful when other alternatives have been tried with poor results. If the risks are not too great, a supervisor may choose a new alternative because of an intuitive feeling that a fresh approach might bring positive results. Even if the hunch does not work out well, the supervisor has tried something different. Supervisors will remember doing so and can draw upon those experiences in future decisions.

## ADVICE FROM OTHERS

Although a supervisor cannot shift personal responsibility for making decisions in the department, the burden of decision making often can be eased by seeking the advice of others. The ideas and suggestions of employees, other supervisors, staff experts, technical authorities, and the supervisor's own manager can be of great help in weighing facts and information. Seeking advice does not mean avoiding a decision because the supervisor still must decide whether to accept the advice of others.

Many believe that two heads are better than one and that input from others improves the decision process.[18] The following four guidelines can help the supervisor decide whether groups should be included in the decision-making process:

1. If additional information would increase the quality of the decision, involve those who can provide that information.
2. If acceptance of the decision is critical, involve those whose acceptance is important.
3. If people's skills can be developed through participation, involve those who need the development opportunity.
4. If the situation is not life-threatening and does not require immediate action, involve others in the process.[19]

Generally, the varied perspectives and experiences of others add to the decision-making process.

## EXPERIMENTATION

In the scientific world, where many conclusions are based on tests in laboratories, experimentation is essential and accepted. In supervision, however, experimentation is often too costly in terms of people, time, and materials. Nevertheless, in some instances a limited amount of testing and experimenting is advisable. For example, a supervisor may find it worthwhile to try several different locations for a new copy machine in the department to see which location employees prefer and which location is most convenient for the workflow. There also are instances in which a certain amount of testing is advisable to allow employees to try new ideas or approaches, perhaps of their own design. While experimentation may be valid from a motivational standpoint, it can be a slow and relatively expensive method of reaching a decision.

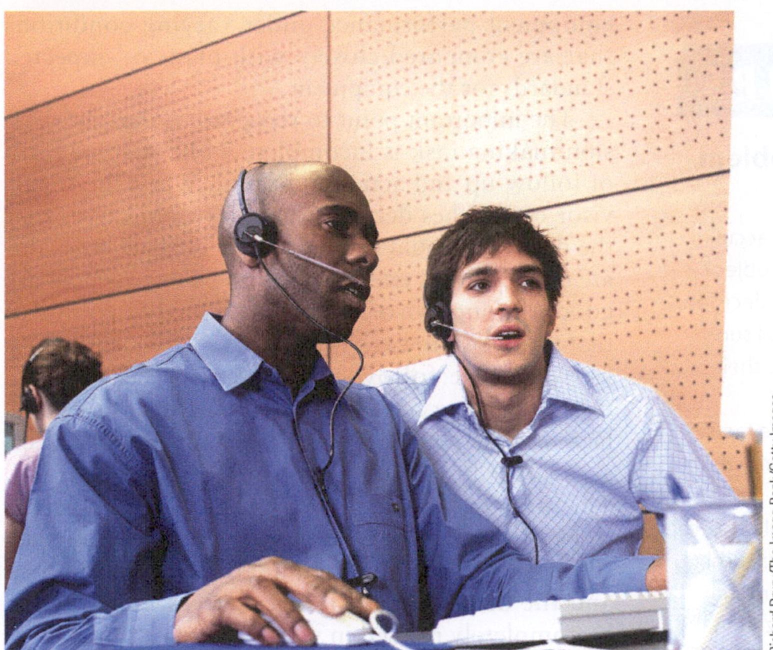

Richard Drury/The Image Bank/Getty Images

*In decision making, two heads can be better than one*

## QUANTITATIVE DECISION MAKING

Numerous quantitative techniques and models are available for helping managers improve the quality of their decision making. Decision trees, operations research, payback analysis, probability, and simulation models are but a few of these tools.[20] They require the decision maker to quantify most of the information that is relevant to a decision. But one desirable feature of quantitative decision making is the ability of the user to perform what if scenarios—the simulations of business situations over and over using different data for select decision areas.

For many supervisors, these quantitative decision-making techniques are not practical. For example, the decision that the pharmacy manager, Brey Yancey, needs to make in the You Make the Call! feature of this chapter cannot be made using statistical or quantitative models.

## STEP 7: FOLLOW UP AND APPRAISE THE RESULTS

After a decision has been made, specific actions are necessary to carry out that decision. Follow-up and appraisal of a decision's outcome are part of decision making.

Follow-up and appraisal of a decision can take many forms, depending on the decision, timing, costs, standards, personnel, and other factors. For example, a minor production-scheduling decision could be evaluated easily based on a short written report or perhaps even by the supervisor's observation or a discussion with employees. In contrast, a major decision involving the installation of complex new equipment requires close and time-consuming follow-up by the supervisor, technical employees, and high-level managers. This type of decision usually requires the supervisor to prepare numerous detailed, written reports of

## SUPERVISORY TIPS

### Suggestions for Improving Problem Solving and Decision Making

1. Take enough time to state the problem accurately and concisely and to identify the objectives you want to accomplish with your decision.
2. Whenever appropriate, seek opinions and suggestions from others who can contribute their ideas toward solving the problem.
3. Before deciding what to do, gather ample facts and information that will help define/clarify the problem and suggest solutions.
4. Stretch your mind to develop numerous alternative solutions; brainstorm with others when practical.
5. Make your decision based on objective criteria; avoid letting personal biases and organizational political considerations direct your choice.
6. When implementing and following up on your decision, do not hesitate to admit and rectify errors in the decision, even if doing so causes some personal embarrassment. (Admitting mistakes early is prudent and builds your integrity with others.)

equipment performance under varying conditions that are compared closely with plans or expected standards for the equipment.

The important point to recognize is that the decision-making task is incomplete without some form of follow-up and action appraisal. When the supervisor establishes decision criteria or objectives that the decision should accomplish, it is easier to evaluate the decision's effects. When the consequences are good, the supervisor can feel reasonably confident that the decision was sound.

When the follow-up and appraisal indicate that something has gone wrong or that the results have not been as anticipated, the supervisor's decision-making process must begin all over again. This may even mean going back over each of the steps of the decision-making process in detail. The supervisor's definition and analysis of the problem and the development of alternatives may have to be completely revised in view of new circumstances surrounding the problem. In other words, when follow-up and appraisal indicate that the problem has not been solved, the supervisor should treat the situation as a completely new problem and go through the decision-making process from a completely fresh perspective. See the accompanying Supervisory Tips box for some specific suggestions for improving your decision-making process.

**3 Identify and describe various decision-making styles.**

## Decision-Making Styles

Decision making is influenced by many forces, making it difficult to formulate a simple to-do checklist that applies to every situation in the same way. Earlier in this chapter, we stressed that when supervisors are faced with complex, unusual, or new problems, they must use good judgment, intuition, and creativity in the decision-making process. What processes do managers actually use when making decisions? We know from observing others and our own experiences that people make decisions differently. We have observed the two extremes: some people are like the "waffler" (see Team Skill Builder 8-2) who takes forever to study the problem and never makes a decision, while others like the "gunner" pull the trigger (fire-aim-ready) quickly, and if things don't go the intended way, they fire again and again until they hit the target (achieve the intended results).

We feel it is important for supervisors to know that different types of decisions require different decision-making styles. Supervisors are continually being asked to make decisions, and how they make those decisions is under constant scrutiny. Supervisors have many people looking over their shoulders, not necessarily to get their cues on how to make decisions but to criticize the decisions made. What can we learn from the decisions that we made earlier in our careers? How many times have you heard someone say, "If I had been in that situation, I would have done . . ." Our current scientific method focuses almost exclusively on identifying what worked best or what went wrong. Few have studied the decision-making process. When asked to think of words that describe one's decision-making process, what comes to mind?

Relying heavily on the social styles model, Mike Lynch and Harvey Lifton developed the decision-making styles model to describe how people make decisions. Think of the most recent major purchase that you or someone in your family made. What process did you or they go through to make the final decision? To help you analyze your decision-making style, see Figure 8.7.

**FIGURE 8.7 What is your decision-making style?**

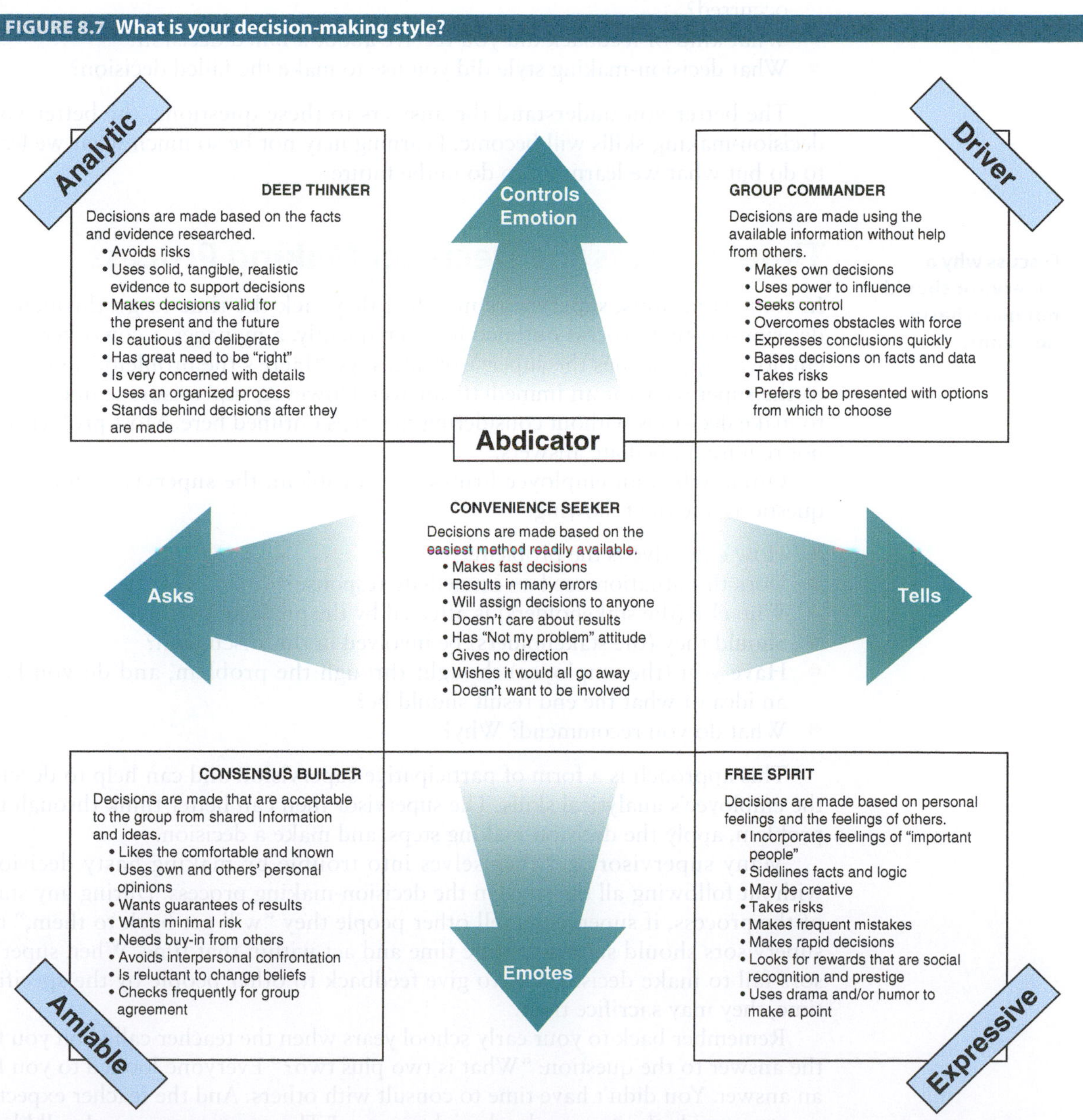


*Source:* Reprinted from *Training Clips: 150 Reproducible Handouts, Discussion Starters*, and Job Aids, by Mike Lynch and Harvey Lifton, copyright © 1998. Reprinted by permission of the publisher: HRD Press, Amherst, MA (800-822-2801), http://www.hrdpress.com.

To assist you in understanding how you make decisions, look back at your recent decisions. Analyze them from the following perspectives:

- What worked?
- What actually happened as a result of the decision?
- What kind of feedback did you receive about the success of a decision?
- What style did you use to make the successful decision?
- What didn't work?
- Why didn't it work?
- How much tweaking did you have to do to make it work?
- What caused the differences between the intended outcome and what actually occurred?
- What kind of feedback did you receive about a failed decision?
- What decision-making style did you use to make the failed decision?

The better you understand the answers to these questions, the better your decision-making skills will become. Learning may not be so much what we learn to do but what we learn not to do in the future.

**4 Discuss why a supervisor should not make hasty decisions.**

## Time Impacts the Decision-Making Process

In some situations, supervisors may feel they lack the time to go through the decision-making process outlined here. Frequently, a manager, a coworker, or an employee approaches the supervisor and says, "Here's the problem," and looks to the supervisor for an immediate answer. However, supervisors cannot afford to make decisions without considering the steps outlined here. Most problems do not require immediate answers.

Often, when an employee brings up a problem, the supervisor should ask questions like the following:

- How extensive is the problem?
- Does the situation need an immediate response?
- Who else (the stakeholders) is affected by the problem?
- Should they (the stakeholders) be involved in this discussion?
- Have you (the employee) thought through the problem, and do you have an idea of what the end result should be?
- What do you recommend? Why?

This approach is a form of participative supervision and can help to develop the employee's analytical skills. The supervisor then can better think through the problem, apply the decision-making steps, and make a decision.

Many supervisors get themselves into trouble by making hasty decisions without following all the steps in the decision-making process. During any stage of the process, if supervisors tell other people they "will get back to them," the supervisors should state a specific time and act within that time. When supervisors fail to make decisions or to give feedback to other people by the specified time, they may sacrifice trust.

Remember back to your early school years when the teacher called on you for the answer to the question: "What is two plus two?" Everyone looked to you for an answer. You didn't have time to consult with others. And the teacher expected you to provide the "one and only right answer." The pressure was on. In all likelihood, you paused, gathered your wits, thought of the alternatives, drew a deep breath, and answered "Four!" How did you feel? The joy that comes from doing the right thing at the right time is priceless. Even if you had given the incorrect answer, you would have learned "what not to do in the future."

## Introducing Change

**5 Suggest approaches for introducing change to employees and for proposing changes to higher-level managers.**

Often when a decision is made by a leader or a supervisor, that decision will indicate that a change is imminent in the department or the whole organization. Change is expected as part of life, and the survival and growth of most enterprises depend on change and innovation. Many books and articles have been written concerning the imperatives for change faced by most organizations. Indeed, the survival of a firm may depend on the abilities of its managers to make fundamental changes in virtually all aspects of operations while facing the risks of an uncertain future. The impact of change has become so common that security and stability are often concepts and practices related to the past.[21]

We are all familiar with planned change. For example, at some point in the term, students will start planning their schedules for the next term. After having met with their advisers, they may have a list of four courses they need to take to finish the degree. Two of those are required courses, and the others are electives. Now imagine they browse through the course schedule to find when those two required courses are offered, and discover that one of the courses they need to complete the degree requirements is not being offered next term. They didn't plan on that. Their blood pressure rises, and their frustration level increases. Why? Because they did not anticipate this situation. **Unplanned change** comes as a result of circumstances beyond our control. For example, a hurricane hits the Gulf Coast and destroys your manufacturing plant; a competitor launches a new product that makes your best-seller obsolete; or a colleague or close friend dies unexpectedly. As mentioned in Chapter 3, we can have a crisis plan in place, but only minimal precautions can be taken. The student's situation discussed above presents a new challenge along with fears—the fear of not being able to graduate at the end of next term. Then they pause, collect their thoughts, and ponder a strategy for coping with the unexpected situation.

**Unplanned change**
An unexpected situation causes you to initiate a strategy for change

*People don't resist change—they resist being changed*

Bruce Laurance/The Image Bank/Getty Images

### MAKING CHANGE MEANS SUPERVISORY INVOLVEMENT

Despite the emphasis on change, there still appear to be numerous problems and considerable resentment concerning both the introduction and effects of many organizational changes. There is an adage that says, "All progress is change, but not all change is progress." In some cases this is true, particularly when managers identify problems, initiate change, then look for a quick response in their organizations, and they become frustrated when expected results are not achieved. Mediocrity is then tolerated, and the net result is that the more things have changed, the more they have stayed the same. Conversely, well-performing organizations can potentially exist for years without making any changes, but they run the risk of eroding employee motivation and effectiveness as organizational silos, departmental routines, and entrenched interests begin to weigh down organizational processes. In situations like this, restructuring business units or employees' responsibilities can energize a stagnant company.[22] These contrasting perspectives reinforce that supervisors *must* consider the pervasiveness of change in organizations, the goals of change, and its impact on employees, bringing to mind another adage we can translate to the organizational context, "Change is the only constant."

Our focus in the remaining part of this chapter is not on comprehensive strategies for total organizational change,[23] but rather on the introduction and management of change from the supervisory perspective. This is another challenging aspect of a supervisor's leading function of management. As with so many other areas of concern, the introduction of change, such as a new work method, a new product, a new schedule, or a new human resources policy, usually requires implementation at the departmental level. In the final analysis, whether a change has been initiated by upper management or by the supervisor personally, it is the supervisor who has the major role in effecting change. The success or failure of any change is usually related to a supervisor's ability to anticipate and deal with the causes of resistance to change.

## REASONS FOR RESISTANCE TO CHANGE

Some supervisors are inclined to discount the existence and magnitude of human resistance to change. What may seem like a trifling change to the supervisor may bring a strong reaction from employees. Supervisors should remember that employees seldom resist change just to be stubborn. They resist because they believe a change threatens their positions socially, psychologically, or economically. Therefore, the supervisor should be familiar with the ways in which resistance to change can be minimized and handled successfully.

Most people pride themselves on being up to date. As consumers, they expect and welcome changes in material goods such as automobiles, convenience items, electronic appliances, and computers. As employees, however, they may resist changes on the job or changes in personal relationships, even though such changes are vital for the operation of the organization. If an organization is to survive, it must be able to react to prevailing conditions by adjusting.

Change disturbs the environment in which people exist. Employees become accustomed to a work environment in which patterns of relationships and behavior have stabilized. When a change takes place, new ideas and new methods may be perceived as a threat to the security of the work group. Many employees fear change because they cannot predict what the change will mean in terms of their positions, activities, or abilities (Figure 8.8). It makes no difference whether the change actually has a negative result. What matters is that the employees believe that the change will have negative consequences. For example, the introduction of new equipment is usually accompanied by employee fears of losing jobs or skills. Even if the supervisor and higher-level managers announce that no employees will be laid off, rumors circulate that layoffs will occur or that jobs will be downgraded. Employee fears may still be present months after the change.

Change affects individuals in different ways. Remember that a change that greatly disturbs one person may create only a small problem for another, while it may actually inspire or energize some. A supervisor must learn to recognize how changes affect different employees and observe how individuals develop patterns of behavior that serve as barriers to accepting change.

**FIGURE 8.8 Many people fear change because they cannot predict what the change will mean in terms of their future in the organization**

## OVERCOMING RESISTANCE TO CHANGE

Probably the most important factor in gaining employee acceptance of new ideas and methods is the relationship between the supervisor who is introducing the change and the employees who are affected by it. If the relationship has confidence and trust, employees are more likely to accept the change.[24] This relates to our earlier discussion of trust and its role in reducing employees' fear of change. If a supervisor has regularly interacted with employees with constancy, caring, candor, and competence, all of which lead to a trusting relationship, employees are more likely to proceed confidently with the directives they are given because they will trust that the change being proposed will be facilitated with those same virtues.

## PROVIDING ADEQUATE INFORMATION

In the final analysis, it is not the change itself that usually leads to resistance, but rather the way the supervisor introduces the change. Resistance to change, when it comes from fear of the unknown, can be minimized by supplying all the information employees consciously and subconsciously need to know. Presenting employees with the vision, or idealized picture of the future once a change is fully implemented, can help supervisors introduce change. In a study of the reactions of 102 employees to organization-wide restructuring, most employees tended to adapt more readily to the change and became proactive in the change process when supervisors shared a clear, compelling view of the future and how it would be different.[25]

Whenever possible, a supervisor should explain what will happen, why it will happen, and how the employees and the department will be affected by the change. If applicable, the supervisor should emphasize how the change will leave employees no worse off or how it may even improve their present situation. This information should be communicated as early as appropriate to all employees who are directly or indirectly involved, either individually or collectively. Only then can employees assess what a change will mean in terms of their activities. This result will be facilitated if the supervisor has made consistent efforts to give ample background information for all directives.

Robert H. Miles warns that the information dissemination process must take place rapidly and sequentially throughout all levels of an organization once a change is announced in order to get all employees to accept and commit to the initiative. He describes a global semiconductor company that spent three months equipping top management to execute a change and then sent an HR team out for five days to train 50,000 employees across the globe. It wasn't until two years later that all employees had participated in the engagement, alignment, and commitment follow-up program. By that time, the company had already started the next phase of the transformation, while many employees still weren't quite sure how they were supposed to engage to the first phase. Miles suggests that organizations **cascade** key information and skills related to the change, a process in which employees at all levels of the organization are rapidly engaged with their direct supervisors in education, training, and the establishment of clear line-of-sight accountability for change processes and tasks. In his second example, Miles described a 40,000-employee organization that was educated, engaged, and committed in less than a month to a transformation that was successfully rolled out to 800 stores simultaneously, crediting the cascade process for building employee buy-in and capacity.[26]

**Cascade**
Rapidly engaging supervisors and employees at all levels of an organization in education, training, and the establishment of clear accountability for change processes and tasks

Employees who are well acquainted with the underlying factors of departmental operations usually understand the need for change. They will probably question a change, but they then can adjust to that change and go on. When employees have been informed of the reasons for a change, what to expect, and how their jobs will be affected, they usually make reasonable adaptations. Instead of insecurity, they feel relatively confident and willing to comply.

A change that involves closing certain operations and losing jobs should be explained openly and frankly. It is especially important to discuss which employees are likely to be affected and how the job cuts will be made. If higher-level managers have decided not to identify which individuals will be terminated until it actually happens, the supervisor should explain this as a reality and not try to hide behind vague promises or to raise unrealistic expectations.[27]

## ENCOURAGING PARTICIPATION IN DECISION MAKING

Another technique for reducing resistance to change is to permit the affected employees to share in making decisions about the change. If several employees are involved in a change, group decision making is an effective way to reduce their fears and objections. When employees have an opportunity to work through new ideas and methods from the beginning, usually they will consider the new directives as something of their own making and will give those changes their support. The group may even apply pressure on those who have reservations about going along with the change, and it is likely that each member of the group will carry out the change once there is agreement on how to proceed. According to organizational anthropologist Judith Glasser, "When successful change occurs, employees feel like *authors* not *objects* of change. They feel fully invested, accountable and energetic about the future, regardless of challenges."[28]

Group decision making is especially effective when the supervisor is indifferent about the details of the change. In these cases, the supervisor must set limits for the group. For example, a supervisor may not care how a new departmental

Masterfile

*Employee involvement and empowerment are the keys to overcoming resistance to change*

work schedule is divided among the group as long as the work is accomplished within a prescribed time, with a given number of employees, and without overtime.

Change affects every aspect of what the organization does and how it does it. Typically, employee responses to changes taking place in the organization have been lukewarm at best. Figure 8.9 provides a guide for supervisors to use to help overcome the barriers to change.

## PROPOSING CHANGE TO HIGH-LEVEL MANAGERS

In many organizations, high-level managers complain that supervisors are too content with the status quo and are unwilling to suggest new and innovative ways to improve departmental performance. Supervisors, on the other hand, complain that higher-level managers are not receptive to ideas they suggest for their departments. There is probably some truth to both allegations. In Chapter 9, we discussed the concept of the learning organization. Author Peter Senge says that big companies that wish to succeed must start acting like gardeners: "I have never seen a successful organizational-learning program rolled out from the top. Not a single one. Conversely, every change process that I've seen that was sustained and that spread has started small. Just as nothing in nature starts big, start creating change with a pilot group—a growth seed."[29]

It should be clear that top management's job is to pollinate those seeds (ideas) and help them to bear fruit. Unfortunately, that is not the way it works. If supervisors wish to propose changes, it is important that they understand how to present ideas not only to their employees, but to higher-level managers as well. "Selling" an idea to a manager involves the art of persuasion, much as a good salesperson uses persuasion to sell a product or service to a reluctant customer. What do I really do about my boss, if he or she is a tough sell? Cartoonist Scott Adams of *Dilbert* fame makes the following suggestion:

FIGURE 8.9 Overcoming the barriers to change

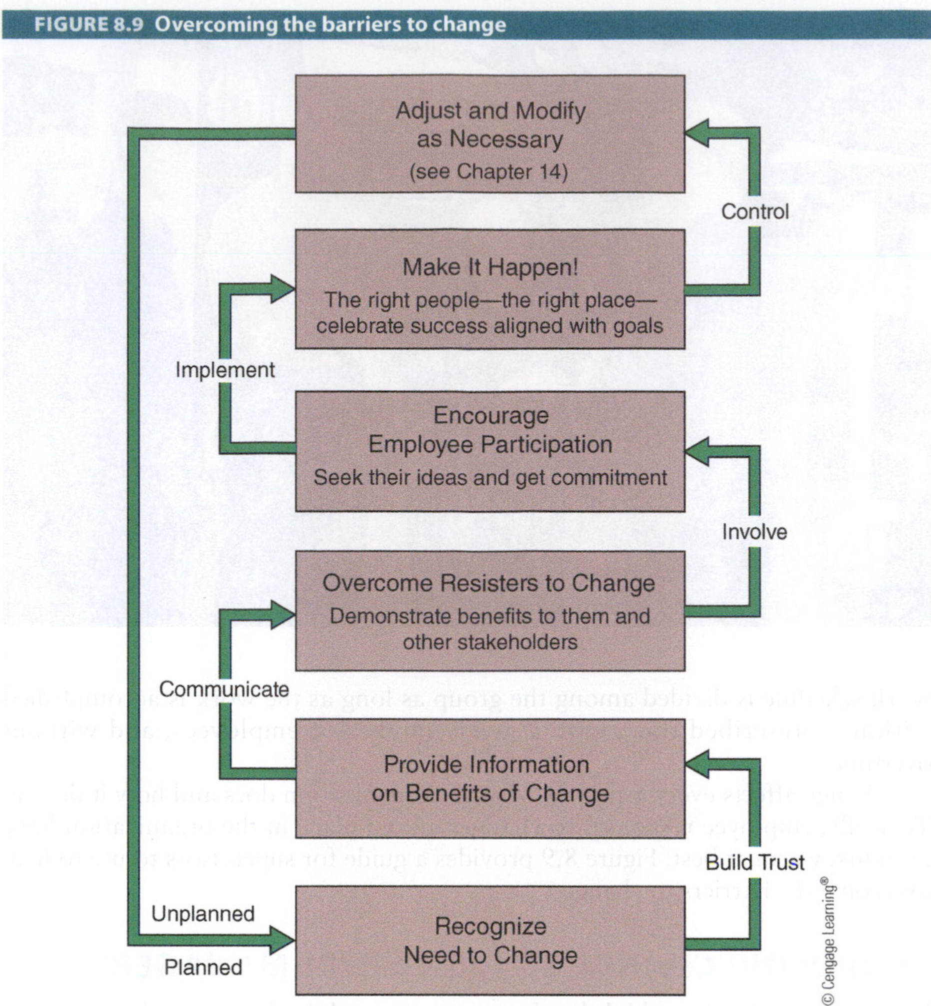


> *Whatever you do, never use the so-called direct approach: "I have an idea. Let's do this." Dilbert would take exactly that approach because he's an engineer and totally ignorant of the human condition. But the only way that a boss will respond to a reasonable suggestion is unreasonably—like with some of those great-idea-sinker questions: "If this is such a good idea, why isn't everybody doing it?" Or, "Have you asked everybody in the organization—all 1,000 of them—to buy into your idea?" The worst thing you can do is assume that your boss is a thoughtful person who will immediately recognize a good idea and take a personal risk to implement it. Instead, I suggest using the hypnosis approach. Lead your boss to your idea through subtle questioning—giving the impression that it was his idea in the first place.*[30]

As unlikely as it may seem, at times the supervisor must use various strategies to convince the boss that a proposal was the boss's idea.

## OBTAINING NEEDED INFORMATION

A supervisor who has a good idea or who wishes to suggest a change should first ask, "What aspects of the idea or change will be of most interest to the boss?" Higher-level managers usually are interested if a change might improve production, increase sales and profits, improve morale, or reduce overhead and other costs. It is important to do considerable homework to see whether a proposed change is feasible and adaptable to the departmental operation. By thinking through the idea carefully and getting as much information as possible, the supervisor will be better positioned to argue strong and weak points of the proposal. In addition, the supervisor should find out whether any other departments or organizations have used the proposed idea—successfully or unsuccessfully. The manager will be impressed that the supervisor has invested time and effort to investigate the best practices of other organizations.

## CONSULTING WITH OTHER SUPERVISORS

To get an idea or a proposal beyond the discussion stage, the supervisor should consult with other supervisors and personnel who might be affected and get their reactions to the proposed change. Checking an idea out with them gives them a chance to think the idea through, offer suggestions and criticisms, and work out some of the problems. Otherwise, some supervisors may resist or resent the change if they feel they have been ignored.

If possible, it is helpful to get the tentative commitment of other supervisors. It is not always necessary to obtain total approval, but higher-level managers will be more inclined to consider an idea if it has been discussed at least in preliminary form with knowledgeable people in the organization.

## FORMAL WRITTEN PROPOSAL

At times, a manager may ask a supervisor to put a proposed idea in writing so that copies may be forwarded to higher-level managers, other supervisors, or other personnel. This requires effort. The supervisor may have to engage in considerable study outside of normal working hours to obtain all the needed information. Relevant information on costs, prices, productivity data, and the like should be included in the proposal, even if some data are only educated guesses. Highly uncertain estimates should be labeled as tentative, and exaggerated claims and opinions should be avoided. Risks, as well as potential advantages, should be acknowledged in the formal proposal.

## FORMAL PRESENTATION

If a supervisor is asked to formally present the proposal, ample planning and preparation are required (see the tips presented in Chapter 5 for managing up). The presentation should be made thoroughly and unhurriedly, allowing sufficient time for questions and discussion.

A supervisor who has carefully thought through an idea should be unafraid to express it in a firm and convincing manner. The supervisor should be enthusiastic in explaining the idea, but at the same time should be patient and empathetic with those who may not agree with it. A helpful technique in a formal presentation is to use some type of chart, diagram, or visual aid.

## ACCEPTANCE OR REJECTION OF CHANGE BY HIGH-LEVEL MANAGERS

A supervisor who can persuade higher-level managers and other supervisors to accept a proposed change will likely feel inner satisfaction. Of course, any good idea requires careful implementation, follow-up, and refinement. Rarely does a change follow the suggested blueprint. Following up and working out the problems with others are important aspects of making a change effective.

However, despite a supervisor's best efforts, an idea may be rejected, altered greatly, or shelved. This can be frustrating, particularly to supervisors who have worked diligently to develop ideas they believed would lead to positive results. The important thing is to avoid becoming discouraged and developing a negative outlook. There may be valid reasons for the rejection of an idea, or the timing may not have been right. A supervisor should resolve to try again and perhaps to further refine and polish the idea for resubmission.

A supervisor who has developed an idea for change, even if it has not been accepted, usually will find that higher-level managers appreciate such efforts. Moreover, the experience of having worked through a proposal for change will make the supervisor a more valuable member of the organizational team, and there will be many other opportunities to work for change.

**6 Understand the formula for organizational renewal.**

## A Formula for Organizational Renewal

We must accept the reality that organizations must change or die. Many organizations, like people, wait until they are near death before they recognize the need to make changes. Harvard professors Michael Tushman and Charles O'Reilly pointed out that "leading an organization is an ongoing process."[31] One of your authors has found that when he asks a business leader what his or her most formidable challenge is, the answer is usually, "Figuring out how to do a better job of doing what we are doing." Unfortunately, that answer is only partially right. Are they doing the right things that will position their organizations for tomorrow? Renewal requires doing the right thing today so that they are prepared to meet the challenges of tomorrow. In short, **organizational renewal** means that management must improve upon and sustain what they are doing today while creating processes for long-term success.

**Organizational renewal**
A continuous process for long-term success

Think of it this way. A good friend—let's call him Alex—goes to the doctor for his annual physical examination. You know that Alex is carrying a few extra pounds. When the two of you dine out, you always order smaller portions, but Alex orders the king-size portions. After conducting a series of tests, the doctor tells Alex that he must shed 30 or more pounds, take blood pressure medicine, and commence a rigorous, supervised exercise program. For the past several years, everyone could see that Alex was having problems, but he was either ignoring the reality or couldn't see it. The same is true for certain persons in leadership positions. Hopefully, Alex will be up to the challenge and will make the appropriate changes. It is difficult to do. Alex must be willing to accept the recommendations and implement the change strategy or suffer the consequences.

Throughout this chapter, we have discussed various leadership styles and methods for overcoming the barriers to change. The following section provides a conceptual framework of initiating and implementing the process of organizational renewal and the SKAs needed to accomplish it.

### RECOGNIZING THE NEED FOR RENEWAL: ONE ORGANIZATION'S QUEST FOR EXCELLENCE

Let's rewind to 1996. At that time, Jim Vickary was president of Baptist Health Care (the system) in Pensacola, Florida, and Al Stubblefield was president of Baptist Hospital, Inc. (the hospital). Vickary created a new position of executive vice president (of the system) and promoted Stubblefield, leaving the administrator position for the hospital open. Stubblefield recruited Quint Studer from Holy Cross Hospital in Chicago to replace him as administrator of Baptist Hospital.

When Studer arrived at Baptist Hospital in 1996, admissions were flat and patient satisfaction, as measured by a national survey, was slightly below average. Stubblefield had hired Studer to implement many of the organizational change tools that were developed during Studer's tenure at Holy Cross. The goal was to improve both patient and employee satisfaction. Studer refined those tools and developed others while at Baptist.[32]

Studer left Baptist Hospital, in 2000 and formed the Studer Group to take his methods of cultural change to other organizations. He now coaches other organizations on how to create a culture of excellence.[33] Jim Collins, author of *Good to Great*, wrote, "Great organizations benefiting from the Flywheel effect where the power of continued improvement and the delivery of results creates momentum."[34] The Studer Group developed the Healthcare Flywheel (see Figure 8.9) to help organizations understand their role in creating great places for employees to work, physicians to practice, and patients to receive care. Working in healthcare organizations for over 20 years and studying "the best of the best," Studer found that what motivates people is the accomplishment of desired results. By tying results back to purpose, worthwhile work, and making a difference, the organization is inspired to follow more prescriptive behaviors to achieve even greater results, thereby creating a self-perpetuating culture of excellence, fueled by the momentum of the flywheel.[35]

According to Studer, the beginning of the journey starts with a focus on the organization's core values. The five-pillar resources (Figure 8.10) serve as a

**FIGURE 8.10 A process for organizational renewal**[1]

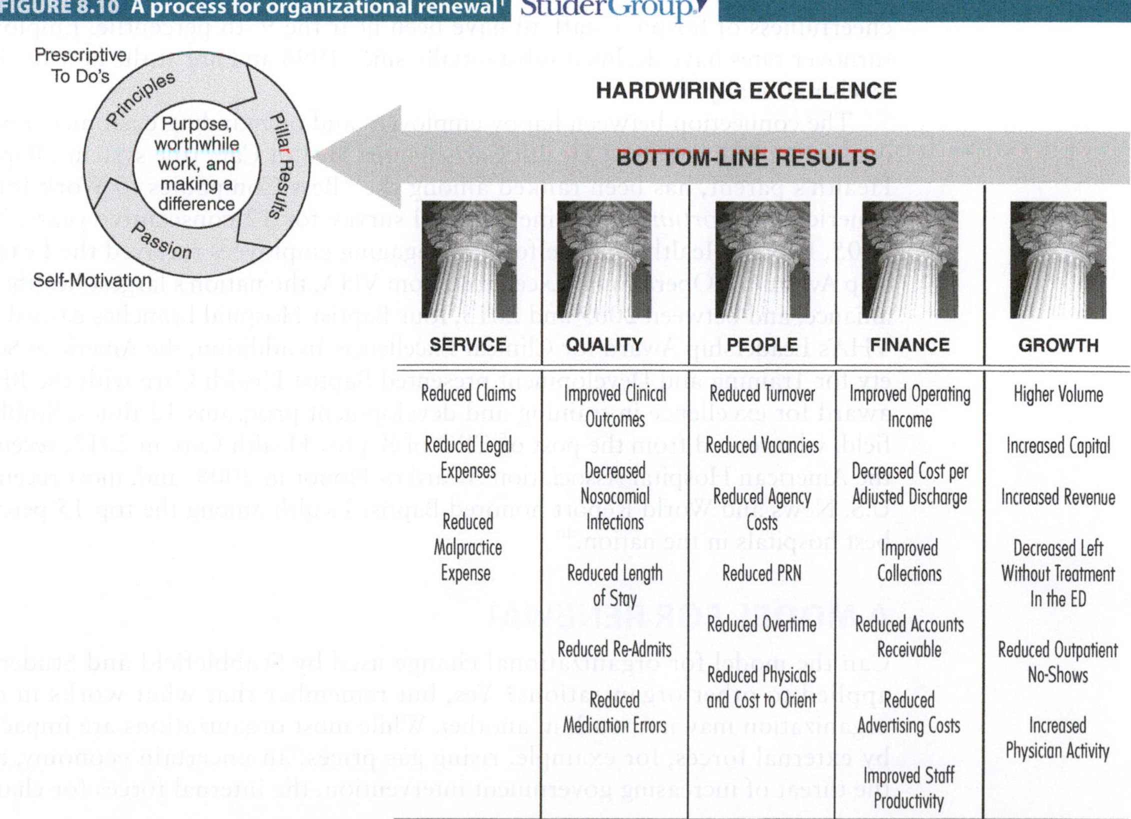


*Source:* Adapted from Hardwiring Excellence Copyright 2003, Studer Group, All Rights Reserved, Used with Permission.

starting point for establishing organizational objectives: service, quality, people, finance, and growth. Once objectives are set for each pillar, they are cascaded throughout, from division to department to unit to individual. These pillars then lay the metrics and framework for consistent evaluations. Studer suggests that additional pillars can be added to meet the uniqueness of a particular organization.[36]Studer believes that you create movement by connecting the dots to the hub so that people truly know they can make a difference. This allows organizations to implement initial changes.[37]

Among the true tests of leadership are (1) whether anyone follows and (2) the legacy the leader leaves. That is, what does the organization look like three years after they leave? At this point, you are probably wondering what has happened to Baptist Hospital, Inc. Did Studer leave a legacy? You be the judge.

The rest of the story: As of mid-2011, the Baptist Health Care system included four hospitals—Atmore Community Hospital, a 49-bed facility; Baptist Hospital, a 492-bed tertiary-care and referral hospital; Gulf Breeze, a 60-bed medical and surgical hospital; and Jay Hospital, a 55-bed facility—as well as Andrews Institute for Orthopaedics and Sports Medicine Baptist Manor, a 51-bed long-term skilled nursing and rehabilitation facility; Lakeview Center for residential and outpatient behavioral health, vocational, and child protective services; Baptist Medical Park, an ambulatory-care complex that delivers an array of outpatient and diagnostic services; and Baptist Leadership Group, a consulting practice that provides custom, individualized coaching, training, and learning resources for patient care facilities across the United States. During this century, patient satisfaction has been near or above the 99th percentile every quarter. Patient surveys of staff sensitivity, attitude, concern, and overall cheerfulness of hospital staff all have been near the 99th percentile. Employee turnover rates have declined substantially since 1996 and are at the best-in-class levels nationally.[38]

The connection between happy employees and outstanding customer service is most evident at Baptist Health Care. Baptist Health Care (the system), Baptist Health's parent, has been ranked among the "Best Companies to Work for in America" by *Fortune* magazine's annual survey for 12 consecutive years.[39] In 2005, Baptist Health Care's efforts in engaging employees received the Leadership Award for Operational Excellence from VHA, the nation's largest healthcare alliance, and between 2009 and 2013, four Baptist Hospital branches earned the VHA's Leadership Award for Clinical Excellence. In addition, the American Society for Training and Development presented Baptist Health Care with the BEST award for excellence in training and development programs 12 times; Stubblefield, who retired from the post of CEO of Baptist Health Care in 2012, received the American Hospital Association Award of Honor in 2008, and, most recently, U.S. News and World Report honored Baptist Health among the top 15 percent best hospitals in the nation.[40]

## A MODEL FOR RENEWAL

Can the model for organizational change used by Stubblefield and Studer be applied to other organizations? Yes, but remember that what works in one organization may not work in another. While most organizations are impacted by external forces, for example, rising gas prices, an uncertain economy, and the threat of increasing government intervention, the internal forces for change vary greatly. If we could look inside two organizations, we would find them to be very different. Each organization has its own culture. Managers vary in leadership styles and communication skills. Employees bring different values and SKAs to the workplace. Clearly, when the need for change is recognized, management will respond in radically different ways. Ordinarily, management may agree that change is needed but may have difficulty agreeing on the process to follow. To that end, we offer the following to point you in the right direction:

- Remember that as leader of the team, you are also a member of the team.
- Identify the issues confronting the organization.
- Analyze how those issues prevent goal attainment.
- Recognize the difference between needed change and change for the sake of change.
- Identify metrics that will be used to monitor and evaluate the change process.
- Communicate to and involve all who have a stake in the change.
- Understand what needs to be changed.
- Seek consensus, but recognize when to sacrifice unanimity for decisiveness.
- Confront the resisters to change.
- Establish clear targets.
- Take risks, experiment, and innovate.
- Spend money to develop (train) employees so they have the competencies to implement the change.
- Focus on the outcome(s).
- Monitor progress and make adjustments as necessary.
- Provide feedback and encouragement.
- Guarantee total commitment to organizational renewal—to be the "best of the best."
- Celebrate victories.

Noted leadership theorist John Kotter said, "Behavior change happens mostly by speaking to people's feelings."[41] Clearly, Studer and Stubblefield created passionate, empowered employees who made a difference in their organization and, ultimately, in the lives of those they serve.

## SUMMARY

**1.** **Everything we do revolves around the decisions we make. Supervisors like Lori, the college student, encounter many situations that force them to carefully analyze the available information and ponder various courses of action. Supervisors must find solutions for problems that result from changing situations and unusual circumstances. Decision making is a choice between two or more alternatives, and the decisions made by supervisors significantly affect departmental results.**

**Appreciative inquiry (AI) is a cooperative search for the best in people, their organizations, and the environment around them. At the heart of AI is asking questions.**

**Decision making is a skill that can be learned. Organizations are giving employees a more active role in decision making today. A decision made today often sets a precedent for decisions made tomorrow.**

**2.** **Better decisions are more likely to occur when supervisors follow these steps of the decision-making process:**

1. **Define the problem.**
2. **Gather facts and information and analyze the problem.**
3. **Establish decision criteria.**
4. **Develop a sufficient number of alternatives.**

5. Evaluate alternatives by using the decision criteria or by thinking of the alternatives as if they had already been placed into action and considering their consequences.
6. Select the alternative that has the greatest number of wanted consequences and the least number of unwanted consequences.
7. Implement, follow up, and appraise the results.

Corrective action may be necessary if the decision is not achieving the desired objective.

The supervisor should develop a problem statement that answers the questions of what, how, where, when, and who. Proper problem definition clarifies the difference between the way things are and the way they should be.

After defining the problem, the supervisor must gather information. Decision criteria, which are measures or standards of what the supervisor wants to accomplish with the decision, should be specified. In developing alternatives, supervisors can use brainstorming and creative thinking techniques.

Only alternatives that are lawful and ethical within the organization's guidelines should be considered. In the process of evaluation and choice, a supervisor can be aided by ethical guidelines, personal experience, intuition, advice, experimentation, and quantitative methods.

Once the decision has been made, specific actions are necessary to carry it out. Follow-up and appraisal are essential.

**3.** Supervisors constantly make decisions that vary in scope, complexity, and impact on stakeholders. Figure 8.7 is used to illustrate five decision-making styles: *abdicator, free spirit, amiable, analytic,* and *driver*. Most supervisors will use all of the styles depending on the complexity of the problem, who is involved, and how much time the supervisor has. The key to effectiveness is matching the appropriate style to the situation.

**4.** Supervisors risk getting themselves into trouble unless they follow the steps of the decision-making process, which is time-consuming. Most problems do not require immediate answers. It is often valuable to allow subordinates to help make decisions. They may see the problem from a different perspective, and they may have information that bears on the problem.

**5.** To cope with employees' normal resistance to change, supervisors must understand why resistance surfaces and what can be done to help employees adjust to and accept changes. Preparing employees for change by being open and honest, providing information and training early in the process, and encouraging participation in decision making will help employees take ownership of changes and make the transition more smoothly to new tasks and processes. A supervisor also should learn the principles of selling change to higher-level managers. Sometimes, supervisors may have to subtly convince their managers that changes were the managers' ideas. Regardless of the approach, the supervisor must persuade all affected personnel that accepting proposed change will benefit them and the organization.

**6.** Organizational renewal is a continuous process, often resulting from the synergy of leadership and change. Baptist Health Care serves as an example of how one organization consistently responds over time to the swiftly changing healthcare environment and effectively manages the changes necessary to achieve success. Striving for a culture of continuous improvement where employees understand their role is a critical component. The process is cyclical, beginning with setting objectives (the five pillars). Then metrics are established against which to measure progress. Once progress is made and measured, new objectives are set, based on internal and external changes, and the cycle of improvement continues. The implications for supervisors are that they need to fix the problems of today while focusing on where they want to be tomorrow.

## KEY TERMS

Appreciative inquiry (AI) (p. 285)
Brainstorming (p. 292)
Cascade (p. 304)
Decision criteria (p. 289)
Decision making (p. 285)
Decision-making process (p. 286)
Electronic brainstorming system (EBS) (p. 292)
Ethical "tests" (p. 292)
Fishbone technique (cause-and-effect diagram) (p. 289)
Nominal group technique (NGT) (p. 292)
Optimizing (p. 294)
Organizational renewal (p. 308)
Satisficing (p. 294)
Unplanned change (p. 301)

## WHAT HAVE YOU LEARNED?

1. Define the decision-making process. Why should supervisors write problem statements when defining the problem? What pitfalls should the supervisor avoid at each step of the process?
2. Think of a major decision you have made in your life. For example, why did you decide to go to college? Why did you choose the college you selected? How did you select a major? Explain how you applied the steps in the decision-making process. What factors might you have considered to have made a better choice?
3. "None of us is as smart as all of us." Think of a situation in which you would prefer to solve a problem in a group setting rather than by yourself. Why would you rather "not go it alone?"
   a. What are the advantages of involving others in the decision-making process? The disadvantages?
   b. Identify the major elements in the brainstorming approach.
4. Define and discuss the factors a supervisor should consider when developing and evaluating alternatives in the decision-making process. To what degree should the ethical tests come into play in any decision?
5. Discuss how a decision to take no action to a problem might be most appropriate?
6. Consider the following statement, "People don't resist change; they resist being changed." To what extent is this statement true? Discuss strategies for overcoming resistance to change. Discuss the principles of proposing change to higher-level managers.
7. What are the major ways in which the concepts and principles of organizational renewal might be incorporated into every supervisor's job?

## EXPERIENTIAL EXERCISE FOR SELF-ASSESSMENT

### EXPERIENTIAL EXERCISE FOR SELF-ASSESSMENT 8—Assess Your Problem-Solving Skills

This exercise is designed to help you identify key areas where your problem-solving skills could be improved.

1. Directions: Beside each statement, indicate the number that best describes your agreement or disagreement.

   Key:

   4 = Strongly Agree 3 = Agree 2 = Disagree Somewhat 1 = Strongly Disagree

   1 2 3 4 1. I always ask, "Is this problem worth solving?" before beginning to solve it.

   1 2 3 4 2. I try to break big problems into manageable pieces instead of trying to solve the whole problem at once.

   1 2 3 4 3. To determine the cause of a problem, I gather enough data to know exactly where, when, and under what circumstances the problem occurs.

   1 2 3 4 4. I have a network of contacts within my company and elsewhere with whom I discuss the problems in my area.

   1 2 3 4 5. I usually use experience, advice from others, or experimentation to help me solve problems.

   1 2 3 4 6. I involve others in problem solving when I need their help to implement a major decision.

   1 2 3 4 7. During "crunch" times, when time is of the essence, I solve problems with little input from others.

   1 2 3 4 8. It's impossible for me to have all the information about a problem before taking action.

   1 2 3 4 9. I involve others when they know more about a situation than I do, even though it usually takes longer to solve the problem.

   1 2 3 4 10. I usually use brainstorming techniques to generate ideas for solving problems.

   1 2 3 4 11. When I have a big problem to solve, I talk to everyone who has knowledge of the problem, those affected by the problem, and those who will have to implement the problem, before I come up with a solution.

   1 2 3 4 12. Once a solution is implemented, I have a follow-up plan to ensure that the solution fixes the problem.

   Total (add your scores)

2. Interpretation:

   **12–23**: Your present problem-solving skills thwart your attempt to reach a solution. Improve your problem-solving approach by following the suggestions in this chapter.

   **24–35**: Your problem-solving skills are satisfactory but could be improved.

   **36–48**: Your problem-solving skills are good. With a little improvement, they could be outstanding.

3. Carefully review the five decision-making styles in Figure 5.7. Based on your responses to questions 1–12 above, which

style would most appropriately describe your approach to decision making? Why?

4. Write a one-page paper detailing how you will continually look for ways to improve your problem-solving skills.

*Source*: From MESCON GROUP. *Techniques for Problem Solving*, 1E. 1995 South-Western, a part of Cengage Learning, Inc.

## PERSONAL SKILL BUILDING

### PERSONAL SKILL-BUILDER 8-1: You Make the Call!

Refer to this chapter's You Make the Call! You are Brey, the manager, and you know that you need to make a decision regarding Molly's actions. You are in a quandary, as you know that if she loses her job at the pharmacy, she will not be able to find another job easily.

1. Write a problem statement that addresses what, how, where, when of Molly's actions in the past week. Make sure that your statement includes the impact on customer service and the other employees.
2. Is Molly worth saving as an employee in your store? Why or why not?
3. Find at least two current articles or reports that indicate why employee absenteeism is a serious problem in our society. Based upon your findings and your personal work experiences, what should an organization such as Kincaid Pharmacies do to help employees such as Molly get to work on time and show up when she is scheduled?

### PERSONAL SKILL BUILDER 8-2: Computer Rules

Suppose that your company has a rule prohibiting the use of the company computer for personal business.

1. Is it realistic for your boss to expect you to abstain from conducting personal business on the company computer? Why or why not?
2. Early today, you notice that one of your coworkers is using the computer to surf porn sites. What would you do? Why would you take this course of action?
3. As the supervisor, you notice one of your subordinates using the computer for information on the fantasy football league. What would you do? Discuss the "ethical tests" that might help you make your decision?

### PERSONAL SKILL BUILDER 8-3: Identifying Supervisory Problems

1. Interview three people in supervisory or management positions. Ask them to identify (a) the major problem facing their organization today and (b) the major problem they have in doing their job.
2. Compare the problems identified by the supervisors. Did they state the problems in a way that make them understandable to you, or did you have to ask them questions in order to fully comprehend?
3. In your opinion, which of the organizational problems identified is most critical to organizational success?
4. Based on your analysis of the problems, would the supervisors be better off solving the problems themselves or eliciting input from others? Why?
5. Think of the week ahead. What is the major problem that you must deal with? What ideas from the Supervisory Tips Box will provide you the most guidance in dealing with your problem?

## TEAM SKILL BUILDING

### TEAM SKILL BUILDER 8-1: Technology Tool—Decision-Making Apps Can Help You Make Data-Driven Decisions

INTERNET ACTIVITY

What kind of decision maker are you? Do you look at your options and choose the best fit? Do you make a quick decision using gut feelings? Do you have a hard time making decisions? Do you count on others to make decisions for you? Do you use a strategy or a set of steps to guide your decision making like the process described in this chapter? Both in organizations and in our personal lives, we have to make many decisions. In the workplace it is likely that you will have a decision-making protocol and a certain level of discretion that

guides which decisions are yours to make and which ones you need to defer to someone higher up in the organization. Often, though, you will need to make workplace, career, and personal decisions that are not guided by a protocol. Technology tools have emerged that can help with the decision-making process.

In this activity, you will investigate several different decision-making software applications in two categories (1) decision-processing applications and (2) polling applications. Decision-processing applications present a series of steps during which the user inputs information (data) about the decision and the application uses statistical processes to "crunch the numbers" and come up with a decision that fits criteria that the user specifies. Polling applications enable users to pose a question or a set of choices to their social network and collect others' opinions to help inform a decision. Lists of several examples of each type of application are listed below. You can learn more about each one by putting the application name into your Internet browser.

**Decision-Processing Applications**

- Ethical Decision Making
- ChoiceMap
- Decision Buddy
- The Decision App
- Best Decision

**Polling Applications**

- Seesaw
- Loop
- Deciderr
- PeepAdvice
- Polar

1. Locate and review the Web sites for at least three of the software applications listed above.
2. Watch the demo videos and/or download the trial versions of the applications you chose to review.
3. Reflect on the kind of decision making help each of the applications provides. Do you think the applications would be helpful to you in making decisions? Why or why not?
4. Think of something about which you would like to make a decision. It could be a big, life-changing decision like which job to choose, or it could be a simple decision like which flavor of ice cream to buy.
5. In a group of four to five students, each student should describe the decision he or she want to make. Ask the others in the group which decision they think you should make by taking a poll. Did you feel comfortable with their responses? Would you take their advice?
6. In a one- to two-page paper, discuss the value and the challenges of using technology to help make decisions. Contrast that with the value and challenges of asking friends or colleagues to help make decisions. Then describe the process you find to be most helpful when making decisions (it does not need to be one of the two you contrasted above.).

## TEAM SKILL BUILDER 8-2: Dealing with People that Make Your Life Difficult—The "Indecisive" Waffler

This is another in a series of skills-building exercises that introduce you to the people who might make your life difficult.

1. Read the following statement from Kelly Klemm, a student at Southwest Tech:

   I had a friend, Henry, who wanted everyone to like him. I really liked him and thought we might have a future together. Most of the time he would say, "That is a great idea. Let me think about it and get back to you." When pressured, he would say, "I really don't know. Life seems so complicated. There are too many choices. I'll just go with the flow." That drove me up the wall. He felt that he needed to please everyone by acting as if each person's latest idea was the best he'd ever heard. Whether it was going to a movie or out to eat, he never had an opinion of where he wanted to go or what he wanted to see, but every alternative I came up with sounded like the best idea he had ever heard. When forced to make a decision, he took forever, and sometimes it seemed like it was torturing him inside as he was debating the options.

   One time, a bunch of us decided to go on a camping trip. Henry really acted like he wanted to go. He listened to all the details and acted excited about it. The day we all met to go, he never showed up and left a message saying he couldn't make it. This was not the first time he had done something like this.

   Henry was always "on the fence." He could not make a decision to save his life. He never wanted to take any action or make a choice that might hurt someone or make someone else uncomfortable. I recall another time when we needed to decide where to spend New Year's Eve. Some of our friends wanted to go to Holly Hall for dinner and dancing while others wanted to go to the Savoy for dinner and then to the Rave for a movie. I told Henry that we needed to make a decision so that reservations could be made. One person could persuade him that one idea was the right way, then I could come along, and he would just "climb to the other side of the fence" and agree with me. One minute we were going to Holly Hall, and the next minute, we were going to the Savoy. Two hours later, it would be Holly Hall again.

   Guess what? We ended up at his apartment, munching on some popcorn and watching an old movie. That was the last straw. Even though Henry was one of the kindest, gentlest people I'd ever met, I knew that Henry would never make a decision. So I made one. I decided I didn't have a future with him. I couldn't cope with him always sitting on the fence.

2. 
   INTERNET ACTIVITY
   Using the Internet, find at least three sources of information for coping with a "waffler." Carefully review each site for suggestions.
3. ROLE PLAY
   Divide the class into groups of three to five students. One student in each group is assigned the role of Kelly Klemm and the others are a group of her close friends. (a) The friends have

read Kelly's story, and each of them should write a problem statement in 30 words or less. Compare the problem statements. What are the similarities? Then the group should collectively write a problem statement. (b) Identify at least three suggestions for Kelly to use to cope with her problem. (c) Kelly should then share with the group what she is going to do to solve her problem with Henry. (d) The group could write a one-page paper that summarizes how Kelly can deal with Harry.

4. Optional activity: Students could write a one-page paper explaining how this skills application increased their working knowledge of coping with the behaviors of the "waffler."

## TEAM SKILL BUILDER 8-3: Becoming an Agent for Change

For the purpose of this team skill-building activity, students will be placed into groups of four to eight individuals and will be assigned one of the following situations:

a. Your mission is to renovate this classroom. There is no money to spend.
b. Your mission is to renovate this classroom. You cannot spend more than $1,000.
c. Your mission is to renovate this classroom. You cannot spend more than $10,000.
d. Your mission is to renovate this classroom.

1. Working as a group, address the following:
   a. Identify reasons for resistance to any change(s) you might propose.
   b. Develop your renovation blueprint.
   c. Outline a strategy for presenting your recommended changes to whoever has final decision authority. This may be your instructor, a dean, the financial officer, the physical plant manager, or others.
2. After your group has developed a strategy for change, your instructor will have you formally present it to the class. Your instructor will designate persons to play the following specific roles: instructor, dean of the college, chief financial officer, physical plant manager, and others as appropriate for your situation. The persons in these designated roles are encouraged to ask probing and clarifying questions, suggest alterations to the proposal, and express why they can or cannot accept the proposal. Other class members will act as observers.
3. Debriefing session: After all groups have presented their strategy for change, answer the following questions:
   a. To what extent did you personally own the recommendation that your group made?
   b. To what extent were you personally committed to seeing the recommendation "bear fruit"?
   c. Was your recommendation a success or failure? Why?
   d. What could you have done to make it easier for others to accept your group's recommendations?
4. Each group could be assigned a collaborative writing project (maximum of two pages): "*This is what we would do differently if we had to do it over again.*"

## SUPERVISION IN ACTION

The video for this chapter can be accessed from the student companion website at www.cengagebrain.com. (Search by authors' names or book title to find the accompanying resources.)

## ENDNOTES

1. BillySwan's "I Can Help," accessed at http://www.oldielyrics.com/-lyrics/billy_swan/i-can_help.html. You may want to review the article by June Fabre, "The Importance of Empowering Front-line Staff," *SuperVision* 71, No. 12 (December 2010), pp. 6–7
2. David Cooperrider, under the guidance of his Ph.D. advisor, Suresh Srivastva, laid out the framework for appreciative inquiry (AI). See David L. Cooperrider and Diana Whitney, *Appreciative Inquiry* (San Francisco: Berrett-Koehler Publishers, 1999), p. 10.
3. Definitions from *The American Heritage Dictionary of the English Language*, 3rd ed. (Boston: Houghton Mifflin Co., 1992). The idea for including the definitions came from Appreciative Inquiry Commons, http://appreciativeinquiry.cwru.edu/intro/whatisai.cfm.
4. David L. Cooperrider and Diana Whitney quote on Appreciative Inquiry Commons, "What Is Appreciative Inquiry?" Also see David L. Cooperrider, Diana Whitney, and Jacqueline Stavros, *Appreciative Inquiry Handbook* (San Francisco, CA: Berrett-Koehler, 2008); Cooperrider and Whitney, *A Positive Revolution in Change: Appreciate Inquiry* (San Francisco: Berrett-Koehler, 2000). Also see the following: Whitney and Amanda Trosten-Bloom, *Power of Appreciative Inquiry* (San Francisco: Berrett-Koehler Publishers, Inc., 2002); James D. Ludema, Whitney, Bernard J. Mohr, and Thomas J. Griffin, *Appreciative Inquiry Summit* (San Francisco: Berrett-Koehler Publishers, Inc., 2003).
5. Review *Fortune*'s yearly listing of the "100 Best Companies to Work For," or "The World's Most Admired Companies." The top five most

admired in 2014 were Apple, Amazon.com, Google, Berkshire Hathaway, and Starbucks. See *Fortune* "World's Most Admired Companies," http://money.cnn.com/magazines/fortune/most-admired / and use the pull-down menu to view the past several years.

For a listing of the "Best Small and Medium-sized Businesses to Work For," go to www.greatplacetowork.com (Great Place to Work Institute, Inc.). Generally, the companies are selected, in part, on the basis of trust that exists between management and employees, perceptions of fairness, availability of employee empowerment, and a management style that engages employees.

6. For more information on the fishbone or cause-and-effect diagram, go to: http://www.miatx.net/PDF/Pitoolbox/fishbone.pdf or http://en.wikipedia.org/wiki/Ishikawa_diagram.
7. See Roger von Oech, *A Whack on the Side of the Head* (Menlo Park, CA: CreativeThink, 1992) or von Oech, *A Whack on the Other Side of the Head* (New York: Warner Books, 1998), p. 178.
8. For more quotes from Thomas A. Edison, go to http://www.thomasedison.com/quotes.html. It should be noted that Edison's various electric companies were brought together to form Edison General Electric. Later the company was known simply as GE.
9. Thinking strategically is a high-level decision-making skills according to Jill Fowler and Jeanette Savage, "Ask 'What,' Not 'How,'" *HR Magazine* (August 2011), pp. 85–86.

   For more information on brainstorming and creative problem solving, see Alex F. Osborn (with Alex Faickney), *Applied Imagination*, 3rd rev. ed. (Buffalo, NY: Creative Education Foundation, 1993). Also see Alan G. Robinson and Sam Stern, *Corporate Creativity: How Innovation and Improvement Actually Happen* (San Francisco: Berrett-Koehler Publishers, 1997). For a list of ways to disrupt a brainstorming session, see Tom Kelley, "Six Ways to Kill a Brainstormer," *Across-the-Board* (March/April 2002), p. 12.

   Also see the following for ideas on how to "think outside the box": Micahle Michalko, *Cracking Creativity: Secrets of a Creative Genius* (Berkeley, CA: Ten Speed Press, 2001); and James C. Adams, *Conceptual Blockbusting: A Guide to Better Ideas* (Cambridge, MA: Perseus Publishing, 2001).

   Still another type of group brainstorming approach that has gained some acceptance in recent years is called storyboarding. Originally attributed to Walt Disney and his organization for developing animated cartoons, storyboarding can be especially helpful in generating alternatives and choosing among them. Depending on the nature of the problem, it may be appropriate to use a neutral party to manage the team process when alternatives, ideas, and other information are listed on index cards and arranged on "storyboards."
10. Our students have found that an Internet search for Nominal Group Technique (NGT) provides a more expanded discussion than any of the contemporary management texts. John A. Sample (1984) "Nominal Group Technique: An Alternative to Brainstorming" *Journal of Extension* 22, No. 2, http://www.joe.org/joe/1984march/iw2.php provides the steps for using NGT and the advantages and disadvantages of using the approach.
11. For more information on electronic brainstorming, go to http://en.wikipedia.org/wiki/brainstorming. It appears that this author is among the first to use the EBS. See also Alan Dennnis, Randal Minas, and Akshay Bhagwatwar, "Sparking Creativity: Improving Electronic Brainstorming with Individual Cognitive Priming," a paper presented at the 45th Hawaii International Conference on System Sciences in 2012, available at http://www.hicss.hawaii.edu/hicss_45/bp45/cl2.pdf
12. During the past decade, we have witnessed so many business scandals and management misdeeds that one has to wonder if upper-level management can really walk the talk? See Roger Higgs, Michael Smith, and George Mechling, "Making Better Business Decisions," *SuperVision* (February 2010), pp. 10–12; or David T. Ozar, "The Gold Standard for Ethical Education and Effective Decision Making in Healthcare Organizations," *Organizational Ethics: Healthcare, Business, and Policy* 1, No. 1 (Spring 2004), pp. 58–63.
13. For excellent discussions on both the theory and practice of sound business ethics, see Kyle Scott, "Business Ethics: Do What's Right, or What's Right Now," *SuperVision* 72, No. 7 (July 2011), pp. 8–9; or T. J. Stanley, "Ethics in Action," *SuperVision* 69, No. 4 (April 2008), pp. 14–16; or Archie B. Carroll and Ann L. Buchholtz, *Business and Society: Ethics and Stakeholder Management*, 8th ed. (Mason, OH: South-Western, 2012). See also Kris Maher, "Wanted: Ethical Employer," *The Wall Street Journal* (July 9, 2002), pp. B1, B8.
14. Rotary International whose members represent a wide variety of religious and cultural beliefs is committed to the four-way test. It is a simple checklist for ethical behavior.
15. Some management theorists distinguish between the terms *risk* and *uncertainty* in decision making. According to Stephen Robbins, risk involves conditions in which the decision maker can estimate the likelihood of certain alternatives occurring, usually based on historical data or other information that enables the decision maker to assign probabilities to each proposed alternative. Uncertainty involves a condition in which the decision maker has no reasonable probability estimates available and can only "guesstimate" the likelihood of various alternatives or outcomes. See Stephen P. Robbins, *Managing Today*, 2nd ed. (Upper Saddle River, NJ: Prentice-Hall, 2000), pp. 64–65.
16. Herbert Simon developed the normative model of decision making to identify the process that managers actually use in making decisions. As opposed to the rational decision model illustrated in Figure 5.2, Simon's normative model is characterized by limited information processing, the use of rules of thumb (intuition) or shortcuts, and satisficing. See J. G. March and H. A. Simon, *Organizations* (New York: John Wiley & Sons, 1958), pp. 10–12.
17. See Jones Loflin and Todd Musig, *Juggling Elephants—An Easier Way to Get Your Most Important Things Done Now!* (New York: Portfolio, 2008). Life is a three-ring circus: work, relationships, and self. You need to be a ringmaster, and you can only be in one ring at a time. For a recap of the problem-solving approach, see William W. Hull, "What's the Problem?" *SuperVision* 65, No. 5 (May 2004), pp. 5–7.
18. See Glen Llopis, "The 4 Most Effective Ways Leaders Solve Problems," *Forbes* (November 4, 2013), http://www.forbes.com/sites/glennllopis/2013/11/04/the-4-most-effective-ways-leaders-solve-problems/. See also Dean Gano, "Are You a Good Problem Solver?" *Quality Progress* 44, No. 5 (May 2011), pp. 30–35; Anne Houlihan, "Empower Your Employees to Make Smart Decisions," *SuperVision* 68, No. 7 (July 2007), pp. 3–5; and "Harnessing Employee Creativity," *The Worklife Report* (2001), p. 14; or Jim Perrone, "Moving from Telling to Empowering," *Healthcare Executive* (September/October 2001), pp. 60–61.
19. The guidelines were adapted from Robert Kreitner and Angelo Kinicki, *Organizational Behavior*, 9th ed. (Homewood, IL: Richard D. Irwin, 2009), pp. 354–360. Also see Kreitner, *Management*, 12th ed. (Mason, OH: Cengage Learning, 2013), Chapter 8.
20. For a general overview of several quantitative approaches to decision making, see Ricky W. Griffin, *Management*, 10th ed. (Mason, OH: Cengage Learning, 2011).
21. See *Stretch! How Great Companies Grow in Good Times & Bad* (New York: Wiley, 2004). Vice presidents of A.T. Kearney, a global

consulting firm, present in-depth illustrations of how short-term cost-cutting strategies don't work but how *stretch* creates new products, new markets, and new customer opportunities. Also see Jeremy C. Short and G. Tyge Payne, "First Movers and Performance: Timing Is Everything," *Academy of Management Review* (January 2008), pp. 267–269.

22. See Richard Roberts, "You Want to Improve? First You Must Change," *SuperVision* (January 2011), pp. 11–13, and Donald Chrusciel, "What Motivates the Significant/Strategic Change Champion(s)," *Journal of Organizational Change Management* 21, No. 2 (2008), p. 148. You may want to see "Masters of Design," *Fast Company* (June 2004), pp. 60–75, for an overview of 20 individuals who have changed the way their organizations innovate, create, and compete.

    For general discussions on change and overcoming resistance to change, the following are recommended: Judith E. Glasser, *Conversational Intelligence: How Great Leaders Build Trust and Get Extraordinary Results* (Brookline Village, MA: Bibliomotion, 2013); Jeffrey D. Ford, Laurie W. Ford, and Angelo D'Amelio, "Resistance to Change: The Rest of the Story," *Academy of Management Review* 33, No. 2 (April 2008), pp. 341–361; Tom R. Tyler and David De Cremer, "Process-based Leadership: Fair Procedures and Reactions to Organizational Change," *The Leadership Quarterly* (August 2005), pp. 529–546; "Case Study: Modeling How Their Business Really Works Prepares Managers for Sudden Change," *Strategy and Leadership* 32, No. 2 (2004), pp. 28–35. We urge you to read Alan Deutschman, "Change or Die!" *Fast Company* (May 2005), pp. 52–62. Deutschman asks, "Why is it so darn hard to change our ways?" Our students have found that the article provides some practical recommendations on how leadership has been used to change people's behavior and improve the organization's effectiveness.

23. Oren Harari, "Why Don't Things Change?" *Management Review* (February 1995), pp. 30–32. Author Jim Collins presents an interesting aspect of change. He says that while many experts say "'Change or die—the reason to get better is that bad things will happen to you if you don't.' Is that kind of fear a good motivator? Not for long." See Collins, "Fear Not," *Inc.* (May 1998), pp. 30–40. This perspective is countered by Freek Vermeulen, Phanish Puranum, and Ranjay Guliati, who suggest that change for change's sake is beneficial, even necessary, in organizations that are performing well. See Vermeulen et al., "Change for Change's Sake," *Harvard Business Review* (June 2010), pp. 71–77.

    For overviews of strategic organizational change approaches, see Frank Heller, "The Levers of Organizational Change: Facilitators and Inhibitors," in Charles De Wolff, P. J. D. Drenth and Theirry Henk, *A Handbook of Work and Organizational Psychology* 4 (East Sussex, UK: Psychology Press, 2013), pp. 229–252; John P. Cotter & Dan S. Cohen, *The Heart of Change: Real-Life Stories of How People Change Their Organizations* (Cambridge, MA: Harvard Business Press Books, 2012); Linda A. Anderson and Dean Anderson, *The Change Leader's Roadmap* (San Francisco, CA: Wiley, 2010); A. G. Lafley and Ram Charan, "Making Inspiration Routine," *Inc.* (June 2008), pp. 98–104; Lotte S. Lushcer and Marianne W. Lewis, "Organizational Change and Managerial Sensemaking: Working through Paradox," *Academy of Management Journal* 51, No. 2 (April 2008), pp. 221–240; Jean Ann Larson, "Using Conceptual Learning Maps and Structured Dialogue to Facilitate Change at a Large Hospital System," *Organizational Development Journal* 25, No. 3 (Fall 2007), pp. 25–32.

24. For discussions on building trust between supervisors and employees when changes are being made, see Jim Dougherty, "The Best Way for New Leaders to Build Trust," *Harvard Business Review.Org* (December 13, 2013), http://blogs.hbr.org/2013/12/the-best-way-for-new-leaders-to-build-trust/; JoEllen Vrazel, *Managing Change and Leading through Transitions: A Guide for Community and Public Health Practitioners* (Spring 2013), http://www.leveragepoints.net/RESOURCES/Managing_Change_Leading_Transitions.pdf; and Max Messmer, "Leading Your Team through Change," *Strategic Finance* (October 2001), pp. 8–10.

25. Mark A. Griffin, Sharon K. Parker, and Claire M. Mason, "Leader Vision and the Development of Adaptive and Proactive Performance: A Longitudinal Study," *Journal of Applied Psychology* 95, No. 1 (2010), pp. 174–182.

26. Robert H. Miles, "Accelerating Corporate Transformations (Don't Lose Your Nerve!): Six Mistakes That Can Derail Your Company's Attempts to Change," *Harvard Business Review* (January–February 2010), pp. 73–74.

27. The Worker Adjustment and Retraining Act (WARN) requires that employers must give at least 60 days notice before closing or layoffs are carried out. For an overview of the requirements, go to http://www.doleta.gov/programs/factsht/warn.htm. An opportunity to observe and analyze how past Levi Strauss USA president Pete Thigpen addressed employee inquiries about an imminent plant closure is provided in "Walking the Line" (2007), a Stanford Graduate School of Business Leadership in Focus video case, available for instructor download from the Center for Leadership Development and Research Web site (http://www.leadershipinfocus.net).

28. Judith E. Glasser, in "Change Management: 4 Factors that Distinguish Successes from Failures," *Huffington Post* (April 19, 2014), http://www.huffingtonpost.com/judith-e-glaser/change-management-4-facto_b_5179944.html.

29. Peter Senge in Alan M. Webber, "Learning for Change," *Fast Company* (May 1999), pp. 178+. Also see Senge's *The Dance of Change: The Challenges of Sustaining Momentum in Learning Organizations* (New York: Doubleday/Current, 1999).

30. Scott Adams in Anna Muoio, "Boss Management," *Fast Company* (April 1999), pp. 91+.

31. Interview with Michael Tushman and Charles O'Reilly, "Leading Change and Organizational Renewal," *Harvard Business School Working Knowledge* (November 16, 1999), http://hbswk.hbs.edu/item/1156.html, accessed August 27, 2008. Also see Tushman and O'Reilly, *Leading Change in Organizational Renewal* (Cambridge, MA: Harvard Business School Press, 1997).

    See Drew Stevens, "Increase Employee Productivity without Additional Time and Resources," *SuperVision* (October 2007), pp. 7–11. *Note:* There is an organization of professionals committed to organizational renewal: ACCORD—Association for Creative Change in Organizational Renewal and Development (www.accord.org).

32. Adapted from interviews with Chris Roman (Studer Group representative) and Quint Studer. (Visit their Web site at http://www.studergroup.com.) Also see Studer, *Hardwiring Excellence* (Gulf Breeze, FL: FireStarter Publishing, 2005).

33. Nancy J. Lyons, "The 90-Day Checkup," *Inc.* (March 1999), pp. 111–112.

34. Jim Collins, *Good to Great: Why Some Companies Make the Leap . . . and Others Don't* (New York: HarperCollins, 2001).

35. Adapted from Quint Studer, "Healthcare Flywheel," Studer Group; and Bill Bielanda, "Rules for Developing Effective Leader Goals," Studer Group, with permission.

36. Adapted after interviews with Chris Roman (Studer Group representative) and Quint Studer. (Visit their Web site at http://www.studergroup.com.) For a detailed description of cascading objectives and SKAs throughout all levels of an organization during a change initiative, see Miles, "Accelerating Corporate Transformations (Don't Lose Your Nerve!)."
37. Studer, *Hardwiring Excellence*, with permission.
38. Baptist Health Care History Web page, http://www.ebaptisthealth-care.org/BHC/History.aspx
39. Baptist Health Care Awards & Recognition Web page, http://www.ebaptisthealthcare.org/Awards/
40. Ibid. For comprehensive information about Baptist Health Care, Inc., visit its Web site (http://www.ebaptisthealthcare.org); also see Kerry Vermillion et al., "Innovations in Performance Management" (May 2010), http://www.bhclg.com/contentdocuments/-hfmarticle_042010.pdf; Richard C. Huseman and Pamela A. Bilbrey, "BreakOUT!" (http://www.LeaderExcel.com); Baptist Hospital Baldrige Application (http://www.nist.gov/public_affairs/releases/bhitrauma .htm); and "Within Reach" (www.healthexecutive.com/features/sept_2005_coverstory).
41. Robert Levering and Milton Moskowitz compiled a listing of the best companies to work for. See, for example, the 2011 list at http://money.cnn.com or see the February 7, 2011, issue of *Fortune* magazine. BHI's parent organization's ranking has varied between 10th and 59th during the past seven years. That is among all organizations in America.

# PART 2 Critical Incidents

The critical incidents below each present a supervisory situation based on real events to be used for educational purposes. The identities of some or all individuals, organizations, industries, and locations, as well as financial and other information may have been disguised to protect individual privacy and proprietary information. In some cases fictional details have been added to improve readability and interest.

---

Critical Incident 2-1

## IT'S NOT WHERE YOU START BUT WHERE YOU FINISH: THE LIFE OF OPRAH WINFREY

Oprah was born in Mississippi to an unmarried teenager. Until she was six years old, Oprah was raised in poverty by her grandmother. Living for a while in inner city Milwaukee, Wisconsin, Oprah said that she was molested by a cousin, an uncle, and a family friend beginning when she was nine years old. At age 13, she ran away from home.

Oprah ended up in Nashville, Tennessee, and earned many honors at East Nashville High School. She won an oratory contest, which helped her get a scholarship to Tennessee State University where she majored in communication. After working as the first black female news anchor in Nashville, she moved to Baltimore and co-anchored the 6 o'clock news.

In 1983, Oprah relocated to Chicago. The authors first became aware of Oprah Winfrey when she co-starred in Stephen Spielberg's *The Color Purple* as a distraught housewife, Sofia. She was nominated for an Academy Award as the best-performing actress for her performance in that movie. Oprah became a millionaire at age 32 and is the only black billionaire according to *Forbes* magazine. In 2004, Oprah became the first black person to rank among the 50 most generous Americans. She has given millions of dollars to educational causes.

The one Oprah quote that we like to share with our students is:

"The greatest discovery of all time is that a person can change his or her future by merely changing their attitude."

Lisa Werner/Alamy

### QUESTIONS FOR DISCUSSION

We suggest that you review the following resources to learn more about Oprah Winfrey:

http://en.wikipedia.org/wiki/Oprah_Winfrey

http://www.biography.com/people/oprah_winfrey-9534419/

http://www.forbes.com/sites/clareoconnor/2012/09/17/the-oprah-effect-charity-edition/

Petrone, Paul. "What Oprah Taught the World About Hiring". *http://www.business2community.com*. (July 31, 2014).

Jackson, David. "Obama Awards Medal of Freedom to Oprah, others", *USA Today*, (November 20, 2013).

Oprah Winfrey Network, *FastCompany.com* (June 2011) p.90.

Taylor, Candace. "Oprah Winfrey Buys About 60 Acres in Telluride for $10.85 Million", The Wall Street Journal (March 21, 2014) p.2.

1. Go online and find at least two sources that will give you additional information about the "Life and Legend of Oprah Winfrey."
2. If Oprah came into your classroom, what questions would you ask her?
3. What responses do you think she would give to your questions?
4. Some of Oprah's educational causes have been in other countries. If you were to ask her to explain how she became involved in those situations, how do you think she would respond? How would her answer help you as you journey through life?
5. How do you think Oprah would respond if you asked her what she learned about leadership and managing others from working on national TV versus having her own station?
6. Food for Thought: Lupita Amondi Nyong'o won the 2014 Academy Award for Best Supporting Actress for her role in *12 Years a Slave*. She thought about becoming an actress after seeing Whoopi Goldberg and Oprah Winfrey in *The Color Purple*. Visit your local video store and get a copy of *12 Years a Slave* or *The Color Purple*. After reviewing the movies, answer the following questions: (a) In what ways were some of the people ruthless? (b) In what ways did the actress correctly use the various communication and supervisory techniques discussed in the first eight chapters of this book?

## ETHICAL EXPENSE REPORTING

Critical Incident 2-2

Ron Bush was supervisor of a merchandise sales department at the headquarters of a major retail store chain operation. He had been hired several years previously, and he was currently pursuing an MBA degree on a part-time basis. His salary had been adjusted upward because of his good performance at the firm, and he was participating in the company profit-sharing plan.

Ron was planning a business trip to Washington, D.C., that was to occur in about two months. In a conversation with another merchandise sales department supervisor, Kristy Whitcomb, he mentioned his forthcoming trip. Kristy proceeded to tell him she had just returned from a business trip to Florida on which she had taken her husband along with her. Kristy said they stayed an extra weekend and "really painted the town red on Saturday night." She confided in Ron that she put the entire weekend through as part of her expense report.

Ron pointed out to Kristy that the employee handbook stated that only "business-related expenses" were to be reimbursed by the company. Kristy responded that she figured that all of her expenses, including entertainment, were part of a business trip. She rationalized that the plane fare did not cost the company any more by not leaving until Sunday, and she had been working very hard. Why shouldn't the company pay for her husband to stay with her and have a good time relaxing? Besides, she had been working long hours and had been out of town frequently; she was due some additional "rest and recreation." Kristy also told Ron that her manager did not reject any of the expenses she had turned in, so it must have been all right; otherwise her manager would not have approved it.

A week or so after their discussion, there was a company reorganization. Kristy Whitcomb was promoted to a position of division marketing manager. With the departmental changes, Ron Bush was now a supervisor reporting directly to Kristy. Nothing more had been said about the conversation they had had regarding business expenses.

Several weeks later, Ron Bush went on his business trip to Washington, D.C., and he decided to invite his wife along for the weekend. Ron's wife had always wanted to go there and it was close to their anniversary date. Ron rented a car and enjoyed the weekend entertaining his wife and seeing the sights. He saved all of their travel and other expenses and entertainment receipts. As he was relaxing on the flight home, Ron wondered whether he should submit all of the expenses he had incurred on this trip to Washington, D.C.

## QUESTIONS FOR DISCUSSION

1. Why would Kristy have shared with Ron the information she did regarding putting personal expenses on her business trip report?
2. What are some of the ethical issues facing Ron Bush in this situation?
3. What are the possible benefits and the consequences of Ron's taking the actions that were modeled by Kristy?
4. Put yourself in Ron's shoes. What will you do to solve the problem at hand?

---

Critical Incident 2-3

## SUPERVISORY HUMOR

Don Fitzgerald, supervisor of customer service at Software-n-More, was articulate and possessed a dry sense of humor. He could be counted on for occasional practical jokes, but he was not discrete in his selection of targets.

Software-n-More was a major computer software, supplies, and services firm. The company had over 300 employees spread over five states. Like most retail firms, the company was having tough financial times. Staples, the largest U.S. office-supply retailer, forecast a fall in sales as customers were moving to mass-market chains and to e-retailers. The company said it would be closing 250 stores in the United States in the next year. In the last several years retailers were particularly hard hit by hackers.

Software-n-More, as a result of the hard times in the retail market, had laid off employees, several supervisors, and one middle-level manager. This restructuring had resulted in a consolidation of positions. The surviving supervisors were assigned additional employees and duties. Virtually everyone felt stressed about seeing colleagues depart and having more to do in the same amount of time.

Fitzgerald decided to write a humorous news item to try to boost morale. He wrote and posted on several employee bulletin boards a one-page memorandum titled, "The Chopping Block." A few excerpts follow:

QUESTION: Sharon, what is your reaction to the loss of your beloved supervisor, Karen Cates?
RESPONSE: Ding Dong, the beloved Witch is Gone!

| | |
|---|---|
| QUESTION: | Richard, How do you like taking on the additional responsibilities for the parts department while continuing to supervise the testing lab? |
| RESPONSE: | My boss, Ryan Kohenski, gave me a half hour pep-talk, and now I am up to top speed and on top of things. |
| QUESTION: | Employees, what do you think about our fearless leader's new motto, "Find ways to do more with less"? |
| RESPONSE: | We feel that our president, Bob Swan, can teach us the true meaning of this motto, since he has lived it since birth. |

Fitzgerald also printed multiple copies of his memorandum and put it on the desks of several of his cohorts. One of the employees immediately posted the excerpts on Facebook. Shortly thereafter, a copy made its way to the office of the company president, Bob Swan. Fitzgerald's comments were the talk of the employees and many were laughing.

Not President Swan, who immediately contacted Chandler Mane, HR director, and asked him to arrange a meeting with Don and his boss Bernie Collins. Swan told Mane that he was deeply concerned about the negative remarks posted by Fitzgerald. He stressed that this type of so-called humor was not acceptable. If carried to extremes, which Fitzgerald's postings were, it could result in lawsuits by individuals who felt they were being ridiculed or defamed.

Shortly thereafter, Don Fitzgerald was summoned to Chandler Mane's office. Bernie Collins was also present when Fitzgerald arrived. Mane said, "Don, you have been a good employee, but your behavior in regard to these postings is unprofessional and inappropriate." He replied, "It's just a little joke. Top management needs to lighten up. Everyone is so uptight here about what the future holds that my little memo will be forgotten quickly." Mane replied, "Don, this is serious. You didn't exercise good supervisory judgment. In many organizations a supervisor would be fired on the spot for something like what you did. You made a wrong choice and we will get back to you shortly about our recommendations."

Bernie Collins told Chandler that if Fitzgerald was fired or even disciplined, it would alienate all of the other supervisors and most employees. He continued, "Yes, I feel that Don's humor was a bit sarcastic, but everyone else is saying the same things and worse in private!"

After the meeting, Chandler Mane pondered what her recommendation to Pres. Swan would be.

## QUESTIONS FOR DISCUSSION

1. What are the challenges facing the leadership of Software-n-More?
2. Was Don Fitzgerald's "The Chopping Block" just a bit of humor to improve morale, or was it a serious breach of a supervisor's responsibilities?
3. Evaluate the general positions as stated by each individual in this critical incident. Which of them do you find the most and the least credible?
4. Evaluate the alternatives available to Chandler Mane?
5. If you were Chandler Mane, what will you recommend to President Swan, and why?
6. What are the key lessons you learned for this Critical Incident?
7. Food for Thought Question: In a troubled economy what can managers do to motivate their employees to continuously improve?

Critical Incident
2-4

## WHAT MOTIVATES CALLIE?[1]

What's it like to be a 23-year-old single parent, working at a minimum-level wage to support yourself and your child? Meet Callie Michaels.

In high school, Callie learned that she was pregnant. The father did not want to take any responsibility for the child, and for a time Callie considered giving up her baby, Olivia, for adoption. But instead Callie decided to drop out of school, get a reliable job, and raise the baby herself.

For almost seven years, Callie has worked the front desk at The Highland Golf, Tennis and Ski Resort. Her major duties include welcoming and registering guests. When Callie started, there was always at least one other person on duty with her. At peak periods, at least four employees provided front-desk service. The employees worked well together, and they had become good friends. In fact, several of the employees spent some of their personal time together. The front desk was operational 24/7.

Over the last two years, however, The Highland, like most high-end resorts, started feeling the effects of the depressed economy. Overbuilding in the vacation industry, together with increased competition for tourism dollars, have decreased the resort's profitability. A drop in corporate-travel business has added to the resort's woes.

A year ago, the resort changed ownership. First, the new management felt it could improve occupancy by increasing promotion and advertising expenditures. The expected increase in business did not materialize, however. So more recently, the resort started offering substantial discount packages for groups. While this strategy did increase the occupancy rate slightly, the company still experienced a 9.8 percent decline in revenue per room. In the first six months of this year, the resort's occupancy rate was running at about 55 percent. This paled in comparison with the average rate of 92 percent occupancy that the resort used to see a decade ago. The continued decline in revenue per available room and in profit margins caused the new management to institute a cost-cutting drive.

Included in the attempt to restore profitability were such measures as eliminating and consolidating various management and supervisory positions and curtailing merit increases. Two years ago, there were 12 full-time and six part-time people in front-end guest services. Currently, only nine people are involved directly in front-end guest services, and two of them are part-time. Callie has been fortunate enough to retain her job at The Highland, but several of Callie's good friends have been let go and have not been successful in finding other employment in the area.

When Callie first started, The Highland was considered an excellent employer. At that time, the resort was owned by one of the country's larger hotel real-estate corporations. Thomas, the previous general manager, had instituted a number of family-friendly measures for employees. Among those measures were a full range of alternative work schedules, including flextime (a system whereby employees chose their own work schedules within certain limits). For employees with children, like Callie, the HR department would find quality child care and discount the cost by 10 percent. Employees such as Callie who worked more

[1] Originally prepared as a critical incident by Ed Leonard, IPFW and Claire McCarty Kilian. University of Wisconsin-River Falls and first published in the 2003 *Proceedings of the Society for Case Research* (© 2003 by the authors). Substantially revised for inclusion in *Supervision*, 13th ed.

than 30 hours a week received healthcare benefits. Staying home with a sick child was no problem, given the company's flexible work policies.

As part of an overall reward system, the company also instituted an employee of the week, month, and year program. Employees received "positive stroke" points based on customer evaluations and feedback. Callie and others referred to these as their "report cards," and employees willingly treated customers as "very special people" hoping they would receive good reports from customers. Each week, the top three-point recipients in each work area received $25, $15, or $10 in resort credit, which could be used in any of the resort's facilities, such as the coffee shop, swimming pool snack bar, gift shop, or dining room. The monthly award winner in each area received $50, and his or her photo was prominently displayed on the lobby wall.

Things were very different under the new owners. In addition to eliminating some positions, they initiated a hiring freeze, meaning that the remaining employees had to work much harder. They also discontinued the employee recognition program, but the last round of winners' photos were still prominently displayed for all to see.

Some guests, who were particularly impressed with Callie's customer service, noticed the employee recognition board. Upon leaving the resort, the guests asked Callie, "How come your picture's not on the board? You've been most helpful during our stay!"

"It should have been, but the new management doesn't believe in those things," Callie said. As their discussion continued, it became clear that Callie had lost her enthusiasm for her job. "They're not as flexible as the previous management, so I've had to put work ahead of my child, Olivia. They've cut the child-care supplement, and several of my good friends have left. If business doesn't pick up, I'll probably lose my job! I love most of the people who stay with us. But I'm beginning to wonder if I should do something else."

## QUESTIONS FOR DISCUSSION

1. What do employees such as Callie Michaels want from work?
2. Evaluate Highland Golf, Tennis and Ski Resort's employee recognition program under the previous ownership.
3. What are some actions that the current management of Highland Golf, Tennis and Ski Resort can take to improve employee morale?
4. Discuss the various models of motivation theory that could be relevant to this incident.
5. Explain why Callie is no longer excited about her job and future.
6. If you were Callie Michaels, what would you do? Why?

## IT'S NOT FAIR! GIVING MORE AND GETTING LESS!

Critical Incident 2-5

Elaine Pierce had worked for the city of Metropolis in the water and sewer department for over two decades. She began working at age 17 when she was a junior in high school but she never graduated. Her 20-some years of hard work paid off when she was promoted to second shift supervisor two years ago. She had taken some management training programs offered by the local community college and felt that she had honed her management skills and was deserving of the promotion. She was proud of her accomplishments and was known as being thorough and conscientious to train and develop new hires. She was pleased with her success as a supervisor, but knew she still had a lot to learn. She reflected on the events of the past 24 hours.

In recent years, the city had struggled in balancing its budget. Therefore, there had been no raises, and employees were paying a higher medical premium. The local area was known as a place that attracted a large number of Bosnian, Asian, and other refugees. With the help of churches and social service agencies, the city had brought a large number of them into city employment. These employees were offered English as a second language course and other professional development and social skills courses. In addition to paying the cost of these courses, the city paid each employee for four hours of training each week.

Last night, Elaine was approached by Faith Newman, who expressed her concern about not having a raise for the last two years and her disagreement and frustration with the city's pay policies. Newman was upset because she had learned that Hu Twong was making $0.50 per hour more than she. According to Newman, Twong had been employed by the city for four months, and she had been employed for 12 years. In addition, Twong was getting four extra hours of pay each week because he did not speak English well.

"I was under the impression that pay is a reward for doing the job well and working for the city a long time," Newman said. "Experience doesn't seem to matter. It's not fair!"

After consulting HR director Evan Maloney, Elaine was really confused. Maloney explained that the HR department determined all pay rates. The mayor and the city council had dictated that no raises would be given in the last two years. Each job classification had a wide wage range, but seniority and experience differences had become nonexistent. Maloney confirmed that some of the new employees had been hired at higher rates than longer-term employees. Maloney explained to Elaine that city administration looked unfavorably on discussing wages with current employees. Maloney reminded Elaine to reaffirm that the city administration had been pleased with Newman's work performance and that the pay situation was beyond the city's control at this time. In conclusion, Maloney asked Elaine to try to soothe her employees' feelings about pay as much as possible and to be patient. "Things will change sooner or later, and the more senior employees will be taken care of," Maloney assured Ellen.

## QUESTIONS FOR DISCUSSION

1. What are the problems and ethical issues facing Elaine Pierce?
2. Search the Internet to ascertain the extent of company policies prohibiting wage discussions among employees.
3. Are policies against wage discussion among employees just to protect supervisors and HR managers from having to explain differences in wages? Why or why not?
4. After hearing what Evan Maloney had to say, what should Elaine Pierce do?
5. What should Elaine Pierce do to soothe Faith Newman's feelings?
6. Pierce thought that Maloney's response to her inquiries was inaccurate. Do you agree? If so, how might the situation have been better handled?
7. Why is communication so important in employee pay and motivation?

## FACEBOOK AND SOCIAL MEDIA SLIP-UP

Critical Incident 2-6

The supervisory position in healthcare has become a very difficult and demanding job. Trying to understand the Patient Protection and Affordable Care Act (ACA), and not seeing employers provide education and incentives for employees to improve their health, has created stress for many healthcare professionals. More healthcare professionals know that employees who exercise, eat right, stop smoking, and adopt proactive preventative behaviors are healthier, happier, and do better work. Employers should find a way to reward their employees' good health behaviors. These are challenging times for the healthcare field and some departments and managers are expected to do more with less.

On Monday's early morning management meeting, it was reported that a survey found that 53 percent of Pine Valley Medical Center (CMC) nurses "have high levels of stress, with feelings of extreme fatigue and being out of control." Management toyed with the following short-run strategies: (1) keep reasonable work hours, (2) allow nurses to have a full 30-minute lunch time and several 15 minute breaks during the day, (3) be realistic when assigning tasks, and (4) create a supportive culture. A group of managers were chosen to work with the HR department and a consulting group would be developing a plan of action. As the CEO said, "We must ensure that our patients receive the best care in a safer environment and we must enable our staff (nurses) to be the best they can be!" As the management team went out the door they agreed to provide all employees with more ample feedback.

Charlotte Kelly had been the CMC ER (emergency room) supervisor and had a very divisive group of employees who were operational 24/7. Like more supervisors, Charlotte believed when people come to work some cannot leave their personal feelings at the door. Some folks need help to understand the consequences for the way they act and the adverse effect it has on coworkers and patients. She looked to accentuate the positive and she hated to deal with challenges for bad acts.

Later that week, things went from bad to worse! Marty Johnson, an eight year ER veteran posted his feelings on Facebook. "I am drowning here in the emergency room at CMC. I HATE THEIR GUTS! The supervisor, Charlotte, and doctors, nurses and techs are the devils from hell!"

One of Marty's Facebook friends, who was a hospital employee, contacted the hospital HR department and noted concerns about the impropriety of the postings. Management launched an investigation. Marty claimed he had not written the offending comments and that a friend had access to his Facebook account and had posted them. A member of the HR department interviewed the friend who at first stated that she was the author of the comments. This friend was not a CMC employee but after being warned that she could be charged with perjury, she admitted that Marty had told her to take responsibility so than he (Marty) would not lose his job.

Marty told Charlotte, Carol Holbrook (CMC's director of HR), and Bob Rentz (the executive VP for administration) that he was merely venting his frustration after several hard days at work. He had deleted the post shortly thereafter and comments were directed to his online friends only, not to hospital patients, other employees, or fellow workers. He did not intend for the comments to be published or viewed by the public at large. Charlotte told

Marty he was suspended for two days with loss of pay. She said that management would continue to investigate the situation and tell him at that time about his future with the hospital. As she pondered, she looked at the CMC's Cultural Beliefs on the wall, "People Matter: I value people as I want to be valued, holding myself and others accountable." What should Charlotte and the CMC administration do?

## QUESTIONS FOR DISCUSSION

1. What are the issues in this critical incident?
2. Do you think that some employees, managers, patients, and other stakeholders will be outraged if Marty's comments become public knowledge?
3. Why should the problem with Marty be solved quickly?
4. What suggestions would you make to help management on how to best deal with Marty?
5. What might management do to increase the levels of trust, cooperation, and cohesiveness among employees?
6. Explain why a manager should look at every disciplinary action as if it will eventually end up in the court room?

PART 3

Feature Photo Service/Newscom

# Organizing, Staffing, Managing and Measuring for Success

Chapter 9

# The Principles of Organizing

© Don Bannister/Blend Images/Corbis

**After studying this chapter, you will be able to:**

1. Describe the organizing function of management.
2. Discuss the impact of the informal organization and informal group leaders and how supervisors should deal with them.
3. Explain the unity-of-command and the span-of-management principles and their applications.
4. Justify why a supervisor should strive for the "ideal" organizational structure and work toward this objective.
5. Compare and contrast departmentalization and alternative approaches for grouping activities and assigning work.
6. Assess the implications of downsizing for restructuring and suggest alternatives.
7. List the major factors contributing to organizing effective meetings, especially the supervisor's role.
8. Appraise the importance of self-organization, that is, effective use of your time and talents.

## YOU MAKE THE CALL!

*Tom Hayes was recently appointed as plant manager of Waldo Electronics by the principal owner and president, Bill Sanders. Tom had worked for more than 20 years in various engineering and managerial positions at the company. The core values of Waldo can be summed up as follows:*

- Make a profit
- Do the job right the first time
- Come up with and try new ideas
- Respect others
- Service to customers
- Be fair to all stakeholders
- Tell the truth
- Look for ways to cut costs

In reviewing all of Waldo's operations, Tom ascertained that the following were among the firm's major policies and approaches:

1. All employees are paid salaries instead of hourly wages.
2. Machine operators inspected their own output, made work rules, and participated in the decision-making process.
3. After initial training, a machine operator was trusted to know what needed to be done and then do it with limited direction.
4. Every job was stressed as being important.

Tom was grateful that his predecessor George Dean had left the business in good shape. Tom knew that there would be many areas that would need his attention and that there would be some challenges to address and opportunities to improve upon what had previously existed.

Tom spent his first week wandering around the organization. He met with all 110 employees, first in small groups and then each one individually. In the individual meeting, he gave each employee a piece of paper on which there were two questions: (1) What can I do to help you do a better job? (2) What should we be doing as an organization to get more customers and improve our bottom line?

Before he analyzed the employees' answers to the questions he wondered whether there was something else he could have done during his first week on the job.

The above scenario presents a supervisory situation based on real events to be used for educational purposes. The identities of some or all individuals, organizations, industries, and locations, as well as financial and other information may have been disguised to protect individual privacy and proprietary information. Fictional details may have been added to improve readability and interest.

YOU MAKE THE CALL!

## Organizing as an Essential Managerial Function

1 **Describe the organizing function of management.**

It's a new era, and the economy appears to be a bit rocky. Organizations have been looking for ways to increase their efficiency by making adjustments to the way they do business. For many, this has meant the elimination of jobs and the restructuring of those that remain. The challenge for many managers has become that of how to organize so that they can do more with less.

As one of the five major functions of management, organizing requires every manager to be concerned with building, developing, and maintaining working relationships that will help the organization achieve its objectives. Although organizations may have varied objectives and may operate in many kinds of environments, the fundamental principles of organizing are universal.

A manager's organizing function consists of designing a structure for grouping activities and assigning them to specific work units (e.g., departments, teams). Organizing includes establishing formal authority and responsibility relationships among activities and departments. To make such a structure possible, management must delegate authority throughout the organization and establish and clarify authority relationships among departments. We use the term **organization** to refer to any group structured by management to carry out designated functions and accomplish certain objectives.

**Organization**
Group structured by management to carry out designated functions and accomplish certain objectives

Management should design the structure and establish authority relationships based on sound principles and organizational concepts, such as unity of command, span of supervision, division of work, and departmentalization. In Chapter 2, we briefly discussed managerial authority and the process of delegation. In Chapter 5, we expanded on those concepts, which reflect how management establishes authority and responsibility relationships in organizational structures.

Although organizing the overall activities of the enterprise is initially the responsibility of the chief executive, it eventually becomes the responsibility of supervisors. Therefore, supervisors must understand what it means to organize. Although the range and magnitude of problems associated with the organizing function are broader at higher managerial levels than for supervisors, the principles are the same.

## ORGANIZATIONS ARE PEOPLE

Throughout this chapter's discussions of the concepts and principles of organizing, it should not be forgotten that people are the substance and essence of any organization, regardless of how the enterprise is structured. Managers and supervisors may become so preoccupied with developing and monitoring the formal structure that they neglect the far more important aspects of relationships with and among their employees, which affect the workers and the workplace. For example, in its most recent Global Workforce Study of over 32,000 workers worldwide, Towers Watson found that just over a third (35%) of workers have a high level of **engagement** with their workplace,[1] which author Kevin Kruse defines as "the level of emotional commitment the employee has to the organization and its goals,"[2] and, moving down on the scale, 22 percent feel unsupported, 17 percent feel detached, and 26 percent feel disengaged. Engagement,

**Engagement**
The level of emotional commitment the employee has to the organization and its goals

**FIGURE 9.1** Disgruntled workers can easily broadcast their unhappiness throughout their organizations

according to the survey report, is influenced by employees' level of belief in the company's goals, their perceived emotional connection with the employer, the number of obstacles to success they find in their day-to-day work, the availability of resources, the ability to maintain energy, whether the workplace has a supportive social environment and whether they have feelings of accomplishment. When we couple these findings with those of other surveys that show many employees seem to be hanging on until the job market gets better, the challenge for supervisors becomes clear. Employees are generally not in the best of spirits, and some are being threatened by the organizational changes they and others have experienced. Figure 9.1 illustrates how disgruntled workers broadcast dissatisfaction with organizations that don't "walk the talk."

"Ultimately, most employees would much rather be part of a team they're committed to, not just a member of an organization. Developing and maintaining a consistent management approach that engenders *esprit de corps* is a key link in the productivity process. Such management—balancing appropriate levels of results-orientation with an understanding of employee needs—is neither easy nor unattainable."[3] Where are those organizations in which employee needs and concerns are truly given top-priority attention by managers and supervisors? Our focus in this chapter is on building sound organizational structures that form the building blocks and foundations supporting the mutual goals of effective work performance and high job satisfaction. Although following good and accepted organizational principles will not ensure organizational success, it usually prevents many problems and irritations.

## Informal Organization

**2** **Discuss the impact of the informal organization and informal group leaders and how supervisors should deal with them.**

Every enterprise is affected by a social subsystem known as the **informal organization**, sometimes called the "invisible organization." The informal organization reflects the spontaneous efforts of individuals and groups to influence their environment. Whenever people work together, social relationships and informal work groups inevitably arise. Informal organization develops when people are in frequent contact, but their relationships are not necessarily a part of formal organizational arrangements. Their contacts may be part of or incidental to their jobs, or they may stem primarily from the desire to be accepted as a group member.

**Informal organization**
Informal gatherings of people, apart from the formal organizational structure, that satisfy members' social and other needs

At the heart of the informal organization are people and their relationships, whereas the formal organization primarily represents the organization's structure and the flow of authority. Supervisors can create and rescind formal organizations they have designed; they cannot eliminate an informal organization because they did not establish it.

Informal groups arise to satisfy the needs and desires of members that the formal organization does not satisfy. Informal organization particularly satisfies members' social needs by providing recognition, close personal contacts, status, companionship, and other aspects of emotional satisfaction. Groups also offer their members other benefits, including protection, security, and support. Furthermore, they provide convenient access to the informal communications network, or grapevine, as discussed in Chapter 6. The grapevine provides a communication channel and satisfies members' desires to know what is going on. The informal organization also influences the behavior of individuals in the group. For example, an informal group may pressure individuals to conform to the performance standards to which most group members subscribe. This phenomenon may occur in any department or at any level in the organization.

## THE INFORMAL ORGANIZATION AND THE SUPERVISOR

At different times, the informal organization makes the supervisor's job easier or more difficult. Because of their interdependence, the attitudes, behaviors, and customs of informal work groups affect the formal organization. Every organization operates in part through informal work groups, which can positively or negatively impact departmental operations and accomplishments.

The informal group has the potential to influence employees to strive for high work performance targets or restrict production, and to cooperate with or work against supervisors, to the point of having those supervisors removed. Supervisors must be aware that informal groups can be very strong and can even shape employee behavior to an extent that interferes with supervision. So-called organizational negativity has become a major area of concern for many organizations as it pollutes overall organizational culture, increases stress and employee turnover, and reduces quality of work.[4] The negative attitudes that lead to negative behavior patterns are often traced to the work groups that influence their members to conform to the groups' norms. The pressures of informal groups can frustrate the supervisor trying to get the results that higher-level managers expect.

To influence the informal organization to play a positive role, the supervisor first must accept and understand it. The supervisor should group employees so that those most likely to compose harmonious teams work on the same assignments. Moreover, the supervisor should avoid activities that would unnecessarily disrupt those informal groups whose interests and behavior patterns support the department's overall objectives. Conversely, if an informal group is influencing employees negatively, and to the extent that the department is seriously threatened, a supervisor may have to do such things as redistribute work assignments or adjust work schedules.

## SUPERVISING AND INFORMAL WORK-GROUP LEADERS

Most informal work groups develop their own leadership. An informal leader may be chosen by the group because he or she is well-liked or very knowledgeable, or the leader may assume leadership by being an effective spokesperson for the group. Work group leaders play significant roles in both formal and informal organizations; without their cooperation, the supervisor may have difficulty controlling the performance of the department. A sensitive supervisor, therefore, will make every effort to gain the cooperation and goodwill of informal leaders of different groups and will solicit their cooperation in furthering departmental objectives. When approached properly, informal leaders can help the supervisor, especially as channels of communication. Informal leaders may even be viable candidates for supervisor understudies. However, it is questionable whether these people can function as informal leaders once they have been designated as understudies.

Instead of viewing informal leaders as "ringleaders," supervisors should consider them employees who have influence and who are "in the know," and then try to work with them. For example, to try to build good relationships with informal leaders, a supervisor may periodically give them information before anyone else or ask their advice on certain problems. However, the supervisor must be careful to avoid having informal leaders lose status in their groups because the leaders' close association with the supervisor is being observed and could be interpreted negatively by employees. Similarly, the supervisor should not extend unwarranted favors to informal leaders as this could undermine their leadership. Rather, the supervisor should look for subtle approaches to have informal groups and their leaders dovetail their special interests with the department's activities. We discuss this and other aspects of work groups in Chapter 11.

## Unity of Command

3 **Explain the unity-of-command and span-of-management principles and their applications.**

As stated many times in this text, employees need to know what is expected of them and to whom they report. Generally, people cannot serve two masters, and the masters can effectively manage only a limited number of people. In the following paragraphs we will discuss two important foundations for organizing; unity of command and span of management.

The chief executive groups the activities of the organization into divisions, departments, services, teams, or units and assigns duties accordingly. Upper-level management places managers and supervisors in charge of divisions and departments and defines their authority relationships. Supervisors must know exactly who their managers and subordinates are. To arrange authority relationships this way, management normally follows the **unity-of-command principle**, which holds that each employee should report directly to only one immediate supervisor. That is, there is only one person to whom the employee is directly accountable. While formal communication and the delegation of authority normally flow upward and downward through the chain of command, there are exceptions, such as in functional authority and the matrix organizational structure, which are discussed later in this chapter. Similarly, task forces, project groups, and special committees may blur the unity-of-command concept. Committees and problem-solving groups are discussed in later chapters.

**Unity-of-command principle**
Principle that holds that each employee should directly report to only one supervisor

As shown in Figure 9.2 the employee is torn when the unity-of-command principle is violated. Having more than one boss usually leads to unsatisfactory performance by the employee due to confusion over who is in charge. Therefore, a supervisor should make certain that, unless there is a valid reason for an exception, only one supervisor should direct an employee.

**FIGURE 9.2 The unity-of-command principle is violated**

## THE SPAN-OF-MANAGEMENT PRINCIPLE

Departments and managerial levels are not solutions; they are the sources of numerous difficulties. Departments are expensive because they must be staffed by supervisors and employees. Moreover, as more departments and levels are created, communication and coordination problems arise. Therefore, there must be valid reasons for creating levels and departments. The reasons are associated with the **span-of-management principle**, which holds that there is an upper limit to the number of employees a supervisor can manage effectively. This principle is also called the span of control (see Figure 9.3).

**Span-of-management principle**
Principle that there is an upper limit to the number of subordinates a supervisor can manage effectively

Because no one can manage an unlimited number of people, top-level managers must organize divisions and departments as separate operating units and place middle-level managers and supervisors in charge. Top-level managers then delegate authority to those middle-level managers, who delegate authority to supervisors, who, in turn, supervise the employees.

The principle that a manager can effectively supervise a limited number of employees is as old as recorded history.[5] However, it is impossible to state how many subordinates a manager should have. It is only correct to say that there is some upper limit to this number. In many industries, a top-level executive has from three to eight subordinate managers, and the span of management usually increases the lower a person descends in the managerial hierarchy. A span of management between 15 and 25 is not uncommon at the first level of supervision.

There has long been a question concerning the link between organizational size and organizational performance. The economic law of diminishing returns has been applied to suggest that size can impact organizational efficiency. However, the "optimal size" for a firm has never been defined; the answer remains elusive.

**FIGURE 9.3 A manager can effectively supervise a limited number of employees**

## FACTORS INFLUENCING THE SPAN OF MANAGEMENT

The number of employees one person can supervise effectively depends on a number of factors (see Figure 9.4), such as the supervisor's abilities, the types and amounts of staff assistance, employees' capabilities, employees' locations, the kinds of activities, and the degree to which departments have objective performance standards.

In most situations, there must be a weighing, or balancing, of the factors listed in Figure 9.4, to arrive at an appropriate span of management for each supervisor.

## HOW MANAGERIAL LEVELS, UNITY OF COMMAND, AND SPAN OF MANAGEMENT ARE RELATED

It is generally accepted that "one-person–one-boss" should be the standard. But some organizations have created another level, the lead person, sometimes called the "working supervisor." A **lead person** is not usually considered part of management, especially in unionized firms. Although the authority of these individuals is somewhat limited, particularly in employee evaluation and discipline, they perform most managerial functions.

**Lead person**
Employee in charge of other employees who performs limited managerial functions but is not considered part of management

While it may be desirable to use "leads," it is not without disadvantages. One can easily see how an employee might view the lead person as a great communicator, with greater skills, knowledge, abilities (SKAs) and competency than the supervisor. Suddenly, the lead person becomes the unofficial supervisor and lines of leadership and authority are blurred. These authors have problems with assigning the lead person supervisory responsibilities without also giving him or her a title

**FIGURE 9.4 A list of factors that influence span of supervision**

**Supervisory competence:** The number of employees that can effectively be managed depends to a large degree on the supervisor's managerial capabilities and the advance planning he or she has done.

**Specialized staff assistance:** If the human resources staff helps the supervisor recruit, select, and train employees, the supervisor will have more time to devote to departmental activities.

**Employee abilities:** The greater the employees' skills, knowledge, abilities (SKAs), and capacity for self-direction, the broader the supervisor's span can be.

**Location:** When employees are in the same area or in close proximity, the supervisor can supervise more employees because observation and communication are relatively easy. When employees are widely dispersed, as they are when they work in different parts of the world (offshoring), work at home (telecommuting), or work in outdoor crews (highway workers), the span of supervision may be somewhat limited because face-to-face communication and coordination are more difficult.

**Nature and complexity of activities:** The simpler, more routine, and more uniform the work activities, the greater the number of people one supervisor can manage. When activities are varied or interdependent, or when errors could have serious consequences, the span may be as few as three to five.

**Objective performance standards:** When each well-trained employee knows exactly what is expected, such as a certain number of customer calls each week, the supervisor may not need to have frequent discussions with the employee about performance. Well-communicated expectations and performance standards will permit a larger span of supervision.

and commensurate pay. But most importantly, making someone a "lead" without properly preparing that person for the task is a sure prescription for failure.

In summary, other things being equal, the narrower the spans of management, the more managerial levels are needed. Stated another way, organizational structures tend to be taller when spans of management are narrower, and structures tend to be flatter when spans of management are wider, especially at the supervisory level. Of course, this may vary because of other organizational considerations. Adding or reducing levels of management may or may not be desirable. For example, adding levels can be costly and can complicate communication and decision making. On the other hand, reducing levels may widen the spans of management to the extent that supervisors become overburdened and cannot maintain adequate control of employees and departmental activities. A trade-off exists between the span and the number of levels.

The managerial problem is to decide which is better: a broad span with few levels or a narrow span with more levels. This important question often confronts upper management. A first-line supervisor does not normally face this question, but supervisors should understand how it influences the design and structure of their organizations.

**4 Justify why a supervisor should strive for the "ideal" organizational structure and work toward this objective.**

## Planning the "Ideal" Departmental Structure

It has often been said that the organizational structure is not an end but the means to an end. Thus, just because Old Ivy is structured in a certain way does not mean that an identical or a similar structure will work for other institutions. Comparing two organizations illustrates this point.

When Hewlett-Packard (HP) was started, the founders formulated a vision:

> *The achievements of the organization are the results of the combined efforts of each individual in the organization working toward common objectives. The objectives should be realistic, should be clearly understood by everyone in the organization, and should reflect the organization's basic character and personality.*[6]

This became known as the "HP Way." In 2007, HP's CEO Mark Hurd was selected as *BusinessWeek*'s Businessperson of the Year. Hurd was quoted as saying, "It's easy to get motivated when you're behind, but when business is going well, that takes the pressure off. HP's growth is a journey, but it's one with a sense of urgency. I focus all my energy on one and only one task: leading HP."[7]

> *Hurd was a classic example of a no-nonsense operator hammering away at a struggling business to get it moving in the right direction again. The marching orders: squeeze out costs and improve efficiency.*[8]

Three years after making those statements, Hurd abruptly resigned amid allegations of sexual harassment and other misconduct. In the past ten years, HP has experienced a shareholder battle over its controversial acquisition of Compaq Computer; the ouster of CEO Carly Fiorina; a congressional investigation into allegations of spying on board members and reporters; and most recently, the Hurd indiscretions. Within months after the Hurd resignation, ten other executive or senior vice presidents were out of the door.[9] In August 2011, HP announced that it would discontinue its tablet computer and smartphone products, sell or spin off its PC division, and look to buy a business software maker.[10]

Less than a month later, former eBay CEO, Meg Whitman replaced an embattled Lew Apotheker as CEO. In her first two years leading HP, Whitman directed steps to revisit mobile devices, move into cloud computing and big data markets, and cut 22,700 jobs to reduce costs, moves that have helped HP turn itself around and achieve revenue stabilization after several years of decline.[11] With five CEOs in the past 13 years, the reorganization appears to be a continuous, circular journey.

In 2011, "the itty bitty machine company" (IBM) celebrated its one-hundredth anniversary. "A century of corporate life has taught us this truth: *To make an enduring impact over the long term, you have to manage for the long term*."[12]

Thomas Watson Sr., a man with a fervor for instilling company pride and encouraging employees to "THINK," served as president/CEO of IBM, originally known as C-T-R (the Computing-Tabulating-Recording Company), for 42 years.[13] Truly this was time enough to plan and see those plans bear fruit.

Watson's son, Thomas Watson Jr., succeeded him as president. Some of the products developed by IBM were the punchcard system, the IBM 701 (a large computer based on vacuum tubes), the magnetic hard disk for data storage, Fortran, the Selectric Typewriter, the floppy disk, bar codes, and the personal computer.[14] Watson Jr. said, "I believe that if an organization is to meet the challenges of a changing world, it must be prepared to change everything about itself, except its beliefs."[15] Figure 9.5 lays the foundation for IBM values and how they impact employee actions and company structure.

Pause for a moment and try to imagine the burdens that fall on HP's or IBM's front-line supervisors who were charged with designing and managing the production operations. Designing and redesigning is not a one-and-done thing. It is a journey that requires starts, stops, and restarts. Typically, managers ask, "How

**FIGURE 9.5 IBM's core values**

Watson's more enduring contribution to business was his intentional creation of something that would outlast him—a shared corporate culture. He showed how the basic beliefs and values of an organization could be perpetuated—to become its guiding constant through time. This is why we have never defined IBM by what we make, no matter how successful the product or service.

By values we do not mean ethics or morals, which are requisites for every enterprise. We mean the characteristics that identify what is both unique and enduring for a particular enterprise. And by deliberately building a culture, we don't mean memorializing the routine of what the founder did. Rather, it's about institutionalizing *why* the organization does what it does—getting to the essential truths of what makes you, *you*. Grounding a culture in such values and purpose is about how employees, anywhere around the globe, at this very moment and for generations, honor and deliver on that.

Values therefore force choices: Whom you hire. The ways you serve the customer. How you develop talent at all levels. Which businesses you create, enter and exit, and when. How much risk taking you promote.

When we have lived our values, IBMers and our company have thrived. When we haven't, it hurt us.

*Source*: From International Business Machines Corporation, (2011)

*Note*: Also see: "Nearly All the Companies Our Grandparents Admired Have Disap-peared," The Wall Street Journal (June 16, 2010), pp. A10–13. This ad summarizes the history, vision, and mission of IBM.

should we organize this department based on the people we have?" But the question should instead be, "What organizational structure will efficiently and effectively allow us to achieve our objectives and strategies?" In short, organizational structure decisions should follow strategy choice.

Supervisors should think of an ideal departmental structure—a structure the supervisor believes can best achieve the department's objectives. The supervisor should plan the departmental structure based on sound organizational principles, not personalities. If the organization is planned primarily to accommodate current employees, shortcomings will likely persist. When a department is structured around one employee or a few, serious problems can occur when key employees are promoted or leave.[16] When departments are organized according to activities and functions, the company can seek qualified employees. For example, when a supervisor relies heavily on one or two key, versatile employees, the department will suffer if one or both of these employees leave. Conversely, if a number of weak employees do not carry their share of the load, the supervisor may assign too many employees to certain activities to compensate for the poorly performing individuals. Therefore, supervisors should design structures that best serve departmental objectives; then, employees can be best matched with tasks.

This is easier said than done, however. It frequently happens, particularly in small departments, that employees fit the "ideal" structure poorly. In most situations, the supervisor is placed in charge of a department without having had the chance to decide its structure or to choose its employees. In these circumstances, the supervisor can gradually adjust to the capacities of employees. As time goes on, the supervisor can make the personnel and other changes that will move the department toward fitting the supervisor's concept of an "ideal" structure. In all this, of course, the supervisor's primary focus still should be on finding, placing, and motivating the best employees.

**Learning organization**
Employees continually strive to improve their SKAs while expanding their efforts to achieve organizational objectives

While CEOs continually search for ideal organizational structure, they often neglect a key component, that is, the concept of a **learning organization** that fosters employee collaboration and sharing of information. In *The Fifth Discipline*, Peter Senge describes learning organizations as places "where people continually expand their capacity (SKAs) to create the results they truly desire, where new and expansive patterns of thinking are nurtured, where collective aspiration is set free, and where people are continually learning to see the whole together."[17]

A culture is created in which all employees take responsibility for identifying and resolving work-related issues. Ideally, the learning organization will more quickly be able to adapt and respond to change. The most effective organizational structure is one in which the supervisor aligns his or her department's goals with the organization's vision and engages all employees in the pursuit of being the "best of the best."

**5 Compare and contrast departmentalization and alternative approaches for grouping activities and assigning work.**

## Approaches to Structuring Work

It is important for managers, supervisors, and employees to understand how their positions and responsibilities relate to the positions and responsibility of other employees. Organization charts and manuals, job descriptions, and job specifications can help employees understand their positions and the relationships among various departments and jobs.

In planning their organizational structures, many companies develop organizational charts for all or parts of their operations. An **organizational chart** is a graphic portrayal of organizational authority and responsibility relationships using boxes or other depictions. The graphic elements of organizational charts are usually interconnected to show the grouping of activities that make up a department, division, or section. Each box normally represents one position category, although several employees may be included in a position category. By studying the relationships of categories, anyone can readily determine who reports to whom. Historically, organization charts have been constructed vertically, arranged in a pyramid shape reflective of a hierarchical organization structure. In the past decade, however, an increasing number of firms' organization charts, primarily those with a focus on innovation, reflect a "flattened" structure, one with fewer hierarchical levels and decision-making authority distributed across whole levels of the organization.[18] The arrangement of an organization chart can provide a great deal of insight about how power is distributed, how decisions are made, and how work and information flows throughout an organization.

**Organizational chart**
Graphic portrayal of a company's authority and responsibility relationships

A **job description** identifies the job's principal elements, duties, and scope of authority and responsibility. **Job specifications** refer to the skills, capacities, and qualities—personal qualifications—that are needed to perform the job adequately. As mentioned in previous chapters, these personal qualities are referred to as SKAs. Many organizations include job specifications as part of each job description. These will be discussed in more detail in Chapter 10.

**Job description**
Written description of the principal duties and responsibilities of a job

**Job specifications**
Written description of the personal qualifications needed to perform a job adequately

The question of how to develop an organizational chart begins with an analysis of what work needs to be done by when and by whom. The organizational structure is influenced largely by the principle of **division of work (specialization)**. This principle holds that jobs can be divided into smaller components and specialized tasks to increase efficiency and output. Technological advances and increasing complexity make it difficult for employees to keep current with their work or specialty responsibilities. Dividing work into smaller tasks allows employees to specialize in narrower areas of their fields. Employees can then master these smaller tasks and produce more efficiently. For example, as cars become more complex and diverse, it becomes more difficult for a mechanic to know how to fix everything on every type of car. As a result, specialty repair shops, such as muffler shops, oil-change services, and foreign-car specialists, have sprung up. Even in shops that do many types of repairs, mechanics often specialize. By specializing, employees can become expert enough in their areas to produce efficiently.

**Division of work (specialization)**
Dividing work into components and specialized tasks to improve efficiency and output

**Departmentalization** is the process of grouping activities and people into organizational units, usually known as departments. A **department** is a set of activities and people over which a manager or supervisor has responsibility and authority. The terminology organizations use for this entity varies. A department may be called a division, an office, a service, or a unit. Most organizations have departments because division of work and specialization enhance efficiency and results.

**Departmentalization**
The process of grouping activities and people into distinct organizational units

**Department**
An organizational unit for which a supervisor has responsibility and authority

The **formal organizational structure** is based on a company's number and types of departments, positions and functions, and authority and reporting relationships. Whereas an organization's major departments are established by top-level managers, supervisors are primarily concerned with activities in their own areas. From time to time, supervisors confront the need to departmentalize their areas, so they should be familiar with the alternatives for grouping activities. These are the same options available to top-level managers when those managers define the company's major departments. Departmentalization is usually done according to function, products or services, geographic location, customer, process and equipment, or time.

**Formal organizational structure**
Departments, positions, functions, authority, and reporting relationships as depicted on a firm's organizational chart

## THE PROJECT MANAGEMENT STRUCTURE

**Project management–type organizational structure**
A hybrid structure in which regular, functional departments coexist with project teams made up of people from different departments

The need to coordinate activities across departments has contributed to the development of the **project management–type organizational structure**, also called matrix structure. The project management–type structure, which is superimposed on the line-staff organization, adds horizontal dimensions to the normally vertical (top-down) orientation of the organizational structure. It is a hybrid in which both regular (functional) line and staff departments coexist with project teams or group assignments across departmental lines.

Many high-tech firms employ project structures to focus special talents from different departments on specific projects for certain periods. Project structures enable managers to undertake several projects simultaneously, some of which may be of relatively short duration. Each project is assigned to a project manager who manages the project from inception to completion. Employees from different functional departments are assigned to work on each project as needed, either part-time or full-time.

Although the complexity of project structure varies, a basic matrix form might resemble the chart shown in Figure 9.6. This chart illustrates how some managers have been given responsibility for specific projects in the firm while departmental supervisors are primarily responsible for supervising employees in their regular departments. Project managers A and B are responsible for coordinating activities on their designated projects. However, the project managers must work closely with the departmental supervisors of functions X, Y, and Z. The employees who work in these departments report directly (functionally) to the departmental supervisors, but their services are used under the authority and responsibility of the project managers to whom they are assigned for varying periods.

**FIGURE 9.6 Basic project management–type organizational structure**

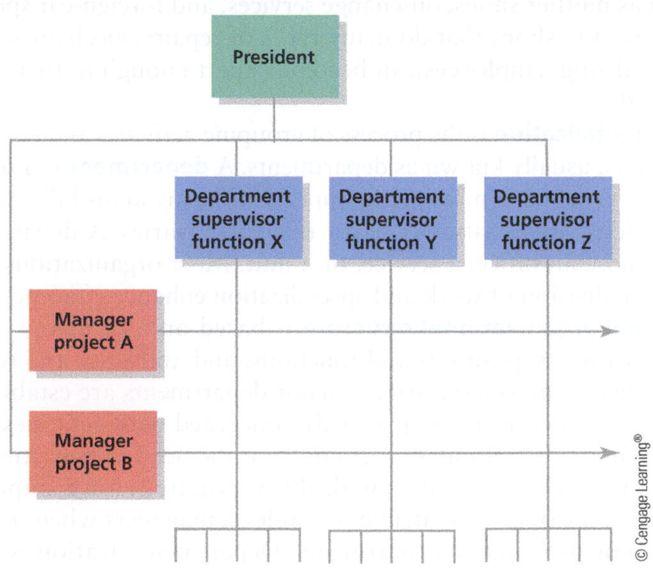

Several problems are associated with the project management–type organizational structure. The most frequent is direct accountability. The matrix structure violates the principle of unity of command because departmental employees are accountable to a departmental supervisor and project managers. Other problems involve scheduling employees who are assigned to several projects. These problems can be avoided, or at least minimized, by planning properly and clarifying authority relationships before the project starts.

Despite such problems, this structure is increasingly common because organizations find it advantageous. Successful project teams are generally those where someone dreamed big, created a vision, aligned the project team's goals with the overall strategy, inspired and informed team members, and made changes as necessary.[19] It also requires the willingness of project managers (sometimes referred to as project team leaders) and departmental supervisors and their employees to coordinate activities and responsibilities to complete projects. Such coordination is vital to work scheduling, and it is imperative to employees' performance appraisals. Consider the suggestions in the accompanying "Supervisory Tips" box when managing project teams.

## WORK ASSIGNMENTS AND ORGANIZATIONAL STABILITY

Supervisors are challenged much more frequently by the problem of how and to whom to assign work than by the problem of how to organize departments. How and to whom to assign work always involve differences of opinion. Nevertheless, the assignment of work should be justifiable and explainable on the basis of good management rather than on personal likes and dislikes or intuition. The supervisor is subject to pressures from different directions. Some employees are willing and want to assume more work, while others believe they should not be burdened by additional duties. One of the supervisor's most important responsibilities is to assign work so that everybody has a fair share and all employees do their parts equitably and satisfactorily (see Figure 9.7).

**FIGURE 9.7 Work should be assigned equitably, but supervisors sometimes rely too much on certain employees**

**SUPERVISORY TIPS**

### Getting Home with Project Management Teams

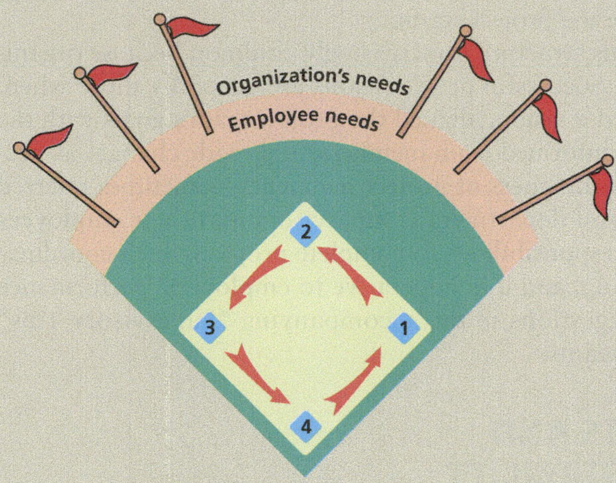


**A good project team design enables employees to be the best they can be so they can achieve both high performance and satisfaction in their work.**

1. You reach first base when you create a vision.
   - Define the project and set project objectives that can be measured.
   - Communicate the vision to everyone.
   - Know the importance of getting people to buy into and commit to the project.
2. You reach second base when you have a well-qualified, well-trained employee group committed to company objectives.
   - Use employee SKAs to their fullest when brainstorming alternative strategies.
   - Develop a plan.
   - Break the project into steps or units and set performance standards for each step or unit.
3. You reach third base when the team is working together on the project.
   - Implement the plan and control work-in-progress.
   - Share information, resolve conflicts, support, and encourage teamwork.
   - Be an enabler (see Chapter 2).
4. You score when the goal is accomplished and both team and individual performers are appropriately recognized.
   - Complete and evaluate the project.
   - Learn from the experience and make suggestions for future projects.
   - Celebrate the victory.

**Principle of organizational stability**
Principle that holds that no organization should become overly dependent on one or several "indispensable" individuals

As emphasized previously, a supervisor's task of assigning departmental work is easier when the supervisor consistently uses the strengths and experiences of all employees. However, supervisors are often inclined to assign heavier and more difficult tasks to capable employees who are the most experienced. Over the long term, it is advantageous to train and develop less experienced employees so that they, too, can perform difficult jobs. When supervisors rely too much on one employee or a few employees, a department becomes weaker because top performers can call in sick, take promotions, or leave the enterprise. The **principle of organizational stability** advocates that no organization should become overly dependent on one or several key "indispensable" individuals whose absences or departures would disrupt the organization. Organizations need enough employees who have been trained well and have flexible skills. One way to develop such flexibility is to assign employees to different jobs in the department temporarily, such as during vacation periods or employee absences. In this way, there is usually someone to take over any job if the need arises.

At times, a supervisor may have to hire temporary employees to meet workload demands for a project or other needs. As discussed in Chapter 3, temporary employees can be helpful when given work assignments they can complete and when they do not cause disruptions or disagreements with permanent employees. Some temporary employees prove themselves so competent that supervisors seek to hire them for permanent positions.[20]

## AUTHORITY AND ORGANIZATIONAL STRUCTURES

Once management establishes departments, it must set and clarify relationships among and within the departments. In Chapter 2, we briefly defined managerial authority and the process of delegation. We expanded on those concepts in Chapter 5. The following discussion serves as a basis for discussing how management establishes authority and responsibility relationships in organizational structures. Every organization has a vertical, direct line of authority that can be traced from the chief executive to departmental employees. **Line authority** provides the right to direct others and requires them to conform to company decisions, policies, rules, and objectives. Supervisors directly involved in making, selling, or distributing the company's products or services have line authority. Line authority establishes who can direct whom in the organization. A primary purpose of line authority is to make the organization work smoothly.

**Line authority**
The right to direct others and to require them to conform to decisions, policies, rules, and objectives

With organizational downsizings, activities tend to become less specialized and more complicated. Line supervisors cannot be expected to direct subordinates adequately and expertly in all phases of operations without some assistance. In order to perform their managerial functions, line supervisors need the assistance of specialists who have been granted staff authority. **Staff authority** refers to the right and duty to provide counsel, advice, support, and service regarding policies, procedures, technical issues, and problems in a person's areas of expertise. Certain specialists are granted staff authority because of their positions or specialized knowledge. Staff people assist other members of the organization whenever the need arises. For example, human resource specialists often screen candidates for line managers to interview. While human resource managers can direct the work of employees in their own departments (line authority), they can only advise managers in other departments in human resource matters (staff authority).

**Staff authority**
The right to provide counsel, advice, support, and service in a person's areas of expertise

Most organizations use a **line-and-staff-type organizational structure**. Certain departments, such as human resources and accounting, usually are classified as staff since they mainly support other departments. For example, human resource managers are responsible for seeing the line departments carry out certain policies and procedures. For the most part, staff supervisors lack the direct authority to order line employees to conform to policies and procedures. They primarily counsel and advise. Line supervisors can accept the staff person's advice, alter it, or reject it, but because the staff person is usually the expert in the field, line supervisors usually accept, and even welcome, the staff person's advice.

**Line-and-staff-type organizational structure**
Structure that combines line and staff departments and incorporates line and staff authority

*A line supervisor is usually open to a staff person's feedback and input because the staff person is considered an "expert in the field"*

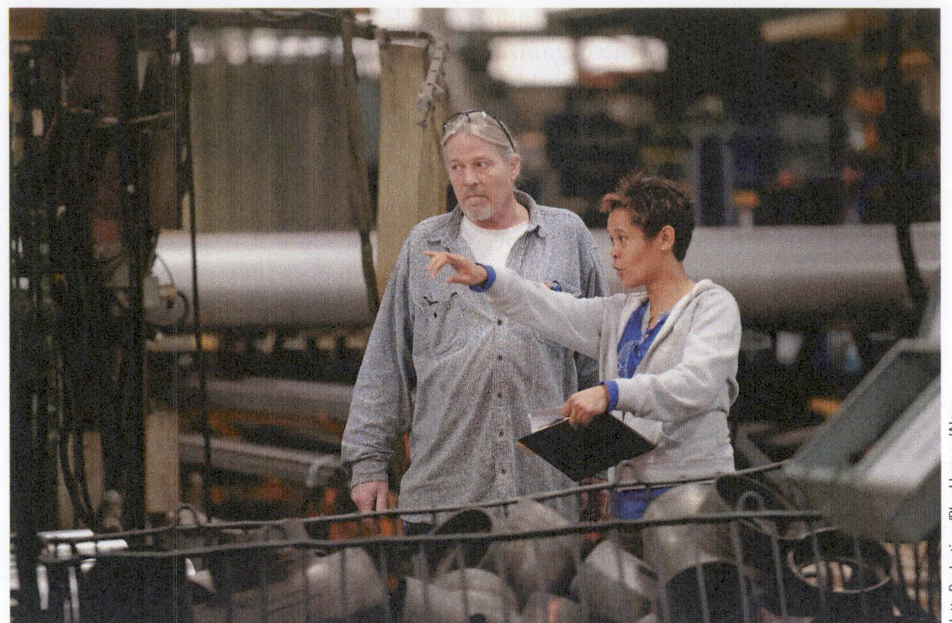

Jetta Productions/Blend Images/Alamy

The day-to-day usefulness and effectiveness of the human resources staff depends primarily on their abilities to develop close working relationships with line managers and supervisors. The quality of these line/staff relationships, in turn, depends on how clearly top-level managers have defined the scope of activities and authority of the staff.

There is no one best way to organize. Organizational theorists contend that structure should follow strategy. In recent years, there has been significant change in the way business is conducted. Pick up a current copy of *Fortune*, *BusinessWeek*, or the *Wall Street Journal* and read about how one organization or another is announcing plans to modify its organizational structure. Why? Intense competition for the consumer dollar, rising resource costs, globalization, and a search for ways to increase profitability is leading many organizations to alter their strategies. As you read the articles in these publications, ascertain how the organization has changed its strategy. To the consternation of these authors, most top managers have forgotten a fundamental principle: "organizations tend to be more effective when they are structured to fit the strategic change and the demands of the situation."

**6 Assess the implications of downsizing for restructuring and suggest alternatives.**

## Organizational Principles in an Era of Organizational Downsizings

**Downsizing, restructuring, or right-sizing**
Large-scale reduction and elimination of jobs in a company that usually reduces middle-level managers, removes organizational levels, and widens the span of management for remaining supervisors

Among the most publicized aspects of corporate business in recent years has been the large-scale reduction and permanent elimination of thousands of jobs in many major companies. Many companies have eliminated large segments of their workforces. This process, called **downsizing, restructuring, or right-sizing**, has been accomplished through such things as plant and office closings, the sales of divisions, extensive employee layoffs, attrition, and early retirements.

Typically, management resorts to restructuring in order to reduce costs, streamline operations, and become more efficient and competitive. In some industries, external factors force reductions in staff. In the health care field, for example, over 41,000 employees were laid off in 2013 due to reductions in income from Medicare reimbursements, research funding, and decreased length of inpatient stays, layoffs that were "shortsighted," according to J. P. Fingado, CEO of API Healthcare "because the providers will likely have to add staff as soon as next year to handle increased patient volumes from the health care law."[21] With a predicted trend of continued reductions in funding, though, remaining hospital employees will be expected to do more with less staff as well as face more layoffs.[22] Similarly, Radio Shack, which at one time supplied consumer electronics in 5,000 community stores across the United States, closed over 1,000 retail outlets in 2014 primarily due to buyers' shift to online purchasing behavior.[23] Noted author H. James Harrington contends that employment security is one of the most critical and complex issues facing top management. According to Harrington:

> *Corporate America has been on a downsizing kick since the late 1980s. The answer to business pressure has been to slow down and lay off, with the hope of raising stock prices, but that doesn't work. Large layoffs produce sudden, substantial stock gains because the effects of a reduced workforce don't immediately reach the customer, and the savings from reduced wages make the organization appear more profitable than it really is. But in the long run, downsizing has a negative effect.*[24]

The companies that are repeatedly restructuring do particular damage because employee productivity declines dramatically as a result. However, downsizing doesn't just affect corporate America. When University of Michigan cut 50 administrative support positions and relocated 275 positions to an off-campus location and discouraged employees from discussing the impending change, the organization received a letter from its faculty asserting that the process led to "rumors that have increased staff and faculty anxiety; and that the process amounts to a dehumanization of the workplace."[25] Even layoff survivors feel no added security or commitment.

One major organizational impact of downsizing is a reduction of middle-level managers and the removal of one or more organizational levels. For supervisors and other managers who survive downsizing, the span of management usually widens. Many supervisors are stretched because they are required to add unfamiliar departments or functions to their responsibilities.[26]

Some middle-level management and staff positions have been eliminated because information technology (IT) has made it possible for higher-level managers to acquire data and information quickly and to keep in close touch with operations. Not surprisingly, the authors are familiar with many situations where the IT function has been offshored to India or another lower-cost country, although this trend has begun to reverse in recent years.[27] As a result, supervisors and employees usually have to become more knowledgeable about more aspects of operations. Peter Drucker argued that the knowledge/information explosion requires restructured organizations to depend on remaining employees throughout the firm, rather than on traditional "command-and-control structures," to make decisions.[28]

The firms that have downsized most effectively appear to be those that have planned for it systematically and have tried to harmonize, as much as possible, previous and new organizational structures and operations in ways that are compatible and acceptable to those who remain. Usually, this means involving human resources staff specialists early in downsizing plans. Workforce planning, training and skills assessment, and widespread communication of what will happen throughout the organization are typical areas that require the skills and major participation of the human resources department.[29] In addition, ideas about authority and the use of authority must be reshaped to give supervisors and employees greater decision-making responsibility.[30] Even with a weakened organizational structure, most individuals need clear lines of accountability for their performance to be evaluated. These lines are vital if reward systems are to be meaningful and motivational.[31]

Most organizational theorists predict that downsizing will continue indefinitely and that in some firms there will be radical restructuring. Is there an answer? The authors believe so! It begins with top management creating a vision for the organization that goes outside the conventional. All organizations, including federal, state, and local governments and various agencies, must "think outside the box" by developing creative strategies. Then they should strive to design organizational structures that put the right person in the job to do more with less. Clearly, the "do more with less" concept may be a guiding principle for planning and organizing.

## ALTERNATIVES TO DOWNSIZING

Proponents of downsizing and restructuring have typically advocated employee empowerment and engagement. Empowerment, as identified in a number of places in this text, essentially means delegating sufficient authority to employees to allow them to make decisions and become more involved in achieving organizational objectives. Engagement, as discussed earlier in this chapter as well as in Chapter 11, means that the employee is fully involved in, and enthusiastic about, his or her work. Nothing is more important than getting employees committed to the expanding opportunities that reorganization might bring. Studies show that job satisfaction increases if employees have more opportunities to use their SKAs and if career development and skills training accompany the reorganization.[32]

When employee groups are given wide latitude and considerable authority to make job-related decisions, empowerment is associated with the creation of **self-directed (self-managed) work teams (SDWTs)**. We discuss team concepts further in Chapter 11.

**Self-directed (self-managed) work teams (SDWTs)**
Employee groups that are given wide latitude and considerable authority to make many of their own job-related decisions

Some firms have tried **reengineering**, whereby they restructure based more on process (e.g., meeting customer orders and requirements) than on department or function (e.g., sales and production). Reengineering requires supervisors and employees to focus on customer needs and services rather than on their own functions and specialties. Little Caesars, for example, worked with a consulting company to reengineer pizza preparation processes, such as the distance a worker has to walk each week while making and serving pizzas, in order to increase efficiency and customer satisfaction. Rearranged kitchens in targeted stores cut the distance from 15 miles to 10.5 miles per week, which decreased production time per pizza, increased the number of pizzas available for immediate purchase, and ultimately, decreased customer wait time. Happier customers who don't have to wait have translated to return visits and increased orders.[33] Focusing on the customer may enhance a firm's efforts to be more efficient and competitive in the marketplace, but it also can mean blurring line and staff functions and roles. Some authorities have suggested that reengineering will require

**Reengineering**
Concept of restructuring a firm based on processes and customer needs and services rather than on departments and functions

"process managers," who will manage key processes and whose broadened responsibilities will cut across line and staff functions and organizational levels.[34] A number of major corporations already have restructured parts of their organizations along customer-process dimensions. When carried out, reengineering could create what has been called the **horizontal corporation**, in which organizational structures flatten markedly and managerial authority relationships are minimal.[35]

**Horizontal corporation** A very flat firm resulting from restructuring by customer process and organizational structure

Making the decision to downsize an organization is not easy, and sometimes strategies are put in place that can produce increased efficiency and effectiveness without the need to eliminate workers. William Martin and Audrey Davis encourage decision makers to resist making drastic personnel changes without first exploring other options that will keep workers engaged. Their analysis of the research has shown that the presumed economic advantages of downsizing are not always realized, and often organizations are left with a demoralized workforce, which can breed a whole new collection of problems. They suggest 50 alternatives to downsizing, organized into seven categories, which can be applied systematically in consideration of how to cut costs and increase efficiencies.

- Modifying compensation and benefits by, for example, eliminating overtime, freezing salaries, or reducing hours;
- Talent management strategies such as job sharing, creation of new teams, and removing underperforming employees;
- Training and development processes such as helping employees launch complementary businesses or retraining workers for new tasks;
- Business process/operations changes that could include employing new technologies or, as discussed previously, reengineering processes;
- Organizational structure modifications, including sharing ownership with employees, consolidating locations, or, as suggested above, flattening the organization;
- Supply chain management tactics such as collaborating with customers, suppliers, and competitors; and
- Revenue enhancements that can include selling assets and moving employees into new revenue-producing positions.[36]

The past decade has seen a tremendous growth in a new conceptualization of the corporate organization, the **virtual organization** in which independent organizations, including customers, suppliers, and even competitors are linked together temporarily, typically through the use of IT, to share costs, skills, employees, and access to each other's markets in order to respond to exceptional market opportunities.[37] The values of the virtual organization design are that participating entities can be brought together rapidly to realize a shared objective without having to invest time and resources in creating extensive infrastructure, and there is no commitment to keeping it going once the objective is achieved, which are what make it a viable option for organizations seeking ways to contain costs while seeking sustaining opportunities.

**Virtual organization** Companies linked temporarily to take advantage of marketplace opportunities

Four principles guide the formation of a virtual organization. First, the boundaries of the organization are conceptual, rather than tangible—the organizations are bound solely by their common purpose. Second, technology is used to link people, assets, and ideas. Third, each participating entity is included by virtue of its expertise or specialization. Fourth, once the common purpose is realized, the virtual organization disbands. One example of a virtual organization relationship is one between Proctor and Gamble and Clorox, competitors who came together to create GLAD Press and Seal plastic wrap specifically to compete with Dow-Brands's Saran Wrap. P&G invented the wrap in its labs, and Clorox marketed it under the well-known GLAD brand.[38] Likewise, Symbian, a mobile phone software development company, was originally set up as a virtual organization by Nokia, Sony Ericsson, Samsung Electronics Co., Panasonic, and Siemens AG to create a common smartphone operating system. With newer, more nimble operating systems coming online, Symbian has been disbanded and support agreements handed off to a management company.[39]

The character of the virtual organization requires a high level of trust and collaboration, as the structure often operates with no organizational chart, hierarchy, or vertical integration. When this trust is maintained, innovations and shared success result. However, virtual organizations do have challenges, which include an increase in communication load for each of the partners as they manage the networked relationships, the danger of eroding trust if communication and coordination are not well maintained, and the difficulty in defining and maintaining employee reporting relationships. As more and more organizations explore the flexibility of the virtual organization design and become more adept at working virtually, supervisors will see an increase in the need to manage these challenges.

**Lean manufacturing** Techniques that enable a company to produce more product with fewer resources (lower costs)

Although beyond the scope of this text, lean manufacturing or lean production as it would apply to service-related industries is a concept that allows employees greater authority to make decisions based on customer needs. **Lean manufacturing** is not about laying off people. It is about planning and organizing to use resources more efficiently. Streamlining production, cross-training employees so they can do multiple tasks, and building on advances in robotics, software, and other manufacturing technologies are usually part of the system. Decreasing distance between, or even colocating manufacturing, research and development, and supply chain facilities is another lean manufacturing strategy. All employees, from the CEO to the floor sweeper, must rethink how they work and must eliminate non-value-added time.[40]

Regardless of whether we want them, radical company restructurings will become more commonplace. It is unclear whether reengineering or the other interventions mentioned above differ significantly from what many firms try to concentrate on, with or without downsizing. What seems likely is that organizational principles will always be part of supervision and that any organizational change will require supervisors to understand how to apply and adapt certain organizational principles.

**7 List the major factors contributing to organizing effective meetings, especially the supervisor's role.**

## Organizing for Effective Meeting Management

Electronic messaging or instant messaging (IM) systems are not the complete answer to effective supervision. But they have become a form of real-time direct communication. Corporate intranets, chat rooms, and IM are forms of synchronous communications. The sessions are live, and each user can respond to the others in real time. While these, along with e-mail and the wide collection of collaboration software available, are ways to supply information people need to perform their jobs and to share ideas and opinions, face-to-face meetings can sometimes be the most effective way to achieve organizational objectives.

Many work teams have experimented with meeting facilitators. In this case, the group leader or the supervisor does not conduct the meeting. This role falls to the facilitator, a function that is often rotated among team members. This approach allows the supervisor, for example, to observe, listen, and ask probing questions of team members. In addition, team members gain leadership experience. A downside of this approach is that all team members must be adept at meeting management. Furthermore, the note-taking responsibility is rotated among team members.

Meetings should be called only when necessary. In his TED Talk, "Why Work Doesn't Happen at Work," Jason Fried suggests that meetings are actually very expensive to an organization. If a supervisor calls a one-hour meeting, it actually is not a one-hour meeting if ten people are in attendance—it is a ten-hour meeting. This perspective, of the productivity cost of meetings, should cause a manager to pause and consider whether a face-to-face meeting is necessary, if an entire department needs to be involved, if the information could be shared electronically, or whether it would be more efficient for a few key people to get together to address a targeted objective or specific problem. When a supervisor decides that a meeting is necessary, however, the purpose for the meeting, the topics, and the intended outcome should be communicated to meeting participants, and the participants' roles should be clarified.[41]

## SUPERVISORY TIPS

### Guidelines for Planning and Leading a Meeting[42]

1. Select participants who will bring knowledge and expertise to the meeting.
2. Notify participants well in advance of the meeting.
3. Have a plan and an agenda.
4. Begin the meeting on time.
5. Present the problems and issues to be discussed and the meeting's objectives.
6. Encourage all group members to participate fully in the discussion.
7. Allow sufficient time for participants to offer information and discuss alternative proposals.
8. Strive to find consensus and areas of agreement before voting on the proposal.
9. Try to stay on the subject and adjourn on time, but make adjustments as necessary.
10. Follow up, including distributing a summary of the meeting (minutes) and actions to be taken.

The accompanying "Supervisory Tips" box outlines guidelines for planning, organizing, and leading a meeting.

The meeting chairperson or facilitator must be skilled at keeping the meeting focused. Many successful work teams have adopted ground rules for their meetings. Suggested ground rules might include the items presented in Figure 9.8.

The meeting chairperson is ultimately responsible for the meeting's effectiveness. Figure 9.9 provides a useful list of questions to consider when planning and organizing a meeting.

**FIGURE 9.8 Suggested meeting ground rules**

- Everyone will be candid and specific.
- Everyone will have a say.
- Everyone will stop what they are doing and listen carefully to other team members' comments.
- Everyone will avoid electronic distractions.
- All team members must support their opinions with facts.
- No one will be allowed to interrupt another; we will hear each other out.
- We are a TEAM—Together Everyone Achieves More!

**FIGURE 9.9 Questions to consider when planning a meeting**

What is the purpose (goal) of the meeting?

What are the opportunities, threats, conflicts, problems, concerns, issues, or topics that should be considered?

What information must be disseminated before the meeting?

What information must be gathered before the meeting?

What preparation is needed on the part of the participants?

What work must be completed before the meeting?

What additional resources will be needed to accomplish the purpose?

What are the ground rules for conducting the meeting?

Who is involved with the concerns, issues, or topics?

Who must do advance work or make decisions regarding the agenda?

Who should be invited because they can provide information needed for problem solving or discussing the issue?

Who will develop and distribute the agenda?

Who must attend?

Who will facilitate the meeting?

Who will be assigned as the note-taker?

How much time do we need to allot to each topic?

How should the meeting room be arranged?

How do we strive to find consensus and areas of agreement?

How do we stay focused on the subject(s)?

When and where should the meeting be scheduled?

When should the meeting end?

When and how should the meeting be evaluated?

When and what follow-up is needed to the meeting (e.g., distribute a summary of the meeting and the actions to be taken)?



The chairperson's general approach is crucial. He or she sets the tone for the meeting and should model expected meeting etiquette and behaviors. One particularly important behavior the chairperson should model is avoiding electronic distractions during the meeting. The authors have seen exponential growth in the number of meeting attendees and even meeting leaders who only attend meetings "part way" because they are busy checking their messages and sending emails during discussions. Shane Atchison, CEO of Possible global digital ad agency, asserts that when the smartphone arrived, meetings got longer and less got done. In an attempt to change this trend, when Atchison convenes or enters a meeting, "I take my phone out of my pocket, switch it off in front of everyone, and place it face down on the table. It sits there for the whole meeting. I don't even pick it up if we take a break." That simple act, he asserts, puts pressure on all in attendance to be fully present.[43] Along with ensuring that attendees are tuned in, the chairperson should also encourage everyone to be involved. Initially, everyone's contribution should be accepted without judgment, and everyone should feel free to participate. The chairperson may have to ask controversial questions to start the discussion and participation. This is sometimes done by asking provocative, open-ended questions that use words like *who*, *what*, *why*, *where*, and *when*. Questions that can be answered with a simple "yes" or "no" should be avoided.

As you may remember from our discussion of communication in Chapter 6, the supervisor is responsible for giving and getting information. To get information or to open discussion on a particular topic, the supervisor might want to ask the W questions—what, where, why, when, and who—before getting to the how. For example, the chairperson could use questions to get and keep the discussion going, such as, "What is the relationship between quality and machine setup times?" "Jason, what would be your suggestion?" "Where did the problem occur?" "Why is that important to you, Heather?" "When will we have the new machine on line?" "Who might have the experience to handle such an assignment?" "Who would like to comment on Michelle's question?" and "How can we exceed the customer's expectations?"

Another technique is to start at one side of the conference table and ask members to express their thoughts on the problem in turn. While this approach forces everyone to participate, it discourages spontaneous participation and allows the rest of the group to sit back and wait until called upon. This approach also may cause some individuals to take a stand on an issue before they are mentally prepared to do so.

As a general rule, the chairperson should appoint someone, for example, a scribe or note-taker, to record what happened during the meeting. Before adjourning the meeting, the chairperson may have the scribe orally summarize the key points of the meeting, describe the chosen action, and ascertain that participants are in agreement on the gist of the meeting. This process gives all participants a chance to review and agree on what took place.

The chairperson should see to it that every participant gets the written summary, or minutes. The summary should also be distributed to all other personnel who have a need to know what took place or who and what is essential in accomplishing the necessary actions. In short, the meeting action summary lists the actions to be taken by the group, assigns accountability (who is to do what by when), and becomes a record for follow-up and feedback.

The written summary also serves as a permanent record or guideline for future situations involving similar circumstances. If some matters are left undecided, the summary can provide a review of the alternatives that were discussed and help to crystallize the thinking of participants. For permanent standing committees, such as the organization's safety committee, it is advisable to use the summary to announce when the group shall meet next.

Remember: None of us is as smart as all of us! A group of individuals exchanging information, opinions, and experiences will usually develop a better solution to a problem than could any one person who thinks through a problem alone. While meetings at the departmental level are important, supervisors often will meet with others to discuss, plan, and decide on issues and to determine what actions must be carried out. The meeting management tips and suggestions offered here should become a part of every supervisor's toolbox.

## How to Use Time More Effectively

**8 Appraise the importance of self-organization, that is, effective use of your time and talents.**

World-renowned leadership author and speaker Stephen Covey passed away in 2012. Recognized as one of twenty-five most influential Americans by *Time* magazine, Covey coined seven principles, *The 7 Habits of Highly Effective People*, the

FIGURE 9.10 Plan your work—work your plan!

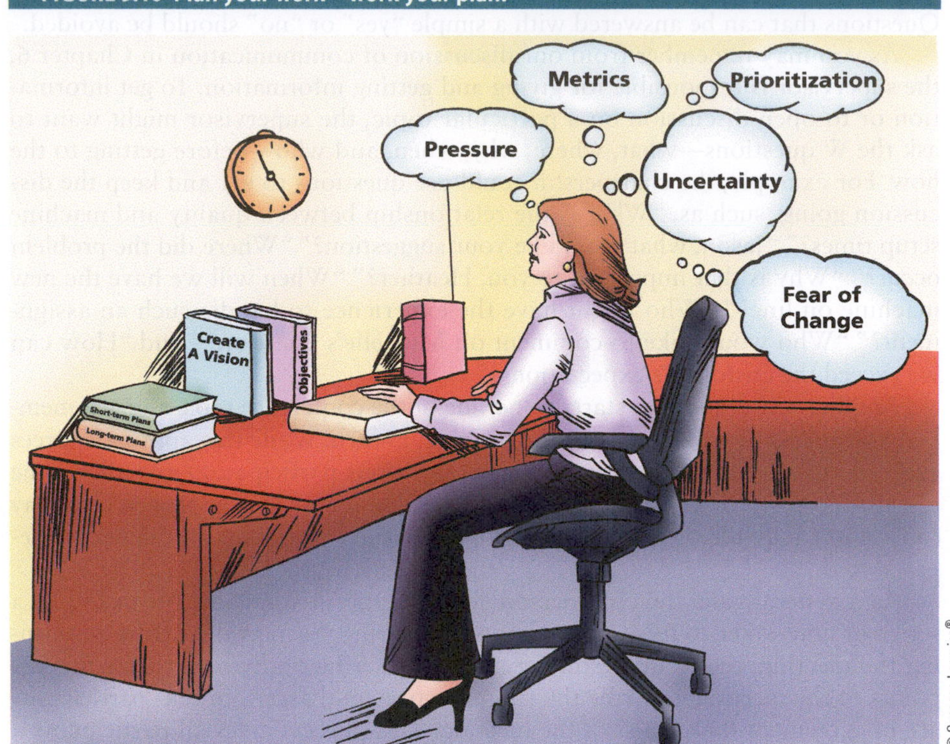


first three of which can help guide our decisions about how to best use our time. Habit 1, "be proactive," Habit 2, "begin with the end in mind," and Habit 3, "put first things first" suggest that in order to effectively use the time we have, we need to take charge of our time, know where we are going, and prioritize the things we need to do.[44] Each of us has the same finite amount of time. There are still 24 hours in a day and 168 hours in a week. No one has yet found a way to "save time" or store it for another day. How many times have you heard someone say, "I wish I had more time"? The phrase "making time" is a myth. Everyone has the same amount of time. We need to be deliberate and focused in planning, organizing, and managing our activities in order to use our time effectively (see Figure 9.10).

Many of you have learned to balance family, school, and work. You have, with varying degrees of success, learned how to identify those tasks that are most important and urgent. As President Dwight D. Eisenhower said, "What is important is seldom urgent and what is urgent is seldom important."[45] Think about how you study for this course. Do you allocate blocks of regular study time, or do you pull all-nighters? Most of you probably study in blocks of time. How long before your mind turns to other things? Some of us need more frequent breaks for a variety of reasons.

Technology use has become second nature to students and workers alike, and it has become yet one more thing to balance in the productivity equation. It might seem logical to consider computers and mobile devices as time savers that can boost efficiency. However, productivity research has shown that after an initial increase in workers' output per hour at the beginning of this century as technology became part of day-to-day tasks, in the past decade worker productivity has declined to levels equal to that of the 1980s and 1990s. Northwestern University economist Robert Gordon asserts that technology innovations such as the iPad, the smartphone and their engine, the Internet, "were enthusiastically adopted, but they provided new opportunities for consumption on the job and in leisure hours rather than a continuation of replacing human labor with machines."[46] Have you ever found yourself working on a class or work assignment on the computer, then taking "just a minute" to check Facebook or e-mail, a minute that turns into an hour or two? Technology now requires us to be even more diligent in structuring and managing our time because of all of the information, options, and distractions that are available to us instantly on our devices. These authors acknowledge the challenge of balancing the value of the Internet with its potential for distraction. The Technology Tools activity at the end of this chapter provide an opportunity for you to consider ways you can avoid wasting valuable time with online distractions.

When studying, do you begin with your most difficult subject or task? Do you review the text and the last lecture material immediately before class? Do you review lecture material immediately after class, when it is fresh in your mind? Do you schedule time to review the more important activities? If you answered "yes" to most of these questions, how did you develop these habits? Most of us learn by a system of trial and error. To help you, we have offered some practical tips for making more effective use of time:

- Have a daily, weekly, and long-term planner. Use them to identify the most important items.
- Make a list of the major tasks that need to be completed. This is your to-do list. Also, make note of the reason for doing them and the timeline for getting them done. Listing some tasks wastes time.
- Determine priorities. Focus on the most important tasks, those that support your objectives. Do not be afraid to ask your boss if a new task takes priority over other assignments.
- Use technology wisely. Avoid distractions that are instantly and widely available on the Internet and mobile devices. Give yourself a set amount of time for recreational technology use then get back to the task at hand.
- Clarify duties with a time-use chart. Identify which of your regular duties most directly relate to departmental objectives.
- Set up a reminder system. Use your iPad, smartphone calendar, day-time-planner, or another system to alert you to what needs to be done by when.
- Know your prime time. This is the time of day when you are most alert, think most clearly, and work most effectively. Schedule your most complex tasks for this period.
- Refer to your to-do list regularly. Interruptions will arise; deal with those emergencies, then go back to the high-priority task.
- Schedule routine duties at times when you have low energy.
- Schedule time at the end of the day to make tomorrow's to-do list.
- Write everything down. Document what, when, who, and where. Use an iPad, smartphone, or pocket or desk calendar to note activities that need major attention.
- Use commonsense organizational and time-management techniques. For example, handle papers only once, keep your desk or workstation clear, finish one job before starting another, avoid distractions, and say "no."

- Deal with interruptions. If someone asks you for a minute on a non-life-threatening matter, tell that person you want to give the matter your undivided attention and ask to schedule a brief meeting later. It is acceptable to tell someone you will call back; wasting valuable time is not acceptable.
- Be adaptable. Don't be afraid to reschedule in the face of unexpected events.
- Enable subordinates to be the best they can be. Encourage them to take responsibility and to make decisions in their power to make. Do not let subordinates pass these decisions on to you.
- Delegate. See Chapter 10 for tips on delegating successfully.
- Get the most from meetings. See this chapter's supervisory tips box for additional suggestions on managing meetings.
- Overcome procrastination. Plan habitually and continuously, break difficult tasks into small and doable units, and work on unpleasant tasks immediately.
- Use the two-hour rule. That is, if you have been working on a problem for more than two hours without making progress, get help. Often, by explaining a problem to someone else, you get a different perspective.
- Follow the 80/20 principle. Eighty percent of achievement comes from 20 percent of time spent.
- Remember, if you don't know what is important, you will continue to wander without much accomplishment.

Only by developing a vision about what the end result should be, developing plans, organizing, and prioritizing activities will supervisors be able to use their available time effectively.

## SUMMARY

**1.** **The organizing function of management is to group and assign activities to work areas so as to achieve established objectives, in other words, to create a structural framework for getting the work done. To organize is to establish authority relationships among managers, supervisors, and departments. The most effective organizing practices create structures that help workers feel engaged, committed to the organization and its goals, and find satisfaction in their work.**

**2.** **The informal organization interacts with, yet is apart from, the formal organizational structure. The informal organization can positively or negatively influence individual and group work performance. In order to engage the informal organization in productive ways, supervisors should seek to identify and understand the groups and their leaders and find ways to enlist their participation in promoting and accomplishing departmental objectives.**

**3.** **Normally, an organization should adhere to the unity-of-command principle. This principle requires that everyone be directly accountable to only one supervisor and that formal communication flows through the chain of command.**

**The span-of-management principle should be observed when assigning employees to supervisors. Also known as the span of supervision or the span of control, this principle recognizes that there is an upper limit to the number of employees a supervisor can manage effectively. The span of management is determined by such factors as the competence of the supervisor, the training and experience of employees, employees' work locations, and the amount and nature of work to be performed. Other things being equal, the narrower the span of management is, the greater the number of levels of management that are needed; the broader the span of management is, the fewer levels that are needed.**

**4.** **Hewlett-Packard (HP) and IBM are two of the world's larger and best known organizations. Their vision and time-honored culture set the foundation for how they are structured and managed.**

**When organizing a department, the supervisor should envision the ideal arrangement based on the assumption that all required and qualified employees are available. Because there are seldom employees with all the desired qualifications, available employees must be fit to the structure. Over time,**

the supervisor should make changes to move the department toward its ideal structure. Supervisors who strive for superior performance should adopt the concepts instrumental in creating a "learning organization." Because structure should follow strategy, as strategy changes, structures should be reviewed and modified appropriately.

**5.** Departmentalization is the process of grouping activities and people into distinct organizational units. Departmentalization is most often done according to function, but it can be determined by geographic line, product or service, customer, process and equipment, or time. Rather than being able to design new departments, supervisors most often must assign activities and employees to existing departments to achieve efficiency and stability.

A project- or matrix-type organizational structure places managers in charge of project teams whose members are drawn from different departments or even from outside the organization, that is, temporary employees. Line supervisors manage the employees in regular departments. This structure facilitates more efficient use of employees on multiple projects with a minimum disruption of regular assignments. However, a matrix structure may create problems of priority scheduling and employee accountability.

To perform effectively, a supervisor must have authority. In their own departments, supervisors have line authority to direct their employees. Employees in staff-authority positions furnish counsel, guidance, advice, and service in a specialized field. Staff supervisors with specialized knowledge and skills support line managers and others throughout the organization. They often take responsibility for ensuring that certain policies and procedures are uniformly and consistently carried out. Line-and-staff-type organizational structures are the norm in large-scale enterprises.

**6.** Downsizing usually involves eliminating job positions and levels of management. Supervisors who survive downsizings must adapt organizational principles to the changes, as well as provide support to layoff survivors in their department. This usually includes widening the span of management, giving employees more latitude in decision making. To empower employees, supervisors should structure their departments to allow for more employee participation. Various changes, such as restructuring, SDWTs, lean manufacturing, and horizontal and virtual organizational structures, can help companies reduce costs and be flexible in meeting customer demands.

**7.** Historically, meetings were always face to face, because supervisors and employees want to know what is going on right now. Supervisors usually call meetings to get or give information or to discuss and solve problems. Face-to-face meetings are the best for bringing together the people who are responsible for solving a problem or discussing an issue. Social and electronic media have enabled people to share and exchange information instantaneously. Supervisors should consider the purpose of a meeting and the productivity costs of meeting face-to-face versus using virtual alternatives when choosing the best meeting modality. Numerous tips and suggestions are available to help supervisors achieve group participation and make meetings more productive and relevant. The success of any meeting depends largely on effective leadership.

**8.** "Work smarter, not harder" should become an integral part of your management vocabulary. Every supervisor needs to make effective use of time. Identifying the most important tasks is the most important step. The effective supervisor must plan, organize, prioritize, and diligently strive to complete the things that are most important. Short-range plans must dovetail with your long-term plans. Technology must be used in ways that increase efficiency and productivity, and avoided when it can distract you from the task at hand.

## KEY TERMS

Department (p. 341)
Departmentalization (p. 341)
Division of work (specialization) (p. 341)
Downsizing (restructuring, right-sizing) (p. 346)
Engagement (p. 332)
Formal organizational structure (p. 341)
Horizontal corporation (p. 349)
Informal organization (p. 333)
Job description (p. 341)
Job specifications (p. 341)
Lead person (p. 337)
Lean manufacturing (p. 350)
Learning organization (p. 340)
Line authority (p. 345)
Line-and-staff-type organizational structure (p. 345)
Organization (p. 331)
Organizational chart (p. 340)
Principle of organizational stability (p. 344)
Project management-type organizational structure (p. 342)
Reengineering (p. 348)
Self-directed (self-managed) work teams (SDWTs) (p. 348)
Span-of-management principle (p. 336)
Staff authority (p. 345)
Unity-of-command principle (p. 335)
Virtual organization (p. 349)

## WHAT HAVE YOU LEARNED?

1. Define the organizing function.
2. What are the advantages of the informal organization? What are the challenges of the informal organization? Discuss the approaches the supervisor can take to foster cooperation with informal groups and their leaders. How can the leader(s) of the informal organization help the supervisor achieve departmental goals? Hinder their attainment?
3. Think of your most recent visit to a restaurant or coffee house. From the time you pulled into the parking lot until the time you pulled out, what were your impressions? What was done well or exceeded your expectations? What could they have done better? What was your assessment of how well they were organized? To what extent do the principles of organizing have on performance?
4. Discuss the advantages and disadvantages of the project management structure. What needs to be done so that the unity of command is not violated?
5. Explain the trade-off between the number of levels of management and the span of management. How does this problem typically affect a first-line supervisor?
6. How have downsizing and the restructuring of organizations affected you, your family, friends, and the country? Are the downsizings and radical organization restructurings likely to render organizational principles obsolete? Discuss.
7. Why is the ability to conduct effective and productive meetings important for a supervisor? What should supervisors consider when deciding whether a face-to-face meeting is necessary? What steps should supervisors take to ensure that the meetings they participate in or chair succeed?
8. What do you need to do to better manage your time? Why is creating and prioritizing a "to-do" list important? How can technology help and hinder your effective use of time? What are your personal and professional goals for the week ahead? What time management strategies should you use to achieve them?

## EXPERIENTIAL EXERCISE FOR SELF-ASSESSMENT

### EXPERIENTIAL EXERCISE FOR SELF-ASSESSMENT 9—How do your time management skills measure up?

Building time management skills by trial and error, while common, can waste a lot of time and energy. The first step in building those critical self-management skills is assessing areas in which you are strong and areas you can improve. The Time Management Self-Assessment below can help pinpoint areas for skill-building.

1. For the first set of statements, answer each with "yes" or "no."

   ________ The tasks I work on during the day begin with the ones with the highest priority.

   ________ I set aside time for planning and scheduling.

   ________ I know how much time I am spending on the various tasks I have to accomplish.

   ________ I use goal setting to decide what tasks and activities I should work on.

   ________ I leave contingency time in my schedule to deal with "the unexpected."

   ________ I know whether the tasks I'm working on are high, medium, or low value.

   ________ When given a new assignment or task, I analyze it for importance and prioritize it accordingly.

   ________ I prioritize my "To Do" list or Action Plan.

   ________ Before I take on an extra responsibility or obligation, I consider whether the time investment will be worth the results.

   Number of "yes" answers ________

2. For the next set of statements, answer each with "yes" or "no."

   ________ I often find myself dealing with interruptions.

   ________ I am stressed about deadlines and commitments.

   ________ Distractions often keep me from working on critical tasks.

   ________ I find I have to work through the night or weekends to get work done.

   ________ I find myself completing tasks at the last minute or asking for extensions.

   Number of "no" answers ________

3. Add the number of "yes" answers from the first set of questions to the number of "no" answers from the second set of questions. Your Assessment Score: ________

   Score Interpretation:

   If you scored between 11 and 14, you manage your time effectively. Keep up the good work, and look for ways to continue to improve.

   If you scored between 7 and 10, you are beginning to develop a time management toolbox. Each month you should choose one or two "no" statements from the first section, or one or two "yes" statements from the second section to work on transforming to increase your time management skills.

If you scored below a 7, yikes! On the positive side, you've identified many opportunities to grow (the "no" statements in the first section, the "yes" statements in the second section). However, in order to be successful in your work as a student and an employee, you will need to start building those time management skills right away.

4. To start working on filling your time management toolbox, revisit the list of time management strategies on page ________ in this chapter and select strategies that fit areas in need of improvement. You can also visit the Time Management page on the Mindtools website, http://www.Mindtools.com/pages/main/newMN_NTE.htm# to find additional tools and strategies. Create a list of the tools and strategies you will use, along with resources (websites, books) that can guide you in putting them into practice. For each strategy, set a date that you will start using it. Check the list every few months to see how you're doing on filling your time management toolbox.

5. Think of someone you consider to be a great time manager. What strategies does he or she use to stay on schedule and get things done? Write a 200-word paper describing your time management role model.

Assessment items adapted from: Mind Tools, Ltd. (2014), "How Good Is Your Time Management,"http://www.mindtools.com/pages/article/newHTE_88.htm

## PERSONAL SKILL BUILDING

### PERSONAL SKILL BUILDER 9-1: Organizing a Company

The Dried Foods Solution Company produces and sells a variety of freeze-dried products in stores throughout the Unites States and Canada. The company does not have an online sales division. Following is a list of job titles for the organization as well as the number of people in each position. Sales have been growing at about 2 percent a year, slightly above the inflation rate. As a result of the slow growth, projections reveal no new job openings except for replacements.

**Dried Foods Solution Personnel**

| Job Title | Number of Employees |
|---|---|
| Production Worker | 60 |
| Production Supervisor | 6 |
| Production Manager | 1 |
| Vice President—Production | 1 |
| Bookkeeper | 6 |
| Accountant | 3 |
| Accounting Supervisor | 6 |
| Vice President—Finance | 1 |
| Clerk | 4 |
| Payroll Coordinator | 2 |
| Compensation Manager | 1 |
| Benefits Specialist | 1 |
| Vice President Human Resources | 1 |
| Salesperson | 100 |
| Area Sales Manager | 8 |
| District Sales Manager | 8 |
| Vice President—Marketing | 1 |
| President | 1 |
| Staff Specialist | 6 |
| Chemists | 3 |
| Technicians | 6 |
| Research & Development Supervisor | 2 |
| Vice President—Research & Development | 1 |
| Personnel Manager | 1 |

1. From this information, construct an organizational chart. You may use a template from any source you wish, and you may use a hierarchical, flat, project management, or other structure. Templates are available in Microsoft Word and a variety of online sources. You may eliminate or change the job titles but do not reduce the number of people working for the company.

2. After developing your organizational chart, define the departments and the relationships that you believe could most likely be downsized (restructured) in the event that growth slows or stops. Explain your proposed restructuring and your rationale for the restructuring strategy you've chosen.

**FOOD FOR THOUGHT QUESTIONS**

3. What would be the advantages to the company if the production operations were transferred to an offshore location such as China? What would be the disadvantages?

4. What would be the advantages and challenges to the company if it chose to incorporate an online sales division?

5. What if the production operations were subcontracted? The disadvantage?

6. Should the organization, as many firms have done; subcontract the human resources functions? Why or why not?

7. 
INTERNET ACTIVITY

Using your choice of Internet search engine, search for examples of organizational charts using the key words "organizational chart." Select three organizational charts to compare and contrast. In a one-page paper, describe the authority and responsibility relationships illustrated in each chart, then suggest what you believe are strengths and weaknesses of each organizational structure, based on the charts.

## PERSONAL SKILL BUILDER 9-2: Managing Virtually

Many of today's supervisors will be asked to manage virtual employees or workgroups. In fact, the American Society for Training and Development (ASTD) and the Society for Human Resource Management (SHRM) estimate between 30 and 45 percent of employees work from home or off-site.[47] Gil Gordon Associates' website (www.gilgordon.com) and the U.S. Office of Personnel Management telecommuting guidance website (www.Telework.gov) both specifically address the topics of telecommuting and working in a virtual environment for both managers and employees. After using these or other sites, find information regarding telecommuting and working in a virtual environment. Then answer the following questions.

1. As a supervisor, what specific management issues will you have to address?
2. What specific concerns might a supervisor have about managing telecommuters?
3. If you were an employee proposing a transition to telecommuting, how would you address these concerns?

## PERSONAL SKILL BUILDER 9-3: Technology Tools—Prevent Yourself From Web-surfing to distraction

**INTERNET ACTIVITY**

We have all heard one place or another that technology is meant to save time and effort. In some ways it does, but studies have shown that technology, specifically using the Internet, can become a time waster, particularly for people who use computers on a daily basis or have smartphones or mobile devices.[48] The technology sector itself realizes that the sheer volume of information and activities available on the Internet has become a serious distraction. To help minimize distraction and help people control and focus their use of the Internet on things they must get done, several companies have created tools that can keep our technology use productive. These tools come in the form of applications, or apps, as well as add-on programs that operate within specific Internet browsers like Firefox or Google Chrome. All of the tools below are available for free or trial versions. The tools may be helpful to you, so this exercise enables you to check them out, evaluate their usefulness and decide for yourself.

1. When using the Internet, what are some habits you have that cause you to procrastinate or use time unwisely? If you don't have any of these kinds of habits, what are some time-wasting habits you've observed in other Internet users?
2. Investigate the technology tools listed below by visiting the website where they can be accessed, trying demonstration versions, viewing videos or installing trial versions of a few of them. You can locate the tools by searching their names in your Internet browser, or you can access links to each of the tools on the Chapter 9 Technology Tools section of the companion website for this textbook.
3. Choose two of the tools and, in a one- to two-page paper, evaluate whether they would be useful for a person who tends to waste time using the Internet. Discuss the benefits and drawbacks of each tool and explain why you would or would not suggest using them.
   - **Internet locks** prevent access to the Internet for up to 8 hours at a time. Two examples of Internet locks are *Freedom* and *Internet Lock*.
   - **Page savers** allow users to collect and archive articles or sites to read later. *Instapaper, Pocket, and Readability* are examples of page saver applications.
   - **Tab controllers** limit the number of tabs open on your browser. Three extensions are available for download that install tab controllers within specific Web browsers: *Controlled Multi-Tab Browsing Extension for Google Chrome, Window and Tab Limiter Extension for Firefox*; and *Tab Limit Extension for Mac.*
   - **Website blockers** allow users to block particular URLs (Web addresses) of sites that they don't want to or shouldn't visit during work times, such as Facebook or Twitter, for specific periods of time. Several website blockers are available, some of which are add-ons to Web browsers, and some which are stand-alone applications: *BlockSite, Facebook Nanny, LeechBlock, Nanny for Google Chrome, and SelfControl.*

# TEAM SKILL BUILDING

## TEAM SKILL BUILDER 9-1: YOU MAKE THE CALL!

Read this chapter's "You Make the Call!"

1. Pair up with another classmate. Discuss the following:
   a. Why would you like to work at Waldo Electronics? Why or why not?
   b. What do you think of the way that Waldo has organized its operations?
2. We have not shared with you the responses that the employees gave Tom. Please think of your current job or most recent job, and answer the questions that Tom asked each of the employees. Please write out your answers to those two questions and then share those answers with several of your classmates.

a. Assuming that you all work for different organizations and have different job responsibilities, what are the similarities to your responses to these questions?
b. What are the differences?

3. Based on the group's responses, collaboratively write a one-page paper sharing what you learned from this "You Make the Call!"

## TEAM SKILL BUILDER 9-2: Dealing with People Who Make Your Life Difficult—"The Boss's Favorite"

This is another in a series of exercises that introduces you to people who might make your life difficult.

1. Read the following statement from Steve Vincent, an employee at Harding Hardware:

    Bill Allen is the model employee—or at least, upper management thinks so. The store manager always notes that he contributes significantly during customer service meetings, and they always give him positive feedback for his contributions. Allen excels at giving his supervisor feedback. The supervisors have been overheard describing Allen as "warm and supporting." Allen is very well organized, gets his work done promptly, and often offers to help various supervisors on their sales orders or special projects.

    Allen excels at flattery. He is adept at making every detail of the boss's life (e.g., clothes, house, wife, grandkids, and talents) a workplace event. Allen does not care who hears his praise, as long as they have authority. According to Allen, everything that comes from the owner's mouth is the best thing said. Allen's compliments are almost always directed toward the owner. "Oh, Mr. Harding, I'm glad you think that customer feedback reporting system is a good idea." Allen might say. "I will do everything possible to make it work."

    To say that Allen is agreeable is an understatement. Problems arise when he does not follow through because other employees must honor his commitments. Allen, however, is first in line to take credit when things go well, and he is always willing to do special favors for Harding. Last summer, all we heard about was how Allen was building a deck on Harding's lake cottage.

    However, Allen is chilly to any request from someone lower than him on the company ladder. This presented a problem for Bessie Colicho, one of our timid colleagues. Colicho and Allen were responsible for putting together the monthly advertising flyer. Somehow, Allen was always too busy with more important projects, like helping Harding become familiar with the new inventory control system. Colicho had tried to talk to Harding about the problem, but she was told that Allen was the model employee and that her perceptions of him were unrealistic. I know that when the assistant store manager, George Sutherland, retires next year, Allen will be the first in line for his job. It's not fair! He'll get the promotion not on merit but by being the boss's favorite.

2. Have you ever worked with someone like Allen? If so, what effect did it have on your performance? How did you cope with the situation?
3. 

Using the Internet, find at least three sources for coping with a boss's favorite. Carefully review each site for suggestions that deal with this type of behavior.
4. Pair up with three or four classmates.
    **a.** Share your research findings on suggestions on how to deal with someone like Allen.
    **b.** Share your story from question 2 above. Get guidance from your classmates on how you should have handled the situation. Then state how you handled the person who made your life difficult. Is there a common thread? If so, what is it?
5. Based on the group's findings, what suggestions would you give to Vincent for working with Allen?
6. Collaboratively, write a one-page paper explaining how this team skill-building exercise increased your working knowledge of coping with the behaviors of this type of person who makes like difficult for certain people.

## TEAM SKILL BUILDER 9-3: Investigating Factors that Influence Span of Supervision

Midway through this chapter you read about the span-of-management principle and learned about factors that influence the number of employees one person can effectively supervise.

In this activity, you and two or three of your classmates will use this list to investigate those factors in action and compare your findings.

1. Revisit Figure 9.4 and review the list of factors that influence a supervisor's span of supervision.
2. Go to a local business or organization and ask to speak for a few minutes with a supervisor about organizational management concepts.
3. Ask the supervisor how many employees he or she supervises, then ask what factors he or she feels influence the number of employees that can be effectively supervised. You may use the factors listed in Figure 9.4 to provide some food for thought.
4. Using your notes and the factors, summarize your discussion in preparation for a small group discussion.
5. As a small group, compare your findings and compose a one- to two-page paper describing which factors you found to have the greatest influence and why you believe they have the greatest influence.

## SUPERVISION IN ACTION

The video for this chapter can be accessed from the student companion website at www.cengagebrain.com. (Search by authors' names or book title to find the accompanying resources.)

## ENDNOTES

1. Towers Watson *2012 Global Workforce Study,* (2012), p. 4, targeted full-time employees working in medium- and large-sized organization across twenty-nine world markets using an online questionnaire. It is one in a collection of studies that identifies the factors and attitudes that influence employee attraction, retention, productivity, and engagement. The survey's findings suggest that workers are being forced to do more with less, they are beginning to doubt the level of support from their supervisors and retaining workers has everything to do with the overall work experience, not just the task at hand. The drivers of sustainable engagement were identified as leadership, workload balance, clear goals and objectives, effective supervision, and an ethical, highly regarded organizational image. http://www.towerswatson.com/en-CA/Insights/IC-Types/Survey-Research-Results/2012/07/2012-Towers-Watson-Global-Workforce-Study. See also the Gallup 2013 *State of the Global Workplace: Employee Engagement Insights for Business Leaders Worldwide* report, http://www.gallup.com/strategicconsulting/164735/state-global-workplace.aspx
2. Kevin Kruse, "What Is Employee Engagement?" Forbes.com (July 22, 2012), http://www.forbes.com/sites/kevinkruse/2012/06/22/employee-engagement-what-and-why/. See also K. Kruse, *Employee Engagement 2.0* (2012, CreateSpace Independent Publishing Platform, 2nd ed.)
3. See "7 Management Practices that Can Improve Employee Productivity," *Forbes* (July 2013); See also "Management Practices That Work," *The McKinsey Quarterly* (September 2007); T. Craig Williams and Juliet Rains, "Linking Structure to Strategy: The Power of Systematic Organizational Design," *Organizational Development Journal* 25, No. 2 (Summer 2007), pp. 163–170; John R. Graham, "Seven Ways to Differentiate Your Company That Makes a Difference to the Customer," *Supervision* (August 2005), pp. 14–16; and T. L. Stanley, "The Best Management Ideas Are Timeless," *SuperVision* (June 2004), pp. 9–11.
4. Guarav Bagga further asserts that when a substantial number of employees behave negatively, communication and coordination suffers in "Positive Steps to End Negativity in the Workplace," *Human Resource Management International Digest* 2, No. 6 (2013) pp. 28–29. Also see Maria Sanchez-Bueno and Isabell Suarez-Gonzalez, "Towards New Organizational Forms," *International Journal of Organizational Analysis* 18, No. 2 (2010), pp. 340–357; Thomas Head, Theresa Yaeger, and Peter Sorenson, "Global Organization Structural Design: Speculation and a Call for Action," *Organizational Development Journal* 28, No. 2 (Summer 2010), pp. 41+;
5. See "Exodus" in the Bible for the story of Moses and Jethro. We like to refer to Jethro as the "world's first management and organization consultant."
6. David Packard and William R. Hewlett first put the statement in writing in 1957. See "David Packard: The Legacy Endures," Hewlett-Packard 1996 Annual Report (Palo Alto, CA: January 1997). Go to http://www.hp.com/country/us/en/uc/welcome.html for current information on HP.
7. See Louise Lee, "BW's Businessperson of the Year: Hewlett-Packard CEO Mark Hurd's Single-Mindedness Is Paying Off for the Tech Company in Profits That Will Be Hard to Beat in 2008," *Business Week* (January 2008), pp. 21–25; or Cliff Edwards, "How HP Got the WOW! Back," *BusinessWeek* (December 2008), pp. 60–61. Jena McGregor, "When Service Means Survival," *BusinessWeek* (March 2, 2009), pp. 26–40, reported that HP was ranked 8th in customer service.
8. Lee, "BW's Businessperson of the Year." Also see David Kirkpatrick, "HP's Grand Vision: Measure Everything," *Fortune* online (July 18, 2008); Gary Bradt, "5 Simple Steps to Build a Winning Corporate Culture," *Supervision* 69, No. 3 (March 2008), pp. 13–15. Go to Hewlett-Packard's Web site to see current press releases.
9. Ben Worthen and Joann Lublin, "Executives Churn at Hewlett-Packard," *The Wall Street Journal* (May 26, 2011), pp. B1–B2. Also see Jon Swartz, "Will Hurd's Sexual-Harassment Scandal Tarnish HP?" (August 9, 2010) 1B; or "Hurd" Successor Inherits Strong Company, Big Challenges," *USA Today* (August 10, 2010), p. 3B. You can access these articles at http://online.wsj.com.
10. Jordan Robertson, "HP to End Mobile Products," Associated Press as reported in the *Fort Wayne, IN Journal Gazette* (August 19, 2011), p. 12B. Also see: Nick Wingfiled, "Whitman New HP Chief," *The New York Times* (September 22, 2011, www.nytimes.com).
11. Quentin Hardy, "Meg Whitman's Toughest Campaign: Retooling H.P.," *The New York Times* (September 29, 2012, www.nytimes.com); Chris O'Brien, "HP Stock Rises on CEO Meg Whitman's Optimistic Outlook," *Los Angeles Times* (October 19, 2013, www.latimes.com)
12. IBM ad in *The Wall Street Journal* (June 16, 2011), pp. A9–A12.
13. Ibid. Also see Michael Hill and Jordan Robertson, "IBM: From Clocks to Computers," Associated Press, reported in the *Fort Wayne, IN Journal Gazette* (June 19, 2011), p. 3H.
14. See http://www.ibm.com to get more information about the company and their products. IBM has identified six imperatives of a smarter planet: (1) Turn information into insights, (2) drive enterprise operations' effectiveness and efficiency, (3) increase agility, (4) connect and empower people, (5) enable business service and product innovation, and (6) manage risk, security, and compliance. See http/www.ibm/smarterplanet. The authors would like to note that IBM has reduced its U.S. workforce by about 50,000 employees in the past ten years. Increasingly, IBM, like many U.S. firms, has increased its employee base in countries such as India.

15. Thomas J. Watson Jr.'s quote in the IBM ad, *The Wall Street Journal* (June 16, 2011), p. A10. In 1987, *Fortune* called him "The Greatest Capitalist in History" (August 31, 1987).
16. This type of problem is inherent in the "principle of organizational stability," which states that no organization should become overly dependent on the talents and abilities of one individual or a few individuals. That is, no one should be indispensable to the enterprise. Today's organizations need to manage the agility–stability paradox by being fluid in allocating human resources. For an interesting viewpoint, see Columbia Business School professor Rita Gunther McGrath's *The End of Competitive Advantage* (Boston: Harvard Business School Press, 2013), pp. 49–51; see also Jon Aarum Andersen, "An Organization Called Harry," *Journal of Organizational Change Management* 21, No. 2 (2008), pp. 164–187.
17. Adapted from Peter M. Senge et al., *The Fifth Discipline Fieldbook: Strategies and Tools for Building a Learning Organization* (New York: Doubleday, 1994). Senge said, "You can't fix things, at least permanently. You can apply theories, methods, and tools, increasing your own skills in the process. You can find and instill new guiding ideas. You can experiment with redesigning your organization's infrastructure. If you proceed in all these ways, you can gradually evolve a new type of organization" (p. 4).
18. See Tim Kastelle, "Hierarchy Is Overrated" (November 20, 2013), Harvard Business Review Blog, http://blogs.hbr.org/2013/11/hierarchy-is-overrated/. See also Steve Denning's discussion of Holacracy, an emerging organizational structure paradigm, in "Making Sense of Zappos and Holacracy" (January 15, 2014), Forbes.com, http://www.forbes.com/sites/stevedenning/2014/01/15/making-sense-of-zappos-and-holacracy/. The structure has been promoted as a system in which there are "no job titles and no managers," which Denning points out as not quite accurate. Hierarchy and varied levels of authority exist in all organizations; the processes for exercising authority and making decisions are just different. The jury is still out regarding whether flattening an organization is always beneficial in terms of increasing competitiveness and response to customers, and improving accountability and morale, which are the primary reasons organizations choose to adopt this type of structure, according to Julie Wulf, "The Flattened Firm: Not as Advertised," *California Management Review* 44, No. 1 (Fall 2012), pp. 5–23.
19. For information on Project Management, see Hadi Minavand, Spideh Farahmandian, and Vahid Minaei, "HR Challenges of Project Managers," *IOSR Journal of Business and Management* 11, No. 5 (2013), pp. 40–45; "The Five Pillars of Project Management Infrastructure: An Interview with Glenn Ferrell," *Journal of Digital Asset Management* 6, No. 2 (2010), pp. 83–96; Kevin Fulk and Reginald Bell, "Not Everyone Sees Technology the Same Way: How Project Managers Can Improve Their Interactions With Stakeholders," *SuperVision* 71, No. 12 (December 2010), pp. 8–12; James Patterson, "Leadership: The Project Management Essential," *Production and Inventory Management Journal* 46, No. 2 (2010), pp. 73–75; M. Alam et al., "The Importance of Human Skills in Project Management Profession Development," *International Journal of Managing Projects in Business* 3, No. 3 (2010), pp. 494–516; and Wendy Bliss et al., *The Essentials of Project Management* (Boston: SHRM and Harvard Business School Press, 2006).
20. As the United States moves out of its recession, conversion of temporary employees to full-time employees is beginning to rise after a significant decline. According to Manpower Group CEO Jeffrey Jorres, "In good times, 60% to 70% of our people will receive a full-time offer while on assignment. Right now, it's around 30%, and the tepid economy is driving that. Permanent recruitment is up about 10% on a year-over-year basis in the U.S.," shared by Lauren Weber in "ManpowerGroup CEO: What's Next for the Job Market," *Wall Street Journal* (June 18, 2013, online.wsj.com). See also J. Shapiro, P. Morrow, and I. Kesslerm, "Serving Two Organizations: Exploring the Employment Relationship of Contracted Employees," *Human Resource Management* 45, No. 4 (2006), pp. 561–583; J. Zapper, "Temp-to-Hire Is Becoming a Full-time Practice at Firms," *Workforce Management* (June 2005), pp. 82–85.
21. See Paul Davidson and Barbara Hansen, "A Job Engine Sputters as Hospitals Cut Staff," *USA Today* (October 13, 2013), www.usatoday.com/story/money/business/2013/10/13/hospital-job-cuts/2947929/
22. Predictions include large penalties being assessed to hospitals with large numbers of readmissions due to hospital errors and other preventable causes, as well as continued reductions in Medicare reimbursements of up to 15 percent for hospitals, skilled nursing facilities, and home health agencies by 2019, as reported by Kimberly Leonard, "Is Obamacare to Blame for Hospital Layoffs?" U.S. News and World Report (September 20, 2013), http://health.usnews.com/health-news/hospital-of-tomorrow/articles/2013/09/20/is-obamacare-to-blame-for-hospital-layoffs/
23. See *Time* (March 17, 2014), p. 2 and Ricardo Lopez, "Radio Shack to Close Up to 1,100 'Underperforming' Stores," *Los Angeles Times* (March 4, 2014), http://www.latimes.com/business/money/la-fi-mo-radioshack-closing-stores-20140304,0,1629242.story#axzz2vfbsgSI9
24. See H. James Harrington, "Rightsizing, Not Downsizing: Layoffs Are Costlier than You Think," *QualityDigest* (July 2005), p. 12. Visit his Web site at http://www.harrington-institute.com.
25. See Kellie Woodhouse, "University of Michigan Staff 'Demoralized' in Downsizing Effort," *Ann Arbor News* (November 12, 2013), http://www.mlive.com/news/ann-arbor/index.ssf/2013/11/university_of_michigan_downsiz.html.
26. See John Graham, "Outsourcing a Company's Marketing: A Better Way to Meet Competitive Challenges," *SuperVision* (May 2007), pp. 15–17; Thomas N. Duening and Rick L Click, *Essentials of Business Process Outsourcing* (New York: John Wiley & Sons, 2005); Amelia Kohn and David La Piana, *Strategic Restructuring for Non-profit Organizations: Merger, Integration and Alliances* (Westport, CT: Praeger, 2003); "Organize for Efficiency," *Supervision* (October 2004), pp. 25–26.
27. According to the 2013 Grant Thornton *Realities of Reshoring* study, 42 percent of executives indicated that they were likely to bring IT functions back to the United States that had previously been sourced to overseas service providers, as summarized by Walter D. Gruenes, "Reshoring Likely to Radically Reshape U.S. Economy Next Year" (November 19, 2013) on the advisory agency's Web site, www.grantthornton.com/issues/library/survey-reports/manufacturing/2013/11-survey-reshoring.aspx. Reshoring, or returning manufacturing and services to the location from which they were initially outsourced, is beginning to bring jobs back to the U.S. PlanetMagpie IT Consulting Services reported in "The Argument for ReShoring American IT: The Risks of Outsourcing Offshore and Why 'IT ReShoring' is Growing" (2012), available at www.planetmagpie.com/ReShoringAmericanIT.pdf, that its clients have found several factors are contributing to this reversing trend: increased labor costs in offshore destinations, rising energy costs, absence of consistent quality control, political risk, theft of customer identities and sensitive data, and domestic job losses.

28. Peter F. Drucker as cited by Jennifer Reingold, "The Power of Cosmic Thinking," *BusinessWeek* (June 7, 1999), p. 17. Review Figure 9.3 in Chapter 1 for more of Drucker's thoughts on management.
29. See Andrew Kinder, "Five Ways HR Can Support 'Survivor' Employees during Redundancies," *Personnel Today* (September 27, 2013), http://www.personneltoday.com/hr/five-ways-hr-can-support-survivor-employees-during-redundancies. See also C. K. Prahalad, "The Art of Outsourcing," *The Wall Street Journal* (June 8, 2005), p. A14; and Stephanie Crane, "Outsourcing's Newest Niche," *BusinessWeek on-line* (June 11, 2004).
30. See James C. Cooper and Kathleen Madigan, "Manufacturing May Already Be on the Mend," *BusinessWeek* (May 30, 2005), pp. 25–26; Jeff Higley, "La Quinta Restructures to Increase Growth *Rate," Hotel and Motel Management* (November 18, 2001), pp. 1–2; K. S. Cameron, S. J. Freemand, and A. K. Mishra, "Best Practices in White Collar Downsizing: Managing Contradictions," *Academy of Management Executive* (August 1991), pp. 57–73; and Susan Sonnesyn Brooks, "Managing a Horizontal Revolution," *HR Magazine* (June 1995), pp. 52–58.
31. See Alexandra Kaleva, "How You Downsize Is Who You Downsize," *American Sociological Review* 79, No. 1 (2014), pp. 109–135; Amar Gupta, "Expanding the 24-Hour Workplace," *The Wall Street Journal* (September 15–16, 2007), p. R9; and Sandra O'Neal, "Reengineering and Compensation: An Interview with Michael Hammer," *ACA Journal* (Spring 1996), pp. 6–11.
32. In their examination of burnout and engagement in layoff survivors, Elizabeth Cotter and Nadya Fouad found that workers with the highest social support, optimism, and effective personal career management skills were most engaged after surviving a reduction in force at their companies, "Examining Burnout and Engagement in Layoff Survivors," *Journal of Career Development* 40, No. 5 (2012), pp. 424–444. This suggests that managers can help layoff survivors remain engaged by providing a supportive, optimistic culture with opportunities for employees to learn self-management skills. Also see Nancy Lockwood, "Leveraging Employee Engagement for Competitive Advantage: HR's Strategic Role," *HR Magazine* (March 2007), pp. 1, 11.
33. See Ashlee Vance, "The Smarter Pizza Makers," *Bloomberg Business Week* (March 17, 2014), pp. 42–44.
34. See, Robert Marshall and Lyle Yorks, "How Supervisors Can Use the 'Critical Zone' to Revitalize Employees After a Reorganization," *SuperVision* (November 2010), pp. 9–11. Our students have found Vincent P. Barrabba, *Surviving Transformation: Lessons from GM's Surprising Turnaround* (New York: Oxford University Press, 2004) to be most interesting reading, particularly in light of GM's recent continuing problems.
35. See Lizabeth Yacovone, "Organizational Design for a Supply Chain Transformation: Best Practice at Johnson & Johnson Health Care Systems Inc.," *Organizational Development Journal* 25, No. 3 (Fall 2007), pp. 105–112; John A. Byrne, "The Horizontal Corporation," *BusinessWeek* (December 20, 1993), pp. 76–81, and Frank Ostroff, *The Horizontal Corporation: What the Organization of the Future Actually Looks Like and How It Delivers Value to Customers* (New York: Oxford University Press, 1999).
36. See William M. Martin and Audrey C. Davis, "Alternatives to Downsizing: An Organizational Innovation Approach," *International Journal of Business and Social Research* 3, No. 7 (2013), pp. 19–27.
37. John A. Byrne, "The Virtual Corporation," *BusinessWeek* (February 8, 1993), pp. 98–103.
38. See N. Anand and Richard L. Daft, "What is the Right Organization Design?" *Organizational Dynamics*, 36, No. 4 (2007), pp. 329–344.
39. See Christopher Null, "The End of Symbian: Nokia Ships Last Handset with the Mobile OS," *PC World* (June 14, 2013).
40. Kevin G. Hall describes how lean manufacturing is helping turn around U.S. industries in "'Lean' Manufacturing Bringing Industry Back From Depths," *McClatchyDC* (December 24, 2013). To learn more about "How Manufactures Can Achieve Real Lean and Real Result," from INFOR Corporation download the free report (http://go.infor.com/introtoinfor2) or see Steve Minter, *How to Implement Lean Manufacturing* (New York: McGraw-Hill, 2010). Lean manufacturing is often identified with the Toyota Production System, "a business practice that allows workers to identify waste in operations and to focus on tasks that add value to the product." See Jerry Feingold, "Lean Roots—A Quick History Lesson," *QualityDigest* (May 2008), pp. 35–39 for a roadmap on how the Toyota Production System began and what it means today.

    Also see the following: Preston J. McCreary, "Unlocking the Value of Lean: Successful Lean Planning," *APICS Magazine* (May/June 2010), pp. 38–41; or "The Need for Lean Flow," *American Machinist* (October 13, 2009), pp. 14–16. McCreary contends that "Companies that adopt Lean flow in the warehouse are not only reducing inventories, but are also improving their service levels."
41. Jason Fried (2010). "Why Work Doesn't Happen at Work" [video] available at the TEDTalks website, http://www.ted.com/talks/jason_fried_why_work_doesn_t_happen_at_work.html ; See also Anton Guinea, "Meetings Must Have Meaning, Clearly Define the Purpose," *The Gladstone Observer* (May 7, 2013), http://www.gladstoneobserver.com.au/news/meetings-must-have-meaning/1857038/
42. Someone once said, "The best way to get the most from a meeting is—don't go!" Unfortunately, for most of us that is not an option. For discussions on meeting management tips and skills, see Edgar Staren and Chad Eckes, "Optimizing Organizational Meeting Management," *Physician Executive Journal* (November–December 2009), pp. 80–83; Don Schmincke, "Do Your Meetings Sabotage Profits?" *SuperVision* 68, No. 10 (October 2007), pp. 5–6; T. L. Stanley, "Making Meetings Count," *SuperVision* (August 2004), pp. 6–8; Bryan R. Fisher, "Listen to What's Really Going On," *SuperVision* (August 2004), pp. 9–11; Jann Dyer, "Meetings, Meetings, Meetings," *Chartered Accountants* (May 2004), pp. 64–65; Craig Harrison, "Meeting Monsters," *Executive Excellence* (January 2004), p. 18
43. See Shane Atchison, "Productivity Hacks: The Face-Down Phone Trick" (January 21, 2014), LinkedIn.com, http://www.linkedin.com/today/post/article/20140121123921-224083-productivity-hacks-the-face-down-phone-trick
44. Stephen R. Covey's, *The7Habits of Highly Effective People: Restoring the Character Ethic* (New York: Simon & Schuster, 1989) is a foundational book the authors recommend as a must-read for every working person. To learn more about Stephen Covey's legacy and his additional works on principle-driven leadership and effective management, see https://www.stephencovey.com/about/about.php. Also, Kevin Kruse has distilled ten of Stephen Covey's quotes that can serve as powerful principles for managers and supervisors in "Stephen Covey: 10 Quotes That Can Change Your Life" *Forbes* (July 16, 2012), http://www.forbes.com/sites/kevinkruse/2012/07/16/the-7-habits/. For additional ideas on time management principles, see Jared Sandberg, "To Surrender All My Days," *The Wall Street Journal* (September 11, 2007), p. 1B, or Covey, A. Roger Merrill, and Rebecca R. Merrill, *First Things First* (New York: Simon & Schuster,

1994). For additional insights on time management, see Aaron Guerrero "7 Tips to Stop Procrastination," *U.S. News and World Report* (May 8, 2013), p. 1; Danita Johnson-Hughes, "Managing Interruptions and Your Time," *Super-Vision* 72, No. 7 (July 2011), pp. 13–14; Daniel Markovitz, "Time Management Training: A Waste of Time," *SuperVision* 72, No. 3 (March 2011), pp. 3–5.

45. Hundreds of quotes from President Dwight D. Eisenhower can be found at http://www.brainyquotes.com. Two other interesting quotes are: "I have only one yardstick by which I test every major problem and that yardstick is: Is it good for America?" and "It is far more important to be able to hit the target than it is to haggle over who makes the weapon or who pulls the trigger."

46. See John Cassidy, "What Happened to the Internet Productivity Miracle?," *New Yorker* (April 2, 2013), http://www.newyorker.com/online/blogs/johncassidy/2013/04/what-happened-to-the-internet-productivity-miracle.html; see also Rhiannon Williams, "Internet Fuels Procrastination and Lowers Productivity" (February 23, 2014), Telegraph.co.uk, http://www.telegraph.co.uk/technology/internet/10654987/Internet-fuels-procrastination-and-lowers-productivity.html.

47. See Meghan M. Biro, "Telecommuting Is the Future of Work" (January 12, 2014), Forbes.com, http://www.forbes.com/sites/meghanbiro/2014/01/12/telecommuting-is-the-future-of-work/. See also Alina Tugend, "It's Unclearly Defined, but Telecommuting Is Fast on the Rise," NYTimes.com (March 7, 2014), http://www.nytimes.com/2014/03/08/your-money/when-working-in-your-pajamas-is-more-productive.html.

48. John Cassidy, "What Happened to the Internet Productivity Miracle?" *New Yorker* (April 2, 2013), http://www.newyorker.com/online/blogs/johncassidy/2013/04/what-happened-to-the-internet-productivity-miracle.html. See also Kate Bratskeir, "How the Internet can Help You Stop Wasting Time on the Internet," HuffingtonPost.com (August 23, 2013), http://www.huffingtonpost.com/2013/08/02/stop-procrastinating-online_n_3672495.html; Witson Gordon, "Read Later Apps Compared: Pocket vs. Instapaper vs. Readability," Lifehacker.com (August 27, 2013), http://lifehacker.com/5894995/bookmark-and-read-later-apps-compared-read-it-later-vs-instapaper-vs-readability

Chapter

# 10 Empowering Employees for Success

Blend Images/Alamy

**After studying this chapter, you will be able to:**

1. Discuss the interaction between the supervisor and the human resources department in empowering employees for success.
2. Describe actions the supervisor should take to prepare for the selection process.
3. Identify what the supervisor can do to ensure that the most qualified applicant is chosen.
4. Describe the hiring process and the importance of documentation.
5. Understand how to conduct an effective onboarding program.
6. Explain approaches to training and the supervisor's role in employee development.

## YOU MAKE THE CALL!

*Bonnie Minnick is a supervisor in the electronics department at King Appliances. The store specializes in appliance sales to retail and commercial customers. The company has a reputation for extensive involvement in community activities including working on Habitat for Humanity's building projects. The store is open from 8 to 8 every day of the week except on Christmas, Easter, the Fourth of July, and Thanksgiving.*

King Appliances's annual Fourth of July picnic was always well attended. It was a well-planned and organized day-long family affair for all employees of the firm. The event gave everyone an opportunity to informally interact with others. The event concluded with an outstanding fireworks display. At the picnic, Bonnie had a long chat with her boss, James Staker, the general manager of the store.

They talked about many things, including some of the economic problems that the country was facing in the competitive nature of their industry.

Staker talked about the need for the company to find ways to cut costs and improve sales, and generally the need to strengthen the firm's finances. He told Minnick that he had received some text messages and written suggestions and plans from some of the supervisors on how to improve efficiencies. He highly praised the efforts of employees and found their efforts to be helpful.

Three weeks after the picnic, Bonnie received a text message from her boss asking her why her "report on ideas to improve sales and cut costs had not been received." At first, she wondered what James Staker was referring to, and then she remembered the conversation at the company picnic. She went through all of her e-mails and text messages and realized that was the only time James had discussed the issue with her. Bonnie pondered what she should do.

The above scenario presents a supervisory situation based on real events to be used for educational purposes. The identities of some or all individuals, organizations, industries, and locations, as well as financial and other information may have been disguised to protect individual privacy and proprietary information. Fictional details may have been added to improve readability and interest.

YOU MAKE THE CALL!

## The Human Resources Department and the Supervisor's Staffing Responsibilities

**1 Discuss the interaction between the supervisor and the human resources (HR) department in empowering employees for success.**

Everyone in an organization is affected by human resources (HR) issues. Regardless of the organization, a qualified workforce must be attracted and maintained in order for the organizations to be competitive and successful. The management of human resources is the supervisor's most important activity, and it begins with staffing. As Chapter 2 discusses, staffing involves the recruitment, selection, placement, orientation, and training of employees. These activities are part of every supervisor's responsibilities, although in large organizations staff specialists provide help and support. The supervisory staffing function also includes the evaluation of employees' performance and input regarding how employees will be rewarded for their performance.

In a broad sense, **human resource management (HRM)** encompasses the philosophy, policies, procedures, and practices related to the management of people in an organization. To perform the activities necessary to accomplish its goals, every organization must have human resources and use them effectively. To facilitate these activities, many firms have a **human resources (HR) department**. See Figure 10.1 for an overview of the HR functions.

**Human resource management (HRM)**
Organizational philosophies, policies, and practices that strive for the effective use of employees

**Human resources (HR) department**
Department that provides advice and service to other departments on human resource matters

Many HR personnel are members of the Society for Human Resources Management (SHRM), which is the world's largest HR professional association. SHRM suggests the following guideline for human resources personnel: "As HR professionals, we are responsible for adding value to the organizations we serve and contributing to the ethical success of those organizations. We accept

FIGURE 10.1 An overview of the role of the HR department[50]

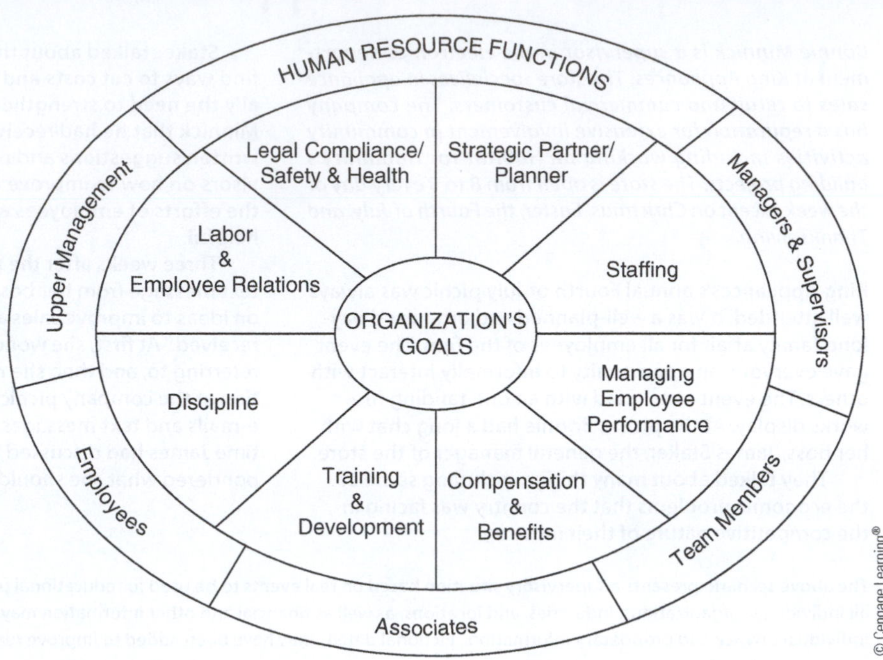


professional responsibility for our decisions and actions. We are also advocates for the profession by engaging in activities that enhance its creditability and value."[1]

For many organizations, the role and size of the HR department has expanded, in part, because of the need to comply with government regulations. At the same time, some organizations have found it cost-effective to contract out, or outsource, some HR activities.[2]

## HUMAN RESOURCES ADVICE AND SUPERVISORY DECISIONS

Regardless of its official name, the usefulness and effectiveness of any HR department depends on its ability to develop close working relationships with managers and supervisors. The quality of these line-staff relationships, in turn, depends on how clearly top-level managers have defined the scope of activities and the authority of the HR department. Effective HR professionals are responsible for developing and implementing strategies, policies, and procedures that enable the organization's employees to be the best they can be. The HR professionals must

- monitor the external environment for forces that are beyond the control of the organization but could affect long-term performance,
- develop and initiate strategic initiatives that support the organization's mission and objectives,
- manage the HR process ranging from recruiting and training to compensating and coordinating employee–management relations' activities, and
- deal with day-to-day supervisor/employee issues that could impede organizational effectiveness.[3]

The HR department often is given primary responsibility for certain activities, and supervisors must follow HR requirements with little or no discretion. For example, certain policies and practices regarding Equal Employment Opportunity (EEO), labor relations, and wage rates are typically formulated and directed by the HR department, but there are many areas and situations in which supervisors must make the decisions.

Because employee problems arise continually, supervisors should consult with the HR department staff for assistance, information, and advice. HR staff members usually prefer to offer suggestions to line supervisors, who, in turn, must decide whether to accept, alter, or reject those suggestions or recommendations. Whenever a member of the HR staff has expertise and knowledge directly related to a decision, the supervisor will usually follow that person's advice and recommendations.

When supervisors conclude that a recommendation of the HR staff is not feasible, those supervisors should make their own decisions. For the most part, line supervisors will accept the recommendations of human resources staff members because they are considered experts in employee relations matters.

Some situations pit the supervisor against the HR department. HR executive Paul Falcone shares a number of examples from his experiences, such as a supervisor avoiding taking an employee problem to HR and threatening to fire his team if they don't keep quiet about it; or a manager failing to disclose discrimination or potential violence to HR because an employee shared information "off the record." Falcone has seen "[m]anagers often wait until a land mine has detonated to go to the HR department," rather than working in tandem with HR to solve problems.[4] Situations such as these expose employees, the supervisor, and the organization as a whole to substantial legal and other risks. Proactively working with the HR department helps ensure that policies, guidelines, and federal and state requirements are followed both in spirit and in letter for the well-being of everyone in the organization.

Some supervisors readily welcome the willingness of the HR staff to make certain decisions for them so that they will not have to solve difficult employee problems in their own departments. These supervisors reason that their own departmental tasks are more important than dealing with issues the human resources staff can handle just as well or better than they can. Other supervisors may accept the staff's advice based on the premise that if the decision later proves to be wrong or dubious (e.g., in disciplinary cases), they can say, "It wasn't my choice; human HR made the decision—not me!" For them, it is a relief to rely on the staff's advice and consider it a decision. In so doing, these supervisors defer to the HR department in the hope that they will not be held accountable for the decision. However, even when supervisors follow the advice of the HR staff, they are still accountable for their decisions.[5]

Although it is easy to understand why some supervisors are reluctant to reject the advice of an HR staff member, those supervisors should recognize that the staff person may see only part of the picture. The HR director is not responsible for the performance of a supervisor's department. Usually, the departmental supervisor will have a better understanding of unique factors than anyone else.

## DETERMINING THE NEED FOR EMPLOYEES

The staffing function is an ongoing process for the supervisor; it is not something that is done only when a department is first established. It is more realistic to think of staffing in the typical situation in which a supervisor is placed in charge of an existing department. Although it has a nucleus of employees, the department will undergo changes due to employee separations from the workforce, changes in operations or growth, or other reasons. Because supervisors depend on employees for results, they must make certain that there are enough well-trained employees to fill all positions.

An ongoing aspect of the supervisory staffing function is that of determining the department's need for employees, both in number and job positions. Supervisors should become familiar with departmental jobs and functions and should consult the organizational chart or manual if one is available. For example, the supervisor of a maintenance department may have direct reports who are painters, electricians, and carpenters, each with different skills. The supervisor should study each of these job categories to determine how many positions are needed to get the work done and how employees should work together. The supervisor may have to compromise by adjusting a preferred arrangement to existing realities or by combining several positions into one if there is not enough work in a particular function to keep one employee busy. By carefully studying the department's organization, the supervisor can reasonably determine how many employees and what skills are needed to accomplish the various work assignments.

## DEVELOPING JOB DESCRIPTIONS AND JOB SPECIFICATIONS

After determining the number of positions and skills that are needed, the supervisor's next step is to match jobs with individuals. This usually is done with the aid of job descriptions (as discussed in Chapter 9), which indicate the duties and responsibilities of each job. A supervisor may have access to existing job descriptions; however, when such descriptions are not available, they can be developed with the assistance of higher-level managers or the HR staff. Similarly, when a new job is created, the supervisor should determine its duties and responsibilities and develop an appropriate job description.[6]

The supervisor may find it helpful to ask departmental employees to write down the tasks they perform during a given period, such as in a day or a week. This task list gives the supervisor considerable information from which to develop a job description. While the final job description may be written by a HR staff person, the supervisor is responsible for determining what goes into it.[7]

A supervisor should at least annually compare each job description with what each employee does. Outdated job descriptions that no longer fit job duties should be corrected. When the supervisor finds that some of the duties assigned to a job no longer belong to it, then these duties should be deleted or assigned elsewhere. Supervisors should not take the preparation of job descriptions lightly because job descriptions can be used to explain to applicants the duties and responsibilities of a job. Job descriptions that describe jobs accurately help supervisors provide realistic job previews, develop performance standards, conduct performance appraisals, and perform other staffing functions. As part of the annual job evaluation, supervisors should review what the employee needs to know and the qualifications necessary to perform the designated activities.

After the content of each job has been determined or reevaluated, the supervisor should next identify the knowledge and skills required of employees who are to perform the job. As discussed in Chapter 9, a written statement of required knowledge, skills, and abilities is called a job specification. Typically, the job description and job specification are combined into one document.

## DETERMINING HOW MANY EMPLOYEES TO HIRE

Supervisors seldom have to hire large numbers of employees at the same time. Large-scale hiring usually occurs when a new department is created or when a major expansion takes place. The more typical pattern is to hire one or a few employees as the need arises. Of course, some supervisors constantly request additional employees because they feel pressured to get their work done on time. In many cases, however, a supervisor's problems are not solved by getting more help. In fact, the situation may become worse. Instead of reducing problems, overstaffing causes inefficiencies and so may give rise to new problems.

Normally, a supervisor must hire a replacement when a regular employee leaves the department for reasons such as promotion, transfer, resignation, dismissal, or retirement. In such cases, there is little question that the job must be filled. However, if major technological changes or a downsizing are anticipated, a replacement may not be needed. There are other situations in which additional employees must be hired. For example, if new functions are to be added to the department and no one in the department possesses the required knowledge and skills, it may be necessary to go into the labor market and recruit new employees. Sometimes, a supervisor will ask for additional help because the workload has increased substantially and the department is under extreme pressure. Before requesting additional help, the supervisor should make certain that the employees currently in the department are being used fully and that any additional help is necessary and in the budget.

Francisco Cruz/Superstock

*Failing to hire the right number of employees can cause problems for the business and its customers*

Two interesting phenomena are present in today's economy. First, today when an employee retires, is laid off, or terminated, the organization does not generally replace the person. Instead, the person's job duties are consolidated and the remaining workers' responsibilities are expanded, forcing departments to do more with less. Second, it should be noted that the number of part-timers, temps, or whatever the organization calls them, has increased substantially in the past several years. Prospective employees, unable to find full-time work, have been forced to take part-time work for "economic reasons." Often, the organization can hire part-timers at a substantially lower wage and with few, if any, benefits.[8]

## SOLICITING RECRUITMENT AND SELECTION ASSISTANCE

When supervisors have open positions in their departments, they normally ask the HR department to recruit qualified applicants. Whether a job will be filled by someone from within or outside the organization, the HR department usually knows where to look to find qualified applicants. Most organizations try to fill job openings above entry-level positions through promotions and transfers. Promotions reward employees for accomplishments; transfers can protect employees from layoffs or broaden their job knowledge. Internal applicants already know the organization, and the costs of recruitment, orientation, and training are usually less than those for external applicants. Hiring from within sends two clear messages:

- There is a future for someone in the long-term, not only to grow within the current job but also within the company.
- If you continue to learn more and more about the business and add skills to your toolbox, there are always opportunities waiting for you.

Generally, internal applicants can be found through computerized skills inventories or job postings and biddings. Information on every employee's skills, educational background, work history, and other pertinent data can be stored in a database that can be reviewed to determine quickly whether any employees qualify for a particular job. This procedure helps ensure that every employee who has the necessary qualifications is identified and considered. Most organizations communicate information about job openings by posting vacancy notices on bulletin boards or in newsletters. Interested employees apply or bid for vacant positions by submitting applications to the HR office and copies to the supervisors. Posting job openings makes all employees aware of job opportunities. Job posting and job bidding are common where labor unions represent employees.

Outside sources for job applicants vary depending on the type of job to be filled. For example, Apple's strategy for recruiting its vice presidents is very different from its process for staffing retail stores. Advertising, professional recruiting, social networks like LinkedIn, college career centers, public or private employment agencies, employee referrals, walk-ins, and contract or temporary-help agencies are some of the sources companies may use, although organizations are finding that in the past five years, the use and effectiveness of social media for recruiting candidates has grown exponentially, making it the most widely used recruiting tool. Some organizations use technology in yet a different way, employing applicant tracking systems to identify their best hires and go back to the same sources to get more of the same.[9]

To select from among job seekers, usually the HR department first has applicants fill out applications, and then it conducts preliminary interviews to determine whether the applicants' qualifications match the requirements of the positions. The HR department also conducts reference checks of the applicants' employment and background. For certain positions, the department may administer one or more tests to determine whether applicants have the necessary skills and aptitudes.[10] Eventually, applicants who lack the required qualifications are screened out. Those who do have the qualifications are referred to the supervisor of the department where the job is open.

**2 Explain how the supervisor should prepare for the selection process.**

## Preparing for Selection

Because the purpose of the selection process is to choose the most qualified person to fill the needs of the organization, supervisors with the help of HR must plan and prepare. First, the job description and specifications should be reviewed to make sure that they clearly and thoroughly address the current duties, responsibilities, and expectations of the position.

Legislation has somewhat restricted the recruiting and selection process. With the aid of HR personnel, the supervisor should always review the EEO laws.

## UNDERSTANDING THE INFLUENCE OF EQUAL EMPLOYMENT OPPORTUNITY LAWS

EEO legislation restricts the questions employers may ask job applicants. The overriding principle to follow in employee selection interviews is to ask job-related questions. Questions on topics not related to a person's ability to perform the job should be avoided. For example, asking an applicant for a data-entry clerk position about keyboarding experience is valid. However, asking applicants whether they own or rent their homes is questionable. Employee selection procedures must ensure that legally protected groups, such as minorities and women, are treated fairly. Information that would adversely affect members of protected groups can be used only if it is directly related to the job. For example, the question, "Who cares for your children?" is potentially discriminatory because traditionally it has adversely affected women more than men. On the other hand, the question, "Do you speak Spanish?" is legitimate if speaking Spanish is a job requirement. It would be wrong to ask the question selectively. The same basic questions must be asked of every applicant for a job. When the questions and the selection criteria differ, the hiring decision cannot be justified if it is challenged. Figure 10.2 lists some of the most common areas of unlawful and potentially unlawful inquiry.

Applications, tests, interviews, reference checks, and physical examinations must be nondiscriminatory and must focus on job-related requirements. To determine whether a selection criterion is appropriate and complies with the law, one consulting firm has suggested the OUCH test.[11] OUCH is a four-letter acronym that represents the following:

*O*bjective

*U*niform in application

*C*onsistent in effect

*H*as job relatedness

A selection criterion is objective if it systematically measures an attribute without being distorted by personal feelings. Examples of objective criteria include work sample test scores, number of years of education, degrees, and length of service in previous positions. Examples of subjective criteria include a supervisor's general impression about a person's interest in a job or feelings that a person is "sharp."

A selection criterion is uniform in application if it is applied consistently to all job candidates. Asking only female applicants a question such as, "Would working on weekends conflict with your childcare arrangements?" is not uniform application. However, it would be permissible to ask all applicants, "Would you be able to meet the job's requirement to work every third weekend?"

A selection criterion is consistent in effect if it has relatively the same proportional impact on protected groups as it does on others. For example, criteria such as possessing a high school diploma or living in a certain area of town may be objective and uniformly applied to all job candidates, but they could screen out proportionately more members of minority groups. When a selection criterion is not consistent in effect, the burden of proof is on the employer to demonstrate that the criterion is job-related.

A selection criterion has job relatedness if it can be demonstrated that it is necessary to perform the job. For example, in most cases, it would be

**FIGURE 10.2 Areas of unlawful or potentially unlawful questions in applications and employment interviews**

| Subject of inquiry | Unlawful or potentially unlawful questions |
|---|---|
| Applicant's name | 1. Maiden name<br>2. Original name (if legally changed) |
| Civil and family status | 1. Marital status<br>2. Number and ages of applicant's children<br>3. Childcare arrangements<br>4. Is applicant pregnant, or does she contemplate pregnancy? |
| Address | 1. Foreign addresses that would indicate the applicant's national origin |
| Age | 1. Before hiring, requests for birth certificate, baptismal certificate, or statement of age |
| Birthplace | 1. Birthplace of applicant (national origin)<br>2. Birthplace of applicant's spouse, if any, and parents<br>3. Lineage, ancestry, or nationality |
| Race and color | 1. Any question that would indicate the applicant's race or color |
| Citizenship | 1. Country of citizenship, if not the United States<br>2. Does the applicant intend to become a U.S. citizen?<br>3. Citizenship of spouse, if any, and of parents |
| Disabilities | 1. Preemployment physical examinations or questions about an applicant's physical or mental condition |
| Religion | 1. Religious denomination<br>2. Clergyperson's recommendation or references<br>3. Any inquiry into willingness to work a particular religious holiday |
| Arrests and convictions | 1. Numbers and kinds of arrests |
| Education | 1. Nationality, race, or religious affiliation of schools<br>2. Native tongue or how foreign-language skills were acquired |
| Organizations | 1. Is the applicant a member of any association other than a union and/or a professional or trade organization? |
| Military experience | 1. Type of discharge from the U.S. armed forces<br>2. Did the applicant have military experience with governments other than the U.S. government? |
| Relatives | 1. Names and/or addresses of any relatives |

*Source:* Vivian Gang, "11 Common Interview Questions that are Actually Illegal", BusinessInsider.com (July 5, 2013), derived in part from the U.S. Equal Employment Opportunity Commission (EEOC) Prohibited Employment Policies /Practices listed on the EEOC website, www.eeoc.gov/laws/practices/

extremely difficult to prove that a selection criterion such as marital status is job-related. Job-related criteria should stress the skills required to perform the job.

Supervisors who do not understand the reasons for some of the restrictions imposed on them by the EEO policies of their organizations should not hesitate to consult with specialists in the HR department for explanations and guidance in this regard.

## REVIEWING THE APPLICANT'S BACKGROUND

Before interviewing a job applicant, the supervisor should review all background information that has been gathered by the HR office. By studying whatever is available, the supervisor can develop in advance a mental impression of the job applicant's general qualifications. The application will supply information concerning the applicant's schooling, experience, and other relevant items.

When studying the completed application, the supervisor should always keep in mind the job for which the applicant will be interviewed. If questions come to mind, the supervisor should write them down to remember them. For example, if an applicant shows a gap of a year in employment history, the supervisor should plan to ask the applicant about this gap and why it occurred.

A supervisor should also review the results of any employment tests taken by the applicant.[12] An increasing number of organizations are administering job performance, integrity/honesty, and drug tests before the interview stage. Tests should be validated before they are used to help make hiring decisions.

As part of their normal procedures to screen out unqualified applicants, HR departments often administer job performance tests that measure skill and aptitude for a particular job. The HR department must be able to document that these tests are valid, job-related, and nondiscriminatory. This typically involves studies and statistical analyses by staff specialists—procedures that are normally beyond the scope of a supervisor's concern. Applicants whose test scores and other credentials appear to be acceptable are referred to the departmental supervisor for further interviewing. It is essential for the supervisor to understand what a test score represents and how meaningful it is in predicting an applicant's job performance. By consulting with the HR department, the supervisor can become more familiar with the tests that are used and can learn to interpret the test scores.[13]

References provide additional information about the applicant. Generally, telephone or e-mail checks are preferable because they save time and allow for greater feedback. For the most part, information obtained from personal sources,

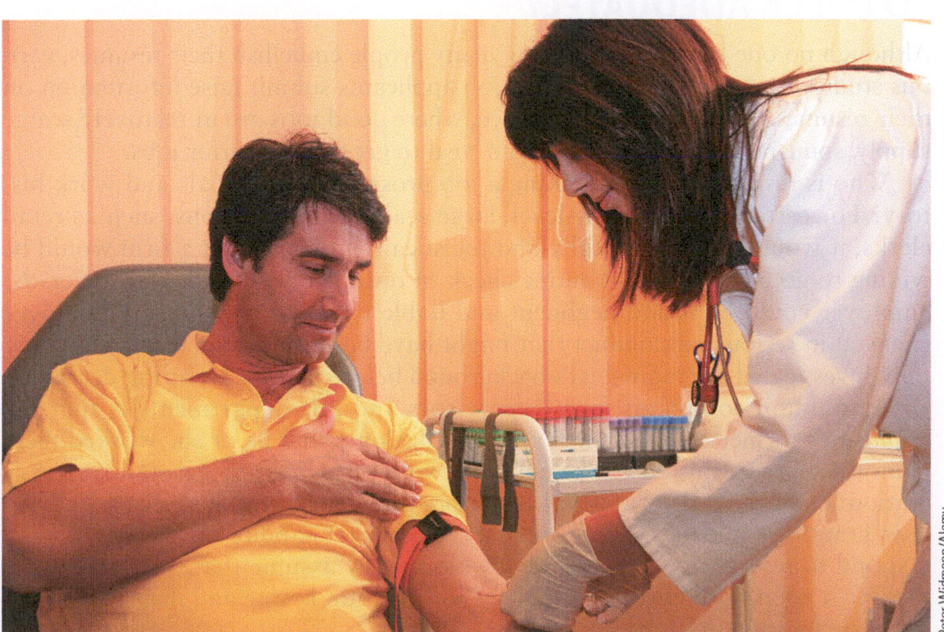

*A realistic job preview might include showing the job candidate the actual work environment in which he or she will work*

Peter Widmann/Alamy

such as friends or character references, will be positively slanted because applicants tend to list only people who will give them good references. Information from previous supervisors who were in positions to evaluate the applicant's work performance is best. However, because of emerging personal privacy regulations and potential damage claims, an employment background investigation is usually conducted by the HR department. If possible, job references should be obtained in writing, should deal with job-related areas, and should be gathered with the knowledge and permission of the applicant. After reviewing all available background information, the supervisor should be able to identify areas in which little or no information is available and areas that require expansion or clarification.

Social media screening is a fairly new practice some employers choose to use to learn more about applicants' backgrounds and activities. Scanning a potential hire's Facebook or LinkedIn page may provide a wealth of positive and negative insight, which many students are warned about by professors and career service staff as they prepare for their job search. However, the appropriateness of this strategy is challenged both by legislation and reactions of job candidates. Laws passed in several states prohibit employers from requesting passwords or access to applicants' social media sites to protect individual privacy, and a North Carolina State University research study found that applicants who learn that a potential employer has been "creeping" on their social media are sometimes driven away by what they feel is an unfair breach of privacy. Further, the practice doesn't add value to the screening process, as much of the information gained from social media sites, such as leisure time behavior, relationship status, and political beliefs, cannot be used to make employment-based decisions under federal, state, and local anti-discrimination laws.[14] Accordingly, it is best for employers to steer clear of social media as a preemployment information source to avoid the liability of knowing too much about a candidate.

## THE CONSEQUENCES OF FAILING TO CHECK ADEQUATELY

Although no one knows exactly how many people embellish their résumés, various studies have reported that many job applicants submit false information on their résumés.[15] In today's marketplace, where good jobs are in relatively scarce supply, some people will lie, cheat, and steal to get these superior jobs.

Who is responsible for checking a job prospect's credentials and work history? For certain types of low-level, large-scale hiring positions, such as retail clerks, it would be economically and logistically unlikely that a firm would be willing to go beyond just a routine check of résumé information. However, the employer could be found negligent and liable if, at some point, an employee engaged in serious misconduct that might have been avoided had the employer fully investigated the individual's background before making its hiring decision.

A common complaint from supervisors and HR departments is that the applicant's former employer will acknowledge only that he or she worked there from this date to this date. The company won't provide any substantive information. As of the time of this writing, more than half of the states have enacted laws granting some measure of immunity from legal liability for employers who respond to reference requests. The laws generally assume that the employer is making a good-faith effort and that the information is true and dispensed without malicious intent.[16]

The message in all of this seems to be, "Employers beware! Your employees and potential employees may not be what they claim to be, and there may be trouble ahead if you are negligent in taking some steps to deal with résumé exaggeration and fraud." So, is background checking fruitless? No! Businesses today can turn to many companies for conducting educational, employment, and criminal background checks on applicants. Some managers will contend that the cost of checking is too expensive; we maintain that the costs of not checking can potentially bankrupt the organization.

Consultant and author Bradford Smart recommends using threat of reference check (TORC). He suggests using the question, "If I were to ask you to arrange an interview with your last boss, and the boss was very candid with me, what's your best guess as to what he or she would say were your strengths, weaker points, and overall performance?" The interviewer then may gain insight into what makes this applicant tick and how the person is apt to function in the job.[17]

The importance of verifying reference or application form data cannot be overemphasized. Various organizations have been charged with negligently hiring employees who later commit crimes. Typically, the lawsuits charge that the organizations failed to adequately check the references, criminal records, or general background information that would have shown the employee's propensity for deviant behavior. The rulings in these cases, which range from theft to homicide, should make employers more aware of the need to check applicants' references thoroughly. Not surprisingly, you can be held liable if you knew or should have known that the person you were hiring was a potential risk to others.

As a safeguard, organizations should make sure that the job application includes a statement to be signed by the applicant stating that all information presented during the selection process is truthful and accurate. The statement should note that any falsehood is grounds for refusal to hire or for termination.[18]

## PREPARING KEY QUESTIONS

In preparing for the interview, the supervisor should develop a list of key questions, which may include directive and nondirective components.[19] It is preferable that the supervisor list six to ten directive and nondirective questions that are vital to the selection decision and are job-related. It is important that all applicants be asked the same set of key questions so that responses can be compared and evaluated. For example, the supervisor may want to know technical information about an applicant's work experience, why the applicant left a previous employer, and whether the applicant can work alternative shift schedules and overtime without difficulty.

Some organizations appear to have changed their focus from fixed job descriptions and job specifications to the competencies that differentiate average performers from superior ones. Ron and Susan Zemke, nationally known HR specialists, contend that "[i]f you can identify the key skills, knowledge, (abilities), and personal attributes that make a master performer successful at a given job, and then group these things into appropriate clusters, then you have a set of **competencies**. Link each of these broad competencies to a set of behaviors that answer the question, 'How do we know it when we see it?' and they can serve as sort of a blueprint to help you hire, train, and develop people."[20] A thorough plan for the employment interview is well worth the time spent preparing it.

**Competencies**
The set of skills, knowledge, and personal attributes possessed by the superior performer

**3 Identify what the supervisor can do to ensure that the most qualified applicant is chosen.**

## Interviewing and Choosing from among Qualified Applicants

After the HR department has screened and selected qualified applicants for a job opening, the departmental supervisor normally interviews each candidate before any decision is made. Supervisors should make, or at least should have considerable input in making, the final hiring decisions for jobs in their departments. However, supervisors should not make staffing decisions without considering the legal ramifications of their decisions. It is easy to understand why supervisors are confused by the numerous laws, executive orders, regulations, and guidelines that they may have heard or read about. As discussed in Chapter 1, Title VII, of the Civil Rights Act of 1964 prohibits employment discrimination. Figure 10.2 gives an overview of what cannot be asked in the interview. The laws regarding the so-called protected classes are discussed extensively in Chapter 4.

Under EEO and affirmative action programs, employers must make good-faith efforts to recruit, hire, and promote members of protected classes so that their percentages in the organization approximate their percentages in the labor market. Although it is difficult to be current on all aspects of the law, effective supervisors are acquainted with the Uniform Guidelines on Employee Selection Procedures because these guidelines apply to all aspects of supervisors' staffing responsibilities.[21]

Corporate restructuring or downsizing—the temporary or indefinite removal of employees from the organization—has created serious staffing concerns. Supervisors are being asked to do more work with fewer employees. Consolidating various job activities may not be the supervisor's decision, but it is one the supervisor must live with. Employees may be transferred from one job to another, or additional responsibilities may be added to existing ones. Some employees may even be involuntarily demoted from supervisory or staff positions. Unfortunately, supervisors sometimes find themselves with little or no authority in staffing decisions. In general, however, the supervisor should make the decision to hire or not.

**Selection criteria**
Factors used to choose among applicants who apply for a job

Regardless of who makes the final hiring decision, however, selection criteria must be developed. **Selection criteria** are the factors used to differentiate applicants. Education, knowledge, experience, test scores, application forms, background investigations, and interpersonal skills often serve as selection criteria.

### THE SELECTION PROCESS

**Selection**
The process of choosing the best applicants to fill positions

**Selection** is the process of screening applicants in order to choose the best person for a job. Once job applicants have been located, the next step is to gather information that will help determine who should be hired. Usually, the HR staff or the supervisor reviews résumés or applications to determine which applicants meet the general qualifications of the position. Then, qualified applicants may be further screened with tests, reference or background checks, and interviews to narrow down the pool of applicants.

For supervisors, the most frequently used selection criterion, and often the most important part of the selection process, is the employee selection interview.[22] It is difficult to accurately appraise a person's strengths and potential during a brief interview. If there are several applicants for a position, the supervisor must ascertain which applicant is the most qualified, meaning which applicant is most likely to perform best on the job and to stay with the company long-term. The employment interview plays a very important role in the selection process.

Depending on the type of job, the applicant may be interviewed by one person, by several members of a work team, or by even external stakeholders. A Florida children's hospital, for example, formed a Family Advisory Council comprises parents of patients. The parents were trained by the hospital's HR staff in interviewing practices and laws and then they participated, accompanied by an HR professional, as part of the second round interview team. The parent interviewers were able to bring a previously absent family/client perspective into the doctor recruitment process, which resulted in higher than ever positive consumer feedback.[23]

While the organization seeks to learn as much as possible about a candidate through an interview, the applicant also is interviewing the organization (see Figure 10.3).

**FIGURE 10.3 Setting the stage of an effective employment interview**

**Set the Stage (HR department and the Supervisor)**

1. Arrange a meeting with HR, the supervisor, and other key employees before the interview to review the interview and selection process.
2. Make sure that all the interviewers know the "do's and don'ts" of interviewing, for example, appropriate protocol and questions.
3. Remind all interviewers of the implications of EEO laws during the interview process to avoid discriminatory bias.
4. Review the "hard data," that is, the application form, résumé, references, test scores, and, if appropriate, the background check.
5. Make sure the applicant knows what to expect during the interview process.
6. Give the interview the time it takes to "sell the organization" and ascertain the applicant's suitability for the open position.

**Goals of the Applicant (the Interviewee)**

1. Obtain information about the job.
2. Obtain information about the organization.
3. Ascertain how the opening or vacancy occurred.
4. Determine whether the job matches my needs.
5. Determine whether I want the job.
6. Communicate important information about myself.
7. Favorably impress the employer (the interviewer).

**Goals of the Employer (the Interviewer)**

1. Involve those who will be working closely with the applicant to provide input into the selection process.
2. Serve as a public relations tool by promoting the organization.
3. Gather information about the applicant.
4. Assess how well the applicant's qualifications match the job requirements.
5. Determine whether the applicant will fit well with the organization and other employees.
6. Differentiate among the applications.
7. Hire the applicant with the most potential.

*Note:* Ideas for this figure were adapted from those presented in Kristen Weirick, "The Perfect Interview," *HR Magazine* (April 2008), pp. 85–88 and Northeastern University's Career Services "Successful Interviewing" website. Students may wish to visit http://www.northeastern.edu/careers/ for tips on interviewing..

How can one reconcile a major employer goal—to promote the organization—with a survey report that 20 percent of job applicants say they were "insulted" in job interviews?[24] The supervisor and team members must properly prepare for the interview and remember that they are "selling" the organization. Interviewing is much more than a technique; it is an art every supervisor must learn. Although our focus in this chapter is on the employee selection interview, over time, every supervisor will conduct or be involved in other types of interviews. Among these are appraisal and counseling interviews, interviews regarding complaints and grievances, interviews concerned with disciplinary measures or discharge, and exit interviews when employees quit voluntarily. The basic techniques are common to all interview situations.

There are two basic approaches to interviewing: directive and nondirective. These approaches are classified primarily according to the amount of structure the interviewer imposed on the interview. Regardless of the approach used, it is essential that all applicants be asked the same questions and that interviewers receive training in how to conduct legally defensible interviews.[25]

## THE DIRECTIVE INTERVIEW

**Directive interview**
Interview approach in which the interviewer guides the discussion along a predetermined course

In a **directive interview**, the interviewer guides the discussion with a predetermined outline and objectives in mind. This approach is sometimes called a patterned or structured interview. An outline helps the interviewer ask specific questions to cover each topic on which information is wanted. It also allows the interviewer to question and expand on related areas. For example, if a supervisor asks about the applicant's work experience, it may lead to questions about what the applicant liked and did not like about previous jobs. The supervisor guides and controls the interview but does not make it a rigid, impersonal experience. If all applicants are asked the same questions, it makes it easier to compare applicants fairly.

## THE NONDIRECTIVE INTERVIEW

**Nondirective interview**
Interview approach in which the interviewer asks open-ended questions that allow the applicant latitude in responding

The purpose of a **nondirective interview** is to encourage interviewees to talk freely and in depth. The applicant has freedom to determine the course of the discussion. Rather than asking specific questions, the supervisor may stimulate the discussion by asking broad, open-ended questions, such as "Tell me about your work in the computer field." Generally, the supervisor will develop a list of possible topics to cover and, depending on how the interview proceeds, may or may not ask related questions. This unstructured approach to interviewing allows for great flexibility, but it is generally more difficult and time-consuming to conduct than directive interviews. For this reason, the nondirective interview is seldom used in its pure form in employee selection.

## BLENDING DIRECTIVE AND NONDIRECTIVE APPROACHES

Ultimately, the purpose of any interview is to promote mutual understanding—to help the interviewer and interviewee understand each other better through open communication. In employee selection interviews, the directive approach is used most often because supervisors find it convenient to obtain information by asking the same direct questions of all applicants. At times, however, supervisors should strive to blend directive and nondirective techniques to obtain additional information that might help them reach a decision. Often, interviewers use situational questions to assess what the applicant would do in a certain situation. All applicants are given a specific situation to which to respond. For example, the question, "How would you assign daily work when two employees are absent?" allows the applicants to organize and express their thoughts about a realistic work situation. The supervisor may gain deeper insight into applicants' abilities to think and solve problems that could make the difference in choosing which applicant to hire.

Would it surprise you that "What computer skills do you have?" is a commonly asked interview question? Regardless of the approach used, the initial questions about computer skills should lead to the development of additional, relevant, job-related questions. For example, questions such as the following allow applicants to reveal their skills, knowledge, or abilities (SKAs) and values more clearly than could be ascertained from other sources: "What is your knowledge of the various Software as a Service (SaaS) solutions for managing a worldwide workforce?" or "Explain how you trained other employees in the use of a quality improvement software program," or a situational interview question such as, "Just as you are walking out the door to take your family on a scheduled vacation, you receive a phone call from me explaining that a problem has arisen with the computer system and that you are the only one who might be able to come in and take care of things. What would you do?" The supervisor should avoid using judgmental questions, such as, "Do you think that IT geeks are a detriment to our goals?" Also, answers to questions that require a "yes" or "no" response, such as, "Do you like to work with figures?" reveal very little about the applicant's ability to perform a job. It is better for the supervisor to ask why the applicant does or does not like to work with figures.

## CONDUCTING THE SELECTION INTERVIEW

Remember, the purpose of the selection interview is to collect information and arrive at a decision concerning the job applicant. As stated earlier, the directive interview is the most common approach for getting this information. Many organizations have forms and procedures to guide supervisors in the interview process. For example, often interviewers will be required to fill out detailed forms on all applicants who are interviewed. Other firms use a standard interview form that more or less limits supervisors to only the questions on the form. These forms are intended to prevent supervisors from asking questions that might be considered discriminatory or in violation of the law.

All those in the interview progress must know what can be asked and what should not be asked of job applicants during the interview. A general rule is to seek information that is related to job qualifications and the candidate's ability to do the job. Guidelines for conducting the selection interview are found in the accompanying Supervisory Tips box.

## ESTABLISHING A CONDUCIVE PHYSICAL SETTING

Privacy and some degree of comfort are important components of a good interview setting. When a private room is not available, the supervisor should at least

## SUPERVISORY TIPS

### Supervisory Guidelines for Conducting an Employee Interview

- Carefully review the application, the applicant's résumé, and other background information about the job candidate.
- Determine the objectives and the form of interview to be conducted (i.e., directive and/or nondirective); develop specific questions to ask.
- Find a quiet, private place to hold the interview where interruptions will not occur.
- After a cordial warm-up, explain the nature of the job and its requirements; do not attempt to oversell the job or what is needed.
- Ask directive questions to verify information and qualifications on the application as well as to fill in any gaps that may be significant to the hiring decision.
- Ask the candidate to state what he or she could most contribute to the job in question; ask the applicant to provide examples of previous job situations that might be relevant.
- Encourage the candidate to speak freely and to ask as many questions as necessary.
- Take notes of the candidate's statements and comments that are most pertinent to meeting the requirements of the job.
- Avoid judging the candidate's suitability until the interview is completed; be aware of possible biases and stereotypes that could unfairly influence the hiring decision.
- Close the interview positively by thanking the candidate and indicating when a hiring decision will be made.

create an atmosphere of semiprivacy by speaking to the applicant in a place where other employees are not within hearing distance. This much privacy, at least, is necessary.

In some interviewing situations, employers choose a virtual setting for interviews, using web-based one-way or two-way video to conduct interviews with potential hires. Dave Zielinski writes in *HR Magazine* that in the past few years, the use of virtual interviewing has jumped nearly 300 percent, with some companies using the tool for first or screening interviews and others recording and capturing an interview conversation to share with internal stakeholders who may not be able to come together physically as an interview team. He asserts that the primary reasons for using virtual interviewing include the cost-savings of not having to bring candidates onsite for in-person interviews, which can reach upward of $1,000 per candidate; the convenience of not having to schedule a room and bring in a team of interviewers, all of whom can participate virtually from their own desks behind closed doors; and the opportunity to review recorded interviews if questions arise during the decision-making process. The physical setting of both the interviewer and the interviewee being on their home turf is also a benefit that can lead to more relaxed exchanges. Figure 10.4 provides suggestions for both employers and potential employees on how to reflect their best in a virtual interview. This new approach to interviewing may be a stretch for HR traditionalists and managers who prefer a face-to-face modality, but its benefits can help an organization's bottom line.[26]

**FIGURE 10.4 Virtual interviews: Tips for employers and job candidates**

**Tips for Employers:**

- Decide on a live or prerecorded format—You can either provide a list of questions to all candidates and ask them to record and submit their responses, or you can host a live interview with each. Is it important to collect the same information from each candidate? Choose prerecorded. Or do you wish to interact with the candidates? Choose live.
- Schedule wisely—Choose a time that is convenient for you and the candidate, one during which you are not likely to be disturbed, and one that respects each party's time zone.
- Prepare your technology—Ensure that your Internet connectivity, recording device, and sound are working correctly before the interview begins. While you are interviewing the candidate, he or she is also interviewing you. Technology failures can send an unwanted message about the state of technology in your organization.
- Establish the purpose of the interview—Is it a first, screening interview, or an opportunity to learn more about the candidate in order to make hiring decisions? The interviewee will benefit from knowing the purpose as he or she prepares.
- Record with permission—You may wish to record a live interview so that you can share it with colleagues involved with the decision-making process or have it available for review. Before pressing "record," explain that you would like to record the interview, tell the candidate how you will use the recording, and then get the candidate's permission to record. Once you start recording, ask the candidate to give permission again verbally so that it is contained in the recording.
- Close with next steps—At the end of a live interview, thank the candidate for his or her time, and then describe what he or she can expect in terms of follow-up to the interview. If the interview is a recorded response submitted to you, follow up promptly by acknowledging that you've received the recording, thanking the candidate for the submission and describing next steps.[27]

**Tips for Candidates:**

- Prepare your technology—At least an hour before your interview, set up and test your Internet connectivity, webcam, and sound. Technology glitches can quickly cut short the interview and your chances of getting the job.
- Create a professional environment—The best background for an interview is a blank background, one without visual or sound distractions. Choose a quiet place (find a friend or neighbor to keep pets and children engaged elsewhere) and a static background, such as a blank wall or bookshelf.
- Dress professionally—Dress for this interview as you would for a traditional, face-to-face interview. Avoid bright colors and busy patterns, as they may translate poorly on others' monitors.
- Manage yourself—Practice good posture and eye contact before the interview. Look at the webcam, not at the screen image, and don't fidget or fiddle with things on your desk.
- Practice, practice, practice—Recruit a family member or friend to for a trial run of the interview. Provide them with a few interview questions and ask them to evaluate your webcast technology, the physical environment and lighting, and your clothing, speech, and mannerisms. Practice responding clearly and succinctly with good grammar and no "ums."
- Be enthusiastic and professional—Even if you aren't in the same room as the interviewer, you can communicate a great deal with nonverbal cues, voice inflection, and expressions.
- Be yourself and don't sweat it—Highlight your best qualities by sharing relevant experiences in a positive way and be confident! It will come through in the interview.
- Say thank you—Just as though you were in a face-to-face interview, smile and thank the interviewer for his or her time, and follow up with a written thank you.[28]

*Note:* Content for this figure was adapted from suggestions presented in Megan McMonagle, "Bring Your Interview Into the Virtual Age," Comere-commended.com http://comerecommended.com/2011/02/bring-your-interview-into-the-virtual-age/ (February 18, 2011) and Dawn Dugan, "8 Tips for Acing Virtual Job Interviews: Know What You Need to Succeed When a Firm Handshake Isn't Possible," Salary.com, http://www.salary.com/8-tips-for-acing-virtual-interviews/.

## OPENING THE INTERVIEW

Remember that the employee selection interview is not just a one-way questioning process; the applicant also will want to know more about the company and the job. The interview should enable job seekers to learn enough to help them decide whether to accept the position if it is offered. The supervisor must conduct the interview professionally by opening the interview effectively, explaining the job requirements, and using good questioning and note-taking techniques.

The experience of applying for a job is often filled with tension for an applicant. It is to the supervisor's advantage to relieve this tension. Some supervisors try to create a feeling of informality by starting the interview with social conversation about the weather, city traffic, a recent sports event, or some broad interest but noncontroversial topic. The supervisor may offer a cup of coffee or make some other appropriate social gesture. An informal opening can help reduce an applicant's tensions, but it should be brief and then the discussion should move quickly to job-related matters.

Many supervisors begin the employee selection interview with a question that is nonthreatening and easily answered by the applicant but that contains job-related information the supervisor might need. An example is, "How did you learn about this job opening?"

The supervisor should avoid excessive informal conversation because studies of employee selection interviews have revealed that frequently an interviewer makes a favorable or an unfavorable decision after the first five minutes of the interview. If the first ten minutes are spent discussing items not related to the job, the supervisor may be basing the selection decision primarily on irrelevant information.

## EXPLAINING THE JOB

During the interview, the supervisor should discuss details of the job, working conditions, wages, benefits, and other relevant factors in a realistic way. A **realistic organizational preview (ROP)** includes sharing complete information about the organization: its mission, philosophy, opportunities, and other information that gives applicants a good idea of where the job fits in and why it is important. In discussing the job, a **realistic job preview (RJP)** informs applicants about the desirable and undesirable aspects of the job. To make a job look as attractive as possible, the supervisor may be tempted to describe conditions in terms that make it more attractive than it is in reality. For example, a supervisor might oversell a job by describing in glowing terms the possible career progression that is available only for exceptional employees. If the applicant is hired and turns out to be an average worker, this could lead to disappointment and frustration. Applicants who are given realistic information are more likely to remain on the job because they will encounter fewer unpleasant surprises.[29]

**Realistic organizational preview (ROP)**
Sharing information by an interviewer with a job applicant concerning the mission, values, and direction of the organization

**Realistic job preview (RJP)**
Information given by an interviewer to a job applicant that provides a realistic view of both the positive and negative aspects of the job

## ASKING EFFECTIVE QUESTIONS

Even though the supervisor will have some knowledge of the applicant's background from the application and from information the applicant volunteers, the need still exists to determine the applicant's specific qualifications for the job. The supervisor should not ask the applicant to repeat information on the application. Instead, the supervisor should rephrase questions to probe for additional details. For example, the question, "What was your last job?" is likely to

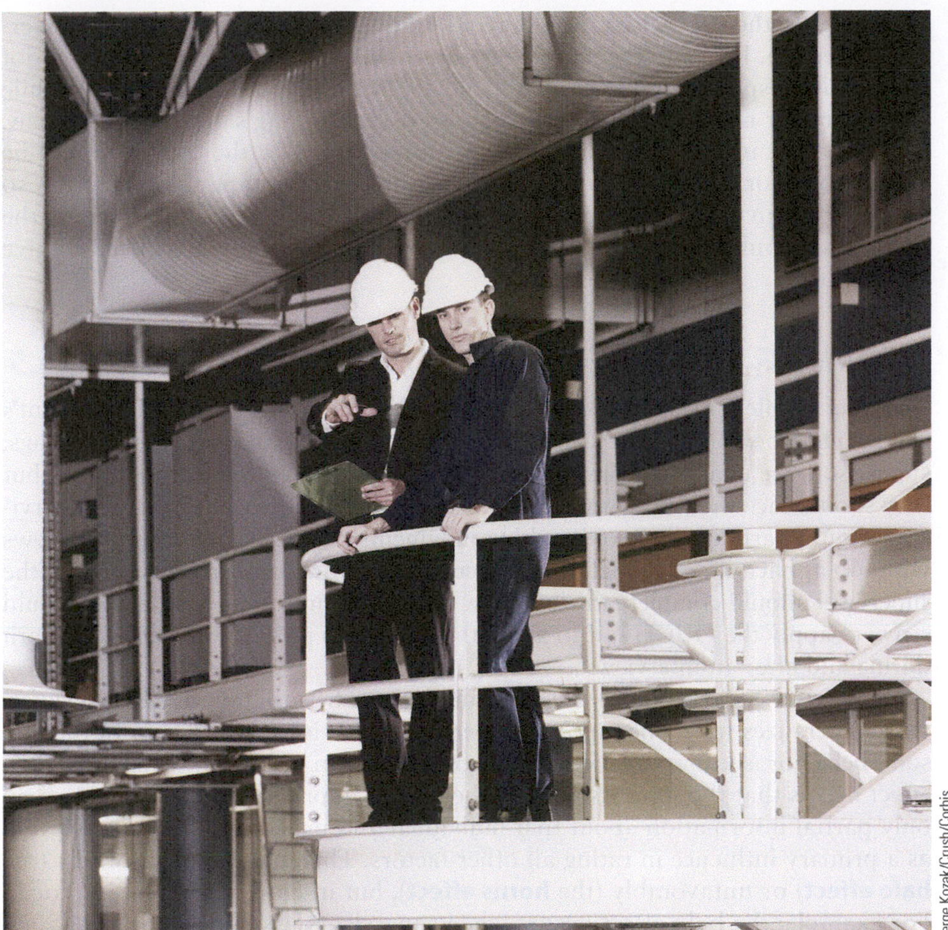
Serge Kozak/Crush/Corbis

*HR managers sometimes ask job candidates to take one or more types of tests as part of the screening and selection process*

be answered on the application. This question could be expanded as follows: "As a computer technician at Omega, what type of computer problems did you most frequently encounter?" Then a follow-up question would be, "How did you solve that problem?"

A supervisor must use judgment and tact when questioning applicants and so should avoid such leading or trick questions as, "Do you have difficulty getting along with other people?" or "Tell me about a person in your last work situation who you would describe as your least preferred co-worker." Interviewers sometimes use questions like these to see how applicants respond to difficult personal questions. However, these questions may antagonize the applicants. By no means should the supervisor pry into personal affairs that are irrelevant or removed from the work situation.

## TAKING NOTES

In their efforts to make better selection decisions, many supervisors take notes during or immediately after the interview. Written information is especially important when a supervisor interviews a number of applicants. Trying to remember what several applicants said during their interviews and exactly who said what is virtually impossible.

However, the supervisor should avoid writing while an applicant is answering a question. Instead, it is more courteous and useful for the supervisor to jot down brief response summaries after the applicant has finished talking. While the supervisor is not required to take notes on everything said in the interview, key facts that might aid in choosing one applicant over the others should be noted. Food for thought: Managers might want to videotape the interviews so that others can review the applicants' responses and reactions. Of course, the applicants would need to be informed of the purpose and would need to give permission.

## AVOIDING INTERVIEWING AND EVALUATION PITFALLS

The chief problem in employee selection usually lies in interpreting the applicant's background, personal history, and other pertinent information. As human beings, supervisors are unable to eliminate their personal preferences and prejudices, but they should face their biases and make efforts to avoid or control them. Supervisors should particularly avoid making judgments too quickly during interviews with job applicants. Although it is difficult not to form an early impression, the supervisor should complete the interview before making any decision and should strive to apply the OUCH test to avoid the numerous pitfalls that can occur both during and after an interview.

Supervisors also should avoid generalizations. The situation in which a supervisor generalizes from one aspect of a person's behavior to all aspects of the person's behavior is known as the halo or horns effect. In practice, the halo or horns effect means that the supervisor bases the overall impression of an individual on only partial information about that individual and uses this limited impression as a primary influence in rating all other factors. This may work favorably (the **halo effect**) or unfavorably (the **horns effect**), but in either case, it is improper. For example, the halo effect occurs when supervisors assume that if applicants have superior interpersonal skills, they also will be good at keyboarding, working with little direction, and so forth. On the other hand, when supervisors judge applicants with hearing impairments as being low on communication skills and allow this assessment to serve as a basis for low ratings on other dimensions, the horns effect prevails. The process we have suggested does not guarantee that the supervisor will not form erroneous opinions. However, objectivity minimizes the chances of making the wrong choice.

**Halo effect**
The tendency to allow one favorable aspect of a person's behavior to positively influence judgment on all other aspects

**Horns effect**
The tendency to allow one negative aspect of a person's behavior to negatively influence judgment on all other aspects

## CLOSING THE INTERVIEW

At the conclusion of the employee selection interview, the supervisor will likely have a choice among several alternatives, ranging from hiring the applicant to deferring the decision to rejecting the applicant. The supervisor's decision will be guided by the organization's policies and procedures. Some supervisors have the authority to make selection decisions independently, others are required to check with their managers or the HR department, and still others may have the authority only to recommend which applicant should be hired. For purposes of brevity, we assume in the following discussion that the supervisor has the authority to make the final selection decision. Under these circumstances, the supervisor can decide to hire an applicant on the spot. All the supervisor has to do is tell the applicant when to report for work and provide any additional, pertinent instructions.

If the supervisor wishes to defer the decision until several other candidates for the job have been interviewed, the applicant should be informed that he or she will be notified later. The supervisor should indicate a time frame within which the decision will be made. However, it is unfair to use this tactic to avoid the unpleasant task of telling an applicant that he or she is not acceptable. By telling the applicant that a decision is being deferred, the supervisor gives the applicant false hope. While waiting for the supervisor's decision, the applicant might not apply for other jobs, thereby letting opportunities slip by. Therefore, if a supervisor has made the decision not to hire an applicant, the supervisor should tell the applicant tactfully. Some supervisors merely say that there was not a sufficient match between the needs of the job and the qualifications of the applicant. Tony Lee, editor in chief at CareerJournal.com, said it best:

> *Although rejecting all but one applicant is part of the process, employers should be cautious in how they communicate with potential new hires. Remember that those applicants may buy your products and services and have long memories of how they're treated. Nothing can damage a company's reputation faster than bad word of mouth.*[30]

Regardless of its outcome, applicants should leave interviews feeling that they have been treated fairly and courteously. It is every supervisor's managerial duty to build as much goodwill as possible because it is in the organization's self-interest to maintain a good image.

### COMPLETING THE POST-INTERVIEW EVALUATION FORM

Some organizations have the supervisor and other members of the interview team complete an evaluation form shortly after the interview while the information is still fresh in their minds. Figure 10.5 is an adaptation of a form used by one retail store.

Its approach increases the likelihood that the same selection criteria are applied to each applicant. Other firms may require that supervisors submit a written evaluation that summarizes their impressions of and recommendations for each job candidate.

## Making the Hiring Decision

**4 Describe the hiring decision and the importance of documentation.**

The decision to hire can be challenging when the supervisor has interviewed several applicants and all appear qualified for the job. There are no definite guidelines a supervisor can use to select the best-suited individual. At times, information from the applications, tests, and interviews indicate which applicants should be hired.[31] However, at other times such information may be unconvincing or perhaps even conflicting. For example, an applicant's aptitude test score for a sales job may be relatively low, but the person has favorably impressed the supervisor in the interview by showing an enthusiastic interest in the job and a selling career.

At this point, supervisory judgment and experience come into play. The supervisor must select employees who are most likely to contribute to good departmental performance. The supervisor may consult with members of the HR staff for their evaluations, but, in the final analysis, it should be the supervisor's responsibility to choose. Before the final decision is made, the supervisor should evaluate each applicant against the selection criteria. By carefully analyzing all

**FIGURE 10.5 A post-interview evaluation form**

| POST-INTERVIEW EVALUATION FORM | | |
|---|---|---|
| **Position** | Major Job Requirements | |
| | (List major job requirements here.) | |
| **Applicant's Name:** | (Evaluate SKAs here.) | (Total) |
| **Strengths:**<br>**Weaknesses:** | | |
| **Applicant's Name:** | (Evaluate SKAs here.) | (Total) |
| **Strengths:**<br>**Weaknesses:** | | |
| **Applicant's Name:** | (Evaluate SKAs here.) | (Total) |
| **Strengths:**<br>**Weaknesses:** | | |

**Instructions to Interviewers**

1. The interviewer(s) may decide that some job requirements are more important than others. Therefore, it may be appropriate to assign weights to those requirements to illustrate their relative importance.
2. Evaluate each applicant's skills, knowledge, or abilities (SKAs) for each of the major job requirements:
   1 = Unacceptable 2 = Moderately acceptable
   3 = Acceptable 4 = Strongly acceptable
3. Total the rating for each applicant. (By totaling the ratings, the interviewer[s] will have a system by which to make a more objective choice.)
4. Record each applicant's strengths and weaknesses.
5. Make a copy of the form: (a) Retain one copy for documentation. (b) Deliver one copy to HR.

the information and keeping in mind previous successes and failures in selecting employees, the supervisor should be able to select applicants who are most likely to succeed.

Of course, hiring decisions always involve uncertainties. There are no exact ways to predict how individuals will perform until they are placed on the job. A supervisor who approaches the hiring decision thoroughly, carefully, and professionally is likely to consistently select applicants who will become excellent employees.

### INVOLVING EMPLOYEES IN THE HIRING DECISION

The degree to which employees are involved in the selection process differs among organizations. Generally, subordinates, peers, or work-team members meet with the applicant and give their impression to the ultimate decision maker. Members of employee work teams, for example, are generally most knowledgeable about job responsibilities and challenges. They can offer valuable insight into the employee selection process. Even without formal teams, some organizations allow employees to fulfill various roles, from assisting with the definition of job responsibilities to having a direct say in the final hiring decision. However, it is important to note that the downside of involving employees in the hiring decision is the possibility of favoritism and violation of EEOC regulations. Supervisors must be aware of company policies regarding **nepotism**. The practice of hiring relatives may eliminate other applicants from consideration.[32]

**Nepotism**
The practice of hiring relatives

### DOCUMENTING THE HIRING DECISION

Documentation is necessary to ensure that a supervisor's decision to accept or reject an applicant is based on job-related factors and is not discriminatory. At times, a supervisor's hiring decision will be challenged; the supervisor must be able to justify that decision or risk its reversal by higher-level managers. Similarly, sometimes higher-level managers or HR staff members will strongly encourage supervisors to give preferential hiring considerations to minority or female applicants, especially if the organization is actively seeking such employees. Some supervisors resent this type of pressure, but they should recognize that the organization may be obligated under various laws to meet certain hiring goals. In general, when supervisors follow the approaches suggested in this chapter, they should be able to distinguish the most qualified people from among applicants and also be prepared to justify their employment selections.

## Bringing New Employees Onboard

**5 Understand how to conduct an effective onboarding program.**

According to author Carole Fleck, "Some organizations use the terms *orientation* and *onboarding* interchangeably, but there is a difference."[33] In large organizations, when new employees report for their first day of work, HR usually conducts an initial session that familiarizes the new hire with the organization's vision, structure, culture, handbook, policies, and procedures, and perhaps includes a quick tour of the facilities. This initial phase is called orientation. **Orientation** is a process designed to help new employees become acquainted with the organization and understand the organization's expectations. In short, orientation helps the employee develop a sense of belonging to the organization.

**Orientation**
The process of smoothing the transition of new employees into the organization

**Onboarding**
A continuous process of assimilation and growth within the organization for new hires

**Onboarding** occurs when the new employee begins and it continues indefinitely. It is about helping employees to understand their roles, effectively perform their jobs, learn new tasks, gain new SKAs, and acquire the attitudes, behaviors, and knowledge needed to be a successful member of the team. Helping new employees to feel comfortable in their new work environment is a supervisory responsibility. The supervisor sets the stage for building working relationships within the department and may want to select a couple of employees to serve as guides or resources for the new hire. A chain hardware and building supply company, for example, has hitched its new hires to several of its "stars." The stars model the desired behaviors and can serve as mentors or coaches for the new employee. Some organizations have found it beneficial to add a preboarding component that provides information online so that the new hire can sign up for benefits, computer passwords, and other necessities before they show up the first day.[34] As shown in Figure 10.6, the supervisor must consider several important aspects to help the employee become a star.

The manner in which the supervisor welcomes new hires and introduces them to other employees in the department may have a lasting effect on their future performance. The first days on the job for most new employees are disturbing and anxious. They typically feel like strangers in new surroundings among people whom they have just met. It is the supervisor's responsibility to make the transition as smooth as possible by leading new employees in the desired directions and helping them become productive as soon as possible.

A supervisor can use several approaches to bringing new employees onboard. The supervisor may choose to escort new employees around the

**FIGURE 10.6 Getting new hires onboard**

department personally, showing them equipment and facilities and introducing them to other employees. Instead, the supervisor may prefer to assign new employees to an experienced, capable employee and have this person do all the orienting, perhaps even instructing new employees on how to perform their jobs.

## USING A CHECKLIST

A useful technique to ensure that new employees are well-oriented is to use a checklist. When developing an orientation checklist, the supervisor should strive to identify all the things that a new employee ought to know. The supervisor should ask the question: "To do this job well, what does a new employee need to know?" Without some type of checklist, the supervisor is apt to skip some important items. Checklists can also be used to help new employees understand the company and its objectives, and to build a more positive attitude toward the supervisor, fellow employees, and the company.

## DISCUSSING THE ORGANIZATION

In most firms, the HR department provides booklets that give general information about the firm, including benefits, policies, and procedures. There may even be a formal class that provides this type of information to employees and includes a tour of the firm's facilities. In small firms, it may be appropriate to introduce new employees to the owner or top-level managers. In large firms, this may not be practical, so these firms may videotape an interview with the CEO and other members of top management. This is one way the company's vision for the future, corporate philosophy, market and product development, management styles, and so forth may be shared.[35] Employees should receive an explanation of what they can expect from the organization. Realistic organization and job previews should clarify employee expectations. The key is that the information must be accurate and that all employees must receive the same information.

A common mistake supervisors make when onboarding new employees is to give them too much information on the first day. Presenting too many items in a very short time may result in information overload. New employees are unlikely to remember many details presented in the first two hours of the first day. Consequently, the supervisor should spread different aspects over a new employee's first few weeks or months. Also, the supervisor should schedule a review session several days or weeks later to discuss any problems or questions the new employee might have.

## BEING SUPPORTIVE

More important than the actual techniques used to orient new employees are the attitudes and behaviors of the supervisor. When a supervisor conveys sincerity in trying to make the transition period a pleasurable experience and tells new employees that they should not hesitate to ask questions, it will smooth the early days on the job. Even when the HR department provides formal orientation, it remains the supervisor's responsibility to help each new person quickly become an accepted member of the departmental work team and a contributing, productive employee.

## SETTING THE STAGE

Supervisory responsibility goes beyond making sure that the employee has received a handbook and department work rules. The supervisor should inform the other employees that someone new is joining the group and should let them know something positive about the new person. Imagine how difficult it would be for a person to be received into the work group if the employees had been told "we had to hire this person." The supervisor needs to set the stage for the new employee's arrival so that the new employee is socialized properly into the work group.

Organizations that use work teams believe in spreading authority, responsibility, and accountability throughout the organization. For many employees, this has meant learning to work more closely with others as team members and depending on each other for the completion of assigned tasks. Over time, effective teams develop open communication and relationships. New employees need to understand the purpose and goals of the work group, why the job is important, and where the job fits in. They also need to understand the roles various team members fulfill. Supervisors must make certain that members of the work team understand that it is their responsibility to communicate and contribute to this understanding.

Part of the onboarding process is to shape positively the new employee's behavior. Because people observe and imitate others' behavior, it is not enough for a supervisor simply to state what is expected of the employee. People tend to act—productively and counterproductively—like those with whom they closely identify. Effective work-team members model positive norms for the new employee. An effective technique designed to perpetuate excellent performance is to place the new employee with an outstanding performer who acts as a coach or mentor. Finally, as discussed in Chapter 4, all employees need positive feedback on performance, and an effective supervisor reinforces the new employee's early successes by giving sincere praise.

## MENTORING

**Mentoring**
An experienced employee guiding a newer employee in areas concerning job and career

Since the publication of the classic *Harvard Business Review* article "Everyone Who Makes It Has a Mentor," researchers have explored the roles that mentors or sponsors play in employee development.[36] **Mentoring** is the process of having a more experienced person provide guidance, coaching, or counseling to a less experienced person. Broadly defined, the mentor teaches "the tricks of the trade," gives the new employee all the responsibility he or she can handle, thrusts the new employee into new areas, directs and shapes performance, suggests how things are to be done, and provides protection.

Mentoring should be looked upon as one way to smooth the transition of new employees into the organization and develop them into productive employees. New employees can build a network of people who can collectively provide the many benefits of a mentor. The ultimate question for the new employee is, "How do I attach myself to a role model who will guide my career?" Professor Kathy Kram suggests, "Putting all your eggs in one basket is a mistake. I think people ought to think in terms of multiple mentors instead of just one. Peers can be an excellent source of mentorship."[37]

To expand on the idea of "multiple mentors," mentors can be identified for the following purposes: a mentor for life, a mentor for the season, and a mentor for a specific reason. Ask someone you respect and trust about their mentors, and you will probably get the following responses:

1. "I have several people who have always been there for me. I can go to them anytime day or night, and after I tell them the situation, they ask me questions to clarify the situation. They never tell me what to do, but ask me questions to get me to think through the problems. They are not critical, but supportive. They will always be there for me."
2. "As a college student, there were two professors that I could always go to for help and guidance. They not only helped guide me, but they provided advice. They were there for me during the semester (season)."
3. "When I got my first job and had a specific problem or concern, I had a supervisor that would help and guide me. Sometimes it was a co-worker that provided help when needed on a specific project."[38]

Each of these levels will require a mentor with a set of SKAs, and you will need to recognize those persons who can help you grow. Sometimes, that person may be a peer.

Increasingly, new employees are responsible for their career development. How does one go about selecting a mentor? Kram says, "Would-be mentors are most receptive to people who ask good questions, listen well to the responses, and demonstrate that they are hungry for advice and counsel. Mentoring is a chance for the mentors to revitalize their own learning."[39] Should supervisors mentor? Yes, they should mentor when they feel comfortable doing so. In Chapter 5, we discussed the delegation of authority, which the supervisor can do to add to the employee's knowledge base and which can be considered a form of mentoring.

## Training and Developing Employees

**6 Explain approaches to training and the supervisor's role in employee development.**

In today's world, we like to see every person as a potential coach. While that may seem farfetched, think back over the last ten years of your life. Who provided you with an opportunity to add SKAs to your toolbox? Who encouraged you to get into situations that caused you to learn something new and unusual? Who forced you to think independently or gave you an opportunity to make a difference (contribute in ways that you never thought possible)? Was there a person who helped unlock your potential? Your success is a tribute to all of those who helped you along the way. The supervisor/coach does not have to be a solution provider, but rather one who engages employees in activities that help them to reach their potential and the organization to reach or exceed its goals.[40]

In most job situations, new employees require general and specific training. When skilled workers are hired, the primary training need may be in the area of company and departmental methods and procedures. When unskilled or semi-skilled workers are hired, they (the trainees) must understand the importance of the job and why each step must be done correctly. The supervisor or another capable employee should demonstrate the proper way to do the job. It is critical to the learning process that the supervisor frequently monitor the work being performed, answer questions, make adjustments, provide additional guidance as necessary, and encourage them. We will discuss the supervisor's coaching responsibilities further in Chapter 12 (see Figure 12.9 for an overview of the supervisor's coaching responsibilities).

*When supervisors do on-the-job training, they can get to know their new employees*

Walter Hodges/The Image Bank/Getty Images

Formal training methods vary among organizations and depend on the unique circumstances of each situation. According to a SHRM employee skills and training survey, 81 percent of employees receive training onsite, 57 percent attend off-site training, and approximately 40 percent gain skills at technical colleges or universities.[41] At the department level, helping employees improve their SKAs to perform current and future jobs is an ongoing responsibility of the supervisor.[42] Remember, if the "trainee fails, the supervisor/coach fails."

## PROVIDING ON-THE-JOB TRAINING

Most training at the departmental level takes the form of on-the-job training. The supervisor may prefer to do as much of the training as time permits. Doing on-the-job training provides the advantage of helping the supervisor get to know the new employees while they are being trained. It also ensures uniform training, because the same person is training everyone. When the supervisor lacks the time or the technical skills to do the training, the training should be performed by one of the best employees. The supervisor should assign the training task only to experienced employees who enjoy this additional assignment and are qualified to do it. The supervisor should follow up periodically to see how each new employee is progressing.

Programs may also be offered within the firm during or outside of working hours. For example, safety training meetings and seminars are commonly scheduled during working hours for supervisors and employees alike.

## PROVIDING OFF-THE-JOB TRAINING

Many training programs for new and existing employees are conducted outside of the immediate work area. Some of these training programs may be coordinated or taught by HR staff or training departments. For skilled crafts involving, for example, electricians, machinists, or toolmakers, a formal apprenticeship training program may be established.[43] Usually these programs require employees to be away from the job for formal schooling and work part of the time.

Increasingly, business firms are initiating college-campus-based programs for employee training. Generally, college representatives work together with the firm's supervisors to develop a curriculum for employees. Employees attend classes on the campus during nonworking hours. The firm pays the tuition, and employees receive credit for taking classes related to their jobs. A continual process of curriculum review and assessment of employees' on-the-job performance ensures that the program meets the firm's needs.

E-learning as an employee development strategy has made consistent gains in popularity over the past decade. In its biannual survey of nearly 9,000 HR professionals, SHRM found that 59 percent of respondents' organizations plan to increase the use of e-learning in 2014 and beyond.[44] Webinars, tutorials, online video, simulations, free massive open online courses (MOOCs), and instructional programs delivered through learning management systems allow an employee to work on company time or during free time at their own speed to build SKAs. These approaches allow the company to bring the training directly to the employees, to give specialized training suited to individual needs, to report and track completion as part of ongoing professional development. An expectation, and sometimes a challenge, of e-learning is that the participant must be self-directed and able to learn independently. Therefore, it is important for supervisors to ensure that workers have the basic skills necessary to navigate the e-learning environment and workers know exactly what is expected of them in terms of participation and completion, otherwise the training may not be effective or even completed. A best practice before implementing an e-learning initiative is to engage HR or the training and development department in providing an orientation to the e-learning environment. A well-designed e-learning training program delivered to well-prepared employees can be as effective in building employee skills as through face-to-face training.[45]

## ENSURING ONGOING EMPLOYEE DEVELOPMENT

Supervisors should continually assess the skills and potential of existing employees and should provide opportunities for the ongoing development of employee skills so that those employees can perform better now and in the future. When supervisors believe that training is needed that cannot be provided at the departmental level, those supervisors should go to higher-level managers or to the HR department to see whether courses outside the organization can meet training needs.

Many organizations have tuition-aid programs to help employees further their education. A supervisor should be aware of course offerings at nearby educational institutions and encourage employees to take advantage of all possible educational avenues. These learning experiences can help employees develop the SKAs that improve their performance and prepare them for more demanding responsibilities.

## UNDERSTANDING THE SUPERVISOR'S ROLE IN EMPLOYEE DEVELOPMENT

The impetus for a training program can come from many directions, but generally, operating problems and the failure to accomplish organizational objectives may highlight the need for training. Training activities should be based on identification of the combined needs of the organization and the employees.

Training must be viewed as an ongoing developmental process, not a simple solution to a short-term problem. Therefore, training must be relevant, informative, interesting, and applicable to the job, and it must actively involve the trainee. As Confucius put it:

*I hear and I forget;*
*I see and I remember;*
*I do and I understand.*

**Cross-training**
Training employees to do multiple tasks and jobs

**Reductions in force (RIFs)**
Termination of jobs due to changes in funding or work requirements

Skills that employees need to perform essential departmental tasks should be the initial training focus. However, in the current business environment, **cross-training** is becoming essential. Downsizings, outsourcing, or **reductions in force (RIFs)**, termination of jobs due to changes in funding or work requirements, have left millions of employees wondering what the future holds. Consolidation of job duties suggests that supervisors must identify the jobs that are important to the ongoing performance of their departments and that other employees can learn. Employees will need to learn new skills that will make them more valuable to their organizations. Cross-trained employees learn how to do a variety of jobs within the organization. An employee's ability to perform a variety of tasks makes him or her more valuable and able to assume additional responsibilities in the future.

In formulating an employee development program, supervisors should seek answers to the following types of questions:

- Who, if anyone, needs training?
- What training do they need?
- What are the purposes of the training?
- What are the instructional objectives that need to be incorporated into the training program? (Instructional objectives are basically what the employee will know or be able to do upon completing the training.)
- Which training and development programs best meet the instructional objectives?
- What benefits are anticipated to be derived from the training?
- What will the program cost?
- When and where will the training take place?
- Who will conduct the training?
- How will the training effort be evaluated?[46]

Efficient and effective training should contribute to the achievement of organizational objectives. Instructional objectives are essential to an evaluation plan.

## MAKING YOURSELF MORE VALUABLE

The need for training and development is not limited to departmental employees. Supervisors also need training and development to avoid obsolescence or status-quo thinking. By expanding their perspectives, supervisors are more likely to encourage employees to improve their knowledge and abilities and to keep up to date.

Most supervisors attend supervisory management training and development programs as well as courses in the technical aspects of company and departmental operations. Supervisors may want to belong to one or more professional or technical associations whose members meet periodically to discuss problems and topics of current interest and to share experiences. In addition, supervisors should subscribe to technical and managerial publications and should read articles of professional interest.

We contend that today, more than at any other time, supervisors are responsible for their own destinies. To survive, supervisors must give some thought to their long-term career development. Ambitious supervisors will find it helpful to formulate career plans by writing down the goals that they would like to achieve in the next three to five years. Such plans include a preferred pattern of assignments and job positions and a listing of educational and training activities that will be needed as part of career progression.

Our former students have reported that Richard Bolles's *What Color Is Your Parachute? A Practical Manual for Job-Hunters and Career-Changers* helped them to think and rethink their career options and opportunities. In an interview, Bolles outlined his career development strategies:

> *Sending out resumes doesn't work. Neither does answering ads. Employment agencies? No way. What does work is figuring out what you like to do and what you do well—and then finding a place that needs people like you. Contact organizations you're interested in, even if they don't have known vacancies. Pester others for leads.*[47]

Bolles has a free site, JobHuntersBible, which provides guidance in the following areas: The Internet, Research, Contacts, Counseling, Job Hunting, and Jobs and Résumés. His purpose is to provide free and expert help for job seekers.[48]

## SUMMARY

**1.** **Managing human resources (HR) should be one of the supervisor's top priorities. In fulfilling staffing responsibilities, the supervisor can be substantially aided by the HR department. Increasingly, many organizations use firms that supply temporary workers to do some of the staffing work.**

**One ongoing process of staffing is determining how many employees and what skills are needed to accomplish various work assignments. Job descriptions indicate the duties and responsibilities of the job and must be reviewed periodically. Job descriptions that accurately describe jobs help supervisors provide realistic job previews, develop performance standards, conduct performance appraisals, and other staffing functions. Job specifications detail the SKAs an employee should have to perform a job adequately. Applicants are recruited and screened based on the job specifications.**

**HR advertises the opening, recruits a pool of applicants, screens, tests, and checks references, and conducts background checks. The departmental supervisor and those who will be working with the new hire either make or will have the most say in the final hiring decision.**

**2.** **The pervasive presence of EEO laws and regulations has resulted in the HR staff assuming much of the responsibility to ensure that an organization's employment policies and practices comply with these laws. The supervisor should review the applicant's application, test scores, and other background materials. Hopefully, HR verified the applicants' past work performance so that negligent hiring does not take place.**

**With a list of key questions, the supervisor should be able to cover the most important areas in which more information is needed. By preparing questions in advance, the supervisor can make certain that all applicants are asked the same questions. Supervisors should develop job-related questions. Situational questions may be used to assess how an applicant would act in a given situation. Remember, ask job-related questions that foster nondiscriminatory and fair treatment of all applicants. All aspects of the selection process must comply with the OUCH test—objective, uniform in application, consistent in effect, and have job relatedness.**

**3.** **Selection is the process of choosing the best applicant to fill a particular job. After job applicants are located, information must be gathered to help in determining who should be hired.**

**Supervisors will use either a directive or nondirective interview approach, or some combination of the two. The directive interview is highly structured; the supervisor asks each applicant specific questions and guides the discussion. In the nondirective interview, the supervisor allows the applicant freedom to determine the course of the discussion.**

The supervisor is tasked with establishing a setting for the interview that is private and comfortable for the applicant. In some cases, the most appropriate setting is a virtual setting.

The supervisor may open the employee selection interview by using an approach that reduces tension, such as asking a question that is easily answered. The supervisor should explain the job, use effective questioning techniques, and take appropriate notes. When evaluating an applicant, the supervisor should avoid such common pitfalls as making hasty judgments; allowing generalizations, such as the halo or the horns effect; or forming impressions based on personal biases or preferences. The OUCH test will help the supervisor minimize judgmental errors.

At the conclusion of the interview, the supervisor should remember that the applicant is entitled to a decision as soon as possible. The supervisor should strive to have the applicant leave with an impression of fair and courteous treatment.

4. The supervisor wants to select employees who will contribute to excellent departmental performance. A review of the selection criteria is critical to identifying the best applicant. Depending on the organization, subordinates, peers, or team members may have a say in determining who is hired. This involvement varies from assistance in defining job duties to having a say in the final decision.

The hiring decision will never make everyone happy. Documentation of the selection process is critical in helping to demonstrate that the process is based on job-related factors and is nondiscriminatory.

5. Efficiently and effectively bringing employees onboard should be the supervisor's top priority. Traditionally, orientation means helping new employees become acquainted with the organization and its policies and procedures. This is done with the help of the HR department. The supervisor ensures that new hires understand what is expected in the way of job duties. A checklist can ensure that each new employee receives the same information. In most large organizations, the HR department helps the supervisor with the basic orientation process. Effective onboarding is a process that continues beyond the first day on the job. The supervisor's supportive attitude and the involvement of other employees are significant. Using other employees as mentors is an effective way to shape the new employee's behavior positively. Positive role models, coaches, or mentors should be used to perpetuate excellent performance standards.

6. Every supervisor should see himself or herself as a coach and mentor with responsibility to help each employee be the best he or she can be. When supervisors lack the time or technical skills to do the training personally, they can delegate the task to an experienced employee with excellent job performance. Off-the-job and online training programs also can help employees perform better. Training and development is a continual process, not just a one-time effort.

Supervisors must determine the skills employees need to do their jobs better. Factors such as failure to meet organizational objectives, operating problems, introduction of new machines and equipment, and addition of new job responsibilities to a position can help the supervisor pinpoint training needs. The supervisor should constantly monitor the training that each person needs. Instructional objectives and a procedure for evaluating the effectiveness of training are essential.

Also, supervisors must recognize the need for their own training and development, and they should explore all opportunities for career development. Supervisors should consider having career plans to help them chart and monitor their long-term career progression.

## KEY TERMS

- Competencies (p. 377)
- Cross-training (p. 396)
- Directive interview (p. 380)
- Halo effect (p. 386)
- Horns effect (p. 386)
- Human resource management (HRM) (p. 367)
- Human resources (HR) department (p. 367)
- Mentoring (p. 392)
- Nepotism (p. 389)
- Nondirective interview (p. 380)
- Onboarding (p. 390)
- Orientation (p. 389)
- Realistic job preview (RJP) (p. 384)
- Realistic organizational preview (ROP) (p. 384)
- Reduction in force (RIF) (p. 396)
- Selection (p. 378)
- Selection criteria (p. 378)

## WHAT HAVE YOU LEARNED?

1. What are some of the major activities of the HR department that can assist the line supervisor in the staffing function? What should be the primary responsibility of the HR staff and of line supervisors for various employment and other staffing activities? Is there a clear dividing line of responsibility? Discuss.
2. Define some of the major laws and regulations governing equal employment opportunity (EEO). Why have many organizations assigned to the HR department the primary responsibility for making sure that their employment policies and practices are in compliance?
3. What is the role of job descriptions and job specifications in an effective employee recruitment development program?
4. In what ways do Equal Employment Opportunity laws restrict employers? How do they protect employers? How do they protect potential employees?
5. How would you define "the selection process"? Why is adequate supervisory preparation for an employee selection interview crucial to the interview's success? Discuss each of the following aspects of conducting an employee selection interview:
   a. Opening the interview
   b. Explaining the job
   c. Using effective questioning techniques
   d. Taking notes
   e. Concluding the interview
6. Do you remember your first day on your current or most recent job?
   a. What were your feelings? Most of our students admit to being nervous as well as concerned about their ability to measure up.
   b. Describe the type of orientation program you received. What could the organization have done to do a better job of bringing you onboard?
   c. Why do many employers fail to adequately socialize or orient their new hires to the organization?
   d. How is onboarding for a new employee related to future performance? Discuss the approaches a supervisor may take in onboarding a new employee.
7. What are the different approaches to training and development at the departmental level?
   a. If you had the opportunity to choose between the different training modalities described in the chapter, which would you prefer? Why?
   b. Why should training programs be evaluated?
   c. Do you believe that on-the-job (face-to-face) training and development will become more or less important in the future? Why or why not?

## EXPERIENTIAL EXERCISES FOR SELF-ASSESSMENT

### EXPERIENTIAL EXERCISE FOR SELF-ASSESSMENT 10: Exploring Preemployment Assessments

An important part of the employee selection process is determining the level of SKAs a potential employee can bring to the organization. As discussed in this chapter, one strategy for assessing applicants' skills and aptitudes is by administering preemployment tests. While this task is typically relegated to the HR department, it is important for supervisors to be knowledgeable about the content of the test and what the test scores represent relative to how they can predict a potential employee's job performance. This assessment activity provides you with the opportunity to explore and sample a variety of hypothetical preemployment assessments. (Note: These tests have not been validated and are not appropriate for use in an actual employment situation.) The value of this activity is twofold. It will build your understanding of the types of test results an HR department might share with you as a supervisor and, as you complete your degree program and possibly consider a change in your own career, the assessments will give you an idea of what kinds of tests you may be asked to complete.

1. Visit one or more of the following websites, which each provide links to a variety of hypothetical practice tests:
   a. SHL Talent Measurement: Practice Tests: http://www.shldirect.com/en/practice-tests
   b. Practice Aptitude Tests: http://www.practiceaptitutedtests.com
   c. The Riley Guide: Self Assessment: http://www.rileyguide.com/assess.html
2. Complete at least three practice tests.
3. In a one- to two-page response, reflect on the process and results of the tests. List the name of each test, followed by answers to the following questions:
   a. What information could the results provide about the future performance of an employee taking this test?
   b. What would the results *not* tell you that would be important to know about a potential employee?
   c. How would you characterize the experience of taking this test? Hard? Easy? Confusing? Tedious? Other descriptors?

## PERSONAL SKILL BUILDING

### PERSONAL SKILL BUILDER 10-1: What Call Will You Make?

You are Bonnie Minnick, supervisor at King Appliances. Please review this chapter's opening You Make the Call!

1. Identify what James Staker might have done differently to get Bonnie to offer suggestions on ways to improve the store's efficiency?
2. Was it appropriate for Staker to give to Bonnie a directive in a social, off-the-job setting? Why or why not?
3. What might you have done differently at the picnic as you listened to your boss's comments?
4. In this chapter, we talk about empowering employees for success. After reviewing the chapter and this you make the call, if you were James Staker what would you have done differently to get Bonnie on board, that is, help her to be the best employee possible?
5. What should Bonnie do now?

### PERSONAL SKILL BUILDER 10-2: Ethical Issues

INTERNET ACTIVITY

It is unlawful to ask certain personal questions before making an employment offer. Legislation on equal opportunity employment (EEO) has restricted the questions employers can ask job applicants.

1. Using the Internet, identify a number of unlawful and potentially unlawful areas of inquiry.
2. James Staker (see this chapter's You Make the Call!) is interviewing Alan Hunter, who is confined to a wheelchair, for a data processing position in his store. Hunter has passed the usual selection criteria. Using the Internet to aid you in identifying a list of accommodations for Staker to consider before deciding whether to offer Hunter the position.
3. Why is it important for supervisors to be up to date on legislation that affects staffing decisions?

### PERSONAL SKILL BUILDER 10-3: Successful Interviewing

INTERNET ACTIVITY

You may have heard people say, "I know a good person when I see one." Look around the classroom or virtual course room and identify one person whom you do not know.

1. Based on your first impression—just by observing the person or reading his or her first discussion posts—make a list of adjectives that describe your impression.
2. Assume that you would be interviewing this person for an assistant store manager position at Sanders Supermarkets Store #6. Using at least three different Internet resources or resources found in your institution's career center, identify a list of questions that you might use for successful interviewing.
3. Ask the person identified in question number 2 whether you may interview him or her for three to five minutes. You may have to arrange a phone interview, Skype or Facetime meeting with an online classmate. Use the questions you developed above as an outline for the interview.
4. How did your interview evaluation of this person compare with your first impression?
5. Summarize in a one-page essay what you learned from this skill builder.

### PERSONAL SKILL BUILDER 10-4: Personal Career Development

1. Think back to a time in your life when you were exuberant because you or a group to which you belonged accomplished something that others thought was nearly impossible. List four to six things that you have accomplished that make you extremely proud.
2. Write a paragraph describing each accomplishment.
3. Carefully analyze each paragraph to identify specific SKAs that you used to accomplish those things.
4. Now look at your list of SKAs. What SKAs appear most often? These are your "proven" SKAs, and no one can take them away from you. Remember: We build on strengths!
5. Take a moment to close your eyes and develop a mental picture of where you will be five years from now. What will you be doing? Where will you be doing it? Who will you be doing it with?
6. You know where you have been. You know where you are currently. You now have a vision of where you want to be five years from now. What is it going to take to get you there?
7. How can you use your "proven SKAs" to get there?
8. What forces inside you (weaknesses) will interfere with you getting there? What will you do over the next five years to shore up your weaknesses?
9. In one page or less, outline a plan (your career plan) for getting where you want to go.

TEAM SKILL BUILDING

## TEAM SKILL BUILDER 10-1: Technology Tools—LinkedIn Can Help You Build Your Social Capital

Social capital, according to Harvard University's BetterTogether.org initiative, is "the collective value of all social networks and the inclinations that arise from these networks to do things for each other."[49] In organizations we build social capital by building relationships, sharing information, and helping one another. Technology has provided a myriad of applications that can help us build social capital by connecting and doing things together with our friends, family, colleagues, and like-minded individuals.

LinkedIn is one such application that focuses on building connections between organizations and individuals within those organizations. You may be familiar with LinkedIn, you may have already created a LinkedIn profile, or you may be new to this electronic network. This activity provides opportunities for you to learn about the features of LinkedIn and how it can help you build your social capital.

Based on your level of experience with LinkedIn, you will choose and do at least three of the following exercises. First, join up with a team of five to six people. After exploring LinkedIn and doing the exercises, share your experiences with your team, then write a one- to two-page chronicle and reflection of your activities. What did you do? What did you learn? Reflect on how LinkedIn can be helpful to you in at least two of the following ways:

- In a job search
- To build your career and personal SKAs
- As a supervisor or manager
- To engage with your industry sector
- To engage with your local community

1. Visit LinkedIn.com and join the network. It is free to join using either your e-mail address or Facebook identity.
2. Create a LinkedIn Profile. Your profile is your engine for building social capital. LinkedIn will help you build your profile by suggesting content you should add in each section. The Education portal of LinkedIn, found under the Interests tab, specifically the Students section, can also provide hints for building your profile. If you want to energize your profile even more, type "make a great LinkedIn profile" into your search engine and you will be answered with dozens of suggested links. Focus on suggestions that come from companies and individuals in your sector. In other words, if you are a business major, take advice from business people and sites, and if you are preparing to become an engineer, take advice from engineers.
3. Build your network. Start with the people on your team, then move on to other people you know. Once you connect to a few people, you can view their connections or view LinkedIn's recommendations of other people like them with whom you may want to connect. To find possible connections, type a person's name into the Search Bar, select "people" from the pull-down connected to the search bar and click the magnifying glass. Connect away!
4. Follow big ideas and thought leaders using Pulse. Under the Interests tab, choose Pulse. The Channels feature of Pulse allows you to select and follow topics you are interested in. The Influencers feature lists the most active LinkedIn users by number of followers. The influencers share big ideas about specific content on a regular basis. Richard Branson, founder of Virgin Group, for example, posts on entrepreneurship. Jack Welch posts on leadership and management. Deepak Chopra posts on health, wellness, and fitness. Following influencers will bring their big ideas straight to your news feed.
5. Build your knowledge. The Home tab will take you to a news feed that is populated by information that is shared by people with whom you are connected and those who you follow. As you scroll down the news feed you will see articles that are written and recommended by your connections.
6. Discover jobs. By clicking the Jobs tab you can do a general search of what jobs are out there, or you can use advanced features to get more specific. In the Search for Jobs bar, type in job title keywords or a specific company you are interested in to see what's available. Or, customize your search by clicking Advanced Search to designate industries, functions, or zip codes.
7. Learn about companies. Do you have an assignment that requires you to find out more about a company? Is there a company you would love to work for? Do you want to find out how to blaze a new career path? The Companies network, located in the Interests tab, will connect you to every company that belongs to LinkedIn.
8. Join groups to interact with like-minded folks. LinkedIn Groups are available for every imaginable interest and industry. Individuals choose groups based on personal and professional interests. You can join groups that your connections participate in or search the LinkedIn Groups Directory to see if any seem interesting to you. The Interests tab will take you to Groups, where you can choose to join any you wish.

## TEAM SKILL BUILDER 10-2: People Who Make Life Difficult—the Embellisher!

Chance Fisher was hired a little over a year ago for an accounting analyst position at Wedgewood Credit Union. Wedgewood has more than 30 branches located throughout northern Indiana. When Chance was hired, the Credit Union posted the opening internally, contacted local colleges, and advertised the position in area papers. The Credit Union required three years of experience in finance/accounting and a college degree in accounting.

Chance was a storyteller and could always one-up others. When Carrie returned from her grandparents' fiftieth anniversary to Disney, Chance had to take charge of the group and talk about his trip to the Great Wall of China. One evening, at a social function, Dave asked Chance's wife about their trip to China. Her response was "What trip to China? We have never been out of the country!" When David and others confronted Chance about the Great Wall trip, he admitted that he had made up the story, but then added that "everyone embellishes a little bit."

Chance's performance was good, and his most recent performance appraisal showed him to be a "good or better" performer in relevant categories, except for "teamwork." Basically, Chance performed most tasks assigned in a satisfactory manner. Bob Harmeyer had spent time discussing Chance's storytelling and the need for open and honest communications.

On Tuesday night, Michele Kay was with a friend at the local college library. As she looked across the room, she saw Chance and he appeared to be studying. When Michele's friend asked who she was staring at, she responded, "One of the guys I work with." The friend inquired, "Do you mean Chance? He is in two of my accounting classes."

Michele and a couple of the accountants at Wedgewood were talking the next day about what, if anything, Michele should do with the information. It appears that Chance might not have the degree that he needed to get the job.

Arrange the class into groups of three or four. Ask each group to reflect on the following questions:

1. How pervasive is the embellishment of résumés?
2. It appeared that someone failed to check Chance's résumé! Who should have the responsibility for verifying that the information applicants submit is honest?
3. If you were Michele or one of the other coworkers who believe Chance got the job under false pretences, what would you do? Why?
4. If you were one of Chance's coworkers, what would you want the Credit Union management to do? Why?
5. You are Chance's immediate supervisor. HR, after investigation, has discovered that Chance did cite a baccalaureate degree in accounting on his résumé, and again when he filled out the company personal record sheets. What will you recommend as a course of action? Why?

*FOOD FOR THOUGHT QUESTIONS*

6. When hiring an employee, which is more important: (a) the past work performance of the potential employee, (b) the way the individual will fit in with other employees in the accounting department, or (c) the employee's honesty and trustworthiness? Why might there not be a clear answer to this question?
7. If Chance is retained in his current position, what might be the reaction of the other employees?

## SUPERVISION IN ACTION

The video for this chapter can be accessed from the student companion website at www.cengagebrain.com. (Search by authors' names or book title to find the accompanying resources.)

## ENDNOTES

1. Figure 10.1 is adapted with permission from Edwin C. Leonard Jr. and Roy A. Cook, *Human Resource Management: 21st Century Challenges* (Mason, OH: Thompson Custom Publishing, 2005), p. 2
2. Megan Biro, "Top 5 Reasons HR is on the Move" (December 1, 2015), Forbes.com, http://www.forbes.com/sites/meghanbiro/2013/12/01/top-5-reasons-hr-is-on-the-move/, estimates that 50 percent of larger companies contract out HR tasks. Biro and Suzanne Lucas, "Should You Hire or Outsource HR?" (May 22, 2013), Inc.com, http://www.inc.com/suzanne-lucas/should-you-hire-or-outsource-hr.html, assert that HR outsourcing frees companies up to concentrate on "core competencies"; it saves money by reducing the number of HR staff, enabling companies to use specialist services on an as-needed basis, to help improve specific tasks such as compliance and recruitment. Also, contracting out HR gives companies access to current technologies that are maintained by the service suppliers, rather than the companies themselves. Lucas maintains that while HR outsourcing can be effective, it may be best to maintain a basic HR department in-house and contract specialized services so that a human is available on site to deal with HR issues.
3. "About SHRM," the Society for Human Resources Management (http://www.shrm.org). Also visit the SHRM Web site at www.shrm.org to see the types of resources available and find research reports and white papers on current HR-related topics. *Note:* For some reports and information, one must be a SHRM member, while other information is available. The *HR Magazine* is available in most college libraries.

4. See Paul Falcone, "Lessons from the HR Trenches," *HR Magazine* (May 2013), pp. 84–85.
5. Leonard and Cook, *Human Resource Management*, p. 4. For an excellent overview of the history and future of HR management, see Richard Vosburgh, "The Evolution of HR: Developing HR as an Internal Consulting Organization," *Human Resource Planning* 30.3 (2007), pp. 11–23. See also Michael R. Losey and Susan R. Meisinger, *The Future of Human Resource Management* (Alexandria, VA: SHRM, 2005); Michael Losey, Dave Ulrich et al., *HR Competencies* (Alexandria, VA: SHRM, 2008); William J. Rothwell, Robert K. Prescott and Maria W. Taylor, *Human Resource Transformation: Demonstrating Strategic Leadership in the Face of Future Trends* (Alexandria, VA: SHRM, 2008).
6. Leonard and Cook have identified a simplistic job analysis approach. They suggest asking the incumbent employee(s) or those doing similar work the following questions:
   - What are your duties and responsibilities?
   - What is the most important thing you do during the day?
   - What is the toughest assignment you face in doing this job?
   - What are the three biggest challenges you face in doing this job?
   - What are you doing that you shouldn't be doing?
   - What should you be doing that you currently are not doing?
   - What is the most personally rewarding thing you did in the past week?

   After gathering employee inputs, ask the same questions of managers and other employees who are familiar with the job, only phrase them in such a way that you get an impression of what they believe the job is, ought to be, and is not. Then determine the qualifications necessary to perform these tasks. This can be a starting point for development and/or revision of the job description. See Leonard and Cook, *Human Resource Management*, pp. 30–31.
7. For an extended discussion of job analysis, including job descriptions and job specifications, see M. T. Brannick, E. L. Levine, and F. P. Morgeson, *Job and Work Analysis* (Thousand Oaks, CA: Sage, 2007). The National Employer Technical Assistance Network's Employer Assistance and Resource Network (EARN), "Job Analysis," AskEarn.org (March 14, 2014), http://askearn.org/refdesk/Supervision_Management/Job_Analysis provides guidance for job analysis, which includes consideration of requests for accommodation of disabilities, a concept discussed in Chapter 4.
8. See Allen Smith, "The Rise of the 'Part-Time Society,'" *HR Magazine* (August 2013), p. 66.
9. See Society for Human Resource Management, "SHRM 2013 Workplace Forecast" (May 2013), pp. 38–39, which can be downloaded from http://www.shrm.org/research/futureworkplacetrends/pages/topworkplacetrends2013.aspx; Tamara Lytle, "College Career Centers Create a Vital Link," *HR Magazine* (May 2013), pp. 34–41; Dave Zielinski, "Referral Booster," *HR Magazine* (March 2013), pp. 63–66; Steven Hunt and Susan Van Clink, "How to Source and Select the Best Hires," SuccessFactors White Paper (2011), available at www.successfactors.com; Jennifer Salopek, "Employee Referrals Remain a Recruiter's Best Friend," *Workforce Management Online* (December 2010), http://www.workforce.com/articles/employee-referrals-remain-a-recruiters-best-friend; Joshua Ramey-Renk, "The Ins and Outs of Applicant Tracking," *HR Magazine* (May 2013), pp. 50–52.
10. See Adrienne Fox, "Upon Further Assessment…," *HR Magazine* (August, 2013), pp. 39–45; see also Eric Krell, "The Global Talent Mis-Match," *HR Magazine* (June 2011), pp. 68–73. You might want to review the following: Patrice Mareschal and Joel Rudin, "E-Government Versus E-Business: A Comparison of Online Recruitment in the Public and Private Sectors," *The American Review of Public Administration* 41, No. 4 (2011), pp. 453–467; Emma Parry and Hugh Wilson, "Factors Influencing the Adoption of Online Recruitment," *Personal Review* 38, No. 6 (2009), pp. 655–673; Jennifer C. Berkshire, "Social Network Recruiting," *HR Magazine* (April 2005), pp. 95–98; or Stacy Foster, "The Best Way To … Recruit New Workers," *The Wall Street Journal* (September 15, 2003), p. R8.

    Also see Robert Kimmitt and Matthew Slaughter, "Insourcing: The Secret to Job Growth," *The Wall Street Journal* (December 6, 2010), p A19; K. H. Ehrhart and J. C. Ziegert, "Why Are Individuals Attracted to Organizations?" *Journal of Management* 31, No. 6 (2005), pp. 901–919; and D. S. Chapman et al., "Applicant Attraction to Organizations and Job Choice: A Meta-Analytic Review of the Correlates of Recruiting Outcomes," *Journal of Applied Psychology* 90, No. 5 (2005), pp. 928–944.
11. See Bill Roberts, "Hire Intelligence," *HR Magazine* (May 2011), pp. 63–67. According to John T. Neighbours, "Seventh Circuit Rejects Use of MMPI for Applicant Screening," *Indiana Employment Law Letter* (August 2005), pp. 1–2: "Preemployment testing is one technique used to screen applicants for such things as intellectual ability, physical ability, aptitude in specific skill areas, personality, and honesty. Tests are generally allowed as long as they don't have a disparate impact on a protected status or characteristic. Additional limitations apply, however, if the tests qualify as medical examination under the Americans with Disabilities Act (ADA). The Seventh Circuit Court rejected Rent-A-Center's use of MMPI for applicant screening."
12. The OUCH concept was part of a training program developed by Jagerson Associates, Inc., for the Life Office Management Association and has been presented in earlier editions of this text. Students may want to see Mary-Kathryn Zachary, "Discrimination Laws Provide Protection to Job Applicants," *SuperVision* (July 2011), pp. 21–24, or Zachary, "Labor Law—Judgments: People with Disabilities," *SuperVision* (January 2011), pp. 23–26.
13. Work sample tests (skills tests) are a relatively inexpensive and objective way to measure whether the applicant meets minimum requirements for the job. Selection criterion of pre- and postemployment testing must be validated by the test—that is, the selection criterion bears directly on job success.

    The Bureau of National Affairs and CCH published a series of papers related to preemployment testing: (1) "Policy Issues in Pre-Employment Testing" (2008). (2) "Developing and Administering Pre-Employment Tests" (2008). Also see Jonathan Katz, "Rethinking Drug Testing," *Industry Week* (March 2010), pp. 16–81; Dino di Mattia, "Testing Methods and Effectiveness of Tests," *SuperVision* (August 2005), pp. 4–5 or Leslie A. Weatherly, "Reliability and Validity of Selection Tests," *SHRM Research Report* (June 2005).

    A note of caution is illustrated by Allen Smith, "Tests Raise Flags," *HR Magazine* (June 2008), p. 36: "Pre-employment testing cases have become an area of emphasis for the EEOC because every test has an adverse impact against somebody."
14. See Stuart Tochner, "California Restricts Employer Access to Workers' Social Media," *HR Magazine* (December, 2012), p. 18. See also Gregory M. Saylin, and Tyson C. Horrocks, "The Risks of Pre-employment Social Media Screening," SHRM.Org (July 18, 2013); Roni Jacobson, "Facebook Snooping on Job Candidates May Backfire for Employers," Scientific American.com (January 13, 2014).
15. See *Employment Screening Benchmarking Report,* 2010 Edition, HireRight (www.hireright.com), "Resume Fraud by Job Applicants on the Rise," *Employment Digest online* (May 30, 2004); "Surfeit of False CVs as Tech Job Demand Is Up," *Economic Times* (December 18, 2004). Also see Joey George and Kent Marett, "The Truth about Lies," *HR Magazine* (May 2004), pp. 11–14. Also see the final rules: http://www/federalregister.gov/articles/2011/04/15/2011-9152/documents-acceptable-for-employment-eligibility-verification. Federal law requires companies to inform job applicants that they intend to get credit reports, and to get the applicants' permission. The law requires companies to let applicants know they wouldn't hire them

because of what they found on the reports and to give them a chance to correct the erroneous information. The law does not require companies to keep a job open while an applicant fixes the mistake.

16. See Joanne Deschenaux, "States Seek to Limit Credit Checks for Hiring," *HR Magazine* (April 2011), p. 20. Also see "State Reference Regulations," Feature Report, Alexander Hamilton Institute, Inc. (2004).
17. Bradford Smart as interviewed by Geoffrey Colvin, "How GE Topgrades: Looking to Hire the Very Best? Ask the Right Questions. Lots of Them," *Fortune* (June 21, 1999), p. 194.
18. From "Beware of Resumania," *Personnel Journal* (April 1996), p. 28. See also Nick Saffieri, "Interviewing Techniques: Looking for That Perfect Employee," *SuperVision* 68, No. 5 (May 2007), pp. 3–5; "The Right Staff Survey: Resume Review, Asking Good Questions, Top Hiring Challenges," *SuperVision* (August 2005), pp. 17–18; William C. Byham, "Can You Interview for Integrity? Yes, and You Don't Need a Lie Detector to Do It," *Across the Board* (March/April 2004), pp. 35–38.
19. Patricia M. Buhler identified ten keys to better hiring in "Managing in the New Millennium," *SuperVision* 68, No. 11 (November 2007), pp. 17–20. She argued that "[i]f the applicant was not dressed appropriately for the interview or did not display signs of enthusiasm, chances are that they will not change once they are on the job." Buhler strongly suggests the use of behavioral or situational questions during the interview. An example of a question that could be asked a prospective hardware and building materials supervisor might be, "If you were approached by an employee who contended that another employee was stealing merchandise from the store and selling it on eBay, what would you do?"

    For lists of questions that might be asked during the employment interview, see Fred S. Steingold, *Hiring Your First Employee* (Berkeley, CA: Nolo, 2008).
20. Ron Zemke and Susan Zemke, "Putting Competencies to Work," *Training* (January 1999), pp. 70+.
21. A thorough discussion of equal employment opportunity and applications is the major substance of Chapter 12. For an overview about protected classes of people, see http://www.eeoc.gov/; *Employer EEO Responsibilities* (Washington, DC: Equal Employment Opportunity, U.S. Government Printing Office, 1996).

    "Employment disability is defined as a physical, mental, or emotional condition lasting six months or more that causes difficulty working at a job or business," as quoted by Susan J. Wells, "Counting on Workers with Disabilities," *HR Magazine* (April 2008), pp. 45–49. For specific information on recruiting, hiring, and accommodating individuals with disabilities, a federal Web site (http://www.disAbility.gov) is available. See also Linda Wasmer Andrews, "Hiring People with Intellectual Disabilities," *HR Magazine* (July 2005), pp. 72–77.

    In 2011, the U.S. Citizenship and Immigration Services published a "final rule" regarding the employment eligibility verification. See Allen Smith, "Final Rule on Form 1-9 Issued," *HR Magazine* (June 2011), p. 16; Roy Maurer, "Job Seekers Can Check Eligibility," *HR Magazine* (May 2011), p. 12; and David Zielinski, "Automating I-9 Verification," *HR Magazine* (May 2011), pp. 57–60.
22. See Susan Grant, "Technology Streamlines Recruitment," *Canadian HR Reporter* 24, No. 7 (April 11, 2011), p. 14; Bob Schultz, "Recruiting, Interviewing, and Hiring: The Ultimate Game of 'Survivor,'" *SuperVision* 69, No. 3 (March 2008), pp. 3–4; Patricia M. Buhler, "Interviewing Basics: A Critical Competency for all Managers," *SuperVision* (March 2005), pp. 20–22; "It's Not Your Grandfather's Hiring Interview," *SuperVision* (April 2005), pp. 21–22; Martha Frase-Blunt, "Dialing for Candidates," *HR Magazine* (April 2005), pp. 78–82; Clifford M. Koen Jr., "Supervisor's Guide to Effective Employment Interviewing," *SuperVision* (November 2004), pp. 3–6.

    "Any job interview can be a nerve-wracking experience. However, nothing is quite as intimidating as being interviewed by two or more people at the same time." For tips on how the job hunter can manage the interview process, see Kemba J. Dunham, "The Jungle/Career Journal," *The Wall Street Journal* (April 20, 2004), p. B8.
23. Rick Kennedy, "When Customers Help Select the Staff," *HR Magazine* (December 2012), pp. 42–44.
24. Frederic M. Biddle, "Work Week," *The Wall Street Journal* (September 28, 1999), p. A1. Will "textspeak" become the language of the workplace? For an interesting view, see "Casual Job Seekers Turn Off Interviewers," *The Wall Street Journal* (July 29, 2008), pp. D1, D4.
25. Bohlander and Snell, among others, contend that the structure of the interview and the training of interviewers strongly influence the success of the hiring process. Interviews range from highly structured (the supervisor controls the course of the interview) to less structured (the applicant plays a larger role in determining the direction of the interview). See Scott Snell and George Bohlander, *Managing Human Resources*, 15th ed. (Mason, OH: South-Western/ Cengage Learning, 2010). Regardless of the approach used, Professor Leonard contends that each applicant must be given equal opportunity, that is, be asked the same questions and evaluated on the same criteria.
26. See Dave Zielinski, "The Virtual Interview," *HR Magazine* (July 2012), pp. 55–57.
27. John P. Wanous, "Installing a Realistic Job Preview: Ten Tough Choices," *Personal Psychology* (Spring 1989), pp. 117–133. Also see Gordon Amsler et al., "Performance Monitoring: Guidance for the Modern Workplace," *SuperVision* (January 2011), pp. 16–22; Carol Hymowitz, "How to Avoid Hiring the Prima Donnas Who Hate Teamwork," *The Wall Street Journal* (February 15, 2000), p. B1.
28. Adapted from Dawn Dugan, "8 Tips for Acing Virtual Job Interviews: Know What You Need to Succeed When a Firm Handshake Isn't Possible," Salary.com, http://www.salary.com/8-tips-for-acing-virtual-interviews/. See also
29. John P. Wanous, "Installing a Realistic Job Preview: Ten Tough Choices," *Personal Psychology* (Spring 1989), pp. 117–133. Also see Gordon Amsler et al., "Performance Monitoring: Guidance for the Modern Workplace," *SuperVision* (January 2011), pp. 16–22; Carol Hymowitz, "How to Avoid Hiring the Prima Donnas Who Hate Teamwork," *The Wall Street Journal* (February 15, 2000), p. B1.
30. See Tony Lee, "Companies Should Treat Job Seekers Well," Business Monday, *Fort Wayne, Indiana News Sentinel* (August 26, 2004), p. 1. Visit the Career Journal Web site (http://www.onlinewsj/com/-career) for recruitment tips. Also see http://www.monster.com for interviewing techniques.
31. To understand how to evaluate the effectiveness of the hiring function, see Charlotte Garvey, "The Next Generation of Hiring Metrics," *HR Magazine* (April 2005), pp. 70–77. For a general discussion on making the hiring decision, see T. L. Stanley, "Hire the Right Person," *SuperVision* 68, No. 7 (July 2007), pp. 11–12; or Max Messmer, "Finalizing the Hiring Decision," *Strategic Finance* (November 2001), pp. 8–10. AHI's Web site (http://www.ahipubs.com) provides reports and other employment-related information

    For a good review of the hiring process, see Jonathan Segal, "Hiring Days Are Here Again: Brush Up on Hiring Skills in 10 Areas," *HR Magazine* (July 2011), pp. 58–60. Also see John Shipman, Joe Light, and Paul Vigna, "No Rush to Hire Even as Profits Soar," *The Wall Street Journal* ( February 7, 2011), pp. B1, B7.
32. For a discussion of the pros and cons of hiring relatives, see Jo Palazzolo, Christopher M. Matthews and Serena Ng, "Nepotism: Is It a Crime?" Wall Street Journal Online, online.wsj.com (August 19, 2013); Mary S. Yamin, "Think Long and Hard before Hiring Relatives and Friends," *Capital District Business Review* (June 1998), pp. 26–27; Kevin Steel, "Nepotism Is a Human Right," *Western Report* (June 15, 1998), pp. 17–19;
33. SHRM reports that each year, nearly 25 percent of the working U.S. population undergo some sort of career transition. See Talya N. Bauer, *Onboarding New Employees: Maximizing Success*, SHRM Foundation's

Effective Practice Guidelines (2010), and Carole Fleck, "Now Boarding New Hires," *SHRM Tools and Techniques* 3, No. 3 (July–September 2007). Also see "Welcome On Board: Press 1 for Training," *SHRM Online Technology Focus Area* (July 2006); or Derek Moscato, "Using Technology to Get Employees on Board," *HR Magazine* (April 2005), pp. 107–109.

34. The SHRM *Onboarding Practices Survey* (released April 13, 2011) reported that more than 80 percent of organizations "roll out the welcome mat for new hires." For an expanded discussion of new-hire orientation, see Catherine Fyock, "Managing the Employee Onboarding and Assimilation Process," *SHRM Research Article* (revised September 2010); Jennifer Taylor Arnold, "Ramping Up Onboarding," *HR Magazine* (May 2010), pp. 75–80; Kathryn Ullrich, "Hiring and Retaining Talent: Three E's for Creating an Attractive Work Environment," *Industry Week* (November 2010), pp. 31–32; Kevin Martin and Jayson Saba, "All Aboard: Effective Onboarding Techniques and Strategies," *The Aberdeen Group* (January 2008); Kathy Gurchiek, "Orientation Programs Help New Hires Find Bearings," *SHRM Home* (May 25, 2007); D. G. Allen, "Do Organizational Socialization Tactics Influence Newcomer Embeddedness and Turnover?" *Journal of Management* 32, No. 2 (2006), pp. 237–256; and M. J. Wesson and C. I. Gogus, "Shaking Hands with a Computer: An Examination of Two Methods of Newcomer Orientation," *Journal of Applied Psychology* 90, No. 5 (2005), pp. 1018–1026.
35. See Peter Vanden Bos, "How to Build an Onboarding Plan for a New Hire," *Inc. online* (April 26, 2010), http://www.inc.com/guides/2010/04/building-an-onboarding-plan.html; or Belin Tai and Nancy R. Lockwood, "Organizational Entry: Onboarding, Orientation and Socialization," *SHRM Research* (November 2006).
36. See Franklin J. Lunding, "Everyone Who Makes It Has a Mentor," *Harvard Business Review* (July–August 1978), pp. 91–100. See also Laura DiFlorio, "How Do We Build Loyalty in New Employees?" Workforce.com (May 1, 2013), which suggests steps for creating a mentor program for new employees that will ease fears and make connections that can help them transition into the culture of their new workplace. The organization should determine the objectives of the program, enlist a champion to promote it, equip mentors with coaching skills, communicate about the program so everyone knows its purpose and importance, measure the success of the program through surveys and interviews and use the evaluation data to continually improve it.
37. See Nancy D. O'Reilly, "Women Helping Women: How Mentoring Can Help Your Business," *SuperVision* 69, No. 1 (January 2008), pp. 12–13; Pam Slater, "Careers Can Be Made or Derailed over Choice or Absence of a Mentor," *Knight-Ridder Tribune Business News: The Sacramento Bee* (August 9, 1999).
38. From Karen Dillon, "Finding the Right Mentor for You," *Inc.* (June 1998), p. 55. Patricia Buhler contends that the mentoring process is changing because there are four generations working in the typical organization today and they were socialized differently. Buhler argues that the mentor–mentee alignment is crucial to the success of the arrangement. See Patricia M. Buhler, "Managing in the New Millennium, *SuperVison* 68, No. 5 (May 2005), p. 18. Marina Khidekel, "The Misery of Mentoring Millennials," *Bloomberg Businessweek,* (March 11, 2013) suggests that Millennials seek a different type of mentoring from a legion of mentors who provide a variety of career insights across shorter tenures, more like "speed-dating" than long-term relationship-building. Further, she describes Millennials' pursuit of "sponsors" who will promote them in the workplace, rather than just come alongside in support. Donna M. Owens contends that online mentoring can offer you better matches from a wider pool of mentors. See Owens, "Virtual Mentoring," *HR Magazine* (March 2006), pp. 105–107.

    The 2013 Sodexo Workplace Trends Report, available at http://www.multivu.com/players/English/59261-sodexo-workplace-trends-2013/, echoes this finding in its discussion of "21st Century Mentoring," which presents a variety of fluid, flexible-term and often virtual mentoring approaches employers should consider when equipping and supporting new workers.
39. The authors use the notion of multiple mentors in a supervisory training program. An article by Larry Burlew, "Multiple Mentor Model: A Conceptual Framework," *Journal of Career Development* 17, No. 3 (Spring 1991), pp. 213–221 suggested that mentoring is not a single event but many occurrences with different levels of mentors.
40. Dillon, "Finding the Right Mentor for You," p. 55.
41. See SHRM survey findings, "Changing Employee Skills and Education Requirements," SHRM.org (October 3, 2012)
42. For an interesting perspective on coaching, read about how Bill Campbell, a former college football coach, is coaching, mentoring, and advising at multiple levels in Jennifer Reingold, "The Secret Coach," *Fortune* (July 21, 2008), pp. 125–134. Also see, David Zoogah, "Why Should I Be Left Behind? Employees' Perceived Relative Deprivation and Participation in Development Activities," *Journal of Applied Psychology* 95, No. 1 (2010), pp. 159–173; Jean Thilmany, "Passing on Know-How," *HR Magazine* (June 2008), pp. 100–104; or Mary Massad, "The Benefits of Employee Coaching," *Entrepreneur.com* (May 23, 2005).
43. See Kathryn Tyler, "The American Apprenticeship," *HR Magazine* (November 2013), pp. 33–36.
44. Society for Human Resource Management, "SHRM 2013 Workplace Forecast" (May 2013) can be downloaded from http://www.shrm.org/research/futureworkplacetrends/pages/topworkplace-trends2013.aspx
45. In its 2013 survey, "Grade Change: Tracking Online Education in the Unites States," (January 2014), Babson Survey Research Group found that for 2,500 colleges and universities 75 percent of academic leaders viewed the learning outcomes for online learning as the same or better than the outcomes for face-to-face instruction. The survey is available at http://sloanconsortium.org/publications/survey/grade-change-2013. Likewise, the U.S. Department of Defense's Advanced Distributed Learning Initiative, in cooperation with the University of Tulsa, analyzed 96 studies comparing e-learning with traditional, face-to-face learning and found no difference in the effectiveness of the modalities when the content and learners were the same, as reported by Traci M. Sitzmann, Robert A. Wisher, David Stewart and Kurt Kraiger, "Moderators of the Effectiveness of Web-Based Instruction," 20th Annual Conference on Distance Teaching and Learning (May 2006).

    See Jeanette Brooks, "How Experian Used E-Learning to Transform New-Hire Orientation (assessed August 24, 2011 from the articulate blog, http://www.articulate.com/blog. Also see Bob Hanson, "Using Social Media to Advance Your Online Training Program," GoToTraing (April 2010); Candice G. Harp, Sandra C. Taylor, and John W. Satzinger, "Computer Training and Individual Differences: What Really Matters?" *Human Resources Development Quarterly* (Fall 1998), pp. 271–83; Allison Rossett and Lisa Schafer, "What to Do about E-Dropouts?—What If It's Not the e-Learning But the e-Learner," *Training and Development* (June 2003), pp. 40, 42–46.
46. Adapted from Edwin C. Leonard Jr., *Assessment of Training Needs* (Chicago: U.S. Civil Service Commission under Intergovernmental Personnel Act (P.L. 91–648), 1974), pp. 36–40.
47. See Daniel H. Pink, "Richard Bolles: What Happened to Your Parachute?" *Fast Company* (September 1999), p. 241. Also see Bolles's latest annual edition of *What Color Is Your Parachute*? (Berkeley, CA: Ten Speed Press, 2014).
48. See Bolles's Web site at http://www.jobhuntersbible.com. You might also want to see Jenny Wood-Young and Marlin Ruhl, "Are You Promotable?" *SuperVision* (February 2011), pp. 13–16.
49. Social capital is defined at http://www.bettertogether.org/socialcapital.htm.
50. Figure 10.1 is adapted with permission from Edwin C. Leonard Jr. and Roy A. Cook, *Human Resource Management: 21st Century Challenges* (Mason, OH: Thompson Custom Publishing, 2005), p. 2

Chapter

# 11 Building and Managing Effective Teams

©SergeBertasiusPhotography/Shutterstock.com

**After studying this chapter, you will be able to:**

1. Describe the form and function of the different types of work groups and the unique relevance of each to the supervisory role.
2. Explain the relevance of research findings about work groups.
3. Distinguish the relationships between employee morale, engagement, teamwork and productivity, and identify factors that influence employee engagement
4. Discuss techniques for assessing employee morale, including observation and employee attitude surveys.
5. Understand why counseling is an important part of the supervisor's job.
6. Identify programs that organizations use to help employees with personal and work-related problems.

## YOU MAKE THE CALL!

*Don Brockman had just begun his first official day on the job at Lighthouse Financial. He was 27 years old, had spent three years in active military service, and finished his degree in business administration in May of this year. He had taken eighteen hours of various HR management courses and had had an internship in HR at the local hospital. The intern position helped him to hone his interviewing and communication skills and his military experience had matured him and helped him to deal with difficult people.*

The company was in the process of building a new operation center next to the corporate headquarters. Lighthouse will be adding 250 new positions and many of them will be customer service employees. Don will have primary responsibility for interviewing candidates for various positions the company needs to fill. His job would be screening, interviewing, and referring potential employees to the appropriate unit managers. Charlie Bright, vice president of HR, told him that he needed to look at becoming a member of the local SHRM chapter. Bright also said, "If you have any questions, come see me. My door is always open."

After spending a couple of hours reviewing company policies and procedures on recruiting, screening interviewing, and the like, Don wandered down to the break room. Betty Seward, HR specialist for compensation and benefits, sat down across the table from him. Seward asked him how his morning was going. Don responded, "O.K." "Let me give you some motherly advice," Betty began, "I've been working here for nine years and have learned to go with the flow—if you know what I mean? It took me a while to learn how you play the game. No one ever told me—I had to learn without anyone to guide me. Remember when dealing with Charlie, you must be willing to say anything to him as long as it's something he wants to hear."

Pausing to sip coffee, Betty continued, "Saying what he wants to hear is more important than the truth. Remember, it's the only way to survive in this game. Charlie wants staff members who always take their cue from him. You need to listen carefully and watch him closely—take his ideas and make them work. If there is any doubt about what to do, take your cue from him. Without question, accept his decisions and if you have an idea of your own, find a way to make him think it is his idea. Let him take credit. You make him look good and he will take care of you. Gosh, I've got to run, see you later."

Don was startled by Betty's comments. He wondered how reliable her advice was. Back in his own cubicle, Don continued to review the company handbook but Betty's comments continued to interrupt his train of thought. Don recounted, "Lighthouse Financial has a good reputation in the area, and I like what I've been hired to do. I wonder if Betty's comments are personal to her alone or if others feel the same way. Time will tell." At lunch that day, Ken Howard, a member of the accounting team for Lighthouse , came over to the table and said, "You must be new here. Welcome." Don replied, "I'm Don Brockman. This is my first day here and I work in human resources." Ken said, "Oh, you're the new guy. Welcome aboard to Charlie's ship. I will be praying for you." Don wondered what he had gotten into and what he might do to be the best employee for Lighthouse Financial.

**Disclaimer:** The above scenario presents a supervisory situation based on real events to be used for educational purposes. The identities of some or all individuals, organizations, industries, and locations, as well as financial and other information may have been disguised to protect individual privacy and proprietary information. Fictional details may have been added to improve readability and interest.

YOU MAKE THE CALL!

## Understanding Work Groups and Their Importance

**1 Describe the form and function of the different types of work groups and the unique relevance of each to the supervisory role.**

In Chapter 9, we presented an overview of the informal organization, with particular reference to the supervisor's relationship with informal work groups and their leaders. We mentioned that informal work groups can positively or negatively influence employee motivation and performance. Throughout this book, we have emphasized that a supervisor must be concerned not only with employees as individuals but also with how those employees relate to groups both inside and outside the supervisor's department.

An individual's motivations and behavioral clues are often found in the context of the person's associates, colleagues, and peers. On the job, an employee's attitudes and morale can be shaped to a large degree by co-workers, at times even more than by the supervisor or other factors in the work environment. Therefore, a supervisor should be aware of work groups and how those groups function.

Moreover, a supervisor must understand how morale influences employee performance and what can be done to maintain a high level of morale at the departmental level.

## WHY WORK GROUPS FORM AND FUNCTION

Work groups form and function in work settings for many reasons.[1] Among the most common reasons are the following:

- ***Companionship and identification.*** The work group provides a peer relationship and a sense of belonging, which can help satisfy the employee's social needs.
- ***Behavior guidelines.*** People tend to look to others, especially their peers, for guides to acceptable workplace behavior.
- ***Problem solving.*** The work group may be instrumental in providing a means by which an employee may solve a personal or minor work-related problem.
- ***Protection.*** Employees often look to the work group for protection from outside pressures, such as those pressures placed by supervisors and higher-level managers.

Much behavioral research has focused on factors that make work groups tightly knit, cohesive, and effective. A work group is usually most cohesive when it

- has members who perceive themselves as having higher status than other employees, as in job classification or pay;
- is small;
- shares similar personal characteristics, such as age, gender, ethnic background, and off-the-job interests;
- is relatively distant from other employees, as in geographically dispersed work groups and groups away from the home office;
- has formed due to outside pressures or for self-protection, such as a layoff or disciplinary action taken by management;
- has members who communicate relatively easily; and
- has succeeded in some group effort, which encourages members to seek new group objectives.

**Groupthink**
The tendency of members of a group to make faulty decisions because of group pressures, even in the face of red flags or better, more logical alternatives

The most effective teams are those that have *shared cognition*, or a common level and depth of knowledge that allows all team members to anticipate and execute actions toward meeting the group's goals. In other words, in order to reach their goal, every team member must be on the same page of the playbook.[2] However, sometimes having all team members stuck on the same page can be detrimental to team performance and organizational outcomes if the team engages in **groupthink**, the tendency of members of a group to make faulty decisions because of group pressures, even in the face of red flags or better, more logical alternatives. Groupthink can have dire consequences, as was seen in the *Challenger* and *Columbia* space shuttle disasters, the failures of corporate powerhouses Enron and WorldCom, and most recently in the 2008 financial crisis.[3] For that reason, it is important for supervisors to consider ways to encourage diverse opinions and opposing points of view, as well as check in with the team regularly to ensure they are steering toward appropriate outcomes. Of course, the supervisor will never be completely aware of the kinds of forces that are most prevalent in the department's group dynamics. However, regular interaction with teams, as well as sensitivity to employee needs and individual concerns, can help the supervisor guide work groups more effectively.

Ron Haviv/VII/Corbis News/Corbis

*Members of a cohesive work group enjoy their group affiliation.*

## Classifications of Work Groups

Four major types of employee work groups can be identified in most organizations:

1. Command
2. Task
3. Friendship
4. Special interest[4]

Because these classifications overlap, a supervisor should recognize that employees may be members of several such groups.

The **command group** consists of employees classified according to the authority relationships on the formal organizational chart. Members of this group work together daily to accomplish regularly assigned work. For example, at the departmental level, a command group consists of the supervisor and the employees who report to the supervisor. Throughout the organization are interrelated departments or command-group divisions that reflect the formal authority structure.

**Command group**
Grouping of employees according to authority relationships on the formal organization chart

### TASK GROUP OR CROSS-FUNCTIONAL TEAM

A **task group or cross-functional team** consists of employees from different departments brought together to accomplish a particular task or project. For example, for a telephone to operate in a customer's home, the telephone company's employees and supervisors from a number of departments, such as customer service, construction, plant installation, central office equipment, accounting, and testing, may work together to accomplish the job. Another example is a hospital in which numerous interdepartmental task relationships and communications

**Task group or cross-functional team**
Grouping of employees who come together to accomplish a particular task

take place among hospital personnel, from such departments as admitting, nursing, laboratory, dietary, pharmacy, physical therapy, and medical records, to care for a patient.

A specialized subset of the task group is the customer-satisfaction team. Members of this team represent many different functions and may include customer and supplier representatives. Team members come together to solve a specific problem, and they disband once the solution is put in place. For example, 3M empowers self-directed work teams (SDWTs) to develop systems and processes that help them do their jobs. The use of SDWTs to monitor and take action when needed to correct problems frees upper-level managers to do other things that contribute to 3M's success rather than tending to daily routine chores.[5] Simply put, 3M's use of task groups or cross-functional teams brings groups of people together so that they can apply their combined talents to continuously improve quality and ultimately increase customer satisfaction.

**Friendship group**
Informal grouping of employees based on similar personalities and social interests

The **friendship group** is an informal group of people who have similar personal characteristics and social interests. Many friendship groups are related primarily to such common factors as age, gender, ethnic background, outside interests, and marital status. Command and task groups may be instrumental in bringing friendship groups together. Also, preexisting friendships often serve as a catalyst for increased productivity and performance of newly formed teams, primarily because the team does not need to spend much time becoming oriented and building the relationships necessary to work effectively together.[6]

**Special-interest group**
Grouping of employees that exists to accomplish something as a group that would not likely be pursued individually

The **special-interest group** accomplishes in a group things that individuals feel unable or unwilling to pursue individually. A temporary special-interest group might be a committee of employees who wish to protest an action taken by a supervisor or management, promote a charitable undertaking, or organize an employee picnic.

A labor union is an example of a more permanent special-interest group because it is legally and formally organized. A labor union brings together employees from different departments and divisions as they strive to achieve economic and other objectives. A labor union official once made the following comment: "Labor unions don't just happen, they're caused. And it's the management, not labor unions, that cause them!" This official was quite candid in expressing his opinion that labor unions were a direct response to management's failure to respond to employee needs. The sentiments (morale) of workers are usually determined more by conditions existing in their work situations and the need to fulfill unmet needs. Thus, employees may join a labor union primarily to obtain economic objectives such as higher wages and greater benefits. Or they may join a group to satisfy psychological or sociological objectives, such as feeling a greater sense of identity. Some employees believe that membership in a group provides them with greater security and better control over their jobs. Other employees believe that the presence of a labor union in matters of grievances and complaints promotes a fairer settlement of disputes.

As stated earlier, an employee may belong to a number of groups in the workplace, and the supervisor who understands these different groups is more likely to influence these groups. Some research studies have suggested that a supervisor has a better chance of influencing an employee's behavior as a member of a work group than individually without the work group's influence. Some of these concepts are discussed later in this chapter.

## Research Insights for Managing Work Groups

**2 Explain the relevance of research findings about work groups to their supervision and management.**

Numerous behavioral studies have been conducted on work groups and on how they function. These studies have suggested a number of approaches for managing work groups effectively. While these approaches will not guarantee the desired results, they are consistent with behavioral research findings concerning work-group dynamics and group behavior.

### FINDINGS FROM GROUP (TEAM) RESEARCH

The work-group studies that have probably had the most lasting influence during the twentieth century and beyond were conducted in the late 1920s and early 1930s at Western Electric Company's Hawthorne plant near Chicago, Illinois.[7] Known as the **Hawthorne Studies**, they remain a comprehensive and definitive source on the subject of work-group dynamics as they relate to employee attitudes and productivity. Many of the lessons of the Hawthorne Studies still apply to supervisory practice today, supporting the adage that the more things change, the more they stay the same.

**Hawthorne Studies**
Comprehensive research studies that focused on work-group dynamics as they related to employee attitudes and productivity

Throughout the text, we have mentioned various organized participative management programs. Regardless of what these programs are called, they share certain characteristics. For the most part, these programs try to build effective work teams that foster the continual improvement of work processes, project tasks, and customer service. One of the most comprehensive surveys was conducted by Jon Katzenbach and Douglas Smith, two management consultants who interviewed hundreds of team members in dozens of organizations that had used teams to address various problems. Katzenbach and Smith identified principles that are most closely associated with effective work teams, including the following:

- Team members must be committed to the group and its performance.
- Teams function better when they are small, usually consisting of ten or fewer members.
- Teams should be composed of individuals with skills that are complementary and sufficient to deal with the problem.
- Teams should be committed to objectives that are specific and realistic.[8]

Much also can be learned from the case studies reported in Steven Jones and Michael Beyerlein's *Developing High Performance Work Teams*. One such study, which describes Eastman Chemical Company's decision to move to a team management approach at its Kingsport, Tennessee, facility, delivered the following findings:

- Because supervisors must take on more responsibility and receive less recognition, they feel threatened by transitions to teams. Therefore, supervisors must be coached, supported, and encouraged in their new roles.
- Team members must be held accountable for their actions to increase feelings of personal responsibility for the team's success.
- New team leadership roles for supervisors include coaching and facilitating.
- Communication becomes more important. Team leaders must be process-oriented and have meetings to clarify team roles.[9]

The Kingsport facility employs almost 7,000 of Eastman's 14,500 employees and is one of the largest chemical manufacturing facilities in the country.[10]

## INSIGHTS INTO THE GROUP DEVELOPMENT PROCESS

When the need to convene a work group arises, the supervisor's work is just beginning. The first step in the process is identifying the task the group needs to accomplish or the problem that needs to be solved. Then, the supervisor needs to identify work-group members who will fulfill the SKA needs of the task or problem, or delegate this role to an employee who is familiar with the skills and abilities of others in the department or company. Once the group is built, it may seem logical for the supervisor to step out of the way and let the team do its work. However, Tuckman and Jensen's classical research on the process of group development asserts that when new work groups are formed, the supervisor remains a key player. They describe five specific stages small groups go through: *forming, storming, norming, performing*, and *adjourning*.

- Forming—When a group first convenes, individuals meet, agree on goals, and begin the task at hand. At the same time, members are often on their best behavior as they gather information and impressions about the rest of the group's personalities, motivations, and orientation to the task. During this stage, the supervisor's role is directive in outlining roles, responsibilities, the task, and its deliverables.
- Storming—As the work progresses, group members begin to share ideas and perspectives about the task and the group itself, some of which may be in competition or conflict. The supervisor should remain accessible to the team during this stage to provide feedback, suggest decision-making strategies, give explicit direction regarding next steps, and coach employees in the use of professional behavior when competing ideas and personalities begin to hamper productivity. It is possible for groups to get stuck in this stage if conflict overtakes the group's goal as a primary focus of its activities, which illustrates why it is important for the supervisor to stay indirectly involved in a supportive monitor role.
- Norming—Once group members establish their roles and responsibilities and a shared understanding of the goal, they tend to move forward productively with the work. At this point in the group development process, the supervisor should expect, receive, and review regular reports of progress from the group and provide feedback and support when appropriate.
- Performing—Groups at this stage run like clockwork. They can work independently, make decisions, and establish new goals with little or no supervision. Group members have established processes for resolving conflict and changing direction when necessary. The group's supervisor should remain active in holding the group accountable for deliverables, providing feedback, and approving changes as they are proposed.
- Adjourning—At some point, an existing group may no longer be necessary, particularly in the case of task or special-interest groups that have achieved the goals for which they were originally established. In order to help group members transition to new roles, either in new groups or back to their original positions, the supervisor should be directive in providing explicit guidance to each employee about his or her new responsibilities. While it may again seem logical to simply disband the group, it is important for supervisors to recognize that employees' levels of power and discretion may change as they move into different roles. Accordingly, orienting employees to new expectations will help them transition out of work groups smoothly.[11]

## EXAMPLES OF HIGHLY EFFECTIVE TEAMS

Highly effective teams are hard to find, and they are inspiring. The Japan women's national soccer team demonstrated teamwork and perseverance against all odds in 2011. Members of the nonprofessional league team, many of whom work day jobs in hot spring resort hotels and train in the evenings,[12] stunned the world and inspired their earthquake-ravaged homeland as it stood on the brink of nuclear and economic disaster when they became the first Asian team to win the FIFA Women's World Cup.

The road to victory was treacherous, but the Japanese women's team was prepared. Finishing second behind England to reach the quarter finals, the team shocked the host nation and defending champion Germany with a 1-0 victory. Prior to the match against Germany, Japanese coach Norio Sasaki showed the team a video of the crippled Fukushima power plant. Karina Maruyama, who had worked at the plant from 2005 to 2009, scored the match's only goal.[13] Japan then handily defeated Sweden 3-1 in the semifinal. A 2-2 tie in the championship match against the United States sent the competition into extra time, but Japanese players didn't get discouraged when the referee sent off one of their players with a red card for a questionable tackle. Instead, their coach set a celebratory tone for the team, smiling, clapping, and embracing the thrill of the moment as the women proceeded to astonish their opponents and spectators with an unlikely 3-1 penalty shootout victory.[14]

Kumiko Fukushi, a Tokyo music studio owner, believes the tragedy of the earthquake bolstered the resolve and initiative of the team as they prepared for their international challenge. "It shows the true bravery of Japanese women. Even when we are under intense pressure, in life or on the soccer field, we don't panic. We just think about trying our best to reach our goal." [15]

The Japan women's team, nicknamed "Nadeshido," or beautiful flower,[16] captured hearts worldwide as it brought joy to a devastated country. The team

Tony Feder/Getty Images

*Japan's women's soccer team, who won the 2011 FIFA Women's World Cup, give tribute to 2011 tsunami victims on March 14, 2014, continue to work to as a team.*

was awarded the People's Honor Award by the prime minister of Japan, Naoto Kan. "With firm teamwork and the spirit of never giving up, you accomplished a great achievement of becoming No. 1 in the world for the first time in the history of Japanese soccer," Kan shared with the women. "To the disaster victims and all the people of Japan who are trying to recover from the Great East Japan Earthquake, you gave them the courage to face hardships and moved them with your eloquent victory." Its victory in the face of adversity has made the Japan women's team iconic, a national treasure that continues to inspire the country and lend support through ongoing recovery.[17]

Think back also to the 2008 Olympics and the performance of the U.S. men's volleyball team. The underdog team overcame tragedy to win the Olympic gold medal. The team claimed the gold with a four-set win over the defending champion, Brazil. Coach Hugh McCutchen's father-in-law was stabbed to death in Beijing on the eve of the team's first game. He turned the reins over to his assistant for the first three matches.[18]

Having lost the first game 20–25, the Americans' backs were against the wall. They came back to win the next two games and, when the Brazilian star player popped the ball out of bounds, the Brazilians crouched on the floor in disbelief. The U.S. team rushed the court and savored the moment and what they had just accomplished.[19] In volleyball, every player is intensely involved in each and every play. What each one does or doesn't do is critical to the success of the team.

The highly effective team is the one whose members are always supporting and encouraging one another. Chris Widener, president of Made for Success, said it well: "The coach always does a pre-game talk, laying out the vision. During the game, the coach is always updating the team as to where they are and what changes need to be made. He or she coaches and communicates throughout the game. When you watch a great team, they are talking to each other all of the time, helping one another out, encouraging one another, praising one another, and telling each other how they can make changes so the same mistakes aren't made again."[20]

Regardless of the activity, good communication skills are needed to create trust and collaboration among the various players. Remember, there is no "I" in the word team.

## THE IMPORTANCE OF TEAM MEMBERS

In Chapter 9, we postulated various organizational designs, but many forces in the marketplace can rapidly change even our best guesses. Nevertheless, we expect that teamwork will be as important tomorrow as it was yesterday and perhaps even more so. The American Management Association's 2012 Critical Skills Survey found that 72 percent of managers and executives surveyed want employees who are compatible in a team setting, supporting the notion that very little is accomplished without strong collaboration.[21]

When asked about effective teams, another illustration from professional and amateur sports comes to mind. Why? Few organizations, their leaders, and members are as well-documented as sports teams. Legendary basketball coach John Wooden won ten national championships at UCLA, including an unbelievable seven in a row from 1966 to 1973. Coach Wooden's team won over 80 percent of their games.[22] Imagine making the right choice at the right time that turns out the right way—the way it was intended—eight out of ten times. This former basketball coach believes that "Coach" was able to get a diverse group of individuals to work together and satisfy the needs of each member of the team because "Coach" was able to recruit individuals who were willing to put aside individual differences and focus on the goals he set for the team. "Coach" prepared his players with a "we will win!" mentality, and the team members made it happen again and again and again![23]

Yet another factor may help to explain the difference between winning and losing. Synergy! A **synergistic effect** takes place when the whole is greater than the sum of the parts. Many organizations like great sports teams lose their competitive advantage when key team members leave or the coach retires. Since Coach Wooden's retirement in 1975, the team has won just one NCAA basketball championship. Clearly, success increases the appetite for additional success. If you don't win it all every year, people are clamoring for the coach's head. The same is true for the CEO who doesn't meet Wall Street expectations.

**Synergistic effect**
The interaction of two or more individuals such that their combined efforts are greater than the sum of their individual efforts

Astute sports fans can recall some of the stars from these winning teams, but for every star, there are dozens of unheralded support players, sometimes called role players. These role players show up for work every day, clearly understand their roles, are trained so that they know how to perform and continuously improve on their jobs, and want to feel that they are contributing meaningfully to the effectiveness of their teams. As author Kenneth Turan said, "Team sports could not exist without, well, teams. Competent, superbly professional role players, the good soldiers who do what's asked of them and don't bask in anyone's attention, are the *sine qua non* of the organizations that win year after year."[24]

Several observations are pertinent here. First, a team is made up of a group of individuals who *must work together* to meet their individual and team objectives.[25] It is important to remember that people are more motivated to achieve goals they help set. Second, strong leadership and effective communication are key ingredients for successful teams. As stated previously, the ability to trust a leader (or for that matter, an upper manager) is more important today than at any time in recent history. Perhaps nothing is more important to the success of a team than the leader's ability to build an environment of mutual trust and respect. Finally, not everyone is suited for team play. Throughout this text we have introduced people, who, at best, are not team players, and they make your life difficult. As one engineering vice president related, "Some people can leave their ego at the door, and some can't, and you will immediately know who is on (board) and who isn't."[26] The key is to identify people who can work in teams and those who cannot.

## COLLABORATIVE WORKPLACE

None of the great sports teams or business organizations could have succeeded without **teamwork**—people working cooperatively to solve problems and achieve goals important to the group. Stated succinctly, a **collaborative workplace** means that, throughout the organization, employees and management share authority for decision making. Teamwork processes promote trust, integrity, consensus, and shared ownership as team members strive to achieve common objectives. Collaboration recognizes that people want and need to be valued for their contributions and that improvements and changes are best achieved by those who are responsible for implementing changes and are committed to making those changes work.[27]

**Teamwork**
People working cooperatively to solve problems and achieve goals important to the group

**Collaborative workplace**
Work environment characterized by joint decision making, shared accountability and authority, and high trust levels between employees and managers

Noted quality writer H. James Harrington wrote:

> *The disadvantage with teams is that they are inwardly focused. They are small groups that, if functioning properly, strive to be better than other teams. Teams by their very nature are competitive. . . . In well-managed organizations, trust runs high and people are empowered to make decisions on their own. These organizations focus on promoting teamwork between individuals. It's an attitude of "How can I help?" "What can I do to make your job easier?" and "How can we work together to produce more value for the whole organization?"*[28]

Figure 11.1 summarizes the characteristics of effective work teams. While no one approach succeeds in all situations, a group must know where it is going. Throughout this text, we have stressed the importance of setting goals and the

**FIGURE 11.1 Characteristics of effective work teams**

**Keys to Effective Work Teams**

- Top management removes the barriers, that is, clears the roadblocks.
- Team members receive training on how to work together.
- Group members agree on team goals and objectives and commit to those goals.
- All members participate actively in team meetings and discussions.
- All team members follow team rules, guidelines, and procedures.
- All members are valued and treated with respect and dignity.
- Team members share vital information and ensure that everyone is informed on a need-to-know basis.
- Members express their ideas without fear of retribution. Team members also feel free to disagree, and the group grows with differences of opinion.
- The team uses a systematic problem-solving approach, but members are encouraged to think "outside the box" (i.e., alternative ways of thinking are encouraged).
- All members are included in solving problems, developing alternatives, and institutionalizing decisions.
- Decisions are made by consensus (i.e., all team members support decisions, even though they may not totally agree with those decisions; therefore, every team member feels ownership for the team's decisions and responsibility for the team's success).
- The team is cohesive—openness, trust, support, and encouragement are always present.
- Conflict is viewed as healthy and is brought out into the open and addressed in a timely manner.
- Group members give each other honest feedback on performance; constructive feedback is used to improve performance.
- Team training and peer helping are essential elements of the team process. Peers help team members who may need individualized attention.
- The team continually evaluates its performance and uses that information as the basis for improvement.
- Team members take pride in team accomplishments. Challenging tasks, recognition of accomplishments, and continued support from top management fuel the drive for continued success.
- Members enjoy their team affiliation.

notion that the supervisor must provide direction. As noted in Chapters 1 and 2, if supervisors want their work groups to perform at higher levels, there must be a shared purpose and values, and the supervisor must constantly strive to balance employees' needs with the organization's needs.

## VIRTUAL TEAMS

As many companies have expanded their operations domestically and internationally, they have found that virtual teams can help them focus on meeting customer requirements. A virtual team is one that has members who rarely, if ever, meet face to face, even though they work on a project or in an area of operations with a common goal. In a **virtual team**, also known as a **geographically dispersed team (GDT)**, members share a common purpose, but are physically separated by time and/or space and primarily interact electronically.[29] GDTs are a variant of work teams that present unique supervisory challenges at every stage of development and performance.

**Virtual or geographically dispersed team (GDT)**
Geographically separated people who are working on a common project and linked by communication technologies

Workforce surveys across multiple sectors indicate that the number of employees who participate in virtual teams is increasing every day, and with that increase comes a need to address the specific SKAs that are necessary for workers to effectively contribute to organizational goals. Consider these statistics:

- Approximately 25 million people telecommute at least one day per month as of September 2013.[30]
- By 2015 an additional 300 million virtual workers will join the global workforce.[31]
- 85 percent of HR professionals expect that the use of virtual global teams will change the face of the U.S. workplace in the next five years.[32]
- While over 60 percent of respondents to a *Training Magazine* survey believe that virtual team management is an emerging skill need, less than 40 percent believe their managers have this skill.[33]

Virtual teams function primarily through technological tools that enable them to communicate and share documents. Most prominent are audio and video web conferencing, instant messaging, online collaboration software, document storage and file sharing applications, co-creation tools, social networking applications, scheduling applications, and project management software.[34] Virtual teams require their members to receive specialized training in technology use. They also demand careful planning and organization to establish regular times for group interaction as well as other communication needs. One advantage of virtual teams is that members can communicate quickly when needed to bring team members up to date on events and to keep each other informed. Scheduling becomes critical as one team member may be located, for example, in Ohio and another in Australia. Communication must cross several time zones, with 12 or more hours of difference. When one employee is working, the other may be sleeping.

While technology serves as the primary facilitator for the growth of virtual teamwork, it also has been indicated as a significant challenge to productivity and the achievement of team goals. In a study of collaboration breakdowns of thirty virtual team projects, investigators found that most problems stemmed from technology policy restrictions, mandated technology changes, and inadequate or malfunctioning technology tools.[35]

However, technology is not the only challenge in geographically dispersed teams. This study, as well as an investigation of eighteen teams working worldwide for a Fortune 500 company, also identifies trust (see Chapter 5) and power (see Chapter 2) as barriers to success. In virtual teams that rated themselves as having a high level of trust among members, employees indicated that sharing and shifting power based on the needs of the group and specific tasks helped them succeed in reaching their goals. In virtual teams with low levels of trust, power battles, coercion, misunderstandings, and conflicts of interest kept teams from performing effectively.[36]

These findings illustrate that virtual teams share some of the same challenges as face-to-face teams, but at the same time they encounter barriers that are not typically found in the traditional office setting. During more than a decade of working with virtual teams in business, government, and military environments, Professors Jay Nunamaker, Bruce Reinig, and Robert Briggs identified some challenges that are unique to virtual teams. Nonverbal communication, such as eye-rolling or nodding in agreement, cannot be seen by virtual teammates unless, of course, they are videoconferencing. Informal conversations and friendships forged in hallways and break rooms do not take place when employees are not in the same building or town, although they can take place through FaceTime, Google Hangouts, texting or instant messaging. When different work processes, cultures, and time zones are added to the mix, we can envision the potential for miscommunication and misunderstanding, as well as the difficulties virtual teams might find in building consensus and establishing shared understandings about tasks and goals.[37] However, as virtual work becomes more commonplace and technology is able to facilitate more seamless communication, high-performing teams are finding success in translating their skills to the virtual environment. See Figure 11.2 for some specific strategies that you can use to make a virtual team more successful.

**FIGURE 11.2 Twelve principles for making virtual teams work**

- *Get the team together physically, or at least in a videoconference, early on.* Having a get-to-know-you session or two will help establish relationships and give the opportunity to create guiding principles and a shared vision for the team. Reconnect regularly.
- *Clarify processes and tasks, not just roles and goals.* It is important for everyone to know who needs to do what, so roles and goals should be established within the first few meetings, as they would be for any team project. It is equally important to come to agreement on how and when individual and collaborative tasks will take place, how documents will be shared, who will facilitate processes, and who is accountable for specific deliverables. Virtual teams do not have the benefit of being able to "do what has always been done," so work processes need to be clearly defined, reviewed, and revised to ensure they are efficient and effective.
- *Commit to a communication charter.* To avoid the pitfalls of miscommunication that can emerge on virtual teams due to less rich, less frequent, and less nonverbal communication, create a clear set of expectations for communication. Norms of behavior such as reducing background noise, when to mute, balancing conversations, and when to use certain communication modalities, for example when to reply via e-mail versus calling or going online to collaborate on a document, should be established and distributed to the team.
- *Leverage the best communication technologies.* Collaborative technologies are improving every day and, for the most part, are becoming more and more affordable.

(continued)

**FIGURE 11.2 Twelve principles for making virtual teams work *(continued)***

When deciding what communication vehicles to employ, opt for those that are most reliable and easy to use to avoid wasting time on learning all the features or troubleshooting.

- *Build a team with rhythm.* When working remotely, it is easy to get disconnected from the rhythms of the workplace. Establishing and enforcing systems and schedules for virtual team work, such as weekly meetings and set collaboration sessions, will help get everyone moving forward together on projects. When a team is distributed across time zones, rotate the schedule so that the load is spread equitably.
- *Agree on a shared language.* Virtual teams can be distributed across the entire world, so it is likely that different cultures will be represented. When working on technical topics, science and engineering language usually sets a good foundation for language. When working on social or relational issues or problem solving, translations may not mesh. Accordingly, come to agreement on shared interpretations of important words and phrases, for example, "when we say 'yes,' we mean . . ." and post the list in the virtual workspace.
- *Create a virtual staff lounge or water cooler.* Gathering around the water cooler is an adage used to describe informal exchanges in the workplace. The virtual workspace is often very task-focused with little shared downtime. In order to prevent burnout, reinforce team cohesion and give team members opportunities to casually share ideas, carve out time during each meeting for a "check-in" or "personal update, " use virtual team-building activities to add a bit of fun, or embed social networking features like a newsfeed, a chat room, or a video portal into the workspace.
- *Clarify and track commitments.* In the virtual workspace, unlike the office hallway, it is uncommon for team members to check in to ask, "How's it going?" Even after establishing tasks, processes, roles and responsibilities, it is important to establish a mechanism for tracking progress. Scheduling regular status meetings, posting and reporting on a shared work plan, or creating a deliverables dashboard visible to all members can ensure that everyone is on track. Avoid micromanaging.
- *Foster shared leadership.* Designing work plans and defining and tracking deliverables provides push to keep members focused and productive. Leadership provides the pull of motivation, encouragement, and support. Appoint specific virtual team members to serve as coaches, share best practices, run virtual team-building exercises, and lead special projects so that everyone has an opportunity to lead.
- *Don't forget the 1:1s.* One-on-one coaching and performance management are fundamentally sound practices on any team and should be incorporated into the rhythm of the virtual team. As you lead, use them to check status, provide feedback, listen to frustrations, and focus on each member's contribution to the work.
- *Visit the past to define the future.* If you are taking over a team, take the time to learn about the structures, processes, and culture of the team so you can quickly step into the communication and coordination role.
- *Realign reward structures for virtual teams.* A virtual team member doesn't get a pat on the back for staying late or arriving early. Find ways to incentivize consistency and participation or share deliverables with management so distributed employees are recognized for their efforts.

*Adapted by Kelly A. Trusty from:* Michael Watkins, "Making Virtual Teams Work: Ten Basic Principles," HBR Blog Network (June 27, 2013), http://blogs.hbr.org/2013/06/making-virtual-teams-work-ten/ and and Surinder Kahai, "What Leads to Effective Virtual Teamwork?" LeadingVirtually.com (April 18, 2009), http://www.leadingvirtually.com/what-leads-to-effective-virtual-teamwork/

Virtual teams require strong management support, which typically means that managers and supervisors have less direct control over team members. Nevertheless, the need for supervisory feedback and evaluation is paramount. The challenge for a manager or supervisor of a virtual team is to hold team members together and keep them motivated, even though they are separated geographically. The focus must be on overall results rather than on the specific activities of team members. Managers of virtual teams have tried various techniques to help team members stay focused on their projects and to strengthen their functioning and team spirit. Among these techniques are giving the project team a name or logo, rotating the hosting of conference calls, and recognizing accomplishments.

In essence, managing virtual teams, while it has some unique challenges and problems, is not completely unlike managing teams that are close geographically. Regardless of the team approach used, supervisors must be adept at applying their managerial skills with appropriate human relations approaches. Remember, the manager's challenge is to build commitment, cooperation, and collaboration through effective communication.

**3 Distinguish the relationships between employee morale, engagement, teamwork and productivity, and identify factors that influence employee morale and engagement.**

## Understanding and Maintaining Employee Morale and Engagement

**Morale**
A composite of feelings and attitudes that individuals and groups have toward their work, working condition, supervisors, top-level management, and the organization

Most definitions of morale recognize that it is essentially a state of mind. For example, Merriam-Webster's online dictionary defines *morale* as "the mental and emotional condition of an individual or group with regard to the function or tasks at hand." We consider **morale** to be the attitudes and feelings of individuals and groups toward their work, their environment, their supervisors, their top-level management, and the organization. Morale is not one single feeling or attitude but a composite. It can affect employee performance and willingness to work, which in turn can affect individual and organizational objectives. When employee morale is high, employees usually do what the company wants them to do; when it is low, the opposite tends to occur.

Engagement, which we introduced in Chapter 9, is the level of emotional commitment the employee has to the organization and its goals. If we consider these two terms side by side, we might conjecture that the two mean essentially the same thing, but they do not. Morale is the general feeling toward the workplace, and engagement focuses on its goals. Cari Turley provides us with an illustration that shows the difference:

> *Treating everyone on your staff to ice cream would surely improve morale for the afternoon. But that's about it. Consider, however, promising an ice cream social for the afternoon to your sales team as a reward for closing the big account they've been after. You get the same morale boost on ice cream day, but you also get the incentive to close the deal, the anticipation of the event, and the message that good work is noticed and rewarded. That's much likelier to translate to business results than the impromptu dessert, and for no additional cost.*[38]

Numerous articles have suggested that today's employees are less happy with many aspects of their jobs than were employees of earlier decades, a significant problem because it has long been recognized and documented that the reasons employees stay with or leave employers are more frequently attributed to factors other than pay.[39] However, an organization's employees can have high morale, love their boss and their job, but never get anything done, which can put them at risk of being let go or becoming "dead wood." When employees are highly engaged, by contrast, they invest more time, effort, and sometimes creativity and passion into the work they do in order to do their best and help the company achieve its objectives.

The idea of workplace morale has been discussed for decades, but increasingly workplaces are finding that unpacking the black box of morale by considering its roots in engagement is key to keeping employees happy and productive. Building employee engagement increases trust, loyalty, and, ultimately organizational performance more so than just creating a feel-good environment. According to the Towers Watson 2012 Global Workforce Study, which covers more than 32,000 full-time employees of large and midsized organizations in twenty-nine markets around the world, highly engaged employees have 25 percent less absenteeism than those who are disengaged; 18 percent of highly engaged workers reported being likely to leave their jobs compared to 40 percent of disengaged workers; and 72 percent of highly engaged workers would stay at their current workplace if they were offered a similar job elsewhere compared to 28 percent of disengaged workers. Further, Gallup's nearly two decades of research on employee engagement has linked its levels to nine performance outcomes: customer ratings, profitability, productivity, turnover, safety incidents, theft, absenteeism, patient safety, and product quality. Additionally, the Gallup research has found that workers who rate themselves as highly engaged at work view their lives as better, report having better moods and better relationships with colleagues, and are four times as likely as actively disengaged workers to say they like what they do at work every day.[40]

Based on these findings, these authors contend that the happiest workers are highly engaged workers. But what does a highly engaged worker look like?

Highly engaged workers, which comprise approximately one-third of those surveyed, cooperate, are enthusiastic about their work, understand their jobs, and look for ways to improve. Workers who are not engaged andaren't concerned about customers, productivity, safety, or the organization's purpose, whereas actively disengaged workers are out to damage the company, waste managers' time, are often absent, have more accidents, and quit more often than nonengaged workers. Nonengaged and actively disengaged workers make up the other two-thirds of those surveyed.[41]

## FACTORS INFLUENCING ENGAGEMENT AND MORALE

The research on engagement has identified a number of things workers need in order to feel engaged with their work and committed to their organization's mission. They need to know what is expected of them; have the appropriate materials and equipment to do their jobs and opportunities to do things they are good at; and they need to be recognized for their achievements. Employees engage and thrive when their supervisors show that they care about them, encourage them to develop their strengths, value their opinions, and promote an organizational mission that makes workers feel important. Further, workers who have colleagues who are committed to doing good work and are genuinely friendly enjoy and invest in their work, and they are inspired to contribute new ideas when they are given feedback about their performance and provided with opportunities to grow in new ways. When an organization provides this type of work environment, workers become more trusting of management, more willing to put in extra effort, and more likely to recommend their company to others.[42]

The description of engaged workers above sounds much like a Cinderella story, as though engagement is a glass slipper that can be slipped on to transform an entire workforce. Increasing engagement requires a great deal of concentrated, coordinated effort by an organization, starting with hiring managers who genuinely care for people and are committed to high performance and can balance the two by motivating and rewarding engaged behaviors; also, managers must be held accountable for their efforts to engage workers. Managers also need to invest extra time in assessing workers' strengths and assigning them to positions that best fit their strengths. When employees are regularly asked to do low-value work—tasks that don't use their talents, are a waste of time, don't contribute to organizational success, and wouldn't be missed if they weren't done—they tend to become frustrated, less effective, and resentful toward their employer.[43]

We discussed training and development in Chapter 10, and this is another area where managers can build engagement—by identifying and developing employees' strengths. Think about the last time your performance was evaluated, whether it was in a work role, at home, or at school. Did the evaluation focus on everything you did wrong, or everything you did right? Research shows that when performance evaluations and coaching focus on a person's weaknesses, even if just one or two, the person walks away from the process feeling worse than before. When developmental interactions focus on the positives or strengths, a person's morale is much higher and engagement and performance increase.[44] If we translate this approach to employee engagement, it is easy to conjecture that when managers focus on employees' strengths, give them opportunities to use their strengths, and help them build those strengths to an even greater extent, the employees will feel good about their contribution to the organization and grow in their commitment to their work. As workers become more engaged, they become more productive, and the organization also reaps benefits. If managers just focus on what employees do wrong, they tend to get more of the same or even worse performance.

These findings encourage supervisors to focus on strengths and find ways to help employees build on those strengths. The Gallup research also found that investing in workers' well-being also contributes to higher levels of engagement. Placing a high priority on helping workers maintain a healthy balance between work and family, providing a sense of job security, and ensuring sufficient health and retirement benefits also encourages worker loyalty, commitment, and investment in the company's mission.[45] Wellness programs, which are discussed later in this chapter, also boost engagement.[46]

Virtually any factor can influence employee morale, positively or negatively (see Figure 11.3). Some of these factors are within the supervisor's control, while others are not. Influences outside the organization are generally beyond the supervisor's control. Nevertheless, they may significantly affect employee morale. Examples of such external factors are family relationships, care of children or elderly parents, financial difficulties, problems with friends, vehicle breakdowns, and sickness or death in the family. What happens at home can change an employee's feelings very quickly. An argument before work may set the tone for the rest of the day. Even headlines in the morning newspaper may depress or uplift.

Company conditions can also influence morale. Examples of internal factors are compensation, relations with co-workers, and working conditions. These factors are partially or fully within the supervisor's control. For example, when

FIGURE 11.3 Dark clouds affect on-the-job performance

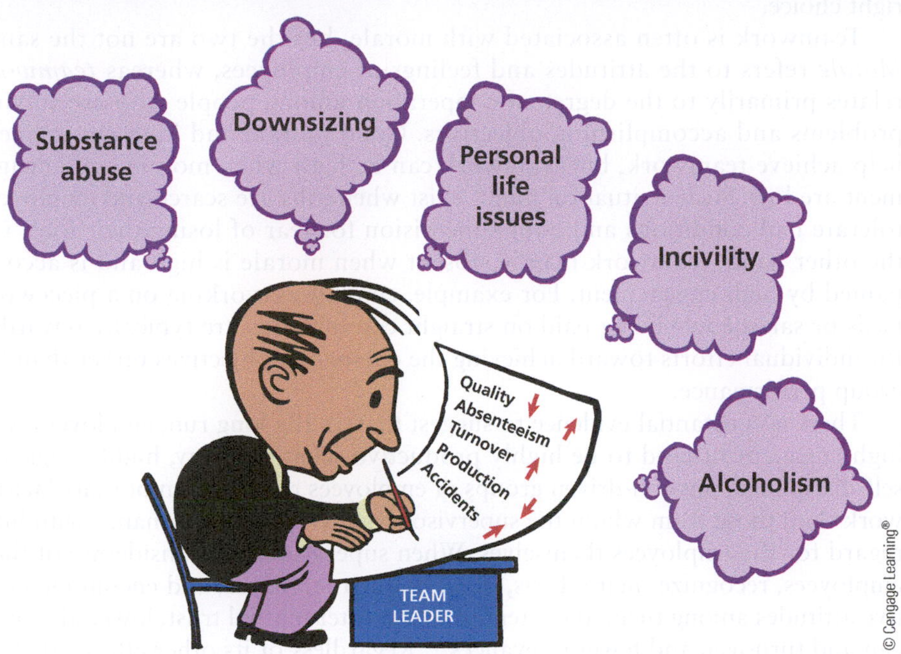


compensation is adequate, other factors may be more significant, but even when wages are good, morale can sink quickly when working conditions are neglected. The critical factor is whether the supervisor tries to improve working conditions. Employees often will perform well under undesirable conditions and still maintain high morale and engagement when they believe their supervisors are seriously trying to improve work conditions.

## MORALE, ENGAGEMENT, TEAMWORK, AND PRODUCTIVITY RELATIONSHIPS

Workplace morale tends to be contagious, as does engagement, and this contagion works in both positive and negative ways. When managers select and hire employees who are enthusiastic and interact with those workers using the strategies described earlier, the workers become committed and driven as they gain tenure in the company. If supervisors provide those workers with opportunities to influence others in their work groups, their positive morale and work ethic often rubs off. Recall our discussion of informal organizations in Chapter 9. In most organizations, informal groups form organically, and certain people in those groups naturally emerge as leaders. When supervisors position informal leaders where they can share their energy and commitment and inspire others, entire teams' engagement levels are often elevated. Further, in a team environment, managers can create teams whose members have different strengths and assign team roles based on strengths and encourage co-workers to understand and engage each others' strengths so that the team's talents complement each other, thereby increasing the team's performance. In a similar way, when actively disengaged workers emerge as leaders in teams and informal groups, they model behaviors and attitudes such as complaining, absenteeism, and negativity toward management that can frustrate and demotivate others in the group, thus decreasing everyone's productivity. Clearly, choosing engaged team leaders is the right choice.

Teamwork is often associated with morale, but the two are not the same. *Morale* refers to the attitudes and feelings of employees, whereas *teamwork* relates primarily to the degree of cooperation among people who are solving problems and accomplishing objectives. Good morale and high engagement help achieve teamwork, but teamwork can be high when morale and engagement are low. Such a situation might exist when jobs are scarce and employees tolerate bad conditions and poor supervision for fear of losing their jobs. On the other hand, teamwork may be absent when morale is high and is accompanied by high engagement. For example, employees working on a piecework basis or salespeople being paid on straight commissions are typically rewarded for individual efforts toward achieving the company's objectives rather than for group performance.

There is substantial evidence to suggest that, in the long run, employees with high engagement tend to be highly productive. That is to say, highly engaged, self-disciplined, mission-driven groups of employees tend to do more satisfactory work than those from whom the supervisor tries to force performance with little regard for the employees themselves. When supervisors are considerate of their employees, recognize their efforts, build on their strengths, and encourage positive attitudes among them, there tends to be greater mutual trust, lower absenteeism and turnover, and fewer grievances.[47] Regardless of its other effects, there is little question that a high level of engagement tends to make work more pleasant for employees and their supervisors.

## THE IMPACT OF DOWNSIZING AND OUTSOURCING ON MORALE

The magnitude of downsizing is nothing compared with the impact of outsourcing. According to recent studies, 75 percent of U.S. and European multinational companies now use outsourcing to support administration of their retirement plans, 52 percent use outsourcing to manage health and welfare plans, and many expect to increase their use of outsourcing.[48] Outsourcing is not limited to the financial field. Information technology (IT), call center operations, and production processes have been a favorite targets of the outsourcers.

Consider the following scenario: It was a beautiful morning, on August 5, 2011, when Gary, aged 39, married with two small children, ages 7 and 4, left home for his software development job. He usually arrived at work early on Friday so that he could leave early and get home to spend some time with his children. Shortly after 8:00 A.M., Gary and thirty-one of his software development and IT team members were summoned into the conference room. The announcement came as a shock. Effective immediately, his job, as well as those of his colleagues, was eliminated. That day was his last day of work. The employees were escorted from the facility, told that their personal effects would be boxed up, and that they could come back for them at 4:30 P.M. They were informed of the day and time for their scheduled exit meetings with human resources. Their meetings with HR would clarify what severance they might be entitled to, if any. The work would still need to be done, but not in the United States. Their work projects had been offshored to India. The story of Gary and his colleagues has been repeated over and over during the last several years. After thirteen years of service with the same company, what would he do? Where would he go?

Clearly, these events have disturbed workers deeply. Many downsized and/or outsourced employees feel they might never again find jobs like those they had. The survivors—those who remain in the downsized workplace—worry about being laid off and are concerned about the future of their firms. Employees have lost trust in their organizations and their leadership. As one study reported:

> *A worker's ability to form "best" friendships at work is among the most powerful of twelve indicators of a highly productive workplace. Workplaces with low turnover and high customer satisfaction, productivity, and profitability also tended to be places where employees reported having a best friend present.*[49]

Downsizings and outsourcings force employees to sever workplace friendships. Those who remain suffer from what has been termed survivors' syndrome. Few companies are prepared to address widespread employee fears and insecurities. However, some firms have developed training programs and have provided counseling services to plan for and implement job reductions and to help surviving employees cope with the aftereffects of downsizing. A detailed discussion of these types of programs is beyond the scope of this text, but among the recommended strategies are (1) early and ample communication with clear and specific details concerning which jobs have been eliminated and, more important, why they have been eliminated, and (2) working with surviving employees to develop the new short-term objectives that will help those employees focus on activities and targets over which they have some control.[50] Here, as in many other situations, first-line supervisors play a crucial role in influencing employee morale.

## ENGAGEMENT SHOULD BE EVERYONE'S CONCERN

Jim Clifton, chairman and CEO of the Gallup, Inc., contends that "How employees feel about their job starts and ends with their direct supervisor. If employees feel, among other things, that their supervisor takes a real interest in their development or offers frequent [authentic] recognition, they are very likely to be engaged."[51] Every manager, from the chief executive down to the supervisor, should be concerned with the engagement level of the workforce. It should be a priority to develop and maintain employee engagement at as high a level as possible.

It should be clear that the actions of the first-line supervisor, probably more than anyone else, influences engagement and morale in day-to-day contact with employees. Bringing engagement to a high level and maintaining it is a continuous process; engagement cannot be achieved simply through short-run devices, such as pep talks or contests. High engagement is slow to develop and difficult to maintain. The level of morale can vary considerably from day to day. Morale is contagious in both directions because both favorable and unfavorable attitudes spread rapidly among employees. Unfortunately, it seems to be human nature for employees to quickly forget the good and long remember the bad when it comes to factors influencing their morale.

The supervisor is not alone in desiring high engagement and positive morale. Employees are just as concerned with engagement because it is paramount to their work satisfaction and achievement. Feeling engaged helps to make the employee's day at work a pleasure, not a misery. Positive morale and high engagement are also important to an organization's customers. Customers can usually sense whether employees care about their satisfaction and are serving them enthusiastically or are just going through the motions.

**Workplace spirituality** Organizational efforts to make the work environment more meaningful and creative by relating work to employees' personal values and spiritual beliefs

Because of widespread concern about deteriorating employee morale and the disengagement of many workers, many firms have launched programs and efforts that collectively have been called **workplace spirituality**. This term essentially covers organizational efforts that are designed to make the work environment more meaningful and creative by recognizing and tapping into people's deeply held values and spiritual beliefs. Some believe that spirituality can improve employees' personal lives and mental outlook and that this outlook might translate to a better work environment.[52]

Listen carefully to what Ben Cohen, co-founder of Ben & Jerry's Homemade Ice Cream Company, had to say: "At Ben & Jerry's, we learned that there's a spiritual life to businesses as there is in the lives of individuals. As you give, you receive. As you help others, you are helped in return."[53] When some people accused Cohen and co-founder, Jerry Greenfield, of doing "nice things" only to sell more ice cream, Cohen responded, "We did what we believed in; it just happened to sell more ice cream. Our actions are based on deeply held values. We are all interconnected, and as we help others, we cannot help but help ourselves. Creating a consonance of values with employees and customers builds loyalty and even more value."[54]

**4 Discuss techniques for assessing employee morale, including observation and employee attitude surveys.**

## Assessing Employee Engagement

Most firms believe that, if they are to succeed, employee engagement is important in the long run. That said, we can only manage what we can measure. Measuring engagement is complicated and somewhat elusive because, as Kevin Kruse, author of *Employee Engagement 2.0*, states, "Engagement is a feeling just like love is a feeling. And how in the world can we measure the amount of love someone feels? It would be silly to say, 'Today the amount of love I feel for my wife is 3.8.'"[55] Kruse explains that like with other emotional states, an observer would know engagement if he or she saw it. There are behaviors that demonstrate engagement or lack of it, in other words, proxy measures.

An employer can observe when a worker puts in extra effort, is proactive and creative in solving problems, and encourages co-workers. A number of surveys comprised of proxy measures for engagement have been developed and are widely used to assess organizations', teams', and individuals' levels of engagement. The survey data, along with real-time, observable measures of engagement provide supervisors with a relatively strong measure of employee engagement. Employers can then analyze these measures relative to employee and organization performance in areas such as attendance, turnover, sick leave use, productivity, and profit margins to create action plans for improvement. Supervisors are advised to approach engagement measurement systematically to assess prevailing levels and trends. The two most frequently used techniques—(1) observation and study and (2) engagement surveys—warrant a closer look.

### OBSERVATION AND STUDY

By observing, monitoring, and studying patterns of employee behavior, a supervisor often can discover evidence of employee engagement. The supervisor should closely monitor such key indicators as job performance levels, tardiness and absenteeism, the amount of waste or scrap, employee complaints, and accident and safety records. Any significant changes in these indicators should be analyzed because often they are related to engagement. For example, excessive tardiness and absenteeism seriously interfere with job performance. If the reasons are related to the employee's feelings of engagement, the supervisor should determine, through conversation with the employee, whether the causes are within the supervisor's span of control and follow-up accordingly.

Specific behaviors in the workplace also provide insight into employee engagement levels. Entrepreneur Lisa Horan suggests that supervisors should consider the extent and character of employee communication—are employees pleasant and fair, do they engage in conversation, and share ideas? Also, Horan advises supervisors to study employee choices on a day-to-day basis to observe the decisions they make on a consistent basis to see the extent to which decisions are appropriate and focused on achievement and performance.[56] Gazelle CEO Verne Harnish proposes that real-time assessment of employee engagement is critical to organizational performance because using just surveys to assess engagement is "like driving your car by only looking in the rearview mirror. By the time you get the results, most of the 'accidents' have already happened: grumpy employees have already alienated customers, incompetent managers have killed productivity, and the best talent has left for the competition." Harnish recommends that supervisors adopt analytic tools such as NetPromoter System to track progress toward goals and priorities and MoodApp or TINYPulse to quickly measure morale on-the-spot through daily questions on touch pads or mobile devices. He cautions that those practices cannot substitute for regular conversations with employees and suggests three simple questions managers should ask at least one employee each week: "What do we need to start doing, stop doing and keep doing?"[57] The combination of data can provide a rich, timely perspective of employee engagement, which can be combined with engagement survey data to be used for organizational planning and development.

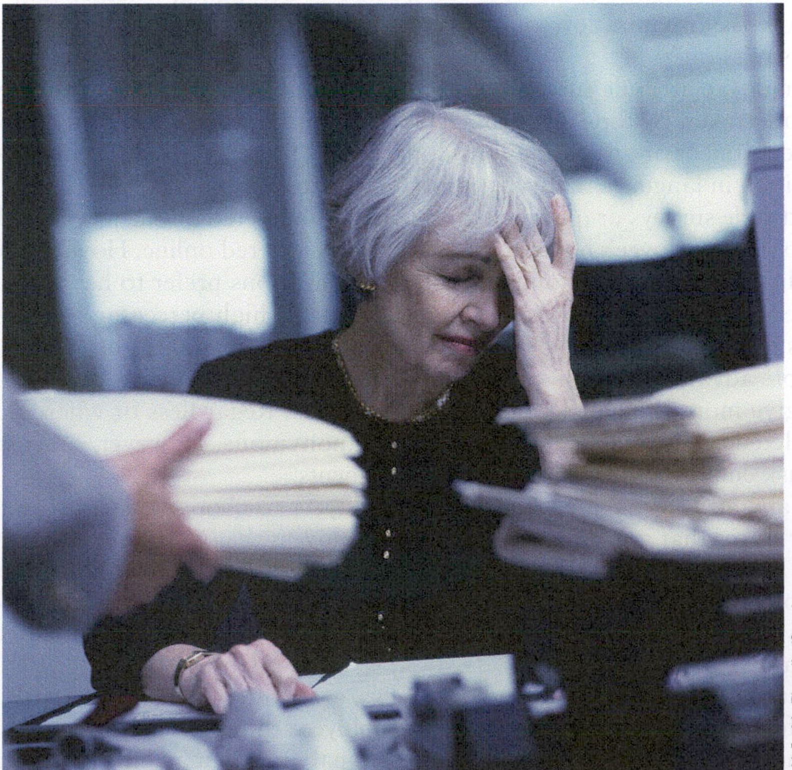

Keith Brofsky/Photodisc/Getty Images

*Overloading an employee with too much work can deflate his or her morale*

Daily working relationships offer numerous opportunities for a supervisor to observe and analyze changes in employee engagement and morale. However, many supervisors do not take time to observe; others do not analyze what they observe. It is only when engagement and/or performance clearly drops that some supervisors first take note. By then, the problems that caused the changes probably will have magnified to the point that major corrective actions are necessary. As is often the case in supervision, an ounce of prevention is worth more than a pound of cure.

**Exit interviews**
Interviews with individuals who leave a firm that are used to assess morale and the reasons for employee turnover

Many companies conduct exit interviews with individuals leaving their employ. **Exit interviews** are usually conducted by a HR staff person, although sometimes, especially in small firms, the supervisor may fill this role. The interviewer asks why the person is leaving and about the person's perceptions of the firm's conditions. Results of exit interviews are used to assess morale in the firm as a whole or in certain departments of the firm, as well as to identify reasons for employee turnover.

## ATTITUDE SURVEYS

**Attitude survey**
Survey of employee opinions about major aspects of organizational life that is used to assess engagement and morale

Another technique to assess employee engagement is an **attitude survey**, also called an engagement survey or morale survey. All employees, or a sample of the employees, are asked to express their opinions about major aspects of organizational life, usually in the form of answers to questions or rating scales printed on a survey form or presented in electronic format to be completed online using a computer or mobile device. The survey questionnaire elicits employee opinions about such factors as management and supervision, job conditions, job satisfaction, rewards and incentives, recognition, co-workers, pay and benefits, job security, and advancement opportunities. Often engagement surveys also include items asking whether employees feel a sense of belonging, whether they would promote the organization to others, and if they feel committed to the company and its mission.[58]

Employee attitude surveys are rarely initiated by a supervisor. Usually, they are undertaken by top-level management and are prepared with the help of the HR department or an outside consulting firm.[59] The survey questionnaire should be written in language that is appropriate for most employees.

Attitude surveys or questionnaires may be completed on the job or in the privacy of the employee's home, and they are often offered online. However, if using a traditional paper questionnaire, some organizations prefer to have employees answer these questionnaires on the job because a high percentage of questionnaires that are taken home or mailed are never returned. On the other hand, a possible advantage of completing the questionnaire at home is that employees may give more thoughtful and truthful answers. Regardless of where they are completed, questionnaires should remain anonymous. However, some surveys may ask employees to indicate their departments.

Many attitude survey forms allow employees to choose answers from a list. Other forms that are not so specific give employees the opportunity to answer as freely as they wish. Because some employees may find it difficult to express their opinions in sentences or to fill in answers, better results usually are obtained with survey forms on which employees simply check the responses that correspond to their answers.

Attitude surveys, like any other surveys, are limited by their ability to report workforce engagement and summarize employee sentiments at a specific moment in time. An isolated incident or organizational change may have temporary effects on morale or long-term impacts on engagement, neither of which can be measured with a single survey. Supervisors might consider using attitude surveys on an annual or semiannual basis as part of continuous improvement processes to monitor shifts in organizational or departmental culture and climate that might erode engagement over time. This long-term data can be used to identify specific problems and make proactive changes accordingly.

## FOLLOW-UP OF SURVEY RESULTS

The tabulation and analysis tasks of questionnaires usually are assigned to the HR department or to an outside consulting firm. Survey results are first presented to top-level and middle-level managers and eventually to departmental supervisors. In some organizations, survey results are used as discussion materials during supervisory training. What happens to the survey results next can have dramatic impact on employee engagement. If the survey results are then put on a shelf, the survey has done nothing to help the organization. Survey results should be used as a tool, a baseline for problem solving and action planning efforts that will increase engagement and morale across the organization.

Attitude surveys may reveal deficiencies the supervisor can eliminate. For example, a complaint that there is a lack of soap in the washroom can be resolved easily. Frequently, however, responses are difficult to evaluate, such as a complaint that communication channels are not open to employees. Such complaints raise more questions than answers and may necessitate a careful study of existing policies and procedures to see whether corrective actions are warranted.

If the attitude survey reveals that the problem can be corrected at the departmental level—perhaps with a supervisor—the solution should be developed and implemented by the involved supervisor. A broader problem, however, that requires the attention of higher-level managers should be reported to the appropriate manager for action. When supervisors and higher-level managers do not make needed changes as a result of a survey, the survey wastes time and money. In fact, if no changes materialize, or if changes are not communicated to employees, morale may decline after the survey and engagement levels will not change. Employees may feel that their problems and suggestions have been ignored. Therefore, whenever possible, concerns or dissatisfactions expressed in an attitude survey should be addressed promptly by managers and supervisors. At a minimum, employees should be informed that management is aware of the dissatisfactions and will work to change things by some future date.

## ORGANIZATIONAL DEVELOPMENT

Many companies follow up their attitude surveys with feedback meetings and conference sessions with groups of employees and supervisors. Typically these meetings are conducted by outside consultants or by staff members from HR or some other department. In these meetings, the results of attitude surveys are discussed and debated openly. The groups are expected to recommend improvements, which are forwarded anonymously to higher-level management for consideration and possible implementation.

This approach is often part of a broader concept that also has become widespread in large enterprises. Known as **organizational development (OD)**, or process consultation, this concept usually involves group meetings under the guidance of a neutral conference leader. The groups may consist of only employees, employees and supervisors, only supervisors, only higher-level managers, or whatever composition is appropriate. For the most part, these meetings focus on

**Organizational development (OD)**
Meetings with groups under the guidance of a neutral conference leader to solve problems that are hindering organizational effectiveness

solving problems that may be hindering work performance or causing disruption, poor coordination, inadequate communication, or strained personal relations. When there is frank discussion in a relatively open and informal atmosphere, individuals tend to open up about what really is on their minds and what might be done to solve problems and reduce conflict. OD can take numerous forms that are beyond the scope of this text.[60] However, supervisors may be involved in OD efforts because these programs can improve morale and organizational effectiveness.

**5 Understand why counseling is an important part of the supervisor's job.**

## The Supervisor's Counseling Role

**Counseling**
An effort by the supervisor to deal with on-the-job performance problems that are the result of an employee's personal problems

**Counseling interview**
Nondirective interview during which the supervisor listens empathetically and encourages the employee to discuss problems openly and to develop solutions

Counseling is not the same as coaching. In **counseling**, the supervisor tries to address on-the-job performance problems that result from an employee's personal problems.[61] As described in Chapter 12, an employee's performance problems may stem from a job-related personal problem, such as the failure to get a promotion, or from an off-the-job situation, such as a financial crisis due to divorce. When not addressed, these problems can impede morale, engagement, and quality of work. Therefore, the supervisor must help the employee return to productivity. The most effective way to get an employee back on track is to counsel—to ask, listen, reflect, and encourage. A **counseling interview** is essentially nondirective; the supervisor serves primarily as an empathetic listener, and the employee is encouraged to discuss the problem frankly and to develop solutions.

By being a good listener, the supervisor can find out what happened and may help the employee develop alternatives. For example, consider Laura, an X-ray technician at Anderson Memorial Hospital, who is upset because of a personal financial crisis. She and her husband recently filed bankruptcy under Chapter  of the federal Bankruptcy Code. To compound the problem, Laura's bankruptcy filing was listed in the local newspaper, announcing to the community her family's current debt of $140,000 and assets of $20,000.[62] This public information has resulted in Laura's fellow employees giving her pitying looks and shaking their heads as they pass her in the hallway. She can just imagine them thinking to themselves, "How can Laura be so stupid?" Because of this crisis, Laura's work performance is showing a marked decline. She spends more of her time thinking about how to solve her financial problems than she does thinking about her work.

Laura's counseling interview might begin when the supervisor addresses a performance problem and expresses concern: "Laura, I'm concerned about your performance. You were late for work two days last week, and the Finegan report did not get done. Could you explain?" The supervisor should listen carefully and without interruption to understand Laura's perspective. In Chapter 6, we discussed the importance of paraphrasing and reflecting to improve understanding. Paraphrasing involves expressing, in different words, Laura's response, such as, "Let me see if I understand what you're saying. . . ." A follow-up question might be, "Why do you feel that way?" Through reflection, the supervisor can help Laura talk about her feelings.

The supervisor may discuss with Laura possible ways to obtain financial assistance. The supervisor should not offer specific advice because it might bring unwanted repercussions. If Laura is dissatisfied with the results of following a supervisor's advice, for example, she might blame the supervisor, which would complicate an already difficult situation. If Laura's problem is beyond the supervisor's expertise, perhaps the supervisor can arrange for Laura to get help from a professional or refer her to the HR department where assistance may be available. For example, many employers provide assistance and referral services for employees with personal problems. Many large employers also have employee assistance programs (EAPs), which are discussed later in this chapter. Regardless, the supervisor's job is to help the employee explore alternatives and choose the course of action that is best for the particular situation.

Aside from conducting a private counseling interview or referring the employee to some source of assistance, there may be little else the supervisor can do to cope with the factors affecting an employee's morale. The supervisor's main role is to help get the employee's performance back to an acceptable level. Figure 11.4 presents a roadmap to guide your steps when dealing with employee problems.

**FIGURE 11.4 Steps in the counseling process**

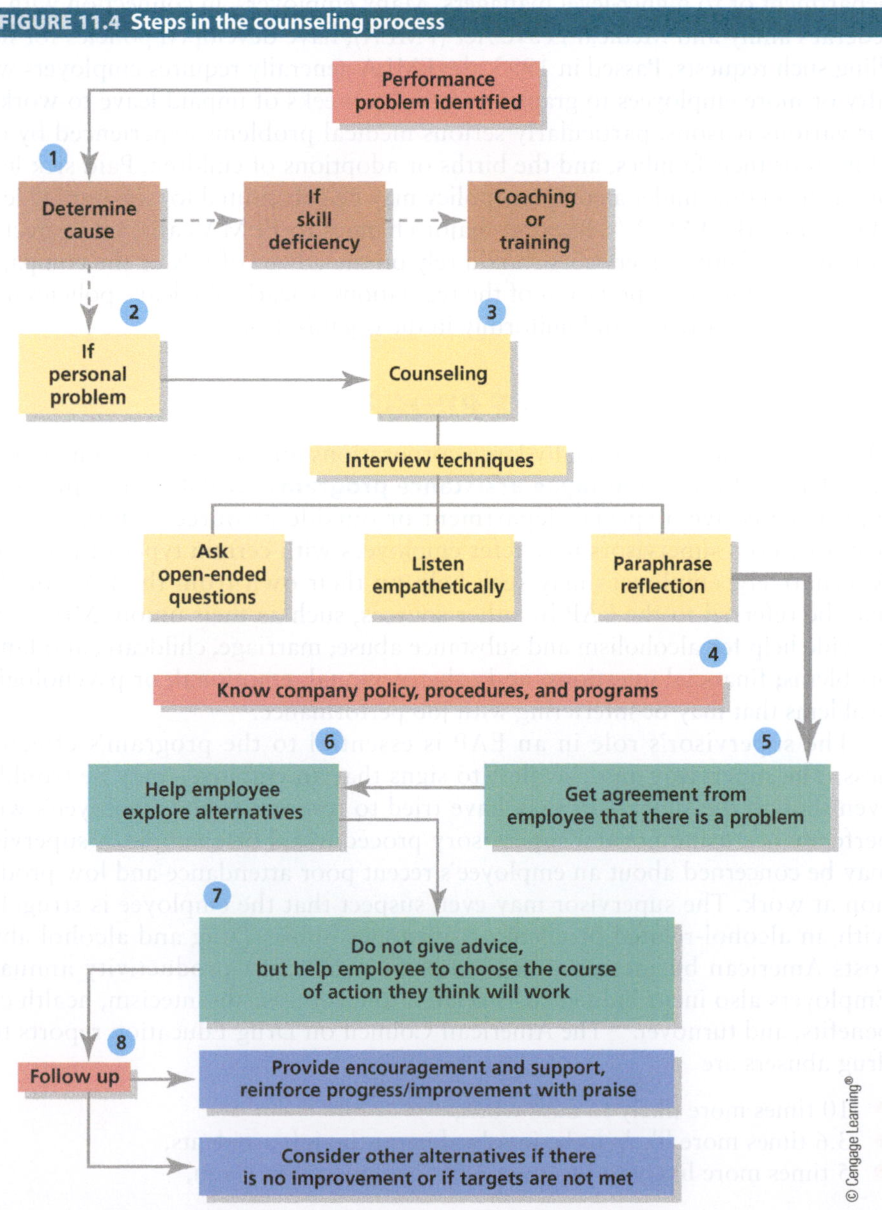

**6 Identify programs that organizations use to help employees with personal and work-related problems.**

## Supporting and Helping Employees with Personal and Work-Related Problems

As discussed previously, the supervisor may refer an employee to the HR department or to a designated manager who will conduct the counseling interview and make helpful suggestions.

### FAMILY AND MEDICAL LEAVE PROVISIONS

If the employee's problem involves requesting a leave of absence due to sickness or family considerations such as childbirth or caring for a seriously ill member of the immediate family, the supervisor normally should refer the request to the HR department or to higher-level managers. Many employers, in connection with the federal Family and Medical Leave Act (FMLA), have developed policies for handling such requests. Passed in 1993, the FMLA generally requires employers with fifty or more employees to grant up to twelve weeks of unpaid leave to workers for various reasons, particularly serious medical problems experienced by employees or their families, and the births or adoptions of children. Paid sick leave or vacation time under a company policy may be substituted for the unpaid leave allowed by the FMLA.[63] Because major changes to FLMA came into effect on January 16, 2009, supervisors should rely on the advice of HR or the company's legal counsel for interpretation of the regulations. Clearly, the leave policies must be applied consistently and uniformly in the organization.

### EMPLOYEE ASSISTANCE PROGRAMS

**Employee assistance programs (EAPs)**
Company programs to help employees with personal or work-related problems that are interfering with job performance

Many organizations, especially large corporations and major government agencies, have adopted **employee assistance programs (EAPs)**. These programs typically involve a special department or outside resources retained by the firm to whom supervisors may refer employees with certain types of problems. Alternatively, employees may seek help on their own from the EAP, or they may be referred to the EAP by other sources, such as their union. Most EAPs provide help for alcoholism and substance abuse; marriage, childcare, and family problems; financial questions; and other personal, emotional, or psychological problems that may be interfering with job performance.

The supervisor's role in an EAP is essential to the program's effectiveness. The supervisor must be alert to signs that an employee may be troubled, even though the supervisor may have tried to respond to the employee's work performance using normal supervisory procedures. For example, a supervisor may be concerned about an employee's recent poor attendance and low production at work. The supervisor may even suspect that the employee is struggling with an alcohol-related problem or substance abuse. Drug and alcohol abuse costs American businesses almost $100 billion in lost productivity annually. Employers also incur hidden costs related to tardiness, absenteeism, health care benefits, and turnover.[64] The American Council on Drug Education reports that drug abusers are

- 10 times more likely to miss work,
- 3.6 times more likely to be involved in on-the-job accidents,
- 5 times more likely to file a workers' compensation claim,

- two-thirds as productive, and
- responsible for health care costs that are three times as high.[65]

When talking with the employee, the supervisor should focus primarily on the person's poor or deteriorating job performance and then suggest the EAP services that might be of help.

Most EAPs emphasize the confidential nature of the services. Supervisors should discuss this confidentiality with employees and assure them that no stigma will be associated with their seeking EAP help. However, the supervisor should inform an employee who refuses EAP assistance and whose work performance continues to deteriorate that such a refusal might be a consideration in a termination decision.

## WELLNESS PROGRAMS

Another approach used by some firms, often where EAPs are in place, is the wellness program. The Towers Watson 2013 Global Benefits Attitude Survey found that workers' wellness is directly related to performance, both employee performance and organizational performance. The survey identified seven lifestyle risk factors that decrease productivity even in the best-equipped workforces: stress, obesity, lack of physical activity, poor nutrition, tobacco use, presenteeism, and substance abuse, which have dire, yet often preventable consequences for workers and organizations.[66]

**Wellness program**
Organized effort by a firm to help employees get and stay healthy to remain productive
© Michael Newman/PhotoEdit

In order to comprehensively empower workers for success, employers are forced to consider how they can address these risk factors by promoting and supporting employee wellness. Companies are recognizing this growing challenge and are committed to helping by providing wellness programs for employees. A **wellness program** is essentially a firm's organized effort to help employees stay healthy physically and mentally so they can stay productive and engaged, and to reduce employer health costs. Wellness programs vary, but they often focus on areas of recovery and prevention of chronic, preventable health problems. Wellness programs can include exercise facilities, counseling, and other resources, both on company premises and elsewhere. New wellness technologies provided within contracted wellness services can actively engage workers with wellness programs by providing tools to build healthy habits, incentives for participation, and tracking tools to manage chronic health conditions, as well as securely report data to employees' medical providers. For just a few dollars per employee, companies can help workers be proactive in improving their health and substantially reducing health care costs for the organization.[67] In some firms, corporate wellness programs are viewed as an employee benefit, but for the most part, they are directed efforts by the firm to improve employee health and safety, which should positively impact engagement and work performance.[68]

*A wellness program might include a gym membership to encourage exercise and overall good health.*

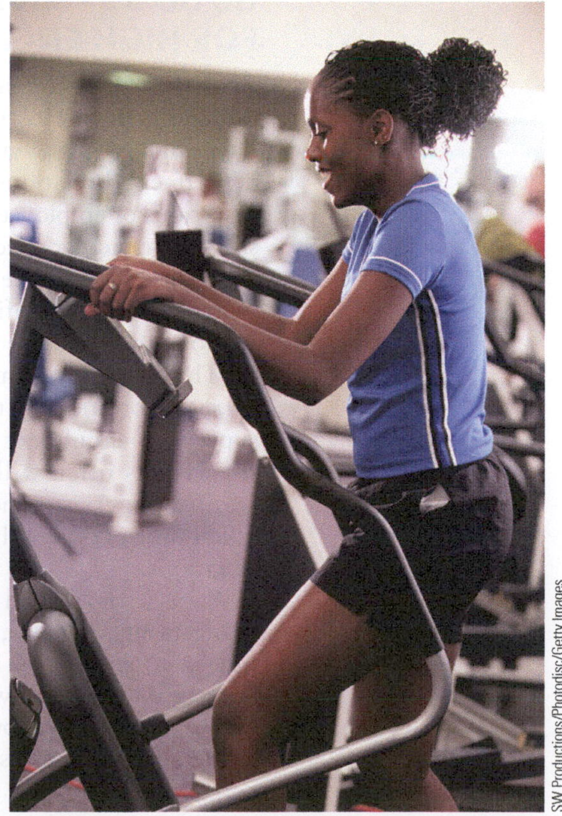

SW Productions/Photodisc/Getty Images

## PAID TIME OFF (PTO)

It is well known that all work and no play will negatively impact the best of us. We all need time to pause, relax, and recharge our batteries. Did you ever wonder why schools have a spring break? How do you spend your time off? We suspect that you use it for personal reasons. The same is true for employees. Did you ever know an employee who used a sick day to tend to personal business? Of course, we all do. Anderson Memorial Hospital recently eliminated the distinction between vacation, sick, and personal days by granting employees *paid time off*.

**Paid time off (PTO) program** PTO allows employees to establish a personal time-off bank that they can use for any reason they want

Increasingly, companies are developing **paid time off (PTO) programs** where employees can use their accrued time off for personal reasons rather than solely for illnesses or vacations. PTO programs are in place at about one-third of the companies that responded to a recent SHRM Benefits Survey.[69] Under the PTO plan, employees can take time off with pay as needed without the restrictions imposed by traditional time-off policies. Anderson Memorial employees get days in their personal leave bank and make withdrawals as needed. At Anderson, the average employee previously received ten days of paid vacation, five sick days, and three personal days. Now employees receive eighteen days of personal time to use as they wish. It eliminates the problem of employees calling in sick when they want to play golf. PTO plans should be coordinated with FMLA, and employees have more control over how they use their time-off days.

## GOOD SUPERVISION IS THE FOUNDATION FOR HIGH ENGAGEMENT

All aspects of good supervision impact employee engagement as it relates to job conditions. However, perhaps the most significant day-to-day influence on employee engagement is the supervisor's general attitude and behavior in departmental relationships. When a supervisor's behavior indicates he or she is suspicious of employees' motives and actions, low morale will likely result. When supervisors act worried or depressed, employees tend to follow suit. When supervisors lose their temper, some employees also may lose theirs. Conversely, supervisors who show confidence in their employees' work and commend employees for good performance reinforce their positive outlook.

This does not mean that a supervisor should overlook difficulties that are present from time to time. Rather, it means that if something goes wrong, the supervisor should act as a leader who has the situation in hand. For example, supervisors often will be called on to mediate conflict among their employees. The supervisor should demonstrate the attitude that the employees will be relied on to correct the situation and do what is necessary to prevent similar situations.

Supervisors should not relax their efforts to build and maintain high employee engagement. However, they should not become discouraged if morale drops from time to time, because many factors impacting morale are beyond their control. Supervisors should always maintain a focus on building high engagement in the long-term. We have found that effective supervisors embrace that old saying, "If it [high engagement] is to be, it is up to me!"

## SUMMARY

1. Work groups are typically formed to provide companionship and identification, behavioral guidelines, problem-solving help, and protection. Various factors can contribute to the cohesiveness and functioning of the work group, including the group's status, size, personal characteristics, location, and previous successes. Work groups can significantly influence employee attitudes and job performance, a reality supervisors must recognize and be prepared to address.

   At any time, an employee may be a member of a command group, a task group or cross-functional team, a friendship group, or a special-interest group. Command and task groups are based primarily on job-related factors. Friendship and special-interest groups mainly reflect personal relationships and interests. Employees who are dissatisfied with their jobs or working conditions, or fear losing their jobs due to outsourcing or economic downturn, may be attracted to form a special-interest group, for example, a labor union. As a supervisor, you need to be aware of any hint of employee dissatisfaction that may lead to a unionizing effort. There is increasing use of customer-satisfaction teams, which may include customer and supplier representatives. Participation in each of these work groups can influence worker attitudes and productivity in different ways. Supervisors should be sensitive to all these groups and how they impact their employee members.

2. The Hawthorne Studies demonstrated that work groups can positively or negatively influence employee performance. To influence work groups positively, supervisors should review the keys to effective team building. Teams should be relatively small, and members must have the necessary skills and be committed to specific and realistic objectives. Organized participative management programs primarily involve building effective teams to work on tasks that will improve work performance and customer service. While work teams are convened with the expectation that the group will take charge of accomplishing a specific task, the supervisor still plays an important role in providing direction, feedback, accountability measures, and coaching during the team development process of forming, storming, norming, performing, and adjourning.

   Virtual or geographically dispersed work teams (GDTs) are a way for organizations to leverage the SKAs from workers located in all parts of the world. For such programs to be effective, top-level and other managers must give their full support and encouragement.

   Members of these teams communicate electronically, so they rarely or never meet face to face. Thus, the supervisor's ability to communicate, build commitment, and encourage collaboration is fundamental to the success of these teams.

3. Employee engagement is the level of emotional commitment the employee has to the organization and its goals. Morale is a composite of feelings and attitudes of individuals and groups toward their work environment, supervision, and the organization as a whole. Morale can vary from very high to very low and can change considerably from day to day. Engagement is a more stable characteristic that is driven by the level of support, encouragement, and opportunity provided by supervisors and managers. Everyone in the organization should be concerned about engagement, although it is primarily the direct supervisor who is, and should be responsible for creating a climate that encourages engagement. Morale can be influenced by factors from outside the organization as well as by on-the-job factors. Morale, engagement, and teamwork are not synonymous, but high morale usually contributes to high productivity. The converse is also true; employees with low morale seldom put forth their best effort. Further, individuals with high levels of engagement who assume leadership positions on teams can positively influence the engagement level and productivity of the entire team. Workplace spirituality is an effort to improve employees' personal lives and mental outlook.

   Downsizing and corporate restructuring during the past decade have created a legacy of fear among workers. Supervisors must be aware of employee needs, feelings, and perceptions because they impact morale. In general, a supervisor's attitude and behaviors can significantly influence employee engagement and morale.

4. Perceptive supervisors who regularly interact with employees can detect changes in engagement by monitoring employee behaviors and such key indicators as absenteeism and performance trends. The attitude survey is another method of assessing engagement and, when used over time, monitoring trends that reflect engagement changes in the workforce. When possible, supervisors and higher-level managers should correct problems that have been brought to their attention through the survey. A participative approach is desirable when considering attitude survey data, in which the supervisor discusses the results with supervisors and employee groups and encourages them to recommend changes and improvements.

**5.** **Supervisors adopt the counseling role when they deal directly with employee performance problems that are influenced by personal problems. If these problems are not addressed, employee morale, work quality, and productivity can be negatively affected. When a supervisor recognizes an employee performance problem, it is important to use empathetic listening, reflective questioning, and direct communication, and refer the employee to additional sources of assistance as directed in established employee support policies. Sound interviewing and communication practices are the foundation of counseling.**

**6.** **Supervisors should be aware of the Family and Medical Leave Act (FMLA) and the company's related policies in case an employee requests a leave of absence due to personal sickness, childbirth, or other family medical concerns. To help employees with personal and work-related problems a supervisor would not be competent to handle, some organizations have employee assistance programs (EAPs) and wellness programs. EAP efforts typically help employees solve problems that detract from job performance, with the goal of restoring those employees to full capabilities that meet acceptable work standards. Wellness programs aim to promote and maintain proper physical condition and other personal or health habits that will tend to keep employees healthy and productive on the job. Paid time off (PTO) programs are increasing in popularity as employers recognize the need of employees to take time off for personal reasons rather than solely for illnesses and vacations.**

## KEY TERMS

Attitude survey (p. 428)
Collaborative workplace (p. 415)
Command group (p. 409)
Counseling (p. 430)
Counseling interview (p. 430)
Employee assistance programs (EAPs) (p. 432)
Exit interviews (p. 428)
Friendship group (p. 410)
Groupthink (p. 408)
Hawthorne Studies (p. 411)
Morale (p. 420)
Organizational development (OD) (p. 429)
Paid time off (PTO) program (p. 434)
Special-interest group (p. 410)
Synergistic effect (p. 415)
Task group or cross-functional team (p. 409)
Teamwork (p. 415)
Virtual or geographically dispersed team (GDT) (p. 417)
Wellness program (p. 433)
Workplace spirituality (p. 426)

## WHAT HAVE YOU LEARNED?

1. What are some of the most common reasons for forming work groups? What are some factors that make a work group cohesive? Is work-group cohesiveness always desirable? Discuss.
2. Consider a team (work group) of which you are presently a member.
   a. Describe the group dynamics of this team. Use Tuckman and Jensen's stages of group development to identify the current stage of the group.
   b. Is your team successful? Why?
   c. What are some reasons that your team might not be achieving to its full potential?
   d. What steps should you be taking to make the team more successful, that is, a high-performance team?
3. Imagine that you are located in El Paso, Texas, with responsibility for managing a customer-service call center. Your team members are located in El Paso; Calcutta, India; and Teresopolis, Brazil. What are the strengths and shortcomings of using GDTs to provide customer service? Suggest specific leadership and team-building strategies you will use to facilitate the development and performance of your team.
4. Define and differentiate between employee morale and employee engagement. What are the factors that influence employee engagement? Morale?
   a. What is the direct supervisor's role in building and maintaining employee engagement?
   b. What should a supervisor do to minimize the influence of external factors on an employee's work?
   c. Discuss the impact of downsizing on employee engagement and supervisory responses to the effects of downsizing.
5. Picture yourself as a newly hired X-ray department manager in a regional health care system. During your first few weeks of conversations with employees, you notice an undertone of fatigue and frustration and you notice productivity dropping. What steps can you take to identify the causes of this low engagement, and how might you go about improving the climate of your workplace?
6. Discuss the use of employee assistance programs (EAPs) and wellness programs. What should a supervisor do when an employee requests a family or medical leave?

# EXPERIENTIAL EXERCISE FOR SELF-ASSESSMENT

## EXPERIENTIAL EXERCISE FOR SELF-ASSESSMENT 11: Team Assessment

1. Describe the most effective team with which you have ever been associated.
   a. What did you like most about being a member of that team?
   b. Why were you able to perform successfully on the team?
   c. What did the team leader do to blend the team members into an efficient and effective group?
   d. Provide specific examples to illustrate how team members used feedback to help you grow, develop, and improve.
   e. Have you ever been part of the team or group that, in retrospect, you wish that you had never been a part of? What are the major differences between this team and the one described in (a) above?

# PERSONAL SKILL BUILDING

## PERSONAL SKILL BUILDER 11-1: Is this the best way to get people on board your team?

In this skill building exercise, you are assigned the role of Don Brockman, the newest member of Lighthouse Financials HR team (refer to this chapter's You Make the Call!)

1. Discuss why morale may not be high in Lighthouse Financials' HR department.
2. Do you think that the employees in the HR department can be an effective team? Why or why not? If not, what must management do to get HR professionals to function as a team?
3. Please think back to the information in Chapter 5 ("Leadership and Followership"). Develop a list of the concepts and principles of leadership that might be useful to help Charlie do a better job of supervising his team and building a more effective HR team.
4. Would you want to work for a manager like Charlie? Why? Why not?
5. Please go to this link to see Alan Cavaiola's study (www.shrm.org/1013-Cavaiola-personal-problems-at-work.)

INTERNET ACTIVITY

   a. What are the potential impacts of dissatisfied team members for the organization?
   b. After reading this chapter's You Make the Call! and Cavaiola's study, would you want to work for Charlie? Why or why not?
   c. Cavaiola' study found that high achievers were often dissatisfied. If the senior leadership of Lighthouse Financials becomes aware that dissatisfaction occurs among various teams in the organization, what actions would you recommend they take?

## PERSONAL SKILL BUILDER 11-2: The Law Is the Law!

Most of us would like to work for an organization that is family-friendly.

1. Review either your university's, employer's, or another organization's handbook or policy manual to determine what their policies and procedures are for handling employees' personal and work-related problems.
2. If the organization has an employee assistance program (EAP):
   a. What are the procedures for a supervisor to follow when they suspect that an employee's personal or work-related problems are hindering job performance?
   b. What assistance services are available for your referral?
   c. Do the policies provide procedures regarding the steps the supervisor should take if the employee's on-the-job performance does not improve?
   d. If so, what actions should the supervisor take?
3. The EEOC provides fact sheets to help supervisors and employees understand the Family and Medical Leave Act (FMLA), ADA, and workers' compensation compliance. Managing leaves of absence is complicated enough for the supervisor without having to consider state law. See Joanne Deschenaux, "Managing Leave of Absence in California Is Complicated," *HR Magazine* (June 2011), p. 23.

**FOOD FOR THOUGHT QUESTIONS:** (a) Does the California law make the supervisor's job of managing and scheduling employees easier or more difficult? (b) Is the California law more or less in line with the concepts and examples for effectively supervising employees in *SuperVision?*

### PERSONAL SKILL-BUILDER 11-3: Technology Tools—Virtual Team Collaboration

Imagine that you meet a group of three new friends while on vacation in Cozumel, Mexico, over spring break. While hanging out at the beach, you come up with a great idea for a new kind of low-profile, water-resistant headphones that would be perfect for the beach. The discussion continues throughout the week. On the last day of the trip, you exchange numbers so you can keep working on developing a prototype and business plan for the idea. Once you leave Cozumel, you will become a virtual team. What technology tools could help the team collaborate to make the headphones a reality?

Thousands of software applications exist to bring people together for virtual work. You may already be using some of them in your day-to-day life. Hassan Oman, Senior Program Manager at Cisco and part-time webpreneur, has curated a list of productivity applications he feels are the "ultimate" virtual team collaboration tools.

Visit the list of tools here: http://www.thecouchmanager.com/2013/05/ or use your Internet browser to find another list of reviews of "virtual team technology tools."

1. Consider the interactions you will need to have with the team as you work on your design and business plan. Will you need to have video conferences? Share documents? Manage a timeline? Instant message?
2. Visit Oman's Ultimate List of Virtual Team Technology Tools here: http://www.thecouchmanager.com/2013/05/21/
3. Explore at least ten different tools. Click the links and read the specifications of the different applications.
4. Create a work plan for the next year that incorporates at least five different technology tools from the list and, if applicable, your experience. Using Microsoft Excel or a Word table, show the monthly timeline, what tools you will use, and what you will accomplish with each tool. Along with the work plan, write a 200-word assessment of what you think the biggest challenges will be for the virtual team and suggest ways to overcome them.

## TEAM SKILL BUILDING

### TEAM SKILL BUILDER 11-1: Dealing with People Who Make Your Life Difficult—"The Deadweight"

This is another in a series of skills exercises that introduce you to people who might make your life difficult.

1. Read the following statement from Chandra Morris, a pet shop employee:

   *I love working at the pet shop—mostly. I enjoy what I do, but I do not look forward to coming to work when I'm scheduled to work the same shift as Jay. Jay goes around as if nothing is ever wrong and nothing has to be done on time. Yesterday, I arrived at work at 8:00 A.M. to get things organized for our opening at 10:00 A.M. Jay was supposed to be here at 8:00 A.M., but he didn't show up until 9:15 A.M. We're supposed to clean cages and feed and water the animals. Every morning, I end up cleaning the cages by myself. Jay said it was too early in the morning for him to deal with animal droppings. He says he'll get around to it later, once he wakes up. I asked him if he could start filling food and water bowls while I finished cleaning cages. To my surprise, he actually started filling the bowls. At 9:30 A.M., the phone rang, and Jay answered it. We're not supposed to answer the phone until after 10:00 A.M. as the message system clicks in to tell people our hours of operation, but it was Jay's girlfriend. After he talked for about 15 minutes, I asked Jay if he would hurry up and feed the animals as we were about ready to open the store. He said not to worry about it, that it would get done.*

   *I should have known better. As I opened the doors at 10:00 A.M., the customers started to come in. Jay got off the phone, but he didn't finish his duties. I proceeded to answer the customers' questions and work the cash register until my shift was over at 4:00 P.M. I've asked Jay if he ever worries about losing his job because of the lack of effort, and his responses have included, "What? Me worry? No way!" and "Don't sweat the small stuff. Everything works out in the end."*

   *I've talked with the other employees, and they have expressed the same concern. During the week, there are only two of us on duty, so we have to work as a team to get everything done. I have lots of responsibility, including opening and closing the store, but no authority. I've reported my concerns to the owner, Aaron Minnick, but he only says, "Figure out a way to work together." I'm starting to feel like the Lone Ranger. It's always the same thing: Every time I'm scheduled to work with Jay, I end up carrying the entire load.*

2. 

   Using the Internet, find at least three sources of information for working with people who fail to carry their loads. Carefully review each site for suggestions on how to deal with this type of person.
3. Pair students into groups of three or more. In the group, each student should share his or her research finding for how to cope with someone like the deadweight.

4. After reviewing the research findings and discussing the possible courses of action, the group must reach a decision as to how Chandra Morris should deal with Jay—the deadweight.
5. Evaluate the role of the leader—the owner, Aaron Minnick—in getting members of the team to play the game so that all can be winners.
6. As a group, write a one-page paper explaining how this exercise increased your working knowledge of coping with the behaviors of this type of difficult person.

## TEAM SKILL BUILDER 11-2: Thinking Outside the Box—Advantages of Teamwork

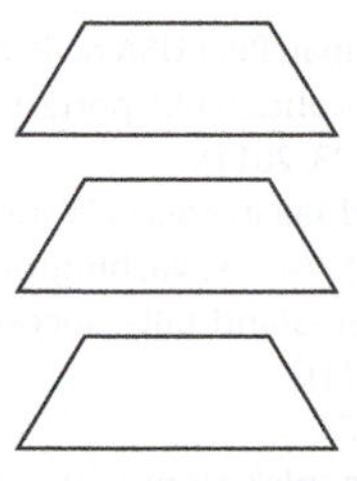

1. Your instructor will randomly organize the class into a team of four to six persons.
2. Each team should decide how it will arrange these three identical pieces into one figure that forms a triangle. Compare your team's final solution with the solution that the instructor will provide.
3. At the conclusion of the exercise, each member of the team should list the advantages and limitations of working as a team on this project as opposed to doing it as an individual.
4. Each group should select one individual to be its reporter. The reporter should take notes and report what the group decided was the major benefit of working as a team on this project and the major obstacle the team faced in completing the task. Your instructor will then develop a composite listing of the advantages and limitations of team problem solving.
5. In conclusion, analyze the dynamics of your team.
   a. Were you satisfied with the solution your team developed?
   b. How did you arrive at the solution?
   c. Did anyone just sit there and refuse to participate? If so, why?
   d. What were the patterns of communication within the group?
   e. Did the group work well together?
   f. Who was the person with the most influence?
   g. Did you feel welcome in the group?
   h. Did you personally make an effort to involve everyone in the process?
   i. Would you like to work with this group of individuals on another project? Why? Why not?

*Source:* Adapted from QCI International, from QCI International's Timely Tips for Teams, a monthly Internet newsletter (November 2004).

## SUPERVISION IN ACTION

The video for this chapter can be accessed from the student companion website at www.cengagebrain.com. (Search by authors' names or book title to find the accompanying resources.)

## ENDNOTES

1. For an expanded discussion of group processes in organizations, see Debra L. Nelson and James Campbell Quick, *Organizational Behavior: Science, the Real World, and You* (Cincinnati, OH: South-Western Cengage Learning, 2011), pp. 292–324; John M. Ivancevich, Robert Konopaske, and Michael T. Matteson, *Organizational Behavior and Management* (Boston: McGraw-Hill Irwin, 2005), pp. 321–346; Steven L. McShane and Mary Ann Von Glinow, *Organizational Behavior* (Boston: McGraw-Hill Irwin, 2005), pp. 264–288.
2. Leslie De Church and Jessica Mesmer Magnus undertook a meta-analysis of sixty-five studies of team cognition and its relationship to teamwork processes in their investigation, "The Cognitive Underpinnings of Effective Teamwork: A Meta-Analysis," *Journal of Applied Psychology* 95, No. 1 (2010), pp. 32–53. They found that team cognition has strong positive relationships to team behavioral processes, motivational states, and team performance.
3. See a comprehensive discussion of the characteristics of groupthink, its precursors, and results in Roland Benabou, "Groupthink: Collective Delusions in Organizations and Markets," *Review of Economic Studies* 80, No. 2 (2013), pp. 429–462. See also Sallie Krawcheck, "Diversify Corporate America" *Time* (March 13, 2014), pp. 36–38.
4. See Nelson and Quick, *Organizational Behavior,* pp. 304–310; or McShane and Von Glinow, *Organizational Behavior,* pp. 294–318. Also see Natasha Calder and P. C. Douglas, "Empowered Employee Teams: The New Key to Improving Corporate Success," *Quality Digest* (March 1999), pp. 26–30, for a discussion of empowered teams.

Access the Web site http://www.teambuilding.com for information on teams.

5. Go to www.3M.com for information on their self-directed team approach. See Dave Gray, "3M Is Podular" (http://www.dachisgroup.com), posted May 9, 2011; or Larry Edmonds, "The Self-Directed Work Team," *National Work Place Issues* (January 24, 2010) (http://www.examiner.com). To understand how Johnson & Johnson uses the team approach, see "What Makes Good Teams Better: Research-Based Strategies That Distinguish Top-Performing Cross-Functional Drug Development Teams," *Organizational Development Journal* 25, No. 2 (Summer 2007), pp. 179–186.
6. See Salvatore Parise and Keith Rollag, "Emergent Network Structure and Initial Group Performance: The Moderating Role of Pre-existing Relationships," *Journal of Organizational Behavior* 31 (2010), pp. 877–897.
7. For discussion of the Hawthorne Studies and their impact, see Ivancevich, *Organizational Behavior and Management*, pp. 12–13. See Fritz J. Roethlisberger and W. J. Dickson, *Management and the Worker* (Cambridge, MA: Harvard University Press, 1939); and Elton Mayo, *The Social Problems of Industrial Civilization* (Boston: Harvard University Press, 1945), for a complete picture of the works of Mayo, Roethlisberger, and Dickson at the Hawthorne Works.
8. Jon R. Katzenbach and Douglas K. Smith, *The Wisdom of Teams: Creating the High-Performance Organization* (Boston: Harvard Business School Press, 1993). Review Chapters 4, 7, 8, and 11 of this text for useful checklists for building team performance, leading teams effectively, and overcoming team obstacles. Also see Diane McLain Smith, *Divide or Conquer—How Great Teams Turn Conflict into Strength* (New York: Portfolio, 2008); Casimer DeCusatis, "Creating, Growing and Sustaining Efficient Innovations Teams," *Creativity and Innovation Management* 17, No. 2 (June 2008), pp. 155–164; Maria Isabell Delgado Pina, Ana Maria Romero Martinez, and Luis Gomez Martinez, "Teams in Organizations: A Review on Team Effectiveness," *Team Performance Management* 14, No. 1–2 (2008), pp. 7–21; or Nancy R. Lockwood, "Teams—Just the Basics," *Journal of Organizational Behavior* 22, No. 3 (August 2004), pp. 309–328.
9. "From Supervisor to Team Manager," by Allen Ferguson, Amy Hicks, and Steven D. Jones, is one of the case studies in *Developing High-Performance Work Teams*, ed. Jones and Michael M. Beyerlein (Washington, DC: ASTD, Part 1, 1998, and Part 2, 1999). Also visit the Center for the Study of Work Teams Web site (http://www.workteams.unt.edu) for additional information. Also see Phred Dvorak, "Munchausen at Work: Employees Advances by Fixing Problems They Had Created," *The Wall Street Journal* (August 25, 2008), p. B4.
10. For information on Eastman's Kingsport, Tennessee, facility and operations, go to www.eastman.com.
11. See Bruce W. Tuckman, "Developmental Sequence in Small Groups," *Psychological Bulletin* 63, No. 6 (1965), pp. 384–399, as well as Bruce W. Tuckman and Mary Ann C. Jensen, "Stages of Small-Group Development Revisited," *Group and Organization Studies* 2, No. 4 (December 1977), pp. 419–428. This pair of classical descriptions of the group development process remains as relevant today as it was nearly fifty years ago as described in Daniel Levi's *Group Dynamics for Teams* (San Francisco: Sage Publications, 2010), pp. 39–41; and Jorg Finsterwalder and Sven Tzovic, "Quality in Group Service Encounters: A Theoretical Exploration of a Simultaneous Multi-customer Co-creation Process," *Managing Service Quality* 20 No. 2 (2010), pp. 109–122. Students can view the stages as depicted in the popular football film, *Remember the Titans* (2000), in an annotated set of video clips from the AlphaGeneral YouTube channel (http://www.youtube.com/watch?v=6M6pAhHhMc&feature=mfu_in_order&list=UL and http://www.youtube.com/watch?v=sgK_r_nnkc&feature=channel_video_title).
12. Benjamin Gottlieb, "Women's Soccer a 'Beautiful Flower' for Post-Disaster Japan," CNN International Edition (July 17, 2011) (http://edition.cnn.com/2011/SPORT/football/07/15/japan.world.cup.final/index.html, retrieved September 23, 2011).
13. Charlie Smith, "Fukushima Disaster Inspired Japanese Women to Defeat Germany in Women's World Cup," Straight.Com: Vancouver's Online Source (July 15, 2011) (http://www.straight .com/article-404121/vancouver/fukushima-disaster-inspired--japanese-women-defeat-germany-womens-world-cup, retrieved September 23, 2011).
14. Saj Chowdhury, "Women's World Cup Final: Japan Beat USA on Penalties," *BBC Sport* (July 17, 2011) (http://news.bbc.co.uk/sport2/hi/football/14168601.stm, retrieved September 23, 2011).
15. Christopher Johnson, "Japan's Women Stand Tall in Soccer World," *The Washington Times* (July 18, 2011) (http://www.washington-times.com/news/2011/jul/18/japans-women-stand-tall—soccer-world/?page=all, retrieved September 23, 2011).
16. Gottlieb, "Women's Soccer a 'Beautiful Flower.'"
17. Masami Ito, "Women's Soccer Team Gets People's Honor Award," *Japan Times Online* (August 19, 2011) (http://search.japantimes .co.jp/cgi-bin/nn20110819a4.html, retrieved September 23, 2011). See also Mike Cardillo, "Japanese Soccer Team Remembers 2011 Tsunami with Unique Goal Celebration," TheBigLead.com (March 11, 2014).
18. See Associated Press, "Hugh McCutcheon Ends Olympic Volleyball Run," ESPN Sports (August 13, 2012), http://sports.espn.go.com/espn/wire?id=8263934
19. One of our IPFW graduates, Lloy Ball, was the setter on the 2008 U.S. gold medal volleyball team. Ball had appeared in three previous Olympics without success. See Anne M. Peterson, "Ball, U.S. Strike Volleyball Gold," *Fort Wayne, Indiana Journal Gazette* (August 25, 2008), pp. 1B, 7B; Also see Nancy R. Lockwood, "High-Performance Teams," *Team Performance Management SHRM Research* (August 2004), pp. 123–135; or T. L. Stanley, "The Challenge of Managing a High-Performance Team," *SuperVision* (June 2003), pp. 10–13.
20. Adapted from Chris Widener, "Secrets of Successful Teams," *IJR Business* (www.insiderreports.com, accessed September 1, 2008). Widener spent seven years working for the Seattle Supersonics.
21. See AMAnet.org, for details of the *2012 Critical Skills Survey* (December 2012) for details of the survey conducted by the American Management Association (AMA).
22. Review the following: Coach Wooden's Web site at www .coachjohnwooden.com; and his two books: John Wooden and Steve Jamison, *Wooden on Leadership* (New York: McGraw-Hill, 2005) and *My Personal Best: Life Lessons from an All-American Journeyman* (New York: McGraw-Hill, 2004).
23. Dr. Ed Leonard was the first basketball coach at Indiana University—Purdue University Fort Wayne (IPFW), an NCAA Division I school and is their Athletics Hall of Fame. Coach Wooden was my "hero!" See John Zarr, "No I in Team," *SuperVision* (June 2011), pp. 12–13; Eric Bigelow, "A Team Environment," *SuperVision* (April 2010), pp. 16–17; and Russell Adams, "The Culture of Winning," *The Wall Street Journal* (October 5, 2005), pp. B1, B4.
24. Kenneth Turan, "Tales from the Trenches: Role Players," *ESPN Sports Century* (December 12, 1999), p. 19.
25. The emphasis is on the word *must*, from the Mescon Group, Inc., *Strengthening Teamwork* (Cincinnati: Thomson Executive Press, 1995), p. 19. As teams work together, each member must use his or her SKAs to fulfill specific tasks that together will achieve the team's goal. Edward

DeBono likens this synergy to the wheels of a car, the legs of a horse, or organs in the human body—if one is missing, the object won't work. See "Teamwork and Creativity" (December 9, 2010). Retrieved from Management Issues Web site (http://www.management-issues.com/2010/12/9/opinion/teamwork-and-creativity.asp). Also see T. L. Stanley, "Taking on the Challenges of High-Performance Work Teams," *SuperVision* (December 2004), pp. 10–12; and W. H. Weiss, "Team Management," *SuperVision* (November 2004), pp. 19–21.

26. As quoted in Randi Brenowitz and Tracy Gibbons, "Workforce Collaboration: Building a Strong Team Foundation," *Information Executive* (January/February 2002), pp. 5–6.
27. See Jacob Morgan, "The 12 Habits of Highly Collaborative Organizations," Forbes.com (July 30, 2013), http://www.forbes.com/sites/jacobmorgan/2013/07/30/the-12-habits-of-highly-collaborative-organizations/. See also Edward M. Marshall, "The Collaborative Workplace," *Management Review* (June 1995), pp. 13–17.
28. H. James Harrington, "Beyond Teams: Teamwork," *Quality Digest* (August 1999), p. 20. Also see Harrington, "Horsing Around: A Parable about Teamwork," *Quality Digest* (November 2004), p. 16; and Harvey Robbins and Michael Finley, *The New Why Teams Don't Work: What Went Wrong and How to Make It Right* (San Francisco: Berrett-Koehler Publishing, 2000).
29. See Terri L. Griffith, Elizabeth A. Mannix, and Margaret A. Neale, "Conflict and Virtual Teams," in *Virtual Teams That Work* (San Francisco: Jossey-Bass, 2003). They contend that the virtual team model can be used in any organization. Also see Philip L. Hunsaker and Johanna S. Hunsaker, "Virtual Teams: A Leader's Guide," *Team Performance Management* 14, No. 1–2 (2008), pp. 86–101; Nancy R. Lockwood, "Global Virtual Teams," *SHRM Research* (August 2004).
30. See Jay Nunamaker; Bruce Reinig, and Robert Briggs, "Principles for Effective Virtual Teamwork," *Communications of the ACM Magazine*, 52, No. 6 (April 2009), pp. 113–117. See GlobalWorkplaceAnalytics.com/telecommuting_statistics for current telework statistics.
31. Unify (2013). *A New Way To Work*, No. 1 In Thought Leadership Series (2013), www.unify.com/NW2W.
32. See *SHRM 2013 Workplace Forecast Survey*, http://www.shrm.org/research/futureworkplacetrends/pages/topworkplacetrends2013.aspx. See also Bill Leonard, "Managing Virtual Teams," *HR Magazine*, 56, No. 6 (June 2011), pp. 38–42.
33. "Developing Successful Global Leaders," *Training Magazine* (May/June 2011), pp. 58–63. Also see, Ellen Toogood, *The Invisible Workforce* (Tampa, FL: AchieveGlobal, August 2011). You can review at article at www.achieveglobal.com.
34. See Hassan Osman, "The Ultimate List of Virtual Team Technology Tools," Couchmanager.com (May 21, 2013), http://www.thecouchmanager.com/2013/05/21/the-ultimate-list-of-virtual-team-technology-tools/.
35. Dominic M. Thomas, Robert P. Bostrom, and Marianne Gouge, "Making Knowledge Work in Virtual Teams," *Communications of the ACM* (November 2007), pp. 85–90.
36. Niki Panteli and Robert Tucker, "Power and Trust in Virtual Teams," *Communications of the ACM* 2, No. 12 (December 2009), pp. 113–115.
37. For more detailed discussion of the challenges virtual teams face, and strategies managers can use to help them succeed, see Wendy Combs and Stephanie Peacocke, "Leading Virtual Teams: How to Successfully Manage Virtual Team Productivity Online," *Training and Development (T&D)* (February 2007), pp. 27–28. Keith Dixon and Niki Panteli assert that technology-mediated interactions can complement face-to-face interactions and suggest that managers facilitate "virtual continuity" to mitigate the discontinuities found in virtual work environments, in "From Virtual Teams to Virtuality in Teams," *Human Relations* 63, No. 8 (August 2010), p. 1177.
38. Cari Turley, "Does Your CFO Know the Difference between Engagement and Morale?" Employee Success Blog (April 30, 2013), http://blog.achievers.com/2013/04/does-your-cfo-know-difference-between-engagement-and-morale/
39. Towers Watson *2012 Global Workforce Study*, available at the TowersWatson website, http://www.towerswatson.com/Insights/IC-Types/Survey-Research-Results/2012/07/2012-Towers-Watson-Global-Workforce-Study
40. The Gallup *State of the Global Workforce (2013)* report is one of a series of survey findings spanning from 1996 to 2012 chronicling the extent of employee engagement in businesses around the world. Gallup has collected engagement data from 25 million respondents from 2.8 million workgroups in 16 major industries in 195 countries around the world between 1996 and 2012, on which the above figures are based. The survey report is available for download at http://www.gallup.com/strategicconsulting/164735/state-global-workplace.aspx
41. The 2013 Towers Watson survey (see above) parallels the findings of the Gallup report. Towers Watson reports that 63 percent of workers are not engaged because of an unsupportive workplace and a lack of positive connections with their supervisors.
42. Ibid. See also Dov Seidman, "(Almost) Everything We Think about Employee Engagement Is Wrong"Forbes.com (September 9, 2012), http://www.forbes.com/sites/dovseidman/2012/09/20/everything-we-think-about-employee-engagement-is-wrong/
43. See "Building Team Resilience by Increasing Effectiveness" (December 2010) for a comprehensive definition of "low-value" work, which was found in a 2004 study to reduce worker morale and effectiveness and increase stress and work–life conflicts. Retrieved from the Ceridian Web site (http://www.ceridian.com/www/-content/10/12487/16991/17005/20101215_building_tea.htm).
44. Kathy Toogood, "Strengthening Coaching: An Exploration of the Mindset of Executive Coaches Using Strengths-Based Coaching," *International Journal of Evidence-Based Coaching and Mentoring* 6 (June 2012), pp. 72–87. See also Llewellyn E. Van Zyl and Marious W. Stander, "A Strengths-Based Approach toward Coaching in a Multicultural Environment," *Interdisciplinary Handbook of the Person-Centered Approach* (2013), pp. 245–257.
45. According to a survey of 470 companies across the United States and Canada, Mercer, "As Workforce Hiring Increases, Organizations Stay Focused on Employee Engagement" (October 2, 2012), http://www.mercer.com/press-releases/focused-on-engagement, found in its *2012 Attraction and Retention Survey* results related to employee engagement were similar to those of the Gallup (2013) and Towers Watson (2013) surveys.
46. Gallup, *State of the Global Workforce* (2013), Washington, DC: Gallup, pp. 38–48.
47. See Robert Ramsey, "Bad Times Are Good Times to Show Appreciation for Employees," *SuperVision* (November 2010), pp. 12–14. For a comprehensive source on how to develop and maintain a positive work environment, see Jim Harris, *Getting Employees to Fall in Love with Your Company* (New York: AMACOM, 1996).
48. See Stephen Miller's report "SHRM Asks: 'Is HR Outsourcing Here to Stay'"(January 2009) for the latest statistics on HR outsourcing as summarized from Watson Waytt's (2008) *Changing Strategies in HR Technology and Outsourcing* survey at the SHRM Web site (http://www.shrm.org/hrdisciplines/benefits/Articles/Pages/SHRMAsks%27IsHROutsourcingHeretoStay%27.aspx. Also see *AccountingWeb*,

"Survey Says Less than Half of Companies Consider Outsourcing to Be Cost Effective" (October 29, 2004) for details of the survey conducted by PricewaterhouseCoopers' Management Barometer Survey.

49. Sue Shellenbarger, "An Overlooked Toll of Job Upheavals: Valuable Friendships," *The Wall Street Journal* (January 12, 2000), p. B1; and Michael T. Brannick, *The Necessary Nature of Future Firms: Attributes of Survivors in a Changing World,* reviewed by Walter R. Nord, *Academy of Management Review* (October 2005), pp. 873–875.
50. Jacqueline Gish, "Taking Responsibility for Your Employees' Morale," *SuperVision* (May 2005), pp. 8–10; and Robert J. Grossman, "Damaged, Downsized Souls: How to Revitalize the Workplace," *HR Magazine* (May 1996), pp. 54–61.
51. The Gallup *State of the Global Workforce (2013)* report is one of a series of survey findings spanning from 1996 to 2012 chronicling the extent of employee engagement in businesses around the world. Gallup has collected engagement data from 25 million respondents from 2.8 million work groups in 16 major industries in 195 countries around the world between 1996 and 2012, on which the above figures are based. The survey report is available for download at http://www.gallup.com/strategicconsulting/164735/state-global-workplace.aspx
52. A 1999 Gallup Poll reported that 78 percent of U.S. citizens felt they needed to experience spiritual growth. See George Gallup Jr. and Tim Jones, *The Next American Spirituality* (Washington, DC: Gallup National Opinion Research Center, 2000); Chris Beakey, "Spirituality in Higher Education." Visit www.spirituality.ucla.edu for more recent data; Kent Rhodes, "Six Components of a Model for Workplace Spirituality," *Graziadio Business Report* (http://gbr .pepperdine.edu/062/workplace.html, retrieved September 1, 2008); Michelle Conlin, "Religion in the Workplace: The Growing Presence of Spirituality in Corporate America," *BusinessWeek* (November 1, 1999), pp. 153+; and Nancy K. Austin, "Does Spirituality at Work Work?" *Working Women* (March 1995), pp. 26–28.
53. Ben Cohen, co-founder of Ben & Jerry's Homemade Ice Cream Company with Jerry Greenfield, as quoted at a Babson College symposium. Also see, Frederica Saylor, "Businesses Benefit from a Low-Key Spirituality," www.northway.org (retrieved May 12, 2005), August 2008.
54. Cohen, ibid.
55. Kevin Kruse, "How Do You Measure Love (Or Employee Engagement)?" Forbes.com (July 14, 2013), http://www.forbes.com/sites/kevinkruse/2013/07/14/how-do-you-measure-engagement/. See also Kevin Kruse, *Employee Engagement 2.0: How to Motivate Your Team for High Performance* (2012), CreateSpace Independent Publishing Platform.
56. Lisa Horan, "6 Tips for Successfully Measuring Employee Engagement," Businessbee.com (2014), http://www.businessbee.com/resources/operations/6-tips-for-successfully-measuring-employee-engagement/
57. Verne Harnish, "A Better Way to Measure Employee Engagement," SmartCEO.com (January 2014), http://www.smartceo.com/better-measure-employee-engagement/. See also Kathryn Tyler, "Keeping Employees in the Net," *HR Magazine* (March 2013), pp. 55–57.
58. Two widely used engagement surveys are the Gallup G[12] Survey administered by Gallup (www.gallup.com), which asks employees to respond to twelve items, the responses to which group them into one of the three engagement categories and the Sirota Employment Survey, which is customized to the mission and sector of the organization. http://www.sirota.com/employee-engagement-surveys.
59. See Elaine McShulkis, "Employee Survey Sins," *HR Magazine* (May 1996), pp. 12–13. Many organizations choose to develop their own engagement surveys modeled after a tool they've found on the Internet or in a business strategy book. This practice, while convenient and inexpensive, is not recommended. Effective survey design requires specific knowledge that informs creating and testing questions to ensure they are appropriate, valid, and will measure what the organization intends to measure.
60. For a detailed explanation of OD, see Warren G. Bennis's classic, *Organizational Development: Its Nature, Origins, and Perspectives* (Reading, MA: Addison-Wesley, 1969). Also see Oleen Miranda-Stone and Michael C. Leary, "Organizational Development: Acting as One with the Business—Best Practices at Chevron Corporation," *Organizational Development Journal*, 25, No. 3 (Fall 2007), pp. 77–82; or Carol Pledger, "Building Manager Effectiveness by Combining Leadership Training and Organizational Development," *Organizational Development Journal* 25, No. 2 (Summer 2007), pp. 77–80.
61. The National Employment Counseling Association (NECA), a division of the American Counseling Association, provides employers with education and resource links related to employment and workforce counseling. Visit the NECA Web site at http://www.employmentcounseling .org. See Marianne Minor, *Coaching and Counseling: A Practice Guide for Managers* (Seattle, WA: Crisp Publications, 1989).
62. Local newspapers regularly list bankruptcies filed by individuals, families, and businesses. While these listings, like police reports, are often reviewed out of sheer curiosity, employers who scan them for workers' names can gain valuable insights into employee struggles outside of the workplace and be prepared for possible impacts on job performance and the need for counseling or other intervention.
63. Eligible employees covered under the Family and Medical Leave Act (FLMA) must be granted up to a total of twelve work weeks of unpaid leave during any twelve-month period for one or more of the following reasons: for the birth and care of a newborn child of the employee; for placement with the employee of a child for adoption or foster care; to care for an immediate family member (spouse, child, or parent) with a serious health condition; or to take medical leave when the employee is unable to work because of a serious health condition.

    The U.S. Department of Labor (DOL) updated the FMLA effective January 16, 2009. See the FMLA Web site (http://www.dol.gov/esa/whd/fmla/ndaa_fmla.htm) or FMLA Final Rule Web site (http://www.dol.gov/esa/whd/fmla).

    Also see James Thelen, "The New Bermuda Triangle: New Federal Disability and Leave Laws Become Infinitely More Complex, so Does Coordinating Compliance," *HR Magazine* (August 2010), pp. 85–88; Diane Cadrain, "A Leave Law That Just Won't Go Away," *HR Magazine* (July 2010), pp. 49–52; and Cadrain, "Noble Headache: The Family and Medical Leave Act Achieves a High Purpose—at a Price," *HR Magazine* (July 2008), pp. 54–59.
64. As reported in Diane Cadrain, "Helping Workers Fool Drug Tests Is a Big Business," *HR Magazine* (August 2005), pp. 29, 32. The Drug-Free Workplace Act of 1988 requires companies receiving $25,000 or more in federal government contracts to maintain a drug-free workplace, which includes establishing policies and conducting awareness programs to achieve this objective. See "Best Practices: How to Establish a Workplace Substance Abuse Program," U.S. Department of Labor Web site (http://www.dol.gov).

    Also visit the following Web sites:

    American Council on Drug Education (http://www.acde.org)

Center for Substance Abuse Prevention (http://www.drugfree-workplace.gov)

Drug-Free America Foundation (http://www.dfaf.org)

National Institute on Alcohol Abuse & Alcoholism (http://www.niaaa.nih.gov)

National Institute on Drug Abuse (http://www.nida.nih.gov)

65. Ibid.
66. Towers Watson Global Benefits Attitude Survey (GBAS) reached this conclusion by surveying over 5,000 U.S. workers in 2013. The survey found that stress, the number one risk factor (reported by 78% of respondents), has its roots in the lack of work–life balance, technologies that make workers available 24/7, inadequate staffing, unclear job expectations, and low pay increases, among others. The survey report is available at http://www.towerswatson.com/DownloadMedia.aspx?media=%7BF71EA970-260B-4CAB-A4C9-EA53BDAED77B%7D. The seven risk factors have dire consequences, as together they have forced the United States to near the bottom in rankings of many health areas including injuries and homicides, drug-related deaths, obesity and diabetes, heart disease, lung disease, and disability, according to the National Academy of Sciences report, "U.S. Health in International Perspective: Shorter Lives, Poorer Health" (January 2013), available at http://sites.nationalacademies.org/DBASSE/CPOP/US_Health_in_International_Perspective/index.htm.
67. See Dave Zielinski, "Help Employees Get Healthy," *HR Magazine* (July 2013), pp. 53–56.
68. One study found that 85 percent of surveyed companies offered wellness programs. See Susan J. Wells, "The Doctor Is In-House," *HR Magazine* (April 2006), pp. 38–54; Francis P. Alvarez and Michael J. Soltis, "Preventive Medicine: Employee Wellness Programs Are Prone to Legal Maladies That Require Careful Monitoring," *HR Magazine* (January 2006), pp. 105–109; "Here's to Your Health," *HR Focus* (January 1996), p. 18; and Paul L. Cerrato, "Employee Health: Not Just a Fringe Benefit," *Business and Health* (November 1995), pp. 21–26.
69. "Time Off from Work," *SHRM Home—Knowledge Center* (November 3, 2005). According to John Reh, "Sick Leave vs. PTO," *Your Guide to Management Newsletter—New York Times* (accessed November 3, 2005), "PTO invites abuse. Since a company no longer knows why an employee takes off, and officially doesn't care, employees are gone more frequently." However, Alexander Hamilton Institute's (AHI) 2008 Survey of Traditional Time Off (TTO) and PTO Program Practices stated that more than two-thirds (69%) of PTO users reported that, on average, an employee missed four workdays or fewer due to unscheduled absences each year versus only 57 percent for TTO users. Almost half of the PTO users indicated that the number of unscheduled absences dropped by more than 10 percent after converting to a PTO program. You should review the literature and determine whether PTO is appropriate for you and your organization.

Chapter

# 12 Performance Management

©Photographee.eu/Shutterstock.com

**After studying this chapter, you will be able to:**

1. Describe the roles and responsibilities of a supervisor in a system of performance management.
2. Summarize the management tasks required in the performance appraisal process and describe the purposes of a formal appraisal system.
3. Explain the factors, techniques, and challenges involved in measuring and documenting performance.
4. Discuss the process of conducting a sound appraisal meeting.
5. Give examples of coaching strategies that can be used as follow-up to performance appraisal.
6. Identify the benefits and challenges of a promotion-from-within policy.
7. Discuss the supervisor's role in employee compensation and outline the goals of an effective compensation program.

## YOU MAKE THE CALL!

*You are Rita Sheldon, manager of the customer service department for the Community Medical Center (CMC) Hospital in Angola. You started as a customer service rep 14 years ago and worked your way up to become manager four years ago. Because of the uncertainties in health care related to Obamacare and other factors, you are working harder and longer hours but still feel that your job is fulfilling and rewarding.*

You are preparing yourself for a meeting with Fred Young, an employee who reports to you. You are somewhat apprehensive about this meeting. Under the hospital's policies, performance evaluations are required every six months or as needed to ensure that employees can be the best they can be. Although the hospital has a performance appraisal form that must be used, the appraisal review form is left to the discretion of each manager to follow according to his or her own needs and preferences. Before this year, your approach was to fill out the appraisal form for each employee. You then would meet individually with each employee, show the employee the evaluation that had been made, and discuss the evaluation and suggest areas for improvement.

About three months ago, you attended a mandatory supervisory training program for all hospital supervisors. The seminar was conducted by a university professor hired by CMC to provide a new approach for doing performance evaluations. The professor advocated using a self-appraisal technique in which the employee was given an opportunity to evaluate himself or herself in advance of the meeting with the manager. The manager would then compare his or her evaluation with the employee's self-appraisal and then discuss the two with the employee. The professor shared research that had indicated that when employees are allowed to evaluate themselves, they tended to be more critical of themselves than their managers. According to the professor, with this approach, employees usually are more receptive to suggestions for improvement.

You have decided to try this approach with your employees. About a week ago, you sent several of your employees, including Fred Young, a copy of CMC's appraisal form and asked them to fill it out in order to evaluate their own job performance over the past six months. You asked them to send their evaluation form back to you a day or two before their scheduled performance appraisal meeting. Fred Young filled out an appraisal form for himself and gave it to you yesterday.

You were astounded to find out that Fred's self-ratings were much different from everyone else's. He had given himself a "superior" or "outstanding" rating in every category on the performance appraisal. Further, under the section entitled "Areas for Improvement," Fred Young had left this section entirely blank. You realized this was not the outcome you had hoped for, nor was it consistent with what the professor had stated in the training program. Your own personal appraisal of Fred Young is that his performance was certainly average at best, with several areas of serious deficiencies that needed improvement. He will be coming to your office this afternoon for his performance appraisal review. You wonder how you should handle this unexpected situation.

**Disclaimer:** The above scenario presents a supervisory situation based on real events to be used for educational purposes. The identities of some or all individuals, organizations, industries, and locations, as well as financial and other information may have been disguised to protect individual privacy and proprietary information. Fictional details may have been added to improve readability and interest.

YOU MAKE THE CALL!

## The Performance Management Process

**1 Describe the roles and responsibilities of a supervisor in a system of performance management.**

This section reintroduces some of the key concepts in understanding what causes people to behave the way they do. As stated throughout this text, *management* is the process of getting things accomplished with and through people by guiding and motivating their efforts toward common objectives. Clearly, people are an organization's most important assets and as such must be managed effectively to achieve organizational objectives. In previous chapters, we addressed the importance of effective communication, the ABCs of employee behavior, a participatory approach for setting measurable objectives, and various tips for ensuring employee success. In this chapter, we focus on the process of employee appraisal, but before we begin, let us look at how the concepts are related.

Professor Alan Cardy of Towson University has stated that "employers are interested in more than simply controlling behavior; they are looking to maximize employee productive performance that should in turn lead to better organizational performance" and the "bedrock ingredient to effective performance is a skilled and motivated worker."[1] Cardy asserts that a combination of effective executive leadership, organizational culture and infrastructure, appropriate human resources policies, and, most importantly, positive, engaging working conditions come together to build employee skills and motivation. Once an employee joins the work group, the task for supervisors becomes one of creating and maintaining conditions that will enhance employee SKAs. Ongoing communication with employees, along with various coaching and mentoring activities, are opportunities to provide information as well as feedback to employees about their job performance.

**System of performance management**
All those things a supervisor must do to enable an employee to achieve prescribed objectives

Our **system of performance management** (see Figure 12.1) identifies all those things a supervisor must do to enable an employee to achieve the organization's objectives. The system of performance management begins with the supervisor setting the stage for employee success.[2] While the system is presented in a detailed, straightforward form, we caution that no system survives without feedback and controls. To ensure that the necessary work is done, the supervisor must monitor performance regularly and provide support, guidance, and direction as needed.

**FIGURE 12.1 Performance management**

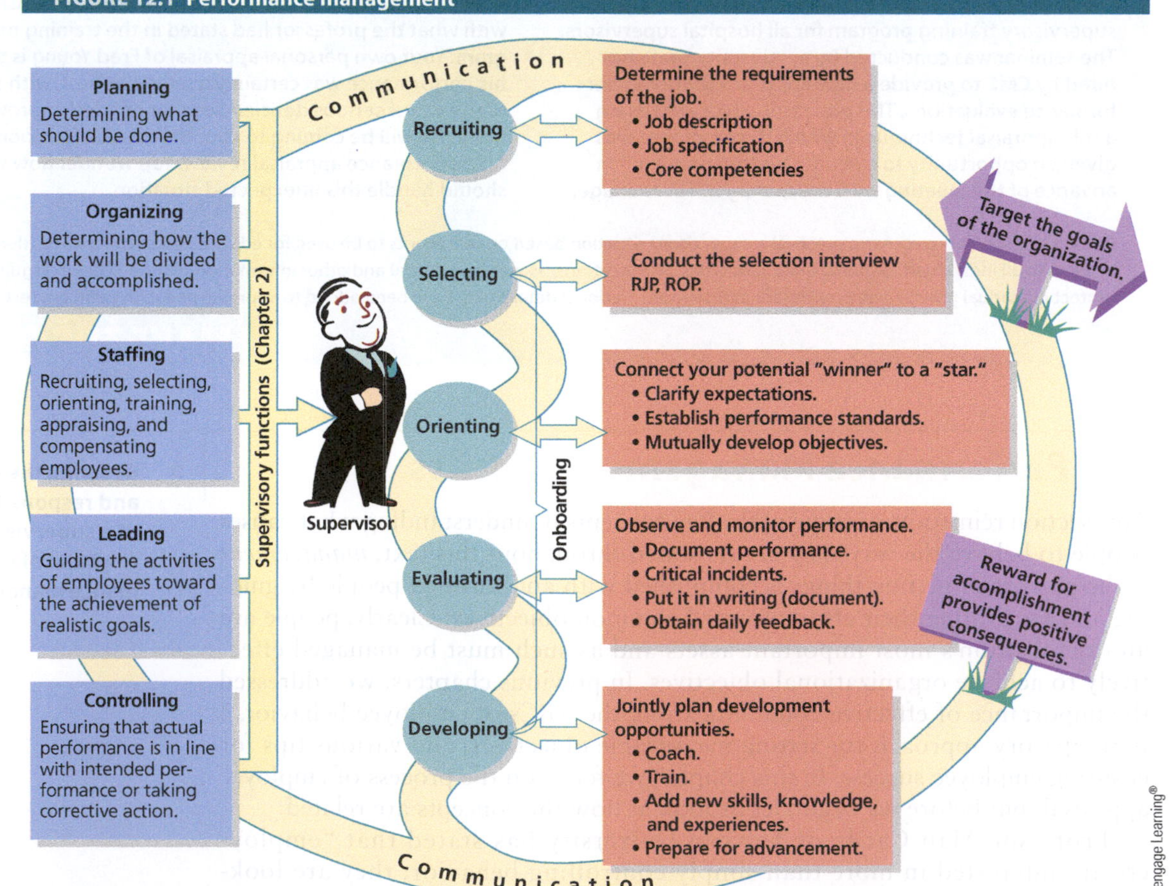
Communication
Planning
Determining what should be done.
Organizing
Determining how the work will be divided and accomplished.
Staffing
Recruiting, selecting, orienting, training, appraising, and compensating employees.
Leading
Guiding the activities of employees toward the achievement of realistic goals.
Controlling
Ensuring that actual performance is in line with intended performance or taking corrective action.
Supervisory functions (Chapter 2)
Supervisor
Recruiting
Selecting
Orienting
Evaluating
Developing
Onboarding
Determine the requirements of the job.
• Job description
• Job specification
• Core competencies
Conduct the selection interview
RJP, ROP.
Connect your potential "winner" to a "star."
• Clarify expectations.
• Establish performance standards.
• Mutually develop objectives.
Observe and monitor performance.
• Document performance.
• Critical incidents.
• Put it in writing (document).
• Obtain daily feedback.
Jointly plan development opportunities.
• Coach.
• Train.
• Add new skills, knowledge, and experiences.
• Prepare for advancement.
Target the goals of the organization.
Reward for accomplishment provides positive consequences.
Communication

## The Employee Performance Appraisal

From the time employees begin their employment with a firm, the supervisor is responsible for evaluating the employees' job performances. **Performance appraisal** is the systematic assessment of how well employees are performing their jobs and the communication of that assessment to them. As discussed in earlier chapters, supervisors establish performance standards or targets that subordinates are expected to achieve. Performance appraisal includes comparing the employee's performance with the standards. Often these standards may be referred to as metrics. For example, processing customer transactions with zero errors might be a metric for a bank teller. The metrics used should enable management to compare the employee's performance to others and how he or she contributes to the overall team success. Effective supervisors provide their subordinates with day-to-day feedback on performance. Regular feedback on performance is essential to improve employee performance and to provide the recognition that will motivate employees to sustain satisfactory performance (see Figure 12.2).

**Performance appraisal**
A systematic assessment of how well an employee is performing a job and the communication of that assessment

Most organizations require supervisors to evaluate their employees' performance formally. These evaluations become part of an employee's permanent record and play an important role in management's training, promotion, retention, and compensation decisions. Figure 12.3 summarizes the reasons for evaluating performance on a regular and systematic basis.

Supervisors should approach the appraisal process from the perspective that it is an extension of the planning, organizing, leading, and controlling functions. When employees understand what is expected of them and the criteria on which they will be evaluated, they will also believe the process is administered fairly and then that performance appraisal serves as a powerful motivational tool. While

**FIGURE 12.2 The effective supervisor avoids these comments by providing regular positive feedback on performance**

**FIGURE 12.3 Reasons for evaluating performance on a systematic basis**

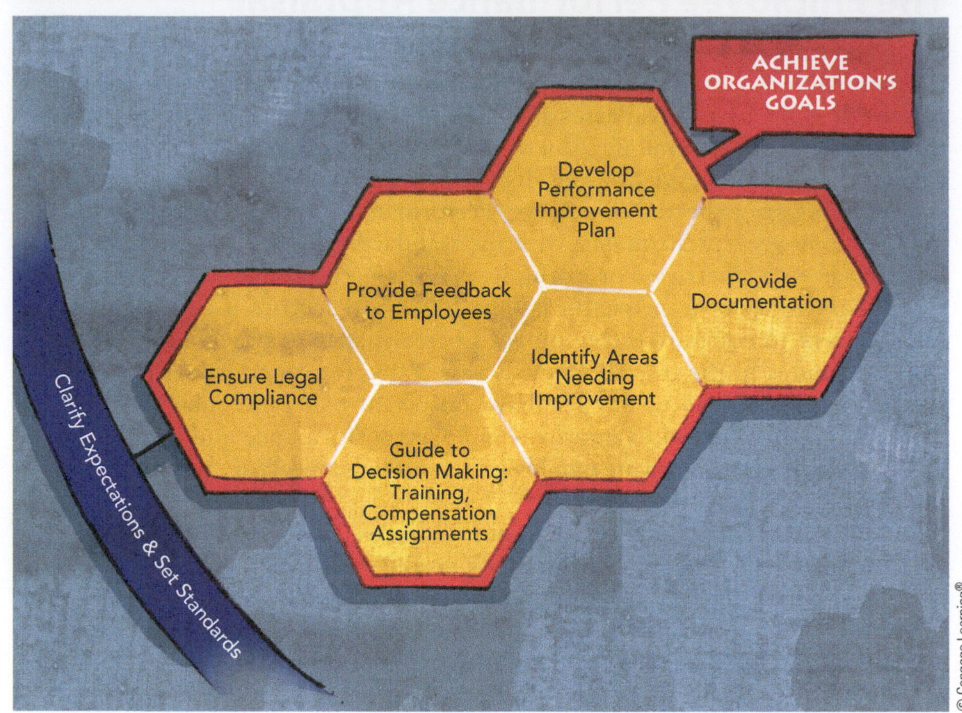




performance appraisals are frequently used to determine compensation, supervisors also use performance appraisals to provide feedback to employees so that they know where they stand and what they can do to improve their performance as well as to develop to their full potential.

The importance of documenting personnel decisions cannot be overemphasized. It is becoming increasingly important for organizations to maintain accurate records to protect themselves against possible charges of discrimination in connection with promotion, compensation, and termination.

While employee performance appraisal is a daily, ongoing aspect of the supervisor's job, the focus of this chapter is on the formal performance appraisal system. The purpose of the formal system is to evaluate, document, and communicate job achievements in understandable and objective terms, as well as secondary results of employee effort compared with job expectations. This is done by considering such factors as the job description, performance standards, specific objectives, and critical incidents for the evaluation period. The evaluation is based on direct observation of the employee's work over a set period.[3]

Clearly, the long-term success of an organization depends to a substantial degree on the performance of its workforce. We have learned that to get employees to work smarter, they first must know what is expected in the way of performance, and then they must receive regular feedback on their performance. Effective supervisors should subscribe to the notion that "[t]here is no substitute for daily feedback on performance." Unfortunately, some supervisors either fail to recognize performance problems or feel uncomfortable engaging employees in conversations about performance expectations and how to achieve those expectations. We contend that most employees want to know how well they have performed relative to the organization's expectations or performance standards. Generally, the supervisor should recognize and comment on a particular aspect of performance when that aspect occurs. The supervisor may glean this information from direct observation of the employee's work or from other sources. Because it is impossible for supervisors to observe everything employees do, they must rely on performance feedback from other sources—customers, peers, attendance records, production data, sales data, or customer feedback surveys.[4]

Regardless of the information source, it is essential that the information is reliable. Imagine, for example, that a percentage of your course grade is determined by your class participation. The instructor sometimes records attendance and sometimes does not. At the end of the course, the instructor uses attendance data to determine your participation grade. As luck would have it, the only three days you missed class during the term were among the days the instructor took attendance. Another student was rarely in attendance but was fortunate enough to be there on the days the instructor took attendance. Even though your test scores were similar, the other student received a higher grade than you did. Obviously, from your point of view, this method is not fair. The instructor can reduce the probability of a grade appeal in several ways, such as (1) by ensuring that students understand from the start of the course that attendance will be integral in determining their course grades and (2) by recording attendance regularly—that is, recording all absences. Many problems have occurred because some supervisors record performance data selectively.

## THE SUPERVISOR'S RESPONSIBILITY TO DO PERFORMANCE APPRAISALS

A performance appraisal should be done by an employee's immediate supervisor because the immediate supervisor is usually in the best position to observe and judge how well the employee has performed on the job. In some situations, a "consensus" or "pooled" appraisal may be done by a group of supervisors. For example, if an employee works for several supervisors because of rotating work-shift schedules or because the organization has a matrix structure, a consensus appraisal may be done. Some organizations have implemented work teams that expand the supervisor's span of control, and some have become leaner and have eliminated middle-level management positions. It is impractical for a supervisor to track the performance of twenty, thirty, or even fifty workers and evaluate their performance objectively. Consensus or pooled appraisals could lead to inequities in the performance appraisal system. To ensure that employees feel that the appraisal process is fair, each evaluator must understand what is needed for successful job performance and apply the standards uniformly. Performance improvement professor Mary Lanigan suggests three practices evaluators should follow in order to provide accurate representations of their assessments in reports to management:

1. Establish and clearly understand benchmarks for what constitutes optimal performance for all areas being evaluated—in other words, know what they are measuring.
2. Support the findings of evaluations with multiple sets of data rather than making generalizations from one or two comments.
3. Be impeccable with words, ensuring that evaluative comments accurately portray what was observed and reported.[5]

## PEER EVALUATIONS

**Peer evaluation**
The evaluation of an employee's performance by other employees of relatively equal rank

A **peer evaluation** is the evaluation of an employee's performance by other employees of relatively equal rank. Peers usually have close working relationships and know more than the supervisor about an individual's contributions. However, safeguards must be built in to ensure that peers are basing their evaluations on performance factors and not on bias, prejudice, or personality conflicts. Having an individual's performance evaluated anonymously by a team of peers is one way to encourage candid evaluation. To protect employees from prejudice or vendettas, the organization should establish an appeals mechanism to allow ratings review by upper-level managers.

Generally, employees work cooperatively to achieve common goals. Consider the situation in which members of work teams evaluate other team members' performance. On the one hand, because a peer rating system uses a number of independent judgments, peer evaluations can be more reliable than supervisory evaluations. On the other hand, when employees are forced to criticize their teammates via the performance appraisal system, their appraisals could have undesirable consequences for the cooperative culture and could defeat the purposes of teamwork. Imagine what could happen to morale and spirit among team members when one worker gets a low evaluation from an unknown co-worker and wonders who was responsible. To safeguard the peer rating process, supervisors can incorporate the input from all peers into one composite evaluation. Then, ratings that may be high due to friendship or low due to bias will cancel each other out. Safeguards that ensure confidentiality and minimize bias are critical to the effective use of peer evaluations.[6]

**360-degree evaluation**
Performance appraisal based on data collected from all around the employee—from customers, vendors, supervisors, peers, subordinates, and others

Increasing numbers of organizations are using a type of evaluation called a **360-degree evaluation**, which is based on evaluative feedback regarding the employee's performance collected from everyone around the employee—from customers, vendors, supervisors, peers, subordinates, and others. These 360-degree evaluations give employees feedback on their skills, knowledge, and abilities (SKAs) and on job-related effectiveness from sources that see different aspects of their work.[7] This approach gives employees a broader perspective of what they do well and where they need to improve.

## SELF-EVALUATIONS

Many effective supervisors find it appropriate to supplement their judgments with self-ratings from subordinates. About a week before the performance review, the employee is asked to conduct a self-evaluation. The supervisor compares the two evaluations to make sure to discuss all important performance specifics in the appraisal meeting. As mentioned previously, if the supervisor has provided ongoing feedback to the employee, the employee's self-ratings should be very close to the supervisor's ratings. However, research done at Cornell University revealed that self-appraisal is often inaccurate; top performers tend to rank their performance lower than it actually is, while less competent individuals tend to overestimate their skills and abilities.[8] Widely divergent ratings could mean that performance expectations are not clearly defined or supervisors are giving too little feedback throughout the year for the employees to have clear pictures of how well they are doing.

Regardless of the approach, the ultimate responsibility for completing the appraisal form and conducting the appraisal meeting lies with the immediate supervisor. If peer and self-evaluations are used, the supervisor still must reconcile the appraisals and communicate the information to the employee. The formal appraisal meeting usually takes place at a set time each year and should summarize what the supervisor has discussed with the employee throughout the year.

## Managing the Appraisal Process

**2 Summarize the management tasks required in the performance appraisal process and describe the purposes of a formal appraisal system**

As stated before, performance evaluation should be a normal part of the day-to-day relationship between a supervisor and employees. If an employee is given ongoing feedback, then the appraisal process should contain no surprises. The supervisor who communicates frequently with employees concerning how they are doing will find that engaging employees in formal appraisal is primarily a matter of reviewing much of what has been discussed during the year. Figure 12.4 illustrates how regular feedback, by removing uncertainty, can reduce the natural apprehension surrounding performance appraisals.

### TIMING PERFORMANCE APPRAISALS

Upper-level management decides who should appraise and how often. Most organizations require supervisors to formally appraise all employees at least once a year. Traditionally, this has been considered long enough to develop a reasonably accurate record of the employee's performance and short enough to provide current, useful information. However, if an employee has just started or if the employee has been transferred to a new and perhaps more responsible position, it is advisable to conduct an appraisal within the first couple of weeks.

**FIGURE 12.4 Regular feedback reduces the natural apprehension surrounding appraisals**

In an ideal world, the supervisor should meet with the new hire at the conclusion of his or her first day on the job. The purpose of this meeting is to review expectations, get input from the employee regarding "how his or her day went," provide feedback on performance, and coach and train as necessary. If the mind-set of the supervisor is such that *onboarding* is a continuous process to help new hires to reach their full potential and contribute to the department's objectives, then performance appraisal meetings should be scheduled on an as-needed basis.

For an employee who is new to the organization, the supervisor should do appraisals periodically during the employee's probationary period. This will fulfill the employee's need to know how he or she is doing. Ultimately, these appraisals will determine whether the employee will be retained. The performance evaluation of the probationary employee is critical. Employees are usually on their best behavior during the probationary period, and if their performance is less than acceptable, the organization should not make a long-term commitment to them.

After the probationary period, the timing of appraisals varies. In some organizations, appraisals are done on the anniversary of the date the employee started; in other organizations, appraisals are done once or twice a year on fixed dates. If an employee exhibits a serious performance problem during the evaluation period, the supervisor should schedule an immediate meeting with the employee. This meeting should be followed by another formal evaluation within a week to review the employee's progress. If the performance deficiency is severe, the supervisor should meet daily with the employee to completely document the performance deficiency and the supervisor's efforts to help the employee.

Ongoing feedback throughout the year, both positive and negative, rewards good performance and fosters improvement. Over time, ongoing feedback, as well as formal appraisals, can become an important influence on employee motivation and morale. Appraisals reaffirm the supervisor's genuine interest in employees' growth and development. Most employees would rather be told how they are doing—even if it involves some criticism—than receive no feedback from their supervisors.

## ADVANTAGES OF A FORMAL APPRAISAL SYSTEM

A formal appraisal system provides a framework to help the supervisor evaluate performance systematically. It forces the supervisor to scrutinize the work of employees from the standpoint of how well those employees are meeting established standards and to identify areas that need improvement.

Organizations that view their employees as long-term assets worthy of development adhere to the philosophy that all employees can improve their performance. Employees have the right to know how well they are doing and what they can do to improve. Most employees want to know what their supervisors think of their work. This desire can stem from different motives. For example, some employees realize they are doing relatively poor jobs, but they hope that their supervisors are not too critical and will help them improve their performance. Other employees feel that they are doing outstanding jobs and want to ensure that their supervisors recognize and appreciate their services.

Appraisals should become part of employees' permanent employment records. These appraisals serve as documents that are likely to be reviewed and even relied on in decisions concerning promotion, compensation, training, disciplinary action, and even termination. Performance appraisals can answer such questions as:

- Who should be promoted to department supervisor when the incumbent retires?
- Who should get merit raises this year?
- What should be the raise differential between employees?
- Who, if anyone, needs training?
- What training do employees need?
- This behavior has happened before. Does the employee need additional coaching, or is the behavior serious enough for disciplinary action?
- If an employee is appealing our termination decision, do we have adequate documentation to support the decision?

A formal appraisal system serves another important purpose: An employee's poor performance and failure to improve may be due in part to the supervisor's inadequate supervision. A formal appraisal system provides clues to the supervisor's own performance and may suggest where the supervisor must improve. Even when designed and implemented with the best intentions, performance appraisal systems are often sources of anxiety for the employee and the supervisor alike. Formal performance appraisal systems can be misused as disciplinary devices rather than as constructive feedback tools aimed at rewarding good performance and helping employees improve. As shown in Figure 12.5, not all supervisors fully understand the importance that performance appraisals play in employee morale. Why does Ralph have to leave his employees feeling bruised, desolate, dejected, or confused about their future with the organization? We would offer the following words of advice to him: "The purpose of the annual performance review is to direct employee attention to new targets."[9]

**FIGURE 12.5 Sally and her coworkers would wholeheartedly agree: Everyone is still doing annual performance reviews—but not the right way**

Sally, King Features Syndicate

3 **Explain the factors, techniques, and challenges involved in measuring and documenting performance.**

# The Performance Appraisal Process

Typically, a formal employee performance appraisal by a supervisor involves (a) completing a written appraisal form and (b) conducting an appraisal interview.

## COMPLETING AN APPRAISAL FORM

To facilitate the appraisal process and make it more uniform, most organizations use performance appraisal forms. There are numerous types of forms for employee evaluation. These forms are usually prepared by the HR department with input from employees and supervisors. Once the forms are in place, the HR department usually trains supervisors and employees in their proper use. Often, supervisors are responsible for informing new employees about the performance appraisal process as part of the onboarding process.

## FACTORS IN MEASURING PERFORMANCE

Most appraisal forms include factors that serve as criteria for measuring job performance, skills, knowledge, and abilities. Following are some of the factors that are most frequently included on employee appraisal rating forms:

- Job knowledge
- Timeliness of output
- Positive and negative effects of effort
- Suggestions and ideas generated
- Dependability (absenteeism, tardiness, work done on time)
- Safety
- Amount of supervision required (initiative)
- Aptitude
- Cooperation (effectiveness in dealing with others)
- Adaptability
- Ability to work with others
- Ability to learn
- Quantity and quality of work
- Effectiveness of resource use
- Customer service orientation
- Judgment
- Appearance

*Remember, regardless of the factors, performance appraisal criteria must relate to employees' jobs!* Factors that enable the supervisor to make objective performance evaluations rather than personality judgments should be used whenever possible. For each of these factors, the supervisor may be given a "check-the-box" choice or a place to fill in the employee's achievements. Some appraisal forms offer a series of descriptive sentences, phrases, or adjectives to help the supervisor understand how to judge the rating factors. Generally, the "check-the-box" forms are somewhat easier and less time-consuming for supervisors to complete. Ideally, the supervisor should write a narrative to justify the evaluation. There should be no shortcuts to performance appraisal. Supervisors should give it as much time as it needs.

Typically, the supervisor reads each item and checks the appropriate box. The supervisor identifies the outstanding aspects of the employee's work as well as

FIGURE 12.6 Begin with a blank sheet of paper and answer these questions

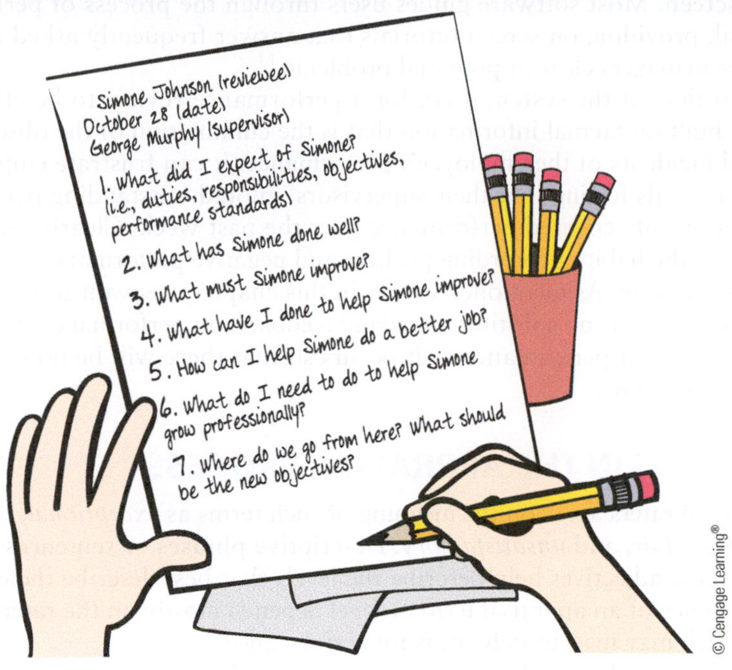
Simone Johnson (reviewee)
October 28 (date)
George Murphy (supervisor)
1. What did I expect of Simone? (i.e., duties, responsibilities, objectives, performance standards)
2. What has Simone done well?
3. What must Simone improve?
4. What have I done to help Simone improve?
5. How can I help Simone do a better job?
6. What do I need to do to help Simone grow professionally?
7. Where do we go from here? What should be the new objectives?
© Cengage Learning®

specific performance characteristics that need improvement (weaknesses) and suggests several things that might be done to improve performance. Most forms provide space for additional comments about the various aspects of an employee's performance. Many organizations continue to search for the "one best form." Unfortunately, one does not exist.[10] One of the authors preferred that supervisors (evaluators) start with a blank sheet of paper. See Figure 12.6 for how to use a blank sheet of paper to ask questions and record vital information related to an employee's performance.

If the system calls for employee self-appraisal, the employee's form is usually identical to the regular appraisal form except that it is labeled as a self-appraisal. Self-appraisals give employees an opportunity to think about their achievements and prepare for the appraisal meeting.[11]

## PERFORMANCE APPRAISAL SOFTWARE

"Point and click" has become a way of life for many people. Various vendors have developed software that allows supervisors to move beyond the often cumbersome paper-based performance appraisal process. A majority of performance appraisal software applications are integrated with or are part of a comprehensive human resource management package. In most situations in which such software is used, human resource managers work with supervisors to identify the features and functions needed in the software, then the supervisors inform HR of the specific SKAs they would like included in the appraisal form.[12]

On some performance appraisal forms, the supervisor can choose from the list of factors for a given job (e.g., personal efficiency, job knowledge, judgment). Software can weight each factor according to its importance to the employee's job. Then, to determine whether the employee has met, exceeded, or failed to meet the performance standard, the supervisor can rate statements that appear on the screen. Most software guides users through the process of performance appraisal, providing on-screen tutorials that answer frequently asked questions and steer managers clear of potential problems.[13]

Regardless of the system used, for a performance review to be effective, it must be built on factual information that is the culmination of the observed and reported incidents of the employee's performance. It can frustrate employees to leave appraisals feeling that their supervisors ignored outstanding performance incidents or only covered performance over the past week. Clearly, supervisors must get in the habit of recording positive and negative performance information as incidents occur. As mentioned earlier in this chapter, we want to reinforce the notion that there is no substitute for daily feedback on performance. Supervisors should document performance as it occurs so that there will be no surprises at annual review time.

## PROBLEMS IN THE APPRAISAL PROCESS

First, not all raters agree on the meaning of such terms as *exceptional, very good, satisfactory, fair*, and *unsatisfactory*. Descriptive phrases or sentences added to each of these adjectives help describe the levels that best describe the employee, but the choice of an appraisal term or level depends mostly on the rater's perceptions, which may inaccurately measure performance.

Another problem is that one supervisor may be more severe than another in the appraisal of employees. A supervisor who gives lower ratings than other supervisors for the same performance is likely to damage the morale of employees, who may feel they have been judged unfairly. One such supervisor stated that because no one is perfect, no one should ever be evaluated as above average. Another supervisor felt that if he rated his employees too high, those employees would be considered for promotions elsewhere in the organization and would be lost to his department. As a result, this supervisor rated his employees much lower than was fair. In the long run, the supervisor lost the employees' trust and respect or lost them to other firms.

**Leniency error**
Error that occurs when supervisors give employees higher ratings than they deserve

In contrast to this supervisor, some supervisors tend to be overly generous or lenient in their ratings.[14] The **leniency error** occurs when supervisors give employees higher ratings than they deserve. Some supervisors give high ratings because they believe that poor evaluations may reflect negatively on their own performance, suggesting that they have been unable to elicit good performance from their employees. Other supervisors do not give low ratings because they are afraid that they will antagonize their employees and make them less cooperative. Some supervisors are so eager to be liked by their employees that they give out only high ratings, even when such ratings are undeserved.

In addition to leniency errors, supervisors should be aware of the problems of the halo effect and the horns effect (described in Chapter 10), each of which causes a rating in one factor to inspire similar ratings in other factors. One way to avoid the halo or horns effect is for the supervisor to rate all employees on only one factor and then proceed to the next factor for all employees. This suggestion only works, however, if the supervisor is rating several employees at once. If that is not the case, the supervisor should pause and ask, "How does this employee compare on this factor with other employees?" For each factor, the supervisor must rate each employee relative to a standard or to another employee.

The above examples of errors that can be made in assessing performance are examples of **rater bias**, the influence our unconscious thinking processes can have on the decisions and judgments we make. Rater bias can substantially affect the ways in which supervisors evaluate employees' work. The supervisor's values, stereotypes, experiences, culture, background, personality differences with individual workers, understanding of the assessment process, or even simply being distracted can affect how he or she assesses individual employee performance. The supervisor's resulting biases can negatively impact the fairness and equity of performance assessment. Performance management consultant Leslie Traub instructs managers to "recognize any potential bias well before the review process begins. Recognizing our biases and their power over our decision making gives us the opportunity to pause, question and reassess our decisions so we may strive for objectivity".[15]Figure 12.7 provides strategies supervisors should take into consideration to reduce bias in the assessment process.

**Rater bias**
The influence unconscious thinking processes have on an individual's decisions and judgments.

The supervisor should ask what conditions exist when the job is done well. These conditions, called **performance standards**, are the job-related requirements by which the employee's performance will be evaluated. They should be described in terms of *how much, how well, when*, and *in what manner*. Effectiveness and efficiency measures are part of these standards. The positive and negative effects of performance also should be considered. Consider, for example, the most prolific salesperson in a store, whose product knowledge and selling ability are second to none. However, this salesperson always expects the cashiers to enter his sales first. The cashiers are frustrated, and the other salespeople are not as able to give good service. In addition, this salesperson always has the stockroom personnel running errands for him. This salesperson receives accolades on selling, but every one of his sales is a rush project, and others are expected to

**Performance standards**
The job-related requirements by which the employee's performance is evaluated

**FIGURE 12.7 Strategies for preventing bias when assessing employee performance**

- Know your biases and identify them before the review begins.
- When soliciting input from others about an individual's review, such as when using peer or 360 degree assessment, explore views that are opposite from your own. Adopt an open mind rather than dismissing opposing views.
- Check your assumptions prior to the performance appraisal meeting, especially those concerning work style and other differences.
- Give performance reviews the time and importance they deserve. Haste and distraction can negatively impact the assessment process.
- Be conscious of potential cultural or gender differences in self-ratings and look for accurate means of comparing accomplishments.
- Understand that employees can both overrate and underrate, and both can be damaging. Help employees use objective performance data to rate their performance.
- If ratings are weighted, have clear and transparent rating and weighting processes.
- Be conscious of informal groups and each group's dominance in the organization, avoiding bias toward one group over another.
- Create clear norms for decision-making that mitigate power dynamics.

Adapted from Leslie Traub, *Bias in Performance Management Review Process: Creating an Inclusive Talent Pipeline by Understanding Our Filters* (Silver Spring, MD: Cook Ross, Inc., 2013). This resource is available for download from Cook Ross, Inc., http://www.cookross.com/docs/unconsciousbiasinperformance2013.pdf

juggle their schedules to accommodate him. While this salesperson is proficient in the process of getting his job done, he negatively impacts the organization. His supervisor must broaden the performance standards to include more than product knowledge and selling.

To reiterate, every appraisal should be made in the context of each employee's job, and every rating should be based on the employee's total performance. It would be unfair to appraise an employee based on one assignment that had been done recently, done particularly well, or done very poorly. The appraisal should be based on an employee's total record for the appraisal period. All relevant factors must be considered. Moreover, the supervisor must continuously strive to exclude personal biases for or against individuals because they can be serious appraisal pitfalls.

Although performance appraisal results are by no means perfect, they can be objective and positive forces influencing employee performance.

**4 Discuss the process of conducting a sound performance appraisal meeting.**

## The Appraisal Meeting

The second major part of the appraisal process is the evaluation or appraisal meeting. After supervisors complete the rating form, they arrange to meet with employees to review the employees' ratings. Because these meetings are the most vital part of the appraisal process, the supervisor should develop a general plan for carrying out appraisal discussions. When handled poorly, appraisal meetings can lead to considerable resentment and misunderstanding. The conflict that develops may be irreparable.

### THE RIGHT PURPOSES

The primary purposes of appraisal meetings are to let employees know how they are doing and help them set goals for future performance. In the interest of maintaining employees' productive behaviors, supervisors formally praise employees for their past and current good performance. Supervisors also use appraisal meetings to help employees develop good future performance. Emphasizing the strengths on which employees can build supports employees' career plans. Supervisors can explain the opportunities for growth in the organization and can encourage employees to develop needed skills. Finally, supervisors use appraisal meetings to explain behavior that needs to be corrected and the need for improvement. Even when improvement is needed, supervisors should take the approach that they believe the employee can improve and that they will do everything possible to help. It is important that supervisors conduct appraisal meetings for the right purpose.

### THE RIGHT TIME AND PLACE

Appraisal meetings should be held shortly after the performance rating process has been completed, preferably in a private setting. To enable employees to prepare for their appraisal meetings and to consider what they would like to discuss, supervisors should make appointments with employees several days in advance. Privacy and confidentiality of the appraisal meeting should be ensured because this discussion could include criticisms, personal feelings, and opinions.

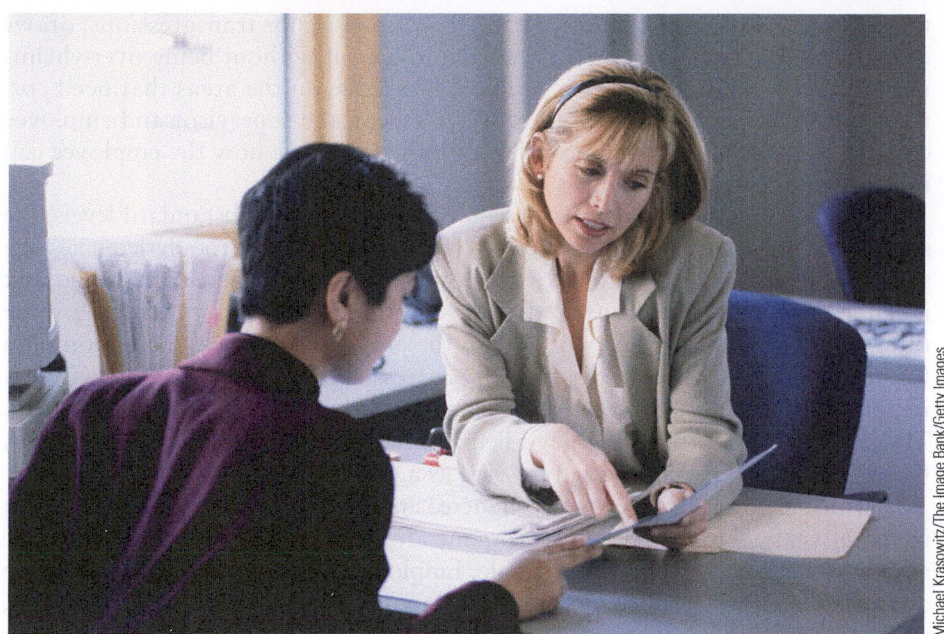


*At appraisal meetings, supervisors emphasize employees$ strengths to help them improve performance*

It is a good idea for the supervisor to complete the official rating form by compiling and summarizing all assessment data several days before the meeting and then review it a day or two before the meeting to analyze it objectively and to ensure that it accurately reflects the employee's performance.

## CONDUCTING THE APPRAISAL MEETING

Most of the interviewing discussion in Chapter 10 applies to the appraisal meeting. While appraisal meetings tend to be directive, they can take on nondirective characteristics because employees may bring up issues that supervisors did not expect or of which they were unaware. It is easy for most supervisors to communicate the positive aspects of job performance, but it is difficult to communicate major criticisms without generating resentment and defensiveness. There is a limit to how much criticism an individual can absorb in one session. If there is a lot of criticism to impart, dividing the appraisal meeting into several sessions may ease the stress.

The manner in which the supervisor conducts the appraisal meeting influences how the employee reacts. After a brief, informal opening, the supervisor should state that the purpose of the meeting is to assess the employee's performance in objective terms. During this warm-up period, the supervisor should state that the purpose of the performance appraisal is to recognize the employee for his or her achievements, to help the employee improve, if necessary, and to set goals for future performance. The supervisor should review the employee's achievements during the review period, compliment the employee on those accomplishments, identify the employee's strengths, and then proceed to the areas that need improvement. A secret of success is to get the employee to agree on his or her strengths first because it is easier to build on strengths than weaknesses. Unfortunately, not every employee performs at the expected level. Limiting criticism to just one or two major points, rather than to all minor transgressions, draws attention to the major areas that need improvement without being overwhelming. The supervisor must get the employee to agree on the areas that need correction or improvement. When there is agreement, the supervisor and employee can use a problem-solving approach to jointly determine how the employee can improve performance.

When dealing with an employee who is performing at substandard levels, the supervisor must clearly communicate to the employee that the deficiencies are serious and that substantial improvement must be made. Supervisors should mix in some positive observations so that the employees know they are doing some things right. The supervisor works with the employee to create an action plan for improvement with expectations and progress checkpoints along the way. It is important that the employee leaves the meeting feeling able to meet expectations. The supervisor must be available to help, assist, coach, and advise the employee. Often, a co-worker will be asked to serve as a coach or trainer.

Performance appraisals have been increasingly scrutinized by the legal system in recent years.[16] It is essential that organizations ensure that their performance appraisal systems are legally defensible. Employees often disagree with negative aspects of the performance appraisal because the ratings later affect their jobs, specifically their compensation and potential for promotion. The supervisor must be certain that each employee fully understands the standards of performance that serve as the basis for appraisal. Also, the appraisal must accurately represent the employee's performance and must be free of bias. The employee must know that the review is fair, is based on job-performance factors, and is supported by proper documentation.[17]

Most mature employees are able to handle deserved, fair criticism. It is important, therefore, for the supervisor to provide authentic and specific feedback comments, which is sometimes easier said than done. Harvard Law School lecturers Douglas Stone and Sheila Heen cite research that 63 percent of executives report "their managers lack courage to have the difficult performance discussions."[18] By the same token, those who merit praise want to hear it, and again the supervisor should be authentic and specific. In both cases, the conversation should be clear and concise with the goal of making sure that the employee understands the full meaning of the information being provided. Figure 12.8 includes suggestions for relieving the uncertainty of the performance appraisal process through preparation.

During the appraisal meeting, the supervisor should emphasize that everybody in the same job in the same department is evaluated using the same standards. The supervisor must be prepared to support or document ratings by citing specific illustrations and instances of good or poor performance. In particular, the supervisor should indicate how the employee performed or behaved in certain situations that were especially crucial or significant to the performance of the department or achievement of organizational objectives. This is sometimes called the **critical incident method**. To use this method, the supervisor must keep a file of notes describing situations in which employees performed in an outstanding fashion or situations in which their work was clearly unsatisfactory. An example of a positive critical incident would be the following: "Shortly before closing on October 22, an employee realized that a customer had received an item of lesser value than she had paid for. The employee called the customer to verify that a mistake had been made, apologized for the error, and offered

**Critical incident method**
Supervisors record specific examples of outstanding and below-average performance on the part of each employee

**FIGURE 12.8 Comprehensive performance appraisal checklist**

***Supervisors are trained in the performance appraisal system***

- The forms
- Use of job standards
- Timing of appraisal
- Monitoring employee progress
- Contracting for performance improvement
- Using developmental methods and action plans
- Providing feedback
- Rating scales and dimensions
- Linkages with personnel decisions
- Objective performance assessment
- Documentation
- Interviewing techniques
- Rewarding performance
- Both the supervisor and the employee understand the purpose of the appraisal process.

***The supervisor clarifies employee expectations through a job description that lists duties and responsibilities.***

- An updated job description serves as the foundation for the appraisal.
- The supervisor makes the employee aware of performance standards and specific areas of accountability.
- The supervisor provides ongoing feedback on performance. Remember: *There is no substitute for daily feedback on performance!*
- The supervisor gives at least one official performance appraisal per year—within the first thirty workdays for new employees or transfers and as required for problem employees.
- As soon as a performance problem is observed, the supervisor works with the employee to try to determine the cause of the problem and corrective action.
- The supervisor keeps a regular record of all unusual behavior—a critical incident file.
- The supervisor schedules the appraisal meeting several days in advance.
- The supervisor puts the employee at ease at the beginning of the appraisal meeting.
- The supervisor allows the employee to engage in self-evaluation. (The supervisor may ask the employee to complete the evaluation form.)
- The supervisor reviews the written appraisal with the employee, stating both standards and/or objectives met and not met.
- The supervisor criticizes performance, not the person, and tells the employee specifically what he or she did wrong.
- The supervisor objectively emphasizes work behaviors rather than personal traits (the O of OUCH).
- The supervisor provides positive as well as negative feedback.
- The supervisor uses specific examples to illustrate the employee's accomplishments. (The employee knows that the supervisor is using factual information that is well-documented.)
- The supervisor asks probing questions to get additional information and to seek clarification of misunderstandings or views that differ. This gives the employee an opportunity to bring forth mitigating circumstances or to discuss items of interest or concern (e.g., "What is my opportunity for advancement or specialized training?").
- The supervisor summarizes the discussion and overall rating.
- The supervisor allows the employee to summarize the interview in his or her own words.
- The employee knows that the organization has an audit procedure to review the supervisor's appraisal decisions in the event of disagreement; that is, the decision is audited to ensure that feedback is related to job performance (the H of OUCH).
- Personnel decisions are made consistent with the written results of the appraisal (the C of OUCH).
- The system is periodically reviewed to ensure that there is uniformity throughout the organization and that protected classes are not adversely impacted by the performance appraisal system (the U of OUCH).
- Performance ratings are linked to organizational objectives.

to either credit the customer's account or send the correct item and a prepaid return envelope to the customer in order to process an exchange. The exchange was completed through U.S. mail without incident. Identification and correction of the problem enabled the store to maintain customer confidence and to develop a system to prevent recurrence." When the critical incident method is used, employees know that the supervisor has a factual record on which to assess performance.

If the supervisor chooses to use the employee self-rating approach mentioned earlier, the discussion primarily centers on the differences between the employee's self-ratings and those of the supervisor. These differences may involve considerable back-and-forth discussion, especially if there are major differences of opinion regarding various parts of the appraisal form. Typically, this is not a major difficulty unless employees have exaggerated notions of their abilities or feel that the supervisor's ratings were unjustified. The impact of downsizing and a tight job market may lead to greater disagreement over performance appraisal if there are now more people competing for fewer jobs. Conflict is particularly likely when employees perceive that the supervisor's appraisal may jeopardize their jobs.

Regardless of how supervisors approach the appraisal meeting, they must include a discussion about plans for improvement and possible opportunities for the employee's future. The supervisor should mention any educational or training plans that may be available. The supervisor should be familiar with advancement opportunities open to employees, requirements of future jobs, and each employee's personal ambitions and qualifications. When discussing the future, the supervisor should be careful to make no promises for training or promotion that are uncertain to materialize in the foreseeable future. False promises are a quick way to lose credibility.

The evaluation meeting also should give the employee an opportunity to ask questions, and the supervisor should answer those questions as fully as possible. When the supervisor is uncertain about an answer, it is better to say, "I don't know, but I'll find out and get back to you with an answer tomorrow." Employees lose trust in supervisors who evade subjects, are dishonest, and fail to return with answers in a timely fashion. In the final analysis, the value of an evaluation meeting depends on the employee's ability to recognize the need for self-improvement and the supervisor's ability to stimulate in the employee a desire to improve and facilitate opportunities for improvement, actions that together help build employee engagement. It takes sensitivity and skill for a supervisor to accomplish these outcomes, and it is frequently necessary for the supervisor to adapt to each employee's reactions as they surface during the meeting.

In the previous paragraph, we discussed things that might be described as "must do things." Every performance evaluation will be different for every supervisor, and some will bring unexpected issues and challenges for the supervisor. With regard to the chapter-opening You Make the Call! Rita had to prepare for an appraisal meeting with an employee who clearly overestimated his performance and did not recognize any need for self-improvement. How can a supervisor help an employee grow if, during his one yearly opportunity to reflect on his performance, the employee reports that he is already at the top of the chart? This critical incident brings to light the importance of viewing the performance assessment meeting as just one facet of performance management, one that must be part of an ongoing conversation between supervisors and employees about performance.

## CLOSING THE APPRAISAL MEETING

When closing the appraisal meeting, the supervisor should be certain that employees clearly understand their performance ratings. In situations in which an employee's performance needs improvement, the supervisor and employee should agree on some mutual skill-building goals. When employees who are performing at a high level express the desire for more challenge or additional responsibilities during the appraisal meeting, the supervisor can use the opportunity to gather information on the employee's interests and aspirations and, where appropriate, work with the employee to set stretch goals to accommodate those requests and advance the work of the department.[19] If there are presently no such opportunities, the supervisor should communicate that clearly and let the employee know that information will be provided when and if opportunities become available. Returning to the discussion of employee engagement in Chapter 11, ultimately it is the direct supervisor's responsibility to continually help employees assess and maximize their strengths. The performance appraisal meeting is the perfect venue in which to facilitate this process. After setting SMART (specific, measurable, attainable, realistic and time-limited) goals, the supervisor should set a date with the employee, perhaps in a few weeks, to discuss progress toward the new goals. This reinforces the supervisor's stated intent to help the employee improve and gives the supervisor an opportunity to praise the employee for progress.

Many organizations ask that employees sign their performance appraisal forms after the meetings. If a signature is requested as proof that the supervisor held the appraisal meeting, the supervisor should so inform the employee. The supervisor should ensure that the employee understands that signing the form does not necessarily indicate agreement with the ratings on the form. Otherwise, the employee may be reluctant to sign the form, especially if the employee disagrees with some of the contents of the appraisal. Some appraisal forms have a line above or below the employee's signature stating that the signature only confirms that the appraisal meeting has taken place and that the employee does not necessarily agree or disagree with any statements made during the appraisal.

Some organizations require supervisors to discuss employee appraisals with managers or the HR department before they place the appraisal documents in individuals' permanent employment records. A supervisor may be challenged to justify certain ratings if, for example, the supervisor has given very high or very low evaluations to most departmental employees. For the most part, if the supervisor has appraised employees carefully and conscientiously, such challenges will be infrequent.

Many organizations have an audit or a review process to review supervisors' appraisal decisions. The purposes of this audit are to ensure that evaluations are done fairly and to give employees a means of resolving conflicts arising from the appraisal process.

With or without a formal appraisal system, supervisors must provide regular feedback on performance. Most employees want to know how they are doing. We have known a few bosses who believe that "No news is good news. If I'm not yelling at you, then you're doing a good job." Supervisors are obligated to provide regular feedback on performance. See the accompanying Supervisory Tips box for some practical suggestions on appraising performance.

## SUPERVISORY TIPS

### Practical Suggestions for Improving Employee Performance

The Supervisory Challenge:

*Good, better, best, never let it rest, until your good is better, and your better is the very best!*

- Let people know what is expected of them in the way of performance.
- Set clear and high goals and clarify performance standards.
- Find out what you can do to help the employee do the job.
- Supervise and coach employees so that they can succeed.
- Find out what people perceive as desirable consequences for good performance.
- Observe performance and record observations.
- Catch people doing something right and provide desirable consequences.
- Give timely feedback on performance and help the employee improve.
- Do not make good performance extinct by ignoring it.
- Thoroughly document employee performance; keep a list of critical incidents.
- Tie employee development to organizational goals. Be a coach.
- Encourage employee participation in the appraisal and development process.
- Take responsibility for soliciting feedback about your own performance.
- Remember: *There is no substitute for daily performance feedback.*

**5 Give examples of coaching strategies that can be used as follow-up to performance appraisal.**

**Coaching**
The frequent activity of the supervisor to give employees information, instruction, and suggestions relating to their job assignments and performance

## Managing Performance Appraisal Results: Coaching Employees

Effective supervisors use periodic performance evaluations as a way to develop their employees' competence. **Coaching**, a frequent supervisor activity, gives employees information, instructions, and suggestions relating to their job assignments and performance. In addition to being a coach, the supervisor should be a cheerleader and a facilitator who guides employee behaviors toward desired results. If you want your people to be high performers (winners), then you need to help them get there (coach).[20] As a coach, the supervisor must identify activities that prepare employees for greater depth and breadth in their current or future jobs, reinforce employees' positive behaviors, and correct negative behaviors positively. In addition, by coaching, the supervisor can inspire employees toward a shared vision and remove barriers along the way.

The supervisor's follow-up role in performance appraisal varies with the assessment. As a rule, supervisors use coaching to help superior employees prepare for greater responsibility as well as to improve the performance of all employees. In both cases, the purpose of coaching is to help employees become more productive by developing action plans. Even though a plan may be jointly determined with the employee, the supervisor is ultimately responsible for providing the plan and the instructions for carrying it out. The questions in Figure 12.9 may serve as guidelines for the supervisor's coaching effort.

Effective supervisors recognize that ongoing employee skill development is critical to the organization's success. Instruction, practice, and feedback are

**FIGURE 12.9 Questions to determine coaching strategies**

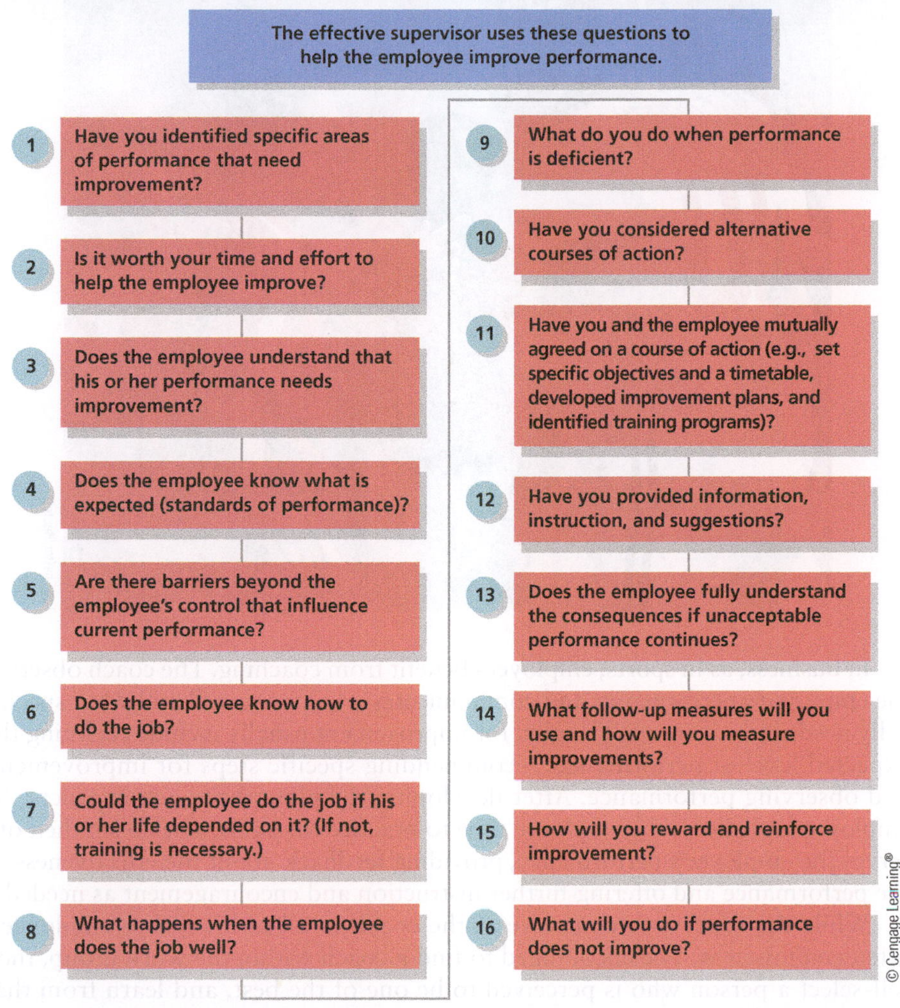




essential elements of development. Imagine playing in a football tournament game without first receiving instruction and having a chance to practice throwing, catching, blocking, and running plays. Many football players start playing in their neighborhoods as kids, but they seek the guidance of a coach and the structure of a team because they want to achieve a goal—winning against real opponents in games that matter. However, Alabama Crimson Tide coach Nick Saban would tell you that preparation, hard work, and doing the right things right all the time, not just winning, are the marks of a championship team. Saban, five-time National Coach of the Year who has coached teams to four NCAA championships and brought three Alabama teams to visit the White House after their victories, coaches players using what he calls the process, a clear set of expectations for performance and conduct, and he and his staff invest nearly every waking hour guiding the athletes through highly disciplined drills and exercises so they can execute the right things right, all the time.[21] While the Tide players are gifted with fundamental ability, they continually look to their coach for support, wisdom, and guidance.

The effective supervisor uses these questions to help the employee improve performance.
1 Have you identified specific areas of performance that need improvement?
2 Is it worth your time and effort to help the employee improve?
3 Does the employee understand that his or her performance needs improvement?
4 Does the employee know what is expected (standards of performance)?
5 Are there barriers beyond the employee's control that influence current performance?
6 Does the employee know how to do the job?
7 Could the employee do the job if his or her life depended on it? (If not, training is necessary.)
8 What happens when the employee does the job well?
9 What do you do when performance is deficient?
10 Have you considered alternative courses of action?
11 Have you and the employee mutually agreed on a course of action (e.g., set specific objectives and a timetable, developed improvement plans, and identified training programs)?
12 Have you provided information, instruction, and suggestions?
13 Does the employee fully understand the consequences if unacceptable performance continues?
14 What follow-up measures will you use and how will you measure improvements?
15 How will you reward and reinforce improvement?
16 What will you do if performance does not improve?

*Effective coaches use a variety of tactics to motivate individuals and teams*

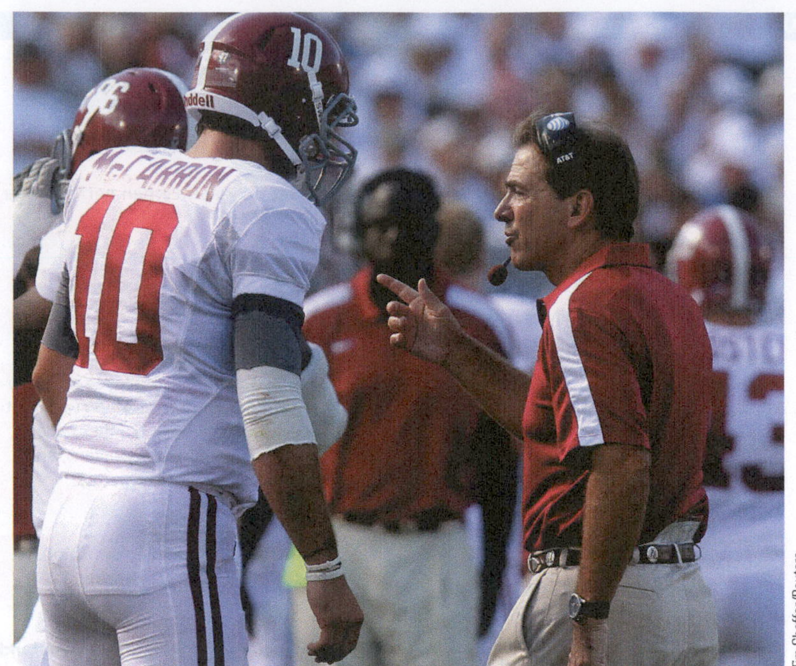

Tim Shaffer/Reuters

In business, as in sports, employees benefit from coaching. The coach observes the employee's performance and communicates what went well and what specifically needs improvement. The plan for improvement usually includes defining the expected level of performance, recommending specific steps for improvement, and observing performance. After developing the plan, the coach instructs the employee and allows the employee time to practice the skills. The coach then observes the employee's performance, providing feedback about the effectiveness of the performance and offering further instruction and encouragement as needed.

While the supervisor can serve as the coach to all of his or her employees, often employees will be encouraged to find a coach within the work group, then self-select a person who is perceived to be one of the best, and learn from that person. Consider again the Crimson Tide football team—the athletes who signed in 2014 to play for Saban comprised a recruiting class that was ranked first in the nation by ESPN, 247Sports, Rival.com, and Scout.[22] The best athletes in the nation chose to play for the best coach so they could experience "the process" and continue to learn, grow, and, of course, win.

Generally, though, the employees who benefit most from coaching are the average performers, not the superstars. The average performers must develop their skills and learn the fundamentals. It is important for supervisors to realize that coaching employees takes time, and in order for a coach to be effective, the supervisor must be willing to factor that time into both the coach's (or his or her own) and the employee's work schedule. Also, specific practices recommended in the *HBR Guide to Coaching Your Employees* can help the time invested in coaching result in greater performance gains:

- The supervisor should match employees' skills with the needs of the department so that employees can focus on using their strengths.
- The supervisor should work with employees to create realistic, yet inspiring plans for growth by setting "stretch" goals that are attainable but encourage the employee to challenge him- or herself.

- The supervisor should provide the resources and support employees need to do their job well.
- The coach should customize the coaching approach to the personality style of the employee.
- The coach should prompt the employee with questions before dispensing advice.
- The coach should give the employee ongoing, constructive feedback they'll actually apply, feedback that is specific and authentic.
- The coach should design instruction to match the employee's learning style. If the employee learns best with visual diagrams, draw them. If he or she learns by listening to instructions, give them completely and repeat as necessary.
- After giving instruction and time for practice, the coach should give the employee room to grapple with problems and discover solutions.
- The coach should move the employee toward independence.[23]

Employee performance usually improves when specific improvement goals are established during the performance appraisal. It is important that supervisors realize that they are responsible for improving the performance of deficient employees. The supervisor must remember that employees cannot improve unless they know exactly what is expected.

Rarely, when action plans fail to improve performance and unsatisfactory performance continues, termination may be necessary. The termination option is time-consuming, risks litigation if not defensible,[24] and can devastate an employee and family. Also, employee replacement is very expensive in terms of the costs of onboarding the new employee. Good coaching can avoid termination in many cases. (The role of the supervisor in the positive discipline of less proficient employees is discussed in Chapter 15.)

## Managing Performance Appraisal Results: Promoting Employees

**6 Identify the benefits and challenges of a promotion-from-within policy.**

Given proper encouragement, many employees strive to improve their performance and eventually be promoted. A promotion usually means advancement to a job with more responsibility, more privileges, higher status, greater potential, and higher pay.

Most, but not all, employees want to improve or advance. Some employees may feel that increased responsibility would demand too much of their time and energy, or they may be content with their present positions. Most employees, however, want promotions. For them, starting at the bottom and rising in status and income is a normal way of life.

### PROMOTING FROM WITHIN

Most organizations have policies for promoting employees. The policy of promoting from within is widely practiced, and it is important to both an organization and its employees. For the organization, it means a steady source of trained personnel for higher positions; for employees, it is a major incentive to perform better. When employees work for organizations for a long time, more is usually known about them than even the best selection processes and interviews could reveal about outside applicants for the same job. Supervisors should know their employees well; they do not know individuals hired from outside until those individuals have worked for them for some time.

Occasionally, a supervisor might want to bypass an employee for promotion because the productivity of the department will suffer until a replacement is found and trained. However, this thinking is shortsighted. It is better for the organization in the long run to have the best qualified people in positions where they can make the greatest contributions to the organization's success.

There would be little reason for employees to improve if they believed that the better and higher-paying jobs were reserved for outsiders. Additional job satisfaction results when employees know that stronger efforts on their part may lead to more interesting and challenging work, higher pay and status, and better working conditions. Most employees are more motivated when they see a link between excellent performance and a reward they covet.

When considering promotion for an employee, the supervisor should recognize that what management considers a promotion may not always be perceived as such by the employee. For example, an engineer may believe that a promotion to administrative work is a hardship, not an advancement. The engineer may feel that administrative activities are less interesting or more difficult than technical duties, and he or she may be concerned about losing or diluting professional

*Employee satisfaction increases when there are opportunities for advancement*

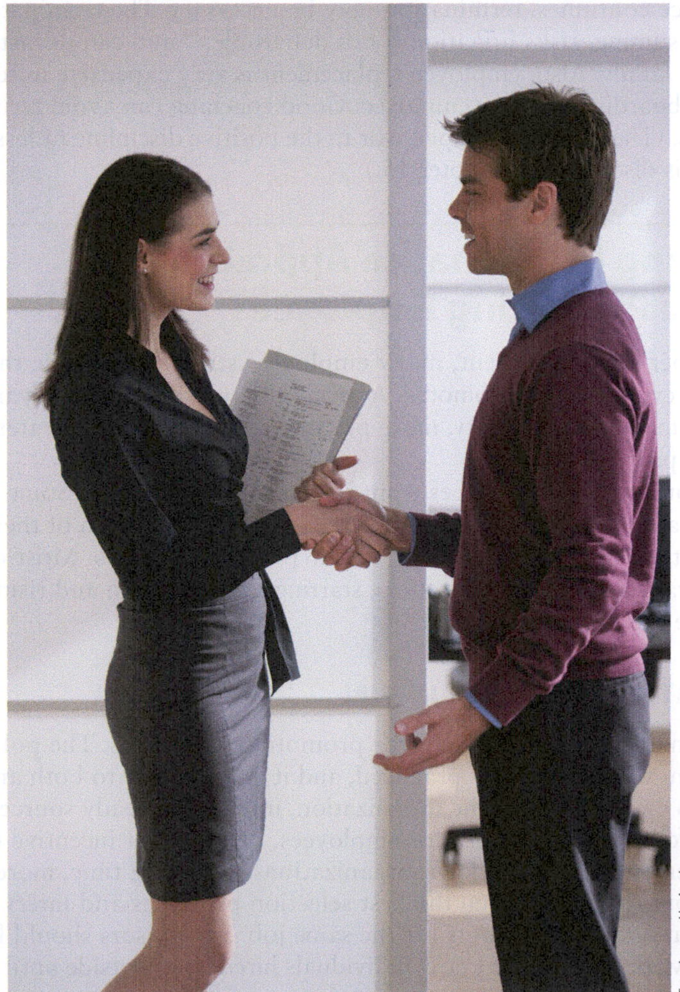
Tetra Images/Jupiter Images

engineering skills. Such an attitude is understandable, and the supervisor should try to suggest promotional opportunities that do not require unacceptable compromises.

Also, the supervisor should be sensitive to employees who appear to be satisfied in their present positions. Such employees may prefer to stay with their fellow employees and to retain responsibilities with which they are familiar and comfortable. The supervisor should not pressure them to accept higher-level positions. However, if the supervisor believes that such an employee has excellent qualifications for promotion, the supervisor should offer all the encouragement and counsel that may make a promotion attractive to the employee for current or future consideration. When the employee agrees to accept the promotion, it is essential for both the supervisor and employee to recognize that the dynamics between the employee and his or her peers will change dramatically. The employee will be required to make staffing and workload decisions that may not always be well-received by others who were previously "buddies." In *From Bud to Boss*, Kevin Eikenberry and Guy Harris encourage newly promoted supervisors to "adopt the mindset of a leader and develop the skills needed to communicate change, give feedback, coach employees, lead productive teams and achieve goals."[25] The supervisor can play a significant role in facilitating a successful transition by providing time, resources, and coaching to help the new leader acquire and apply new SKAs.

## MODIFYING A PROMOTION-FROM-WITHIN POLICY

Generally, it is preferable to apply a promotion-from-within policy whenever possible. However, in some cases strict adherence to this policy might not be sensible and might even harm an organization. If there are no qualified internal candidates for a position, then someone from the outside must be recruited. For example, if an experienced computer programmer is needed and no existing employee has programming expertise, the departmental supervisor will have to hire one from outside the organization.

At times, bringing a new employee into a department may be desirable because this person brings different ideas and fresh perspectives to the job. Another reason for recruiting employees from the outside is that an organization may not be in a position to train its own employees in the necessary skills. A particular position may require long, specialized, or expensive training, and the organization may be unable to offer or to afford such training. To cover these contingencies, a promotion-from-within policy must be modified as appropriate. For this reason, most written policy statements concerning promotion from within include such qualifying clauses as "whenever possible" or "whenever feasible."

## CRITERIA FOR PROMOTING FROM WITHIN

Typically, more employees are interested in being promoted than there are openings. Because promotions should be incentives for employees to perform better, some supervisors believe that employees who have the best records of production, quality, and cooperation are the ones who should be promoted. In some situations, however, it is difficult to measure such aspects of employee performance accurately or objectively, even when supervisors have made a conscientious effort in the form of merit ratings or performance appraisals.

## SENIORITY

**Seniority**
An employee's length of service in a department or an organization

One easily measured and objective criterion that has been applied extensively in an effort to reduce favoritism and discrimination is seniority. **Seniority** is an employee's length of service in the department or organization. Labor unions have emphasized seniority as a major promotion criterion. Its use is also widespread among organizations that are not unionized and for jobs that are not covered by union agreements. Many supervisors are comfortable with the concept of seniority as a basis for promotion. Some supervisors feel that an employee's loyalty, as expressed by length of service, deserves to be rewarded. Basing promotion on seniority also assumes that an employee's abilities tend to increase with service. Although this assumption is not always accurate, it is likely that, with continued service, an employee's skills and knowledge will improve. If promotion is to be based largely on seniority, then the initial selection procedure for new employees must be followed carefully, and each new employee should receive considerable training in various positions.

Probably the most serious drawback to using seniority as the major criterion for promotion is that it discourages young employees—those with less seniority. Younger employees may believe that they cannot advance until they too have accumulated years of service on the job. Consequently, they may lose enthusiasm and perform at only average levels. Another serious drawback is that the best performer is not always the most senior. If seniority is the only criterion, then there may be no incentive to perform well.

## MERIT AND ABILITY

Seniority alone does not guarantee that an individual either deserves promotion or is capable of advancing to a higher-level job. In fact, some employees with high seniority may lack the educational or skill levels needed for advancement. Consequently, most unions understand that length of service cannot be the only criterion for promotion. They agree that promotion should be based on seniority combined with merit and ability, and this type of provision is therefore included in many union contracts.

**Merit**
The quality of an employee's job performance

**Ability**
An employee's potential to perform higher-level tasks

**Merit** usually refers to the quality of an employee's job performance. **Ability** means an employee's ability or potential to perform or to be trained to perform a higher-level job. Supervisors often are in the best position to determine the degree to which merit and ability are necessary to compensate for less seniority. However, seniority is frequently the decisive criterion when merit and ability are relatively equal among several candidates seeking a promotion.

## BALANCING CRITERIA

Good supervisory practice attempts to attain a workable balance among merit, ability, and seniority. When selecting from among the most qualified candidates available, the supervisor may decide to choose essentially on the basis of seniority. Or the supervisor may decide that, in order to be promoted, the employee who is most capable but who has less seniority will have to be far better than those with more seniority. This is sometimes referred to as the head-and-shoulders concept. Otherwise, the supervisor will promote the qualified employee with the greatest seniority, at least on a trial basis.

Because promotion decisions can have great significance, the preferred solution would be to apply all criteria equally. However, promotion decisions often involve gray areas or subjective considerations that can lead rejected employees to be dissatisfied and file grievances. Realistically, unless there are unusual circumstances, it is unlikely that a supervisor will choose to promote an employee based solely on merit and ability without some thought to seniority.

## Managing Performance Appraisal Results: Compensating Employees

**7 Discuss the supervisor's role in employee compensation and outline the goals of an effective compensation program.**

Although it is not always recognized as such, a supervisor's staffing function includes helping to determine the relative worth of jobs. Typically, wage rates and salary schedules are formulated by higher-level management, by the HR department, by union contract, or by government legislation or regulation. In this respect, the supervisor's authority is limited. Nevertheless, the supervisor is responsible for determining appropriate compensation for departmental employees.

The question of how much to pay employees poses a problem for many organizations. It is possible, however, to establish a compensation program that is objective, fair, and relatively easy to administer. The objectives of a compensation program should be to

- eliminate pay inequities to minimize dissatisfaction and complaints among employees;
- establish and/or maintain sufficiently attractive pay rates so that qualified employees are attracted to and retained by the company;
- conduct periodic employee merit ratings to provide the basis for comparative performance rewards;
- control labor costs with respect to productivity gains; and
- reward employees for outstanding performance or for the acquisition of additional skills or knowledge.[26]

Generally, the HR department establishes compensation levels that will attract and retain competent employees. Too often, wage rate schedules simply follow historical patterns, or they are formulated haphazardly. At the departmental level, wage rate inequities often develop over time due to changes in jobs, changes in personnel, and different supervisors using varying standards for administering compensation. Because wage inequities and concerns arise, supervisors should immediately address them and, on balance, strive for a wage system that is uniform, consistent, and meets the aforementioned objectives.

### THE SUPERVISOR'S ROLE IN COMPENSATION DECISIONS

Although a sound and equitable compensation structure should be of great concern to everyone in management, it is an area in which supervisors typically have limited direct authority. However, supervisors should try to make higher-level managers aware of serious compensation inequities at the departmental level. This often can be done when supervisors make their recommendations for wage and salary adjustments for individual employees.

It is imperative that both supervisors and employees know the "lay of the land" as it relates to the relationship between performance evaluation and salary increases. Generally, an individual employee or team of employees will be given a merit raise when they achieve some performance objective. As you will recall from Chapter 7, employees are willing to put forth more effort when they perceive the following linkages: making greater effort will lead to achievement, which will lead to a desirable outcome: a merit raise.[27] It is imperative that supervisors be able to justify and document performance evaluations regardless of whether the employee exceeded expectations, met expectations, or did not meet expectations, and be able to explain how the performance evaluation relates to the raise an employee might receive.

## RECOMMENDING WAGE ADJUSTMENTS

**Pay for performance**
Compensation, other than base wages, that is given for achieving employee or team goals.

**Gain-sharing plans**
Group incentive plans that have employees' share in the benefits from improved performance

Some organizations use pay for performance plans. While a detailed presentation of compensation issues is beyond the scope of this text, we will briefly discuss two plans that if appropriately used have been found to reward good works. In **pay for performance**, compensation is based on employee or group performance goals. Among these approaches are special cash awards, bonuses for meeting performance targets, or cost-cutting targets.

**Gain-sharing plans** are group reward programs. Group or team rewards are often used when the individual contributions are not easily identifiable. They are particularly important when the outstanding performance depends on team working and cooperation of all team members. Employees share the monetary benefits (gains) of improved productivity, cost reductions, or improvement in quality or customer service that improve the bottom line. Most plans use an easy-to-understand formula to calculate the gains and the resulting bonus.[28]

Unfortunately, too often supervisors automatically recommend full wage increases without seriously considering whether each employee deserves such a raise. Here is where employee performance evaluation is crucial. If an employee's work has been satisfactory, then the employee deserves the normal increase. If the employee has performed at an unsatisfactory level, the supervisor should suspend the recommendation for an increase and discuss this decision with the employee. The supervisor might outline specific targets for job improvement that the employee must meet before the supervisor will recommend a wage increase. If an employee has performed at an outstanding level, the supervisor should not hesitate to recommend a generous, above-average wage increase if this can be done within the wage structure. Such a tangible reward will encourage the outstanding employee to continue striving for excellence.

## COMPENSATION CONCERNS

Employees commonly compare their compensation to that of others. This becomes a serious motivational problem for the supervisor when the organization has wages or benefits that are considerably lower than those for similar jobs at other firms in the community. What does the company owe a great employee, and what does the employee expect in return for doing a great job? Figure 12.10 illustrates one employee's perceptions.

Two-tier wage systems and contract employees are additional concerns for the supervisor who is trying to maintain a perception of fairness.[29] Depending on a firm's arrangement with a temporary agency, the temporary employee may be paid more or less than regular employees performing the same job. In organizations using a two-tier wage system, new employees are paid less than present employees performing the same or similar jobs. Unfortunately, lower-paid

FIGURE 12.10 "Freshly Squeezed" by Ed Stein Universal Uclick

Universal Uclick

employees can develop feelings of inequity when working under these systems. Again, supervisors should make every effort to stay informed about their organization's compensation systems and should consult the HR or benefits office when questions arise. As easy as it might be to disregard employee concerns about compensation, supervisors must recognize that this is an important area of concern for most employees.

We cannot emphasize enough the importance of communication. Again, if the supervisor does not have the answer to the employee's question, the supervisor should say so and then should strive to find the answer. Moreover, supervisors should permit and even encourage employees to visit the HR department or the appropriate manager for advice and assistance concerning benefits and compensation problems. This practice is particularly desirable when employees have personal problems or questions about sensitive areas, such as medical and other health benefits and retirement and insurance programs.

## SUMMARY

**1.** **Performance management consists of all those things a supervisor must do to enable an employee to achieve organizational objectives. As illustrated in Figure 12.1, the supervisor establishes goals and objectives, coaches, gives feedback, helps the employee adjust performance or take corrective action, documents performance, and rewards performance.**

**Supervisors are responsible for using two-way and frequent informal communication to appraise employee performance on a day-to-day basis and formally at predetermined intervals. Supervisors must keep accurate records of employee performance.**

**Evaluators must understand what is necessary for successful job performance in order to ensure that employees feel the appraisal process is fair. Peer evaluations and 360-degree performance evaluations are ways to provide performance feedback from a wider range of perspectives than just the supervisor's, which can reduce real or perceived bias, and they can contribute to a more complete performance picture. Including self-rating in the process can facilitate the open discussion of employees' perceptions of their strengths and weaknesses.**

**2.** **Supervisors ideally spend time each day providing performance feedback to employees. As stressed throughout the chapter, there is no substitute for daily feedback on performance.**

**Most organizations require formal performance appraisals at least once each year. Because the decision to retain a new employee is critical, the performance assessment of probationary employees should be done at the end of the probationary period. When there is a serious performance problem, the supervisor should provide immediate feedback. However, ongoing feedback, both positive and negative, should be a regular part of the supervisor's routine. If the employee is given ongoing feedback, then the annual appraisal should contain no**

surprises. It should be a review of what the supervisor and employee have discussed during the year.

If done properly, formal performance appraisals benefit both the employee and the organization. Companies use performance appraisals as a basis for important decisions concerning promotions, raises, terminations, and the like. Performance appraisals reward employees' good performance and inform them of strategies they can use to become more productive.

The major advantage of a formal appraisal system is that it provides a framework to help the supervisor systematically evaluate performance and communicate to employees how they are doing. Formal appraisals can be employee incentives. They get positive feedback about their performance and know that the formal system documents their performance.

Criticism of performance appraisal process dwells on the fact that it often focuses only on past accomplishments or deficiencies. Supervisors can counteract this criticism by emphasizing developmental aspects of performance appraisal.

3. Appraisal forms may vary in format and approach, but they should allow supervisors to identify the outstanding aspects of the employee's work, specify performance areas that need improvement, and suggest ways to improve performance.

Supervisors should be consistent in applying the terms used to describe an employee's performance. Not all supervisors judge employees' performance accurately, and sometimes a supervisor can damage an employee's morale by giving lower ratings than the employee deserves. Additional perceptual errors include the leniency error, the halo and horn effects, and other rater biases.

When completing the appraisal form, the supervisor should focus on the employee's accomplishments. The results should be described in terms of *how much, how well*, and *in what manner*. Whatever the choice of appraisal form, it is important that every appraisal be made in the context of the employee's job and be based on the employee's total performance.

4. Although the appraisal meeting may be trying, the entire employee performance appraisal system is of no use if the meeting is ignored or is carried out improperly. The supervisor should begin by stating that the overall purpose of the appraisal meeting is to let employees know how they are doing. The supervisor should give positive feedback for good performance, emphasize strengths the employee can build on, and identify performance aspects that need improvement.

The meeting should be conducted in private shortly after the form is completed. How the meeting proceeds depends to a large extent on the employee's performance. Supervisors should limit criticism to those areas that need correction or improvement. An employee performing at a substandard level must clearly understand that the deficiencies are serious and that substantial improvement is needed. Employees are more apt to agree with an appraisal when they understand the standards of performance and recognize that the appraisal is free of bias.

The supervisor should emphasize that the same standards are used to evaluate all employees in the same job. Supervisors may use a critical incident method for documenting employee performance that is very good or unsatisfactory. Employees should be given opportunities to ask questions, and the supervisor should answer them honestly. The supervisor should anticipate questions, potential areas of disagreement, and difficult responses that may arise during the appraisal meeting.

Employees should clearly understand their evaluations. New objectives should be set and areas for improvement described. Generally, the employee is asked to sign the appraisal form to prove that the meeting took place. Organizations should have an audit process to resolve conflicts arising from the appraisal.

5. Supervisors should serve as coaches in the conduct of their daily activities. During the performance appraisal process, supervisors should provide employees with information, instruction, and suggestions relating to their job assignments and performance.

Supervisors can use a coaching approach to prepare high-performing employees for greater responsibility as well as to improve the performance of all employees. Ongoing employee skill development is essential. Based on the performance appraisal, the coach develops a plan for improvement. Specific improvement goals are set. The employee receives instruction and is given an opportunity to practice. The coach provides feedback and encouragement.

6. Most employees want to improve and advance in the organization. Promotion from within is a widely practiced personnel policy that is beneficial to the organization and to employee morale. Supervisors know their employees' strengths and abilities; they do not know as much about individuals hired from outside. When employees know they have a good chance of advancement, they will have an incentive to improve their job performance. In short, promotion from within rewards employees for their good performance and serves notice to other employees

that good performance will lead to advancement. At the same time, promotion from within requires the supervisor to provide support to individuals who are promoted so they can successfully make the transition from a peer to a supervisor.

Although organizations should promote from within whenever possible, strict adherence to a promotion-from-within policy is not always practical. When internal employees have not received the necessary training, an external candidate may be preferred. Sometimes, too, an outsider may be needed to introduce innovative ideas.

Because promotions should serve as an incentive for employees to perform better, it is generally believed that employees with the best performance records should be promoted. Nevertheless, seniority still serves as a basis for many promotions. Seniority is easily understood and withstands charges of favoritism and discrimination. However, a promotional system based solely on seniority removes the incentive for junior employees who want to advance.

Although it is difficult to specify an exact basis for employee promotion, there should be appropriate consideration of ability and merit on the one hand and length of service on the other.

**7.** The supervisor's staffing function includes making certain that a department's employees are compensated properly. Many compensation considerations are not within the direct domain of a supervisor.

Additional monetary compensation serves, in part, to reward employees who perform at outstanding levels. Some organizations may utilize a pay for performance or gain-sharing program to reward productivity and other gains.

Because supervisory responsibility and authority are limited in these areas, supervisors should work closely with the human resources staff to maintain equitable compensation offerings and to ensure that departmental employees are informed and treated fairly in regard to benefits and any bonus plans that may be available.

## KEY TERMS

360-degree evaluation (p. 450)
Ability (p. 470)
Coaching (p. 464)
Critical incident method (p. 460)
Gain-sharing plans (p. 472)
Leniency error (p. 456)
Merit (p. 470)
Pay for performance (p. 472)
Peer evaluation (p. 450)
Performance appraisal (p. 447)
Performance standards (p. 457)
Rater bias (p. 457)
Seniority (p. 470)
System of performance management (p. 446)

## WHAT HAVE YOU LEARNED?

1. What are the major purposes of a performance management system? How do appraising, coaching, promoting, and compensating employees fit into the system?
2. What are some of the factors most frequently included on employee performance appraisal forms? Why should most performance appraisal forms include space for supervisors to write comments about the employee being evaluated?
3. What are the benefits and drawbacks of using peer ratings, 360-degree evaluations, or an employee self-rating approach?
4. What are the characteristics of effective performance feedback?
5. What are some of the challenges involved in measuring and documenting employee performance?
6. Describe the major components of an appraisal meeting. What are some of the challenges that can arise during this type of meeting?
7. Outline a coaching program for an employee who exhibits unsatisfactory behaviors. How will your program meet the needs of both the organization and the employee?
8. What are the benefits and challenges of a promotion-from-within policy?
9. What are the advantages and disadvantages of promotion based on seniority?
10. Explain the following statement: "Wage increases should be based solely on performance measures." How does the supervisor develop clear guidelines for determining who gets a raise and how much they should get?

EXPERIENTIAL EXERCISE FOR SELF-ASSESSMENT

## EXPERIENTIAL EXERCISE FOR SELF-ASSESSMENT 12: Recognizing Personal Bias

In the discussion of *rater bias* in this chapter, we listed many different facets of unconscious thinking processes that contribute to individuals' biases. For each of us, our values, stereotypes, experiences, culture, background, personality differences, and distractions can lead us to view situations and people in unique and sometimes unfair ways and make decisions that are unfairly based on our own biased perspective. In order to avoid bias in our interactions with others, it is important to first recognize our own biases.

This assessment activity provides you with an opportunity to assess and mitigate your own biases so that you can ensure that your actions are fair, objective and bias-free. As a journal entry or free-writing activity, respond to the questions below while thinking about a person who you find hard to work with or get along with. You may also want to save the questions and use them as a tool to continually assess and address your biases as you widen your network and work among a greater variety of people and contexts.

1. What kind of biases have I experienced myself? How have those experiences affected me?
2. What part of my own agenda is being served by the decisions I am making?
3. Does this person or their situation remind me of someone else? Is that association applicable to this situation?
4. Are there differences in style or opinion between me and the person I am working with? If so, are they wrong, or just different? Are these differences influencing how I am acting toward this person? Might their style or opinion yield the same results?
5. Are there cultural, gender, religious, or lifestyle differences between us? Are the differences influencing how I am acting toward this person?
6. What do I imagine are this person's values, dreams, and aspirations? Is this what I imagine, or what he or she has told me?
7. Considering my answers to these questions, am I approaching this person in a way that is unfairly influenced by my own biased perspective?
8. If so, what strategies and tactics can I put in place to engage fully and consciously, putting my biases aside? (See Figure 12.7 on page 443.)

Adapted from Leslie Traub, *Bias in Performance Management Review Process: Creating an Inclusive Talent Pipeline By Understanding Our Filters.* (2013). Silver Spring, MD: Cook Ross, Inc., http://www.cookross.com/docs/unconsciousbiasinperformance2013.pdf, p. 8

PERSONAL SKILL BUILDING

## PERSONAL SKILL BUILDING 12-1: Develop Guidelines for Performance Appraisal

1. Select two persons who are currently employed full-time. Ask each of them the following questions:
   a. Have you ever had a performance appraisal that has had a positive effect on your morale or development as an employee? Describe the circumstances of that appraisal.
   b. Have you ever had a performance appraisal that has had a negative effect on your morale or development as an employee? Describe the circumstances of that appraisal.
   c. If you were a supervisor and had to conduct a performance appraisal of your employees, what one thing would you do to ensure that the appraisal had a positive impact on employee morale and/or development?
2. In a one- to two-page paper, summarize your findings and describe circumstances and supervisor actions that contribute to positive employee morale and development.

## PERSONAL SKILL BUILDING 12-2: Identify Strengths and Build on Them

1. Think of the best teacher you have ever known. Make a list of his or her strengths. Should these become standard for all teachers? Why or why not?
2. If your instructor informed you that you will be responsible for conducting the next class meeting in his or her absence, what tactics and techniques that you observed in your best teacher might help you to lead the class?
3. Have you ever written that best teacher a letter or sent him or her a note of thanks? If not, write that teacher a letter or send an e-mail, thanking the teacher for the great job he or she did.
4. How hard was it for you write that letter of praise? Why do you suppose that some managers find it difficult to give praise?
5. What about the worst teacher you ever had? Did you take action to try to improve his or her performance? Why or why not?

## PERSONAL SKILL BUILDING 12-3: Technology Tools—Picking Performance Assessment Software

INTERNET ACTIVITY

Many organizations are currently making the transition from paper-based performance appraisal forms to HR management software that includes performance appraisal applications. Hundreds of such software exists for companies to choose from. Often companies will engage a team of managers from across departments to help evaluate a number of software applications before deciding on the tool that will best meet the needs of the organization. Imagine you are a member of such an evaluation team. Your job is to make a recommendation based on an abbreviated review of several performance appraisal software applications.

1. Visit the web sites of at least three performance appraisal software applications and view the video tour, demonstration or screenshots of the software. Examples of such software include the following (links are available on the text's student companion website):
   a. Cornerstone On Demand:
   b. Employee Appraisals 1.0
   c. Empxtrack
   d. Insperity
   e. PerformSmart
   f. Promantek
   g. People
   h. Small Improvements
   i. Success Factors
2. As you review the limited information on the applications, evaluate your first impressions of each relative to the following criteria:
   a. Available features
   b. Ease of understanding
   c. Ease of use by manager
   d. Ease of use by employee
   e. Cost (if information is available)
3. Rank your three choices in order of preference by listing each application and writing a 100- to 200-word review of each.
4. Reflect on the evaluation experience. Was it easy or difficult to rate the applications with only the available information? What would have made the evaluation experience more valuable to you? After this experience, would you recommend that the company further investigate any of the applications? Why or why not?

## PERSONAL SKILL BUILDER 12-4: Batty the Scatterbrain

This is another in the series of exercises introducing a person who may make your life difficult.

1. Read the following statement from John Peters, an accounting department supervisor for the Citizens National Bank:

   *Wilma is a real dingbat. Everybody loves her, but she is scatterbrained. She forgets appointments all the time. We all try to help her because we know she means well, but we sometimes wonder how she got hired. I recognize that some people have bad days, but Wilma always has trouble. When I talk about Wilma at home, my kids say she is an "airhead," and I tell them that some of the employees call her "Batty" behind her back. She is always making silly mistakes and lacks common sense. Unorganized is probably the word that best describes Wilma.*

   *Wilma can be truly endearing and completely frustrating. She has potential but is lost in her own world, so she can't be relied on. She's easily distracted by peripheral issues and has trouble working with the team. She should probably be fired because she always misses deadlines, but I'm not certain that we can find anyone better to replace her.*

   *I've tried to explain what needs to be done and how to do it and to let Wilma know that I'm available if she has any questions. I even leave her a "punch list" of what needs to be done by when, and she still messes up. Just last week, she misplaced the list.*

   *Yesterday, Wilma asked me about a customer's account that needed to be reconciled. We spent at least an hour going over the "how's" and "where's." Today, she asked me the same questions about another customer's account. I don't know if she's just dumb or just doesn't care. I don't think I can continue to be a babysitter, but what do I do?*

2. 

   INTERNET ACTIVITY

   Using the Internet, find at least three sources for how to deal with people who are scatterbrained. Carefully review each site for suggestions on how to deal with this type of person.
3. Based on your findings, what suggestions would you make to John Peters on how to deal with Wilma?
4. Write a one-page paper explaining how this exercise increased your working knowledge of coping with the behaviors of this person who makes life difficult for others.

## TEAM SKILL BUILDING

### TEAM SKILL BUILDER 12-1: What Would You Do at CMC?

1. Before beginning this activity, carefully reread this chapter's opening You Make the Call!
2. Work together with three other students on this activity. Using the Internet, each student should find one current article that deals with getting employees to be the best they can be. Share your findings so that the group can find ways that the information in the articles might apply to this You Make the Call! and help Rita deal with the situation. Working together you should develop a strategy that Rita Sheldon can use in the appraisal meeting with Fred Young.

INTERNET ACTIVITY

3. Food for thought questions:
   a. What do you think about Rita Sheldon's strategy for performance appraisal?
   b. What would be the advantages and disadvantages of having several colleagues answer the following questions about Fred:
      (i) What does Fred Young do well?
      (ii) What one thing does Fred Young need to improve on?
   c. What other questions might Rita ask of Fred's colleagues to help her to help Fred be the best employee he can be?
4. Based on your readings in this chapter, what suggestions would you make to Rita?

### TEAM SKILL BUILDER 12-2: I Hate Performance Management!

ROLE PLAY

Form groups of three, with one person acting as the employee, the second as the supervisor, and the third as the observer. The supervisor will evaluate the employee using the information in one of the following situations. The supervisor role will require imagination and creativity to provide feedback.

The observer will observe the interview relationship, make notes and, at the end of the interview, the observer will provide feedback on the effectiveness of the interview.

Next review the scenario:

*Tony Becker had been a regional supervisor for Sanders Supermarkets. When the organization consolidated operations, Becker was demoted and transferred to an assistant store manager position at the Pridemore location. Becker has been with Sanders for more than thirty years and is much older than you, his supervisor. Becker shows up for work early and stays late. Becker's knowledge of the supermarket industry is second to none. However, he is unwilling to share it with anyone. He is very angry about his demotion and is very difficult to work with in general. He is belligerent toward younger employees, resents your authority, and insists on doing things his way. He refers to the younger female employees and to customers as "Honey." You have constantly counseled Becker on his inappropriate behavior, and he reminds you that he started at Sanders before you were born. Some employees try to avoid him. Several have threatened to quit unless he changes. Becker has made some serious errors when scheduling deliveries. You approach the interview knowing the following circumstances:*

a. Becker's performance is unsatisfactory on most factors.
b. The supervisor questions whether Becker should be retained. Your perspective is clouded, however, because they know that your immediate supervisor trained under Becker and has said on several occasions that Becker taught him everything he knows and that if Becker had not helped him, he would not have such a great job.

1. The person playing the role of the supervisor is to give Becker a performance review. The supervisor should focus on one or two key points. (It is to be expected that the supervisor will develop examples of critical incidents that need attention.) The person playing the role of Becker may want to play the age-discrimination card during the review.
2. At the conclusion, the observer is to identify the things that the supervisor did well and conclude with a simple comment about what he or she might have done differently.

## SUPERVISION IN ACTION

SUPERVISION IN ACTION

The video for this chapter can be accessed from the student companion website at www.cengagebrain.com. (Search by authors' names or book title to find the accompanying resources.)

## ENDNOTES

1. Alan Cardy, "A General Framework for Performance Management Systems," *Performance Improvement* 52, No. 2 (February 2013), pp. 6–15.
2. One of the authors cannot remember when he first heard that "managing performance to achieve organizational objectives is what supervision is all about." Peter M. Glendinning used the terms *performance management* and *performance appraisal* synonymously in his article "Performance Management: Pariah or Messiah," *Public Personnel Management* (Summer 2002), pp. 161+. He said, "Performance management, or performance appraisal, is defined as the process through which companies ensure that employees are working toward organizational goals."

   In an interview in *Performance Management Magazine*, Aubrey C. Daniels offered this definition: "In simplest terms, performance management is a way of getting people to do what you want them to do and to like doing it" (November 13, 2000), accessed at http://www.pmezine.com/article_dtls.asp?NID=68. Adrienne Fox, in "Prune Employees Carefully," *HR Magazine* (April 2008), pp. 66–70, says that firms need to get their performance management systems in order to engage top performers and to prepare for an economic rebound.

   Author Ram Charan asserts that less than 10 percent of companies conduct rigorous, quarterly reviews of key players in order to keep them engaged and focusing on continuous improvement, as reported by Joann Lublin in "Message to CEO's: Do More to Keep Your Key Employees," *The Wall Street Journal* (December 27, 2010), p. B5. Lin Grensing-Pophal, "Performance Management Opportunities for HR Consultants," *Society for Human Resource Management* (February 2, 2010), http://www.shrm.org, provides insight from a study of 556 HR professionals and line managers. Less than 50 percent believed their companies' performance management (PM) systems delivered value to the business, or that time spent on performance management was worth the investment. Only 30 percent believed that their PM systems achieved their intended objectives. This tells us that supervisors should consider examining PM as they look for ways to help improve their organizations. Also see "Parallels between Performance Management Quality and Organizational Performance," *SuperVision* (August 2005), pp. 19–20.
3. Many employees dislike performance reviews. See Scott Sleek, Andrew Merluzzi, and Anna Mikulak, "The Perils of Performance Appraisal," Psychological Science.com (January 9, 2013), http://www.psychologicalscience.org/index.php/news/minds-business/the-perils-of-performance-appraisals.html. See also Satoris S. Culbertson, Jaime B. Henning, and Stephanie C. Payne, "Performance Appraisal Satisfaction: The Role of Feedback and Goal Orientation," *Journal of Personnel Psychology* 12, No. 4 (2013), pp. 189–195; Rachel Silverman, "Yearly Reviews? Try Weekly," *The Wall Street Journal* (September 6, 2011), p. B6; Jared Sandberg, "Performance Reviews Often Miss the Mark," *The Wall Street Journal* (December 4, 2007), p. 6B.
4. A comprehensive discussion of the variety of tools and strategies supervisors can use to monitor performance, including suggested contexts for each, is presented by Gordon Amsler, Henry Findley, and Earl Ingram, "Performance Monitoring: Guidance for the Modern Workplace," *SuperVision* 72, No. 11 (January 2011), pp. 16–22.
5. Mary L. Lanigan, "Evaluating the Evaluator: A Case Study Illustrating Three Critical Mistakes No Evaluator Should Make," *Performance Improvement* 49, No. 10 (November/December 2010), pp. 39–45.
6. A 2004 survey by Novations Group, Inc., found that 44 percent of HR professionals said that their firms' forced ranking systems damaged morale and generated mistrust of leadership, a finding that holds true a decade later according to Elizabeth G. Olsen, "Microsoft, GE, and the Futility of Ranking Employees," CNNMoney (November 18, 2013), http://management.fortune.cnn.com/2013/11/18/microsoft-ge-ranking-employees/. Forced ranking systems assess employee performance relative to peers rather than against predetermined goals. For a comprehensive overview, see Dick Grote, *Forced Ranking Making Performance Management Work* (Boston: Harvard Business School Press, 2005).

   For a discussion of peer appraisals, see Arvind Sudarsan, "Concurrent Validity of Peer Appraisal of Group Work for Administrative Purposes," *IUP Journal of Organizational Behavior* 9, No. 1 (2010), pp. 71–86 and Angelo Dennisi and Caitlin E. Smith, "Performance Appraisal, Performance Management, and Firm-Level Performance: A Review, a Proposed Model, and New Directions for Future Research," *The Academy of Management Annals* 8, No. 1 (2014), pp. 127–179. See also Josh Bersin, "Time to Scrap Performance Appraisals," Forbes.com (May 6, 2013), http://www.forbes.com/sites/joshbersin/2013/05/06/time-to-scrap-performance-appraisals/. An alternative to traditional peer appraisals, "crowdsourced" performance reviews have recently emerged as a real-time, ongoing process of collecting feedback from across an organization that are shown to boost employee engagement levels and create more accurate, actionable results. A description of this strategy is provided in Eric Mosley's *The Crowdsourced Performance Review: How to Use the Power of Social Recognition to Transform Employee Performance* (New York: McGraw-Hill Education, 2013).
7. 360-degree appraisals are controversial. HR experts caution that their use should be considered carefully, particularly when the results influence pay and promotion decisions because they are not meant as a rating tool, but as a development tool, according to Steve Taylor, "Assess Pros and Cons of 360-Degree Performance Appraisal," *Society for Human Resource Management* Web site (July 12, 2011), www.shrm.org. Dennis Coates says, "You can use 360-degree feedback for performance management, but not for performance appraisal. Why not? Because it undermines trust."

   For an extended discussion of the pros and cons of 360-degree appraisals, see David W. Bracken, "The 'New' Performance Management Paradigm: Capitalizing on the Unrealized Potential of 360 Degree Feedback," *People & Strategy* 36, No. 2, (2013), pp. 34–40; Himanshu Rai and Manjari Singh, "A Study of Mediating Variables of the Relationship between 360 Degree Feedback and Employee Performance," *Human Resource Development International* 16, No. 1 (February 2013), pp. 56–73; Kenneth M. Nowack and Sandra Mashihi, "Evidence-Based Answers to 15 Questions about Leveraging 360-Degree Feedback," *Consulting Psychology Journal: Practice and Research* 64, No. 3 (September 2012), pp. 157–182. *Leanne* Atwater and Joan F. Brett, "Antecedents and Consequences of Reactions to 360-Degree Feedback," *SHRM Home* (2005); Nathalie Towner, "Turning Appraisals 360 Degrees," *Personnel Today* (February 17, 2004), p. 18.
8. Justin Kruger and David Dunning, "Unskilled and Unaware of It: How Difficulties in Recognizing One's Own Incompetence Lead to Inflated Self-Assessments," *Journal of Personality and Social Psychology* 77, No. 6 (December 1999), pp. 1121–1134. See also Dick Grote, "Let's Abolish Self-Appraisal," HBR Blog Network (July 11, 2011),

http://blogs.hbr.org/2011/07/lets-abolish-self-appraisal/, in which Grote suggests that employers provide clear guidance on the purpose and process of self-evaluation, explaining that it is just one of many sources of data for evaluating performance and that the supervisor's document is the "official performance appraisal." Further, Grote suggests that asking employees to send a list of their most significant achievements and accomplishments may have more value than completing a standardized rating form because it provides concrete examples of performance (or lack thereof) and can reduce some of the stress that comes with discussing potentially divergent ratings. Management professors Peter Massignham and Thi Ngueyet Que Nguyen, and accounting professor Rada Massignham, suggest that companies combine 360-degree peer review with self-reporting in order to validate the self-ratings; see "Using 360 Degree Peer Review to Validate Self-reporting in Human Capital Measurement," *Journal of Intellectual Capital* 12, No. 1 (2011), pp. 43–74.

9. The noted quality guru, the late W. Edwards Deming, contended that performance appraisal is the premier American management problem. "It takes the average employee six months to recover from it." Deming, *Out of Crisis* (Cambridge, MA: MIT, 1982), p. 37. Also see Tom Peters, *Thriving on Chaos* (New York: Alfred A. Knopf, 1987), p. 495.
10. A survey of research and company literature found seventy-six perceived problems with typical performance appraisal, to which Jack Kondrasuk responded with five proposed changes to the performance appraisal process in "So What Would an Ideal Performance Appraisal Look Like?" *Journal of Applied Business and Economics* 12, No. 1 (2011), pp. 57–71. Kondrasuk suggests (1) clarifying the goals of the performance appraisal, (2) focusing on both results and behavior appraisals, (3) adding a category that describes the present environment or situation, (4) better timing between evaluation and appraisal discussions, and (5) including the employee, peers, customers, and HR specialists in the appraisal process.
11. Organizations that choose to use self-appraisal as part of the performance management process provide employees with the opportunity to have ownership in the appraisal process, according to Neil Boyd in "Oppression in the Mundane of Management: An Example from Human Resources," *Administrative Theory and Practice* 3, No.3 (September 2010), pp. 445–449. Boyd criticizes appraisal processes that fail to consider employees' reflection on their own performance, and he asserts that one-sided "performance appraisal systems contain power and control issues that are rooted in hierarchy." Employees can provide valuable insight into their strengths, challenges, motivations, decisions, and work habits that employers often cannot overtly observe. Supervisors are encouraged to find ways to involve employees in the process of performance assessment and improvement.
12. Erin Osterhaus, managing editor of SoftwareAdvice.com provides a list of the most commonly used systems in "Top 10 Most Recommended Employee Performance Appraisal & Review Software Systems," SoftwareAdvice.com (March 4, 2014), http://www.softwareadvice.com/hr/performance-review-software-comparison/. Success Factors, Inc., for example, provides an automated, paperless performance management software system that incorporates appraisal, performance evaluation, compensation, and organizational goal-setting functions that can be accessed by all levels of management, as described in "Taking the Performance Review Process from Painful to Proactive,"*SuccessFactors HR Insider Series* (2009).
13. See James Michael Brodie, "Optimizing HR Software Demonstration," *HR Magazine* (April 2006), pp. 99–101. Each month, *HR Magazine* provides a "What's New" guide to HR products and services to make organizations aware of various resources available to assist with the performance management process.
14. Barbara Holmes, "The Lenient Evaluator's Hurting Your Organization," *HR Magazine* (June 1993), pp. 75–77.
15. Leslie Traub, *Bias in Performance Management Review Process: Creating an Inclusive Talent Pipeline by Understanding Our Filters* (Silver Spring, MD: Cook Ross, Inc., 2013). This resource is available for download from Cook Ross, Inc., http://www.cookross.com/docs/unconsciousbiasinperformance2013.pdf
16. The courts have held that employers must have fully documented, authentic, and accurate performance deficiencies in order to avoid costly lawsuits. For example, in *Sandell v. Taylor-Listug Inc.,* 188 Cal. App. 4th 297 (2010), the court held that if organizational performance is outside an employee's control and unrelated to his or her actual performance, then negative performance evaluations could be reasonably inferred as being motivated by discrimination, rather than performance itself and the lawsuit can go to the jury. Also see Timothy S. Bland, "Supreme Court Decision Makes Giving Truthful Reasons for Discharge Critical," *SHRM White Paper* (October 2002), pp. 1–13.
17. Failure of supervisors to follow a consistent, established performance management process can result in significant issues, including litigation, if an employee believes that discriminatory or unfair missteps were taken in appraisal and documentation leading to termination. Jonathan Segal describes seven common performance management mistakes supervisors should avoid in order to minimize risk in "Performance Management Blunders," *HR Magazine* (November 2010), pp. 75–78.
18. Katie Van Syckle, "Don't Let Feedback Crush You," *Bloomberg Businessweek* (March 6, 2014), pp. 75–77. See also Douglas Stone and Sheila Heen, *Thanks for the Feedback: The Science and Art of Receiving Feedback Well,* (New York: Penguin Group, 2014); WorldatWork and Sibson Consulting, *2010 Study on the State of Performance Management* (Scottsdale, AZ: WorldatWork). The study can be downloaded from http://www.worldatwork.org/waw/adimLink?id=44473.
19. Robert Liddell, "Employee Crafted Goals Pay Off," *HR Magazine* (July 2013), p. 63.
20. One of the supervisor's important roles is to coach—that is, to help employees learn how to become better employees. For an enlightening discussion on the supervisor's role as a coach, see Wendy Bliss, "Coaching in a Business Environment," Society for Human Resource Management (SHRM) Toolkit (March 21, 2013), available from the SHRM website, http://www.shrm.org/templatestools/toolkits/pages/coachinginabusinessenvironment.aspx; Issie Lapowsky, "The Lost Art of Tough Love," *Inc.* (February 2014), pp. 46–48; Robert Paxton, "Training Managers to Lead Innovation," *HR Magazine* (February 2014), pp. 38–40; Jean Thilmany, "Passing on Know-How," *HR Magazine* (June 2008), pp. 100–104; J. Richard Hackman and Ruth Wageman, "A Theory of Team Coaching," *Academy of Management Review* (April 2005), pp. 269–287;
21. Warren St. John, "Nick Saban: Sympathy for the Devil," GQ.com (September 2013), http://www.gq.com/entertainment/sports/201309/coach-nick-saban-alabama-maniac. See also Rolltide.com's profile of Coach Nick Saban, http://www.rolltide.com/sports/m-footbl/mtt/saban_nick00.html; Sharon Terlep, "The Other Half of Team Saban," WSJ.com (November 26, 2013), http://

online.wsj.com/news/articles/SB10001424052702303281504579220393805048908

22. WHNT News, "Crimson Tide Finishes with No. 1 Recruiting Class in 2014," WHNT.com (February 5, 2014), http://whnt.com/2014/02/05/crimson-tide-finishes-with-no-1-recruiting-class-in-2014/
23. Adapted from Harvard Business Press Books' *HBR Guide to Coaching Your Employees* (Cambridge, MA: Harvard Business Press, 2013). See also Lee Colan, "4 Keys to Coaching Underperforming Employees," Inc.com (July 23, 2013), http://www.inc.com/lee-colan/4-keys-to-coaching-underperforming-employees.html.
24. Cornell University Law School's Legal Information Institute provides a concise definition of wrongful termination: "A fired employee's claim that the firing breached an employment contract or some public law." http://www.law.cornell.edu/wex/wrongful_termination. An employee can sue for wrongful termination if he or she feels the employer has exercised discrimination, retaliation, illegal acts, ignorance of Family or Medical Leave or other federal law, or if the organization has not followed its own termination procedures. Consequences of firing for employees and families are discussed by Jennifer Merritt, "The Awfulness of Firing an Employee: A Manager's Take," LinkedIn.Com (August 13, 2013), , https://www.linkedin.com/today/post/article/20130813180326-20195722-the-awfulness-of-firing-an-employee-a-manager-s-take. Paul Falcone describes ramifications of firing for co-workers and departments in "The Fired Elephant in the Room," SHRM.org (January 3, 2014), http://www.shrm.org/publications/managingsmart/pages/fired-employees.aspx. An example of steps a supervisor could take to investigate whether performance issues are related to an employee's status as a member of a protected class is shared by Shari Lau, "Performance-Based Discipline, Union Organizing, Bonus Taxation," *HR Magazine* (September 2009), p. 27.
25. Kevin Eikenberry and Guy Harris, *From Bud to Boss: Secrets to a Successful Transition to Remarkable Leadership* (San Francisco, CA: Jossey Bass, 2011). The book also has a companion Web site with free resources and tools, www.budtobosscommunity.com. See also Dori Meinert, "Develop Your Managers' Legal Awareness," SHRM.org (June 17, 2013), http://www.sherm.org/Publications/HRNews/Pages/Develop-Your-Managers'-Legal-Awareness.aspx.
26. The objectives listed here were developed by Professor Leonard for use in the Do it Best Store Management training program. For a discussion of the challenges organizations face in setting compensation levels, see Joanne Sammer, "The Art of Setting Pay," *HR Magazine* (May 2013), pp. 65–67. See also Donna M. Owens' interview of journalist Timothy Noah, winner of the Hillman Prize for public service magazine journalism for his ten-part series on income disparity in *Slade* magazine in 2010, "Why Care about Income Disparity," *HR Magazine* (March 2013), p. 53; Eric Krell, "Manufacturing's Great Salary Divide," *HR Magazine* (November 2012), pp. 41–45.
27. For a discussion of merit pay, see Scott Snell and George Bohlander, *Managing Human Resources*, 16th ed. (Mason, OH: South-Western/Cengage Learning, 2013). Also see Sarah E. Needham, "Tough Times Don't Mean Tough Luck on Salary," *The Wall Street Journal* (April 15, 2008), p. D6; and D. E. Terpstra and A. L. Honoree, "Employees' Responses to Merit Pay Inequity," *Compensation and Benefits Review* (January–February 2005), pp. 51–58.

    While many of the compensation issues are beyond the scope of this test, you might want to see Gerald E. Ledford Jr. and Herbert G. Henneman III, *Skill-Based Pay* (June 2011), Society for Human Resource Management (SHRM). Retrieved from http://www.siop.org/userfiles/image/SIOP_SHRM_Skill_Based_Pay.pdf.
28. See Robert J. Grossman, "The Care and Feeding of High-Potential Employees," *HR Magazine* (August 2011), pp. 34–39. A February 2011 study by Market-Tool, Inc., found that almost two-thirds of organizations have no formal feedback process for compensation decisions. Reported by John Sweeney, *HR Magazine* (July 2011), p. 23.

    For a discussion of pay for performance and gainsharing, also see Scott Snell and George Bohlander, *Managing Human Resources*, 16th ed. (Mason, OH: South-Western/Cengage Learning, 2013).
29. See Sharon Terlep, "GM: Contract Protects Us," *The Wall Street Journal* (September 29, 2011), p. B3; and Matthew Dolan, "GM Talks Take Center Stage," *The Wall Street Journal* (September 16, 2011), p. B 3. GM plans to offer buy-out to 17,000 veteran workers and to hire lower wage workers. Imagine the thoughts of Joe, a newer GM employee, earning $16 per hour, working alongside Sam, a long-term GM employee, making $28 per hour doing the same work. Only time will tell if the two-tiered system works.

# PART 3 Critical Incidents

The critical incidents below each present a supervisory situation based on real events to be used for educational purposes. The identities of some or all individuals, organizations, industries, and locations, as well as financial and other information may have been disguised to protect individual privacy and proprietary information. In some cases fictional details have been added to improve readability and interest.

Critical Incident 3-1

## HALF OF US WOULD LIKE TO LEAVE IF WE COULD

Grove City Regional Hospital CEO, Roy Mitchell, had been married twice and divorced. His first wife and mother of one of his children had recently filed suit for more child support. But that is only half the story. Roy often attended community functions with a beautiful young woman on his arm. Several hospital employees commented that, "a consensual sexual relationship between powerful men and ambitious younger women is commonplace these days." However, Linda Archer, Grove City chaplain and director of social services, has been increasingly critical of Mitchell's alleged liaisons with young women, some of whom are employed by the hospital. Last week in a meeting with Mike Schott, the hospital's director of HR and others, Archer exclaimed, "these relationships hurt morale and can end sourly amid charges of sexual harassment. Some women perceive that they can't get a fair shake around here unless they are the one on Mitchell's arm."

Schott cautioned, "Bite your tongue Linda. It might not be healthy to talk about the boss's business. Whom he takes to the symphony or to the college basketball game is his business, not ours."

On Friday, Schott received word from Mitchell's office that Ahmad Prasad would be transferred to a vacant position in the accounting department. Prasad had served as a deputy director of strategic planning and quality assurance. At the same time, it was announced that Mary Grant would be replacing Prasad as deputy director of planning. Schott was concerned because hospital policy required that vacant jobs be posted internally for five days, and this had not been done.

Later that afternoon, Jeffrey Zimmerman, director of quality assurance assured Schott that this position was now exempt from the internal posting requirement. He confided to Schott that Mitchell's persistent executive vice president of operations, Dennis Mansfield, had dictated the transfer of Prasad and the promotion of Grant. Grant had been working as an assistant admissions counselor at one of the hospital's satellite facilities. Schott walked down to the employee break room to get a cup of coffee wondering, "What qualifications does Mary

Grant have for this job? It pays $15,000 more than she was earning as an admissions counselor. Maybe the rumors are true. She was one of the finalists a couple of years ago in the Steuben County Miss America contest, and she has been seen with Mitchell on numerous occasions around the area."

A review of Ahmad Prasad's most recent performance evaluations indicated that he met or exceeded most of the expectations required for the new position. One of Schott's assistants reported that Prasad claimed that Zimmerman was told to prepare a place for Grant as a favor to Mitchell. Schott thought about the situation as he left to go to his weekly SHRM meeting.

Upon returning from the meeting, Schott was engaged by Terry Dugue, one of his HR clerks. Terry closed the door and said, "We have a problem that is now in center court. A friend just sent me a copy of a Facebook post that appears in several places":

| | |
|---|---|
| QUESTION: | How does one get a great job at Grove City hospital? |
| ANSWER: | On your back! |
| QUESTION: | Who is the employee of the month at Grove City hospital? |
| ANSWER: | Mary Grant, the new Deputy Director for strategic planning and quality sex! |

## QUESTIONS FOR DISCUSSION

1. What are the potential implications of CEO Mitchell's alleged behavior?
2. What, if anything, should Michael Schott do? Why?
3. Go online to see how many sexual harassment suits were filed in the United States last year. How many of them involve allegations of egregious behavior at the top management levels? Similarly, major political and governmental officials have been vilified for extramarital affairs and sexual involvement with subordinates. What kinds of problems do these relationships create for an organization?
4. How can consensual relationships with subordinates become devastating for an organization?
5. If Mary Grant's job performance is not negatively affected by her personal life and the same is true for CEO Roy Mitchell, should Mike Schott and other administrators become involved in this situation anyway?
6. If you were a member of the hospital's Board of Directors and you became aware of these allegations, what would you do to intervene?

## THE RIGHT EMPLOYEES CAN SHAKE THE BLUES OF THE GLOOMY PICTURE!

Critical Incident 3-2

With rumors of his state's economic woes and the federal government's lack of consensus among the various political parties on what to do to get economic growth back on track, Larry Sparks wondered how Paul's Home Center would survive. Sally Paul had two stores in rural communities in Texas. Last month, she purchased a Kmart complex that was closed in a metropolitan area. The store was being renovated and would become the third Paul's Home Center. This facility is about a mile down the road from a Wal-Mart.

Larry Sparks is 48 years old, married with five children ages 7 to 18. Shortly after graduating from high school, Paul enlisted in the Army and spent six years in the military. His tour of duty included three tours in Iraq and other Middle East countries. His military experience helped him to hone maintenance skills and leadership abilities. He returned to the area to marry his childhood sweetheart and has worked for Sally Paul for the past 16 years. He had finished an associate's degree in supervisory leadership at the local community college and Sally Paul had provided him with many opportunities to hone his skills.

Larry had never dreamed of the opportunity that was before him. He was to be the store manager at the new store and have full responsibility for all aspects of its operation. Since this new store was located 60 miles from his home, he knew that there would be many challenges. As he contemplated the future, he knew that finding the best employees and training them to be great was his first challenge. Where will he begin?

## QUESTION FOR DISCUSSION

1. Wander a local Wal-Mart store and look at the type of jobs that employees are doing.
   Would any of those jobs be appropriate for the new store Larry will be managing?
   What kind of skills does an employee need to do the jobs that need to be done in Larry's store?
2. Develop a plan to help Larry staff the store. (Please consider all the aspects discussed in Chapter 3 and in Part 3 of the text.)
3. Once Larry has selected his staff, what type of training is needed to get them to work together as an effective team?
4. Based upon your experiences in the workplace and your reading of the chapters in Part 3, what advice would you have for Larry to help him enable his employees to be the best they can be?

---

Critical Incident 3-3

## THE RIGHT JOB FOR ME!

Wilfred "Will" Reime couldn't believe what he was hearing. He was seated at 9 o'clock on Monday morning in Professor Edwards's management class. On this day the professor had invited a former student, Donnie Sanchez, to speak to the class. Sanchez was holding forth about his experiences as a student that had prepared him for the "real world." Sanchez talked about how four years earlier he was sitting where the students were currently sitting and wondered what the future would hold.

As Will listened intently, he heard echoes of some of Professor Edwards's recent lectures. As Will thought to himself many times, "How can it be that this professor actually knows what he is talking about? He's been a professor for the past 25 years and can't know anything about the real world." Donnie Sanchez continued:

> *Where do you want to go tomorrow was the question that Professor Edwards proposed to his class each week. Every term, he preached that we needed career self-reliance or at least a career self-direction. It was the question facing many of us as we planned to sprint into a full-time*

*job market. The U.S. economy has had the highest level of unemployment since the Great Depression. Good jobs were hard to come by and there were lots of applicants for every job opening. Most of the jobs wanted people that had experience. I had played on the college baseball team and summer leagues, so a co-op program or internship was out of the question for me. I felt that my team experiences have given me pretty good interpersonal skills, persistence, and a high energy level but no real world experience.*

*The college placement officer told me that I would have trouble finding meaningful work. After posting my resume on all social media, I found that restaurants were hiring at a brisk pace. But a major corporation like Darden had cut back most of its employees' hours because of ObamaCare. Even though I love to eat, the restaurant field was not appealing and I lacked many of the technical skills and computer skills to apply for some of the jobs that were available. I am a native of Puerto Rico, and I had braved the cold Midwest winters to play sports and pursue a basic liberal arts degree. Midway through my sophomore year, I heard some of my teammates extolling the virtues of Professor Edwards. After enrolling in his "Principles of Management" class, I changed my major to general management.*

*I don't want to embarrass Professor Edwards in front of his students, but I can honestly say that he was my best professor. He played the role of brain surgeon; he asked thought-provoking questions and demanded a lot from us. He extracted my best efforts and output, even after a strenuous day of practice. Professor Edwards required us to read What Color is Your Parachute. I decided to follow the advice offered by the author, Richard Boles, and contacted James Metzler, the supervisor at a local electronics manufacturing firm, Luxor.*

*At the time, Luxor employed 280 people and manufactured and assembled electronic components for the telecommunication industry. Today, their business has expanded to have over 400 employees. I had an opportunity to shadow Jim Metzler as part of my senior class project in Professor Edwards's "Management of Technological Change" course. Metzler's project team was changing some of Luxor's methods and processes. I learned a lot about the process of change and gained a mentor and a friend in the process. At the end of my shadowing experience, I asked Metzler a simple question: "Do you know of any jobs in general management that might be available for me?"*

*I got the surprise of my life when he told me that we were going down the hall to meet with Philip Lynn, the plant manager, and Jeannie Lerch, HR director. I was hired on the spot; I guess having a recommendation from Professor Edwards didn't hurt. Even though the job was somewhat technical, I began in early June after I graduated and played in my last college baseball game. They put me through a series of tests to show that I was a self-starter and a team player. Mr. Lynn said that he hires for attitude over aptitude. He claims that technical stuff is teachable, but that initiative and ethics aren't. The plant is organized on a self-directed work team approach. Teams elect their own leaders to oversee quality training, scheduling, and communication with other teams. The goals are created by Mr. Lynn and his staff after an in-depth consultation with all teams.*

*The plant follows simple ground rules, such as commit yourself to respect other team members, communicate openly and honestly, continually look for ways to improve on what we do well, and do the right job the right way the first time. The sales staff, customers, engineers, and assemblers consistently "noodle ideas around," and there are no status symbols or an attitude of "us" versus "them." There are no sacred cows in the company. Many procedures are written down, but any employee can propose changes to any process, subject to approval by those whose work it affects. When we change processes or methods, an employee logs onto the network to make it a part of the record—the law of the plant. There is plenty of feedback on performance. Team leaders share the good and the bad. Each day begins with a recap of the previous day's performance. Every employee knows the destination for every product they touch. Each employee puts his or her signature on the part.*

*In conclusion, let me say that I have had a great experience. Thanks, Professor Edwards, for what you did for me. Jim Metzler has served as my mentor and we meet each day to discuss my progress. I enjoy visiting customers to understand how they use our products. The company has a bonus system based upon individual performance, team performance, and ideas generated. Last year my bonus exceeded 25 percent of my yearly pay. I have been given additional job responsibilities and authority and love working there. I am getting an education for a lifetime and getting paid to learn. It doesn't get any better than this!*

## QUESTIONS FOR DISCUSSION

1. As you reflect on Donnie Sanchez's remark, "Is he making this up or are there really companies like", do the research to find the "Best Companies to Work For," and the reasons they are on the list. Did you find a company or two that might be like Luxor?
2. Evaluate the techniques that Donnie Sanchez used that led to his being offered the job at Luxor. How might you use the same "techniques" for finding the best job for you?
3. Would you like to work for a company like Luxor? Why and why not?
4. What do you need to do to hone your skills, knowledge, and abilities to help you find a "great job"?

---

**Critical Incident 3-4**

## UNWANTED HELP!

Most city employees were aware of the city's financial difficulties and the impact Detroit's bankruptcy had on creditors and employees and retirees. The city of Metropolis retirees were well aware of the fact that the bankruptcy judge had stated that pensions were not protected. It was estimated that only a fraction of the $3.5 billion the city of Detroit owed to pension funds would be paid to retirees. Like most cities and counties, Metropolis's city council and administration will have no recourse in future years but to raise property taxes or cut more current services.

The city's purchasing department consisted of six buyers, two clerks, and one supervisor. It is responsible for ordering all supplies needed by all departments.

Mary Sue Beringer is the newest buyer in the department. Included in her responsibilities are purchasing and inventory monitoring of all supplies needed by the city police department. The city's material requirements planning (MRP) system provides daily reports to Mary Sue and the other buyers. These reports identify items and supplies that need to be reordered. During her orientation Mary Sue was instructed that she would need to review the report at the beginning of each day, and place the necessary orders before the end of the day. The city required that all orders in excess of $2,500 needed to have at least three vendors bid and the low bidder was to get the order. This process would take a week and was the exception to filling the orders by the end of the day.

Three years ago, Corey Chesney was promoted from buyer to supervisor of the department. Six months ago, Mary Sue Beringer was his first hire. Corey had worked in the purchasing department for almost 14 years, and he knew the system inside and out. As a supervisor, he reviewed the MPR reports of all his buyers every day.

On Wednesday, several months after Mary Sue was hired, a review of the MRP report revealed to Corey that several necessary items for which Mary Sue was responsible had not been ordered. Since Corey was most familiar with the needed supplies and the appropriate suppliers, he decided to place the orders. Later in the day, he conveyed to Mary Sue that he had placed the orders and was willing to help her in any way possible to do the best job.

On Friday of that week, Mary Sue got a call from one of the suppliers wanting to know why there were duplicate orders placed. They asked her if she really needed to double the amount that she usually ordered, since earlier in the week Corey Chesney had placed orders for similar amounts. Mary Sue was infuriated that Corey had placed orders with her suppliers without informing her. She then confronted Corey about it. He apologized and said, "If you remember we discussed this on Wednesday and reminded her that he told her at the time he was willing to help her in any way."

Mary Sue thought the problem had been solved. But as time progressed, Corey continued placing some of her orders, although he always informed her of what he had done. On one occasion, Corey said. "I know you have been extremely busy and I needed to reduce your workload."

Mary Sue did not say anything about this to any of the other buyers, because she was afraid of what they might think. She thought to herself, "We work well together as a team but I am frustrated by what my supervisor is doing." She wondered how to tell Corey to let her do her job without causing hard feelings. Mary Sue came to realize that her supervisor didn't have confidence in her abilities and that he was unwilling to tell her what might be done differently. Her six-month performance appraisal was scheduled for next week.

Mary Sue was not comfortable with her situation, and wondered if her days in the purchasing department were numbered. She couldn't afford to lose her job. She wondered if she should first go to see the director of HR or Corey Chesney's immediate boss.

## QUESTION FOR DISCUSSION

1. Should a supervisor like Corey do the work of an employee to assist the employee or reduce his or her workload? Discuss.
2. Why would Corey have continued to do some of Mary Sue's job duties even after their initial discussion?
3. Why did Mary Sue resent her supervisor performing some of her job duties?
4. If you were Mary Sue, what would you do? Please consider alternatives.

5. In previous parts of the text we talked about the essentials for effective supervision. Do you think Corey is an effective supervisor? Why or why not?
6. Every supervisor needs to find ways to become more effective. Write a two-paragraph paper indicating some suggestions you have for Corey to improve his supervisory effectiveness.



Critical Incident 3-5

## IS SHE ON OUR TEAM?

Kyle Crawford had been a team leader for the League for the Blind and Disabled the past year, but had worked for a nonprofit organization for about five years. As team leader, Crawford had experienced many new work challenges. The number of people who need help in the community had more than doubled since he began his job. His team was responsible for providing help and direction for those in need.

Recently, some of Crawford's team members complained about Kaylee Depew's slow work pace and her failure to keep up with the needs of the clients. In response, Crawford had told the complaining team members that Kaylee was a silent employee who always shows up for work on time. While she worked a little slower than the rest of the team members, the work she did was well done. She often took longer to do the job and sometimes clients had to wait while she finished the prior project. Crawford's response initially seemed to satisfy the team members.

Yesterday, Paige Mora came to Crawford and said that some of the team members had indicated they also wanted to slow their pace of work if something wasn't done about Kaylee. At that point Crawford asked Mora whether she or other team members had talked or confronted Kaylee about her slow work pace. Mora replied, "Yes, we have told Kaylee on numerous occasions to pick up her speed and get the lead out. Clients don't like to wait and wait, beyond the time of their scheduled appointment with her. But she just continues to work at her usual slow pace. Dorothy Craig has spent an excessive amount of time instructing Kaylee on some of the more effective ways to do the job. Even that hasn't worked. Maybe she's just too fat to do the job here!"

Crawford decided to meet with the director, Lamarr Adams, and his immediate manager, Sabrina Lopez. Adams and Lopez discussed how Crawford's team had been one of the most productive and how Kaylee had joined the team about three years ago. According to Sabrina, "Kaylee's weight had ballooned in the past two years, and she appeared to carry about 300 pounds or more on her 5'6" frame. Work records indicated that Kaylee was not able to keep the pace set by some team members but that the team had been negligent to address the issue and her past performance evaluations." Crawford told Adams and Lopez, "I would be welcome to any advice you can give me."

### QUESTIONS FOR DISCUSSION

1. Every work group has its own personality. Discuss how a group's personality influences its ability to be productive?
2. Why is it important for Crawford to identify the issues that distract from group cohesiveness?
3. What are the issues in this critical incident?
4. If you were Crawford, what would you do? Why?

5. Go online and review the Americans With Disabilities Act Amendment Act (ADAAA), *Neely v. Public Service Enterprise Group Inc.*, 5th Cir., No.12-51074, and see other recent court decisions regarding overweight employees. Is Kaylee a "qualified individual with a disability"?
   a. Define: Essential job functions, reasonable accommodation, and undue hardship.
   b. Is overweight covered by the ADA?
   c. What if Kaylee says "her inability to keep up with the other team members and serve clients in a timely fashion is because of her health?" What should Crawford and the administration do?
6. What recommendations would you make to Crawford to help all team members understand reasonable accommodation for employees that are protected under ADA?

---



Critical Incident 3-6

## BUILDING A BRIGHT FUTURE, LESLIE H. WEXNER'S SECRET!

Feature Photo Service/Newscom

Leslie H. Wexner graduated from the Ohio State University with a bachelor's degree in 1959, briefly attended law school but then left to help his parents run their store in a suburb of Columbus, Ohio. In 1963, Wexner borrowed $5,000 from his aunt to start "The Limited" (so named because the store focused on clothing for younger women). In 1969, he took The Limited brand public (listed as LB on the NYSE). In 2013, Wexner was the longest serving CEO of a Fortune 500 company. Most students are familiar with The Limited and its Victoria's Secret and Bath and Body Works brands.

In 2013 Wexner was recognized as the wealthiest man in the state of Ohio. He served on the board of trustees and chairman of the Ohio State University board for several years. In 2011, Wexner donated $100 million to Ohio State, which was to be allocated to the university's academic medical center and the James Cancer Hospital and Solove Research Institute, with additional gifts to the Wexner Center for the Arts. This is the largest gift in the history of the University. In 2012, the medical center at Ohio State was renamed the Wexner Medical Center.[1] At that time, university president E. Gordon Gee, said, "For more than three decades, Mr. Wexner has been one of the university's most committed leaders and devoted followers. His generous contributions, both in time and resources, have been wholly transformational, but his most valuable gift has been his remarkable leadership."[2]

In October 2013 Wexner was the inaugural speaker at the Columbus Chamber of Commerce's "CEO Insight Series." Wexner offered several observations from his life lessons that may give students some thought.

"John W. Galbraith told me, just pursue things that interest you with an open mind. But what he was really talking about was open-mindedness, to be curious. I have really looked for a working diagram for success."

---

[1] http://www.alumni-osu.org/swfl/wp/pdf/wexner-medicalcenter.pdf
[2] http://www.buckeyeplanet.com/forum/threads/e-gordon-gee-official-thread.599670/page-27

Wexner continued, "My parents taught me to do business the right way! If a customer brought something back I would give them a refund; the proof for me that it was [the]right [thing] to do was that the customer came back!"

"Find the right way to treat people. When I was a young kid my dad and I ran a store and someone was giving the employee a hard time. When that customer left, my dad said 'That is not right.' That employee is in a vulnerable position. If you pick on someone, always pick on someone for the right reason."

On encouraging diversity:

"I grew up on the wrong side of the tracks. I kind of grew up with a chip on my shoulder, and did not think the world was fair. I found it is hard to level the playing field."

On learning from mistakes:

"You are not going to be a 100% hitter all the time. You are going to be wrong more than right. You must adjust your errors quickly."[3]

## QUESTIONS FOR DISCUSSION

1. Go online, and read about Wexner and The Limited Brands. After reading the chapters in Part 2, it should be apparent that managers must find ways to help themselves and their employees continuously improve. Based on your research findings, what are three things that Wexner has done to help himself grow? What one thing did you learn that will help you grow as you journey through life?
2. After reading the Critical Incident and your online findings, would you want to work for Wexner and one of his companies? Why or why not?
3. To what extent do you believe that Wexner's companies have empowered employees to be the best they can be?
4. Make a list of the characteristics of leadership and building effective teams that that Wexner has used to make his companies effective.
5. Visit one of Wexner's stores and ask at least two employees what they like best about working there. Compare your findings with those of three other students. To what degree are your findings similar or different? If there are differences, what you think might be the reasons for this?

[3] http://www.columbusceo.com/content/topic/2013/10/wexner-insights.html

PART 4

© Eugene Parciasepe/Shutterstock.com

# Controlling and Managing Performance and Conflict

Chapter 13

# Fundamentals of Controlling

©Rawpixel/Shutterstock.com

**After studying this chapter, you will be able to:**

1. Describe the nature and importance of the managerial controlling function.
2. Discuss the characteristics of effective controls and their importance based on time factors.
3. Identify the essential steps in the control process.
4. Clarify the supervisor's role in creating budgets and using them as a control device.
5. Examine the supervisor's role in maintaining cost consciousness and in responding to higher-level managers' orders to reduce costs.
6. Explain how the controlling function is closely related to the other managerial functions.

## YOU MAKE THE CALL!

*You are Nick Coy the accounting department supervisor for Lichty Manufacturing. The plant is located in a rural area of Minnesota and employs about 600 people. Directly reporting to you are two accountants and four clerks. All of your staff, except for one accountant, are women. Your department has responsibility for all aspects of internal accounting. All of you work in an office area that is separated from other departments.*

Several new software packages have been successfully implemented in your department. The new streamlined software system for processing accounts payable and receivable was recently project given top priority. It was so important that you were able to develop and carry out this project by yourself. Your boss, the company treasurer, specified a deadline date for completion that was very tight. In introducing the new software package, you met with the treasurer and one of your former professors to make sure it was properly installed. The software company provided help to get it installed. Your staff and others, who would be the software's primary users, were only told recently about the project, the implementation date, and scheduled training sessions.

One of the most interesting aspects of this new software was that you had the privilege to visit some other businesses to see how they were using the software. You visited a nearby nuclear plant, a local hospital, the community college and a food production plant to see how they operated and used the new technology.

This morning, a day after the first training session, one of your accountants and two of your clerks walked into your office quite upset. They claimed that the project's proposed implementation date was "totally unrealistic" and they were not happy because of some flaws in the new software package. They asserted that the new system would create more work than the old system, it would be confusing to employees and some of the customers, and its use would require extra time that was not available with the existing staff. Lori Bell, one of the clerks, summed up the group's feelings by stating, "All of this could have been avoided if you would have made us a part of the planning process from the beginning."

As the group left your office, you wondered whether the other accountant and team members felt the same way. You were feeling rather distressed. The project's scheduled implementation date was a week away and only one more training session remained. As Nick Coy, you pondered what you should do.

**Disclaimer:** The above scenario presents a supervisory situation based on real events to be used for educational purposes. The identities of some or all individuals, organizations, industries, and locations, as well as financial and other information may have been disguised to protect individual privacy and proprietary information. Fictional details may have been added to improve readability and interest.

YOU MAKE THE CALL!

## The Supervisor's Role in Controlling

**1 Describe the nature and importance of the managerial controlling function.**

The word *control* often elicits negative reactions, but control is a normal part of daily life. At home, at work, and in the community, everyone is affected by various controls, such as alarm clocks, thermostats, fuel and electronic gauges, traffic lights, and police officers directing traffic. Controls also play an important role in organizations. Controls ensure that results match plans. Every manager, from the chief executive to the supervisor, must develop and apply controls that regulate the organization's activities to achieve the desired results. What might happen when effective controls are not in place?

Students may remember hearing and reading about how Kweku Adoboli, the 31-year-old UBS AG trader, concealed speculative trading for his bosses and others. The trader incurred $2.3 billion losses betting on U.S. and European stocks, a practice prohibited on his UBS desk. Three years earlier, Lehman Brothers, one of the financial world's giants, went belly-up in part because of the lack of control systems to monitor and respond in a timely manner. These huge financial losses occurred because of unauthorized and flawed transactions and left many asking the question: "Where were the controls?"[1]

On another note, Bank of America (BofA) was a key driver of the financial meltdown that began in 2007 when it misrepresented the quality of $57.5 billion in mortgage securities, selling the bad debts to other financial agencies. The company was in shambles; regulators insisted that BofA bring in a new management team and revamp its management practices to deal with its legal and regulatory problems, which resulted in a nearly $10 million fine for the misrepresentation. BofA's revenues faltered immensely, showing a loss of $8.8 billion in the second quarter of 2011, with a $14.5 billion loss in the consumer real-estate market. Three years later, BofA revealed that it possibly hid up to $4 billion in losses from regulators during the period following the meltdown. Bank analyst Mike Mayo responded to the most recent revelation with the assertion, "Garbage in, garbage out. They have a $2 trillion balance sheet. What other losses are in there? It raises issues about control."[2]

These are just a few of the management malpractice events that have occurred in the past several years. Why did these events happen? The reason in part was greed, but a more important reason was the lack of control systems that alert managers in a timely fashion that something is amiss.

As management guru Peter Drucker stated, "Checking the results of a decision against its expectations shows managers what their strengths are, where they need to improve, and where they lack knowledge or information."[3] Thus, the **managerial controlling** function consists of checking to determine whether operations adhere to established plans, ascertaining whether progress is being made toward objectives, and taking action, where necessary, to correct deviations from plans. In other words, the supervisor acts to make things happen the way they were planned. Controlling is essential whenever a supervisor assigns duties to employees because the supervisor remains responsible for assigned work. If all plans proceeded according to design and without interference, the controlling function would be obsolete. As every supervisor knows, however, this is not reality. Therefore, it is part of the supervisor's job to keep activities in line and, when necessary, to get those activities back on track. This is done by controlling.[4]

**Managerial controlling**
Ensuring that actual performance is in line with intended performance and taking corrective action, if necessary

## NATURE OF THE CONTROLLING FUNCTION

Controlling is one of the five primary managerial functions. It is so closely related to the other functions that the line between controlling and the other functions sometimes blurs. Controlling is most closely related to planning. In planning, the supervisor sets objectives, and these objectives become standards against which performance is appraised. When performance and standards deviate, the supervisor must carry out the controlling function by taking corrective action, which may involve establishing new plans and different standards.

You might think that because controlling is the last managerial function discussed in this book, it might be perceived as something the supervisor performs after all other functions. The notion is far from the truth. You should view controlling as a function that is carried out simultaneously with the other managerial functions. As we discuss later in this chapter, there are control mechanisms for before, during, and after an activity.

## EMPLOYEE RESPONSES TO CONTROLS

Employees often view controls negatively because the amount of control in departments may determine how much freedom employees have to do their jobs. Yet most employees understand that a certain amount of control is essential to regulate performance. They know that a lack of control will result in confusion, inefficiency, and even chaos.

In a behavioral sense, controls and on-the-job freedom seem to conflict. However, when controls are well-designed and properly implemented, they can positively influence employee motivation and behavior. The supervisor should design and apply control systems that employees will accept without resentment but that will also monitor department performance effectively.[5] Interestingly, some firms have at times loosened certain controls and given employees more freedom, only to be disappointed by the outcome and then forced to tighten or return to discarded controls.

Rules about appropriate attire for schools and businesses provide us an example. Casual and informal dress in society certainly has grown dramatically in recent years. Look around you. Is everyone dressed appropriately? Attire such as halter tops, short shorts, t-shirts with offensive slogans, provocative blue jeans, flip-flops, and body piercing are among the types of questionable attire that have shown up in classrooms as well as in many business establishments. Should your instructor, college, or organization have the right to determine appropriate dress? Regardless of what a policy might prescribe, some people will say that it violates their freedom of self-expression or other rights.

What is acceptable dress in the classroom or business world? Several years ago, a teaching colleague announced that he expected all students in his classes to be appropriately dressed, that is, wearing business attire, since his was a business class. Seeking clarification, one student inquired as to what exactly he expected. Without really thinking, my colleague responded, "I expect all male students to wear a tie and suit or sport coat—you are a business student!" The next class session, he got exactly what he prescribed. Most of the male students showed up wearing flip-flops, shorts, T-shirts, ties, and suit coats. Within the bounds of decency, we cannot describe his rants at the next faculty meeting. Of course, that was 30-some years ago, and recently he was seen at a retired faculty meeting dressed very casually. We use this story to illustrate the problems individuals and organizations encounter when they do not draft policies carefully. A couple of sidebar questions are: Should the policy clearly specify ideas of appropriate attire? If so, who decides what is appropriate? How will students (employees) respond when they believe that the policy is not fair?

## CONTROLLING SHOULD BE FORWARD-LOOKING

A supervisor can do nothing about the past. For example, if work assigned to an employee for the day has not been accomplished, controlling cannot correct the day's results. Yet some supervisors believe that the main purpose of controlling is to assign blame for mistakes. This attitude is not sound because supervisors should primarily look forward, not backward. Of course, supervisors should study the past to learn how and why something happened and then take steps to avoid the same mistakes.

Because supervisors should look forward while controlling, it is essential that they identify deviations from standards as quickly as possible. Controls within a process or within an activity's time frame—rather than at its end—will enable the supervisor to take prompt corrective action. For example, instead of waiting until the day is over, the supervisor could check at midday to see whether a job is progressing satisfactorily. Even though the morning is past and nothing can change what has already happened, there may be time to correct the problem before the damage becomes excessive.

## CONTROLLING SHOULD BE CONSISTENT WITH STRATEGY

As you may recall from Chapter 3, strategic planning begins with establishing goals and making decisions that enable an organization to accomplish its objectives. The ultimate question becomes whether the organization achieved what it intended. The Supervisory Tips box in Chapter 3 shows that in order to reach our goal, we must establish feedback controls and monitor progress. Then changes, if necessary, must be made. In Chapter 8, we discussed how top management developed a vision and strategy for turning around the Baptist Health Care system of Pensacola, Florida. (See Figure 8.9 on page 300.)

Managers such as Nick Coy in this chapter's You Make the Call! must first create a vision—a picture of what a finished product, like a new software system, should look like and how it should function when the project is finished—and put a system in place that involves workers and provides feedback and opportunity to take corrective action. See Figure 13.1.

**FIGURE 13.1 You need a blueprint to get from average to outstanding!**

Someone once said that the ultimate criterion of organizational worth is whether or not the organization thrives. Today's healthcare environment is one of the most competitive, scrutinized, and regulated. You can only imagine the intense pressures—both internal and external—that hospital administrators face unless you have walked in their shoes. We believe that Pensacola, Florida-based Baptist Health Care, Inc. is an excellent example of an organization that made a decision about 10 years ago to become the "best of the best" and "walk the talk!"[6]

Baptist Hospital, Inc. (BHI), one of the four Baptist Health Care hospitals, is an example of a dramatic turnaround. In the early 1990s, BHI's morale and finances were in bad shape, and in 1995, the hospital scored in the 18th percentile for patient satisfaction.[7] In 1996, Stubblefield and Studer began to redefine the culture of the organization. Studer believed that some of the lessons he learned as a special-education teacher could be applied to healthcare. "Maximizing an organization's ability is similar to maximizing a child's potential." His first step was to diagnose the situation and then set achievable goals. "The higher the goals, the closer the student—or organization—comes to reaching full potential."[8]

- **Have a Goal:** Studer believed that Baptist needed to have a measurable service goal and a means of comparison. Hiring a large patient-satisfaction-measurement company that compares Baptist to 500 other hospitals across the country was a start. Every patient gets a survey. The feedback allows the hospital to take corrective action, restate goals, and recognize those employees who have received positive comments on the survey.
- **Incorporate Training:** Training played an important role in the turnaround. All nursing managers, supervisors, and department heads go off-site for two days every 90 days for managerial training and development.
- **Seek Employee Input:** Employee forums were held every 90 days. Employees got an opportunity to make their suggestions and concerns known. Employees were encouraged to identify changes in the workplace that would make it better. Studer and the top management team acted on those suggestions. If a suggestion could not be implemented, the employee understood why.
- **Report Cards (Metrics):** Accountability was the key. All leaders got report cards every 90 days. A typical employee had four measurements: customer service (Baptist's goal was to be in the top 1 percent of all hospitals in the country); efficiency (how long

*(continued)*

**FIGURE 13.1** *(continued)*

patients are in their units per diagnosis); expense management (how well managers are controlling costs); and turnover. Everyone got a turnover goal based on his or her unit and its past history.

- **Break a few rules:** Stepping outside the box was encouraged. Studer used the following example: *"One of our nurses, Cyd Cadena, called a lady who was hospitalized to see how she was doing at home. She was in a wheelchair, and she was depressed because she didn't have a wheelchair ramp. Her family was so busy working on home healthcare and a whole bunch of other things that they didn't get a chance to put in a ramp. Cyd called Don Swartz, Baptist's plant manager, and he built a ramp. He didn't ask, 'Can I do it?' He just did it; it was the right thing to do!* We tell the story about Don Swartz all over the whole organization. We tell our people it is OK to break a few rules. Take a few risks. Don is a star. You have to celebrate your legends."[9]

Legendary college basketball coach John Wooden summed it up when he said, "You cannot live a perfect day without doing something for someone who will never be able to repay you."[10] Every organization has the potential to create many Don Swartzs, but will they do it?

Within a few years, Baptist ranked number two in the country for all hospitals in patient satisfaction. Employee satisfaction had improved 30 percent, and physician satisfaction had risen from 72.4 to 81.3 percent. Job turnover for nurses declined from 30 to 18 percent.[11] A short-term miracle, a one-time blip on the radar screen, or building the foundation built in the late 1990s allows BHI to sustain those accomplishments over the long haul. In his book, *Hardwiring Excellence*, Quint Studer explains that once systems and processes are in place to sustain service and operational excellence, an organization is no longer dependent on a particular leader to ensure continued success. Results are *hardwired*![12] In 2000, Studer moved on to form the Studer Group, which coaches hospitals on service and organizational excellence. And yet Baptist's success lives on.

*The Moral of the Story*: A commitment to excellence requires creating a culture that demonstrates a commitment to employees, setting high but achievable goals, holding people accountable, appraising performance on a regular basis, and taking corrective actions. Our suggestion: "Try it—you will like it!"

*Sources:* A special thanks to Christina Roman of the Studer Group for her assistance in developing this Contemporary Issue. Material contained in this Contemporary Issue box pertaining to Quint Studer (http://www.Studergroup.com).

If you have active, hands-on, fully informed employees, who have the authority to see things that need to be done and the right to tackle any problem, ask any question of anyone, and apply their knowledge consistent with the organizational mission and culture, then the possibilities are limitless. The essence of Studer's system is the report card.[13] Unless people know how they are doing, they won't know what to change or accelerate. Remember, in the end, the goal is to satisfy customers and other stakeholder needs.

## CONTROLLING AND CLOSENESS OF SUPERVISION

Supervisors must know how closely to monitor employees' work. The closeness of supervisory follow-up is based on such factors as an employee's experience, initiative, dependability, and resourcefulness. Permitting an employee to work on an assignment without close supervision is both a challenge and a test of a supervisor's ability to delegate. This does not mean, however, that the supervisor should leave the employee alone until it is time to inspect the final results. It does mean that the supervisor should avoid watching every detail of every employee's work. By familiarizing themselves with employees' abilities, supervisors can learn how much leeway to give and how closely to follow up and control.

2 **Discuss the characteristics of effective controls and their importance based on time factors.**

## Characteristics of Effective Controls

For control mechanisms to work effectively, they should be understandable, timely, suitable and economical, indicational, and flexible. These characteristics are required of the controls used in all supervisory jobs—in manufacturing, retail, office work, healthcare, government service, restaurants, nonprofit organizations, banks, and other services. Because department activities are so diverse, these characteristics are discussed here only generally.

### UNDERSTANDABLE

All control mechanisms—feedforward, concurrent, and feedback—must be understood by the managers, supervisors, and employees who use them. At higher management levels, control mechanisms may be rather sophisticated and based on management information systems, mathematical formulas, complex charts and graphs, and detailed reports. At the top levels, such controls should be understandable to all managers who use them. At the departmental level, controls should be much less complicated. For example, a supervisor might use a brief, one-page report as a control device. In a dry-cleaning store, this report might show the number of different types of clothes cleaned and the number of employee hours worked on a given day. This control is uncomplicated, straightforward, and understandable. In an afterschool program run by a community organization, the report might show the number of youth served, the number of programs run, the number of participant disciplinary issues that arose, and the number of employees on duty during the day. When controls are confusing or too sophisticated for employees, the supervisor should devise new controls that meet departmental needs and are understandable to everyone who uses them.

### TIMELY

Controls should indicate deviations from standards without delay, and such deviations should be reported to the supervisor promptly, even when substantiated only by approximate figures, preliminary estimates, or partial information. It is better for the supervisor to know when things are about to go wrong than to learn that they are already out of control. The sooner a supervisor knows about deviations, the more quickly the deviations can be corrected.

For example, assume that a project that requires the installation of equipment must be completed on a tight schedule. The supervisor should receive regular reports (e.g., hourly or daily) that detail project status and that compare project progress to the schedule. Roadblocks (e.g., missing parts or work absences) that might delay the project should be included in these reports. The supervisor needs this type of information early to take corrective steps—before a situation gets out of hand. This does not mean that the supervisor should jump to conclusions or hastily resort to drastic action. Generally, a supervisor's experience and familiarity with a job will help determine when a job is not progressing as it should.

## SUITABLE AND ECONOMICAL

Controls must be suited to activities. For example, a complex information system control that is necessary for a large corporation would not apply to a small department. The small department needs controls, but controls of a different magnitude. The controls the supervisor applies must also be economical for a job. There is no need to control a minor assignment as elaborately as a manager would control a major capital-investment project.

For example, the head nurse in a hospital will control narcotics more carefully and frequently than bandages. In a small company with three clerical employees, it would be inappropriate and uneconomical to assign a full-time worker to check the clerks' work for mistakes. It would be better to make employees check their own work or, possibly, to check their co-workers' work. In contrast, in a large department of several hundred employees who are mass producing a small-unit product, it makes considerable sense to employ full-time inspectors or quality-control specialists to check results. Typically, these employees take samples because it is impossible to check every item in production.[14] For the many in-between situations that supervisors face, good judgment helps determine the suitability of controls.

Stefan Kiefer/imagebroker/Alamy

*Employees dedicated to inspecting items are expensive but may be well worth the value they add in discovering deviations and preventing problems.*

Even though it may be difficult to determine how much controls cost and how much they are worth, they must be worth their expense. To determine the value of controls, supervisors should consider the consequences of having no controls. For example, compare an elaborate, expensive control system in a pharmaceutical company with controls in a rubber-band manufacturer. Defective rubber bands are an inconvenience, but defective drugs can kill people. The risks to the pharmaceutical company make elaborate controls worth their expense.

## INDICATIONAL

It is not enough for controls just to expose deviations as those deviations occur. A control also should indicate who is responsible for the deviation and where the deviation occurred. When several subassemblies or successive operations comprise a work process, the supervisor may need to check performance before and after each step. Otherwise, if results are below standards, the supervisor may not know where to take corrective action.

## FLEXIBLE

Because work operations occur in a dynamic setting, unforeseen circumstances can wreak havoc with even the best-laid plans and systems. Therefore, controls should be flexible enough to cope with unanticipated patterns and problems.

Control mechanisms must permit changes when such changes are required. For example, when an employee encounters significant condition changes early in a work assignment, such as an equipment failure or a materials shortage, the supervisor must recognize the changes and adjust plans and standards accordingly. If these difficulties are due to conditions beyond the employee's control, the supervisor also must adjust the criteria by which the employee's performance is appraised. Supervisors must tailor controls to the activities, circumstances, and needs for their departments. But more importantly, they must understand how time impacts what they do when.

## TIME FACTOR CONTROL MECHANISMS

Before we discuss the steps of the controlling process, it is important to distinguish among the following three types of control, which are classified according to time:

1. Feedforward (preliminary, preventive, anticipatory)
2. Concurrent (in-process)
3. Feedback (after-the-process)

## FEEDFORWARD (PRELIMINARY, PREVENTIVE, ANTICIPATORY) CONTROLS

**Feedforward control**
Anticipatory action taken to ensure that problems do not occur

Because controlling has forward-looking aspects, the purpose of a **feedforward control** is to anticipate and prevent potential sources of deviation from standards by considering, in advance, the possibility of any malfunctions or undesirable outcomes. A preventive maintenance program, designed so that equipment will not break down at the height of production, is an example of a feedforward control. The produce clerk who checks samples of bananas to ensure their acceptability is another example. The clerk selects a sample from the crates before the crates are unloaded and the merchandise is placed on display. Requiring assemblers to ascertain components' quality before installation and to signify that they have done so is becoming increasingly common. Other examples of feedforward controls include such devices as safety posters; fire drills; disciplinary rules; checklists to follow before starting equipment; and the policies, procedures, and methods drawn up by managers when planning operations. Everyone uses feedforward controls at one time or another. For example, a person who checks a car's tires, oil, and gas gauge before a trip is using feedforward controls.

## CONCURRENT (IN-PROCESS) CONTROLS

**Concurrent control**
Corrective action taken during the production or delivery process to ensure that standards are being met

A control that is applied while operations are proceeding and that spots problems as they occur is called a **concurrent control**. The traveler who notices that the fuel gauge is below half full or that the fuel warning light has just come on, and who pulls into the next gas station for a fill-up uses a concurrent control. Other examples of concurrent controls are online monitoring systems, numerical counters, automatic switches, gauges, and warning signals.

To illustrate, let's consider the Fisherman's Wharf, a bait, tackle, and convenience store in a lake resort town. Vacationers frequent the store to buy fishing, boating, and camping supplies, t-shirts, snacks, beverages, souvenirs, and the typical things people forget to bring when they go on vacation; and they can rent pontoon boats and canoes by the day or week. Locals typically buy gas, bait, and candy. The store is owned by Caitlyn Robbins, an avid outdoorswoman who took over the business when her parents retired. Suppose the Wharf cashiers optically scan each customer's purchases. The customers get printouts of their purchases and the prices they paid (sales receipts). At the same time, the store's inventory automatically decreases by the numbers just sold. The store's computer records the items sold. The computer has been programmed to alert Robbins at the close of business each day of items that are close to sold-out, and to automatically place a purchase order when the store's inventory reaches a specified level. As a result, stock is replenished as needed, and the store risks no shortages. When these types of concurrent control aids are absent, supervisors such as Robbins have to monitor activities by observation, often with the assistance of employees.

Even with feedforward controls, concurrent controls are necessary to catch the problems that feedforward controls cannot anticipate. Consider the traveler who fills the fuel tank before a trip and estimates, based on experience, that she should be able to travel the 300 miles to her destination without refueling. Unexpectedly, the weather turns unseasonably warm, and the traveler experiences a lengthy delay due to a highway accident. For the convenience of her passengers, the traveler runs the air conditioner while waiting in traffic, both of which unexpectedly increase fuel consumption. Unless the driver periodically checks the fuel gauge or is alerted by the low-fuel warning light (both concurrent controls), she might run out of fuel before reaching the destination.

### FEEDBACK (AFTER-THE-PROCESS) CONTROLS

The purpose of a **feedback control** is to evaluate and, when necessary, correct the results of a process or an operation and to determine ways to prevent deviations from standard. The traveler who calculates average miles per gallon and uses that feedback when planning the budget for the next trip uses a feedback control. Other examples of feedback controls include measurements of the quality and quantity of units produced, various kinds of statistical information, program satisfaction surveys, accounting reports, and visual inspections. Because feedback controls are applied after a task, process, service, or product is finished, they are the least desirable control mechanisms when damage or mistakes occur, because nothing can be done after the fact. When no damage or mistakes occur, feedback controls are used to further improve the process or product.

**Feedback control**
Actions taken after the activity, product, or service has been completed

Feedback controls are probably the most widely used category of controls at the supervisory level. Too often, however, they are used primarily to determine what went wrong and where to place blame rather than to prevent the problem from recurring.

## Steps in the Control Process

**3 Identify the essential steps in the control process.**

The control process involves three sequential steps. The first step, which is usually part of the planning function, is to set standards appropriate to the task. In the second step, performance is measured against these standards. If performance does not meet the standards, the third step is to take corrective action. These three steps must be followed in sequence if controlling is to achieve the

FIGURE 13.2 Steps in the control process

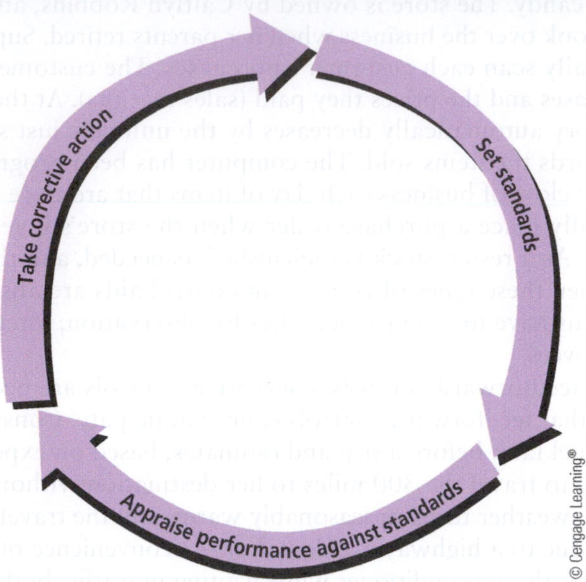


desired results (see Figure 13.2). The accompanying Supervisory Tips box provides selected do's for supervisors as they carry out control responsibilities with their employees.

## SETTING STANDARDS

**Standards**
Units of measure or criteria against which results are evaluated

Standards may be defined as the units of measure or the criteria against which performance or results are judged. **Standards** are targets; they are the criteria to which performance is compared in order to exercise control. Standards must be set before a person's work, a finished product, or a service can be meaningfully evaluated. In Chapter 3, we described goals and objectives as the foundations of planning. Objectives give employees specific targets. However, the presence of objectives does not mean targets will be attained. The effective supervisor must follow up to ensure that the actions that are supposed to be taken are being taken and that the objectives are being achieved.

**Tangible standards**
Standards for performance that are identifiable and measurable

**Intangible standards**
Standards for performance results that are difficult to measure and often relate to human characteristics (e.g., attitude, morale)

There are many types of standards, depending on the areas of performance or results to be measured. **Tangible standards** are performance targets for results that are identifiable and measurable. These standards can be set to measure such things as quantity of output, quality of output, market share, labor costs, overhead expenses, and time spent producing a unit or providing a service. (The tangible standards included on employee appraisal rating forms are identified in Chapter 12.) **Intangible standards** are targets for results that have no physical form; these standards may cover such areas as an organization's reputation, level of employee engagement, or quality of care in a healthcare center or nursing home. It is usually more difficult to establish intangible standards in numerical or precise terms.

The most frequent tangible standards that supervisors determine or must follow pertain to departmental operations. For example, in a production department, standards can be set for the number of units to be produced; the labor hours per unit; and product quality in terms of durability, finish, and closeness of dimensions.[15] In a sales department, standards might be set for the number of customers contacted, the sales dollars realized, and the number and types of customer complaints.[16] In an Indiana Superior Court that hears child welfare cases, performance standards may include the time it takes to for a child abuse or neglect case to be heard in court after initial filing, the time it takes for parental rights to be terminated, the number of children placed in foster care, the number of foster children placed permanent homes, the time it takes to place foster children in permanent homes, and the number of children who reenter foster care.[17] As more and more organizations are incorporating social media into their efforts to attract, engage, and maintain stakeholders, cross-industry standards are being developed to help measure the extent to which those efforts are actually bearing fruit.[18] In the examples above, standards measure the extent to which the intended work is being done, according to the organizations' established goals.

In setting standards, a supervisor can use experience and job knowledge as guides. Through experience and observation, most supervisors have general ideas of how much time it takes to perform certain jobs, the resources that are required, and what constitutes good or poor quality. By studying and analyzing previous budgets, past production and service delivery, and other departmental records, supervisors should be able to develop workable standards of performance for most aspects of their departments' operations.

**SUPERVISORY TIPS**

### Supervisory Do's for Controlling Employee Performance

- Do be very clear when communicating the objectives and specifics of work assignments.
- Do get agreement, if possible, on the standards and measures of performance assessment.
- Do solicit employees' ideas for improvement.
- Do use employee ideas and suggestions whenever appropriate.
- Do concentrate on those issues that most need attention.
- Do take corrective action with improvement as the primary goal.
- Do demonstrate consistently with all personnel that budgets, standards, and strategic control points are considered necessary components of effective supervision.
- Do convey by words and deeds that in no area of your supervisory responsibilities will you compromise or accept any work performance that is unsatisfactory.
- Do use praise and encouragement daily

## MOTION AND TIME STUDIES

A more thorough and systematic way to establish standards for the amount of work employees should accomplish in a given time frame is to apply work measurement techniques, preferably performed by, or with the assistance of, industrial engineers.[19] The most prominent techniques are motion and time studies. In a **motion study**, engineers analyze how a job is performed to identify ways to improve, eliminate, change, or combine steps to make the job easier and faster. After thoroughly studying work motions and layout, the industrial engineers or analysts develop what they consider the best methods for doing the jobs.

**Motion study**
An analysis of work activities to determine how to make a job easier and quicker to do

Once the best current method has been identified, a **time study** is performed to determine a time standard for the job. This is accomplished in a systematic and largely quantitative manner by selecting certain employees for observation; observing the time needed to accomplish various parts of the job; applying correction factors; and making allowances for fatigue, personal needs, and unavoidable delays. When all these factors are combined properly, the result is a time standard for the job.

**Time study**
A technique for analyzing jobs to determine time standards for performing each job

While the time study approach attempts to be objective, considerable judgments and approximations are part of the process. A time standard is neither wholly scientific nor beyond dispute, but it does provide a sound basis on which a supervisor can set realistic standards. The standards developed through motion and time studies can help the supervisor distribute work more evenly and judge each employee's performance fairly. Such standards also help the supervisor predict the number of needed employees and the probable job cost.

Most supervisors work in organizations without industrial engineers. When a new job is to be performed in the department, the supervisor can set tentative standards based on similar operations in his or her department or other departments. When no comparison standard is readily available, the supervisor should identify the key tasks necessary to accomplish the job and then observe employees directly or ask employees to record the time required to complete their tasks. From these data, a reasonable standard can be calculated.

To illustrate, suppose a shift supervisor in a fast-food restaurant must determine how long it takes employees to prepare a new menu item. The supervisor lists all the steps necessary to complete the job. Then, the supervisor can perform the task under several different circumstances and record the required times. The supervisor also can select several employees to perform the task under various conditions. From these several observations, the supervisor can determine the average time required to complete the task. Such an approach will not only establish realistic standards but also might uncover better ways of doing the job.

There are, of course, numerous ways to measure workers' productivity to reflect the unique nature of a department's operations and its products or services. Some worker productivity standards are expressed relative to overall sales volume, profitability, and other aggregate figures—factors over which a supervisor has limited or no control.[20]

## EMPLOYEE PARTICIPATION

Some employees resent standards, especially those standards arrived at through motion and time studies. This resentment is part of a long-standing fear that so-called efficiency experts and supervisors use motion and time studies primarily to increase workers' output. However, the main purpose of performance standards should be to create realistic targets, that is, objectives that can be achieved and are considered fair by both the supervisor and the employees. Workers are more apt to accept standards as reasonable and fair when they help formulate the standard.[21] Figure 13.3 provides an interesting illustration to support the notion that those who have responsibility for achieving the targets should be involved in setting standards.

**FIGURE 13.3 Whose job is it?**

United Features Syndicate

One technique for including employees in standards establishment is to form a committee of workers to help the supervisor or industrial engineer carry out a work-measurement program. The employees selected for this committee should be those who, in the supervisor's judgment, consistently do a fair day's work.

When adopting this approach, the supervisor and industrial engineer should explain to all employees what is involved in motion and time studies, including areas in which judgment is involved. Employees should be allowed to challenge any standard they consider unfair and perhaps even be allowed to request that a job be restudied or retimed. Most workers accept performance standards when they feel the supervisor has tried to help them understand the basis for the standards and has been willing to reconsider and adjust standards that appear to be unreasonable. There are a number of examples where employees, or employees and their union, help set productivity standards. They jointly participate in budgeting, pricing, designing product, marketing, sourcing decisions, and appraising results.

## STRATEGIC CONTROL POINTS

As mentioned previously, a metric or standard is nothing more than a measure to assess the department's performance in a particular area.[22] For example, Caitlyn Robbins, the owner of the Fisherman's Wharf store introduced earlier in this chapter, might want to consider developing metrics for the following:

- Customer satisfaction
- Market share
- Inventory measures
- Sales per square foot or sales of various product lines
- Revenue per hour per employee. Some firms might use income per full-time equivalent (FTE)
- Associate (employee) satisfaction
- Delivery time against customer requirements
- Service quality
- Advertised items in stock in sufficient supply to meet customer demand
- Performance of suppliers against their requirements
- Profitability
- Employee suggestions asked for, listened to, and incorporated

In the Supervisory Tips box in Chapter 3, we introduced the notion of SMART goals. Caitlyn Robbins needs to develop goals in those areas where she can get "the biggest bang for her buck." When you play a game, do you keep score? Why? Because the score card is a way to keep track of how one is doing. The score is only good for those things that we are able to measure. Developing strategic control points or metrics for which you cannot collect accurate or timely data is a waste of time.

For supervisors, the number of standards needed to determine performance quantity and quality may grow as a department expands. As operations become more complex and as the number of department functions increases, it becomes time-consuming and impractical for the supervisor to constantly check against every conceivable standard. Therefore, the supervisor should concentrate on certain strategic control points against which overall performance can be monitored. **Strategic control points**, or **strategic standards**, are a limited number of

**Strategic control points (strategic standards)**
Performance criteria chosen for assessment because they are key indicators of overall performance

key indicators that give the supervisor a good sampling of overall performance. There are no rules for selecting strategic control points. Because the nature of the department and the makeup of the supervisor and employees differ in each situation, only general guidelines can be suggested.

One major consideration that may render one standard more strategic than another is timeliness. Because it is essential to control time, the sooner a deviation is discovered, the better it can be corrected. A supervisor must recognize at what critical step operations should be checked. For example, a strategic control point might be after a subassembly operation but before the product is assembled with other parts and spray painted. A similar approach can be applied to the dry cleaning process of a soiled dress. In this example, a strategic control point can be established shortly after stain remover is applied. Imagine the cost if a stain is still present when all other dry-cleaning operations have been completed.

A supervisor should be careful to choose strategic control points that do not significantly impede other important standards. For example, excessive control to increase production quantity might erode product quality.[23] Likewise, if labor expenses are selected as a strategic control point, supervisors might try to hold down wage expenses by hiring too few workers, thereby causing both quality and quantity standards to deteriorate. Similarly, a laundry department supervisor in a nursing home must not sacrifice standards for preventing infections simply to reduce the cost of laundering linen. To some extent, decisions about strategic control points depend on the nature of the work. What serves well as a strategic control point in one department will not necessarily serve well in another.

Another example of strategic control points is the supervisor who wishes to assess departmental employee relations. The supervisor might decide to use the following indicators as strategic control standards, which are often described as employee engagement measures:

- Number of employees' voluntary resignations and requests for transfer
- Levels of absenteeism, tardiness, and turnover
- Accident frequency and severity rates
- Number and types of employee grievances and complaints
- Number and types of customer complaints
- Amount of scrap and rejects and unexplained losses of materials and inventory
- Number of employee suggestions for methods or operations improvement
- Employee responses to satisfaction surveys conducted by the human resources department or an outside firm.

By closely watching trends and changes in these indicators, the supervisor should be able to spot problems requiring corrective action. If the trends of most or all of these indicators are unfavorable, major supervisory attention is needed.

Consider a wire manufacturer who used simple statistics to track the productivity of machine operators. During the preceding hour, scrap exceeded the acceptable standard by 10 percent. Using strategic control points in a timely fashion, the supervisor working with the operators and the maintenance department knew it was time to check production. A check of the diamond dies, pressure settings, and quality of the raw stock led to action so that scrap rates increased no further and could be returned to their lower levels. Strategic control points should be established so that corrective action can be taken early in production.[24]

As mentioned previously, areas of an intangible nature also should be monitored closely, even though it is difficult to set precise standards for these areas. For example, employee engagement is typically an important element of departmental operations that a supervisor may decide to appraise and assess as a strategic control standard. This is particularly important in an era when workplace anger and employee discontent are reportedly widespread and the potential for these feelings to erupt into violence is real. Techniques for measuring and evaluating employee engagement were discussed extensively in Chapter 11.

## CHECKING PERFORMANCE AGAINST STANDARDS

The second major step in the control process, an ongoing activity for every supervisor, is to check performance against standards. The primary ways for a supervisor to do this are to observe, study oral and written reports, spot check, and use statistical sampling. Figure 13.4 takes a lighthearted look at tracking performance. Unfortunately, the supervisor did not give praise when Tuesday's performance exceeded expectations and did not take corrective action on the other days. We ask you, who is at fault that Friday's performance fell to the bottom?

## PERSONAL OBSERVATION

When monitoring employee performance, there is no substitute for a supervisor's direct observation and personal contact. The opportunity to inspect and closely observe employee performance is an advantage the supervisor has over top-level

**FIGURE 13.4 After developing performance standards, the supervisor must be alert for any deviations from these standards**

managers because the further a manager is from employees' work, the more that manager must depend on reports from others. The supervisor, however, has ample opportunity to observe directly all day long.

When supervisors find deviations from standards, they should assume a questioning, though not necessarily a fault-finding, attitude. A problem could be due to something outside the employees' control, such as a malfunctioning machine or faulty raw materials. Supervisors should question mistakes in a positive, helpful manner. For example, instead of criticizing, a supervisor should first ask what caused the problem and whether there is any way in which the supervisor can help the employees do their jobs more easily, safely, or efficiently. Supervisors also should ask employees what should be done to correct problems. When standards are stated primarily in general terms, supervisors should look for specific unsatisfactory conditions, such as inadequate output, poor quality work, or unsafe practices. It is not enough just to tell employees that their work is "unacceptable" or "unsatisfactory." When the supervisor can point to specific instances or cite recent examples, the employee is more likely to acknowledge the deficiencies that must be corrected.[25]

To identify the causes of poor performance that are not employees' fault, such as inadequate training, problems with workflow design, or an unusual increase in workload, supervisors can use personal observation and questioning. For example, if a retail-store supervisor discovers that customers are being processed by the cashier too slowly, the reason may be that an unusually large number of customers entered the store at once. Therefore, instead of chastising employees, the proper corrective action may be to open another checkout lane. Also, the supervisor may need to hire backup cashiers or to find a better way to predict customer traffic. The supervisor may include alternative ways of doing the job in his or her plans. Employees may have valuable ideas for preventing this problem.

Checking employee performance through personal observation has limitations. It is time-consuming, and it may require supervisors to spend hours away from other activities. Also, it may be impossible for the supervisor to observe some important activities at critical times. Some employees will perform well while being observed but will revert to poorer, less diligent habits when the supervisor is not present. Nevertheless, personal observation is still the most widely used and probably the best method of checking employee performance at the supervisory level.

Suppose that as part of Caitlyn Robbins's vision for her Fisherman's Wharf, she wanted her associates to be engaged in all aspects of the operation. What are some things she might have done? As part of the onboarding process, she could have developed a strategic map explaining the Wharf's goals such as building customer loyalty and team spirit, and treating others with respect. The associates would be accountable to the customer and each other. Everyone needs to have a stake in the game. When a culture like this is created, the employees will work together for the good of the team.

Unfortunately, however, recent research shows that not all employees are willing to help a fellow employee who is struggling (see Figure 13.5). With the increasing use of the team approach, tying compensation to team performance, and supervisors being expected to do more with less, we would have thought that more colleagues would have reached out to help their fellow workers.

**FIGURE 13.5 Would you "rat" on an associate?**

If a colleague on your team is seriously underperforming, would you report him or her to a supervisor, even if the colleague is a friend?

No, I would help my friend catch up and perform better. 58%

Yes, if the team's success is on the line. 27%

No, it's not my concern. 11%

Yes, if I thought it would help me get ahead. 4%

*Sources:* Jae Yang and Sam Ward, USA Today Snapshots® *USA Today* (September 21, 2011), page 1B; Laura Chamberlain, "One Third of Workers Would Report Underperforming Colleagues," *Personnel Today* (August 15, 2011), personneltoday.com; Leigh Steere, "Only One-Third of Workers Report Underperforming Colleagues," *Ragan's HR Communication* (August 18, 2011), hrcommunication.com

## ORAL AND WRITTEN REPORTS

When a department is large, operates in different locations, or works around the clock, oral and written reports are necessary. For example, when a department operates continuously and its supervisor has responsibility for more than one shift, to appraise the performance of shifts when the supervisor is not present, the supervisor must depend on reports submitted by employees. When a department operates multiple shifts and different supervisors are in charge of different shifts, each supervisor should arrive early to get a firsthand report from the supervisor who is completing the previous shift.

Whenever reports are required, the supervisor should insist that those reports are clear, complete, concise, and correct. When possible, oral presentations should accompany written reports. Reports are more effective when they are substantiated with statistical or comparative data.

Most employees submit reasonably accurate reports, even when those reports contain unfavorable outcomes. Report accuracy depends largely on the supervisors' reactions to reports and their relations with employees. When supervisors handle adverse reports constructively and helpfully, appreciating honesty instead of just giving demerits, employees are encouraged to submit accurate reports, even when those reports show them unfavorably.

When checking reports, supervisors usually find that many activities have been performed according to standards and can be passed over quickly. As a result, many supervisors use the **exception principle**, which means concentrating on those areas in which performance is significantly above or below standard. Supervisors may even ask employees to forgo reporting on activities that have, for the most part, attained standards and to report only on activities that are exceptionally below or above standard. When performance is significantly below standard, the supervisor must move to the third stage of the control process—taking corrective action. When performance is significantly above standard, the supervisor should praise the employees and encourage the exceptional performance to be repeated.[26]

**Exception principle**
Concept that supervisors should concentrate their investigations on activities that deviate substantially from standards

## SPOT CHECKS

When the employees' work routine does not lend itself to reports, the supervisor may have to rely on periodic spot checks. For example, a data-systems supervisor who is responsible for a centralized computer department that works around the clock, six days a week, should report to work at varying times to assess the department during different shifts. Supervisors with little or no opportunity to spot check usually must depend on reports.

## SAMPLING TECHNIQUES

**Sampling**
The technique of evaluating some number of items from a larger group to determine whether the group meets acceptable quality standards

Sampling techniques are really supplements to strategic control points and spot checks. In some firms, each part or product is inspected to determine whether it meets standards. Inspecting every item is time-consuming and costly. While a detailed discussion is beyond the scope of this book, it is becoming increasingly crucial for supervisors, particularly in production facilities, to acquaint themselves with statistical quality control (SQC). SQC is a method to help supervisors determine not only which products, product components, or services to inspect, but also how many to inspect.[27] **Sampling** is the process of inspecting some predetermined number of products from a batch to determine whether the batch is acceptable or unacceptable. To illustrate, suppose that a store manager has been concerned with the quality of produce received from a distributor. The store manager and the produce manager use SQC to determine how many items in an incoming produce shipment should be inspected. Rather than inspecting the entire lot, the store manager and produce manager compare random samples against a predetermined quality standard. If a certain number of the samples fail to meet the standard, the managers reject the entire lot. Note that if the distributor used this technique before shipping the produce, it would be feedback control. The same process used by the store manager would be feedforward control. While SQC saves time and inspection costs, the supervisor must ensure that the inspected units accurately represent all units.

## TAKING CORRECTIVE ACTION

When no deviations from standards occur, the process of control is fulfilled by the first two steps of control: (1) setting standards and (2) checking performance against standards. When, however, deviations are noted through personal

Ryan Pyle/Corbis

*A supervisor should analyze the causes of a deviation before determining the best course of corrective action.*

observation, reports, or spot checks, the supervisor must take the third step: taking corrective action to bring performance back into line.

Before taking corrective action, the supervisor should remember that deviations from standards can occur in any job for various reasons. Following are some of these reasons:

- Standards were based on faulty forecasts or assumptions.
- Unforeseen problems arose and distorted results.
- Failure occurred in some preceding job or activity.
- Employee who performed the job was unqualified or was given inadequate directions or instructions.
- Employee who performed the job was negligent or failed to follow directions or procedures.

Therefore, before taking corrective action, the supervisor should determine the causes of the deviation by analyzing the situation. Only after identifying specific causes can the supervisor decide which remedial actions will obtain better results. For example, if the reason for the deviation lies in the standards themselves, the supervisor must revise the standards. If the employee who performed the job was unqualified, additional training and closer supervision might be the answer. If the employee was given improper instructions, the supervisor should accept the blame and improve techniques for giving directives. In the case of employee negligence or insubordination, corrective action may consist of a discussion with the employee or a verbal or written reprimand. At times, more serious forms of discipline, including employee suspension or replacement, may be needed. Under such circumstances, the supervisor should follow the disciplinary procedures discussed in Chapter 15.

## Budgetary Control

**4 Clarify the supervisor's role in creating budgets and using them as a control device.**

Among the tools for financial control, the budget is usually the one with which supervisors have the most frequent contact. A **budget** is a written plan expressed in numerical terms that projects anticipated resources and expenditures for a period, such as a month, a quarter, six months, or one year. Firms usually prepare various budgets. Supervisors are most familiar with the operating budget. The **operating budget** projects the dollar amounts of the various costs and expenses needed to run the business, given projected revenues. Operating budgets, which may be developed for every department, usually show how much is allocated for inventory, salaries, supplies, travel, rent, utilities, advertising, and other expenses.

**Budget**
A financial plan that projects expected revenues and expenditures during a set period

**Operating budget**
The assignment of dollar allocations to the costs and expenses needed to run the business, based on expected revenues

At times, it is convenient to express budgets in terms other than dollars. Budgets pertaining to employment requirements, for example, may be expressed in the number of employee-hours allocated for certain activities or the number of workers needed for each job classification. Eventually, however, such nonfinancial budgets are converted to monetary figures—operating budgets. These statements summarize organizations' overall activities and serve as foundations on which managers can plan and control the use of financial and other resources.[28]

All managers, from the CEO to supervisors, must learn how to develop budgets, live within budgetary limits, and use budgets for control purposes. The term *budgetary control* refers to the use of budgets by supervisors, accountants, and higher-level managers to control operations so that they comply with organizational standards for making budgets.

## SUPERVISORY PARTICIPATION IN BUDGET MAKING

Budget making falls under the managerial function of planning, but carrying out the budget, or living within the budget, is part of the controlling function. As is true in so many other areas of management, the planning and controlling aspects of the budget process are interrelated. Preparing a budget, whether it is expressed in monetary or other terms, requires the budget-maker to quantify estimates by attaching numerical values to each budgetary item. The numerical figures in the final budget become the desired financial standards of the organization. Similarly, the numerical figures in the final departmental budgets become the standards to be met by each department and departmental supervisors.

**Incremental budgeting**
A technique for projecting revenues and expenses based on history

**Zero-base budgeting**
The process of assessing, on a benefit-and-cost basis, all activities to justify their existence

Most annual budgets are projections for the following year based on the previous year's budget. This approach for making a budget is known as **incremental budgeting**. Another approach, which has gained some acceptance in recent years, is zero-base budgeting. When an organization practices **zero-base budgeting**, all budgets must begin "from scratch," and each budget item must be justified and substantiated. In zero-base budgeting, the previous budget does not constitute a valid basis for a future budget. The advantage of zero-base budgeting, sometimes called zero-base review, is that all ongoing programs, activities, projects, products, and the like are reassessed by management in terms of their benefits and costs to the organization. This avoids the tendency of simply continuing expenditures from a previous budget period without much consideration. The disadvantage of zero-base budgeting is that it involves a large amount of paperwork and is very time-consuming. Moreover, in practice, it is difficult to apply the concept to some departments and types of operations.[29]

The budget that most concerns supervisors is usually the departmental expense budget, which covers the expenditures incurred by the department. In the discussion that follows, we presume that a firm uses incremental budgeting practices. To many supervisors, budgets have a negative connotation of arbitrariness, inflexibility, conflicts, and problems. When the budget is perceived in this way, it tends to breed resentment. To facilitate acceptance, expense budgets should be prepared with the participation and cooperation of those responsible for executing them. Preferably, supervisors should help make their departmental budgets. When they are allowed to do this, supervisors must be familiar with both general and detailed aspects of budget preparation. Even when a budget is just handed down to supervisors by higher-level management, supervisors should understand the budget and the reasoning behind each budget figure.

To participate successfully in budget making, supervisors must demonstrate the need for each amount they request and document their requests with historical data whenever possible. The final budget frequently contains lower figures than those that are submitted. A supervisor should not consider this as a personal rejection because other supervisors also make budget requests and have them cut. It is rarely possible for higher-level management to grant all budget requests. Much depends on how realistic the supervisors have been and how well their budgetary needs are documented or substantiated. Supervisors can only hope that the final budget will be close to what they requested and will give them sufficient resources to operate their departments efficiently.

## SUPERVISING WITHIN THE BUDGET

Supervisors must manage their departments within budget limits and refer to their budgets to monitor their expenditures during the operating period. When a budget is approved by higher-level management, the supervisor is allocated specific amounts for each item in the budget. Expenditures in the supervisor's department must be charged against various budget accounts. At regular intervals (perhaps weekly), the supervisor must review budgetary figures and compare them with expenses. Cost and revenue data are usually reported to the supervisor by the accounting department. Many, if not most, firms use computer-based cost and financial control systems. Income and cost projections and reports are produced in the form of computer printouts or dashboards. With the advent of company-wide integrated technology, which connects finance departments with production or program departments, budget reports and projections are often available in real time, which is helpful to supervisors when making decisions.

If the expenditures for an item greatly exceed the item's budgeted amount, the supervisor must find out what happened. Investigation could reveal a logical explanation for the discrepancy. For example, if the amount spent on labor in a manufacturing department exceeded the budgeted amount, it could be due to an unanticipated demand for the firm's product, which required overtime. When supervising programs, sometimes supply costs can run over budget, especially if more individuals participate than expected, and the supervisor must deal with the overage when planning for future programs. When the deviation from the budgeted amount cannot be justified, the supervisor must take whatever actions are necessary to bring the out-of-control expenditures back to where they should be, at least from that point on. Usually, the supervisor must explain excessive deviations to higher-level managers or to the accounting department. To avoid this unpleasant task, a supervisor is well advised to regularly compare expenditures with budgeted amounts and to keep expenses close to the budget.

A supervisor's budget should not be so detailed and rigidly applied that it becomes a burden. The budget should allow the supervisor some freedom to accomplish departmental objectives. Flexibility does not mean that the supervisor can change budget figures unilaterally or take them lightly. Rather, it means that the supervisor should not be led to believe that budget figures are rigid (see Figure 13.6). Budgets are guides for management decisions, not substitutes for good judgment.[30]

To prevent budgets from becoming a burden, most organizations have budgets regularly reviewed by supervisors and higher-level managers or the accounting department. These reviews should take place about every week, or at least every month, to ensure a proper degree of flexibility. When operating conditions change appreciably once a budget is established, or when there are valid indications that the budget cannot be followed, a revision is in order. For example, unexpected price increases or major fluctuations in the general economic climate might be reasons to revise a budget. Usually, there is enough flexibility in a budget to permit the commonsense departures that accomplish the objectives of the department and the organization.

FIGURE 13.6 Budgetary flexibility means that budget figures are not rigid

**5 Examine the supervisor's role in maintaining cost consciousness and in responding to a higher-level manager's orders to reduce costs.**

## Cost Control and the Supervisor

Intense competition and an uncertain economic environment require all organizations to strive continuously to control their costs. Sooner or later, most supervisors become involved in some way with cost control because higher-level managers expect supervisors to control costs at the departmental level to help meet organizational cost goals. Therefore, cost consciousness should be an ongoing supervisory concern. Sporadic efforts to reduce costs and eliminate various processes seldom have lasting benefits. Although many large organizations employ consultants trained in work efficiency and cost control, in the final analysis, it remains the supervisor's duty to look at cost consciousness as a permanent part of the managerial job.

### SHARING INFORMATION AND RESPONSIBILITY WITH EMPLOYEES

Robert Levering examined 20 top U.S. firms and concluded that managers can turn a bad workplace into a good one by granting employees more responsibility for their jobs. According to Levering, this means "establishing a partnership with employees rather than acting as adversaries."[31] In forging a partnership with its employees, a firm should be willing to share financial information with them. However, it is not enough for a firm just to share financial information with employees. Employees must understand financial data and have a basis for comparing their firms' financial information with that of previous years and competitors.

**Transparency**
Open-book management in which all financial information is shared with employees and other stakeholders

Many organizations practice **transparency**, a form of open-book management in which all financial information is shared with employees and other stakeholders. Employees receive timely information on all aspects of the business ranging from revenues and purchasing costs to labor and management expenses. Every employee learns to understand the information; that part of their job is to move those numbers in the right directions and learn how their day-to-day decisions and actions impact revenues, costs, and the bottom line. Further, transparent organizations make organizational financial data available to the public, typically on their Web site or upon request, in order to build public trust and confidence.

When employees have relevant financial data, they may act more conscientiously when making decisions with cost consequences. Similarly, employees with responsibility to make choices about certain expenditures can promote a sense of cost awareness that otherwise might not occur. If all financial information is out in the open, there is no place for unscrupulous dealings to hide.

## MAINTAINING COST AWARENESS

Because cost consciousness is of ongoing concern to the supervisor, plans should be made to achieve cost awareness throughout the department. Here is where planning and controlling again become closely interrelated. By setting objectives and specific results for a certain time frame, costs can be prioritized.

When setting cost objectives, the supervisor should involve the employees who will be most affected. Employees often can make valuable contributions. The supervisor should fully communicate cost-reducing objectives to employees and get as much input from them as possible. The more employees contribute to a cost-control program, the more committed they will be to meeting objectives. It also may be advisable to point out to employees that eventually everyone benefits from continuous cost awareness. Supervisors should help employees see cost containment as part of their jobs and as being in their long-term interest. Firms that do not control costs cannot remain competitive, which could mean job loss. When their supervisors approach them positively, most employees will try to do the right thing and to reduce waste and costs.

## RESPONDING TO A COST-CUTTING ORDER

Reducing costs, a natural objective of most organizations, is frequently brought on by competition. It is likely that within an enterprise at one time or another, an order will come from top-level managers to cut all costs across the board by a certain percentage. At first glance, such a blanket order could be considered fair and just. However, this may not be so because such an order could affect some supervisors more severely than others. Some supervisors are constantly aware of costs and operate their departments efficiently; others are lax and perhaps even wasteful. How should a supervisor react to such a blanket order?

Some supervisors will read a blanket order to mean that everything possible should be done immediately to bring about the desired cost reduction. They might hold "pep rallies" with employees or, at the other extreme, harshly criticize employees and others. Some supervisors might stop buying supplies, eventually leading to work delays. Others might eliminate preventive maintenance work, even though doing so could lead to equipment breakdowns and workflow interruptions. While these actions may reduce some costs, they could be more expensive in the long run.

Other supervisors will follow cost-cutting directives halfheartedly. They will make minimal efforts here and there to give the appearance that they are doing something about costs. Such efforts are unlikely to impress employees, who also may make only halfhearted efforts. This type of supervisory response contributes inadequately to cost control.

An across-the-board cost-reduction order may present a hardship to the diligent, cost-conscious supervisor whose department is working efficiently. Nevertheless, this supervisor may strive to take some action by looking again at areas where there is still room to reduce expenses. This supervisor will call for employee suggestions because employees can bring about results. For example, it may be possible to postpone some paperwork indefinitely, or to eliminate certain operations that are no longer necessary. The supervisor should point out to employees which operations are most expensive and let them know what those operations actually cost. An employee might suggest a less expensive way of doing a job. If so, the supervisor should welcome the suggestion. The supervisor should commit to the cost-reduction campaign and should set a good example whenever possible. While it may be difficult to come up with large savings, at least the supervisor will have made a diligent effort to support the organization's cost-cutting drive. While supervisors play a key role in cost reduction, they cannot succeed without employee involvement and commitment.

Effective supervisors constantly seek ways to eliminate costs by questioning the necessity of everything done in their departments. It has been our experience that in times of economic downturns, organizations focus on cutting costs. Costs are associated with internal process activities and inventory. Working with her accountant and associates, Caitlyn Robbins, the Fisherman's Wharf owner, might focus on ways to reduce costs, but these authors

*The greater the number of employees who contribute to a cost-control program, the more committed they will be to meeting objectives.*

Jupiter Images/Comstock Premium RF/Alamy

offer another alternative. Get ideas from employees on how to increase sales revenue, expand the sales effort, and increase margins on certain products and services. Caitlyn and her key personnel should wander through other local bait stores, big-box stores with bait and tackle departments, and other service organizations to see how they ascertain customer needs, and find a way to serve those needs. The next time you go to a restaurant, observe what they do "great" to serve their customers, then come back to your place of work and working with the other employees, figure out ways that your organization can improve on those practices. Food for thought question for Caitlyn's staff: What else can we do to make people want to shop our store? How can we demonstrate that doing business with us can fulfill their needs? What should we be doing to make it easy for them to do business with us?

Even when an organization lacks a formal suggestion program, supervisors can establish a climate of mutual trust and respect that encourages employee suggestions. The supervisor can formally and informally encourage employees during departmental meetings to emphasize the value of suggestions. For example, when an employee or a group of employees complains about a policy or practice, the supervisor might turn the complaint into a challenge by saying, "You may be right. Why don't you do something about it? Perhaps we need a change. Think of a better way, and we'll take it to top management. Any credit for the idea will be yours."

Whether for changing policies or controlling costs, employee suggestions can be a valuable source of ideas. Employees like to see their ideas put into effect and are more committed to goals they help set.

## Controlling Is Part of a Continuous Process

**6 Explain how the controlling function is closely related to the other managerial functions.**

Everything that a person does should be reviewed—and when appropriate—changes should be made. In addition to accounting and budgetary controls, there are other areas of management control in many organizations. As students, you will periodically review where you are on the timetable for completing this course. Maybe you have to have an assignment turned in by tomorrow, and you have not yet given any thought to the assignment. We suspect that you will immediately make a change in your plans and take corrective action. But we all know of "one of those other people" who will not make the changes necessary to get the assignment done and done well.

In most organizations there are specialists who can help the supervisor get things back on track. It is imperative that supervisors be aware of how various staff specialists can help them do a better job.

### SPECIALIZED CONTROLS

*Inventory control* means keeping watch over raw materials, supplies, work-in-process, finished goods, and the like. Maintaining sufficient, though not excessive, inventory; keeping status records of all inventory; ordering economic lot sizes; and many other tasks are part of inventory control.[32]

*Quality control* means maintaining the quality standards a firm sets for its products or services. Products and services must be monitored and improved continually to ensure that quality is maintained. As discussed earlier in this chapter, the quality control of products is often accomplished by testing randomly selected samples to determine whether quality standards are being met. A commitment to total quality management (TQM), as described in Chapter 3, means making an overall effort to respond to customer needs by preventing defects or errors, correcting errors when they occur, and continuously building better overall quality into goods and services as dictated by market and other conditions.[33]

*Production control* usually consists of a number of activities that are designed to keep overall operations on schedule. It involves routing operations, scheduling, and, when necessary, expediting workflow. Elaborate charts and network analyses may be used. For example, the production-control department may start with a Gantt chart, which is a diagram or pictorial representation of the progress and status of various jobs in production. When practical, this can lead to a computerized network analysis. Two of the most widely used analyses—program evaluation review technique (PERT) and Gantt charts were discussed in Chapter 3.[34]

## CONTROLLING AND THE OTHER MANAGERIAL FUNCTIONS

Throughout this book, we have discussed, from different perspectives, numerous aspects of effective managerial controls. At this point, we review several of those aspects as they relate to the controlling function.

In Chapter 3, we discussed management by objectives (MBO) in connection with motivation and planning. MBO provides another mechanism for providing feedback. It involves a "co-partnership" approach and calls for high involvement and accountability.

In Chapters 5 and 7, we discussed the positive aspects of participative management. In general, this management style means that employees share the objectives and plans of top managers guiding the organization. Often, this is accomplished through programs and systems that involve employees in many phases of planning how best to meet customer needs. Employees are urged to search for new ways to help customers, and employees are given timely information about their performance accomplishments and any problems that require correction.[35] Such approaches, sometimes called commitment-to-excellence programs, are consistent with the principles of control discussed in this chapter and with the principles of motivation discussed in Chapter 7.

In Chapter 3, we discussed standing (repeat-use) plans, such as policies, procedures, methods, and rules, primarily in regard to managerial planning. When standing plans do not work or are not followed, the supervisor must take the necessary corrective actions to bring the department's operations back in line. Therefore, these types of standing plans may be seen as forward-looking control devices. Performance appraisal, which was discussed under the staffing function in Chapter 12, also has a place as a control mechanism. During a performance appraisal meeting, the supervisor evaluates an employee's performance against predetermined objectives and standards. At the same time, the supervisor and the employee may agree on steps for corrective action, as well as on new objectives and standards. The element of supervisory control can be detected throughout a performance-appraisal cycle. In Chapter 15, we will discuss employee discipline. When a supervisor takes disciplinary measures because employees do not follow established rules, such measures serve as control techniques.

These managerial activities show how intrinsically related the controlling function is to all the other managerial functions. As stated previously, controlling is typically performed simultaneously with the other managerial functions. The better supervisors plan, organize, staff, and lead, the better their ability to control activities and employees. Controlling takes a forward-looking view, even though it has been discussed as the final managerial function in this book.

## SUMMARY

1. Controlling is the managerial function that determines whether plans are being followed and whether performance conforms to standards. Every manager must develop and apply controls that monitor the organization's activities to achieve the desired results. The controlling function is most closely related to the planning function. Supervisors set the objectives that become the standards against which performance is checked. Well-designed controls can positively influence employee motivation. Controls should be forward-looking because nothing can be done about the past. The closeness of supervisory control depends, in part, on employees' experience, initiative, dependability, and resourcefulness.

2. To be effective, controls should be understandable to everyone who uses them and should yield timely information so that problems can be corrected before situations get out of hand. Also, controls should be suitable to, and economical for, situations. The more serious the consequences of mistakes, the tighter the controls should be, despite the expense. Further, controls should indicate where trouble lies in the process and should be flexible enough to adjust to changing conditions.

   Control mechanisms can be categorized as feedforward, concurrent, or feedback based on when they are implemented in the control process. Feedforward, or preliminary, controls are used to anticipate and prevent undesirable outcomes. The person who checks the tires, oil, gas gauge, and the like before a trip uses a feedforward control. The traveler who notices that the fuel gauge is below half full or that the fuel warning light has just come on and pulls into the next gas station for a fill-up uses concurrent control. Feedback controls are employed after the fact; they are the basis for correction and improvement. The traveler who calculates average miles per gallon and uses that information when planning the budget for a next trip uses feedback control. Generally, effective supervisors rely on all three types of controls to improve the control process or to prevent problems.

3. When performing the controlling function, a supervisor should follow three basic steps:
   1. Set standards.
   2. Check performance against standards.
   3. Take corrective action when necessary.

   The age-old question: "How's it going?" can only be answered if you know where you want to go and how you will know if you got there. In recent years, there has been a greater emphasis on metrics. A metric or standard is a measure to assess how you are doing in a particular area. Standards may be set for tangible and intangible areas. A supervisor's experience and knowledge can help that supervisor develop performance standards. More precise work standards can be set through motion and time studies and workflow charts. Employee participation in setting standards is crucial to employee acceptance of those standards. Many supervisors focus their control efforts on selected strategic control points, or strategic standards, which are major performance indicators.

   The supervisor should continuously check performance against standards. In some instances,

**the supervisor must depend on reports, but in most cases, personal observation and inspection are appropriate for checking employee performance. At times, the supervisor may apply the exception principle, which means concentrating on areas in which performance is significantly below or above standards. Sampling can help the supervisor determine whether products meet standards. When discrepancies arise, the supervisor must take the necessary corrective actions to bring performance back in line and to prevent other deviations.**

**4.** **The most widely used financial control is the budget. Budget preparation is primarily a planning function. However, applying, supervising, and living within a budget are part of the controlling function. Supervisors should help prepare their departmental budgets, regardless of whether the enterprise practices traditional or zero-base budgeting. Virtually all budgets need some built-in flexibility to allow for adjustments, when necessary. When significant deviations from the budget occur, the supervisor must investigate and take whatever actions are appropriate to bring expenditures back in line.**

**5.** **Cost control and cost consciousness should be the continuing concerns of all supervisors. When top-level managers issue cost-cutting orders, supervisors should avoid extreme measures that may in the long run be more costly than the reductions themselves.**

**Involving employees in cost-reduction efforts is one way the effective supervisor creates cost awareness. Suggestion programs can be used to solicit employee ideas for potential cost-reduction areas. The supervisor should constantly seek ways to eliminate costs. Periodically, the supervisor should look at the department "through the eyes of a stranger" and question the necessity of everything done in the department.**

**6.** **Many organizations have specialists who concentrate on inventory control, quality control, and production control. These types of control systems are not usually under the direct authority of most departmental supervisors but are handled by staff specialists. Other managerial concepts, techniques, and approaches used by departmental supervisors contain aspects of the controlling function. Among these are MBO, standing plans, discipline maintenance, and the employee performance appraisal. Thus, controlling is intimately interrelated with all other managerial functions.**

## KEY TERMS

Budget (p. 511)
Concurrent control (p. 500)
Exception principle (p. 509)
Feedback control (p. 501)
Feedforward control (p. 500)
Incremental budgeting (p. 512)
Intangible standards (p. 502)
Managerial controlling (p. 494)
Motion study (p. 503)
Operating budget (p. 511)
Sampling (p. 510)
Standards (p. 502)
Strategic control points (strategic standards) (p. 505)
Tangible standards (p. 502)
Time study (p. 503)
Transparency (p. 514)
Zero-base budgeting (p. 512)

## WHAT HAVE YOU LEARNED?

1. Define the managerial controlling function, and discuss its relationship to the other managerial functions. Why do many people view controls negatively?
2. After reviewing Figure 13.1, ponder the following statements:
   a. "It's OK to break the rules."
   b. "If in doubt, check with your boss."
   c. "Rules exist to make things work consistently, but when rules get in the way of meeting customer needs, it is appropriate to question the rule."
   d. "You should always be willing to take a risk!"
   e. "Celebrate your successes!"

   Do you agree with the statements? Why or why not? Recall an instance where you followed each of these statements. Did the situation turn out OK? If not, why not?
3. Define and give examples of each of the following controls:
   a. Feedforward
   b. Concurrent
   c. Feedback
4. Define and discuss each of the following primary steps in the control process:
   a. Setting standards
   b. Checking performance against standards
   c. Taking corrective action

5. To what degree should supervisors be permitted to prepare budgets for their departments? What are the advantages and disadvantages of allowing employees to participate in the budget-making process?

6. Discuss the supervisor's duty to take appropriate action when accounting reports indicate that expenditures are significantly above or below budget allocations. How do effective supervisors reduce costs? Increase revenues?

## EXPERIENTIAL EXERCISES FOR SELF ASSESSMENT

### EXPERIENTIAL EXERCISE FOR SELF-ASSESSMENT 13—Can A Personal Time Study Boost Your Personal Effectiveness?

Just as organizations can increase their effectiveness by using a time study to determine the time it should take for a job to get done, then schedule just the right amount of time for each task that needs to be done in order to reach organizational goals, each of us can use the time study technique to ensure that we are meeting our own personal goals.

In this exercise, you will spend a few days assessing how you use the 24 hours in a day we each have to work with, then you will analyze the data you collected to see how you spend your time and envision how you might be able to increase your own personal efficiency and effectiveness.

1. Time Use Assessment—Using a spreadsheet program or a sheet of paper, keep a log of every task you do for the next three days, for each 24-hour period, and how much time it takes, in minutes. Your log might look like this:

   Monday
   12:00–7:00 A.M.—Sleep
   7:00–7:30 A.M.—Eat breakfast ( 30 min.)
   7:30–8:15 A.M.—Get ready for the day (shower, dress, etc.) (45 min.)
   8:15–8:35 A.M.—Drive to work (20 min.)
   8:35–9:00 A.M.—Coffee and chitchat with colleagues (25 min.)
   9:00–10:30 A.M.—Program reports (90 min.)
   10:30 A.M.– 12:00 P.M.—Staff meeting (90 min.)
   12:00–12:45 P.M.—Lunch (45 min.)
   12:45–1:00 P.M.—Check FB and LinkedIn (15 min.)

2. Time Use Analysis: On a separate piece of paper or spreadsheet, make a new list of all the things or tasks you do each day. Leave space for four columns next to your list.
   a. Using the data you collected, determine an average amount of time per day you spend doing each of the tasks you listed. Next to each task, write the average time (in minutes) you calculated. (For example, if you took 30 minutes to get ready on Monday, 50 minutes on Tuesday, and 45 minutes on Wednesday, the average amount of time it takes you to get ready is 45 minutes.)
   b. In the second column of your Time Use Analysis chart, input the number of days per week you normally do that task (if you don't do the task on the weekends, you would input five days, rather than seven).
   c. In the third column of the chart, input an equals (=) sign.
   d. In the fourth column of the chart, multiply the average time for the task (Column 2) by the number of days per week you do that task (Column 3). The resulting number is the average number of minutes you spend each week doing that task.
   e. At the bottom of the chart, add up the total number of minutes you use each week. Then divide that number by 60 to convert the total to hours. Now, subtract that number from 168, which is the total number of hours in each week. How many hours are left over? Technically, that number is the amount of free time you have left during the week? Is it a negative number? A positive number?

3. Boosting Efficiency: Based on your analysis, you may have found that you should either have time left over at the end of the week, you're using up all of your time, or you're working overtime, trying to cram too much into your days. Does your schedule feel comfortable? Are you accomplishing all that you hope to accomplish each week? If so, you are already pretty efficient. If not, then you may want to make some changes. Here are some suggestions:
   a. Revisit your first list, the Time Use Assessment. Are there things on that list that you could do differently, such as spend less time on visiting, shopping or doing time-wasters online? Are there things you would like to do that you do not have time for, like exercise or more studying? Could you combine them with others, such as reading for class while doing laundry, running errands once per week rather than three times, walking during lunchtime, or doing calisthenics while watching TV?
   b. Create a new list, a schedule that includes blocks of time for things you want to do and eliminates the things that you've found to be time-wasters.
   c. Challenge yourself to follow the schedule for one week. Make copies of the schedule for each day of the week, either on paper or on your mobile device, and check off each item as you do it, so you feel a sense of accomplishment for staying on track with your schedule.
   d. Assess the changes. At the end of the week, do you feel like you've been more efficient in using your time? If so, congratulations! Keep up the good work. If not, go back to your Time Use Assessment and see if there are other changes you can make.

## PERSONAL SKILL BUILDING

### PERSONAL SKILL BUILDER 13-1: What Should Nick Do?

After reading this chapter's opening You Make the Call!, please answer the following questions.

1. INTERNET ACTIVITY Evaluate the way that Nick Coy introduced the new software program.
2. Search the Internet to find at least two suggestions on how an organization such as Lichty Manufacturing should provide employees with needed information about forthcoming organizational change. You may want to search for information on the botched 2013 rollout of the HealthCare.gov enrollment Web site, and software implementation suggestions made in articles that provide analyses of the problems. Based upon your research, what suggestions would you make to Nick and on how to effectively bring about the desired change?
3. If you were Nick Coy, what safeguards would you have used to make sure that the new system was accepted by the employees and that they would feel that they had responsibilities for its success?

### PERSONAL SKILL BUILDER 13-2: Technology Tools—Motion and Time Study Software Applications

INTERNET ACTIVITY

As we learned in this chapter, organizations sometimes do motion studies to analyze how a job is performed to identify ways to improve, eliminate, change or combine steps to make the job easier or faster. Time studies are used to determine how much time it should take to get something done in an organization. This data is used to help managers make adjustments in order to meet departmental goals, and ultimately contribute to organizational goals. This data can also be used to determine whether an organization is able to create new "space" in order to implement new initiatives to help reach existing goals. While large organizations often have the resources to hire an industrial engineering firm or consultant to perform motion and time studies, many must figure out this information on their own in order to make changes to improve performance.

For example, what if Valley Boat Works, a small boat dealership, found that it had a consistent backlog in service work and customers had to wait more than a week to get their boats fixed or pick up their new boats? The owner would need to determine whether the current service processes being used in the shop could be changed to improve efficiencies, or if he needed to hire another boat mechanic to meet the shop's demands.

Likewise, what if the local Crisis Pregnancy Center wanted to implement a social media strategy to raise awareness of its services and engage more community members in its education and advocacy events? The executive director would have to determine whether the existing staff could take on the added work of managing social media, or if a new staff member or volunteer would need to be brought on board to take the desired growth step.

In another example, what if, after a hard winter, a city streets department found that it wasn't able to make all the necessary spring road repairs in a timely manner while also performing required spring and summer roadway maintenance? The streets department manager would need to determine if the problem was due to too few workers, inefficiencies in their repair processes or workers who were slacking off. The department would need to identify the source of the problem so it could make internal changes or request additional city funds for contracted street crews to help with the work.[36]

Technology tools are available to help organizations of all sizes, in all sectors, analyze employees' time and effort so decisions can be made about how to best achieve organizational goals. In this exercise, you will put yourself in the role of decision-maker in one of the organizations above and decide whether a motion and time study technology tool could help you make the right decision.

1. After reading the three scenarios above, choose whether you will consider the tools from the perspective of the owner of Valley Boat Works, the executive director of the Crisis Pregnancy Center, or the streets department manager.
2. Learn about available time and motion study technology tools by exploring Web sites of at least three of the tools listed below. Use the name of the tool in your search engine to find the tool's Web site or app store page.
3. Watch the demonstration videos and/or download the trial versions of the software applications you chose to review.
4. Reflect on the types of data and information the applications can provide. Would that type of information be helpful to you in making a decision about whether to change processes or hire more employees? What other information would you need to know in order to use the tools you've investigated?
5. Create a one- to two-page software review, an annotated list of the software applications you reviewed. For each application, provide the name of the software, a link to its website or app store page, and a 100- to 150-word description in which you provide insights based on your answers to the questions in #4.

**Examples of Motion and Work and Time Study Software Applications**

- ISampler by Springfield Controls, Inc. (iTunes mobile application)
- ProTime Estimation by ProPlanner (PC)
- Time Motion Study by Graphite, Inc. (GoogleApps mobile application)
- Timer Pro Professional by Applied Computer Services, Inc. (PC and mobile application)
- TimeStudy by nuVIzz (iTunes mobile application)
- TimeStudy StopWatch by LeanMfgApps (Google mobile application)
- UMT Plus by Laubrass (PC and mobile application)
- WorkStudy+ by Quetech (PC software and mobile application)

## PERSONAL SKILL BUILDER 13-3: Preparing a Budget

Budgets are both a planning and controlling tool. They help supervisors determine the best use of available funds and controlling spending.

1. Identify and list your major expense categories—for example, tuition, books, supplies, transportation, lodging, food, fees, healthcare costs, recreation and entertainment, past credit card charges, and the like. (*Note*: Many of you are part-time students and have family expenses and other costs that are not typical for the full-time college student.)
2. Estimate your expenditures in each of these categories for the next three months.
3. Identify your sources of revenue for the next three months.
4. Will you need to secure additional sources of income (loans, etc.) or reduce your expenses. Why or why not?
5. Keep a log of revenue and expenses for the next three months.
   a. How accurate do you expect your budget to be?
   b. Why might deviations occur?
6. Compare your budget categories with those of several other students. Did you fail to include some possible expenses? If so, why did you forget about them?
7. How difficult will it be to live within the budget?

# TEAM SKILL BUILDING

## TEAM SKILL BUILDER 13-1: Where Should Caitlyn Robbins Go from Here?

ROLE PLAY

Divide the class into groups of five or six students. One is to play the role of Caitlyn Robbins, owner of the Fisherman's Wharf store described in this chapter, another is to be accountant Lynn Green, another is Caitlyn's husband Richard, and the others are to be a couple of her most valued associates.

**Task 1:** Caitlyn wants the group to develop strategies for increasing sales revenue. The group has five minutes to develop a list of the target markets (customer segments) and other promotion and sales strategies that Caitlyn might want to consider.

**Task 2:** Each group should be given 10 minutes to develop two SMART sales objectives and the specific standards (metrics) that will be used to determine how Caitlyn's shop is progressing. (Students may want to review the guidance on SMART goals in the Supervisory Tips box on page 80 in Chapter 3.)

**Task 3:** The groups then have ten minutes to develop specific strategies (actions) for achieving your objectives. The team is to brainstorm specific strategies that might be implemented to increase sales revenue. They may want to consider how social media could help reach specific target markets.

**Task 4:** The instructor will ask each group to briefly summarize their number one strategy for increasing sales revenue.

## TEAM SKILL BUILDER 13-2: Help Caitlyn Understand Her Financials

The most recent financial report for Fisherman's Wharf just arrived. The company accountant, Lynn Green, is not available to answer questions Caityn, the owner, has about the financials. In groups of three or so, help Caitlyn understand the financials.

**Income Statement for Fisherman's Wharf (in thousands)**

| | Most Recent Quarter | Past Quarter |
|---|---|---|
| Sales & rental | $1450 | $1,167 |
| Cost of goods sold | | |
| Beginning inventory | $165 | $176 |
| Purchases | $1,180 | $851 |
| Shipping | $31 | $18 |
| Goods available | $1,376 | $1,045 |
| Ending inventory | ($172) | ($165) |
| Cost of goods sold | $1,204 | $ 880 |
| Operating expenses | | |
| Payroll | $121 | $113 |
| Rent, utilities | $30 | $25 |
| Advertising | $26 | $18 |
| Other operating expenses | $49 | $45 |
| Total operating expenses | $226 | $201 |
| Net income for operations | $20 | $86 |
| Other revenues and expenses | $20 | $14 |
| Income before income taxes | $40 | $100 |
| Income tax expense | ($16) | ($42) |
| Net income | $24 | $68 |

1. Working together, help Caitlyn understand her most recent financial report.
2. What are some appropriate financial ratios that might be used to demonstrate how Fisherman's Wharf is really doing? What would they reveal?
3. Based on the group's analysis of the most recent financials, what suggestions would the group make to Caitlyn?
4. The pressure on small-business owners, like Caitlyn, to increase sales and control costs has increased dramatically in the past few years. What dimensions of organizational renewal and change might Caitlyn want to consider?

## TEAM SKILL BUILDER 13-3: Wise the "Know-It-All"

This is the latest exercise that introduces you to another person who has the potential to make your life difficult.

1. Read the following statement from Dick Warfield, the operations supervisor at the New America facility of Barry Automotive:

   *Every time we have a quality meeting, Brenda Wise, our plant manager, constantly interrupts the discussion. She hears a portion of the discussion and quickly puts in her two cents. Here's an example: Michael, who's from the design engineering department, and I were discussing the high percentage of product returns on Part 35A1206 from Ford's assembly plant in Lorain. Wise jumped into the middle of the conversation with the statement that the assembly workers weren't following instructions. She then stated that she had looked at the blueprints and knew that if they followed directions there would be no problem. When we tried to explain other possible causes for the returns, Wise emphatically stated that inaccurate measurement was the problem and that we were both wrong.*

   *Wise is very opinionated and demands that you follow her directions. One-way communication is her style—top-down. In her defense, Wise is very intelligent and organized. She throws facts and figures out so quickly that we are buried by her arguments. When she can't sway us with her interpretation of the facts, she tries to "bulldoze" her ideas and solutions through the entire organization. It's clear that Wise's management style is "my way or the highway." If we were unionized, the union reps would be filing grievances left and right.*

   *Wise even butts in where she has no business. Last week, several of us were discussing my daughter's upcoming wedding. Wouldn't you know it? Wise was passing by the breakroom table, heard the discussion, and proceeded to tell me how everything ought to be done—the "Wise Way" is the only way, according to her.*

   *I know that Wise is very knowledgeable in some aspects of work, but she hasn't realized that "none of us is as smart as all of us!" Her sarcasm and know-it-all attitude are driving me crazy. I'd like to look for another job, but I feel I'm trapped here. What do I do?*

**INTERNET ACTIVITY**

2. Using the Internet, find at least three sources of information on how to deal with Brenda Wise. Carefully review each site for suggestions on how to deal with the "know-it-all."
3. Based on your findings, what suggestions would you make to Dick Warfield on how to cope with Wise?
4. Write a one-page paper explaining how this skills exercise increased your working knowledge of coping with the behaviors of this type of difficult person.

## SUPERVISION IN ACTION

The video for this chapter can be accessed from the student companion website at www.cengagebrain.com. (Search by authors' names or book title to find the accompanying resources.)

## ENDNOTES

Students have found D. Quinn Mills's book, *Wheel, Deal, and Steal* (Upper Saddle River, NJ: FT Prentice Hall, 2003) to be an interesting read.

1. The unauthorized activities at UBS AG in 2011 resulted in a mega-billion dollar loss for the company. See Deborah Ball et al., "UBS Trader Faces Expanded Case," *The Wall Street Journal* (September 23, 2011), p. C3; Carrick Mollenkamp and Dana Cimilluca, "UBS Loss Reveals Gaps," *TheWall Street Journal* (September 20, 2011), pp. C1–2. Ultimately rogue trader Adoboli was sentenced to seven years in prison under two counts of fraud by abuse of position, and his associate, John Christopher Hughes, the most senior trader on the desk in question during Adoboli's trades and someone who was expected to report any misguided trading, was banned for life from working in the financial industry by the Financial Conduct Authority in 2014. See Julia Rampen, "FCA Bans Former USB Trader Linked to $2bn Adoboli Fraud," INvestmentweek.co.uk (May 1, 2014), http://www.investmentweek.co.uk/investment-week/news/2342543/fca-bans-ubs-trader-associated-with-usd23bn-adoboli-fraud. A chronicle of the Lehman Brothers' scandal is provided by Christopher Harress and Kathleen Caulderwood in "The Death of Lehman Brothers: What Went Wrong, Who Paid the Price and Who Remained Unscathed through the Eyes of Former Vice President," *International Business Times* (September 13, 2013), http://www.ibtimes.com/death-lehman-brothers-what-went-wrong-who-paid-price-who-remained-unscathed-through-eyes-former-vice.
2. Who bears the costs of lack of controls? On September 12, 2011, Bank of America (BofA) announced the elimination of more than 30,000 jobs in their consumer banking and global technology areas by the end of 2013. The cost-cutting measure is to be carried out at the end of 2013, See Dan Fitzpatrick, "BofA Readies the Knife," *The Wall Street Journal* (September 13, 2011), pp. C1–2. See also Sheelah Kolhatkar, "Billions in Fines, but No Jail Time for Bank of America," *Bloomberg Businessweek* (March 27, 2014), http://www.businessweek.com/articles/2014-03-27/billions-in-fines-but-no-jail-time-for-bank-of-america; and Stephen Gandel, "How Bank of America Lost Billions and Forgot to Tell Regulators," *Fortune* (April 29, 2014), http://finance.fortune.cnn.com/2014/04/29/bank-of-america-error/.
3. Adapted from Peter F. Drucker, American Businessman Quotes, "Brainy Quotes." [We substituted the word *manager* for Drucker's *executive.*]
4. For expanded discussions on the controlling function, see Richard L. Daft, *Management*, 10th ed. (Mason, OH: Southwestern/Cengage, 2012), Chapters 19 and 20; or Ananya Rajagopal, "Team Performance and Control Processes in Sales Organizations," *Team Performance Management* 14, No. 1/2 (2008), pp. 70–85; or Gary Bradt, "We've Merged or Reorganized, Now What?" *SuperVision* (February 2008), pp. 16–17.
5. See Robert Ramsey, "How to Start Over," *SuperVision* (April 2011), pp. 3–5; Richard Roberts, "You Want to Improve? First You Must Change," *SuperVision* (January 2011), pp. 11–13; Allison Stein Wellner, "You Know What Your Company Does. Can You Explain It in 30 Seconds?" *Inc.* (July 2007), pp. 92–97; David K. Lindo, "Tell Them What You Expect," *SuperVision* (June 2005), pp. 16–18; and William Cottringer, "Setting the Standards," *SuperVision* (April 2005), pp. 6–7.
6. For a discussion comparing incremental versus zero-based budgeting and other budgeting approaches, see Richard L. Daft and Dorothy Marcic, *Understanding Management*, 8th ed. (Mason, OH: South-Western/Cengage, 2012), Chapter ; or O. C. Ferrell and Geoffrey Hirt, *Business: A Changing World*, 5th ed. (Boston: McGraw-Hill Irwin, 2006), Chapter.

   The notion behind *open-book management* is that by opening financial records to employees and getting them to think and act as business owners by setting financial and operating targets in sales, production, and revenues, the result can be greater profits, greater efficiency, better morale, and a more engaged workforce can. The open-book concept requires education to understand the financial data and other relevant business information and then actively engage them in setting goals, establishing metrics and encouraging them to strive for improvement. For a discussion of open-book management, see John Case, "The Open-Book Revolution," *Inc.* (June 1995), pp. 44–50; and *The Coming Business Revolution* (New York: Harper-Business, 1995).
7. While Figure 13.6 shows a manager changing the figures, we contend that there is a huge difference between making budget adjustments and "cooking the books." Andy Fastow, former Enron CFO, said, "What I did was reprehensible, and it is not easy to look at yourself and to admit it. . . . All I can do is ask for forgiveness." As quoted in Bethany McLean and Peter Elking, "Guilty Conscience," *Fortune* (April 3, 2006), pp. 34–36. Also see Harry Markopolos, "Spot a Fraud," *Bloomberg Businessweek* (September 26, 2011), p. 88; or Martin Kenney, "Hide (And Find) Assets," *Bloomberg Businessweek* (September 26, 2011), p. 93.

   We contend that organizations need to have a confidential, anonymous reporting mechanism in place to serve as an early warning system operated by an independent third party who can quickly investigate allegations of fraud and other charges. The foundation of the control system is that employees need to believe that someone will respond quickly to charges of malfeasance or other unethical behavior.
8. From Beth Brophy, "Nice Guys (and Workshops) Finish First," *U.S. News & World Report* (August 22, 1988), p. 44. Also see Robert Levering and Milton Moskowitz, "The 100 Best Companies to Work

For," in *Fortune* (published each year); or visit their Web site (http://resources.greatplacestowork.com); and "Special Report: The Best (& Worst) Managers of the Year," *BusinessWeek* (January 13, 2003), pp. 58–92. You may want to visit Robert Levering's Web site (http://www.greatplacetowork.com).

9. "Squandered capital and wasted efforts are a major problem of entrepreneurs," according to Eric Ries. See "Build, Measures, Learn," *Inc.* (October 2011), pp. 56–63 and Ries, *The Lean Startup: How Today's Entrepreneurs Use Continuous Innovation* (New York: Crown Business, 2011). For expanded information on inventory control, see Krajewski and Ritzman (2002), *Operations Management: Strategy and Tactics*, 3rd ed., Upper Saddle River, NJ: Prentice Hall, pp. 667–689.
10. For expanded information concerning quality control and TQM, see Gillian Campbell, "Taking Quality to the Customer," *Quality* (March 2011), pp. 46–51; Jim Smith, "A Tribute to Dr. Joseph M. Juran: The Greatest Quality Management Consultant." *Quality* (March 2011), p. 20; or Nicole Torka, Marianne Van Woerkon, and Jan-Kees Looise, "Direct Employment Involvement Quality (DEIQ)." *Creativity and Innovation Management* 17, No. 2 (June 2008), pp. 147–154.
11. For expanded information on production control and service quality, see Donald Miller, "Q-u-a-l-i-t-y: Realities for Supervisors," *SuperVision* (April 2011), pp. 14–16; Craig Cochran, "Measuring Service Quality: Even If You Can't Heft or Gauge It, You Can Still Assess It," *Quality Digest* (March 2008), pp. 30–33; Jack West, "Controlling Production and Service Provision," *Quality Digest* (September 2007), p. 20; Laurie Brown, "What Your Customers Really Want: Seven Goals of Customer Care," *SuperVision* (June 2007), pp. 20–21; Krajewski and Ritzman, *Operations Management Strategy and Tactics*, pp. 194–227; Thomas E. Vollmann, William L. Berry, David C. Whybark, and F. Robert Jacobs, *Manufacturing Planning and Control for Supply Chain Management* (Boston: McGraw-Hill Irwin, 2005); E. M. Goldratt and J. Cox, The Goal: *A Process of Ongoing Improvement* (Great Barrington, MA: North River Press, 1992).

    If you have a healthcare orientation, you might want to read Jeffrey C. Bauer and Mark Hagland, *Paradox and Imperatives in Health Care: How Efficiency, Effectiveness, and E-Transformation Can Conquer Waste and Optimize Quality* (New York: Taylor & Francis, 2007).
12. For illustrations of outstanding customer service, see Stanley A. March, "Understanding Change Management," *Quality Digest* (December 2002), p. 18; John Guaspari, *Switched-on-Quality* (Chico, CA: Paton Press, 2002); Susan Greco, "Real-World Customer Service," *Inc.* (October 1994), pp. 36–45; and Torben Hansen, "Quality in the Marketplace: A Theoretical and Empirical Investigation," *European Management Journal* (April 2001), pp. 203–211. Also see Thomas Pyzdek, "What Does Your Customer Expect?" *Quality Digest* (July 2008), pp. 14–15.

    Southwest Airlines led the industry in passenger satisfaction for the 15th consecutive year. CEO Kelly acknowledged that the airline still had room to improve. It should be noted that SWA is one of the most unionized airlines. See "Airlines Face More Gripes about Service," *The Wall Street Journal* (May 20, 2008), p. D6. For more information about unhappy fliers, visit www.jdpower.com/corporate/news/releases/pressrelease.aspx?ID=2008050.
13. Visit Quint Studer's Web site for information on what the Studer Group does and how they do it. Also see, Quint Studer, *Hardwiring Excellence* (Gulf Breeze, FL: Firestarter Publishing, 2003). A special thanks to Christina Roman of the Studer Group for her assistance in developing Figure 13.1 for this edition. Material contained in Figure 13.1 pertaining to Quint Studer was adapted with his permission and the permission of the Studer Group (http://www.studergroup.com).
14. Baptist Hospital, Inc. and its parent Baptist Health Care, Inc. (BHI) have distinguished themselves in the healthcare field. *Inc., Fortune, HealthLeaders, Healthcare, Health Executive,* and many other magazines, newspapers, and healthcare trade journals have contained articles on BHI's efforts in creating and sustaining outstanding operational and service excellence by implementing and maintaining effective controls.
15. "Within Reach," *Health Executive* (September 2005 cover story—http://www.healthexecutive.com/features/sept_2005/sept05_coverstory.asp).
16. Nancy Lyons, "The 90-Day Checkup," *Inc.* (March 1999), pp. 111–112. Lyons's interview with then-president of BHI, Quint Studer, illustrates how Studer used quarterly evaluations to help BHI reach its goal of becoming an employer of choice.
17. Judge Charles Pratt and Assistant Chief Juvenile Probation Officer Kathleen Rusher, *Court Performance Measures in Child Abuse and Neglect Cases: Report of Allen County's Court Performance Pilot Project,* (November 7, 2012), http://courts.in.gov/cip/files/cip-allen-report.pdf
18. The SMMStandards.com Web site defines six different social media standards that are currently being developed by a conclave of representatives from business, public agencies, marketing, communications, and nonprofit organizations. The standards go beyond measuring how many "likes" or "clicks" to assessing and analyzing an organization's social media efforts relative to (1) engagement and conversation, (2) content sourcing, (3) reach and impressions, (4) sentiment, opinion, and advocacy, (5) influence and relevance, and (6) impact and value. Organizations can use the defined standards to create measures that fit their organization's character and goals.
19. Nancy Lyons, ibid.
20. Lyons, "The 90-Day Checkup."
21. See Studer, *Hardwiring Excellence.* Also see the Malcolm Baldrige award recipient profiles (http://www.nist.gov/malcolmbaldrige and http://www .nist.gov/public_affairs/releases/bhitrauma.htm).
22. Often this is accomplished through some form of statistical quality control (SQC). See Lloyd S. Nelson, "Test on Quality Control Statistics and Concepts," *Journal of Quality Technology* (January 2001), pp. 115–117.
23. A survey of over 700 manufacturing firms revealed that, among the identified "leading" firms, the following areas of performance measurement were used by over 90 percent of firms: manufactured or delivered costs per unit, inventory levels, worker productivity, manufacturing cycle time, and cost efficiencies in operations. See "Survey in Manufacturing," *Management Review* (September 1999), pp. 18–19.
24. See Debra Smith and Chad Smith, *Demand Driven Performance: Using Smart Metrics*(New York: McGraw-Hill Professional, 2013); Adrian Slywotzky, David J. Morrison and Bob Andelman, *The Profit Zone: How Strategic Business Design Will Lead You to Tomorrow's Profits* (New York: Crown Publishing Group, 2007); Erin White, "Quest of Innovation: Motivation Inspires Gurus," *The Wall Street Journal* (May 6, 2008), p. B6; John R. Graham, "Seven Ways to Differentiate Your Company that Make a Difference to the Customer," *SuperVision* (August 2005), pp. 17–18; Carol Hymowitz, "Use Technology to Gather Information, Build Customer Loyalty," *The Wall Street Journal* (October 26, 2004), p. B1; and Dara Mirsky, "Good, Bad, and Close Customer Service as 2001 Ends," *Customer Interaction Solutions* (February 2002),

pp. 44–45. Go to www.sap.com/bestrun for information on what it means to be a best-run business. See also "20 Common HR Metrics and Their Formulas," Great Workplace (October 13, 2010), assessed at http://greatworkplaces.wordpress.com; "HR Metrics," assessed at http://www.mrdashboard.com/HR; and Karen M. Kroll, "Repurposing Metrics for HR," *HR Magazine* (July 2006), pp. 64–69.

25. For expanded descriptions of job-design and work-measurement techniques, see F. Richard Jacobs and Richard Chase, *Operations and Supply Management*, 11th ed. (Boston: McGraw-Hill Higher Education: 2011), pp. 181–205; or Fred E. Meyers, *Motion and Time Study* (Boston: Pearson Education, 2002).

26. See William J. Stevenson, "Work Design and Measurement" in *Operations Management*, 11th ed. (New York: McGraw-Hill, 2011); M. A. Robinson, "Work-Sampling: Methodological Advances and New Applications," *Human Factor and Ergonomics in Manufacturing and Service Industries* 20, No. 1 (2010), pp. 42–60, or A. Ampt et al., "A Comparison of Self-Reported and Observational Work Sampling Techniques for Measuring Time in Nursing Tasks," *Journal of Health Services Research and Policy* 12 (2007), pp. 18–24. See Rick Rutter, "Work Sampling: As a Win/Win Management Tool," *Industrial Engineering* (February 1994), pp. 30–31.

27. For a discussion of worker productivity measurement, see "A Company's Most Challenging Asset: Its People," *Quality Digest* (December 2002), p. 6; "Value at Work: The Risks and Opportunities of Human Capital Measurement and Reporting" (http://www .conference-board.org). Also see Jim Carbone, "It Takes a Lot of Hard Work to Reach Top Plus Quality," *Purchasing* (November 15, 2001), pp. 244–245; or Edwin R. Dean, "The Accuracy of Bureau of Labor Statistics (BLS) Productivity Measures," *Monthly Labor Review* (February 1999), pp. 24–34.

28. Employee and management co-participation is a key ingredient in any improvement effort. See H. James Harrington, "Management Participation," *Quality Digest* (July 2008), p. 12; Thomas R. Cutler, "Bored by Lean: Apathy Is a Cancer that Affects Lean Continued Process Improvement," *Quality Digest* (May 2008), pp. 46–48; Robert J. Grossman, "Steering a Business Turnaround," *HR Magazine* (April 2008), pp. 73–80; and Alberto Bayo-Moriones and Javier Marino-Diaz de Cerio, "Quality Management and High Performance Work Practices: Do They Coexist?" *International Journal of Production Economics* (October 13, 2001), p. 251.

29. For a detailed explanation of Zero-based budgeting, see Jim Wilkinson, "Zero-Based Budget," StrategicCFO.com, (July 24, 2013). North Carolina Representative Timothy Moffitt provides a rationale for using zero-based budgeting in government in his blog, "Zero-based Budgeting", nchouse116.com, (May 24, 2013), while Michael D. LaFaive, director of fiscal policy for the Mackinack Center for Public Policy encouraged the Michigan House Appropriations Subcommittee to consider the pros and cons of using this strategy in government in "The Pros and Cons of Zero Based Budgeting," Mackinac.org (November 4, 2003). The pros include the need for greater budgetary constraint, reduction of entitlement mentalities, and increasing the meaningfulness of budget discussions; the cons include increased time and expense in budget preparation, presentation of solutions that are too radical, and the possibility of making the budget worse if the strategy isn't done correctly. Personal finance coach Dave Ramsey provides an explanation of how zero-based budgeting can also work well for households. Visit his Web site for suggestions, http://www.daveramsey.com/blog/zero-based-budget-what-why/?ictid=lm2.130308.zbbudget?atid=davesays

30. For additional information on productivity measurement, see Robert O. Brinkerhoff and Dennis E. Dressler, *Productivity Measurement: A Guide for Managers and Evaluators,* Applied Social Research Methods Series, Volume 19 (Newbury Park, CA: Sage Publications, 1990). Also see Peter Dickin, "Find Mistakes Where They Can Be Corrected," *Quality Digest* (May 2008), pp. 31–34; Kostas N. Dervitsiotis, "Looking at the Whole Picture in Performance Improvement Programmers," *Total Quality Management* (September 2001), pp. 687–700; and Otis Port, "How to Tally Productivity on the Shop Floor," *BusinessWeek* (November 23, 1998), p. 137.

31. In the major manufacturing survey cited in note 17, manufacturers were asked to identify the "critical practices" they used to compare their operations with those of competitors. The five most often cited were (1) cost efficiencies in operations, (2) speed time-to-market, (3) research and development, (4) rapid supply from suppliers, and (5) delivery logistics.

32. See Susan Oakland and John S. Oakland, "Current People Management Activities in World-Class Organizations," *Total Quality Management* (September 2001), pp. 773–788. Also see Leander Kahney, *Inside Steve's Brain* (New York: Portfolio, 2008). Kahney describes how the late Steve Jobs, co-founder of Apple, learned from his mistakes and applied solid management skills. Also see, Walter Isaacson, book excerpt, "*Steve Jobs: The Biography,*" Fortune (November 7, 2011), pp. 96–112; or "Steve and Me," *Fortune* (November 7, 2011), pp. 115–123.

33. See Rita Zeidner, "Questing for Quality: For High-Performing Organizations. 'Good Enough' Is Not Good Enough," *HR Magazine* (July 2010), pp. 24–28.

34. For expanded discussions on statistical quality control, see Jacob and Chase, *Operations and Supply Management*, pp. 318–371; or on statistical process control, see Lee J. Krajewski and Larry P. Ritzman, *Operations Management: Strategy and Tactics*, 3rd ed. (Upper Saddle, NJ: Pearson Prentice Hall, 2005), pp. 202–221.

35. See Norm Brodsky, "Keeping Your Company Healthy: Balance-Sheet Blues," *Inc.* (October 2011), p. 34. For an expanded discussion of short-term financial analysis, including budgets and budgetary control, see Thomas P. Edmonds et al., *Fundamentals of Financial Accounting* (Boston: McGraw-Hill Irwin, 2006), pp. 314–335; or Jacob and Chance, Operations and Supply Management, pp. 750–766.

36. Bill Leukhardt, "Southington Plans Spring Road Repairs," *The Hartford Courant* (March 5, 2014).

Chapter

# 14 Resolving Conflicts

© iStock.com/ Steve Debenport

**After studying this chapter, you will be able to:**

1. Recognize that handling disagreements and conflicts in the workplace is a component of supervision.
2. Describe strategies for addressing bullying in the workplace.
3. Identify and contrast five styles that are inherent in conflict-resolution approaches.
4. Distinguish between supervisory handling of employee complaints in any work setting and grievances in a unionized situation.
5. Explain the major distinctions between grievance procedures, complaint procedures, and alternative dispute resolution (ADR) procedures.
6. Describe the supervisor's role at the initial step in resolving a complaint or grievance.
7. Analyze and understand supervisory guidelines for resolving complaints and grievances effectively.

# YOU MAKE THE CALL!

*A supervisory position in healthcare has become a difficult and demanding job. Trying to understand the Patient Protection and Affordable Care Act (ACA) and not seeing many employers providing education and incentives for their employees to improve their health has created stress and conflict for many healthcare professionals. Most healthcare professionals know that people need to exercise, eat right, stop smoking, and adopt proactive preventative behaviors to become healthier, happier, and do better work. Employers should find a way to reward their good health behaviors. Some hospitals have made significant reductions in staff and many healthcare professionals have been expected to do more with less. Alas, these are challenging times for the healthcare field.*

During Monday's morning management meeting, it was reported that a survey found 53 percent of Community Medical Center (CMC) nurses "had high levels of stress, feelings of extreme fatigue and felt they had no control in providing quality healthcare." A group of managers were chosen to work with the human resources (HR) department and a consulting group to develop an action plan. Management brainstormed the following short run strategies: (1) assign reasonable work hours, (2) allow nurses to have a full 30-minute break and several 15-minute breaks during the day, (3) configure realistic assignment of tasks, and (4) create a management culture that would support the nurses' activities.

The CEO said, "We want to ensure that our patients receive the best care in a safe environment and we want to ensure that the nurses can be the best they can be!" As the management team walked out of the door, they agreed to provide all employees with ample feedback and find ways to recognize their contributions.

Charlotte Kelly was the emergency room (ER) supervisor and had a diverse group of employees who were operational 24/7. Like many supervisors, Charlotte believed that "when employees came to work, they should leave their personal problems at home. Some employees need to work to understand the consequences of the way they act and the adverse effect their words and actions may have on coworkers and patient care. I have tried to accentuate the positive, but I often have challenges dealing with adversity."

Near the end of one week, things went from bad to worse. Marty Johnson, an eight-year ER veteran posted some comments on Facebook. "I am drowning in the emergency room at CMC. I HATE THEIR GUTS! My supervisor Charlotte, the doctors, other nurses and techs are devils from hell!"

One of Marty's Facebook friends, a hospital employee, contacted the HR department and noted her concerns about the impropriety of the postings. Bob Renty, executive VP for administration and the HR department, conducted an investigation. In a meeting with Renty and Carol Holbrook, HR director, Marty Johnson claimed that he had not posted the offending comments and a friend, who had access to his Facebook account, might have posted them. A representative of the HR department interviewed the friend who at first stated that she was the author of the comments. The friend was not a CMC employee and after being warned that she might be charged with perjury, she admitted that Marty had told her to take responsibility for the postings because he was afraid that he might lose his job.

In a meeting with Charlotte, Renty, and Holbrook, Marty said he was merely venting his frustrations after several long and hard days at work. He said he had deleted the post and the comments had been directed for his online friends only, not for hospital patients or fellow workers. He did not intend for his comments to become public or be viewed by the public at large.

Management told Marty they would get back with him later in the day. Renty and Holbrook asked Charlotte to make a recommendation on what to do about Marty's actions. As Charlotte pondered what to do, she looked at CMC's Cultural Belief Statement on her wall, "people matter! I value people the way I want to be valued, holding myself and others accountable!"

Charlotte thought about what recommendations she should make.

**Disclaimer:** The above scenario presents a supervisory situation based on real events to be used for educational purposes. The identities of some or all individuals, organizations, industries, and locations, as well as financial and other information may have been disguised to protect individual privacy and proprietary information. Fictional details may have been added to improve readability and interest.

YOU MAKE THE CALL![1]

## Disagreements and Conflicts Are Part of the Workplace

**1 Recognize that handling disagreements and conflicts in the workplace is a component of supervision.**

Most of us grew up in a world full of conflict situations. Perhaps as children we fought with our siblings or with others over whose turn it was to play with a certain toy, or we argued with our parents over bedtime hours. These disagreements over what should be done or what should occur are called **substantive conflict**.[2]

**Substantive conflict**
Conflict between individuals because of what should be done or what should occur

However, many of us grew up disliking disagreements unless we won. Often, because we saw the dispute from only one point of view—our own—and were unwilling to compromise or to accommodate the other party, the dispute escalated and the relationship between the two parties deteriorated. Growing up, we played games in which there could be only one winner. Sometimes, the winners arrogantly touted their success. Other times, the losers pouted, ranted, and raved, or cried. Someone may have countered, "You're a sore loser." The competitive nature of our society, which tends to reward and revere winners, carries over into the workplace.

How did the preceding actions impact the people they involved? The winners wanted to win, sometimes at any cost. Some of the losers lost interest in playing the game. Still others learned to intensely dislike the arrogance of the winners or the childlike behavior of the losers. The parties may have argued for any reason, or no reason, just because they did not like each other. **Personalized conflict**, in which two people simply do not like each other, is laden with emotions. According to author Todd Bowerman,

**Personalized conflict**
Conflict between individuals that occurs because the two parties do not like one another

> *A personalized conflict is fueled primarily by emotions. Anger, jealousy and any other number of human responses can cause this type of conflict, and indulging in it is rarely productive for you or your workforce. Personalized conflict is dangerous in that it often escalates rather than fades away, and it must be addressed early or the problems might fester before erupting again.*[3]

As you recall from earlier chapters, personalized conflict, including bullying and other forms of incivility, appears to be on the rise. Personalized conflict that cannot be resolved leads to "dysfunctional conflict." The end result is that communications between individuals break down. The workplace may become politicized as other team members either choose sides or withdraw. Energy and effort that should be devoted to the accomplishment of objectives is diverted as a result of the conflict. Thus, **dysfunctional conflict** prevents the team from accomplishing its goals because communication breaks down and individual pride becomes more important than team pride.

**Dysfunctional conflict**
Conflict that arises when communication between individuals breaks down and the lack of teamwork causes the team to stray from its chosen path

## BULLIES AT WORK

During childhood, many of us experienced the playground bully. In some instances, the playground bully has grown up and now works alongside us. The dilemma for many employees is learning to work with such a person. The findings of various studies, which report that "rude behavior is on the rise in the workplace and can undermine an organization's effectiveness," are summarized as follows:

- Incivility has worsened in the past 10 years.
- Thirty-five percent of U.S. workers have been bullied at work, and an additional 15 percent have witnessed bullying.
- Bullying is four times more prevalent than illegal forms of harassment.
- Women are targeted by bullies more frequently (in 58 percent of cases), especially by other women (in 80 percent of cases).
- Rude people are three times more likely to be in higher positions than their targets.
- Men are seven times more likely to be rude or insensitive to the feelings of their subordinates than to superiors.
- Twelve percent of people who experience rude behavior quit their jobs to avoid the perpetrators.
- Forty-five percent of bullied targets report that the actions affect their health.

- Fifty-two percent of respondents reported losing work time worrying.
- Nearly half of respondents said they are sometimes angry at work.
- Twenty-two percent of respondents deliberately decreased their work efforts as a result of rudeness.
- One out of six employees reported being so angered by coworkers that they felt like hitting those coworkers.
- Forty percent of bullied targets never complain.[4]

Almost everyone has been on the receiving end of a rude person's temper or a bully's wrath. Whether the crude or impolite behavior takes place behind closed doors or in the open, it directly affects the recipient and lowers group morale. Psychologist Dr. Michelle Callahan contrasts bullying with the boss having a bad day every once in a while. She describes **bullying** as a recurring behavior that can include yelling, intimidation, humiliation, or sabotage.[5]

**Bullying**
Recurring behavior directed at individuals that can include yelling, intimidation, humiliation, or sabotage

For years, workers' rights groups have advocated legislation that would protect employees from workplace bullies. At present, workers who are abused or bullied because of their race, religion, sex, or other protected status can confront bullying through existing civil rights laws, and 49 states in the United States have passed school anti-bullying legislation, but no laws exist to prevent or protect all employees from hostile treatment on the job. Twenty-six states have introduced the Healthy Workplace Bill (HWB) and New York advocates have succeeded in bringing it through the state senate. If it is passed in New York, it will be the first piece of legislation to let workers sue for "physical, psychological, or economic harm due to abusive treatment on the job." Although some employers fear such a law could lead to frivolous lawsuits, the bill and others like it proposed in 22 states would cover "repeated, offensive, and deliberate abuse done with malice."[6] Throughout the text, we have provided various skill-building and activities that focus on workplace behaviors that deter teamwork. These Internet activities and experiential exercises should help you work with those people who make your life and the lives of their coworkers difficult.

## ADDRESSING WORKPLACE INCIVILITY

Who determines "good behavior" in the workplace? Have you ever been confronted by a workplace bully? How did you respond? Did you try to gain an advantage by "going one up," that is, retaliating with equally rude behavior? Or did you respond in a courteous and civil manner? *Workplace incivility* occurs when one acts in a discourteous, rude, or demeaning manner. Bullying is one form of incivility. Verbally abusing, swearing, making fun of you, or giving you impossible jobs for which you either lack the SKAs or the time to get them done are all forms of psychological incivility. Physical incivility occurs when the employee is physically attacked, touched, or threatened.

In recent years, **workplace violence**, defined as violent acts, including physical assaults and threats of assaults directed toward employees at work or on duty, has increased dramatically in both large-scale enterprises and small businesses. The National Census of Fatal Occupational Injuries (CFOI) reported 4,547 fatal workplace deaths in 2010. Unfortunately, more than one in 10 workplace deaths was a homicide. While overall workplace homicides fell by 7 percent in 2010, homicides involving women were up 13 percent.[7] Homicides are perennially among the top three causes of workplace fatalities. "Robberies committed by total strangers—not crimes of passion committed by disgruntled coworkers or spouses—are the cause of a majority of these incidents."[8]

**Workplace violence**
Assaults or threats of assaults against employees in the workplace

Although experts agree that it is impossible to accurately predict violent behavior, some studies have identified certain behavioral problems that may portend serious problems on the job. Supervisors are typically best positioned to identify the warning signals, which include an individual's extreme interest in weapons or bringing weapons to the workplace; paranoid behavior, such as panicking easily or perceiving that the "whole world is against me"; reacting to or failing to take criticism, either from a supervisor or a colleague; and unexplained dramatic changes in an individual's productivity, attendance, or hygiene.[9] Often, incidents of workplace incivility escalate to violent actions. Studies of violent acts in the workplace have shown that these acts typically start as verbal disputes and involve people who know each other. Disputes may be over trivial matters, or they may involve major disagreements with supervisors or employees. The supervisor should address problem behaviors immediately, before they escalate. The accompanying Supervisory Tips box presents some strategies for addressing workplace incivility.[10] A supervisor should be alert to those employees who have difficulty adjusting to their coworkers or who make the lives of others unbearable. Through private counseling sessions with such individuals, the supervisor may be able to uncover the reasons for problem behaviors and to help individuals stop those behaviors. The supervisor should also work with the HR department to determine whether individuals who are behaving in uncharacteristically hostile or inappropriate ways should be referred to the Employee Assistance Program to access additional help and support to deal with personal or mental health issues. In many instances, however, disagreements mushroom and intensify despite the supervisor's best efforts to solve the problems.[11]

## SLACKERS CAUSE STRESS

**Slacker**
A person who withholds effort and could be much more productive but makes a persistent, conscious decision not to be

In recent years, employees have begun to reference coworkers of a certain type of character as particularly frustrating and demoralizing to work with. The office **slacker**, or person who withholds effort and could be much more productive but makes a persistent, conscious decision not to be,[12] aggravates and angers hardworking colleagues. High performers who see others loafing, freeloading, sandbagging, or even sabotaging others' efforts simply because they do not want to put forth more effort can begin to scale back their work, too. Furthermore, if slacker behavior is not addressed by the supervisor and changed through performance management efforts, conflict between employees typically increases and the level of communication and information sharing decreases. In some instances, coworkers have been known to cover up or accommodate others' slacking in order to protect the group, which leads to increased tension. It is in the supervisor's best interest to observe work habits carefully over time and immediately address slacker behavior in order to encourage productivity and reduce this potential source of personalized and dysfunctional conflict.

**Constructive or functional conflict**
The end result of conflict that is a win–win situation for all concerned

Sometimes, through experience, we recognized that conflict was good because we learned a great deal by talking out our differences and settling on a course of action that met the needs of both parties. Good conflict, often called **constructive conflict** or "**functional conflict**," is healthy for the organization and helps improve performance. Various researchers have contended that "[t]eam leaders (supervisors) need to encourage team members to express disagreement, keep the disagreement constructive, find points of agreement, and build a commitment to the team decision."[13] When the needs of the employees and the organization are met, constructive conflict results in a win–win situation for all concerned.

## SUPERVISORY TIPS

### Strategies for Addressing Workplace Incivility

- Eliminate the problem behavior.
- Help the team accomplish its goals.
- Preserve team cohesiveness.
- Maintain the self-esteem of team members.

Pause and evaluate what was really said (content, context, tone).

Be assertive.

Stay in control when attacked; do not counterattack.

Speak clearly and calmly and choose your words carefully.

Address the person by name.

Take action—stop problem behavior when it happens.

State how you feel: "David, when you do _______, I feel _______."

State why you feel: "... because ... it may be discrimination, it may be harassment, it is inappropriate."

State your expectations: "David, I expect this behavior to stop immediately."

Ask the individual to commit to ceasing the behavior.

State the repercussions if the behavior happens again.

Document the discussion and, if appropriate, report the incident to the HR department, security, or higher management.

If you think that you can go through a day without conflict, you're wrong. Conflict is inevitable, and to some it seems that workplace conflict has increased. Organizational development consultant Arlyne Diamond suggests three main reasons for the increase. First, the workplace has flatter chains of command, and workers have more decision-making latitude, which can cause power issues. Second, the world has gotten smaller, and people from all cultures and backgrounds bring a wider variety of experiences and expectations to work with them, which can cause misunderstandings, differential treatment, and discord. Third, the workplace is populated by equal numbers of males and females, whose behavioral and communication styles may not always be compatible.[14] In order to effectively deal with the impact of these and other interpersonal aspects of your workplace, you will need to develop conflict-resolution strategies. In this chapter, we will discuss some of the most important conflict, grievance, and complaint considerations.

## WORKPLACE CONFLICT MUST BE RESOLVED

In the workplace, many supervisors become irritated and confused when employee complaints or grievances challenge their authority. Some supervisors find it difficult to function because they feel that disagreements with employees reflect on supervisory performance or perhaps that there is something wrong with their supervisory abilities. At times, supervisors must act like referees to resolve employee conflicts. Most supervisors do not like conflict because they may be drawn into the fray and they must guard against losing their tempers. When conflicts are handled improperly, employee disputes can turn into further anger and conflict that is directed toward the supervisor.

Many workplace events can trigger complaints and conflicts. Communication breakdowns, competition over scarce resources, unclear job boundaries ("That isn't my responsibility!"), inconsistent policy application ("You didn't punish Joe when he was late, and now you're picking on me!"), unrealized expectations ("I didn't know you expected me to do that!"), and time pressures ("You didn't give us enough notice!") are workplace events that commonly lead to irritations, disagreements, and complaints.

For these and other reasons, many supervisors view workplace conflict as dysfunctional because it distracts and detracts from the completion of objectives. However, employee conflicts, complaints, and grievances should be viewed as expected parts of workplace relationships. Of course, it is undesirable for supervisors to confront a constant flood of employee disagreements because this would probably indicate severe departmental problems. Yet supervisors should understand that, as they carry out their managerial responsibilities, it is normal that supervisory perspectives and decisions will at times conflict with those of employees or the labor union. Further, employees are human beings who, like anyone else, are not immune to the irritations and frustrations that can lead to conflict. Therefore, a supervisor should recognize that handling conflicts and resolving employee complaints and grievances are natural components of departmental relationships and the supervisory position.

Consider dealing with slackers—one of a tremendous variety of sources of conflict—as an example of the necessity of supervisory involvement in conflict prevention. Authors Laura Martin, Meagan Brock, M. Ronald Buckley, and David Ketchen Jr. assert that slacker behavior can be demonstrated in four different ways and that supervisors must address these behaviors differently. *Sandbaggers* look like they are working, but are simply holding up the appearance of doing so by attending meetings or carrying papers. Supervisors should use reward systems to rechannel their efforts toward desired behaviors. *Parasites* align themselves with a group and put in less effort than the rest of the members. Upon reporting this type of behavior, workgroup members should be encouraged by the supervisor to set performance goals that increase in magnitude over time. If the parasites don't pull their weight, they should be dismissed. *Weasels* do the minimum amount of work required to complete a task and manipulate work systems to keep output expectations low. Supervisors can provide incentives for

**FIGURE 14.1 When it comes to resolving conflict, the ball is in your court!**

increased outputs to boost these workers' productivity levels. Finally, *mercenaries*, often engaged in highly structured jobs, waste time with jokes or tardiness and slow down the pace of the whole work process. Supervisors can set up self-managed teams and encourage them to compete with each other to achieve specific outcomes, and teams can direct slackers to stay on task. Supervisors should consider the situation and the individuals involved and use strategies that will help all workers achieve common goals, which will build cohesiveness and reduce the potential for conflict.[15]

Remember, passivity, silence, or wishful thinking will not cause the conflict to go away. There are times when the supervisor must respond to the situation on the spot. Here are some thoughts on how that can be done (see Figure 14.1). First, pause and survey the situation. Often, conflict is caused by misunderstanding. Ask yourself these questions: What is your approach to resolving conflict? Are you the person who "shoots from the hip," or do you take another approach (such as: "Angie, I want to run something by you. I could be wrong, so I need your input.")? Do you look at each situation with an open mind? Do you want to discuss this right now? If not, do you set a specific time for dialogue and discussion? Who should be involved in the discussion? Are you willing to show them the harm or potential harm that the conflict is causing? To what extent are you willing to work with them on developing alternatives and a solution? As motivational speaker and author Dale Carnegie said, "If you want to gather honey, don't kick the beehive."[16]

## Resolving Conflicts Successfully Requires Effective Communication

**2 Identify and contrast five styles that are inherent in conflict-resolution approaches.**

Our primary focus in this chapter is the effective handling of complaints and grievances that usually result from workplace disagreements or conflicts. However, before discussing the handling of complaints and grievances, it is appropriate to identify, in general terms, some approaches, and to discuss why communication is crucial to effective conflict resolution.

Although supervisors may approach conflict resolution differently, they should understand the five basic conflict-resolution or negotiation styles (see Figure 14.2).

The horizontal axis on Figure 14.2 indicates the degree of cooperativeness, ranging from low to high. A high degree of cooperativeness implies that one desires a long-term, harmonious relationship with the other party. A customer tells a sales supervisor that a competitor can provide the same services for a substantially lower price. The price is just slightly above the supervisor's breakeven point. A conflict arises between what the supervisor is willing to sell the product for and what the customer is willing to pay. If the customer is a long-time purchaser of large quantities of the product, the supervisor would be high on the cooperativeness scale. On the other hand, if the customer purchased very little and only purchased when other suppliers could not fill the orders, the supervisor might rate a moderate to low score on the scale. An important question can serve as a guide when you have a conflict with someone else: "Is this relationship worth saving?" If the answer is *yes*, then you are higher on the horizontal axis than if the answer is *no*.

Low to high concern for self, or degree of assertiveness, is found on the vertical axis of Figure 14.2. To determine location on this scale, the supervisor must ask: "What is really important to me?" For example, many supervisors have stated that employee safety and product quality are their top priorities. In other words, they will not compromise their high standards of quality and safety. Various combinations of these concerns yield five **conflict-resolution styles**:

**Conflict-resolution styles** Approaches to resolving conflict based on weighing desired degrees of cooperativeness and assertiveness

1. *Withdraw/avoid:* The withdraw/avoid approach may be appropriate when the issue is perceived to be minor and the costs of solving the problem are greater than the benefits. For example, a student leaves class and sees an altercation in the parking lot. Two students unknown to her are arguing. Withdrawal is probably the best strategy because the student's potential costs outweigh the potential benefits.

    However, workplace conflict between two employees must be addressed when noticed by a supervisor. When left alone, conflict tends to fester. We have all known the person who believes that if you ignore the problem, it will go away. That may be true for the thunderstorm that occurred the other day—the day you forgot your umbrella. You got soaked on your way from

**FIGURE 14.2 Conflict-resolution or negotiation styles**

the parking lot to class. What did you learn from that situation? Whose fault was it that you got wet? Our point here is simple: One needs to assess each situation or potential situation and accept personal responsibility for withdrawing, avoiding, going with the flow, or taking proactive action to deal with the situation (or at least putting a plan in place for dealing with future situations). Supervisors must assess each situation and decide whether to address the conflict or avoid it. Ask this question: "If I do nothing, what is likely to happen?" If avoidance might result in declining performance or create long-term fear, resentment, or dissatisfaction in the work group, then you must take action.

2. *Accommodate/oblige:* The primary strength of the accommodate/oblige style is that it encourages cooperation. For example, Sam goes home one evening and is greeted by his wife, Mary, who says, "I thought we'd go out for dinner tonight. I'd really like to go to the seafood restaurant." Sam had his mind set on having a quick dinner at home and watching football on television. Sam decides to oblige Mary to preserve the relationship over the long term. This style is thought of as "I lose, you win." Sam wins by losing because his wife may love him more or reciprocate the next time. Because no one wants to lose all the time, this style implies the rule of reciprocity, or the **reciprocity reflex**—that is, you give up something now to eventually get something of value in return.

   No one wants to give in all the time. Some use this style because it is easy. You do not have to communicate your preferences or provide data to support your "real stance" on a situation. Supervisors who rely on this style may be well-liked but not respected.

**Reciprocity reflex**
The rule that one good turn deserves another in return

3. *Compromise:* The compromise style is called "win some, lose some." What is wrong with splitting the difference? Consider the story of King Solomon in the Bible.[17] "Two women argued that the living child was theirs and that the dead one belonged to the other. After listening to their arguments, the King said to his aides, 'Bring me a sword.' They brought the king a sword. Then he said, 'Cut the living baby in two—give half to one and half to the other.'"

   In that case, who would be the winner? Clearly, it would have been an illustration of "everyone loses." In the long term, this approach is not in the best interests of either party since neither gets what she really wants.

   But the real mother said, "On no! Give her the whole baby alive; don't kill him." The other one said, "If I can't have him, you can't have him—cut away!" The wise King said, "Give the whole baby to the first woman. No one is going to kill this baby. She is the real mother." We could all use the wisdom of King Solomon.

   Labor-management negotiations often make use of compromise. Unfortunately, when one party knows that the other always compromises, that party will bring inflated demands to the bargaining table. As a result, valuable time is wasted trying to identify the real issues.

   Remember, there are certain items for which there should be no compromise. What would be the long-term results if a company used a lower quality component in the braking systems of the automobiles they produced? What if a supervisor bent company policies to accommodate an employee's request? The policies were written for a purpose. In every organization there are certain things for which there is no compromise.

4. *Compete/force/dominate:* The compete/force/dominate style is characterized as "I win, you lose." This style may be appropriate to resolve the following

type of conflict: Employees have not been wearing their safety glasses because they are uncomfortable in humid weather. The supervisor could force a decision on the employees because the potential safety factor is deemed more important than employees' feelings. However, the question that arises is why the supervisor had to force the solution on the employees. When supervisors foster open and participative climates, they can use good communication skills to gain understanding rather than decide by edict. The forcing style may foster resentment and cause long-term problems.

There is nothing wrong with competition as long as it is healthy. As one manager was heard to say, "Now, we all know that competition between work groups is healthy. But remember, the goal is to get the work done. I want competition to be fun and a learning experience for all. If we all work to become better, the plant becomes better."

However, think back to that playground bully. He or she wants to be in control of each and every situation. Power is important to this person. Some of you have experienced the boss whose style was "my way or the highway!" What was the impact of such a style of leadership?

5. *Collaborate/integrate/problem-solve:* The collaborate/integrate/problem-solve style is usually characterized as "I win, you win." In essence, collaborative problem solving, or **interest-based negotiating**, means that you first must seek to determine what the other person really wants and then find a way or show that person how to get the desired result. At the same time, you can get what you want. This style gives the supervisor an opportunity to question the other parties to ascertain their interests and needs. Joint problem solving leads all parties to understand the issues and constraints and to consider options. Solutions are developed collaboratively, and mutual trust and respect can be primary gains of this style.

**Interest-based negotiating**
Understanding why the other party wants what he or she wants, and then working toward a solution that satisfies those needs as well as one's own

According to Louis Manchise, director of mediation services—Midwest for the Federal Mediation and Conciliation Service (FMCS), "Interest-based negotiating is about the process to find a solution, and not as much about

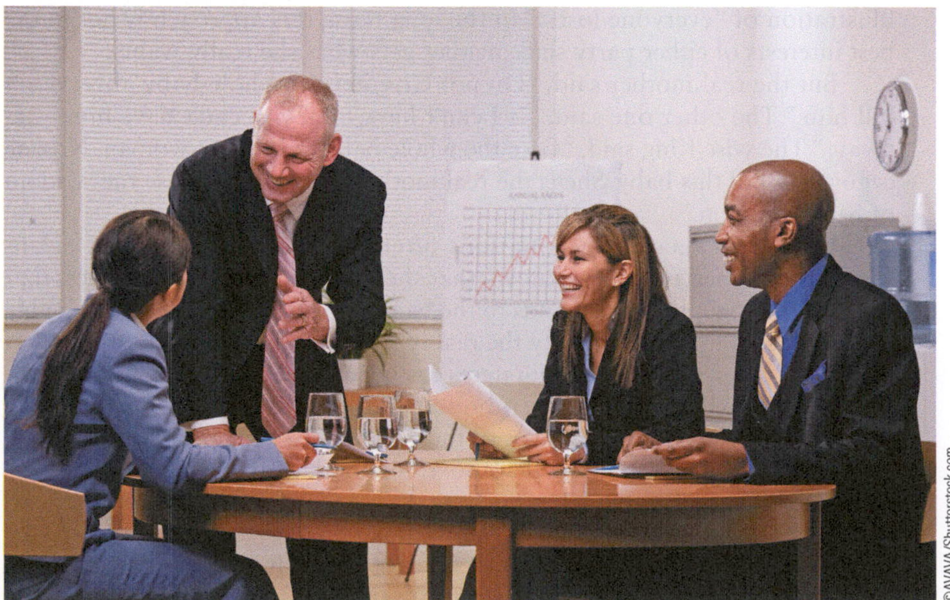

*Collaborative problem solving means finding out what other people want, showing them how to get it, and getting what you want*

the substance of the negotiations, like wages or which restaurant to go to for dinner. One side doesn't use its power to force an agreement. It's an option that satisfies both interests."[18] Although this style of conflict resolution is ideally best, it tends to be the most time-consuming. Also, not every issue can be resolved with a "win–win" solution; some conflict resolutions clearly have winners and losers.

## COMMUNICATION IN RESOLVING CONFLICTS

One of the first lessons students learn is that one need not shout to get attention. Suppose, however, that a production worker approaches a supervisor and is really angry that a material handler has let some inferior-quality material get through quality checks. The angry production employee is shouting. To defuse the employee's anger and to gain control of the situation, some communication experts advocate the following: Get the employee's attention by shouting back, "You have every right to be angry, and I'm as angry as you are." Then continue in a normal tone of voice: "Now that we both agree that this is a serious problem, what can we do about it, and how can we prevent it from happening again?" This approach puts the employee back on track by focusing on the issues. The objectives of the organization and the needs of the employee may then be met through collaborative problem solving. See Figure 14.3 for suggestions for resolving conflict.[19]

In all this, it should be apparent that the most effective communication and problem solving take place when people try to share perspectives. When employees are on the same team and want to do a good job—and when supervisors are clear in their objectives and work to improve human relations—there is a better chance of making the organizational climate conducive to the effective resolution of most complaints, grievances, and conflicts that will inevitably occur. Remember, employees need to know where they stand and what is expected. A sincere, genuine compliment from the other party (or boss) may go a long way toward resolving conflict.

**FIGURE 14.3 Suggestions for resolving conflicts**

- Take responsibility for resolving the conflict—do not let it escalate.
- Identify the issue(s).
    - Explore all sides of the issue(s).
    - Become aware of each party's position, needs, and feelings.
    - Ask open questions—probe.
    - Use paraphrasing and reflective questioning to ensure understanding (see Chapter 3).
    - Establish ground rules for the meeting management (see Chapter 8) (e.g., everyone will have a chance to be heard, there will be no interruptions, and feelings will be supported with facts).
- Do not be quick to use your authority or position power.
- Help parties to agree on the issue or problems.
- Ask all parties to commit to working with you to solve the problem.
- Create a climate of open communication so that you can help the parties explore "win-win" alternatives.

*(continued)*

**FIGURE 14.3 (*continued*)**

- Develop fallback alternatives if the parties cannot reach consensus; you may have to use your authority or position of power to force a solution if the participative approach does not work.
- Follow up to make certain the conflict has been resolved or, at the very least, minimized.

**3 Distinguish between supervisory handling of employee complaints in any work setting and grievances in a unionized situation.**

**Complaint**
Any individual or group problem or dissatisfaction employees can channel upward to management, including discrimination

**Grievance**
A formal complaint presented by the union to management that alleges a violation of the labor agreement

## Complaints and Grievances in Supervision

For supervisors at the departmental level, resolving conflicts largely involves handling and settling employee complaints and grievances. The terms *complaint* and *grievance* are not synonyms. As commonly understood, a **complaint** is any individual or group problem or dissatisfaction that employees can channel upward to management. A complaint can normally be lodged in any work environment, and the term can be used to include legal issues, such as a complaint of racial or sexual discrimination. Typically, a **grievance** is defined more specifically as a formal complaint involving the interpretation or application of the labor agreement in a unionized setting. This usually means that it has been presented to a supervisor or another management representative by a steward or some other union official.

In earlier chapters, we discussed at some length the terminology used in union–management situations and the important relationship between the supervisor and the union steward at the departmental level. The number and types of grievances that arise in a department can reflect the state of union–management relations. Of course, grievances also can be related to internal union politics, which are usually beyond a supervisor's control.

In this chapter, we use the terms *complaint* and *grievance* somewhat interchangeably. Whether employees are unionized, every supervisor should handle employee complaints and grievances systematically and professionally. Doing so requires skills and efforts that are major indicators of a supervisor's overall managerial capabilities. The underlying principles for handling complaints and grievances are basically the same, even though the procedures for processing them may differ. The supervisory approaches suggested here should generally be followed, regardless of the issue or whether the work environment is unionized.

**4 Explain the major distinctions between grievance procedures, complaint procedures, and alternative dispute resolution (ADR) procedures.**

## Procedures for Resolving Grievances and Complaints

Although the procedures for resolving grievances and complaints are similar, there are some important distinctions supervisors should understand. This section discusses these distinctions.

## GRIEVANCE PROCEDURES

Grievances usually result from a misunderstanding, a different interpretation of the labor agreement, or an alleged violation of a provision of the labor agreement. Virtually all labor agreements contain a **grievance procedure**, which is a negotiated series of steps for processing grievances, usually beginning at the departmental level. If a grievance is not settled at the first step, it may be appealed to higher levels of management or to the HR department. The last step typically involves having a neutral arbitrator render a final and binding decision in the matter.

**Grievance procedure**
Negotiated series of steps in a labor agreement for processing grievances, beginning at the supervisory level and ending with arbitration

## COMPLAINT PROCEDURES

Many nonunion organizations have adopted formal problem-solving or complaint procedures to resolve the complaints employees bring to their supervisors. A **complaint procedure**, which may be called a "problem-solving procedure," is a management-designed procedure for handling employee complaints that usually provides for a number of appeal steps before a final decision is reached. A complaint procedure is usually explained in an employee handbook or a policies and procedures manual. Even when no formal system is spelled out, it is usually understood that employees have the right to register a complaint with the possibility of appealing to higher-level management. A procedure for handling complaints differs from a union grievance procedure in two primary respects. First, the employee normally must make the complaint without assistance in presenting or arguing the case. Second, the final decision is usually made by the chief executive or the HR director rather than by an outside arbitrator.

**Complaint procedure**
A management-designed series of steps for handling employee complaints that usually provides for a number of appeals before a final decision

Figure 14.4 presents an edited excerpt of one firm's problem-solving procedure. Note that it involves a series of steps that begins at the supervisory level and ends with the company president or executive vice president. It is important to note the *Freedom from Retaliation* statement in Figure 14.4. Increasingly, the courts have taken a negative view of employer actions that hint of retaliation against employees who exercised their rights under company handbook policy or state and federal legislation.[20]

**FIGURE 14.4 A problem-solving procedure for complaints**

**PROBLEM-SOLVING PROCEDURE**

**Objective**

Our purpose is to give employees an effective means of bringing problems to the attention of management and getting those problems solved. A problem may be any condition of employment an employee feels is unjust or inequitable. Employees are encouraged to air any concern about their treatment or conditions of work over which the company might be expected to exercise some control.

**Normal Procedure**

Step 1—*Supervisor.* Problems are best solved by the people closest to them. Employees are therefore asked to first discuss their concerns with their immediate supervisors. Supervisors should, of course, seek satisfactory resolutions. If the employee feels the supervisor is not the right person to solve the problem, the employee can ignore this step.

Step 2—*District Manager.* If the problem is not resolved after discussion with the supervisor, the employee should be referred to the district manager or assistant district manager.

Step 3—*Division Manager.* If the problem has not been settled by the supervisor or the district manager, the employee should be referred to higher-level divisional management.

Step 3—*Alternate—The HR Staff.* As an alternative, the employee can discuss the problem with a member of the HR staff rather than higher-level divisional management.

*(continued)*

**FIGURE 14.4 (*continued*)**

Step 4—*The President.* If the matter is not adjusted satisfactorily by any of the foregoing, the employee may request an appointment with the president or executive vice president, who will see that a decision is finalized.

**Policies**

1. *Freedom from Retaliation*—Employees should not be discriminated against for exercising their right to discuss problems. Obviously, any retaliation would seriously distort the climate in which our problem-solving procedure is intended to operate.
2. *Prompt Handling*—A problem can become magnified if it is not addressed promptly. Supervisors are expected to set aside time to discuss an employee's concerns within one working day of an employee's request. Supervisors should seek to solve a problem within three working days of a discussion.
3. *Fair Hearing*—Supervisors should concentrate on listening. Often, hearing an employee out can solve a problem. Supervisors should objectively determine whether the employee has been wronged and, when so, seek a satisfactory remedy.

**President's Gripe Box**

The president's "Gripe Box" is on each floor of our home office buildings. Employees should feel free to use the "Gripe Box" to get problems to the president's attention expeditiously. Employees may or may not sign gripes. Written responses will be sent for all signed gripes.



## ALTERNATIVE DISPUTE RESOLUTION PROCEDURES

In recent years, some companies have offered their employees assistance in processing complaints by providing a neutral person or a counselor to serve as an intermediary. Other companies offer the services of a mediator—usually a third party who facilitates communication but who has no direct authority to decide outcomes.

Numerous companies have adopted "juries" or "panels" of employees and managers who serve as arbitration boards in the final step of complaint procedures. This approach, often called peer review, can be adapted as an alternative to litigation to resolve various disputes.

Some organizations use outside arbitrators as the final step to resolve complaints.[21] When outside arbitrators are used, all parties agree to abide by the arbitrator's decisions. The arbitrator is a neutral third party, and policies for the arbitrator's selection, fee, and hearing procedure are specified and agreed on before the case is heard. A number of firms have combined mediation and arbitration, called "med-arb." Under med-arb procedures, the parties' first attempt to resolve a dispute is through some form of mediation. If mediation fails to achieve a satisfactory solution, then there is recourse to an outside arbitrator.[22]

**Alternative dispute resolution (ADR)**
Approaches to processing and deciding employee complaints internally as an alternative to lawsuits, usually for disputes involving discharge or employment discrimination

Collectively, these approaches have been labeled **alternative dispute resolution (ADR)**, which generally means processing and deciding employee complaints internally as an alternative to lawsuits, usually in discharge or employment discrimination cases. ADR approaches are becoming more common, driven primarily by the desire of employers to expedite dispute resolution and avoid the high costs of litigation.[23]

**Online dispute resolution (ODR)**
An alternative approach similar to ADR but with the dispute process handled online

There may eventually be legislation to expand ADR to millions of workers with no union or legal protection. Already, many organizations and individuals are experimenting with **online dispute resolution (ODR)** techniques. ODR is purported to be more cost-effective and results in quicker adjudication of disputes and, in situations of disputes that span multiple geographic areas, ODR can help avoid complex jurisdictional issues. You may have already used ODR if you've ever dealt with a deal gone bad on eBay or Amazon Marketplace. If so, how did the process go? ODR does have disadvantages, including the ability to address just a limited range of disputes, particularly when fully automated techniques, with no human intervention, are used; possible accessibility issues related to Internet availability, cost, and individuals' computer skills; and confidentiality of case information, which can be easily shared outside of the ODR environment.[24]

Recall our discussion in Chapter 6 about the challenges of electronic communication. If sharing basic information electronically in the workplace has the potential to cause miscommunication and conflict, imagine the challenge of trying to solve a conflict solely through electronic means. You will have an opportunity to think about whether you would be comfortable using ODR to solve a workplace dispute in this chapter's Personal Skill Builder 14-2. While everyone has different levels of comfort with technology, particularly as it increasingly mediates our relationships, it appears inevitable that ODR is finding its place in the conflict resolution continuum.

In a major organizational policy statement, the Society for Human Resource Management (SHRM), a national organization of HR professionals, has strongly endorsed ADR procedures that "provide employees a process that is accessible, prompt, and impartial, and that results in reduced dispute resolution costs and more timely resolution of complaints as an alternative to costly litigation." In the same policy statement, SHRM has recognized that for ADR to be effective, certain standards of fairness and due process must be met. Included among these standards are:

- The opportunity for a hearing before one or more neutral, impartial decision makers
- The opportunity to participate in the selection of decision makers
- Participation by the employee in assuming some portion of the costs of the dispute resolution
- The opportunity to recover the same remedies available to the employee through litigation and confidentiality of proceedings.[25]

It appears that most private-sector employers prefer that ADR be voluntary rather then required by law. Yet, a major question remains: Does ADR work? One government report cautioned that "no comprehensive evaluative data" exist on the effectiveness of ADR.[26]

A review of management literature, particularly arbitration decisions, indicates that many disputes could be prevented if supervisors practiced good communication skills and displayed genuine concern for employee problems.[27] Time and again, workers complain that they do not know their employers' expectations, lack the materials to do their jobs, and cannot get timely responses from their supervisors.[28]

In summary, if ADR is to succeed, companies must train supervisors to respond positively to employee requests, concerns, and complaints, and to address conflict and resolve complaints to ensure that fairness prevails.

## MANDATORY ARBITRATION MAY INCREASE

Buoyed by several recent court decisions, some large companies have instituted mandatory complaint-resolution procedures whose final step is private arbitration.[29] Figure 14.5 summarizes a dispute-resolution procedure put into effect by a major corporation for its salaried and nonunion hourly employees.

**FIGURE 14.5 The dispute resolution program for employees that includes mandatory, binding arbitration as a final step**

**THE DISPUTE RESOLUTION PROGRAM SUMMARY**

The dispute resolution process (DRP) is a structured process that is not intended to replace or infringe on a supervisor's communication responsibilities in the resolution of work-related issues. The three levels of DRP are in logical sequence, and employees must complete each level of the process before proceeding to the next.

**Level 1—Local Management Review**

At Level 1, an employee and the management team attempt to resolve the employee's dispute or complaint to a satisfactory conclusion.

1. An employee initiates Level 1 by completing a written complaint on the DRP Level 1 Form, Part 1—Notice of Dispute.
2. On the form, the employee details the dispute, complaint, or issue, as well as the desired resolution.
3. The employee identifies all individuals who may have information regarding the dispute. The employee should provide copies of other pertinent information relating to the dispute.
4. The employee should give the completed form and copies of relevant information to the employee's supervisor, the department head, or corporate HR, and retain a copy.

The company's management will ensure that an appropriate investigation is conducted, that all information is evaluated carefully, and that a decision is made promptly. All information presented during the review process and the final determination is handled on a need-to-know basis. HR representatives will be involved in each claim to discuss disputes with employees, supervisors, or management personnel.

When a final determination is made, the Level 1 Form, Part II, will be completed and a copy will be given to the employee, the DRP administrator, and corporate HR.

When the complaint is a covered claim and an employee wishes to appeal the decision made at Level 1, the employee may request mediation (Level 2) and binding arbitration (Level 3).

**Level 2—Nonbinding Mediation**

When the dispute cannot be resolved at Level 1, and the complaint is a covered claim, an employee can request Level 2—Nonbinding Meditation by submitting the appropriate form to the DRP administrator within applicable time limits. Level 2 is described fully in the DRP Policy Statement and the DRP Guide.

**Level 3—Binding Arbitration**

When the employee's dispute cannot be resolved at Level 2, the employee may request Level 3—Binding Arbitration by submitting the appropriate form to the DRP administrator within applicable time limits. Level 3 is described fully in the DRP Policy Statement and the DRP Guide.

**Employees Covered under the DRP**

The DRP applies to all salaried and nonunion hourly employees. Effective January 2, 2012 all employees agree, as a condition of employment, that all covered claims are subject to the DRP.



The primary objectives of such a procedure are to handle complaints—including discrimination charges—internally and to avoid costly litigation. It is expected that more organizations will adopt such procedures. However, a number a legal issues remain to be clarified by statues or the courts—principally standards for fairness and other elements of basic due-process protection when private arbitration is mandatory.[30]

## The Supervisor and the Significant First Step in Resolving Complaints and Grievances

**5 Describe the supervisor's role at the initial step in resolving a complaint or grievance.**

In the following discussions, we focus primarily on the resolution of employee complaints and grievances, with the role of the supervisor uppermost. As in so many other areas, the supervisor's role in handling employee complaints and grievances is often the most crucial part of the outcome. Supervisors also become involved in ADR procedures and in the resolution of other types of conflict at the departmental level. The principles of complaint and grievance handling apply to most workplace conflicts.

As the first step in a unionized firm, the departmental steward usually will present a grievance to the supervisor, and the aggrieved employee or employees may be present.[31] The supervisor should listen to these parties very carefully. He or she may speak with the employee directly in front of the steward. There should be frank and open communication among the parties. If the steward does not bring the employee, the supervisor should listen to the shop steward.

It is unusual for an aggrieved employee to present a grievance to a supervisor in the absence of the steward. However, if this should happen, it is appropriate for the supervisor to listen to the employee's problem and to determine whether the problem involves the labor agreement or the steward, or whether the union should be involved at all. Under no circumstances should supervisors give the impression that they are trying to undermine the steward's authority or relationship with the employee. When the labor agreement or union interests are involved, the supervisor should notify the steward concerning the employee's presentation of the problem.

When a grievance is not settled at the first step and when the steward believes the grievance is justified, the grievance proceeds to the next step. The steward may carry the grievance further with some other objective in mind. The steward is usually an elected representative of the employees, is familiar with the labor agreement, and is knowledgeable in submitting grievances. The steward may be eager to receive credit for filing a grievance. By making a good showing or by winning as much as possible for the employees, stewards enhance their chances of reelection.

When a firm is not unionized, some employees may be afraid to bring their complaints to their supervisors, even when the complaints are legitimate. They may fear that complaining may be held against them and that there may be retaliation if they dare to challenge a supervisor's decision. At the other extreme are employees who resent supervisory authority and who take every opportunity to complain about departmental matters. They may relish making the supervisor uncomfortable by lodging complaints. Because they lack union representation, these employees may approach the supervisor as a group, believing that doing so gives them strength and protection.

The importance of the supervisor's handling of employee complaints at the first step cannot be overemphasized. Open and frank communication between all parties is usually the key element in amicable resolution of a problem. When such communication does not occur, disagreement, resentment, and possibly an appeal to higher levels of management are likely.

6 **Analyze and understand supervisory guidelines for resolving complaints and grievances effectively.**

## Supervisory Guidelines for Resolving Complaints and Grievances

For the most part, the supervisor should handle grievances and complaints with the same general considerations and skills. Regardless of the nature of an employee complaint or grievance, a supervisor should fully investigate the problem and determine whether the problem can be solved quickly. It is always better to settle minor issues before they grow into major ones. While some cases will have to be referred to higher-level managers or to the HR staff (such as complaints involving charges of discrimination prohibited by law), the supervisor should endeavor to settle or resolve the issues at the first step. When many complaints go beyond the first step, supervisors probably are failing to carry out their duties appropriately. Unless circumstances are beyond the supervisor's control, complaints and grievances should be handled within reasonable time limits and brought to fair conclusions within the pattern of supervisory guidelines as discussed in the following sections. The accompanying Supervisory Tips box lists major guidelines for resolving complaints and grievances, which are expanded on in the following discussion.

### MAKE TIME AVAILABLE

The supervisor should find time to hear a complaint or grievance as soon as possible. This does not mean the supervisor must drop everything to meet with the employee or steward immediately. Rather, it means making every effort to set a time for an initial hearing. When the supervisor makes it difficult for an employee to have a hearing as expeditiously as possible, the employee could become frustrated and resentful. A long delay could be interpreted to mean that the supervisor does not consider the problem important. It could even be interpreted as stalling and indifference.

**SUPERVISORY TIPS**

**Guidelines for Resolving Complaints and Grievances**

- Do it as soon as possible; make time available.
- Do it privately, not publicly.
- Listen patiently and with an open mind.
- Distinguish facts from opinions.
- Determine the real issue(s).
- Focus on one issue at a time.
- Deal with the behaviors the person can change.
- Check and consult.
- Avoid setting precedents.
- Exercise self-control.
- Minimize delays in reaching a decision.
- Explain decisions clearly and sensitively.
- Keep records and documents.
- Do not fear a challenge.
- Don't forget the compliments. End on a positive note.
- And remember: *When it is over, it is over!*

### LISTEN PATIENTLY AND WITH AN OPEN MIND

Often, supervisors become preoccupied with defending themselves and trying to justify their positions. As a result, they fail to give stewards or employees ample time to present their cases. Supervisors should bear in mind that all the principles discussed in the chapters on communication and interviewing apply to complaints and grievances. All people involved should be encouraged to say whatever they have on their minds. When employees believe the supervisor is willing to listen to them and wants to provide fair treatment, problems may seem less serious. Also, the more a person talks, the more likely that person is to make contradictory remarks that weaken the argument.[32] Employees may even uncover solutions as they talk out problems. Sometimes, employees simply want to vent frustrations. After allowing them to do so, attention can be focused on the real problem. Therefore, by listening empathetically, the supervisor can minimize tensions and even solve some problems in the initial hearing.

## DISTINGUISH FACTS FROM OPINIONS

Distinguishing facts from opinions means weighing hearsay and opinions cautiously. In this process, the supervisor should avoid confusing the employee or shop steward. The supervisor should ask factual, pointed questions regarding who or what is involved; when, where, and why the alleged problem took place; and whether there is any connection between this situation and some other problem. Frequently, it is impossible to gather all relevant information at once, which makes it difficult to settle a complaint or grievance immediately. Under such conditions, supervisors should tell the employees or the stewards that they will gather the necessary information within a reasonable time and by a definite date. The supervisor should not postpone a decision with the excuse of needing more facts when the relevant information can be obtained without delay.

## DETERMINE THE REAL ISSUE

In both union and nonunion work settings, employee complaints are sometimes symptoms of deeper problems. For example, a complaint of unfair work assignments may really reflect personality clashes among several employees. A complaint that newly installed machinery prevents employees from maintaining their incentive rates may indicate that employees actually are having a difficult time adjusting to the operation of the new equipment after years of operating old machines. Unless the real issue is clearly defined and settled, complaints of a similar nature are likely to be raised again.

## CHECK AND CONSULT

Checking and consulting are among the most important aspects of a supervisor's role in handling employee complaints and grievances. We cannot emphasize too strongly that the labor agreement, as well as company policies and procedures, must be administered fairly and uniformly. In a unionized setting, the supervisor may be unsure whether a grievance is valid under a labor agreement, or the provisions of a labor agreement that relate to the alleged violation might be unclear. In all cases, the supervisor should make decisions only after carefully reviewing the company's policies and procedures and labor agreement.

As stated previously, grievances revolve around interpretation of the labor agreement, and complaints in nonunion settings may include questions of employment policies. Complaints that involve allegations of discrimination and other aspects of equal employment opportunity (EEO) have legal implications.[33] Therefore, whenever a grievance or complaint requires contractual, policy, or legal interpretation, the supervisor should tell the complaining individuals that it will be necessary to look into the matter and that an answer will be given by a definite date. Subsequently, the supervisor should consult with the HR department and higher-level managers for advice and guidance. Seeking assistance from HR staff or higher-level managers is not passing the buck or revealing ignorance, nor should it be considered showing weakness. The supervisor is usually not authorized or qualified to make the policy or legal interpretations necessary to respond to certain employee complaints and grievances.

## AVOID SETTING PRECEDENTS

The supervisor should consult settlement records and ensure that any proposed decision is consistent with established practices. If an issue has not been encountered before, the supervisor should seek guidance from other supervisors or staff personnel who may have experienced similar, though not necessarily identical, problems. When circumstances require a departure from previous decisions, the supervisor should explain to the employee or steward why, as well as whether any exception will create a new precedent.

Unless there is a valid reason, or unless there has been prior approval from higher-level management or the HR department, the supervisor should avoid making exceptions to policies. Exceptions set precedents, and precedents often haunt supervisors and the organization. In labor-arbitration issues, most arbitrators believe that precedents can become almost as binding on an organization as if they were negotiated in the labor agreement. Therefore, a supervisor should be very careful about making an exception in a union grievance because a grievance settlement may become part of a labor agreement.

## EXERCISE SELF-CONTROL

Emotions, arguments, and personality clashes sometimes distort communication between the supervisor and complaining employees. The worst thing the supervisor can do in these situations is to engage in a shouting match or to "talk down" to the employees. Emotional outbursts usually impede constructive thinking. Arguing and shouting may escalate a problem to far more serious proportions. Of course, a supervisor's patience is limited. When an employee or a steward persists in loud arguments, profanity, or the like, the supervisor should terminate the meeting and schedule another, hoping that the problem can be discussed later in a calm and less emotional manner.

When a complaint or grievance is trivial or invalid, the supervisor must be careful to show no animosity toward the steward or the complaining employee. Instead, the supervisor should explain why a grievance has no merit. The supervisor cannot expect the steward to explain because the steward is the employee's official representative.

Sometimes, an employee or a steward may deliberately provoke an argument to put the supervisor on the defensive. Even this tactic should arouse no hostility on the supervisor's part. When supervisors do not know how to handle these types of situations, they should consult higher-level managers or the HR department for assistance.

## MINIMIZE DELAYS IN REACHING A DECISION

Many labor agreements require grievances to be answered within set periods. The same principle should hold true in nonunion work situations. When an employee raises a complaint, that employee should be entitled to know, within a reasonable time, exactly when management will make a decision concerning that complaint. When the complaint can be handled immediately, and when the supervisor is authorized to do so, this should be done immediately. When, however, the complaint requires consultation with higher-level managers or HR staff, the supervisor should close the hearing with a definite commitment as to when an answer or a decision will be given.

While postponing a decision in the hope that a grievance will disappear can invite trouble and more grievances, speedy settlements should not outweigh sound decisions. When delay is necessary, the supervisor should tell the parties the reason for the delay and not leave them thinking that they are being ignored. Because delayed decisions can frustrate all parties, prompt handling is crucial.

## EXPLAIN DECISIONS CLEARLY AND SENSITIVELY

The supervisor should make every effort to give a straightforward, clear answer to a complaint or grievance. The supervisor also should communicate, as specifically as possible, the reasons for the decision, especially when the decision is not in the employee's favor. It is frustrating for an employee to get just a "no" with no explanation other than that management feels it does not have to comply with the employee's request.

Even when a complaint is not justified, the supervisor should in no way convey to the employee that the problem is trivial or unnecessary. The employee likely has good reasons for raising the complaint. Therefore, the supervisor should be sensitive to the employee's perspective.

When a labor agreement requires a written reply to a grievance, the supervisor should restrict the reply to the grievance and ensure that the response relates to the case. References to labor-agreement provisions or plant rules should be confined to those in question. So that the reply is worded appropriately, the supervisor is well advised to first discuss the written reply with higher-level managers or the HR department.

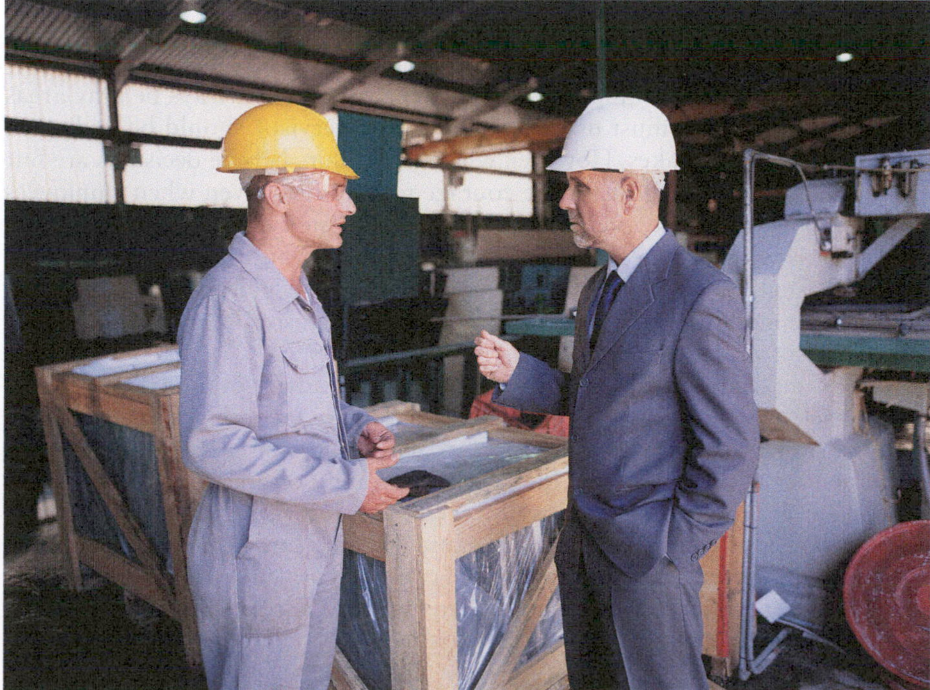

John Rowley/Digital Vision/Getty Images

*The supervisor should answer complaints and grievances in a straightforward, reasonable manner*

## KEEP RECORDS AND DOCUMENTS

Despite the good-faith efforts of supervisors or higher-level managers to settle complaints or grievances, an employee may choose to appeal a decision. When a complaint involves discrimination, the employee may file a formal complaint with a government agency. When there is a union grievance, it may go all the way to arbitration. In a nonunionized firm, the firm's complaint procedures may provide several steps for appeal, which is why it is important for a supervisor to document all evidence, discussions, and meetings. In any appeal process, written evidence is generally superior to oral testimony and hearsay.

Many firms have policies for the confidential handling of certain employee records and documents. Supervisors must be careful to adhere to any such policies, especially when documents involve issues of employee job performance and company disciplinary actions.

Keeping good records is especially important when a complaint or a grievance is not settled at the supervisory level. The burden of proof is usually on management. Therefore, a supervisor should be ready to explain actions without having to depend solely on memory. Documentation can be very supportive in this regard.

## DO NOT FEAR A CHALLENGE

A supervisor should make every effort to resolve a complaint or grievance at the first step without sacrificing a fair decision. Unfortunately, supervisors are at times tempted to grant questionable complaints or grievances because they fear challenges or want to avoid hassles. By giving in to an employee or the union just to avoid an argument, the supervisor may invite others to adopt the "squeaky-wheel-gets-the-grease" theory. That is, other employees or stewards will be encouraged to submit minor complaints because they feel that by complaining often and loudly they have a better chance of gaining concessions. In this way, a supervisor can establish a perception that may lead to even greater problems.

In efforts to settle a complaint or grievance, there will always be gray areas in which a supervisor must use judgment. The supervisor should be willing to admit and rectify mistakes. However, when supervisors believe decisions are fair and objective, they should have the courage to hold firm, even when employees threaten to appeal. That an employee appeals a decision does not mean that the supervisor is wrong. Even if higher-level managers or arbitrators reverse a supervisor's decision, poor handling on the supervisor's part is not implied. Some decisions will be modified or reversed during appeal for reasons that may go beyond the supervisor's responsibility.

For example, upper management, perhaps on the advice of the HR staff or legal counsel, may decide to settle a case on terms more favorable to the employee than the supervisor believes is appropriate. This occurs because management is concerned about possibly losing the case in arbitration or litigation and incurring excessive extra costs in the process. Reversal of a supervisor's decision by higher management is usually not desirable because doing so can weaken a supervisor's position with departmental employees and cause resentment. It occasionally happens, however, sometimes for political reasons, and a supervisor should avoid becoming too frustrated or distressed as a result.

Supervisors who generally follow the guidelines in this chapter and who do their best to reach equitable solutions will enjoy the support of higher-level management in most cases. At the very least, a supervisor should be able to handle a complaint or grievance professionally and to prevent minor issues from escalating into major ones.

In summary, handling employee complaints and grievances is another of the many skills of effective supervision. It requires sensitivity, objectivity, and sound analytical judgment, the same qualities required in most other areas of supervisory management.

## SUMMARY

1. As supervisors manage their departments, it is natural that their perspectives and decisions at times conflict with those of employees or the union. Resolving employee conflicts and handling employees' complaints and grievances is part of each supervisor's job. The supervisor's effectiveness in doing so is another indicator of a supervisor's overall managerial capabilities.

2. Incivility in the workplace has gotten worse in the past ten years and is more prevalent than the illegal forms of harassment we've learned about elsewhere in the text. Bullying is a recurring behavior that can include yelling, intimidation, humiliation, or sabotage. Although workers who are bullied on the basis of their race, religion, sex, or other protected status can fight back through civil rights laws, at present there is no law to protect all employees from hostile treatment in the workplace. Workplace incivility is a more general term to describe discourteous, rude, or demeaning behavior, which can sometimes escalate to workplace violence—violent acts, assaults, and physical threats directed toward employees. Supervisors should address problem behaviors immediately before they escalate and work closely with the HR department to connect individuals who are behaving in dangerous ways to seek help to deal with personal issues that are contributing to such behavior.

3. An understanding of the five conflict-resolution or negotiation styles can help supervisors address conflicts. The five styles are (1) withdraw/avoid, (2) compromise, (3) accommodate/oblige, (4) compete/force/dominate, and (5) collaborate/integrate/problem-solve. Different issues and individuals in the workplace may require supervisors to use all these styles. The collaborative style is preferred in that it develops a "win–win" mentality, that is, the needs and wants of all parties are fulfilled. This style also is referred to as interest-based negotiations, the process that helps to develop a climate of mutual trust and respect that is essential to attaining long-term departmental objectives.

4. An employee complaint can occur in any work environment. Complaints may involve individual or group dissatisfactions that can be initiated with a supervisor and possibly appealed further. A grievance is normally identified as a complaint involving the interpretation and application of a labor agreement where employees are represented by a union.

5. Conflict-resolution procedures have a number of steps that begin at the supervisory level. A grievance procedure in a unionized setting and a complaint procedure in a nonunionized setting differ in two major ways. In the nonunionized setting, the employee normally must make a complaint without assistance; an employee who files a union grievance has the assistance of a steward or some other union representative. Second, the final decision is usually made by the chief executive or the HR director in a nonunionized firm, and some firms use other ways to resolve complaints. In a union grievance matter, an outside neutral arbitrator may make the decision at the final step.

   Alternative dispute resolution (ADR) procedures take various forms, including mediation, arbitration, and panel, or peer review. ADR is especially used to expedite and resolve discharge and discrimination cases to avoid high litigation costs. Online dispute resolution (ODR) has become a viable option for some dispute adjudication. Some organizations are mandating procedures for processing employee complaints, especially for nonunion personnel and salaried staff. These types of procedures may include mandatory arbitration of disputes when preliminary steps do not resolve the issues.

6. During the initial step in handling grievances, there should be open, frank communication between the supervisor and the complaining employee and the steward. When the grievance is not settled at this step, the steward probably will carry the grievance further, and it may eventually be submitted to an outside arbitrator. The same need for open and frank communication exists in hearing and resolving employee complaints at the supervisory level.

**Employee complaints should be settled amicably by the supervisor whenever possible rather than having them appealed and decided at higher levels.**

**7.** **Whether or not employees are represented by labor unions, the supervisor should follow the same general guidelines to resolve complaints or grievances. Among the most important supervisory considerations are to make time available, listen patiently and with an open mind, distinguish facts from opinions, determine the real issue, check and consult, avoid setting precedents, exercise self-control, minimize delay in reaching a decision, explain the decision clearly and sensitively, keep records and documents, and do not fear a challenge.**

## KEY TERMS



## WHAT HAVE YOU LEARNED?

1. Why is it important for a supervisor to understand the difference between substantive and personalized conflicts? Before reading this chapter, what did workplace conflict mean to you? Do you view it differently now? Why or why not?
2. Have you ever had to deal with a bully, either in school or in the workplace? What strategies should a supervisor use to address bullying? What are the dangers of not addressing workplace incivility immediately?
3. Why should employee conflicts, complaints, and grievances be considered natural components of supervision? Define and discuss the five conflict-resolution styles.
4. Distinguish between a union grievance procedure and a complaint or problem-solving procedure.
5. What is meant by alternative dispute resolution (ADR)?
6. Why should most complaints and grievances be settled by the supervisor at the departmental level? Which complaints and grievances should be referred to higher-level managers or the HR staff? Discuss.
7. Why is the satisfactory handling of complaints or grievances a major component of effective supervisory management?

## EXPERIENTIAL EXERCISES FOR SELF-ASSESSMENT

### EXPERIENTIAL EXERCISE FOR SELF-ASSESSMENT 14—What is Your Conflict Resolution Style?

Each of us has our own way of dealing with interpersonal conflict. Our approach to conflict is based on our personality, our environment, our character, and where we are in our life journey. Generally speaking, most people use one of the five approaches discussed in this chapter when dealing with conflict. None of the approaches can be considered better than the others. Each has its own contexts in which it is most effective. In this exercise, you will assess your predominant conflict resolution style and learn about the pros and cons of using each of the five styles when dealing with conflict.

**Instructions**

Each of the statements below describes a way in which a person reacts when faced with an interpersonal conflict. Read, then rate each statement on a scale of 1 to 4 based on how likely you would be to react to a conflict situation in that way.

Please answer the questions by indicating how you would behave, rather than how you think you should behave.

Key: 1 = rarely 2 = sometimes 3 = often 4 = always

1 2 3 4 1. If a group is at an impasse during a conflict, I encourage everyone to try to meet halfway.

1 2 3 4 2. During a conflict, I gather information about all sides and keep communication flowing.

1 2 3 4 3. I work hard to keep the peace, realizing that it might not result in getting what I need or want.

1 2 3 4 4. During a conflict I ask myself what I need and what the other person needs in an attempt to see both sides of the issue.

1 2 3 4 5. I feel I am right most of the time and I am good at figuring out what needs to be done to solve a problem.

1 2 3 4 6. During a disagreement I try to say as little as possible and get out of the situation quickly.

1 2 3 4 7. Conflict situations make me feel anxious and uneasy.

1 2 3 4 8. I use a give-and-take approach to negotiate solutions so that each person gets something.

1 2 3 4 9. I would champion my point of view and argue my case strongly.

1 2 3 4 10. I discuss issues with the group in order to find solutions to meet everyone's needs.

1 2 3 4 11. My goal is to meet others' expectations.

1 2 3 4 12. If I disagree with someone, I try to keep it to myself so that I won't start an argument.

1 2 3 4 13. I tend to approach problem solving as compromise, finding something to appease each party then moving on.

1 2 3 4 14. I always try to accommodate the desires of others.

1 2 3 4 15. I thrive on conflict. I find battles of the minds thrilling and energizing.

**Scoring:**

To identify your most prominent conflict resolution style, total the ratings for each question in the respective categories below. The style with the highest score indicates your most commonly-used style. The style with the lowest score indicates that you prefer to use it least. If you deal with conflict on a regular basis in a variety of contexts, you may find that your style is a blend of two or more styles that have high scores. Read the pros and cons of all the styles listed below and review the descriptions of each style contained in this chapter to see whether your approach is the most effective for the situations you most often find yourself in. Would other approaches be helpful to you?

| Style | Statement Numbers | Total score of the statement ratings |
|---|---|---|
| Accommodate/Oblige | 3, 11, 14 | _____ |
| Collaborate/Integrate/ Problem-solve | 2, 4, 10 | _____ |
| Compete/Force/Dominate | 5, 9, 15 | _____ |
| Compromise | 1, 8, 13 | _____ |
| Withdraw/Avoid | 6, 7, 12 | _____ |

**Pros and Cons of the Five Conflict Management Styles**

**Accommodating/Obliging Style:**

- Pros: Encourages cooperation and preserves relationships
- Cons: Giving something up now may lead to resentment if there is no reciprocity later

**Collaborating/Integrating/Problem-solving Style**:

- Pros: Maintains positive relationships, collaboration builds trust, respect and buy-in
- Cons: Time consuming, requires trust, some resolutions can only have a winner and loser

**Competing/Forcing/Dominating Style:**

- Pros: Achieves a specific goal, generally resolves the conflict quickly
- Cons: May foster hostility, resentment, and cause long-term problems

**Compromising Style**:

- Pros: Power is balanced among parties, everyone achieves something they want.
- Cons: Valuable time is wasted trying to identify the real issues, no one fully "wins"

**Withdrawing/Avoiding Style:**

- Pros: Postpones the conflict and the accompanying negative feelings and actions
- Cons: If a solution is not found, performance can decline or more problems may arise

PERSONAL SKILL BUILDING

## PERSONAL SKILL BUILDER 14-1: You Make the Call!

Refer to this chapter's opening You Make the Call!

1. 

Using the Internet, find other examples of bad or irresponsible conflict in organizations, and describe the impact this conflict has on limiting the organization's ability to achieve its goals.
2. What are the issues in this You Make the Call!?
3. Assume that one of your loved ones was a patient at CMC and you became aware of Marty Johnson's comments. What might you do to ensure that your loved one gets the best care while a patient in CMC?
4. 

Conduct an Internet search to gather information to find information on the extent to which employees have been disciplined for venting on social media (complaining about their bosses, their working conditions, and other work-related activities). Disagreements at work are commonplace. Would you use social media to blast a coworker or a boss?
5. The bottom line in this You Make the Call! is, "What should Charlotte Kelly and the hospital administration do about Marty's postings?"

Adapted with permission from Reginald Adkins, Ph.D., http://elementaltruths.blogspot.com/2006/11/conflict-management-quiz.html

## PERSONAL SKILL BUILDER 14-2: Technology Tool—Online Dispute Resolution Services

Online dispute resolution (ODR), discussed in this chapter as an emerging means to address workplace disputes, involves using technology to facilitate the diagnosis, negotiation, mediation, and arbitration of workplace, personal, financial disputes. In some ODR services, the process is entirely technology-driven, and in others it is mediated by a neutral decision maker, a mediator, employed by the company who facilitates the service. The decision rendered through the process is a final and binding decision that, in most cases, is globally enforceable. ODR services can be provided by for-profit companies that act as a third party, some companies, like eBay, provide their own, in-house ODR services to arbitrate disputes between sellers and buyers, and some ODR services are public entities. The array of services provided by ODR spans from arbitrating disputed dollar figures using a mathematical process with no humans involved, to elaborate negotiation and case management services facilitated by trained mediators. The costs for ODR are based on the services provided.[34]

The Internet hosts a myriad of ODR services. If you were to type the term or the acronym into your search engine, you would find many options. That said, when the authors researched ODR services online, over 50 percent of the companies listed on ODR review sites were no longer in operation, which indicates that the service life of ODR providers may not necessarily be stable. (You may have found the same to be true when you've watched law and other professional offices come and go in your community.) For this exercise, the authors have identified a list of ODR services that have been in existence for at least five years and are referenced in multiple law reviews, in an attempt to provide examples of ODR service providers that are successful based on their longevity. That said, this activity makes no claims about the appropriateness or quality of the services provided by the companies listed below.

In this exercise, you will be investigating the functions of ODR services and evaluating whether you would feel comfortable using such services in the event that you are involved in a workplace dispute. Consider the following hypothetical situation:

*You have been sick and unable to work on and off for two months, during which your supervisor has reacted in reproachful ways and is threatening to fire you. You feel as though you are being harassed because you have followed the policies and procedures regarding sick leave. You register a formal complaint with the human resource department, which recommends mediation.[35] HR gives you the option to work with a mediator face-to-face or use the services on an ODR service to work through the problem in order to try to resolve the problem peacefully and quickly, before it elevates to a possible harassment claim. You can choose the process with which you are most comfortable. In order to make an informed decision, you decide to go online to learn more about ODR. The following list of ODR providers comes up in your browser window.*

- *Cybersettle.com*
- *Juripax.com*
- *ODR.Info—National Center for Technology and Dispute Resolution*
- *Mediate.com*
- *Modria.com*
- *National Arbitration and Mediation (NAMADR.com)*
- *Smartsettle.com*
- *TheADRCenter.org*
- *Virtual Courthouse.com*

Choose three or four of the above service providers to investigate. View their Web sites, any demonstration videos, or tutorials. Then answer the following questions in a one- to two-page narrative that you would send as an e-mail message to the HR department indicating your choice of traditional mediation or ODR to address the problem you are having with your supervisor:

1. What types of services are provided by the ODR Web sites you reviewed?
2. Do you think those ODR providers can be effective in mediating your current problem? Why or why not?
3. Would you rather have your situation mediated face to face or through ODR? Why or why not?

## PERSONAL SKILL BUILDER 14-3: Conflicts! Conflicts! Conflicts! Or Teamwork?

A decade ago, the last original daily *Peanuts* comic strip appeared in newspapers coast to coast. As the creator, Charles M. Schulz said of the farewell piece: "I have been fortunate to draw Charlie Brown and his friend for almost 50 years. … Unfortunately, I am no longer able to maintain the schedule demanded by a daily comic strip, therefore, I am announcing my retirement. … Charlie Brown, Snoopy, Linus, Lucy … How can I ever forget them. …"

1. 

Using the Internet, find at least three *Peanuts* comic strips, perhaps on the Snoopy or Peanuts Collector Club Web sites.
2. Look carefully at each strip. What does the particular strip teach about conflict, teamwork, and life?

3. Show one of the strips to a supervisor or manager. Ask them to describe the extent to which the strip presents a realistic reflection of their workplace.
4. Take one of the strips and answer the following questions:
   a. Is the key player a manipulator or one who empowers others?
   b. Does the key player encourage or control others?
   c. How good a listener is the key player?
   d. How sensitive to other people's feelings is the key player?
   e. Is this a situation where the key player should show empathy to others?
   f. If you were the key player in the strip, what would you have done differently?

## TEAM SKILL BUILDING

### TEAM SKILL BUILDER 14-1: What to Do with Marty Johnson?

Before beginning this activity, please carefully reread this chapter's opening you make the call.

Form groups of three to five people, one of you play the role of Charlotte Kelly, another HR director Carol Holbrook, another the role of Bob Renty, executive VP for administration, and the others are members of CMC's administration team. Depending upon your class size, you may want to have a student play the role of observer, making notes so at the end of this exercise they can provide the group with feedback on what they did well and what they could have done better.

1. Assuming that the participants have already done Personal Skill Builder 14-1, have each of them identify what they saw as the issues in this you make the call.
2. Do you think that some of CMC's stakeholders will be outraged if Marty Johnson's comments became public knowledge?
3. What would you do to quickly resolve the problems that the survey identified and were exemplified by Marty's postings?
4. What might management do to increase the levels of trust, cooperation, and cohesiveness among employees?
5. Refer to question 5 of Personal Skill Builder 14-1.
   **a.** Assuming that Marty's performance has been satisfactory according to all factors used in CMC's performance evaluations, should he be retained as an employee? What restrictions would you place on him, if any?
   **b.** Assuming that Marty's performance was less than satisfactory, to what extent will his overall job performance affect the decision the group makes?

### TEAM SKILL BUILDER 14-2: The Stinky Employee

Several employees in your patient-billing section of CMC Health Center have complained about the hygiene problems of two fellow employees. In one case, to state it bluntly, this is not just some hot summer body odor; this is from not bathing. In the other, the employee goes too far in masking body odor with heavy cologne. To address these earlier complaints, you had put up a general notice, asking people to be more considerate of their fellow employees and patients and (1) to shower more regularly and (2) to refrain from bathing in perfume and cologne. But apparently this notice has not solved the problem.

Today, a group of four employees, including your very best, told you that the smell from two employees is overwhelming and that they will no longer work in the same area. Transfer or relocation is not an option. You must now sit down and have a conversation with each employee and resolve this conflict.

**Role-play # 1: Meet Molly.** Molly is a good worker but she is a throwback to the "hippie era" of the 1960s. To her, cleanliness is not important. She does not appear to bathe, brush her teeth, or wash her hair. She often wears the same clothes for several days in a row, and on a couple of occasions you were able to smell her from a couple of cubicles away.

**Role-play Format**: After reading the scenario, assign the roles of supervisor, employee, HR manager, and observers. The person playing the role of the employee with the body odor should be excused from the room while the other participants prepare for the role play. The person playing the role of the HR manager should discuss the legal and practical implications confronting them in the conflict-resolution (counseling) session. After a plan of action has been developed, the "stinky" employee should be invited back into the room to complete the role-play exercise.

At the conclusion of the activity, each participant should prepare a critique of how effectively this situation was handled. Suggestions for improvement should be offered.

**Role-play # 2: Meet Wai.** Wai is a relatively new employee. According to his fellow employees, he appears to douse himself in cologne. The smell is unpleasant. Early in the day, it smells like disinfectant.

**Role-play Format**: After reading the scenario, assign the roles of supervisor, employee, HR manager, and observer. The person playing the role of the employee with the excessive cologne should be excused from the room while the other participants prepare for the role-play. The person playing the role of the HR manager should discuss the legal and practical implications involved in the conflict-resolution (counseling) session. After a plan of action has been developed, the "stinky" employee should be invited back into the room to complete the role-play exercise.

At the conclusion of the second role-play, observers should prepare a critique of the exercise indicating what the participants did well and what could have been done better.

Write a one-page paper indicating what you learned from this skills exercise.

*Source:* Adapted with permission from Edwin C. Leonard Jr. and Roy A. Cook, *Human Resource Management: 21st Century Challenges* (Mason, OH: Thomson Custom Publishing, 2005), pp. 23–24 (Case 1-12: The Stinky Employee).

## TEAM SKILL BUILDER 14-3: Nedra "the Negativist"

This is the last exercise introducing you to another of those folks who will make your life difficult. As you read Fred's story, you will find that Nedra is somewhat similar to a couple of previous characters who were introduced to you. We hope you have enjoyed exploring ways to cope with these people who have the potential to make your life difficult.

1. Read the following statement from Fred Roberts, operations supervisor at Barry Automotive's Dublin plant:

   *The most challenging person I work with is Nedra. She has so many redeeming features. For one, she is a workaholic and has a passion for quality work. But she is a pessimist and sees only the worst in every situation. Recently, there was a quality discrepancy reported by a customer, and we were asked to solve the problem. As a member of the quality-improvement team, instead of working with us to figure out ways to improve the production process, Nedra claimed the production operators do not know how to use their brains to do the work right. In a whining and complaining tone, I can still hear her say, "It's such a simple procedure, and we have to deal with their inability to read the spec sheets. It's just not right! Those people in personnel can never find us any good employees."*

   *Everyone is fair game for Nedra's complaints. About a month ago, the company experienced a major machine downtime due to a mechanical failure. I can hear Nedra now: "It's either the lousy people, the old equipment, or the incompetent maintenance supervisor." She stores mistakes from the past and can't let go of them. For example, two years ago, Lee Kim, a good employee in the maintenance department, made a serious setup error that resulted in over $50,000 of product being run with the wrong specs. We ended up with two bins of scrap. Lots of people could have caught the mistake in a timely fashion, but no one did. Kim was suspended without pay for two weeks, and we used the mistake to illustrate why we need to follow our in-process controls. But Nedra won't let up. It's been over two years, and she is still obsessed with "Kim's mistake."*

   *I've tried to deal with Nedra by developing a positive attitude and smiling. But that doesn't seem to work. Nedra's negativity is destroying the team's spirit.*

   *Yesterday was the last straw. Three months ago I was chosen to head a project team to develop a new database to improve our customer tracking. Initially, Nedra suggested that we strive for the "optimal" solution rather than a "satisficing" one.*

   *The team worked diligently despite Nedra's negativity. I did everything I knew to try to get her off the bench and into the game. She was not open to any of our ideas and was unwilling to make any suggestions of her own. Her only contribution was to develop the worst-case scenarios of every suggestion we came up with. I made some notes on the words Nedra used during the past week in team meetings: "We can't do it!" "Our people aren't intelligent enough to do anything that sophisticated." "The machines will break down." "It's not possible." "We don't have enough money to do the job right." I came very close to losing it.*

   *I've never known anyone with such a bad outlook on life. Nowhere in my college or professional training did I have anything to prepare me for this. What should I do?*

2. 
   INTERNET ACTIVITY
   Using the Internet, find at least three sources for how to work with negative people. Carefully review each site for suggestions on how to cope with this type of behavior.

3. Pair up with three to six other students.
   a. Share your research findings.
   b. Based on the findings, make a list of the three best options for Fred Roberts.
   c. Select one student to play the role of Fred Roberts. Your mission is to help Fred decide which of these options he could use to help him and others cope with Nedra.
   d. Fred Roberts's job is to take that best suggestion and explain to the group his strategy for dealing with Nedra.

4. The group is asked to collaboratively write a one-page paper explaining how this exercise increased their working knowledge of how to better cope with the behaviors of this difficult person—Nedra.

## SUPERVISION IN ACTION

The video for this chapter can be accessed from the student companion website at www.cengagebrain.com. (Search by authors' names or book title to find the accompanying resources.)

## ENDNOTES

1. The opening You Make the Call! feature adapted with permission from Roy Cook and Ed Leonard, "Whose Money Is It?" critical incident presented at the March 2011 Society of Case Research annual meeting in Chicago.
2. Adapted from Robert Bacal, "Conflict and Cooperation in the Workplace," *Institute for Conflict Prevention* (http://www.conflict911.com/conflictarticles/in-communication1.htm). Robert Bacal has written many books and articles on conflict resolution. Visit the Bacal & Associates Web site (http://www.work911.com/conflict/index.htm) to access some of his suggestions on conflict resolution.
3. Adapted from Todd Bowerman, "Typical Conflict Situations in the Workplace," *eHowMoney* (October 23, 2010), http://www.ehow.com/list_7383094_typical-conflict-situations-workplace.html. See also Robert Bacal, *Conflict Prevention in the Workplace* (Winnipeg, AL: Institute for Cooperative Communication, 1998); *Defusing Hostile Customers Workbook for the Public Section* (Winnipeg, AL: Institute for Cooperative Communication, 1998).
4. Access the detailed results of the 2010 Workplace Bullying Institute U.S. Workplace Bullying Survey at the WBI Web site (http://www.workplacebullying.org/wbiresearch/2010-wbi-national-survey/). See also Danita Johnson Hughes, "A Return to Civility," *SuperVision* (February 2011), pp. 17–19. Kate N. Grossman, "Boys Behaving Badly: Men Mostly at Fault for Rising Incivility at Work," Associated Press (August 11, 1999); this news release summarized the work of University of North Carolina professor Christine M. Patterson et al., "Workplace Incivility: The Target's Eye View," presented at the Academy of Management's Annual Meeting (Tuesday, August 10, 1999). Jim Owen, "Workplace Incivility: Bullying and Rudeness on the Rise," *Career Builder, Inc.* (1999). See also Dyane Holt, "HR Solutions," HR Magazine (November 2003), p. 42. Holt discusses how to cope with bullying behavior.

   *The U.S. Workplace Bullying Survey* (September 2007) reported that bullying is a top-down phenomenon: 55 percent of targets are nonsupervisory employees; 45 percent of targets have stress-related health problems; 40 percent never report it; only 3 percent sue; and 4 percent complain to state or federal agencies. See complete survey report at www.bullyinginstitute.org.

   A more recent study found that employees who experience bullying, incivility, or interpersonal on-the-job conflict were more likely to quit their jobs. See "Study Spotlights Workplace Bullying," SHRM Home Business and Legal Reports, Inc. (April 10, 2008). Also see Robert Caldwell, "Work to Reduce Exposure to Workplace Violence Threats," SHRM Home (April 2008); and Pauline Wallin, Taming Your Inner Brat: A Guide for Transforming Self-Defeating Behavior (Dallas, TX: Wildcat Press, 2004).
5. See Michelle Callahan, "10 Tips for Dealing with Bullies at Work," *Huffington Post: Living* (March 13, 2011), http://www.-huffingtonpost.com/dr-michelle-callahan/work-bullies_b_833977.html.
6. As reported by Adam Cohen in "New Laws Target Workplace Bullying," Time (July 21, 2010). Retrieved from Time Web site (http://www.*time*.com/time/nation/article/0,8599,2005358,00.html). See also the Healthy Workplace Bill Campaign Web site (http://www .healthyworkplacebill.org/).
7. In August 1986, a U.S. Postal Service employee shot and killed 14 coworkers and wounded six others in Edmond, Oklahoma. Since that incident, the news media has created an awareness of workplace violence concerning employees killed by fellow employees as "going postal."

   In 2007, there were 4,547 fatal workplace injuries, and 506 of those were homicides. See the following: National Census of Fatal Occupational Injuries (CFOI) (http://www.bls.gov/news.release/pdf/cfoi.pdf), National Institute for Prevention of Workplace Violence, Crisis Prevention Institute, Inc. (www.crisisprevention.com), National Institute for Occupational Health and Safety, National Center for Analyzing Violent Crime (www.fbi.gov/publications/violence.pdf or www.worktrauma.com.)
8. The study by Prince & Associates as reported in Kathy Gurchiek, "Workplace Violence Is on the Upswing, Say HR Leaders," *SHRM Home* (May 12, 2005). Also see Philip S. Deming, "Workplace Violence: Trend and Strategic Tools for Mitigating Risk," *SHRM White Paper* (March 2006). It is estimated that 70 percent of employers do not have a program or policy addressing workplace violence.
9. See Sandra J. Kelley, "Making Sense of Violence in the Workplace," *Risk Management* (October 1995), pp. 50–57. A recent Reuter-Ipsos global survey reported that nearly 10 percent of workers worldwide reported they had been harassed sexually or physically at work. See Bill Leonard, "Survey," *HR Magazine* (October 2010), p. 18.
10. Many authors have applied their own terms to problem behaviors. As cited in Rita Zeidner, "Problem of Workplace Bullying Demands Attention, Researchers Say," SHRM Home (March 2008): M. Sandy Hershcovis and Julian Barling distinguished among different forms of workplace aggression:

    *Incivility included rudeness and discourteous verbal and nonverbal behaviors. Bullying included persistently criticizing employees' work, yelling, repeatedly reminding employees of mistakes, spreading gossip or lies, ignoring or excluding workers, and insulting employees' habits, attitudes, or private life. Interpersonal conflict included behaviors that involved hostility, verbal aggression, and angry exchanges.*

    Regardless of the terms used, there is no place for inappropriate behavior in the society.

    Those practicing incivility (bullying) in the workplace may be called *atomic bombs, unguided missiles, backstabbers, jabbers, ridiculers, hotheads, showoffs, tyrants, Sherman tanks, hostile aggressives,* and *snipers*, among others. When left unchecked, this behavior will destroy a team. Underlying strategies for dealing with difficult people are the notions of self-esteem, assertiveness, and trust.

Also see Teresa A. Daniels, "Managing Difficult Employees and Disruptive Behaviors," *SHRM Research Articles* (December 23, 2010), http://www.shrm.org/Research/Articles/Articles/Pages/ManagingDifficultEmployees.aspx; Linda Wasmer Andrews, "Hard-Core Offenders," *HR Magazine* (December 2004), pp. 43–48; Rick Brinkman and Rick Kirschner, *Dealing with People You Can't Stand: How to Bring Out the Best in People at Their Worst* (New York: McGraw-Hill, 1994); and Muriel Solomon, *Working with Difficult People* (Englewood Cliffs, NJ: Prentice-Hall, 1990).

11. See Christine McGovern, "Take Action, Heed Warnings to End Workplace Violence," *Occupational Hazards* (March 1999), pp. 61–63, and John W. Kennish, "Violence in the Workplace," *Professional Safety* (November 1995), pp. 34–36.
12. Adrienne Fox, "Taking Up Slack," *HR Magazine* (December 2010), 26–31, presents the psychology of slacking, strategies supervisors can use to identify slacker behavior, and a menu of interventions that can be used to address and reduce slacker behavior. Also see Ben Leichtling, "Slacker Management: What to Do If You Recognize a Slacker," *HR Magazine* (December 2010), pp. 101–102.
13. See Nancy R. Lockwood, "Workplace Conflict: Reasons, Reactions and Resolution," *SHRM Research* (November 2007); T. R. Harrison and M. L. Doerfel, "Competitive and Cooperative Conflict Communication Climates," *International Journal of Conflict Resolution* 17, No. 2 (2006), pp. 129–153; G. R. Massey and P. L. Dawes, "The Antecedents and Consequences of Functional and Dysfunctional Conflict between Marketing Managers and Sales Managers" (Elsevier, Inc. 2006, accessed September 2008 at http://www.sciencedirect.com); F. J. Medina, L. Nunduate, M. A. Dorato, L. Martinez, and J. M. Guerra, "Types of Intragroup Conflict and Affective Reactions," *Journal of Management Psychology* 20, No. 3/4 (2005), pp. 219–230; F. McGrane, J. Wilson, and T. Cammock, "Leading Employees in One-to-One Dispute Resolution," *Leadership & Organizational Development Journal* 26, No. 3/4 (2005), pp. 263–279. Also see an article from *Harvard Business School's Working Knowledge*, "Don't Listen to 'Yes'" (June 6, 2005), where Martha Lagrace talks with Professor Michael Roberto on why it's essential for leaders to spark conflict in their organizations, as long as it is constructive (,http://www.thepracticeofleadership.net or http://hbswk.hbs.edu/item/4833.html, accessed September 2008). Also see Michael A. Roberto, *Why Great Leaders Don't Take Yes for an Answer* (Upper Saddle River, NJ: Pearson Education, 2005).
14. Organizational development consultant Arlyne Diamond identifies three reasons for what seems to be more conflict in the workplace and suggests nine strategies supervisors can use to help workers mitigate conflict in "Workplace Conflict Resolution: What's Creating Workplace Conflict and 9 Easy Ways to Resolve It," *Teamtemps Personnel Staffing, Inc.* (February 7, 2007), pp. 227–228.
15. As reported by Adrienne Fox, "Taking Up Slack."
16. Dale Carnegie quote accessed from http://www.brainyquote.com, September 2008. Carnegie (1888–1955), a pioneer in public speaking and seminar development, wrote *How to Win Friends and Influence People* (New York: Simon & Schuster, 1934, revised 2009) and *How to Stop Worrying and Start Living* (New York: Pocket Books, 1944, revised 2004).
17. See 1 Kings, Chapter 3, verses 16–28, for the story of King Solomon's approach for deciding which woman was the mother of the living child.
18. As quoted in Jeff Segal, "Mutual Satisfaction: Interest-Based Negotiation Means Getting What You Want by Knowing What They Want," *Southwest Airlines Spirit* (September 2004), pp. 54–57. Louis Manchise was director of mediation services (FMCS) in Cincinnati for 33 years and is currently a faculty member at Northern Kentucky University.
19. For extensive discussions of various approaches to conflict resolution and dealing with disgruntled employees, see Meridith Levinson, "Workplace Conflict: How to Diffuse Battles with Co-Workers," *NetworkWorld* (August 22, 2011), http://www.networkworld.com; Kathy Gurchiek, "Don't Let Conflict Go Unchecked," *SHRM Home* ( www.shrm.org, accessed August 2008); Mark A. Hyde, "5 Keys to Resolving Employee Conflict," *SuperVision* 69, No. 4 (April 2008), pp. 3–6; Ronnie Moore, "Communicating through Conflict," *SuperVision* 68, No. 10 (October 2007), pp. 12–13; Rob Walker, "Take It or Leave It: The Only Guide to Negotiating You Will Ever Need," *Inc.* (August 2007), pp. 75–82; Tina Nabatchi, Lisa B. Bingham, and David H. Good, "Organizational Justice and Workplace Mediation: A Six Factor Model," *International Journal of Conflict Management* 18, No. 2 (2007), pp. 148–174; S. Parayitam and R. S. Dooley, "The Relationship between Conflict and Decision Outcomes: Moderating Effects of Cognitive and Affect-based Trust in Strategic Decision-Making Teams," *International Journal of Conflict Management* 18, No. 1 (2007), pp. 42–73; Jonathon A. Segal, "Resolve or Report: Give Supervisors Detailed Directions to Help Them Avoid Making Wrong Turns," *HR Magazine* (October 2005), pp. 125–130; Mable H. Smith, "Grievance Procedures Resolve Conflict," *Nursing Management* (April 2002), p. 13; Mike Frost, "Resolving Conflicts at Work," *HR Magazine* (November 2001), pp. 136–137.
20. The California Supreme Court has upheld a ruling in favor of a woman who accused L'Oreal USA Inc. of retaliating against her because she refused to carry out an order to fire a female sales associate who a supervisor said was not "hot" enough. See *Yankowitz* v. *L'Oreal USA, Inc.* as reported *in BLR Business and Legal Reports* (August 12, 2005).
21. See "Using Arbitration to Resolve Legal Disputes," http://adr.findlaw.com/arbitration/using-arbitration-to-resolve-legal-disputes.html; and "What is Mediation," http://adr.findlaw.com/mediation/what-is-mediation-html.
22. See Allen Smith, "ADR Is Underused Tool for Resolving Disputes," SHRM.org (April 13, 2011), http://www.shrm.org/legalissues/federalresources/pages/adrisunderusedtool.aspx; and "Complaints through Alternatives to Litigation," *Employee Relations Weekly* (November 25, 1991), pp. 1–2.
23. For expanded discussions of ADR approaches, see Nancy R. Lockwood, "Alternative Dispute Resolution," *SHRM Briefly Stated* (February 2004); Michael Netzley, "Alternative Dispute Resolution: A Business and Communication Strategy," *Business Communication Quarterly* (December 2001), pp. 83–89; Lee A. Rosengard, "Appreciating Client Constituencies in Fashioning an ADR Solution," *Dispute Resolution Journal* (August–October 2001), pp. 56–60; and Bennett G. Picker, "ADR: New Challenges, New Roles, and New Opportunities," *Dispute Resolution Journal* (February–April 2001), pp. 20–23.
24. For a discussion of ODR techniques, see Joseph W. Goodman, "The Pros and Cons of Online Dispute Resolution: An Assessment of Cyber-Mediation Websites," *Duke Law & Technology Review,* 1(2) (February 18, 2003) http://scholarship.law.duke.edu/dltr/vol2/iss1/2; and Amy S. Moeves and Scott C. Moeves, "Two Roads Diverged: A Tale of Technology and Alternative Dispute Resolution," *William & Mary Bill of Rights Journal* 12, No. 3 (2014), pp. 843–872. See also Gabrielle Kaufman-Kohler and Thomas Schultz, *Conflict Resolution in the Age of Internet Online Dispute Resolution (ODR): Challenge for Contemporary Justice* (The Hague, Netherlands: Kluwer Law Institute, 2004).

25. See Douglas M. McCabe and Jennifer M. Rabil, "Administering the Employment Relationship: The Ethics of Conflict Resolution in Relation to Justice in the Workplace," *Journal of Business Ethics* (March 2002), pp. 33–48; and Dominic Bencivenga, "Fair Play in the ADR Arena," *HR Magazine* (January 1996), pp. 51–56.
26. Reported in Michael Barrier, "A Working Alternative for Settling Disputes," *Nation's Business* (July 1998), pp. 43–46. Because ADR is used in nearly every workplace setting, each sector and industry has its own data related to ADR. In agencies that report ADR evaluation efforts, the benefits appear to outweigh the costs. The Environmental Protection Agency, for example, has found ADR to result in significant time and money savings, as well as improved relationships and broader stakeholder support, "Evaluation of Alternative Dispute Resolution" (2007), http://www.epa.gov/adr/cprc_evaluation.html; the Department of Justice has seen an average 75 percent resolution rate in voluntary ADR proceedings between 2008 and 2013, http://www.justice.gov/olp/adr/doj-statistics.htm; and the EEOC found that 87 percent of federal agencies were successfully using mediation as their primary ADR technique, "Federal Sector Alternative Dispute Resolution Fact Sheet," http://www.eeoc.gov/federal/adr/facts.cfm. For more information on ADR implementation, go to www.autoissues.org/arbitration_fag.htm, or see Eric Krell, "Process Affects Sense of Fairness in ADR Systems," *HR Magazine* (November 2010), p. 18.
27. There are many differences reported in the research literature. For example, the 2013 Gallup Employee Engagement Index reported that only 30 percent were engaged in their job, 52 percent were not engaged, and 18 percent were actively disengaged. See Gallup's 2013 *State of the American Workplace: Employee Engagement Insights for U.S. Business Leaders,* http://www.gallup.com/strategicconsulting/163007/state-american-workplace.aspx, p. 13. The BlessingWhite "2013 Employee Engagement Report" (http://www.blessingwhite.com, accessed April 2014) reported that only 40 percent of employees are fully engaged in their work, 15 percent are actually disengaged, 74 percent trust their immediate supervisors, and only 57 percent trust top management.

    See Eric Krell, "Do They Trust You?" *HR Magazine* (June 2006), pp. 58–65.
28. See Rebecca R. Hastings, "Loyalty Built on Communication, Not Compensation," *SHRM Home* (April 2008), http://www.shrm.org/hrdisciplines/staffingmanagement/articles/pages/loyaltybuiltoncommunication.aspx S. Rama Iyer, "Driving Engagement through Targeted HR Communication," *SHRM White Paper* (2008); ; and Carlos Tejada, "Disengaged at Work?" *The Wall Street Journal* (March 13, 2001), p. A1. Also see *2008 Quarterly CEO Survey* (Management Action Programs [MAP]), which stressed that open communication, employee recognition, and involvement in decision making are the prime drivers of employee loyalty and retention.
29. For a comprehensive discussion of the regulation of dispute resolution process, see the entire spring 2013 issue of the American Bar Association Section of Dispute Resolution's *Dispute Resolution Magazine* 19, No. 3, titled "Considering Regulation of ADR," available at http://maestro.abanet.org/trk/click?ref=zpqri74vj_3-1c021x31f85fx01&#page=16. See also Barry M. Rubin and Richard S. Rubin, "Creeping Legalism in Public Sector Grievance Arbitration: A National Perspective," *Journal of Collective Negotiations in the Public Sector* 30, No. 1 (2003), p. 3; Tony Mauro, "A Victory for Mandatory Arbitration," *The Record* (American Lawyer Media) (March 22, 2001) p. 1, or Maria Coyle, "Arbitration Heaven Ahead," *The National Law Journal* (April 2, 2001), p. B1.
30. See Charles H. Smith, "When Is Arbitration Not an Arbitration?" *Dispute Resolution Journal* (August–October 2005); Mark A. Hofmann, "Court Upholds Binding Arbitration," *Business Insurance* (March 26, 2001), p. 1; Carlos Tejada, "Supreme Court Ruling Doesn't Answer Vexing Questions about Arbitration," *The Wall Street Journal* (March 27, 2001), p. A1; or Carolyn Hirschman, "Order in the Hearing," *HR Magazine* (July 2001), pp. 58–62.
31. For extensive discussions of grievance–arbitration procedures under a labor agreement, see *Grievance Guide, 13th ed.* (Washington, DC: BNA, 2012), and Fred Whitney and Benjamin J. Taylor, *Labor Relations Law* (Englewood Cliffs, NJ: Prentice-Hall, 1998). For a condensed discussion of the grievance–arbitration process, see David A. Dilts, *Cases in Collective Bargaining and Industrial Relations: A Decisional Approach*, 11th ed. (New York: McGraw-Hill Irwin, 2007), pp. 165–183.

    *Note:* Since 2000, unions have won slightly over half of the union representation elections held in the United States. The rate is remarkably low since unions usually pick the time and place for elections and typically hold them only if they think they can win. Nevertheless, organizations address worker needs on a daily basis and work to engage employees in the affairs of the business.
32. See Alison Stein Wellner, "Making Amends: Apologizing in Part for Doing Business," *Fast Company* (June 2006), pp. 41–42; and Aaron Lazare, *On Apology* (New York: Oxford University Press, 2004). Both authors look at why some apologies work and others fail, and why they are important in opening the door for conflict resolution.
33. To learn more about the EEOC laws, go to www.eeoc.gov and click on "Laws and Guidelines."
34. Scott J. Schackelford and Anjanette H. Raymond, "Building the Virtual Courthouse: Ethical Considerations for Design, Implementation, and Regulation in the World of ODR," *Wisconsin Law Review (2014),* pp. 1–52.
35. This hypothetical situation is based on a case study described in "ODR for Organizational Conflict," ADRhub.com (October 15, 2010), http://www.adrhub.com/forum/topics/odr-for-organizational

Chapter 15

# Positive Discipline

©Tatty/Shutterstock.com

**After studying this chapter, you will be able to:**

1. Discuss the basis and importance of positive discipline in an organization.
2. Identify disciplinary situations that violate standards of conduct and discuss the need to confront those situations appropriately.
3. Identify approaches that ensure proper action for just cause.
4. Describe and discuss the application of progressive discipline.
5. Explain the "hot stove rule" approach to discipline.
6. Discuss the need to document disciplinary actions and to provide the right of appeal.
7. Differentiate between the "discipline without punishment" approach and other alternatives to progressive discipline.
8. Recognize the importance of "fairness" in the disciplinary process.

# YOU MAKE THE CALL![1]

*You are Karissa Dawson, general manager of the Marion Hotel in rural North Carolina. For years families have loved to come and spend time in the hotel. The Marion Hotel was a three-diamond property and the 218-room facility was the place to stay in western North Carolina. The hotel had a full-service restaurant that was a training center for the local college students. Employees were expected to exceed guests' expectations and use their skills to carefully exceed the opportunities and challenges that would occur on a daily basis.*

Four and half years ago, you hired Michael May as your purchasing manager. May was 57 years old at the time. His past work experiences met your needs and his references were outstanding. He and his wife wanted to move to this part of the country so this position would be beneficial for him and the Marion Hotel. As purchasing manager, May was required to negotiate with vendors and suppliers for a variety of hospital supplies including furniture, bed linens, bathroom amenities, food and beverage items, cleaning supplies, and other supplies and equipment as needed in the daily operations of the hotel. May also handled incoming shipments and acquired an off-site warehouse where inventory could be stored. May's performance evaluations had ranged from very good to excellent.

Yesterday, the hotel operator received a call from a woman who identified herself as Becky Reimbold. She explained that she was an associate with KBA Property Preservation a company that was hired to remove property from May's residence as he was being evicted from it. According to Reimbold, the company had run across items that appeared to be Marion Hotel property.

The receptionist attempted to transfer the call to you, or Bette Haver, the HR director, or director of security Jim Hartman, but you were all in the same meeting. The receptionist recorded the details of the call from Reimbold for you, Haver, and Hartman and provided the information to the three of you in sealed envelopes.

Later in the day, Hartman contacted Reimbold at KBA Property Preservation, who told him that the company had found numerous boxes of commercially packaged washcloths and towels, food items including vacuum packed steaks; assorted toiletries and cleaning supplies, and other items that appeared to be property of the Marion Hotel. Hartman was told that the nonperishable property had been moved to a storage facility and Reimbold asked Hartman to come to the facility so he could verify that the items belonged to the Marion Hotel.

Hartman and Andrew Logan traveled to the storage facility to examine the property. Hartman had Logan take pictures of the items. Hartman wrote a report summarizing his findings: "After looking through the items we found six boxes of hotel logo bathroom amenities and numerous washcloths and towels that were clearly unused hotel property. There were three vacuum cleaners of the same brand and model number used by the hotel." KBA's Becky Reimbold stated, "We threw away numerous items because they were perishables and could not be stored in the storage shed by law."

After Hartman presented his findings to top management, you (the general manager), Bette Haver (HR director), and Kip Williams (legal counsel) met with Michael May to inform him of your findings. Williams explained the sequence of events that had led to this meeting. May vehemently denied that he had stolen anything from the hotel. He did admit, however, that he had been given samples of many items from vendors. He was reminded by Bette Haver that the Marion Hotel policies require all employees to report gifts that they receive from those doing business with the hotel.

You told Michael May that he was suspended effective immediately and that the hotel's leadership team would meet with him two days later after they had discussed the actions he had taken as an employee. Later in the day, you reviewed the hotel's policies. One thing in particular stuck in your mind: "The Marion Hotel will not tolerate stealing, nor will it tolerate the possession of company property or other employees' property without prior permission."

You had a sleepless night and wondered what you might have done to prevent things like this from happening. More importantly you wondered what to do with Michael.

**Disclaimer:** The above scenario presents a supervisory situation based on real events to be used for educational purposes. The identities of some or all individuals, organizations, industries, and locations, as well as financial and other information may have been disguised to protect individual privacy and proprietary information. Fictional details may have been added to improve readability and interest.

YOU MAKE THE CALL!

## The Basis and Importance of Positive Discipline

**1 Discuss the basis and importance of positive discipline in an organization.**

**Discipline**
State of orderliness; the degree to which employees act according to expected standards of behavior

The term *discipline* is used in several different ways. Many supervisors associate discipline with the use of authority, force, or punishment. Throughout the book, we consider **discipline** as a condition of orderliness—that is, the degree to which members of an organization act properly and observe the expected standards of behavior. **Positive discipline** exists when employees generally follow the rules and meet the standards of the organization. Discipline is negative, or bad, when

**Positive discipline**
Condition that exists when employees generally follow the organization's rules and meet the organization's standards

**Morale**
A composite of feelings and attitudes that individuals and groups of workers have toward their work environment

**Positive self-discipline**
Employees regulating their behavior out of self-interest and their normal desire to meet reasonable standards

employees follow organizational rules reluctantly or when they disobey regulations and violate prescribed standards of acceptable behavior.

**Morale** is a composite of people's attitudes and feelings toward their work, whereas discipline is primarily a state of mind. However, some relationship exists between morale and discipline. Normally, fewer disciplinary problems arise when morale is high; conversely, low morale is usually accompanied by a higher number of disciplinary problems. However, a high degree of positive discipline could be present despite low morale; this could result from insecurity, fear, or sheer force. It is unlikely, however, that a high degree of positive employee discipline will be maintained indefinitely unless there is an acceptable level of employee morale. The past few years have been very different. Morale and job satisfaction have been at low levels, but employee turnover is low. Why? Many employees are dissatisfied, but know that they may not be able to find a job that is nearly as good as the one they dislike.[2] We will discuss morale and its impact on teamwork and productivity in greater detail in Chapter 11.

The best type of discipline is **positive self-discipline** in which employees essentially regulate themselves out of self-interest. This type of discipline is based on the normal human tendency to do what needs to be done, to do one's share, and to follow reasonable standards of acceptable behavior. Even before they start to work, most people accept the idea that following instructions and observing fair rules of conduct are among the normal responsibilities of any job.

Positive self-discipline relies on the premise that most employees want to do the right thing and can be counted on to exercise self-control. They believe in performing their work properly, coming to work on time, following the supervisor's instructions, and refraining from fighting, using drugs, drinking liquor, or stealing. They know it is natural to subordinate some of their personal interests to the needs of the organization. As long as company rules are communicated and are perceived as reasonable, most employees will observe those rules.

## POSITIVE EMPLOYEE DISCIPLINE REQUIRES SUPERVISORY EXAMPLE

Unfortunately, there are always some employees who, for one reason or another, fail to observe established rules and standards, even after they have been informed of them.

Occupational fraud, more commonly known as employee theft, amounts to billions of dollars of loss annually.[3] Companies with fewer than 100 employees suffer the greatest percentage of employee theft.[4]

What do you think the cost to U.S. business is if one considers other forms of employee dishonesty, including habitual misuse or "stealing" of company time by unwarranted absenteeism and tardiness, doing personal business, and socializing on company time? Social networking sites were relatively unknown a few years ago. About half of the employees surveyed in one study admitted that they regularly visit sites such as Facebook, Twitter, and LinkedIn during their work hours.[5] Do employees care if the boss sees what's on their computer screens? All of us know coworkers who use e-mail and the Internet at work for personal reasons. It is estimated that employees spend at least two hours a day on non–work-related Internet matters.[6] Look at the person sitting next to you in class—is she concentrating on the lecture, playing games, or texting her friends? Do you know of anyone who receives inappropriate transmissions, such as pornography and sexist and racist materials, at work or at school?[7]

Today, an employer can legally use electronic devices to monitor employees. Not all companies that monitor their employees let them in on the secret during training or orientation. Most employers monitor their employees' e-mails.[8] Common sense dictates that employers notify employees that surveillance devices may be used, how they are being used, and the purpose they are intended to serve. Employees also should be assured that any information learned from such surveillance will be kept confidential.

Supervisors should maintain a balanced perspective since employees at the departmental level will take most of their cues for self-discipline from their supervisors and managers (see Figure 15.1). Ideally, positive self-discipline should exist throughout the management team, beginning at the top and extending through all supervisors. Supervisors should not expect their employees to practice positive self-discipline if they themselves do not set good examples. As we have stated several times previously, a supervisor's actions and behavior are easy targets for employees to either emulate or reject. Furthermore, if the supervisor can encourage the vast majority of employees in the department to show a strong sense of self-discipline, those employees usually will exert group pressure on the dissenters. For example, if a no-smoking rule is posted for a building, usually someone in the work group will enforce this rule by reminding smokers to leave the premises before lighting a cigarette. As a result, the supervisor has little need for corrective action when most employees practice positive self-discipline. Oren Harari, a professor and management consultant, has commented that good employee discipline depends mostly on the supervisor's daily behavior and on aligning decisions in the same positive direction and with consistency of actions. He states, "Discipline is the daily grind that makes things happen and lets people know that you're worthy of your word. In short, it's about honor and integrity."[9]

**FIGURE 15.1 Self-discipline must exist at the supervisory level before it exists at the employee level**

**2 Identify disciplinary situations that violate standards of conduct and discuss the need to confront those situations appropriately.**

# Identifying and Confronting Disciplinary Situations

Because individuals do not always agree on what constitutes acceptable standards of conduct, top-level managers must define the standards for supervisors and employees. In many companies, standards are defined in statements of ethical codes and rules of conduct.

## ETHICAL CODES AND POLICIES

In Chapter 1, we discussed ethical considerations, ethics was one of the major focuses of Chapter 5's discussion of leadership, and in Chapter 8, we introduced ethical tests and guidelines for decision making. We mentioned that many organizations have developed statements of ethical standards or ethical codes. Such codes usually outline in broad, value-oriented terms the norms and ideals that are supposed to guide everyone in the organization. Figure 15. 2 presents an example of a statement of values and code of ethics for Darden Restaurants. The seven principles that make up this code are expanded upon in Darden's policy manual that guides employees as to the meaning of those principles and the importance of complying with them.

A code of ethics alone does not ensure ethical conduct. Some codes are documents that primarily outline legal requirements and restrictions, and they provide only limited guidance for solving moral and ethical dilemmas at work. Have you ever observed workplace conduct that was unlawful or that violated the employer's standards of ethical business conduct? If so, you are not alone. Have you or do you know of someone who has been pressured at times by other employees or managers to compromise their organization's business ethics standards to achieve business objectives? What did you do about it? If you observed a manager or another top-level employee turn his eyes and ears away from what is right, what message did he or she send to all the other employees?

Because ethical standards and ethical behavior can be interpreted in varying ways, some firms have developed their ethical codes and policies with major input from teams of employees and supervisors. Furthermore, some major firms have established hotlines or ethics-reporting systems by which employees are encouraged to report questionable situations or individuals who they believe are acting unethically, improperly, or illegally. These firms may have a "corporate ombudsman" who investigates the allegations and takes appropriate action. The person who reported the alleged wrongdoing, usually called a **whistleblower**, should be afforded anonymity. There is supposed to be no retaliation, regardless of whether the report is substantiated by facts and evidence.[10] In this regard, it is generally recognized that a hotline or an ethics-reporting system requires top-level management's commitment to make the system credible—that is, both to deal firmly with wrongdoing when it is reported and to prevent retaliation against the messenger who delivers an unwelcome message.[11]

**Whistleblower**
A person who reports alleged wrongdoing

Of course, an unfounded or a false report with malice may require a disciplinary response by management.

In addition to the preceding tools, some firms have developed statements and policies for addressing conflicts of interest. These statements may be part of, or in addition to, ethical codes. Conflict-of-interest statements usually define situations and employee behaviors that are inconsistent with an individual's

**FIGURE 15.2 A corporate values and code of ethics statement**

**OUR CORE VALUES**

At Darden, we believe building and maintaining a strong, people-focused culture is the single most important reason we've become the world's largest full-service restaurant operating company—a $8.5 billion enterprise. Our 40-plus years of success have come largely as a result of our employees, who create great dining experiences for our guests. That is why we work so hard to provide a nurturing and sustaining environment for our 200,000 employees.

We understand that in order to encourage superior performance from our employees, we must create and maintain a compelling place to work—a place where people can grow and learn enduring life skills. Our goal is to make working at Darden more than just a job, but a place where people can realize their personal and professional dreams.

Developing our people is a cornerstone of our business model. We are constantly striving to foster a team of exceptional leaders at all levels of our company, so we can create a positive workplace for all of our employees. Our company's vibrant culture impacts everything we do, from how we treat our employees and what we value, to how we recognize and reward a job well done.

**OUR STRENGTH COMES FROM OUR STRONG VALUES**

We believe our strong corporate values and culture help our employees learn, thrive and grow. In fact, we believe our vibrant culture gives our company a competitive advantage. Our core values have been forged over a 70-plus-year history, starting with our founder, Bill Darden, who opened his first restaurant in 1938. We look to these values as we endeavor to deliver on Darden's core purpose—To nourish and delight everyone we serve.

- ***Integrity and fairness.*** It all starts with integrity. We trust in the integrity and fairness of each other to always do the right thing, to be open, honest, and forthright with ourselves and others, to demonstrate courage, to solve without blame, and to follow through on all our commitments.
- ***Respect and caring.*** We reach out with respect and caring. We have a genuine interest in the well-being of others. We know the importance of listening, the power of understanding, and the immeasurable value of support.
- ***Diversity.*** Even though we have a common vision, we embrace and celebrate our individual differences. We are strengthened by a diversity of cultures, perspectives, attitudes, and ideas. We honor each other's heritage and uniqueness. Our power of diversity makes a world of difference.
- ***Always learning—always teaching.*** We learn from others as they learn from us. We learn. We teach. We grow.
- ***Being "of service."*** Being of service is our pleasure. We treat people as special and appreciated by giving of ourselves, doing more than expected, anticipating needs, and making a difference.
- ***Teamwork***. Teamwork works. By trusting one another, we bring together the best in all of us and go beyond the boundaries of ordinary success.
- ***Excellence***. We have a passion to set and to pursue, with innovation, courage, and humility, ever higher standards.

*Source:* Darden.com, "Our Culture, " http://www.darden.com/careers/culture.asp. Used here with permission of Darden Restaurants, Orlando, Florida (April 25, 2014).

primary obligations to the employer. Figure 15.3 is an excerpt from 3M's Conflict of Interest Policy.[12] In the final analysis, a firm's commitment to high standards of ethical behavior must go far beyond just codes and policy statements. An ethical commitment requires everyone in the organization, especially those

**FIGURE 15.3 Excerpt from a conflict-of-interest policy statement**

**Principle Statement:**

Employees and third parties to which this Principle applies must be free from conflicts of interest that could adversely influence their judgment, objectivity, or loyalty to the company in conducting 3M business activities and assignments. Employees must avoid situations where their personal interests could inappropriately influence, or appear to influence, their business judgment. This is called "conflict of interest." Even the perception that personal interests influence business judgment can hurt 3M's reputation and business. Employees may take part in legitimate financial, business, charitable, and other activities outside their 3M jobs, but any real, potential, or perceived conflict of interest raised by those activities must be promptly disclosed to management and updated on a periodic basis. Local policies and procedures may require employees to provide timely and complete conflict of interest certifications.

**Purpose:**

Our reputation and business can be damaged when personal interests influence or appear to influence business judgment.

This Principle applies globally to all employees and may apply to those acting on behalf of 3M. See the Compliance Principle for information on when a third party might be covered by the Code of Conduct Principles.

**Additional Guidance:**

- Employees who have friends or other personal or business relationships with people who are government officials must carefully consider whether those relationships create conflicts of interest with their 3M jobs. "Government officials" include government employees, appointed and elected officials, and others, including, but not limited to political parties and high ranking party members, professors and health care professionals who work at public universities and healthcare programs, employees of government-owned or government-controlled companies or public international organizations like the Red Cross and United Nations. Determining whether someone is a "government official" can be difficult, so employees must consult with their assigned business unit's legal counsel or 3M Compliance & Business Conduct Department if they have questions.
- 3M employees must disclose any outside activities, financial interest, or relationship that may pose a real, potential, or perceived conflict of interest. Disclosures may be to a supervisor, manager, or Human Resources professional and will vary depending on the job or role of the employee making the disclosure. Obtain management approval before accepting any position as an officer or director of an outside business.
- Remember that management approval is subject to ongoing review, so employees must periodically update their management regarding any activity that has previously been disclosed pursuant to this Principle.
- Employees must notify management before serving on the board of a charitable, educational, or other nonprofit organization. Employees are encouraged to advise 3Mgives, which may connect them with volunteer resources such as 3M Volunteer Match or additional training.

**This Principle also requires that employees avoid:**

- Accepting outside employment that is inconsistent with 3M's interests, such as working for a competitor or starting your own line of business that competes with 3M.
- Mixing personal relationships and business—for example, hiring a family member as an employee or vendor; buying goods or services from a family business on 3M's behalf; or selling 3M goods to a family business on any basis for which others might compete.
- Accepting gifts, meals, or entertainment that could appear to affect objectivity and judgment. Turn down expensive dinners or gifts that would be considered extravagant by anyone.

*(continued)*

**FIGURE 15.3 (continued)**

- Accepting a gift that does not meet the standards in the 3M Gifts, Entertainment, and Travel Principle.
- Personal relationships with other 3M employees where being in that relationship may result in one of the persons receiving or giving unfair advantage, or preferential treatment because of the relationship.
- Actions or relationships that might conflict or appear to conflict with job responsibilities or the interests of 3M.
- Having a direct or indirect financial interest in or a financial relationship with a 3M competitor, supplier or customer (except for insignificant stock interests in publicly-held companies).
- Taking part in any 3M business decision involving a company that employs a spouse or family member.
- Having a second job where the other employer is a direct or indirect competitor, distributor, supplier or customer of 3M.
- Having a second job or consulting relationship that affects the employee's ability to satisfactorily perform 3M assignments.
- Using nonpublic 3M information for personal gain or advantage, or for the gain or advantage of another, including the purchase or sale of securities in a business 3M is interested in acquiring, selling or otherwise establishing or terminating business relations with.
- Investing in an outside business opportunity in which 3M has an interest, except for having an insignificant stock interest in publicly-held companies.
- Receiving personal discounts or other benefits from suppliers, service providers or customers that are not available to all 3M employees.
- Receiving personal honoraria for performing services that are closely related to the employee's work at 3M. Employees must have their supervisor approve occasional honoraria, such as for a university presentation or symposium.
- Having romantic relationships with certain other employees where:
  - There is an immediate reporting relationship between the employees.
  - There is no direct reporting relationship between the employees, but where a romantic relationship could cause others to lose confidence in the judgment or objectivity of either employee, or the relationship could cause embarrassment to the company.

*Source:* 3M Conflict of Interest Principle, http://solutions.3m.com/wps/portal/3M/en_US/businessconduct/bcmain/policy/principles/beloyal/conflictinterest/, reprinted with permission, May 2014.

in management and supervision, to show daily, by word and deed, that behaving ethically at work is not optional. There is ample evidence that good ethics means good business, a sentiment expressed eloquently by Nicholas Moore, retired global chair of PricewaterhouseCoopers and current director of Wells Fargo Company, as follows:

> *When companies stand up for what's right, day in and day out, it has a positive impact. Positive in terms of whom it attracts, because good people want to work in ethical environments. It simplifies decision making. We know what we won't even think about doing. And, in the process, we earn the respect of our competitors, our clients, and our people. In the long term, that's very, very important. So ethical behavior is at the core of the way we do business, and it's the only way we're going to do business.*[13]

## RULES OF CONDUCT

Not every organization has a published code of ethics or conflict-of-interest statement. However, virtually every large firm, and probably most other firms and organizations, have some formal statements or lists of rules of behavior to which employees are expected to conform.

In Chapter 3, we discuss the need for policies, procedures, methods, and rules to cover many aspects of ongoing operations. These tools are vital in informing employees which standards of behavior are expected and which behaviors are unacceptable.

Most organizations give their employees written lists of rules or codes of conduct. These lists are sometimes included in employee handbooks; sometimes they are provided as separate booklets or as memoranda posted in departments. Supervisors must ensure that employees read and understand general and departmental rules, which may include safety and technical regulations, depending on a department's activity.

Written rules and regulations provide a common basis and standards that should help the supervisor encourage employee self-discipline. Some organizations provide very detailed lists of rules and infractions; these lists may include classifications of the likely penalties for violations. Other organizations, probably most, prefer to list their major rules and regulations but not the consequences of rule violations. Such a list appears in Figure 15.4. Regardless of what type of list is used, the supervisor is the person most responsible for the consistent application and enforcement of company and departmental rules. In fact, the degree to which employees follow corporate rules in a positive, self-disciplined way is usually more attributable to the supervisor's role and example than to any other factor.

Rules of conduct and policy statements in employee handbooks and manuals are often subject to review and change because of legal problems and interpretations. While the review and revision of employee handbooks are usually the responsibility of human resources staff, supervisors should be very familiar with the content of employee handbooks. Supervisors should not hesitate to suggest revisions when those revisions appear justified.[14]

### Confronting Disciplinary Situations

Despite their best efforts to prevent infractions, supervisors will at times confront situations requiring some type of disciplinary action. The following require immediate action by the supervisor:

- Infractions of rules regarding time schedules, rest periods, procedures, safety, and so forth.
- Excessive absenteeism or tardiness.
- Defective or inadequate work performance.
- Poor attitudes that influence the work of others or damage the firm's public image.

A supervisor may at times experience open insubordination, such as when an employee refuses to carry out a legitimate work assignment. A supervisor may even confront disciplinary problems stemming from employee behavior off the job. For example, an employee may have a drinking problem or may be taking illegal drugs. Whenever an employee's off-the-job conduct affects on-the-job performance, the supervisor must be prepared to respond to the problem

**FIGURE 15.4 Partial list of one company's rules and regulations**

**COMPANY RULES AND REGULATIONS**

The efficient operation of our plants and the general welfare of our employees require certain uniform standards of behavior. Accordingly, the following offenses are considered violations of these standards. Employees who refuse to accept this guidance subject themselves to appropriate disciplinary action.

- Habitual tardiness and absenteeism (see no-fault attendance policy)
- Theft or attempted theft of company or another employee's property
- Fighting or attempting bodily injury upon another employee
- Horseplay, malicious mischief, physically threatening word or gestures, or any other conduct affecting the rights of or could potentially damage other employees
  - Smoking or tobacco usage and alcohol is not allowed on company properties or in company vehicles
  - Using of company telephone, computers (e-mail) systems, or other company property for personal use
- Intoxication or drinking on the job or being in a condition that makes it impossible to perform work satisfactorily
- Refusal or failure to perform assigned work or refusal or failure to comply with supervisory instructions
- Inattention to duties; carelessness in performance of duties; loafing on the job, sleeping, or reading non-work-related material during working hours
- Violation of published safety or health rules
- Possessing, consuming, selling, or being under the influence of illegal drugs on or off the job
- Unauthorized possession of weapons, firearms, or explosives on the premises
- Requests for sexual favors, sexual advances, and physical conduct of a sexual nature toward another employee on the premises
- Verbal and physical abuse, including threatening others

*Note to all employees:* Closed-circuit security cameras closely monitor the interior and exterior of our facilities. Safety training, including fire drills, emergency evacuation, and other contingency exercises, is conducted quarterly so that staff and associates are properly prepared and forewarned.



appropriately. In Chapter 11, we discuss a number of ways to help employees with personal and work-related problems.

Situations that require disciplinary action are unpleasant, but the supervisor must have the courage to deal with those situations. If the supervisor does not take action when required, borderline employees might be encouraged to try similar violations.

A supervisor should not hesitate to draw on some of the authority inherent in the supervisory position, even though it might be easier to overlook the matter or to pass the matter to higher-level managers or the human resources department. Supervisors who ask the human resources department to assume all departmental disciplinary problems shirk their responsibility and undermine their own authority.

Normally, good supervisors will not have to take disciplinary action very frequently. When such action is necessary, however, the supervisor should be ready to act, no matter how unpleasant the task may be.

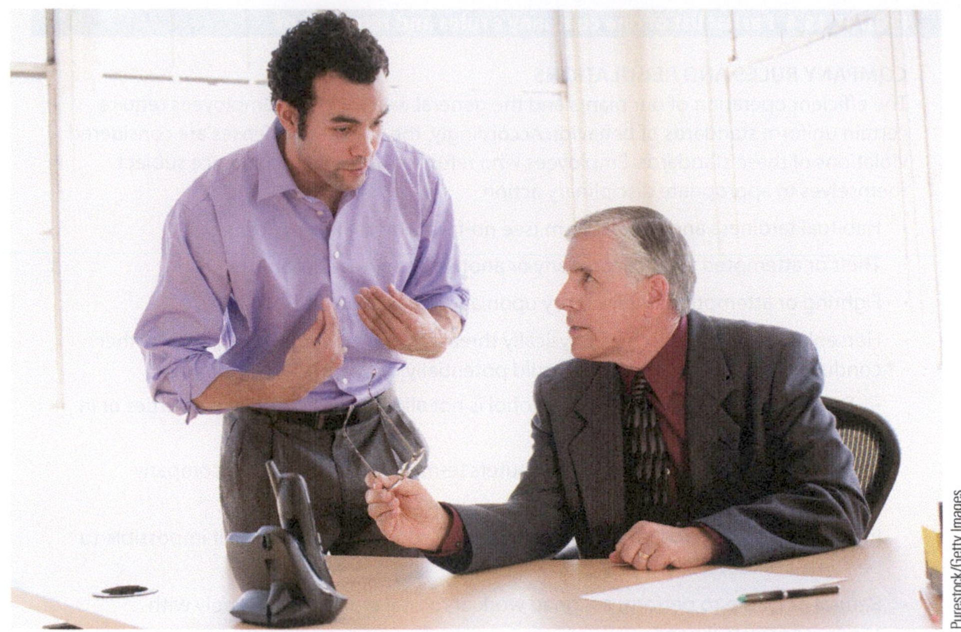

*Every supervisor must be prepared to occasionally confront insubordination or other situations that require some type of disciplinary action*

Purestock/Getty Images

**3 Identify approaches that ensure proper action for just cause.**

# The Disciplinary Process and Just Cause

Supervisors must initiate any disciplinary action with sensitivity and sound judgment. The purpose of disciplinary action should not be to punish or to seek revenge but to improve employees' behavior. In other words, the primary purpose of disciplinary action is to prevent similar infractions. In this text, we do not consider directly those situations in which union contracts may restrict the supervisor's ability to take disciplinary action. The ideas discussed here apply generally to most unionized and nonunionized organizations.

## DISCIPLINARY ACTION SHOULD HAVE JUST CAUSE

As discussed in Chapter 2, most employers accept the general premise that disciplinary action taken against an employee should be based on "just cause." Generally, to be viewed as "just," the disciplinary action must consider all the facts in the individual case and be consistent with past practice. Figure 15.5 lists eight questions arbitrators ask in union–management disciplinary-type grievance matters. A "no" answer to one or more of these questions means that the just-cause standard was not fully met. As a result, the arbitrator or court might set aside or modify management's disciplinary action.

The preponderance of labor-union contracts specify a just-cause or proper cause standard for discipline and discharge. Similarly, many cases decided by government agencies and by the courts have required employers to prove that disciplinary actions taken against legally protected employees (discussed in Chapter 4) were not discriminatory but were for just cause. Even under various forms of alternative dispute resolution (ADR) (discussed in Chapter 14), a just-cause standard, or something approximating it, typically is applied in resolving disciplinary case matters.[15] It would seem almost certain that a just-cause standard would prevail throughout most organizations. Although the ramifications of a just-cause

**FIGURE 15.5 Eight tests for just cause**

**EIGHT TESTS FOR JUST CAUSE**

1. Did the company give the employee forewarning of the possible or probable disciplinary consequences of the employee's behavior? (Give Advance Warning)
2. Was the company's rule or managerial order reasonably related to (a) the orderly, efficient, and safe operation of the company's business and (b) the performance the company might properly expect of the employee? (Clarify Expectations—Everyone Needs to Know the Rules of the Game)
3. Did the company, before administering discipline to an employee, make an effort to discover whether the employee did, in fact, violate or disobey a rule or an order of management? (Investigate Immediately)
4. Was the company's investigation conducted fairly and objectively? (Be Objective)
5. After investigation, was there substantial evidence or proof that the employee was guilty as charged? (Analyze the Evidence)
6. Has the company applied its rules, orders, and penalties evenhandedly and without discrimination? (Be Consistent, Uniform, and Impersonal)
7. Was the degree of discipline administered by the company in a particular case reasonably related to (a) the seriousness of the employee's proven offense and (b) the record of the employee's service with the company? (Punishment in Relation to the Offense)
8. Has the company kept records of the offense committed, the evidence, and the decision made, including the reasoning involved in the decision? *(Cover Your Rear—Be Sure to Document Specifically the Who, What, Where, When, Why, and How)*

*Source:* Presented Edwin C. Leonard Jr. and Roy A. Cook, *Human Resource Management: 21st Century Challenges* (Mason, OH: Thomson, 2005), p. 133. Seven tests were originally adapted from a list suggested by arbitrator Carroll R. Daugherty. They are included in many texts and arbitral citations.

standard for disciplinary action can be rather complicated, the guidelines presented in this chapter are consistent with the principles and requirements needed to justify any disciplinary or discharge action. The supervisor who follows these guidelines conscientiously should be able to meet a just-cause standard, regardless of whether the case involves a unionized firm, a nonunionized organization, or a potential area of legal discrimination.[16]

## PAUSE BEFORE TAKING ACTION

As a first consideration in any disciplinary situation, a supervisor should guard against undue haste or unwarranted action based on emotional response. A supervisor should answer and follow a number of precautionary questions and measures before deciding on any disciplinary action in response to an employee's alleged offense.

## INVESTIGATE THE SITUATION

Before doing anything else, the supervisor should investigate what happened and why. The questions in the accompanying Supervisory Tips box can serve as a checklist as supervisors consider what to do.

For certain serious violations, such as stealing, illegal substance use, and violence, an organization may call in law-enforcement authorities to investigate and take appropriate action. Some firms employ consultants to administer polygraph tests in an effort to determine who committed the violations, particularly in matters involving theft. Polygraph use, however, has been restricted by a federal law. This statute permits an employer with "reasonable suspicion" of employee wrongdoing to use a polygraph. The employer should not force an employee to take a polygraph test.[17]

There may even be situations in which investigation of possible wrongdoing requires some form of personnel surveillance. An outside private investigator may be hired to conduct electronic surveillance or perhaps become part of the workplace as an undercover "employee." The supervisor may or may not be informed that such surveillance is taking place.[18] However, federal regulations require employers to notify workers if the company intends to have an outside party investigate or probe the alleged workplace wrongdoings. Such disclosure is required if an inquiry could lead to an adverse decision against an employee, such as discipline, termination, or job movement.[19] When an employee is injured on the job, many firms require the employee to take a drug-and-alcohol screening test. Such tests usually are given by a qualified person in the firm's first-aid room or by someone at an occupational-health clinic where the employee is treated. Safeguards concerning employee privacy and test result validation usually are followed, although the results may be used as part of management's investigation and decision-making process.[20]

## SUPERVISORY TIPS

### Checklist of Questions to Ask during a Disciplinary Investigation

1. Are all or most of the facts available, and are they reported accurately? That is, can the alleged offense be proved by direct or circumstantial evidence, or is the allegation based merely on suspicion?
2. How serious is the offense (minor, major, or intolerable)?
3. Were others involved in or affected by the offense?
4. Were company funds or equipment involved?
5. Was there damage to the organization's reputation, product or service quality, personal injury, or other identifiable harm?
6. Did the employee know the rule, standard, and/or expectations?
7. Does the employee have a reasonable excuse, and are there any extenuating circumstances?
8. What is the employee's disciplinary record, length of service, and performance level?
9. Does the offense indicate carelessness, absentmindedness, or loss of temper?
10. How does this employee react to constructive criticism?
11. Should the employee receive the same treatment others have had for the same offense? If not, is it possible to establish a basis for differentiating the present alleged offense from past offenses of a similar nature?
12. Is all the necessary documentation available in case the matter leads to outside review?

## INVESTIGATORY INTERVIEWS

As part of the supervisor's investigation of an alleged infraction, it may be necessary to question the employee involved as well as other employees who may have relevant information. In general, such interviews should be conducted privately and individually, perhaps with a guarantee of confidentiality. These situations are usually less threatening to employees who may otherwise be reluctant to tell what they know. Such situations also help prevent employees from being unduly influenced by another's version or interpretation.

If a union employee is to be interviewed concerning a disciplinary matter, that employee may ask that a union representative or coworker be present during the interview. Normally, the supervisor should grant such a request. Under federal labor law (the Weingarten rights), a union employee has the right to have a union representative present during an investigatory interview if the employee reasonably believes the investigation may lead to disciplinary action.[21] However, a union representative or coworker cannot disrupt an investigatory interview or answer questions for the employee under investigation. Of course, if the employee is to have a witness present, the supervisor is well advised to have a fellow supervisor present to serve as a supervisory witness to the interview.

Occasionally, a nonunion employee will ask that a fellow worker or another supervisory witness be present during an investigatory interview. Recent court decisions have generally extended to nonunionized employees the right to have coworkers present in investigatory interviews that may lead to discipline. When faced with such a request, the supervisor should probably consult with the human resources department or a higher-level manager for guidance. Normally, such a request should be granted, but there may be reasons such a request should be denied or the interview voided.[22]

Most of the principles of interviewing and effective communication discussed throughout this text apply to investigatory interviewing. The supervisor should ask both directive and nondirective questions that are designed to elicit specific answers about what happened and why. Above all, the supervisor should avoid making final judgments until all interviews have been conducted and other relevant information assembled.

## MAINTAINING SELF-CONTROL

Regardless of the severity of an employee's violation, a supervisor must maintain self-control. This does not mean a supervisor should face a disciplinary situation halfheartedly or indifferently, but if supervisors feel they are in danger of losing control of their tempers or emotions, they should delay the investigatory interviews and take no action until they regain control. A supervisor's loss of self-control or display of anger could compromise fair and objective judgment.

Generally, a supervisor should never lay a hand on an employee in any way. Except for emergencies, when an employee has been injured or becomes ill, or when employees who are fighting must be separated, any physical gesture could easily be misunderstood. A supervisor who engages in physical violence, except in self-defense, normally is subject to disciplinary action by higher-level management.

## PRIVACY IN DISCIPLINING

When supervisors decide on disciplinary actions, they should communicate those actions to the offending employees in private. A public reprimand not only can humiliate the employee in the eyes of coworkers but also can erode department morale or inspire a grievance. If, in the opinion of other employees, a public disciplinary action is too severe for the violation, the disciplined employee might emerge as a martyr.

We have learned through experience that it is always desirable to have another management person present (such as the supervisor, the supervisor's superior, and perhaps the human resources director) to witness any discussion that might require corrective action. It is also essential that the witness confirm the discussion and actions that took place. In a litigious society, it is most important to document all of your discussions and actions, which some people refer to as "covering your rear" (CYR).[23]

Only under extreme circumstances should disciplinary action be taken in public. For example, a supervisor's authority may be challenged directly and openly by an employee who repeatedly refuses to carry out a reasonable work request, or an employee may be drunk or fighting on the job. In these cases, the supervisor must reach a disciplinary decision quickly (e.g., send the offending employee home on suspension pending further investigation). Supervisors may have to act in the presence of other employees to regain control of situations and to maintain their respect.

### DISCIPLINARY TIME ELEMENT

When a supervisor decides to impose discipline, the question arises as to how long the violation should be held against the offending employee. Generally, minor or intermediate offenses should be disregarded after a year or so has elapsed since those offenses were committed. Therefore, an employee with a record of defective work might be given a "clean bill of health" by subsequently compiling a good record for six months or one year. Some companies have adopted "point systems" to cover certain infractions, especially absenteeism and tardiness. Employees can have points removed from their records if they have perfect or acceptable attendance during later periods.

In some situations, time is of no importance. For example, if an employee is caught brandishing a knife in a heated argument at work, the supervisor need not worry about the punishment period or previous offenses. Such an act is serious enough to warrant immediate discharge.

**4 Describe and discuss the application of progressive discipline.**

## Practicing Progressive Discipline

**Progressive discipline**
System of disciplinary action that increases the severity of the penalty with each offense

Unless a serious violation, such as stealing, physical violence, or gross insubordination, has been committed, rarely is the offending employee discharged for a first offense. Although the type of disciplinary action varies according to the situation, many organizations practice **progressive discipline**, which increases the severity of the penalty with each offense. The following stages compose a system of progressive disciplinary action:

- Informal discussion with the employee. (At this stage and subsequent stages, place documentation of discussion in the employee's file, including the reason for discussion; the date and time of discussion and who was present; and how the employee was strongly encouraged to modify his or her behavior.)
- Oral warning including counseling.
- Written warning.
- Disciplinary layoff. (Suspension without pay, usually for one to three days. The more serious the infraction, the longer the suspension.)

- Transfer or demotion.
- Discharge. (Very serious infractions may warrant termination in the first and only step.)
- Figure 15.6 details a company's progressive discipline policy, and Figure 15.7 illustrates its use.

Many disciplinary situations can be handled solely or primarily by the supervisor without escalating those situations to difficult confrontations. In the early stages of progressive discipline, the supervisor communicates with the employee about the problem and how to correct it.

**FIGURE 15.6 A hospital's progressive disciplinary policy**

**Corrective Action Policy**

Corrective action shall progress from verbal counseling to written reprimand, suspension, and termination. All actions shall reference the policy or procedure that has been violated, the adverse consequence resulting from the violation, the type of behavior expected in the future, and the corrective action that will be taken if further violations occur. A copy of the completed corrective action form shall be given to the employee.

Following are guidelines for the corrective action procedure:

- **Verbal counseling**—Verbal counseling shall be given for all minor violations of hospital rules and policies. More than two verbal counseling sessions in the past 12-month period regarding violations of any rules or policies warrants a written reprimand.
- **Written reprimand**—Written reprimands shall be given for repeated minor infractions or for first-time occurrences of more serious offenses. Written reprimands shall be documented on the "Notice of Corrective Action" form, which is signed by the department head or supervisor and the employee.
- **Suspension**—An employee shall be suspended without pay for one to four scheduled working days for a critical or major offense or for repeated minor or serious offenses.
- **Termination**—An employee may be terminated for repeated violations of hospital rules and regulations or for first offenses of a critical nature.



**FIGURE 15.7 A disciplinary action program often begins with informal talk. With repeated offenses, penalties become more severe**

## INFORMAL DISCUSSION

If the offense is relatively minor and the employee has no disciplinary record, a friendly and informal talk will clear up the problem in many cases. During this talk, the supervisor should try to determine the underlying reasons for the employee's unacceptable conduct. At the same time, the supervisor should reaffirm the employee's sense of responsibility and acknowledge previous good behavior. Regardless of the offense, the supervisor should record the "date, place, time, and nature" of the incident. If others witnessed the incident, their names also should be noted. See Figure 15.8 for an illustration of the type of information the supervisor should record.

## ORAL COUNSELING (WARNING)

If a friendly talk does not take care of the situation, the next step is to provide the employee with counseling (sometimes known as oral warning). Here, the supervisor emphasizes in a straightforward manner the undesirability of the employee's repeated violation. While the supervisor should stress the preventive purpose of discipline, the supervisor also should emphasize that unless the employee improves, more serious disciplinary action will be taken. In some organizations, a record of this oral warning is made in the employee's file. Alternatively, the supervisor may simply write a brief note in a supervisory logbook to document that an oral warning was given on a particular date. This can be important evidence if the employee commits another infraction.

At times, a supervisor may believe that the substance of verbal counseling should be put in writing so that the message is documented and, more likely,

**FIGURE 15.8 Supervisors should record information on a regular basis. We suggest you begin with a blank sheet of paper and answer the following questions**

is impressed on the employee. In such a situation, the supervisor may resort to what is called a letter of clarification. Such a letter should clearly state that it is not a formal disciplinary document and that its primary purpose is to reiterate to the employee what was communicated verbally by the supervisor. In general, letters of clarification tend to apply most often when dealing with minor employee infractions in the early stages of progressive discipline.[24] If oral warnings and letters of clarification are carried out skillfully, many employees will respond and improve at this stage. The employee must understand that improvement is expected and that the supervisor believes the employee can improve and is ready to help the employee do so.

## WRITTEN REPRIMAND

A written reprimand contains a statement of the violation and the potential consequences of future violations. It is a formal document that becomes a permanent part of the employee's record. The supervisor should review with the employee the nature of this written warning and should once again stress the need for improvement. The employee should be placed on notice that future infractions or unacceptable conduct will lead to more serious discipline, such as suspension or discharge.

Written warnings are particularly necessary in unionized organizations because they can serve as evidence in grievance procedures. Such documentation also is important if the employee is a member of a legally protected group. The employee usually receives a duplicate copy of the written warning, and another copy is sent to the human resources department. Figure 15.9 is a written warning used by a supermarket chain. This form even provides space for the supervisor to note if the employee refuses to sign it.

Even at this stage in the disciplinary process, the supervisor should continue to express to the employee a belief in the employee's ability to improve and the supervisor's willingness to help in whatever way possible.[25] The primary goal of disciplinary action up until discharge should be to help the employee improve and add value to the organization.

## SUSPENSION (DISCIPLINARY LAYOFF)

Unfortunately, not every employee responds to the supervisor's counseling and warnings to improve job behavior. In progressive discipline, more serious disciplinary actions may be administered for repeated violations, with discharge being the final step.

If an employee has offended repeatedly and previous warnings were of no avail, a disciplinary layoff may constitute the next disciplinary step. Disciplinary layoffs involve a loss of pay and usually extend from one day to several days or weeks. Because a disciplinary layoff involves loss of pay, most organizations limit a supervisor's authority at this stage. Most supervisors can only initiate or recommend a disciplinary layoff. The layoff must then be approved by higher-level managers after consulting with the human resources department.

Employees who do not respond to oral or written warnings usually find a disciplinary layoff to be a rude awakening. The layoff may restore in them the need to comply with the organization's rules and regulations. However, managers in some organizations seldom apply layoffs as disciplinary measures. They believe that laying off trained employees will hurt their production, especially in times of

**FIGURE 15.9 Written warning used by a supermarket chain**

**EMPLOYEE CORRECTIVE ACTION NOTICE**

Employee's name ____________________ Date of notice ____________________

Store # ________ Dept. ________ Classification ________

This notice is a: First warning ☐ Second warning ☐ Third warning ☐ Final warning ☐

Reason for corrective action: (Check below)

| | | |
|---|---|---|
| ☐ Non-team worker | ☐ Cash register discrepancy | ☐ Insubordination |
| ☐ Quality/quantity of work | ☐ Dress code | ☐ Time-card violation |
| ☐ Tardiness/absenteeism | ☐ Disregard for safety | ☐ Other cause(s) (Explain) |

Tardiness/absenteeism Disregard for safety Other cause(s) (Explain)

Explanation must accompany reason checked above:

________________________________________

________________________________________

________________________________________

**I HEREBY SIGNIFY THAT I HAVE RECEIVED A FULL EXPLANATION OF MY FAILURE TO PERFORM AS EXPECTED. THE COMPANY AND I UNDERSTAND THAT FURTHER FAILURE ON MY PART WILL BE DUE CAUSE FOR DISCIPLINARY ACTION UP TO, AND INCLUDING, DISCHARGE.**

| | | | |
|---|---|---|---|
| Employee's signature | Date | Supervisor's signature | Date |
| | | Store manager's signature | Date |

**REFUSAL OF EMPLOYEE TO SIGN THIS NOTICE SHOULD BE SO NOTED HEREON.**

*Note:* Prepare original and four copies. Send original and one copy to the human resources director. Send one copy to the store manager and one copy to the employee. Retain one copy.



labor shortages. Furthermore, these managers reason that the laid-off employees may return in an even more unpleasant frame of mind. Despite this possibility, in many employee situations, disciplinary layoffs are an effective disciplinary measure.

## TRANSFER

Transferring an employee to a job in another department typically involves no loss of pay. This disciplinary action is usually taken when an offending employee seems to be experiencing difficulty working for a particular supervisor, working in a current job, or associating with certain employees. The transfer may markedly improve the employee if the employee adjusts to the new department and the new supervisor. When transfers are made primarily to give employees a final chance to retain their jobs with the company, those employees should be told that they must improve in the new job or be subject to discharge. Of course, the supervisor who accepts the transferred employee should be informed of the circumstances surrounding the transfer. This information helps the supervisor facilitate a successful transition for the transferred employee.

## DEMOTION

Another disciplinary measure, the value of which is questionable, is demotion (downgrading) to a lower-paying job. This course of action is likely to bring about dissatisfaction and discouragement because losing pay and status over an extended period is a form of ongoing punishment. The dissatisfaction of the demoted employee also can spread to other employees. Therefore, most organizations avoid demotion as a disciplinary action.

Demotion should be used only in unusual situations in which disciplinary layoff or discharge is not a better alternative. For example, when a long-service employee is not maintaining the standards of work performance required in a certain job, this employee may accept a demotion as an alternative to discharge to retain seniority and other accrued benefits.

## TERMINATION (DISCHARGE)

The most drastic form of disciplinary action is termination or discharge. The discharged employee loses all seniority and may have difficulty obtaining employment elsewhere. Discharge should be reserved only for the most serious offenses and as a last resort.

A discharge means having to train another employee to do the job and disrupting the makeup of the work group, which may affect the morale of other employees. Moreover, in unionized organizations, management becomes concerned about possible prolonged grievance and arbitration proceedings. Management knows that labor arbitrators are unwilling to sustain discharge except for severe offenses or for a series of violations that cumulatively justify the discharge. If the discharge involves an employee who is a member of a legally protected group, management will have to be concerned about meeting appropriate standards for nondiscrimination.

In recent years, many organizations are being sued by former employees who allege that they were terminated or discriminated against unlawfully, which led to their discharge. Because of the serious implications and consequences of discharge, most organizations have removed the discharge decision from supervisors and have reserved it for higher-level managers. Other organizations require that any discharge recommended by a supervisor must be reviewed and approved by higher-level managers or the human resources department, often with the advice of legal counsel.

Because of legal and other concerns, the final termination interview with the discharged employee may be conducted by a member of the human resources department. When supervisors conduct the termination interview, however, they should be careful to focus on the reasons for the termination and to respond to the questions of the employee being terminated. The supervisor should not lose emotional control or engage in a heated debate about the fairness of the termination decision. With luck, the supervisor will be able to close the termination interview by suggesting avenues or options the discharged employee should consider for possible employment elsewhere.[26]

Generally, all of the preceding considerations should be observed, even by employers who traditionally have had the freedom to dismiss employees at will, at any time, and for any reasons, except for unlawful discrimination, union

**FIGURE 15.10 Sample employment-at-will policy from a bank**

**EMPLOYMENT-AT-WILL POLICY**

Citizens Bank is an at-will employer. This means that employees may resign from the bank if they choose to do so. Similarly, the bank may discharge an employee at any time, for any reason, with or without notice. Nothing in this handbook or any other policy adopted by Citizens Bank in any way alters the at-will nature of Citizens Bank employment.

The separation decision is not to be made without serious consideration by either the employer or employee. Ideally, an employee choosing to leave will give two weeks notice so that customer needs can be fulfilled without disruption. Downsizings, reduction in force, and discharges are not likely to occur precipitously.



**Employment-at-will**
Legal concept that employers can dismiss employees at any time and for any reason, except unlawful discrimination and contractual or other restrictions

activity, or where contracts, policy manuals, or some form of employment agreements impose restrictions. This has been called **employment-at-will**, and it still is generally considered applicable from a legal point of view.[27] Figure 15.10 is an employment-at-will policy statement from a bank's employee handbook.

As stated before, most employers recognize that a discharge action should have a rational basis, such as economic necessity, or should be for just cause or at least for good cause, as it has been sometimes called.[28] When employers follow the principles of progressive disciplinary action and couple them with good supervisory practices, those employers usually do not have to resort to employment-at-will to decide whether to terminate an employee who has not performed acceptably.

**5 Explain the "hot stove rule" approach to discipline.**

## Applying the Hot Stove Rule

**Hot stove rule**
Guideline for applying discipline analogous to touching a hot stove: advance warning and consequences that are immediate, consistent, and applied with impersonality

Taking disciplinary action may place the supervisor in a strained or difficult position. Disciplinary action is an unpleasant experience that tends to generate employee resentment. To help the supervisor apply the disciplinary measure so that it will be least resented and most likely to withstand challenges from various sources, some authorities have advocated the use of the **hot stove rule**. This rule equates touching a hot stove with experiencing discipline. Both contain the following four elements:

1. Advance warning
2. Immediacy
3. Consistency
4. Impersonality

Everyone knows what happens if they touch a red-hot stove (advance warning). Someone who touches a hot stove gets burned right away, with no questions of cause and effect (immediacy). Every time a person touches a hot stove, that person gets burned (consistency). Whoever touches a hot stove is burned because the stove treats all people the same (impersonality). The supervisor can apply these four elements of the hot stove rule when maintaining employee discipline.

### ADVANCE WARNING

For employees to accept disciplinary action as fair, they must know in advance their expectations as well as rules and regulations. Employees must be informed clearly that certain acts will lead to disciplinary action, and supervisors should clarify any questions that arise concerning rules and their enforcement.

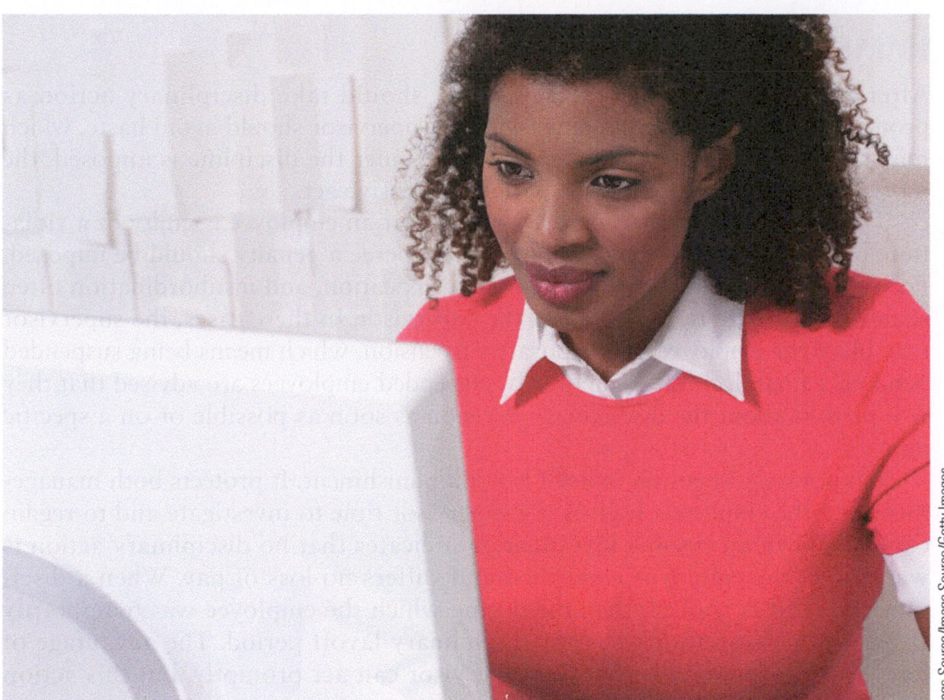

Image Source/Image Source/Getty Images

*An employee handbook is an excellent tool for ensuring that employees are kept clearly informed about behaviors that will lead to disciplinary actions*

Most firms document their rules in employee handbooks that are given out to all new employees, either in print or electronic formats. As part of orientation, the supervisor should explain to each new employee the departmental rules and the rules that are part of the employee handbook. All organizations should require employees to sign documents stating that they have (a) received, (b) read, and (c) understood the company handbook and that they are willing to comply with the rules and regulations contained therein. For example, because of the numerous legal and performance problems associated with substance abuse, many firms give their employees detailed information about the firm's policies and procedures for dealing with employees who are found to have alcohol or drugs in their systems. Such policies and procedures may specify information and warnings that spell out the firm's intentions regarding testing, treatment, and disciplinary responses, including possible termination. The basic premise requires that you have written documentation to prove that the employees have been forewarned.[29] When an employee violates a company policy or when his or her behavior does not meet expectations, you note information rather than rely on your memory.

Unfortunately, in some organizations rules are not enforced. For example, smoking may be prohibited in a certain area, but the supervisor has not enforced the rule. Of course, it is improper for the supervisor to suddenly decide it is time to enforce this rule strictly and to try to make an example of an employee found smoking in an unauthorized area by taking disciplinary action against that employee. That a certain rule has not been enforced does not mean it can never be enforced. To enforce such a rule, the supervisor must warn the employees that the rule will be strictly enforced from a certain point onward. It is not enough just to post a notice on a bulletin board because not all employees look at the board every day. The supervisor must issue a clear, written notice and supplement that notice with oral communication.

## IMMEDIACY

After noticing an offense, the supervisor should take disciplinary action as promptly as possible. At the same time, the supervisor should avoid haste, which might lead to unwarranted reactions. The sooner the discipline is imposed, the more closely it will be connected with the offensive act.

There will be instances when it appears that an employee is guilty of a violation, but the supervisor may doubt to what degree a penalty should be imposed. For example, incidents such as fighting, intoxication, and insubordination often require immediate responses from the supervisor. In these cases, the supervisor may place the employee on temporary suspension, which means being suspended pending a final decision. Temporarily suspended employees are advised that they will be told about the disciplinary decision as soon as possible or on a specific date.

Temporary suspension in itself is not a punishment. It protects both management and the employee. It gives the supervisor time to investigate and to regain control. When an ensuing investigation indicates that no disciplinary action is warranted, the employee is recalled and suffers no loss of pay. When a disciplinary layoff is applied, the time during which the employee was temporarily suspended constitutes part of the disciplinary-layoff period. The advantage of temporary suspension is that the supervisor can act promptly, but this action should not be used indiscriminately.

## CONSISTENCY

Appropriate disciplinary action should be taken each time an infraction occurs. The supervisor who feels inclined to be lenient every now and then is, in reality, doing employees no favor. Inconsistent discipline leads to employee anxiety and creates doubts as to what employees can and cannot do. This type of situation can be compared to the relations between a motorist and a traffic police officer in an area where the speed limit is enforced only occasionally. Whenever the motorist exceeds the speed limit, the motorist experiences anxiety knowing the police officer can enforce the law at any time. Most motorists would agree that it is easier to operate in areas where the police force is consistent in enforcing or not enforcing speed limits. Employees, too, find it easier to work in environments in which their supervisors apply disciplinary action consistently.

**No-fault attendance policy** Policy under which unscheduled absences and tardiness are counted as occurrences and their accumulation is used in progressive discipline

Because of the numerous difficulties associated with inconsistently enforced absenteeism and tardiness policies, many firms have adopted no-fault attendance policies, especially for blue-collar employees. A **no-fault attendance policy** counts any unscheduled absence or tardiness as an "occurrence," and the accumulation of occurrences or assessed points during designated time frames is used to invoke progressive discipline ranging from warnings to suspension and finally termination. Supervisors often prefer a no-fault approach because they do not have to assess or determine the legitimacy of an employee's unscheduled absence. A firm's no-fault attendance policy may provide for rewarding good attendance and may designate certain absence exceptions. These provisions are spelled out so that employees and supervisors have a well-understood and consistent framework by which absences and tardiness are evaluated and handled.[30] Figure 15.11 is an excerpt from a manufacturing firm's "Absenteeism and Tardiness Policy," which is a no-fault system that applies to this firm's unionized plant employees.

**FIGURE 15.11 Excerpt from a manufacturing plant's no-fault attendance policy**

**Absenteeism and Tardiness Policy**

1. All employees are expected to report to work in sufficient time to receive job assignments as scheduled and to work their scheduled hours and necessary overtime. Employees will be charged with "absence occurrences" when they fail to report for scheduled work hours. Employees will be considered tardy and charged with "partial absence occurrences" when they report to work past their scheduled starting times. Similarly, workers who leave early will be charged with partial absence occurrences.
2. Absences for which employees will be charged with occurrences consist of failure to work a scheduled shift, except for the following exclusions:
    - Jury or military duty
    - Work-related injuries or illnesses
    - Scheduled time off for vacations and holidays
    - Disciplinary suspension
    - Temporary layoff
    - Approved union business
    - Court-ordered appearances
    - Authorized bereavement leave
3. No-Fault Attendance System

    Absences are recorded as following:

    - Each absence = 1 point (Absences lasting several consecutive days due to non-work-related illness and injury of the employee will be treated as one occurrence. Nonconsecutive partial occurrences related to the same medical or dental condition also will be treated as one partial occurrence with pre-notification to the company. The employer has the right to require a worker to submit a doctor's note or to undergo a physical examination to verify a claim of illness or injury.)
    - Each time late to work (tardy) or leaving before end of work day = ½ point
    - Each no-show for work (failing to call in 1 hour before scheduled time) = 2 points

    If an employee earns:

    - 3 points = verbal warning
    - 5 points = written warning
    - 7 points = 3 day suspension
    - 10 points = termination

    Points are accumulated in a 12-month period (not a calendar year).

    The human resources department will provide counseling at each step of this progressive procedure and will refer employees for outside counseling and assistance in dealing with medical, physical, or personal difficulties related to their attendance problems, if necessary.



Applying disciplinary action consistently does not necessarily mean treating everyone in the same manner in all situations. Special considerations surrounding an offense may need to be considered, such as the circumstances, the employee's productivity, job attitudes, and length of service. The extent to which a supervisor can be consistent and yet consider the individual's situation can be illustrated with the following example. Assume that three employees become involved in some kind of horseplay. Employee A just started work a few days ago. Employee B has been warned once before about this type of behavior, and Employee C has been involved in numerous cases of horseplay. In taking disciplinary action, the supervisor could decide to have a friendly, informal talk with Employee A, give Employee B a written warning, and impose a two-day disciplinary layoff on Employee C. Thus, each case is considered on its own merits, with the employees judged according to their work histories. Of course, if two of these employees had the same number of previous warnings, their penalties should be identical.

Imposing discipline consistently is one way a supervisor demonstrates a sense of fair play, but it may be easier said than done. There are times when the department is particularly rushed and the supervisor may be inclined to overlook infractions. Perhaps the supervisor does not wish to upset the workforce or does not wish to lose the output of a valuable employee at a critical time. This type of consideration is paramount, especially when it is difficult to obtain employees with the skills the offending employee possesses. Most employees, however, accept exceptions as fair if they know why the exception was made and if they consider the exception justified. However, employees must feel that any other employee in the same situation would receive similar treatment.

## IMPERSONALITY

All employees who commit the same or a similar offense should be treated the same way. Penalties should be connected with the offense, not with the offending employee. It should make no difference whether the employee is white or black, male or female, young or old, or a member of any other group. The same standards of disciplinary expectations and actions should apply uniformly.

When a supervisor is imposing discipline, impersonality can help reduce the amount of resentment that an employee is likely to feel. At the same time, supervisors should understand that employee reactions to discipline will vary, just as individuals who get burned touching a hot stove react differently. One person may shout, another may cry, another may reflexively inhale, and one may simply "push away" from the stimulus of the pain. Regardless of the individual, there will always be a reaction to being burned.

*When a supervisor is imposing discipline, impersonality can help reduce the employee's resentment*

The optimal reaction to discipline is acceptance of responsibility for the wrongdoing and a change in behavior by the employee to the desired standards with no severe side effects, such as loss of morale, disruption of other employees, or a negative portrayal of the company to customers or external business associates.

Making a disciplinary action impersonal may reduce the level of resentment felt by the employee, but it is difficult to predict an employee's reaction. Personality, acceptance of authority, the job situation, and circumstances surrounding the offense all factor into an employee's reactions. A supervisor may have to deal with an employee's reactions if they are detrimental. However, assuming the employee's reactions are not severe, the supervisor should treat the employee the same before and after the infraction and disciplinary action, without apologizing for what had to be done.

## Documentation and the Right to Appeal

**6 Discuss the need to document disciplinary actions and to provide the right of appeal.**

Whenever a disciplinary action is taken, the supervisor must record the offense and the decision, including the reasoning involved in the decision. This is called **documentation**, and it may include keeping files of the memoranda, minutes of meetings, and other documents that were part of the case handling. Documentation is necessary because the supervisor may be asked to justify the action, and the burden of proof is usually on the supervisor. It is not prudent for the supervisor to depend on memory alone. This is particularly true in unionized firms where grievance-arbitration procedures often result in challenges to the disciplinary actions imposed on employees.

**Documentation**
Records of memoranda, documents, and meetings that relate to a disciplinary action

The **right to appeal** means it should be possible for an employee to request a review of a supervisor's disciplinary action from higher-level management. If the employee belongs to a labor union, this right is part of a grievance procedure. In most firms, the appeal is first directed to the supervisor's boss, thereby following the chain of command. Many large firms have hierarchies of several levels of management through which appeals may be taken. The human resources department may become involved in an appeal procedure. Complaint procedures in nonunion firms and grievance procedures in unionized organizations are discussed in Chapter 14.

**Right to appeal**
Procedures by which an employee may request higher-level management to review a supervisor's disciplinary action

The right to appeal must be recognized as a real privilege and not merely a formality. Some supervisors tell their employees they can appeal to higher-level management but that doing so will be held against them. This attitude reflects the supervisors' insecurity. Supervisors should encourage their employees to appeal to higher-level management if the employees feel they have been treated unfairly. Supervisors should not feel that appeals threaten or weaken their positions as department managers. For the most part, a supervisor's manager will be inclined to support the supervisor's action. If supervisors do not foster an open appeal procedure, employees may enlist outside aid, such as a union would provide. Management's failure to provide a realistic appeal procedure is one reason some employees resort to unionization.

During an appeal, the higher-level manager may reduce or reverse the disciplinary penalty imposed or recommended by a supervisor. The supervisor's decision might be reversed because the supervisor imposed disciplinary action inconsistently or failed to consider all the facts. Under these circumstances, supervisors may become discouraged and feel their managers failed to back them up. Although this situation is unfortunate, it is better for the supervisor to be disheartened than for an employee to be penalized unjustly. This is not too high a price to pay to provide every employee with the right to appeal. Situations like these can be avoided when supervisors adhere closely to the principles and steps discussed in this chapter before taking disciplinary action.

**7 Differentiate between the "discipline without punishment" approach and other alternatives to progressive discipline.**

**Discipline without punishment**
Disciplinary approach that uses coaching and counseling as preliminary steps and a paid decision-making leave that allows employees to decide whether to improve and stay or to quit

## Discipline without Punishment

A growing number of companies have adopted disciplinary procedures called **discipline without punishment**. The major thrust of this approach is to stress extensive coaching, counseling, and problem solving and to avoid confrontation. A significant (and controversial) feature is the paid decision-making leave, in which employees are sent home for a day or more with pay to decide whether they are willing to commit to meeting performance standards previously not met. If an employee commits to improving but fails to do so, the employee is terminated.

In general, this approach replaces warnings and suspensions with coaching sessions and reminders by supervisors of expected standards. The decision-making leave with pay is posed as a decision to be made by the employee, namely, to improve and stay or to quit.

Organizations that have implemented this approach successfully have reported various benefits, particularly reduced complaints and grievances and improved employee morale. It is questionable whether discipline without punishment programs will be adopted extensively because it is unclear that these programs are all that different in concept and outcome from progressive disciplinary action as discussed in this chapter. What is clear is that a discipline without punishment approach requires commitment from all management levels—especially from supervisors—if it is to be carried out successfully.[31]

**8 Recognize the importance of "fairness" in the disciplinary process.**

**Norms**
Standards shared by most employees for how one should act and be treated in the organization

## It's Not Fair!

Every individual brings certain expectations to work. The values, beliefs, and perceptions are unique to that person. However, each work group has a set of norms. **Norms** are the organized and shared ideas regarding what members should do and feel, how this behavior should be regulated, and what sanctions should be applied when behavior does not coincide with organization or group expectations.[32] When an employee encounters a situation, whether new or old, his or her behavior is guided by past experiences and expectations. He or she may react in several different ways depending on how he or she perceives the situation and is impacted by it.

What is fair? What is just? What is not fair? Just the use of these questions conjures up memories. Some of these memories go back to our early childhood and revolve around getting into or out of trouble. Trouble may have led to discipline, and discipline usually meant punishment. To begin, imagine the following scenario:

> *You and a group of friends were playing in the street. Someone threw your ball, someone else hit the ball, and the batted ball went further than anyone could imagine. Like the Energizer battery, it just kept going and going until it shattered Charlie's window. Unfortunately, you all knew Charlie—the meanest man on the block. What bad luck! Of all the windows in the neighborhood, it had to be ill-tempered Charlie's window.*

What would you have done in that situation? I suspect that you might have been the one to calmly and politely ring Charlie's doorbell, apologize for the damage done, and offer to make amends. Perhaps one of the hardest things you ever had to do was to offer a sincere, heartfelt apology while bearing the brunt of Charlie's rage. In reality, you and all the others involved fled the scene of the "crime."

What happened in your home when the angry Charlie arrived to tell your parents that he saw you running from the scene and you had broken his window? Holding the ball in hand—and it was your ball, though you did not throw it or hit it—he demanded restitution. What would your parents have done in this situation? We know that actions taken by parents will vary greatly, but for the sake of this illustration we will assume that your parents presumed you guilty—it was your ball, and you were playing in the street. They may have presumed that Charlie's assessment of the situation was correct and did not bother to get your side of the story. You expected the worst and you got it. You were assigned extra chores including mowing Charlie's yard for the rest of the summer. You were grounded for a couple of weeks. Thus, you were going to miss a couple of fun activities. Your friends got off without even a reprimand.

How did you feel? "It's not fair" was probably foremost in your mind. But what did you learn from this experience? Was the discipline effective? How did you feel about your parents who meted out the punishment? What about your friends who got off scot-free? Because the parents (the supervisors) did not listen to your view or attempt to reach a mutual understanding of the severity of the group's actions, you had great difficulty accepting responsibility for what happened. No one likes negative outcomes, particularly when they are not warranted. In this scenario, the punishment was not fair. While your parents did not follow the proper protocol in applying discipline, it is to be hoped that they followed up by clearly communicating future behavioral expectations.

How did you respond? Were you angry? If so, toward whom was your anger directed? Your playmates? Charlie? Yourself? Your parents? Various writers purport that one's sense of **fair treatment** is contingent upon the following: the interactions that one has with one's supervisors (parents), the procedures used to arrive at the action taken (punishment or other supervisory actions), and outcomes (the punishment or reward). In retrospect, you may conclude that your parents' actions were appropriate in light of the offense, but when you compared your punishment (outcomes) with that of your playmates who got off scot-free, fair treatment did not prevail.[33] Some of you are thinking about how a brother or sister might have been treated differently in the same or similar situation. The lack of consistency in disciplinary action or the inconsistency in meting out rewards may have led you to conclude that "life is not fair." Dissatisfaction is a potential source of trouble for parents (supervisors). All too often instances like this occur in organizations, but the employee has an outlet—a grievance or appeal procedure. With a grievance procedure, supervisors are able to respond to employee concerns in a timely fashion. Without an appeal procedure, the dissatisfaction festers and can lead to bigger problems.

**Fair treatment**
Impartial and appropriate actions taken that are free of favoritism and bias

Consider some other aspects of our parent–child illustration. Did your parents take the time to let you know how they determined the appropriate punishment? Did they treat you politely and courteously to help you understand that there may have been other options than fleeing the scene? Did they pause and ask you what might have been a fair solution to the problem? Were your parents always clear as to how they arrived at the degree and severity of your punishment?

What could they have done to be more sensitive to the situation and your role in what happened? When you were treated unfairly in the disciplinary process, how did you respond? Before succumbing to the temptation to place all the blame on the parents, remember you were playing the game when things went awry.

Have you ever been treated unfairly? How did you respond? Perhaps you recognized the errors of your behavior. We call this the "I really screwed up" syndrome. Feelings of embarrassment and shame may have led you to shed a few tears of remorse. Another response is to argue that you have been wronged; it was all those other people who were at fault. (This is a very common employee response.) Feelings of anger and being misunderstood (unfairly treated) are very common. Would you have stepped back, looked at the situation objectively, and bit your tongue to keep from saying some things that might have made the situation worse?

In a most basic sense, people react to unfair treatment in three ways:

- Fight
- Flight
- Go with the flow[34]

How does one get adjudication for situations they deem to be "not fair"? Employees should first use the organization's grievance procedure to deal with (fight) the perception of unfairness.

In numerous situations the punished child will run away from home. The flight response is one used by "wronged" employees. The "I'll show them—they can take this job and shove it!" response is still prevalent in today's society. Many employees know that they probably cannot get another job or a job that pays as well as the one they have, so they do not quit. So they psychologically disappear from the job.

This is where understanding the ABCs (see Chapter 7) becomes most important. The feeling of unfairness causes a person to stay with the organization and go with the flow. They simply accept the situation and stay with the organization. If the feelings of unfairness are great, the employee may talk with others about how badly they were treated. This may bring up visions of personal situations that at the time might not have been important but, coupled with other

© Ljupco Smokovski/ShutterStock.com

*Discipline should focus on the behavior, not the person; otherwise some employees will perceive discipline as "unfair" treatment, which can lead to anger and resentment*

illustrations of unfairness, may fester and escalate. Clearly, supervisors must be vigilant for feelings of employee dissatisfaction.

All too often, when a sense of "it's not fair" arises in the workplace, a worker will combine these responses. Recently, an employee who thought that he had been treated unfairly stayed with the organization, complained to any person—both inside and outside the organization—who would listen, and then brought a firearm to work. The end result—the supervisor, three other employees, and the disgruntled employee were dead.

*Remember, people need to know what is expected in the way of performance.* Dealing with employees who are not performing to expected standards requires taking corrective actions. Focus on performance. Not everyone will accept the fact that they must change their behavior. When problems occur, deal with them immediately and fairly.

## SUMMARY


1. **Employee discipline can be thought of as the degree to which employees act according to expected standards of behavior. If employee morale is high, discipline will likely be positive and the supervisor will probably not have to take disciplinary action. Supervisors should recognize that most employees want to do the right thing. Positive self-discipline means that employees essentially regulate their own behaviors out of self-interest and their normal desires to meet reasonable standards. Supervisors should be role models and project positive examples for their employees to emulate. Unfortunately, employee theft and fraud have been increasing dramatically, and some CEOs and managers have not set a good example for their employees to follow.**

2. **Many employers have codes of ethics that describe in broad terms their enterprise values and ethical requirements. Ethical codes and conflict-of-interest policies usually include procedures for reporting possible violations.**

3. **Most organizations have written rules and regulations with definitions of infractions and possible penalties for infractions. Rules typically address areas of attendance, work scheduling, job performance, safety, and improper behavior. When infractions occur, supervisors must take appropriate disciplinary action. When ignored, problems do not go away.**

4. **Supervisors should take disciplinary action with the objective of improving employees' behavior. Before disciplining, the supervisor must first investigate the situation thoroughly. Disciplinary actions should be for just (proper) cause. Emotional and physical responses should be avoided. The supervisor should determine whether there is sufficient evidence to conclude that the employee knew about the rule or standard and, in fact, violated it. The supervisor should consider the severity of the violation, the employee's service record, and other relevant factors. If disciplinary action is necessary, normally it should be administered in private.**

5. **A number of progressively severe disciplinary actions, ranging from an informal talk to a warning, suspension, and discharge, are open to a supervisor as choices, depending on the circumstances and nature of the infraction. The supervisor's purpose in taking disciplinary action should be to improve the employee's behavior and to maintain proper discipline throughout the department. Progressive discipline is also desirable and applicable.**

6. **Taking disciplinary action can be unpleasant for both the employee and the supervisor. To reduce the distasteful aspects, disciplinary action should fulfill as much as possible the requirements of the hot stove rule. These requirements are advance warning, immediacy, consistency, and impersonality.**

7. **Documentation of a supervisor's disciplinary action is important to substantiate the reasons for the action. This is especially important if there is appeal of the disciplinary decision to higher-level management through a grievance or complaint procedure. In the interest of fairness, an appeal procedure gives the employee a review process through which the supervisor's disciplinary decision may be sustained, modified, or set aside.**

8. **The discipline without punishment approach uses extensive coaching and counseling as preliminary steps. If there is no improvement in the employee's performance, a paid decision-making leave may be**

**imposed on the employee to force the employee to decide whether to commit to improving or to be terminated.**

**9.** **Another challenge for supervisors is to treat people fairly in the workplace. Finding answers to the question, "What is fair?" is not an easy task. Supervisors need to use good communication skills to understand what employees perceive as fair. Supervisors need to understand how employees might react when they are treated unfairly. Disciplining employees is not one of the supervisor's favorite tasks. Remember, applying the concepts of progressive discipline requires consistent application of practical and sound supervisory skills.**

## KEY TERMS

Discipline (p. 561)
Discipline without punishment (p. 586)
Documentation (p. 585)
Employment-at-will (p. 580)
Fair treatment (p. 587)
Hot stove rule (p. 580)
Morale (p. 562)
No-fault attendance policy (p. 582)
Norms (p. 586)
Positive discipline (p. 561)
Positive self-discipline (p. 562)
Progressive discipline (p. 574)
Right to appeal (p. 585)
Whistleblower (p. 564)

## WHAT HAVE YOU LEARNED?

1. Identify appropriate standards and expectations; progressive discipline and due process are linked to employee disciplinary actions.
2. During a major exam, you notice that the student sitting across the aisle from you is apparently cheating. It appears that he (your school's star athlete) is using his cell phone to get information to answer the questions. What would you do, if anything? Why? If he is caught and confesses to the "crime," what should the discipline be?
3. Discuss the relationship between discipline and morale. Evaluate the following statement: "Discipline should be directed against the act and not against the person."
4. Why should supervisors be unafraid to confront disciplinary situations when they occur? What is meant by "disciplinary action should have just cause"?
5. Define and evaluate each of the following elements of the hot stove rule:
   **a.** Advance warning
   **b.** Immediacy
   **c.** Consistency
   **d.** Impersonality
6. Why is fair treatment important to people? How might thoughts of "It's not fair!" affect an employee's behavior? Look at **question 2** above; the student who is apparently cheating does not get caught. He gets an A and you get a C.
   **a.** On the next exam, it appears that he is cheating. What would you do? Why?
   **b.** Thorndike's law of effect (discussed in Chapter 4) states that "behavior with favorable consequences tends to be repeated." Assume that in question 2 above you reported your suspicions to the instructor and nothing happened. Assume that the student appears to continually cheat, goes unpunished, and gets better grades than you. What are the consequences of the cheater's actions?
7. Why should employees or a student have the right to appeal any disciplinary action that is taken? Look at your school's handbook. Does it prescribe an appeal procedure? In your opinion, does it provide fairness? If not, what changes would you suggest?

## EXPERIENTIAL EXERCISES FOR SELF-ASSESSMENT

### EXPERIENTIAL EXERCISE FOR SELF-ASSESSMENT 15—How Full is Your Supervisory Toolbox?

As we wrap up the *Supervision* learning experience, we would like to invite you to envision the future and your place in it as an excellent supervisor. Through the self-assessment exercises you have completed after each chapter, it is likely that you've learned many things about yourself and ways you can fill your SKA toolbox in preparation for opportunities to lead and inspire employees in your field. In this last self-assessment, you have an opportunity to put your new SKAs to work as you envision yourself as a supervisor and choose the best approaches to issues you will likely face in a supervisory role.

**Instructions**

Read each of the 10 questions below and choose the answer that best describes how you would respond as a supervisor.

1. Understanding and relationship-building: How could you get to know the people you supervise and what motivates them?
   A. It's enough to know what shifts they're on and whether they show up.
   B. Invite them to a company picnic.

C. Count the number of people who complain about money and the number that don't.
D. Meet with each one for coffee monthly, or at least a 10 minute conversation.

2. Interaction: How often should you "manage by walking around"?
   A. Never. It isn't appropriate to interact casually with subordinates.
   B. At least once a week to touch base, answer questions, recognize achievements, assess progress, and see what can be improved around the organization.
   C. During special events.
   D. Only when the restroom near my office is broken.
3. Appreciation: How would you communicate to your team that you appreciate them?
   A. With a paycheck. If they get paid well, what else do they want?
   B. I would bring coffee in for everyone about once every six months.
   C. I would praise my staff and share their accomplishments with my boss.
   D. I thank people out loud when they bring in treats.
4. Delegation: How do you feel about delegating work to subordinates?
   A. I would actively delegate, starting with simple tasks, then increasing their complexity as employees increase their proficiencies.
   B. I don't think I would trust subordinates to work independently.
   C. I wouldn't delegate. It is easier to do things myself and I know they'll be done right.
   D. I would watch them work until the task is finished.
5. Unity of Command: How would your team know that you are the leader?
   A. If they made one mistake and they'd be out the door.
   B. I would be buddies with them and try not to let them know I'm watching them.
   C. They would see the word "Manager" next to my name in the company directory.
   D. They would know they can count on me for direction, swift action and firm, fair decisions.
6. Empowerment: Would you let your staff make important decisions?
   A. I would let them decide who is going to make the coffee.
   B. Only if we were doing well. Otherwise they would just make things worse.
   C. Yes, starting with decisions that have small impacts. We would evaluate their rationale and the outcomes of smaller decisions before moving to bigger ones.
   D. Yes, but if they mess something up they have to deal with it on their own.
7. Recognition: If YOUR boss praised a report done by one of your subordinates, what would you do?
   A. Affirm the feedback, thank your boss, and share the praise with your employee.
   B. Take credit for the report and thank your boss for her kind words.
   C. Act surprised and explain that you are astonished that they could actually put something that good together.
   D. Disguise your jealousy and make a plan to get revenge on the employee for "kissing up".
8. Empathy: An employee seems stressed out and begins to tell you about the marital problems he has been dealing with.
   A. Shout "Get back to work! The project needs to get done right away. I don't have time to give you a pity party."
   B. Start listening, rest your head on your hand, shuffle papers on your desk, and try to guess what he is going to say next.
   C. Look up from your mobile phone, stop texting, and ask if he'll start from the beginning.
   D. Hear him out, thank him for sharing, ask if needs to take a sick day to deal with it, and suggest contacting the EAP office if he needs more support.
9. Taking action: How effectively can you deal with problems among the workers?
   A. Can I let you know next week?
   B. I listen to the situation, gather information quickly, act promptly, consistently, and objectively, then I document my actions
   C. I typically ignore them. They can work it out themselves. They're grownups.
   D. When they start yelling, I usually step in.
10. Self-assessment: How would you like your team to describe your leadership and management skills?
   A. I just want them to know who I am.
   B. I'd like them to think I'm one of the gang.
   C. I'd like to be known as a hard worker who is fair, firm, encouraging and learns from mistakes.
   D. The person in charge who gets things done.

**Correct Answers**

1. D – Every worker is different. If you work to understand what motivates each one and adapt your leadership to help them excel, they will become loyal, high performers.
2. B – Management by walking around (MBWA) is one of the most valuable things a supervisor can do to build rapport, assess processes, and identify issues that can be fixed before they turn into problems.
3. C – Praise is free, and it pays off tremendously in increased employee engagement.
4. A – Effective delegation frees up the supervisor to lead, inspire, and design and implement improvements.

5. D – Workers need to know who they report to, what is expected of them, and who they can come to when they have a problem.
6. C – Every worker can grow by taking risks, finding success and making mistakes, provided they are given the opportunity to learn what they can do differently in the future.
7. A – Recognition increases workers' self-esteem, confidence and motivation, which together increase employee engagement, team cohesion and employee performance.
8. D – Taking a few minutes to be an effective listener can help employees feel valued and supported, and learning about and helping them find help for their problems can prevent larger problems down the road.
9. B – It is always effective to address a problem promptly, fairly and consistently. Problems that are ignored or are dealt with unfairly can escalate into substantial conflicts.
10. B – A good leader knows his or her strengths, weaknesses, and the perceptions of the team.

**Scoring and Interpretation**

Add up the number of items you answered correctly. Use the scoring system below for guidance as you move forward in your supervision journey:

**9–10** correct – You have the makings of a great boss! Keep your supervisory toolbox full.

**7–8** correct – You're on the right path. Note the items on which you did not answer correctly and continue seeking opportunities to grow those skills.

**6 or less** correct – You have a new SKA toolbox and you are starting to fill it. Seek out as many opportunities as you can to read, talk, and learn about effective supervision and leadership practices.

## PERSONAL SKILL BUILDING

### Personal Skill Builder 15.1: You Make the Call!

Read this chapter's You Make the Call! then respond to the following questions.

1. Visit the following Web sites
   - www.dol.gov and review age discrimination
   - www.eeoc.gov (correct website is www.eeoc.gov) and review the most current facts on age discrimination
2. Question: What are some of the legal and ethical issues in this call particularly as they relate to potential age discrimination?
3. Review the hot stove rule discussed in this chapter. How might the four rules apply to the actions you might take with Michael?
4. Based on your assessment of Jim Hartman's and Betty Haver's findings, do you think that Michael should be discharged? Why or why not? Remember that this is his first offense.
5. Contact to two practicing supervisors (or managers). Briefly share with them the essentials of this You Make the Call! and ask them to recommend what management should do. Was there a difference in the two supervisors' recommendations? If so, how do you account for the difference?
6. Write a two-paragraph paper indicating what you learned from this skill builder.

### Personal Skill Builder 15.2: Disciplinary Action for Just Cause

1. From the information in this chapter, develop a list of requirements and considerations that you believe are the most essential for ensuring that a disciplinary action taken against an employee has a just cause basis.
2. Contact two practicing supervisors who are willing to be interviewed. One supervisor should be in a unionized organization and have subordinates working under a union–management contract. The other supervisor should be from an organization whose employees are not represented by a union.
   **a.** Ask each supervisor to identify what he or she believes to be the half-dozen or so most important requirements and considerations when a supervisor takes disciplinary action. (*Note*: Do not use the term "just cause" when making your request.)
   **b.** Ask each supervisor to respond to the following hypothetical situation: "You discover an employee sound asleep at his or her work station, which is isolated from the view of other employees. It is two hours after the shift began. What would you do? Why?"
3. Compare your list (see question 1 above) with the lists of the two practicing supervisors. To what degree were these lists similar? Different? If there were major differences, what do you feel would be the most likely explanation?
4. Compare each supervisor's response to the hypothetical situation posed in question 2b. If there are many differences, how might they be explained.
5. Write a 50-word or less paper, sharing what you learned from this activity.

## Personal Skill Builder 15.3: Technology Tool—Whistleblower Software

INTERNET ACTIVITY

Rules are rules, put in place to help ensure safety and integrity in the workplace and in life. The reality exists that some individuals choose to break the rules and, in some cases, breaking the rules can have disastrous consequences, as we've seen in corporate scandals and cover-ups. Individuals who have the ethical values and courage to stand up and speak out when they see or hear about illegal, dangerous, or improprietous behavior should be celebrated because they are taking the lead in doing the right thing. However, we learned in this chapter that *whistleblowers,* individuals who report alleged wrongdoing, are sometimes retaliated against by the rule-breaker or a supervisor who might want to cover up the problem, and they may jeopardize opportunities for future employment. Accordingly, it is important for organizations to have a system in place, sometimes termed an "ethics reporting system" or "anonymous incident reporting/management system" that will allow individuals to report what they believe is wrongdoing in a way that will protect them from retaliation and ensure that the information is received and acted upon appropriately.[35]

In this activity, you will have the opportunity to explore a variety of software applications that organizations can put in place that facilitate anonymous reporting and management of ethics, rules, safety, and other violations. Your task is to review and evaluate a few of the applications and assess whether they would be useful in an organization with which you are familiar. Please follow the instructions below to complete the activity.

1. Think of an organization you are very familiar with. It could be your company, your school, or a community organization. Keep in mind that in every organization that deals with people and money, individuals have the capacity to break the rules.
2. Choose at least three incident reporting or management software applications below to review, or search for additional applications using information from the exercise as keywords.
   - Anonymous Incident Management (dnv.com)
   - Compliance 360 (saiglobal.com)
   - ConfidenceLine (confidenceline.net)
   - EthicsPoint (ethicspoint.com, navexglobal.com)
   - Globaleaks (globaleaks.org)
   - Hotline (tnwinc.com)
   - IViewSystems (iviewsystems.com)
   - TipSoft and TipSoft for Education (www.publicengines.com)
3. Explore the Web sites, demonstration videos, and/or trial versions of the applications. While you are exploring them, consider the following questions:
   - Do the features of this software match the structure and scope of the organization I am considering?
   - If I saw something happening at this organization that I felt was illegal, unsafe, or improper, would I feel comfortable using this technology?
   - Would the leaders of the organization feel that investing in an incident reporting or management software application is a worthwhile use of the organization's resources? Why or why not?
4. Using the insight you gained through the review, write a one-page summary of your review experience.
   - List the three applications you reviewed.
   - Discuss whether you would recommend an incident reporting or management software application to the organization you considered for this exercise, and, if so, which one you would choose, describing specific features of the software that made it your first choice.
   - If you would not recommend the use of incident reporting or management software, explain your rationale, using specific examples of features or processes from the software you reviewed as justification.

# TEAM SKILL BUILDING

## Team Skill Builder 15-1: You Make the Call!

ROLE PLAY

This chapter's You Make the Call! can be used as a team role-playing exercise. One student should play the role of general manager Karissa Dawson, another the role of HR director Bette Haver, another of security director Jim Hartman, and another the role of legal counsel Kip Williams.

1. Did the management of Marion Hotel conduct an investigation fairly and objectively?
2. Was there substantial evidence that purchasing manager Michael May was guilty of stealing from the company?
3. Should Michael May have known the rules of the company?
4. What would be a proper course of action for management to take?
5. If you decide that the appropriate course of action is to fire Michael May for just cause, what actions should management take to make sure that you have everything in order in case he would file an age discrimination charge?

Food for thought: If you fired Michael May and three months later you received a phone call from an organization in another part of the country, saying that May has applied for a position of responsibility in their organization, what would be your response? Why would you do that rather than another alternative?

## Team Skill Builder 15-2: Would You Blow the Whistle?

Divide students into groups of three, four, or five.

As a relatively new group of employees in MSU, you are faced with an ethical dilemma involving your boss. It appears to all of you that he is misusing university funds. For example, you all know for a fact that he filed a travel form to attend a conference in Arizona last month. All of you were at the conference, and he was nowhere to be seen, nor was his name on the roster of attendees. Another example involved the purchase of an expensive TV for the employee break room that somehow never got delivered to the break room.

1. In your group, using the concepts presented in this and previous chapters, outline an approach you would use to determine whether your assumptions are true.
2. If these assumptions can be proven to be true and you believed them to violate university standards of conduct, what would you as a group do? Why?
3. In your group, discuss why most employees would not like to be known as the whistleblower.
4. If you witnessed another employee taking home office supplies to stock their children's school supplies, what would you do? In the group's opinion, does taking office supplies warrant the same concerns as the boss's behaviors? Explain your reasoning.
5. As a group, write a one-page paper explaining what supervisors should do to help employees fully understand the consequences of their actions.

## Team Skill Builder 15-3: Dealing with People Who Make Your Life Difficult—"The Backstabber"

This is the fourth in a series of exercises that introduces you to people who might make your life and job difficult.

1. Have students read the following statement from Rex Duncan, an employee at Alvey Electric, a medium-sized parts-manufacturing firm in Tennessee:

   *Working with Brutus sure is frustrating. He has the uncanny ability to pull off any work assignment given to him. Not long ago, Brutus was on my project team to develop a new electrical harness system for a classic car. Paul had been given the assignment of researching other successful efforts so that we didn't spend all our time reinventing the wheel. At the meeting when Paul presented his findings, Brutus waited until just the right moment before jumping in with his own research findings. Several of the things Brutus found flew in the face of Paul's research and made Paul appear incompetent.*

   *I don't trust Brutus. He is very controlling, greedy, and driven by his hunger for power. He is always behind the scenes, maneuvering and manipulating to get what he wants. Brutus knows just what to do to get the work done and always has his own agenda. He never volunteers suggestions or ideas to the group's planning meetings. If the meeting includes people from corporate, Brutus is really great at sabotaging the group's plan. He always seems to have a plan or two in his hip pocket to spring on the group. His surprises mean you always have to be on your guard.*

   *I've learned not to turn my back on Brutus. He is always spreading rumors and will try his best to ruin your career to promote his. You're always on your guard with him. His team spirit is minimal, but he steps forward to take credit for any successes. He'll double-cross teammates for personal gain and make excuses for any missed work. We work in an organization where the rewards aren't great, but Brutus is still there, trying to figure out a way to "work the system."*

2. 

Using the Internet, find at least three sources for coping with a backstabber in the workplace. Carefully review each site for suggestions for dealing with this type of behavior. Based on your findings, what suggestions would you give to Rex Duncan for coping with Brutus?
3. 

Group students into small groups of at least four. One of the students will play the role of Rex Duncan, another will be his immediate supervisor, and the others are coworkers who have similar observations about Brutus. (a) The student playing the role of Duncan should share his or her observations about Brutus, and those playing the roles of coworkers should add supportive comments to the conversation. (b) If the supervisor investigated and found all the allegations to be true, what should the supervisor do?
4. Discipline should be directed against the act and not against the person. Does the group believe that disciplinary action is warranted? Why? Why not?
5. Why might disciplinary or corrective action be difficult for the supervisor?
6. Collaboratively, write a one-page paper explaining how this Team Skill-Builder increased your knowledge of the difficulties of changing undesirable behaviors via positive discipline.

## SUPERVISION IN ACTION

The video for this chapter can be accessed from the student companion website at www.cengagebrain.com. (Search by authors' names or book title to find the accompanying resources.)

## ENDNOTES

1. This You Make the Call! was adapted from "Old Age or Just Bad Judgment?" Case presented by Ed Leonard and Roy Cook at the 2010 Society for Case Research Summer Workshop. It has been adapted here with permission of the Leonard and Cook.
2. Job dissatisfaction data varies depending on the survey and reporting agency. Several studies report that 65 percent of workers are not satisfied with their job. Blessing White's *Employee Engagement Report 2011* reports that more currently employed workers are looking for new opportunities outside their current organization than anytime this century (http://www.blessingwhite.com/EEE-report.asp). Also see Towers Watson *2013–2014 Talent Management and Rewards Study*(http://www.towerswatson.com); and *2014 Employee Job Satisfaction Survey* (http://www.shrm.org), which reports that nearly two-fifths of workers plan to look for work in the near future. The Society of Human Resources Management (SHRM) study reports that job security is the most important contributor to job satisfaction.

   Mercer's *What's Working* survey, reported in June 2013, confirmed the Blessing White survey and reported that 21 percent of employees were not looking to leave but viewed their employers unfavorably (http://inside-employees-mind.mercer.com/reference-content.htm?idContent=1419320). Younger workers were more likely to be seeking other opportunities. As reported in *HR Magazine* (August 2011), p. 20.
3. Estimates of employee theft in the United States vary and are hard to verify since some employers don't want other employees, customers, or shareholders to know that controls were not in place. The National Retail Security Survey estimated that retail theft in 2010 was $37.1 billion, and employee theft made up the largest category of thefts.
4. The Association of Certified Fraud Examiners (ACFE) *Report to the Nation on Occupational Fraud and Abuse* (www.acfe.com, 2011) reported that around the world fraud loss amounted to more than $3.5 billion, and more than 75 percent of the crimes were committed by accounting, operations, sales, executive/upper management, customer service, or purchasing department employees. Employee theft is the same as occupational fraud.
5. As more and more people use social networks, problems will continue to arise. See Aliah Wright, "Guard against Data Breaches," *HR Magazine* (August 2011), p. 24; Rob Cross et al., "The Collaborative Organization: How to Make Employee Networks Really Work," *MIT Sloan Management Review* (Fall 2010), pp. 83–87; Rita Zeidner, "Security Policies: Problem or Protection?" *HR Magazine* (December 2010); Bill Roberts, "Developing a Social Business Network," *HR Magazine* (October 2010), pp. 54–60; Roberts, "Mind Employees' Social Media Manners," *HR Magazine* (December 2010), p. 70; Yvette Lee, "Electronic Harassment," *HR Magazine* (September 2010), p. 24; and Nicole Kamm, "Bodyguard for Electronic Information," HR Magazine (January 2010), pp. 57–59.

   Employers appear to have an increased interest in how their employees are using the computer. Many organizations have developed policies to prevent workers from accessing "bad" Web sites and importing harmful viruses. See Joanne Deschenaux, "Europeans Demand Greater Privacy: Standards for Protecting Electronic Communication Vary around the World," *HR Magazine* (June 2010), pp. 99–104.
6. Numerous studies have reported that the typical employee spends an hour or two each workday on non-work-related computer activities. The following provide insight into the e-mail problems: B. Roberts, "Avoiding the Perils of Electronic Data," *HR Magazine* (January 2007), pp. 72–77; and Allen Smith, "Federal Rules Define Duty to Preserve Work E-Mails," *HR Magazine* (January 2007), pp. 27, 36.
7. During 2013, the cyber war escalated. Target Corporation had its databases hacked to the tune of 40 million customer credit card numbers (see Michael Riley, Ben Elgin, Dune Lawrence, and Carol Matlack, "Missed Alarms and 40 Million Stolen Credit Card Numbers: How Target Blew It," *Bloomberg Businessweek* (March 13, 2014), http://www.businessweek.com/articles/2014-03-13/target-missed-alarms-in-epic-hack-of-credit-card-data. In July 2011, two U.S. congressmen resigned after their actions were featured on various Web sites. Also see Tim Gould, "Employee Internet Management: Now an HR Issue," *HR Magazine* (accessed April 24, 2014), http://www.shrm.org/publications/hrmagazine/editorialcontent/pages/cms_006514.aspx; or "Employers Can Restrict Employee Web Surfing," Lawyers.com (accessed August 2, 2011), http://labor-employment-law.lawyers.com/human-resources-law/employers-can-restrict-employee-web-surfing.html.
8. The *2012 National Business Ethics Survey of Social Networkers (NBES-SN)* survey found that 67 percent of people use social networks when they're supposed to be working (see Curtis C. Verschoor, "Social Networking at Work Is a Major Risk with Large Costs," Accountingweb.com (December 20, 2013). Robert Half Technology survey reported the following results: "Which of the following most closely describes your company policy on visiting social networking sites, such as Facebook and Twitter, while at work?"

| | 2010 | 2009 |
|---|---|---|
| Prohibited completely | 31% | 54% |
| Permitted for business purposes only | 51% | 19% |
| Permitted for limited personal use | 14% | 16% |
| Permitted for any type of personal use | 4% | 10% |

   (" Social Networking on the Job," http://www.hrcomplaincee.cerdian.com, accessed June 20, 2011). Also see Mary-Kathryn Zachary, "Social Networking Sites in a Union Setting," *SuperVision* (February 2011), pp. 20–23
9. From Oren Harari, "U2D2: The Rx for Leadership Blues," *Management Review* (August 1995), pp. 34–36.
10. All supervisors should know that it is unlawful to retaliate against an employee for engaging in activity protected by civil rights laws. The question of what constitutes "retaliation" will be for the courts to decide. In 2007, the Supreme Court provided guidance in the case of *Burlington Northern and Santa Fe Railway Co. v. White* (548 U.S. 53); in 2013 two Supreme Court cases were decided that increased the level of proof an employee is required to provide to file and sustain a retaliation claim against an employer. See *Vance v. Ball State University* 133 S.Ct. 2434 (2013) and *University of Texas Southwestern Medical Center v. Nassar* 133 S.Ct. 2517 (2013); see also Joanne Deschenaux, "Supreme Court Reins in Retaliation Claims," SHRM.com (June 25, 2013), http://www.shrm.org/legalissues/federalresources/pages/supreme-court-reins-in-retaliation-claims.aspx.

    See Barrett Brooks, Gail Farb, and Mandi Ballard, "The Future of Retaliation Claims: Retaliation Claims Are Increasing, So Take Steps to Limit Them," *HR Magazine* (January 2011), pp. 69–71. In 2013, over 76 percent of the almost 94,000 charges workplace discrimination charges filed with the EEOC alleged retaliation and race discrimination. Reported on the EEOC Web site, http://www.eeoc.gov/eeoc/statistics/enforcement/charges.cfm

11. See Dori Meinert, "High Court Extends Employee Whistle-Blower Protections," SHRM.com (March 5, 2014), http://www.shrm.org/legalissues/federalresources/pages/high-court-extends-employee-whistle-blower-protections.aspx; and Meinert, "Whistle-Blowers: Threat or Asset?" *HR Magazine* (April 2011), pp. 26–32.
12. See Benjamin Schneider and Karen B. Paul, "In the Company We Trust: Follow the Lead of 3M's HR Managers and Strive to Strengthen Employee's Trust," *HR Magazine* (January 2011), pp. 40–43. 3M Corporation is well known to most students for its development of Post-It notes. The company recently was named a 2014 World's Most Ethical Company by Ethisphere® (http://solutions.3m.com/wps/portal/3M/en_US/businessconduct/bcmain/) Visit its compliance and ethics page to see many of 3M's policies and procedures that clarify what it expects in the way of employee behavior. See Figure 15-3 for a portion of one of 3M's policies.
13. From Nicholas G. Moore, *Ethics: The Way to Do Business*, published pamphlet of his Sears Lectureship in Business Ethics at Bentley College (February 9, 1998), p. 9. (For more information on Nicholas Moore, see http://people.forbes.com/profile/nicholasg-moore/36988.)
14. Many organizations have developed handbooks for communicating information about employment practices and procedures. See Susan Milligan, "The Employee Handbook: A Perennial Headache," SHRM.com (April 1, 2014) for guidance on being diligent in updating the employee handbook to reflect emerging HR trends and legal decisions that affect employment and personnel decisions. Social media is one example. In Charla Bizios Stevens's "Your Company's Social Media Policy—Fair or Foul," Mondaq.com (March 24, 2014), a caution is given regarding policies that govern employees' reference to their workplace outside of work time, as the National Labor Relations Board (NLRB) ruled that employees' rights of freedom of speech are protected on social media. When making updates, be sure to ensure the legality of the changes by referencing employment law or consulting a legal advisor. See also Aliah D. Wright, "Agenda: Social Media—Polish Your Social Media Policy, Set Clear Expectations about Social Media Use, but Be Aware of Being Intrusive," *HR Magazine* 58(8) (August 2013), pp. 71-72.
15. See Robert K. Wrede, "What HR Professionals Should Know about Alternative Dispute Resolution," *SHRM Hawaii Chapter Newsletter* (July 2006).
16. For expanded information on grievance-arbitration procedures, particularly as related to discipline/discharge cases, see Susan E. Jackson, Randall S. Schuler, and Steve Werner, *Managing Human Resources*, 11th ed. (Mason, OH: South-Western/Cengage Learning, 2012); and Scott Snell and George Bohlander, *Managing Human Resources*, 16th ed. (Mason, OH: South-Western/Cengage Learning, 2013).
17. The Employee Polygraph Protection Act of 1988 (EPPA) stated that employers generally cannot require or request an employee to take a lie detector test, or to discharge, discipline, or discriminate against an employee for refusing to take a test. (http://www.dol.com/compliance/laws/comp-eppa.htm)
18. See Paul Falcone, *101 Sample Write-ups for Documenting Employee Performance Problems,*, 2nd ed. (Saranack Lake, NY: AMACOM, 2010), or James G. Vigneau, "To Catch a Thief . . . and Other Workplace Investigations," *HR Magazine* (January 1995), pp. 90–95.
19. See Philip W. Turner, "Top Ten Tips for Conducting Effective Internal Investigations," Association of Corporate Counsel, ACC.com (November 9, 2010) http://www.acc.com/legalresources/publications/topten/internalinvestigations.cfm; and Albert R. Karr, "Some Employers Are Alarmed about Disclosing Employee Investigations," The *Wall Street Journal* (June 1, 1999), p. A1.
20. Many companies conduct random and other drug tests on their employees, especially federal government contractors and employers as mandated by the Drug-Free Workplace Act of 1988. Companies usually have policies and procedures that outline how tests will be taken, safeguards, and possible penalties for violations.

    Also see Mary-Kathryn Zachary, "Alcohol Use and Work Part 1," *SuperVision* (April 2011), pp. 21–25, and "Part 2" (May 2011), pp. 21–25.
21. This is called a unionized employee's Weingarten rights, based on a U.S. Supreme Court decision. See Martha B. Pedrick, "Weingarten Rights in Non-Union Settings," *Labor Law Journal* (Winter 2001), pp. 195–201.
22. See C. R. Deitsch, D. A. Dilts, and Francine Guice, "Weingarten Rights in the Non-Union Workplace," *Dispute Resolution Journal* (May/July 2006), p. 46; Victoria Roberts, "Court Upholds Extending Weingarten Rights to Nonunion Workers," *HR News* (December 2001), p. 13; or Margaret M. Clark, "Nonunion Employers Face Charges in Investigating Misconduct," *HR News* (January 2002), p. 9.
23. One of the authors first heard the term *CYR (cover your rear)* while an ROTC student in 1958. CYR clearly reinforces the notion that supervisors must investigate before acting and document all aspects of the incident. The author is familiar with too many cases in which the supervisor acted without getting the employee's side of the story. For an interesting article that discusses the advantages of CYR, see Jared Sandberg, "Covering Yourself Is Counterproductive but May Save Your Job," *The Wall Street Journal* (June 8, 2005), p. B1.
24. For discussion of the technique and applications of letters of clarification, see Paul Falcone, "Letters of Clarification: A Disciplinary Alternative," *HR Magazine* (August 1999), pp. 134–140.

    Jonathan A. Segal argues that "progressive discipline lays a paper trail that can minimize an employer's exposure to discrimination claims." See Segal, "A Warning about Warnings," *HR Magazine* (February 2009), pp. 67–69. Also see Reginald Bell and Jeanette Martin, "Techniques for Writing a Reprimand: How to Modify the Behavior of a Rule-Breaker at Work," *SuperVision* (April 2010), pp. 8–12.
25. Jonathan A. Segal, "A Warning about Warnings," *HR Magazine* (February 2009), pp. 67-70, cautions employers to carefully consider the actions taken during the discipline process, particularly issuing a written warning, as inappropriate or excessive employer actions can be construed as retaliation, as found in *Witte v. Moffe*,C.A. No. 03-CV-971A (W.D.N.Y. Feb 6, 2008).
26. See Paul Falcone, "After They're Gone: Communicating about Employee Departures with Remaining Staff Is Critical," *HR Magazine* (October 2013), pp. 76-77. See also Dennis L. Johnson, Christie A. King, and John G. Kurutz, "A Safe Termination Model for Supervisors," *HR Magazine* (May 1996), pp. 73–78; and Gary Bielous, "How to Fire," *SuperVision* (November 1996), pp. 8–10.
27. See Melinda J. Caterine (Ed.), *Employment at Will: A State-by-State Survey, 2013 Supplement*, (Bethesda, MD: Bloomberg BNA, 2013). See also Liz Ryan, "How At-Will Employment Hurts Business," *Forbes* (May 1, 2014), http://www.forbes.com/sites/lizryan/2014/05/01/how-at-will-employment-hurts-business/; Michael J. Phillips, "Toward a Middle Way in the Polarized Debate over Employment at Will," *American Business Law Journal* (November 1992), pp. 441–483, or Kenneth Gilberg, "Employers Must Protect against Employee Lawsuits," *SuperVision* (November 1992), pp. 12–13.
28. See Dawn M. Kaiser, "The Implications of At-Will versus Just-Cause Employment," *Proceedings of the Academy of Organizational Culture, Communications and Conflict* 10(2) (Las Vegas, NV: 2005), pp. 33–36; and Matt Siegel, "Yes, They Can Fire You," *Fortune* (October 26, 1998), p. 301.

29. See Deandra Corinthios, "Cheating the System: Faking a Drug Test," NBC26 News (May 12, 2014), http://www.jrn.com/nbc26/news/Beating-Drug-Tests-Labs-Getting-tougher-Employeers-Getting-Smarter-258957231.html; see also Diane Cadrain, "Helping Workers Fool Drug Tests Is a Big Business," *HR Magazine* (August 2005), pp. 29, 32.
30. For an expanded discussion of no-fault and other employee attendance policies, see M. Michael Markowich, "When Is Excessive Absenteeism Grounds for Disciplinary Action?" *ACA News* (July/August 1998), pp. 36–39. See also Jon Hyman, "The FMLA, the ADA and No-Fault Attendance Policies," Workforce.com (July 2, 2013), in which the author encourages employers to balance benefits of such a policy against the risk of violating FMLA or ADA.
31. Tom Watson summarizes the discipline without punishment approach and provides examples of companies finding success, including a 200 percent decrease in written warnings over a three-year period, a 63 percent reduction in grievances, and a 50 percent reduction in sick leave usage, "Discipline without Punishment: A Best Practices Approach to Disciplining Employees," Watson-training.com (April 15, 2014), http://www.watson-training.com/blog2/46-discipline-with-punishment-a-best-practices-approach-to-disciplining-employees.html. For a thorough discussion of the pros and cons and applications of discipline-without-punishment approaches, see Dick Grote, *Discipline without Punishment* (New York: American Management Association, 1995). See also Dick Grote, "Discipline without Punishment," *Across-the-Board* (September/October 2001) pp. 52–57; and Jathan Janove, *Managing to Stay out of Court* (Berrett-Kohler, 2005). Janove reaffirms that the following will likely land you in court: acting inconsistently, treating one employee differently from another, treating employees differently from what documented policies require, letting documents conflict with one another, or treating one person in different ways over time.
32. Definition of norms adapted from discussion by Don Harvey and Robert Bruce Bowin, *Human Resource Management; An Experiential Approach* (Upper Saddle River, NJ: Prentice Hall, 1996), pp. 15–21.
33. For a discussion of what fairness means to employees, see Susan E. Jackson, Randall S. Schuler, and Steve Werner, *Managing Human Resources*, 11th ed. (Mason, OH: South-Western/Cengage Learning, 2012). Also See Maurice A. Ramirez, "Outrage of Enthusiasm: The Choice Is Yours," *SuperVision* 69, No. 4 (April 2008), pp. 17–19; Bill Catlette and Richard Hadden, "Consistency Does Not Equal Fairness," *SuperVision* 69, No. 2 (February 2008), pp. 19–21; T. Simons and Q. Roberson, "Why Managers Should Care about Fairness: The Effects of Aggregate Justice Perceptions on Organizational Outcomes," *Journal of Applied Psychology* 88, No. 3 (2006), pp. 432–443; and M. L. Williams, M. A. McDonald, and N. T. Nguyen, "A Meta-Analysis of the Antecedents and Consequences of Pay Level Satisfaction," *Journal of Applied Psychology*, 91 (2006), pp. 392–413.
34. Many psychology and biology texts discuss the psychological and biological aspects of stressful situations. For an expanded discussion of the fight-or-flight responses, see Bronston T. Mayes and Daniel C. Ganster, "Exit and Voice: A Test Hypothesis Based on the Fight/Flight Response to Job Stress," *Journal of Organizational Behavior* 9, No. 3 (July 1998), pp. 199–216 (published online November 20, 2006). Also see S. E. Taylor et al., "Biobehavioral Responses to Stress in Females: Tend-and-Befriend, not Fight-or-Flight," *Psychological Review* 107 (2000), pp. 411–429; or H. S. Friedman and R. C. Silver, *Foundations of Health Psychology* (New York: Oxford University Press, 2007).

    Final Note: For a general overview of the disciplinary process, see the following: Susan E. Jackson, Randall S. Schuler, and Steve Werner, *Managing Human Resources*, 11th ed. (Mason, OH: South-Western/Cengage Learning, 2012); Kathryn W. Hegar, *Modern Human Relations at Work*, 11th ed. (Mason, OH: Thomson/South-Western, 2012); Robert L. Mathis and John H. Jackson, *Human Resource Management*, 13th ed. (Mason, OH: Thomson/South-Western, 2011); and Scott Snell and George Bohlander, *Managing Human Resources*, 16th ed. (Mason, OH: South-Western/Cengage Learning, 2013).
35. Erika Kelton, "Seven Ingredients for a Successful Whistleblower Program," Forbes.com (March 21, 2012).

# PART 4 Critical Incidents

The critical incidents below each present a supervisory situation based on real events to be used for educational purposes. The identities of some or all individuals, organizations, industries, and locations, as well as financial and other information may have been disguised to protect individual privacy and proprietary information. In some cases fictional details have been added to improve readability and interest.

---

Critical Incident 4-1

## "TOP GUN!"

Sitting in her office late on Friday afternoon, CEO Nancy Warner thought about how happy she was to have this job. "The opportunity to do what I love to do and find ways to make Community Hospital a great place to work has given me purpose in life," she thought. Community Hospital in rural Oklahoma is the only hospital immediately accessible to the area's 40,000 inhabitants.

Nancy Warner grew up on a farm in the area, went to a local community college to be a nurse, got a master's degree in healthcare management, and a year and a half ago became the CEO of Community Hospital. She loved the opportunity and believed that part of her job was to make employees feel appreciated and enable them to be good employees.

Late on Friday afternoon, Nancy's good week changed suddenly. HR director Ted Perry brought to her attention a problem with employee Joe Trosh. Joe, a maintenance worker, had been reprimanded by his supervisor for tardiness, and during a meeting with Perry to discuss his attendance problems, Perry noticed a bulge under Joe's work jacket. Upon his inquiry, Joe stated that he had a permit to carry a concealed handgun. He went on to say that several of his fellow employees were not easy to get along with and on occasion they might "fly off the handle."

He wanted to be prepared just in case something happened. He pointed out most of the maintenance workers were "good old boys" with gun racks in their pickup trucks that they had parked in the employee parking areas. Joe told Perry and his supervisor, "the law allows me to carry a concealed weapon for self-defense purposes." Joe Trosh was a Native American who on occasion had been subject to "Indian jokes" from fellow employees. Some of the hospital employees did not appreciate the presence of a gambling casino at a nearby Indian reservation because the casino provided little tax revenue to the local community yet promoted an unhealthy, addictive behavior.

Joe had worked for the hospital for approximately five years and was considered to be a competent employee. An investigation revealed that several other native American employees said they had been "harassed by coworkers." Nancy Warner was disturbed about these developments and wondered about whether the hospital was treating its Native American employees and other employees fairly.

(Critical Incident was adapted of a case developed by Ed Leonard, Ray Hilgert, and Mitchell Sherr, and published in *Annual Advances in Business Cases* 1996, by the Society for Case Research (SCR). It was adapted with permission of the original authors and SCR for use in the 13th edition of *Supervision Concepts and Practices of Management.)*

## QUESTIONS FOR DISCUSSION

1. The Second Amendment to the United States Constitution says, "A well regulated Militia, being necessary to the security for a free State, the right of the people to keep and bear Arms, shall not be infringed."
   Go on line and find excerpts of Oklahoma's self-defense act. After reading the act, do you believe that Joe Trosh has the right to carry a concealed handgun in the hospital.
2. Assuming that the hospital has a written policy prohibiting possession of weapons on company property, what should Nancy Warner do? Consider alternatives that may be open to her.
3. Why have Nancy Warner and other members of the hospital's administrative team been insensitive to the actions of some employees to the Native American employees?
4. What does the hospital administration need to do so that more incidents of discrimination to Native Americans does not occur?

---

Critical Incident 4-2

## SANDERS SUPERMARKETS: WHAT HAPPENED TO CONTROL?

Sanders Supermarkets operated 50 stores in the Midwest. Faced with significant challenges from Wal-Mart, Kroger and Meijer, and in an attempt to regain market share, the company had embarked on a program to do some renovation of its stores. Juan Sanchez was a store manager of Store #16. Three months ago, Sanchez was talking with his district manager, Norm Greenberg, about a major renovation in the grocery section of his store, but had heard no more about it. Finally, Greenberg called Sanchez to tell him about a meeting at the corporate main office that would be held to discuss his proposed renovation project.

The meeting was attended by Sanchez, Greenberg, management from corporate sales, the maintenance department, several district managers, and the corporate operations manager. At the end of the meeting, they generally agreed that Store #16 would be reorganized (called "reset" in the language of the maintenance department), including relocating various main aisles. The supervisor of the reset crew and the maintenance department were to submit final plans and a cost estimate a week later.

During his next visit to Store #16, Greenberg told Sanchez about the plans for his store. He said that not everything had been finalized and apparently failed to mention that part of the reset would include moving some of the aisles.

The next week, completed plans and cost were submitted and given final approval by the corporate operations manager. Since new shelving had to be ordered and schedules made, the supervisor of the reset crew and the construction supervisor would be assigning the job of putting the necessary paperwork into motion. Greenberg then called Sanchez and said, "The restart project for your store has been approved. We will be getting back to you later with more information."

A month later, Sanchez took a five-day vacation with his family. Normally, this would have been a great time, but he constantly thought about the frustrating work environment. The last day of his vacation, he sent Greenberg a text message asking about a starting date for the project.

Store #16 opened at 7 AM daily and closed at 10 PM. When Sanchez arrived at the store at 6:30 A.M., on his first day back from vacation, he soon forgot about the project. He walked into the store to find three major problems: the frozen food case was broken down, the floor scrubber was malfunctioning, and the grinder in the meat department was not working. After some checking, he found that no maintenance calls had been made, because each of his two assistant store managers, Jane Oliver and Wally Weathers, thought that the other was going to do it. The floor scrubber had not been working for several days, the frozen food case had broken down the previous afternoon, and the meat grinder was not functioning.

"It doesn't pay to take five days off and spend time with your family," Sanchez pondered to himself as he headed toward his office. He called the maintenance department, explained what happened, and requested immediate help. While waiting for the maintenance person, Sanchez called Oliver and Weathers to talk with them about letting him and each other know about the problems and how to control them. "All it takes," he said, "is working together, communicating, and following up to be sure that our customers get the best possible service. We can't be out of merchandise, especially in the frozen food department. We have to make sure that when we are busy, as we will be this week, our customers aren't stepping alongside workers in the aisles."

About that time, Sanchez was called to his office. When he arrived, he was greeted by four carpenters and three laborers, who told him, "We just wanted to tell you that we are here and are ready to get started on the renovation project right away."

"How come it takes this many people to fix a frozen food case?" asked Sanchez.

"We're not here to fix a frozen food case," said one of the carpenters. "We're here to remove the shelving in the aisles and begin to reset your store."

"Today?" Questioned Sanchez. "Nobody told me that you guys were coming to do this today. I can't have you moving aisles during the day. What are my customers going to do? I thought you would be doing the renovation project after hours."

Sanchez immediately called Greenberg, "Norm, why didn't you tell me you were going to start the reset project in my store today?"

"What," said Norm, "I wasn't notified either."

"Why wasn't I consulted by someone on this?" exclaimed Sanchez. "First of all, the first week of a month is always too busy a time for laborers to be working in the aisles of my store. Second, I thought this type of work would be done at night. Some of our other stores might be able to handle this in the daytime, but our customers will not tolerate this type of inconvenience."

"OK," said Greenberg, "it sounds like things are really out of control at your store right now. What are you going to do about it?"

"Norm, don't you mean, what are we going to do about it?"

## QUESTIONS FOR DISCUSSION

1. Analyze Juan Sanchez's discussion with the two assistant store managers, particularly when he said that "all it takes is working together, communicating and follow through." Are these the only factors that Sancheznees to address, or does good supervision require something more? Discuss.
2. Review the chapter on resolving conflicts. What suggestions would you make to Sanchez to help him resolve the problems he is facing?
3. What should Greenberg and Sanchez do in regard to the immediate problem of the carpenters and laborers in the store?
4. Identify various places in this critical incident where members of Sanders Supermarkets' management team did not plan on how to control for the unexpected?
5. In Chapter 2, we define "Management is getting things done through others." How can Juan Sanchez do a better job of leading his two assistant store managers?
6. Food for Thought: "Would you like to work for Sanders Supermarkets?" Why or why not?

---

## COPING WITH THE NEW MANAGER

Critical Incident 4-3

Phyo Thu Htet was a supervisory training facilitator at Blan's automotive plant in Tennessee. The plant made composite plastic components for the automotive industry. Plastic components were more durable and resisted dents and scratches better than ones made with steel. The nonunionized plant employed about 450. Eight years ago, Phyo began as a second shift entry level worker in the molding department. After a series of advancements she was promoted to production supervisor and then to training facilitator, a position she has had the last 16 months.

New hires are assigned to her section for orientation and training which usually lasts two weeks. Depending on the company's needs, employees are then reassigned to a specific production department. The unemployment rate in the area recently lowered to less than 6 percent. In recent months, 25 percent of new hires quit within six weeks of hire. Part of the problem is the company's high expectations of its employees.

Three months ago, Don Patterson became the new operations manager. His predecessor had been Alan Seitz. Even though the Tennessee plant had missed delivery deadlines and labor costs were escalating, Seitz appeared to have been content with what was going on. He had the reputation of expecting departmental managers to correct problems when they occurred, and "crisis management" was the prevalent style.

Donald Patterson, a former colonel in the 82nd Airborne Division, was expected to turn the plant around. Under his direction, the culture of the plant changed overnight. He immediately announced to all supervisors that he was not willing to accept a high rate of product rejects. Patterson practiced management by wandering around (MBWA), and he met and talked with all supervisors, group leaders, and facilitators one-on-one. Further, he met with small groups of employees and listened to their concerns. Initially, Patterson was positively received, but that soon changed.

Shortly after assuming the operations manager position, Donald Patterson informed all managers and supervisors that they were being placed on a salary and bonus system. He told them that their hard work was appreciated and would be rewarded. Yet, because of costly work production delays and over time for hourly employees, the bonus system did not yield any tangible benefits. Among the supervisory complaints: "You told us that the new system would result in increased compensation, and it hasn't. We're making less than before the change. We would be better off financially if we were hourly production workers!"

Most supervisors were now working six days a week, 10 hours a day. Employees and equipment was being stretched to the limit. Some supervisors had quit within the last month and had taken less demanding factory jobs in the area. Phyo and her one remaining employee (five had been assigned to fill the vacant supervisory positions and another was placed in the quality department) were directed by Patterson to cut the normal two-week training time to one day.

The most recent customer quality audit was a disaster. There were rumors that some of the work would be transferred to other of the company's plants or even to competitors. To Phyo Thu Htet, it was like someone had pulled the plug. Every supervisor that you spoke with said that Donald Patterson had "lost their respect." Her blood pressure went up every time someone questioned her about what Patterson was doing. Most supervisors were afraid to say anything. To Phyo, supervisors appeared to be "mindless robots going through the motions."

Later in the day, Phyo got a text message from Amy, Patterson's assistant. Amy and Phyo were good friends and did things together outside the workplace. Amy said, "Patterson has been meeting and interviewing with several of the supervisors and some employees. He wants to get the scoop on everyone. I even heard him tell the plant manager Bill Arnold that he would get rid of all the malcontents."

Phye felt betrayed after all her years with the company and wondered what the future held for her.

## QUESTIONS FOR DISCUSSION

1. Assess Donald Patterson's leadership style. How might his past military experiences govern the way he tries to lead Blan's Tennessee plant?
2. How would you evaluate Phyo's situation in terms of job stress and conflict?
3. Have you, a family member or close friend, ever experienced a situation like the one described in this critical incident. If so, how did you or they handle the problems?
4. What should Phyo do? Why?
5. Go online to find at least two websites that discuss disgruntled employees, and find at least two sources where managers have used abusive controlling and created conflicts for employees. Write a one-page report, giving some suggestions that you might use if you were in Phyo's situation. We suggest that you use the last paragraph to suggest ways in which the effective supervisor can prevent employees from becoming disgruntled.
   (You may want to go to www.YouTube.com, and view Angelina Leigh in the *Disgruntled Employee* movie.)

## WHO MADE THE EAT FRESH SUBWAY SANDWICH?

Critical Incident 4-4

Professor Edwards and two of his former students were having a meeting at one of their Subway Restaurants when his cell phone went off; there was a message to the professor from his 15-year-old granddaughter. "'Ouch! You should see this,' he said to Mark and Jake. It appeared that two Subway employees near my granddaughter's home in Ohio had posted images on a social networking site."

One of the photos showed a male employee with his genitals on what appeared to be a loaf of subway bread. The other photo showed a hand holding a water bottle that's half filled with a cream-colored substance. The caption said, "At work today I froze my pee!"

Mark and Jake own about 40 Subway Stores in the Midwest. The good news was that the photos were not from one of their stores. Subway Systems is a franchise operation that they bought into almost 25 years ago, while both were working in the financial industry. At the time of this on-line posting, Subway was ranked the most popular fast food restaurant in the United States (go to www.subway.com to learn more about the company that 17-year-old Fred DeLuca started while trying to raise money to pay for college).

Mark and Jake had created a culture that said: "Working with us is something you can be proud of. At our Subway Restaurants, we don't serve food; we serve fresh, healthy food. We will train you to be a Subway sandwich artist so you can make a sandwich that looks and tastes great. We schedule your work hours around your needs."

Several years ago with Professor Edwards's help, Jake and Mark had developed an orientation/onboarding program to help every new associate identify with Subway System's purpose. More importantly, their motto is, "We hire for attitude, as we can teach and train you to be a great Subway sandwich artist." They believe that the employees' beliefs and attitudes should align with what is expected of the artist each day. While the turnover rate in the food service industry is high, Subway Systems' turnover rate is less than 13 percent.

Mark, Jake, and the six area managers met with all associates one-on-one every three months. Most of the time was spent on ideas that the associates had for improving the business. In advance of the meeting, the associate was given a 3 × 7 card on which she or he should answer two questions: (1) If you were the supreme commander of Subway Systems, what one thing would you do differently? (2) What would you do to improve profitability?

The owners took responsibility for listening to and acting on the suggestions and ideas that came out of the meetings. Mark and Jake collected information on all members of the management team including themselves.

Early the next morning, Professor Edwards thought about the dinner and the events of the previous day. Mark had asked him to go back and look at the employees' attitudes and needs survey that the professor had done three years ago. Jake had asked the professor to think about whether the survey should be redone now. Mark said, "We are very lucky to have great associates. What else might we do to enable them to be the best of the best?"

(This critical incident was developed by Ed Leonard, Lisa Koss, and Lori Leonard for this edition of *Supervision*.)

## QUESTIONS FOR DISCUSSION

1. See this blog by Katherine Luster, The 10 Most Egregious Restaurant Crimes (http://www.restaurants.com/blog/employees-behaving-badly-the-10-most-egregious-restaurant-crimes/#.U81YyvldVD4)
2. Using the Internet, try to find at least three other incidents where employees in the fast food industry have posted what you would consider inappropriate activities at their place of work. In your opinion, why would employees do such a thing?
3. Are there some ways for Professor Edwards, Mark, and Jake to find out if the images are real or fake?
4. What is meant by the term "Subway sandwich artist?" Assume that you are the franchise owner of the store where this posting took place, how would you respond to a person that asked you the following question: "I saw on Facebook a posting of how you train one of your employees to be a Subway sandwich artist!"
5. The next time associates are given the 3 × 5 card with the two questions, which Jake and Mark had come up with, the associates were asked to add a third question and provide an answer. If you work for Subway Systems, based upon your previous work experiences, what question would you ask and what would your answer be? (We suggest that instructors have students share their questions and answers in small groups.)
6. If you were the manager of the store where the employees posted the offensive photos, how would you deal with the situation?
7. Most organizations do not have a specific rule that would address what the employees did. Why should organizations have an employee policy that would allow them to immediately and effectively address the actions that these employees had allegedly taken?

---

**Critical Incident**
**4-5**

## DISCHARGE FOR ABSENTEEISM?

Absenteeism has been a major problem for the city of Metropolis. The overall absenteeism rate has been about 6 percent for the past year. However, no unionized employee has been disciplined or discharged for excessive absenteeism under the provisions of labor contract. At the first week of September's department heads meeting (department heads meet early every Thursday to discuss various issues), the discussion centered on absenteeism. The general consensus expressed by supervisors and managers was that the city administration was unwilling to "back" managers who might try to enforce the rules. The labor contract between the city and the union that represented most of the employees contained the following provisions:

Section 4.1. The city of Metropolis maintains the exclusive right to discipline an employee for just cause.

Section 8.3. The city of Metropolis has the right to discipline an employee for absenteeism. Excessive absenteeism may result in discharge.

During the meeting, the mayor's chief administrative assistant, Nicole Powers, stated that the mayor didn't want any adverse publicity regarding city personnel matters since the next year was the election year. However, Shane Dwight, the director of HR, took a more hard-line approach, saying. "Work rules need to be uniformly and consistently enforced throughout the city.

Department heads should build their cases, and if the suspension without pay or being discharged is unwarranted, then so be it!" Several managers and supervisors remarked that union leaders would be hostile to any suspension or discharge for absenteeism.

Ricardo Moreno-Varela, director of utility administration, said, "We need to be objective, but if someone is a habitual offender, document your case. We'll throw the disciplinary action on the wall and see if it will stick."

Shane Dwight then added, "Most employees want to do the right thing and only a small minority are abusing our attendance policies. When infractions occur, we must take disciplinary action with the objective of improving the employees' future behavior. Remember to investigate thoroughly before recommending disciplinary action."

*The Discharge of Charlie Pulfer*: Pulfer had been an employee in the sanitation department for almost 15 years. A review of his personnel file revealed the following: (1) he had the ability and experience to do the assigned work; (2) his overall performance has been satisfactory; (3) he had received annual pay advances as prescribed by union contract; and (4) his work performance the past several years has not been good. On Friday, September 18, he failed to show up for work or call in. He was given an oral warning. The second Friday in October, he did the same thing, and was given a day off without pay. His manager and the HR manager told him and the union steward that they were not going to tolerate such behavior.

On October 30, he called in two hours before a scheduled shift and said that he was not feeling well and would not be in to work that day. A review of his personnel records from January to October revealed that Pulfer had missed 16 of the days that he was scheduled to work. Any time he worked overtime during the week, he would fail to show up for his next regularly scheduled Friday or Monday. On only three occasions, he brought in notes from a doctor indicating that he had been sick; the other were for a variety of personal reasons.

The first Friday in December was the last straw. He failed to show up for work and failed to call in. This was his regularly scheduled work day. At a meeting, with union representatives and Charlie Pulfer, the administration informed him that he was being discharged for excessive absenteeism and failure to call in again.

This maintains that Charlie was terminated for just cause, because he had failed to carry out his responsibilities as an employee. His recent absences were a glaring example of a total disregard of his responsibilities.

*The union's position*: Charlie Pulfer admitted that he failed to report to work last Friday. He said he didn't feel good, tried to call in, and all the lines were busy. He admitted that he never thought about sending an e-mail. He maintained that he had a valid excuse, and when he arrived on Monday, he explained to a supervisor, "I'm sorry about Friday, the darn furnace went out on me. One of my kids was sick, and I needed to get heat in the house. You know, it was less than 10° that day. It took me most of the day to overhaul the blower."

The union reminded management that Charlie had worked for the city for many years, and until recently, he had never been disciplined. Charlie Pulfer would not be able to find comparable work in today's economy, and he and his family would suffer severe economic hardships. The union requested that he not be discharged and that the city reinstate him with back pay and full benefits, since this was "an unjust action" by the city administration.

## QUESTIONS FOR DISCUSSION

1. Internet activity: What is the average absenteeism rate in American industry today? How does city Metropolis' absenteeism rate of 6 percent compare with the absenteeism rate of other city and county governmental units and industry?
2. Based on your findings, how serious is the city's absenteeism problem?
3. What should the city do to minimize absenteeism?
4. This case will probably go to arbitration. The arbitrator will have a number of possible options, such as:

   —The city would be correct in terminating Pulfer.

   —The city's tally of discharge was too severe (e.g. five days off without pay. What would be more appropriate?).

   —The city should not have penalized Pulfer in any way because of his reasons for his latest absence.

   —Other possibilities for the arbitrator might be… you make the call.

   If you were the arbitrator, how would you rule and why?

   *Note*: Instructors may want to have the students do this in teams, so that they can compare their ideas and thoughts.

---

**Critical Incident 4-6**

## CHANGING THE WORLD

© Eugene Parciasepe/Shutterstock.com

William Henry "Bill" Cosby, Jr. was born on July 12, 1937 in Philadelphia, Pennsylvania. The stand-up performer started the Hungry I in San Francisco and various other clubs. Cosby became the first African American actor to co-star in a television drama in 1965. *I Spy* with costar Robert Culp was a hit.

From 1984 to 1992, Cosby produced and starred in "The Cosby Show." It was the number one show in America for five straight years. The sitcom highlighted the experiences and growth of an affluent African American family. He also produced a "Different World," and other shows. Cosby still lectures at churches and universities about his frustrations with problems prevalent in underprivileged urban communities and how we have failed to live up to the ideals of Martin Luther King Jr., and others.

Don Steinberg, in a 2013 interview with Cosby, asked him the following question: "When you came to comedy in the 1960s, there were comedians trying to influence politics and race relations. You were a political comedian, but you tried to change things."

Cosby responded, "There were routines I was doing in those days, working 'til 4 o'clock in the morning in Greenwich Village. I did a routine about slavery. My stuff was all in the storytelling. But I never believed that after laughing at what was said on stage, about what was going on offstage, racially, was going to change anybody's minds. The thing that I do with helping people identify was enough. I felt that if you hear me talk about my mother, and your mother did the same thing, what's the difference? But it still doesn't change anybody's racism. Racism is a mental illness."[1]

---

[1] Steinberg, Don, "How Bill Cosby Changed the World," *The Wall Street Journal*, November 15, 2013, p. D6.

Cosby has made public remarks pleading for African American families to educate their children in the various aspects of the American culture. Cosby has come under sharp criticism for admonishing apathetic blacks for not assisting or conducting themselves as individuals who are involved in crime or have counterproductive aspirations. Georgetown University sociology professor Michael Eric Dyson suggested that Cosby's comments "betray classist, elitist viewpoints rooted in generational warfare."[2]

Princeton's Cornel West defended Cosby's remarks, and said, "He is speaking out of great compassion and trying to get folks to get on the right track. He is trying to speak honestly and freely and lovingly and I think that's a very positive thing."[3]

## QUESTIONS FOR DISCUSSION

We suggest you review the following resources to learn more about Bill Cosby:

http://www.billcosby.com

http://www.free-times.com/arts/112013-bill-cosby-still-going-strong

"Bill Cosby": http://esperstamps.org/t61.htm

Cosby, Bill (2011). *I Didn't Ask to Be Born (But I'm Glad I Was)*. New York: Center Street. ISBN 978-0-89296-920-3. OCLC 707964887.

Video: Bill Cosby: Far From Finished. Available on Blu-Ray-DVD. Severance

Students may want to review: Larry Getlen, "Pudding Pop. The maddening pardox of America's favorite TV dad." Time (September 29, 2014), p. 54. Ann Hornaday, "Review: Cosby: His Life and Times" The Washington Post. (September 19, 2014) or review the book by Mark Whitaker: "Cosby: His life and Times), Simon and Schuster (2014).)

1. Conduct an Internet search to learn more about Bill Cosby's life and his social and economic views. After reading this case and doing research on Cosby's life and views, do you think that the university professor's comment about Cosby is appropriate? Or do you think that Cornell West's defense is more appropriate?
2. Years ago, poet William Wordsworth, wrote about the loss of a child's insight, security, and creativity.
   "What though the radiance which was once so bright
   Be now for ever taken from my sight
   Though nothing can bring forth the hour
   Of splendour in the grass, for glory is in the flower."
   Many people in America today have lost their insight, security, and creativity. Based upon Bill Cosby's views and the words of Wordsworth, what are you doing to provide comfort for yourself?
3. What did you learn from the experiences and life of Bill Cosby that will help you to develop a plan to enable you to be the best you can be?
4. If Bill Cosby was invited to your college as a guest speaker, what question would you ask him?

[2] http://www.nytimes.com/2004/05/22/arts/22COSB.html
[3] http://www.npr.org/templates/story/story.php?storyId=1910649

# GLOSSARY

## A

**360-degree evaluation** Performance appraisal based on data collected from all around the employee—from customers, vendors, supervisors, peers, subordinates, and others.

**Ability** An employee's potential to perform higher-level tasks.

**Acceptance theory of authority** Theory that holds that the manager only possesses authority when the employee accepts it.

**Accountability** The obligation one has to one's boss and the expectation that employees will accept credit or blame for the results achieved in performing assigned tasks.

**Administrative skills** The ability to plan, organize, and coordinate activities.

**Aesthetic needs** The need to create something that is useful and pleasing.

**Alternative dispute resolution (ADR)** Approaches to processing and deciding employee complaints internally as an alternative to lawsuits, usually for disputes involving discharge or employment discrimination.

**Appreciative inquiry (AI)** The cooperative search for the best in people, organizations, and the world around them.

**Arbitrator** Person selected by the union and management to render a final and binding decision concerning a grievance.

**Attitude survey** Survey of employee opinions about major aspects of organizational life that is used to assess engagement and morale.

**Austerity** Harsh and severe times requiring a tightening of the belt and budget.

**Authority** The legitimate right to direct and lead others.

**Autocratic (authoritarian) supervision** The supervisory style that relies on formal authority, threats, pressure, and close control.

## B

**Benchmarking** The process of identifying and improving on the best practices of leaders.

**Body language** All observable actions of the sender or receiver.

**Brainstorming** A free flow of ideas in a group, while suspending judgment, aimed at developing many alternative solutions to a problem.

**Budget** A plan that expresses anticipated allocations and results in numerical terms, ultimately financial terms, for a stated period.

**Bullying** Recurring behavior directed at individuals that can include yelling, intimidation, humiliation, or sabotage.

**Bureaucratic style of supervision** The supervisory style that emphasizes strict compliance with organizational policies, rules, and directives.

## C

**Cascade** Rapidly engaging supervisors and employees at all levels of an organization in education, training, and the establishment of clear accountability for change processes and tasks.

**Coaching** The frequent activity of the supervisor to give employees information, instruction, and suggestions relating to their job assignments and performance.

**Cognitive dissonance** The state of being out of balance because of conflicting goals, job assignments, expectations, or knowledge.

**Cognitive needs** One's need to know and understand.

**Collaborative workplace** Work environment characterized by joint decision making, shared accountability and authority, and high trust levels between employees and managers.

**Command group** Grouping of employees according to authority relationships on the formal organization chart.

**Communication skills** The ability to give—and get—information.

**Communication** The process of transmitting information and understanding.

**Comparable worth** Concept that jobs should be paid at the same level when they require similar skills or abilities.

**Competencies** The set of skills, knowledge, and personal attributes possessed by the superior performer.

**Competitive advantage** The ability to outperform competitors by increasing efficiency, quality, creativity, and responsiveness to customers and effectively using employee talents.

**Complaint procedure** A management-designed series of steps for handling employee complaints that usually provides for a number of appeals before a final decision.

**Complaint** Any individual or group problem or dissatisfaction employees can channel upward to management, including discrimination.

**Conceptual skills** The ability to obtain, interpret, and apply information.

**Concurrent control** Corrective action taken during the production or delivery process to ensure that standards are being met.

**Conflict-resolution styles** Approaches to resolving conflict based on weighing desired degrees of cooperativeness and assertiveness.

**Consistency needs** Being in harmony and free from variation and contradiction.

**Constructive or functional conflict** The end result of conflict that is a win–win situation for all concerned.

**Contingency-style leadership** No one leadership style is best; the appropriate style depends on a multitude of factors.

**Contingent workforce** Part-time, temporary, or contract employees who work schedules dependent primarily on employer needs.

**Controlling** Ensuring that actual performance is in line with intended performance and taking corrective action.

**Cooperation** The willingness of individuals to work with and help one another.

**Coordination** The synchronization of employees' efforts and the organization's resources toward achieving goals.

**Corporate culture** Set of shared purposes, values, and beliefs that employees hold about their organization.

**Corporate social responsibility (CSR)** A notion that organizations consider the interests of all stakeholders.

**Counseling interview** Nondirective interview during which the supervisor listens empathetically and encourages the employee to discuss problems openly and to develop solutions.

**Counseling** An effort by the supervisor to deal with on-the-job performance problems that are the result of an employee's personal problems.

**Crisis** A critical point or threatening situation that must be resolved before it can cause more harm.

**Critical incident method** Supervisors record specific examples of outstanding and below-average performance on the part of each employee.

**Cross-training** Training employees to do multiple tasks and jobs.

**Cultural competency** The ability to understand and adapt to a variety of cultural communities.

## D

**Dashboard** A visual presentation of the current status of an organization's key performance metrics relative to its goals.

**Decision criteria** Standards or measures to use in evaluating alternatives.

**Decision making** Defining problems and choosing a course of action from among alternatives.

**Decision-making process** A systematic, step-by-step process to aid in choosing the best alternative.

**Delegation** The process of entrusting duties and related authority to subordinates.

**Department** An organizational unit for which a supervisor has responsibility and authority.

**Departmentalization** The process of grouping activities and people into distinct organizational units.

**Directive interview** Interview approach in which the interviewer guides the discussion along a predetermined course.

**Directive** The communication approach by which a supervisor conveys to employees what, how, and why something is to be accomplished.

**Discipline without punishment** Disciplinary approach that uses coaching and counseling as preliminary steps and a paid decision-making leave that allows employees to decide whether to improve and stay or to quit.

**Discipline** State of orderliness; the degree to which employees act according to expected standards of behavior.

**Diversity** The cultural, ethnic, gender, age, educational level, racial, and lifestyle differences of employees.

**Division of work (specialization)** Dividing work into components and specialized tasks to improve efficiency and output.

**Documentation** Records of memoranda, documents, and meetings that relate to a disciplinary action.

**Downsizing, restructuring, or right-sizing** Large-scale reduction and elimination of jobs in a company that usually reduces middle-level managers, removes organizational levels, and widens the span of management for remaining supervisors.

**Dysfunctional conflict** Conflict that arises when communication between individuals breaks down and the lack of teamwork causes the team to stray from its chosen path.

## E

**Electronic brainstorming system (EBS)** Using technology to share and evaluate ideas.

**Emotional contagion** Transfer of emotion and attitudes between people who are in close contact.

**Emotional intelligence skills** The ability to use your emotions intelligently.

**Employee assistance programs (EAPs)** Company programs to help employees with personal or work-related problems that are interfering with job performance.

**Employee entitlement** The belief that the organization "owes" them.

**Employment-at-will** Legal concept that employers can dismiss employees at any time and for any reason, except unlawful discrimination and contractual or other restrictions.

**Empowerment** Giving employees the authority and responsibility to accomplish their individual and the organization's objectives.

**Enabler** The person who does the things necessary to enable employees to do the best possible job.

**Engaged employees** An employee who has a strong emotional bond to his or her organization and is committed to its objectives.

**Engagement** The level of emotional commitment the employee has to the organization and its goals.

**Equity theory** Explains how people strive for fairness in the workplace.

**ERG Theory** Existence, relatedness, and growth needs.

**Ethical "tests"** Considerations or guidelines to be addressed in developing and evaluating ethical aspects of decision alternatives.

**Ethics** The system of moral principles that guide the conduct of an individual, group, or society.

**Exception principle** Concept that supervisors should concentrate their investigations on activities that deviate substantially from standards.

**Exit interviews** Interviews with individuals who leave a firm that are used to assess morale and the reasons for employee turnover.

**Expectancy theory** Theory of motivation that holds that employees perform better when they believe such efforts lead to desired rewards.

**Extinction** Good behavior occurs less frequently or disappears because it is not recognized.

## F

**Fair treatment** Impartial and appropriate actions taken that are free of favoritism and bias.

**Feedback control** Actions taken after the activity, product, or service has been completed.

**Feedback** The receiver's verbal or nonverbal response to a message.

**Feedforward control** Anticipatory action taken to ensure that problems do not occur.

**Filtering** The process of omitting or softening unpleasant details.

**Fishbone technique (cause-and-effect diagram)** Cause-and-effect approach to consider the potential interrelatedness of problem causes in decision making.

**Flextime** Policy that allows employees to choose their work hours within stated limits.

**Followership** The capacity or willingness to follow a leader.

**Formal organizational structure** Departments, positions, functions, authority, and reporting relationships as depicted on a firm's organizational chart.

**Friendship group** Informal grouping of employees based on similar personalities and social interests.

**Frustration-regression principle** If higher-needs are not satisfied, individuals will regress to a lower-order need that is more easily fulfilled.

**Functional approach** School of management thought that asserts that all managers perform various functions in doing their jobs, such as planning, organizing, staffing, leading, and controlling.

## G

**Gain-sharing plans** Group incentive plans that have employees' share in the benefits from improved performance.

**Gantt chart** A graphic scheduling technique that shows the activity to be scheduled on the vertical axis and necessary completion dates on the horizontal axis.

**Gender stereotyping** Use of demeaning language, judgments, or behavior based on a person's gender.

**General supervision** The style of supervision in which the supervisor sets goals and limits but allows employees to decide how to achieve goals.

**Glass ceiling** Invisible barrier that limits the advancement of women and minorities.

**Glass walls** Invisible barriers that compartmentalize women and minorities into certain occupational classes.

**Going green** Voluntary steps taken by organizations and individuals to conserve energy and protect the environment.

**Grapevine** The informal, unofficial communication channel.

**Grievance procedure** Negotiated series of steps in a labor agreement for processing grievances, beginning at the supervisory level and ending with arbitration.

**Grievance** A formal complaint presented by the union to management that alleges a violation of the labor agreement.

**Groupthink** The tendency of members of a group to make faulty decisions because of group pressures, even in the face of red flags or better, more logical alternatives.

## H

**Halo effect** The tendency to allow one favorable aspect of a person's behavior to positively influence judgment on all other aspects.

**Hawthorne effect** The fact that personalized interest shown in people may cause them to behave differently.

**Hawthorne Studies** Comprehensive research studies that focused on workgroup dynamics as they related to employee attitudes and productivity.

**Hierarchy of needs** Maslow's theory of motivation, which suggests that employee needs are arranged in priority order such that lower-order needs must be satisfied before higher-order needs become motivating.

**Horizontal corporation** A very flat firm resulting from restructuring by customer process and organizational structure.

**Horns effect** The tendency to allow one negative aspect of a person's behavior to negatively influence judgment on all other aspects.

**Hot stove rule** Guideline for applying discipline analogous to touching a hot stove: advance warning and consequences that are immediate, consistent, and applied with impersonality.

**Human relations movement / behavioral science approach** Approach to management that focuses on the behavior of people in the work environment.

**Human relations skills** The ability to work with and through people.

**Human resource management (HRM)** Organizational philosophies, policies, and practices that strive for the effective use of employees.

**Human resources (HR) department** Department that provides advice and service to other departments on human resource matters.

**Hygiene factors** Elements in the work environment that, if positive, reduce dissatisfaction but do not tend to motivate.

## I

**Inclusion** Providing opportunities for every worker to fully participate and valuing every worker's skills, experiences, and perspectives.

**Incremental budgeting** A technique for projecting revenues and expenses based on history.

**Informal organization** Informal gatherings of people, apart from the formal organizational structure, that satisfy members' social and other needs.

**Intangible standards** Standards for performance results that are difficult to measure and often relate to human characteristics (e.g., attitude, morale).

**Interest-based negotiating** Understanding why the other party wants what he or she wants, and then working toward a solution that satisfies those needs as well as one's own.

**ISO 9001** International quality standard.

## J

**Jargon** Words that are specific to an occupation or a specialty.

**Job description** Written description of the principal duties and responsibilities of a job.

**Job enrichment** Job design that helps fulfill employees' higher-level needs by giving those employees more challenging tasks and more decision-making responsibility for their jobs.

**Job redesign** The belief that well-designed jobs lead to increased motivation.

**Job rotation** The process of switching job tasks among employees in a work group.

**Job sharing** Policy that allows two or more employees to perform a job normally done by one full-time employee.

**Job specifications** Written description of the personal qualifications needed to perform a job adequately.

**Just or proper cause** Standard for disciplinary action requiring tests of fairness and elements of normal due process, such as proper notification, investigation, sufficient evidence, and a penalty commensurate with the nature of the infraction.

**Just-in-time (JIT) inventory control system** A system for scheduling materials to arrive precisely when they are needed in the production process.

## K

**Kanban** Another name for a just-in-time (JIT) inventory-control system.

**KISS technique** An acronym that stands for keep it short and simple.

**Knowledge management** The systematic storage, retrieval, dissemination, and sharing of information.

## L

**Labor agreement** Negotiated document between union and employer that covers the terms and conditions of employment for represented employees.

**Labor union / labor organization** Legally recognized organization that represents employees and negotiates and administers a labor agreement with an employer.

**Law of effect** Behavior with favorable consequences is repeated; behavior with unfavorable consequences tends to disappear.

**Lead person** Employee in charge of other employees who performs limited managerial functions but is not considered part of management.

**Leadership skills** The ability to engage followers in all aspects of the organization.

**Leadership** The process of influencing the opinions, attitudes, and behaviors of others toward the achievement of a goal.

**Leading** The managerial function of guiding employees toward accomplishing organizational objectives.

**Lean manufacturing** Techniques that enable a company to produce more product with fewer resources (lower costs).

**Learning organization** Employees continually strive to improve their SKAs while expanding their efforts to achieve organizational objectives.

**Leniency error** Error that occurs when supervisors give employees higher ratings than they deserve.

**Line authority** The right to direct others and to require them to conform to decisions, policies, rules, and objectives.

**Line-and-staff-type organizational structure** Structure that combines line and staff departments and incorporates line and staff authority.

## M

**Malcolm Baldrige National Quality Award** America's highest quality award.

**Management by objectives (MBO)** A process in which the supervisor and employee jointly set the employee's objectives and the employee receives rewards upon achieving those objectives.

**Management** Getting objectives accomplished with and through people.

**Managerial controlling** Ensuring that actual performance is in line with intended performance and taking corrective action, if necessary.

**MBWA (management by walking around)** Asking employees, customers, and others what one can do to help them to be the very best they can be.

**Mentoring** An experienced employee guiding a newer employee in areas concerning job and career.

**Merit** The quality of an employee's job performance.

**Method** A standing plan that details exactly how an operation is to be performed.

**Metrics** A standard of measurement used to determine that performance is in line with objectives.

**Mission statement** A statement of the organization's basic philosophy, purpose, and reason for being.

**Morale** A composite of feelings and attitudes that individuals and groups have toward their work, working condition, supervisors, top-level management, and the organization.

**Motion study** An analysis of work activities to determine how to make a job easier and quicker to do.

**Motivation factors** Elements intrinsic to the job that promote job performance.

**Motivation** A willingness to exert effort toward achieving a goal, stimulated by the effort's ability to fulfill an individual need.

**Motivation-hygiene theory** Herzberg's theory that factors in the work environment primarily influence the degree of job dissatisfaction while intrinsic job content factors influence the amount of employee motivation.

**Multinational corporation** A company that establishes locations, manages production, and delivers services in more than one country and most often directs management policies and practices from one home country.

**Multitasking** When an employee performs several tasks simultaneously.

## N

**Needs for power (nPOW)** The need to exert influence over others or to be in position of control.

**Negative reinforcement** Making behavior occur more frequently by removing an undesirable consequence.

**Nepotism** The practice of hiring relatives.

**Networking** Individuals or groups linked by a commitment to a shared purpose.

**No-fault attendance policy** Policy under which unscheduled absences and tardiness are counted as occurrences and their accumulation is used in progressive discipline.

**Noise** Obstacles that distort messages between people.

**Nominal group technique (NGT)** A group brainstorming and decision-making process by which individual members first identify alternative solutions privately and then share, evaluate, and decide on an approach as a group.

**Nondirective interview** Interview approach in which the interviewer asks open-ended questions that allow the applicant latitude in responding.

**Norms** Standards shared by most employees for how one should act and be treated in the organization.

## O

**ODR (Online dispute resolution)** An alternative approach similar to ADR but with the dispute process handled online.

**Onboarding** A continuous process of assimilation and growth within the organization for new hires.

**Operating budget** The assignment of dollar allocations to the costs and expenses needed to run the business, based on expected revenues.

**Optimizing** Selecting the best alternative.

**Organization** Group structured by management to carry out designated functions and accomplish certain objectives.

**Organizational chart** Graphic portrayal of a company's authority and responsibility relationships.

**Organizational development (OD)** Meetings with groups under the guidance of a neutral conference leader to solve problems that are hindering organizational effectiveness.

**Organizational renewal** A continuous process for long-term success.

**Organizing** Arranging and distributing work among members of the work group to accomplish the organization's goals.

**Orientation** The process of smoothing the transition of new employees into the organization.

## P

**Paid time off (PTO) program** Allows employees to establish a personal time-off bank that they can use for any reason they want.

**Participative management** Allowing employees to influence and share in organizational decision making.

**Pay for performance** Compensation, other than base wages, that is given for achieving employee or team goals.

**Peer evaluation** The evaluation of an employee's performance by other employees of relatively equal rank.

**Performance appraisal** A systematic assessment of how well an employee is performing a job and the communication of that assessment.

**Performance standards** The job-related requirements by which the employee's performance is evaluated.

**Personal power** Power derived from a person's SKAs and how others perceive that person.

**Personality** The knowledge, attitudes, and attributes that make up the unique human being.

**Personalized conflict** Conflict between individuals that occurs because the two parties do not like one another.

**Physiological needs** Basic physical needs (e.g., food, rest, shelter, and recreation).

**Planning** The process of deciding what needs to be done by whom and when.

**Policy** A standing plan that serves as a guide to making decisions.

**Political skills** The ability to understand how things get done outside of formal channels.

**Position power** Power derived from the formal rank a person holds in the chain of command.

**Positive discipline** Condition that exists when employees generally follow the organization's rules and meet the organization's standards.

**Positive Mental Attitude (PMA)** Seeing the positive side of things, rather than the negative, which helps individuals deal with challenges and adapt more easily to changes.

**Positive reinforcement** Making behavior occur more frequently because it is linked to a positive consequence.

**Positive self-discipline** Employees regulating their behavior out of self-interest and their normal desire to meet reasonable standards.

**Principle of organizational stability** Principle that holds that no organization should become overly dependent on one or several "indispensable" individuals.

**Procedure** A standing plan that defines the sequence of activities to be performed to achieve objectives.

**Program evaluation and review technique (PERT)** A flowchart for managing large programs and projects that shows the necessary activities, with estimates of the time needed to complete each activity and the sequential relationship of activities.

**Progressive discipline** System of disciplinary action that increases the severity of the penalty with each offense.

**Project management–type organizational structure** A hybrid structure in which regular, functional departments coexist with project teams made up of people from different departments.

**Project** A single-use plan for accomplishing a specific, nonrecurring activity.

**Protected-group employees** Classes of employees who have been afforded certain legal protections in their employment situations.

**Punishment** Making behavior occur less frequently because it is linked to an undesirable consequence.

## Q

**Qualified disabled individual** Defined by the Americans with Disabilities Act (ADA) as someone with a disability who can perform the essential components of a job with or without reasonable accommodation.

**Quantitative/systems approaches** Field of management study that uses mathematical modeling as a foundation.

## R

**Rater bias** The influence unconscious thinking processes have on an individual's decisions and judgments.

**Realistic job preview (RJP)** Information given by an interviewer to a job applicant that provides a realistic view of both the positive and negative aspects of the job.

**Realistic organizational preview (ROP)** Sharing information by an interviewer with a job applicant concerning the mission, values, and direction of the organization.

**Reasonable accommodation** Altering the usual ways of doing things so that an otherwise qualified disabled person can perform the essential job duties, but without creating an undue hardship for the employer.

**Reciprocity reflex** The rule that one good turn deserves another in return.

**Reductions in force (RIFs)** The temporary or permanent elimination of positions.

**Reengineering** Concept of restructuring a firm based on processes and customer needs and services rather than on departments and functions.

**Responsibility** The obligation to perform certain tasks and duties as assigned by the supervisor.

**Reverse discrimination** Preference given to protected group members in hiring and promotion over more qualified or more experienced workers from non-protected groups.

**Right to appeal** Procedures by which an employee may request higher-level management to review a supervisor's disciplinary action.

**Rule of reciprocity** The rule of reciprocity implies paying back a good deed or retaliating when one experiences a wrongdoing.

**Rule** A directive that must be applied and enforced wherever applicable.

## S

**Sampling** The technique of evaluating some number of items from a larger group to determine whether the group meets acceptable quality standards.

**Satisfaction** An emotional state or affective response toward various factors associated with one's work.

**Satisficing** Selecting the alternative that meets the minimal decision criteria.

**Scientific management approach** School of management thought that focuses on determining the most efficient ways to increase output and productivity.

**Security needs** Desire for protection against danger and life's uncertainties.

**Selection criteria** Factors used to choose among applicants who apply for a job.

**Selection** The process of choosing the best applicants to fill positions.

**Self-directed (self-managed) work teams (SDWTs)** Employee groups that are given wide latitude and considerable authority to make many of their own job-related decisions.

**Self-fulfillment needs** Desire to use one's abilities to the fullest extent.

**Self-respect needs** Desire for recognition, achievement, status, and a sense of accomplishment.

**Seniority** An employee's length of service in a department or an organization.

**Servant leadership** The notion that the needs of followers are looked after so they can be the best they can be.

**Sexual harassment** Unwelcome sexual advances, requests, or conduct when submission to such conduct is tied to the individual's continuing employment or advancement, unreasonably interferes with job performance, or creates a hostile work environment.

**Single-use plans** Plans to accomplish a specific objective or to cover a designated time period.

**SKAs** A person's skills, knowledge, and abilities.

**Slacker** A person who withholds effort and could be much more productive but makes a persistent, conscious decision not to be.

**Social needs** Desire for love and affection and affiliation with something worthwhile.

**Society of Human Resources Management's (SHRM)** A professional organization for HR professionals.

**Span-of-management principle** Principle that there is an upper limit to the number of subordinates a supervisor can manage effectively.

**Special-interest group** Grouping of employees that exists to accomplish something as a group that would not likely be pursued individually.

**Staff authority** The right to provide counsel, advice, support, and service in a person's areas of expertise.

**Staffing** The tasks of recruiting, selecting, orienting, training, appraising, promoting, and compensating employees.

**Standards** Units of measure or criteria against which results are evaluated.

**Standing plans** Policies, procedures, methods, and rules that can be applied to recurring situations.

**Status** The degree of responsibility and power afforded by a person's professional or social position.

**Stereotyping** The perception that all people in a group share attitudes, values, and beliefs.

**Strategic control points (strategic standards)** Performance criteria chosen for assessment because they are key indicators of overall performance.

**Strategic plan** Long-term plans developed by top management.

**Strategic planning** The process of establishing goals and making decisions that enable an organization to achieve its long- and short-term objectives.

**Stretch targets** Targeted job objectives that present a challenge but are achievable.

**Substantive conflict** Conflict between individuals because of what should be done or what should occur.

**Supervisors** First-level managers in charge of entry-level and other departmental employees.

**Synergistic effect** The interaction of two or more individuals such that their combined efforts are greater than the sum of their individual efforts.

**System of performance management** All those things a supervisor must do to enable an employee to achieve prescribed objectives.

## T

**Tangible standards** Standards for performance that are identifiable and measurable.

**Task group or cross functional team** Grouping of employees who come together to accomplish a particular task.

**Teamwork** People working cooperatively to solve problems and achieve goals important to the group.

**Technical skills** The ability to do the job.

**Telecommuting** Receiving work from and sending work to the office from home via a computer and modem.

**Theory X** Assumption that most employees dislike work, avoid responsibility, and must be coerced to do their jobs.

**Theory Y** Assumption that most employees enjoy work, seek responsibility, and can self-direct. The belief that well-designed jobs lead to increased motivation.

**Time study** A technique for analyzing jobs to determine time standards for performing each job.

**Total quality management (TQM)** An organizational approach involving all employees to satisfy customers by continually improving goods and services.

**Tragedy** A disastrous event or misfortune that negatively impacts the lives of people.

**Transcendence needs** Achieving even higher goals and peak experiences once all of the self-actualization needs have been met.

**Transparency** Open-book management in which all financial information is shared with employees and other stakeholders.

**Trust** The belief that someone or something is reliable, good, honest, and effective.

## U

**Underemployment** Situations in which people are in jobs that do not use their SKAs.

**Unity-of-command principle** Principle that holds that each employee should directly report to only one supervisor.

**Unplanned change** An unexpected situation causes you to initiate a strategy for change.

## V

**Virtual or geographically dispersed team (GDT)** Geographically separated people who are working on a common project and linked by communication technologies.

**Virtual organization** Companies linked temporarily to take advantage of marketplace opportunities.

**Vision statement** Management's view of what the company should become; reflects the firm's core values, priorities, and goals.

## W

**Wellness program** Organized effort by a firm to help employees get and stay healthy to remain productive.

**Whistleblower** A person who reports alleged wrongdoing.

**Working supervisors** First-level individuals who perform supervisory functions but who may not be legally or officially be part of management.

**Workplace spirituality** Organizational efforts to make the work environment more meaningful and creative by relating work to employees' personal values and spiritual beliefs.

**Workplace violence** Assaults or threats of assaults against employees in the workplace.

## Z

**Zero-base budgeting** The process of assessing, on a benefit-and-cost basis, all activities to justify their existence.

# INDEX

## D

## E